KT-528-746

Tuscany
& Umbria

THE ROUGH GUIDE

There are more than one hundred and fifty Rough Guide titles
covering destinations from Amsterdam to Zimbabwe

Forthcoming titles include
Beijing • Cape Town • Croatia • Ecuador • Switzerland

Rough Guide Reference Series
Classical Music • Drum 'n' Bass • English Football • European Football
House • The Internet • Jazz • Music USA • Opera • Reggae
Rock • Techno • World Music

Rough Guide Phrasebooks
Czech • Dutch • Egyptian Arabic • European Languages • French • German
Greek • Hindi & Urdu • Hungarian • Indonesian • Italian • Japanese
Mandarin Chinese • Mexican Spanish • Polish • Portuguese • Russian
Spanish • Swahili • Thai • Turkish • Vietnamese

Rough Guides on the Internet
www.roughguides.com

ROUGH GUIDE CREDITS

Text editor: Cameron Wilson
Series editor: Mark Ellingham
Editorial: Martin Dunford, Jonathan Buckley, Jo Mead, Kate Berens, Amanda Tomlin, Ann-Marie Shaw, Paul Gray, Helena Smith, Judith Bamber, Orla Duane, Olivia Eccleshall, Ruth Blackmore, Sophie Martin, Geoff Howard, Claire Saunders, Gavin Thomas, Alexander Mark Rogers, Polly Thomas, Joe Staines, Lisa Nellis, Andrew Tomičić, Claire Fogg, Richard Lim, Duncan Clark, Peter Buckley (UK); Andrew Rosenberg, Mary Beth Maioli (US)
Production: Susanne Hillen, Andy Hilliard, Link Hall, Helen Ostick, Julia Bovis, Michelle Draycott, Katie Pringle, Robert Evers, Neil Cooper

Cartography: Melissa Baker, Maxine Repath, Nichola Goodliffe, Ed Wright
Picture research: Louise Boulton, Sharon Martins
Online editors: Kelly Cross, Loretta Chilcoat (US)
Finance: John Fisher, Gary Singh, Edward Downey, Mark Hall, Tim Bill
Marketing & Publicity: Richard Trillo, Niki Smith, David Wearn, Jemima Broadbridge (UK); Jean-Marie Kelly, Myra Campolo, Simon Carloss (US)
Administration: Tania Hummel, Charlotte Marriott, Demelza Dallow

ACKNOWLEDGEMENTS

Tim Jepson would like to thank Duncan and Amanda Baird, Marella Caracciolo, Michael Sheridan, and the hardworking updaters of this fourth edition, Tom Bruce-Gardyne and Sarah Stephens.
Tom extends his gratitude to Alessandro and Elisa Sappupo for their hospitality in giving him a place to stay.

The editor would like to thank David Price for eagle-eyed proofreading, Neil Cooper for typesetting, Maxine, Nichola and also The Map Studio for superb cartography, and Rob Mackey and Henry Barrkman for their help in updating Basics. Many thanks to Jonathan Buckley for ideas and advice and for casting a critical eye over photos, and to Paul Gray and Susanne Hillen for the securing of loose ends. A special thankyou also to Candy MacMahon.

PUBLISHING INFORMATION

This fourth edition published February 2000 by Rough Guides Ltd, 62–70 Shorts Gardens, London, WC2H 9AB.
Distributed by the Penguin Group:
Penguin Books Ltd, 27 Wrights Lane, London W8 5TZ
Penguin Books USA Inc., 375 Hudson Street, New York 10014, USA
Penguin Books Australia Ltd, 487 Maroondah Highway, PO Box 257, Ringwood, Victoria 3134, Australia
Penguin Books Canada Ltd, 10 Alcorn Avenue, Toronto, Ontario, Canada M4V 1E4
Penguin Books (NZ) Ltd, 182–190 Wairau Road, Auckland 10, New Zealand
Typeset in Linotron Univers and Century Old Style to an original design by Andrew Oliver.
Printed by Clays Ltd, St Ives PLC
Illustrations in Part One and Part Three by Edward Briant.

Illustrations on p.1 & p.593 by Henry Iles
© Jonathan Buckley, Mark Ellingham and Tim Jepson, 2000
No part of this book may be reproduced in any form without permission from the publisher except for the quotation of brief passages in reviews.
656pp – Includes index
A catalogue record for this book is available from the British Library
ISBN 1-85828-518-6

Tuscany
& Umbria

THE ROUGH GUIDE

written and researched by

Jonathan Buckley, Mark Ellingham
and Tim Jepson

with additional research by

Tom Bruce-Gardyne and Sarah Stephens

THE ROUGH GUIDES

TRAVEL GUIDES • PHRASEBOOKS • MUSIC AND REFERENCE GUIDES

 We set out to do something different when the first Rough Guide was published in 1982. Mark Ellingham, just out of university, was travelling in Greece. He brought along the popular guides of the day, but found they were all lacking in some way. They were either strong on ruins and museums but went on for pages without mentioning a beach or taverna. Or they were so conscious of the need to save money that they lost sight of Greece's cultural and historical significance. Also, none of the books told him anything about Greece's contemporary life – its politics, its culture, its people, and how they lived.

So with no job in prospect, Mark decided to write his own guidebook, one which aimed to provide practical information that was second to none, detailing the best beaches and the hottest clubs and restaurants, while also giving hard-hitting accounts of every sight, both famous and obscure, and providing up-to-the-minute information on contemporary culture. It was a guide that encouraged independent travellers to find the best of Greece, and was a great success, getting shortlisted for the Thomas Cook travel guide award, and encouraging Mark, along with three friends, to expand the series.

The Rough Guide list grew rapidly and the letters flooded in, indicating a much broader readership than had been anticipated, but one which uniformly appreciated the Rough Guide mix of practical detail and humour, irreverence and enthusiasm. Things haven't changed. The same four friends who began the series are still the caretakers of the Rough Guide mission today: to provide the most reliable, up-to-date and entertaining information to independent-minded travellers of all ages, on all budgets.

We now publish more than 150 titles and have offices in London and New York. The travel guides are written and researched by a dedicated team of more than 100 authors, based in Britain, Europe, the USA and Australia. We have also created a unique series of phrasebooks to accompany the travel series, along with an acclaimed series of music guides, and a best-selling pocket guide to the Internet and World Wide Web. We also publish comprehensive travel information on our web site:

www.roughguides.com

HELP US UPDATE

We've gone to a lot of effort to ensure that the fourth edition of *The Rough Guide to Tuscany and Umbria* is accurate and up-to-date. However, things change — places get "discovered", opening hours are notoriously fickle, restaurants and rooms raise prices or lower standards. If you feel we've got it wrong or left something out, we'd like to know, and if you can remember the address, the price, the time, the phone number, so much the better.

We'll credit all contributions, and send a copy of the next edition (or any other Rough Guide if you prefer) for the best letters. Please mark letters: "Rough Guide Tuscany and Umbria Update" and send to:
Rough Guides, 62–70 Shorts Gardens, London WC2H 9AB, or Rough Guides, 375 Hudson St, New York NY 10014.
Or send email to: mail@roughguides.co.uk
Online updates about this book can be found on Rough Guides' Web site at **www.roughguides.com**

THE AUTHORS

Jonathan Buckley first visited Italy in 1979 and has returned every year since. He has written The Rough Guide to Venice, and co-authored The Rough Guide to Florence.

Tim Jepson's career began with street busking and work in a slaughterhouse. Having acquired fluent Italian, he went on to do better things as a Rome-based journalist and a leader of walking tours in Umbria. He is also an author of the Rough Guide to Florence, the Rough Guide to Canada and the Rough Guide to the Pacific Northwest.

Mark Ellingham wrote the first Rough Guide – to Greece – and has written and edited numerous titles in the series since. He found his ideal landscape south of Siena but continues to live mainly in South London.

READERS' LETTERS

Thanks to all those readers who sent us their comments on the previous edition of this guide:

Richard Andrews; Dr Andrew Bamji; Reverend Dominic Barrington; Jane S. Benjamin; Lisa Bentley and Mark Youngman; Reverend and Mrs R.J. Blakeway-Phillips; E.C.A. Bloem; Andrew Brociner; Roland and Joan Brown; John and Elizabeth Buckell; Roger Carter; Alan Castle; David Clement-Davies; Richard Colebourn; Anne Copland; Roger G. Dean; Sybille Decoo; Julia A. DeLancey; Professor John W. Dixon; Professor Sir Anthony Epstein; Maria Pettoello Mantovani Fano; Kathleen M. Fox; Frances Hartnett Gajano; Reverend Vincent and Mrs Carys Gillett; Kate Growtt; Holly Haisty; Pam Harris and Andrew Wella; Alice Jacobs; Jacky Jenkins; David A. Katz and Lee Katman; Ellen Kearns; Glen Keywood; Simon Kyte; J.C. Lewis; Dr Christopher G. Male; John Masi; Alan G. McDonald; Herman Meilak; Jilly Merton; N.J. Mills-Hicks; Walter O. Moeller; Gordon Moran; Coralie A. Moynihan; Christopher Oh; Nina Ørum; Alicia Parry; Irene Perri; Helen and Andrew Phillips; Bertin Quaghebeur; Hans Reitsma; Peter Richards; Laura Schmulewitz; Pamela Schöne; Eileen and Tim Shirley; John Sidgwick; Joanna Slade; Roger Stafford; Bobbi Stauffer; Susan L. Stonard; Anthony Twist; Andrew Walker; Andrew L. Walker; Kate Walsh; John Watterson; Petra and Adrian Whatmore; Lorna Wilson and Terry Jack

CONTENTS

Introduction x

LIST OF MAPS

MAP SYMBOLS

▬▬▬ Railway	▲	Mountain peak	ℂ	Telephone
▭▭▭ Motorway	◆	Point of interest	H	Hospital
═══ Road	⊥⊥	Town wall	✕	Airport
≡≡≡ Road tunnel	•—	Gate	P	Car park
▭▭▭ Steps	�	Castle	★	Bus stop
- - - Footpath	✕	Battlefield	▬	Building
─── River	†	Church (regional maps)	⊞	Church (town maps)
— — Ferry route	◉	Accommodation	▦	Park
- - - - Chapter division boundary	△	Campsite	▦	National Park
—•— Regional boundary	⊠	Post office	⊞	Cemetery
↟↟ Mountains	ⓘ	Tourist office	∷	Beach

INTRODUCTION

Tuscany and Umbria harbour the classic landscapes of Italy, familiar from a thousand Renaissance paintings, with their backdrop of medieval hill-towns, rows of cypress trees, vineyards and olive groves, and artfully sited villas and farmhouses. It's a stereotype that has long held an irresistible attraction for northern Europeans. Shelley referred to Tuscany as a "paradise of exiles", and ever since his time the English, in particular, have seen the region as an ideal refuge from a sun-starved and overcrowded homeland.

The expatriate's perspective may be distorted, but the central provinces – and especially Tuscany – are indeed the essence of Italy in many ways. The national language evolved from Tuscan dialect, a supremacy ensured by Dante, who wrote the *Divine Comedy* in the vernacular of his birthplace, Florence. Other great Tuscan writers of the period – Petrarch and Boccaccio – reinforced its status, and in the last century Manzoni came to Tuscany to purge his vocabulary of any impurities while working on *The Betrothed*, the most famous of all Italian novels. But what makes this area pivotal to the culture not just of Italy but of all Europe is, of course, the **Renaissance** period, whose masterpieces of painting, sculpture and architecture are an intrinsic part of any tour. The very name by which we refer to this extraordinarily creative era was coined by a Tuscan, Giorgio Vasari, who wrote in the sixteenth century of the "rebirth" of the arts with the humanism of Giotto and his successors.

Florence was the most active centre of the Renaissance, flourishing through the patronage of the all-powerful Medici, of a multitude of religious bodies and of the guilds, whose merchants and manufacturers laid the foundations of the city's prosperity. Every eminent artistic figure from Giotto onwards – Masaccio, Brunelleschi, Alberti, Donatello, Botticelli, Leonardo, Michelangelo – is represented here, in an unrivalled gathering of churches, galleries and museums.

If Florence tends to take the limelight, however, rivalry between the towns of both provinces – still an important factor in a region whose inhabitants feel a strong loyalty to their particular locality – ensured that pictures and palaces were sponsored by everyone who could afford them. Exquisite Renaissance works adorn almost every place of any size from the Tuscan coast to the Apennine slopes of eastern Umbria, while the largest towns can boast artistic projects every bit as ambitious as those to be seen in the Tuscan capital – the Piero della Francesca frescoes in **Arezzo**, for example, or those by Luca Signorelli in **Orvieto** or Giotto in **Assisi**.

Moreover, the art of the Renaissance did not spring out of thin air – Tuscany and Umbria both can boast a cultural lineage that stretches back unbroken to the time of Charlemagne and even beyond. **Lucca** is one of the handsomest Romanesque cities in Europe, and **Pisa** – whose Campo dei Miracoli, with its Leaning Tower, is one of Europe's most brilliant monumental ensembles – is another city whose heyday came in the Middle Ages. **Siena**'s red-brick medieval cityscape, arranged around its fabulous scallop-shaped Campo, makes a refreshing contrast with the darker tones of Florence, while a tour through Umbria can seem like a procession of magnificent ancient hill-towns. The attractions of **Assisi** (birthplace of St Francis), **Spoleto** and the busy provincial capital of **Perugia** are hardly secrets, but other Umbrian towns remain more obscure – such as **Gubbio** and the backwater delights of **Bevagna** and **Todi**. Many of the Umbrian towns retain a fair showing of their ancient past, too, with Etruscan and Roman walls and tombs to be seen on sites left undisturbed for centuries.

Even though the percentage of the population who make their living from the land has plummeted since the last war – in Umbria the figure fell from nearly sixty percent in 1950 to just over ten percent in 1980 – both Tuscany and Umbria are predominantly **rural** provinces. Just as the hill-towns mould themselves to the summits, the terraces of vines follow the lower contours of the hills and open fields spread across the broader valleys, forming a distinctive balance between the natural and human world. The towns may have grown and industrial estates may have blocked in some of the outskirts, but great tracts of land still look much as they did half a millennium ago.

The variety of **landscape** within this comparatively small area is astounding. A short distance from central Florence spread the thickly wooded uplands of the **Mugello** and the **Casentino**, much of the latter still maintained by the monasteries to which the forests were entrusted hundreds of years ago. Lucca is a springboard for the **Alpi Apuane**, whose mountain quarries have supplied Europe's masons with pure white marble for centuries. Along the Tuscan shoreline the resorts are interspersed by some of Italy's best-kept wildlife reserves, including the fabulous **Monti Uccellina**, the last stretch of virgin coast in the whole country. Out in the **Tuscan archipelago**, the island of **Giglio** is unspoilt by the sort of tourist development that has infiltrated – though certainly not ruined – nearby **Elba**. The pastoral archetype is perhaps most strikingly subverted in the **deep south** of the province, where the agricultural hinterland of Siena soon gives way to the bleak *crete* and the sulphurous pools of Saturnia.

Landlocked Umbria may not be as varied as its neighbour, but the wild heights of the **Valnerina**, the **Piano Grande**'s prairie-like expanse and the savage peaks of the **Monti Sibillini** all contrast with the tranquil, soft-contoured hills with which the region is most often associated. In **Lago Trasimeno** the province has the largest body of water on the Italian peninsula, while in the south there's the **Cascate delle Marmore**, a spectacular if sporadic waterfall.

When to go

Midsummer in central Italy is not as pleasant an experience as you might imagine: the heat can be stifling, and from May to September you'll require luck to find accommodation in all but the most out-of-the-way spots. If at all possible, the month to **avoid** is **August**, when the great majority of Italians take their holidays. As a result many town restaurants and some hotels are closed for the entire month and the beaches are jammed solid. As the standard Italian idea of an enjoyable summer break is to spend a few weeks towel-to-towel on the sand, Umbria escapes the worst of the rush, but the problem of limited opening remains.

Florence throughout the summer is such a log jam of tour groups that the major attractions become a purgatorial experience – a two-hour queue for the Uffizi is not unusual. To enjoy a visit fully, go there shortly **before Easter** or in the **late autumn** – times of the year that are the best for Tuscany and Umbria as a whole, as the towns are quieter and the countryside is blossoming or taking on the tones of the harvest season. The Umbrian climate is slightly more extreme than Tuscany's, chiefly because of its distance from the sea; temperatures in summer are fractionally higher, while the hill-top locales of many towns can make them surprisingly windy and cool at other times. Winter is often quite rainy, but the absence of crowds makes this a good option for the cities on the major art trails. Bear in mind, however, that the high altitude of much of the region means many roads are impassable in midwinter, and in places like the upper Casentino or the Sibillini the snow might not melt until March or even April.

Festivals

It's always worth checking when each town has its **festivals** or pilgrimages. Accommodation is always tricky during these mini peak seasons, but some of the festivities are enjoyable enough to merit planning a trip around. Many have been crucial

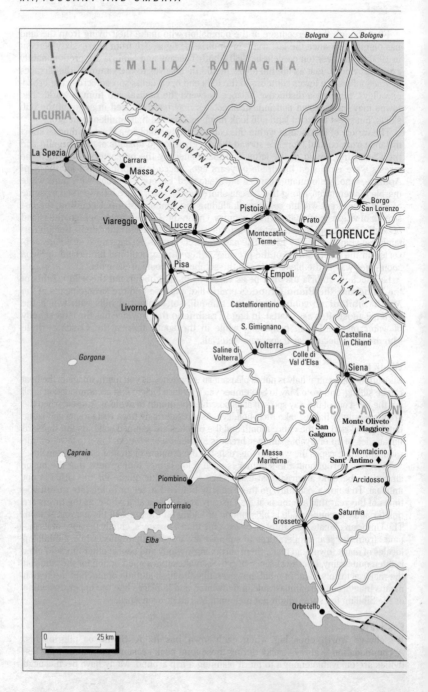

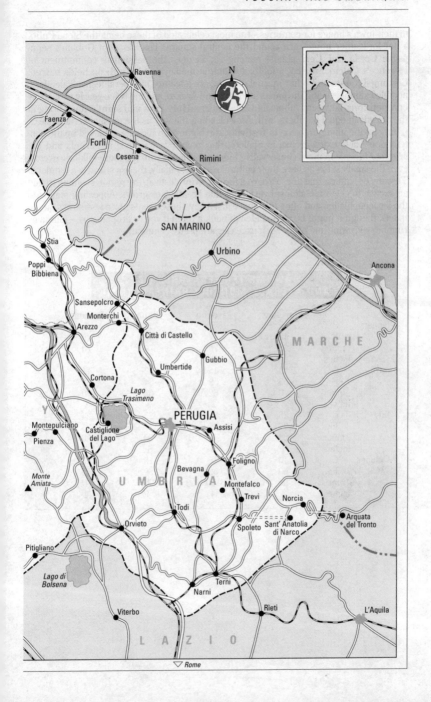

to their town's image for centuries – the most celebrated of these being the Siena **Palio**, a hell-for-leather horse race round the central square. The frenzy of Gubbio's semi-pagan **Corsa dei Ceri** almost matches it, as does the passionate commitment of Florence's **Calcio Storico**, a football match in medieval attire with no holds barred. Costumed **jousts** and other martial displays are a feature of several festive calendars, notable examples being the jousts in Pistoia and Arezzo, and the twice-yearly **crossbow competitions** between Gubbio and Sansepolcro. **Holy days** and **saint's days** bring in the crowds in equal numbers, with Assisi leading the way as the most venerated site.

Among the innumerable **arts festivals**, the highest profiles are achieved by the contemporary arts extravaganza in Spoleto, the *Umbria Jazz* festival in Perugia and the *Maggio Musicale* in more conservative Florence – but as with the more folkloric events, even the smallest towns have their cultural *stagione*. Finally, there's scarcely a hamlet in Tuscany or Umbria that doesn't have a **food** or **wine** festival, the region seeming to find an excuse to celebrate almost everything that breathes or grows. Appealing mainly to the local population and often lasting for just a day, these events place less stress on the hotels, though it might be a good idea to book a room if you're dropping by – fountains running with wine and other such excesses are pretty common.

DAYTIME TEMPERATURES (°C) AND AVERAGE MONTHLY RAINFALL (MM)				
		Florence	**Livorno**	**Siena**	**Perugia**
January	°C	6	9	5	5
	°F	42	47	40	40
	mm	62	70	70	70
	inches	3	3	3	3
April	°C	13	15	12	11
	°F	55	59	54	52
	mm	70	62	62	70
	inches	3	3	3	3
July	°C	25	24	25	24
	°F	77	75	77	75
	mm	23	6	20	30
	inches	1	0	1	1
October	°C	16	15	15	13
	°F	60	59	59	55
	mm	96	110	110	115
	inches	4	4	4	4

PART ONE

THE
BASICS

GETTING THERE FROM BRITAIN AND IRELAND

The easiest way to get to Tuscany and Umbria from Britain is to fly. The main destinations are Pisa, Rome and Bologna, though the smaller airports at Florence and Perugia are also served by an increasing number of flights from the UK. Flight times from London are about two hours. Prices for charter and discounted scheduled flights compare well with those for the long rail journey. Fares inevitably fluctuate with the seasons – Easter and June to September are the peak times – but special offers can be picked up at short notice at any time of year.

BY PLANE FROM BRITAIN

The main airlines operating **scheduled flights** to central Italy are British Airways, Alitalia, Meridiana, Virgin Express, Ryanair, Go and KLM UK (see box on next page for contact information and flight frequency). In choosing a flight you should be guided by price, but also by the convenience of the Italian airports served by each carrier.

The biggest choice of flights, discounted tickets and operators is to **Rome**, but this also leaves you the longest and most complicated onward journey to Tuscany (around three hours by road or rail to Florence), slightly less to Umbria (about two hours by road or rail to Perugia and Spoleto). Fiumicino, the common name for Rome's main Leonardo da Vinci airport is about 30km west of Rome's city centre. The best way into the city is on the express rail service, which leaves the airport hourly between about 7.30am

and 10pm, taking 30 minutes to reach Stazione Termini, Rome's principal railway station. The smaller **Ciampino** airport, to the southeast of the city, is linked by hourly buses (25min, L3500) to the Rome metro system at Anagnina, whence you pick up a train to Termini railway station.

Only Meridiana currently flies directly to the small hub airport in **Florence** from London (Gatwick). The much bigger airport at **Pisa**, which can accommodate far larger planes, is otherwise the best bet for Florence and most of Tuscany. It has a large choice of scheduled and charter operators (including British Airways and Alitalia) and an easy one-hour rail trip directly from the airport to the centre of Florence (see p.237). British Airways and Alitalia also fly to **Bologna**, which is one hour by road and rail from Florence, but is less convenient and takes longer if you're relying on trains; unlike Pisa you have to allow for a shuttle bus service from the airport to Bologna's main railway station.

Giving an idea of precise **fares** is difficult, as all airlines – even the major carriers – offer a plethora of cheap but constantly changing deals throughout the year. Competition among the low-cost airlines such as Go and Ryanair also helps keep prices down. Among the low-cost carriers, fares start from about £100, rising to around £300 depending on the season and flexibility in your choice of flight times. Seasons are: low (October through to the end of March); shoulder (April to June and September to October); and high (July and August, as well as periods at Christmas and Easter). Advertised prices can be much lower (from £79), but in practice it is almost impossible to secure flights at these prices unless you book well in advance and travel at inconvenient times. As a rule, the more flexibility you require and the closer to the day of departure you book, the more expensive the flight.

As a general guide, the cheapest British Airways or Alitalia ticket is an **Apex** return fare, which to Pisa, Rome and Bologna, costs around £236 during shoulder season: low and high season prices may be up to £50 higher or lower. Restrictions are generally that you must book a minimum of seven or fourteen days in advance, and there are no refunds or changes to return flights after departure: they're also rarely valid for more than a month. Prices for all types of tickets

AIRLINES AND AGENTS IN BRITAIN

AIRLINES

Alitalia (☎020/7602 7111; *www.alitalia.it*). London Heathrow–Rome (6 daily); London Gatwick–Pisa (1 daily); London Gatwick–Rome (1 daily); London Gatwick–Bologna (2 daily); London Stansted–Rome (2 daily, code-share with KLM UK).

British Airways (☎0345/222 111; *www.british-airways.com*). London Heathrow–Rome (6 daily); London Heathrow–Bologna (2 daily); London Gatwick–Rome (2 daily); London Gatwick–Pisa (2 daily); Manchester–Rome (1 daily except Sat).

Go (☎08456/054 321; *go-fly.com*). London Stansted–Rome (4 daily); London Stansted–Bologna (2 daily).

KLM UK (☎08705/074 074; *www.klm.nl*). London Stansted–Rome (2 daily).

Meridiana (☎020/7839 2222). London Gatwick–Florence (2 daily).

Ryanair (☎0541/569 569; *www.ryanair.com*). London Stansted–Pisa (2 daily).

Virgin Express (☎020/7744 0004; *www.virgin-express.com*). London–Rome (15 flights daily from Heathrow, Gatwick and Stansted combined). All flights via Brussels.

TRAVEL AGENTS

Alpha Flights, 37 King's Exchange, Tileyard Rd, London N7 9AH (☎020/7609 8188).

APA Travel, 138 Eversholt St, London NW1 1BL (☎020/7387 5337).

Council Travel, 28a Poland St, London W1V 3DB (☎020/7437 7767).

CTS Travel, 44 Goodge St, London W1P 2AD (☎020/7290 0620).

Flight File, 49 Tottenham Court Rd, London W1P 0NH (☎020/8296 0309).

Italflights, 125 High Holborn, London WC1V 6QA (☎020/7405 6771).

Italia nel Mondo, 6 Palace St, London SW16 5HY (☎020/7828 9171).

Italy Skybus, 24 Earls Court Gardens, London SW5 0SZ (☎020/7631 3444).

Italy Sky Shuttle, 227 Shepherds Bush Rd, London W6 7AS (☎020/8748 1333).

LAI, 185 King's Cross Rd, London WC1X 9DB (☎020/7837 8492).

Mundus Air Travel, 5 Peter St, London W1V 3RR (☎020/7437 2272).

North South Travel, Moulsham Mill Centre, Parkway, Chelmsford, Essex CM2 7PX (☎01245/492 882).

Primrose Travel, 25 Rose St, London WC2 9EA (☎020/7497 9347).

STA Travel, 86 Old Brompton Rd, London SW7 3LQ; 117 Euston Rd, London NW1 2SX; 38 Store St, London WC1E 7BZ; 11 Goodge St, London W1P 1FE (☎020/7361 6161); 30 Upper Kirkgate, Aberdeen AB10 1BA (☎01224/658 222); 34 North St, Brighton BN1 1EB (☎01273/728 282); 25 Queen's Rd, Bristol BS8 1QE (☎0117/929 4399); 38 Sidney St, Cambridge CB2 3HX (☎01223/366 966); 184 Byres Rd, Glasgow G12 8SN (☎0141/338 6000); 88 Vicar Lane, Leeds LS1 7JH (☎0113/244 9212); 14 Oxford Rd, Manchester M1 5QA (☎0161/834 0668); 9 St Mary's Place, Newcastle NE1 7PG (☎0191/233 2111); 36 George St, Oxford OX1 2BJ (☎01865/792 800): plus branches on university campuses throughout Britain. *www.statravel.co.uk*

Travel Bug, 597 Cheetham Hill Rd, Manchester M8 5EJ (☎0161/721 4000; *www.travel-bug.co.uk*).

Usit CAMPUS, 52 Grosvenor Gardens, London SW1W 0AG (☎020/7730 3402); 110 High St, Old Aberdeen AB24 3HE (☎01224/273 559); 541 Bristol Rd, Selly Oak, Birmingham B29 6AU (☎0121/414 1848); 61 Ditchling Rd, Brighton BN1 4SD (☎01273/570 226); 39 Queen's Rd, Clifton, Bristol BS8 1QE (☎0117/929 2494); 5 Emmanuel St, Cambridge CB1 1NE (☎01223/324 283); 20 Fairfax St, Coventry CV1 5RY (☎01203/225 777); 53 Forrest Rd, Edinburgh EH1 2QP (☎0131/668 3303); 122 George St, Glasgow G1 1RF (☎0141/553 1818); 166 Deansgate, Manchester M3 3FE (☎0161/833 2046); 105–106 St Aldates, Oxford OX1 1DD (☎01865/242 067); 340 Glossop Rd, Sheffield S10 2HW (☎0114/275 2552); branches also in YHA shops and on university campuses all over Britain. *www.campustravel.co.uk*

are invariably lower if you travel midweek: Friday and Saturday flights are the most expensive.

Direct charter flights may very occasionally be a better bargain. It's worth checking with a specialist agent, or sources such as the classified sections in the weekend newspapers – the *Daily Telegraph* and *Sunday Times* especially – and, if you live in London, *Time Out* magazine and the *Evening Standard*. Or contact one of the big youth/student travel specialists like STA Travel or Campus Travel, good for cheap deals if you're **under 26** or a **student**. There are also a number of specialist Italian agents (addresses below), who will normally have a range of fares.

Most agents offer "**open-jaw**" deals, whereby you can fly into one Italian city and back from another – a good idea if you want to make your way across the country, and generally no more expensive than a standard charter return. Consider also a **package deal** (see below), which takes care of flights and accommodation for an all-in price. Package operators can also be a source of cheap one-off flights.

BY TRAIN

Travelling by **train** to Italy won't save much money. The beauty of train travel and the ticketing, however, is that you can break your journey en route.There are two basic ways to go: by ferry across the Channel and then train, or on Eurostar via the Channel Tunnel.

The simplest and quickest route is to take a **Eurostar** service from Waterloo to Paris (Gare du Nord), cross Paris by metro and then pick up a train for Florence from the Gare du Lyon. The cheapest current through fare is £246 return (subject to availability): it requires booking seven days

in advance, staying at least one Saturday, and includes a couchette (bunk-bed) on the sleeper-only overnight service from the Gare du Lyon. A fully flexible fare comes in at a staggering £406. If you are 25 or under, the cheapest option is a no-restrictions "Youth Ticket" at £212.

Crossing the Channel by **ferry** gives you a different set of options: it costs more to travel via Switzerland, less via France (changing in Paris). Journey time is around 22 hours to Florence via France, a little less via Switzerland. And since the advent of Eurostar, onward connections in Paris tend to work in favour of that service and not the trains meeting ferries in Calais. Many arrive too late for the evening connecting train in Paris, meaning an overight stay the city.

The fare to Florence currently starts from £185 return via Switzerland, or £164 by the other route. If you're under 26, you can get a slightly discounted ticket from student and youth agents and some high-street travel agents; these tickets are valid for up to two months and include as many stopovers as you like.

Whichever route or method you plump for, it's well worth reserving a seat or couchette (around £12) for your trip to Italy – something you should do well in advance for travel in high season.

If you are 25 or under and planning a trip through Europe, and travelling around Italy once you're there, it might be a better idea to invest in an **InterRail** pass. These come in four categories: one-zone (£159), two-zone (£209), three-zone (£229) and global (£259). The one-zone pass is valid for 22 consecutive days of travel; the other three passes are valid for a calendar month.

To get to and travel in Italy, you'll need at least a two-zone pass. The passes also give discounts

---

RAIL TICKET OFFICES

Citalia, Marco Polo House, 3–5 Landsdowne Rd, Croydon, Surrey (☎0891/715 151: premium-rate line). Enquiries for Italian rail travel and rail passes.

Eurostar, Eurostar House, Waterloo Station, London SE1 8SE (☎0990/186 186).

Rail Europe (☎0990/848 848). Call centre only that sells rail journeys for Italy, sleepers and couchettes, as well as InterRail and Euro-Domino (see p.27) passes. Handles Eurostar only – no rail connections involving Channel ferries. Expect a long wait on the phone.

Rail Europe, 179 Piccadilly, London W1V 0BA. Sells the same range of tickets as the call centre, but to personal callers only: no telephone bookings.

Ultima Travel, 424 Chester Rd, Little Sutton, Ellesmere CH66 3RB (☎0151/339 6171). Books rail tickets (Eurostar and ferry-rail routes) from the UK and for national rail networks across Europe.

Wasteels, Victoria Station (by platform 2), London SW1V 1JY (☎020/7834 7066).

on cross-Channel services, including Eurostar, and some ferry routes in Europe; note that all supplements, such as those on some high-speed or Inter-City-type trains, and seat reservations and couchettes, are extra.

An **InterRail 26+** ticket is available for those 26 and over in the same four categories and with the same validity: one-zone (£229), two-zone (£279), three-zone (£309) and four-zone £349). Senior citizens holding a Senior Citizen Railcard can purchase a Rail Europe Seniors Card (£5), which allows 30-percent discounts on rail fares throughout Europe, as long as the journey crosses an international boundary, plus 30 percent off most ferry crossings. InterRail and other passes are available from main railway stations, Rail Europe and youth/student travel agents; to qualify, you need to have been resident in Europe for at least six months.

Once in Italy, the rail system is comprehensive and efficient, and much the best way of getting around the country. See pp.26–28 for full details, as well as information on Italian rail passes.

BY ROAD

It's difficult to see why anyone would want to travel to Italy by **bus**. But if you do have a phobia about trains and planes, there are direct services to Florence, taking a gruelling 32 hours and costing around £112, with reductions of around 10 percent for under-26s and students. Occasional promotional fares can bring the fare down to around £70 return. Run by National Express Eurolines (☎0990/143 219), coaches leave three times weekly in winter and daily in summer (excluding Tues) from London's Victoria Coach Station. If you are really keen on bus travel, and plan to see other countries en route, then the **Eurolines Pass** offers unlimited travel across sixteen countries for either 30 or 60 days: high-season prices for under-26s and over-60s are £199 for 30 days, or £249 for 60 days; full adult fares are £229 and £279 respectively. Low season rates are £159 (30 days) or £199 (60 days) for

---

CROSS-CHANNEL TICKETS

Hoverspeed Dover (☎01304/240 241). To Boulogne and Calais.

Eurotunnel (☎0990/353 535). To Calais.

P&O Stena Line and Sea France (☎0990/980 980). To Calais.

---

under-26s and over-60s, or £159/£249 for other adults.

There's no one fixed route to Italy if you're travelling with **your own vehicle**. The best cross-Channel options for most drivers will be the standard ferry/hovercraft links between Dover and Calais (with P&O Stena, Hoverspeed and Sea France), Folkestone and Boulogne (Hoverspeed), or Eurotunnel through the Channel Tunnel (24-hr service, with departures every 15min at peak periods). The last will speed up the initial part of your journey, but in the context of the long trip to Italy may not make a huge difference. Any travel agent can provide up-to-date cross-Channel schedules and make advance bookings – which are essential in season.

As regards routes from northern France, the Alpine route via Germany and Switzerland is probably the quickest and can **save you money** as German motorways – unlike their French equivalents – are generally toll-free. The eastern French route into the Valle d'Aosta in northwest Italy has been compromised by the fire in 1999 in the Mont Blanc tunnel, but for up-to-the-minute information on this and all route-planning problems, contact the RAC premium-rate help-line (☎0891/347 333).

An option that combines a hassle-free journey by train and the flexibility of your own car in Italy, is a **motorail** arrangement from Calais to Rome, Bologna or Livorno. Journey time is about 18 hours, and prices vary according to time of travel: two adults and two children aged four to 11, for example, riding motorail to Bologna would pay £956–996 return in July, including couchettes.

PACKAGES AND ORGANIZED TOURS

Italy stands somewhat apart from other European package destinations: it's not especially cheap and is as much a venue for specialist interest and touring holidays as sun-sand-sea packages. Tuscany and Umbria are prime destinations in most "specialist" Italian programmes, and – a definite plus – most of these holidays are sold by small, independently run travel companies. Holidays on the market mostly fall into one of the following categories:

● **Flight-plus-hotel**. These deals can be excellent value if you want to base yourself in one (or two) places, usually featuring a good three-star hotel. All-in prices for a week's bed and breakfast in Florence, for example, start at around £500 per

SPECIAL INTEREST HOLIDAYS

ART AND CULTURE HOLIDAYS

ACE Study Tours (☎01223/835 055). A variety of mainly art and architectural tours under the guidance of various experts.

British Museum Traveller (☎020/7323 8895). A company that works with the museum's curators: Tuscan jaunts include a five-day trip to Florence and Siena.

Fine Art Travel (☎020/7437 8553). High-cost tours for access to private houses and collections in Florence, Lucca and elsewhere.

Inscape (☎01993/891 726). Art and history trips based on first-hand study of relevant works and cities: Florence and Orvieto feature on the Renaissance cities tour.

Liaisons Abroad (☎020/7376 4020). Agency for tickets to major Italian opera and musical events, timed museum tickets, Siena Palio, Serie A football matches.

Light and Land (☎01737/768 723). Offers week-long photographic holidays in Tuscany and Umbria for camera enthusiasts of all standards. Well-scouted locations, plus time for sightseeing and relaxation: some trips led by Charlie Waite, one of Britain's most distinguished landscape photographers.

Martin Randall (☎020/8742 3355). One of the best operators in the sector: imaginative art, music and cultural tours ranging from three to twelve nights, including Piero della Francesca, Medici Villas & Gardens, Florence & Siena, San Gimignano & Tuscan Hill Towns and Florence Revisited (lesser-known sights and private palaces).

NADFAS (☎020/7873 5027). Cox & Kings run nine Italian, predominantly art and architecture-based tours for the National Association of Decorative & Fine Arts Societies: trips are open to non-members.

Prospect (☎020/8995 2151). Aimed at a broad but inquisitive audience rather than rarified art specialists: the Italian programme includes a tour of the major Umbrian hill towns.

WALKING, CYCLING AND RIDING

Alternative Travel Group (☎01865/310 399). The best all-inclusive escorted walking holidays in Tuscany and Umbria. They also run cheaper self-guided walking and cycling trips: hotel bookings are made for you and luggage is transported.

Equitour (☎01865/511 642). Group riding holidays on trails between hotels in Chianti and the Maremma, or single-centre holidays in bases around Tuscany.

Explore Worldwide (☎01252/760 000). Offers a fortnight's camping and walking between Florence, Siena and Volterra.

Headwater (☎01606/813 399). A variety of guided and independent walking and cycling holidays in both regions.

HF (☎020/8905 9556). A choice of one- and two-week Tuscan walks from a long-established company using bases in Tuscany at Barga and Albiano.

Inntravel (☎01653/628 811). Self-guided walks around the Tuscan hills, plus more demanding hikes such as an Apennine trail from Florence to Bologna.

In the Saddle (☎01256/851 665). Seven-day excursions in the Maremma (Tuscany) for experienced riders, and gentler day rides for all levels and ages from Montieri, south of Florence.

Sherpa (☎020/8577 2717). Offers a selection of self-guided walks and cycles in Tuscany and Umbria.

Waymark (☎01753/516 477). One of the longer-established companies, with walks across Italy, including Tuscany.

WINE AND COOKERY HOLIDAYS

Alternative Travel Group (☎01865/310 399). Truffle-hunts in Umbria, plus language, cookery and painting courses based at a delightful ninth-century house in the countryside outside Colle di Val d'Elsa.

Arblaster & Clarke (☎01730/893 344). Up-market wine tours in Tuscany and Umbria, staying at four- and five-star hotels and with tastings at the premier estates.

Italian Cookery Weekends (☎020/7620 2121). Seven-night cookery courses run by Susan Gelmetti in Umbria, flights and full board included.

Tasting Places (☎020/7460 0077). By far the best of several companies offering cooking courses in the region. Leading chefs such as Alistair Little and Sophie Braimbridge lead one-week residential courses at country houses in Tuscany and Umbria.

Winetrails (☎01306/712 111). Exercise and indulgence combine: tours link vineyard visits with guided walks and good food. An independent programme is also available.

GENERAL PACKAGE OPERATORS

Abercrombie & Kent (☎020/7559 8686). Tailor-made holidays and grand hotels for the top end of the market.

Citalia (☎020/8686 5533). Mid-range three-star and smarter four-star hotel and villa packages from a major and long-established company: also offers city-break packages, escorted tours, good rural hotels, apartments and a tailor-made "Freedom" programme.

Italian Connection (☎07071/303 030). Interesting brochure-less company which sends out personalized information and suggestions in response to a questionnaire. Has a database of over 2000 hotels and 2500 villas, plus a wide range of activity and escorted holidays.

Italiatour! (☎01883/621 900). Package deals, city breaks, winter sun holidays and specialist Italian cuisine tours. Also offers tailor-made itineraries and can book local events and tours.

Magic of Italy (☎020/8748 7575). With Citalia this is the frontrunner among the plethora of

multi-service Italian operators. Hotel and villa packages, individual properties, "City Break" deals (under the Magic Cities label), tailor-made itineraries and a booking service for opera, events, train and other tickets.

Room Service (☎020/7636 6888). Dedicated booking service for hotels in all categories across most of northern and central Italy.

Solo's Holidays (☎020/8951 2811). Holidays in Tuscany for singles or groups of friends, the former arranged in age bands (28–55 and 45–69).

Sunvil Holidays (☎020/8568 4499). City breaks and hotel and villa packages, but especially strong on tailor-made fly-drive packages in cheaper two- and three-star hotels in both regions.

Thermalia Travel (☎020/7586 7725). Spa holidays are big business in Tuscany: this company will set you up for de-tox and pampering at Monsummano near Montecatini.

person per week, rising by about £50 upwards in high season. Prices are slightly lower for stays in some provincial towns, like Siena and Assisi.

● **Villas and farmhouses**. Numerous companies offer villa or farmhouse accommodation in rural Tuscany and Umbria; charter flights, ferry crossings or fly-drives are usually available as part of a package deal, but it's generally possible to book just the house if you prefer. This is one of the boom markets for Italian tourism, so book well in advance for the summer season.

Properties vary enormously, from small, simple farmhouses sleeping four to eight people right up to castles fitted out to accommodate groups of 25 or more; reckon on paying at least £75 per person per week for the former and from £350 per person per week for the latter. Properties in Umbria might cost a touch less, and rates drop considerably outside July and August – often a day or so either way can make a difference of hundreds of pounds. Rental prices usually include insurance, water and electricity, and sometimes linen, cooking and maid service in the more posh places. Check carefully what is and isn't included. Italian villa companies are **notorious** for their added "extras", so read all printed information diligently. The same property often appears in several

brochures, so shop around. The term "villa" is also a loose one – your dream medieval retreat may turn out to be a concrete monstrosity. Villas and farmhouses often form part of complexes, with apartments and wings rented out to various groups, so privacy can become an issue (it's common too for the owner to live on or near the property). Check that the swimming pool attached to the villa is for your sole use – the "shared pool" is very common.

● **Specialist holidays**. Several operators offer walking tours, riding holidays, cycling trips, art and archeology holidays, and food and wine jaunts. Many are group tours and most don't come cheap: accommodation, food, local transport and the services of a guide are nearly always included, and a week's half-board holiday can cost £1000 or more per person. As a result there is a growing trend for smaller packaged and self-guided activity trips for individuals or groups of friends, particularly among walking and cycling companies. Such trips may be half the price of escorted trips – "transparent pricing" policies should enable you to see just how much you're spending and where your money's going.

● **Short-break deals**. Florence is a standby in major holiday companies' "Italian City Break" pro-

VILLAS, FARMHOUSES AND APARTMENTS

Bridgewater (☎0161/787 8587). A company with over 25 years' experience of apartments in Florence, Pisa and Lucca, *agriturismo* and country hotels in Umbria, farmhouses and villas: especially strong on mostly modern houses on the Tuscan coast.

Carefree Italy (☎01293/552 277). Farmhouses and villas, often in shared complexes, in Tuscany and Umbria: also has a range of small hotels and city apartments.

Cottages to Castles (☎01622/726 883). Over 100 properties, cottages, villas and apartments in Tuscany alone, plus a more limited selection in Umbria.

CV Travel (☎020/7581 0851). Expensive and well-chosen villas and farmhouses at the top of the market, usually with private pool, in Tuscany and Umbria.

Hello Italy (☎01483/284 011). Village properties, studios and farmhouses, including hideaways in the little-known Lunigiana region in northern Tuscany.

Ilios Travel (☎01403/240 843). Ask for the *Italian Collection* brochure: strong on quality Umbrian villas with pools; also some Tuscan properties in good rural locations.

Invitation to Tuscany (☎020/7603 7111). Villas with pools, apartments in villa, farm and historic property complexes, plus the chance to hire these complexes (sleeping up to 25) in their entirety.

Italian Chapters (☎020/7722 9560). The largest of the villa specialists, handling bookings for major Italian holiday home companies.

Italian Life (☎0113/281 8811). Villas and farms across the region in the mid- and top range: also apartments on wine estates.

Landmark Trust (☎01628/825 925). Stay in the Brownings' Casa Guidi in Florence, but book early.

Simply Tuscany & Umbria (☎020/8995 9323). A good selection of mostly small, stylish apartments, usually sleeping 2–6, plus a few villas and a selection of small family-run rural hotels. Also offers fly-drive options and short breaks in Florence.

Solemar (☎020/8371 8540). One of the biggest companies, with over 1000 properties on their books: covers areas such as the Mugello in Tuscany – often untouched by other operators.

Traditional Tuscany (☎01877/382 999). Offers B&B in Florentine palaces and on working farms and vineyards, plus a selection of some 25 villas and converted farms at competitive prices.

Tuscan Holidays (☎015394/31120). A small company with carefully selected homes in central Tuscany, most with pools in working vineyards.

Tuscany Now (☎020/7272 5469). This company's 60 or so villas are among the most luxurious in either region: also has cheaper but high-quality apartments in farmhouse and hamlet complexes.

Vacanze in Italia (☎08700/772 772). Some 420 mainly upmarket properties (modern and traditional) in both provinces.

Veronica Cotgrove (☎020/7267 2423). Carefully chosen villas and apartments in both regions, including some very exclusive properties.

---

grammes; reckon on spending about £250–450 per person for three nights, depending on season and the class of hotel. Always check precisely where your hotel is located: cheaper places may be some way from the city centre. More adventurous companies such as Citalia, Kirker and Magic Cities (Magic of Italy) offer breaks to smaller centres such as Lucca, Assisi and elsewhere.

● **Fly-drive deals**. If you want to hire a car in Italy, it's well worth checking with tour operators before you leave as most deals work out a lot cheaper than hiring on the spot. Italian Escapades and Citalia have good prices (from £250 per week), and check out also Sunvil and Italiatour!, who both offer some kind of fly-drive deal. If you

have bought your own flight through a regular agent, they can (or you can) book a car in advance through companies like Holiday Autos (see p.30).

● **Language courses**. An excellent way of learning Italian is to take a package, combining accommodation with tuition. There are a great many places where you can do this, usually offering courses of varying levels of intensity for between one and three months. Reckon on paying around £600 for a four-week course, including accommodation, which will normally be with an Italian family. For details, contact the British Institute of Florence, Palazzo Lanfredini, Lungarno Guicciardini 9, 50100 Florence, or Università Italiana per Stranieri, Palazzo Gallenga, Palazzo

Fortebraccio 4, 06100 Perugia – both of which are long-established and run regular courses. In the UK, try Euro-Academy (☎020/8686 2363), which runs Italian language lessons in small groups at Florence's Università Europa, or CESA Languages Abroad (☎01872/225 300).

GETTING THERE FROM IRELAND

No airline offers direct flights from Ireland to Tuscany or Umbria, but there are direct Aer Lingus and Alitalia flights to Milan from **Cork** and **Dublin**, with at least one flight daily between Ireland and Italy. The least expensive way of flying from Ireland to central Italy is to get to London and then catch a Pisa- or Florence-bound plane from there. For example, there are numerous daily flights from Dublin and other Irish airports (Cork, Kerry and Knock) to London operated by Ryanair, with connections on to their Stansted to Pisa flights. Aer Lingus and British Midland also offer cheap flights to London which cost from around IR£60 for a return to Luton or Stansted, though the cost of the bus and underground journeys across London may make the total cost greater than an Aer Lingus or British Midland fare to Heathrow.

From Belfast, there are British Airways and British Midland flights to Heathrow, but the cheapest service is the Jersey European run to Luton, at around £85 return. From Dublin you can slightly undercut the plane's price by getting a **Eurotrain** ticket (IR£45 return), but from Belfast you'll save nothing by taking the train and ferry. For the best youth/student deals from either city, go to USIT (see box below).

AIRLINES, AGENTS AND TOUR OPERATORS IN IRELAND

AIRLINES

Aer Lingus, 46 Castle St, Belfast (☎028/9024 5151); 40 Upper O'Connell St, Dublin (☎01/737 7470); 2 Academy St, Cork (☎021/327 155); 136 O'Connell St, Limerick (☎061/474 239).

Alitalia, 63 Dawson St, Dublin (☎01/677 5171; *www.alitalia.it*).

British Airways, Belfast reservations, 9 Fountain Centre, College St, Belfast (☎0345/222 111); Dublin reservations (☎1800/626 747). *www.british-airways.com*

British Midland, Belfast reservations (☎0345/554 554); Dublin reservations (☎01/282 8833).

Jersey European Airways, Belfast reservations (☎0990/696 696).

Ryanair, Belfast reservations, call London (☎00541/569 569; *www.ryanair.com*) or Dublin; Dublin reservations (☎01/609 7800).

AGENTS AND TOUR OPERATORS

Budget Travel, 134 Lower Baggot St, Dublin 2 (☎01/661 1866). Flight-only charters.

Thomas Cook, 11 Donegall Place, Belfast BT1 5AJ (☎028/9055 4455); 118 Grafton St, Dublin (☎01/677 1721). Mainstream package holiday and flight agent, with occasional discount offers.

United Travel, Stillorgan Bowl, Stillorgan, Dublin (☎01/288 2555). Scheduled flights, charters and packages to Italy.

USIT, branches at: 19 Aston Quay, O'Connell Bridge, Dublin 2 (☎01/602 1777); 10–11 Market Parade, Patrick St, Cork (☎021/270 900); Fountain Centre, College St, Belfast BT1 6ET (☎028/9032 4073). Student and youth specialist.

GETTING THERE FROM NORTH AMERICA

There are no direct flights from North America to Tuscany or Umbria, but you can fly to Rome (or less conveniently, Milan) from a number of US and Canadian cities, then move on by internal flight or by land. There are regular flights to Pisa and Florence from Milan and Rome, plus flights from Milan to Perugia, as well as a host of rail connections, including a twice-daily direct service between Florence and Rome's Fiumicino airport.

SHOPPING FOR TICKETS

Barring special offers, the cheapest of the airlines' published fares is usually an **Apex** ticket, although this will carry certain restrictions: you have to book – and pay – at least 21 days before departure, spend at least seven days abroad (maximum stay three months), and you tend to get penalized if you change your schedule. On transatlantic routes, there are also winter **Super Apex** tickets, sometimes known as "Eurosavers" – slightly cheaper than an ordinary Apex, but limiting your stay to between seven and 21 days. Some airlines also issue **Special Apex** tickets to people younger than 24, often extending the maximum stay to a year. Many airlines offer youth or student fares to **under 26s**; a passport or driving licence are sufficient proof of age, though these tickets are subject to availability and can have eccentric booking conditions. It's worth remembering that most cheap return fares involve spending at least one Saturday night away and

that many will only give a percentage refund if you need to cancel or alter your journey, so make sure you check the restrictions carefully before buying a ticket.

You can normally cut costs further by going through a **specialist flight agent** – either a **consolidator**, who buys up blocks of tickets from the airlines and sells them at a discount, or a **discount agent**, who in addition to dealing with discounted flights may also offer special student and youth fares and a range of other travel-related services such as travel insurance, rail passes, car rentals, tours and so on. Bear in mind, though, that penalties for changing your plans can be stiff. Remember too that these companies make their money by dealing in bulk – don't expect them to answer lots of questions. Some agents specialize in **charter flights**, which may be cheaper than anything available on a scheduled flight, but again departure dates are fixed and withdrawal penalties are high (check the refund policy). If you travel a lot, **discount travel clubs** are another option – the annual membership fee may be worth it for benefits such as cut-price air tickets and car rental.

Don't automatically assume that tickets purchased through a travel specialist will be cheapest – once you get a quote, check with the airlines and you may turn up an even better deal. Be advised also that the pool of travel companies is swimming with sharks – exercise caution and *never* deal with a company that demands cash up front or refuses to accept payment by credit card.

Regardless of where you buy your ticket, **fares** will depend on the season: highest from June through to the end of August; fares drop during "shoulder" season (roughly April–May, and September–October), and further still during the low season, between the end of October and the end of March – excluding Christmas and New Year. Note also that flying on Friday, Saturday or Sunday will add about US$40–60 (Can$60–90); price ranges quoted below assume midweek travel. Taxes usually run an extra US$30–40 (Can$50–80), depending on the airports involved.

FLIGHTS FROM THE US

Alitalia, the international airline of Italy, flies the widest choice of routes between the US and Italy.

AIRLINES IN THE US AND CANADA

Air Canada (in BC ☎1-800/663-3721; in Alberta, Saskatchewan and Manitoba ☎1-800/542-8940; in eastern Canada ☎1-800/268-7240; in US ☎1-800/776-3000; www.aircanada.ca). Most Canadian cities to Rome (via various European capitals), in partnership with Alitalia.

Air France (in US ☎1-800/237-2747; in Canada ☎1-800/667-2747; www.airfrance.fr). Major US and Canadian cities to Rome and Florence (via Paris).

Alitalia (☎1-800/223-5730; in New York ☎1-800/442-5860; in Canada ☎1-800/361-8336; www.alitalia.com). Boston, Chicago, Los Angeles, Miami, Newark, New York/JFK and Toronto to Rome and Milan, with connecting flights to Florence, Pisa and Perugia.

Canadian Airlines (in Canada ☎1-800/665-1177; in US ☎1-800/426-7000; www.cdnair.com). Toronto and Vancouver to Rome.

Continental Airlines (☎1-800/231-0856; www.continental.com). Newark to Milan and Rome nonstop.

Delta Airlines (in US ☎1-800/241-4141; in Canada, call directory enquiries, ☎1-800/555-1212 for local toll-free number; www.delta-air.com). New York to Rome nonstop; flights from Atlanta, Cincinnati, Los Angeles and Orlando in co-operation with Sabena (via Brussels).

KLM (in US ☎1-800/374-7747; in Canada ☎1-800/361-5073; www.klm.com). In partnership with Northwest, flies from many US and Canadian cities to Rome and Florence (via Amsterdam).

Lufthansa (in US ☎1-800/645-3880; in Canada ☎1-800/563-5954; www.lufthansa.com). Many US and Canadian cities to Rome, Florence and Pisa (via Frankfurt).

Northwest Airlines (☎1-800/447-4747). See KLM.

Sabena (☎1-800/955-2000; www.sabena-usa.com). Atlanta, Boston, Chicago and New York to Rome and Florence (via Brussels).

Swissair (in US ☎1-800/221-4750; in Canada ☎1-800/267-9477; www.swissair.com). Many US and Canadian cities to Rome (via Zurich or Geneva).

TWA (☎1-800/892-4141; www.twa.com). New York/JFK to Rome nonstop.

United Airlines (☎1-800/538-2929; www.ual.com). Many US cities to Milan nonstop.

US-based carriers United, Delta and TWA fly from many cities to Rome or Milan, and several other European carriers fly via their respective capitals (see box above).

Standard round-trip fares vary a little between airlines, although the only true variations start with the special offers that may be available, and even these have a tendency to be mirrored from one carrier to another. At the time of writing, the cheapest Apex fares **to Rome** were: from New York, US$680 in low season, $1020 in high season; from Chicago or Miami, $770/$1110; from Los Angeles or San Francisco, $920/$1260.

However, consolidators will always be able to beat these prices, typically by $100–150; more if you're a student or under 26. The airlines themselves occasionally offer special promotional fares that are even cheaper. When available, these start at around $450 round-trip from New York to Rome, flying midweek in low season, through around $650 during the shoulder season and rising to about $750 in the peak months.

Florence is "common-rated" with Rome in most airlines' fare schedules, meaning the standard fares are identical, but that's only a deal if you're prepared to pay the standard rate. In practice, there are fewer discounted deals to Florence because there's less competition in that market. That said, consolidators like Skylink can often produce fares to Florence that match those to Rome. **Pisa** and **Perugia** are also common-rated with Rome, but fares to those cities are hardly ever discounted.

FLIGHTS FROM CANADA

The only airline to fly direct to Italy from Canada is Alitalia, which flies from Toronto to Rome, with the usual connections to other cities in Italy. Canadian Air and Air Canada fly from more Canadian cities, but their flights entail a stop in one of various European hubs en route. Several other European airlines also fly from the major Canadian cities by way of their capitals (see box above).

Flights **to Rome** from Toronto are invariably cheapest: Apex fares tend to come in at around Can$860 in low season, $1350 in high season. From Montreal, figure $900/1100; from Vancouver, $1250/1520. However, as explained

DISCOUNT TRAVEL COMPANIES IN THE US AND CANADA

Air Courier Association, 191 University Blvd, Suite 300, Denver, CO 80206 (☎303/278-8810; *www.aircourier.org*). Courier flight broker.

Airhitch, 2641 Broadway, New York, NY 10025 (☎1-800/326-2009 or 212/864-2000; *www.airhitch.org*). Standby-seat broker. For a set price, they guarantee to get you on a flight as close to your preferred destination as possible, within a week.

Airtech, 584 Broadway, Suite 1007, New York, NY 10012 (☎1-800/575-TECH or 212/219-7000; *www.airtech.com*). Standby-seat broker; also deals in consolidator fares and courier flights.

Council Travel, 205 E 42nd St, New York, NY 10017 (☎1-800/226-8624 or 212/822-2700; *www.counciltravel.com*), and branches in many other US cities. Student/budget travel agency.

Educational Travel Center, 438 N Frances St, Madison, WI 53703 (☎1-800/747-5551 or 608/256-5551; *www.edtrav.com*). Student/youth and consolidator fares.

International Student Exchange Flights, 5010 E Shea Blvd, Suite 104A, Scottsdale, AZ 85254 (☎602/951-1177; *www.isecard.com*). Student/youth fares, student IDs.

New Frontiers/Nouvelles Frontières, 12 E 33rd St, New York, NY 10016 (☎1-800/366-6387); 1001 Sherbrook East, Suite 720, Montreal, Quebec H2L 1L3 (☎514/526-8444); and other branches in LA, San Francisco and Quebec City.

French discount travel firm. *www.nouvelles-frontieres.com*

Now Voyager, 74 Varick St, Suite 307, New York, NY 10013 (☎212/431-1616; *www.nowvoyagertravel.com*). Courier flight broker and consolidator.

Skylink, 265 Madison Ave, 5th Fl, New York, NY 10016 (☎1-800/AIR-ONLY or 212/573-8980; e-mail to *skylinkny@msn.com*) with branches in Chicago, Los Angeles, Montreal, Toronto and Washington DC. Consolidator.

STA Travel, 10 Downing St, New York, NY 10014 (☎1-800/777-0112 or 212/627-3111; *www.sta-travel.com*), and other branches in the Los Angeles, San Francisco and Boston areas. Worldwide discount travel firm specializing in student/youth fares; also student IDs, travel insurance, car rental, rail passes, etc.

Travac Tours, 989 6th Ave, New York NY 10018 (☎1-800/872-8800 or 212/563-3303; *www.thetravelsite.com*). Consolidator.

Travel CUTS, 187 College St, Toronto, ON M5T 1P7 (☎416/979-2406; *www.travelcuts.com*), and other branches all over Canada. Organization specializing in student fares, IDs and other travel services.

UniTravel, 1177 N Warson Rd, St Louis, MO 63132 (☎1-800/325-2222 or 314/569-2501; *www.flightsforless.com*). Consolidator.

above, consolidators will usually be able to beat these fares, and airline promotional fares, when available, are the best deals of all.

For advice on fares to **Florence**, **Pisa** and **Perugia**, see the USA section.

ORGANIZED TOURS

There are dozens of companies operating **group travel** and tours in Italy, ranging from full-blown luxury escorted tours to small groups sticking to specialized itineraries; if you're happy to stay in one (or two) places, you can also of course simply book a hotel-plus-flight deal, or, if you're keener to self-cater, rent a villa or a farmhouse for a week or two. Prices vary wildly, so check what you are getting for your money (many don't include the cost of the airfare). Reckon on paying at least $1500 for a ten-day touring vacation, up to as much as $3000 for a fourteen-day city package.

Tour operators (like tourists) generally focus more on Tuscany than Umbria, and most tours are based around walking itineraries in Tuscany (not only because it's a nice way to experience this area, but also because the logistics of inn-to-inn walking are the sort of thing best left to a tour company). These hiking and biking tours typically cost $1500–2500 a week (excluding air fare) because they're all pretty luxurious and gastronomic. Package bus/train tours of northern Italy, which usually take in Florence and often Pisa (and rarely Perugia), may cost anywhere from $1000 to $3000 for two weeks, depending on the standard of accommodation. Independent tours and city breaks include accommodation and transportation, but beyond that they leave you to your own devices – nightly double room rates can range from $60 for small city hotels to $200 or more for country villas.

NORTH AMERICAN TOUR OPERATORS

Although phone numbers are given here, you're better off making tour reservations through your local travel agent. An agent will make all the phone calls, sort out the snafus and arrange flights, insurance and the like – all at no extra cost to you.

Abercrombie & Kent (☎1-800/323-7308; *www.abercrombiekent.com*). Deluxe village-to-village hiking and biking tours, rail journeys.

Adventure Center (☎1-800/227-8747; *www.adventurecenter.com*). Walking/camping in Tuscany.

Backroads (☎1-800/462-2848; *www.backroads.com*). Deluxe village-to-village hiking and biking tours.

BCT Scenic Walking (☎1-800/473-1210; *www.bctwalk.com*). Village-to-village.

Classic Journeys (☎1-800/200-3887; *www.classicjourneys.com*). More village-to-village walking.

European Incoming Services (☎1-800/443-1644). Independent tours, villa stays.

Mountain Travel-Sobek (in US ☎1-800/227-2384; in Canada ☎1-800/282-8747; *www.mtsobek.com*). Village-to-village perambulating.

New Frontiers (☎1-800/366-6387; *www.nouvelles-frontieres.com*). City breaks and independent packages.

Saga Holidays (☎1-800/343-0273; *www.sagaholidays.com*). "Road Scholar" educational tours for seniors include a 12-day intensive stay in Florence.

Wilderness Travel (☎1-800/368-2794; *www.wildernesstravel.com*). Inn-to-inn walking through Tuscany.

TRAVELLING VIA BRITAIN

It might be a good idea to transit via Britain, since there's a broad range of well-priced flights available to London from all North America, and there is a wide choice of options to Italy once there. Flying is the most straightforward way to get from Britain to Italy, and prices are competitive; see above (pp.3–6) for full details of flights and rail deals from Britain and Ireland.

If you're interested in seeing more of Europe en route to Italy, travelling by train from Britain may be more appealing, though be prepared for prices comparable to air fares if you're over 26, and a shortest possible journey time of at least 18 hours from London. If you're under 26, however, a range of youth fares is available, which have to be bought in Britain, or – the most attractive option – a **Eurail Youthpass**, which gives unlimited travel in seventeen countries and costs $499 for 21 days, $623 for one month or $882 for two months. It must be bought before leaving home (outlets are given below), as must the other kinds of Eurail passes. For over-26s there's the standard **Eurail pass**, giving 15 consecutive days' first-class travel for $554, 21 days for $718, 1 month for $890 or 2 months for $1260. The **Eurail Flexipass** entitles you to 10 days' first-class travel within a two-month period for $654, or 15 days for $862; the under-26s' **Eurail Youth**

Flexipass costs $458 for 10 days, $599 for 15. If you're travelling in a group, it might be worth buying the **Eurail Saverpass**, which for $470 per person gives 15 days' first-class travel for 2 or more people travelling together – or 3 or more from April to September; the 21-day version costs $610 and the one-month $756. Finally, the **Eurail Drive Pass**, valid for any 7 days within a period of 2 months, gives you 4 days' first-class rail travel plus 3 days' car rental for around $350, with options for additional days at large discounts.

Canadians can also buy Eurail passes, though they must again be purchased before arrival in Europe.

For details on rail passes issued by the Italian train company, see p.27.

RAIL CONTACTS IN NORTH AMERICA

CIT Tours, 342 Madison Ave, Suite 207, New York, NY 10173 (☎1-800/223-7987; *www.fs-on-line.com*).

DER Travel, 9501 W Divon Ave, Suite 400, Rosemont, IL 60018 (☎1-800/421-2929; *www.dertravel.com*).

Rail Europe, 226 Westchester Ave, White Plains, NY 10604 (in US ☎1-800/438-7245; in Canada ☎1-800/361-7245; *www.raileurope.com*). Official Eurail Pass agent in North America.

GETTING THERE FROM AUSTRALIA & NEW ZEALAND

Carriers flying directly (though not nonstop) from Australia to Rome include: Alitalia, who, in conjunction with other airlines, have six flights weekly from Sydney and Melbourne (via Bangkok); Qantas, who have three flights weekly from Melbourne (via Bangkok) plus two flights weekly from Sydney (via Bangkok); Garuda, with one flight weekly from Melbourne (via Denpasar); Thai Airways, with two flights weekly from Melbourne and six from Sydney (via Bangkok). In addition, KLM have six flights weekly from Sydney with a change in Amsterdam; and Lauda Air have three flights weekly from Melbourne and Sydney with a change in Vienna to a connecting flight on either Lauda Air or Austrian Airlines. There are also indirect services available with, among others, Malaysia Airlines and Japan Airlines (with an overnight stop in Kuala Lumpur or Tokyo), Singapore Airlines (via Singapore), Cathay Pacific (via Hong Kong), and British Airways (various southeast Asian routes).

There are no direct flights to Rome **from New Zealand**. Indirect flights are with Alitalia in conjunction with other carriers, from Auckland via Sydney and Hong Kong/Singapore; Garuda, from Auckland via Denpasar; British Airways from

AIRLINES IN AUSTRALIA AND NEW ZEALAND

Alitalia, 455 Bourke St, Melbourne (☎03/9670 0171); 118 Albert St, Milson's Point, North Sydney (☎1300/653 757); 229 Queen St, Auckland (☎09/379 4457). *www.alitalia.it*

British Airways, Level 4, 50 Franklin St, Melbourne (☎03/9603 1133); Level 19, 259 George St, Sydney (☎02/8904 8800); 154 Queen St, Auckland (☎09/356 8690). *www.british-airways.com*

Cathay Pacific, Level 12, 8 Spring St, Sydney (☎13 1747); Level 3, 31 Queen St, Melbourne (☎13 1747); Floor 11, 205 Queen St, Auckland (☎09/379 0861).

Garuda, 45 Bourke St, Melbourne (☎03/9654 2522); 55 Hunter St, Sydney (☎1300/365 331); 120 Albert St, Auckland (☎09/366 1855).

Japan Airlines, Floor 14, Darling Park, 201 Sussex St, Sydney (☎02/9272 1111); Level 6, 250 Collins St, Melbourne (☎03/9654 2733); Floor 12, 120 Albert St, Auckland (☎09/379 9906). *www.jal.co.jp*

KLM, Nauru House, 80 Collins St, Melbourne (☎03/9654 5222; toll-free 1800/500 747); 5 Elizabeth St, Sydney (☎02/9231 6333; toll-free 1800/500 747). *www.klm.com*

Lauda Air, Level 7, 84 William St, Melbourne (☎03/9600 4000; toll-free 1800/642 438); Level 11, 143 Macquarie St, Sydney (☎02/9251 6155; toll-free 1800 642 438). *www.laudaair.com*

Malaysia Airlines, 388 George St, Sydney (☎1300/656 566); Floor 12, Swanson Centre, 12–26 Swanson St, Auckland (☎09/373 2741). *www.malaysiaairlines.co.my*

Qantas, 50 Franklin St, Melbourne (☎13 1211); 70 Hunter St, Sydney (☎13 1211); 154 Queen St, Auckland (☎09/357 8900; toll-free 0800/808 767). *www.qantas.com.au*

Singapore Airlines, 17–19 Bridge St, Sydney (☎13 1011); 414 Collins St, Melbourne (☎13 1011); West Plaza Building, cnr Fanshawe and Albert streets, Auckland (☎09/303 2129). *www.singaporeair.com*

Thai Airways, 250 Collins St, Melbourne (☎1300/651 960); 75–77 Pitt St, Sydney (☎1300/651 960); 22 Fanshawe St, Auckland (☎09/377 3886). *www.thaiair.com*

Anywhere Travel, 345 Anzac Parade, Kingsford, Sydney (☎02/9663 0411).

Budget Travel, 16 Fort St, Auckland; other branches around the city (☎09/366 0061; toll-free 0800/808 040).

CIT, 422 Collins St, Melbourne (☎03/9670 1322); 263 Clarence St, Sydney (☎02/9299 4754), as well as Brisbane, Adelaide and Perth.

Destinations Unlimited, Level 7, 220 Queen St, Auckland (☎09/373 4033).

European Travel Office (ETO), 122 Rosslyn St, West Melbourne (☎03/9329 8844); 20th Floor, 133 Castlereagh St, Sydney (☎02/9267 7727).

Flight Centres, Australia: 82 Elizabeth St, Sydney (☎02/9229 6611); 19 Bourke St, Melbourne (☎03/9650 2899); plus other branches nationwide (☎13 1600 for nearest branch). New Zealand: 205–225 Queen St, Auckland (☎09/309 6171); other branches countrywide (0800/FLIGHTS for nearest branch).

Italia Mia, 101 Bridport St, Melbourne (☎03/9682 8098).

Northern Gateway, 22 Cavenagh St, Darwin (☎08/8941 1394).

Passport Travel, 401 St Kilda Rd, Melbourne (☎03/9867 3888).

STA Travel, Australia: 855 George St, Sydney (☎02/9212 1255); 256 Flinders St, Melbourne (☎03/9654 7266); other offices in state capitals and major universities (phone ☎13 1776 for nearest branch). New Zealand: Travellers' Centre, 10 High St, Auckland (☎09/309 0458); also branches in Wellington, Christchurch, Dunedin, Palmerston North, Hamilton and major universities.

Thomas Cook, Australia: 175 Pitt St, Sydney (☎02/9231 2877; toll-free 1800/801 002); 257 Collins St, Melbourne (☎03/9282 0222); branches in other state capitals (phone ☎13 1771 for nearest branch). New Zealand: 159 Queen St, Auckland (☎09/379 3924; toll-free 0800/353 535).

Tymtro Travel, Level 8, 130 Pitt St, Sydney (☎02/9223 2211; local call-charge 1300/652 969).

Ya'lla Tours, 661 Glenhuntly Rd, Caulfield, Vic. (☎03/9523 1988; local call-charge 1300/362 844).

Auckland via Singapore/Bangkok; Qantas from Auckland, Christchurch or Wellington via Bangkok; Japan Airlines from Auckland with overnight stop in Tokyo/Osaka; and Thai from Auckland via Bangkok.

The lowest **standard return fare** from Australia to Rome via Bangkok is A$2300/3200 (low/high season) with Alitalia; however fares as low as A$1800 are periodically on offer from travel agents. The lowest standard return fare from New Zealand (via Bangkok) to Rome is NZ$2500/3000 (low/high season) with Thai Airways.

Agencies such as those listed in the box above might well be able to undercut the prices offered directly by the airlines – STA is a particularly good and long-established company. Alternatively you could investigate a package

with an outfit such as Thomas Cook or with one of the airlines (the Italian tourist board – see p.23 – can supply names of companies offering good packages). In addition, more specialized packages are available from Rushdown Travel (mainly gastronomic tours, A$4500 per person including air fares, accommodation, transport, meals and cooking classes), Italia Mia (15-day gastronomic and cultural tours, A$8000 per person including air fares, accommodation, transport, meals and cooking classes), CIT (villa accommodation from A$600 per week for two people, and a large range of other deals), European Travel Office (villa and farmhouse accommodation, with olive oil and wine tours, all meals, plus sightseeing excursions, from A$1500 per person for eight days), and Ya'lla Tours (villa accommodation from A$400 per week for two people).

RED TAPE AND VISAS

British and other EU citizens can enter Italy, and stay as long as they like, simply on production of a valid passport. Citizens of the United States, Canada, Australia and New Zealand need only a valid passport, too, but are limited to stays of ninety days. All other nationals should consult the relevant embassies about visa requirements.

Legally, you're required to register with the police within three days of entering Italy, though if you're staying at a hotel this will be done for you. Some policemen are more punctilious about this than ever, though others would be astonished by any attempt to register yourself at the local police station while on holiday.

ITALIAN EMBASSIES AND CONSULATES

AUSTRALIA Embassy: 12 Grey St, Yarralumla, ACT 2600 (☎02/6273 3333). Consulates: 509 St Kilda Rd, Melbourne, VIC 3000 (☎03/9867 5744); Level 45, 1 Macquarie Place, Sydney, NSW 2000 (☎02/9392 7900). .

CANADA Embassy: 275 Slater St, 21st Floor, Ottawa (☎613/232-2403). Consulates: 3489 Drummond Ave, Montreal (☎514/849-8351); 136 Beverley St, Toronto (☎416/977-1566); 1200 Burrard St, Suite 705, Vancouver (☎604/684-5575); and others in Quebec City and Edmonton.

IRELAND 63–65 Northumberland Rd, Dublin (☎01/601 744); 7 Richmond Park, Belfast (☎028/9066 8854).

NEW ZEALAND 34 Grant Rd, Thorndon, Wellington (☎04/473 5339).

UK Embassy: 38 Eaton Place, London SW1 (☎020/7235 9371). Consulates: 32 Melville Crescent, Edinburgh EH3 7HA (☎0131/226 3631); 111 Piccadilly, Manchester M1 2HY (☎0161/236 9024).

USA Embassy: 1601 Fuller St, Washington, DC 20009 (☎202/328-5550). Consulates: 690 Park Ave, New York, NY (☎212/737-9100 or 439-8600); 12400 Wilshire Blvd, Suite 300, Los Angeles, CA (☎310/820-0622)

COSTS, MONEY AND BANKS

The days are long gone when Italy was a relatively inexpensive country to visit: the economic boom and the glut of visitors have conspired to make prices roughly on a par with the UK, and in certain cases even more expensive – Florence is one of the three priciest Italian cities, with Milan and Venice. However, prices do vary a lot in Tuscany and Umbria, and even as popular a place as Siena is noticeably less costly than Florence.

AVERAGE COSTS

Most **basic things** are inexpensive compared with Britain: delicious picnic meals can be put together for under £5/$8, and a pizza or plate of pasta with a glass of wine will set you back around £7/$10 on average – though in some of the larger towns, Florence in particular, such budget places can be difficult to find. **Buses** and **trains** are comparatively cheap too, the 97-kilometre rail journey from Florence to Siena, for instance, is L16,400 (around £6/$9) for a second-class return. Wine is cheap, but other **drinks** are not: soft drinks or coffee all cost around the same price as in Britain, if not more, and a glass of beer can cost £3/$5 in central Florence (less elsewhere), even more if you decide to sit down.

Room rates start at £20/$30 for a double room in a one-star hotel, though again in Florence you won't find much under £30/$45. Overall, if you're really watching your budget – camping, hitching a little, buying food from shops and markets – you could get by on around £20/$35 per person per day; a more realistic **average minimum daily budget** for a couple staying in one-star hotels, taking trains and eating one modest-priced meal out a day, would be in the region of £50/$75 per person. If you want to allow yourself the occasional extravagance or an intensive bout of museum-visiting, then you'll need £60/$90 per day – and in view of the disproportionate cost of single hotel rooms, a person travelling alone can expect this figure to go about 20 percent higher.

Time of year makes a big difference. During the height of summer, from Easter to September, hotel prices tend to escalate; outside the season, however, you can often negotiate lower rates in the smaller towns, and should find rooms in the cheapest hotels in the bigger places. State-owned museums offer **reductions** to people under 18 and for over-60s, but only a handful of other attractions accept International Student ID Card (ISIC) cards, and buses and trains never do – though Alitalia's domestic routes are subject to a 25-percent reduction if you're **under 26 or a student**.

LIRE AND EUROS

The Italian unit of money is the lira (plural lire), always abbreviated as L; for some time the relatively weak lire has meant the rate has hovered around L2800 to the pound sterling, about L1600 to the US dollar. Banknotes come in denominations of L1000, L2000, L5000, L10,000, L50,000, L100,000 and L500,000, and coins as L50, L100, L200, L500 and L1000. You might also be given a telephone token or *gettone* in change, which is worth L200.

Italy is one of eleven European Union countries which on January 1, 1999, formed an economic union and started using a single currency, the **euro**, whose value is fixed at L1936.27, US$1.0418, and £0.6425. Initially, it will only be possible to make paper transactions in the new currency, and the lira will remain, in effect, the normal unit of currency in Italy. Euro notes and coins will be issued at the beginning of 2002, and will replace the lira entirely by the end of that year.

TRAVELLERS' CHEQUES

The easiest and safest way to carry your money is as **travellers' cheques**, available for a small commission (1 percent of the amount ordered) from any major bank and some building societies, whether or not you have an account. You'll usually – though not always – pay a small commission, too, when you exchange money using travellers' cheques – again around 1 percent of the amount changed, although some banks will make a standard charge per cheque regardless of its denomination – usually around L6000. Thomas Cook offices don't charge for cashing their own cheques, and American Express offices don't charge for cashing anyone's cheques. Alternatively, most banks in Britain can issue current account holders with a **Eurocheque card** and chequebook, with which you can get cash from the majority of banks in Italy (including from cash-dispensing machines, which can help to avoid the queues); you'll pay a few pounds service charge but usually no commission on transactions.

CREDIT AND CHARGE CARDS

Major **credit and charge cards** – Visa, Access/Mastercard, American Express and Diner's Club – are accepted in many shops, and for cash advances in many banks. However, it's an idea to have at least some Italian money for when you first arrive, and you can buy lire in advance from nearly all banks, though you're not supposed to exceed L400,000 in cash.

In Italy, the best place to change money is at a **cash machine** or ATM, known as *bancomat* in Italian, found in all but the smallest towns and villages. Visa, American Express and, less commonly, Mastercard, can be used in the cash-dispensing machines. If you intend to withdraw cash on your card, make sure you have a personal identification number (PIN) that's designed to work overseas. The minimum single withdrawal is usually L50,000, the maximum daily amount L300,000–500,000. Credit card **cash advances** are treated as a loan and interest accrues on your account from the day of withdrawal. Cards can also be used for payment (for a fee of 1.5 percent) in most larger city stores, hotels and restaurants, but petrol stations and smaller establishments may still be reluctant to accept plastic – cash still reigns supreme in much of Italy, so check first before embarking on a big meal out.

BANKS

An increasing number of places with large numbers of tourists have machines that change money automatically (notes only). Otherwise the place to change money or travellers' cheques is at a **bank**, though the process can sometimes be excruciatingly slow. There are a few banking chains that you'll find nationwide, the Banca Nazionale del Lavoro, Banca d'Italia and Cassa di Risparmio, as well as regional chains like the Monte die Paschi di Siena. **Banking hours** are normally Monday to Friday mornings from 8.30am until 1pm, and for an hour in the afternoon (usually 3–4pm), though there are local variations on this – and larger banks in bigger towns and cities also increasingly open on a Saturday morning. Outside these times, the larger hotels will change money or travellers' cheques, although if you're staying in a reasonably large city the rate is invariably better at the train station exchange bureaux – normally open evenings and weekends.

EMERGENCY CASH

If you run out of money, or there is some kind of emergency, the quickest way to get **money sent out** is to contact your bank at home and have them wire the cash to the nearest bank. You can do the same thing through Thomas Cook or American Express if there is a branch nearby. You can also have cash sent out through Western Union to a nearby bank or post office – a process which takes two to five days; this is a last-ditch option, though, since commission rates are punitive.

WIRE SERVICES

Australia: American Express MoneyGram (☎9886 0666 in Sydney, elsewhere toll-free 1800/230 100); Western Union (☎3229 8610 in Brisbane, elsewhere toll-free 1800/649 565).

Britain: American Express MoneyGram (☎0800/894 887); Western Union (☎0800/833 833).

New Zealand: American Express MoneyGram Auckland (☎09/379 8243), Wellington (☎04/499 7899 or 473 7766); Western Union Auckland (☎09/302 0143).

USA and Canada: American Express MoneyGram (☎1-800/543-4080); Western Union (☎1-800/325-6000).

HEALTH AND INSURANCE

As an EU country, Italy has free reciprocal health agreements with other member states. You'll need to pick up an E111 form, available from major post offices. There's a similar arrangement with Australia, but nonetheless you're strongly advised to take out separate travel insurance. This way, you're covered against things being lost or stolen during your travels. For all non-EU citizens, some kind of travel insurance is essential.

Before you purchase insurance, check what cover you already have in other areas: Americans and Canadians, in particular, will often find they have some cover (see below). Some **home policies** cover your possessions abroad, for example; and if you pay for your trip with a credit card, some form of limited travel insurance may well be offered automatically by the **credit card company**. This can be quite comprehensive, anticipating anything from lost or stolen baggage and missed connections to charter companies going bankrupt, but check the small print carefully. For **medical treatment and drugs**, keep all receipts and claim the money back later. If you **have anything stolen** (including money), register the loss immediately with the local police – without their report you won't be able to claim. This also applies to North American policies – even if it's your best friend who has lost your prized possessions, you still have to report the loss to the police. The office to go to is the *Questura*, not the *carabinieri*.

If you plan to participate in any "**high-risk activities**" – and, depending on the insurer, this can extend to water sports, skiing, or even just hiking – you'll probably have to pay an extra premium; check carefully that any insurance policy you are considering will cover you in case of an accident.

BRITISH AND IRISH COVER

Most travel agents and tour operators will offer you insurance when you book your flight or holiday, and some will insist you take it. Note that if you have a good "all-risks" **home insurance** policy it may well cover your possessions against loss or theft even when overseas, and many **private medical schemes** also cover you when abroad – make sure you know the procedure and the helpline number. Otherwise, travel insurance schemes are sold by almost every travel agent or bank, and by specialist insurance companies (see box opposite). Most policies provide two weeks' basic cover in Italy for around £20, one month for around £25; in **Ireland**, a standard fourteen-day policy for travel in Europe will set you back around IR£21. Some banks and agents also offer an annual **multi-trip policy** with twelve months' cover for £50.

NORTH AMERICAN COVER

Before buying an insurance policy, check that you're not already covered. **Canadian provincial health plans** typically provide some overseas medical coverage, although they are unlikely to pick up the full tab in the event of a mishap. Holders of official **student/teacher/youth cards** are entitled to accident coverage and hospital in-patient benefits – the annual membership is far less than the cost of comparable insurance. **Students** may also find that their student health coverage extends during the vacations and for one term beyond the date of last enrolment. Bank and credit cards (particularly American Express) often provide certain levels of medical or other insurance, and travel insurance may also be included if you use a major credit or charge card to pay for your trip. **Homeowners' or renters'** insurance often covers theft or loss of documents, money and valuables while overseas. After exhausting the possibilities above, you might want to contact a specialist **travel insurance** company; your travel agent can usually recommend one, or see the box opposite.

Travel insurance **policies** vary: some are comprehensive while others cover only certain risks (accidents, illnesses, delayed or lost luggage, cancelled flights, etc). In particular, ask whether the policy pays medical costs up-front or reimburses you later, and whether it provides for medical evacuation to your home country. For policies that include lost or stolen luggage, check exactly what is and isn't covered, and make sure that the per-article limit will cover your most valuable possession.

The best **premiums** are usually to be had through student/youth travel agencies – ISIS policies, for example, cost around $70 for fifteen days (depending on level of coverage), $115 for a month, $165 for two months, $700 for a year.

AUSTRALIAN AND NEW ZEALAND COVER

Travel insurance in Australia and New Zealand is available through the airlines and travel agent groups or direct from insurance companies (see box below). A typical policy for Europe will cost A$190/NZ$220 for one month, A$270/NZ$320 for two months and A$330/NZ$400 for three months.

HEALTH PROBLEMS

If you're going to use your **E111** to get free treatment and prescriptions for medicines at the local rate, there's a complicated process to go through first. You have to go to the local **Unita Sanitaria**

Locale to exchange the E111 for a "certificate of entitlement" and a list of doctors and dentists that provide a service free of charge. The E111 will only get you immediate unconditional treatment if you're rushed into a hospital. If you're looking for repeat medication, take any empty bottles or capsules with you to the doctors – the brand-names often differ.

An Italian **chemist** (*farmacia*) is well qualified to give advice on minor ailments, and to dispense prescriptions, and there's generally one open all night in the bigger towns and cities. They work on a rota system, and you should find the address of the one currently open on any *farmacia* door. If you do require a **doctor** (*médico*), ask at your hotel for help in the first instance (or the local tourist office). Alternatively look in the Yellow Pages (*Pagine Gialle*): some larger towns have English-speaking doctors specifically earmarked to help visitors. Follow a similar procedure if you have dental problems. Keep any receipts for treatment or medicines for later insurance claims.

If you are taken **seriously ill** or involved in an accident, hunt out the nearest hospital and go to the *Pronto Soccorso* (casualty) section; in a real emergency phone ☎113 and ask for *ospedale* or *ambulanza*. Major train stations and airports

---

TRAVEL INSURANCE COMPANIES

BRITAIN AND IRELAND

Columbus Travel Insurance (☎020/7375 0011).
Endsleigh Insurance (☎020/7436 4451).
Liverpool Victoria (☎01202/292 333).

Royal & Sun Alliance – Dublin (☎01/677 1851).
Note: *Good-value policies are also available through Usit CAMPUS and STA (see p.4 for addresses).*

NORTH AMERICA

Access America (☎1-800/284-8300).
Carefree Travel Insurance (☎1-800/323-3149).
Desjardins Travel Insurance (Canada only; ☎1-800/463-7830).

International Student Insurance Service (ISIS), sold by STA Travel (☎1-800/777-0112).
Travel Guard (☎1-800/826-1300).
Travel Insurance Services (☎1-800/937-1387).
Worldwide Assistance (☎1-800/821-2828).

AUSTRALIA AND NEW ZEALAND

AFTA (☎02/9956 4800).
Cover More (☎9202 8000 in Sydney; elsewhere in Australia toll-free 1800/251 881).

Ready Plan, Australia (☎1300/555 017); New Zealand (☎09/379 3208).
UTAG, (☎9819 6855 in Sydney; elsewhere in Australia toll-free 1800/809 462).

CONTACTS FOR TRAVELLERS WITH DISABILITIES

BRITAIN AND IRELAND

Disability Action Group, 2 Annadale Ave, Belfast BT7 3JH (☎028/9049 1011). Information on access for disabled travellers abroad.

Holiday Care Service, 2nd Floor, Imperial Buildings, Victoria Rd, Horley, Surrey RH6 7PZ (☎01293/774 535). Provides information on all aspects of travel.

Irish Wheelchair Association, Blackheath Drive, Clontarf, Dublin 3 (☎01/833 8241). A national voluntary organization working with disabled people and offering related services for holidaymakers.

RADAR, 12 City Forum, 250 City Rd, London EC1V 8AS (☎020/7250 3222). A good source of advice on holidays and travel abroad.

Tripscope, The Courtyard, Evelyn Rd, London W4 5JL (☎ & Minicom 020/8994 9294, or 0345/585 641). National telephone information service offering transport and travel advice, free of charge.

USA AND CANADA

Access First, 45-A Pleasant St, Malden, MA 02148 (☎1-800/557-2047). Specializes in trips to Italy.

Directions Unlimited, 720 north Bedford Rd, Bedford Hills, NY 10507 (☎1-800/533 5343 or 914/241-1700). Specializes in customized tours for people with disabilities.

Jewish Rehabilitation Hospital, 3205 Place Alton Goldbloom, Montreal, PQ H7V 1R2 (☎450/688 9550, ext 226). Guidebooks and travel information.

Mobility International USA, PO Box 10767, Eugene, OR 97440 (☎541/343-1284; www.miusa.org). Information and referral services, access guides, tours and exchange programmes. Annual membership $35 (includes quarterly newsletter).

Society for the Advancement of Travel for the Handicapped (SATH), 347 5th Ave, Suite 610, New York, NY 10016 (☎212/447-7284 or 447-0027; www.sath.org). Non-profit travel-industry referral service that passes queries on to its members as appropriate; allow plenty of time for a response.

Travel Information Service, Moss Rehabilitation Hospital, 1200 West Tabor Rd, Philadelphia, PA 19141 (☎215/456-9603; www.mossresourcenet.org). Information and referral service.

Twin Peaks Press, Box 129, Vancouver, WA 98666; ☎360/694-2462 or 1-800/637-2256; www.pacifier.com/twinpeak). Publisher of the Directory of Travel Agencies for the Disabled ($19.95), listing more than 370 agencies worldwide; Travel for the Disabled ($14.95); the Directory of Accessible Van Rentals; and Wheelchair Vagabond ($9.95), loaded with personal tips.

Wheels Up!, (☎1-888/389-4335; www.wheelsup.com). Provides discounted air-fare, tour and cruise prices for disabled travellers, and also publishes a free monthly newsletter.

AUSTRALIA AND NEW ZEALAND

ACROD (Australian Council for the Rehabilitation of the Disabled), PO Box 60, Curtin, ACT 2605 (☎02/6282 4333); 24 Cabarita Rd, Cabarita, NSW (☎02/9743 2699).

Disabled Persons Assembly, 173 Victoria St, Wellington (☎04/801 9100).

---

often have first-aid stations with qualified doctors on hand.

The inhabitants of the Chianti and Umbrian hills are quite neurotic about the danger of **vipers** (*viperi*), to the extent of keeping serum in their fridges. The chances of being bitten by a snake are negligible, but if you want to be prepared for every eventuality, serum is available from most local chemists (less useful than it sounds, as it has to be kept chilled).

Should you be rummaging around in old farm buildings or collecting timber from a woodpile, keep an eye out for small **scorpions**, which can deliver nasty but not life-threatening stings. Low-lying zones on or near the coast, especially the once-swampy Maremma and Pisa areas, are plagued by mosquitoes (*zanzari*) and other insects from March till the end of the autumn. You can buy cheap little machines or sprays to zap them.

INFORMATION AND MAPS

Before you leave, it's well worth dropping in at the Italian State Tourist Office (ENIT) or writing to them for a selection of their free maps and brochures, though don't go mad – much of what they have is available in Italy itself. Worth grabbing are any accommodation listings they may have for the area you're interested in, town plans and maps of the regions. Note that many of these offices, however, can be laborious to deal with – phone lines, especially, are often constantly engaged. ENIT is on the Web at *www.enit.it*.

TOURIST OFFICES

Most Italian towns, and main city train stations and airports have a **tourist office**, known by any one of a number of acronyms: an APT (Azienda Promozione Turistica), an EPT (Ente Provinciale per il Turismo) – a provincial branch of the state organization – an IAT (Ufficio di Informazione e Accoglienza Turistica), or an AAST (Azienda Autonoma di Soggiorno e Turismo), a smaller local outfit. When there isn't one of any of these, there will sometimes be a Pro Loco office, usually in the smaller villages, which will have much the same kind of information but generally keep much shorter hours. All of these vary in degrees of usefulness, and apart from the main cities and tourist areas the staff aren't likely to speak English. But you should always be able at least to get a free town plan and a local listings booklet in Italian, and some will reserve you a room and sell places on guided tours. **Opening hours** vary, but larger city and resort offices are likely to be open Monday to Saturday 9am to 1pm and 4 to 7pm, and sometimes for a short period on Sunday mornings; smaller offices may open weekdays only, while Pro Loco times are notoriously erratic – some open for only a couple of hours a day, even in summer. If the tourist office isn't open and all else fails, the local telephone office, most hotels, and bars with phones should all have a copy of the local *Tuttocittà* or similar (a supplement to the main telephone directories), which carries listings and phone numbers of essential services and adverts for restaurants and shops, together with indexed maps of the appropriate city.

INTERNET ADDRESSES

Italian Web sites have proliferated in recent years and provide a wealth of information – be warned, however, that not all of it is entirely accurate: we've listed a few of the more useful and reliable ones on page 25.

ITALIAN STATE TOURIST OFFICES ABROAD

UK: 1 Princes Street, London W1R 8AY (☎020/7408-1254, fax 7493-6695).
Ireland: 47 Merrion Square, Dublin 2 (☎01/766 397).
US: 630 Fifth Avenue, Suite 1565, New York NY 10111 (☎212/245-4822, fax 586-9249); 500 North Michigan Avenue, Suite 2240, Chicago, Il 60611 (☎ 312/644-0990, fax 644-3109); 12400 Wilshire Boulevard, Suite 550, Los Angeles, CA 90025 (☎310/820-0098, fax 820-6357).

Canada: 1 Place Ville-Marie, Suite 1914, Montreal PQ H3B 2C3 (☎514/866-7667, fax 392-1492).
Australia: Italian Consulate, Level 26, 44 Market St, Sydney, NSW 2000 (02/9262 1666).
New Zealand: Italian Embassy, 34 Grant Rd, Thorndon, Wellington (☎04/473 5339).

MAP OUTLETS

BRITAIN AND IRELAND

Blackwell's Map and Travel Shop, 53 Broad St, Oxford OX1 3BQ (☎01865/792 792).

Daunt Books, 83 Marylebone High St, W1M 3DE (☎020/7224 2295); 193 Haverstock Hill, NW3 4QL (☎020/7794 4006).

Easons Bookshop, 40 O'Connell St, Dublin 1 (☎01/873 3811).

Fred Hanna's Bookshop, 27–29 Nassau St, Dublin 2 (☎01/677 1255).

Heffers Map Shop, 3rd Floor, 19 Sidney St, Cambridge CB2 3HL (☎01223/568 467).

Hodges Figgis Bookshop, 56–58 Dawson St, Dublin 2 (☎01/677 4754).

Italian Bookshop, 7 Cecil Court, London WC2N 4EZ (☎020/7240 1635).

James Thin Melven's Bookshop, 29 Union St, Inverness IV1 1QA (☎01463/233 500).

John Smith and Sons, 57–61 St Vincent St, Glasgow G2 5TB (☎0141/221 7472).

National Map Centre, 22–24 Caxton St, London SW1H 0QU (☎020/7222 4945).

Newcastle Map Centre, 55 Grey St, Newcastle-upon-Tyne NE1 6EF (☎0191/261 5622).

Stanfords,* 12–14 Long Acre, London WC2E 9LP (☎020/7836 1321); at Usit CAMPUS, 52 Grosvenor Gardens, London SW1W 0AG; 156 Regent St, London W1R 5TA (☎020/7434 4744); 29 Corn Street, Bristol BS1 1HT (☎0117/929 9966).

The Map Shop, 30a Belvoir St, Leicester LE1 6QH (☎0116/247 1400).

The Travel Bookshop, 13–15 Blenheim Crescent, London W11 2EE (☎020/7229 5260).

Waterstone's, 91 Deansgate, Manchester M3 2BW (☎0161/832 1992); Queens Bldg, 8 Royal Ave, Belfast BT1 1DA (☎028/9024 7355); 7 Dawson St, Dublin 2 (☎01/679 1415); 69 Patrick St, Cork (☎021/276 522).

*Note: maps by **mail or phone order** are available from Stanfords, ☎020/7836 1321.

USA AND CANADA

Book Passage, 51 Tamal Vista Blvd, Corte Madera, CA 94925 (☎415/927-0960).

California Map & Travel Center, 3312 Pico Blvd, Santa Monica, CA 90405 (☎310/396-6277).

The Complete Traveler Bookstore, 199 Madison Ave, New York, NY 10016 (☎212/685-9007); 3207 Fillmore St, San Francisco, CA 94123 (☎415/923-1511).

Curious Traveller Travel Bookstore, 101 Yorkville Ave, Toronto, ON M5R 1C1 (☎1-800/268-4395).

International Travel Maps, 555 Seymour St, Vancouver, BC V6B 3J5 (☎604/687-3320).

Open Air Books and Maps, 25 Toronto St, Toronto, ON M5C 2R1 (☎416/363-0719).

Phileas Fogg's Books, Maps and More, #87 Stanford Shopping Center, Palo Alto, CA 94304

(☎1-800/233-FOGG in California; ☎1-800/533-FOGG elsewhere in US).

Rand McNally,* 444 N Michigan Ave, Chicago, IL 60611 (☎312/321-1751); 150 E 52nd St, New York, NY 10022 (☎212/758-7488); 595 Market St, San Francisco, CA 94105 (☎415/777-3131; 7988 Tysons Corner Center, Maclean, VA 22102 (☎202/223-6751).

Sierra Club Bookstore, 6014 College Ave, Oakland, CA 94618 (☎510/658-7470).

Travel Books & Language Center, 4437 Wisconsin Ave NW, Washington, DC 20016 (☎1-800/220-2665).

Traveler's Bookstore, 22 W 52nd St, New York, NY 10019 (☎212/664-0995).

*Note: Rand McNally now has 24 stores across the US; call ☎1-800/333-0136 (ext 2111) for the location of your nearest store.

AUSTRALIA AND NEW ZEALAND

Mapland, 372 Little Bourke St, Melbourne, VIC 3000 (☎03/9670 4383).

The Map Shop, 16a Peel St, Adelaide, SA 5000 (☎08/8231 2033).

Perth Map Centre, 884 Hay St, Perth, WA 6000 (☎08/9322 5733).

Speciality Maps, 58 Albert St, Auckland (☎09/307 2217).

Travel Bookshop, Shop 3, 175 Liverpool St, Sydney, NSW 2000 (☎02/9241 3554).

Worldwide Maps and Guides, 187 George St, Brisbane, QLD 4000 (☎07/3221 4330).

Alitalia *www.alitalia.it* Routes and schedules in English.

Firenze Online *www.fionline.it/wel_eng.htm* Classy site from one of Florence's main service providers, with information on art, music, theatre, cinema, shopping and finding a job.

Firenze Net *english.firenze.net/* Smart, stylish site packed with info and links. Allows you to take a virtual reality tour of the Uffizi courtyard, Ponte Vecchio and other sights.

Florence Art Guide *www.italink.com/eng/egui/hogui.htm* A pictorial map showing the city's galleries and museums: click for photos and information.

Italian State Railways *www.fs-on-line.com* Rail and timetable information in English.

Italian Yellow Pages *www.paginegialle.it*

Museums *www.beniculturali.it/home.htm* Web site of the Italian arts and culture ministry.

Travel
The following sites have a miscellany of travel, shopping, transport and other information aimed at visitors to Italy.
www.visiteurope.com/Italy
www.itwg.com
www.initaly.com
www.wel.it
www.traveleurope.it
www.tour-web.com

Uffizi Gallery *www.uffizi.firenze.it/ welcome E.html* The Uffizi's official Web site, with images of paintings, news, historical notes, index of artists and a virtual reality tour of several rooms.

Umbria *www.regione.umbria.it/turismo* Web site of Umbria's regional tourist authority: current events, news, museums, galleries and other visitor information.

Your Way to Florence *www.arca.net/florence/htm* A visitor-orientated site with news, transport, accommodation, information, opening times and a map.

MAPS

The **town plans** we've printed in this book should be fine for most purposes, and most tourist offices give out maps of their local area for free. But if you want an indexed town plan, Studio FMB covers the main towns, and Falk and several other companies do a decent, fold-open plan of Florence. The best **road maps** are those published by the TCI (Touring Club Italiano); they have excellent 1:200,000 scale maps for both Tuscany (*Toscana*) and Umbria (*Umbria Marche*).

For **hiking**, go for the ever-expanding Kompass 1:50,000 series. So far they produce two Tuscany maps (*Florence-Chianti* and *Siena-Colline Senesi*) and four in Umbria – *Perugia-Deruta, Assisi-Camerino, Gubbio-Fabriano* and *Monti Sibillini*. The Orecchiella and Apuan mountains north of Lucca are covered by the excellent 1:25,000 Multigraphic-Wanderkarte series. Even more detailed maps are beginning to appear in recognized walking areas, most notably in the Siena hills and around Monte Amiata. These include the 1:16,000 sheet put out by the caving, climbing and walking club at Costacciaro in Umbria (northeast of Gubbio), and the 1:25,000 Universo map for the area around Norcia and the Sibillini. Both are available in local shops.

GETTING AROUND

Use of a car is a major advantage if you want to travel extensively around Tuscany and Umbria. You can still get to all the major places by public transport, especially by train in Umbria, but away from main routes services can be slow and sporadic. In general, trains are most use for longer journeys, buses for local routes. We have detailed bus, train and ferry routes in the "Travel Details" section at the end of each chapter, with more specific information, where appropriate, in the main body of the guide.

TRAINS

Rail travel in Italy is operated by Italian State Railways, the Ferrovie dello Stato (FS). The service is relatively inexpensive, reasonably comprehensive and – despite its reputation – fairly efficient. At first glance, however, the variety of different train categories can be bewildering. Essentially they divide into three types: trains requiring pre-reservations and payment of a supplement (*supplemento*) on top of the normal ticket price (you are usually issued with separate ticket and supplement); trains requiring payment of supplement; and "ordinary" trains requiring purchase of a normal first- or second-class ticket.

There are no fewer than nine categories of train: **EuroStar Italia** (ES), which are super-fast trains between major cities (such as Rome–Florence–Bologna) that require obligatory reservations and payment of a supplement; **Cisalpino Pendolino**, a trans-Alpine service requiring reservations and supplement; **InterCity** (IC), fast trains requiring a supplement; **InterCityNight** (ICN), InterCity trains running at night with couchette and sleeper service; **EuroCity** (EC), like InterCity trains but in service across national borders; **Euronight** (EN), like EuroCity trains but with couchette and sleeper facilities (and generally no ordinary seating); **Espresso** (EX), medium-fast trains with no supplement that stop at major towns and cities; **Interregionali** (IR), similar to the Espresso, but usually with more stops; and **Regionali** (Reg), slow trains that generally stop at every station.

In addition to the routes operated by FS, there are a number of privately run lines, often using separate stations though charging similar fares; in cases where a private line uses an FS station (such as Arezzo or Terni), there may often be a separate ticket counter. Where these lines are worth using, notably in Umbria, they're detailed in the text.

TICKETS AND FARES

Fares are simply calculated by the kilometre and a return fare (*andata e ritorno*) is exactly twice that of a single (*andata*), except for journeys of under 250km in total, for which you get a fifteen-percent reduction. Timetables such as the *Pozzorario Generale* (see next page) contain a full breakdown of distances between all stations and a table of corresponding first-class (*prima classe*) and second-class (*seconda classe*) fares and supplements. You can thus work out exactly how much any trip will cost. Note that **supplements** for EuroStar (ES) trains are higher than those for InterCity (IC) trains. Bear in mind, too, that children aged four to twelve qualify for fifty-percent discount on all journeys. Children under four not occupying a seat travel free.

A ticket (*un biglietto*) can be bought from station ticket offices (*la biglietteria*), from some travel agents, and – vitally – from many station news kiosks or bars where the journey is a short one (often avoiding long queues). Note that in Florence the queues for tickets can be extremely long, so either buy a ticket the day before, or allow plenty of time before your train departs. All **tickets must be validated just before travel** (see next page): once validated, tickets for journeys up to 200km are valid for six hours; tickets for journeys over 200km are valid for 24 hours.

TICKET MACHINES

All stations have small yellow or gold machines at the end of the platforms or in ticket halls in which passengers must stamp all tickets immediately before embarking on a journey. Do not validate return portions of tickets until you embark on the return journey. If you fail to validate your ticket you may be given a spot fine in the region of L50,000.

Make sure you pay your supplement before getting on board as the supplement is higher if you pay the ticket-collector.

A **reservation** (*una prenotazione*) is obligatory on EuroStar trains, but as these services proliferate and with computer bookings, it is usually possible to buy a ticket and make your reservation up to a few minutes before the departure of your chosen service. Note that it can be worth making reservations in summer for InterCity trains as well. At larger stations there may be a separate window for ordinary and sleeper reservations, so check you're in the right queue. **Sleepers** are available on most long-distance services; expect to pay about an extra L30,000 for a couchette or *cuccetta* (a place in a six-berth compartment) and much more for one- or two-bed berths in first class, for which you need to be holding a first-class ticket for travel on top of the extra supplement.

RAIL PASSES

The Europe-wide **InterRail** and **Eurail** passes (see p.5 and p.14) allow unlimited travel on the FS network, although you'll be liable for all supplements and reservation requirements on EuroStar, InterCity and similar fast trains. If you're travelling exclusively in Italy, however, you might want to invest in one of the rail passes available on the FS system. Travellers from the UK have a choice of three **Euro-Domino** passes for the Italian network, giving three days' unlimited second-class rail travel for £119, five days' for £149, or ten days' for £239; the under-26 versions cost £89, £109 and £179 respectively. Passes are available from agents in the UK (see p.5) and must be bought a week before you make your first journey.

For North Americans, these passes are slightly different and can be purchased for either first- or second-class travel. A pass for 15 days' unlimited travel costs US$341 for first class, $228 for second class; 21 days is $396/254; 30 days $478/318. A variant of this pass, the **Flexicard**, allows 4 days travel within a 30-day period for $215 first class, $144 second class; the 8-day Flexicard is $302/202, the 12-day $389/259. See p.14 for details of rail contacts in North America (Australasian travellers should apply through their travel agent).

There are two **Italian passes** available from agencies abroad and at major city train stations and some travel agents within Italy. The **Italy Railcard** (also known as the *Biglietto Turistico Libera Circolazione*) is valid for unlimited travel on all FS trains, except the Pendolino; for eight days it costs £110/$176, for fifteen days £136/$218, for 21 days £158/$253 and for 30 days £190/$304. The second option is the **Biglietto Chilometrico**, a ticket that gives up to five people 3000 kilometres' worth of travel on a maximum of twenty separate journeys (valid for two months from validation on the first journey); it costs L206,000 in second class, L338,000 in first, but you have to pay supplements on faster trains. With both cards, you must get the ticket office to validate the journey you're about to make before getting on the train.

There are two discount cards that come into their own if you're going to be spending a long time in the country. For under-26s there's the **Carta Verde**, which is valid for one year, gives twenty-percent discount on any fare, and costs L40,000 ; it's available from any main train station in Italy. Stations also issue the **Carta d'Argento**, for people over 60, which has the same validity, price and percentage discount. Note that neither of these passes is valid for the periods June 25 to August 31 and December 24 to 31.

TIMETABLES AND INFORMATION

Timings and route information are posted up at train stations. Separate posters are used for arrivals (*Arrive* – usually white) and departures (*Partenze* – usually yellow), so be careful not to confuse the two. Florence station also has a large information centre. In the larger stations, in addition to departure boards, there are video machines into which you can tap your destination and desired arrival time to get a breakdown of the best services, routes and fares. Many are invariably broken.

You can save a lot of time and hassle by picking up a **timetable** if you are going to be doing a lot of travelling by train. The best bet is the small *Pozzorario*, which comes in two versions – you want the *Pozzorario Generale* (L10,000), which covers the whole country (the other one covers north and central Italy only). It's available from virtually every station and street kiosk in the country, and is packed with maps, prices and all train times. Note that train timetabling changes with the season: timetables run from May to September, and from October to April – don't consult an out-of-date one.

Pay extremely careful attention to the **timetable notes**, which may specify the dates between which some services run (*Si effetua dal. . .al. . .*), or whether a service is seasonal (*periodico*); *giornaliero* means the service runs daily, *feriale* is the phrase for Monday to Saturday (*lavorativi* – literally 'working days' – also covers Monday to Saturday, and is indicated by a crossed hammer symbol), and *festivo* means a train only runs on Sundays and holidays. Look out, too, for other small footnotes – some trains only run in the summer, or for a few days either side of Easter and Christmas.

TRAIN SERVICES IN TUSCANY

Not surprisingly, **Florence** is the centre of the Tuscan rail network. Two lines run westward from the city, one of them passing through **Prato**, **Pistoia**, **Montecatini** and **Lucca** on its way to the coast at **Viareggio**, the other going through **Empoli** and **Pisa** before reaching the sea at **Livorno**. A picturesque line runs through the Garfagnana from Lucca to **Aulla**, providing access to the Lunigiana region and connections to La Spezia and Milan. To the east, a line rises through the **Mugello** district and then loops out of Tuscany towards Faenza, roughly parallel to the route through the mountains to Bologna. South of Florence, the train follows the River Arno towards **Arezzo**, from where there's a private line up into the **Casentino** region, while the FS services continue south past Cortona to Chiusi, Orvieto and Rome. Just beyond Cortona, at **Terontola**, there's the junction for the branch line east to Perugia, the fulcrum of Umbria's network. Several trains go directly from Florence to Perugia, Foligno and Spoleto each day.

Siena can also be reached directly from Florence – though you may occasionally have to change at Empoli. From Siena itself there's a choice of two main routes – southeast to Chiusi, or southwest to Grosseto.

A **coastal service** between Rome and the Ligurian town of La Spezia links the Tuscan coastal towns of **Orbetello**, **Follonica**, **Cecina**, **Livorno** and **Viareggio**, swerving inland to call at **Grosseto** in the south of the province and **Pisa** in the north. Above Pisa it serves the resorts of the Versilia coast, calling principally at **Massa** and **Carrara**. At Cecina there's a spur inland to within a few kilometres of **Volterra**, where the line abruptly ends.

TRAIN SERVICES IN UMBRIA

All Umbria's major towns, with the exception of Gubbio, are easily accessible by train. In the west, the **Rome–Florence** route is the main artery, with branch-line connections throughout the region. Most of the high-speed services between the two cities stop at no Umbrian stations other than **Orvieto**; you will probably have to board a slower service to connect with the **Ancona line** at **Orte**, with the **Siena line** at **Chiusi**, or with the **Perugia and Foligno line** at **Terontola**.

More useful for the heart of the region, especially if you're coming from Rome, is the **Rome–Ancona** line, which meets the Rome–Florence line at Orte. This line gives direct access to **Narni**, **Terni** (connections for Rieti, the Abruzzo and the Ferrovia Centrale Umbra – see below), **Spoleto**, **Foligno** (connections to Spello, Assisi, Perugia and Terontola), **Nocera Umbra** and **Gualdo Tadino**.

Terni's FS station is shared with the **Ferrovia Centrale Umbra** (FCU), a private railway that fills some crucial gaps left by the state network. Using ramshackle, bone-crunching carriages, it runs through **Terni**, **Todi**, **Deruta**, **Perugia**, **Umbertide** and **Città di Castello** before reaching the terminus at **Sansepolcro**. Services are frequent, though trains are often replaced by buses over certain sections.

The line between **Foligno** and **Terontola** (on the Rome–Florence route) goes by **Spello** and **Assisi** then intersects with the FCU line at Perugia, continuing along the northern shore of Lago Trasimeno. In addition, there are a couple of direct trains daily between Perugia and both Rome and Florence.

BUSES

If you're limited to public transport and want to get to know Tuscany and Umbria thoroughly, sooner or later you'll have to use **regional**

MAJOR BUS COMPANIES

GENERAL

Lazzi, Piazza della Stazione 1, Florence (☎055.351.061; 24-hr recorded message ☎166.845.010).

SITA, Via Santa Caterina da Siena 15, Florence (regional services ☎055.214.721; inter-regional services ☎055.483.651).

TUSCANY

CAP, Largo Fratelli Alinari 9, Florence (☎055.214.637). Northern Tuscany.

CAT, Via Fiume 2, Florence (☎055.283.400). Central and southern Tuscany.

CLAP, Piazza Stazione 15, Florence (☎055.283.734). Northern Tuscany.

CLAP, Piazzale Giuseppe Verdi, Lucca (☎0583.587.897). Services from Lucca to Barga and the Garfagnana.

COPIT, Piazza Santa Maria Novella 22, Florence (☎055.215.451). Northern Tuscany.

Lazzi, Piazzale Giuseppe Verdi, Lucca (☎0583.584.876). Long-distance regional buses from Lucca.

Nardini, Via Roma 7, Barga (☎0583.73.050). From Barga and around the Garfagnana.

RAMA, Via Topazio 12, Grosseto (☎0564.456.745). Around Grosseto and the Maremma.

TRA-IN, Piazza San Domenico, Siena (☎0577.221.221 or 0577.204.205). Siena province.

UMBRIA

APM, Pian di Massiano, Perugia (☎075.506.781). Perugia, Gubbio, Assisi and northern Umbria. Also connections to Tuscany.

ATC, Piazzale della Rivoluzione Francese, Terni (☎0744.492.711). From Terni through southern Umbria, Orvieto and the Valnerina.

ASP, Pian di Massiano, Perugia (☎075.751.145). Perugia, Assisi, Todi and northern Umbria.

SIT, Via Flaminia, Km 127, Spoleto (☎0743.212.211). Around Spoleto and the Valnerina.

SULGA, Pian di Massiano, Perugia (☎0500.9641). Perugia to Rome and Florence.

---

buses (*autobus* or *pullman*). Almost everywhere is connected by some kind of bus service, but schedules can be sketchy, and are drastically reduced – sometimes nonexistent – at weekends, something the timetable won't always make clear. Bear in mind also that in rural areas schedules are often designed with the working and/or school day in mind, meaning a frighteningly early start if you want to catch that day's one bus out of town, and occasionally no buses at all during school holidays.

There isn't a national **bus company**, though Lazzi and SITA – both of which have a major presence in Tuscany and Umbria – cover much of Italy and there are a few other companies that operate services beyond their own immediate area (see the box above). **Bus terminals** in larger towns are often next door to the train station; in smaller towns and villages most buses pull in at the central piazza. We've detailed the whereabouts of all bus terminals in the text, but, if you're not sure, ask for directions to the *autostazione*.

Timetables are worth picking up if you can find one, from the local company's office, bus stations or on the bus. You generally buy tickets on the bus or from the station bar or newsagents, though on longer hauls you should buy them from the bus company office, which will invariably be right by the stop; there are no seat reservations. On most routes it's usually possible to flag a bus down if you want a ride: the convention, when it stops, is to get on at the back, off at the front. If you want to get off, ask *posso scendere?* The next stop is *la prossima fermata*.

City buses are always cheap, usually a L1000–1500 flat fare: in some places each ticket is valid for a single journey, in others it may be valid for any number of journeys within a set period (typically 20 or 40 minutes). Invariably you need a ticket **before** getting on the bus. Buy them in *tabacchi* or from the kiosks at bus terminals and stops, and cancel in the machine inside the bus. Arriving at railway stations, tickets for buses (especially shuttle buses to the town centre) are sold at the station bar or newspaper kiosk. The whole thing works on a basis of trust, though in most cities checks are regularly made, and hefty spot fines issued to offenders.

DRIVING

Travelling **by car** in Italy is relatively painless. The roads are good, the motorway, or *autostrada*, network very comprehensive, and Italian drivers rather less erratic than their reputation suggests – though their regard for the rules of the road is sometimes in doubt. The secret, if driving, is to make it very clear what you're going to do, using your horn as much as possible, and then do it with conviction. Don't assume you're safe as a pedestrian, either, and *never* step off the pavement without looking first: Italian drivers aren't keen on stopping when they can simply swerve, and even on pedestrian crossings you can undergo some close calls.

Most motorways are toll-roads. Take a ticket as you come on and pay on exit; the amount due is flashed up on a screen in front of you. Rates aren't especially high but they can mount up on a long journey.

As regards **documentation**, if you're bringing your own car you need a valid driving licence and an international green card of insurance, available from your insurer (sometimes free, usually for a fee). You'll also need to get a translation of your licence from the state tourist board, unless you've got one of the new pink EU-style licences. It's compulsory to carry your car documents and passport while you're driving, and you may be required to present them if stopped by the police – not an uncommon occurrence. **Rules of the road** are straightforward: drive on the right; at junctions, where there's any ambiguity, give way to vehicles coming from the right; observe the speed limits – 50kph in built-up areas, 110kph on country roads and on motorways during the week, 130kph on motorways at weekends; and *don't* drink and drive.

If you **break down**, dial ☎116 at the nearest phone and tell the operator where you are, the type of car and your registration number: the nearest office of the Automobile Club d'Italia (ACI), Via Marsala 8, 00185 Rome (☎06.499.8234), the Italian national motoring organization, will be informed and they'll send someone out to fix your car – although it's not a free service, and can work out very expensive if you need a tow. For peace of mind, you might prefer to join the ACI outright, and so qualify for their discounted repairs scheme. Any ACI office in Italy can tell you where to get **spare parts** for your particular car.

Never leave anything visible in the car when you're not using it, including the radio. If you're taking your own vehicle, consider installing a detachable car radio, and always depress your aerial or else you might find it snapped off. Most cities and ports have **garages** where you can

---

CAR RENTAL AGENCIES

UK

Avis ☎0990/900 500
Hertz ☎0990/996 699

Holiday Autos ☎0990/300 400
National Car Rental ☎01895/233 300

IRELAND

Avis ☎01/874 5844
Hertz ☎01/676 7476

Holiday Autos ☎01/872 9366

NORTH AMERICA

Auto Europe ☎1-800/223-5555
Avis ☎1-800/331-1084
Europe by Car ☎1-800/223-1516; in New York ☎212/581-3040; in Canada ☎1/800-252 9401

Hertz ☎1-800/654-3001; in Canada except Toronto ☎1-800/263 0600; in Toronto ☎416/620 9620

AUSTRALIA

Avis ☎1-800/225 533
Budget ☎13 2727

Renault Eurodrive ☎02/9299 3344

NEW ZEALAND

Avis ☎09/526 2847
Budget ☎09/375 2222

Hertz ☎09/309 0989

leave your car, a safe enough option. At least your car is unlikely to be stolen if it's got a right-hand drive and a foreign number-plate: they're too conspicuous to be of much use to thieves.

CAR RENTAL

Car rental in Italy is pricey, with costs for a Fiat Panda or Renault Twingo (the standard cheap cars) currently around £300/$480 per week with unlimited mileage. Italian and locally based firms might be a bit cheaper than the multinationals – there are plenty of companies with desks at Pisa airport, and other addresses are detailed in the relevant sections of the guide – but it usually works cheapest to book before leaving, either by arranging a fly-drive package through a travel agent or by going direct to the rental agency. Most operators will only hire to drivers who have held a licence for over a year and are aged over 21.

HITCHING

Getting around exclusively by **hitchhiking** (*autostop*) could be a frustrating experience, but for the odd short hop along a quiet country road, and long hauls between major towns, it's feasible enough. Note that it's illegal to hitch on motorways, and to do so would be to risk a spot fine; stand on a slip-road or at one of the service stations. Also, be aware that few women hitch alone in Italy, and not too many in two-women pairs; if you do it, always ask where the car is headed (*Dovè diretto?*) before you commit yourself. If you want to get out, say *Mi fa scendere?*

CYCLING AND MOTORCYLES

Cycling is seen as more of a sport than a way of getting around in Italy – on a Sunday you'll see plenty of people out for a spin on their Campagnolo-equipped machines, but you'll not come across many luggage-laden tourers. Only in major towns will you find a shop stocking spares

for non-racing bikes, so make sure you take a supply of inner tubes, spokes and any other bits you think might be handy. On the islands, in major resorts and in the larger cities it's usually possible to **rent** a bike, but generally facilities for this are few and far between and you may be better off bringing your own.

An alternative is to tour by **motorbike**, though again there are relatively few places to rent one. **Mopeds** and **scooters**, on the other hand, are relatively easy to find: everyone in Italy, from kids to grandmas, rides one of these, and, although they're not built for long-distance travel, for shooting around towns and islands they're ideal. We've detailed outlets in the text; roughly speaking you should expect to pay up to around L85,000 a day for a machine. Crash helmets are compulsory.

FERRIES

In Tuscany there are three ports with ferry services:

● **Livorno** has services to Corsica (Bastia), and to the northern Tuscan island of Capraia.

● **Piombino** is the point of departure for Elba, connecting to Portoferraio, as well as the smaller ports of Cavo and Rio Marina. There are also ferries from Piombino for Corsica, and from Portoferraio for Capraia.

● **Porto Santo Stefano** on Monte Argentario has ferries to the island of Giglio.

Summer sailings from all ports are heavily subscribed, especially those to Elba, and **booking** is essential if you want to take a car across. In Britain you can book tickets on the Elba ferries through SMS (☎020/7373 6548). Journey **times and frequencies** are detailed in the relevant parts of the guide, along with addresses to contact for latest timetable and ticket information. Out of season, services are drastically reduced, and some stop altogether.

ACCOMMODATION

Accommodation is a major cost in Tuscany and Umbria. The hotels are more upmarket than in most Italian regions, with a preponderance of two- and three-star places, and a tendency for one-stars in the major tourist towns and cities to price themselves ever closer to the plusher places; there are few really inexpensive hotels, only a scattering of hostels, and even campsites are fairly pricey. On the plus side, however, both provinces have plenty of villas for rent, while a rapidly expanding aspect of the tourist industry is *agriturismo* – farmhouse rents, similar to the French *gîtes*.

Accommodation in Italy is strictly regulated. All hotels are **star-rated** from one to five, one being the most basic, five representing luxury class. Prices are set by law for each room (prices can vary within a hotel) and must be posted at the hotel reception and in individual rooms (usually on the back of the door). Ask to see a variety of rooms if the first you're shown is too expensive or not up to scratch – there may be cheaper rooms available, particularly in hotels that have a choice of rooms with and without private bathrooms, the latter always being cheaper.

Most tourist offices carry full **lists of hotels** and other accommodation such as private rooms and *agriturismo* options. They may also be able to help you root out a room at short notice, but few have dedicated accommodation services. In popular areas, resorts and cities, it is essential to **book rooms in advance**, especially for July and August, and around Easter and Christmas. In Florence the high season lasts the best part of the

year, with a relative lull only in November, January and February; to secure a room in Siena for any time between Easter and October now requires booking six months in advance.

HOTELS

Hotels in Italy are known by a variety of often confusing names. Most are simply tagged "**Hotel**" or "**Albergo**". Others may be called a "**Locanda**", traditionally the cheapest sort of inn, but now sometimes rather self-consciously applied to smart new hotels. A **pensione** was also traditionally a cheap place to stay, though the name now lacks any official status: anywhere still describing itself as a "pensione" is probably a hotel in the one-star class.

The star system is the best way to get a rough idea of what you can expect from a hotel, though it's essential to realize the system is based on an often eccentric set of criteria relating to facilities (the presence of a restaurant, phones, TV and so forth) rather than notions about comfort, character or location. A three-star, for example, must have a phone in every room: if it hasn't, it remains a two-star, no matter how magnificent the rest of the hotel. Equally, a two-star hotel may have phones, but lack some other facility that might have taken it up a rating. This said, as a rule of thumb, a two-star will usually be a reliable and reasonably priced option in most towns, while in a four-star you'll be getting something that for most people will be pretty special.

One-star places start on average at about L50,000–70,000 per night for a double room without private bath. In some out-of-the-way spot you may find something slightly cheaper, while in Florence you should assume that prices are around L20,000–70,000 per night higher than anywhere else – it's difficult to find anything at all in Florence for under L90,000, even without a private bathroom.

Two-star hotels cost upwards of L70,000 for a double and facilities won't always be that much better, though you're usually assured of a private bathroom; with **three-star** places you begin to notice a difference – TVs and phones should be standard – in them you'll be paying a minimum of L120,000 (perhaps L200,000 in Florence). **Four-star** hotels are a marked step up, with prices

ACCOMMODATION PRICES

Throughout this guide, **hotel** accommodation is graded on a scale from ① to ⑨, indicating the cost of the **cheapest double room** in each establishment in high season (for **hostels**, rates per person are given in lire, and assume Hostelling International (HI) membership; rates for non-members at some hostels may be a few thousand lire more).

① up to L60,000.	④ L120,000–150,000.	⑦ L250,000–L300,000.
② L60,000–90,000.	⑤ L150,000–200,000.	⑧ L300,000–350,000
③ L90,000–120,000.	⑥ L200,000–250,000.	⑨ over 350,000

starting at around L200,000, much more in cities or major tourist centres. Everything has more polish, and in rural four-stars you'll probably get a swimming pool. **Five-stars** are rare, and represent the real luxury option: a million lire a night is a possibility, though it's not unknown for some of these hotels to rest on their laurels rather, and service and standards can be variable.

In the more popular cities – again, Florence especially – it's not unusual for hotels to have a **minimum stay** of three nights, and many proprietors will add the price of **breakfast** to your bill whether you want it or not; try to resist this – you can always eat more cheaply in a bar. Supplements for showers are also common in cheaper places. You can cut costs slightly by cramming three into a double room, but most hotels will charge you an extra 35 percent for this. Note also that people **travelling alone** may be hit for the price of a double room even when taking a single. It can on occasion work the other way, however, and kindlier hoteliers may give you a double room if no singles are available, but still charge you the single rate.

Wherever you book in, establish the full price of your room before you accept it; out of season you may pay less than the advertised rate – if you ask first. When booking by phone, the phrases at the end of the book should help you get over the language barrier, but in many places you should be able to find someone who speaks some English. Many hotels require a **fax confirmation** of a booking – even if they don't, it's worth making one anyway. Wherever and whenever you've booked, it's *always* worth a phone call a day or so before arrival to confirm again that you're coming. This is especially true if you're arriving late – it's not uncommon for cheaper places, especially in Florence, to let your room go if you've not shown up by lunch: call that morning if you're worried.

PRIVATE ROOMS

With the summer demand for accommodation, **"rooms for rent"** signs are becoming an increasingly common sight in both Tuscany and Umbria. Local tourist offices usually have lists of rooms on offer, though you'll invariably need to ask for these specially – the official name is *affitacamere* (room rentals). Wandering around towns, or driving through the countryside, you'll see signs – often in English or German (*zimmer*), as well as Italian (*camere*). Most are in private houses, rather than the specially constructed blocks that seem to have taken over across the Adriatic in Greece. Increasingly, rooms can be rented – at a discount – by the week. Many, notably in San Gimignano, are also available with kitchenettes, a potentially useful way of keeping down costs.

DAY HOTELS

One peculiar Italian institution is the *albergo diurno* or **day hotel** – not as sleazy as it sounds in fact, but an establishment providing bathrooms, showers, cleaning services, hairdressers and the like for a fixed rate, usually around L10,000. You'll often find them at train stations and they're usually open daily 6am–midnight. Useful for a fast clean-up if you're on the move.

YOUTH HOSTELS AND STUDENT ACCOMMODATION

Youth hostels offer a cut-price way of exploring parts of Tuscany and Umbria. Most charge between L15,000 and L30,000 a night for a dormitory bed; breakfast, when not included comes to around L3000 (usually not terribly good value), and showers may also cost an additional L1000–2000. Most hostels also offer cheap

YOUTH HOSTEL ASSOCIATIONS

England and Wales Youth Hostel Association (YHA), Trevelyan House, 8 St Stephen's Hill, St. Alban's, Herts AL1 2DY (☎01727/845047). London shop and information office: 14 Southampton St, London WC2E 7HY (shop ☎020/7836 8541; information 7379 0597).

Scotland Scottish Youth Hostel Association, 7 Glebe Crescent, Stirling FK8 2JA (☎01786/451 181).

Ireland An Oige, 61 Mountjoy St, Dublin 7 (☎01/830 4555).

Northern Ireland Youth Hostel Association of Northern Ireland, 22 Donegall Rd, Belfast BT12 5JN (☎028/9032 4733).

USA Hostelling International-American Youth

Hostels (HI-AYH), 733 15th St NW, Suite 840, PO Box 37613, Washington, DC 20005 (☎202/783-6161).

Australia Australian Youth Hostels Association, Level 3, 422 Kent St, Sydney, NSW 2000 (☎02/9261 1111).

Canada Hostelling International/Canadian Hostelling Association, Room 400, 205 Catherine St, Ottawa, ON K2P 1C3 (☎613/237-7884 or 1-800/663-5777).

New Zealand Youth Hostels Association of New Zealand, 173 Gloucester St, Christchurch (☎03/379 9970).

Italy Associazione Italiana per la Gioventù (AIG), Vla Cavour 44, 00184 Rome (☎06.487.1152, fax 06.488.0492; *www.hostels-aig.org/*).

half-board and full-board deals (around L60,000 for full-board), though don't expect much by way of culiinary sophistication at this price. When the extras are factored in, hostels don't always represent a massive saving for two people travelling together – especially when you take into acccount that some are inconveniently located and require bus journeys from the towns they serve (Florence is a case in point).

If you're travelling on your own, on the other hand, hostels are certainly more sociable and can work out a lot cheaper; many have facilities such as self-catering kitchens and bargain-basement restaurants that enable you to cut costs further.

Most hostels are members of Hostelling International (formerly International Youth Hostel Federation), and strictly speaking you need to be a member of that organization in order to use them. Many, however, allow you to join on the spot, or simply charge you extra. Whether or not you're an HI member, you'll need to **book ahead** at hostels in the summer months – and for major cities like Florence it's worth doing so at least fifteen days in advance. The most efficient way to book is using Hostelling International's Booking Network: for a small fee this enables you to book at selected hostels from your home country up to six months in advance (see box for details of head offices). For more out-of-the-way hostels, you need to contact the hostel direct, sending a 30-percent deposit (or more) with your booking.

We've listed many hostels in the guide, but for the very latest information, obtain a list from the Italian State Tourist Office in your home country (see p.23) or contact the Associazione Italiana Alberghi per la Gioventù (see above). Tuscany currently has seven hostels (HI and non-HI): at Florence, Siena, Pisa, Volterra, San Gimignano, Lucolena and Tavarnelle (the last two in Chianti); Umbria has six, at Perugia, Assisi, Gubbio, Magione, Poggiodomo and Sigillo.

In the university cities of Florence, Perugia, Siena and Pisa, it's also possible to stay in **student accommodation** vacated by Italian students for the summer (July–Aug), or occasionally at other times. Accommodation is generally in individual rooms and can work out a lot cheaper than a straight hotel room; we've listed possible places in the text. In Florence, once again, contact locations as far ahead as possible to be sure of a room. Beware, however, that the paperwork and bureaucracy involved can be demanding.

RELIGIOUS ORGANIZATIONS

You'll come across **religious organizations** offering cheap accommodation; big centres such as Florence and San Gimignano have them, as do the very smallest villages, such as Spello and Bevagna in rural Umbria. Often the lodgings are annexed to **convents or monasteries**, or pilgrim hostels, and in most cases amount more or less to simple hotels. Most have rooms with and without bathrooms: only a few have dorm rooms with bunks. Some only accept women, others only familes or single travellers of either sex. Most have a curfew, but few, contrary to expectations, pay much heed to your coming and going. Virtually none offer meals – the notable exception is Assisi, where dozens of places offer food and lodgings to the vast pilgrim market. Elsewhere you may have to root convents out: they are often buried in the accommodation listings issued by tourist offices, but for this reason remain relatively unknown to the majority of travellers.

CAMPING

Camping is not especially popular in Tuscany, except on the island of Elba, and the sites that do exist are mostly on the upmarket side – well equipped and expensive. Once you've added the cost of a tent and possibly a vehicle, they don't always work out any cheaper than staying in a hotel or hostel: prices range from L7000 per person per night up to L15,000, plus L7000 for each caravan or tent, plus around L7000 for each vehicle.

Useful sites are detailed in the text. If you're camping extensively it might be worth investing in the TCI's *Campeggi e Villaggi Turistici*, available from the outlets listed on p.24, which gives full **details** of facilities. If you don't need something this detailed, you can obtain an abridged version free of charge from Centro Internazionale Prenotazioni, Federcampeggio, Casella Postale 23, 50041 Calenzano, Florence (☎055.882.391). This is also the place to **book** campsites in advance.

VILLAS AND AGRITURISMO

Travelling with a group of people, or even just in a pair, it's worth considering renting a **villa or farmhouse** for a week or two. These are not too expensive if you can split costs between, say, four people, are of a consistently high standard, and often enjoy marvellous locations. British-based operators who rent villas, either on their own, or as part of a package, are detailed on p.9.

If you want a similar experience, but on a cheaper daily basis, your best bet is an **agriturismo** property, a scheme whereby farmers let out their unused buildings. Usually these have a self-contained flat or building to let, though a few places just rent rooms on a bed-and-breakfast basis. If you're travelling by car or bike, the properties offer enormous scope: virtually every big town or village has one or more within a few miles, which means you can avoid busy town centres in favour of rural tranquillity at a cost usually

equivalent to one- or two-star hotel prices (but occasionally much more).

This market has boomed over the last few years, and while some rooms are still annexed to working farms or vineyards, many are smart rural properties run by disenchanted townies seeking "the good life". Attractions may include home-grown food, swimming pools and a range of **activities** from walking and riding to archery and mountain biking. Most offer daily or weekly rates, many have family rooms or self-catering apartments (invariably weekly lets), and some may have minimum stay requirements in busy periods. It is always possible to call up *agriturismo* places directly, or even follow the (usually yellow) signs and chance your luck.

Tourist offices keep **lists** of local properties, and the Umbria regional tourist authority produces a detailed booklet containing all the region's *agriturismo* options (*Agriturismo Umbria Ospitalità*), available from most larger tourist offices.

MOUNTAIN REFUGES

If you're planning on **hiking** or climbing, or even if you're just touring by car or bike, you may want to make use of *rifugi* (refuges) – mountain and upland huts. Most are owned by the Club Alpino Italiano, who allow non-members to stay for around L20,000 a night, though a few are privately operated and may charge up to double this; most are **open July to August only** and winter weekends. Not all are away from roads: in the Sibillini in Umbria, for example, you can drive or cycle to superbly situated refuges at Forca di Presta and elsewhere and use them as a base for walking, or simply as refreshment stops.

Rifugi in general are fairly spartan, with bunks in unheated dorms, but the sites can be magnificent, and usually leave you well placed to continue your hike the next day. You also do not need to stay: most make their basic living selling snacks and hot meals to people coming in off the slopes. All CAI *rifugi* are obliged to take you if you turn up on the off chance, though this may mean you end up sleeping on the floor or in the chicken shed, so it's always best to **book in advance**, either through the local tourist office, the Club Alpino Italiano (☎02.205.7231; *www.cai.it*), or – best and easiest of all – direct with the *rifugi*. Addresses and phone numbers are given where relevant in the text.

FOOD AND DRINK

The traditional dishes of Tuscany are Italy's most influential cuisine – the ingredients and culinary techniques of the region have made their mark not just on the menus of the rest of Italy but also abroad, even in France. Umbrian cooking may not be accorded quite the same degree of reverence, but the produce of Italy's only landlocked province is of the highest quality, with its truffles and ham being especially prized. And wine has always been central to the area's economy and way of life, familiar names such as Chianti and Orvieto representing just a portion of the enormous output from Tuscan and Umbrian vineyards.

BREAKFAST AND SNACKS

Most Italians start their day in a bar, their **breakfast** consisting of a coffee and the ubiquitous *cornetto* or *brioche* – a jam-, custard- or chocolate-filled croissant, to which you usually help yourself from the counter (unfilled croissants are occasionally hard to find; ask for *un cornetto semplice* or *normale*). Breakfast in a hotel (*prima colazione*) will be a limp affair, usually worth avoiding.

At other times of the day, **sandwiches** (*panini*) can be pretty substantial, a bread stick or roll packed with any number of fillings. Specialized sandwich bars (*paninoteche*) can be found in many larger towns, and grocers' shops (*alimentari*) – who'll make sandwiches to order – are another standard source; you'll pay L2500–L5000

for most varieties. Bars may also offer *panini* and *tramezzini*, ready-made sliced white bread with mixed fillings – tasty and slightly cheaper than the average *panino*. Toasted sandwiches (*toste*) are common too: in a *paninoteca* you can get whatever you want toasted; in ordinary bars it's more likely to be a variation on cheese or ham with tomato.

If you want **takeaway food** there are a number of options. It's possible to find slices of **pizza** (*pizza taglia* or *pizza rustica*) pretty much everywhere (buy it by the *etto* – 100g), and you can get most of the things already mentioned, plus pasta, chips, even full hot meals, in a *tavola calda*, a sort of snack bar that's at its best in the morning when everything is fresh. Some are self-service with limited seating – found mostly in the bigger towns and inside larger train stations. They are, however, a dying breed, as is the *rosticceria*. Here the speciality is usually spit-roast chicken but *rosticcerie* often serve fast foods such as pizza slices, chips and hamburgers. Burger and other fast-food joints are proliferating in Italy at a depressing rate.

Other sources of quick snacks are **markets**, some of which sell take-away food from stalls, including *focacce* – oven-baked pastries topped with cheese or tomato or filled with spinach, fried offal or meat; and *arancini* or *suppli* – deep-fried balls of rice with meat (*rosso*) or butter and cheese (*bianco*) filling. **Supermarkets**, also, are an obvious stop for a picnic lunch: the major department store chains, Upim and Standa, often have food halls. Excellent **co-ops** are also a feature of most Tuscan towns.

ICE CREAM

Italian ice cream (*gelato*) is justifiably famous: a cone (*un cono*) or better-value "cup" (*una coppa*) are indispensable accessories to the evening *passeggiata*. Most bars have a fairly good selection, but for real choice go to a *gelateria*, where the range is a tribute to the Italian imagination and flair for display. You'll sometimes have to go by appearance rather than attempting to decipher their exotic names, many of which don't even mean much to Italians: often the basics – chocolate, strawberry, vanilla – are best. There's no problem locating the finest *gelateria* in town – it's the one that draws the

BASIC FOOD TERMS AND PHRASES

Aceto	Vinegar	*Olio*	Oil
Aglio	Garlic	*Olive*	Olives
Biscotti	Biscuits	*Pane*	Bread
Burro	Butter	*Pane integrale*	Wholemeal bread
Caramelle	Sweets	*Panino*	Bread roll/sandwich
Carne	Meat	*Panna*	Cream
Cioccolato	Chocolate	*Patatine*	Crisps
Focaccia	Oven-baked snack	*Patatine fritte*	Chips
Formaggio	Cheese	*Pepe*	Pepper
Frittata	Omelette	*Pesce*	Fish
Frutta	Fruit	*Pizzetta*	Small cheese and tomato pizza
Frutti di mare	Seafood	*Riso*	Rice
Gelato	Ice cream	*Sale*	Salt
Grissini	Bread sticks	*Uova*	Eggs
Insalata	Salad	*Yogurt*	Yoghurt
Maionese	Mayonnaise	*Zucchero*	Sugar
Marmellata	Jam	*Zuppa*	Soup

USEFUL TERMS

il cameriere	Waiter	*cena*	Dinner
il menù/la lista	Menu	*menù degustazione*	Tasting menu
la lista dei vini	Wine list	*antipasti*	Starters
un coltello	Knife	*primi*	First courses
una forchetta	Fork	*zuppe/minestre*	Soups
un cucchiaio	Spoon	*secondi*	Main courses
senza carne	Without meat	*contorni*	Vegetables
al sangue/	Rare/medium (steaks)	*dolci*	Puddings
al puntino		*coperto*	Cover charge
la colazione	Breakfast	*servizio*	Service charge
pranzo	Lunch		

COOKING TERMS

Affurnicato	Smoked	*Grattuggiato*	Grated
Arrosto	Roast	*Alla griglia*	Grilled
Ben cotto	Well done	*Al Marsala*	Cooked with Marsala wine
Bollito/lesso	Boiled	*Milanese*	Fried in egg and breadcrumbs
Brasata	Cooked in wine	*Pizzaiola*	Cooked with tomato sauce
Cotto	Cooked (not raw)	*Ripieno*	Stuffed
Crudo	Raw	*Sangue*	Rare
Al dente	Firm (not overcooked)	*Allo spiedo*	On the spit
Ai ferri	Grilled without oil	*Surgelato*	Frozen
Fritto	Fried	*Umido*	Steamed/stewed

USEFUL PHRASES

I'd like to reserve a table	*vorrei riservare una tavola*	I'd like…	*vorrei…*
		It's good	*è buono*
Have you a table for two?	*avete una tavola per due?*	It's delicious	*è squisito*
		The bill, please	*il conto, per favore*
I'd like to order	*vorrei ordinare*	Is service included?	*Il servizio è incluso?*
I'm a vegetarian	*sono vegetariano/a*		

A LIST OF FOOD AND DISHES

PIZZAS

Calzone	Folded pizza with cheese, ham and tomato
Capricciosa	Literally "capricious"; topped with whatever they've got in the kitchen, usually including baby artichoke, ham and egg
Cardinale	Ham and olives
Frutta di mare	Seafood; usually mussels, prawns and clams
Funghi	Mushroom; the tinned sliced variety, unless it specifies fresh mushrooms (funghi freschi)
Margherita	Cheese and tomato
Marinara	Tomato, anchovy and olive oil
Napo/Napoletana	Tomato
Quattro formaggi	"Four cheeses", usually including mozzarella, fontina and gruyère
Quattro stagioni	"Four seasons"; the toppings split into four separate sections, usually including ham, green pepper, onion, egg, etc

ANTIPASTI

Antipasto misto	Mixed cold meats and cheese	Insalata russa	Russian salad; diced vegetables in mayonnaise
Bruschetta	Garlic bread, often topped with tomatoes and olive oil	Melanzane in parmigiana	Aubergine in tomato and parmesan cheese
Caponata	Mixed aubergine, olives, tomatoes	Peperonata	Green and red peppers stewed in olive oil
Caprese	Tomato and mozzarella cheese salad	Pomodori ripieni	Stuffed tomatoes
Crostini	Mixed chicken liver canapés	Prosciutto	Ham
Insalata di mare	Seafood salad	Salame	Salami
Insalata di riso	Rice salad		

THE FIRST COURSE (PRIMO): SOUPS, PASTA. . .

Brodo	Clear broth	Penne	Smaller pieces of rigatoni
Cannelloni	Large tubes of pasta, stuffed	Ravioli	Ravioli
Farfalle	Literally "butterfly"-shaped pasta	Rigatoni	Large, grooved tubular pasta
Fettucine	Narrow pasta ribbons	Risotto	Cooked rice dish, with sauce
Gnocchi	Small potato and dough dumplings	Spaghetti	Spaghetti
		Spaghettini	Thin spaghetti
Lasagne	Lasagne	Stracciatella	Broth with egg
Maccheroni	Tubular spaghetti	Tagliatelle	Pasta ribbons, another word for fettucine
Minestrina	Any light soup		
Minestrone	Thick vegetable soup	Tortellini	Small rings of pasta stuffed with meat or cheese
Pasta al forno	Pasta baked with minced meat, eggs, tomato and cheese		
Pasta fagioli	Pasta soup with beans	Vermicelli	Very thin spaghetti ("little worms")
Pastini in brodo	Pasta pieces in clear broth		

. . . AND PASTA SAUCE (SALSA)

Arabiata	Spicy tomato sauce, with chillies	Parmigiano	Parmesan cheese
Bolognese	Meat sauce	Peperoncino	Olive oil, garlic and fresh chillies
Burro	Butter	Pesto	Green basil and garlic sauce
Carbonara	Cream, ham and beaten egg	Pomodoro	Tomato sauce
Funghi	Mushroom	Ragù	Meat sauce
Matriciana	Cubed pork and tomato sauce	Vongole	Clam and tomato sauce
Panna	Cream		

THE SECOND COURSE (SECONDO): MEAT (CARNE). . .

Agnello	Lamb	*Maiale*	Pork
Bistecca	Steak	*Manzo*	Beef
Cervello	Brain	*Mortadella*	Salami-type cured meat
Cinghiale	Wild boar	*Ossobuco*	Shin of veal
Coniglio	Rabbit	*Pernice*	Partridge
Costolette	Chops	*Pancetta*	Bacon
Cotolette	Cutlets	*Pollo*	Chicken
Fagiaon	Pheasant	*Polpette*	Meatballs
Faraona	Guinea fowl	*Rognoni*	Kidneys
Fegatini	Chicken livers	*Salsiccia*	Sausage
Fegato	Liver	*Saltimbocca*	Veal with ham
Involtini	Meat slices, rolled and	*Spezzatino*	Stew
	stuffed	*Tacchino*	Turkey
Lepre	Hare	*Trippa*	Tripe
Lingua	Tongue	*Vitello*	Veal

. . . FISH (PESCE) AND SHELLFISH (CROSTACEI)

Acciughe	Anchovies	*Merluzzo*	Cod
Anguilla	Eel	*Ostriche*	Oysters
Aragosta	Lobster	*Pescespada*	Swordfish
Baccalà	Dried salted cod	*Póoipo*	Octopus
Calamari	Squid	*Sarde*	Sardines
Céfalo	Mullet	*Sgombro*	Mackerel
Cozze	Mussels	*Sogliola*	Sole
Dentice	Dentex	*Tonno*	Tuna
Gamberetti	Shrimps	*Triglie*	Red mullet
Gámberi	Prawns	*Trota*	Trout
Granchio	Crab	*Vóngole*	Clams

VEGETABLES (CONTORNI) AND SALAD (INSALATA)

Asparagi	Asparagus	*Cávolo*	Cabbage	*Melanzane*	Aubergine
Basílico	Basil	*Cetriolo*	Cucumber	*Orígano*	Oregano
Broccoli	Broccoli	*Cipolla*	Onion	*Patate*	Potatoes
Capperi	Capers	*Fagioli*	Beans	*Peperoni*	Peppers
Carciofi	Artichokes	*Fagiolini*	Green beans	*Piselli*	Peas
Carciofini	Artichoke	*Finocchio*	Fennel	*Pomodori*	Tomatoes
	hearts	*Funghi*	Mushrooms	*Radicchio*	Chicory
Carotte	Carrots	*Insalata*	Green salad/	*Spinaci*	Spinach
Cavolfiori	Cauliflower	*verde/mista*	mixed salad	*Zucchini*	Courgettes

SWEETS (DOLCI), FRUIT (FRUTTA), CHEESE (FORMAGGI) AND NUTS (NOCE)

Amaretti	Macaroons	*Gorgonzola*	Soft blue-veined	*Pesche*	Peaches
Ananas	Pineapple		cheese	*Pignoli*	Pine nuts
Anguria/	Water melon	*Limone*	Lemon	*Pistacchio*	Pistachio nut
Coccómero		*Macedonia*	Fruit salad	*Provolone*	Hard strong
Arance	Oranges	*Mandorle*	Almonds		cheese
Banane	Bananas	*Mele*	Apples	*Ricotta*	Soft white
Cacchi	Persimmons	*Melone*	Melon		sheep's cheese
Cilliegie	Cherries	*Mozzarella*	Bland soft white	*Torta*	Cake, tart
Fichi	Figs		cheese used on	*Uva*	Grapes
Fichi d'India	Prickly pears		pizzas	*Zabaglione*	Dessert made
Fontina	Northern Italian	*Nespole*	Medlars		with eggs, sugar
	cooking cheese	*Parmigiano*	Parmesan cheese		and Marsala
Fragole	Strawberries	*Pecorino*	Strong hard		wine
Gelato	Ice cream		sheep's cheese	*Zuppa Inglese*	Trifle
		Pere	Pears		

crowds, and we've noted the really special places in the text. The procedure is to ask for a *cono* or *coppa*, indicating the size you want: prices go up in L500 increments, usually from a modest two-scoop L2000 to a whopping L4500 or more. Often you'll be asked if you want a dollop of (usually free) cream (*panna*) on top.

PIZZA

Everywhere in Italy, **pizza** comes thin and flat, not deep-pan, and the choice of toppings is fairly limited – none of the pineapple and sweetcorn variations that have taken off in Britain and America. Most are cooked in the traditional way, in wood-fired ovens (*forno a legna*), rather than in the squeaky-clean electric ones, so that they arrive blasted and bubbling on the surface, and with a distinctive charcoal taste.

Pizzerie range from a stand-up counter selling slices (*alla taglia*) to a fully-fledged sit-down restaurant, and on the whole they don't sell much else besides pizza and drinks, though in large towns you'll come across a pizzeria that also does simple pasta dishes. Some straight restaurants often have pizza on the menu too. A basic cheese and tomato pizza (*margherita*) costs around L4000, a fancier variety anything up to L15,000, and it's quite acceptable to cut it into slices and eat it with your fingers. Check the food glossary (see box on pp.38–39) for a rundown of varieties.

RESTAURANTS

Tuscan and Umbrian restaurant meals (lunch is *pranzo*, dinner is *cena*) are traditionally long and pretty solid affairs, starting with an *antipasto*, followed by a risotto or a pasta dish, leading on to a fish or meat course, cheese, and finished with fresh fruit and coffee. Even everyday meals are a miniaturized version of this. The minimalist ethic of *nouvelle cuisine* has made inroads into the more expensive restaurants, but the staple fare at the majority of places is exactly what it might have been a century ago. Vegetarianism is a concept that's also been slow to catch on – outside Florence you're unlikely to find any vegetarian places, and they are pretty scarce even there.

TYPES OF RESTAURANT

Restaurants are most commonly called either **trattorie** or **ristoranti**. Traditionally, a trattoria is a cheaper and more basic purveyor of home-style cooking (*cucina casalinga*), while a *ristorante* is

---

---

more upmarket, with aproned waiters and table-cloths. These days, however, there's a fine line between the two, as it's rather chic for an expensive restaurant to call itself a trattoria. It's in the rural areas that you're most likely to come across an old-style trattoria, the sort of place where there's no written menu (the waiter will simply reel off a list of what's on) and no bottled wine (it's straight from the vats of the local farm). A true *ristorante* will always have a written menu and a reasonable choice of wines, though even in smart places it's standard to choose the ordinary house wine. In popular tourist towns (again, Florence is a sinner in this) you may well find restaurants willing to serve full meals only – no lunchtime restraint of a pasta and salad allowed.

Increasingly, too, you come across *osterie*. These used to be old-fashioned places specializing in home cooking, though recently they have had quite a vogue and the *osteria* tag more often signifies a youngish ownership and clientele and adventurous foods. Other types of restaurant include *spaghetterie* and *birrerie*, restaurant-bars which serve basic pasta dishes, or beer and snacks, and are again often youngish hang-outs.

THE MENU AND THE BILL

The cheapest – though not the most rewarding way – to eat in bigger city restaurants is to opt for a set price *menù turistico*. This will give you a first course (pasta or soup), main course, pudding (usually a piece of fruit) and half a litre of water and a quarter litre of wine per person. **Beware** the increasingly common *prezzo fisso* menu, which excludes cover, service, dessert and beverages.

Working your way through an Italian menu (*la lista*, or sometimes *il menù*) is pretty straightforward. *Antipasto* (literally "before the meal") is a course generally consisting of various cold cuts of meat, seafood and various cold vegetable dishes. *Prosciutto* is a common *antipasto* dish: it's ham either cooked (*cotto*) or just cured and hung (*crudo*), served alone or with melon, figs or mozzarella cheese. Also very common are *crostini*, canapés of minced chicken liver or minced sautéed spleen (. . .*di milza*).

The next course, *il primo*, consists of a soup, risotto, polenta or pasta dish. This is followed by *il secondo* – the meat or fish course, usually served alone, except for perhaps a wedge of lemon or tomato. Watch out when ordering fish or Florence's famous *bistecca alla fiorentina,* which will usually be served by weight: 250g is usually plenty for one person, or ask to have a look at the fish before it's cooked. Anything marked *S.Q.* or *hg* means you are paying by weight (hg = 100g, or around 4oz).

Vegetables – *il contorno* – or salads – *insalata* – are ordered and served separately, and often there won't be much (if any) choice: most frequent are beans (*fagioli*), potatoes (*patate*), and salads either green (*verde*) or mixed (*mista*).

For afters, you nearly always get a choice of fresh fruit (*frutta*) and a selection of **puddings** (*dolci*) – often focused on ice cream or a selection of usually dull home-made flans (*torta della casa*).

At the end of the meal ask for **the bill** (*il conto*). In many *trattorie* this amounts to no more than an illegible scrap of paper, and if you want to be sure you're not being ripped off, ask to have a receipt (*ricevuta*), something all bars and restaurants are legally bound to provide anyway. Bear in mind that almost everywhere you'll pay a **cover charge** on top of your food – the *pane e coperto* or just *coperto* – of L2000–3000 a head. There have been legally backed efforts to do away with this, given that it amounts to charging extra for what should really be incorporated in a restaurant's margins – they've not yet noticeably succeeded. As well as the *coperto*, service (*servizio*) will often be added, generally about ten percent. If service isn't included you should perhaps tip about the same amount, though *trattorie* outside the large cities won't necessarily expect this.

TUSCAN CUISINE

The most important ingredient of Tuscan cooking is **olive oil**, which comes into almost every dish – as a dressing for salads, a medium for frying, or simply poured over vegetables and into soups and stews just before serving. The olive picking begins around November, before the olives are fully ripe; the oil produced from the first pressing is *extra virgine*, the purest and most alkaline oil, with less than one-percent acidity. The other categories of good-quality oil, in descending order of excellence and ascending order of acidity, are *soprafino virgine, fino virgine* and *virgine*. Top-quality oil is now an even more precious commodity than it used to be – a terrible frost in 1985 killed so many olive trees that several of Tuscany's oil producers have to use oil from other parts of the country in their blends.

The biggest influences on Tuscan cooking are the simple rustic dishes of **Florence**, the most famous of which is *bistecca alla fiorentina*, a thick T-bone steak grilled over charcoal, usually served rare. The meat for true Florentine *bistecca* comes from the Valdichiana area, south of Arezzo, from an animal no more than two and a half years old.

The Florentines are also fond of the unpretentious *arista*, roast pork loin stuffed with rosemary and garlic, and of *pollo alla diavola*, a flattened chicken marinated with olive oil and lemon juice or white wine, then dressed with herbs before grilling. Wild hare features on many menus, as *lepre in dolce e forte* – cooked in wine and tomatoes with raisins, pine nuts, candied orange peel and herbs – or as *pappardelle con lepre* – noodles topped with hare, fried bacon and tomatoes. These are basically peasant meals that have become staples of the regional cuisine, as have dishes like *trippa e zampa* – tripe with calf's feet, onions, tomatoes, white wine, garlic and nutmeg.

Each major Tuscan town has its culinary specialities, too, a vestige of the days when the region was divided into city states. **Pisa**'s treats include black cabbage soup, new-born eels (*cieche*) fried with garlic and sage, and *torta coi bischeri*, a cake filled with rice, candied fruit, chocolate, raisins and pine nuts, and flavoured with nutmeg and liqueur. Many of the specialities of **Siena** date back to the medieval period, including *salsicce secche* (dried sausages) and *panforte di Siena*, the celebrated spicy cake of nuts and candied fruit. **Arezzo** has *acquacotta*, a soup of fried onion, tomato and bread, mixed with

CHECKLIST OF TUSCAN DISHES

ANTIPASTI

Crostini di milza	Minced spleen on pieces of toasted bread
Donzele or *Donzelline*	Fried dough balls
Fettuna or *Bruschetta*	Slab of toast flavoured with garlic and *extra virgine* olive oil
Finocchiona	Pork sausage flavoured with fennel
Pinzimonio	Raw seasonal vegetable in *extra virgine* olive oil, with salt and pepper
Prosciutto di cinghiale	Cured wild boar ham
Salame toscano	Pork sausage with pepper and cubes of fat
Salsicce	Pork or wild boar sausage

PRIMI

Acquacotta	Onion soup served with toast and poached egg
Cacciucco	Fish stew with tomatoes, bread and red wine
Carabaccia	Onion soup
Garmugia	Soup made with fava beans, peas, artichokes, asparagus and bacon
Gnocchi di ricotta	Dumplings filled with ricotta and spinach
Minestra di farro	Wheat and bean soup
Minestrone alla fiorentina	Haricot bean soup with red cabbage, tomatoes, onions and herbs
Panzanella	Summer salad of tomatoes, basil, cucumber, onion and bread
Pappa al pomodoro	Tomato soup thickened with bread
Pappardelle	Wide, short noodles, often served with hare sauce (*con lepre*)
Pasta alla carrettiera	Pasta with tomato, garlic, pepper, parsley and chilli
Penne strasciate	Quill-shaped pasta in meat sauce
Ribollita	Winter vegetable soup, based on beans and thickened with bread
Risotto nero	Rice cooked with cuttlefish (in its own ink)
Zuppa di fagioli	Bean soup

SECONDI

Arista	Roast pork loin with garlic and rosemary
Asparagi alla fiorentina	Asparagus with butter, fried egg and cheese

egg and cheese, while **Livorno** offers *cacciucco*, a mixture of fish with bread, tomatoes, garlic and white wine, and *brodatino*, a red bean and black cabbage soup.

Everywhere in the province, **soups** are central to the cuisine, the most famous being *ribollita*, a thick vegetable concoction traditionally including left-over beans (hence "reboiled"). *Pappa al pomodoro* is a popular broth with bread and tomatoes and basil cooked to a sustaining stodge. As *secondi*, you'll find a lot of **"hunters' dishes"** (*cacciatore*), most commonly *cinghiale* (wild boar) or *pollo* (chicken). White *cannellini* **beans** are the favourite vegetables, boiled with rosemary and doused with olive oil, or cooked with tomatoes (*all'uccelletto*). Broad beans, peas, artichokes and asparagus are other much-used vegetables, but none is as typically Tuscan as **spinach**. It's served as a side vegetable, or in combination with

omelettes, poached eggs or fish, or mixed with ricotta to make *gnocchi*, or used as a filling for *crespoline* (pancakes). Don't be surprised if spinach or green beans come cold – they're often eaten this way, usually with a squeeze of lemon.

Despite some crop reductions caused by outbreaks of tree disease, wild **chestnuts** remain another staple of Tuscan cooking, and there is a long tradition of specialities based on dried chestnuts and chestnut flour – such as the delicious *castagnaccio* (chestnut cake), made with pine nuts, raisins and rosemary.

Sheep's milk *pecorino* is the most widespread Tuscan **cheese**, but the most famous is the oval *marzolino* from the Chianti region, which is eaten either fresh or ripened, and is often grated over meat dishes. **Pudding** menus will often include *cantuccini*, hard biscuits which are dipped in a glass of Vinsanto, or *zuccotto*, a brandy-soaked

Baccalà alla livornese	Salt cod with garlic, tomatoes and parsley
Bistecca alla fiorentina	Thick grilled T-bone steak
Cibreo	Chicken liver and egg stew
Cieche alla pisana	Small eels cooked with sage and tomatoes, served with Parmesan
Lombatina	Veal chop
Peposo	Peppered beef stew
Pollo alla diavola or *al mattone*	Chicken flattened with a brick, grilled with herbs
Scottiglia	Stew of veal, game and poultry, cooked with white wine and tomatoes
Spiedini di maiale	Skewered spiced cubes of pork loin and liver, with bread and bay leaves
Tonno con fagioli	Tuna with white beans and raw onion
Trigile alla livornese	Red mullet cooked with tomatoes, garlic and parsley
Trippa alla fiorentina	Tripe in tomato sauce, served with Parmesan

CONTORNI

Fagioli all'olio	White beans served with olive oil
Fagioli all'uccelletto	White beans cooked with tomatoes, garlic and sage
Frittata di carciofi	Fried artichoke flan

DOLCI

Brigidini	Anise wafer biscuits
Buccellato	Anise raisin cake
Cantucci or *Cantuccini*	Small almond biscuits, served with Vinsanto wine
Castagnaccio	Unleavened chestnut-flour cake containing raisins, walnuts and rosemary
Cenci	Fried dough dusted with powdered sugar
Frittelle di riso	Rice fritters
Meringa	Frozen meringue with whipped cream and chocolate
Necci	Chestnut-flour crêpes
Panforte	Hard fruit, nut and spice cake
Ricciarelli	Marzipan almond biscuits
Schiacciata alla fiorentina	Orange-flavoured cake covered with powdered sugar, eaten at carnival time
Schiacciata con l'uva	Grape- and sugar-covered bread dessert
Zuccotto	Sponge cake filled with chocolate and whipped cream

sponge cake filled with cream mixed with choco-late powder, almonds and hazelnuts – like *tiramisù* elsewhere in Italy.

UMBRIAN CUISINE

Like that of Tuscany, Umbria's cooking relies heav-ily on rustic staples – pastas and roast meats – and tends to the simple and homely. It is, howev-er, the only region in Italy apart from Piemonte to offer **truffles** in any abundance. Traditionally the white truffle is the most highly prized on account of its aroma, but locals swear by the Umbrian grey-white (*bianchetto*) variety and the black truf-fle that's most common to the area around Spoleto and Norcia in the east. You're most likely to come across them with *tagliolini* (a super-fine thread of pasta that enables you to taste the truf-fle), as a modest sprinkling over your *tagliatelle* or meat, or on *crostini* – at a price that prohibits

overindulgence. Producing truffles in controlled conditions remains the culinary Holy Grail, and until there's success in this field they will remain a treasured commodity. (For more on truffles, see box on p.544).

Meat, and in particular **pork**, is the staple of the Umbrian main course, usually grilled or roast-ed. The region's small, free-range black pigs are famous, and have lately been joined by wild boar (*cinghiale*) – apparently *emigrés* from Tuscany, now reproducing at a prodigious rate. Norcia is the heart of pig country, with a superb selection of all things porcine, though other towns boast their own specialities. Città di Castello produces a *salame* made with spices and fennel seed; Cascia and Preci are known for their *mortadella*; Foligno has a distinctive dry *salame*; and Gualdo Tadino does a special sausage, the *soppressata*. Also look out for the extraordinary fruit-and-nut-

CHECKLIST OF UMBRIAN DISHES

ANTIPASTI

Bruschetta	Garlic toast with olive oil
Prosciutto di' Norcia	Cured raw ham from Norcia
Salame mezzafegato	Sausage spiced with a mixture of pine nuts, pork liver, candied orange, sugar and raisins
Schiacciata	Flat bread baked with olive oil, or flavoured with onions or cooked greens
Torta al testo	Unleavened bread baked on a slab of stone

PRIMI

Manfrigoli	Rustic pasta made from emmer, a coarse type of wheat introduced into the region by the Romans
Minestra di farro	Tomato, wheat and vegetable soup
Pici, stringozzi or *ceriole*	Thread-like spaghetti, usually served with garlicky tomato sauce
Spaghetti alla norcina	Spaghetti with an oily sauce of black truffles, garlic and anchovies
Umbrici	Large, heavy noodles

SECONDI

Anguilla alla brace	Grilled eel
Anguilla in úmido	Eel cooked with tomatoes, onions, garlic and white wine
Frittata di tartufi	Black truffle omelette
Gobbi alla perugina	Deep-fried cardoons (like artichokes) with meat sauce
Lepre alle olive	Hare cooked with herbs, white wine and olives
Palombe or *palombacci*	Wood pigeon, usually spit-roasted
Pollo in porchetta	Chicken cooked in the same way as suckling pig
Porchetta	Suckling pig cooked in a wood oven with fennel, garlic, mint and rosemary
Regina in porchetta	Lago Trasimeno carp, cooked as above
Salsiccia all'uva	Pork sausage cooked with grapes
Tegamaccio	Freshwater-fish stew with white wine and herbs

DOLCI

Cialde	Paper-thin sweet biscuits
Fave di morte	Almond biscuits
Pinoccate	Pine nut biscuits
Serpentone, torcolato or *torcolo*	Almond and dried fruit dessert in the shape of a coiled snake

flavoured *salame mezzafegato*. Endemic to the region, too, is *porchetta*, a whole roast suckling pig stuffed with herbs and spices and eaten sliced in crusty white rolls. It's an Umbrian concoction that's spread through most of central Italy, and is widely available as a snack from markets and roadside stalls.

Game may crop up on some menus, most often as pigeon, pheasant or guinea fowl. It's not unknown to be offered *tordo* (thrush), usually as a paté, so if this offends your sensibilities, watch out; other songbirds are hunted, often illegally, but they're unlikely to find their way into a restaurant. Despite the lack of a coast, some restaurants make the effort to bring in fresh **fish**, and

there's a reasonably wide selection of freshwater specimens close to lakes and mountain rivers. Trout are pulled out of the Nera, Clitunno and Sordo rivers, while lakes Piediluco and Trasimeno yield pike, tench and grey mullet.

The region's minor specialities are the tiny **lentils** of Castelluccio, the **beans** of Trasimeno, the **peas** from Bettona, and the **celery** and **cardoons** from around Trevi. Umbrian **olive oil**, though not hyped quite as the Tuscan oils, has a high reputation, especially that from around Trevi and Spoleto. *Monini* is the best producer.

Umbria offers the standard Italian selection of exotically named **desserts**, most of them glorified sponges or tarts. *Perugino* chocolate is outstanding, but it's available throughout Italy. One genuine novelty are the white **figs** of Amelia, mixed in a tooth-rotting combination of almonds and chocolate. **Cheeses** follow the standard variations, with the only genuine one-offs to be found in the mountains around Norcia and Gubbio.

DRINKING

Drinking in Tuscany and Umbria – as in Italy as a whole – is essentially as an accompaniment to food. There is little emphasis on drinking for its own sake. Locals sitting around in bars or cafés will spend hours chatting over just the one drink – whatever their age. And even in bars, most people you see imbibing one of the delicious Italian grappas or brandies will roll in just for the one shot, then be on their way. It's a pleasant change from the culture in Britain – the one snag being that, since Italians drink so little, prices are high in any place you sit to be served a drink.

WHERE TO DRINK

Bars are often very functional, brightly lit places, with a chrome counter, a *Gaggia* coffee machine and a picture of the local football team on the wall. You'll come here for **ordinary drinking** – a coffee in the morning, a quick beer, a cup of tea – but people don't generally idle away the day or evening in bars. Indeed in some, more rural places it's difficult to find a bar open much after 9pm. Where it does fit into the general Mediterranean pattern is that there are no set licensing hours

and children are always allowed in; there's often a telephone and you can buy snacks and ice creams as well as drinks.

Whatever you're drinking, the **procedure** is the same. It's nearly always cheapest to drink standing at the counter (there's often nowhere to sit anyway), in which case you often pay first at the cash desk (*la cassa*), present your receipt (*scontrino*) to the barperson and give your order; sometimes you simply order your drink and pay as you leave. If you don't know how much a drink costs, there's always a list of prices (*listino prezzi*) behind the bar. It's customary to leave an extra L100 on the counter for the bar staff. Slap it down with your till receipt to guarantee prompt service. If there's waiter service, sit where you like, though bear in mind that to do this will cost perhaps twice as much, especially if you sit outside (the different prices are shown on the price list as *bar*, *tavola* and *terrazza*).

COFFEE AND TEA

One of the most distinctive smells in an Italian street is that of fresh **coffee**, usually wafting out of a bar. The basic choice is either small and black (*espresso*, or just *caffè*), or white and frothy (*cappuccino*), but there are other varieties. If you want a longer *espresso* ask for a *caffè lungo*; a double *espresso* is *una doppia*, whilst an extra-strong *espresso* is *un ristretto*. A coffee topped with unfrothed milk is a *caffè latte*; with a drop of milk it's *caffè macchiato*; with a shot of alcohol it's *caffè*

DRINKING ESSENTIALS

zucchero	Sugar	*Limonate*	Lemonade
tazza	Cup	*Selz*	Soda water
limone	Lemon	*Spremuta*	Fresh fruit juice
aperitivo	Pre-dinner drink	*Spumante*	Sparkling wine
digestivo	After-dinner drink	*Succo di Frutta*	Concentrated fruit juice with
Acqua minerale	Mineral water		sugar
Aranciata	Orangeade	*Tè*	Tea
Bicchiere	Glass	*Tonico*	Tonic Water
Birra	Beer	*Vino*	Wine
Bottiglia	Bottle	*Rosso*	Red
Caffè	Coffee	*Bianco*	White
Cioccolata calda	Hot chocolate	*Rosato*	Rosé
Frappé	Milk-shake made with	*Secco*	Dry
	ice cream	*Dolce*	Sweet
Frullato	Milk-shake	*Litro*	Litre
Ghiaccio	Ice	*Mezzo*	Half
Granita	Iced drink, with coffee or fruit	*Quatro*	Quarter
Latte	Milk	*Salute!*	Cheers!

corretto. Although most places let you help yourself, some will lace your black coffee with sugar; if you don't want it, you can make sure by asking for *caffè senza zucchero*. Many places also now sell decaffeinated coffee (ask for *Hag*, even when it isn't); in summer you might want to have your coffee cold (*caffè freddo*). For a real treat, ask for *caffè granita* – cold coffee with crushed ice, usually topped with cream.

Hot **tea** (*tè caldo*) comes with lemon (*con limone*) unless you ask for milk (*con latte*); or in summer you can drink it cold (*tè freddo*). **Milk** itself is drunk hot as often as cold, or you can get it with a dash of coffee (*latte macchiato*) and sometimes as milk-shakes – *frappé*.

SOFT DRINKS

There are numerous **soft drinks** (*analcoliche*). A *spremuta* is a fresh fruit juice, squeezed at the bar, usually orange, lemon or grapefruit. You might need to add sugar to the lemon juice (. . . *di limone*) but the orange (. . . *d'arance*) is invariably sweet enough on its own, especially the crimson variety, made from blood oranges. A *succo di frutta* is a bottled fruit juice, widely drunk by Italians at breakfast. There are also crushed-ice *granite*, coming in several flavours other than coffee, and, of course, the usual range of fizzy drinks and concentrated juices: Coke is as prevalent as it is everywhere, while the home-grown Italian version, Chinotto, is less sweet – good with a slice of lemon. An excellent thirst-quencher is Lemon Soda (the brand name), a widely available bitter lemon drink – the Orange Soda is not as good. **Tap water** (*acqua normale*) is quite drinkable, and free in bars: ask for *un bicchiere d'acqua dal rubinetto*. **Mineral water** (*acqua minerale*) is a more common choice, either still (*senza gas, liscia, non gassata* or *naturale*) or sparkling (*con gas, gassata* or *frizzante*).

BEER AND SPIRITS

Beer (*birra*) is nearly always a lager-type brew which usually comes in one-third (*piccola*) or two-third (*grande*) litre bottles. Commonest and cheapest are the Italian brands Peroni and Dreher, both of which are very drinkable; if this is what you want, either state the brand name or ask for *birra nazionale* – otherwise you may be given a more expensive imported beer. In most bars you have a choice of this or draught beer (*alla spina*), measure for measure more expensive than the bottled variety. You may also come across darker beers (*birra nera* or *birra rossa*), which have a sweeter, maltier taste and resemble stout or bitter.

All the usual **spirits** are on sale and known mostly by their generic names. There are also Italian brands of the main varieties: the best Italian brandies are Stock and Vecchia Romagna. A generous shot of these costs about L3000, much more for imported stuff or in smart city bars. The home-grown Italian firewater is **grappa**, originally from Bassano di Grappa in the Veneto but now made just about everywhere: the best Tuscan varieties are from Montalcino (Brunello) and Montepulciano. Grappas are made from the leftovers of the winemaking process (skins, stalks and the like) and drunk as *digestifs* after a meal; they're delicious – as well as being perhaps the cheapest way of getting plastered and savagely hung over.

You'll also find **fortified wines** like Martini, Cinzano and Campari; ask for a "Campari-soda" and you'll get a ready-mixed version from a little bottle. If you want a real Campari, ask for *un Campari bitter*. Lemon Soda (see above) and Campari bitter makes a delicious and dangerously drinkable combination. The non-alcoholic Crodino, easily recognizable by its lurid orange colour, is also a popular *aperitivo*. A slice of lemon is a *spicchio di limone*, ice is *ghiaccio*. You might also try Cynar, an artichoke-based sherry often drunk as an aperitif.

There's also a daunting selection of **liqueurs**. Amaro is a bitter after-dinner drink, and probably the most popular way among Italians to round off a meal. The top brands, in rising order of bitterness, are Montenegro, Ramazotti, Averna and Fernet-Branca. Amaretto is a much sweeter concoction with a strong taste of marzipan. Sambuca is a sticky-sweet aniseed brew, often served with a coffee bean in it and set on fire. Strega is another drink you'll see in every bar – the yellow stuff in elongated bottles: it's as sweet as it looks but not unpleasant. Also popular, though considered slightly naff in Italy, is *limoncello*, a bitter-sweet lemon spirit that's becoming increasingly trendy outside the country.

WINE

Pursuit of wine is as good a reason as any for a visit to Tuscany. The province constitutes the heartland of Italian wine production, with sales of Chianti accounting for much of the country's wine exports, and the towns of Montalcino and

Montepulciano producing two of the very finest Italian vintages (Brunello and Vino Nobile respectively). Umbria, by contrast, is low-key, except for the white Orvieto – a long-established bevvy developed by the Etruscans – but is increasingly producing top-quality but as yet little-known wines.

Until the last decade or so, most Tuscan wines – including Chianti – were criticized by wine buffs for methods geared principally to high yields, low prices, and never mind the quality. However, nudged along by the DOC laws standards have steadily risen. Besides the finer tuning of established names, there's a good deal of experimentation going on, with French grape varieties such as Chardonnay, Sauvignon and the Pinots being added to the blends of Tuscan wines, and producers using the French technique of *barriques*, 225-litre oak casks, for ageing reds and whites.

The snobbery associated with "serious" wine drinking remains for the most part, mercifully absent. Light reds such as those made from the *dolcetto* grape are hauled out of the fridge in hot weather, while some full-bodied whites are drunk at near room temperature. Wine is also still very cheap. In bars you can get a glass of good local produce for L500 or so, and table wine – often decanted from the barrel – in restaurants is rarely charged at more than L12,000 a litre. Major-name bottled wine is pricier but still very good value; expect to pay from around L20,000 a bottle in a restaurant, and less than half that from a shop or supermarket.

TUSCAN WINE

The wines of Tuscany are predominantly based on the local Sangiovese grape, the foundation of heavyweights such as Chianti, Brunello di Montalcino and Vino Nobile di Montepulciano. Tuscan wine is traditionally red, but new techniques have boosted the quality of many whites, especially Vernaccia di San Gimignano and Bianco di Montecarlo.

Chianti, the archetypal Italian wine, is also the most difficult to characterize, as the vintages produced by the seven Chianti districts (see box p.174) vary from the lightest swillable stuff to deep-toned masterpieces aged in the cellars of ancient castles. The core of Chianti country is the Chianti Classico region between Florence and Siena, and even within this well-defined zone there are so many variables of climate and terrain

that the character of the wine bottled in one estate might be entirely distinct from the neighbouring product. The variety makes it as difficult to get a full grasp of the subject of Chianti wine as it is to master the intricacies of Bordeaux, but it does make a tasting tour a highly rewarding experience.

The greatest Tuscan red – **Brunello di Montalcino** – is produced just outside the Chianti region, around a hill town to the south of Siena. First created just over a hundred years back, Brunello is a powerful, complex and long-lasting wine, whose finest vintages sell at stratospheric prices. More accessible is the youthful **Rosso di Montalcino**, offering a cut-price glimpse of Brunello's majesty.

The mighty if inconsistent **Vino Nobile di Montepulciano** completes the upper tier of the Tuscan wine hierarchy, and the town again has a good regular red produced by less complex methods. **Carmignano**, from near Florence, traces its pedigree back to 1716 and is also highly regarded. Equally ancient and consistently good is **Pomino**, from the Mugello region, available as an excellent red and as a white made from Chardonnay and Pinot grapes. A rapidly improving alternative red DOC is **Morellino di Scansano**, from the coastal Maremma vineyards.

Non-DOC wines include some of the most fashionable Tuscan products at the moment. **Sassicaia**, produced near Livorno from Cabernet Sauvignon grapes, was described by Hugh Johnson as "perhaps Italy's best red wine". The Chianti-based Antinori estate, a pillar of the Tuscan wine establishment, joined the experimental wave in merging Sangiovese and Cabernet Sauvignon to make the top-rated **Tignanello**.

Cabernet-based wines have tended to steal the limelight from other innovations in recent years, with Castello dei Rampolli's **Sammarco**, Antinori's **Solaia**, and **Tavernelle** from the Villa Banfi doing especially well in blind tastings. However, Merlot and Pinot Noir grapes have begun to thrive in Tuscany, while **white-wine** producers are achieving excellent results with Chardonnay, Sauvignon Blanc, the Pinot varieties, and even Riesling and Gewurztraminer, usually considered to be best suited to cooler zones.

UMBRIAN WINE

Umbria has only a handful of DOC regions, many producing cheap, serviceable wine that rarely

A WINE CHECKLIST

TUSCANY

Bianco di Pitigliano Delicate dry white from southern Tuscany.

Bianco Vergine della Valdichiana Soft dry white from the area south of Arezzo.

Brunello di Montalcino Full-bodied red from south of Siena; one of Italy's finest wines.

Carmignano A dry red produced in the region to the west of Florence; this area also produces Vin Ruspo, a fresh rosé.

Chianti Produced in seven distinct central Tuscan districts, Chianti ranges from the roughest table wine to some of the most elegant reds bottled in Italy. (More details appear in the box on Chianti wines on p.174.)

Colline Lucchesi A soft and lively DOC red from the hills east of Lucca.

Galestro Light, dry summer white – a recent development, motivated partly by the need to find some use for the surplus of low-grade white wine produced in Chianti.

Grattamacco Produced in the area to the south-east of Livorno, this non-DOC wine comes as a fruity white and as a full, dry red.

Montecarlo A full and dry white – one of Tuscany's finest – from the east of Lucca.

Morellino di Scansano A fairly dry, robust DOC red, made to the southeast of Grosseto; an up-and-coming wine.

Pomino New DOC from near Rúfina; red, white and Vinsanto.

Rosso di Montalcino A full-bodied DOC from the Montalcino area, aged less than the great Brunello di Montalcino.

Rosso di Montepulciano Excellent-value red table wine.

Sammarco Big Cabernet wine from the Chianti region.

Sassicaia Full ruby wine, best left a few years; from near Livorno.

Solaia Another Cabernet Sauvignon from the Antinori estate.

Spumante Sparkling wines are a relatively new departure in Tuscany, but vineyards all over the province are now using the *champenoise* or *charmat* method to produce quality vintages.

Tavernelle California-style red from western Chianti.

Tignanello Traditional Sangiovese Chianti, again from Antinori.

Vernaccia di San Gimignano Subtle dry white DOC from the hills of San Gimignano.

Vino Nobile di Montepulciano A full, classy red DOCG from around Montepulciano, south of Siena.

Vinsanto Toscano Aromatic wine, made from semi-dried grapes and sealed in casks for at least three years. Produced all over Tuscany (and Umbria too), it ranges from dry to sweet, and is often served at dessert.

UMBRIA

Cabernet Sauvignon di Miralduolo Purplish dry red from Torgiano.

Cervaro della Sala A new white wine, aged in French oak.

Chardonnay di Miralduolo Flowery, dry white from Torgiano, also aged in wood.

Colli Altotiberini Tiber valley DOC; promising new arrival, best drunk young.

Colli Amerini Another new DOC, best known for its reds.

Colli Perugini Umbria's newest DOC – red, white and rosé.

Colli del Trasimeno Huge area producing reds and whites of ever-rising standard.

Decugnano dei Barbi Rosso Fruity red from near Lago di Corbara.

Montefalco From the hills close to Foligno: Montefalco Rosso, a soft, dry red, and the more robust Sagrantino di Montefalco, plus Sagrantino Passito, a superb red dessert wine.

Orvieto Umbria's most famous DOC wine, a dry, light white, or a lightly sweet dessert wine (*abboccato*).

San Giorgio A bold, full-bodied red, made in Torgiano.

Solleone Dry, sherry-like aperitif.

Torgiano DOC region, southeast of Perugia, producing both red and white wines; look out for the fruity and dry white Torre di Giano, the wood-aged white Torre di Giano Riserva, and the opulent Rubesco Riserva, one of Italy's finest red wines.

finds its way outside the region. Most are made from similar grapes and in similar ways to the workaday reds of Tuscany; however, innovation is producing ever more interesting high-quality vintages, and there's a trove of little-known wines that repay searching out.

The region's most famous liquid export, **Orvieto**, has in recent times been reduced to a shadow of its former self, as local producers realized that the world market was turning to dry, crisp wines. In response they transformed the venerable vintage of antiquity – traditionally a semi-sweet *abboccato* – into a mass-produced plonk for the supermarket shelf. More ambitious producers, however, are returning to the old wine, and with patience you'll find samples of the revamped product in and around the town. Orvieto's pre-eminence in Umbria itself has been taken over by **Grechetto**, made by countless producers across the region from the eponymous grape. It's a cheap and almost unfailingly reliable white.

Amongst the most famous of the region's new names is Giorgio **Lungarotti** at Torgiano (near Perugia), employing new grape varieties and innovative techniques to produce some of Italy's finest wines. Anything with his name on a label should be good, and in some cases – the *Rubesco Riserva* – of almost unparalleled excellence. Other key names include **Antinori**, the big Tuscan producers, who in Umbria make wine at Sala to the north of Orvieto: look out for their *Cervaro della Sala*.

Other exponents of Umbria's quest for quality are concentrated in the new **Montefalco** DOC region, a tiny area whose wines are at last becoming obtainable outside its environs; the reds are excellent, and the key producer is Adanti. Similar progress is being made in the Upper Tiber above Perugia, where much is expected of the **Colli Altotiberini** DOC, and the region around Assisi and Amelia (**Colli Amerini**) is also producing ever-improving wines. Again, most of the vintages are reliable, and few of them available anywhere but Umbria. The **Colli Perugini** and **Colli del Trasimeno** wines are the region's most humble; the latter include offerings from the Lamborghini vineyard – he of sports-car fame.

COMMUNICATIONS, POST, PHONES AND THE MEDIA

Opening hours of main post offices are usually Monday to Saturday 8.30am to 7.30pm, but most post offices are open mornings only, Monday to Friday 8.30am to 1.50pm, Saturday 8.30am to noon, and offices in smaller towns may close altogether on Saturday. If you want stamps (*francobolli*) you can buy them in *tabacchi* too, as well as in some gift shops in the tourist resorts; they will often also weigh your letter. Airmail letter rates to Britain are L850; to North America, L1300; to Australia and New Zealand, L1400; postcard rates are around L50 less. The Italian postal system is one of the worst in Europe: if your letter is urgent consider spending the extra L3000 required to send it express. Letters can be sent poste restante to any Italian post office, by addressing them "Fermo Posta" followed by the name of the town; advise friends to double-underline your surname on any envelope for easier identification, as filing is often diabolical. When picking something up take your passport, and make sure they check under middle names and initials.

TELEPHONES

Public **telephones**, run by **Telecom Italia**, come in various forms, usually with clear instructions printed on them (in English too). In the major towns, the most common type takes L100, L200 and L500 coins, as well as **telephone cards** (*carte telefoniche*), available from tobacco shops and newsstands for L5000, L10,000 or L15,000; note that the perforated corner of these cards must be torn off before they can be used. Some phones do take phonecards only, but there's always one that takes coins nearby, usually adjacent. You will also come across phones, normally in bars, that only take a *gettone* (L200), available from telephone offices, *tabacchi*, bars and some newsstands, although these are really only useful for making local calls. If you can't find a phone box, bars will often have a phone you can use (look for the red phone symbol).

Telephone numbers change with amazing frequency in Italy, as the phone system is overhauled. If in doubt, consult the local directory — there's a copy in most Italian bars, hotels and, of course, telephone offices. Note, too, that in Italy all former area codes are now part of the subscriber numbers, and must be included whether you're calling from within the same town or from another country. Thus, dialling a number in Florence from within that city you must include the old 055 area code as part of the number, and when calling Italian numbers from abroad, you must now include the initial zero.

You can make **international calls** from any booth that accepts cards, and from any other booth labelled *interurbano*; put in at least L2000 to be sure of getting through. The cheapest way to make international calls, however, is to get hold of a phone card before you leave from **British Telecom** (☎0800/345 144) or **Cable & Wireless** (☎0500/00505); in the US, similar cards are issued by **AT&T** (☎1800/543 3117) or **MCI** (☎1800/444 3333). All the cards are issued free, and work in much the same way: from most major cities, just ring the company's international "Country Direct" operator (see numbers in box above), who will connect you free of charge and add the cost of the connected call to your domestic bill. You can also make international collect calls by dialling ☎172 followed by your home country code (see box below); this will connect you to an operator in that country.

Another alternative is to find a main **Telecom Italia office**, where you make your call from a kiosk and pay for it afterwards. A lot of Telecom "offices", however, are unstaffed and simply consist of ranks of normal phones. Some bars have a pay-after facility too — it's called a *cabina a scatti*. Finally, you can also make metered calls from hotels, but this will cost you at least 25 percent more, unless you make the call using a charge card.

Phone **tariffs** are highest on weekdays between 8am and 1pm, and cheapest between 10pm and 8am all week and all day Sunday. **Mobile phones** work on the GSM European standard — make sure you have the necessary arrangements for using phones abroad before you leave.

INTERNATIONAL TELEPHONE CODES

The country **code for calling Italy** is ☎39. For direct **international calls from Italy**, dial 00 followed by the country code (given below). the area code (minus its first 0), and finally the subscriber number. **Country Direct** services enable you to speak to an operator in your home country, and to make collect (reverse-charge) calls.

UK: 44   Ireland: 353   US & Canada: 1   Australia: 61   New Zealand: 64

COUNTRY DIRECT SERVICES

UK:	BT ☎172 0044; Cable & Wireless ☎172 054
Ireland:	☎172 0353
US:	AT&T ☎172 1011; MCI ☎172 1022; Sprint ☎172 1877
Canada:	☎172 1001
Australia:	Telstra ☎172 1061; Optus ☎172 1161
New Zealand:	☎172 1064

NEWSPAPERS

The major **newspaper** in Tuscany is the Florence-based national paper *La Nazione*. This is technically a national paper but its sales are concentrated in the central provinces of Italy. It produces local editions, with supplements, including informative entertainments listings, for virtually every major Tuscan town. Umbria's intensely provincial and very widely read tabloid-format paper is the *Corriere dell'Umbria*.

Of the other national papers, the centre-left *La Repubblica* and authoritative right-slanted *Corriere della Sera* are the two most widely read and available. *L'Unità*, the Democratic Left (PDS) party organ, has experienced hard times, even in the party's Tuscan strongholds; it now seems to have regained some lost ground under new editorship.

The most avidly read papers of all, however, are without question the pink *Gazzetta dello Sport* and *Corriere dello Sport*; essential reading for the serious Italian sports fan, they devote as much attention to players' ankle problems as most papers would give to the resignation of a government. News magazines are also widely read in Italy, from the virtually indistinguishable *L'Espresso* and *Panorama* to the brain-candy offerings of *Gente*, *Oggi* and *Novella 2000*.

English and US newspapers can be found for around L4500 a time (L7000 for Sundays) in all the larger towns and established resorts, usually on the day of issue in bigger cities like Florence and Siena; the European editions of the *Guardian* and *Financial Times* and the Rome editions of the *International Herald Tribune* and *USA Today* are also usually available on the day of publication.

TV AND RADIO

The three main national television channels are RAI 1, 2 and 3. Silvio Berlusconi's Fininvest runs three additional nationwide channels – Canale 5, TG4 and Italia 1. Although all are blatantly pro-Berlusconi, the degree of sycophancy displayed on the TG4 news has reached such ludicrous heights (newscaster Emilio Fede is variously overcome by tears of joy or despair, depending on the fortunes of Berlusconi) that Italians now tune in solely for a giggle. The seventh main channel is Telemontecarlo, currently reaching seventy percent of the country.

If you get the chance, try and watch some Italian TV, if only to size up the pros and cons of deregulation. Although the stories of stripping housewives are overplayed, the output is pretty bland across the board, with the accent on quiz shows and soaps, and a heavy smattering of American imports. The RAI channels carry less advertising and try to mix the dross with above-average documentaries and news coverage. Numerous channels concentrate on sport; if you want to see the weekend's Italian League football action, settle into a bar from 5pm on a Sunday.

The situation in radio is even more anarchic than that of TV, with the FM waves crowded to the extent that you continually pick up new stations whether you want to or not. There are some good small-scale stations if you search hard enough, but on the whole the RAI stations are again the more professional – though even with them daytime listening is virtually undiluted dance music. For English-language broadcasts, you can pick up the BBC World Service on MW 648kHz (463m).

OPENING HOURS, PUBLIC HOLIDAYS & SIGHTSEEING

Opening times in Italy are becoming more flexible across the board. Most shops and businesses in Tuscany and Umbria open Monday to Saturday from 8 or 9am until around 1pm, and from about 4pm until 7 or 8pm, though in the biggest towns major shops and offices increasingly work to a more standard European 9am to 5pm (or later). Virtually everything except bars and restaurants closes on Sunday, though Sunday opening is now common in bigger tourist centres and you might find *pasticcerie* or bakers open until Sunday lunchtime. Service stations shut on Sunday (except on motorways) and numerous businesses (restaurants included) take their holidays in August. Many non-food shops are closed on Monday mornings.

HOLIDAYS

You may well find your plans disrupted by national holidays and local saints' days. Local religious holidays don't generally close down shops and businesses, but they do mean that accommodation space may be tight. The country's official national holidays, on the other hand, close everything down, except some bars and restaurants. These are:

January 1
January 6 (Epiphany)
Easter Monday
April 25 (Liberation Day)
May 1 (Labour Day)
August 15 (*Ferragosto*; Assumption of the Blessed Virgin Mary)
November 1 (*Ognissanti*; All Saints)
December 8 (Immaculate Conception of the Blessed Virgin Mary)
December 25
December 26

CHURCHES, MUSEUMS AND ARCHEOLOGICAL SITES

Opening times for museums, galleries, churches and archeological zones are more than usually varied and prone to change in Italy. There are a few general rules, especially for state-run galleries and sites, but always plenty of exceptions that disprove the rule. These days, there is a trend for museums to open 9am–7pm from Tuesday to Saturday in summer, retaining the traditional Sunday half-day and all-day Monday closing. Winter hours are almost always shorter – either 9am to 5/6pm, or the older 9am until 1 or 2pm routine. Smaller museums in smaller towns and villages will almost always have shorter hours.

The opening times of state archeological sites are similar: many sites open Tuesday to Saturday from 9am until one hour before sunset. Similar hours are kept by many of the public gardens. Museums and gardens in Florence, however, are a law unto themselves, with places shutting on almost any day of the week. A special trick of some major Florentine museums is to open on alternate Sundays and/or Mondays when they might usually be closed: check all opening times carefully before embarking on any sightseeing ventures.

Churches are equally problematic, though you can generally rely on them being open daily from 7 or 8am to 7pm (shorter hours in winter). They are usually closed for long periods in the afternoon (typically noon to 3.30 or 4pm) and on Sunday morning during services and all Sunday afternoon. In more obscure places, some churches will only open for early morning and evening services, while others are closed at all times except Sundays and on religious holidays. Wherever possible, the precise opening hours of major churches are given in the guide. The etiquette for visiting churches is much as it is all over the Mediterranean: to dress modestly, which means no shorts and covered shoulders, and don't wander around during a service.

Another problem you'll face is that lots of churches and monasteries are closed for restoration (*chiuso per restauro*) or closed simply because there's not enough money to pay people to keep an eye on their treasures. We've indicated in the text the more long-term closures, though you might be able to persuade a workman or priest/curator to show you around even if there's scaffolding everywhere.

Admission prices for most museums vary between L4000 and L8000, but again Florence is a law unto itself – here L12,000 and upwards is the standard for the biggest galleries such as the Uffizi. Under-18s and over-60s get into public museums free on production of documentary proof; student cards are no longer accepted at many places, though possibly worth a try. Some sites, churches and monasteries are nominally free, though there'll be a custodian around to open things up and show you around, whom you are expected to tip – L1000 per person is appropriate.

FESTIVALS AND ANNUAL EVENTS

Both Tuscany and Umbria have a plethora of local celebrations, with saints' days being the usual excuse for some kind of binge. All cities, small towns and villages have their home-produced saint, whose mortal remains or image are normally paraded through the streets amid much noise and spectacle. There are no end of other occasions for a *festa* – either to commemorate a local miracle or historic event, or to show off the local products or artistic talent. Many happen at Easter, in May or September, or around *Ferragosto* (Aug 15); local dates are detailed below – for more on what goes on, see the respective town entries.

There's also been a revival of **carnival** (*carnevale*), the last fling before Lent, although the anarchic fun that was enjoyed in the past has generally been replaced by elegant, self-conscious affairs, with ingenious costumes and handmade masks – at their most extravagant at the coastal resort of **Viareggio**. Carnival usually lasts for the five days before Ash Wednesday; because it's connected with Easter the dates change from year to year.

RELIGIOUS AND TRADITIONAL FESTIVALS

Many of the local **religious processions** have strong pagan roots, marking important dates on the calendar subsequently adopted and sanctified by the church. **Good Friday**, for obvious reasons, is also a popular time for processions, with images of Christ on the Cross paraded through towns accompanied by white-robed, hooded figures singing penitential hymns. The separate motivations to make some money, have a good time and pay your spiritual dues all merge in the celebrations for a town's **saint's day**, where it's not unusual to find a communist mayor and local bishop officiating side by side.

Umbria has the edge over Tuscany in religious festivities. **Assisi** – with its Franciscan associations – has a disproportionate number of events, the biggest being the *Festa di San Francesco* (Oct 3–4), a celebration of the saint's canonization which draws religious leaders and pilgrims from all over Italy. Holy Week in Assisi attracts one of the world's biggest concentrations of nuns, monks and lesser religious fanatics, and *Calendimaggio* is also huge; lasting for a week from the first Tuesday in May, it celebrates Francis's more worldly youth.

In **Cascia** another of the region's foremost saints, Santa Rita (as popular in some parts of Italy as the Virgin), attracts many thousands of devotees – mainly women – to the torchlight *Celebrazioni Ritiane* (May 21–22). Also heavily patronized are *Corpus Domini* in **Orvieto**, celebrated with a costumed procession and a panoply of associated events, and **Gubbio**'s *Corsa dei Ceri* (see p.475).

In **Tuscany**, the best traditional festivals are of a more secular nature. Top honours go to the **Palio** horse races in **Siena** – which sees jockeys careering around the central square in a fiercely contested spectacle. Other towns put on

CALENDAR OF TRADITIONAL AND RELIGIOUS FESTIVALS

JANUARY

Foligno *Festa di San Feliciano* – traditional fair (Jan 24).

Trevi *Festa di Sant'Emiliano* – torchlit procession (Jan 27).

Viareggio *Carnevale* (late Jan/early Feb). Also good *carnevale* processions in San Gimignano.

FEBRUARY/MARCH

Terni St Valentine's Day fair (Feb 14).

Norcia Crossbow competition (March 20–24).

Easter celebrations

Assisi Holy Week celebrations.

Grassina (near Florence), **Gubbio** and **Bevagna** (near Perugia). Good Friday processions.

Florence *Scioppio del Carro* – fireworks in the Piazza del Duomo (Easter Sun).

San Miniato National kite-flying championships (first Sun after Easter).

APRIL/MAY

Terni *Canta Maggio* – parade of illuminated floats (May 1).

Assisi *Calendimaggio* – spring festival (early May).

Gubbio *Corsa dei Ceri* – candle race (May 15).

Foligno *Giostro della Quintana* – medieval joust (May 15).

Massa Marittima *Balestro del Girifalco* – crossbow competition (first Sun after May 19).

Cascia *Celebrazioni Ritiane* – procession in honour of St Rita (May 21–22).

Gubbio Crossbow matches against team from Sansepolcro (last Sun in May).

JUNE

Orvieto and **Spello** *Corpus Domini* procession (early June).

Pisa *Luminaria* – torchlit procession – precedes *Regatta di San Ranieri* boat race (June 16 & 17). Also *Gioco del Ponte* – costumed mock battle (third Sun of month).

Florence *Festa di San Giovanni* marked by fireworks and the Gioco di Calcio Storico football game (week beginning June 24).

JULY/AUGUST

Siena *Palio* (horse races held on July 2 & Aug 16 are preceded by trial races on June 29 & 30, July 1, Aug 14 & 15 – see entry in the guide).

Fivizzano Archery contest (second Sun of July).

Lucca *Festa di San Paolino* – torchlit parade and crossbow contest (third Sun of July).

Pistoia *Giostro dell'Orso* – joust of the bear (July 25).

Massa Marittima Second leg of the crossbow competition (second Sun in Aug).

Lucca *Luminaria di Santa Croce* – torchlit processions (Aug 14).

Florence *Festa del Grillo* – fair in the Cascine park (Aug 15).

Orvieto *Festa della Palombella* – horse race (Aug 15).

Livorno *Palio Marinaro* – boat races (Aug 17).

San Stefano *Palio Marinaro* – parade and rowing race (mid-Aug).

Montepulciano *Bravio delle Botti* – barrel race through the town (last Sun in Aug).

SEPTEMBER

Arezzo *Giostro del Saraceno* – jousting by knights in armour (first Sun).

Cerreto Guidi (near Empoli) Renaissance processions (first Sun).

Florence *Festa delle Rificolone* – torchlit procession (Sept 7).

Prato *Festa degli Omaggi* – costume procession (Sept 8).

Foligno *Torneo della Quintana* – jousting by 600 medieval knights (second weekend).

Lucca *Festa della Santa Croce* – procession of sacred image (Sept 14).

Sansepolcro Return crossbow matches against Gubbio (second Sun).

OCTOBER

Trevi *Palio dei Terzieri* – cart race (Oct 1).

Assisi *Festa di San Francesco* – major religious festival (Oct 3–4).

NOVEMBER

Perugia *Festa dei Ognissanti* – All Saints Fair (Nov 1–5).

DECEMBER

Siena *Festa di Santa Lucia* – pottery fair (Dec 13).

Prato Display of Holy Girdle (Dec 25 & 26).

FOOD, WINE AND ARTS FESTIVALS

FOOD AND WINE

FEBRUARY

Spello Olive and *bruschetta* (garlic toast) festival (Feb 5).

Norcia Truffle and sausage festival (Feb).

APRIL–JUNE

Montecatini Terme *Fettunta* festival – an oil and garlic speciality (April 16).

Città della Pieve *Festa della Fontana* – flooding of the town fountain with wine. A similar event takes place at nearby **Panicale.**

Montespertoli Wine festival (last Sun of May).

Orvieto Wine festival (June).

Amelia and **Bevagna** Wine and food jamborees (June).

Piediluco *Sagra del Pesce* (June).

Campello di Clitunno Trout festival (June).

JULY–SEPTEMBER

Le Ghiaie, Elba Wine festival (last week of July).

Montepulciano Food and Wine festival (second Sun of Aug).

Cortona *Festa della Bistecca* – excessive consumption of local beef (Aug 15).

Greve Chianti Classico festival (second Sun of Sept).

OCTOBER

Piediluco Wine and chestnut show.

Castiglione del Lago *Cucina tipica* and wine festival.

Umbértide *Sagra della Castagna* – chestnut fair.

Todi *Festa Gastronomica*.

ARTS

APRIL–JUNE

Lucca Sacred music festival (April–June).

Florence *Maggio Musicale* – music festival (April–June).

Spoleto *Festival dei Due Mondi* (Festival of the Two Worlds). Internationally renowned, this month-long event is a mixture of classical concerts, films, ballet, street theatre and performance art, with its venue the open spaces of the ancient walled town (June & July).

Narni Experimental theatre season (last ten days of June).

Fiesole *Estate Fiesolana* – music, cinema, ballet and theatre (mid-June to Aug).

San Gimignano Summer festival of music and film (late June to Oct).

JULY–SEPTEMBER

Barga, near Lucca Opera and theatre festival (second half of July).

Siena *Accademia Musicale Chigiana* (July).

Perugia *Umbria Jazz* – one of Europe's foremost jazz events (July–Aug).

Siena *Settimane Musicali* (Aug).

Torre del Lago *Festival Pucciniano* (Aug).

Montepulciano *Il Bruscello* – folkloric song festival (Aug 14–16).

Arezzo International choral festival (last two weeks of Aug).

Città di Castello Chamber music festival (Aug–Sept).

Gubbio *Spettacoli Classici* – long-established series of classical plays staged in the town's Roman amphitheatre (mid-July to mid-Aug).

Città di Castello *Festival delle Nazioni di Musica da Camera* – highly respected festival of chamber music (last week of Aug).

Perugia *Sagra Musicale Umbra* – festival of classical music, established in 1937 and now one of the region's most prestigious cultural events (last week of Sept).

Todi Increasingly well-known arts festival (ten days in Sept).

OCTOBER–APRIL

Prato Drama season at Teatro Metastasio (Oct–April).

Florence Opera and concert seasons at Teatro Comunale (Nov–Jan).

medieval-origin contests, too, though they are somewhat phoney, having been revived for commercial ends over the past decade or two. Among the most enjoyable are the Gioco di Calcio Storico – a rough-and-tumble football game played between the four quarters of **Florence** in June – and the crossbow competitions between teams from **Gubbio** and **Sansepolcro**, held during May and September.

FOOD AND WINE FESTIVALS

Food- and wine-inspired festivals are more low-key affairs than the religious and traditional events, but no less enjoyable for that. They generally celebrate the edible speciality of the region to the accompaniment of dancing, music from a local brass band and noisy fireworks at the end of the evening.

At Easter and through the summer and autumn there are literally hundreds of such events, most of them catering to locals rather than tourists; for details, ask at tourist offices or check the local newspapers – where you will find them listed as *sagre*. The more established or more interesting events are detailed in the box above.

ARTS FESTIVALS

The ancient inter-town rivalries across Tuscany and Umbria – described neatly by the term *campanilismo* (ie the only things that matter are those that take place within the sound of your village's church bells) – find a highly positive expression in the willingness of local councils to put money into promoting their own **arts festivals**. For the size of the towns involved, the events are often almost ludicrously rich, celebrating the work of a native composer or artist by inviting major international names to perform or direct. Many festivals are given an added enjoyment by their sites – in summer, open-air performances take place in restored ancient amphitheatres, churches or town squares.

TROUBLE AND THE POLICE

Tuscany and Umbria are not exactly hotbeds of crime. The only real trouble you're likely to come across are gangs of *scippatori* or "snatchers", often gypsy kids, who have something of a reputation in Florence. Crowded streets or markets, train stations and packed tourist sights are the places to beware. As well as handbags, *scippatori* whip wallets, tear off visible jewellery and, if they're really adroit, unstrap watches.

You can **minimize the risk** of this happening by being discreet: wear money in a belt or pouch; don't put anything down on café or restaurant tables; don't flash anything of value; keep a firm hand on your camera; and carry shoulder bags, as Italian women do, slung across your body. It's a good idea, too, to entrust money and credit cards to hotel managers. Never leave anything valuable in your **car** and try and park in car parks or well-lit, well-used streets. On the whole, it's sensible to avoid badly lit areas at night, and deserted inner-city areas by day.

Italy's reputation for **sexual harassment** of women is based largely on experiences in the south of the country. However, even in the "civilized north", travelling on your own, or with another woman, you can expect to be tooted and hissed at in towns from time to time and may attract occasional unwelcome attention in bars, restaurants or on the beach. This pestering is not usually made with any kind of violent intent, but it's annoying and frustrating nevertheless. There are few things you can do to ward it off. Indifference is often the most effective policy, as is looking as confident as possible, a purposeful stride and directed gaze. Sitting around in **parks** – especially Florence's unsavoury Cascine – it's best to pick a spot close to other people.

THE POLICE

If it comes to the worst, you'll be forced to have some dealings with the **police**. In Italy there are several different branches, ostensibly to prevent any single one seizing power. You're not likely to have much contact with the Guardia di Finanza, who investigate smuggling, tax evasion and other finance-related felonies. Drivers may well come up against the **Polizia Urbana**, or town police, who are mainly concerned with traffic and parking offences, and also the **Polizia Stradale**, who patrol motorways.

If you're unlucky, you may have dealings with the **Carabinieri**, with their military-style uniforms and white shoulder belts (they are in fact part of the army), who deal with general crime, public order and drugs control. These are the ones Italians are most rude about, but a lot of this stems from the usual north–south divide. Eighty percent of the *Carabinieri* are from southern Italy (joining the police is one way to escape the poverty trap). For all the digs, though, they are the most professional of the different police forces, and the ones to head for if you're in deep trouble. The **Polizia Statale**, the other general crime-fighting branch, enjoy a fierce rivalry with the *Carabinieri*, and are the ones to whom **thefts** should be reported. You'll find the address of the **Questura** or police station in the local *Tuttocittà* supplement, and we've included details in the

major city listings. The office will issue you with a *denuncia*, an impressively stamped form confirming thefts and so forth which you will need for any insurance claims on your return home. The *Questura* is also where you're supposed to go to obtain a *permesso di soggiorno* **if you're staying** for any length of time, or a **visa extension** if you require one.

In any brush with the authorities, your experience will depend on the individuals you're dealing with. Apart from **topless bathing** (permitted, but don't try anything more daring) and **camping rough**, don't expect a soft touch if you're picked up for any offence, especially if it's **drugs-related**: it's not unheard of to be stopped and searched if you're young and carrying a rucksack. Drugs are generally frowned upon by everyone above a certain age, and universal hysteria about *la droga*, fuelled by the serious problem of heroin addiction all over Italy, means that any distinction between the "hard" and "soft" variety has become blurred. Theoretically everything is illegal above the possession of a little marijuana "for personal use", though there's no proper definition of what this means. Addresses of consulates in Florence – not always that helpful – are given on p.159.

FLORA AND FAUNA

Tuscany and Umbria's countryside has been worked for centuries, but not all of it is the pastoral hill country of popular imagination. The broad sweep of the Apennines contains areas of considerable wilderness and within the coastal and hill regions there is a huge variety of sub-habitats.

A few of these areas are at last receiving protection as **national parks** (*Parco Nazionale*) or as oases supervised by the World Wide Fund for Nature (WWFN). In Tuscany there are two proposed national parks (Italy currently has just eight): the **Monti dell'Uccellina** (or Parco della Maremma) in the Maremma, currently an excellently run nature park (*parco naturale*), and the **Migliarino-San Rossore** area between Pisa and Livorno – partowned by the state, but subject to huge commercial pressures. Two regional parks (*Parco Regionale*) are already established in the mountains north of Lucca – the excellent **Parco dell'Orecchiella**, and the adjoining, but much more tenuous **Parco delle Alpi Apuane**.

In Umbria, where the hunting lobby is one of the most powerful in the country, there are just four parks, all still more or less paper creations. The **Monti Sibillini** in the east have a concerned lobby of environmentalists arguing their case. **Monte Subasio** above Assisi, **Monte Cucco** northeast of Gubbio and the **Valnerina** east of Spoleto are smaller and still fragile.

Much smaller than the state parks are the WWF sites, which are often little more than a couple of hundred hectares in extent. However, in contrast to the state parks, protection on the ground is total, and for the dedicated naturalist they present the best opportunities for sightings. There are none as yet in Umbria, but three in Tuscany, all on the coast in or near the Maremma: **Bólgheri**, **Lago di Burano** and **Laguna di Orbetello**.

SPECIES

Amongst the larger **mammals**, the **wild boar** is best known, endemic through much of Tuscany and now spreading into Umbria. In the Maremma there is an indigenous breed, smaller than the boar of Eastern European origin common elsewhere. Both types are shy, frugal creatures and difficult to spot casually, though you may well see signs of their passage. **Porcupines** are also common and you often find quills on country walks, though again they are elusive creatures. **Roe deer** have been reintroduced into the reserves at Bólgheri and the Monti dell'Uccellina, and are readily seen. Elsewhere they've been hunted to extinction, along with the bulk of the larger mammals.

Wolves, however, are making some sort of return, drifting into the Valnerina from their heartlands in the Abruzzo mountains to the south. There are an estimated 150 to 200 specimens in Italy, all protected. Their largest threat comes from feral dogs – estimated to number 800,000 nationwide – both because they compete for food and because people deal with the dogs by poisoning or shooting them, killing some wolves in the process.

Wild **mountain goats** are found on the island of Montecristo, a nature reserve closed to the casual visitor. Elsewhere, you may see smaller mammals – hares, rabbits, foxes and weasels – though these too have been much depleted by the hunters' guns. Wilder upland areas are seeing the return of the **wild cat**, but – like the wolf – numbers are tiny, and the chance of seeing them minimal.

You stand far more chance of observing an interesting array of **birds**, not all of which have been blasted from the sky. Coastal areas offer the richest pickings, and in particular the reserves set aside to protect them – Lago di Burano, Laguna di Orbetello and the Monti dell'Uccellina. These closely connected areas draw numerous migrant birds, many of them extremely rare. Inland, birdlife is under threat, but you can still see hoopoes, doves, woodpeckers and run-of-the-mill wrens, thrushes and starlings. **Birds of prey** are comparatively rare, though mountain areas boast a few hawks and buzzards, and perhaps a few pairs of golden eagles.

Snakes, and the viper in particular, are common, particularly around abandoned farmland – of which there's plenty. Small black **scorpions** are also quite common (see p.22 for advice on bites and stings).

The **flora** of Tuscany and Umbria is often exceptional, and spring carpets of flowers – particularly on upland meadows – can be breathtaking. The best areas in Tuscany are the Orecchiella and Alpi Apuane, at the meeting point of Alpine and Mediterranean vegetation zones. These contain the vast majority of the species that grow in Italy. In Umbria, the Martani hills, Monte Subasio and the Piano Grande are blanketed in orchids and fritillaries in May and June. In olive groves and on hillsides – often free of pesticides – all manner of common plants thrive: poppies, primroses, violets, grape hyacinth, cyclamen, irises, cistus and many more. Specially adapted marine species can be found in the reserves of the Maremma.

Cypresses and **parasol pines** are the icons of the Tuscan countryside, while **oak** forests blanket many of the interior hills, Chianti in particular.

Elsewhere there are large tracts of **virgin forest**, especially in the Casentino around Camáldoli, filled with oak, beech and pines, many of them huge ancient specimens. Sweet **chestnut** dominates in the Orecchiella and Alpi Apuane, rolling unbroken across mile after mile of the lower hills. On the higher hills, notably in the Sibillini, there are clumps of high beech forest, the predominant tree of the Apennines and of limestone in general. Coastal areas, especially in the Monti dell'Uccellina, have preserved the classic profiles of Mediterranean *macchia* – dwarf trees (usually oak), and a scrub of laurel, broom, lentisk, heather and fragrant plants.

DIRECTORY

ADDRESSES These are usually written as the street name followed by the number – eg Via Roma 69. *Interno* refers to the flat-number – eg interno 5 (often abbreviated as int.). Confusingly, some towns (notably Florence) have two parallel systems for numbering properties, one for shops and restaurants and another for business and private residences; sometimes a shop or restaurant is suffixed by the letter "r", meaning that Via Garibaldi 15r might be in an entirely different place from Via Garibaldi 15. Watch out for addresses with "s/n" rather than a street number, which refers to the fact that they have no number, or are *senza numero*.

BARGAINING Not really on in shops and restaurants, though you'll find you can get a "special price" for some private rooms and cheap hotels if you're staying a few days, and that things like boat or bike rental and guided tours (especially out of season) are negotiable. In markets, you can in theory haggle for everything except food.

BEACHES You'll have to pay a few hundred lire for access to most of the better beaches (referred to as *lido*), a few thousand to hire a sunbed and shade and use the showers all day. During winter most beaches look like rubbish dumps, which is what they are: it's not worth anyone's while to clean them until the season starts at Easter.

CAMPING GAZ Easy enough to buy for the small portable camping stoves, either from a hardware store (*ferramenta*) or camping/sports shops. You can't carry canisters on aeroplanes.

CHILDREN Children are adored in Italy and will be made a fuss of in the street, and welcomed and catered for in bars and restaurants (though be warned that there's no such thing as a smoke-free environment). Hotels normally charge around thirty percent extra to put a bed or cot in your room. The only hazards when travelling with children in Italy in summer are the heat and sun. Sunblock can be bought in any chemist, and bonnets or straw hats in most markets. Take advantage of the less intense periods – mornings and evenings – for travelling, and use the quiet of siesta-time to recover flagging energy. The rhythms of the southern climate soon modify established patterns, and you'll find it quite natural carrying on later into the night, past normal bedtimes. In summer, it's not unusual to see Italian children out at midnight, and not looking much the worse for it.

CIGARETTES The state monopoly brand – MS – are the most widely smoked cigarettes, strong and aromatic, and selling for around L4000 for a pack of twenty. Younger people tend to smoke imported brands – all of which are slightly more expensive, at around L5000 per pack. You buy cigarettes from shops and bars authorized to sell *tabacchi*, recognizable by a sign displaying a white "T" on a black or blue background.

CONTRACEPTION Condoms (*preservativi, profilàttici*) are available over the counter from all pharmacies and some supermarkets; the Pill (*la píllola*) is available from pharmacies without a prescription.

DEPARTMENT STORES There are two main nationwide chains, Upim and Standa, branches of which you'll see virtually everywhere. Neither is particularly upmarket, and they're excellent places to stock up on toiletries and other basic supplies; both stores sometimes have a food hall attached.

ELECTRICITY The supply is 220V, though anything requiring 240V will work. Most plugs are two round pins: a travel plug is useful.

FOOTBALL Tuscany's premier football team is Florence's Fiorentina, one of the strongest squads in Serie A, Italian football's first division. In 1996 Perugia joined them in the top flight, only to be relegated a year later. Perugia returned to Serie A in 1998, but appear unlikely to match Fiorentina's standards in the near future.

GAY LIFE Homosexuality is legal in Italy, and the age of consent is sixteen. Attitudes are relatively tolerant, though there's little developed gay nightlife, even in Florence. There are a few *spiagge gay* (gay beaches) dotted along the coast.

The national gay organization, ARCI-gay, is affiliated to the youth section of the communist party. Their head office is Piazza di Porta Saragozza 2, PO Box 691, 40100 Bologna (☎051.436.700); in Florence they can be contacted through the Arci office at Via Ponte alle Mosse 61. *Babilonia* is the national gay magazine, published monthly.

LAUNDRIES Coin-operated laundries are rare; far more common is a *lavanderia*, a service-wash laundry, but this will be expensive. Although you can usually get away with it, washing clothes in hotel bathrooms has been known to cause problems, since in some parts of the country the plumbing can't cope with all the water.

PHOTOS You may want to bring film with you as it's fairly expensive in Italy – as is the cost of film processing.

PUBLIC TOILETS Almost unheard of outside train and bus stations, and usually the only alternative is to dive into a bar. In stations and some smarter establishments, there might be an attendant who guards the facilities, dispenses paper (*carta*) – and expects a tip of a few hundred lire. Standards seem to be improving, although it is worth carrying your own toilet roll.

TAX If you are thinking of splashing out on a designer outfit or some other expensive item, bear in mind that visitors from outside the EU only are entitled to an IVA (purchase tax) rebate on single items valued at over L625,000. The procedure is to get a full receipt from the shop, describing the purchase in detail. This receipt must be presented to customs on your return home, and then sent back to the shop within ninety days of the date of the receipt; the shop will then refund the IVA component of the price, a saving of eighteen percent.

TIME Italy is always one hour ahead of Britain (except for one week at the end of September when the time is the same), seven hours ahead of US Eastern Standard Time and ten hours ahead of Pacific Time.

PART TWO

TUSCANY

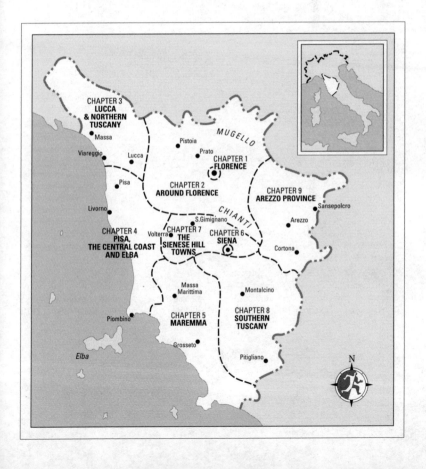

CHAPTER 3
LUCCA
& NORTHERN
TUSCANY

MUGELLO

Massa

Pistoia

Viareggio

Lucca

Prato

CHAPTER 1
FLORENCE

Pisa

CHAPTER 2
AROUND FLORENCE

CHAPTER 9
AREZZO PROVINCE

Livorno

CHIANTI

Sansepolcro

S.Gimignano

Arezzo

CHAPTER 4
PISA,
THE CENTRAL COAST
AND ELBA

Volterra

CHAPTER 7
THE
SIENESE HILL
TOWNS

CHAPTER 6
SIENA

Cortona

Massa
Marittima

Montalcino

Piombino

CHAPTER 5
MAREMMA

CHAPTER 8
SOUTHERN
TUSCANY

Elba

Grosseto

Pitigliano

N

CHAPTER ONE

FLORENCE

Since the early nineteenth century, **FLORENCE** (Firenze) has been celebrated as the most beautiful city in Italy: Stendhal staggered around its streets in a stupor of delight; the Brownings sighed over its idyllic charms; and E.M. Forster's *A Room with a View* portrayed it as the great southern antidote to the sterility of Anglo-Saxon life. For most people Florence comes close to living up to the myth only in its first, resounding impressions. The pinnacle of Brunelleschi's stupendous dome is visible over the rooftops the moment you step out of the train station, and when you reach the Piazza del Duomo the close-up view is even more breathtaking, with the multicoloured **duomo** rising behind the marble-clad **baptistery**. Wander from there down towards the River Arno and the attraction still holds – beyond the **Piazza della Signoria**, site of the immense **Palazzo Vecchio**, the water is spanned by the shopladen medieval **Ponte Vecchio**, with gorgeous **San Miniato al Monte** glistening on the hill behind it.

Yet after registering these marvellous sights, it's hard to stave off a sense of disappointment. For, away from the beaten track, much of Florence is a city of narrow streets and dour, fortress-like houses, of unfinished buildings and characterless squares. Restorers' scaffolding has become an endemic feature of the Florentine scene, and incessant traffic – right through the historic centre – provides all the usual city stresses. Simply roaming the streets is a pleasure in Venice, Rome, Verona – but not in Florence.

The fact is, the best of Florence is to be seen indoors. Under the rule of the **Medici** family – the greatest patrons of Renaissance Europe – Florence's artists and thinkers were instigators of the shift from the medieval to the modern world-view, and the churches, galleries and museums of this city are the places to get to grips with what they achieved. The development of the Renaissance can be plotted stage by stage in the vast picture collection of the **Uffizi**, and charted in the sculpture of the **Bargello**, the **Museo dell'Opera del Duomo** and the guild church of **Orsanmichele**. Equally revelatory are the fabulously decorated chapels of **Santa Croce** and **Santa Maria Novella**, forerunners of such astonishing creations as Masaccio's restored frescoes at **Santa Maria del Carmine**, Fra' Angelico's serene paintings in the monks' cells at **San Marco** and Andrea del Sarto's work at **Santissima Annunziata**.

The Renaissance emphasis on harmony and rational design is expressed with unrivalled eloquence in Brunelleschi's interiors of **San Lorenzo**, **Santo Spirito** and the **Cappella dei Pazzi**. The bizarre architecture of San Lorenzo's **Sagrestia Nuova** and the marble statuary of the **Accademia** – home of the *David* – display the full genius of **Michelangelo**, the dominant creative figure of sixteenth-century Italy. Every quarter of Florence can boast a church or collection worth an extended call, and the enormous **Palazzo Pitti** constitutes a museum district on its own – half a dozen museums are gathered here, one of them an art gallery that any city would envy.

To enjoy a visit fully it's best to ration yourself to a couple of big sights each day (limited opening hours prevent much more anyway), and spend the rest of your hours or days exploring the **quieter spots** on the periphery – such as the **Giardino di Bóboli** behind the Palazzo Pitti – or heading out to one or two of the farther-flung places covered in the next chapter, like Fiesole, the Medici villas or the countryside of Chianti and Mugello.

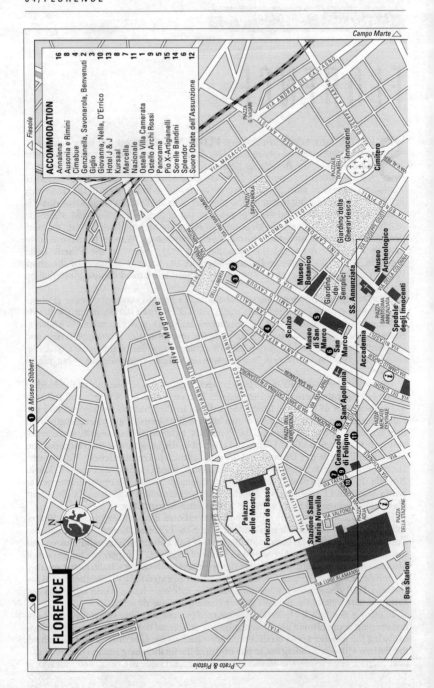

FLORENCE

ACCOMMODATION

Annalena	16
Ausonia e Rimini	8
Cimabue	4
Genzianella, Savonarola, Benvenuti	2
Giglio	3
Giovanna, Nella, D'Errico	10
Hotel J & J	13
Kursaal	8
Marcella	7
Nazionale	11
Ostella Villa Camerata	1
Ostello Archi Rossi	9
Panorama	5
Pio X-Artigianelli	15
Sorelle Bandini	14
Splendor	6
Suore Oblate dell'Assunzione	12

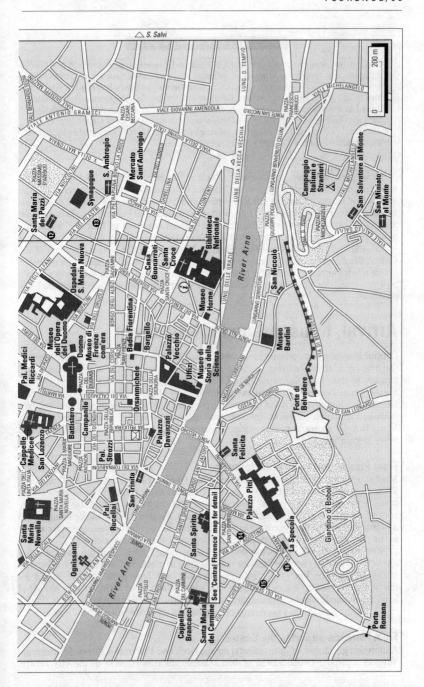

FIRENZE NUOVA

Mass tourism was the inevitable consequence of Florence's rediscovery in the nineteenth century, and today the city's economy has become almost entirely reliant on tourists. An ambitious attempt to break this ever-increasing dependence is the so-called **Firenze Nuova**, a Fiat-underwritten development on the northwestern outskirts that's planned as a viable industrial city, with a view to leaving Florence to flourish as a cultural and small-scale commercial centre. This scheme is still in its early stages, proceeding in the face of objections that it marks a surrender of the city to tourism – just as happened with the development of Venice's industrial twin, Mestre.

Allow some time, too, to involve yourself in the life of the city. Though Florence might seem a little sedate on the surface, its university – and the presence of large numbers of language and art schools – guarantees a fair range of term-time diversions and **nightlife**. The city has some excellent **restaurants** and enjoyable **café-bars** amid the tourist joints, as well as the biggest and liveliest **markets** in Tuscany, and plenty of browsable, high-quality **shops**. And there's certainly no shortage of **special events** – from the high-art festivities of the **Maggio Musicale** to the licensed bedlam of the **Calcio Storico**, a series of costumed football matches held in the last week of June.

For a brief introduction to the history of Florence, see p.597; for the Medici family tree (essential for dispelling confusion in the first few days of church-hopping) see pp.602–5.

Arrival, transport and information

Central Florence is a compact area, and arriving by bus or train will drop you right in the heart of it. If you're flying to Pisa – the routine approach – it's an effortless hour's journey by train from the airport into Florence. Flying to Florence's own ever-expanding airport at Peretola, it's about twenty minutes by shuttle bus or taxi to the city centre. An alternative route is via Bologna airport, though this takes longer and involves both bus and train transfers. International as well as national trains arrive at Santa Maria Novella, a central railway station within a few minutes' walk from the duomo and other key sights.

From Pisa airport to Central Florence
Most scheduled and charter flights fly to **Pisa's Galileo Galilei** airport (☎050.500.707), 95km west of Florence. Getting to Florence from the airport couldn't be simpler. Direct trains leave roughly every hour from a platform at the far left end of the airport concourse, 150m from arrivals. Journey time is an hour. Tickets (L7400) can be bought from an office halfway down the concourse on the right. Remember to **validate your ticket** in the platform machines before boarding the train (see box opposite).

Note that on the return journey you don't have to lug your bags all the way out to the airport, as there's a check-in desk for most airlines by platform 5 at Santa Maria Novella station in Florence, open daily from 7am to 5pm; bags have to be checked in at least thirty minutes before the departure of the train, which must arrive at Pisa airport at least thirty minutes before the departure of the flight. When catching the train, double check it runs through to Pisa Aeroporto – some go no further than Pisa Centrale.

From Florence airport to the Centre
A increasing number of international air services use Florence's **Peretola** (Amerigo Vespucci) airport (☎055.30.615 or 055.373.498), 5km northwest of the city centre.

TRAIN TICKETS

Travelling by train to Florence from Pisa or Bologna airports, be certain to **validate train tickets** in one of the small yellow or gold machines on platforms or in ticket halls. Failure to do so results in a fine. Note that from Bologna, InterCity (IC), EuroCity (EC) or Eurostar (ES) train services require the payment of a supplement (*un supplemento*) on top of the normal ticket price. Pay when purchasing your ticket – rates are higher if you buy it on the train.

The airport has a tiny arrivals hall with exchange machine, half a dozen car rental desks, a lost baggage counter and a small tourist office (daily 8.30am–10.30pm; ☎055.315.874). For information on flights call ☎055.306.1702 (international) or ☎055.306.1700 (domestic).

Light blue SITA buses (☎055.478.2231) provide roughly hourly shuttles into the city from immediately outside the arrivals area. The first bus into the city is 9.15am (last 11.05pm), the first out to the airport at 8.15am (last 8.05pm). Tickets (L6000) can be bought on board. In Florence buses arrive and depart from the main bus terminal on Via di Santa Caterina da Siena, just a few steps west of Santa Maria Novella railway station. Alternatively, the local orange ATAF Florence city bus #62 runs from the airport gate every twenty minutes (6am–10.20pm) to the bays immediately east of the railway station. Tickets (L1500) can be bought from the machine by the exit or the bar on the first floor of the departures area. A taxi costs about L25,000. The journey by bus or taxi takes between fifteen and thirty minutes depending on traffic.

From Bologna airport to Central Florence

A few airlines use Bologna – about the same distance from Florence as Pisa – as a gateway airport for the city. Aerobus shuttles depart every twenty minutes between 7.30am and 11.45pm from outside the airport's Terminal A (Arrivi) to Bologna's main train station (journey time about 25 minutes). From the station, regular trains reach Florence's Santa Maria Novella station in about an hour – tickets cost L8200.

By train

Most trains arrive at Florence's main central station **Santa Maria Novella**, also called Firenze SMN. It's located just north of the church and square of Santa Maria Novella, a couple of blocks west of the duomo (cathedral). A few trains, usually sleepers from southern Italy, may stop at other more outlying stations (Firenze Campo Marte or Firenze Rifredi): if so, wait for a connecting train onwards to SMN.

Santa Maria Novella has an information office just outside (see next page), an accommodation service (see p.72) and left-luggage facilities. For information on trains call ☎147.888.088.

Keep a close eye on your bags at all times – the station's a prime target for thieves and pickpockets. Also avoid the concourse's various taxi and hotel touts, however friendly and reliable they appear: use only licensed cabs from the rank outside, and if you're stuck for a bed, use the station's official accommodation service.

By car and bus

Only residents are allowed to park on the streets in the centre, so you have to leave your **car** in one of the city's main car parks. The most central options are: beneath the train station; Fortezza da Basso (behind the train station); Mercato Centrale; Lungarno Torrigiani; Lungarno della Zecca Vecchia; Piazza della Libertà. You can also find parking spaces alongside the ring roads.

The standard tariff is upwards of L500 per hour for the first hour, and in some spaces anything around L5000 or more for subsequent hours, and all are greatly over-subscribed; Fortezza da Basso has the most space. If you want to leave your car for a prolonged period, try Piazzale Michelangelo, the nearest substantial **free parking** area to the centre. It's about twenty minutes' walk to the Piazza della Signoria from here, so if you're burdened with luggage it's best to take bus #12 or #13 into town. Reports suggest you should watch out for a **scam** in which bogus car-park attendants direct you into a parking space, thus implying there is a charge – there isn't.

Half a dozen **bus** companies run to Florence from various parts of Tuscany. The main operator is SITA, which has a terminal right opposite the train station at Via Santa Caterina da Siena. All the other companies are based nearby: for addresses and routes see pp.159–160.

Orientation and transport

Finding your way around central Florence is straightforward – it's just ten minutes' walk from **Santa Maria Novella** to the central **Piazza del Duomo**, along Via de' Panzani and Via de' Cerretani. You can't really miss these roads: stand with your back to the train station and they form the main thoroughfare sweeping away in front of you and to the left. The great majority of the major sights are within a few minutes of the duomo.

Within the historic centre, walking is generally the most efficient way of getting around, and the imposition of the **zona a traffico limitato** (ZTL) – which limits traffic in the centre to residents' cars, delivery vehicles and public transport – has reduced the once unbearable pollution and noise. On the other hand, the ZTL has increased the average velocity of the traffic, so you should be especially careful before stepping off the narrow pavements.

If you want to cross town in a hurry, or to visit some of the peripheral sights featured in Chapter Two, your best option is to use one of the frequent and speedy orange ATAF **buses**. **Tickets** are valid for 60 minutes (L1500) or three hours (L2500), and can be bought from shops displaying the ATAF sign and from automatic machines all over Florence. The main **ticket and information office** (daily 7am–8pm; ☎055.565.0222) is in the bays to the east of Santa Maria Novella. From this and other outlets and machines you can buy a *Biglietto Multiplo*, which gives you four 60-minute tickets for L5800. Also available is a 24-hour pass (L6000); two-day pass (L8000); three-day pass (L11,000) and one-week pass (L19,000). The **only** time tickets can be bought on board buses is between 9pm and 6am, when tickets cost a flat L3000: exact change is required.

Tickets have to be stamped in a machine on board; there's a hefty on-the-spot fine for any passenger without a validated ticket – inspectors work in plain clothes, attaching their identity badge only at the last minute, and they will accept no excuses. Passes should be validated just at the start of the first journey.

Four of the most **useful bus routes** (A, B, D, P) are covered by special electric buses: Line A runs from SMN station past Orsanmichele and Borgo degli Albizzi to the northeast; Line B runs back and forth along the north bank of the Arno; Line D runs in a circle enclosing the historic centre, Oltrarno and the south bank of the Arno; and Line P runs up and down the Cascine park (Sun only). The following are the handiest of the other routes. Most city **bus routes** originate at or pass by the train station and either Piazza del Duomo or Piazza San Marco.

#7 Train station–San Domenico–Fiesole.
#10 Train station–San Marco–Settignano.
#12 Train station–Porta Romana–Piazzale Michelangelo.
#13 Train station–Campo Marte–Piazzale Michelangelo.

#14 Train station–Duomo–Santa Croce or Piazza dei Ciompi.
#17 Train station–Duomo–San Marco–Salviatino (for the *Villa Camerata* hostel).
#20 Fortezza da Basso–Piazza San Marco.
#25 Train station–San Marco–Piazza della Libertà–Pratolino.
#28 Train station–Via Giuliani–Castello–Sesto Fiorentino.
#52 Train station–football stadium (match days only).
#70 Train station–Duomo–San Marco.
#62 Train station–Ponte di Mezzo–Peretola airport.

Taxis are white with yellow trim. It's relatively difficult to flag one down on the street, but there are central ranks at the station, Piazza della Repubblica, Piazza del Duomo, Piazza Santa Maria Novella, Piazza San Marco, Piazza Santa Croce and Piazza Santa Trinita. The owner-drivers are generally an honest breed and all rides are metered; expect to pay L10,000–15,000 for a short hop within the centre. (Booking a cab costs an extra L3000 – see p.159 for phone numbers of taxi firms).

Information

For information about Florence's sights and events, the city's **main tourist office** is at Via Cavour 1r just north of the duomo (Mon–Sat 8.15am–7.15pm, Sun 8.15am–1.45 pm; ☎055.290.832 or 055.290.833). There's also a quieter and newer office a couple of minutes from Santa Croce at Borgo Santa Croce 29r (Mon–Sat 8.30am–7.15pm; ☎055.234.0444). The most convenient tourist office if you're arriving by train is right outside the train station in **Piazza della Stazione** – it's the stunted tower at the end of the line of bus stops, as you exit the station to the east (Mon–Sat 8.30am–1.45pm; ☎055.212.245).

All of these provide an adequate map and various leaflets, though you may have to ask for the duplicated sheets which give the latest opening hours and entrance charges. The office at Via Cavour also handles information on the whole Florence province. None of these offices will book accommodation – see below for the agencies that do. Another excellent source of information is *Firenze Spettacolo* (L3000), a monthly listings magazine available from most bookshops and larger newsstands.

Florence also has a **youth information line** the *Informagiovanni*, (Tues & Thurs 3–6pm, Wed & Fri 10am–1pm; ☎055.218.310).

Accommodation

Accommodation in Florence can be a problem: hotels are plentiful but prices are high and standards often less than alluring. "Cheap" and "budget" are relative terms in this city. Worse still, the tourist invasion has scarcely any slack spots. Between March and October book your room well in advance, or reconcile yourself to staying some way from the centre. It may even be worth considering staying out of the city altogether:

FLORENTINE ADDRESSES

Note that there is a double address system in Florence, one for businesses and one for all other properties. Business addresses are followed by the letter **r**, and are marked on the building with a red number on a white plate. There's no connection between the two series – thus no. 20 might be several buildings away from no. 20r.

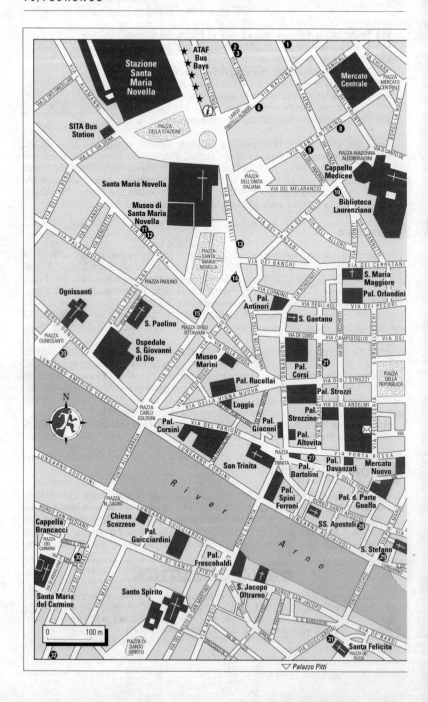

Stazione Santa Maria Novella

★ ATAF Bus Bays ★

② ③

①

Mercato Centrale

PIAZZA MERCATO CENTRALE

VIA CHIARA

VIA PANICALE

VIA NAZIONALE

VIA FIUME

VIA VALFONDA

VIA ALAMANNI

VIA DELL'ARIENTO

BORGO LA NOCE

PIAZZA DELLA STAZIONE

ℹ️

⑥

LARGO FRATELLI ALINARI

VIA FAENZA

SITA Bus Station

VIA S. C. DA SIENA

VIA DELL'ALBERO

VIA DEL SANTO ANTONINO

⑧

⑨

VIA NAZIONALE

PIAZZA MADONNA ALDOBRANDINI

VIA D'CANTO DE

Cappelle Medicee

Santa Maria Novella

PIAZZA DELL'UNITÀ ITALIANA

VIA DEL MELARANCIO

⑩

Biblioteca Laurenziana

VIA DE' CONTI

VIA FANTETTI

Museo di Santa Maria Novella

⑪ ⑫

VIA DELLE BELLE DONNE

VIA DELLA SCALA

VIA DEGLI AVELLI

VIA DEL GIGLIO

VIA DELL'ALLORO

VIA DE' CANACCI

VIA DE BENEDETTA

VIA PALAZZUOLO

PIAZZA SANTA MARIA NOVELLA

⑬

VIA DEI PANZANI

VIA DEI CERRETANI

S. Maria Maggiore

Pal. Orlandini

VIA DEI BANCHI

⑭

VIA DEI PECORI

VIA CORNINO

Ognissanti

VIA DEL PORCELLANA

VIA DEI FOSSI

PIAZZA PAOLINO

Pal. Antinori

VIA RONDINELLI

VIA DEGLI AGLI

S. Gaetano

VIA DE' VECCHIETTI

VIA BRUNELLESCHI

PIAZZA OGNISSANTI

⑳

BORGO OGNISSANTI

S. Paolino

PIAZZA DEGLI OTTAVIANI

⑮

Ospedale S. Giovanni di Dio

VIA DELLA SPADA

VIA DELLE BELLE DONNE

VIA DE' CORSI

VIA CAMPIDOGLIO

VIA DE'

VIA DEL MORO

Museo Marini

Pal. Corsi

VIA DE' PESCIONI

VIA DE' TORNABUONI

PIAZZA DELLA REPUBBLICA

LUNGARNO AMERICO VESPUCCI

VIA DE' FEDERIGHI

Pal. Rucellai

VIA DELLA VIGNA NUOVA

VIA DELLA SOLE

㉑

VIA DEGLI STROZZI

Pal. Strozzi

VIA DEGLI ANSELMI

N

Loggia

PIAZZA CARLO GOLDONI

VIA DEL PARIONE

Pal. Giaconi

Pal. Strozzino

VIA DE' SASSETTI

Pal. Corsini

Pal. Altovita

VIA PORTA ROSSA

LUNGARNO CORSINI

San Trinita

PIAZZA S. TRINITA

Pal. Bartolini

Pal. Davanzati

VIA PELLICCERIA

Mercato Nuovo

LUNGARNO SODERINI

River

Arno

Pal. Spini Ferroni

Pal. d. Parte Guelfa

㉗

VIA DELLE TERME

BORGO SAN

PIAZZA N. SAURO

Chiesa Scozzese

LUNGARNO GUICCIARDINI

Pal. Guicciardini

SS. Apostoli ㉘

LUNGARNO ACCIAIUOLI

BORGO SAN FREDIANO

Cappella Brancacci

PIAZZA DEL CARMINE

VIA DI SANTO SPIRITO

Pal. Frescobaldi

S. Stefano

㉙

PONTE VECCHIO

㉚

S. Jacopo Oltrarno

VIA POR S. MARIA

Santa Maria del Carmine

Santo Spirito

S. Jacopo

BORGO SAN JACOPO

VIA DE' BARDI

PIAZZA DI SANTO SPIRITO

0 ———— 100 m

㉛ Santa Felicita

PIAZZA DE' ROSSI

㉜

▽ Palazzo Pitti

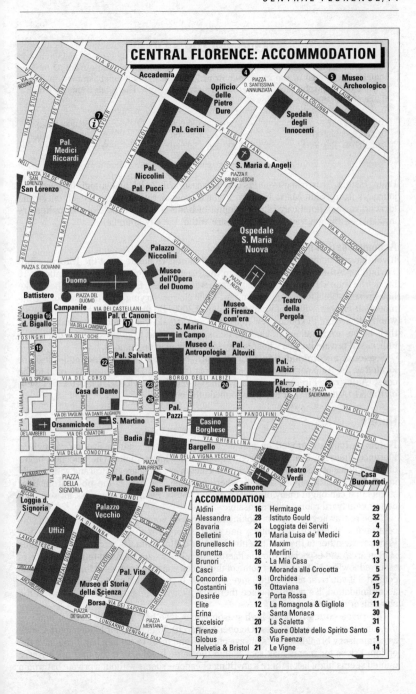

CENTRAL FLORENCE: ACCOMMODATION

ACCOMMODATION

Aldini	16	Hermitage	29
Alessandra	28	Istituto Gould	32
Bavaria	24	Loggiata dei Serviti	4
Belletini	10	Maria Luisa de' Medici	23
Brunelleschi	22	Maxim	19
Brunetta	18	Merlini	1
Brunori	26	La Mia Casa	13
Casci	7	Moranda alla Crocetta	5
Concordia	9	Orchidea	25
Costantini	16	Ottaviana	15
Desirée	2	Porta Rossa	27
Elite	12	La Romagnola & Gigliola	11
Erina	3	Santa Monaca	30
Excelsior	20	La Scaletta	31
Firenze	17	Suore Oblate dello Spirito Santo	6
Globus	8	Via Faenza	1
Helvetia & Bristol	21	Le Vigne	14

ACCOMMODATION PRICES

Throughout this guide, **hotel** accommodation is graded on a scale from ① to ⑨, indicating the cost of the **cheapest double room** in each establishment in high season (for **hostels**, rates per person are given in lire). The price bands to which these codes refer are as follows:

① up to L60,000	④ L120,000–150,000	⑦ L250,000–300,000
② L60,000–90,000	⑤ L150,000–200,000	⑧ L300,000–350,000
③ L90,000–120,000	⑥ L200,000–250,000	⑨ over L350,000

Prato, Pistoia, Arezzo and even Pisa are all reasonably quick and straightforward train journeys from Santa Maria Novella. If you're considering a package deal, check the location of your hotel carefully. A handful of **hostels** and a couple of **campsites** are available for budget travellers, but few are within the city boundaries.

Accommodation booking services

If you haven't booked ahead, the easiest solution is to queue up at the **Informazioni Turistiche Alberghiere** (ITA) next to the Farmacia Comunale opposite platform 16 inside the train station (daily 8.30am–9pm; ☎055.282.893, fax 055.288.429). They make hotel reservations for incoming tourists, their charge varying with the class of accommodation chosen – the minimum is around L3000. Be wary of using the hotel touts, who hang around the queues for this office and around the station in general. Some of their hotels are genuine but likely to be expensive or far from the centre – others are unlicensed private houses whose safety standards may be dubious.

Seasonal accommodation offices (April–Nov daily 10.30am–1pm & 3–7pm) are located at the Agip service station at Peretola (☎055.421.1800) on the A11 road to the coast (Autostrada Firenze Mare), and at the Chianti Est service station (☎055.621.349), on the A1 (Autostrada del Sole) just outside the city.

Hotels

Hotels in Italy are graded on a scale running from one-star to five-star, though in Florence there's a dearth of decent places in the lower ranks. The selection below offers a choice of places over several price categories. Most are central and within walking distance of the sights, and all, where possible, are free of the **noise** from busy streets that can blight many otherwise decent hotels. Even so, always ask for rear, garden or courtyard rooms where possible.

If you're trawling the streets looking for places on your own, there are two main concentrations of lowish-cost hotels: one to the north of the station, centred on **Via Faenza**; the other to the south, centred on **Via della Scala**. Be warned that the whole station area, and especially the Via Faenza zone, has a sizeable night-time population of assorted lowlife. Note also that some of the places you come across in this area are unlicensed – if you're at all doubtful, give it a miss. If you can afford to pay more for your accommodation, it's worth it, since there are plenty of colourful places to stay in the city's nicer districts.

Our **price codes** relate to high-season prices (see box above for details) and you may find lower off-season rates (October to March). Watch out for hidden extras, such as compulsory breakfasts – it's always cheaper and nicer to eat in a bar if you have the option. Prices for rooms may vary within the same hotel – so if the first price you're quoted seems high, ask if there's anything cheaper – rooms without a private bathroom always cost less. The maximum cost of a room, plus any charge for breakfast, should be posted on the back of the door; if it isn't, or if you have any other complaints, contact the tourist office.

Budget

Ausonia e Rimini, Via Nazionale 24 (☎055.496.547). Nicely refurbished one-star with 11 rooms, near the station in the same building as the co-owned and more expensive two-star *Kursaal* (see p.75). ③.

Brunetta, Borgo Pinti 5 (☎055.247.8134). Just a few steps up Borgo Pinti on the left as you head north from Via dell'Oriuolo; ten doubles and one single, shared bathrooms. No breakfast. ②.

Brunori, Via del Proconsolo 5 (☎055.289.648). A short walk east from the duomo, on a busy road, this potentially noisy and slightly run-down place has the compensation of especially friendly and informative owners; one double room with private bathroom, eight without. ③.

Concordia, Via dell'Amorino 14 (☎055.213.233, fax 055.213.337). Cheap and extremely convenient one-star, being located at the back of San Lorenzo church; it has 16 rooms, including four pricier ones with private bathrooms, and doesn't do breakfast. ③.

Genzianella (☎055.573.909), **Savonarola** (☎055.587.824) and **Benvenuti** (☎055.572.141), all Via Cavour 112, all same fax 055.586.727. Three different *pensioni* in one building, virtually in the Piazza della Libertà, which means a bus or long walk to the sights. Two entrances (the other's on Viale Matteotti) lead to a single reception. All are dependable if unthrilling: the two-star, 14-room *Benvenuti* is best; the other two are similarly sized one-stars. ③.

Giovanna (☎055.238.1353), **Nella** (☎055.265.4346) and **D'Ericco** (☎055.215.531), all Via Faenza 69. The first two are small, tidy and as cheap as any on Via Faenza; the third is OK, but no more than that. All have just seven rooms each, none with private bathrooms. ②.

La Mia Casa, Piazza Santa Maria Novella 23 (☎055.213.061). Free showers, occasional film shows on summer evenings and an excellent location make this one-star place a regular sell-out, despite its lack of polish and boarding-school atmosphere. Only three of the 21 rooms have private bathrooms, for which you pay an extra L10,000. ②.

La Romagnola (☎055.211.597, fax 055.211.597) and **Gigliola** (☎055.287.981), both Via della Scala 40. These two one-star hotels, which share the same reception, would unquestionably be the pick of the bunch on Via della Scala if it weren't for a curfew. With a total of 42 rooms, they often have space when the others are full. Some rooms with own bath. ②.

Maria Luisa de' Medici, Via del Corso 1 (☎055.280.048). Slightly run-down one-star, with painting-by-numbers portraits of the Medici in the rooms. But it is comfortable, central, small (nine rooms, two with private bathroom) and quiet. ③.

Merlini, Via Faenza 56 (☎055.212.848, fax 055.283.939). Cheapest of the *pensioni* at this address near the station. Ten one-star rooms, though just one has a private bathroom. ③.

Nazionale, Via Nazionale 22 (☎055.238.2203, fax 055.238.1735). An average but serviceable one-star place with nine rooms, six with private bathroom, halfway between the train station and the San Lorenzo market. ③.

Orchidea, Borgo degli Albizi 11 (☎ & fax 055.248.0346). Lovely twelfth-century building, with half a dozen big rooms, including three doubles, none with private bathroom; a bargain. ②.

Ottaviani, Piazza degli Ottaviani 1 (☎055.239.6223, fax 055.293.355). The best of this one-star's 19 rooms (only two with private bathrooms) overlook Piazza Santa Maria Novella, others aren't so great, but still cheap and convenient. ②.

Via Faenza 56, Via Faenza 56. The upper three floors of this address contain no fewer than five one-star *pensioni*: the eight-room *Anna* (☎055.239.8322); seven-room *Armonia* (☎055.211.146); 12-room *Azzi* (☎ & fax 055.213.806); 12-room *Marini* (☎055.284.824); and seven-room *Paola* (☎055.213.682). With most of its rooms overlooking the garden, the *Azzi* is probably the nicest. The *Anna* is friendly but has a 1am curfew; *Paola* has no curfew but is the scruffiest of the quintet; *Armonia* and *Marini* are comfortable but bland. All come in at around L100,000, but only *Marini* and *Azzi* have rooms with private as opposed to shared bathrooms. ③.

Inexpensive

Bavaria, Borgo degli Albizi 26 (☎ & fax 055.234.0313). A simple and acceptable one-star with just eight rooms, most with shared bathroom, near the city centre. The hotel occupies part of a sixteenth-century palazzo built for a follower of Eleonora di Toledo. Be sure to book, as it's often full of long-stay language students. No credit cards. ④.

Costantini, Via dei Calzaiuoli 13 (☎055.213.995, fax 055.215.128). This 14-room two-star has a great location, on the city's main pedestrian street close to the duomo and Piazza della Signoria. ④.

Elite, Via della Scala 12 (☎ & fax 055.215.395). A two-star run by one of the most pleasant managers in town – and has no curfew. All four double rooms have private bathrooms. ④.

Firenze, Piazza dei Donati 4 (☎055.214.203, fax 055.212.370). The no-frills *Firenze* is a clean and central one-star hotel with 61 rooms, so there's a better chance of finding space here than in some of the smaller places. Virtually all rooms have private bathrooms. Rooms on top floors enjoy a touch more daylight. Three-, four- and five-bed rooms are available. No credit cards. ④.

Giglio, Via Cavour 85 (☎055.486.621, fax 055.461.163). A small eight-room two-star reasonably close to the cheaper *Panorama*, and a touch more pleasant, but at the very inconvenient northern end of this busy road. ④.

La Scaletta, Via Guicciardini 13 (☎055.283.028, fax 055.289.562). An 11-room two-star hotel in the Oltrarno in similar vein to the nearby *Sorelle Bandini*, though more expensive; from the rooftop terrace you look across the Bóboli gardens in one direction and the city in the other. ④.

Marcella, Via Faenza 58 (☎ & fax 055.213.232). Just seven good-sized rooms in this one-star, two without private bathrooms at L10,000 cheaper than other rooms. ④.

Maxim, Entrances at Via dei Calzaiuoli 11 (lift) and Via de' Medici 4 (stairs) (☎055.217.474). Few one-star hotels offer a better location than this friendly 22-room place just a minute from the duomo. Rooms are clean, some with own bath; the quietest look onto a central courtyard. ④.

Panorama, Via Cavour 60 (☎055.238.2043, fax 055.264.404). A 33-room two-star that's a favourite with school groups, in the university area just north of San Marco on the city's main north-running road. ④.

Moderate

Aldini, Via dei Calzaiuoli 13 (☎055.214.752, fax 055.291.621). A 14-room two-star at a very convenient but potentially busy address. All the doubles come with private bathrooms; the singles come with and without. The *Costantini* (see above) at the same address, however, is almost half the price. ⑤.

Alessandra, Borgo Santi Apostoli 17 (☎055.283.438). One of the best of the central two-stars, its 25 rooms occupy a sixteenth-century palazzo and are furnished in a mixture of antique and modern styles; used by the fashion-show crowd, so booking is essential in Sept. ⑤.

Annalena, Via Romana 34 (☎055.222.402, fax 055.222.403). Situated in the Oltrarno, this 20-room three-star, once owned by the Medici, passed to a young Florentine noblewoman (Annalena) who retired from the world after a disastrous love affair and bequeathed the building to the Dominicans. The best rooms open onto a gallery with garden views, and a sprinkling of antiques lend a hint of old-world charm. ⑥.

Belletini, Via dei Conti 7 (☎055.213.561, fax 055.283.551). The warm welcome of owner Signora Gina counts for much in this 27-room two-star; so too do her copious breakfasts. Most of the simple rooms have private bathrooms, around half have TVs and all have air-conditioning. ⑤.

Casci, Via Cavour 13 (☎055.211.686, fax 055.239.6461). It would be hard to find a better two-star in central Florence than this 24-room hotel. Only two (sound-proofed) rooms face the busy street: the rest are wonderfully quiet, clean and fitted out in a manner that wouldn't disgrace a four-star. The welcome is warm and the owners are unfailingly helpful and courteous. The big buffet breakfast in the vaulted and frescoed reception area is a major plus. ⑤.

Cimabue, Via Bonifacio Lupi 7 (☎055.471.989, fax 055.475.601). Like the similarly priced *Casci* (see above), this 16-room hotel offers more than the usual two-star establishment, though its location is not as good. Some of the double and triple rooms have frescoed ceilings, and all are kitted out with antiques and pleasant fabrics. All rooms have (mostly small) private bathrooms; the family atmosphere is welcoming and the breakfasts more than generous. ⑤.

Desirée, Via Fiume 20 (☎055.238.2382, fax 055.291.439). Completely overhauled two-star – stained-glass windows, simulated antique furniture, and a bath in each of the 18 rooms. Located one block east of the station, so there are better-situated hotels at this price. ⑤.

Erina, Via Fiume 17 (☎055.288.294). A two-star hotel located on the third floor of an old palazzo; open mid-July to mid-September. Has just seven double rooms, six with private bathrooms. ⑤.

Globus, Via Sant'Antonino 24 (☎055.211.062, fax 055.239.6225). Friendly but unremarkable, the chief merit of this 23-room place is its location, close to San Lorenzo. It is only a one-star, however, so a touch over-priced (three doubles only with private bathroom). ⑤.

Kursaal Via Nazionale 24 (☎055.496.324, fax 055.474.014). Welcoming and nicely refurbished small nine-room two-star, with the same management as the cheaper *Ausonia e Rimini*. ⑤.

Le Vigne, Piazza Santa Maria Novella 24 (☎055.294.449, fax 055.230.263). Well-refurbished two-star – the nicest of several hotels on this square. ⑤.

Porta Rossa, Via Porta Rossa 19 (☎055.287.551; fax 055.282.179). Florence has smarter three-star hotels, but none as venerable as the 81-room Porta Rossa, which has been a hotel since the four-teenth century and hosted, among others, Byron and Stendhal. You come here for character and nineteenth-century ambience, rather than luxurious modern touches. ⑤.

Sorelle Bandini, Piazza Santo Spirito 9 (☎055.215.308). Some of the ten rooms in this one-star *pensione* are vast and have marble fireplaces, but other rooms are grim – so make sure you inspect before paying. Location is a plus: the hotel is in the Oltrarno on Piazza Santa Spirito, one of the city's more happening squares. ⑤.

Splendor, Via San Gallo 30 (☎055.483.427, fax 055.461.276). A 31-room three-star, occupying a quiet palazzo in the university area (very convenient for San Marco): frescoed and antique-furnished; breakfast is included in the price. Eight cheaper rooms without private bathroom. ⑥.

Expensive

Brunelleschi, Via dei Calzaiuoli-Piazza Santa Elisabetta 3 (☎055.290.311; toll-free in Italy 1678.60076; fax 055.219.653). Designed by leading architect Italo Gamberini, the four-star, 96-room hotel is built around a Byzantine chapel and fifth-century Pagliazza tower. A small in-house muse-um displays Roman and other fragments found during building work. Decor is simple and stylish, with the original brick and stone offset by lots of wood; rooms are spacious – the best, on the fourth floor, have views of the duomo and campanile. ⑦.

Excelsior, Piazza Ognissanti 3 (☎055.264.201; toll-free in Italy 1678.35035, fax 055.210.278). This five-star, 158-room luxury hotel is marginally the better of the two grand old hotels on this unin-spiring piazza. The antique-filled rooms ooze old-world elegance, while the public areas are on the grandest imaginable scale – a vision of columns, marble floors and decorated wooden ceilings. However, the atmosphere is unstuffy and the service impeccable. Some of the best rooms (fifth floor) have terraces and views, but you pay extra for a glimpse of the Arno. ⑨.

Hermitage, Vicolo Marzio 1-Piazza del Pesce (☎055.287.216, fax 055.212.208). Pre-booking is still essential to secure one of the 28 rooms in this superbly located three-star hotel right next to the Ponte Vecchio, with unbeatable views from some rooms as well as from the flower-filled roof gar-den. The service is friendly, and rooms are cosy, decorated with the odd antique flourish; bathrooms are small but nicely done. Double-glazing has removed the noise problems once suffered by the front rooms, but go for courtyard rooms to be sure. ⑧.

Helvetia & Bristol, Via dei Pescioni 2 (☎055.245.247; toll-free in Italy 1670.10058, fax 055.288.353). Florence's finest and most exclusive five-star hotel has been in business since the 18th century. Guests have included Pirandello, Stravinsky and Bertrand Russell. The public spaces and 49 individually decorated rooms are faultless, the latter beautifully appointed with antiques and period paintings. Facilities and bathrooms are modern – many have jacuzzis – but the overall tone is traditional and hyper-tasteful. ⑨.

Hotel J & J, Via di Mezzo 20 (☎055.234.5005, fax 055.240.282). The bland exterior of this former fifteenth-century convent, located in the Sant'Ambrogio district close to Santa Croce, conceals a romantic 18-room four-star hotel. Some rooms are vast split-level affairs – but all have charm and are furnished with modern fittings, attractive fabrics and a few antiques. Common areas are decked in flowers and retain frescoes and vaulted ceilings from the original building. In summer breakfast is served in the convent's lovely old cloister. ⑨.

Loggiata dei Serviti, Piazza Santissima Annunziata 3 (☎055.289.592, fax 055.289.595). This elegant and extremely tasteful three-star hotel is situated on one of Florence's most celebrated squares. Its 29 rooms have been stylishly incorporated into a building originally designed by Brunelleschi; their rel-ative plainness reflects something of the sixteenth-century convent that once occupied the *palazzo*. All are decorated with fine fabrics and antiques and look out either onto the piazza or peaceful gardens to the rear: top floor rooms have glimpses of the duomo. ⑧.

Morandi alla Crocetta, Via Laura 50 (☎055.234.4747, fax 055.248.0954). An intimate three-star gem, whose small size and friendly ex-pat welcome – owner Katherine Doyle has lived in Florence since she was 12 – ensure a home-from-home atmosphere. Rooms are tastefully decorated with antiques and old prints, and vivid carpets laid on parquet floors. Two rooms have balconies opening onto a modest garden: the best room – with fresco fragments and medieval nooks and crannies – was converted from the site's former convent chapel. ⑦.

Hostels

Florence has only a handful of **hostels** and the best of these is some distance from the centre. To help matters a little, there are a number of places run by religious bodies, plus student institutions which provide beds for non-natives at the city universities. Out of term time (June–Oct) some of these places are open to young tourists, and a few even have accommodation throughout the year. In addition to the houses listed below, there are also a number of *Case dello Studente*, which are run by the university authorities and occasionally made available to visitors; for latest information on these, ask at the tourist office (see p.69).

Santa Monica, Via Santa Monica 6 (☎055.268.338, fax 055.280.185). In Oltrarno, close to Santa Maria del Carmine. Privately owned, it's open to check-in 9.30am–12.30pm and 2pm–midnight: there's a 1am curfew. Kitchen facilities, free hot showers and no maximum length of stay. The noticeboard is useful for information on lifts. To get here from the station it's a 15-minute walk: otherwise take bus #36 or #37 to the second stop after the bridge. No credit cards. L23,000.

Ostello Archi Rossi, Via Faenza 94r (☎055.290.804, fax 055.230.2601). A five-minute walk from the train station, this privately owned hostel is very clean but decorated from top to bottom with guests' wall-paintings and graffiti. Open 6.30–11.00am for reservations in person – the 96 places fill up quickly – and to deposit luggage; no reservations by phone. Closed 11.00am–2.30pm; curfew is 12.30am. Breakfast and evening meals are available; spacious dining room with satellite TV and films on request in the evening. No credit cards. Single rooms L35,000. Dorm beds L24,000–27,000 (Nov–March) or L26,000–33,000 (April–Oct).

Ostello Villa Camerata, Viale Augusto Righi 2–4 (☎055.601.451, fax 055.610.300). Take bus #17b from the train station (approx. 30min). Tucked away in a beautiful park, the Villa Camerata is one of Europe's most attractive hostels, a sixteenth-century house with frescoed ceilings, fronted by lemon trees in terracotta pots. Doors open at 2pm; if you'll arrive later, call ahead to make sure there's space. You'll need an HI card, or you can buy a guest card that's valid in other Italian HI hostels. Breakfast and sheets are included; dinner from L14,000 (no kitchen facilities); films every night; curfew 11.30pm. L24,000; family rooms also available at L70,000–78,000.

Pio X – Artigianelli, Via dei Serragli 106 (☎055.225.044 or 055.225.008). Don't be put off by the huge picture of Pope Pius X at the top of the steps – the management is friendly and the atmosphere relaxed. Open all day, but it's best to get there by 9am, as the 64 beds are quickly taken. Midnight curfew; free showers. L25,000, or L22,000 if you're staying more than one night.

Istituto Gould, Via dei Serragli 49 (☎055.212.576). Reception is on the second floor of this former seventeenth-century palazzo – the doorbell is easily missed. Open for check-in Mon–Fri 9am–1pm & 3–7pm, Sat 9am–1pm; closed Sun. *The Gould's* 110 beds are extremely popular, so it's wise to book in advance, especially during the academic year. Street front rooms can be noisy – rear rooms are better – but the old courtyard, terracotta floors and stone staircases provide atmosphere throughout. Singles (with/without private bathroom) L55,000/L38,000; doubles (per person) L39,000/L36,000; triples L35,000/L28,000; quads and quins are also available.

Suore Oblate dell'Assunzione, Via Borgo Pinti 15 (☎055.248.0583). Not far from the duomo, run by nuns but open to both men and women as long as rooms are not required by the nuns or their visitors. 11.30pm curfew; no breakfast. Singles L50,000, doubles L100,000, both with private bathrooms. Triple and quad rooms are also available.

Suore Oblate dello Spirito Santo, Via Nazionale 8 (☎055.239.8202). Again run by nuns, this clean and pleasant hostel a few steps from the station is open mid-June to October to women, families and married couples only: minimum stay two nights. Breakfast included, curfew 11pm. L40,000 per person for doubles or triples, L30,000 per person in four-bed rooms; all with private bath.

Campsites

The situation for campers in Florence isn't very good: summer arrivals are almost certain to find that the only available spaces are at the *Area di Sosta*, an emergency accommodation area sometimes set aside by the city authorities – it usually amounts to a patch of ground sheltered by a rudimentary roof, with a shower block attached. Contact the tourist offices for details, if any, of the latest location. An alternative would be to try the site in Fiesole, to the north of the city (see p.164).

Italiani e Stranieri, Viale Michelangelo 80 (☎055.681.1977). Open April–Oct, this 320-pitch site is always crowded, owing to its superb hillside location. Kitchen facilities and well-stocked, if expensive, shop nearby. Take #13 bus from the station.

Villa Camerata, Viale Augusto Righi 2–4 (☎055.600.315). Basic 55-pitch site in hostel grounds.

THE CITY

Greater Florence now spreads several kilometres down the Arno valley and up onto the hills north and south of the city, but the major sights are contained within an area that can be crossed on foot in little over half an hour. A short walk from the train station brings you to the **Baptistery** and **duomo**; the area south from here to **Piazza della Signoria** – site of the **Palazzo Vecchio** and the **Uffizi** gallery – is the inner core, into which most of the tourists are packed. A square drawn so that the duomo and Uffizi stood in the centre of opposite sides would cover many of the best-preserved of Florence's medieval streets and the majority of its fashionable streets.

Immediately north of the duomo is the **San Lorenzo** quarter, where market stalls surround one of the city's first-rank churches, in effect the chapel of the Medici dynasty. Within a short radius of here are the monastery of **San Marco**, with its paintings by Fra' Angelico, the **Accademia**, residence of Michelangelo's *David*, and **Piazza Santissima Annunziata**, Florence's most attractive square.

The Uffizi backs onto the Arno River, across which lies the district known as **Oltrarno**, where the **Palazzo Pitti** and Masaccio's church of **Santa Maria del Carmine** exert the strongest pull, followed by the churches of **Santo Spirito** and the colourful **San Miniato al Monte**.

Close to the eastern side of Piazza del Duomo stands the **Bargello**, the main museum of sculpture; farther east, the area around the Franciscan church of **Santa Croce** forms a nucleus of activity. On the western side of the city, directly opposite the train station, the unmissable attraction is **Santa Maria Novella**, Florentine base of the rival Dominican order.

Piazza del Duomo

From the train station, all first-time visitors gravitate towards **Piazza del Duomo**, beckoned by the pinnacle of Brunelleschi's dome, which lords it over the cityscape with an authority unmatched by any architectural creation in any other Italian city. Yet even though the magnitude of the **duomo** is apparent from a distance, first sight of the church and the adjacent **baptistery** still comes as a jolt, their colourful patterned exteriors making a startling contrast with the dun-toned buildings around.

Florence doesn't make the most of these two bravura buildings: the Piazza del Duomo is not so much a square as a bit of clear space in the midst of the traffic. There are few cafés from which to admire the view, and most are a little too close for comfort to the traffic roaring past in Via Cerretani. Worse, the square and cathedral steps are almost constantly blanketed with

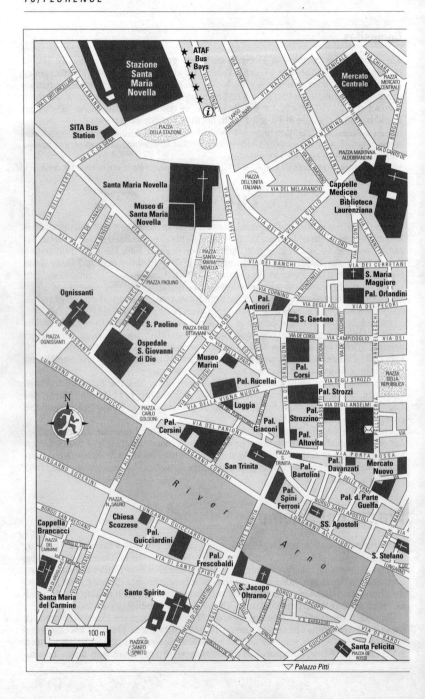

▽ Palazzo Pitti

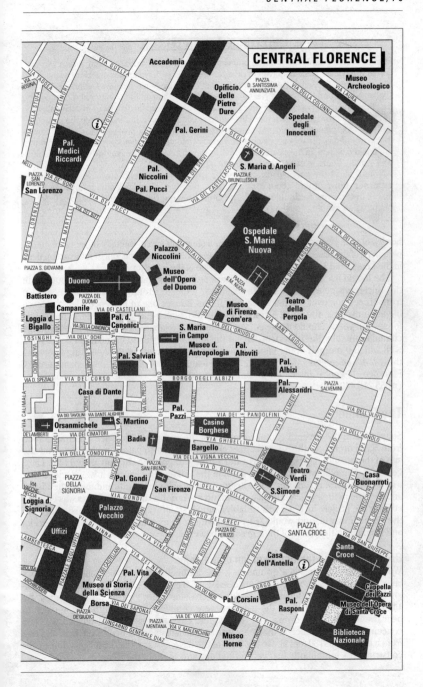

---

hordes of tour groups. And unless you're on a shopping spree, the only other place on the periphery of the piazza that you might drop in at is the summertime tourist information desk in the **Loggia del Bigallo**, opposite the south side of the baptistery.

The loggia itself was built for the Misericordia, a charitable organization founded in the thirteenth century and still in existence today, operating an ambulance service from offices just over Via dei Calzaiuoli. It now houses one of Florence's least accessible art museums, the small **Museo del Bigallo**, which has been closed to the public for several years. Should it reopen, you'll find that it contains several religious paintings commissioned by the Misericordia and the similarly altruistic Compagnia del Bigallo, with which it merged in the fifteenth century. Works include a 1342 painting known as the *Madonna of the Misericordia*, which features the oldest known panorama of Florence. If you're intent on getting in, you could try ringing for an appointment (☎055.215.440).

The Duomo

Some time in the seventh century the seat of the Bishop of Florence was transferred from San Lorenzo to the sixth-century church of Santa Reparata, which stood on the site of the present-day **Santa Maria del Fiore** – to give the **duomo** its full title. Later generations modified that building until, in the thirteenth century, it was decided that a new cathedral was required, to do justice to the wealth of the city and to put the Pisans and Sienese in their place. The plan drawn up by **Arnolfo di Cambio**, who was entrusted with the project in 1294, was suitably immodest – it was to be the largest church in the Catholic world, and would "surpass anything of its kind produced by the Greeks and Romans in the times of their greatest power".

Brunelleschi and the construction of the dome

Work on Arnolfo's basilica ground to a halt immediately after his death eight years later, then was resumed under a succession of architects, each of whom roughly followed his plan, which focused on a domed crossing embraced by three tribunes. By 1418 the nave was finished, the tribunes were complete, and a drum was in place to bear the weight of the **dome** that Arnolfo had envisaged as the church's crown. The conception was magnificent: the dome was to span a distance of nearly 140 feet, and rise from a base some 180 feet above the floor of the nave. It was to be the largest dome ever constructed – but nobody had yet worked out how to build the thing.

A committee of the masons' guild was set up to ponder the problem, and it was to them that **Filippo Brunelleschi** presented himself. His arrogant insistence that only he could possibly redeem the situation, and his refusal to say much more about his solution other than that he could build the dome without the use of exterior scaffolding, did little to endear him to his prospective patrons. Various alternative schemes were considered, including – according to Vasari – the ingenious notion of supporting the dome on a vast mound of earth that would be seeded with thousands of coins; when the dome was finished, the mound would be cleared away by inviting Florence's citizens to excavate the money. In the end, however, Brunelleschi was given the job on condition that he work jointly with his rival Ghiberti (see p.86) – a partnership that did not last long, though Ghiberti's contribution to the project was probably more significant than his colleague ever admitted.

The key to Brunelleschi's strategy turned out to be a technique of laying the brickwork in cantilevered rings, a procedure that ensured the dome supported itself as it grew. On March 25, 1436 – Annunciation Day, and the Florentine New Year – the completion of the dome was marked by the consecration of the cathedral, a ceremony conducted by the pope himself. Yet the topmost piece, the lantern, was still not in place, and many were sceptical about the structure's capability to bear the weight. Other architects were consulted, but Brunelleschi again won the day, and this final stage commenced in 1446, a few months before the architect's death; the colossal lantern was completed in the late 1460s, when the gilded ball and cross, cast by Verrocchio, were hoisted into place. One part of the dome remains incomplete, however: the gallery around the base was abandoned with only one face finished, after Michelangelo compared it to "cages for crickets".

Marble quarried from three different sources was used to clad the **exterior** of the duomo – white from Carrara, red from Maremma and green from Prato. The flanks date back to Arnolfo's era and the succeeding century or so; the overblown and pernickety main facade, however, is a nineteenth-century simulacrum of a Gothic front. The south side is the oldest part of the exterior, but the most attractive adornment is the **Porta della Mandorla**, (**33** on plan) on the other side. It takes its name from the almond-shaped frame (or *mandorla*) that contains the relief of *The Assumption of the Virgin*, sculpted by Nanni di Banco and Donatello around 1420.

The interior

The duomo's interior (Mon–Sat 10am–5pm, except first Sat of the month 10am–3.30pm; Sun 1–5pm; free) is the converse of the exterior – a vast, uncluttered enclosure of bare masonry. The fifth most capacious church in the world, it once held a congregation of 10,000 to hear Savonarola preach against the tyranny of the Medici and the soul-corrupting decadence of Renaissance Florence. Its ambience is more that of a great assembly hall than a devotional building, and it's not surprising to find that the most conspicuous decorations in the main body of the church are a pair of memorials to *condottieri* (mercenary commanders) on the wall of the left aisle.

MUSEUMS ADMISSION

You can buy a "Carnet" for L10,000 that includes a small printed guide and a fifty-percent reduction on entry to the Palazzo Vecchio, Cappella Brancacci, Museo di Santa Maria Novella, Museo di Firenze com'era, Raccolta A. Della Ragione, Cenacolo di Santo Spirito, Museo Stibbert and Museo Marino Marini. If you only visit the first four sights, you'll save L2500.

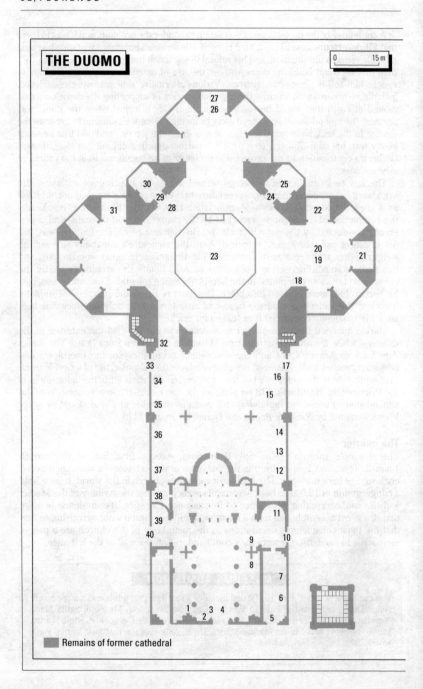

THE DUOMO

0　　　　15 m

27
26

30
29
28
31

25
24
22

23

20
19
21

18

32

33
34
35
36
37
38
39
40

17
16
15
14
13
12
11
10
9
8
7
6
5

1　2　3　4

■ Remains of former cathedral

1 Stained glass: St Stephen (left), Assumption (centre) and St Lawrence (right), Lorenzo Ghiberti
2 Tomb of Antonio d'Orso, bishop of Florence (1323), Tino da Camaino
3 Mosaic: Coronation of the Virgin (1300), attributed to Gaddo Gaddi
4 Clock (1443) – decoration, Paolo Uccello
5 Stained glass: St Lawrence and Angels, Lorenzo Ghiberti
6 Tondo: Bust of Brunelleschi (1447), Andrea Cavalcanti
7 Bust: Giotto at Work (1490), Benedetto da Maiano
8 Gothic water stoup (1380), attributed to Urbano da Cortona
9 Entrance and steps to Santa Reparata
10 Porta del Campanile
11 Painting: St Bartholomew Enthroned (1408), Rossello di Jacopo Franchi
12 Painted sepulchral monument: Fra Luigi Marsili (1439), Bicci di Lorenzo
13 Statue: Isaiah (1427), Bernardo Ciuffagni
14 Painted sepulchral monument: Archbishop Pietro Corsino of Florence (1422), Bicci di Lorenzo
15 Stained glass: Six Saints (1395), Agnolo Gaddi
16 Bust: Marsilino Ficino (1521), philosopher friend of Cosimo I, holding a copy of Plato's works
17 Porta dei Canoncini: sculpture (1395–99), Lorenzo d'Ambrogio
18 Eight statues of the Apostles (1547–72) against the pillars of the octagon
19 Tribune: each tribune has five chapels; each chapel has two levels of stained glass, most by Lorenzo Ghiberti
20 Frescoes below windows of west and east tribunes: Saints (1440), attributed to Bicci di Lorenzo
21 Altar, attributed to Michelozzo
22 Fresco fragment: Madonna del Popolo (13th-century), attributed to Giotto
23 Dome fresco cycle: The Last Judgement (1572–79), Giorgio Vasari and Federico Zuccari
24 Enamelled terracotta (above door): Ascension (1450), Luca della Robbia
25 Sagrestia Vecchia (Old Sacristy)
26 Bronze reliquary (1432–42) of St Zenobius (below altar), Lorenzo Ghiberti
27 Candle-holders: Two Angels (1450), Luca della Robbia
28 Enamelled terracotta: Resurrection (1444), Luca della Robbia
29 Bronze doors (1446–67), Luca della Robbia and Michelozzo
30 Sagrestia Nuova (New Sacristy): intarsia (inlaid wood, 1436–45), Benedetto and Giuliano da Maiano
31 Former site of Michelangelo's Pietà, currently in the Museo dell'Opera
32 Entrance and stairs to the dome
33 Porta della Mandorla: sculpture, Nanni di Banco and Donatello
34 Painting: Dante with the Divine Comedy (1465), Domenico di Michelino
35 Fresco: SS. Cosmas and Damian (1429), Bicci di Lorenzo; two windows by Agnolo Gaddi
36 Statue (in recess) designed for old cathedral facade: King David (1434), Bernardo Ciuffagni
37 Equestrian portrait: Sir John Hawkwood (1436), Paolo Uccello
38 Equestrian portrait: Niccolò da Tolentino (1456), Andrea del Castagno
39 Bust: Antonio Squarcialupi (former cathedral organist, 1490), Benedetto da Maiano
40 The Prophet Joshua (1415), Nanni di Bartolo; the head is by Donatello

Paolo Uccello's **monument to Sir John Hawkwood (37)**, created in 1436, is often cited as the epitome of Florentine mean-spiritedness; according to local folklore – unsupported by any evidence – the mercenary captain of Florence's army was promised a proper equestrian statue as his memorial, then was posthumously fobbed off with this trompe l'oeil version. It features a strange shift of perspective, with the pedestal depicted from a different angle from what's on it; it's known that Uccello was ordered to repaint the horse and rider, presumably because he'd shown them from the same point of view as the base, which must have displayed the horse's belly and not much else. Look back at the entrance wall and you'll see another Uccello contribution to the interior – a clock adorned with four rather abstracted Evangelists.

Andrea Castagno's **monument to Niccolò da Tolentino (38)**, created twenty years later, is clearly derived from Uccello's fresco, but has an aggressive edge that's typical of this artist. Just beyond the horsemen, Domenico do Michelino's *Dante Explaining the Divine Comedy* **(34)**, painted in 1465, gave Brunelleschi's recently completed dome a place only marginally less prominent than the mountain of Purgatory.

Judged by mere size, the major work of art in the duomo is the fresco of **The Last Judgement (23)**. At the time of its execution a substantial body of opinion thought Vasari and Zuccari's combined effort did nothing but deface Brunelleschi's masterpiece; quite a few people today would have preferred the painting to have been stripped away rather than cleaned up. Below the fresco are seven stained-glass roundels designed by Uccello, Ghiberti, Castagno and Donatello; they are best inspected from the gallery

THE PAZZI CONSPIRACY

The **Pazzi Conspiracy**, perhaps the most compelling of all Florence's murkier acts of treachery, had its roots in the election in 1472 of **Sixtus IV**, a pope who distributed money and favours with a largesse remarkable even by papal standards. Six of his nephews were made cardinals, one of them, the uncouth **Girolamo Riario**, coming in for particularly preferential treatment, probably because he was Sixtus's son. Sixtus's plan was that Riario should take over the town of Imola as a base for papal expansion, and accordingly he approached Lorenzo de' Medici for the necessary loan. Aware that Imola was too close to Milan and Bologna to be allowed to fall into papal hands, Lorenzo rebuffed the pope, despite the importance of the Vatican account with the Medici bank, and the family's role as agents for the papacy's alum mines in Tuscany (alum was a vital part of the dyeing industry, and therefore essential to Florence's textile trade). Enraged by the snub, and by Lorenzo's refusal to recognize **Francesco Salviati** as archbishop of Pisa (Sixtus had ignored an agreement by which appointments within the Florentine domain could only be made by mutual agreement), Sixtus turned to the Pazzi, the Medici's leading Florentine rivals as bankers in Rome.

Three co-conspirators met in Rome in the early months of 1477: Riario, now in possession of Imola but eager for greater spoils; Salviati, incandescent at Lorenzo's veto and desperate to become archbishop of Florence; and **Francesco de' Pazzi**, head of the Pazzis' Rome operation and determined to usurp Medici power in Florence. Any plot, however, required military muscle, and the man chosen to provide it, a plain-speaking mercenary called **Montesecco**, proved intensely wary of the whole enterprise – "beware of what you do," he counselled, "Florence is a big affair." In the end he made his co-operation conditional on papal blessing, a benediction that was readily obtained. "I do not wish the death of anyone on any account," was Sixtus's mealy-mouthed observation, "since it does not accord with our office to consent to such a thing"; yet he knew full well Lorenzo's death was essential if the plot was to succeed. "Go, and do what you wish," he added, "provided there be no killing." **Jacopo de' Pazzi**, the Pazzis' wizened godfather, was also won over by Sixtus's disingenuous immediately below them, which forms part of the route to the **top of the dome** (Mon–Sat 8.30am–6.20pm, first Sat of the month 8.30am–3.20pm, closed Sun; L10,000). If you're queasy about confined spaces, the narrow gallery might be troublesome, but it's the only tricky part of the ascent: most of the climb winds between the brick walls of the outer and inner shells of the dome, while at the summit the view is so amazing it takes your mind off everything else.

When you finally come back down to earth, be sure to take a look at the entrances to the two **sacristies**, on each side of the altar. Enamelled terracotta reliefs (**24, 28**) by Luca della Robbia are placed over both, and the doors (**29**) of the north sacristy were his only works in bronze. Lorenzo de' Medici took refuge in the north sacristy (**30**) after his brother Giuliano had been mortally stabbed on the altar steps by the Pazzi conspirators (see box below), the bulk of these new doors protecting him from his would-be assassins; small portraits on the handles commemorate the brothers.

The relics of St Zenobius, fourth-century bishop of Florence, are preserved underneath the altar of the middle **apse**, in a beautifully sculpted bronze reliquary (**26**) designed by Ghiberti, who also executed the stained glass (**19**) in all three apses. The apse is often reserved for prayer, so use your discretion.

SANTA REPARATA

In the 1960s, remnants of the duomo's predecessor, **Santa Reparata** (same hours as the dome; L5000), were uncovered underneath the west end of the nave – the remains

---

support, despite being on good terms with the Medici – indeed, one of his nephews was married to Lorenzo's sister.

After numerous false starts, it was decided to **murder Lorenzo and Giuliano** whilst they attended Mass in the cathedral. The date set was Sunday, April 26, 1478. Montesecco, however, now refused "to add sacrilege to murder", so Lorenzo's murder was delegated to two embittered priests, **Maffei** and **Bagnone**, whereas Giuliano was to be dispatched by Francesco de' Pazzi and **Bernardo Baroncelli**, a violent Pazzi sidekick deeply in debt to the family. Salviati, meanwhile, accompanied by an armed troop, was to seize control of the Palazzo della Signoria.

It all went horribly wrong. Giuliano was killed in a crazed frenzy, his skull shattered and his body rent with nineteen stab wounds, but Lorenzo managed to escape, fleeing wounded to the duomo's new sacristy, where he and his supporters barricaded themselves behind its heavy bronze doors. Across the city, Salviati was separated from his troops, thanks to newly installed secret doors and locks in the Palazzo della Signoria, and arrested by the *Gonfaloniere*, Cesare Petrucci.

Apprised of the plot, a furious mob dispensed summary justice to several of the conspirators: Salviati's troops were massacred to a man, whilst Salviati and Francesco de' Pazzi were hanged from a window of the Palazzo della Signoria. Of the latter execution, Poliziano, the eminent humanist, noted that "as the archbishop rolled and struggled at the end of his rope, his eyes goggling in his head, he fixed his teeth into Francesco de' Pazzi's naked body". Maffei and Bagnone, the bungling priests, were castrated and hanged. Baroncelli escaped to Constantinople but was extradited and executed. Montesecco was tortured, but given a soldier's execution in the Bargello. Jacopo's end was the most sordid. Having escaped Florence, he was recaptured, tortured, stripped naked, and hanged alongside the decomposing Salviati. He was then buried in Santa Croce, but exhumed by the mob, who blamed heavy rains on his evil spirit. His corpse was dragged through the streets, tipped in a ditch, and finally propped up outside the Pazzi palace, where his rotting head was used as door knocker. Eventually the putrefying body was thrown in the Arno, fished out, flogged and hanged again by a gang of children, and finally cast back into the river.

are extensive, as the nave of the duomo was built several feet above that of the old church, which was thus not fully demolished. Subsequent excavations have revealed a complicated jigsaw of Roman, paleochristian and Romanesque remains, plus fragments of mosaic and fourteenth-century frescoes. The explanatory diagrams tend to intensify the confusion: to make sense of it all, you'll have to keep referring to the detailed model in the farthest recess of the crypt.

Also discovered in the course of the dig was the **tomb of Brunelleschi**, the only Florentine ever honoured with burial inside the duomo – his tombstone can be seen, without paying, through a grille to the left of the foot of the stairs.

The Campanile

The **Campanile** (daily: April–Oct 9am–6.50pm; Nov–March 9am–4.20pm; L10,000) was begun in 1334 by Giotto and continued after his death by Andrea Pisano and Francesco Talenti, who rectified the deficiencies in the artist's calculations by doubling the thickness of the walls. Erosion caused by atmospheric pollution has made it necessary to replace the tower's sculptures with copies – the originals are all in the Museo dell'Opera del Duomo (see opposite).

The first storey, the only part of the tower built exactly as Giotto designed it, is studded with two rows of remarkable bas-reliefs; the lower, illustrating the *Creation of Man* and the *Arts and Industries*, was carved by Pisano himself, the upper by his pupils. Donatello and others created the figures of *Prophets* and *Sibyls* in the second-storey niches – too high to be really appreciated. The parapet at the top of the tower is a less lofty viewpoint than the dome, but a good deal more vertiginous – it feels like you're perched on top of a flagpole.

The Baptistery

Generally thought to date from the sixth or seventh century, the **Baptistery** is the oldest building in Florence, and was the city's cathedral before Santa Reparata. Though its origins lie in the depths of the Dark Ages, no building better illustrates the special relationship between Florence and the Roman world. The Florentines were always conscious of their Roman ancestry, and throughout the Middle Ages they chose to believe that the baptistery was originally a Roman temple to Mars, a belief bolstered by the interior's inclusion of Roman granite columns. The pattern of the marble cladding – applied in the eleventh and twelfth centuries – is clearly classical in inspiration, and the baptistery's most famous embellishments, its gilded bronze **doors**, mark the emergence of a more scholarly, self-conscious interest in the art of the ancient world.

The doors

The **south door** was cast in 1336 by **Andrea Pisano**; twenty of its 28 panels form an exquisite narrative on the life of St John the Baptist, patron saint of Florence and, the baptistery's dedicatee. Years of financial and political turmoil, and the ravages of the Black Death, prevented any work on the other entrances to the baptistery until 1401, when a competition was held for the commission to make a new set of doors, each entrant being asked to create a panel showing the Sacrifice of Isaac.

Finding themselves equally impressed by the pieces produced by Brunelleschi and **Lorenzo Ghiberti** (both now displayed in the Bargello), the judges suggested that the pair should become partners. To this Brunelleschi replied that if he couldn't do the job alone he wasn't interested in doing it at all – whereupon the contract was handed over to Ghiberti, and his rival stomped off to study architecture in Rome. Ghiberti, barely twenty years old, was to devote much of his time over the next half-century to this one project, and his fame rests almost entirely on the extraordinary result.

His **north doors** (1403–24), depicting scenes from the life of Christ, the four Evangelists and the four Doctors of the Church, show a new naturalism and classicized sense of composition, but their innovation is fairly timid in comparison with the sublime **east doors** (1425–52), which were ordered from Ghiberti as soon as the first set was finished. They have always been known as "The Gates of Paradise", supposedly because Michelangelo once remarked that they were so beautiful they deserved to be the portals of heaven. In fact, the name almost certainly comes from the fact that the area between the baptistery and Santa Reparata was called the *Paradiso*.

As with so many exterior art works in Florence, what you now see is a reproduction: the original panels are being restored and then placed in the Museo dell'Opera as they are finished. The replicas will remain too garish until pollution and the elements do their work, but they give a reasonable idea of the grand scheme. Unprecedented in the subtlety of their carving, the scenes are a primer of early Renaissance art, using rigorous perspective, gesture and sophisticated groupings to intensify the drama of each scene. Ghiberti has included an understandably self-satisfied self-portrait in the frame of the left-hand door: his is the fourth head from the top of the right-hand band – the bald chap with the smirk.

The pair of marble columns to the side of the east doors were presented by the city of Pisa in the twelfth century, and would have been slotted into the walls if they had not turned out to be too weak to bear any weight. Another marble column on the outside is decorated with bronze branches and leaves to commemorate the miracle brought about by the body of St Zenobius; as the corpse was being carried into Santa Reparata it brushed against a barren elm here, which thereupon sprang into leaf.

The interior

The baptistery **interior** (Mon–Sat noon–6.30pm; Sun 8.30am–1.30pm; L5000) is equally stunning, with its black and white marble cladding and ancient Roman columns below a blazing mosaic ceiling. Both the semi-abstract mosaic floor and the magnificent scenes in the cupola – including a fearsome platoon of demons at the feet of Christ in judgement – were created in the thirteenth century. The empty octagon in the centre of the floor marks the spot once occupied by the huge font in which every child born in the city during the previous twelve months would be baptized on New Year's Day. To the right of the altar is the **tomb of John XXIII**, the schismatic pope who died in Florence in 1419 while a guest of his financial adviser and close friend, Giovanni di Bicci de' Medici – the man who established the family at the political forefront of Florence. The papal monument, draped by an illusionistic marble canopy, is the work of Donatello and his pupil Michelozzo.

The Museo dell'Opera del Duomo

Since the early fifteenth century the maintenance of the duomo has been supervised from the building at Piazza del Duomo 9, behind the east end of the church; nowadays this also houses the **Museo dell'Opera del Duomo** (April–Oct Mon–Sat 9am–6.50pm; Nov–March Mon–Sat 9am–5.20pm; L10,000), the repository of the most precious and fragile works of art from the duomo, baptistery and campanile. As an overview of the sculpture of Florence it's second only to the Bargello, and is far easier to take in on a single visit.

A family of sculptures by **Arnolfo di Cambio**, including an eerily glassy-eyed *Madonna*, are the most arresting works in the first few rooms; they were rescued from Arnolfo's unfinished facade for the duomo, which was pulled down in the sixteenth century. Preceding rooms are dedicated to Brunelleschi, displaying his death mask and a variety of tools and machines devised by the architect. At the other end of the main room, steps lead up to a collection of models of suggested facades for the duomo, and an assembly of reliquaries that can boast the jaw of St Jerome and the index finger of John the Baptist.

On the mezzanine level is **Michelangelo's** anguished *Pietà*, moved here while restoration of the dome is in progress, but probably fated to stay. This is one of his last works, and was intended for his own tomb – Vasari records that the face of Nicodemus is a self-portrait. Dissatisfied with the quality of the marble, Michelangelo mutilated the group by hammering off the left leg and arm of Christ; his pupil Tiberio Calcagni restored the arm, then finished off the figure of the Magdalene, turning her into a whey-faced supporting player.

Although he's represented on the lower floor as well, it's upstairs that **Donatello**, the greatest of Michelangelo's precursors, really comes to the fore. Of the figures he carved for the campanile, the most powerful is that of the prophet Habbakuk, the intensity of whose gaze is said to have prompted the sculptor to seize it and implore "Speak, speak!" Opposite poles of Donatello's temperament are represented by the bedraggled wooden figure of Mary Magdalene and his ornate *cantoria* (choir-loft) from the duomo, with its playground of boisterous putti. Facing it is the *cantoria* created at the same time by **Luca della Robbia**; the earnest young musicians embody the text from Psalm 33 inscribed on the frame: "Praise the Lord with harp. Sing unto Him with the psaltery and instrument of ten strings."

Pisano's bas-reliefs from the campanile are on show nearby, depicting the spiritual refinement of humanity through work, the arts and, ultimately, the sacraments. Another room is evolving into a showcase for the restored panels from the Gates of Paradise, and also contains a dazzling silver-gilt altar from the baptistery, completed in 1480 after more than a century of labour by such master craftsmen as Antonio del Pollaiuolo and Verrocchio.

Between the Duomo and the Signoria

Unless you want to construct a serpentine back-alley route, getting from Piazza del Duomo to Piazza della Signoria comes down to a choice between two streets: **Via del Proconsolo**, which leads from the eastern side of the duomo, or **Via dei Calzaiuoli**, from the campanile. Even the shortest stay in Florence should find time for a stroll along both, but the initial choice depends on whether it's the art you're after – in which case the former gets the nod – or the streetlife.

Via del Proconsolo: from the Duomo to the Badia

The top of **Via del Proconsolo**, just a few yards from the Museo dell'Opera del Duomo, forms a major junction with Via dell'Oriuolo, the most direct route from the duomo to the Sant'Ambrogio quarter (see p.128). If you've got a spare hour or so, it's worth a diversion down here for the **Museo di Firenze com'era** at Via dell'Oriuolo 24 (Mon–Wed, Fri & Sat 9am–2pm, Sun 8am–1pm; L5000).

Charting the growth of Florence and its environs from the fifteenth century, the museum contains a wealth of maps, prints, photos and topographical paintings, none of them masterpieces but most of them at least informative. Perhaps the most impressive item comes right at the start: a meticulous reproduction of the colossal 1470 aerial view of Florence called the *Pianta della Catena* (Chain Map), the original of which is in Berlin. The Medici villas at the end of the sixteenth century are recorded in the sequence of twelve pictures painted by Giusto Utens for the Villa dell'Artimino (see p.167), while eighteenth-century Florence is perpetuated by the elegiac engravings of Giuseppe Zocchi.

There's a poignant section recounting the destruction of the city's ancient heart to make space for the Piazza della Repubblica, and a new section dedicated to the old Roman city.

Dante's district

Take a right turn at Via Dante Alighieri and you'll soon come to the small piazza that fronts the **Casa di Dante** (March–Oct daily except Tues 9am–6pm; Nov–Feb same days 10am–4pm; free), marketed as the birthplace of the author of *The Divine Comedy*, the foundation stone of Italian literature. The museum is a homage to the poet rather than a shrine: it contains nothing directly related to his life, and in all likelihood he was born not here but somewhere in the street that bears his name. Numerous editions of the *Divina Commedia* are on show – including a poster printed with the whole text in minuscule type – along with copies of Botticelli's illustrations to the poem.

DANTE

Dante signed himself "Dante Alighieri, a Florentine by birth but not by character", a bitter allusion to the city he served as a politician but which later cast him into exile and was to inspire some of the most vitriolic passages in his epic poem, *La Divina Commedia* (The Divine Comedy). He was born in 1265, into a minor and impoverished noble family, then was educated at Bologna and later at Padua, where he studied philosophy and astronomy. Long before his academic career had blossomed, however, his romantic life had been forever blighted by an encounter with the eight-year-old **Beatrice Pratinari**. Boccaccio described the young girl as possessed of "habits and language more serious and modest than her age warranted". Her features, furthermore, were "so delicate and so beautifully formed, and full, besides mere beauty, of so much candid loveliness that many thought her almost an angel". Dante (himself just nine when he met Beatrice), described his own feelings after the encounter: "Love ruled my soul . . . and began to hold such sway over me . . . that it was necessary for me to do completely all his pleasure. He commanded me often that I should endeavour to see this so youthful angel, and I saw in her such noble and praiseworthy deportment that truly of her might be said these words of the poet Homer – *She appeared to be born not of mortal man but of God."*

Sadly for Dante, Beatrice's family had decided their daughter was to marry one Simone de' Bardi – the ceremony took place when she was seventeen, and after just seven years of marriage, Beatrice was dead. Dante, for his part, was also forced into an arranged marriage, to one Gemma Donati; agreed when Dante was twelve, the wedding finally took place in 1295, when the poet was thirty.

His romantic hopes dashed, Dante settled down to a political career, joining the apothecaries' guild and serving on a variety of minor civic committees. In 1300 he was dispatched to San Gimignano, entrusted with the job of coaxing the town into an alliance against Pope Boniface VIII, who had designs on Tuscany, and in June of the same year he sought to settle the widening breach between the city's **Black** (anti-imperial) and **White** (more conciliatory) factions of Florence's ruling **Guelph** party. The dispute, inevitably, had its roots in money: the Whites contained leading bankers to the imperial powers (the Cerchi, Mozzi, Davanzati and Frescobaldi); the Blacks, by contrast, counted the Pazzi, Bardi and Donati amongst their number, all prominent papal bankers. Boniface, not surprisingly, sided with the Blacks, who eventually emerged triumphant.

Dante's White sympathies sealed his fate. In 1302, following trumped-up charges of corruption, he was sentenced with other Whites to two years' exile. Whilst many of the deportees subsequently returned, Dante rejected his city of "self-made men and fast-got gain". He wandered instead between Forlì, Verona, Padua, Luni and Venice, writing much of *The Divine Comedy* as he went, finally settling in Ravenna, where he died in 1321.

As contentious as the Casa di Dante's claim is the story that Dante got married in **Santa Margherita de' Cerchi**, the ancient little church up the street on the right. It does, however, have a nice altarpiece of the *Madonna and Four Saints* by Neri di Bicci.

Over Via Dante Alighieri from the poet's house, on Piazza San Martino, the tiny **San Martino del Vescovo** (Mon–Sat 10am–noon & 3–5pm) was once the headquarters of the charitable body called the Compagnia di Buonomini. It was they who commissioned the church's frescoes showing scenes from the life of St Martin and other altruistic acts; painted by the workshop of Ghirlandaio, they are as absorbing a record of daily life in Renaissance Florence as are the better-known works by Ghirlandaio himself in Santa Maria Novella. The chapel also contains a couple of *Madonnas* – one Byzantine, the other possibly by Perugino.

Opposite San Martino soars the thirteenth-century **Torre della Castagna**, meeting place of the city's *priori* before they decamped to the Palazzo Vecchio. This is one of the most striking remnants of Florence's medieval townscape, when over 150 such towers rose between the river and the duomo, many of them over two hundred feet high. Allied clans would link their towers with wooden catwalks, creating a sort of upper-class promenade above the heads of the lowlier citizens. In 1250 the government of the *Primo Popolo* ordered that the towers be reduced by two-thirds of their height; the resulting rubble was voluminous enough to extend the city walls beyond the Arno.

The Badia

On Via dei Magazzini, which runs south from San Martino, there's an entrance to the huge **Badia Fiorentina** (irregular opening hours: generally Mon–Sat 5–7pm, Sun 7.30–11.30am; free). Founded late in the tenth century by Willa, widow of the margrave of Tuscany, the Badia was one of the focal buildings in medieval Florence – the city's sick were treated in a hospital here and the main bell marked the divisions of the working day.

The Badia is a more authentic place of reverence for admirers of Dante than his house: this was the parish church of **Beatrice Pratinari**, for whom he conceived a life-long love as he watched her at Mass here (see previous page). Furthermore, it was here that Boccaccio delivered his celebrated lectures on Dante's theological epic.

In the 1280s the church was overhauled, probably under the direction of Arnolfo di Cambio, architect of the duomo and Palazzo Vecchio; later work has smothered much of the old church, but the narrow **campanile** – Romanesque at its base, Gothic higher up – has come through intact. Inside, the church itself is unremarkable save for Filippino Lippi's *Madonna and St Bernard*, and the monument to Willa's son Ugo, carved around 1480 by Mino da Fiesole, on the wall of the left transept. However, a staircase leads from the right (south) side of the high altar to the upper storey of the **Chiostro degli Aranci** (Orange Cloister – from the fruit trees that used to be grown here), brightened by a fifteenth-century fresco cycle of the life of St Benedict.

The Bargello

To get a full idea of the Renaissance achievement in Florence, two museum calls are essential: one to the picture galleries of the Uffizi, the other to the sculpture sections of the **Museo Nazionale del Bargello** (Tues–Sat, second and fourth Sun of month, & first, third and fifth Mon of month 8.30am–1.50pm; L8000), installed over the road from the Badia in the daunting Palazzo del Bargello. In Renaissance Florence, sculpture assumed an importance unmatched in any other of the numerous states of the Italian peninsula – this most public form of artistic expression was perfectly suited to a city with so highly developed a sense of itself as a special community. On a less abstract level, Florence is surrounded by quarries, and the art of stonecutting had always been nurtured here. Ponderings over the reason aside, the Bargello's collection of sculpture from this period is the richest in Italy.

The palazzo was built in 1255, immediately after the overthrow of the aristocratic regime, and soon became the seat of the *podestà*, the chief magistrate of the city. Numerous malefactors were tried, sentenced and executed here, the elegant courtyard being the site of the gallows and block. It became a bizarre Florentine tradition for the city authorities to commission portraits of the executed criminals, usually to be painted on the outside walls. One of Andrea Castagno's first commissions from Cosimo il Vecchio was to depict the members of the Albizzi family, hanged for subversion; according to Vasari, the painter's skill in this gruesome genre earned him the nickname "Andrea degli Impiccati" – Andrea of the Hanged Men. Even Botticelli took payment for this kind of work, painting the corpses of the Pazzi conspirators for the edification of his fellow citizens. (Leonardo da Vinci, meanwhile, stood in the street to make a drawing of one of the Pazzi felons, who had been hung from the windows as an example to all traitors.) The building acquired its present name in the sixteenth century, when the chief of police – the *bargello* – was based here.

Unfortunately, the Bargello is notoriously prone to closures of whole sequences of rooms. The Donatello and Michelangelo halls will almost certainly be open, but it's common for the entire second floor to be locked – so check the notice by the ticket desk if there's something you're particularly set on seeing.

The collection

You've no time to catch your breath at the Bargello: the first room focuses on **Michelangelo**, in whose shadow every Florentine sculptor laboured from the sixteenth century onwards. The tipsy, soft-bellied figure of *Bacchus* was his first major sculpture, carved at the age of 22 – a year before his great *Pietà* in Rome. A decade later, Michelangelo's style had evolved into something less immediately seductive, as is shown by the *Pitti Tondo*, its stern grandeur prefiguring the prophets of the Sistine Chapel ceiling, which he was then about to commence. The square-jawed *Bust of Brutus*, which dates from 1540, is Michelangelo's sole work of this kind; a powerful sketch in stone, it's a coded celebration of anti-Medicean republicanism, having been made soon after the murder of the nightmarish Duke Alessandro de' Medici (see p.116). Works by Michelangelo's followers and contemporaries are ranged in the immediate vicinity; some of them would command prolonged attention in different company.

The shallower and more flamboyant art of **Cellini** and **Giambologna** is exhibited in the adjacent sections of the hall. Cellini's huge *Bust of Cosimo I*, his first work in bronze, was a sort of technical trial for the casting of the *Perseus*, his most famous work. Alongside the preparatory model for the *Perseus* are displayed the original relief panel and four statuettes from the statue's pedestal; the reproductions that took their place look rather better, seen from the intended distance. Close by, Giambologna's voluptuous *Florence Defeating Pisa* – a disingenuous pretext for a glamour display if ever there were one – takes up a lot of space, but is eclipsed by his best-known creation, the *Mercury*, a nimble figure with no bad angles. Comic relief is provided by the reliably awful Bandinelli, whose coiffured *Adam and Eve* look like a grandee and his wife taking an *au naturel* stroll through their estate.

Part two of the sculpture collection is on the other side of the Gothic courtyard, which is plastered with the coats of arms of the *podestà* and contains, among many other pieces, six allegorical figures by Ammannati from the fountain of the Palazzo Pitti courtyard. This second section, formerly a motley array of fourteenth-century pieces, is now getting better with the arrival of some statues which have been removed from Orsanmichele (see p.93).

THE FIRST FLOOR

At the top of the courtyard staircase, the first-floor loggia has been turned into an aviary for Giambologna's bronze birds, imported from the Medici villa at Castello. The nearer doorway to the right opens into the fourteenth-century Salone del Consiglio Generale, where the presiding genius is **Donatello**, the fountainhead of Renaissance sculpture.

Vestiges of the sinuous Gothic manner are evident in the drapery of the marble *David*, created in 1408, but there's nothing antiquated in the *St George*, carved just eight years later for the tabernacle of the armourers' guild at Orsanmichele and installed in a replica of its original niche at the far end of the room. If any one sculpture could be said to embody the shift of sensibility that occurred in quattrocento Florence, this is it – whereas St George had previously been little more than a symbol of valour, this alert, tensed figure represents not the act of heroism but the volition behind it. The slaying of the dragon is depicted in the badly eroded small marble panel underneath, a piece as revolutionary as the figure of the saint, with its seamless interweaving of foreground and background.

Donatello's sexually ambiguous bronze *David*, the first freestanding nude figure since classical times, was cast in the early 1430s, a decade in which he later produced the strange prancing figure known as *Amor-Atys*. The *Amor-Atys* was later mistaken for a genuine antique, the highest compliment the artist could have wished for – as is attested by the story of Michelangelo's heaping soil over one of his first works, a sleeping cupid, in order to give it the appearance of an unearthed classical piece. Donatello was just as comfortable with portraiture as with Christian or pagan imagery, as his breathtakingly vivid *Bust of Niccolò da Uzzano* demonstrates; and when the occasion demanded he could produce a straightforwardly monumental piece like the nearby *Marzocco*, Florence's heraldic lion.

Donatello's master, **Ghiberti**, is represented by his relief of *The Sacrifice of Isaac*, his entry in the competition for the baptistery doors, easily missed on the right-hand wall; the treatment of the theme submitted by Brunelleschi, effectively the runner-up, is hung alongside. Set around the walls of the room, **Luca della Robbia**'s simply sweet-natured humanism is embodied in a sequence of glazed terracotta *Madonnas*.

The rest of this floor is occupied by a collection of European and Islamic applied art, with dazzling specimens of ivory carving from Byzantium and medieval France – combs, boxes, chess pieces, devotional panels featuring scores of figures crammed into a space the size of a paperback page.

THE SECOND FLOOR

Sculpture resumes upstairs, with works from the della Robbia family forming a prelude to the **Sala dei Bronzetti**, Italy's best assembly of small Renaissance bronzes – providing plentiful evidence of Giambologna's virtuosity at table-top scale.

Lastly, there's a room devoted mainly to **Renaissance portrait busts**, including Mino da Fiesole's busts of Giovanni de' Medici and Piero il Gottoso (the sons of Cosimo il Vecchio), Francesco Laurana's *Battista Sforza* (an interesting comparison with the Piero della Francesca portrait in the Uffizi), and the *Woman Holding Flowers* by Verrocchio. The centre of the room is shared by Verrocchio's *David*, clearly influenced by the Donatello figure downstairs, and a powerful small bronze group of *Hercules and Antaeus* by Antonio del Pollaiuolo, who – like Leonardo – unravelled the complexities of human musculature by dissecting corpses.

Along Via dei Calzaiuoli

Connecting the western side of the duomo to the Signoria, **Via dei Calzaiuoli** is the unchallenged catwalk of the Florentine *passeggiata*. Two distinct economies operate along here: in the daytime the street's jewellery shops and boutiques trawl in lire by the million, but after dark the mainly Senegalese **street traders** move in, laying out their groundsheets with counterfeit designer clothes, posters and tacky paintings. Every now and then the police move the hawkers on, a ritual that sometimes takes into its sweep the buskers, acrobats and dreadful mime artists who perform here on summer evenings. For some reason an exemption seems to have been granted to Via dei Calzaiuoli's nocturnal palmists and tarot-readers, presumably because the Florentine police are as superstitious as the general populace are reputed to be.

The street seems fairly congenial and self-satisfied but there's a nasty undercurrent to life on Via dei Calzaiuoli. Racist gangs have been known to take the law into their own hands, attacking the foreign traders with knives, chains and other lumps of dangerous metalware – and it appears that the thugs have allies in the Florentine business community. Naturally, Florence's politicians and media deplore the violence, characterizing it as an aberration in a country that prides itself on its racial tolerance. Yet this tolerance has only been put to the test in the last few years with the increase in immigration from North and West Africa, and the tacit attitude of many Florentines can be surmised from the fact that the traders are generally known as *marocchini* (Moroccans), a tag that displays a blithe contempt for their identity.

Piazza della Repubblica

Halfway down the street, Via dei Speziali connects with the great expanse of the pedestrianized **Piazza della Repubblica**. Impressive solely for its size, this square was created in the nineteenth century in an attempt to give Florence the sort of grand public space that is a prerequisite for any capital city. On the west side a vast arch bears the triumphant inscription: "The ancient city centre restored to new life from the squalor of centuries." Most people would have preferred a few more traces of the squalor: this was once the site of the Roman forum, before becoming the city's Jewish quarter and central marketplace. In 1431 Donatello was commissioned to make a statue of *Abundance* to top a column amid the stalls, and a bell was mounted underneath the figure to ring the start and close of trading. The column was taken down during the piazza's creation, long after the statue had rotted away; replaced in 1956, it stands as the sole reminder of the square's more active past.

Maintaining the flat tone, the piazza's four large and once-fashionable cafés – *Donnini*, *Giubbe Rosse*, *Gilli* and *Paszkowski* – similarly lack the charisma to which they aspire. The *Paszkowski* in recent years brought attention to bear on racism in the upper economic echelons of Florentine society, through its pioneering employment of a black waiter; itself perhaps an instance of mere radical chic, the move prompted abusive letters and boycotts.

Orsanmichele

Standing foursquare like a truncated military tower at the southern end of Via dei Calzaiuoli, **Orsanmichele** (daily 9am–noon & 4–6pm; closed first and last Mon of the month; free) is the oddest-looking church in Florence. Not only is the church itself a major monument but its exterior was once the most impressive outdoor sculpture gallery in the city. Several pieces will usually be away for restoration, their places at Orsanmichele taken by replicas.

From the ninth century until the thirteenth the church of San Michele ad hortum stood here – hence the compacted form of Orsanmichele. Towards the end of that century a grain market was raised on the site, which was in turn replaced, after a fire in 1304, with a vast loggia that served as an oratory and a trade hall for the *Arti Maggiori*, the Great Guilds which governed the city. In 1380 the loggia was walled in and dedicated exclusively to religious functions, while two upper storeys were added for use as emergency grain stores. Not long after, each guild was charged with decorating one of the exterior tabernacles of the building, a scheme which spanned the emergent years of the Renaissance.

THE EXTERIOR

Beginning on the far left of the Via dei Calzaiuoli side, and moving round the building to the right, the first tabernacle should soon be occupied by a replica of Ghiberti's *John the Baptist*, the earliest life-size bronze statue of the Renaissance period. It was made for the *Calimala*, the guild of the wholesale cloth importers, who were the wealthiest of the guilds but nonetheless very cautious patrons; doubtful whether Ghiberti could cast the figure in one piece as planned, they made him liable for the cost of the metal should he fail. In the event it did come out intact, except for one toe, which had to be welded on. The other niches on this side are soon to be occupied by replicas of *The Incredulity of St Thomas* by Verrocchio and Giambologna's *St Luke*.

Round the corner, Donatello's *St Peter* is followed by two works from Nanni di Banco, *St Philip* and the so-called *Quattro Coronati* – four Christian sculptors executed by Diocletian for refusing to make a pagan image. The story goes that Nanni slightly miscalculated the size of the available space, and found that he could fit only three of the figures into the niche; to solve the crisis he is said to have consulted his friend Donatello, who simply had his assistants chip away at the four saints until they were slim enough to occupy their slot. A copy of Donatello's own *St George* comes next – the original is in the Bargello.

On the west side stand *St Matthew* and *St Stephen* by Ghiberti and *St Eligius* by Nanni di Banco; the *St Matthew*, posed and clad like a Roman orator, makes a telling comparison with the same artist's *St John*, cast just ten years before but still semi-Gothic in its sharp-edged drapery and arching lines.

Earlier than either is Donatello's *St Mark*, made in 1411 when the artist was twenty-five; this is often considered the first freestanding statue of the Renaissance, a title based on the naturalism of his stance and the brooding intensity of his gaze. A replica of Pietro Lamberti's *St James* precedes an uncomplicatedly benign *Madonna and Child*, probably by Giovanni Tedesco. It was damaged in 1493 when one Signor Marrona went berserk and set about axing lumps out of every statue of the Madonna he could find. Retribution in the form of a lynch mob of Savonarola's monks caught up with him just after he'd gouged out one of the eyes of the infant Christ. The weakest of Orsanmichele's sculptures brings up the rear, Baccio da Montelupo's *John the Evangelist*.

THE INTERIOR

Inside Orsanmichele, the centrepiece is the pavilion-sized glass and marble **tabernacle** by Orcagna, the only significant sculptural work by the artist. It frames a *Madonna* painted in 1347 by Bernardo Daddi as a replacement for a miraculous image of the Virgin that was destroyed by the 1304 fire, and whose powers this picture is said to have inherited. The brotherhood that administered Orsanmichele paid for the tabernacle from thanksgiving donations in the aftermath of the Black Death; so many people attributed their survival to the Madonna's intervention that the money received was greater than the annual income of the city coffers. Other paintings can be seen on the pillars – devotional images commissioned by the guilds, they are the low-cost ancestors of the Orsanmichele statues.

The vaulted halls of the **upstairs granary** – one of the city's most imposing medieval interiors – are entered via the footbridge from the Palazzo dell'Arte della Lana; they are usually open only when being used as an exhibition space.

Piazza della Signoria

Even though it sets the stage for the Palazzo Vecchio, Florence's main civic square – the **Piazza della Signoria** – doesn't quite live up to its role. Too many of the buildings round its edge are bland nineteenth-century efforts, now occupied by banks, and the surface of the square itself resembles nothing so much as the deck of an aircraft carrier.

It should look better than it does. Back in the 1970s it was decided to restore the piazza's ancient paving stones. The government minister in charge of archeological work decided that, since the stones were coming up anyway, it might be an idea to turn it into a full-blown dig to uncover the traces of Roman Florence. Unappreciative of the disruption, the city authorities tussled with their political bosses, and the excavation proceeded on a stop-start basis, turning the piazza into a part-time building site. Then a double scandal broke. When the company in charge of cleaning the old slabs returned the first batch, it was found that they had simply sandblasted great chunks off them, rather than rinsing them carefully in the prescribed manner; it turned out that they were not actually conservation experts – and the chief engineer of the city was promptly accused of taking a bribe to award the contract. Then some of the slabs turned up in the yard of a stone merchant on the city outskirts and on the front drives of a number of Tuscan villas. The contractor was dragged through the courts, and the piazza relaid with what looks like a job lot from a DIY warehouse.

The piazza is liveliest on May Day and other occasions in the political calendar, when speakers address the crowds from the terrace in front of the Palazzo Vecchio. (The terrace is called the *arringhiera*, from the same root as the English word "harangue".) Tempers can get frayed, but the temperature is cooler than it often used to be – in 1343, for example, one inflammatory meeting ended with a man being eaten by a mob. Most famously, it was in the piazza that Savonarola held his "Bonfire of the Vanities" – on the very spot where, on May 23, 1498, he was to be executed for heresy. A plaque near the fountain marks the place.

The statues

Florence's political volatility is encapsulated by the Piazza della Signoria's peculiar array of statuary. The line-up, arranged in the sixteenth century to accentuate the axis of the Uffizi, starts with Giambologna's equestrian statue of Cosimo I, the only such equestrian bronze figure produced in the late Renaissance, and continues with Ammannati's fatuous *Neptune Fountain*, a tribute to Cosimo's prowess as a naval commander. Neptune himself is a lumpen lout, who provoked Michelangelo to coin the rhyming put-down – "Ammannato, Ammannato, che bel marmo hai rovinato" (. . . what a fine piece of marble you've ruined); Ammannati doesn't seem to have been too embarrassed, though in a late phase of piety he did come to regret the lasciviousness of the figures round the base, created with the assistance of Giambologna and other junior sculptors.

After a copy of Donatello's *Marzocco* (original in the Bargello) comes a copy of his *Judith and Holofernes* (original in the Palazzo Vecchio), which freezes the action at the moment Judith's arm begins its scything stroke – a dramatic conception that no other sculptor of the period would have attempted. Commissioned by Cosimo il Vecchio, this statue originally served as a fountain in the Palazzo Medici, but was removed to the Piazza della Signoria after the expulsion of the family in 1494, and displayed as an emblem of vanquished tyranny; a new inscription on the base reinforced the message for those too obtuse to get it.

Michelangelo's *David* (original in the Accademia), at first intended for the duomo, was also installed here as a declaration of civic solidarity by the short-lived Florentine Republic. It was not a trouble-free project: during its four-day journey from Michelangelo's studio to the Palazzo Vecchio the statue was stoned by gangs of Medici supporters, and then the Republic's leaders found themselves somewhat abashed by David's nudity – so they kept him under wraps for a couple of months while a skirt of copper leaves was made for him.

Keeping David company is Bandinelli's *Hercules and Cacus*, a personal emblem of Cosimo I, but dismissed by Benvenuto Cellini as "a sackful of melons". The marble might have ended up as something more inspiring. In the late 1520s, when the

THE FLORENTINE REPUBLIC

Dante compared Florence's constant political struggles to a sick man forever shifting his position in bed, and indeed its medieval history often appears a catalogue of incessant civic unrest. Yet between 1293 and 1534 – bar the odd ruction – the city maintained a republican constitution that was embodied in well-defined institutions. The nucleus of this structure was formed by the city's **merchants** and **guilds**, who covertly controlled Florence as early as the twelfth century and formalized their influence during the so-called **Primo Popolo** (1248–59), a quasi-democratic regime whose ten-year rule, claimed Dante, was the only period of civic peace in Florence's history. During the **Secondo Popolo** (1284), the leading guilds, the *Arti Maggiori*, introduced the **Ordinamenti della Giustizia** (1293), a written constitution that entrenched mercantile power still further and was to be the basis of Florence's government for the next two hundred and fifty years.

The **rulers** of this much vaunted republic were drawn exclusively from the ranks of guild members over the age of thirty, and were chosen in a public ceremony held every two months – the short tenure being designed to prevent individuals or cliques assuming too much power. At this ceremony, the names of selected guild members were placed in eight leather bags (*borse*) kept in the sacristy of Santa Croce, and the ones picked from the bags duly became the **Priori** (or *Signori*), forming a government called the **Signoria**, usually comprising nine men, most of them from the *Arti Maggiori*. Once elected, the *Priori* moved into the Palazzo della Signoria, where they were expected to stay, virtually incommunicado, for their period of office – though they were waited on hand and foot, and enjoyed the services of a professional joke-teller, the *Buffone*.

Headed by the **Gonfaloniere** (literally the "standard bearer"), the *Signoria* consulted two elected councils or **Collegi** – the **Dodici Buonomini** (Twelve Citizens) and **Sedici Gonfalonieri** (Sixteen Standard Bearers) – as well as committees introduced to deal with specific crises (The Ten of War, the Eight of Security, the Six of Commerce . . .). Permanent officials included the Chancellor (Machiavelli once held this post) and the **Podestà**, a chief magistrate brought in from a neighbouring city as an independent arbitrator, and housed in the Bargello. In times of extreme crisis, such as the Pazzi Conspiracy (see p.84), all male citizens over the age of fourteen were summoned to a **Parlemento** in Piazza della Signoria by the tolling of the Palazzo Vecchio's famous bell – known as the *Vacca* (cow), after its deep bovine tone. When a two-thirds quorum was reached, the people were asked to approve a **Balìa**, a committee delegated to deal with the situation as it saw fit.

All this looked good on paper but in practice the set-up was far from democratic. The lowliest workers, the **Popolo Minuto**, were totally excluded, as were the **Grandi**, or nobles. And despite the *Signoria*'s apparently random selection process, political cliques had few problems ensuring that only the names of likely supporters found their way into the *borse*. If a rogue candidate slipped through the net, or things went awry, then a *Parlemento* was summoned, a *Balìa* formed, and the offending person replaced by a more pliable candidate. It was by such means that the great mercantile dynasties of Florence – the Peruzzi, the Albizzi, the Strozzi, and of course the Medici – retained their power even when not technically in office.

Florentines were once again busy tearing the Medici emblem from every building on which it had been stuck. Michelangelo offered to carve a monumental figure of Samson to celebrate the Republic's latest victory over tyranny; other demands on the artist's time put paid to this project, and the stone passed to Bandinelli, who duly vented his mediocrity on it.

The Loggia

The square's grace note, the **Loggia della Signoria**, was built in the late fourteenth century as a dais for city officials during ceremonies; its alternative name, the Loggia dei Lanzi, comes from Cosimo I's bodyguard of Swiss lancers, who used the loggia as their rest room. Though the *Judith and Holofernes* was placed here as early as 1506, it was only in the late eighteenth century that the loggia became exclusively a showcase for melodramatic sculpture.

In the corner nearest the Palazzo Vecchio stands a figure that has become one of the iconic images of the Renaissance, Benvenuto Cellini's *Perseus*. Made for Cosimo I, it symbolizes the triumph of firm Grand Ducal government over the monstrous indiscipline of all other forms of government. The traumatic process of its creation is vividly described in Cellini's riproaring and self-serving autobiography – the project seemed doomed when the molten bronze began to solidify too early, but the ever-resourceful hero saved the day by flinging all his pewter plates into the mixture. Equally attention-grabbing is Giambologna's last work, *The Rape of the Sabine*, epitome of the Mannerist obsession with spiralling forms.

The Ragione museum

Occupying a suite of rooms over the Cassa di Risparmio bank at Piazza della Signoria 5 is the **Collezione A. Della Ragione** (Mon & Wed–Sat 9am–2pm, Sun 8am–1pm; L4000), the nearest thing in Florence to a general collection of modern Italian art. A civil engineer by profession, Alberto della Ragione was an extremely active patron, subsidizing young artists and hustling other collectors to buy their work. Now administered by the *comune*, his gallery includes paintings by many of the people you'd expect to find (de Chirico, Carrà, Morandi), a miscellany of Tuscan landscapes, and sculpture by Manzù and Marini. Not much of a treat by the standards of Paris or London, but it might be a welcome aesthetic break from the world of the Medici.

The Palazzo Vecchio

Florence's fortress-like town hall, the **Palazzo Vecchio** (Mon–Wed, Fri & Sat 9am–7pm, Thurs 9am–2pm, Sun 8am–1pm; L10,000), was begun in the last year of the thirteenth century as the home of the *Signoria*, the highest tier of the city's republican government. Local folklore has it that the eccentric plan was not devised by the original architect (thought to be Arnolfo di Cambio), but is rather a product of factional division – the Guelph government refusing to encroach on land previously owned by the Ghibellines (see p.596).

Changes in the Florentine constitution entailed alterations to the layout of the palace, the most radical overhaul coming in 1540, when Cosimo I moved his retinue here from the Palazzo Medici and grafted a huge extension onto the back. The Medici were in residence for only nine years – they moved to the Palazzo Pitti, largely at the insistence of Cosimo's wife, Eleanor of Toledo – but the enlargement and refurbishment instigated by Cosimo continued throughout the period of his rule. Much of the decoration of the state rooms comprises a relentless eulogy of Cosimo and his relations; the propaganda is made tolerable, though, by some of the palace's examples of Mannerist art – among the finest pieces produced by that ultra-sophisticated and self-regarding movement.

The interior

Giorgio Vasari, court architect from 1555 until his death in 1574, was responsible for much of the sycophantic decor in the state apartments. His limited talents were given full rein in the huge **Salone dei Cinquento**, built at the end of the fifteenth century as the assembly hall for the Great Council of the penultimate republic. Instead of these drearily bombastic murals – painted either by Vasari or under his direction – the chamber might have had one of Italy's most remarkable decorative schemes. Leonardo da Vinci and Michelangelo were employed to paint frescoes on opposite sides of the room; Leonardo's work – *The Battle of Anghiari* – was abandoned after his experimental technique went wrong, and Michelangelo's project – *The Battle of Cascina* – existed only as a fragment when he was summoned to Rome by Pope Julius II in 1506. Michelangelo's *Victory*, by the far wall on the left, was carved for Julius's tomb, and was at some point converted by the sculptor from a female to a male figure; donated to the Medici by the artist's nephew, it was installed here by Vasari to mark Cosimo's defeat of the Sienese.

A door to the right of the entrance to the hall, at the far end, opens onto the most bizarre room in the building – the **Studiolo di Francesco I**. Created by Vasari in the 1570s and decorated by several Mannerist artists, this windowless cell was created as a retreat for the introverted son of Cosimo and Eleanor. Each of the miniature bronzes and nearly all the paintings reflect Francesco's interest in the sciences and alchemy: the entrance wall illustrates the theme of "Earth" and the others, reading clockwise, signify "Water", "Air" and "Fire". The outstanding paintings are the two which don't fit the scheme: Bronzino's portraits of the occupant's parents, facing each other across the room.

Bronzino's major contribution to the palace can be seen on the floor above, reached after the **Quartiere di Leone X**, where each room is slavishly devoted to a different member of the Medici clan. Upstairs, Eleanor of Toledo's tiny **chapel** was decorated by Bronzino in the 1540s; it seems that the artist used a novel and time-consuming technique to give these wall paintings the same glassy surface as his canvases, executing a first draft in fresco and then glazing it with a layer of tempera.

Those who find all this Mannerist stuff unhealthily airless can take refuge in the summery **Sala dei Gigli**, which was fitted out in the decade after 1475. Named after the lilies which adorn the room (the city's symbol), it has a splendid ceiling by the brothers Giuliano and Benedetto da Maiano, and frescoes by Domenico Ghirlandaio. Two small rooms are attached to the Sala dei Gigli: the Cancelleria, once Machiavelli's office and now containing a portrait of the often maligned political thinker, and a chamber decorated with 57 maps painted in 1563 by the court astronomer Fra' Ignazio Danti, depicting the entire known world.

The adjoining **Sala d'Udienza**, originally the audience chamber of the republic, has an equally fine ceiling by Giuliano and assistants, and a magnificent doorway by the brothers in partnership; the Mannerists reassert themselves here, however, with a vast fresco sequence by Cecchino Salviati: this is generally held to be his most accomplished work. In here is also Donatello's *Judith and Holofernes*.

Very occasionally it's possible to climb from this floor to the top of the Palazzo Vecchio's **tower**, passing the cell known as the Alberghinetto (little hotel), where such troublemakers as Cosimo il Vecchio and Savonarola were once imprisoned.

The Uffizi

Florence's prime tourist attraction is housed in what was once a government office block, built by Vasari for Cosimo I in 1560 on a site then occupied by a church and some houses between the Palazzo Vecchio and the river. After Vasari's death, work on the elongated U-shaped building was continued by Buontalenti, who was asked by Francesco I to glaze the upper storey so that it could house his art collection. Each of the succeeding Medici added to the family's trove of art treasures, and the accumulated collection was preserved for public inspection by the last member of the family, Anna Maria Lodovica, whose will specified that it should be left to the people of Florence and never be allowed to leave the city. A large proportion of the statuary was transferred to the Bargello during the nineteenth century, while most of the antiquities went to the Museo Archeologico, leaving the **Galleria degli Uffizi** (May–Sept Tues–Sat 9am–10pm, Sun 8.30am–8pm; Oct–April Tues–Sat 8.30am–6.50pm, Sun 8.30am–1.50pm; L12,000) as essentially a gallery of paintings supplemented with some classical sculptures.

THE UFFIZI BOMBING

At 1am on May 27, 1993, a colossal explosion occurred on the west side of the Uffizi, killing five people, demolishing the headquarters of Europe's oldest agricultural academy, blasting holes through the walls of the Uffizi itself, and damaging numerous paintings inside, some of them irreparably. Initially it was supposed that a gas leak might have been responsible, but within hours the country's head prosecutor, after discussions with forensic experts and the anti-terrorist squad, issued a statement – "Gas does not come into it. We have found a crater one and a half metres wide. The evidence is unequivocal." Fragments of the car that had carried the estimated 100kg of TNT had been found some thirty metres from the rubble.

Instantly it was put about that the Mafia lay behind the atrocity, though it was not explained what the Mafia had to gain from the killing of the academy's curator and her family, or from the mutilation of a few Renaissance paintings. While many were willing to believe that the Mafia may have planted the bomb, most Florentines were convinced that the orders had originated within the country's political and military establishment. Frightened by the political realignments taking place all over Italy, with the rise of northern separatists, the reformed communist party and various newly formed groupings, the old guard were evidently employing the tactics of destabilization – a repeat of the 1970s' "Strategy of Tension", when organized criminals and right-wing politicians colluded in a sequence of terrorist attacks to ensure the public's loyalty to the supposedly threatened state. Just days before the Uffizi bombing, the Italian secret service had been implicated in the murders of Giovanni Falcone and Paolo Borsellino, the country's most powerful anti-Mafia investigators, and it seemed plain that the same unholy alliances had been at work in Florence. The aftermath of the explosion has done nothing to dispel these suspicions: the car that carried the bomb was recorded by video cameras at several places in the city, yet no one has been charged with the outrage to this day.

The superficial damage has been repaired, but structural work will take years, so you can expect areas of the Uffizi to be smothered in scaffolding for some time to come.

Florence can prompt an over-eagerness to reach for the superlatives; in the case of the Uffizi, superlatives are simply the bare truth – this is the finest picture gallery in Italy. So many masterpieces are collected here that it's not even possible to skate over the surface in a single visit; it makes sense to limit your initial tour to the first fifteen rooms, where the Florentine Renaissance works are concentrated, and to explore the rest another time. And as this is the busiest single building in the country, with over one and a half million visitors each year, you should anticipate enormous queues at most times of the day except in the depths of winter; in summer the best way to beat the crowds is to visit for the last couple of hours or try booking tickets in advance (see p.80). Be prepared to find some of the rooms closed for one reason or another – at the height of the summer it's not unusual to find that nearly half the gallery is locked up.

In 1999 there was considerable hoopla when several new rooms were opened, with claims that huge previously unseen tranches of the Uffizi's collection would be displayed. In fact they are mostly old rooms that have been given a makeover, with few substantial new works on show. The bookshop and café are now more smartly appointed, but the core of the gallery and its actual layout remain little changed.

From Cimabue to Uccello

The main picture galleries are ranged on the third floor, but on the ground floor, in rooms that once formed part of the eleventh-century church of San Pier Scheraggio, are shown **Andrea del Castagno**'s frescoes of celebrated Florentines; the imaginary portraits include Dante and Boccaccio, both of whom spoke in debates at the church. Close to a Botticelli *Annunciation*, a lift goes up to the galleries; if you take the staircase instead, you'll pass the entrance to the prints and drawings collection, the bulk of which is reserved for scholarly scrutiny, though samples are often on public show.

Room 1, housing an assembly of antique sculptures, many of which were used as a sort of source book by Renaissance artists, is often shut. The beginnings of the stylistic evolution of that period can be traced in the following room, where three altarpieces of the *Maestà* (Madonna enthroned) by **Cimabue**, **Duccio** and **Giotto**, dwarfing everything around them, show the softening of the hieratic Byzantine style into a more tactile form of representation. Painters from fourteenth-century Siena fill **room 3**, with several pieces by Ambrogio and Pietro Lorenzetti and **Simone Martini**'s glorious *Annunciation*, the Virgin cowering from the angel amid a field of pure gold.

Other trecento artists follow in **rooms 5 and 6**, among them Florence's first-rank Gothic painters, **Orcagna** and **Lorenzo Monaco**, whose majestic *Coronation of the Virgin* and *Adoration of the Magi* catch the eye first. The version of the latter subject by **Gentile da Fabriano** is the summit of the precious style known as International Gothic, spangled with gold that in places is so thick that the crowns of the kings, for instance, are like low-relief jewellery. It's crammed with so much detail that there's no real distinction between what's crucial and what's peripheral, with as much attention lavished on incidentals such as a snarling cheetah as on the supposed protagonists. Also in this room is Starnina's *Thebiad*, a baffling but beguiling little narrative that can perhaps best be described as a monastic fairy tale.

Madonna with SS. Francis, John the Baptist, Zenobius and Lucy is one of only twelve extant paintings by **Domenico Veneziano** (**room 7**), who spent much of his life in Venice but died destitute in Florence. Veneziano's greatest pupil, **Piero della Francesca**, is represented with *Federico da Montefeltro and Battista Sforza*, backed by images of the duke surrounded by the cardinal virtues and his wife by the theological virtues. Elevating the couple to the status of mythic lovers, these panels were painted two years after Battista's death – in the background of her portrait is the town of Gubbio, where she died giving birth to her ninth child and first son, Guidobaldo.

Paolo Uccello's *The Battle of San Romano* once hung in Lorenzo il Magnifico's bedchamber, in company with the depictions of the battle now in the Louvre and London's National Gallery. Warfare is the ostensible subject, but this is really a compendium of perspectival effects: a toppling knight, a horse and rider keeled onto their sides, the foreshortened legs of a kicking horse, a thicket of lances: every object exists in a self-contained space, creating a fight scene with no sense of violence.

Filippo Lippi to Botticelli

Most space in **room 8** is given to **Filippo Lippi**, whose *Madonna and Child with Two Angels* supplies one of the gallery's most popular faces, and one of its least otherworldly devotional images – the model was Lucrezia Buti, a convent novice who became the object of one of his more enduring sexual obsessions (see p.182). There's a fine *Madonna* here by Lippi's pupil **Botticelli**, who also steals some of the thunder in the next room, where the artists centre stage are **Piero** and **Antonio del Pollaiuolo**; their sinewy *SS. Vincent, James and Eustace*, one of their best works, is chiefly the work of Antonio. This room also contains the *Portrait of Young Man in a Red Hat*, sometimes referred to as a self-portrait by Lippi and Lucrezia Buti's son, Filippino, but now widely believed to be an eighteenth-century fraud.

It's in the merged **rooms 10–14** that the greatest of **Botticelli**'s productions are gathered. A century ago most people walked past his pictures without breaking stride; nowadays – despite their elusiveness – the *Primavera* and *The Birth of Venus* stop all visitors in their tracks. The identities of the characters in the *Primavera* are clear enough: on the right Zephyrus, god of the west wind, chases the nymph Cloris, who is then transfigured into the goddess of spring; Venus stands in the centre, to the side of the three Graces, who are targeted by Cupid; on the left Mercury wards off a cloud. The question of what this all means, however, has occupied scholars for decades. Some see it as an allegory of the four seasons, but the consensus now seems to be that it shows the triumph of Venus, with the Graces as the physical embodiment of her beauty and Flora the symbol of her fruitfulness – an interpretation supported by the fact that the picture was placed outside the wedding suite of Lorenzo di Pierfrancesco de' Medici.

Botticelli's most winsome painting, the *Birth of Venus* probably takes as its source the grisly myth that the goddess emerged from the sea after it had been impregnated by the castration of Uranus – an allegory for the creation of beauty through the mingling of the spirit (Uranus) and the physical world. A third allegory hangs close by – *Pallas and the Centaur*, perhaps symbolizing the ambivalent triumph of reason over instinct.

His devotional paintings are generally less perplexing. The *Adoration of the Magi* is traditionally thought to contain a gallery of Medici portraits: Cosimo il Vecchio as the first king, his sons Giovanni and Piero as the other two kings, Lorenzo il Magnifico on the far left, and his brother Giuliano as the black-haired young man in profile on the right. Only the identification of Cosimo is reasonably certain, along with that of Botticelli himself, on the right in the yellow robe. Profoundly influenced by Savonarola's teaching, Botticelli in later life confined himself to devotional pictures and moral fables, and his style became increasingly severe. The transformation is clear when comparing the easy grace of the *Madonna of the Magnificat* and the *Madonna of the Pomegranate* with the more rigidly composed *Enthroned Madonna with Saints* or the *Calumny*, a painting so angular and agitated it seems like a recantation of his former self.

Not quite every masterpiece in this room is by Botticelli. Set away from the walls is the *Adoration of the Shepherds* by his Flemish contemporary **Hugo van der Goes**. Brought to Florence in 1483 by Tomasso Portinari, the Medici agent in Bruges, it provided the city's artists with their first large-scale demonstration of the realism of northern European oil painting, and had a great influence on the way the medium was exploited here.

Da Vinci to Mantegna

Works in **room 15** trace the formative years of **Leonardo da Vinci**, whose distinctive touch appears first in the *Baptism* by his master Verrocchio – the wistful angel in profile is by the eighteen-year-old apprentice, as is the misty landscape in the background. A similar terrain of soft-focus mountains and water occupies the far distance in Leonardo's slightly later *Annunciation*, in which a diffused light falls on a scene where everything is observed with a scientist's precision – the petals of the flowers on which the angel alights, the fall of the Virgin's drapery, the carving on the lectern at which she reads. In restless contrast to the aristocratic poise of the *Annunciation*, the sketch of *The Adoration of the Magi* – abandoned when Leonardo left Florence for Milan in early 1482 – presents the infant Christ as the eye of a vortex of figures, all drawn into his presence by a force as irresistible as a whirlpool.

Usually this room also contains a brace of pictures by **Piero di Cosimo**, the wild man of the Florentine Renaissance. Shunning civilized company, Piero did everything he could to bring his life close to a state of uncompromised Nature, living in a house that was never cleaned, in the midst of a garden he refused to tend, and eating nothing but hard-boiled eggs. Where his contemporaries might seek inspiration in commentaries on Plato, he would spend hours staring at the sky, at peeling walls, at the pavement – at anything where abstract patterns might conjure fabulous scenes in his imagination.

Room 18, the octagonal *Tribuna*, now houses the most important of the Medici sculptures, chief among which is the **Medici Venus**, a first-century BC copy of the Praxitelean *Aphrodite of Cnidos*. She was kept in the Villa Medici in Rome until Cosimo III began to fret that she was having a detrimental effect on the morals of the city's art students, and ordered her removal to Florence. Around the walls are hung some fascinating portraits by **Bronzino** – Cosimo de' Medici, Eleanor of Toledo, Bartolomeo Panciatichi and his wife Lucrezia Panciatichi, all painted as figures of porcelain, placed in a bloodless, sunless world. More vital is Andrea del Sarto's flirtatious *Portrait of a Young Woman*, and there's a deceptive naturalism to Vasari's portrait of Lorenzo il Magnifico and Pontormo's of Cosimo il Vecchio, both painted long after the death of their subjects.

Signorelli and **Perugino** – with some photo-sharp portraits – are the principal artists of **room 19**, and after them comes a room largely devoted to **Cranach** and **Dürer**. Each has an *Adam and Eve* here, Dürer taking the opportunity to show off his proficiency as a painter of wildlife. Dürer's power as a portraitist is displayed in the *Portrait of the Artist's Father*, his earliest authenticated painting, and Cranach has a couple of acute pictures of Luther on show, one of them a double with his wife.

Highlights in the following sequence of rooms (**20–24**) are an impenetrable *Sacred Allegory* by **Giovanni Bellini**, **Holbein**'s *Portrait of Sir Richard Southwell* and a crystalline triptych by **Mantegna** – not in fact a real triptych, but rather a trio of small paintings shackled together after the event. To the side are a couple of other pictures by Mantegna – a swarthy portrait of Carlo de' Medici and the tiny *Madonna of the Stonecutters*, set against a mountain that looks like a gigantic fir-cone.

Michelangelo to Titian

Beyond the stockpile of classical pieces in the short corridor overlooking the Arno, the main attraction in **room 25** is **Michelangelo**'s *Doni Tondo*, the only easel painting he came close to completing. (Regarding sculpture as the noblest of the visual arts, Michelangelo dismissed all non-fresco painting as a demeaning chore.) Nobody has yet explained the precise significance of every aspect of this picture, but plausible explanations for parts of it have been put forward. The five naked figures behind the Holy Family seem to be standing in a half-moon-shaped cistern or font, which would relate to the infant Baptist to the right, who – in the words of St Paul – prefigures the coming of Christ just as the new moon as "a shadow of things to come". In the same epistle, Paul goes on to commend the virtues of mercy, benignity, humility, modesty and patience, which are perhaps what the five youths represent. The tondo's contorted gestures, hermetic meaning and virulent colours were greatly influential on the Mannerist painters of the sixteenth century, as can be gauged from the nearby *Moses Defending the Daughters of Jethro* by **Rosso Fiorentino**, one of the seminal figures of the movement.

Another piece by Rosso is on show in **room 27**, along with several works by Bronzino and his adoptive father, **Pontormo** – one of the very few painters not seen at his best in the Uffizi. Separating the two Mannerist groups is a room containing **Andrea del Sarto**'s sultry *Madonna of the Harpies* and a number of compositions by **Raphael**, including the lovely *Madonna of the Goldfinch* and the late *Pope Leo X with Cardinals Giulio de' Medici and Luigi de' Rossi* – as shifty a group of ecclesiastics as was ever gathered in one frame.

Room 28 is entirely given over to another of the titanic figures of sixteenth-century art, **Titian**, with nine paintings on show. His *Flora* and *A Knight of Malta* are stunning, but most eyes tend to swivel towards the *Venus of Urbino*, the most fleshly and provocative of all Renaissance nudes – or, in the opinion of Mark Twain, "the foulest, the vilest, the obscenest picture the world possesses".

Parmigianino to Chardin

A brief diversion through the painters of the sixteenth-century Emilian school follows, centred on **Parmigianino**, whose *Madonna of the Long Neck* is one of the pivotal Mannerist creations. Parmigianino was a febrile and introverted character who abandoned painting for alchemy towards the end of his short life, and many of his works are marked by a sort of morbid refinement – none more so than this one. The Madonna's tunic clings to every contour, an angel advances a perfectly turned leg, the infant Christ drapes himself languorously on his mother's lap, while in the background an emaciated figure unrolls a scroll of parchment by a colonnade so severely foreshortened that it looks like a single column.

Rooms 31 to 35 feature artists from Venice and the Veneto, with outstanding paintings from **Moroni** (*Portrait of Count Pietro Secco Suardi*), **Paolo Veronese** (*Annunciation* and *Holy Family with St Barbara*), and **Tintoretto** (*Leda*). This is the part of the Uffizi that took the brunt of the terrorist bomb, an explosion which reduced Sebastiano del Piombo's *Death of Adonis* to postage-stamp tatters, though the restorers are confident of retrieving the masterpiece.

In **room 41**, dominated by **Rubens** and **Van Dyck**, the former's *Portrait of Isabella Brandt* makes its point more quietly than most of the stuff around it. Rubens lets rip in *Henry IV at the Battle of Ivry* and *The Triumphal Entry of Henry IV into Paris* – Henry's marriage to Marie de' Medici is the connection with Florence. Rubens's equally histrionic contemporary, **Caravaggio**, has a cluster of pieces in **room 43**, including a screaming severed head of *Medusa*, a smug little bore of a *Bacchus*, and a *Sacrifice of Isaac* – religious art as tabloid journalism.

The next room (**44**) is in effect a showcase for the portraiture of **Rembrandt**. His sorrow-laden *Self-Portrait as an Old Man*, painted five years or so before his death, makes a poignant contrast with the self-confident self-portrait of thirty years earlier. Although there are some good pieces from Tiepolo, portraits again command the attention in the following room of eighteenth-century works, especially the two of Maria Theresa painted by **Goya**, and **Chardin's** demure children at play. On the way out, in the hall at the top of the exit stairs, squats one of the city's talismans, the *Wild Boar*, a Roman copy of a third-century BC Hellenistic sculpture; it was the model for the *Porcellino* fountain in the Mercato Nuovo.

The Corridoio Vasariano

A door on the west corridor, between rooms 25 and 34, opens onto the **Corridoio Vasariano**, a passageway built by Vasari to link the Palazzo Vecchio to the Palazzo Pitti through the Uffizi. Winding its way down to the river, over the Ponte Vecchio, through the church of Santa Felicita and into the Giardino di Bóboli, it gives a fascinating series of clandestine views of the city. As if that weren't pleasure enough, the corridor is completely lined with paintings, the larger portion of which comprises a **gallery of self-portraits**. Once past the portrait of Vasari, the series proceeds chronologically, its roll call littered with illustrious names: Raphael, Andrea del Sarto, Bronzino, Bernini, Rubens, Rembrandt, Velasquez, David, Delacroix, Ingres. **Access** to the Corridoio is one of Florence's most vexed questions. Some years you can visit, others you can't: some years you pay and walk in, others you have to book in advance. At the time of writing it was firmly closed, with no projection of when it might again be open. Contact the tourist office for latest details.

Museo di Storia della Scienza

Down the Uffizi's east flank runs Via dei Leoni, named after the lions housed in this street by the *comune* – the ferocious mascots used to be kept in the Piazza della Signoria, but Cosimo I had problems with the smell, so new quarters were built here. At the river end, the street opens into Piazza dei Giudici, so called from the tribunal that used to meet in the building now housing the city's science museum, or **Museo di Storia della Scienza** (Mon, Wed & Fri 9.30am–1pm & 2–5pm, Tues, Thurs & Sat 9.30am–1pm; L10,000).

Long after Florence had declined from its artistic apogee, the intellectual reputation of the city was maintained by its scientists, many of them directly encouraged by members of the ruling Medici-Lorraine dynasty. Grand Duke Ferdinando II and his brother

Leopoldo, both of whom studied with Galileo, founded a scientific academy at the Pitti in 1657 – called the Accademia del Cimento (Academy of Experiment), its motto was "Try and try again". The instruments made and acquired by this academy are the core of the science museum's collection.

The exhibits take up two upper floors, with a large research library on the lowest floor. Lists of the exhibits in English are handed out to visitors, providing a full background to some of the more extraordinary items.

The first eleven exhibition rooms feature some marvellous **timepieces and measuring instruments** (such as beautiful Arab astrolabes), as well as a massive armillary sphere made for Ferdinando I to provide visual demonstration of the veracity of the earth-centred Ptolemaic system, and the fallacy of Copernicus's heliocentric universe. Galileo's original instruments are on show here, such as the lens with which he discovered the four moons of Jupiter – he tactfully named these the Medicean planets. On this floor you'll also find the museum's religious relic, a bone from one of Galileo's fingers.

On the floor above there are all kinds of **scientific and mechanical equipment** – such as a perpetual motion machine from the quasi-magical realms of scientific endeavour. There are a couple of remarkable outsized pieces: the huge lens made for Cosimo III, with which Faraday and Davy managed to ignite a diamond by focusing the rays of the sun, and the enormous lodestone given by Galileo to Ferdinando II. Other rooms are filled with clocks, or pharmaceutical and chemical apparatus. Finally there is a medical section full of alarming surgical instruments and wax anatomical models for teaching obstetrics. The covered roof-terrace on the third floor sometimes houses temporary exhibitions.

West from the Signoria

Despite the urban improvement schemes of the nineteenth century and the bombings of the last war, several streets in central Florence retain their medieval character, especially in the district to the west of Piazza della Signoria. Forming a border post to this quarter is the **Mercato Nuovo**, or Mercato del Porcellino (summer daily 9am–7pm; winter Tues–Sat 9am–5pm), where there's been a market since the eleventh century, though the present loggia dates from the sixteenth. Having forked out their lire at the souvenir stalls, most people join the small group that's invariably gathered round the bronze boar known as *Il Porcellino* – you're supposed to earn yourself some good luck by getting a coin to fall from the animal's mouth through the grille below his head. This superstition has a social function, as the coins go to an organization that runs homes for abandoned children.

From here, an amble through streets such as Via Porta Rossa, Via delle Terme and Borgo Santi Apostoli will give you some idea of the feel of Florence in the Middle Ages, when every important house was an urban fortress.

Palazzo Davanzati

Perhaps the most imposing exterior in this district is just to the south of the market – the thirteenth-century **Palazzo di Parte Guelfa**, financed from the confiscated property of the Ghibelline faction and later expanded by Brunelleschi. However, for a more complete re-creation of medieval Florence you should visit the fourteenth-century **Palazzo Davanzati** in Via Porta Rossa. In the nineteenth century the palazzo was divided into flats, but at the beginning of the twentieth it was restored to something very close to the modified appearance of the 1500s, when a loggia replaced the battlements on the roof, and the Davanzati stuck their coat of arms on the front. Apart from those haute-bourgeois emendations, the place now looks much as it did when first inhabited.

Nowadays the palazzo is maintained as the **Museo della Casa Fiorentina Antica**. The building was closed in 1995 for a major structural restoration, and a token photographic exhibition of the holdings of the museum has since been on display in the entrance hall (Tues–Sun 9am–2pm; plus fourth Mon of month; closed second and fourth Sun of month). The description that follows gives you an idea of the interior of the museum before closure, but as yet no full opening date has been fixed. Virtually every room is furnished and decorated in predominantly medieval style, using genuine artefacts gathered from a variety of sources. The owners of this house were obviously well prepared for the adversities of urban living, as can be seen in the siege-resistant doors, the private water supply and the huge storerooms for the hoarding of provisions. Upstairs, the Sala Grande reinforces the dual nature of the house – furnished in the best style of the day, it also has hatches in the floor for bombarding the enemy.

Merchants' houses in the fourteenth century would typically have had elaborately painted walls in the main rooms, and the Palazzo Davanzati preserves some fine examples of such decor – especially in the dining room, where the imitation wall hangings of the lower walls are patterned with a parrot motif, while the upper walls depict a garden terrace. Before the development of systems of credit, wealth had to be sunk into tangible assets such as the tapestries, ceramics, sculpture and lacework that alleviate the austerity of many of these rooms; any surplus cash would have been locked away in a strongbox like the extraordinary example in the Sala Piccola, whose locking mechanism looks like the innards of a primitive clock. There's also a fine collection of *cassoni*, the painted chests in which the wife's dowry would be stored.

Plushest of the rooms is the first-floor **bedroom**, with a Sicilian linen bed cover woven with scenes from the story of Tristan. But the spot where the occupants would have been likeliest to linger is the **kitchen**. Located on the top floor to minimize the damage that might be caused by the outbreak of a fire, it would have been the warmest room in the house. A load of ancient utensils are on show here, and set into one wall there is the most civilized of amenities, a service shaft connecting the kitchen to all floors of the building.

Santi Apostoli

Between Via Porta Rossa and the Arno, on Piazzetta del Limbo (the former burial ground of unbaptized children), stands the ancient church of **Santi Apostoli**. Legend has it that this was founded by Charlemagne, but it's not quite that ancient – the eleventh century seems the likeliest date of origin. Santi Apostoli possesses some peculiar relics, in the form of stone fragments allegedly brought from the Holy Sepulchre in Jerusalem by a crusading Florentine; on Holy Saturday sparks struck from these stones are used to light the flame that ignites the "dove" that in turn sets off the fireworks in front of the duomo (see p.153). Orderly and graceful, the interior of grey *pietra serena* against white walls looks like an anticipation of the architecture of Brunelleschi. You would be lucky to see it, though, for the church is hardly ever open.

Around the Piazza Santa Trìnita

Westward of the Palazzo Davanzati, Via Porta Rossa runs into **Piazza Santa Trìnita** – not really a square, just a widening of the city's most expensive street, Via de' Tornabuoni. Sweeping past the Column of Justice – which Pope Pius IV uprooted from the Baths of Caracalla and sent to Cosimo I – the traffic crosses the Arno on the sleek **Ponte Santa Trìnita**, which was built on Cosimo's orders after its predecessor was demolished in a flood. The roads on both sides of the river were raised and widened to accentuate the dramatic potential of the new link between the city centre and Oltrarno, but what makes this the classiest bridge in Italy is the sensuous curve of its arches, a curve so shallow that engineers have been baffled as to how the bridge bears up under the strain. Ostensibly the design was conjured up by Ammannati, one of the Medici's favourite artists, but the curves so closely resemble the arc of Michelangelo's Medici tombs that it's likely the credit belongs elsewhere.

In 1944 the Nazis blew the bridge to smithereens and a seven-year argument ensued before it was agreed to rebuild it using as much of the original material as could be dredged from the Arno. To ensure maximum authenticity in the reconstruction, all the new stone that was needed was quarried from the Bóboli gardens – where the stone for Ammannati's bridge had been cut – and hand tools were used to trim it, as electric blades would have given the blocks too harsh a finish. Twelve years after the war, the reconstructed bridge was opened, lacking only the head from the statue of *Spring*, which had not been found despite the incentive of a hefty reward. At last, in 1961, the missing head was fished from the riverbed; having lain in state for a few days on a scarlet cushion in the Palazzo Vecchio, it was returned to its home.

SANTA TRÌNITA CHURCH

The antiquity of the church of **Santa Trìnita** (Mon–Sat 9am–noon & 4–6pm, Sun 4–6pm; free) is manifest in the Latinate pronunciation of its name – modern Italian stresses the last, not the first syllable. Founded in the eleventh century, it was rebuilt between 1250 and the end of the following century, though the inside face of the entrance wall remains from the Romanesque building. The plainness of the architecture is softened by a number of works of art, the best of which all date from the fifteenth century.

Lorenzo Monaco frescoed the fourth chapel in the right aisle and painted its *Annunciation* altarpiece. The decoration of the Cappella Sassetti, second to the right of the altar, was undertaken by **Ghirlandaio**, who provided an altarpiece of *The Adoration of the Shepherds* and a fresco cycle depicting *Scenes from the Life of St Francis*. Set in the Piazza della Signoria, the scene showing Francis receiving the rule of the order (in the lunette above the altar) includes portraits of Lorenzo il Magnifico and Francesco Sassetti, the patron of the chapel, in the right foreground; on the steps below them are Lorenzo's children and their tutor Poliziano, scholar, philosopher and author of a book on the Pazzi conspiracy – in Latin.

Displayed in the neighbouring chapel is the miraculous Crucifix, formerly in San Miniato church, that bowed to **Giovanni Gualberto** in approval of the mercy he showed to the murderer of his brother. Giovanni went on to found the reforming Vallombrosan order and – notwithstanding the mayhem created on Florence's streets by his militant supporters – was eventually canonized. Frescoes in the fourth chapel of the left aisle show scenes from his life.

A powerful composition by **Luca della Robbia** – the tomb of Benozzo Federighi, Bishop of Fiesole – occupies a wall of the chapel second to the left of the altar; moulded and carved for the church of San Pancrazio, it was transported here in 1896.

Via de' Tornabuoni and the Palazzo Strozzi

The shops of **Via de' Tornabuoni** are effectively out of bounds to those who don't travel first class. Versace, Ferragamo, Gucci and Armani have their outlets here (see pp.155–6), sharing the territory with jewellery and leather showrooms, perfumiers and upmarket cafés.

Conspicuous wealth is nothing new on Via de' Tornabuoni. Looming above everything is the vast **Palazzo Strozzi**, the last, the largest and the least subtle of all Florentine Renaissance palaces, with windows as big as gateways and embossed with lumps of stone the size of boulders. It was begun by the banker Filippo Strozzi, a figure so powerful that he was once described as "the first man of Italy", and whose family provided the ringleaders of the anti-Medici faction in Florence. He bought and demolished a dozen town houses to make space for Giuliano da Sangallo's strongbox in stone, and the construction of it lasted from 1489 to 1536. The **Museo di Palazzo Strozzi** is only open when holding temporary – and sometimes contemporary – art exhibitions; ask at the tourist office for information.

The Palazzo Rucellai

Some of Florence's other plutocrats made an impression with rather more élan. In the 1440s Giovanni Rucellai, one of the richest businessmen in the city and an esteemed scholar too, decided to commission a new house from Leon Battista Alberti, whose accomplishments as architect, mathematician, linguist and theorist of the arts prompted a contemporary to exclaim, "Where shall I put Battista Alberti: in what category of learned men shall I place him?" The resultant **Palazzo Rucellai**, two minutes' walk from the Strozzi house at Via della Vigna Nuova 18, was the first palace in Florence to follow the rules of classical architecture; its tiers of pilasters, incised into smooth blocks of stone, evoke the exterior wall of the Colosseum. Alberti later produced another, equally elegant design for the same patron – the front of the church of Santa Maria Novella (see next page). In contrast to the feud between the Medici and the Strozzi, the Rucellai were on the closest terms with the city's royal family. The frieze on the Palazzo Rucellai features the heraldic devices of the two families, the Medici emblem alongside the Rucellai sail; moreover, the Loggia dei Rucellai, across the street, was in all likelihood built for the wedding of Giovanni's son to the granddaughter of Cosimo il Vecchio.

The Marini museum and Rucellai chapel

Round the corner from the Palazzo Rucellai stands the ex-church of San Pancrazio, deconsecrated by Napoleon, then successively the offices of the state lottery, the magistrates' court, a tobacco factory and an arsenal. It is now the swish **Museo Marino Marini** (June–July & Sept Mon & Wed–Sat 10am–5pm, Thurs also 10am–11pm, Sun 10am–1pm; Oct–May same days 10am–1pm; closed Tues & Aug; L8000), where the attire and demeanour of the attendants might make you think you'd strayed into a well-appointed fashion house. Holding around two hundred works left to the city a few years ago in Marini's will, the museum itself is perhaps the most intriguing artefact and it's debatable whether Marini's pieces can stand up to the reverential atmosphere imposed by the display techniques. Variations on the sculptor's trademark horse-and-rider theme – familiar from tasteful civic environments all over Europe – make up much of the show.

Once part of the church but now corralled off from the museum, the **Cappella di San Sepolcro** is the most exquisite of Alberti's buildings (open Oct–June Saturdays only at 5.30pm for Mass, or by appointment ☎055.287.707). Designed as the funerary monument to Giovanni Rucellai, it takes the form of a diminutive reconstruction of Jerusalem's Church of the Holy Sepulchre.

The Santa Maria Novella district

Scurrying from the platforms in search of a room, or fretting in the queues for a rail ticket, most people barely give a glance to **Santa Maria Novella train station**, but this is a building that deserves as much attention as many of the city's conventional monuments. Its principal architect, **Giovanni Michelucci** – who died in January 1991 just two days short of his hundredth birthday – was one of the leading figures of the Modernist movement, which in Mussolini's Italy was marginalized by the officially approved pomposities of the Neoclassical tendency. Accordingly there was some astonishment when, in 1933, Michelucci and his colleagues won the open competition to design the main rail terminal for one of the country's showpiece cities. Although the obstructiveness of some of the staff goes a long way to disguise the fact, the station is a piece of impeccably rational planning, so perfectly designed for its function that no major alterations have been necessary in the half-century since its completion.

Cross the road from the front of the train station, and you're on the edge of a zone free from the hazards of speeding traffic and petrol fumes. On the other side of the church of Santa Maria Novella – whose back directly faces the station – lies **Piazza Santa Maria Novella**, a square with a lethargic backwater feel, much favoured as a spot for picnic lunches and after-dark loitering.

Santa Maria Novella

From the freshly scrubbed gay green, white and pink patterns of its marble facade, you'd never guess that the church of **Santa Maria Novella** (daily 7–11.30am & 3.30–6pm) was the Florentine base of the Dominican order, the fearsome vigilantes of thirteenth-century Catholicism. A church was founded here at the end of the eleventh century and shortly afterwards was handed over to the Dominicans, who set about altering the place to their taste. By 1360 the interior was completed but only the Romanesque lower part of the facade was finished, a state of affairs that lasted until 1456, when Giovanni Rucellai paid for Alberti to design a classicized upper storey that would blend with the older section while improving the facade's proportions. Running round the cemetery to the right of the church is a feature unique in Florence – an arcade of *avelli*, the collective burial vaults of upper-class families.

The interior

The architects of the Gothic interior were also capable of great ingenuity – the distance between the columns diminishes with proximity to the altar, a perspectival illusion to make the nave seem longer. In the 1560s Vasari and his minions ran amok here, ripping out the rood screen and the choir, and bleaching over the frescoes; restorers in the last century managed to reverse much of his handiwork.

Masaccio's extraordinary fresco of *The Trinity* (**6**), one of the earliest works in which perspective and classical proportion were rigorously employed, is painted onto the wall halfway down the left aisle. Surmounting a stark image of the state to which all flesh is reduced, the main scene is a dramatized diagram of the mechanics of Christian redemption, with the lines of the painting leading from the picture's donors, through the Virgin and the Baptist, to the crucified Christ and the stern figure of God the Father at the pinnacle.

Nothing else in the main part of the church has quite the same innovative impact, but the wealth of decoration is astounding. In the right transept lies the **tomb of the Patriarch of Constantinople** (**7**), who died in the city after unsuccessful negotiations to unite the Roman and Byzantine Churches at the 1439 Council of Florence. The cultural repercussions of the failed mission were enormous, however, with the influx of Greek scholars from Constantinople playing a major part in the introduction of classical texts to the Florentine intelligentsia. Raised above the pavement of the transept, the Cappella Rucellai (**8**) contains a *Madonna and Child* signed by Nino Pisano, and Ghiberti's bronze tomb of the Dominican general Francesco Lionardo Dati.

In 1486 the chapel (**10**) immediately to the right of the chancel was bought by Filippo Strozzi, who then commissioned a fresco cycle on the *Life of St Philip* from **Filippino Lippi**. Before starting the project Filippino spent some time in Rome, and the work he carried out on his return displays an archeologist's obsession with ancient Roman culture. In the bizarre *Exorcism of a Demon from the Temple of Mars*, for example, the figures swooning from the nauseous fumes emitted by the demon are almost overwhelmed by an architectural fantasy derived from the recently excavated Golden House of Nero. Look carefully in the top right-hand corner and you'll see a minuscule figure of Christ, about the same size as one of the vases behind the figure of Mars. Behind the altar of this chapel is **Strozzi's tomb**, beautifully carved by Benedetto da Maiano, who also worked on the Palazzo Strozzi.

As a chronicle of fifteenth-century life in Florence, no series of frescoes is more fascinating than **Domenico Ghirlandaio's** pictures (**11**) around the high altar. The work

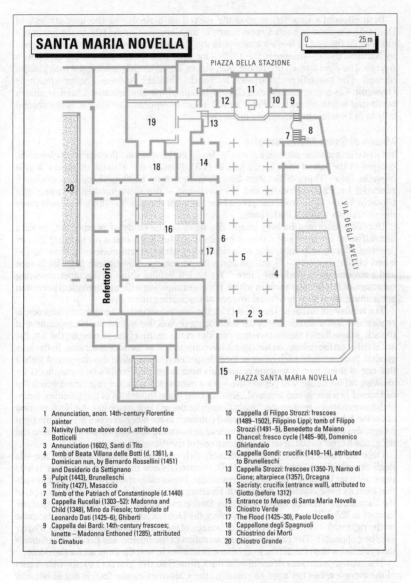

SANTA MARIA NOVELLA

0   25 m

PIAZZA DELLA STAZIONE

11

12   10   9

19   13

7   8

18   14

20

16

6

17   5

4

VIA DEGLI AVELLI

Refettorio

1   2   3

15

PIAZZA SANTA MARIA NOVELLA

1   Annunciation, anon. 14th-century Florentine painter
2   Nativity (lunette above door), attributed to Botticelli
3   Annunciation (1602), Santi di Tito
4   Tomb of Beata Villana delle Botti (d. 1361), a Dominican nun, by Bernardo Rossellini (1451) and Desiderio da Settignano
5   Pulpit (1443), Brunelleschi
6   Trinity (1427), Masaccio
7   Tomb of the Patriarch of Constantinople (d.1440)
8   Cappella Rucellai (1303–52): Madonna and Child (1348), Mino da Fiesole; tombplate of Leonardo Dati (1425–6), Ghiberti
9   Cappella dei Bardi: 14th-century frescoes; lunette – Madonna Enthoned (1285), attributed to Cimabue

10   Cappella di Filippo Strozzi: frescoes (1489–1502), Filippino Lippi; tomb of Filippo Strozzi (1491–5), Benedetto da Maiano
11   Chancel: fresco cycle (1485–90), Domenico Ghirlandaio
12   Cappella Gondi: crucifix (1410–14), attributed to Brunelleschi
13   Cappella Strozzi: frescoes (1350-7), Narno di Cione; altarpiece (1357), Orcagna
14   Sacristy: crucifix (entrance wall), attributed to Giotto (before 1312)
15   Entrance to Museo di Santa Maria Novella
16   Chiostro Verde
17   The Flood (1425–30), Paolo Uccello
18   Cappellone degli Spagnuoli
19   Chiostrino dei Morti
20   Chiostro Grande

was commissioned by Giovanni Tornabuoni, which explains why certain illustrious ladies of the Tornabuoni family are present at the births of both John the Baptist and the Virgin. A sense of well-ordered domesticity pervades the chapel, but there's a nasty disruption with the *Massacre of the Innocents*, its foreground a shambles of severed heads and limbs.

Brunelleschi's Crucifix, supposedly carved as a riposte to the uncouthness of Donatello's version in Santa Croce, hangs in the Cappella Gondi (**12**), to the left of the chancel. At the end of the left transept is the **Cappella Strozzi** (**13**), whose frescoes by Nardo di Cione – painted in the 1350s – incorporate a visual commentary on Dante's *Inferno*. The *Paradise*, on the facing wall, shows Dante already among the ranks of the blessed. The magnificent altarpiece by Nardo's brother Andrea – better known as **Orcagna** – is a propaganda exercise on behalf of the Dominicans: Christ is shown bestowing favour on both St Peter and St Thomas Aquinas, the latter a figure second only to St Dominic in the order's hierarchy.

Museo di Santa Maria Novella

Yet more remarkable paintings are to be found in the spacious Romanesque **cloisters**, entered to the left of the church facade (**15**), housing the **Museo di Santa Maria Novella** (Mon–Thurs & Sat 9am–2pm, Sun 8am–1pm; L5000). These frescoes were executed by **Paolo Uccello** and his workshop – the cloister takes its name, the Chiostro Verde (**16**), from the green base pigment they used – and which now gives the paintings a spectral undertone.

Uccello was driven halfway round the bend by the study of perspective, locking himself away for weeks at a time when he'd got his teeth into a particularly thorny problem. Chronically incapable of looking after his more mundane concerns, he finished his life destitute – "I am old and without means of livelihood. My wife is sick and I am unable to work any more." Yet he left behind some of the most arresting paintings of the Renaissance, in which his preoccupation with mathematical precision sometimes, ironically, produced images of fascinating obscurity.

The windswept image of *The Flood* (**17**), the best preserved of the cloister's frescoes, is rendered almost unintelligible by the telescoping perspective and the double appearance of the ark, whose flanks form a receding corridor in the centre of the picture: on the left, the ark is rising on the deluge, on the right it has come to rest as the waters subside. In the foreground, two men fight each other in their desperation to stay alive; the chequered lifebelt that one of these men is wearing around his neck is one of Uccello's favourite motifs for showing off his mastery of perspective – it's a *mazzocchio*, a wicker ring round which the turbanned headdress was wrapped. Another man grabs the ankles of the visionary figure in the foreground – presumably Noah, though he doesn't look much like the Noah peering out of the ark on the right, nor the bearded patriarch in the other frescoes here. In the right foreground there's a preview of the universal devastation, with tiny corpses laid out on the deck, and a crow gobbling an eyeball from one of the drowned.

Once the chapterhouse of the immensely rich convent of Santa Maria, the **Cappella degli Spagnuoli**, or Spanish Chapel (**18**), received its new name after Eleanor of Toledo reserved it for the use of her Spanish entourage. Presumably she derived constant inspiration from its fresco cycle by **Andrea di Firenze**, an extended depiction of the triumph of the Catholic Church that was described by Ruskin as "the most noble piece of pictorial philosophy in Italy". The sponsors of the project, the Dominicans, appear in emblematic guise on the right wall – the "Domini canes" or hounds of the Lord, unleashed by St Peter Martyr (see box opposite). The prominent representation of the duomo was purely speculative – the cycle dates from the 1360s, long before Brunelleschi won the contract for the dome.

The contemporaneous decoration of the **Chiostrino dei Morti** (**19**), the oldest part of the complex, has not aged so robustly; the Chiostro Grande (**20**) is out of bounds, being the property of the army.

Ognissanti

In medieval times one of the main areas of cloth production – the mainstay of the Florentine economy – was in the western part of the city. **Ognissanti**, the main church

---

THE PATERENES AND SAINT PETER MARTYR

In the twelfth century Florence became the crucible of one of the reforming religious movements that periodically cropped up in medieval Italy. The **Paterenes**, who were so numerous that they had their own clerical hierarchy in parallel with that of the mainstream Church, were convinced that everything worldly was touched by the Devil. Accordingly they despised the papacy for its claims to temporal power and spurned the adoration of all relics and images. Furthermore, they rejected all forms of prayer and all contracts – including marriage vows – and were staunch pacifists.

Inevitably their campaign against the financial and moral corruption of the Catholic Church brought them into conflict with Rome, and eventually the displeasure of the Vatican found its means of expression in the equally zealous but decidedly non-pacific figure of the Dominican known as **St Peter Martyr**. Operating from the monastery of Santa Maria Novella, this papal inquisitor headed a couple of anti-Paterene fraternities, the Crocesegnati and the Compagnia della Fede, which were in effect his private army. In 1244 he led them into battle across the Piazza Santa Maria Novella, where they proceeded to massacre hundreds of the theological enemy. The epicentre of the carnage is marked by the Croce del Trebbio in Via delle Belle Donne, off the eastern side of the piazza.

After this, the Dominicans turned to less militant work, founding the charitable organization called the Misericordia, which is still in existence today (see p.80). In 1252 Peter was knifed to death by a pair of assassins in the pay of a couple of Venetians whose property he'd confiscated, which is why he's usually depicted with a blade embedded in his skull. Allegedly the dying man managed to write out the Creed with his own blood before expiring. Within the year he had been made a saint.

---

of the quarter between Santa Maria Novella and the river, was founded in the thirteenth century by a Benedictine order whose speciality was the weaving of woollen cloth. Three hundred years later the Franciscans took it over, and the new tenure was marked by a Baroque overhaul which spared only the medieval campanile.

The facade of the church is of historical interest as one of the earliest eruptions of the Baroque style in Florence, but the building is made appealing by earlier features – the frescoes by **Domenico Ghirlandaio** and **Sandro Botticelli**. The young face squeezed between the Madonna and the dark-cloaked man in Ghirlandaio's *Madonna della Misericordia*, over the second altar on the right, is said to be that of Amerigo Vespucci – later to set sail on voyages that would give his name to America. Just beyond this, on opposite sides of the nave, are mounted Botticelli's *St Augustine* and Ghirlandaio's more earthbound *St Jerome*, both painted in 1480. In the same year Ghirlandaio painted the *Last Supper* that covers one wall of the **refectory**, reached through the cloister (Mon, Tues & Sat 9am–noon; free). It's a characteristically placid scene, the most animated characters being the birds in flight over the fruit-laden lemon trees above the heads of the disciples.

The San Lorenzo district

Walk a couple of blocks east from the train station and you'll see both the tawdriest and the liveliest aspects of central Florence. Beyond the bustling Via Nazionale and Via Faenza, with their rabbit-hutch hotels and nocturnal hustle, lies the city's main market area, the **Mercato Centrale**, with scores of stalls encircling a vast food hall that rarely sees a foreign face. The racks of T-shirts, leather jackets and belts spread south to and almost engulf the church of San Lorenzo – like Santa Maria Novella, a building of major importance that's often overlooked in the rush to the duomo and the Uffizi.

San Lorenzo

Founded back in the fourth century, **San Lorenzo** (daily 7am–noon & 3.30–6.30pm) has a good claim to be the oldest church in Florence, and for the best part of three hundred years it was the city's cathedral. As this was the Medici's parish church, it inevitably benefited from the family's patronage: in 1420 Giovanni di Bicci de' Medici commissioned Brunelleschi to rebuild San Lorenzo, beginning with the old sacristy, a move which started a long association between the family and the building. Although Michelangelo laboured over a scheme for San Lorenzo's facade, the bare brick of the exterior has never been clad. It's a stark, inappropriate prelude to the powerful simplicity of Brunelleschi's interior, one of the earliest Renaissance church designs.

The church

Close to the entrance of the church, in the second chapel on the right, is **Rosso Fiorentino**'s *Marriage of the Virgin* (**1**), a painting with a uniquely golden-haired and youthful Joseph. Though you might not think so from the acreage of self-congratulatory works in the Palazzo Vecchio, few artists found sixteenth-century Florence a congenial place in which to work, and many followed Rosso's example in leaving the city. No sooner had the Medici returned to the city after the siege of 1530 than he had packed his bags for France, in order – to quote Vasari – "to raise himself . . . out of wretchedness and poverty, which is the common lot of those who work in Tuscany". He eventually found gainful employment with Francis I at Fontainebleau, where he and Primaticcio became the most influential artists in France.

At the end of the right aisle there's a fine tabernacle (**3**) by Desiderio da Settignano, but far more striking are the two **bronze pulpits** (**2**) by **Donatello**, in the centre of the church. Chiefly of scenes preceding and following the Crucifixion, these are the artist's last works, and were completed by his pupils as increasing paralysis limited their master's ability to model in wax. Jagged and discomfiting, charged with more energy than the space can contain, these panels are more like brutal sketches in bronze than conventional reliefs. The overpopulated *Deposition*, for example, has demented mourners screaming underneath crosses which disappear into the void beyond the frame, while in the background a group of horsemen gather on a hill whose contours are left unmarked.

Close by, underneath the dome, an inscription and the Medici arms mark the grave (**5**) of Donatello's main patron, **Cosimo il Vecchio**, bearing the plain dedication "Pater Patriae" – Father of the Fatherland. Donatello is buried in the chapel on the west side of the left transept, currently covered for restoration, where there's also a Filippo Lippi *Annunciation*.

Much of the decorative work in the neighbouring **Sagrestia Vecchia** (**D**) or Old Sacristy (Mon, Wed, Fri & Sat 10–11.45am, Tues & Thurs 4–5.45pm) is by Donatello too: the two bronze doors with their combative pairs of martyrs and disciples, the large reliefs of *SS. Cosmas and Damian* and *SS. Lawrence and Stephen* (high on the wall facing the entrance), and the eight terracotta tondi of the *Evangelists* and *Scenes from the Life of St John the Evangelist*. The table of milky marble in the centre of the room is the tomb (**7**) of Cosimo il Vecchio's parents, Giovanni di Bicci de' Medici and Piccarda Bueri; Cosimo's sons, Piero and Giovanni, are buried in the Verrocchio-designed sarcophagus (**6**) to the left of the entrance.

Biblioteca Medicea-Laurenziana

At the top of the left aisle, beside an enormous Bronzino fresco of *The Martyrdom of St Lawrence* (**10**), a door (**11**) leads out to the cloister, and to a staircase (**12**) going up to the **Biblioteca Medicea-Laurenziana** (Mon–Sat 9am–1pm; free). Wishing to create a

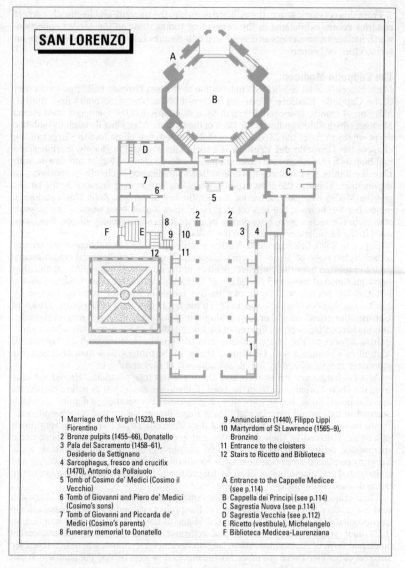

SAN LORENZO

1 Marriage of the Virgin (1523), Rosso Fiorentino
2 Bronze pulpits (1455–66), Donatello
3 Pala del Sacramento (1458–61), Desiderio da Settignano
4 Sarcophagus, fresco and crucifix (1470), Antonio da Pollaiuolo
5 Tomb of Cosimo de' Medici (Cosimo il Vecchio)
6 Tomb of Giovanni and Piero de' Medici (Cosimo's sons)
7 Tomb of Giovanni and Piccarda de' Medici (Cosimo's parents)
8 Funerary memorial to Donatello

9 Annunciation (1440), Filippo Lippi
10 Martyrdom of St Lawrence (1565–9), Bronzino
11 Entrance to the cloisters
12 Stairs to Ricetto and Biblioteca

A Entrance to the Cappelle Medicee (see p.114)
B Cappella dei Principi (see p.114)
C Sagrestia Nuova (see p.114)
D Sagrestia Vecchia (see p.112)
E Ricetto (vestibule), Michelangelo
F Biblioteca Medicea-Laurenziana

suitably grandiose home for the precious manuscripts assembled by Cosimo il Vecchio and Lorenzo il Magnifico, Pope Clement VII (Lorenzo's nephew) asked Michelangelo to design a new Medici library in 1524. The vestibule of the building he came up with is a showpiece of Mannerist architecture, delighting in paradoxical display – brackets that support nothing, columns that sink into the walls rather than stand out from them, a flight of steps so large that it almost fills the room, spilling down like a solidified lava flow.

From this eccentric space, the visitor passes into the tranquil, architecturally correct **reading room**; exhibitions in the connecting rooms draw on the Medici collection, which includes manuscripts as diverse as a fifth-century copy of Virgil and a treatise on architecture by Leonardo.

The Cappelle Medicee

Michelangelo's most celebrated contribution to the San Lorenzo buildings forms part of the **Cappelle Medicee** (Tues–Sat 8.30am–4.50pm, plus same hours first, third & fifth Sun of month, & second & fourth Mon of month; L10,000), entered from Piazza Madonna degli Aldobrandini, at the back of the church. After filing through the subfusc crypt where many of the Medici are actually buried, you climb into the larger of the chapels, the **Cappella dei Principi** (Chapel of the Princes), a gloomy, marble-plated hall built as a mausoleum for Cosimo I and his descendants. Morbid and dowdy, with tank-like tombs, it epitomizes the notion that magnificence is directly proportional to expenditure. This was the most expensive building project ever financed by the family, and the Medici were still paying for it when the last of the line, Anna Maria Ludovica, joined her forebears in the basement. It could have looked even worse – the massive statues in the niches were intended to be made from semiprecious stones, like those used in the heraldic devices set into the walls.

Begun in 1520, the **Sagrestia Nuova** was designed by Michelangelo as a tribute to, and subversion of, Brunelleschi's Sagrestia Vecchia. Architectural connoisseurs go into raptures over the complex cornices of the alcoves, the complex relationship between those alcoves and the plane of the walls, and other such sophistications, but the lay person will be drawn to the fabulous **Medici tombs**, carved by Michelangelo between 1524 and 1533. To the left is the tomb of **Lorenzo, Duke of Urbino**, the grandson of Lorenzo il Magnifico; he is depicted as a man of thought, and his sarcophagus bears figures of *Dawn* and *Dusk*, the times of day whose ambiguities appeal to the contemplative mind. Opposite is the tomb of Lorenzo il Magnifico's youngest son, **Giuliano, Duke of Nemours**; as a man of action, his character is symbolized by the clear antithesis of *Day* and *Night*.

As a contemporary writer recorded, these are not true portraits: "He did not take from the Duke Lorenzo nor from the Lord Giuliano the model just as nature had drawn and composed them, but he gave them a greatness, a proportion, a dignity . . . which seemed to him would have brought them more praise, saying that a thousand years hence no one would be able to know that they were otherwise." They were very much otherwise, flattered by their ducal titles and genealogies as much as by these noble memorials: action man Giuliano was an easy-going but feckless individual, while Lorenzo combined ineffectualness with insufferable arrogance. Both died young and unlamented – Giuliano being killed by tuberculosis, Lorenzo by a combination of the same disease and syphilis.

Their effigies were intended to face the equally grand tombs of Lorenzo il Magnifico and his brother Giuliano; the only part of the project realized by Michelangelo is the preoccupied *Madonna and Child*, the last image of the Madonna he ever sculpted. In 1534, four years after the Medici had returned to Florence in the unfathomably wretched form of Alessandro, Michelangelo decamped to Rome, where he stayed for the rest of his life. There are more Michelangelo drawings behind the altar which can be seen on supervised (free) trips every thirty minutes.

The Palazzo Medici-Riccardi

On the edge of the square in front of San Lorenzo stands the **Palazzo Medici-Riccardi** (Mon, Tues & Thurs–Sat 9am–1pm & 3–6pm, Sun 9am–1pm; L6000), built for Cosimo il Vecchio by Michelozzo in the 1440s, and the family home until Cosimo I installed the

THE MEDICI BALLS

You come across the Medici emblem – a cluster of red balls (*palle*) on a gold background – all over Florence, yet its origins are shrouded in mystery. Legend claims the family descended from a Carolingian knight named Averardo, who fought and killed a giant in the Mugello, north of Florence. During the encounter his shield received six massive blows from the giant's mace, so Charlemagne, as a reward for his bravery, allowed Averardo to represent the dents as red balls on his coat of arms. Others say the balls had less exalted origins, that they were medicinal pills or cupping glasses, recalling the family's origins as apothecaries or doctors (*medici*). Others claim they are *bezants*, Byzantine coins, inspired by the arms of the *Arte del Cambio*, the moneychangers' guild to which the Medici belonged. In a similar vein, some say the balls are coins, the traditional symbols of pawnbrokers.

Whatever the origin, the number of *palle* was never constant. In the thirteenth century, for example, there were twelve. By Cosimo de' Medici's time the number had dropped to seven, though San Lorenzo's Old Sacristy, a Cosimo commission, strangely has eight, while Verrocchio's roundel in the same church's chancel has six and Grand Duke Cosimo I's tomb, in the Cappella dei Principi, has five.

clan in the Palazzo Vecchio. With its heavily rusticated exterior, this monolithic palazzo was the prototype for such houses as the Palazzo Pitti and Palazzo Strozzi, but in the seventeenth century it was greatly altered by its new owners, the Riccardi.

Of Michelozzo's original palazzo only the **chapel** remains intact, its interior covered by lively frescoes by **Benozzo Gozzoli**, of which the centrepiece is the *Journey of the Magi*, painted around 1460 and recently restored to blazing colour. It shows the pageant of the Compagnia dei Magi, the most patrician of the city's religious confraternities; their procession took place on Epiphany, with members of the Medici usually participating. It's known that several of the Medici household are featured in the procession, but putting names to these prettified faces is a problem. The man leading the cavalcade on a white horse is almost certainly Piero il Gottoso, sponsor of the fresco. Lorenzo il Magnifico, eleven years old at the time the fresco was painted, is probably the young king in the foreground, riding the grey horse detached from the rest of the procession, while his brother, Giuliano, is probably the one preceded by the black bowman. The artist himself – almost impossible to find – is in the crowd on the far left, his red beret signed with the words "Opus Benotii" in gold. Finally, the bearded characters in among the gallery of faces might be portraits of the retinue of the Byzantine emperor John Paleologus III, who had attended the Council of Florence twenty years before the fresco was painted.

Stairs ascend to the first floor, where a display case in the lobby of the main gallery contains a *Madonna and Child* by **Filippo Lippi**, one of Cosimo de' Medici's more troublesome protégés. Even as a novice in the convent of Santa Maria del Carmine, Filippo managed to earn himself a reputation as a drunken womanizer: in the words of Vasari, he was "so lustful that he would give anything to enjoy a woman he wanted . . . and if he couldn't buy what he wanted, then he would cool his passion by painting her portrait." Cosimo set up a workshop for him in the Medici palace, from which he often absented himself to go chasing women. On one occasion Cosimo actually locked the artist in the studio, but Filippo escaped down a rope of bed sheets; having cajoled him into returning, Cosimo declared that he would in future manage the painter with "affection and kindness", a policy that seems to have worked more successfully.

The ceiling of the main room is covered by Luca Giordano's fresco of *The Apotheosis of the Medici*, from which one can only deduce that Giordano had no sense of shame. Accompanying his father on the flight into the ether is the last male Medici, Gian Gastone (d. 1737), in reality a man so inert that he could rarely summon the energy to get out of bed in the morning.

The Mercato Centrale and around

The **Mercato Centrale**, the largest covered food hall in Europe, was built in stone, iron and glass by Giuseppe Mengoni, architect of Milan's Galleria, and opened in 1874; a century later it was given a major overhaul, reopening in 1980 with a new first floor. Butchers, *alimentari*, tripe-sellers, greengrocers, pasta stalls, bars – they're all gathered under the one roof, and all charging prices lower than you'll readily find elsewhere in the city. The market is open Monday to Saturday from 7am to 2pm, and in the winter on Saturdays additionally from 4 to 8pm. Get there close to the end of the working day and you'll get some good reductions. And for a taste of simple Florentine food at its best, call in at *Ottavino*, a small bar that's the established meeting place of the market workers – it's on the Via dell'Ariento (southwest) side and is open for incredibly cheap snacks and lunches until 1.30pm.

Each day from 8am to 7pm the streets around the Mercato Centrale are thronged with stalls selling bags, belts, shoes, trousers – everything, in fact, that your wardrobe might need. This is the busiest of Florence's daily **street markets**, and a half-hour's immersion in the haggling mass of customers provides as good a break as any from pursuit of the city's art.

North of the market – the Cenacolo di Foligno and the Fortezza da Basso

One of Florence's more obscure *cenacoli* (Last Suppers), the **Cenacolo di Foligno**, is to be found a short distance west of the market at Via Faenza 42, in the ex-convent of the Franciscans of Foligno (visit has to be booked: ☎055.23.885 for individuals; 055.284.272 for groups). It was once thought to be by Raphael but is now reckoned to have been painted in the 1490s by Perugino. Certainly it shows many of Perugino's stylistic idiosyncrasies – the figures arranged in screen-like ranks, their gestures compiled from the same repertoire of poses that can be seen in his other works.

Beyond Via Faenza, the **Fortezza da Basso** was built to intimidate the people of Florence by the vile **Alessandro de' Medici**, who ordained himself Duke of Florence after a ten-month siege by the army of Charles V and Pope Clement VII (possibly Alessandro's father) had forcibly restored the Medici. The most talented Florentine architect of the day – Michelangelo – had played a major role in the defence of the city during the siege; the job of designing the fortress fell to the more pliant Antonio da Sangallo.

Within a few years the cruelties of Alessandro had become intolerable; a petition to Charles V spoke of the Fortezza da Basso as "a prison and a slaughterhouse for the unhappy citizens". Charles's response to the catalogue of Alessandro's atrocities was to marry his daughter to the tyrant. In the end, another Medici came to the rescue: in 1537 the distantly related **Lorenzaccio de' Medici** stabbed the duke to death as he waited for an amorous assignation in Lorenzaccio's house. The reasons for the murder have never been clear but it seems that Lorenzaccio's mental health was little better than Alessandro's – in his earlier years he and Alessandro had regularly launched lecherous sorties on the city's convents, and he had been expelled from Rome after lopping the heads off the statues on the Arch of Constantine. The assassination, however, had favourable consequences for the city: as Alessandro died heirless, the council proposed that the leadership of the Florentine republic should be offered to **Cosimo de' Medici**, the great-grandson of Lorenzo il Magnifico. Subsequent Medici dukes had no need of a citizen-proof fort, and the Fortezza da Basso fell into dereliction after use as a gaol and barracks.

Since 1978 there's been a vast modern shed in the centre of the complex, used for trade fairs and shows such as the *Pitti Moda* fashion jamborees in January and July. The public gardens by the walls are fairly pleasant, but unless you want an open-air spot to relax before catching a train, you'd be better off on the other side of the Arno, in the Bóboli gardens.

The San Marco district

Much of central Florence's traffic is funnelled along **Via Cavour**, the thoroughfare connecting the duomo area to Piazza della Libertà, a junction of the city's *viale* ring roads. Except as a place to catch buses out to Fiesole and other points north, the street has little to recommend it, but halfway along it lies **Piazza San Marco**, the core of the **university district**. On the square itself stands one of the city's top attractions, the **San Marco** monastery, with its Fra' Angelico paintings; and a couple of minutes away there's the museum that comes second only to the Uffizi in the popularity stakes, the **Accademia**, home of Florence's main assembly of Michelangelo sculptures.

San Marco

A whole side of Piazza San Marco is taken up by the Dominican convent and church of **San Marco**, recipient of Cosimo il Vecchio's most lavish patronage. In the 1430s he financed Michelozzo's enlargement of the conventual buildings, and went on to establish a vast library here. Abashed by the wealth he was transferring to them, the friars of San Marco suggested to Cosimo that he need not continue to support them on such a scale, to which he replied, "Never shall I be able to give God enough to set him down as my debtor." Ironically, the convent became the centre of resistance to the Medici later in the century – Girolamo Savonarola, leader of the government of Florence after the expulsion of the Medici in 1494, was the prior of San Marco (see box on next page).

As Michelozzo was altering and expanding the convent, its walls were being decorated by one of its friars, **Fra' Angelico**, a painter in whom a medieval simplicity of faith was uniquely allied to a Renaissance sophistication of manner. He was born in Vicchio di Mugello (see p.176) some time between the late 1380s and 1400, and entered the Dominican monastery of nearby Fiesole, where he was known simply as Fra' Giovanni da Fiesole. He was then already known as an accomplished artist, but his reputation really flourished when he came to San Marco, where he was encouraged by Antonino Pierozzi – the future St Antonine. By the time Fra' Giovanni succeeded Pierozzi as prior of San Marco, the pictures he had created for the monastery and numerous other churches in Florence had earned him the title "the angelic painter", the name by which he's been known ever since.

The Museo di San Marco

Now deconsecrated, the convent today houses the **Museo di San Marco** (Tues–Sat 9am–1.50pm plus same hours first, third & fifth Mon of month, & second & fourth Sun of month; L8000), in essence a museum dedicated to the art of Fra' Angelico. Around twenty paintings by him are gathered in the **Ospizio dei Pellegrini** (Pilgrims' Hospice) to the right of the entrance, many of them brought here from other churches in Florence. Here a *Last Judgement* and *Deposition* are outstanding, with their typically brilliant colouring and spatial clarity, and their air of imperturbable piety. The so-called *San Marco Altarpiece*, though badly damaged by the passage of time and a disastrous restoration, demonstrates Fra' Angelico's familiarity with the latest developments in artistic theory – its figures are arranged in lines that taper towards a central vanishing point, in accordance with the principles laid out in Alberti's *Della Pittura* (On Painting), which had appeared in Italian only two years before this picture was executed.

Across the cloister, in the **Sala Capitolare**, is a powerful fresco of the *Crucifixion*, painted by Angelico and assistants in 1441. At the rear of this room, the **refectory** – with a lustrous *Last Supper* by **Ghirlandaio** (removed for restoration until further notice) – forms an anteroom to the **foresteria** (guest rooms), which is cluttered with architectural bits and pieces salvaged during the urban improvement schemes of the latter half of the last century.

For the drama of its setting and the lucidity of its composition, nothing in San Marco matches Angelico's **Annunciation** at the summit of the staircase by the entrance to the *foresteria*. The pallid, submissive Virgin is one of the most touching images in Renaissance art, and the courteous angel, with his scintillating unfurled wings, is as convincing a heavenly messenger as any ever painted.

An inscription on this fresco reminds the passing monks to say a Hail Mary as they venerate the image. A less admonitory function is performed by the pictures which Angelico and his assistants painted in each of the 44 **cells** on the upper floor, into which the brothers would withdraw for solitary contemplation and sleep. The outer cells of the corridor on the left almost all have works by Angelico himself – don't miss the *Noli me tangere* (cell 1), the *Annunciation* (cell 3), the *Transfiguration* (cell 6) and the *Coronation of the Virgin* (cell 9). The marvellous *Madonna Enthroned*, on the wall facing these cells, is probably by Angelico too. Several of the scenes include one or both of a pair of monastic onlookers, serving as intermediaries between the occupant of the cell and the personages in the pictures: the one with the star above his head is St Dominic; the one with the split skull is St Peter Martyr. At the end of the corridor adjoining the far end of this one there's a knot of rooms once occupied by **Savonarola**; they are usually closed, but if you're lucky you'll be able to see the portrait of him as St Peter Martyr, painted by his acolyte Fra' Bartolommeo.

SAVONAROLA

Girolamo Savonarola was born in 1452, the son of the physician to the Ferrara court. He grew up to be an abstemious and melancholic youth, sleeping on a bare straw mattress and spending much of his time reading the Bible and writing dirges. At the age of 23 he absconded to a Dominican monastery in Bologna, informing his father by letter that he was "unable to endure the evil conduct of the heedless people of Italy".

Within a few years, the Dominicans had dispatched him to preach all over northern Italy, an enterprise which got off to an unpromising start. Not the most attractive of men – he was frail, with a beak of a nose and a blubbery mouth – Savonarola was further hampered by an uningratiating voice and a particularly inelegant way of gesturing. Nonetheless, the intensity of his manner and his message attracted a committed following when he settled permanently in the monastery of San Marco in 1489.

By 1491, Savonarola's sermons had become so popular that he was asked to deliver his Lent address in the duomo. Proclaiming that God was speaking through him, he berated the city for its decadence, for its paintings that made the Virgin "look like a whore", and for the tyranny of its Medici-led government. Following the death of Lorenzo il Magnifico, the rhetoric became even more apocalyptic. "Wait no longer, for there may be no more time for repentance," he told the duomo congregation, summoning images of plagues, invasions and destruction.

When Charles VIII of France marched into Italy in September 1494 to press his claim to the throne of Naples, Savonarola presented him as the instrument of God's vengeance. Violating Piero de' Medici's declaration of Tuscan neutrality, the French army massacred the garrison at Fivizzano, and Florence prepared for the onslaught, as Savonarola declaimed, "The Sword has descended; the scourge has fallen." With support for resistance ebbing, Piero capitulated to Charles; within days the Medici had fled and their palace had been plundered. Hailed by Savonarola as "the Minister of God, the Minister of Justice", Charles and his vast army passed peacefully through Florence on their way to Rome.

The political vacuum in Florence was filled by the declaration of a republican constitution but Savonarola was now in effect the ruler of the city. Continual decrees were issued from San Marco – profane carnivals were to be outlawed, fasting was to be

Michelozzo's **library**, a design that exudes an atmosphere of calm study, is off the corridor to the right of the *Annunciation*. Cosimo il Vecchio's agents roamed as far as the Near East garnering precious manuscripts and books for him; in turn, Cosimo handed all the religious items over to the monastery, stipulating that they should be accessible to all – thus making it Europe's first public library. Beyond the library is the pair of rooms used by the monastery's benefactor when he came here on retreat.

San Marco church

Greatly altered since Michelozzo's intervention, **San Marco church** is worth a visit for two works on the second and third altars on the right: a *Madonna and Saints* painted in 1509 by Fra' Bartolommeo, and an eighth-century mosaic of *The Madonna in Prayer*, brought here from Constantinople.

Sant'Apollonia, the Scalzo and the Giardino dei Semplici

Within a couple of minutes' stroll of San Marco are two major but little-visited art attractions, one of the city's obscurer parks, and a cluster of specialist museums. Perhaps none would feature in a rushed itinerary, but the first pair in particular are worth the diversion on any high-culture point-to-point.

observed more frequently, children were to act as the agents of the righteous, informing the authorities whenever their parents transgressed the Eternal Law. Irreligious books and paintings, expensive clothes, cosmetics, mirrors, board games, trivialities and luxuries of all types were destroyed, a ritual purging that reached a crescendo with a colossal "Bonfire of the Vanities" on the Piazza della Signoria.

Meanwhile, Charles VIII was installed in Naples and a formidable alliance was being assembled to overthrow him – the papacy, Milan, Venice, Ferdinand of Aragon and the Emperor Maximilian. In July 1495 the army of this Holy League confronted the French and was badly defeated. Charles's army continued northwards back to France, and Savonarola was summoned to the Vatican to explain why he had been unable to join the campaign against the intruder. He declined to attend, claiming that it was not God's will that he should make the journey, and thus set off a chain of exchanges that ended with his excommunication in June 1497. Defying Pope Alexander's order, Savonarola celebrated Mass in the duomo on Christmas Day, which prompted a final threat from Rome: send Savonarola to the Vatican or imprison him in Florence, otherwise the whole city would join him in excommunication.

Despite Savonarola's insistence that the Borgia pope was already consigned to hell, the people of Florence began to desert him. The region's crops had failed, plague had broken out again, and the city was at war with Pisa, which Charles had handed over to its citizens rather than return to Florence's control, as he had promised. The Franciscans of Florence, sceptical of the Dominican monk's claim to divine approval, now issued a terrible challenge. One of their community and one of Savonarola's would walk through an avenue of fire in the Piazza della Signoria: if the Dominican died, then Savonarola would be banished; if the Franciscan died, then Savonarola's main critic, Fra' Francesco da Puglia, would be expelled.

A thunderstorm prevented the trial from taking place, but the mood in the city had anyway turned irrevocably. The following day, Palm Sunday 1498, a siege of the monastery of San Marco ended with Savonarola's arrest. Accused of heresy, he was tortured to the point of death, then burned at the stake in front of the Palazzo Vecchio, with two of his supporters. When the flames had finally been extinguished, the ashes were thrown into the river, to prevent anyone from gathering them as relics.

The Cenacolo di Sant'Apollonia

Running off the west side of Piazza San Marco, Via Arazzieri soon becomes Via XXVII Aprile, where the former Benedictine convent of **Sant'Apollonia** stands at no. 1. Most of the complex has now been turned into flats, but the former refectory houses one of **Castagno**'s masterpieces, the *Last Supper* (Tues–Sat 9am–1.50pm, plus same hours first, third & fifth Mon of month & second & fourth Sun of month; free).

Painted around 1450, after the artist's return from Venice, the *cenacolo* was whitewashed out by the nuns, before being uncovered in the middle of the last century. It is perhaps the most disturbing version of the event painted in the Renaissance. Blood red is the dominant tone, and the most commanding figure is the diabolic black-bearded Judas, who sits on the near side of the table. The seething patterns in the marble panels behind the Apostles seem to mimic the turmoil in the mind of each, as he hears Christ's announcement of the betrayal.

Above the illusionistic recess in which the supper takes place are the *sinopie* of a *Crucifixion*, *Deposition* and *Resurrection* by Castagno, revealed when the frescoes were taken off the wall for restoration.

The Chiostro dello Scalzo

To the north of San Marco, at Via Cavour 69, is **Lo Scalzo**, the home of the Brotherhood of St John, whose vows of poverty entailed walking around barefoot – *scalzo*. The order was suppressed in 1785 and their monastery sold off, except for the **cloister** (Mon and Thurs 9am–1pm; free; ring the bell).

This was the training ground for **Andrea del Sarto**, an artist venerated in the nineteenth century as a painter with no imperfections, but now regarded with slightly less enthusiasm on account of this very smoothness. His monochrome paintings of the *Cardinal Virtues* and *Scenes from the Life of the Baptist* occupied him off and on for a decade from 1511, beginning with the *Baptism*, finishing with the *Birth of St John*. A couple of the sixteen scenes – *John in the Wilderness* and *John meeting Christ* – were executed by his pupil Franciabigio in 1518, when del Sarto was away in Paris.

The Giardino dei Semplici and the university museums

The **Giardino dei Semplici** (Mon, Wed, Fri & Sat 9am–noon & 2.30–5pm, plus mid-April to mid-May Sun 9am–1pm; closed Aug 11–18; free), northeast of San Marco, was set up in 1545 for Cosimo I as a medicinal garden, following the examples of Padua and Pisa. Entered from Via La Pira, it now covers five acres, most of the area being taken up by the original flowerbeds and avenues. It's a shady place to catch your breath.

The garden entrance at Via P. A. Micheli 3 also gives access to a number of museums administered by the university. The **Museo Botanico** (currently open only to scholars; ☎055.275.7462 for information), set up for Leopoldo II of Lorraine, contains over four million botanical specimens, supplemented by plaster mushrooms and wax models of plants; most people will get more fun from the living specimens outside. Masses of rocks are on show in the **Museo di Minerologia e Litologia** (Mon–Sat 9am–1pm, plus first Sun in month 9.30am–12.30pm except July & Aug; closed Aug 13–17; L5000), including a 150-kilo topaz from Brazil and a load of worked stones from the Medici collection – snuff boxes, little vases, a quartz boat. The **Museo di Geologia e Paleontologia** (Mon 2–6pm, Tues–Thurs & Sat 9am–1pm, plus first Sun in month 9.30am–12.30pm except July–Sept; L5000) is one of Italy's biggest fossil shows, featuring such delights as prehistoric elephant skeletons from the upper Valdarno and a skeleton from Grosseto once touted as the missing link between monkeys and Homo sapiens.

Sooner or later all these natural history museums are to be moved into a new home on Via Circondaria, making what will be the largest museum of its kind in Italy.

The Galleria dell'Accademia

Florence's first academy of drawing – indeed, Europe's first – was founded in the mid-sixteenth century by Bronzino, Ammannati and Vasari. Initially based in Santissima Annunziata, this Accademia del Disegno moved in 1764 to Via Ricasoli 66, and soon afterwards was transformed into a general arts academy, the Accademia di Belle Arti. Twenty years later the Grand Duke Pietro Leopoldo founded the nearby **Galleria dell'Accademia** (May–Sept Tues–Sat 9am–10pm, Sun 8.30am–8pm; Oct–April Tues–Sat 8.30am–6.50pm, Sun 8.30am–1.50pm; L12,000), filling its rooms with paintings for the edification of the students. Later augmented with pieces from suppressed religious foundations and other sources, the Accademia has an extensive collection of paintings, especially of Florentine work of the fourteenth and fifteenth centuries.

Yet the pictures are not what draw the crowds in numbers equalled only by the Uffizi. The real attraction is **Michelangelo**, half a dozen of whose major sculptures are here, among them the **David** – symbol of the city's republican pride and of the illimitable ambition of the Renaissance artist. Finished in 1504, when Michelangelo was just 29, and carved from a block of marble whose shallowness posed severe difficulties, it's an incomparable show of technical bravura. But the *David* is a piece of monumental public sculpture, not a gallery exhibit. After being considered as an adornment for the exterior of the duomo, it was instead installed outside the Palazzo Vecchio, where it remained until 1873, when it was removed to the Accademia's specially built tribune. Closely surveyed in this chapel-like space, the *David* appears a monstrous adolescent, with massive head and hands and gangling arms – the ugliest masterpiece of Western sculpture.

Michelangelo once described the process of carving as being the liberation of the form from within the stone, a notion that seems to be embodied by the remarkable unfinished **Slaves** nearby. His procedure, clearly demonstrated here, was to cut the figure as if it were a deep relief, and then to free the three-dimensional figure; often his assistants would perform the initial operation to his instructions, so it's possible that Michelangelo's own chisel never actually touched these stones. Carved in the 1520s, they were intended for the tomb of Julius II, a project that underwent innumerable permutations before its eventual abandonment; in 1564 the artist's nephew gave them to the Medici, who installed them in the grotto of the Bóboli gardens. Close by is another unfinished work, *St Matthew*, which was started immediately after completion of the *David* as a commission from the Opera del Duomo; they actually requested a full series of the Apostles from Michelangelo, but this is the only one he ever began.

The Accademia's **picture galleries** are big but unexciting, with copious examples of the work of "Unknown Florentine" and "Follower of . . . ". The pieces likeliest to make an impact are Pontormo's *Venus and Cupid*, Botticelli's attributed *Madonna of the Sea* and the painted fifteenth-century *Adimari Chest*, showing a Florentine wedding ceremony in the Piazza del Duomo.

Piazza Santissima Annunziata

Nineteenth-century urban renewal schemes left many of Florence's squares rather grim places, which makes **Piazza Santissima Annunziata**, with its distinctive arcades, all the more attractive a public space. It has a special importance for the city, too. Until the end of the eighteenth century the Florentine year used to begin on March 25, the Festival of the Annunciation – hence the Florentine predilection for paintings of the Annunciation, and the fashionableness of the Annunziata church, which has long been the place for society weddings. The festival is still marked by a huge fair in the piazza and the streets leading off it; later in the year, on the first weekend in September, the square is used for Tuscany's largest crafts fair.

The **equestrian statue of Grand Duke Ferdinand I** in the centre of the square was Giambologna's final work, and was cast by his pupil Pietro Tacca from cannons captured at the Battle of Lepanto. Tacca was also the creator of the bizarre **fountains**, on each of which a pair of aquatic monkeys dribble water at two whiskered sea-slugs.

The Spedale degli Innocenti

The tone of the piazza is set by Brunelleschi's **Spedale degli Innocenti**, which was opened in 1445 as the first foundlings' hospital in Europe, and is still an orphanage. Luca della Robbia's ceramic tondi of well-swaddled babies advertise the building's function, but their insouciance belies the misery associated with it. Slavery was part of the Florentine economy even as late as the fifteenth century, and many of the infants given over to the care of the Innocenti were born to domestic slaves. A far from untypical entry in the Innocenti archives records the abandonment of twins "from the house of Agostino Capponi, born of Polonia his slave . . . They arrived half dead: if they had been two dogs they would have been better cared for."

The attached convent, centred on two beautiful cloisters, now contains the **Museo dello Spedale degli Innocenti** (Mon, Tues & Thurs–Sat 8.30am–2pm, Sun 8.30am–1pm, closed Wed; L5000), a miscellany of Florentine Renaissance art that includes one of Luca della Robbia's most charming *Madonnas* and an *Adoration of the Magi* by Domenico Ghirlandaio which has a Massacre of the Innocents going on in the background. No collection of pictures from this period could be entirely unengrossing, but Florence has several museums you should check out before this one.

Santissima Annunziata

Santissima Annunziata (daily 7.30am–12.30pm & 4–6.30pm; free) is the mother church of the Servite order, which was founded by seven Florentine aristocrats in 1234. The church's dedication to the Virgin Annunciate took place in the fourteenth century, in recognition of its miraculous image of the Virgin, which was said to have been completed by an angel when the monastic artist left it unfinished. So many pilgrims came to adore the painting that the church was rebuilt to accommodate them in the second half of the fifteenth century: the architect was Michelozzo (brother of the prior), the paymasters the Medici.

A customary act of devotion was to leave behind a life-size wax effigy of oneself in the **Chiostro dei Voti**, the atrium that Michelozzo built onto the church. None of these ex-votos remains in the now glazed atrium, but it does retain – albeit in battered shape – a fine set of frescoes. Mostly painted in the 1510s, these include a *Visitation* by Pontormo, Rosso Fiorentino's *Assumption*, a bucolic *Nativity* by Baldovinetti, and a *Birth of the Virgin* by Andrea del Sarto that achieves a perfect balance of spontaneity and geometrical order.

Much of the gilt and stucco fancy dress of the main **church interior** was perpetrated in the seventeenth and eighteenth centuries, but the ornate **tabernacle** of the miraculous image (to the left of the entrance) was produced by Michelozzo. His patron, Piero di Cosimo de' Medici, made sure that nobody remained unaware of the money he sank into the shrine – an inscription reads "Costò fior. 4 mila el marmo solo" (The marble alone cost 4000 florins). The painting encased in the marble has been repainted into illegibility, and is usually kept covered anyway.

Far more interesting are the raw-nerved frescoes by **Andrea del Castagno** in the first two chapels on the left, *The Vision of St Jerome* and *The Trinity*. Now restored, they were obliterated after Vasari publicized the rumour that Castagno had poisoned his erstwhile friend, Domenico Veneziano, motivated by envy of the other's skill with oil paint. Castagno was saddled with this guilt until the last century, when an archivist discovered that the alleged murderer in fact predeceased his victim by four years.

Separated from the nave by a triumphal arch is the unusual **tribune**, begun by Michelozzo but completed to designs by Alberti; you get into it along a corridor from the left transept. The chapel at the farthest point was altered by Giambologna into a monument to himself, complete with bronze reliefs and a Crucifix by the sculptor.

The adjoining **Chiostro dei Morti** is worth visiting for Andrea del Sarto's intimate *Madonna del Sacco*, painted over the door leading into the church; the cloister is entered through a gate to the left of the church portico or from the left transept, but both are often locked, so a word with the sacristan might be in order.

The Museo Archeologico – and the Pazzi church

On the other side of Via della Colonna from the side wall of Santissima Annunziata is the **Museo Archeologico** (Tues–Sat 9am–2pm, plus same hours first, third & fifth Mon of month and second & fourth Sun; L8000), the most important collection of its kind in northern Italy. It suffered terrible damage in the flood of 1966 and the task of restoring the exhibits is still not finished, so the arrangement of the rooms is subject to sudden changes.

The museum's special strength is its showing of **Etruscan** finds, many of them part of the Medici bequest. On the ground floor there's a comprehensive display of Etruscan funerary figures, but even more arresting than these is the *François Vase*, an Attic krater from the sixth century BC, discovered in an Etruscan tomb at Chiusi. Pride of place in the first-floor **Egyptian collection** goes to a Hittite chariot made of bone and wood and dating from the fourteenth century BC.

The rest of this floor and much of the floor above are given over to the **Etruscan, Greek and Roman collections**, arranged with variable clarity. Of the Roman pieces the outstanding item is the *Idolino*, probably a copy of a fifth-century BC Greek original. Nearby is a massive Hellenistic horse's head, which once adorned the garden of the Palazzo Medici, where it was studied by Donatello and Verrocchio. In the long gallery you'll find the best of the Etruscan pieces: the *Arringatore* (Orator), the only known Etruscan large bronze from the Hellenistic period; and the *Chimera*, a triple-headed monster of the fifth century BC. A symbol of the three-seasoned pre-Christian Mediterranean year, the *Chimera* was much admired by Cosimo I's retinue of Mannerist artists and all subsequent connoisseurs of the offbeat.

Santa Maria Maddalena dei Pazzi and around

Farther along Via della Colonna, a right turn into Borgo Pinti brings you to the church of **Santa Maria Maddalena dei Pazzi**, named after a Florentine nun who was prone to demonstrating her saintliness by pouring boiling wax over her arms. Her piety was of the uncompromising sort much honoured during the Counter-Reformation: when Maria de' Medici went off to marry Henry IV of France, Maria Maddalena transmitted the news that the Virgin expected her to readmit the Jesuits to France and exterminate the Huguenots, which she duly did.

Founded in the thirteenth century but kitted out in Baroque style, the church is not itself much of an attraction, but its chapterhouse – reached by a strange subterranean passageway – is decorated with a radiant **Perugino** fresco of the *Crucifixion* (Tues–Sun 9am–noon & 5–7pm; L1000). The scene is painted as a continuous panorama on a wall divided into three arches, giving the effect of looking out through a loggia onto a springtime landscape. As always with Perugino, there is nothing troubling here, the Crucifixion being depicted not as an agonizing death but rather as the necessary prelude to the Resurrection.

The enormous building behind the church is the **Synagogue** (April–Sept Sun–Thurs 10am–1pm & 2–5pm, Fri 10am–1pm; Oct–March Mon–Thurs 11am–1pm & 2–5pm, Fri &

Sun 10am–1pm); the ghetto established in this district by Cosimo I was not demolished until the mid-nineteenth century, which is when the present Moorish-style synagogue was built. It contains a small museum that charts the history of Florence's Jewish population (Mon–Thurs & Sun 2–5pm; L6000).

To the north of the Pazzi church, at the end of Borgo Pinti, you come to the **English Cemetery** at Piazza Donatello (daily 9am–noon & 3–6pm). Now a funerary traffic island, this patch of garden is the resting place of Elizabeth Barrett Browning and a number of contemporaneous artistic Brits, among them Walter Savage Landor and Arthur Hugh Clough.

The Santa Croce district

The 1966 flood completely changed the character of the area around **Santa Croce**. Prior to then it had been one of the more densely populated districts, packed with tenements and small workshops. When the Arno burst its banks, this low-lying zone was virtually wrecked, and many of its residents moved out permanently in the following years.

Traditionally the **Piazza Santa Croce** has been one of the city's main arenas for ceremonials and festivities. Thus when Lorenzo il Magnifico was married to the Roman heiress Clarice Orsini, the event was celebrated on this square, with a tournament that was more a fashion event than a contest of skill – Lorenzo's knightly outfit, for instance, was adorned with pearls, diamonds and rubies. During the years of Savonarola's ascendancy, the piazza became the principal site for the execution of heretics. It's still used as the pitch for the *Gioco di Calcio Storico*, a football tournament between the city's four *quartieri*; the game is held three times in St John's week (the last week of June), and is characterized by incomprehensible rules and a level of violence which the sixteenth-century costumes do little to inhibit (see p.153).

The Church of Santa Croce

Though traditionally said to have been founded by St Francis himself, the Franciscan church of Florence, **Santa Croce** (May–Sept Mon–Sat 8am–6.30pm; Oct–April Mon–Sat 8am–12.30pm & 3–6.30pm; Sun year round 3–6pm; free), was probably begun seventy or so years later, in 1294, possibly by the architect of the duomo, Arnolfo di Cambio. In the following century the first of the church's remarkable **fresco cycles** – by Giotto, the Gaddi family and others – were completed. Construction of the building, though, was held up by a split in the Franciscan ranks and not resumed until the early fifteenth century, the period when Santa Croce acquired its status as the mausoleum of Florence's eminent citizens.

Today, more than 270 tombstones pave the floor of the church, while grander monuments commemorate the likes of Ghiberti, Michelangelo, Machiavelli, Galileo and Dante – though the last of the group is actually buried in Ravenna, where he died in exile. The glum statue of the poet outside the church is a nineteenth-century job, as is the facade, which is based on the Orcagna tabernacle in Orsanmichele.

Santa Croce played a significant role in the evolution of Renaissance thought. It was here that the full sessions of the Council of Florence took place in 1439, in an attempt to reconcile the differences between the Roman and Eastern churches. Attended by the pope, the Byzantine emperor and the Patriarch of Constantinople, the council culminated in a compromise that lasted only until the Byzantine delegation returned home. Its more lasting effect was that it brought scores of classical scholars to the city, some of whom stayed on, to provide the impetus behind such bodies as Cosimo de' Medici's academy of Platonic studies, perhaps the single most influential intellectual gathering of the Florentine Renaissance.

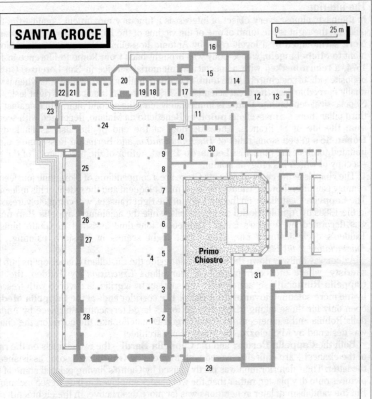

SANTA CROCE

0   25 m

Primo
Chiostro

1. Madonna del Latte (1478), Antonio Rossellino
2. Tomb of Michelangelo (1570), Giorgio Vasari
3. Cenotaph to Dante (1829), Stefano Ricci
4. Pulpit (1472–6), Benedetto da Maiano
5. Monument to Vittorio Alfieri (1810), Antonio Canova
6. Tomb of Niccolò Machiavelli (1787), Innocenzo Spinazzi
7. Annunciation (1435), Donatello
8. Tomb of Leonardo Bruni (1446–7), Bernardo Rossellino
9. Tomb of Giacchino Rossini (1900), Giuseppe Cassioli
10. Cappella Castellani: frescoes (1385), Agnolo Gaddi
11. Cappella Baroncelli: frescoes (1332–8), Taddeo Gaddi
12. Cappella Medici (1434), designed by Michelozzo
13. Madonna and Child altarpiece (1480), Andrea della Robbia
14. Church shop and leather workshop
15. Sacristy
16. Cappella Rinuccini: frescoes (1365), Giovanni da Milano
17. Cappella Velluti: altarpiece, Giovanni di Biondo
18. Cappella Peruzzi: Life of St John and St John the Baptist (1326–30), Giotto
19. Cappella Bardi: Life of St Francis (1315–20), Giotto
20. Chancel: Frescoes and stained glass (1380), Agnolo Gaddi
21. Cappella Pulci-Beradi: Martyrdom of SS Lorenzo and Stefano (1330) frescoes, Bernardo Daddi
22. Cappella Bardi di Vernio: Scenes from the Life of San Silvestro (1340) frescoes, Maso di Banco
23. Cappella Bardi: wooden crucifix (1412), Donatello
24. Monument to Leon Battista Alberti (d. 1472), Lorenzo Bartolini (early 19th-century)
25. Tomb of Carlo Marsuppini (1453), Desiderio da Settignano
26. Pietà (1560), Agnolo Bronzino
27. Tomb of Lorenzo Ghiberti and his son Vittorio (pavement slab)
28. Tomb of Galileo (1737), Giulio Foggini
29. Entrance to the Museo dell'Opera di Santa Croce
30. Cappella dei Pazzi
31. Refectory and museum

The interior

In the nave, almost every object of interest is a funerary monument. Against the first pillar on the right is the tomb of one of the victims of the Pazzi conspiracy, **Francesco Nori**, surmounted by a lovely relief by Antonio Rossellino. Nearby is Vasari's monument to **Michelangelo**, whose body was brought back from Rome to Florence in July 1574, a return marked with a spectacular memorial service in San Lorenzo. On the opposite side of the church is the tomb of **Galileo**, built in 1737, which was when it was finally agreed to give the great scientist a Christian burial. Back in the right aisle, the Neoclassical cenotaph to **Dante** is immediately after the second altar, while against the third pillar there's a marvellous **pulpit** by Benedetto da Maiano, decorated with scenes from the life of St Francis. The side door at the end of the aisle is flanked by **Donatello**'s gilded stone relief of *The Annunciation* and Bernardo Rossellino's much imitated tomb of the humanist **Leonardo Bruni**, author of the first history of the city – a copy of which his effigy is holding.

The chapels at the east end of Santa Croce are a compendium of Florentine fourteenth-century painting, showing Giotto's art at its most eloquent and the extent of his influence. The **Cappella Castellani**, on the west side of the right transept, was completely frescoed in the 1380s by **Agnolo Gaddi** and his pupils, while the adjoining **Cappella Baroncelli** was decorated by Agnolo's father, **Taddeo**, a long-time assistant to Giotto himself. Taddeo's cycle features one of the first night scenes in Western painting, *The Annunciation to the Shepherds*.

A doorway halfway down the corridor, alongside the Castellani chapel, opens into the **sacristy**, where the centrepiece is a marvellous *Crucifixion* by Taddeo; the tiny **Cappella Rinuccini**, separated from the sacristy by a grille, is covered with frescoes by the more solemn **Giovanni da Milano**. The corridor ends at the **Cappella Medici**, open only for those taking Mass, notable for its large terracotta altarpiece by Andrea della Robbia and a nineteenth-century forged Donatello; like the corridor, the chapel was designed by Michelozzo, the Medici's pet architect.

Both the **Cappella Peruzzi** and the **Cappella Bardi** – the two chapels on the right of the chancel – are entirely covered with frescoes by **Giotto**, with some assistance in the latter. Their deterioration was partly caused by Giotto's having painted some of the pictures onto dry plaster, rather than the wet plaster employed in true fresco technique. But the vandalism of later generations was far more destructive. In the eighteenth century they were covered in whitewash, then they were heavily retouched in the nineteenth; restoration in the 1950s returned them to as close to their pristine state as was possible. Scenes from the lives of St John the Evangelist and St John the Baptist cover the Peruzzi chapel, while a better-preserved cycle of the life of St Francis fills the Bardi. Despite the areas of paint destroyed when a tomb was attached to the wall, the *Funeral of St Francis* is still a composition of extraordinary impact, the grief-stricken mourners suggesting an affinity with the lamentation over the body of Christ – one of them even touches the wound in Francis's side, echoing the gesture of Doubting Thomas. The *Ordeal by Fire*, showing Francis about to demonstrate his faith to the Sultan by walking through fire, shows Giotto's mastery of understated drama, with the Sultan's entourage skulking off to the left in anticipation of the monk's triumph. Above the chapel is the most powerful scene of all, *St Francis Receiving the Stigmata*, in which the power of Christ's apparition seems to force the chosen one to his knees.

Agnolo Gaddi was responsible for the design of the stained glass in the lancet windows round the high altar, and for all the chancel frescoes, depicting the Legend of the True Cross (see p.415 for the story). The **Cappella Bardi di Vernio**, the fifth after the chancel, was painted in the 1330s by **Maso di Banco**, perhaps the most inventive of Giotto's followers; as tradition dictated, his *Scenes from the Life of St Sylvester* depict the saint baptizing Emperor Constantine, notwithstanding the fact that Sylvester died some

---

FLORENCE FLOODS

The calamity of the November 1966 flood had plenty of precedents. Great areas of the city were destroyed by a flood in **1178**, a disaster exacerbated by plague and famine. In **1269** the Carraia and Trinita bridges were carried away on a torrent so heavy that "a great part of the city of Florence became a lake". The flood of **1333** was preceded by a four-day storm, with thunder and rain so violent that all the city's bells were tolled to drive away the evil spirits thought to be behind the tempest: bridges were demolished and the original Marzocco – a figure of Mars rather than the leonine figure that inherited its name – was carried away on the raging Arno. Cosimo I instituted an urban beautification scheme after a deluge put nearly twenty feet of muddy water over the city in **1557**; on that occasion the Trinita bridge was hit so suddenly that everyone on it was drowned, except for two children who were left stranded on a pillar in midstream, where for two days they were fed by means of a rope slung over from the bank.

It rained continuously for forty days prior to **November 4, 1966**, with nearly half a metre of rain falling in the preceding two days. When the water pressure in an upstream reservoir threatened to break the dam, it was decided to open the sluices. The only people to be warned about the rapidly rising level of the river were the jewellers of the Ponte Vecchio, whose private nightwatchman phoned them in the small hours of the morning with news that the bridge was starting to shake. Police watching the shopkeepers clearing their displays were asked why they weren't spreading the alarm. They replied, "We have received no orders."

When the banks of the Arno finally broke down, a flash flood dumped around 500,000 tonnes of water and mud on the streets, moving with such speed that people were drowned in the underpass of Santa Maria Novella train station. In all, 35 Florentines were killed, over 15,000 cars wrecked, and thousands of works of art damaged, many of them ruined by heating oil flushed out of basements.

Within hours an impromptu army of rescue workers had been formed – many of them students – to haul pictures out of slime-filled churches and gather fragments of paint in plastic bags. Donations came in from all over the world, but the task was so immense that the restoration of many pieces is still unaccomplished. Some rooms in the archeological museum, for example, have remained closed since the flood, and many possessions of the National Library are still in the laboratories. In total around two-thirds of the 3000 paintings damaged in the flood are now on view again, and two massive laboratories – one for paintings and one for stonework – are operating full time in Florence, developing restoration techniques that are often taken up by galleries all over the world.

---

time before the emperor's actual baptism. At the end of the left chancel, the second Cappella Bardi houses a wooden Crucifix by **Donatello** – supposedly criticized by Brunelleschi as resembling a "peasant on the Cross".

THE CAPPELLA DEI PAZZI, CLOISTERS AND MUSEUM
Brunelleschi's **Cappella dei Pazzi** (March–Oct daily except Wed 10am–12.30pm & 2.30–6.30pm; Nov–Feb same days 10am–12.30pm & 3–5pm; L5000), which stands at the end of Santa Croce's first cloister, typifies the spirit of early Renaissance architecture. Planned in the 1430s and completed in the 1470s, several years after the architect's death, the chapel is geometrically perfect without seeming pedantic, and is exemplary in the way its decorative detail harmonizes with the design. The polychrome lining of the shallow cupola of the portico is by Luca della Robbia, as is the tondo of *St Andrew* over the door; inside, Luca also produced the blue and white tondi of the *Apostles*. The vividly coloured tondi of the *Evangelists* were produced in the Della Robbia workshop, possibly to designs by Donatello.

Off this cloister, the **Museo dell'Opera di Santa Croce** (same hours & ticket) houses a miscellany of works of art, the best of which are gathered in the refectory. Cimabue's *Crucifixion* was very badly damaged in 1966, and has become the emblem of the havoc caused by the flood; the high-water tide mark is still clearly visible on the walls. The other highlights are the detached fresco of the *Last Supper*, valued as the finest work by Taddeo Gaddi, and Donatello's enormous gilded *St Louis of Toulouse*, made for Orsanmichele.

The spacious **second cloister**, another late project by Brunelleschi, is the most peaceful spot in the centre of Florence – or will be once again, when the restoration work is finished.

The Casa Buonarotti and the Sant'Ambrogio area

The enticing name of the **Casa Buonarotti** (Mon & Wed–Sun 9.30am–1.30pm; L12,000), north of Santa Croce at Via Ghibellina 70, is slightly misleading: though Michelangelo Buonarotti owned the property, he never actually lived here. The sculptor's nephew, his sole descendant, was given the house, and his son in turn converted part of the property into a gallery dedicated to his great-uncle. Among the jumble of works collected here – many of them created in homage to him – are a few pieces by the great man himself.

Reproductions of some of Michelangelo's drawings are displayed on the ground floor, the authentic stuff being housed upstairs. The two main treasures are to be found in the room on the left at the top of the stairs: *The Madonna of the Steps* is Michelangelo's earliest known work, carved when he was no older than sixteen, and the similarly unfinished *Battle of the Centaurs* was carved only a few weeks afterwards, when the boy was living in the Medici household. In the adjacent room you'll find his wooden model for the facade of San Lorenzo, while the room in front of the stairs houses the largest of all the sculptural models on display, the torso of a *River God* intended for the Medici chapel in San Lorenzo. To the right is a room containing a slim wooden Crucifix discovered in Santo Spirito in 1963, and now generally thought to be a work whose existence had long been documented, but was feared lost.

The markets

Two of Florence's markets lie within a few minutes of the Casa Buonarotti. To the north, the Piazza dei Ciompi is the venue for the **Mercato delle Pulci** or flea market (Tues–Sat 8am–1pm & 3.30–7pm, plus first Sun of month 9am–7pm). Much of the junk maintains the city's reputation for inflated prices, though you can find a few interesting items at modest cost – old postcards, posters and so on. Vasari's **Loggia del Pesce** gives the square a touch of style; built for the fishmongers of what's now Piazza della Repubblica, it was moved here when that square was laid out.

A short distance to the east, out of the orbit of ninety percent of tourists, is the **Mercato di Sant'Ambrogio** (Mon–Fri 7am–2pm), a smaller, tattier and even more enjoyable version of the San Lorenzo food hall. The *tavola calda* here is one of Florence's lunchtime bargains and – as at San Lorenzo – the stalls bring their prices down in the last hour of trading.

Unassuming on the outside, **Sant'Ambrogio** church is worth a visit for its Orcagna fresco of *The Madonna and Saints* (second altar on the right), and for the chapel to the left of the chancel, containing a tabernacle carved in 1481 by Mino da Fiesole and a fresco by Cosimo Rosselli that's another one of Florence's pieces of Renaissance social reportage. Commemorated by a simple slab, Verrocchio is buried in the fourth chapel of the left aisle.

The Museo Horne

On the south side of Santa Croce, down by the river at Via dei Benci 6, is one of Florence's more recondite museums, the **Museo Horne** (Mon–Sat 9am–1pm, plus Tues 8.30–11pm in summer; L8000). Left to the nation by the nineteenth-century English art historian Herbert Horne, who was instrumental in rescuing Botticelli from neglect, this houseful of paintings, sculptures, pottery, furniture and other domestic objects contains no real masterpieces, but is diverting enough if you've already done the major collections. The building itself is worth a glance even if you're not going into the museum; commissioned by the Corsi family around 1490, it's a typical merchant's house of the period, with huge cellars in which wool would have been dyed, and an open gallery above the courtyard for drying the finished cloth.

The pride of Horne's collection was its drawings, which are now salted away in the Uffizi. Of what's left, the pick is Giotto's *St Stephen* (a fragment from a polyptych), a *Deposition* by Gozzoli, his last work, and Beccafumi's *Holy Family*, shown in its original frame. One of the main exhibits is a piece of little artistic merit but great historical interest – a copy of part of Leonardo's *Battle of Anghiari*, once frescoed on a wall of the Palazzo Vecchio.

Oltrarno

Visitors to Florence might perceive the Arno as just an interruption in the urban fabric, but Florentines still tend to talk as though a ravine runs through their city. North of the river is known as *Arno di quà* (over here), while the other side, hemmed in by a ridge of hills that rises a short distance from the river, is *Arno di là* (over there). More formally, it's known as the **Oltrarno**, a terminology which has its roots in medieval times, when the district to the south was not as accessible as the numerous bridges now make it.

Traditionally an artisans' quarter, Oltrarno has nonetheless always contained more prosperous enclaves – many of Florence's ruling families chose to settle in this area, and nowadays some of the city's plushest shops line the streets parallel to the river's southern bank. Window-shopping is not the principal pleasure of a roam through Oltrarno, however, as this is also the district of the **Palazzo Pitti**, the Masaccio frescoes in **Santa Maria del Carmine**, Brunelleschi's marvellous church of **Santo Spirito** and – looking down from a hill to the southeast – the Romanesque **San Miniato al Monte**.

From the Ponte Vecchio to Santa Felìcita

The direct route from the city centre to the heart of Oltrarno crosses the river on the **Ponte Vecchio**, the only bridge not mined by the retreating Nazis in 1944. Built in 1345 to replace an ancient wooden bridge, the Ponte Vecchio has always been loaded with shops like those now propped over the water, but the plethora of jewellers dates from 1593, when Ferdinando I evicted the butchers' stalls in occupation. Florence had long revered the art of the goldsmith, and several of its major artists were skilled in the craft: Ghiberti, Donatello and Cellini, for example. The third of the trio is celebrated by a bust in the centre of the bridge, the night-time meeting point for Florence's unreconstructed hippies and local lads on the make.

Santa Felìcita

The reason for Ferdinando's objection to the Ponte Vecchio's butchers was that the noisome slabs of meat lay directly beneath the corridor that Vasari had constructed between the Palazzo Vecchio and the Medici's Palazzo Pitti. It was to accommodate this corridor that Vasari stuck a portico onto the nearby **Santa Felìcita**, probably the oldest church in Florence after San Lorenzo. It's now thought that the Syrian Greek tradesmen who came to this district in the second century were the settlement's first practising Christians.

Remodelled in the sixteenth century – when it became the Medici chapel – and again in the eighteenth, the interior demands a visit for the paintings by **Pontormo** in the **Cappella Capponi**, surrounded by irritating railings immediately to the right of the door. Under the cupola are four tondi of the *Evangelists* (Bronzino supplied the *St Mark*), while on opposite sides of the window are the Virgin and the angel of Pontormo's *Annunciation*, the arrangement alluding to incarnation as the means by which the Light came into the world. The low level of light admitted by this window was a determining factor in the startling colour scheme of the weirdly erotic *Deposition*, one of the master-works of Florentine Mannerism. There's no sign of the cross, the thieves, the Roman soldiers or any of the usual scene-setting devices, as the body of Christ is carried like a mournful trophy by androgynous figures clad in billows of acidic sky-blue, green and pink drapery.

Pontormo himself was every bit as strange as this picture suggests. A relentless hypochondriac – his diary is a tally of bowel disorders and other assorted ailments – he seems to have found the company of others almost intolerable, spending much of his time in a top-floor room that could be reached only by a ladder, which he drew up behind him. So eccentric was his behaviour that he was virtually mythologized by his contemporaries, whose stories are often united only by the conviction that Pontormo was a very odd case. Thus one writer attributed to him an all-consuming terror of death, while another insisted that he kept corpses in a tub as models for a *Deluge* that he was painting – an antisocial research project that allegedly brought protests from the neighbours.

Palazzo Pitti

Beyond Santa Felicita, the street opens out at Piazza Pitti, forecourt of the largest palazzo in Florence – the **Palazzo Pitti**. The man for whom this house was built, Luca Pitti, was a prominent rival of Cosimo il Vecchio, and the motive for the commission was in large part a desire to trump the Medici. The building was started around 1457, possibly using a design by Brunelleschi which the architect had intended for the Palazzo Medici but which had been rejected by Cosimo for being too grand. In time the fortunes of the Pitti declined and in 1459 they were forced to sell out to the enemy. The Palazzo Pitti subsequently became the Medici's base in Florence and the building was continually expanded up to the early seventeenth century, when it finally achieved its present gargantuan bulk.

Today the Palazzo Pitti and the pavilions of the **Giardino di Bóboli** contain eight museums, of which the foremost is the **Galleria Palatina**, an art collection second in importance only to the Uffizi. As with the Uffizi, you should anticipate closure of some parts of the Pitti, a building with notorious operational problems; the restoration of the facade, which has been in progress for several years now, was budgeted at around one hundred billion lire – at the time, about one-third of the entire annual government fund for the upkeep of Italy's artistic heritage.

The Galleria Palatina

Many of the paintings gathered by the Medici in the seventeenth century are now arranged in the **Galleria Palatina**, a suite of 26 rooms in one first-floor wing of the palace. Stacked three deep in places, as they would have been in the days of their acquisition, the pictures are not arranged in the sort of didactic order observed by most galleries, but rather are hung to make each room pleasurably varied. You'll need the best part of the morning to see it properly.

The art of the sixteenth century is the Palatina's real strength – in particular, the art of **Raphael** and **Titian**, with eleven pictures by the former, fourteen by the latter. When Raphael settled in Florence in 1505, he was besieged with commissions from patrons delighted to find an artist for whom the creative process involved so little agonizing. In the next three years he painted scores of pictures for such people as Angelo Doni, the man who commissioned Michelangelo's *Doni Tondo* (in the Uffizi); Raphael's portraits of Doni and his wife, hung side by side, display the same unhesitating facility and perfect poise as the *Madonna of the Chair*, in which the figures are curved into the rounded shape of the picture with no sense of artificiality.

The contingent of works by Titian includes a number of his most trenchant portraits. The lecherous and scurrilous Pietro Aretino – journalist, critic, poet and one of Titian's closest friends – was so thrilled by his portrait that he gave it to Cosimo I; Titian painted him on several other occasions, sometimes using him as the model for Pontius Pilate. Also here are likenesses of Philip II of Spain and the young Cardinal Ippolito de' Medici – who fought in the defence of Vienna against the Ottomans only to be poisoned at the age of 24 – and the so-called *Portrait of an Englishman*, who scrutinizes the viewer with unflinching sea-grey eyes.

Andrea del Sarto is represented in strength as well, his seventeen works including a beautifully grave *Annunciation*. Other individual works to look out for are Rosso Fiorentino's *Madonna Enthroned with Saints*, Fra' Bartolommeo's *Deposition*, a tondo of the *Madonna and Child* by Filippo Lippi, his son Filippino's *Death of Lucrezia*, a *Sleeping Cupid* by Caravaggio, and Cristofano Allori's sexy *Judith*. The outstanding piece of sculpture is Canova's *Venus Italica*, commissioned by Napoleon as a replacement for the Venus de' Medici, which he had whisked off to Paris.

Much of the rest of the first floor comprises the **Appartamenti Monumentali**, the Pitti's state rooms. They were renovated by the dukes of Lorraine in the eighteenth century, and then by Vittore Emanuele when Florence became the country's capital, so the rooms display three distinct decorative phases. At the moment, though, a restoration of the chambers keeps this wing shut.

The Pitti's other museums

On the floor above the Palatina is the **Galleria d'Arte Moderna**, a chronological survey of primarily Tuscan art from the mid-eighteenth century to 1945. Most rewarding are the products of the *Macchiaioli*, the Italian division of the Impressionist movement; most startling, however, are the sculptures, featuring sublime kitsch such as Antonio Ciseri's *Pregnant Nun*.

The Pitti's **Museo degli Argenti**, entered from the main palace courtyard, is a museum not just of silverware – as its name implies – but of luxury artefacts in general. The lavishly frescoed reception rooms themselves fall into this category: the first hall, the

Sala di Giovanni di San Giovanni, shows Lorenzo de' Medici giving refuge to the Muses; the other three ceremonial rooms have trompe l'oeil paintings by seventeenth-century Bolognese artists. As for the exhibits, the least ambivalent response is likely to be aroused by Lorenzo il Magnifico's trove of antique vases, all of them marked with their owner's name. The later the date of the pieces, though, the greater the discordance between the skill of the craftsman and the taste by which it was governed; by the time you reach the end of the jewellery show on the first floor, you'll have lost all capacity to be surprised or revolted by seashell figurines, cups made from ostrich eggs, portraits in stone inlay, and the like.

Visitors without a specialist interest are unlikely to be riveted by the two remaining museums currently open. In the Palazzina della Meridiana, the eighteenth-century southern wing of the Pitti, the **Galleria del Costume** provides the opportunity to admire the dress that Eleanor of Toledo was buried in, though you can admire it easily enough in Bronzino's portrait of her in the Palazzo Vecchio. Also housed in the Meridiana is the **Collezione Contini Bonacossi** (free tours usually Thurs & Sat 9.45am – appointments have to be made a week before at the Uffizi ☎055.238.85), on long-term loan to the Pitti. Its prize pieces are its Spanish paintings, in particular Velasquez's *Water Carrier of Seville*.

The **Museo delle Porcellane**, on the other side of the Bóboli, is well laid out but dull, and can generally only be visited by prior arrangement at the Pitti ticket office. The **Museo delle Carrozze** (Carriage Museum) has been closed for years and, despite what the Pitti handouts tell you, will almost certainly remain so for years, to the chagrin of very few.

The Giardino di Bóboli

The creation of the Pitti's enormous formal garden, the **Giardino di Bóboli** (daily: March & Oct 9am–5.30pm; April, May & Sept 9am–6.30pm; June–Aug 9am–7.30pm; Nov–Feb 9am–4.30pm; closed first and last Mon of the month; L4000), began when the Medici took over the house, and continued into the early seventeenth century, by which stage this steep hillside had been turned into a maze of statue-strewn avenues and well-trimmed vegetation. Opened to the public in 1766, it is the only really extensive area of accessible greenery in the centre of the city, and can be one of the pleasantest spots for a midday picnic or siesta. There's a café in the gardens, but it's best to bring your own supplies.

Aligned with the central block of the palazzo, the garden's **amphitheatre** was designed in the early seventeenth century as an arena for Medici entertainments, the site having previously been laid out by Ammannati as a garden in the shape of a Roman circus. For the wedding of Cosimo III and Princess Marguerite-Louise, cousin of Louis XIV, twenty thousand guests were packed onto the stone benches to watch a production that began with the appearance of a gigantic effigy of Atlas with the globe on his back; the show got under way when the planet split apart, releasing a cascade of earth that transformed the giant into the Atlas mountain. Such frivolities did little to reconcile Marguerite-Louise to either Florence or her husband, and after several acrimonious years this miserable dynastic marriage came to an effective end with her return to Paris, where she professed to care about little "as long as I never have to set eyes on the grand duke again".

Of all the garden's Mannerist embellishments, the most celebrated is the **Grotta del Buontalenti**, to the left of the entrance, beyond the hideous and much reproduced statue of Cosimo I's favourite dwarf astride a giant tortoise. Embedded in the grotto's faked stalactites and encrustations are replicas of Michelangelo's *Slaves* – the originals were lodged here until 1908. Lurking in the deepest recesses of the cave, and normally viewable only from afar, is Giambologna's *Venus*, leered at by attendant imps. Another spectacular set piece is the fountain island called the **Isolotto**, which is the focal point of the

THE BIRTH OF OPERA

The Medici pageants in the gardens of the Pitti were the last word in extravagance, and the palace has a claim to be the birthplace of the most extravagant modern performing art, **opera**. The roots of the genre are convoluted, but its ancestry certainly owes much to the singing and dancing tableaux called *intermedii*, with which the high-society Florentine weddings were padded out. Influenced by these shows, the academy known as the Camerata Fiorentina began, at the end of the sixteenth century, to blend the principles of Greek drama with a semi-musical style of declamation. The first composition recognizable as an opera is *Dafne*, written by two members of the Camerata, Jacopo Peri and Ottavio Rinucci, and performed in 1597; the earliest opera whose music has survived in its entirety is the same duo's *Euridice*, premiered in the Pitti palace on the occasion of the proxy marriage of Maria de' Medici to Henry IV.

far end of the gardens; from within the Bóboli the most dramatic approach is along the central cypress avenue known as the **Viottolone**, many of whose statues are Roman originals – or you come upon it quickly if you enter the Bóboli by the Porta Romana entrance, a little-used gate at the southwestern tip of the gardens.

Forte di Belvedere

The **Forte di Belvedere** (daily 9am–one hour before dusk; free except during exhibitions), at the crest of the hill up which the gardens spread, is a star-shaped fortress built on the orders of Ferdinando I in 1590, ostensibly for the city's protection but really to intimidate the grand duke's subjects. The urban panorama from here is incredible, and added attractions are the exhibitions held in and around the shed-like palace in the centre of the fortress, and the summer evening film screenings. The Bóboli gate is very rarely open, so if you want to be certain of the view, approach the fort from the Costa San Giorgio, a lane which begins at the back of Santa Felicita, winding past the villa (at no. 19) that was Galileo's home from 1610 to 1631.

East from the Belvedere stretches the best-preserved stretch of Florence's fortified walls, paralleled by Via di Belvedere. South of the Belvedere, Via San Leonardo leads past olive groves to the rarely open church of **San Leonardo in Arcetri**, now the home of a beautiful thirteenth-century pulpit brought here from the church now incorporated into the Uffizi.

Casa Guidi and La Specola

Within a stone's throw of the Pitti, on the opposite side of the road, on the junction of Via Maggio and Via Romana, you'll find the home of Robert Browning and Elizabeth Barrett Browning, the **Casa Guidi** (summer Mon–Fri 9am–noon & 3–6pm; winter Wed & Sat 3–6pm; free, but donations welcome). It's something of a shrine to Elizabeth, who wrote much of her most popular verse here (including, naturally enough, *Casa Guidi Windows*) and died here, but it's an unatmospheric spot – virtually all the Casa Guidi's furniture went under the hammer at Sotheby's in 1913, and there's just one oil painting left to conjure the missing spirit.

There's more to enjoy on the third floor of the university buildings at Via Romana 17, in what can reasonably claim to be the strangest museum in the city. The first part of the twin-sectioned **Museo di Zoologia** (Mon, Tues & Thurs–Sun 9am–1pm; closed Aug; L6000), popularly known as "La Specola" from the telescope on the roof, is conventional enough – a mortician's ark of animals stuffed, pickled, dessicated and dissected. It includes a hippo given to Grand Duke Pietro Leopardo, which used to reside in the Bóboli gardens, and finishes with a display of wax models of animals and human joints.

This is a hint at what lies behind the door of the section called the **Cere Anatomiche** (Tues & Sat 9am–noon; closed Aug; free). Wax arms, legs, body sections and organs cover the walls, arrayed around satin beds on which recline wax cadavers in progressive stages of de-construction, each muscle fibre and nerve cluster moulded and dyed with absolute precision. Most of the 600 models were made between 1775 and 1814 by the artist Clemente Susini and the physiologist Felice Fontana, and were intended as teaching aids in an age when medical ethics and refrigeration techniques were not what they are today. In a room on their own, however, are some models created by one Gaetano Zumbo, a cleric from Sicily, to satisfy the hypochondriacal obsessions of Cosimo III, a Jesuit-indoctrinated bigot who regarded all genuine scientific enquiry with suspicion. Enclosed in tasteful display cabinets, they comprise four tableaux of Florence during the plague – rats teasing the intestines from green-fleshed corpses, the pink bodies of the freshly dead heaped on the suppurating semi-decomposed. It's the grisliest show in town, and a firm favourite with school parties.

Santo Spirito

Some indication of the importance of the parish of **Santo Spirito** is given by the fact that when Florence was divided into four adminstrative *quartieri* in the fourteenth century, the entire area south of the Arno was given its name. The slightly run-down square in front of Santo Spirito church, with its market stalls and cafés, encapsulates the self-sufficient character of Oltrarno, an area not hopelessly compromised by the encroachments of tourism.

Santo Spirito church

Designed by Brunelleschi as a replacement for a thirteenth-century church, **Santo Spirito church** (daily 8am–noon & 4–6pm; closed Wed pm) was one of his last projects, and was described by Bernini as "the most beautiful church in the world". The paper-smooth facade is just a plastering job to disguise the unfinished front, but inside it's so perfectly proportioned that nothing could seem more artless. Yet the plan is extremely sophisticated – a Latin cross with a continuous chain of 38 chapels round the outside and a line of 35 columns running without a break round the nave, transepts and chancel. Only the Baroque baldachin, about as nicely integrated as garden gnome in a Greek temple, disrupts the harmonics.

The best paintings are in the transepts: in the right there's Filippino Lippi's *Nerli Altarpiece*, and in the left a *St Monica and Augustinian Nuns* by Verrocchio that's virtually a study in monochrome, with black-clad nuns flocking round their black-clad paragon. Also worth a peep is the sacristy, which is entered through a vestibule that opens onto the left aisle; both rooms were designed at the end of the fifteenth century by Giuliano da Sangallo.

A fire in 1471 destroyed all the monastery with the exception of its refectory, now the home of the **Museo Santo Spirito** (Tues–Sat 9am–2pm, Sun 8am–1pm; L4000), a one-room collection comprising an assortment of carvings, many of them Romanesque, and a huge fresco of *The Crucifixion* by Orcagna and his workshop.

Santa Maria del Carmine

Nowhere is the Florentine contrast of exterior and interior as stunning as in the plain brick box of **Santa Maria del Carmine**, a couple of blocks west of Santo Spirito. Outside it's a bleak mess; inside – in the frescoes of the **Cappella Brancacci** – it provides one of Italy's great artistic thrills. The decoration of the chapel was begun in 1424 by **Masolino**

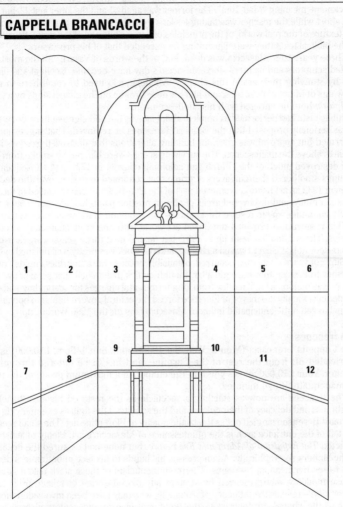

CAPPELLA BRANCACCI

1   The Expulsion
2   The Tribute Money
3   St Peter Preaching
4   The Baptism of the Neophytes
5   The Healing of the Cripple and
    the Raising of Tabitha
6   The Temptation
7   St Paul Visits St Peter in Prison
8   The Raising of the Son of Theophilus
    and St Peter Enthroned
9   St Peter Healing the Sick with his
    Shadow
10 The Distribution of Alms and the
    Death of Ananias
11 The Disputation
12 St Peter Freed from Prison

and a certain Tommaso di Ser Giovanni di Mone Cassai – known ever since as **Masaccio**, a nickname meaning "Mad Tom". The former was aged 41 and the latter just 22, but within a short while the teacher was taking lessons from the supposed pupil, whose grasp of the texture of the real world, of the principles of perspective and of the dramatic potential of the biblical texts they were illustrating far exceeded that of his precursors.

Three years later Masaccio was dead, but, in the words of Vasari, "All the most celebrated sculptors and painters since Masaccio's day have become excellent and illustrious by studying their art in this chapel." Michelangelo used to come here to make drawings of Masaccio's scenes, and had his nose broken on the chapel steps by a young sculptor whom he enraged with his condescension.

Public taste had performed a complete about-face by the mid-eighteenth century, when it was seriously proposed that the Brancacci frescoes be removed. That suggestion was overruled but approval was given for building alterations that destroyed frescoes in the lunettes above the main scenes. The surviving scenes were blurred by smoke from a fire that destroyed much of the church and adjoining convent in 1771, and subsequent varnishings smothered them in layers of grime that continued to darken over the decades. Then in 1932 an art historian removed part of the altar that had been installed in the eighteenth century, and discovered areas of almost pristine paint; half a century later, work finally got under way to restore the chapel to the condition of the uncovered patch.

This **restoration** provided the Italian art world with one of its characteristic controversies. The scaffolding went up in 1981, but for the next three years scarcely a brush was raised. At last Olivetti waved a cheque, and the work was pretty well finished by 1988. A couple of years' delay then occurred, ostensibly because the authorities couldn't decide whether to replace that Baroque altar, though cynics maintained that somebody somewhere was making a lot of money from long-term rental charges for scaffolding and other incidentals. Finally the mayor of Florence forced the central government into opening the chapel to catch the anticipated influx of Masaccio fans for the 1990 World Cup.

The frescoes

The Cappella Brancacci (Mon & Wed–Sat 10am–5pm, Sun 1–5pm; L10,000) is now barricaded off from the rest of the Carmine, and has to be entered through the cloister. Your L10,000 allows you into the chapel, in a maximum group of thirty, for an inadequate fifteen minutes.

The frescoes are now as startling a spectacle as the restored Sistine Chapel, the brightness and delicacy of their colours and the solidity of the figures exemplifying what Bernard Berenson singled out as the tactile quality of Florentine art. The small scene on the left of the entrance arch is the quintessence of Masaccio's art. Plenty of artists had depicted *The Expulsion of Adam and Eve* before, but none had captured the desolation of the sinners so graphically: Adam presses his hands to his face in bottomless despair, Eve raises her head and screams. The monumentalism of these stark naked figures – whose modesty was preserved by strategically placed sprigs of foliage prior to the restoration – reveals the influence of Donatello, who may have been involved in the planning of the chapel. In contrast to the emotional charge and sculptural presence of Masaccio's couple, Masolino's almost dainty *Adam and Eve*, on the opposite arch, pose as if to have their portraits painted.

St Peter is chief protagonist of all the remaining scenes. It's possible that the cycle was intended as propaganda on behalf of the embattled papacy, which was at the time being undermined by the **Great Schism**, with one pope holding court in Rome and another in Avignon; by celebrating the primacy of St Peter, the rock upon whom the Church is built, the frescoes by implication extol the apostolic succession from which the pope derives his authority. Two scenes by Masaccio are especially compelling: the *Tribute Money* (on the upper left wall), a complex narrative showing Peter, under Christ's instruction, fetching money from the mouth of a fish to pay the sum demanded by the city authorities; and the scene to the left of the altar, in which the shadow of the stern and self-possessed saint cures the infirm as it passes over them, a miracle invested with the aura of a solemn ceremonial.

The cycle was suspended when Masaccio left for Rome, where he died, and not resumed for some sixty years, when it was completed by **Filippino Lippi**. He finished the *Raising of the Emperor's Nephew* (lower left-hand wall) and painted the lower part of the wall showing the crucifixion of the saint; his most distinctive contribution, though, is *The Release of St Peter* on the right-hand side of the entrance arch, where there's a touching intimacy in the relationship between saint and counselling angel. Lippi also made a rather odd intervention on the opposite wall. To the right of the enthroned St Peter stands a trio of men, now identified as Masaccio, Alberti and Brunelleschi, who made a trip to Rome together. Masaccio originally painted himself touching Peter's robe, a reference to the enthroned statue of Peter in Rome, which pilgrims touch for good luck. Lippi considered the contact of the artist and saint to be improper and painted out the arm; at the moment, his fastidious addition has been allowed to remain, but you can clearly see where the arm used to be.

East of the Ponte Vecchio

On the tourist map of Florence, the Oltrarno area immediately to the **east of the Ponte Vecchio** is something of a dead zone: as with the opposite bank of the river, blocks of historic buildings were destroyed by mines left behind by the Nazis in 1944. Some characterful parts remain, however, such as the medieval **Via de' Bardi** and its continuation, **Via San Niccolò**. These narrow, palazzo-lined streets will take you past the obsessively eclectic **Museo Bardini** and the medieval church of **San Niccolò**, both perhaps best visited on the way up the hill to San Miniato (see next page).

The Museo Bardini

Like the Horne museum close by across the Arno, the **Museo Bardini** at Piazza de' Mozzi 1 (Mon, Tues & Thurs–Sat 9am–2pm, Sun 8am–1pm; L6000) was founded on the bequest of a private collector. Whereas Horne was just a moderately well-off connoisseur, his contemporary Sergio Bardini was the biggest art dealer in Italy, and was determined that no visitor to his native city should remain unaware of his success. Accordingly he ripped down the church that used to stand here and built a vast house for himself, studding it with fragments of old buildings to advertise his affinity with Florence's past. Doorways, ceiling panels and other orphaned pieces are strewn all over the place: the first-floor windows, for instance, are actually altars from a church in Pistoia. The more portable items on display are equally wide-ranging: musical instruments, carvings, ceramics, armour, carpets, pictures – if it was vaguely arty and had a price tag, Bardini collected it.

On the lower floors Tino da Camaino's *Charity* stands out from the clutter, and there's a room of funerary monuments done out like a crypt, with an altarpiece thought to be by Andrea della Robbia. Upstairs, three pieces grab the attention: a stucco, mosaic and glass relief of the *Madonna* that's probably by Donatello; a beautiful *Virgin Annunciate*, an anonymous piece from fifteenth-century Siena; and a *St Michael* painted by Antonio del Pollaiuolo.

To San Niccolò and the city gates

Beyond the Bardini museum, Via San Niccolò swings towards the church of **San Niccolò sopr'Arno**, this quarter's only interesting church. Restoration work after the 1966 flood uncovered several frescoes underneath the altars, but none is as appealing as the fifteenth-century fresco in the sacristy: known as *The Madonna of the Girdle*, it was painted probably by Baldovinetti.

In medieval times the church was close to the edge of the city, and two of Florence's fourteenth-century gates still stand in the vicinity: the dinky **Porta San Miniato**, set in a portion of the walls, and the huge **Porta San Niccolò**, overlooking the Arno. From either of these you can begin the climb **up to San Miniato** (see below): the path from Porta San Niccolò weaves up through **Piazzale Michelangelo**, with its replica *David* and bumper-to-bumper tour coaches; the more direct path from Porta San Miniato offers a choice between the steep Via del Monte alle Croce or the stepped Via di San Salvatore al Monte, both of which emerge a short distance uphill from Piazzale Michelangelo.

San Miniato al Monte

The brilliant multicoloured facade of **San Miniato al Monte** (daily: May–Sept 8am–noon & 2–7pm, Oct–April 8am–noon, 2.30–6pm; free) lures troops of visitors up the hill from Oltrarno, and the church more than fulfils the promise of its distant appearance. You can take bus #13 up from the station as far as Piazzale Michelangelo and then continue on foot up to the church itself – thereby eliminating the steep uphill climb from the river.

Arguably the finest Romanesque structure in Tuscany, San Miniato is also the oldest surviving church building in Florence after the baptistery. It recently began to show signs of its age, though, and the authorities become so concerned about the dangers of subsidence that a project was initiated to shore up the downhill side of the church and the adjoining cemetery. Then, in a depressing rerun of the Piazza della Signoria fiasco, it was discovered that a degree of financial impropriety may have been involved in awarding the contract; work has now been suspended for an indefinite period.

The church's dedicatee, St Minias, belonged to a Christian community which settled in Florence in the third century. Legend has it that after martyrdom by decapitation the saintly corpse was seen to carry his severed head over the river and up the hill to this spot, where a shrine was subsequently erected to him. Construction of the present building began in 1013, with the foundation of a Benedictine monastery. The gorgeous marble **facade** – alluding to the baptistery in its geometrical patterning – was added towards the end of that century and paid for by the Arte di Calimala (cloth merchants' guild), whose trademark, a gilded eagle, perches on the roof. The mosaic of *Christ between the Virgin and St Minias* dates from the thirteenth century.

The interior

With its choir raised on a platform above the large crypt, the interior of San Miniato is like no other in the city, and its general appearance has changed little since the mid-eleventh century. The main additions and decorations in no way spoil its serenity, though the nineteenth-century recoating of the marble columns is a little lurid. The intricately patterned panels of the **pavement** are dated 1207 on the panel of the zodiac, and the lovely **tabernacle** between the choir stairs was designed in 1448 by Michelozzo, to house the miraculous Crucifix that nodded to Giovanni Gualberto (see p.106).

Dating from a few years later is the **Cappella del Cardinale del Portogallo**, which was built into the left wall as a memorial to Cardinal James of Lusitania, who died in Florence in 1459, aged 25. His chapel is a marvellous example of artistic collaboration: the basic design was by Antonio Manetti, a pupil of Brunelleschi; the tomb itself was carved by Antonio Rossellino; the *Annunciation* was painted by Baldovinetti; Antonio and Piero del Pollaiuolo produced the altarpiece (the original is now in the Uffizi); and the terracotta decoration of the ceiling was provided by Luca della Robbia.

CRIME IN FLORENCE

There's a catchphrase much used by the Florentine press: "Firenze snaturata", meaning "Florence corrupted". It's a cry directed at both the city's violation by tourists and its crime problem – two aspects of the same problem, in many eyes.

Heroin is the source of most anguish: in recent years around seventy percent of all cases heard in the city courts have been drug-related offences, and the percentage shows no sign of decreasing. Piazza Santo Spirito and Piazza Santa Croce became notorious for the detritus of syringes and phials found by the roadsweepers in the morning; these squares were cleaned up, but the operation amounted to little more than window-dressing. Stroll along Via de' Neri, at the back of the Palazzo Vecchio, during the midday siesta, and you'll see gear being set up in doorways and groups waiting for the man. Dealers from the *cosa nostra* strongholds of southern Italy take much of the popular blame, but the poorer half of the country provides as many victims as villains, as young southerners come up to Florence to pick up drugs from foreign dealers.

The other high-profile – and closely associated – problem is **prostitution**, with under-age, transvestite and transsexual prostitutes especially conspicuous round the station area and in the Cascine. Many of the transsexuals come here from Brazil and Argentina – for some reason, more sex-change operations are performed in Florence than in any other Italian city. Their trade covers the entire spectrum of Florentine society; many are caught up in the Florentine underworld, but some of the Florentine smart set also think it's chic to have a South American transsexual hostess for a cocktail party.

Kidnapping, on the other hand, remains a relatively hidden problem. Since 1975 there have been around thirty publicized kidnappings in Florence, but the true statistic is certainly higher. The perpetrators – often Sardinian shepherds based around Prato, up in the Mugello hills or even in bourgeois Chianti – do not mess about, and many hostages have been returned alive but mutilated after their relatives showed reluctance to come up with the ransom. Terrified of retribution if the kidnappers find out that the authorities are party to the negotiations, the families of victims often do not inform the police.

But by far the most sensational crimes of recent decades were the killings committed by the so-called **Mostro di Firenze** (Monster of Florence), one of Italy's few cases of serial murder. Between the mid-1970s and mid-1980s he hacked fourteen people to death, mostly young couples camping out on the hills above the city. Even after the killings had apparently stopped, nobody would risk camping wild in the Florence region, and houses in Chianti were still being shuttered as though to withstand a siege. Towards the end of 1993 a Pietro Pacciani from Mercatale was arrested in connection with the murders. Pacciani was convicted then released on appeal and continues to plead his innocence right up to his death in February 1998, on the eve of his second trial.

Beyond the slender columns of the **crypt** is the church's first altar, containing the relics of Minias. The magnificently carved balustrade and pulpit in the **choir** were both created at the same time as the zodiac pavement; artists from Ravenna executed the mosaic in the apse at the end of that century. Finally, the **sacristy** is completely covered with *Scenes from the Life of St Benedict*, a beguiling fresco cycle painted by Spinello Aretino in 1387.

The city outskirts

The peripheral attractions covered in this section – the **Cascine park**, **Museo Stibbert**, Andrea del Sarto's *cenacolo* at **San Salvi** and **Fiorentina's football ground** – are all a stiff walk from the centre of town, though all can be reached by ATAF bus. Sights lying within the city boundaries but definitely requiring transport – such as the Medici villas – are dealt with in the following chapter.

West: the Cascine

Florence's public park, the **Cascine**, begins close to the Ponte della Vittoria, a half-hour walk west of the Ponte Vecchio (or bus #17e from the duomo, station or youth hostel). It dwindles away three kilometres downstream, at the confluence of the Arno and the Mugnone, where there's a statue of the Maharajah of Kohlapur – he died in Florence in 1870 and the prescribed funeral rites demanded that his body be cremated at a spot where two rivers met.

Once the Medici dairy farm (*cascina*), then a hunting reserve, this narrow strip of green mutated into a high-society venue in the eighteenth century: if there was nothing happening at the opera, all of Florence's *belle monde* turned out to promenade under the trees of the Cascine. A fountain in the park bears a dedication to Shelley, who was inspired to write his *Ode to the West Wind* while strolling here on a blustery day in 1819.

By day, Florentines take their kids out to Cascine to play on the grass or visit the small zoo, and thousands of people come out here on Tuesday mornings for the colossal **market** (see p.157). But the Cascine is not a great park by any stretch of the imagination – and it has a pretty seedy reputation. The situation isn't as bad as it has been, but junkies still shoot up here in the middle of the day, and the Cascine is emphatically not a place for a nocturnal stroll, as it has long been a playground for the city's hookers and pimps (see box on previous page).

North: Museo Stibbert

About a kilometre and a half north of San Marco, at Via Stibbert 26 (bus #4 from the station), is the loopiest of Florence's museums, the **Museo Stibbert** (May–Sept Mon–Wed, Fri & Sat–Sun 10am–1pm & 3–6pm; Oct–April Mon–Wed, Fri 10am–4pm, Sat & Sun 10am–6pm; L8000). This rambling, murky mansion was the home of the half-Scottish half-Italian Frederick Stibbert, who in his twenties made a name for himself in Garibaldi's army. Later he inherited a fourteenth-century house from his mother, then bought the neighbouring mansion and joined the two together, thus creating a place big enough to accommodate the fruits of his compulsive collecting. The 64 rooms contain over fifty thousand items, ranging from snuff boxes to paintings by Carlo Crivelli and a possible Botticelli.

Militaria were Frederick's chief enthusiasm, and the Stibbert **armour** collection is reckoned one of the world's best. It includes Roman, Etruscan and Japanese examples, as well as a fifteenth-century *condottiere*'s outfit and the armour worn by Giovanni delle Bande, retrieved from his grave in San Lorenzo in 1857. The big production number comes in the great hall, between the two houses, where a platoon of mannequins is clad in full sixteenth-century gear. Also on show is the regalia in which Napoleon was crowned king of Italy.

East: San Salvi and Campo Marte

Twenty minutes' walk beyond Piazza Beccaria (or bus #10 from the station, or #6 from Piazza San Marco) is the ex-convent of **San Salvi**, which was reopened in 1982 after the restoration of its most precious possession, the *Last Supper* by Andrea del Sarto (Tues–Sun 9am–2pm; L6000). As a prelude to this picture, there's a gallery of big but otherwise unremarkable Renaissance altarpieces, a gathering of pictures by various del Sarto acolytes, and the beautiful reliefs from the tomb of Giovanni Gualberto, founder of the Vallombrosan order to whom this monastery belonged.

The tomb was smashed up by Charles V's troops in 1530 but they refused to damage the *Last Supper*, which is still in the refectory for which it was painted, accompanied by three del Sarto frescoes brought here from other churches in Florence. Painted around 1520 and evidently much influenced by Leonardo's work, this is the epitome of del Sarto's soft, suave technique – emotionally undernourished for some tastes, but faultlessly carried out.

The Stadio Comunale

As befits the football team of this monument-stuffed city, **AC Fiorentina** play in a stadium that's listed as a building of cultural significance, the **Stadio Comunale** at Campo Marte. It was designed by Pier Luigi Nervi in 1930, as a consequence of two decisions: to create a new football club for Florence and to stage the 1934 World Cup in Italy.

The stadium was the first major sports venue to exploit the shape-making potential of reinforced concrete, and its spiral ramps, cantilevered roof and slim central tower still make most other arenas look dreary. From the spectator's point of view, however, it's far from perfect: for instance, the peculiar D-shape of the stands – necessitated by the straight 200-metre sprint track – means that visibility from some parts of the ground is awful. But the architectural importance of Nervi's work meant that when Florence was chosen as one of the hosts for the 1990 World Cup there could be no question of simply building a replacement (as was done brilliantly at Bari), nor of radically altering the existing one (as happened at most grounds). Much of the seventy billion lire spent on the refurbishment of the Stadio Comunale was thus spent ensuring that the improvements did not ruin the clean modernistic lines, and most of the extra space in the all-seater stadium was created by lowering the pitch a couple of metres below its previous level, in order to insert another layer of seats where the track had been. Visitors familiar with the old ground might notice another couple of additions right behind the goals: they are water hydrants, the latest thing in Italian crowd control.

Their violet shirts are always natty – hence their nickname, the *Viola* – and Fiorentina are usually one of Italy's glamour sides. In the early 1990s they produced one of the most lavishly talented players Italy has seen, the mercurial Roberto Baggio, who transferred to Juventus amid scenes of fervent protest in Florence – for what was then a world record fee of £7,700,000. In 1996, with Argentinian wonderboy **Gabriel Batistuta** (aka "Batigol") attracting the sort of morbid affection that Baggio once commanded, Fiorentina won the Italian cup, and then came close to a league championship in 1999. The *Viola* are probably a couple of players short of the squad needed to finish ahead of mighty Milan and Juventus, but happy days have returned to Campo Marte.

Match tickets cost from L30,000 to over L200,000 and can be bought at the ground itself (information on ticket availability and fixtures ☎055.292.363); you can also sometimes obtain them from the *Toto* booth on the west side of Piazza della Repubblica; to get to Campo Marte, take bus #17 from the station.

CONSUMERS' FLORENCE

Florence might not have the metropolitan dash of Milan or Rome, but it has most of the big-city attractions you'd expect to find – plenty of **cultural events**, scores of **cafés** and **restaurants**, and a lot of very chic **shops** to give focus to the evening *passeggiata*. The main problem is one of identity, in a city whose inhabitants are heavily outnumbered by outsiders from March to October. Restaurant standards are often patchy and prices pitched at whatever level the tourists can bear, while many of the locals swear there's scarcely a single genuine Tuscan place left in the city – an exaggeration, of course, but not altogether groundless. Yet the situation is nowhere near as bad as some reports would have it, and it doesn't require much effort to have a good time in Florence, whatever your budget. As for **nightlife**, the university and the influx of language students keep things lively, and **seasonal events** such as the *Maggio Musicale* maintain Florence's standing as the hub of cultural life in Tuscany.

Cafés and bars

Pavement **cafés** are not a major part of the Florentine scene, though there is no lack of smaller, less ostentatious outdoor venues. Predictably enough, the main concentrations of cafés are found on the big tourist streets – Via de' Tornabuoni, Via de' Panzani, Via de' Cerretani, Via Por Santa Maria, Via Guicciardini and Via dei Calzaiuoli. Many are expensive and characterless, but others, as listed below, are expensive and very good, especially when it comes to cakes and other sweet delicacies. To find places where prices are lower and non-Florentine faces fewer, only a little effort is needed: a short walk north from the duomo gets you into the university area around Piazza San Marco, and it's just as easy to get over into Oltrarno, the most authentic quarter of the historic centre. Most of the places listed in the first two sections below are at their busiest first thing in the morning, as the natives on their way to work stop off for a quick coffee and a pastry such as a *budino di riso* (small rice cake), or a brioche or *cornetto* (croissant). Every other street in the centre has a café or bar of some sort; what follows is a guide to the best and the most popular. **Wine bars** and **late-night bars** are covered under their own headings, while places that have music are listed in the "Nightlife" section (see p.149).

North of the river

Caffè Amerini, Via della Vigna Nuova 63r. The intimate interior's medieval brick arching contrasts with modern furniture and a couple of Art Deco mirrors. Sandwiches, salads and snacks are particularly good – point at what you want from the bar and then sit down to be served: there's only a small premium for sitting down. Closed Sun.

Caffè Cibreo, Via Andrea del Verrocchio 5r. If you're in the Sant'Ambrogio area, it's worth the detour to visit the prettiest café in Florence. Opened in 1989, the wood-panelled interior looks at least 200 years older. Cakes and desserts are great, and the light meals bear the outstanding culinary stamp of the *Cibreo* restaurant kitchens opposite. Closed Sun & Mon.

Caffè Gilli, Piazza della Repubblica 36–39r. Founded in 1733, *Gilli* moved to its present site in 1910, the staggering Belle Epoque interior a sight in itself. Most people, however, choose to sit on the big outdoor terrace. On a cold afternoon try the famous hot chocolate – it comes in five blended flavours: almond, orange, coffee, *gianduia* and cocoa. Closed Tues.

Caffè Italiano, Via della Condotta 56r. *Italiano* is a revelation given its position just off the teeming Via dei Calzaiuoli. Downstairs there's an old-fashioned stand-up bar with lots of dark wood, silver teapots and superb cakes, coffees and teas. Lunch is excellent, as you'd expect from somewhere owned by Umberto Montano, head of the outstanding *Caffè Italiano* restaurants (see p.148). Closed Sun & Aug.

Caffèlatte, Via degli Alfani 39r. Good choice if you're up around Santissima Annunziata; the walls feature temporary exhibitions of paintings and photographs, with laid-back music complementing the vaguely "alternative" mood. There's an organic bakery on site which produces delicious breads and cakes, and the caffè latte is as good as you'd expect given the café's 1920 origins, when a milk and coffee shop opened on the site. Closed Sun.

Capocaccia, Lungarno Corsini 12-14r. This place is about as trendy as it gets for Florentines who tote portable phones and never miss the chance to admire themselves in a convenient mirror. The wood and blue-tiled interior is roomy and has plenty of tables and stools; you'll also be mixing almost entirely with locals, especially later on – it's been voted the Florentines' favourite night-time rendezvous. Tues–Sat noon–4pm & 6pm–1am.

Giacosa, Via de' Tornabuoni 83r. Public living room of Florence's gilded youth, this was the birthplace of the *Negroni* cocktail – equal parts Campari, sweet Martini and gin. Closed Mon.

Procacci, Via de' Tornabuoni 64r. Famous café-shop that doesn't serve coffee, just cold drinks. Its fame comes from the extraordinary truffle rolls (*tartufati*), which are delicious if not exactly filling. Closed Mon.

Rivoire, Piazza della Signoria 5r. If you want to people-watch on Florence's main square, this is the place to do so, and the outside tables are invariably packed. Founded in 1872, the café started life specializing in hot chocolate, still its main claim to fame. Ice creams are also fairly good, but the

THE VINAIO

One of Florence's great – but sadly fast-disappearing – institutions is the tiny street corner or hole-in-the wall wine shop or *vinaio*. Some of these are surprisingly central, and all make fine places for a glass of wine on the hoof. Most are open 8am to 8pm and are closed on Sunday.

Quasigratis Via dei Castellani-corner of Via di Ninna. Little more than a window in a wall and it doesn't say *Quasigratis* ("Almost free") anywhere, just "Vini" and "Lampredotto Caldo". Rolls, nibbles and wine – in tiny glasses called *rasini* – are consumed standing up.

Vineria Via dei Cimatori 38r. A perfect *vinaio* whose survival is all the more remarkable given its location almost immediately off the high-rent Via dei Calzaiuoli.

Vini Via dell'Anguillara. This minuscule place near the corner of Piazza di San Firenze is *literally* a hole in the wall, with just enough room for two people with elbows tucked in to knock back a glass of wine.

---

sandwiches and snacks are run-of-the-mill – this is a place for one pricey beer or cappuccino, just to say you've done it. Closed Mon.

Oltrarno

Hemingway, Piazza Piattellina 9r, off Piazza del Carmine. Self-consciously trendy, but don't let that put you off – there's nothing else like it in Florence. Choose from one of countless speciality teas, sample over 20 coffees, or knock back one of the "tea cocktails". Owners Paul de Bondt and Andrea Slitti are members of the Compagnia del Cioccolato, a chocolate appreciation society – and it shows: the handmade chocolates are sublime. Open Tues–Fri 4pm–1/2am, Sun 11am–8pm. Closed Mon.

Il Caffè, Piazza Pitti 9r. Sit outside or in the old-style interior, nicely done out with wooden floors and subdued gold-yellow walls. *Panini* (from L5000) and other snacks are available, plus two good-value set menus at lunch. In the evenings there's live music (usually jazz or blues), with a full dinner menu until 10pm and light meals later. Daily.

Caffè I Ricchi, Piazza di Santo Spirito 9r. Piazza di Santo Spirito, with its trees and neighbourhood atmosphere, feels like a real old-fashioned Italian square, and the *Ricchi* is the most pleasant and relaxed of its handful of cafés. Menus change daily, and there's a good selection of cakes, ice cream and sandwiches. Closed Sun except second Sun of the month.

Wine bars

Cantinetta dei Verrazzano, Via dei Tavolini 18–20r. Owned by Castello dei Verrazzano, a major Chianti vineyard, this is a good spot for a drink or a slice of pizza. The glass-fronted display inside oozes with outstanding pizza, *focaccia* and cakes – pay at the cash-desk and eat sitting on the bench provided. Otherwise, tables beyond the white-tiled oven or in the pleasant wood-lined room to the left are perfect for an early evening glass of vino. Busy at lunch. Closed Sun & Aug.

Casa del Vino, Via dell'Ariento 16r. Located just west of the Mercato Centrale, *del Vino* is passed by hordes of tourists daily – yet it's probably visited by only a handful. Patrons are mostly Florentines, who pitch up for a drink, a chat with owner Gianni Migliorini and an assault on various *panini, crostini*, and saltless Tuscan bread and salami. Closed Sun & Aug.

Enoteca Baldovino, Via San Giuseppe 18r. An offshoot of the excellent Scottish-run *Baldovino* restaurant just across the road (see p.148), this is a stylish place to buy gastronomic goodies or drink wine at the bar or one of the tables to the rear. The small menu of sandwiches, soups and home-made cakes changes daily. Very convenient for Santa Croce. Closed Mon.

Fiaschetteria, Via degli Alfani 70r, corner of Via dei Servi. The university nearby ensures that this otherwise low-key place is often heaving at lunch time, when students pile in for the pasta-and-a-salad for around L15,000. There's also a fair variety of wines by the glass. Closed Sun.

Fuori Porta, Via del Monte alle Croci. If you're climbing up to San Miniato and regret your decision halfway up, console yourself at this superb wine bar-*osteria*. There are over 400 wines to choose from by the bottle – the choice of wines by the glass changes regularly – as well as a wide selection of grappas and malt whiskies. Bread, cheese, hams and salamis are available, together with a small choice of hot pasta dishes at lunch. Closed Sun & two weeks in August.

Le Volpi e L'Uva, Piazza dei Rossi 1r, off Piazza di Santa Felicita. This discreet little place just over the Ponte Vecchio does good business by concentrating on the wines of small producers and providing tasty snacks to help them down (the selection of cheeses in particular is tremendous). At any one time you can choose from at least ten different wines by the glass. Closed Mon and one week in August.

Zanobini, Via Sant'Antonino 47r. Like the *Casa del Vino*, its rival just around the corner (see above), this is an authentic Florentine place whose feel owes much to the presence of locals and traders from the nearby Mercato Centrale. Food is no great shakes – most people are simply here for a chat over a glass of wine. Closed Sun.

Late-night bars

Art Bar, Via del Moro 4r. A fine little bar near Piazza di Carlo Goldoni. The interior looks like an antique shop, while the club-like atmosphere attracts a rather smart crowd. Don't let that put you off: turn up for the busy happy hour, and the low-priced cocktails enable you to get stuck in before heading on elsewhere. The after-hours ambience is also ideal for a laid-back nightcap. Happy hour 7–9pm. Closed Sun.

Cabiria, Piazza di Santo Spirito 4r. More alternative in look, feel and clientele than the likes of *Dolce Vita* (see below), but still rather cosy. The main seating area is in the room to the rear, but plenty of punters (some locals and lots of foreigners) sit out on the piazza, or crowd into the bar area at the front. There's a DJ-run soundtrack most nights from around 9pm. Closed Tues.

Caracao, Via Ginori 10r. When Florentines aren't drinking in cod-Irish pubs, they're posing in pseudo-Latin American dives, of which *Caracao* is by far the best. A big wooden bar and ranks of tequila bottles create the right look and feel, while a multi-ethnic crowd provides the noise and energy levels. Happy hour is the best and busiest time to show up: cocktails are cheap, and there are snacks and tortillas to help them down. Happy hour 7–10pm. Closed Mon.

Dolce Vita, Piazza del Carmine. A smart, modern-looking and extremely popular bar; aluminium bar stools, sleek black-and-white photos on the walls and the chance to preen with Florence's beautiful things ranged around the tables out on the piazza. *Dolce Vita's* been going for over ten years, and has stayed ahead of the game through constant updating; don't be surprised if the decor's changed by the time you get there. Closed Sun.

Fiddler's Elbow, Piazza di Santa Maria Novella. If you're homesick for an Irish pub, and want to drink in a central location with lots of foreigners, this is the place. There's just one smoky, dark and wood-panelled room, so the place is invariably heaving – fortunately there's also seating out on the piazza. Women travellers are likely to find themselves the object of concerted attention from packs of Guinness-sozzled Italians.

Maramao, Via de' Macci 79r. The well-known *Maramao* is as trendy as you'd expect in the hip Sant'Ambrogio district: this is not the sort of place to turn up in a T-shirt and trainers. The decor, which receives a regular overhaul, is as slick as the punters, who are generally here as much to dance as to drink – the dance floor cranks up most nights from about 11pm.

Rex, Via Fiesola 25r. *Rex* is probably the Florentine bar to visit if you visit no other. One of the city's real night-time fixtures, it's friendly and has a varied clientele. Vast curving lights droop over the central bar, which is studded with turquoise stone and broken mirror mosaics. Big arched spaces to either side mean there's plenty of room, the cocktails are good and the tapas-like snacks excellent. DJs provide the sounds at weekends. Closed July & Aug.

Robin Hood's Tavern, Via dell'Oriuolo. One of the biggest and most successful of several places that try to effect the look of an English pub – probably because it's owned by a former biker from Birmingham. The place really isn't bad if a pub is what you're after: there's lots of wood-panelling, darts, beer barrels and heavy benches. Rents must be high, however, as drink prices are well over the odds.

The Lion's Fountain Borgo degli Albizi 34r. If you must drink in one of Florence's Irish pubs, this small place towards Santa Croce is probably the one to go for. Background music isn't traditional, but it's inoffensive; the decor is pseudo-Irish, and the bar staff and atmosphere are generally friendly. Food is simple and good – lots of salads and sandwiches – and you can catch big sporting events on the TVs. Drinks are reasonably priced, and include a good range of cocktails as well as the ubiquitous Guinness.

Gelaterie

Devotees of Italian **ice cream** will find plenty of occasions to sample some wacky concoctions without straying far off the main drags – though, as with the bars and cafés, the most rewarding spots are less central. Good ice cream is as much a part of the Italian experience as any number of museums and galleries. And in a *gelateria*, or ice-cream parlour, such as Vivoli, Florence can claim to have one of the best purveyors of the stuff in the country (see below). The procedure is the same wherever you buy. First decide whether you want a cone (*un cono*) or a cup (*una coppa*). Then decide how much you want to pay – cone and cup sizes go up in L500 increments from around L2000. Unless you plump for the smallest size you'll usually be able to choose a combination of two or three flavours. Finally, you may be asked if you want a squirt of cream (*panna*) on top – it's usually free.

Badiani, Viale dei Mille 20r. Known for its eggy *Buontalenti* ice cream, the recipe of which is known only to the proprietors. Closed Tues.

Banchi, Via dei Banchi 14r. Close to Santa Maria Novella, this is known not so much for its ice creams as for its wonderful *granite* – fragmented ice soaked in coffee or fruit juice. Closed Sun.

Baroncini, Via Celso 3r. Well-known *gelateria* with rice ice cream its speciality – not as horrible as it sounds. Also does great sorbets. Closed Wed.

Bondi, Via Nazionale 61r. Some of the daftest concoctions in town – rhubarb, for instance, or vanilla-orange-anise. Closed Mon.

Carabe, Via Ricasoli 60r. Wonderful Sicilian ice cream made with Sicilian ingredients as only they know how. Also serves a variety of cakes.

Festival del Gelato, Via del Corso 75r. Over 100 varieties, with some very exotic combinations; good *semifreddi*. Closed Mon.

Frilli, Via San Niccolò 57. Excellent ice creams made from seasonal fruit. Closed Wed.

I Gelati del Righi, Piazza Batoni 18. Around 30 flavours to choose from, ranging from the banal to such unusual ones as green apple.

Il Giardino delle Delizie, Piazza della Felicita 3r. Does a gorgeous chocolate ice cream. Closed Mon.

Perchè No!, Via de' Tavolini 19r. Very central *gelateria*; go for the rum-laced *tiramisù* ice cream. Closed Tues.

Vivoli, Via Isola delle Stinche 7r. Operating from deceptively unprepossessing premises in a side street close to Santa Croce, this is the best ice-cream-maker in Florence – and some say in Italy. At least one daily visit is a must. Closed Mon and Aug.

Food markets and shops

An obvious and enjoyable way to cut down costs is to put together a picnic and retire to the Bóboli gardens or squares such as Piazza Santissima Annunziata, Piazza Santa Croce or Piazza Santa Maria Novella.

For **provisions**, the easiest option is to call in at the **Mercato Centrale** by San Lorenzo church (Mon–Sat 7am–2pm, plus Sat 4–8pm), where everything you could possibly need can be bought under one roof – bread, ham, cheese, fruit, wine. Also comprehensive, and even cheaper, is the **Mercato Sant' Ambrogio** over by Santa Croce (Mon–Fri 7am–2pm). For fresh fruit and vegetables, you could drop by at **Piazza Santo Spirito**, where there are usually a few stalls run by local farmers (Mon–Sat 7am–1pm).

Via dei Tavolini, off Via dei Calzaiuoli, is a good central street where you'll find several shops in which to assemble a picnic: Grana Market at 11r has a fabulous cheese selection, and Semelino at 18r bakes wonderful bread. If you're after wine to take home, check out the wine bars above (see pp.143–4), most of which double as wine shops with a large selection of wines.

Every district has its **alimentari**, which in addition to selling the choicest Tuscan produce often also provide sandwiches. Vera, at the southern end of Ponte Santa Trinita at Piazza Frescobaldi 3r, takes the prize for the ultimate Florentine deli; other excellent central *alimentari* include Tassini, at Borgo Santi Apostoli 24r and Alessi Paride, at Via delle Oche 27–29r.

Restaurants

In gastronomic circles, **Florentine cuisine** is accorded as much reverence as Florentine art, a reverence encapsulated in the myth that French eating habits acquired their sophistication in the wake of Catherine de' Medici's marriage to the future Henry II of France. In fact, Florentine food has always been characterized by modest raw materials and simple technique – beefsteak (*bistecca*), tripe (*trippa*) and liver (*fegato*) are typical ingredients, while grilling (*alla Fiorentina*) is a favoured method of preparation. In addition, white beans (*fagioli*) will feature on most menus, either on their own, garnished with liberal quantities of local olive oil, or as the basis of such dishes as *ribollita* soup.

Unfussy it might be, but quality cooking doesn't come cheap in Florence – most of the restaurants that meet with local approval cost L40,000-plus per person, wine included. Yet there are some decent low-budget places serving food that at least gives some idea of the region's characteristic dishes, and even the simplest **trattoria** should offer *bistecca alla Fiorentina* – though you should bear in mind that this dish is priced per hundred grams, so your bill will be considerably higher than the figure written on the menu. Another thing to be aware of is that many restaurants will only serve full meals – so check the menu outside if you're thinking of just popping in for a quick lunch-time plate of pasta.

As a very rough guideline, the cheapest places tend to be near the station, the best places on or near the main central streets, and the best mid-range restaurants tucked away in alleys on the north of the river or over in Oltrarno.

The **restaurants** below are defined by **area** – west and north of the immediate city centre (around the station, Santa Maria and San Lorenzo), the city centre, east of the city centre (around Santa Croce) and south of the river (Oltrarno). **Prices** are defined as Inexpensive (under L35,000 a head for three courses plus water, wine and cover charge), Moderate (L35,000–65,000) and Expensive (over L65,000), but these are loose definitions, because you can keep costs down even in more expensive places by having just two courses (pasta and main), and retiring to a bar for ice cream or coffee and *digestif*. Remember, too, that you often needn't buy a whole bottle of wine: ask for a half-bottle or quarter-bottle/jug of house wine (*mezza bottiglia* or *un quartino*).

Station and San Lorenzo

Antellesi, Via Faenza 9r (☎055.240.618). Constantly changing menu of Florentine specialities, in a fifteenth-century building just a few steps from the entrance to the Medici chapels. Run by an expat Arizonan and her Florentine chef husband, the food is good, although prices have crept up and reports suggest the place is not quite as friendly as it once was. Closed Sun. Moderate.

Il Contadino, Via Palazzuolo 69r. Simple but very good basic meals at around L25,000 in a no-nonsense trattoria with stark black and white interior; popular with backpackers and you may have to queue. Closed Sat & Aug. Inexpensive.

La Lampara, Via Nazionale 36r (☎055..215.164). Don't be put off by the multilingual menus – the food is very good and the waiters attentive. Packed with locals at lunchtime and evening – so try to book a table. Open daily. Inexpensive to moderate.

Mario, Via Rosina 2r-Piazza del Mercato Centrale. *Mario* has been around for ever, serving generations of students and market workers with high-quality Tuscan food in basic surroundings. It has jazzed up its front, but you don't come here for ambience, you come to fill up at low cost at shared tables. Mon–Sat 12.30–3pm. Closed Sun & Aug. Inexpensive.

Oliviero, Via delle Terme 52r (☎055.240.618). *Oliviero* currently enjoys a reputation for some of Florence's best food, but at a price. It has a welcoming and old-fashioned feel – something like an Italian restaurant of the Sixties. The innovative food is predominantly Tuscan, but includes other Italian dishes, and puddings, for once, are a cut above the usual. The menu includes fresh fish when available, something of a rarity in Florence. Closed lunch, Mon & Aug. Expensive

Palle d'Oro, Via Sant'Antonio 43r (☎055.288.383). Plainest possible type of trattoria; besides full meals, they do sandwiches to take away. Closed Sun. Inexpensive to moderate.

Rose's, Via del Parione 26r (☎055.287.090). The bright, modern, "New York" look here is all but unique in Florence, making a welcome change from wooden beams and brick-vaulted ceilings. This is a great place for a light lunch – the salads are especially good – or tea and cakes in the afternoon. The airy bar and surrounding, intimate rooms are also popular after dark: you can eat sushi or a light supper for around L20,000, and the cocktails are tremendous. Lunch served 12.30–3.30pm. Closed Sun. Inexpensive.

Zà-Zà, Piazza del Mercato Centrale 26r (☎055.215.411). In business over 20 years, *Zà-Zà* is the best of several *trattorie* close to the Mercato Centrale. Unfortunately, it has been patronized by Naomi Campbell and Bill Cosby, which has made it better known – try to book. The interior is dark, stone-walled and brick-arched, with a handful of tables; set-price meals (L20,000) offer a choice of three or four pastas and main courses. Closed Sun & Aug. Inexpensive.

City Centre

Acqua al Due, Via dell'Acqua 2r-Via della Vigna Vecchia 40r (☎055.284.170). Always packed (often with foreigners but with Italians too), chiefly on account of its offbeat decor, lively atmosphere and *assaggio di primi* – a succession of pasta dishes shared by everyone at the table. Closed Mon. Moderate.

Antico Fattore, Via Lambertesca 1–3r (☎055.288.975). Simple Tuscan dishes dominate the menu, and the soups are particularly good; close to the Piazza della Signoria, but not as expensive as the locale might suggest. Grim service though. Closed Sun plus Sat in summer, Mon in winter, and Aug. Moderate.

Belle Donne, Via delle Belle Donne 16r. A tiny trattoria lent a distinctive touch by its banks of fresh flowers and startling mounds of decorative fruit and vegetables. You sit at shared tables and choose from the day's specials chalked up on the blackboard. This may sound off-putting for non-Italian speakers, but the service and atmosphere are friendly. Better for lunch or early supper than dinner. Closed weekends & Aug. Inexpensive.

Birreria Centrale, Piazza dei Cimatori 2r. There's a dearth of decent places to eat (and drink) at a reasonable price right in the city centre. This spot, on a tiny piazza just west of Via dei Calzaiuoli, is a notable exception. It offers snacks, beers and light meals in an old-fashioned room scattered with wooden cabinets and antiques. The interior gets cramped later on, but in summer the tables spill out onto the piazza. Closed Sun. Inexpensive to moderate.

Coco Lezzone, Via del Parioncino 26r, corner of Via del Purgatorio (☎055.287.178). Stumble on this back-street place and you'd swear you'd found one of the great old-world Florentine trattorias. The prices tell a different story, for the place has long attracted slumming politicians, actors and captains of industry. Don't let this put you off, as the food is good and about as Florentine as you'll find: try the *zuppa di lampredotto*, soup made from a veal calf's stomach. Fresh fish is a feature on Fridays. Closed Sun and mid-July to mid-Aug. Moderate to expensive.

Da Ganino, Piazza dei Cimatori 4r, off Via Dante Alighieri (☎055.214.125). One of only a handful of places close to the central Via dei Calzaiuoli. Produces good home-made pastas and desserts; *osteria* atmosphere, *ristorante* prices. In summer, when tables are moved out onto the tiny square, it's essential to book.

Il Latini, Via dei Palchetti 6r (☎055.210.916). Once a trattoria of the old school, the almost legendary *Latini* is now something of a caricature. It still looks the part – hams hanging from the ceiling, family photos on the wall, simple tables and old rush chairs. Food quality, though, is now average at best (the *bistecca* is an honourable exception), and prices well above those of most *trattorie*. Old regulars still eat here, but you'll find the queues in the evenings (booking is difficult) are full of misguided foreigners. Closed Mon & lunch Tues. Moderate.

La Bussola, Via Porta Rossa 58r. Fashionable restaurant-pizzeria with a wonderful long marble bar – handy for the single diner – and exhaustive menu ranging from antipasto to liqueur. Conveniently stays open until past 2am every night except Mon. Inexpensive.

Nuti, Borgo San Lorenzo 39r (☎055.210.410). Massive place that claims to be the oldest trattoria-pizzeria in town; the menu isn't limited to pizzas and prices are reasonable – though the service often isn't. Closed Sun except in summer. Inexpensive.

Santa Croce

Baldovino, Via San Giuseppe 22r (☎055.241.773). *Baldovino* is a superb place, and what makes it more remarkable is the fact that it's run by a charming young Scottish couple. This accounts for the trendy and not-quite Italian look of the place, and for a welcoming atmosphere that sees the place packed with Italians and foreigners alike (be sure to book in the evening). It's known for its pizzas, made in a wood-fired oven according to Neapolitan principles, but the menu is full of excellent Tuscan and Italian dishes. Closed Mon. Moderate.

Benvenuto, Via della Mosca 15r, corner Via de' Neri. *Benvenuto* has been around for years and maintains its reputation for low prices. It may not be a hugely memorable experience food-wise, but you can't go wrong here if all you want is a cheap trattoria-quality meal just a couple of minutes' walk from Piazza della Signora. Closed Wed & Sun. Inexpensive.

Caffè Italiano, Via Isole delle Stinche 11–13r (☎055.289.368). The success of the *Caffè Italiano* bar off Via dei Calzaiuoli (see p.142) prompted the opening of this restaurant "complex", which consists of an informal restaurant-wine bar, a smarter and more expensive restaurant, and a smaller room for lunch round the corner at Via della Vigna Vecchia 2. All the rooms are medieval in appearance: the lunch spot, in particular, with its battered marble tables, looks the part of an old trattoria to perfection. Food is Tuscan and first-rate. Closed Mon. Moderate.

Cibreo, Via de' Macci 118r (☎055.234.1100). First Florentine port-of-call for all self-respecting foodies. *Cibreo* has achieved fame well beyond the city, the original restaurant having spawned a café, trattoria and shop. The recipe for success is simple: superb food with a creative take on Tuscan classics, in a tasteful dining room with friendly and professional service. Prices are set for each course: *primi* L20,000, main L20,000 and sensational puddings at L15,000. You'll need to book days in advance and probably specify a preferred time for dinner. There's a small trattoria section where no bookings are taken and prices are much lower, but while the food's identical, the surroundings are a touch spartan. Closed Sun–Mon & Aug. Expensive.

Danny Rock, Via Pandolfini 13. Looks a bit like a fast-food place with its green metal chairs but employs a French cook who creates marvellous crepes, among other things; large suspended screens show concerts and sporting events. Evenings only. Inexpensive.

Enotecca Pinchiorri, Via Ghibellina 87 (☎055.242.777). No one seriously disputes the *Pinchiorri*'s claim to be Florence's best restaurant, certainly not Michelin, who've given it two of their coveted rosettes. The food is as you'd expect given the plaudits, but the ceremony that surrounds its presentation does strike many as excessive. Choose from 80,000 different wines, including some of the rarest and most expensive vintages on the planet. None of this comes cheap – you could easily spend L250,000 per person – but there's nowhere better for the never-to-be repeated Florentine treat. Closed Mon & Wed lunch, all day Sun & Aug. Very expensive.

Osteria de' Benci, Via de' Benci 13r (☎055.234.4923). First choice in the Santa Croce area after *Baldovino* for a good, modern and reasonably priced *osteria* not yet overrun by tourists. The single dining room is pretty and pleasant, tables have paper tablecloths and you eat off earthy, ceramic plates. The outside tables in summer, too near the road, are less tempting. The food is excellent, well-cooked standards plus innovative takes on Tuscan classics. Staff are young and friendly, and the atmosphere busy and informal. Closed Sun. Inexpensive to moderate.

Pizzaiuolo, Via de' Macci 113r (☎055.241.171). At first glance this tiny place looks no more than a fall-back for those unable to get into *Cibreo* across the road (see above). In fact, a fair few Florentines reckon the pizzas here are the best in the city. Wines and other menu items have a Neapolitan touch, as does the atmosphere, which is friendly and high-spirited. Booking's a good idea, at least in the evening. Closed Sun & Aug. Inexpensive to moderate.

Oltrarno

Alla Vecchia Bettola, Viale Lodovico Ariosto 32–34r (☎055.224.158). Long trestle tables give this place something of the atmosphere of a drinking den, which is what it once was; the menu boasts a good repertoire of Tuscan meat dishes. Closed Sun & Mon. Moderate.

TICKETS

Tickets and information for a wide range of events can be obtained from the **Box Office** agency, which has outlets at Via Almanni 39 (☎055.210.804) and Chiasso dei Soldanieri 8r, off Via Porta Rossa at the corner with Via de' Tornabuoni (☎055.219.402). There is also a number (☎055.264.321) through which you can arrange to have tickets delivered to your hotel.

Angiolino, Via Santo Spirito 36r (☎055.239.8976). Ambience alone makes *Angiolino* worth a visit – it's one of the city's prettiest trattorias. Dried flowers and chillis hang from the ceiling, and colourful strings of tomatoes and pumpkins festoon the bar. The tablecloths are red chequered, and dozens of wicker-clad Chianti bottles are another nice decorative cliché. The menu is short and to the point, featuring Tuscan classics such *crostini, bistecca, ribollita* and *pappa al pomodoro*. Quality is OK one night, exceptional another. Closed Mon. Inexpensive to moderate.

Borgo Antico, Piazza di Santo Spirito 6r (☎055.210.437). Located on one of the Oltrarno's nicest – and increasingly trendy – piazzas, *Borgo Antico* is often very noisy and very crowded, though in summer the tables outside offer relative peace and quiet. Choose from ten different pizzas, a daily set-price menu or a range of interesting Tuscan standards. Salads here are particularly good, and there's often a selection of fresh fish and seafood pastas. Servings – on the restaurant's famous huge plates – are generous to a fault. Open daily. Inexpensive to moderate.

Casalinga, Via del Michelozzo 9r (☎055.218.624). Located in a small side street off Piazza di Santa Spirito, this long-established, family-run trattoria serves up some of the best low-cost Tuscan dishes in town. Fills up with regulars and a good few outsiders, and the paper tablecloths, wine by the jug and brisk service are all as you'd expect. Closed Sun & Aug.

Dante, Piazza Nazario Sauro 10r (☎055.293.215). Popular and very good pizzeria that also serves around a dozen types of pasta. Closed Wed. Inexpensive.

Osteria Santo Spirito, Piazza di Santo Spirito 16r-Via Sant' Agostino (☎055.238.2383). Run by the same people who own the *Borgo Antico*, this *osteria* is part of the new wave of Florentine restaurants. Informal and modern, its walls are painted deep red and blue, and the lighting is bright over hearty Tuscan dishes presented with contemporary flair. Tables are on two floors, and in summer you can eat outdoors on the piazza. Set menus and daily specials are available, and there's no problem ordering a snack or single course. Open daily. Inexpensive to moderate.

Quattro Leoni, Via dei Vellutini 1r-Piazza della Passera (☎055.218.562). A young, relaxed place arranged around a three-roomed medieval interior. The beams are hung with dried flowers, and splashy modern paintings are strung across the rough stone walls. In summer you can also eat under vast canvas umbrellas outdoors in the piazza. A sign saying "We Only Serve Full Meals", meaning a minimum of two courses, points you to the *Caffè degli Artigiani* across the square if all you want is a snack. The menu is very Florentine (the *antipasti* stand out) and you'll usually find one or two interesting seasonal variations amidst the standards. Closed Aug & Wed in winter. Moderate.

Nightlife and cultural events

Florence has a reputation for catering primarily to the middle-aged and affluent, but like every university town it has its pockets of activity, and by hanging around the San Marco area you should pick up news of any impromptu term-time events. Full details of the city's dependable venues are given below; for up-to-the-minute **information** about what's on, call in at Box Office (see box above), the Via Cavour tourist office or pick up a copy of *Firenze Spettacolo* (L3000), a monthly listings magazine available from Feltrinelli (p.155) and bigger news kiosks. Tickets for most events are available at the offices and agencies listed in the box below.

Florence's cultural impresarios make a good job of ensuring that the city doesn't ossify. Art exhibitions are held all through the year in various galleries and palazzi, and seasons of opera, theatre and ballet performances punctuate the year, as do one-off concerts of classical music, folk and jazz. In addition to Box Office, you can usually find information in

English about concerts and shows at tourist offices or the agencies listed in the box below; otherwise, keep your eyes peeled for advertising posters.

The streets of central Florence are generally safe at night, but women should not stroll through the red-light districts alone – the station area, Piazza Santissima Annunziata and Piazza Ognissanti have a particularly dodgy reputation, and kerb-crawling is prevalent on the *viali*, the wide avenues circling the centre. Lone tourists of either gender should stay well clear of the Cascine park at night.

Live music

Many clubs and discos (see below) have **live bands** during the week, or before the DJs take over later in the evening. Check listings magazines, but don't expect much more than some small-time local outfit running though its repertoire. The places listed below are more likely to stick with the bigger names or at least decent acts. Bars recommended elsewhere in the guide where you might also hear live music include *Dolce Vita* (see p.144), *Il Caffè* (see p.143), *Pongo* (see opposite) and *Rex* (see p.144); also check the listings under "Clubs and Discos".

Auditorium Flog, Via Michele Mercati 24 (☎055.490.437). *Flog* is one of the city's best-known mid-sized venues, and a perennial student favourite for all forms of live music (and DJs), but particularly local indie-type bands. It's usually packed, despite being out in the northern suburbs at Il Poggetto – to get here take buses #8, #14, #20 or #28. Opening times vary.

Be Bop, Via dei Servi 28r. No phone. A rather classy rock, jazz and blues bar with bow-tied bar staff and *faux* Art Nouveau decor. Handily placed close to the university district between the duomo and Santissima Annunziata, and often full of local students as a result. No dance floor as such – this is more a place to sit and chill out to the music. Opening times vary.

Chiodo Fisso, Via Dante Alighieri 16r (☎055.238.1290). A good and very central spot for listening to folk, solo guitarists and the occasional jazz musicians – the wine's good as well. Open nightly 9pm till late.

Eskimo, Via dei Canacci 12r, off Via della Scala (no phone). A small but well-established club close to Santa Maria Novella with live music every night. Acts tend to be small-scale – typically Italian solo singers or trios – but the atmosphere is pleasant and you may catch the odd theatre event (punters are occasionally let loose to try their hand on stage). Tues–Sun 9.30pm–3.30am.

Jazz Club, Via Nuova de' Caccini 3 (☎055.247.9700). Florence's foremost jazz venue has been a fixture for some years. The L10,000 "membership" fee gets you into the brick-vaulted basement, where there's live music most nights and an open jam session on Tuesdays. Cocktails are good, and you can also snack on *focaccia* and a range of desserts. Located in a tiny side street a block south of Via degli Alfani at the corner with Borgo Pinti. Tues–Sat 9.30pm–1.30/2.30am.

Kikuya, Via de' Benci 43r (☎055.234.4879). *Kikuya* affects the look and feel of a pub – after a fashion – with brick-vaulted ceiling and red velvet bar stools and banquettes. It's also tiny, which is why it restricts its live music to solo and acoustic acts. Not a bad place for a beer close to Santa Croce. Happy hour 7–10pm: drinks *and* sandwiches are half-price. Mon & Wed–Sun 7pm till late. Closed Tues.

Tenax, Via Pratese (☎055.308.160). *Tenax* is way out near the airport at Peretola, but it's the city's leading venue for new and established bands as well as big-name international acts on the Florentine leg of their European tour. Keep an eye open for posters around town or call at the tourist office for upcoming gigs. The place is enormous and doubles as a disco – a dance session follows every band. There are ranks of bars, pool tables, computer games and plenty of seating on several levels. Tues–Sun 9pm–4am. Bus #29 or #30.

Clubs and discos

Put together balmy summer evenings, a big student population and Florence's huge summer surge of young travellers, and you have a recipe for a happening **club scene**. Not that clubs in the city, or elsewhere in Italy for that matter, resemble their London equivalents. For one thing, most Florentines aren't in clubs to dance or drink – they're there to see and be seen. Foreigners have had an influence, however, and one or two clubs now have a more dedicated and sweaty atmosphere.

Faced with a low income from the bar, most clubs charge a fairly stiff admission – reckon on L25,000 and up for the better-known places – which often includes one or two drinks. Prices at the bar after that are usually pretty steep. Another, more insidious procedure involves a card that gets stamped every time you spend money at the bar. By the end of the night you have to have spent a minimum sum – or you pay the difference before the bouncers will let you out. Alternatively, the card may be used to run a tab, with the bill settled (in cash) at the end of the evening.

Opening hours for clubs and discos are rarely set, though the weekly closed day, if there is one, probably won't vary. Clubs are also notoriously prone to reopening under different names. We've tried to list the established ones, but consult *Firenze Spettacolo* for up-to-the-minute hot spots.

Andromeda, Via dei Cimatori 13 (☎055.292.002). One of the most central clubs, and consequently one of the most popular with foreigners. The place is heaving at weekends. The look changes each year, while the music covers all bases from bland Euro-dance to Caribbean. Admission around L25,000. Closed Mon.

Central Park, Parco delle Cascine (no phone). One of the city's best clubs, with adventurous music from DJs who know what they're doing, and deliver through a superb sound system. A card system operates for drinks, but the minimum spend of L15,000 is more reasonable than most places. Don't wander around the park outside on your own. Midnight till late.

Full Up, Via della Vigna Vecchia 21r (☎055.293.006). Situated close to the Bargello, this is another of the city's major central cubs, and something of a night-time institution. Popular with foreigners, local students and a slightly older Florentine set. Music is fairly anodyne dance stuff, and decor is of the mirror-and-flashing-light disco variety. Admission usually free until midnight and L10,000 after that; around L15,000 for most drinks. Closed Sun–Mon & June–Sept.

Jaragua, Via dell'Erta Canina 12r (☎055.234.6543). Toss aside your inhibitions at this disco with a Latin-American feel. If you want to learn the moves, dance lessons are often available – call for details. Open daily until 3am.

Meccanò, Viale degli Olmi 1–Piazzale delle Cascine (☎055.331.371). Florence's most famous disco and one of its longest-running. The place is labyrinthine, with a trio of lounge and bar areas, and a small, packed dance floor. In summer, when the action spills out of doors, you can cool off in the gardens bordering the Parco delle Cascine. The stiff L30,000 admission (less during the week) includes your first drink. Closed Sun–Mon & Wed, plus two weeks in August.

Pongo, Via Giuseppe Verdi 59r (☎055.234.7880). Located close to Santa Croce, within staggering distance of the city centre. In the afternoon you can sit in the bar and watch satellite TV or fiddle around for free on the Internet. On weekday evenings there's a theme night or – more usually – live music. DJs are some of the city's best, especially if your thing is jungle or drum 'n' bass. Admission is free, but there's a minimum L10,000 spend at the bar before they'll let you out. Bar opens 4.30pm; happy hour 7pm; club 10.30pm till late. Closed Sun & June–Sept.

Space Electronic, Via Palazzuolo 37 (☎055.293.082). Claims to be the largest disco in Europe. True or not, it's got all the clichés you'd expect of a massive Continental club – lasers, glass dance floors and mirrored walls – though the music is surprisingly good. Hipper-than-thou clubbers might be sniffy about the place, but it's popular with foreigners and fine if all you want to do is dance. Admission is L25,000. Daily 10pm till late. Closed Mon in winter.

GAY VENUES

Florence's history is peppered with the names of some of history's greatest gay and bisexual artists – Michelangelo, Leonardo and Botticelli, among others – and the city is, for the most part, tolerant and welcoming for gay and lesbian visitors. The leading gay **bar** is the men-only *Crisco*, Via Sant'Egidio 43r (☎055.248.0580), which is open to members only, though temporary membership is usually available at the door (Mon & Wed–Sun 10pm till late). Another major **club** is the *Tabasco*, Piazza Santa Cecilia 3r (☎055.213.000), daily 10pm till late.

Classical music

Classical music in Florence abounds and is outstanding, with the famous **Maggio Musicale**, Italy's oldest and most prestigious music festival, being the most high profile of several festivals and concert seasons held at venues across the city. The orchestras and associations listed below organize **concerts**, as do churches and theatres such as the Teatro Comunale. Organ recitals are held in the Lutheran church on Lungarno Torrigiani (currently on Wed), while the Lyceum at Via degli Alfani 48, lays on weekly chamber recitals (currently Mon).

For **information** on all events contact the tourist office (p.69), consult listings in the *La Nazione* newspaper and *Firenze Spettacolo*, or keep your eyes peeled for posters outside theatres, churches and elsewhere. **Tickets** for most events can usually be bought from the Box Office outlets (see box on p.149) or individual venues.

Amici della Musica, Via G. Sirtori 49 (☎055.608.420 or 055.607.440). The "Friends of Music" – one of Florence's leading musical associations – organizes a season of chamber concerts with top-name international performers from Jan–April and Oct–Dec. Most concerts take place on Saturday or Sunday at 4pm or 9pm. The vast majority are held in the Teatro della Pergola, built in 1656 and believed to be Italy's oldest theatre. Tickets (L14,000–35,000) and information from Box Office or Teatro della Pergola, Via della Pergola 18 (☎055.247.9651).

Associazione Giovanile Musicale, Via della Piazzuola 7r (☎055.580.996). The A.GI.MUS is devoted to young musicians and holds concerts throughout the year, often in wonderful settings: two of the best are the Concerti di Pasqua, a series of Easter concerts usually held in the church of Orsanmichele, and the Festival Estate, a summer festival held in July in the courtyard of the Palazzo Pitti. Tickets and information from Box Office outlets (see p.149).

Estate Fiesolana. Slightly less high profile and exclusive than the Maggio Musicale, the Estate Fiesolana is a festival that concentrates more on chamber and symphonic music. It's held in Fiesole every summer, usually from June to late August. Films and theatre are also featured, and most events are held in the open-air Teatro Romano. Call ☎055.219.851 for information.

Filarmonica di Firenze G. Rossini, The main concert season of this Florence-based orchestra is in January and February, but it also performs a series of outdoor concerts in June in Piazza della Signoria. Call ☎0338.845.8117 for information.

Maggio Musicale Fiorentino. The highlight of Florence's cultural calendar, the Maggio Musicale Fiorentino is one of Europe's leading festivals of opera and classical music; confusingly, it isn't restricted to May (*Maggio*), but lasts from late April to early July. The festival has its own orchestra, chorus and ballet company, plus guest appearances from foreign ensembles. Events are staged at the Teatro Comunale (or its Teatro Piccolo), the Teatro della Pergola, the Palazzo dei Congressi, the Teatro Verdi and occasionally in the Boboli Gardens. Information and tickets (L25,000–200,000) can be obtained from the Teatro Comunale (see below).

Orchestra Historica di Firenze, Via Palazzuolo 17 (☎0348.602.6167). A new venture in which leading musicians in period dress perform in the beautifully restored Oratorio di San Bernardino. A linked ballet company performs period dance on the same evenings. Concerts are held every few days, April–Sept. Tickets L40,000–60,000.

Orchestra da Camera Fiorentina, Via Enrico Poggi (☎055.783.374). The Florence Chamber Orchestra has a season of concerts and organizes performances by visiting orchestras, quartets and soloists between March and October. Held two or three times weekly at 9pm, they take place in the wonderful setting of Orsanmichele or the Badia Fiorentina. Tickets (from L20,000) are available from Box Office, or from the venues up to an hour before each performance.

Orchestra Regionale Toscana, Via de' Benci 20 (☎055242.767 or 055.234.7355). Tuscany's regional orchestra has its headquarters in Florence, and plays one or two concerts a month in the city during its Dec–May season. Performances are held in the Teatro Verdi at 9pm, usually on a Saturday or Wednesday. Tickets (L10,000–25,000) from Box Office or the Teatro Verdi, Via Ghibellina 99–101 (☎055.212.320 or 055.281.792).

Teatro Comunale, Corso Italia 16 (☎055.27.791 or 055.211.158). The dreary looking Teatro Comunale is Florence's main municipal theatre, and as such hosts many of the city's major classical music, dance and theatre productions. It also has its own orchestra, chorus and dance company whose reputation attracts top-name international guest performers. The main season (concerts, opera and ballet) runs Jan–April and Sept–Dec, with concerts usually held on Friday, Saturday and Sunday evenings.

FLORENCE'S FESTIVALS

Florence's various cultural festivals are covered in the previous sections; what follows is a rundown on its more folkloric events.

Scoppio del Carro

The first major folk festival of the year is Easter Sunday's **Scoppio del Carro** (Explosion of the Cart), when a cartload of fireworks is hauled by six white oxen from the Porta a Prato to the duomo; there, during the Gloria of the midday Mass, the whole lot is set off by a "dove" that whizzes down a wire from the high altar. The origins of this incendiary descent of the Holy Spirit lie with one Pazzino de' Pazzi, leader of the Florentine contingent on the First Crusade. On getting back to Florence he was entrusted with the care of the flame of Holy Saturday, an honorary office which he turned into something more festive by rigging up a ceremonial wagon to transport the flame round the city. His descendants continued to manage the festival until the Pazzi conspiracy of 1478, which of course lost them the office. Since then, the city authorities have taken care of business.

Festa del Grillo

On the first Sunday after Ascension Day (forty days after Easter), the **Festa del Grillo** (Festival of the Cricket) is held in the Cascine park. In amongst the stalls and the picnickers you'll find people selling tiny wooden cages containing crickets, which are then released onto the grass – a ritual that may hark back to the days when farmers had to scour their land for locusts, or to the tradition of men placing a cricket on the door of their lovers to serenade them.

St John's Day and the Calcio Storico

The saint's day of **John the Baptist**, Florence's patron, is June 24 – the occasion for a massive fireworks display up on Piazzale Michelangelo, and for the first game of the **Calcio Storico**. Played in sixteenth-century costume to perpetuate the memory of a game played during the siege of 1530, this uniquely Florentine mayhem is a three-match series played in this last week of June, with fixtures usually held in Piazza Santa Croce (scene of that first match) and Piazza della Signoria. Each of the four historic quarters fields a team, Santa Croce playing in green, San Giovanni in red, Santa Maria Novella in blue and Santo Spirito in grossly impractical white. Prize for the winning side is a calf, which gets roasted in a street party after the tournament and shared among the four teams and the inhabitants of the winning quarter.

Festa delle Rificolone

The **Festa delle Rificolone** (Festival of the Lanterns) takes place on the Virgin's birthday, September 7, with a procession of children to Piazza Santissima Annunziata. Each child carries a coloured paper lantern with a candle inside it – a throwback to the days when people from the surrounding countryside would troop by lantern light into the city for the Feast of the Virgin. The procession is followed by a parade of floats and street parties.

Festa dell'Unità

October's **Festa dell'Unità** is part of a nationwide celebration run by the Italian communists. Florence's is the biggest event after Bologna's, with loads of political stalls and restaurant-marquees. Box Office will have details of venues, while news about the *Feste* and other political events in Florence can be found in *Anteprima*, a local supplement published with Friday's edition of the communist daily *L'Unità*.

Theatre

If your Italian is up to a performance of the plays of Machiavelli or Pirandello in the original, Florence's **theatres** offer year-round entertainment, some of it riskier than the generally conservative repertoire of the city's concert halls and musical associations. In addition to the places listed below, various halls and disused churches are enlisted for one-off performances – keep an eye out for posters, or drop into Box Office or the tourist office for latest information.

Teatro Comunale, Corso Italia 16 (☎055.277.9236). Florence's principal performance space hosts theatre productions as well as dance and classical music concerts (see p.152); offerings here are usually mainstream. Located west of Ognissanti off Lungarno Amerigo Vespucci.

Teatro Niccolini, Via Ricasoli 3 (☎055.239.6653). This is one of the oldest theatres in town, but its repertoire has a decidedly modern look, featuring a mixture of innovative Italian works and classics of contemporary drama. The season runs from October to May.

Teatro della Pergola, Via della Pergola 18 (☎055.247.9651). The beautiful little Pergola is Florence's main classical theatre, and plays host to some of the best-known Italian companies. Productions are usually Italian, or foreign classics in translation. The season runs from October to May. Box office Tues–Sat 9.30am–1pm & 3.45–6.45pm, Sun 9.45am–noon.

Teatro Verdi, Via Ghibellina 99–101 (☎055.212.320). Productions at the Teatro Verdi, another of the city's premier venues, are more or less similar to the mainstream fare of the Teatro Comunale, though you may also catch the odd musical show. Box office 10am–noon & 4–7pm.

Cinema

Florence has a large number of **cinemas**, but very few show subtitled films, and nearly all English-language films are dubbed. See *Firenze Spettacolo* or the listings pages of *La Nazione* for locations and latest screenings. Only one cinema has regular English-language screenings (promoted as *versione originale*), though cinema clubs and more go-ahead mainstream cinemas are gradually realizing the city's foreign tourists and language students offer a ready market for such films (see below for details).

Florence has two major **film festivals**: *Under Florence* (first two weeks of December), which shows Tuscan and other Italian independent films and videos, and the more earnest *Festival dei Popoli* (two weeks in November or December), run by an academic institution concerned with documentary film and its connection with socio-anthropological research. For information on both events contact the Cinema Alfieri Atelier, Via dell'Ulivo 6 (☎055.240.720).

Astro, Piazza San Simeone-Via Isola delle Stinche (near Santa Croce). No phone. Florence's English-language-only cinema; restoration has slightly improved its ramshackle village-hall atmosphere. Usually two shows nightly, six days a week. Tickets L8000, L6000 on Wednesdays or with student ID. Closed Mon.

Cinema Goldoni, Via dei Serragli 109 (☎055.222.437). Towards the Porta Romana, so it's a long way to come for the weekly English-language night (currently Wed). The shows are popular, however, so turn up early to be sure of a seat. Closed June & July. L12,000.

Odeon Original Sound, Via de' Sassetti 1 (☎055.214.068). Films are screened in their original language at this air-conditioned cinema near Piazza della Repubblica once a week, generally on Monday. Closed mid-June to August. L13,000.

Shopping

If you're after high-quality **clothes** and accessories, paintings, prints and marbled paper, or any number of other beautiful or luxury objects, then you'll find them in Florence – though this is not a city for the bargain-hunter. Its best-known area of manufacturing expertise is leather goods, with top-quality shoes, bags and gloves sold across the city. The main concentration of outlets is around **Via de' Tornabuoni** – the city's premier shopping thoroughfare – and the tributaries of Via degli Strozzi and Via della Vigna Nuova, also home to the shops of Italy's top fashion designers. If their prices are too steep, passable imitations (and outright fakes) can be unearthed at the various **street markets**, of which San Lorenzo is the most central. If you want everything under one roof, there's also a handful of up-market **department stores**. Marbled paper is another Florentine speciality, and, as you'd expect in this arty city, Florence is also one of the best places in the country to pick up books on Italian art, architecture and culture.

Books

Alinari, Via della Vigna Nuova 46–48r (☎055.218.950). Alinari was founded in 1852, making it the world's oldest photographic business. Owners of the best archive of old photographs in Italy – 400,000 glass plates and 700,000 negatives – they will print any image you choose from their huge catalogue. They also publish books, calendars, posters and cards. Daily 10am–7.30pm; closed Mon 9am–1.30pm.

BM, Borgo Ognissanti 4r (☎055.294.575). English-language bookshop with a wide selection of guidebooks and general titles, with particular emphasis on Italian literature in translation, as well as books on Italian art, cookery and travel in Italy. Mon–Sat 9am–1pm & 3.30–7.30pm.

Feltrinelli, Via Cerretani 30r (☎055.238.2652). The city's best overall bookshop, Feltrinelli is part of a modern Italy-wide chain. You'll find most Italian titles here, as well as an excellent selection of maps and guides (downstairs) and other English-language titles: there's also a specialist store for foreign-language material (see below). Mon–Sat 9am–7.30pm.

Feltrinelli International, Via Cavour 12r (☎055.219.524). Bright and well staffed, this is by far the best-organized of the large, central bookshops. The first port of call for English or other foreign-language books, newspapers and videos, as well as posters, cards and magazines. Mon–Sat 9am–7.30pm.

Libreria delle Donne, Via Fiesolana 2b (☎055.240.384). A specialist women's bookshop, though most of the titles are in Italian. The noticeboard here is useful for information regarding women's and lesbian groups in Florence. Mon 3.30–7.30pm, Tues–Sat 9am–1pm & 3.30–7.30pm.

Paperback Exchange, Via Fiesolana 31r (☎055.247.8154). A bit remote – north of Santa Croce – but always has a good stock of English and American books, with the emphasis on Italian-related titles and second-hand stuff; also exchanges second-hand books and has informative and friendly staff. Mon–Fri 9am–7.30pm, Sat 9am–1pm & 3.30–7.30pm.

Seeber, Via de' Tornabuoni 68–70r (☎055.215.697). If Feltrinelli's slick operation isn't to your taste, try Seeber, in the view of many the best general bookshop in the city. The art and antiques section alone has over 10,000 titles, while the foreign-language department is also highly renowned. The shop also stocks the full range of Touring Club of Italy titles and a wide variety of other guides in several languages. Mon–Sat 9.30am–7.30pm.

Clothes

Armani, Via della Vigna Nuova 51r (☎055.219.041). Gorgeous clothes from the most astute designer in Italy, at prices that make you think you must have misread the tag. Mon 3.30–7.30pm, Tues–Sat 10am–7.30pm.

Enrico Coveri, Via della Vigna Nuova 27–29r & Via de' Tornabuoni 81r (☎055.211.263). Born in nearby Prato, Coveri specialized in bold multicoloured outfits that contrasted sharply with the prevailing sobriety of Florentine design – the clothes produced by the firm since his death continue in this vein. Mon 3.30–7.30pm, Tues–Sat 10am–1pm & 3.30–7.30pm.

Emporio Armani, Piazza Strozzi 14–16r (☎055.284.315). The lowest-priced wing of the Armani empire, this is really only a place to go if you're desperate to get Italy's #1 label on your back. Mon 3.30–7.30pm, Tues–Sat 10am–1pm & 3.30–7.30pm.

Ferragamo, Via de' Tornabuoni 16r (☎055.292.123). Salvatore Ferragamo emigrated to the US at the age of 14 and became the most famous shoemaker in the world, producing everything from pearl-studded numbers for Gloria Swanson to gladiators' sandals for Cecil B. de Mille. Managed by his widow and children, Ferragamo now produces ready-to-wear outfits, but the company's reputation still rests on its beautiful shoes. Mon 3.30–7.30pm, Tues–Sat 9.30am–7.30pm.

Gucci, Via de' Tornabuoni 73r (☎055.264.011). The Gucci empire was founded at no. 73, which remains the flagship showroom; everything is impeccably made, but even if it weren't, the demand for the linked Gs would probably keep going under its own steam. Mon 3.30–7.30pm, Tues–Sat 9.30am–7.30pm.

Pucci, showroom at Via dei Pucci 6, shop at Via della Vigna Nuova 97r (☎055.294.028). The Pucci family was one of the city's mercantile dynasties, until Marchese Emilio Pucci stunned the fashion world of the 1950s with his vivid, swirling-patterned silks. In 1990, Pucci was the London club-land uniform, and the £400 shirts sold so fast that supply couldn't keep up. The wave has since broken, but the Pucci name still carries considerable clout. Mon 3.30–7.30pm, Tues–Sat 9am–1pm & 3.30–7.30pm.

Department stores

Coin, Via dei Calzaiuoli 56r (☎055.280.531). Clothes-dominated chain store in an excellent central position. Quality is generally high, though styles are fairly conservative except for one or two youth-orientated franchises on the ground floor. Also a good place for linen and other household goods. Mon–Sat 9.30am–8pm, Sun 11am–8pm.

Rinascente, Piazza della Repubblica 1 (☎055.239.8544). Like Coin, Rinascente is part of a country-wide chain, though this store, opened in 1996, is a touch more up-market than its nearby rival. Sells clothing, linen, cosmetics, household goods and other staples. Mon–Sat 9am–9pm, Sun 10.30am–8pm.

Food and drink

Pastificio La Bolognese, Via de' Serragali 24 (☎055.282.318). Come here towards the end of your trip to pick some of the city's best fresh home-made pasta to take home: the variations and specialities are almost endless – truffle pastas and black squids' ink spaghetti are ones to think about. Daily 7am–1pm & 4.30–7.30pm; closed Wed 7am–1pm.

Vera, Piazza de' Frescobaldi 3r (☎055.215.465). Gastronomic heaven: cheese from across Tuscany and the rest of Italy (as well as France), plus a huge range of dried and fresh pastas and all the other great Italian culinary staples, truffles included. You could put together anything from a gourmet picnic to a full five-course dinner with what's on sale here. Daily 8am–8pm; closed Wed afternoon.

Jewellery

The whole **Ponte Vecchio** is crammed with jewellers' shops, most of them catering strictly to the financial stratosphere. Those of more limited means could either take a chance on the counterfeits and low-cost originals peddled by the street vendors on and around the bridge, or check out the places below.

Bijoux Cascio, Via de' Tornabuoni 32r & Via Por Santa Maria 1r. Cascio has made a name for itself over the last 30 years as a maker of imitation jewellery. It takes a trained eye to distinguish much of the stuff from that displayed in the windows on the Ponte Vecchio. Mon 3.30–7.30pm, Tues–Sat 9.30am–1pm & 3.30–7.30pm.

Gatto Bianco, Borgo SS. Apostoli 12r (☎055.282.989). Strange combinations of precious and everyday materials are the signature of this outlet, one of the city's more adventurous jewellery workshops. Mon 3.30–7.30pm, Tues–Sat 9.30am–1pm & 3.30–7.30pm.

Torrini, Piazza del Duomo 10r (☎055.230.2401). Torrini registered its trademark – a distinctive half-clover leaf with spur – as early as 1369. Seven centuries later this store remains one of the premier places to buy Florentine jewellery: gold predominates, but all manner of classic and modern pieces are available, at a price. Mon 3.30–7.30pm, Tues–Sat 9.30am–1pm & 3.30–7.30pm.

Maps and guides

Geografica, Via dei Cimatori 16r (☎055.239.6637). Not only is this Florence's best source of maps, it's the only shop in Italy dedicated to supplying the otherwise highly elusive official Italian 1:25,000 *Istituto Geografico Militare* (Ordnance Survey) series, essential for hiking anywhere away from the most popular areas. Mon–Sat 10am–1pm & 4–7.30pm.

Il Viaggio, Borgo degli Albizi 41r (☎055.240.489). Offers plenty of walking maps, including some *Geografico Militare* sheets, plus a superb selection of guides in English and Italian to Florence,

Tuscany, Italy and the rest of the world. Also an agent for the Italian Alpine Club and Touring Club of Italy. There's also a selection of general travel literature in English and Italian. Mon 3.30–7.30pm, Tues–Sat 9.30am–1pm & 7.30pm.

Markets

Cascine, Parco del Cascine. The biggest of all Florence's markets happens Tuesday morning at the Cascine park near the banks of the Arno (bus #1, 9, 12 or 17c), where hundreds of stallholders set up an alfresco budget-class department store. Fewer tourists make it out here than to San Lorenzo, so prices are keener. Clothes (some second-hand) and shoes are the best bargains, though for cheaper still, you should check out the weekday morning stalls at **Piazza delle Cure**, just beyond Piazza della Libertà (bus #1 or #7), Tues 8am–1pm.

San Lorenzo, Piazza di San Lorenzo. The market around **San Lorenzo** church is another open-air warehouse of cheap clothing, with fake brands accounting for a large percentage of turnover. San Lorenzo is as well organized as a shopping mall: huge waterproof awnings ensure that the weather can't stop the trading, and some of the stallholders even accept credit cards. You'll find plenty of leather jackets, T-shirts and other cheap clothes: it may be what you're looking for, but it may not be that much of bargain. For anything pricey, try to haggle. Daily 9am–7pm.

Mercato Centrale, Piazza del Mercato Centrale. Europe's largest indoor food hall is situated at the heart of the stall-filled streets around San Lorenzo. Great for picnic supplies, but it's well worth a sightseeing and people-watching visit whether you intend to buy anything or not. See also p.116. Mon–Fri 7am–2pm, plus Sat afternoon in winter.

Mercato Nuovo, Loggia del Mercato Nuovo. The Mercato Nuovo, or Mercato del Porcellino market, just to the west of Piazza della Signoria, is the main emporium for straw hats, plastic *David*s and the like. See also p.104. Mon–Sat 9am–7pm.

Piazza dei Ciompi, Piazza dei Ciompi. A flea market, stacked with antiques and bric-a-brac, is pitched every day in Piazza dei Ciompi, near the Sant'Ambrogio food market; you'll also see it referred to as the Mercato dei Pulci (*pulci* – fleas). Mon–Sat 9am–7pm. More serious antique dealers swell the ranks on the last Sunday of each month, from 9am to 7pm.

Music

Alberti, Via de' Pucci 16r. & Borgo S. Lorenzo 45–49r (☎055.284.346). Founded in 1873, this is the city's leading supplier of domestic hi-fi, videos, records and CDs. The Via de' Pucci shop concentrates on contemporary music (dance, rock etc), while the Borgo San Lorenzo store is devoted to opera, classical and jazz. Mon 3.30–7.30pm, Tues–Sat 9.30am–1pm & 3.30–7.30pm.

Kaos, Via della Scala 65r (☎055.282.643). Right now this is the city's trendiest shop for rock, pop and all other genres, as well as obscure imports and half-forgotten vinyl offerings from decades past. Mon 3.30–7.30pm, Tues–Sat 10am–1pm & 3.30–7.30pm.

Paper and stationery

Giannini, Piazza Pitti 37r (☎055.212.621). Established in 1856, this paper-making and book-binding firm has been honoured with exhibitions dedicated to its work. Once the only place in Florence to make its own marbled papers, it now offers a wide variety of diaries, address books and so forth as well. Mon–Sat 9am–7.30pm.

Pineider, Piazza della Signoria 13r & Via de' Tornabuoni 76r (☎055.284.655 or 055.211.605). Florence's gentry would rather die than use anything except Pineider's colour co-ordinated calling cards, handmade papers and envelopes. Napoleon, Stendhal, Byron and Shelley are just a few past customers. Mon 3.30–7.30pm, Tues–Sat 10am–1pm & 3.30–7.30pm.

Il Torchio, Via de' Bardi 17 (☎055.234.2862). A marbled paper workshop that beats many competitors by charging slightly lower prices. Several of the manufacturing techniques are known only to the owner, Signora Anna. Desk accessories, diaries, albums and other items in paper and leather are also available. Mon–Fri 9am–1pm & 3.30–7.30pm, Sat 9.30am–1pm.

Perfume and toiletries

Farmacia Santa Maria Novella, Via della Scala 16 (☎055.216.276). Occupying the pharmacy of the Santa Maria Novella monastery, this sixteenth-century shop was founded by Dominican monks as an outlet for their potions, ointments and herbal remedies. Many of these are still available, including distillations of flowers and herbs, together with face-creams, shampoos, and other more esoteric products. The shop's as famous for its wonderful interior as for its products, which are sold worldwide. Mon 3.30–7.30pm, Tues–Sat 9.30am–1pm & 3.30–7.30pm.

Prints and engravings

Giovanni Baccani, Via della Vigna Nuova 75r (☎055.214.467). You'll see prints and engravings in shops across Florence, but nowhere is the selection as mouthwatering as in Baccani, a beautiful old shop established in 1903, that's crammed with all manner of prints, frames and paintings. Prices range from a few thousand lire into the realms of credit card madness. Mon 3.30–7.30pm, Tues–Sat 9am–1pm & 3.30–7.30pm.

Shoes and accessories

Beltrami, Via de' Tornabuoni 48r (☎055.287.779). Department store selling high-fashion, high-priced shoes, bags, leather, and other clothes for men and women. Mon 3.30–7.30pm, Tues–Sat 9.30am–1pm & 3.30–7.30pm.

Cellerini, Via del Sole 37r (☎055.282.533). Bags, bags and more bags. Everything here is made on the premises under the supervision of the firm's founders, the city's premier exponents of the craft; bags don't come more elegant, durable – or costly. Mon 3.30–7.30pm, Tues–Sat 9.30am–1pm & 3.30–7.30pm.

Desmo, Piazza de' Rucellai 10r (☎055.292.395). Desmo sells virtually every item of clothing and accessory (shoes, belts, bags, wallets, umbrellas) you can imagine – as long they're in leather. The designs combine established classics with more up-to-date contemporary items. Mon 3.30–7.30pm, Tues–Sat 9.30am–7.30pm.

Eusebio, Via del Corso 5r (☎055.292.917). Bargain shoes for men and women, though you'll have to wade through a lot of tat before you uncover any gems. Mon 3–8pm, Tues–Sat 10am–1pm & 3–8pm.

Francesco da Firenze, Via Santo Spirito 62r. (☎055.212.428). Handmade shoes for men and women at very reasonable prices. Designs combine classical footwear with striking designs: the workshop supplies UK chain Hobbs with some if its shoes. Mon–Sat 8.30am–1pm & 3–7.30pm.

Madova, Via Guicciardini 1r (☎055.239.6526). The last word in gloves – every colour, every size, every shape. Mon–Sat 9am–7pm.

Listings

Airlines Air France, Borgo SS Apostoli 9 (☎055.284.304 or 055.308.538); Alitalia, Lungarno Acciaiuoli 10–12r. (☎055.27.881 or 055.278.809; international flight information toll-free on 1678.65642); British Airways, Pisa Airport (☎050.40.866); Lufthansa, Piazza Antinori 2 (☎055.301.375 or 238.1455/6/7); Meridiana, Lungarno Soderini 1 (☎055.32.961 or 055.230.2334); TWA, Via dei Vecchietti 4 (☎055.284.691); United Airlines, Via dei Vecchietti 4 (☎055.289.460).

Airport information Aeroporto Galileo Galilei, Pisa (☎050.500.707 or 050.28.088); information also from the check-in desk at Santa Maria Novella train station, platform 5 (daily 7am–8pm). Peretola-Amerigo Vespucci airport, Via del Termine 11 (☎055.30.615 or 055.373.498): domestic flights ☎055.306.1700; international flights ☎055.306.1702; lost luggage ☎055.373.498.

American Express Via Dante Alighieri 22r (Mon–Fri 9am–5.30pm, Sat 9am–12.30pm; ☎055.50.981, fax 055.509.8220).

Banks and exchange Florence's main bank branches are on or around Piazza della Repubblica, but exchange booths (*cambio*) and ATM cash card machines (*bancomat*) for Visa, Mastercard and Eurocheque advances can be found across the city. Banks generally open Mon–Fri 8.20am–1.20pm and 2.35–3.35pm, though some are open longer hours.

Bike rental Alinari, Via Guelfa 85r (Mon–Sat 9am–1pm and 3–7.30pm, Sun 10am–1pm and 3–7pm, closed Sun in winter; ☎055.280.500). Bikes are L4000 hourly, L12,000 per five hours, L20,000 daily and L40,000 for a weekend (Friday afternoon to Sunday). The same basic rates at Florence by Bike, Via San Zanobi 120–122r (daily 9am–7.30pm in summer; ☎055.488.992), which has a huge variety, plus electric bikes (L10,000 an hour), electric scooters (L45,000 for five hours) and two-person 125cc scooters (L70,000 for five hours). Motorent, Via San Zanobi 9r (daily 8.30am–noon and 2.30–7pm; ☎055.490.113) is marginally cheaper.

Buses Most buses to destinations outside the city (including SITA services to the airport) depart from the bus station immediately west of the train station at Via Santa Caterina da Siena 17. For information contact tourist offices or call the following numbers directly. For city services: ATAF ☎055.565.0222. For services to Peretola airport ☎055.478.2231. For state-run services all over Italy: SITA, Via Santa Caterina di Siena 15 (☎055.483.651 for routes in Tuscany; 055.214.721 for national routes). For services within Tuscany and Umbria: CLAP, Piazza Stazione 15 (☎055.283.734), to Lucca and Lucca province; CAP, Largo Fratelli Alinari 9 (☎055.214.637), to Prato; CAT, Via Fiume 2 (☎055.283.400), to Arezzo, Città di Castello and Sansepolcro; COPIT, Piazza Santa Maria Novella (☎055.215.451), to Pistoia, Poggio a Caiano and Vinci; Lazzi, Piazza Stazione 1 (☎166.845.010), to Empoli, Livorno, Lucca, Pisa, Pistoia, Prato and Viareggio.

Car rental Avis, Borgo Ognissanti 128r (☎055.213.629 or 055.239.8826; airport ☎055.315.558); Europcar, Borgo Ognissanti 53r (☎055.290.437/8; airport ☎055.318.609); Excelsior, Via della Scala 48r (☎055.239.8639 or 055.293.186); Hertz, Via Maso Finiguerra 23r (☎055.239.8205 or 282.260); Italy by Car-Thrifty, Borgo Ognissanti 134r (☎055.287.161 or 055.293.021); Maggiore, Via Maso Finiguerra 31r (☎055.210.238 or 294.578; airport ☎055.311.256); Program, Borgo Ognissanti 135r (☎055.282.916).

Consulates Netherlands, Via Cavour 81 (☎055.475.249); South Africa, Piazza dei Salarelli 1 (no personal callers: telephone appointment essential ☎055.281.863); UK, Lungarno Corsini 2 (☎055.212.594 or 055.284.133); US, Lungarno Amerigo Vespucci 38 (☎055.239.8276). Travellers from Ireland (☎06.697.9121), Australia (☎06.685.2721), New Zealand (☎06.440.2928) and Canada (☎06.445.981) should contact their consulates in Rome.

Doctors The Tourist Medical Service (IAMAT) is a private service used to dealing with foreigners; they have doctors on call 24 hours a day (☎055.475.411), but a visit will cost L90,000 upwards. Alternatively you can visit their clinic at Via Lorenzo il Magnifico 59 (Mon–Fri 11am–noon & 5–6pm, Sat 11am–noon).

Emergencies Police ☎112 or 113; Fire ☎115; Car breakdown ☎116; First aid ☎118. Lost or stolen passports: report loss to police and contact your consulate (see above). Lost credit cards: Amex ☎1678.64.046; Diners Club ☎1678.64.064; Mastercard ☎1867.70.866; Visa ☎1678.77.232.

First aid Misericordia, Piazza del Duomo 20 (☎055.287.788). Otherwise visit the first aid (*pronto soccorso*) department at one of the hospitals listed below. If you need an ambulance call ☎113 or 055.212.222 or 055.215.555.

Hospitals Florence's most central hospital is the Arcispedale di Santa Maria Nuova, Piazza Santa Maria Nuova 1 (☎055.27.581). If you require the services of an interpreter, the Associazione Volontari Ospedalieri can be called out by ringing ☎055.425.0126 or 055.234.4567; it's a volunteer organization, and its services are free.

Laundry Guelfa, Via Guelfa 106n.

Left luggage Santa Maria Novella station by platform 16 (daily 4.15am–1.30am).

Lost property ATAF city buses: Via Circondaria 19 (Mon–Wed & Fri–Sat 9am–noon; ☎055.367.943); take bus #23 to Viale Corsica. Trains: Santa Maria Novella station; the office is on platform 16 next to left luggage; open daily 4.15am–1.30am (☎055.235.2190). Peretola airport call ☎055.373.498.

Pharmacies The main all-night pharmacy (*farmacia*) is the Comunale della Stazione (☎055.216.761) on the train station concourse (no credit cards). Another central late-opening option is Molteni, Via dei Calzaiuoli 7r (☎055.215.472). Normal opening hours for pharmacies are Monday–Saturday 8.30am–1pm and 4–8pm. All pharmacies display a late-night roster in their window; otherwise ring ☎182 for information.

Police Emergency ☎112 or 113; Polizia Urbana ☎055.32.831. The Questura, for passport problems, thefts and so on, is at Via Zara 2 (☎055.49.771). If you do report a theft or other crime, you will have to fill out a form (*una denuncia*): this may be time-consuming, but it's essential if you want to make a claim on your travel insurance.

Post office The most central post office is near Piazza della Repubblica at Via Pellicceria 8 (Mon–Fri 8.15am–6pm, Sat 8.15am–noon; telegram office open 24 hrs); poste restante at counters 23 & 24. Florence's main post office is at Via Pietrapiana 53–55 (same hours). If all you want are stamps (*francobolli*), then it's easier to buy them at a tobacconists (*tabaccaio*), which are marked by a sign outside with a white "T" on a blue background. For postal information ☎160.

Taxis The main ranks are by the train station, Piazza della Repubblica, Piazza del Duomo, Piazza Santa Maria Novella, Piazza San Marco, Piazza Santa Croce and Piazza Santa Trinita. To book a cab call ☎055.4798, ☎055.4242, ☎055.4499 or ☎055.4390.

Thomas Cook Lungarno Acciaiuoli 6–12 (Mon–Sat 9am–6pm, Sunday 9am–2pm; ☎055.289.781).

Tourist offices The city's main tourist office is at Via Cavour 1r, just north of the duomo (Mon–Sat 8.15am–7.15pm, Sun 8.15am–1.45pm; ☎055.290.832 or 055.290.833, fax 055.276.0383). The city council runs another office near Santa Croce at Borgo Santa Croce 29r (Mon–Sat 8.30am–7.15pm; ☎055.234.0444 or 055.226.4524). There's a third, smaller office at Piazza della Stazione – it's the stunted tower at the end of the line of bus stops as you exit the station to the east (Mon–Sat 8.30am–1.45pm; ☎055.212.245, fax 055.238.1226).

Tourist S.O.S. ☎055.217.195 or 055.212.777.

Train information Toll-free ☎166.105050 or 1478.88088.

travel details

TRAINS

Florence to: Ancona (hourly; 2 hr 30min–4hr); Arezzo (hourly; 1hr); Assisi (11 daily; 2hr 35min); Bari (12 daily; 8hr 15min–9hr); Bologna (every 30min; 1hr 5min–1hr 40min); Bolzano (14 daily; 4hr 10min–5hr 50min); Empoli (every 20min; 25min); Foligno (11 daily; 2hr 55min); Genoa (hourly; 3hr 10min–4hr 30min); Lecce (7 daily; 10hr 25min–12hr); Livorno (12 daily; 1hr 30min); Lucca (hourly; 1hr 5min–1hr 50min); Milan (18 daily; 2hr 50min–4hr 50min); Naples (2 daily; 4hr); Perugia (12 daily; 2hr 10min); Pisa airport (hourly; 1hr); Pisa central (every 30min; 55min); Pistoia (hourly; 30–45 min); Prato (every 30min; 20min); Reggio Calabria (from Campo Marte, 4 direct trains daily; 11hr, from Santa Maria Novella, changing at Rome, 7 daily; 11hr); Rimini (hourly; 3hr 30min–6hr); Rome (hourly; 2hr 15min–3hr 30min); Siena (via hourly connection at Empoli; 50min–1hr 20min); Trieste (9 daily, usually changing at Venice-Mestre; 5hr–6hr 15min); Udine (10 daily; 5hr 20min–6hr); Venice central (hourly; 3hr 25min–4hr 10min); Venice-Mestre (10 daily; 2hr 45min–3hr 20min); Verona (14 daily; 2hr 40min–3hr 40min); Viareggio (hourly; 1hr 30min–2hr 25min).

BUSES

In addition to the state-owned SITA, numerous independent bus companies operate from Florence. After the details of SITA routes comes a list of the most useful private routes, with the address and information number of each company. Buses depart from the addresses given in the Directory above.

SITA: to Barberino di Mugello (17 daily; 40min); Bibbiena (8 daily; 2hr 15min); Castellina in Chianti (1 daily; 1hr 35min); Certaldo (4 daily; 1hr 40min); Gaiole (2 daily Mon–Fri; 2hr); Greve (around 30 daily; 1hr 5min); Poggibonsi (10 daily; 1hr 20min); Pontassieve (12 daily; 50min); Poppi (9 daily; 2hr 5min); Radda in Chianti (1 daily Mon–Sat; 1hr 40min); San Casciano (14 daily; 40min); Siena (12 express daily, plus 9 stopping services; 1hr 15min express); Volterra (6 daily; 2hr 25min).

CLAP: to Lucca and Lucca province.

CAP: to Borgo San Lorenzo, Impruneta, Montepiano and Prato.

CAT: to Anghiari, Arezzo, Caprese, Città di Castello, Figline Valdarno, Incisa Valdarno, and Sansepolcro.

COPIT: to Abetone, Pistoia, Poggio a Caiano and Vinci.

Lazzi: to Abetone, Calenzano, Cerreto Guidi, Empoli, Forte dei Marmi, Incisa Valdarno, Livorno, Lucca, Marina di Carrara, Marina di Massa, Montecatini Terme, Montevarchi, Pescia, Pisa, Pistoia, Pontassieve, Pontedera, Prato, Signa, Tirrenia, Torre del Lago and Viareggio.

CHAPTER TWO

AROUND FLORENCE

H aving paid their respects to the sights of Florence, most people doing a Tuscan tour set off for another of the big-league towns, such as Siena or Pisa, leapfrogging the city's immediate surroundings. Yet there's a lot to be gained by lingering a few days in this area, either using Florence as a base, or staying at a couple of the smaller places within the city's orbit.

Inside the boundaries of Greater Florence, city buses run to the village of **Fiesole**, once Florence's keenest rival, and to many of the **Medici villas**, originally countryside retreats but now all but engulfed by the suburbs. Farther afield but readily accessible by train, the busy commercial centre of **Prato** and quiet provincial capital of **Pistoia** each make fine day trips, with their medieval buildings and Florentine-inspired Renaissance art – and either could be used as a springboard for exploring some of the more obscure corners of Tuscany.

West of Florence, an industrialized stretch of the Arno valley leads to **Empoli**, the point of access for a number of upland attractions: **Vinci** (Leonardo da Vinci's village), the imperial settlement of **San Miniato** and the hill-towns of **Castelfiorentino** and **Certaldo**. To the north and the south of Florence lie two rural regions that require independent transport for proper investigation: **Mugello**, the lush agricultural area around the upper valley of the Sieve river; and **Chianti**, Italy's premier wine region and expatriate settlement.

The places covered in this chapter lie on or very near to several of the principal routes through Tuscany, and can easily be visited on a journey between major centres. Three of these routes radiate from Florence: **to Pisa** (via Empoli); **to Lucca** (via Prato and Pistoia); and **to Siena** (via Chianti). The first two can be done by bus or train, the third by bus only. The fourth route – **from Empoli to Siena** via Castelfiorentino and Certaldo – is again possible by bus or train, though if you intend stopping off at San Gimignano, which is really the point of this trip, only the former will do.

Fiesole

The hill-town of **FIESOLE**, which spreads over a cluster of hills above the Mugnone and Arno valleys some 8km northeast of Florence, is conventionally described as a pleasant

ACCOMMODATION PRICES

Throughout this guide, **hotel** accommodation is graded on a scale from ① to ⑨, indicating the cost of the **cheapest double room** in each establishment in high season (for **hostels**, rates per person are given in lire). The price bands to which these codes refer are as follows:

① up to L60,000	④ L120,000–150,000	⑦ L250,000–300,000
② L60,000–90,000	⑤ L150,000–200,000	⑧ L300,000–350,000
③ L90,000–120,000	⑥ L200,000–250,000	⑨ over L350,000

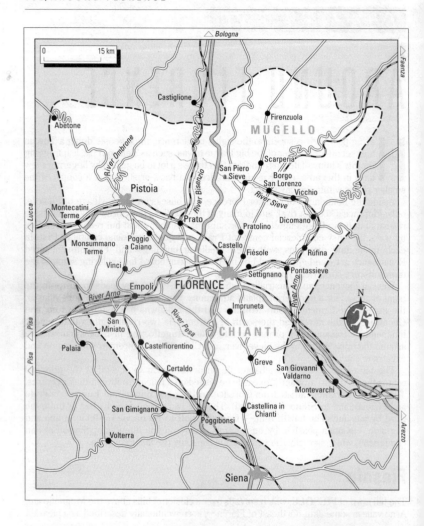

retreat from the crowds and heat of summertime Florence. Unfortunately, its tranquillity has been so well advertised that in high season it's now hardly less busy than Florence itself; you'd probably also need paranormal sensitivity to detect much climatic difference between the two on an airless August afternoon.

That said, Fiesole offers a grandstand view of the city, has something of the feel of a country village, and bears many traces of its history – which is actually lengthier than that of Florence. First settled in the Bronze Age, then later by the Etruscans, and then absorbed by the Romans, it rivalled its neighbour until the early twelfth century, when the Florentines overran the town. From that time it became a satellite, favoured as a semi-rural second home for wealthier citizens such as the ubiquitous Medici.

Fiesole is one of the easiest short trips from the city: the #7 ATAF **bus** runs every quarter of an hour from Santa Maria Novella train station to Fiesole's central Piazza Mino da Fiesole. The journey takes around twenty minutes, and costs the standard city fare of L1500.

The Town

When the Florentines wrecked Fiesole in 1125, the only major building they spared was the **duomo**, on the edge of Piazza Mino. Subsequently, nineteenth-century restorers managed to ruin the exterior, which is now notable only for its lofty campanile. The most interesting part of the bare interior is the raised choir: the altarpiece is a polyptych, painted in the 1440s by Bicci di Lorenzo, and the Cappella Salutati, to the right, contains two fine pieces carved around the same time by Mino da Fiesole – an altar frontal of *The Madonna and Saints* and the tomb of Bishop Salutati. Fiesole's patron saint, St Romulus, is buried underneath the choir in the ancient crypt.

Behind the duomo at Via Dupré 1, the **Museo Bandini** (daily: summer 9.30am–7pm; winter 9.30am–5pm; closed first Tues of every month; L10,000; includes entrance to Fiesole's other museums – see below) possesses a collection of glazed terracotta in the style of the Della Robbias, the odd piece of Byzantine ivory work and a few thirteenth- and fourteenth-century Tuscan pictures – worthy but uninspiring.

Fiesole's other major churches, Sant'Alessandro and San Francesco, are reached by the steep Via San Francesco, which runs past a terrace with a knockout view of Florence. **Sant'Alessandro** was founded in the sixth century on the site of Etruscan and Roman temples; repairs have rendered the outside a whitewashed nonentity, but the beautiful *marmorino cipollino* (onion marble) columns of the basilical interior make it the most atmospheric building in Fiesole.

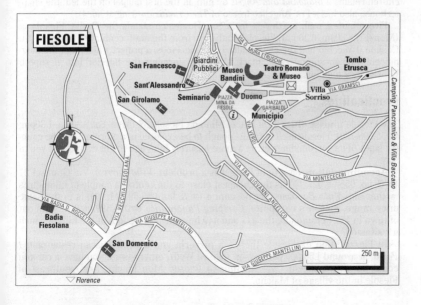

Again, restoration has not improved the Gothic **San Francesco**, which occupies the site of the acropolis – the interior is a twentieth-century renovation, but the tiny cloisters are genuine. The church itself contains an *Immaculate Conception* by Piero di Cosimo (second altar on right), and within the church is a small museum featuring material gathered mainly by missions to the Far East, much of it from China (summer Mon–Sat 10am–noon & 3–6pm; winter same days 10am–noon & 3–5pm; free). From the front of San Francesco a gate opens into a wooded public park, the most pleasant descent back to Piazza Mino.

The Roman Theatre and Etruscan Tombs

Back down in the main part of Fiesole, beyond the duomo in Via Portigiani, are the town's other museums: the **Teatro Romano**, **Museo Archeologico** and the **Antiquarium Costantini** (same hours as Museo Bandini; one ticket covers entrance to all four sites; L10,000). Built in the first century BC, the three-thousand-seat theatre was excavated towards the end of the nineteenth century and is in such good repair that it's used for performances during the Estate Fiesolana festival in July and August. Most of the exhibits in the site's small **museum** were excavated in this area, and encompass pieces from the Bronze Age to Roman occupation.

The **antiquarium** is basically a run-of-the-mill collection of old ceramics. And if you want to wring every last drop of historical significance from Fiesole, you could follow the signposts from here up the hill to the east of the Teatro, to the ruins of a couple of **Etruscan tombs** from the third century BC.

To San Domenico

The most enjoyable excursion from Fiesole is a wander down the narrow **Via Vecchia Fiesolana**, which passes the **Villa Medici** – built for Cosimo il Vecchio by Michelozzo – on its way to the hamlet of **SAN DOMENICO**, 2.5km southwest of Piazza Mino.

Fra' Angelico was once prior of the Dominican **monastery** at this village and the church retains a *Madonna and Angels* by him, in the first chapel on the left; the chapterhouse also has a Fra' Angelico fresco of *The Crucifixion* (ring at no. 4).

Five minutes' walk northwest from San Domenico stands the **Badia Fiesolana** (Mon–Fri 8.30am–6.30pm), Fiesole's cathedral from the ninth century to the eleventh. Cosimo il Vecchio had the church altered in the 1460s, a project which kept the magnificent Romanesque facade intact while transforming the interior into a superb Renaissance building.

Practicalities

The Fiesole **tourist office** is at Piazza Mino da Fiesole 37 (Mon–Sat 8.30am–1.30pm; ☎055.598.720). Fiesole itself is small enough to be explored in a morning, but the country lanes of its surroundings invite a more leisurely tour, and might even tempt you to stay.

Accommodation on a tight budget is a problem. *Villa Sorriso*, Via Gramsci 21 (☎ & fax 055.59.027; ③), is the cheapest close to the centre; a couple of kilometres farther out, *Villa Baccano*, Via Bosconi 4 (☎ & fax 055.59.341; ③), is in the same price range. Fiesole's **campsite**, *Camping Panoramico* (☎055.599.069), is 2km out of town in Via Peramonda; the #47 and #49 bus goes to the foot of the hill on which it's situated.

In Piazza Mino da Fiesole there's a **pizzeria** and a good Tuscan restaurant, *I Polpa*, at around L50,000 per person (closed Wed), otherwise, if you have a car you could try the excellent *Cave di Maiano* (closed Mon lunch), 3km southeast of Fiesole in the village of Maiano.

The Medici villas

The finest country houses of the Florentine hinterland are, predictably enough, those built for the **Medici**. The earliest of these were primarily intended as fortified refuges to which the family could withdraw when the political temperature in the city became a little too hot. In time, as the family grew more secure, the houses became somewhere to show off the humanistic culture of the Medici. In the sixteenth and seventeenth centuries, with the Medici established as unchallenged rulers of the city, the villas became more ostentatious, as if to express the might of the dynasty through their sheer luxuriousness. The land they were built on later became a valuable asset – when Florence's importance as a manufacturing centre was diminished, the Medici were able to divert some resources into agriculture.

Not every Medici villa is covered in this section – just the ones that are easily accessible on a day trip from Florence and whose interior or grounds are open to the public. The villas of Trebbio and Cafaggiolo are described later in this chapter (see p.178), while the Villa Medici at Cerreto Guidi, far closer to Empoli than to Florence, is dealt with on p.192.

Apart from the selection of Medici villas, this section also includes a few sights which can be visited on an excursion to one of the houses – the church at **Carmignano**, for example, with its remarkable Pontormo altarpiece.

Villa Medicea La Petraia

The **Villa La Petraia** (bus #28 from train station to Castello) was adapted from a medieval castle in the 1570s and 1580s by Buontalenti, working to a commission from the future Grand Duke Ferdinando I. Only the watchtower of the fortress was retained, to serve as a high-rise belvedere above the simple two-storey house.

The **interior** (daily: March & Oct 9am–5.30pm; April, May & Sept 9am–6.30pm; June–Aug 9am–7.30pm; Nov–Feb 9am–4.30pm; closed first and last Mon of month); L4000, including admission to gardens of Villa di Castello; ticket office shuts one hour before closing) was altered in turn by Vittorio Emanuele II, who glassed over the interior courtyard to convert it into a ballroom. Its walls are covered by a seventeenth-century fresco cycle glorifying the Medici and the Knights of St Stephen, a pseudo-chivalric order founded by Cosimo I to rid the Tuscan coast of pirates. The suffocating style of the House of Savoy tends to prevail in the villa's apartments, though this is offset by the occasional sixteenth-century tapestry or painting. There is also Giambologna's bronze statue of *Venus*, now transplanted indoors from the fountain on the upper terrace of the garden.

Laid out in geometrical order, in half-hearted imitation of the Castello estate, the garden isn't much to get excited about, but the park behind the villa to the east is glorious, with its ancient cypress trees (grounds close 1hr later than the villa).

Villa Medicea di Castello

From La Petraia follow Via della Petraia past Villa Bel Riposo (where Carlo Lorenzini wrote *Pinocchio*) to the Baroque Villa Corsini, from where Via di Castello leads to the **Villa di Castello**. This house was bought in 1477 by Lorenzo and Giovanni de' Medici, second cousins of Lorenzo il Magnifico, and the principal patrons of Botticelli – the *Birth of Venus* and the *Primavera* both used to hang here. Wrecked after the expulsion of the Medici, it was rebuilt for Cosimo I, and is now the headquarters of the Accademia della Crusca, the society charged with maintaining the purity of the Italian language.

The society doesn't allow visitors into the house, but that's no great hardship, as its Pontormo and Bronzino frescoes perished a long time back, and the villa's fame rests entirely on its **gardens** (same hours as Villa La Petraia, but closed Mondays; L4000), which were laid out by Tribolo for Cosimo and continued by Buontalenti, who also redesigned the house. Had the full scheme been carried out, over fifty sculptural tableaux would have represented the seasons, the virtues, the landscapes of Tuscany and, of course, the triumphs of the Medici. Even in a state of semi-completion, Castello's gardens were astonishing (delighted by their labyrinths, sculptures, fountains and myriad water tricks, Montaigne judged them to be the best in Europe.) Of the surviving eccentricities, the outstanding set pieces are Ammannati's colossal shivering figure of *January*, the triple-bowled fountain topped by the same sculptor's *Hercules and Antaeus*, and the *Grotto degli Animali* – by Giambologna and his school – a man-made cave against the walls of which are stacked a menagerie of plaster birds and animals. (The bronze originals of some of these are now on show in the Bargello in Florence.)

Villa Medicea di Careggi

Originally a fortified farmhouse, the **Villa di Careggi**, 5km northwest of central Florence, came into the possession of the Medici in 1417 and was altered by Michelozzo for Cosimo il Vecchio in the 1430s. It was the old man's favourite home: he brought his private library out here and hung the walls with paintings by his protégés. Cosimo died here, too, as did his son Piero and grandson Lorenzo il Magnifico, with whom the house is particularly associated, as it was here that his academy of Platonic scholars used to meet.

Low-slung and blank-faced, Careggi is not a gracious building, its one amusing touch being a fresco in one of the garden loggias – it depicts a man being thrown down a well, demonstrating the fate of the doctor whose incompetence was (apparently unjustly) alleged to have resulted in the death of Lorenzo.

The villa is now a nurses' home, and written permission to view the interior has to be obtained from Unità Operativa Affari Generali, U.S.L. 10/D, Viale Pieraccini 17, Firenze (☎055.427.9501). The extensive surrounding gardens and woodland can be explored freely, however. The #14C bus runs from Santa Maria Novella train station to the villa, or you can walk from La Petraia (see previous page).

Poggio a Caiano – and Carmignano

For the most complete picture of what life was like in the Medici villas in the family's heyday, you should make the trip to the **Villa Medici di Poggio a Caiano** (daily: March & Oct 9am–5.30pm; April, May & Sept 9am–6.30pm; June–Aug 9am–7.30pm; Nov–Feb 9am–4.30pm; closed second and third Mon of month; L4000), 18km northwest of Florence, on the crest of the main road through the village of Poggio a Caiano. A COPIT bus leaves from Piazza Santa Maria Novella every half-hour, and takes around half an hour to get there; an alternative approach is the #M local CAP service from Prato.

Lorenzo il Magnifico bought a farmhouse on this site in 1480 and commissioned Giuliano da Sangallo to rebuild it as a classical rural palace – the only architectural project instigated by Lorenzo that has survived, and the first Italian house to be built specifically as a place of country leisure. Raised on a kind of arcaded podium, it is the most elegant of the Medici villas and its impact is enhanced by later additions – the entrance loggia, for instance, was commissioned by Lorenzo's son Giovanni, the future Pope Leo X, and the curving double stairway was added in the eighteenth century. The house was often used to accommodate guests of state before they made ceremonial entrance into Florence – Charles V stayed here, and it was at Poggio a Caiano that Eleanor of Toledo was introduced to her future husband, Cosimo I.

You enter the **villa** through the basement, where the plush games room and private theatre hint at the splendour to come. Upstairs, the focal point is the double-height *salone* which Sangallo created out of the courtyard between the two main blocks, and which Vasari pronounced the most beautiful room in the world. Its sixteenth-century frescoes include del Sarto's *Caesar Receiving Egyptian Tribute* (the giraffe shown in the background was a gift to Lorenzo from the Sultan of Egypt), Franciabigio's *Triumph of Cicero* (a reference to Cosimo il Vecchio's return from exile) and, best of the lot, Pontormo's gorgeous *Vertumnus and Pomona*, the perfect evocation of a sun-splashed Tuscan afternoon.

Also on this floor is a reconstruction of the salon from the Villa Topaia built by Cosimo III at Castello and since destroyed. The original villa was set among orchards, and the literal-minded Cosimo duly ordered scores of horticultural paintings to fill the house; the Dutch still-lifes are like ideal fruit stalls, each variety of grape, peach and apple assiduously numbered and labelled. Other such painted images from La Topaia are scattered throughout the main floor.

Many of the rooms were redecorated in the nineteenth century, but one that escaped was the apartment of Bianca Cappello, wife of Francesco I and inspiration of many a romantic tale. Born into an upper-class Venetian family, she fled her native city with a young man, whom she quickly dumped to become Francesco's mistress. Banned from the city by Francesco's first wife, she remained an outcast even after she had become his second, being blacklisted by many of Florence's elite. In October 1587 both she and her husband died here on the same day – perhaps poisoned, perhaps victims of a particularly virulent virus.

In Lorenzo's time the grounds of Poggio a Caiano were far more extensive than they are today, and included a farm and a hunting estate; in the eighteenth century the **gardens** (same days & hours as the villa) were converted into an English-style landscape, now containing some magnificent old trees.

CARMIGNANO

Five kilometres to the west of Poggio a Caiano, the church of San Michele in the village of **CARMIGNANO** contains one of Pontormo's greatest paintings, the *Visitation*. Created in 1530, it's as unusual an interpretation of a common theme as his *Deposition* in Florence – clad in bright pink, green and orange, the women seem to be clutching each other in an almost static dance.

There is a fairly regular CAP bus service to Carmignano from Poggio, the journey taking between ten and twenty minutes. If you feel like staying there's a two-star **hotel**, *Montalbano*, Via Madonna della Valicarda 1 (☎055.879.9008; ②).

Villa dell'Artimino

Some of the buses from Poggio a Caiano to Carmignano stop on the way at Comeana, 3km south, where a couple of large **Etruscan tombs** dating from the seventh century BC have been excavated (Thurs–Sat 9am–2pm; free). A few of these bus services then loop through the walled village of Artimino, site of the Villa dell'Artimino, another 3km on.

Villa dell'Artimino is known as *La Ferdinanda* after Grand Duke Ferdinando I, for whom Buontalenti designed the house as a hunting lodge, with no intervening garden to smooth the transition from civilization to nature. Unlike most of the other Medici villas it's still in the countryside, with brilliant views towards Florence in one direction and west along the Arno in the other.

A white rectangular block with details picked out in grey *pietra serena*, the house has the appearance of a rather dandified fortress, and its most distinctive external feature has earned it the nickname "the villa of the hundred chimneys". Half of the **interior** is open for prearranged visits on Tuesday (☎055.879.2030), though the paintings of the various Medici villas that once hung here are now on show in Florence's *Firenze com'era* museum. In the basement there's a dreary museum of Etruscan finds from the Comeana tombs (daily except Wed 9am–12.30pm; L5000).

While you're here, take a look at the village church of **San Leonardo**, which was put together in the twelfth century from stones recovered from an Etruscan necropolis. And if you can hang around until the evening, you should sample the menu at the village **restaurant**, *Da Delfina* (closed Sun evening, Mon, Aug and first week of Jan), where a wonderful Tuscan meal costs around L75,000.

Pratolino and Monte Senario

Nothing remains of Francesco I's favourite villa at **Pratolino**, 12km north of the city, except for its huge park (April–Oct Thurs–Sun 10am–8pm; L5000) – and even this is but a shadow of its former self. The mechanical toys, trick fountains and other practical jokes that Buontalenti installed in the grounds of Pratolino were the most ingenious ever seen, and required so much maintenance that there was a house in the grounds just for the court plumbers. The only surviving pieces from the original garden are a couple of fountains, a little temple by Buontalenti, and Giambologna's immense *Appennino*, a shaggy man-mountain who gushes water. Nonetheless, the park – known as the **Parco Demidoff**, after the nineteenth-century owners of the estate – is still one of the pleasantest green spaces within a bus ride of Florence (the #25 service).

MONTE SENARIO

If you're travelling under your own steam, you could take an eight-kilometre diversion northeast off the main road into the Mugello to **Monte Senario**, a monastery established by the seven founder members of the Servite order in 1233. The complex is impressive, with gilded Rococo basilica and hermitages scattered up the hill, but the architecture is less rewarding than the views of Mugello from the terrace.

Poggio Imperiale

South of central Florence, Viale del Poggio Imperiale rises from the Porta Romana to the **Villa di Poggio Imperiale**, built by the Salviati family but confiscated by Cosimo I. The Medici did little to improve the place when they enlarged it; nor did the post-Medici rulers of the city, who glued a Neoclassical facade onto the house. The goverment department that now occupies most of the villa allows prearranged visits on Wednesday from 10am to noon, except in August (☎055.220.151; free), but it's a tour for the committed Medicean only.

Chianti

Ask a sample of northern Europeans to define their idea of paradise and the odds are that several will come up with something that sounds much like **Chianti**, the territory of vineyards and hill-towns that stretches between Florence and Siena. Every aspect of life in Chianti seems in perfect balance: the landscape is the sort of terrain beloved of painters evoking the Golden Age; the climate for most of the year is balmy, and even in the pit of winter rarely too grim; and on top of all this there's the wine, the one Italian vintage that's familiar to just about everyone.

The British, and others from similarly ill-favoured zones, were long ago alerted to Chianti's charms, and the rate of immigration has been so rapid since the 1960s that the region is now popularly known as "Chiantishire" or "Surrey in the Sun" (happily, however, foreign residents still only account for five percent of Chianti's 45,000 inhabitants). With up to a million visitors a year, tourism has overtaken wine to become the region's most important cash crop, and has helped push property prices beyond the reach of the local population – thus altering the tone of certain parts irreparably. Tourist handouts might talk of the charm of Chianti's medieval hamlets, but many of them are places

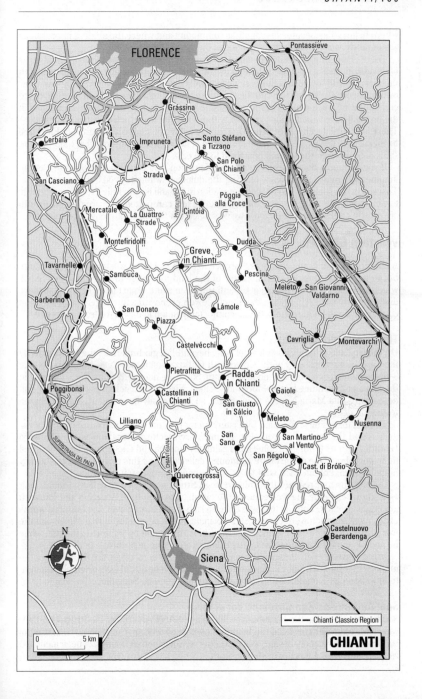

FLORENCE

Pontassiève

Grássina

Cerbáia

Impruneta

Santo Stéfano
a Tizzano

San Polo
in Chianti

San Casciano

Strada

Póggia
alla Croce

Mercatale

La Quattro-
Strade

Cintóia

Montefiridolfi

Dudda

Greve
in Chianti

Tavarnelle

Sambuca

Pescina

Meleto

San Giovanni
Valdarno

Bárberino

San Donato

Lámole

Piazza

Castelvécchi

Cavriglia

Montevarchi

Poggibonsi

Pietrafitta

Radda
in Chianti

Castellina in
Chianti

Gaiole

San Giusto
in Sálcio

Lilliano

Meleto

Nusenna

San
Sano

San Martino
al Vento

San Régolo

Quercegrossa

Cast. di Brólio

Castelnuovo
Berardenga

N

Siena

Chianti Classico Region

0   5 km

CHIANTI

where history has become just another commodity and where the abiding impressions are of newly varnished shutters and locks the size of letter boxes.

There is, nonetheless much to enjoy in Chianti – quiet back roads, hundreds of acres of woodland, and of course the vineyards. Buses from Florence and Siena connect with the main Chianti towns, but the best way to really get to know the region is **by car**. Your own transport allows you to roam the quieter recesses of the hills, and visit any one of the eight hundred **wine producers** to sample the local product. (Every village mentioned in the text will have wine tastings on offer within a few hundred metres of the main street.) There is basically a choice of two main roads to follow through Chianti: the old **Florence to Siena** road (SSN2) along the western edge of the region, or the so-called *Chiantigiana* (SSN222), through the Chianti heartland to the east.

If you pick up a detailed survey map of the region, you can also pick out some of the innumerable miniature **lakes** – offering the quietest swimming you'll find anywhere in Tuscany in the summer. **Hotel** accommodation in Chianti is generally expensive; the only low-budget options are two youth **hostels** and a few **campsites**. The area's **restaurants** are mostly on the pricey side, too – we've singled out the more attractive propositions.

Western Chianti

A stretch of superstrada connects Florence to Siena along the western edge of Chianti, but to get some sense of the character of the land it's better to take the older SSN2, which takes in a few of the major Chianti towns en route. Apart from being a far more diverting drive, it's actually not that much slower: even with a few stops on the way, you could reach San Gimignano or Siena comfortably in a half-day drive from Florence.

The Certosa di Galluzzo
On the city side of the Autostrada del Sole, beyond Poggio Imperiale, the N2 sweeps by the Carthusian monastery of the **Certosa di Galluzzo** (summer Tues–Sun 9am–noon & 3–6pm; winter Tues–Sat 9am–noon & 3–5pm, Sun 9am–noon & 3–6pm; free), founded in the fourteenth century by the Florentine banker Niccolò Acciaioli. Bus #36 and #37 run here from Santa Maria Novella train station, so it can easily be included as an excursion from Florence.

The Certosa is now occupied by Cistercian monks, one of whose number shows visitors round the enormous complex. Its main architectural attraction is the **Chiostro Grande**, with its tondi of prophets and saints by Andrea and Giovanni della Robbia and their workshop. One of the eighteen monks' cells adjoining this cloister is open – a very homely arrangement, each with three rooms and its own patch of garden.

Beyond, the tour reaches the **Palazzo degli Studi**, now a picture gallery, though built as a study centre by the well-educated Acciaioli, who counted Boccaccio and Petrarch among his friends. The Certosa was once so rich that it owned over five hundred works of art, most of which were carried off by Napoleon; the best of those that remain are the five scenes of the Passion, painted for the Chiostro Grande by Pontormo in 1522, while he and his pupil Bronzino were taking refuge from a plague outbreak in the city.

In the **church** itself, down in the crypt of the lay brothers' choir, are the tombs of the monastery's founder and his descendants, including a beautiful slab originally thought to have been by Donatello, now attributed to Francesco da Sangallo.

Sant'Andrea and San Casciano Val di Pesa
South of the Certosa, the N2 passes to the east of **SANT'ANDREA IN PERCUSSINA**, where **Machiavelli** alleviated the boredom of exile by writing *The Prince*, the manual of statecraft that he hoped, in vain, would seal his rehabilitation. A house has been identified as his residence but it is not open to visitors.

SAN CASCIANO VAL DI PESA, 17km from Florence, is the first real town on the road itself. In fact, with a population of around 15,000, it is the only place in Chianti that is really more than an extended village. It is also home to one of the slickest commercial operations in Tuscany, the six-hundred-year-old **Antinori wine house**, as well as one of Chianti's most interesting churches, **Santa Maria del Prato**, which stands by the one surviving gateway in the town walls. The church was built in the fourteenth century and contains some beautiful works of art from the same period: a Crucifix by an anonymous follower of Giotto, an altarpiece of the Madonna and Child, and a pulpit by a pupil of Andrea Pisano.

For **accommodation**, San Casciano town offers the well-appointed *Antica Posta*, Piazza Zannoni 1 (☎055.822.313, fax 055.822.278; ⑤); the attached **restaurant** (closed Tues) offers à la carte meals for around L45,000 – booking is essential. You can also get a fine meal at *Da Nello*, Via IV Novembre 64, where the Friday fish menu is especially good (closed Wed evening & Thurs).

Mercatale and around

The road east from San Casciano passes the Chianti-producing **Villa Le Corti** – one of many Florentine gentry residences in this part of the region – before reaching the once-major market town of **MERCATALE**, 5km from San Casciano. Mercatale has the tiny *Hotel Paradise*, right in the centre at Piazza Vittorio Veneto 28 (☎ & fax 055.821.327, *hotelparad@ftbcc.it*; ②). There's also a couple of good **restaurants**: *Il Salotto del Chianti* on Via Sonnino, at around L60,000 per person (closed Wed); and the somewhat cheaper *Trattoria Da Poldo*, in an old farmhouse along Via Grevigiana (the road from San Casciano); fried rabbit and chicken a speciality.

A couple of kilometres farther east, on the road towards Greve (see next page), stands the eleventh-century **Castello di Gabbiano**, built by the Bardi, the wealthiest Florentine banking dynasty before the coming of the Medici. As with Le Corti, it produces wine – and olive oil, another great Chianti speciality.

Bargino and southwards

Back on the N2 south of San Casciano, you pass the castle of **Bibbione** – home of the Buondelmonte family, who triggered the Guelph versus Ghibelline battles – before coming into **BARGINO**, which has low-cost rooms at the one-star *Bargino*, Via Cassia 122 (☎055.824.9055, fax 055.824.9045; ②). From here it's a short diversion east to the fortified village of **MONTEFIRIDOLFI**, whose castle once belonged to the sons of Ridolfo Buondelmonte (*figli di Ridolfo*).

Beyond Bargino, the N2 rolls into **TAVARNELLE VAL DI PESA**, which expanded as an agricultural centre in the nineteenth century. There's a reasonable **restaurant** here, *La Fattoria* at Via del Cerro 11, and one of two **youth hostels** in Chianti, *Ostello del Chianti*, 300m from the bus-stop at Via Roma 137 (March–Oct; ☎055.807.7009, fax 055.805.0104; L26,000 including breakfast).

A couple of kilometres farther on lies the more ancient **BARBERINO VAL D'ELSA**, site of one of the rare **campsites** in Chianti, *Semifonte*, at Via Ugo Foscolo 4 (☎055.807.5454). The beautiful Romanesque **Pieve di Sant'Appiano**, parts of which date back to the tenth century, is a few kilometres southwest of the village (well signposted); due south, on the main road, is Poggibonsi, hub for buses to San Gimignano and Siena (see p.337).

The Chianti heartland

There's no better way to experience the village life of Chianti than to drive along the **Chiantigiana** (SSN222), which cuts right across the hills from Florence to Siena, connecting with a tangle of minor roads that traverse the most unspoilt parts of the region. If you put your foot down, the twists and turns of the *Chiantigiana* can be negotiated in only a little longer than the major road to the west, but really this is a route to dawdle along, taking turnings on a whim and dropping by at any vineyard that takes your fancy.

Santa Caterina d'Antella and Impruneta

Leaving Florence on the SSN22 (the access road for the *Chiantigiana*), a short detour just before the autostrada will bring you to the village of **PONTE A EMA** and, a kilometre beyond, to the church of **Santa Caterina d'Antella**. This has a fine cycle of scenes from the life of St Catherine of Siena, painted by Spinello Aretino in 1387. Executed immediately prior to his work at San Miniato al Monte, they make an interesting comparison with Agnolo Gaddi's less monumental fresco cycle in Florence's church of Santa Croce, painted at the same time. (For an account of the life of the saint, see p.324.)

Another rewarding detour, this time just south of the autostrada, presents itself at Grássina. Take a right turn here and, after 9km of winding road, you arrive at **IMPRUNETA**. The **Collegiata** here, restored after heavy bomb damage in 1944, was founded in the eleventh century to house a miraculous icon of the Madonna and Child dug up in a nearby field and said to have been painted – as these things often are – by St Luke. It's housed in one of a pair of matching chapels by Michelozzo, the second of which contains a fragment of the True Cross; both have lovely enamelled terracotta decoration by Luca della Robbia. Impruneta has long been a centre of the terracotta industry, and holds a big fair in October on the main square. In nearby Bottai there's a **campsite** at Via San Cristoforo 2 (☎055.237.4704; April–Oct) and a two-star **hotel**: *Scopeti* at Via Cassia 183 (☎ & fax 055.202.2008; ③).

Grássina to Strada

Go east rather than west at Grássina and you'll come to **SANTO STEFANO A TIZZANO**, with its Romanesque church and contemporaneous **Castello di Tizzano**, a producer of good wines but best known for its *extra vergine* olive oil. A couple of kilometres further is **SAN POLO IN CHIANTI**, where a massive iris festival, the *festa del Giaggiolo*, held the second and third Sunday in May, celebrates the village crop of Florence's floral emblem. A good place for a coffee is the *Antica Toscana*.

From San Polo a minor road reconnects with the *Chiantigiana* at **STRADA IN CHIANTI**. The road southeast from Strada to Dudda is overlooked by the mighty **Castello di Mugnana**, which once protected this stretch of road down into the Arno valley and is now the headquarters of a massive wine estate.

Greve and around

For more casual oenophiles, perhaps the best target is **GREVE**, 10km down the *Chiantigiana* from Strada. The venue for Chianti's biggest **wine fair** (usually held during the second weekend in September), this is a town with wine for sale on every street: the best outlets are the Enoteca di Gallo Nero, Piazzetta Santa Croce 8, and the Cantinetta di Checucci Sandro, Via Vittorio Veneto. The hub of the town, and site of the Saturday market, is the funnel-shaped **Piazza Matteotti**, whose irregular arcades are explained by the fact that various merchants paid for their own stretches of colonnade. The statue in the centre is of Giovanni da Verrazzano, the man who discovered New York harbour; he was born in the nearby Castello di Verrazzano.

As the chief town of the *Gallo Nero* region, Greve is equipped with a vineyard-orientated **tourist office** in a building called *La Torre* (The Tower), in Via Luca Cini (Mon–Sat 10am–1pm & 2–5pm, closed Thurs; ☎055.854.5243), and can give information on accommodation in farmhouses, rooms for rent in the area, wine tasting, trekking and local sports facilities. There are also a number of interesting **villas** a stone's throw from Greve, including **Verrazzano**, five minutes drive north of Greti, and **Vignamaggio**, just south of Greve, where Kenneth Branagh filmed *Much Ado about Nothing*. (Check with the tourist office for details). A couple of three-star **hotels** on Piazza Matteotti offer comfortable accommodation: the clean-cut *Del Chianti* at no. 86 (✆ & fax 055.853.763; ⑤) and *Da Verrazzano* at no. 28 (✆055.853.189, fax 055.853.648; ④). The latter also has a very good **restaurant**, at around L50,000 for a full meal (closed Mon & Jan 15–Feb 15). There are several recommended pizzeria-restaurants too: *Gallo Nero*, Via Cesare Battista 9; *La Cantina*, Piazza Trento; and *Torre delle Civette*, Via Veneto. For travellers on a tight rein, there's a **youth hostel** in Lucolena, 10km east of Greve and uncon-nected by public transport – the *Villa San Michele*, Via Casole 42, with a restau-rant and bar (mid-April to Nov; ✆ & fax 055.851.034; L20,000).

Five minutes' drive from Greve, up a steep zigzagging road, lies the much restored hamlet of **MONTEFIORALLE**, where a single elliptical street – Via di Montefioralle – encompasses a few tower houses and a pair of Romanesque churches. This street has one of the nearest approximations to a simple **trattoria** in Chianti, the *Taverna del Guerrino*; a menu of locally produced sausages, beans and vegetables provides a good Tuscan meal for around L40,000.

Continuing west from Montefioralle, the road passes the vestiges of the castle of Montefili – whose owners were benefactors of the **Badia a Passignano**, situated a few kilometres on towards the N2. Once one of the wealthiest religious houses in Tuscany, the Badia a Passignano is now a private residence, but the abbey church of **San Michele** is unaltered; it contains pictures by Ghirlandaio and Alessandro Allori, and a bust of Giovanni Gualberto, founder of the Vallombrosan order, whose arrival here in 1050 led the monastery to dedicate itself to the care of the sick.

South to Castellina

Eight kilometres south of Greve along the *Chiantigiana*, the hill-top town of **PANZANO** overlooks a circle of hills known as the *Conca d'Oro* (Golden Valley) because of their sun-trap properties; the resultant wines can be sampled at the Enoteca del Chianti Classico, Via Giovanni da Verrazzano 8 (closed Mon). Signposted down a branch road, the Romanesque **Pieve di San Leolino**, 3km south of the village, is one of the oldest churches in Chianti, and traces its origins to the first Christian settlers; it's much favoured for local weddings.

The summit of the next main hill, 15km on, is occupied by well-heeled **CASTELLINA IN CHIANTI**, which formerly stood on the front line of the continual wars between Florence and Siena. The walls, fortress and the covered walkway known as the **Via delle Volte** – a kind of gallery looking east from underneath the town – all bear testimony to an embattled past. Marks of a more distant era can be seen ten minutes' walk out of the village, in the form of the **Ipogeo Etrusco di Montecalvario**, a sixth-century BC Etruscan tomb. The power-station bulk of the **wine co-operative** on the main road declares Castellina's modern preoccupations; the local wine and oil are on sale in the compendious Bottega del Vino Gallo Nero, at Via della Rocca 10.

Radda and around

The best of Chianti lies east of Castellina and the *Chiantigiana*, in the less domesticated ter-rain of the **Monti del Chianti** – stronghold of the medieval Lega di Chianti, whose power bases were Castellina itself and the two principal towns of this craggy region. The nearer of these, **RADDA IN CHIANTI**, was the league's capital, and the imprint of that period is stronger here than anywhere else in Chianti. The street plan of this minuscule but historic centre is focused on Piazza Ferrucci, where the frescoed and shield-studded Palazzo Comunale faces a church raised on a high platform. Neither is an outstanding building on its own, but taken together they form an impressive ancient core that gives Radda its appeal.

CHIANTI WINES

Chianti became the world's first officially defined wine-producing area in 1716, the year Cosimo III drew the boundaries within which vineyards could use the region's name on their product. Modern Chianti dates from the 1860s when Bettino Ricasoli, unified Italy's second prime minister, established the classic formula for the wine at his estate at Brolio, based on **Sangiovese** – central Italy's predominant red grape.

White grapes used to be an important part of the mix, as were red grapes imported from southern Italy. This, combined with the huge area of production that extends well beyond the geographical area known as Chianti, meant that the quality and style of the wine varied dramatically – at its worst symbolized by the straw-covered bottle known as a *fiasco*. There was a crisis of confidence and many of the better producers put their efforts into making smart, expensive wines sold as simple *vini da tavola*. The situation improved with Chianti becoming a **DOCG** in 1984 and with the recent change allowing the wine to be made from pure Sangiovese. Total output is presently about 85 million litres per annum, making it Italy's highest-volume DOCG by far. It is split into seven classified **regions** of which the best are Chianti Classico and Chianti Rúfina. The better Chiantis mature in around four to seven years, and the best recent vintages to look out for are the excellent 1997 and 1995, followed by the 1996 and 1994. A *riserva* is a *cru* version aged for a minimum of two and a half years before bottling.

● **Chianti Classico**. The original delineated district (see map on p.169), accounts for a third of the Chianti produced. In 1924 Chianti Classico was institutionalized, taking as its trademark the black cock (*Gallo Nero*) that was once the heraldic symbol of the baronial alliance called the Lega di Chianti. Today the Gallo Nero, to which most producers belong, is really a marketing consortium.

● **Chianti Colli Aretini**. From the hills on the east side of the Arno valley, to the north of Arezzo. Tends to be lighter than Classico and best drunk young.

● **Chianti Colli Fiorentini**. From the area immediately south and east of Florence, and along the Arno and Pesa valleys. Good quaffing wine and staple *Rosso* of many a restaurant in Florence.

● **Chianti Colli Senesi**. The largest Chianti zone, split into three distinct districts: around Montalcino, around Montepulciano, and south of the Classico region east of San Gimignano. Variable quality with the name of the producer all-important.

● **Chianti Colline Pisane**. The lightest Chianti comes from this region, southeast of Pisa around Casciana Terme.

● **Chianti Montalbano**. From the hills west of Florence and south of Pistoia, the wines usually soft and scented.

● **Chianti Rúfina**. From the lower Sieve valley, northeast of Florence, producing some of the most refined and longest-living Chiantis. (Not to be confused with the big Chianti producer Ruffino).

Close to the piazza, at Via Roma 41, there is the simple *Girarrosto* **restaurant** (☎0577.738.010; closed Wed). A few doors down, at no. 46, Elio Pistolesi has rooms and houses to rent (☎0577.738.556), while the *Villa Miranda*, a short distance east of the village in Villa a Radda (☎0577.738.021, fax 0577.738.668; ③) has scruffy rooms and a rather grubby if occasionally inspired restaurant. Meals at around L60,000 per person are served at the *Vignale*, Via XX Settembre 23 (closed Thurs & Jan 10–March 10), and there's a pizza place, *Da Michele*, down the ramp opposite here. Far better are a couple of trattorias in old, isolated farmhouses with spectacular scenery, serving good, local food: *Le Vigne*, just off the road between Villa a Radda and Radda in Chianti, at around L35,000–40,000 and – for about L20,000 more – *Ristorante Vescine*, on the road to Castellina.

Seven kilometres north of Radda is the unspoilt village of **VOLPAIA**, which from the tenth to the sixteenth century was an important military lookout over the valley of the

Pesa. The medieval donjon still stands, but the most interesting structure in Volpaia is the deconsecrated Commenda di Sant'Eufrosino, the unlikely venue for an annual **festival of avant-garde art**, sponsored by the **Castello di Volpaia** wine estate.

The same distance south of Radda is **AMA**, once a fortification on the southern edge of Florentine territory. Round the village are ranged the vineyards of one of Chianti's first-rank wine estates, **Castello di Ama**, which offers tastings throughout the year except in August.

Gaiole and Brolio

Leaving Radda, the first turning left after the *Villa Miranda* passes the foot of the hill on which stands the **Badìa a Coltibuono**, 6km from Radda. This Vallombrosan abbey (see p.412) was founded on the site of an eighth-century hermitage, and its church of San Lorenzo, built in 1050, is one of Tuscany's finest Romanesque buildings; unfortunately, it's rarely open except for daily Mass (4pm in spring, 4.30pm in summer, 3.30pm in autumn, 3pm in winter). The monastic complex is now owned by a wine estate, whose vintages are served at *Badìa a Coltibuono* (✆0577.749.031), the **restaurant** adjoining the abbey – a wonderful meal here will cost upwards of L40,000 per head, depending on which wine you select. Club Alpino **walks** are laid out through the oak and pine woods on the surrounding slopes.

Modern times have caught up with the third of the Lega di Chianti triad, **GAIOLE**, 5km south of Coltibuono. Now a brisk market town, it has a **wine co-operative** at Via Mulinaccio 10, which offers splendid tasting opportunities, as does the Enoteca Montagnani, at Via Bandinelli 9, which has a superlative range of Chianti Classico. The most impressive sights in the immediate area are the ruins of the **Castello di Vertine**, occupying the heights 3km west of the village, and the fortified village of **Barbischio**, up a winding little road to the east. Devotees of military ruins could follow the signposted *Strada dei Castelli* from Gaiole, an itinerary of half a dozen fortresses between Spaltena (1km) and Vistarenni (6km). There are a couple of pricey hotels in the Gaiole vicinity, but it's not the pick of the Chianti towns, so it's better to drive on; the same goes for places to eat.

A couple of kilometres south of Gaiole, the twin circular towers of the **Castello di Meleto** peer from behind a screen of cypresses over the road leading to **Castagnoli**, where the houses form a fringe to a thickset fortress. If you are interested in visiting a classic Chianti *cantina*, perhaps the best place to make for is **Castello di Brolio**, just outside the nearby village of **BROLIO**: from Castagnoli you should take the minor road through San Martino al Vento; or, coming from Gaiole, you could take the turning off the N408 after Meleto.

The building itself passed to the Ricasoli family as far back as the twelfth century, and was the subject of frequent tussles between the Florentines and the Sienese. Demolished by the Sienese army, it was rebuilt in the sixteenth century, then in the nineteenth century it was converted into a colossal mock-medieval country residence by the vinicultural pioneer **Baron Bettino Ricasoli**. The baron's apartments can be visited on a tour of the house (summer Mon–Sat 8am–noon & 1–7pm, Sun 11am–7pm; winter same days 8am–noon & 1–5pm, closed Sun; ✆0577.7301 for bookings) – but a far more rewarding experience is to sample the fruits of his labours in the estate's salerooms. Castello di Brolio wine is the routine accompaniment in the castle's unpretentious *Osteria del Castello* **restaurant**, one of the least expensive places to eat in Chianti (closed Thurs). However, for quality it's surpassed by *Carlino* at San Règolo (just next to Castello di Brolio), a trattoria where you can dine exquisitely for L35,000.

Back on the N408, 9km south of Gaiole there's the option of a diversion to the pleasant *Trattoria Grotta della Nona* in **SAN SANO**, just to the west of the road to Ama (see above) – it's a bar-restaurant and general store, with tables outside.

Mugello

For every ten tourists who give over a day to the vineyards of Chianti, perhaps one will give a few hours to the **Mugello**, the lushly fertile region on the Tuscan side of the Apennine ridge separating the province from Emilia-Romagna. Like Chianti, this is a benign, humanized sort of landscape, with nothing that will take your breath away – but it's easier to avoid the crowds here, even though it's a favourite weekend hangout of the Florentine bourgeoisie. Its celebrated olive groves and vineyards are concentrated in the central Mugello basin, formed by the Sieve and its tributary valleys; elsewhere the vegetation is principally oak, pine and chestnut forest, interspersed with small resorts whose customers tend to be short-stay vacationers from the city. Accommodation is quite expensive – unless you're camping, this is a region to nip into from Florence for the day.

As with Chianti, you'll need a car to see anything much. **Three main roads** run from Florence: the **Via Bologna** (N65), which passes Pratolino on its way to the Passo della Futa, the **N302** direct to Borgo San Lorenzo, and the **N67/551**, which winds up to Borgo San Lorenzo along the Sieve. By public transport, there's choice between the **Sieve valley train line** to Borgo San Lorenzo, or SITA and CAP buses along the same route; buses run from Borgo San Lorenzo to the western and northern parts of Mugello. The layout of this section follows the Sieve upstream.

Eastern Mugello

The Sieve flows into the Arno at the unprepossessing town of **PONTASSIEVE**, which makes its money from the **Rúfina wine** district immediately to the north. From here the N70 clambers over the Passo della Consuma, then drops south into the Casentino district towards Poppi (see p.424). The N67 trails the valley through the moderately industrialized area up to Rúfina, then on through Dicomano, where it veers off towards Forlì (in Emilia-Romagna), passing through the **Alpe di San Benedetto**. The main settlement in this zone of Mugello is San Godenzo, which boasts an eleventh-century abbey and not a lot else.

Hugging the course of the Sieve beyond Dicomano, the N551 runs on through **VICCHIO**, the birthplace of Fra' Angelico. Unsurprisingly, the village makes the most of the Angelico connection, but the **Museo Comunale Beato Angelico** (by appointment only; closed for restoration at the time of writing – for information ☎055.849.7026) in fact possesses nothing directly connected with the man; unless Etruscan bits and pieces sound enticing, it's not worth making the call. Vicchio has a **campsite**, the *Vecchio Ponte*, at Via Costoli 16 (☎055.844.8638; June–Sept).

Next stop along the main road is another exalted birthplace, **VESPIGNANO**, where **Giotto** was born in around 1266. His career started, so the story goes, when Cimabue happened to pass by the spot where the boy was tending his father's flock; Giotto was drawing a picture of one of the sheep on a stone, and Cimabue was so astonished by the shepherd's proficiency that he immediately took him on as an apprentice. The bridge where the crucial encounter is said to have occurred is a few hundred yards out of Vespignano and is well signposted. The farmhouse in which Giotto was actually born – the **Casa di Giotto** (May–Sept Tues & Thurs 4–7pm, Sat & Sun 10am–noon & 4–7pm; Oct–April Tues & Thurs 3–5pm, Sat & Sun 10am–noon & 3–5pm; L2000) – is a kilometre off to the north, also well signposted; as with the homes of Leonardo and Michelangelo, this only has value as a pilgrimage.

Borgo San Lorenzo

With a population of 15,000 or so, **BORGO SAN LORENZO** is the giant of Mugello towns, with industrial plots and tracts of new housing spreading further with each year. Substantially rebuilt after a massive earthquake in 1919, it has just one major building, the church of **San Lorenzo**, an eleventh-century foundation, that was renovated in the sixteenth century but still retains its irregularly hexagonal Romanesque tower. This isn't the most photographed sight in town, though – that honour goes to the ghastly statue of *Fido* in Piazza Dante, a rare example of monumentalized sentimentality. Among the town's hotels try the *Tre Fiumi* in Via Madonna dei Tre Fiumi (☎055.8403.015, fax 055.8403.197; ④) or better still, one of the nearby *agriturismi* – ask at the Comunità Montana, Via Togliatti 45.

If you're travelling by public transport from Florence and want to carry on westward into Mugello, you'll have to change here for the local **bus** route through San Piero a Sieve and Scarperia to Barberino di Mugello. The **rail** line heads north from Borgo San Lorenzo to Faenza, while the road north divides after about 20km, one branch going to the bland resort of Palazzuolo sul Sénio, the other to the similar Marradi. If you're driving that way, or waiting for a train in Borgo San Lorenzo, you could call at **San Giovanni Maggiore** (currently closed for restoration), 3km north of the town at the end of an avenue of cypress trees. Like San Lorenzo, it too has a fine Romanesque campanile, and inside there's a twelfth-century marble pulpit inlaid with symbolic figures.

San Piero a Sieve

The N551 continues up the Sieve from Borgo San Lorenzo to **SAN PIERO A SIEVE**, crossing the N65 coming up from Florence. The Mugello landscape is at its best here, with ploughed fields foregrounding the slopes of tree-crested conical hills. San Piero's Romanesque church, spoiled by an eighteenth-century facade, houses a beautiful terracotta font, possibly by Luca della Robbia; its other main monument is the Medici fortress overlooking the town, built by Buontalenti in 1571.

San Piero has a fine **hotel** in Via Le Mozzette, the *Ebe* (☎055.848.019, fax 055.848.567; ⑤); the hotel **restaurant** is more than acceptable, its menu tending to favour dishes from Emilia-Romagna rather than Tuscany. The *Ebe* has less expensive rooms at its *dipendenza* (annexe), Via di Cafaggio 11 (☎055.849.8333, fax 055.848.567; ③). There's also a **campsite** a short distance outside the town at La Fortezza – the *Mugello Verde* (☎055.848.511; open all year).

Bosco ai Frati

The secluded monastery of **Bosco ai Frati**, reached by taking a left turn off the N503 immediately north of San Piero (it's a rough 4km track), traces its roots back to a community of Greek monks who arrived here in the seventh century. In the early eleventh century the settlement was abandoned, but two centuries later St Francis established his order here. One of the earliest Franciscan saints, **Bonaventure**, was the prior at Bosco ai Frati; a man of exemplary modesty, he refused to put on the cardinal's attire brought to him by a papal delegation until he'd finished washing up his brothers' pots and pans – the tree where the outfit was hung is still there.

Cosimo il Vecchio sank a lot of money into this monastery, hiring Michelozzo to redesign the complex in the plainest early Renaissance style; in the sacristy of Michelozzo's porticoed church (open daily 8.30am–7pm) is the most remarkable work of art in the Mugello: a stripped and pain-racked **Crucifix**, probably carved by Donatello. The Associazione Turismo e Ambiente organizes **tours** of the monastery (for bookings ring Mon, Wed & Fri 9.30am–12.30pm ☎055.84.58.793).

Scarperia and beyond

Beyond the turning for Bosco ai Frati, the N503 continues to **SCARPERIA**, once the biggest producer of cutlery in Tuscany and now a high-quality centre for the industry. Sitting on a platform of rock above a valley 5km from San Piero, it's essentially a one-street town, laid out by the Florentines after they turned it into their chief military base in the region in 1306. The **Palazzo Dei Vicari**, built in the same year along the lines of Florence's Palazzo Vecchio, has a rash of coats of arms on the outside, and extensive frescoes on the inside. None of its churches is remarkable, though one of them bears an unusual dedication, to Our Lady of the Earthquakes.

If you're perplexed by the crowds around the town, they're on their way to the **motor racing track** on the eastern outskirts; built in the 1970s, this is a venue for Formula Three car races and Italy's grand prix motorcycle circuit. The town has a neat little hotel, *Cantagallo*, at Via Kennedy 17 (☎055.843.0442, fax 055.843.0443; ⑤).

A small road climbs northwest to the tiny village of **SANT'AGATA**, where the Romanesque parish church contains some beautiful inlaid panels from a dismantled twelfth-century pulpit, and a tabernacle by Giovanni della Robbia. The N503 becomes a switchback after this turnoff, swooping through the region known as Mugello's "Little Switzerland" to the hill resort of **FIRENZUOLA**, 22km from Scarperia. Rebuilt after a fierce battle in 1944, Firenzuola has few blandishments – only those pressing on into Emilia-Romagna need bother with it.

Trebbio and Cafaggiolo

The Medici were originally from Mugello, and the environs of San Piero contain two rough-hewn villas which encapsulate something of the flavour of the period when the family secured its political ascendancy.

Near Novoli, an unsurfaced road runs west from the Via Bologna to the Medici castle of **Trebbio**, whose fortified tower peeps over a cordon of cypresses from the top of its hill. This fourteenth-century castle was converted into a country abode by Michelozzo in 1461 and became a particular favourite with Giovanni delle Bande Nere and his branch of the clan: it was from here that Giovanni's son, Cosimo, rode down to Florence to assume power after the assassination of Alessandro de' Medici. The small garden is often open to the public, and the house itself can be visited (Tues–Fri; ☎055.84.58.793 for bookings).

A short distance north, right on the Via Bologna, lies the villa of **Cafaggiolo**, which like Trebbio was a fortress converted for less bellicose use by Michelozzo. When Cosimo il Vecchio set about consolidating the family fortune through land acquisition in their ancestral domain, one of his first ventures was to buy this estate, which comprised the castle and tracts of land for hunting and agriculture. It was at Cafaggiolo that Cosimo's immediate descendants Lorenzo il Magnifico and his brother grew up, and Lorenzo's own children – Piero, Giovanni (Pope Leo X) and Giuliano – were taught here by such luminaries as Ficino, Poliziano and Pico della Mirandola. In those days the house would have had an even less suave appearance than it does now – alterations in the nineteenth century did away with the surrounding walls, the moat, the drawbridge and one of its towers. For guided tours ring ☎055.458.793.

Barberino di Mugello – and over the Apennines

North of Cafaggiolo the gradient of the road gets pretty savage as it begins the climb to Passo della Futa; if you don't have enough under the bonnet to do the climb comfortably, there's a less strenuous loop that goes through the main market town of western Mugello, **BARBERINO DI MUGELLO**. In the early fourteenth century this became a Florentine border post, and in later years Michelozzo picked up some work here too, giving the main square its loggia – the **Loggie Medicee**, naturally; the neighbouring, much decorated Palazzo Pretorio and the Castello dei Cattani are the only other buildings to catch the eye.

Barberino has one of the few reasonable Mugello **hotels**, *Il Cavallo* at Via della Repubblica 7 (☎055.841.8144, fax 055.841.8293; ③), and there's a good **restaurant** attached, specializing in seafood, at L55,000–65,000 a head. Another decent restaurant is to be found close to the exit from the autostrada to the west of the village – *Le Capannine*, Viale Don Minzoni 88, Cavallino Mugello (closed Mon). Outside

Barberino, at Via Santa Lucia 24/a in Monte di Fo, is the *Sergente* **campsite** (☎055.842.3018; open all year).

When the Barberino loop rejoins Via Bologna it's an unrelenting haul up to **Passo della Futa**, from whose 900-metre vantage all of Mugello's valleys and ridges are visible. This isn't the highest point on Mugello's road network – Passo della Raticosa, 13km on, is a few metres higher – but it's easily the best viewpoint; there's no reason to go farther unless you're off to Bologna.

Prato

Taking its name from the meadow (*prato*) where the ancient settlement's great market used to be held, **PRATO** has long been a commercial success, and is now the second largest city in Tuscany, after Florence. It's been Italy's chief textile centre since the early Middle Ages, and even though recession has damaged exports, it still produces three-quarters of all the woollen cloth sold from Italy. More recently Prato has found fame as the home town of actor Roberto Benigni, Oscar-winning star of the 1999 hit film, *Life is Beautiful*. It might not feature on a list of the most attractive places in the province, but its long-time wealth has left a fair legacy of buildings and art, including Filippo Lippi's most engaging cycle of frescoes.

A close Florentine connection goes back to 1350, when the self-governing *comune* of Prato was besieged by its neighbour, which by then was becoming alarmed at the economic threat of Prato's cloth mills. The year after, Florence bought the titles to the town from its Neapolitan rulers, thus sealing their union. Thereafter, political events in the capital were mirrored here, a relationship that was to cost Prato dear after Savonarola's example led the Pratese to join him in rejecting the Medici. Under the direction of Leo X, the imperial army sacked Prato in 1512 as a warning to the rebellious Florentines: two days of slaughter and pillage ensued, recorded by historian Guicciardini: "Nothing would have escaped the avarice, lust and cruelty of the invaders had not the Cardinal de' Medici placed guards at the main church and saved the honour of the women who had taken refuge there. More than two thousand men died, not fighting . . . but fleeing or crying for mercy." A more pacific relationship was soon established, and Florence limited its bullying to the imposition of quotas on Prato's factories. Today the balance has shifted: while Prato is fairly self-sufficient, Florence struggles to find some alternative to a service-based economy.

The City

The historic centre remains enclosed within its hexagon of grey stone walls, making orientation very straightforward. Buses from Florence run direct to the Piazza del Duomo; if you're coming from the main train station it's basically a question of following your nose – cross the Ponte della Vittoria over the Bisenzio river, and Viale Vittorio Veneto leads you through the walls at Piazza San Marco.

The Castello area

Directly ahead of the train station, past a Henry Moore sculpture, is the white-walled and sharp-angled **Castello dell'Imperatore** (summer Mon & Wed–Sat 10am–1.30pm & 3.30–7pm, Sun 10am–2pm; winter Mon & Wed–Sat 10am–5pm, Sun 10am–2pm; free), built in the 1230s for Emperor Frederick II as a base for his representative in the city and as a way-station for imperial progresses between Germany and his domains in southern Italy and Sicily. The castle is heavily restored and empty except for the rooms used for temporary exhibitions, but you can wander around the ramparts for views over the old city and the industrial suburbs.

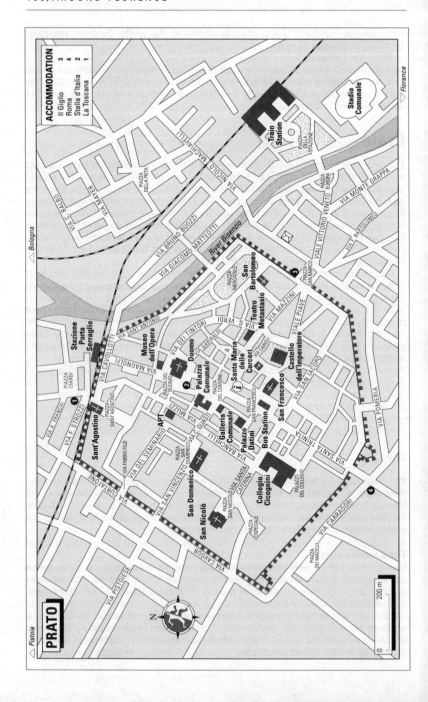

Round the back is Prato's major Renaissance monument, Giuliano da Sangallo's church of **Santa Maria delle Carceri** (daily 6.30am–noon & 4–7.30pm), built to honour a miraculous talking image of the Virgin that was painted on the walls of the gaol here – hence the name "Mary of the Prisons". With its perfect proportions and uncluttered lines, the church feels less like a place for worship than a demonstration of the correctness of the Brunelleschian style. The exterior makes a decorative gesture towards the Romanesque with its half-completed bands of green and white marble, while the interior is lightened by Andrea della Robbia's tondi of the Evangelists and ceramic frieze.

Twin-coloured marble cladding also features on the facade of the thirteenth-century **San Francesco**, which presents one massive flank to the other side of the square. Inside, there are a couple of fine monuments: on the left wall of the single aisle you'll find Bernardo Rossellino's worn-down tomb of Gemignano Inghirami, and set into the floor near the high altar is the slab of **Francesco di Marco Datini**, the city's most celebrated personality. The subject of Iris Origo's classic study, *The Merchant of Prato*, Datini became one of Europe's richest men through his dealings in the cloth trade, and played a crucial role in the rationalization of accounting methods – on his death, his offices were found to contain tens of thousands of scrupulously kept ledgers, all inscribed "To God and profit". Off the cloister, the Cappella Migliatori has lovely frescoes of *The Lives of St Anthony Abbot and St Matthew* and *The Crucifixion*, painted in the 1390s by Niccolò di Pietro Gerini.

Datini's house, **Palazzo Datini** (Mon–Sat 9am–noon, also Tues & Thurs 4–7pm; free), is a couple of minutes from the church, across Piazza San Francesco and up Via Rinascelda. Built in the 1390s, this is now home to the *Ceppo*, a charity Datini established a few years later. The inscrutable frescoes on the facade show scenes from his life; the interior is completely frescoed as well.

The Piazza del Comune and the Duomo

A short distance north of here, Datini is commemorated with a statue and bronze reliefs at the centre of the trim little **Piazza del Comune**; he inevitably crops up again amongst the myriad portraits of local worthies in the **Quadreria Palazzo Comunale** (Sat 4–7.30pm, Sun & holidays 10am–1pm; free). Within the frescoed walls of the same building, the town celebrates its literal rise from rags to riches in the **Museo del Tessuto** (Mon 2.30–6.30pm, Wed–Sun 10.30am–6.30pm; L5000). Amongst the colourful collection of over 5000 fabrics are fifth-century Egyptian tapestries. Across from the Palazzo sits the medieval **Palazzo Pretorio** whose museum, the **Museo Civico**, is currently under restoration, its contents transferred to the Museo di Pittura Murale (see next page).

The wide and lively Piazza del Duomo, a couple of blocks farther in, forms an effective space for the Pisan-Romanesque facade of the **duomo** (7am–noon & 3.30–6.30pm), distinguished by another Andrea della Robbia terracotta over the portal and by Donatello and Michelozzo's beautiful **Pulpit of the Sacred Girdle**. This unique addition was constructed for the ceremonial display of the girdle of the Madonna, a garment handed to the ever-incredulous apostle Thomas at her Assumption. The girdle was supposedly bequeathed by Thomas to a priest, one of whose descendants married a crusader from Prato, who in turn brought it back to his home town in the twelfth century. Replicas have replaced the Donatello reliefs of gambolling children, the originals now being housed in the cathedral museum. Until restoration work is finished on the chapel, the girdle is only displayed five times a year: on Easter Sunday, May 1, August 15, September 8 and Christmas Day.

The story is detailed in the chapel immediately left of the entrance in Agnolo Gaddi's fresco cycle of *The Legend of the Holy Girdle* (1392–95) – though sadly it's all but invisible behind the grating, as is the *Madonna and Child* carved by Giovanni Pisano. Close by, in the left aisle, there's another fine piece of stonework, a chalice-shaped pulpit by Antonio Rossellino and Mino da Fiesole.

Filippo Lippi's famous frescoes, around the high altar, were completed over a period of fourteen years (1452–66) and depict the lives of John the Baptist and St Stephen. (A long-term restoration has hidden much of this cycle for several years; if the work has been completed, you'll need coins for the light boxes.) These are marvellously sensuous paintings in which even the Baptist's wilderness looks enticing, a whisked-up landscape like a confectioner's fantasy. Especially decadent is the *Feast of Herod*, where the decapitation seems like a regrettable incident that needn't ruin the party. There's a scandalous story to the creation of these pictures: during the period of their creation, Lippi – himself a monk, at least in name – became so besotted with a young nun named Lucrezia Buti that he abducted her as she was preparing to attend the ceremony of the girdle. Later to become the mother of Filippino Lippi, Lucrezia is said to have been the model for the dancing Salome. Her lover also depicted himself among those mourning St Stephen – he's third from the right.

The chapel to the right of the high altar has scenes from the *Lives of the Virgin and St Stephen*, still cussedly labelled as being by Paolo Uccello, even though a study of the *sinopie* has established that they can't possibly be.

Housed alongside the duomo, around the cloister of the bishop's palace, the **Museo dell'Opera del Duomo** (Mon & Wed–Sat 9.30am–12.30pm & 3–6.30pm, Sun 9.30am–12.30pm; L8000, includes entrance to the Museo Pittura Murale) contains the Donatello panels from the great pulpit; they are badly cracked and stained by exhaust fumes but their sculpted putti make a sprightly contrast with the lumbering little lads on Maso di Bartolomeo's tiny silver *Reliquary for the Sacred Girdle*, the museum's other main treasure. Also on show is Filippino Lippi's plucky *St Lucy*, unperturbed by the gigantic sword lodged in her neck, and the painting that Filippo Lippi produced to demonstrate his suitability for the fresco commission, *The Death of Jerome*. A doorway on the far side of the cloister opens into the duomo's frescoed **crypt**; beside the altar is the head of one of the city's main wells, which – as the inscription records – was choked with corpses by the barbarian invaders of 1512.

Beyond the duomo

A five-minute walk west of the duomo, in the ex-monastery adjoining the mainly fourteenth-century church of San Domenico, the **Museo Pittura Murale** (Mon & Wed–Sat 10.30am–1pm & 3.30–7pm, Sun 10am–1pm; L8000, includes entrance to the Museo dell'Opera del Duomo) currently houses one of the town's star attractions – Filippo Lippi's *Madonna del Ceppo*. The painting contains portraits of the five men who financed the picture; Datini coughed up more than the other four, so he's the one depicted large-scale. There are also works by Lippi's son Filippino, and a selection of fourteenth-century altarpieces including a predella by Bernardo Daddi narrating the story of Prato's holy relic, the Girdle of the Madonna (see above). The rest of the display features a hotchpotch of minor frescoes, culled mostly from churches in and around Prato.

Practicalities

Prato's **tourist office** is next to the Carceri church in Piazza delle Carceri (summer Mon–Sat 9am–6.30pm; winter Mon–Sat 9am–1pm & 3–6pm; ☎0574.24.112). Prato, half an hour from Florence by bus or train, can be an alternative for **accommodation** when there's nothing available there. It has a one-star hotel, the *Roma*, outside the southern gate at Via Carradori 1 (☎0574.31.777; ③), and three two-stars, the *Stella d'Italia* at Piazza Duomo 8 (☎0574.27.910, fax 0574.40.289; ③), *Il Giglio* at Piazza San Marco 14 (☎0574.37.049, fax 0574.604.351; ③) and *La Toscana* at Piazza Ciardi 3 (☎0574.28.096, fax 0574.25.163; ③).

Prato has plenty of **restaurants**. The *Trattoria Lapo* is a basic local place at Piazza Mercatale 141 (closed Sun); there are two neon-lit *birreria*-pizzeria places on the square as well. Moving upmarket, *Ristorante Osvaldo Baroncelli*, Via Fra Bartolomeo 13 (off Piazza San Marco), offers imaginative variations of traditional Tuscan meat and fish dishes for around L50,000 per head without wine. And for a little more you can eat at one of Tuscany's best seafood restaurants, *Il Piraña*, Via Valentini 110, ten minutes' drive out of the centre (☎0574.25.746; closed Sat lunch, Sun & Aug). Also worth trying are *Lo Scoglio*, Via G. Verdi 40 (closed Mon), which specializes in fish dishes, and *Baghino*, Via dell'Accademia 9, for local food in a traditional atmosphere (closed Sun & Mon lunch): both about L40,000 a head.

A Prato speciality is the *Biscotto di Prato*, a very hard yellow biscuit, traditionally eaten over the Christmas period, and made a touch less resistant by dipping in wine or coffee. The best outlet for these and other Prato pastries is Antonio Mattei, Via Ricasoli 22.

If you're staying, you could check out the art-house Terminale **cinema**, at Via Carbonaia 31, or the **Teatro Metastasio** at Via Cairoli 59, a world-famous venue for concerts and theatre productions (☎0574.608.501; mid-Oct to April). Excellent modern art exhibitions and cultural events are organized year-round by the smart **Centro per l'Arte Contemporanea L. Pecci** (daily except Tues 10am–7pm; L10,000), a kilometre or so southeast of the centre in Viale della Repubblica (☎0574.570.620). Finally, summer concerts are also held in the courtyard.

Pistoia

The provincial capital of **PISTOIA** is one of the least visited cities in Tuscany, an unjustified neglect for this quiet, well-preserved medieval settlement at the base of the Apennines. Just thirty-five minutes by train from Florence (about the same by bus), it is an easy and enjoyable day trip – and also forms the most attractive approach to Lucca and Pisa, with both of which it has strong architectural links.

The Roman forerunner of Pistoia – Pistoria – was where Catiline and his fellow conspirators against the republic were finally run to ground, and the town went on to earn itself a reputation as a lair of malcontents. It was a Ghibelline city until its conquest by Guelph Florence in 1254, whereupon it allegedly brought about the division of the **Guelphs** into the **Black** and **White** factions. According to the folkloric version, one Pistoiese child injured another while playing with a sword; the miscreant's father sent him to apologize, whereupon the father of the injured party chopped the offender's hand off, telling him, "Iron, not words, is the remedy for sword wounds." The city promptly polarized into the Neri and the Bianchi camps (taking the names from ancestors of the two parties), and by some osmotic process the battle names were taken up in Florence. In view of this sort of mayhem, Dante found it entirely appropriate that Pistoia should have been the home of Vanni Fucci, a thuggish factional leader whose exploits included stealing the silver from the cathedral; he's encountered in the *Inferno*, enmeshed in a knot of snakes and cursing God.

Except for a brief spell at the start of the fourteenth century, when Castruccio Castracani held the city for Lucca, Pistoia remained a Florentine fief, yet for centuries the mythology of murderous Pistoia endured, and Michelangelo spoke for many when he referred to the Pistoiese as the "enemies of heaven". It's fitting that, according to one school of thought, the word "pistol" should be derived from this violent town; meaning "from Pistoia", a *pistole* was originally a dagger, but the name was transferred to the first firearms made here in the sixteenth century. These days, Pistoia maintains its industrial tradition with a large rail plant, but is better known for the acres of garden

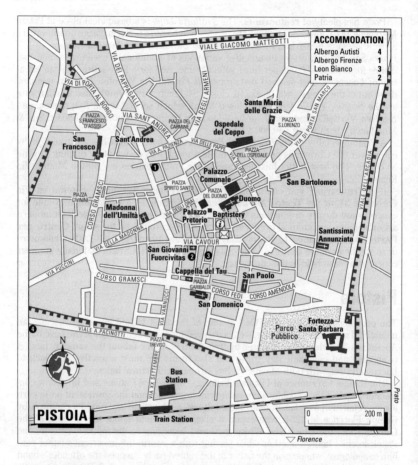

nurseries on the slopes around. In terms of art attractions, its appeal lies in a sequence of Romanesque churches and medieval sculptures, and one of the masterpieces of the della Robbia workshop.

The City

Arriving by train or by bus from Florence you are just a couple of minutes' walk south of the historic centre – Viale XX Settembre points the way through the city walls, which were raised in the fourteenth century and reinforced by the Medici. The interesting part of the city begins one block north of Piazza Treviso, at the junction with the centre's widest avenue, Corso Gramsci.

Around Piazza Garibaldi

A right turn at this junction takes you to Piazza Garibaldi and the thirteenth-century church of **San Domenico**, which was rebuilt in the 1970s after terrible damage during the war. Scraps of medieval frescoes remain inside, where the most arresting feature is the Rossellino brothers' tomb of the teacher Filippo Lazzari, on the right near the door. In the cloister (entered from the aisle) there are remnants of a fresco of *The Journey of the Magi* by Benozzo Gozzoli, who died of the plague in Pistoia and is buried here.

Opposite San Domenico, the **Cappella del Tau** (or Sant'Antonio Abate) preserves a chaos of fourteenth- and fifteenth-century frescoed scenes from the lives of Adam and Eve, Christ and various saints. A couple of doors away, in the Palazzo del Tau, there's the **Museo Marino Marini** (Tues–Sat 9am–1pm & 3–7pm, Sun 9am–12.30pm; L6000), showing a selection of work by Pistoia's most famous modern son. Marini found an early influence in the realism of Etruscan sarcophagi, expressed in the sculptures of horses and riders that he churned out throughout his life; in the 1940s he diversified into portraiture – subjects here include Thomas Mann, Henry Miller and Marc Chagall.

On the same side of the Cappella del Tau, a couple of minutes' walk east, looms the late thirteenth-century facade of **San Paolo**; the front of greenish stone with dark green and white inlays is topped by a statue of St James, possibly by Orcagna.

San Giovanni Fuorcivitas

All streets north from Piazza Garibaldi link with Via Cavour, now the main street of the city's inner core but once the settlement's outer limit – as the name of the majestic **San Giovanni Fuorcivitas** ("outside the walls") proclaims. The church was founded in the eighth century, but rebuilt between the twelfth and fourteenth centuries, when it received the dazzling green and white flank that serves as its **facade**. Rather than being the focal point of the wall, the doorway is just a brief interruption in the infinitely repeatable pattern of the triple arcade – a pattern echoed in the oratory across the alleyway. The **interior**, though only feebly lit by the slit windows, is just as remarkable, as this is one of three Pistoia churches distinguished by pulpits showing state of the art Tuscan sculpture in the thirteenth century. The **pulpit** here was carved in 1270 by a pupil of Nicola Pisano, whose son, Giovanni, executed the four figures of cardinals on the holy water stoup. Just about visible in the murk is a glazed terracotta *Visitation* on the left wall, probably by Luca della Robbia.

From here, a left up Via Roma is the quickest way into the central square, but if you want to make sure you don't miss any of Pistoia's architectural sights, follow the westward arc of Via Cavour into Via Buozzi until you come to **Madonna dell'Umiltà**. This handsome colossus was designed by a pupil of Bramante and finished off by Vasari with a dome so heavy that the walls had to be reinforced to stop the church collapsing.

The direct path from Via Cavour to Piazza del Duomo crosses the **market square**, Piazza della Sala; a marginally more long-winded alternative is to walk through the minuscule **Piazza San Leone**, a few blocks east. This was the centre of the ancient Lombard settlement, and its stocky tower was later the bolt hole of Vanni Fucci.

Piazza del Duomo

The medieval complex of the **Piazza del Duomo** is a superb and slightly eccentric ensemble, reversing the normal priorities of the Italian central square: the ornate baptistery lurks in a recess off one corner and the duomo faces it, turning its unadorned side to the open space and leaving the huge campanile and monolithic civic buildings to take the limelight. There's something odd about the expanse of the piazza too, as if it were conceived for a town considerably larger than present-day Pistoia. Once a year, though, the square is packed to capacity – for the **Giostro dell'Orso** (see p.187), Pistoia's answer to the medieval shenanigans of Siena's Palio.

THE DUOMO

If you have come from Pisa or Lucca, the style of Pistoia's **duomo**, the *Cattedrale di San Zeno*, will be immediately familiar, with its tiered arcades and distinctive Pisan-Romanesque decoration of striped black and white marble. Set into this soberly refined front is a tunnel-vault portico of bright terracotta tiles by Andrea della Robbia, creator also of the *Madonna and Child* above the door.

The **interior** (daily 9am–noon & 4–7pm) has an outstanding array of sculptural pieces, one of which is part of the entrance wall – a marvellous font designed by Benedetto da Maiano, showing incidents from the life of the Baptist. Close by, on the wall of the right aisle, is the monument to Dante's friend, the diplomat, teacher and poet **Cino da Pistoia**; it is said that Boccaccio is one of the pupils to whom he's shown lecturing in the bottom panel.

Just beyond this monument is the Cappella di San Jacopo (Mon–Sat 10am–noon & 4–5.45pm, Sun 11.20am–noon & 4–5.30pm, to fit in around the services; L3000), endowed with one of the richest pieces of silverwork to be seen in Italy, the **Altarpiece of St James**. Weighing almost a ton and populated with 628 figures, it was begun in 1287 and completed in the fifteenth century, when Brunelleschi cast the two half-figures of prophets on the left-hand side. The length of time taken on the work is clear if you compare the scenes on the front with the bolder figures in the scenes from the life of St James on the left-hand flank, where an extra suppleness and vitality is evident. The artist responsible for these latter panels was a certain Leonardo di Ser Giovanni, who immediately after completing them was given the commission to begin the only other piece of silverwork that can stand comparison with this one – the altarpiece now in Florence's Museo dell'Opera del Duomo.

In the chapel to the left of the high altar is Antonio Rossellino's bust of Bishop Donato de' Medici, and the so-called *Madonna di Piazza*, begun by Verrocchio and finished by Lorenzo di Credi (often kept under wraps); Verrocchio, with his workshop, was also responsible for the flurried tomb of Cardinal Forteguerri, in the left aisle by the door.

The duomo's adjacent **Campanile** was originally a Lombard watchtower, then was spruced up with Romanesque arcades in the twelfth century and a Gothic turret in the sixteenth; the swallowtail crenellations near the summit of this bizarre hybrid give away the town's old Ghibelline loyalties.

AROUND THE PIAZZA

Adjoining the duomo is the partly clad Palazzo dei Vescovi, now home of the small **Museo di San Zeno** (guided tours Tues, Thurs & Fri, 10am–1pm & 3–5pm; L7000), where the chief exhibit is Ghiberti's reliquary of St James. The basement has an even more modest archeological collection, with relics from the Roman settlement.

Opposite is the tall, dapper Gothic **baptistery**, designed by Giovanni Pisano, completed in the mid-fourteenth century by Cellino di Nese, creator of the duomo's monument to Cino da Pistoia. There's nothing under the conical brick ceiling but an old font; the vacancy is sometimes filled by commercial art shows.

Though its interior is closed to the public, you can take a look at the courtyard of the **Palazzo del Podestà**, the law-court building to the side of the baptistery. From the stone benches half-sheltered by the portico the Pistoian judges used to pronounce sentences notorious for their severity; a grimly humorous speciality was to sentence the guilty to be elevated to the ranks of the nobility – thus depriving them of any civic rights under the town's republican constitution.

On the far side of the square, the flaking pale limestone facade of the **Palazzo Comunale** bears a black marble head that's probably a portrait of the Moorish king of Majorca whom the Pistoiese defeated in the twelfth century; local folklore, tending to the conspiratorial, prefers to interpret it as the head of a man who betrayed the city to the

THE GIOSTRA DELL'ORSO

The earliest forerunner of the **Giostra dell'Orso** was a peculiar ritual mentioned in a chronicle of 1300. On March 10 of that year, the feast day of San Francesca Romana, a dozen knights fought a ceremonial battle against a bear dressed in the town's coat of arms. The precise form of this joust changed many times over the following centuries but some version of it was fought every year until 1666, when it seems suddenly to have been abandoned. In 1947 it was revived in more humane form and now takes place on July 25, feast of the city's patron, St James. It forms the centrepiece of the festival season known as the *Luglio Pistoiese* – Pistoia July.

The fun begins with a procession of around three hundred standard bearers, trumpeters, knights, halberdiers and assorted costumed extras from the Porta Lucchese to the Piazza del Duomo. These characters represent the villages around Pistoia, the city's crafts and trades, and the four districts of the historic centre. Each of these four districts is represented in the joust by three knights, their regalia bearing the heraldic emblems of the Lion, the Stag, the Griffon and the Dragon. Having led the procession into the arena laid out on the piazza, the knights are separated into pairs, who then ride against each other around the track, scoring points by hitting the two highly stylized "bears" set on bales on opposite sides of the circuit. Points are awarded according to which parts of the target are hit with the lance, and at the end of the day two prizes are awarded – to the highest-scoring district and the highest-scoring knight.

The *giostra* is always a sell-out; to be sure of tickets, contact the regional tourist office at least a month in advance. The address is A.P.T Pistoia, Palazzo dei Vescovi, Piazza del Duomo, Pistoia (☎0573.21.622, fax 0573.34.327).

Lucchesi. The building contains the **Museo Civico** (Tues–Sat 10am–7pm, Sun 9am–12.30pm; L6000), where the customary Tuscan welter of medieval and Renaissance pieces is counterweighted by an impressive showing of Baroque hyperactivity – including a couple of hideous battle scenes by the evidently disturbed Ciccio Napoletano.

There's a **Nuovo Museo Diocesano** (Tues, Thurs & Fri 10am–1pm & 4–7pm, Wed & Sat 10am–1pm; L6000) opened in the Ripa del Sale, next to the Palazzo Comunale, with the furniture and paraphernalia of Pope Clement IX.

From the Piazza to San Francesco

At the back of the Palazzo Comunale, Via Pacini is the obvious route to take to explore the northern part of the town. Across this road, on Piazza San Bartolomeo, is the **Abbazia di San Bartolomeo in Pantano** – "St Bartholomew in the Swamp", from the marshy ground on which it was raised in the eighth century. The semi-complete facade is as appealing as any of the city's more polished fronts, the marble plating giving way to powdery red brick. Inside there's the earliest of Pistoia's trio of pulpits. Executed in 1250 by Guido da Como, and reconstructed from its dismantled parts, it's far less sophisticated than the other two, a rectangular box whose principal scenes are filled with figures arrayed in level ranks like an audience in a stadium.

The most publicized episode of the Pistoia townscape is not a church but a hospital in a square at the end of Via Pacini – the **Ospedale del Ceppo**, which takes its name from the hollowed-out tree stump (*ceppo*) in which alms were traditionally collected. Established in the thirteenth century, it was embellished in the fifteenth with a portico like the one Brunelleschi designed for the Innocenti in Florence. Emblazoned along its length is the feature that makes it famous – Giovanni della Robbia's painted terracotta **frieze** of the *Theological Virtues* and the *Seven Works of Mercy*. Completed in the early sixteenth century, it is a startlingly colourful panoply of Renaissance types and costume: pilgrims, prisoners, the sick, the dead, all committed with a precise attention to domestic realism.

A couple of minutes' walk over to the west, the twelfth-century **Sant'Andrea** has a typically Pisan facade with a pair of Romanesque lions and a panel of *The Journey of the Magi* stuck onto it. The corridor-slim aisle contains the third and greatest of the pulpits, by **Giovanni Pisano**; carved in 1297, it is based on his father's design for the Pisa baptistery pulpit and only marginally less elaborate than his own slightly later work in Pisa cathedral. It shows scenes from the life of Christ and the Last Judgement, the figures carved in such deep relief that they seem to be surging out of a limitless depth. Giovanni was the first to appreciate the glory of his achievement; Nicola Pisano had boasted of being the greatest living sculptor, and Giovanni's inscription brags that he had now surpassed his father. The church also has a second piece by Giovanni – the Crucifix mounted on the wall of the right aisle.

The plainest of the city's churches, the Franciscans' **San Francesco al Prato**, is a little farther to the west, on the edge of one of the main bus terminals. Tattered fourteenth-century frescoes are preserved in the single nave, and some healthier specimens adorn the chapels at the east end, where there's a fine *Triumph of Augustine* in the chapel to the left of the high altar. To the side of the church there's an unusual memorial to Aldo Moro, the Italian prime minister killed by the Red Brigades on May 7, 1978; the bronze plaques are imprinted with the newspaper headlines from the day his body was found.

Out of town – the zoo and the Celle arts centre

Four kilometres southwest of the city at Via Pieve a Celle 160, the **Giardino Zoologico** (daily: summer 9am–7pm; winter 9am–5pm; L14,000) is a good stand-by for anyone with kids who aren't responding to the charms of Romanesque architecture and della Robbia ceramics. Opened in 1970, it's one of Italy's more spacious zoos – though it has to be said that the inmates don't include any rarities.

A short drive east of town at Santomato, the **Fattoria di Celle** holds a remarkable private collection, established in 1982 to give Italy an international forum for contemporary art comparable to such centres as the Kroller-Müller in Holland. Everything here, in the rooms and park of the Villa Celle, could be described as environmental art – the large-scale outdoor pieces are conceived as interactions with the natural world, while the smaller installations inside take their cue from the enclosing space of the rooms.

Artists from all over Europe and the United States have contributed to the sculpture park, devising a variety of responses to its woodlands and grassy slopes, and to the wider cultural environment of Tuscany. Alice Aycock's steel constructions recall such Renaissance mechanisms as the astrolabe, but are built on a scale to echo the curves and angles of the landscape. A labyrinth of polished green and white marble by Robert Morris recalls the Romanesque churches of the region, and is so perfectly placed on the gradient of the hill that it seems to be a single mass of stone until you come to the entrance. An artificial stream and grotto laid out in the last century has been used by Anne and Patrick Poirier to evoke the epic struggle between Zeus and the Giants, with steel lightning flashes and fragments of huge marble heads littering the water course. In hi-tech contrast, Dennis Oppenheim's massive contraption of steel towers, immovable pulleys and functionless wires looks like a visual pun on the ski-lifts of the winter resorts north of Pistoia. Most of the installations date from the inaugural year, but new pieces are being commissioned all the time, maintaining the Fattoria di Celle's status as one of the most vital art centres in the country. The centre is open from April to September and visitors must first write for an appointment: Fattoria di Celle, 51030 Santomato di Pistoia. The entrance gate is not signposted, but rather signalled by a huge spherical metal construction by Alberto Burri.

Practicalities

Pistoia's central **tourist office** is at Piazza del Duomo 4 (Mon–Sat 9am–1pm & 3–6pm, plus June–Sept Sun 9am–1pm & 3–6pm; ☎0573.21.622). The main **post office** is off the south side of Piazza del Duomo at Via Roma 5; the Telecom Italia **telephone** booths are on Corso Gramsci.

The city's low tourist profile means a dearth of **accommodation** – so if you plan to stay, phone ahead. There's just one one-star hotel, the clean and friendly *Albergo Autisti*, Viale Pacinotti 89 (☎0573.21.771; ②), but with semi-permanent guests during the week it is unlikely to have many free rooms; within the city walls there's only one two-star, the *Albergo Firenze*, a short walk west of Piazza del Duomo at Via Curtatone e Montanara 42 (☎0573.21.660, fax 0573.23.141; ③). Central alternatives are the three-star *Leon Bianco*, Via Panciatichi 2 (☎0573.26.675, fax 0573.26.704; ⑤), or the *Patria*, Via Crispi 6 (☎0573.25.187, fax 0573.368.168; ③) – both are within a minute of San Giovanni Fuorcivitas.

The **restaurant** scene in central Pistoia isn't a lot better, with no real rivals for the straightforward Tuscan menu at *Da Mone*, Via Verdi 3, where the set menu for L30,000 changes daily (closed Sun), or *Leon Rosso*, at Via Panciatichi 4 (closed Sun), where a full meal costs around L40,000. For wood-fired oven pizzas and excellent *frutti di mare*, check out *Il Pollo d'Oro*, Via Attilio Frosini 132 (closed Mon). The most interesting food for vegetarians and carnivores is at *S. Jacopo* (closed Sun & Mon lunch), Via Crispi 15, with a likely charge of L40,000 for a full meal.

The liveliest time to be in Pistoia is July, for the *Luglio Pistoiese* – a month-long programme of concerts and events (including the famous *Pistoia Blues* music festival featuring major international jazz and blues artists), culminating in the *Giostra dell'Orso*. Otherwise, the city stirs a little for the morning fruit & veg. **market** (Mon–Sat) in the Piazza della Sala.

Leaving Pistoia, Lazzi **buses** for Florence and Prato run from by the train station; COPIT buses for Empoli, where you can also change for Vinci, from Piazza San Francesco. The route to Vinci goes over beautiful Monte Albano and allows a loop to Florence or Pisa if you set out early in the day.

Montecatini and Monsummano

Known as the **Valdinievole** (Valley of Mists), the area to the west of Pistoia is a region of subterranean streams and springs that now harbours one of Italy's main concentrations of **spa towns**. As with the German spas, such resorts as a rule don't have the same aura of social exclusivity as they do in Britain. But Tuscany has more than its share of the leisured classes, and the two big centres of the Valdinievole, **Montecatini Terme** and **Monsummano Terme**, are definitely not places for the hoi polloi. Dauntless individuals can join the smart set for an afternoon of sweltering and sipping, but most people will probably prefer to spend more time in the old hill- towns above the modern spas.

The Florence to Viareggio **trains** stop at Montecatini; Monsummano is really only worth a call if you're driving through.

Montecatini Terme

No spa in Italy has a glossier reputation than **MONTECATINI TERME**, as can be gauged from the fact that the likes of Gucci and Gianfranco Ferre find it profitable to maintain outlets here. Sedated rather than sedate, most of the town is a leafy grid of indistinguishable apartment blocks and villas where it's eternally siesta.

The centre of the town is delineated by the **Parco delle Terme** (a ten-minute walk from the train station), where each of the nine sulphate springs is encased in its own separate building. Fronting the piazza at the edge of the park is the pompous **Terme Leopoldine**, a shrine to the healing properties of mud baths. North of this is the **Tettuccio**, discovered in the fourteenth century but not exploited to the full until Grand Duke Leopoldo I gave it the works in the eighteenth. Inside, Art Nouveau paintings and ceramics create a suitably sybaritic environment in which to compose your letters in the spa café or imbibe the acrid water. Across the way, the Palladian home of the **Regina** spring suggests more astringent regimes, while at the back of the park, the mock-medieval **Torretta** embodies the straightforwardly escapist element of all spa resorts.

All these spas are open from May to October; there's one establishment, the hybrid Neo-Renaissance-modernist **Excelsior**, that's open all year. For a week's serious wallowing you can buy a book of twelve tickets at the office at Viale Verdi 41, near the entrance to the park, or else individually from each spa: expect to pay, for a half-day pass, somewhere in the region of L10,000–20,000 just for drinking the waters, L30,000 for a bath and L55,000 for mud, depending on the season and time of day.

The non-thermal delights of Montecatini can all be sampled by following Viale Diaz, which curves round the north side of the park. Here, across the road from the Regina spa, you'll find the **Accademia d'Arte** (Mon–Sat 3–6pm; free), a mishmash of gifts from illustrious guests such as Verdi, who composed *Otello* while staying in Montecatini, refining the score on the piano that's kept here. Ten minutes' walk beyond is the relatively unkempt verdure of **Le Panteraie**, a wooded park with a swimming pool and deer reserve.

Halfway between the gallery and the woods is the most enjoyable thing in Montecatini: the **funicular** to **Montecatini Alto**, a few hundred metres above the spa (April–Oct daily every 30min; L4500 single, L8000 return); if you drive, it's a five-kilometre haul. The original Montecatini settlement here offers excellent views, especially of Monsummano, and in summer the tiny Piazza Giusti becomes a pleasant outdoor extension of its cafés and *pizzerie*. If you want to get out of the sun for a while, there's the stalactite-heavy **Grotta Maona** (April–Oct daily 9am–noon & 2–6pm; L7000), a couple of kilometres below Montecatini Alto. Outside you'll find ballroom dancing going on in the afternoons and evenings.

MONTECATINI PRACTICALITIES

The Montecatini **tourist office**, at Via Manzoni 3, just off Viale Verdi (Mon–Sat 9am–12.30pm & 3–6pm, in summer also Sun 9am–noon; ☎0572.772.244) has full details of Montecatini's plentiful **accommodation** – it has around three hundred places to stay, predominantly top-bracket, but with about thirty one-star hotels. In the main town, the best deal is at the *Corallo*, Viale Cavallotti 116 (☎0572.78.288, fax 0572.79.512; full board ⑥) – and there's a pool. Even more reasonable is the one-star *Daniela*, Viale Cavallotti 127 (☎0572.78.858; full board ④) with a garden, while up in Montecatini Alto, *L'Etrusco*, Via Talenti 2 (☎0572.79.645; full board ⑤), is a family-run hotel overlooking the Piazza Giusti with a restaurant offering good-value Tuscan cuisine. With so many choices, the best bet is to go straight to the tourist office for details of vacancies.

Most of Montecatini's **restaurants** are attached to the posh hotels; of the independent places, the best are *Enoteca da Giovanni* at Via Garibaldi 25 (closed Mon & Aug), and *La Rughetta* in Piazza Giusti, Montecatini Alto (closed Tues), both of which will set you back around L70,000 per person. Very nearly as good, and appreciably less expensive, is the *Bolognese* restaurant-pizzeria, Corso Matteotti 90 (closed Mon).

The tourist office organizes various half-day trips to the more inaccessible places in the surrounding area (June–Oct Mon, Wed & Fri leaving 2.30pm; L15,000).

Monsummano Terme

Montecatini's sister spa, **MONSUMMANO TERME**, a few kilometres southeast, has its own speciality act: the steam cave. The family of the satirist Giuseppe Giusti – a native of Monsummano – set the town in motion when they discovered a flooded cave filled with mineral-saturated steam. Divided into chambers tagged *Inferno*, *Purgatorio* and *Paradiso*, the **Grotta Giusti** (April–Oct), on the eastern outskirts, is still the town's big draw – half luxury hotel, half medical centre. Competition is provided by the artificial **Grotta Parlanti** (May–Oct) to the north, whose vapours are allegedly even more efficacious.

The old town of **Monsummano Alto**, three kilometres from the centre up a relentlessly steep and narrow road, is now little more than a twelfth-century church and a few very ruined castle ruins; the panorama is spectacular though, with the massed glasshouses of Pescia catching the sun like a lake (see p.215).

Empoli and around

The N67, tracking the Arno west of Florence, is as dispiriting as the road that follows the river to the east. Busy and slow, it's strung with drab towns, industrial sites, megastores and warehouses, and – apart from a handful of attractions in **Empoli** – is only worth bothering with for the diversions to be found off it.

Empoli

The manufacturing town of **EMPOLI**, purveyor of glass and raincoats to the nation, is a major junction of road and rail routes between Florence, Pisa, the coast and Siena, and thus might well be a place you'll find yourself passing through. Most people limit their exploration to a change of platforms at the train station, or a confused tour of the one-way road system.

If you want to spare time for a quick look around, though, head for the central **Piazza Farinata degli Uberti**, named after the commander of the Ghibelline army of Siena which defeated the Florentine Guelphs at Montaperti in 1260; he's revered not for his military prowess, but for his advocacy at the "parliament of Empoli", when he dissuaded his followers from wrecking Florence. The green and white **Collegiata**, on the square, was founded as far back as the fifth century; its lower portion is the most westerly example of Florentine Romanesque architecture, the top a postwar reconstruction of a nineteenth-century imitation.

Adjacent is the **Museo Collegiata**, entrance in Piazzetta della Propositora (Tues–Sun 9am–noon & 4–7pm; L5000; a L8000-ticket also covers admission on the same day to the town's Museo Archeologico e della Ceramica and the Museo Leonardiano in Vinci, see next page). The Museo Collegiata has a pretty good collection of sculpture and painting: Lorenzo Monaco's *Madonna and Saints*, a couple of panels by local-born Pontormo, a possible Filippo Lippi, a Masolino *Pietà*, sculptures by Bernardo Rossellino and Mino da Fiesole, and Lorenzo di Bicci's *St Nicholas of Tolentino Saving Empoli from the Plague* – with a view of the town in the 1440s. The museum also possesses an item relating to one of Tuscany's stranger Easter rituals, a winged mechanical donkey that used to perform a version of Florence's incendiary dove ceremony – the donkey being propelled from the Collegiata tower down to Piazza Farinata degli Uberti, where it would ignite a pile of fireworks. Nowadays a papier-mâché beast performs the role.

Finally, it's worth recording that Empoli was the birthplace of composer-pianist **Ferruccio Busoni** (1866–1924), a musician of such virtuosity that whenever a new keyboard star emerges, some hack inevitably will remint the phrase "the greatest pianist since Busoni". The town commemorates him with a series of **concerts** from

October to May – details are available from the **tourist office**, at Via Giuseppe del Papa 98, overlooking the piazza (☎0571.76.115), next door to the **Museum of Paleontology** (Mon–Fri 10am–noon & 3.30–6pm, Sat–Sun 10am–noon & 5–7pm; free).

Cerreto Guidi

From the time of Cosimo I to the end of the dynasty, the Medici administered their estates in this northern part of Tuscany from the villa at **CERRETO GUIDI** (daily 9am–7pm, closed second and third Mon of month; ticket office closes 6.30pm; L4000), 8km northwest of Empoli (COPIT bus service). Having converted this former castle into something more domestic, and having got Buontalenti to build the huge approach ramps that remain the villa's most distinctive feature, the clan set about making it the focus of rural life in the Empoli district: they instituted a weekly fair here, with compulsory attendance for the local peasants.

The **villa** is in fact a plain box of a house and the church that Cosimo built next door is no more exciting – though there's a good view from the top of the ramps, with Frederick's tower at San Miniato (see opposite page) standing out in the middle distance. The main point of visiting the **interior** is to see the gallery of Medici portraits, and even these are fairly dull. One section is entitled "Unhappy marriages among the descendants of Cosimo I", and includes a likeness of Cosimo's daughter Isabella, murdered here by her husband in 1576 for her infidelity; the Medici hitmen caught up with her alleged lover in Paris the following year.

Vinci

Sitting on the southern slopes of Monte Albano, 11km north of Empoli, **VINCI** is set amid a rolling swathe of vineyards and olive groves. The landscape is not what draws people along the road between Empoli and Pistoia, however – it's the village's association with **Leonardo da Vinci**, who in April 1452 was born in the nearby hamlet of Archiano, and baptized in Vinci's church of Santa Croce.

Vinci itself is a torpid place but preserves a thirteenth-century castle, Castello dei Conti Guidi, which houses the **Museo Leonardiano** (daily: summer 9.30am–6.30pm; winter 9.30am–5.30pm; L5000, or L8000 including entrance to Empoli's museums, see previous page). Opened on the five-hundredth anniversary of Leonardo's birth, the museum is dedicated to Leonardo the inventor and engineer, with a large and fairly imaginative display of models – tanks, water cannon, flying machines, looms and gear mechanisms. The models were all reconstructed according to Leonardo's notebook drawings, which are reproduced alongside the relevant contraptions. The museum doesn't do Leonardo any favours in giving as much space to his half-baked jottings as to his sounder propositions – thus half a room is wasted on a mock-up of his skis for walking on water. Avoid the museum on a Sunday, when half the population of northern Tuscany seems to come out here.

Leonardo's actual **birthplace** (same hours as Museo Leonardiano; free) is some four kilometres farther north into the hills, a pleasant walk past fields of poppies. The house was owned by his father, a Florentine clerk called Ser Pietro; of his mother little is known except that she was a serving maid and that her name was Caterina. It's now filled with placard-size captions and a couple of reproduction drawings – otherwise there's nothing to see.

San Miniato

The strategic hill-top site of **SAN MINIATO**, more or less equidistant from Pisa and Florence, has been exploited since the era of Augustus, when the Roman settlement of Quarto was founded here. A Lombard town succeeded it, and at the end of the tenth century Otto I made this an outpost of the Holy Roman Empire. A later emperor,

Frederick II, gave the town its landmark fortress, and the imperial connection led to the nickname "San Miniato dei Tedeschi" – San Miniato of the Germans. Today San Miniato is a brusque little agricultural town, good for a couple of hours' break of journey, but unlikely to tempt anyone to give it longer.

The train station and main, predominantly modern, part of town – **San Miniato Basso** – are sited down in the valley. From here it's a steep four-kilometre climb to **San Miniato Alto**, the old quarter. A mini orange **bus** runs from the train station up to San Miniato Alto approximately every thirty minutes (6.30–10.30am & 3.45–7.30pm). It will deposit you just below the walls in **Piazzale Dante Alighieri**, which is also the place to park. From here, once through the town gate, a right turn leads to **Piazza del Popolo**, where a plan of the town is displayed outside the helpful **tourist office** (summer daily 9am–1pm & 4–7.30pm; winter Mon–Sat 9am–1pm & 3–6.30pm, Sun 10am–1pm & 3–7.30pm). At the top end of the square is the much rebuilt **San Domenico**, which contains the fine tomb of a Florentine doctor named Giovanni Chellini. Carved by one Pagno di Lapo Portigiani, it's modelled on the tomb of Leonardo Bruni in Florence's Santa Croce.

From here Via Conti rises to the **Piazza della Repubblica**, which is jazzed up by seventeenth-century *graffiti* on the long facade of the seminary, part of whose ground floor is a row of restored fourteenth-century shops, a rare survival. Opposite the seminary, a flight of steps rises to the **Prato del Duomo**, where a tower of the imperial fortress now houses the expensive *Miravalle* hotel (☎0571.418.075; ⑤) and its more affordable restaurant next door on the site of the **Palazzo dei Vicari dell'Imperatore**. The Palazzo is a relic of the time when San Miniato was the seat of the vicars of the Holy Roman Empire – Countess Matilda of Tuscia, daughter of one of these vicars, was born here (see p.596).

The red-brick **duomo** itself, dedicated to St Genesius, the patron saint of actors, is hacked-about Romanesque, with an interior of Baroque gilding and marbling. Next door, the tiny **museum** (April–Nov Tues–Sun 9am–12.30pm & 3–6.30pm; Dec–March Sat & Sun only, same hours; L3000) has a *Crucifixion* by Filippo Lippi and a terracotta bust of Christ by Verrocchio. At the back of the duomo, the ponderous **Santuario del Crocifisso** was built to house a Crucifix that was thought to have played a part in saving the town from the plague of 1637; the Crucifix is still there, but the sanctuary is rarely open. From the Prato del Duomo it's a short walk up to the tower of the **Rocca**, which was rebuilt by Frederick II and restored brick by brick after damage in the last war; the main point of the climb is the stupendous panoramic view (on a clear day) of the surrounding countryside. Dante's *Inferno* perpetuates the memory of Pier della Vigna, Frederick's treasurer, who was imprisoned and blinded here, a fate that drove him to suicide by jumping from the tower – as the inscription at its foot records. On the first Sunday after Easter this zone is packed with competitors in the national **kite-flying championships**, which competes with a flower festival held the same day.

Below the tower, on the opposite side from the duomo, stands the church of **San Francesco**, occupying the site where the Lombards dedicated the chapel to San Miniato that gave the town its name. The church was altered by the Franciscans, who were given the property after Francis himself had visited the town, and traces of their Romanesque building can still just about be discerned through the later Gothic.

San Miniato boasts a rich cultural calendar between the months of May and October, with a good choice of **concerts and exhibitions**, both in the village itself and in outlying areas. There is also an **antiques market** in the *Loggiata di San Domenico* on the first Sunday of each month. If you want to eat in San Miniato there's a **restaurant** in Piazza Buonaparte, *Da Canapone* (closed Mon), serving local food at reasonable prices, or else try the *L'Antro di Bacco* (closed Wed), in Via IV Novembre.

South of Empoli: Castelfiorentino and Certaldo

The **N429** road and Empoli–Siena **rail line**, which head south between Empoli and San Miniato, provide an easy and direct approach to San Gimignano and Siena. Along the way are two interesting, if modest, hill-town attractions: **Castelfiorentino**, home to a couple of delightful Gozzoli fresco cycles, and **Certaldo**, where Boccaccio spent his last years.

Castelfiorentino

A fief of the bishops of Florence from the twelfth century onwards, **CASTELFIORENTINO** remained in the city's orbit through most of its uneventful history. Today it's a fairly large urban centre, with light industry and block housing spreading out in the modern, lower quarter of town, across the river Elsa. It's not a particularly pretty stop and, for once in Tuscany, you may well find yourself the only visitor in the place.

From the **train station**, the expansive **Piazza Gramsci** can be seen straight ahead. It is flanked by cafés, bars and the only central **hotel**, the two-star *Hotel-Ristorante Lami* at no. 82–83 (☎ & fax 0571.64.076; ③); the town's other hotel, the three-star *La Pieve*, at Via V. Orazio Bacci 2 (☎0571.62.203, fax 0571.64.045; ④), is out on the road for Montespertoli. Best of a dozen or so **restaurants**, most grouped in the area around the square, is *La Magona* at Via Ridolfi 10 (closed Mon and Aug), on the street to your right out of the station.

The Gozzoli frescoes and the town

To look around the **Castello** – the old, upper town – head up the stairs at the corner of Piazza Gramsci, by the Teatro del Popolo, and you'll reach a patch of garden square, to either side of which runs Via dei Tilli. Turn left and you come to the **Biblioteca Comunale** (Tues, Thurs & Sat 4–7pm, Sun 10am–noon & 4–7pm; L3000) where the Gozzoli frescoes are displayed.

The **frescoes** occupy the top floor of the Biblioteca, having been detached from a pair of local sanctuary chapels. To the left of the gallery entrance is a complete reconstruction of the *Madonna della Tosse* chapel, including a frescoed "altarpiece" and side-wall scenes of the death and assumption of the Virgin, their landscapes studded with cypress trees and rolling Tuscan hills. More fragmentary but more interesting are the flood-damaged frescoes and *sinopie* from the *Sanctuary of the Visitation*. These again depict episodes from the life of the Virgin, and of her parents, Joachim (Gioacchino) and Anne, the best of them full of genre detail of everyday fifteenth-century life. Both sets of frescoes were completed in the 1480s, late in Gozzoli's career, possibly during periods when the plague had hit Florence.

Had you turned right along Via dei Tilli, you would have come to the **Piazza del Popolo**, the castello's main square, flanked by the Collegiata of San Lorenzo – built on Lombard foundations – and a nineteenth-century Municipio. The stepped street above the piazza leads to the summit of the town, marked by the Romanesque **Pieve di San Ippolito**. It was here in 1197 that the rectors of the Tuscan League, which was formed to defend the cities against "any emperor, king, or prince", were sworn in – Castelfiorentino's only real episode in the limelight.

Down in the **lower town**, east of Piazza Gramsci (left as you face the station and river), a small park gives onto the Baroque church of **Santa Verdiana**, which houses a museum (Sat 4–7pm, Sun & public holidays 10am–noon & 4–7pm; L5000) displaying paintings from churches in the town and region, including works by Duccio, Taddeo Gaddi and Gozzoli. Many of these panels came from nearby **San Francesco** (usually locked), which has two fragmentary fresco cycles of the *Life of St Francis* – the finest, by Cenno di Cenni, in the nave. As so often in these parts, the church claims foundation by St Francis himself. St Verdiana – the local patron saint – was his contemporary and ordained by him into the order; she is generally depicted with a couple of serpents whose lives she saved, in a pause between other miracles.

San Vivaldo

If you're driving and feel like a rambling, fourteen-kilometre cross-country route down to San Gimignano, follow the road southwest of Castelfiorentino through either Montaione, a quiet little hill-town with a less-than-essential paleontology museum, or through the minor spa of Gambassi Terme – with the lovely Romanesque **Pieve a Chianni** on its outskirts – to the village of **SAN VIVALDO**.

Here, amid the woods, a fourteenth-century Franciscan hermit founded the monastery of **Sacro Monte**, which between 1500 and 1515 was endowed with 34 chapels, representing the Stations of the Cross and other scenes from the life of Christ. The surviving fifteen chapels are not quite the "Jerusalem in Tuscany" the local tourist literature promotes; clustered together by the entrance gate to the monastery, they look more like a miniature cemetery and hardly a credible alternative to a pilgrimage to the Holy Land. However, each of the chapels is endowed with a large-scale painted terracotta tableau, completed with impressive animation by artists from the della Robbia school.

Certaldo

Even without the Boccaccio connection **CERTALDO** would justify a visit. A very striking hill-town – all red-brick towers, battlements and mansions – it is visible for miles along the Elsa valley, and itself has views out to San Gimignano. For a spell in the twelfth century, its rulers, the Alberti, controlled a domain stretching north to the Arno, but subsequent domination by Florence and incursions by Siena led to it assuming a largely provincial role. Nowadays its lower town, built along the N429, is a prosperous place, making its money from wine and agriculture, as well as glass, brick and pasta factories.

Arriving by bus or train, you will find yourself close to the central **Piazza Boccaccio** in the **lower town**. From here, two stone-flagged paths – Costa Alberti and Costa Vecchia – and a road, the Via del Castello, make the steep ascent to the upper town or **Castello**.

Castello

Certaldo's upper town is little more than a single street, predictably dubbed the **Via Boccaccio**. At its western end, by the Piazza Sautissima Annunziata, stands a group of privately owned palazzi. Moving up from here, towards the archetypally Tuscan town hall, or Palazzo Vicariale, you pass the Casa del Boccaccio (on the left) and, fronting a tiny piazza, the church and convent of SS. Jacopo e Filippo.

The **Casa di Boccaccio** (daily 10.30am–12.30pm & 3.30–6.30pm; free) is as likely a candidate for the home of the poet as any of the town mansions, though scholars continue to dispute quite which towers were specified in his will. If indeed it is Boccaccio's home, then it was here that he spent the last twelve years of his life and here that he died – despite a considerable reputation – in very modest circumstances. Giovanni Boccaccio was actually born, according to the account he gave his friend Petrarch, in Paris, probably in 1313. The son of a banker from Certaldo, he returned fairly early in his childhood to Tuscany. As a youth he rejected the banking career planned by his family, instead going to study in Naples, where he fell in love with Fiammetta, an illegitimate princess and the inspiration for numerous of his sonnets. He returned to Florence reluctantly, after the collapse of his father's business, and there – as well as in Milan and Avignon, where he worked as a diplomat – wrote his major works, including the **Decameron**. Aged around fifty, he met a monk who so impressed him with a vision of his death that he decided to reject his worldly excesses of old, and retire to Certaldo. The rest of the years here were spent producing learned volumes on geography, the vanity of human affairs, and mythology, and preparing lectures on Dante. He died on December 21, 1375.

As you'd expect, given the uncertainty over its attribution, the house contains no direct links with Boccaccio, but instead gives an impression of the kind of house he would have lived in. The actual exhibits comprise a colourful group of illustrations from the *Decameron* and a murky display case of drawings from various editions – by Rubens, Hogarth and D.H. Lawrence, among others.

Perhaps more interesting is the church of **SS. Jacopo e Filippo**, alongside, which Boccaccio attended and where he was buried. Between the first and second altars on the right is his **monument** – a sixteenth-century bust and the lines he wrote as an epitaph – on the site of what was, until 1783, his grave. In that year the floor of the church was relaid and the good burghers of Certaldo – having come to the same conclusion as the author that the *Decameron* was an ungodly work – ripped up the original tomb and scattered the ashes. Byron, who came to pay his respects a few years later, was scandalized:

> . . . *even his tomb*
> *Uptorn must bear the hyena bigot's wrong;*
> *No more amidst the meaner dead find room.*

His verses had an effect, prompting the Marquise Lenzoni – a straggler from the Medici family – to buy up and restore the Boccaccio house and arrange the monument. Of some note, also, in the church are a pair of della Robbia tabernacles, an altarpiece by the same family (*Our Lady of the Snow*), and a fourteenth-century Sienese fresco of the Madonna and Child.

Boccaccio aside, the **Palazzo Vicariale** (summer daily 10am–1pm & 2–7.30pm; winter Tues–Sun 10am–12.30pm & 3–7.30pm; L5000) is by far the most interesting building in Certaldo. Arms on its exterior – including further examples of the della Robbia mastery of painted terracotta – attest to its use as the governor's residence, after the decline of its original owners, the Alberti. Inside, the arcaded entrance hall displays further coats of arms and a mostly fragmentary array of frescoes, many either painted or repainted at the end of the fifteenth century by Pier Francesco Fiorentino. The *Doubting Thomas*, over a small door by the stairway, is attributed to Gozzoli. Other fine patches of fresco are to be seen in the "Court of Justice", to the left, including a very faint *Allegory of Truth* on the wall with the door. To the right of the hall was the old civil prison, apparently frescoed by its inmates, and beyond, a series of grim dungeons for serious offenders. Virtually windowless, these retain graffiti etched by prisoners, including a diagram of the sun, each beam numbering a day spent confined.

Upstairs, you move into the more spacious environs of the governor's and servants' chambers, again with the odd faded fresco. These rooms are used on and off for special exhibitions, with an international showing inspired by Boccaccian themes filling the gaps between.

Through the garden to the right of the palazzo, and entered on the same ticket, is the chapel of San Tommaso e Prospero, which was used as a storeroom from the eighteenth century, before restoration after the last war. The work was just in time to save Gozzoli's *Tabernacle of the Condemned* – a group of frescoes of Christ and the two thieves crucified with him, which are now displayed detached from the wall; traces of *sinopie* show their original position.

Practicalities

There's just one **hotel** up in Certaldo Alto, the three-star *Il Castello* at Via della Rena 6 (☎0571.668.250; ④), at the western end of Via Boccaccio, complete with garden and a **restaurant** serving Tuscan food. For eating out, the only competition comes from the *Osteria del Vicario*, in Via Rivellino, just beyond the Palazzo Vicariale. For more choice, head down to the area around Piazza Boccaccio in the lower town, where there are two reasonably priced hotels: *Albergo Gelli*, Via Romana 30 (☎0571.668.135; ②), and *La Speranza*, Via Borgo Garibaldi Giuseppe 80 (☎0571.668.014; ②), close to the piazza.

There's an excellent **campsite** a short distance south of Certaldo in the village of Marcialla – located on the very edge of the Chianti hills, it's called *Toscana Colliverdi*, and is to be found at Via Marcialla 349 (☎0571.669.334).

As for other pursuits, Certaldo runs a **cultural festival** in September, on the first Sunday of which is the Feast of San Giulia della Rena, signal for a reunion of all the town's emigrants. In July there are courses and occasional concerts of **medieval music**, at the *Ars Nova* centre in the Palazzo Vicariale.

Moving south from Certaldo, there are **trains and buses** to Siena. Heading for **San Gimignano** by public transport you need to change at Poggibonsi; by car, the most direct and attractive route is the minor road due south.

travel details

TRAINS

Florence to: Prato (every 30min; 20min); Prato, Pistoia, Montecatini, Lucca, Viareggio (hourly; 20min, 35min, 50min, 1hr 20min, 1hr 40min); Empoli (every 30min; 30min); Borgo San Lorenzo (every 2 hours; 1hr).

Pistoia to: Florence (hourly; 30–45min); Montecatini, Lucca, Viareggio (hourly; 15min, 45min, 1hr 15min); Bologna (hourly; 1hr).

Prato to: Florence (every 30min; 20min); Pistoia, Montecatini, Lucca, Viareggio (hourly; 15min, 30min, 1hr, 1hr 30min); Bologna (10 daily; 1hr).

Empoli to: Florence (every 30min; 25min); Pisa (every 30min; 25min) Castelfiorentino, Certaldo, Poggibonsi, Siena (hourly; 20min, 30min, 40min, 1hr).

BUSES

Florence to: (**ATAF**) La Petraia, Careggi, Pratolino and Fiesole; (**SITA**) Castellina in Chianti, Greve, Radda in Chianti, Gaiole, Barberino di Mugello,

Certaldo, Pontassieve, Borgo San Lorenzo and San Casciano; (**Lazzi**) Cerreto Guidi, Empoli, Incisa Valdarno, Montecatini Terme, Prato, Pistoia and Pontassieve; (**CAP**) Borgo San Lorenzo, Impruneta and Prato; (**COPIT**) Pistoia and Poggio a Caiano.

Prato to: (**Lazzi**) Montecatini, Pistoia, Florence, Lucca, Pisa and Viareggio; (**CAP**) Florence, Siena, Barberino and Mugello.

Pistoia to: (**Lazzi**) Montecatini, Prato, Florence, Lucca, Pisa and Viareggio; (**COPIT**) Montecatini, Poggio a Caiano, Empoli and Vinci.

Empoli to: Cerreto Guidi and Vinci (from outside train station), Castelfiorentino and Certaldo (from Piazza della Vittoria).

Castelfiorentino to: (**SITA**) Empoli, Florence, Certaldo and Volterra.

Montecatini Terme to: (**Lazzi**) Monsummano, Pescia, Collodi, Pistoia, Prato, Florence, Pisa and Livorno.

Borgo San Lorenzo to: (**SITA**) San Piero a Sieve, Scarperia, Barberino di Mugello and other villages in the Mugello.

CHAPTER THREE

LUCCA AND NORTHERN TUSCANY

The north of Tuscany is one of the province's least-known regions. Very few non-Italians holiday on its resort-lined coast, the so-called Riviera della Versilia, and fewer still penetrate inland to the mountains of the Alpi Apuane or the remote hills and valleys of the Garfagnana and Lunigiana. The one city on the Tuscan sightseeing trail is Lucca – and even there tourism, strangely, is very much a secondary consideration.

Lucca's proximity to Pisa – half an hour by road or rail – makes it an excellent first or last Tuscan stop if you're flying in or out of that city's airport. Even if you're not, Lucca is well worth an overnight stay or a day trip from Florence (the train takes around an hour). Contained within vast, park-lined walls, it's an urbane, affluent place, with as rewarding an ensemble of Romanesque churches as any you'll find in Italy.

For a quick break by the sea, the sands of the **Riviera della Versilia** are pleasant enough, and easily reached from Lucca. Though there is often little to distinguish the resorts, where the beaches are usually staked out by private operators, the towns of **Viareggio** and **Forte dei Marmi** have their moments – Viareggio at carnival time, when it mounts Italy's most amazing procession of floats, and in high summer, when it's the first-choice resort for many Florentines having a day out by the sea. And from this coast it is a simple matter to explore the jagged peaks of the **Alpi Apuane**, which run parallel to the sea for some forty kilometres. The mountains are best known for the **marble quarries** around **Carrara**, but head beyond these and you will find yourself amid steep forested valleys, threaded by a network of clearly marked **footpaths**. Many of these can be trekked in a day from their village trailheads, though there are longer trails and accommodation refuges if you fancy something more strenuous. More important still, the area is well mapped, not always the case in Italy.

Equally easy to visit from Lucca is the **Garfagnana**, a lovely rural enclave that focuses on the **Serchio valley** and is flanked by the eastern slopes of the Apuane on one side and the more rounded mountains of the **Orecchiella** on the other. Plenty of trails strike off into these upland regions, each of which is protected by a regional nature reserve. **Castelnuovo di Garfagnana** is the only town of any size, a good base for excursions into the hills or a visit to nearby **Barga**, the one outstanding medieval centre. North of the Serchio is one of the most marginalized areas of Tuscany, the **Lunigiana**, a wild and unspoilt region of rocky, forested landscape peppered with castles and tiny hamlets.

By virtue of their microclimates and a position that puts them at a meeting point of Alpine and Mediterranean vegetation zones, the Apuane and Orecchiella constitute one of the finest **floral** zones in the country: two-thirds of Italy's known species grow here, and in late spring the upland meadows are carpeted with flowers. Besides these and a wide variety of fungi, the reserves here abound in often spectacular **wildlife** such as wolves, red deer and golden eagles. At least 165 bird species have been reported, some 85 of them breeding here, including kestrels, buzzards and sparrowhawks.

ACCOMMODATION PRICES

Throughout this guide, **hotel** accommodation is graded on a scale from ① to ⑨, indicating the cost of the **cheapest double room** in each establishment in high season (for **hostels**, rates per person are given in lire). The price bands to which these codes refer are as follows:

① up to L60,000   ④ L120,000–150,000   ⑦ L250,000–300,000
② L60,000–90,000   ⑤ L150,000–200,000   ⑧ L300,000–350,000
③ L90,000–120,000   ⑥ L200,000–250,000   ⑨ over L350,000

Getting around the region

Lucca is the hub of a broad transport network covering all of the northwest. The **Versilian coast** is extremely accessible, with buses and trains constantly shuttling beach-goers in summer. The **train routes** offer a perfect opportunity for a circular tour – up the coast, then changing at Aulla for the trip down through the Lunigiana and Garfagnana, on the east side of the Apuane. If all you want to do is scan the scenery, it would be feasible to do this in a day from Lucca.

Lucca

LUCCA is the most graceful of Tuscany's provincial capitals, set inside a swathe of Renaissance walls fronted by gardens and huge bastions. The streets are dotted with palazzi and the odd tower and at intervals open onto a church square, invariably overlooked by a brilliantly decorated Romanesque facade. It's quiet without being dull, absorbs its tourists with ease, has a peaceful and self-contained historic centre and offers a range of good restaurants. Henry James's eulogy – "a place overflowing with everything that makes for ease, for plenty, for beauty, for interest and good example" – still holds true.

The city lies at the heart of one of Italy's richest agricultural regions ("half-smothered in oil and wine and corn and all the fruits of the earth", James opined) and has prospered since the Romans, whose gridiron orthodoxy is still obvious in the layout of the streets. Under the Lombards it was the capital of Tuscia (Tuscany), though its heyday was between the eleventh and fourteenth centuries, when banking and the silk trade brought wealth and, for a time, political power. In a brief flurry of military activity Lucca lost its independence to Pisa in 1314, but regained it under the command of a remarkable adventurer, **Castruccio Castracani**, who went on to forge an empire covering much of western Tuscany. Pisa and Pistoia both fell to the Lucchesi, and but for Castracani's untimely death from malaria, Florence might have followed. In subsequent centuries the city remained largely independent – if fairly inconsequential – until passing to Napoleon (and rule by his sister, Elisa Baciocchi), the Bourbons, and, just short of Italian unification, to the Grand Duchy of Tuscany.

Today the city is reckoned among the wealthiest in Tuscany, a prosperity gained largely through silk that was produced here by scores of small family businesses, and on the region's high-quality olive oil and other produce. The Lucchesi themselves have a reputation for tight family links – money never leaves the area – and conservatism; where neighbouring towns are communist, Lucca's political allegiance lies with the Christian Democrats. There is, too, a tradition of decorum, traceable to eighteenth- and nineteenth-century court life; up until the turn of the twentieth century, smart Italian families sent their daughters to the city to pick up the better manners presumed to prevail here.

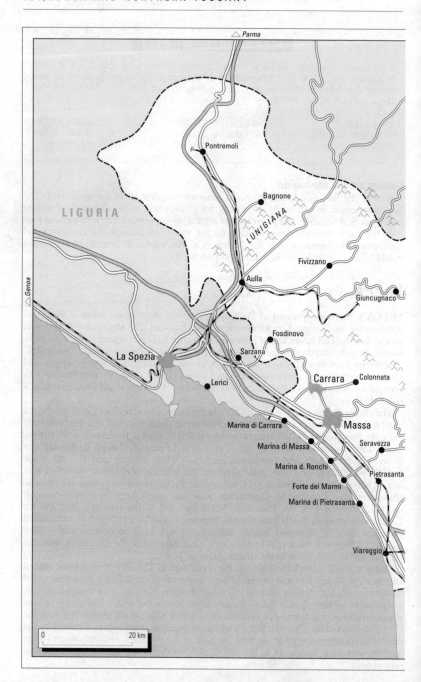

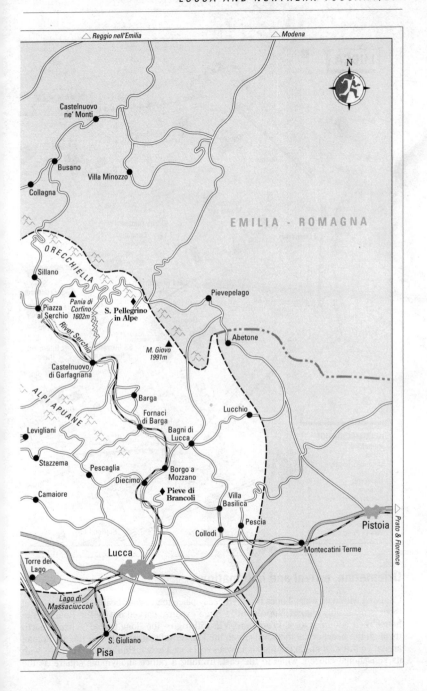

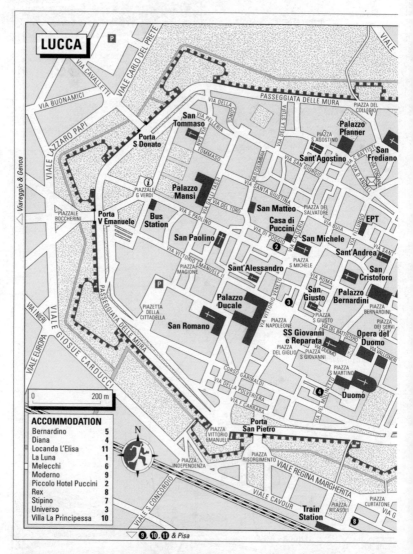

Orientation, arrival and information

Confined within its walls, Lucca is a pretty easy place to get your bearings. The centre of town is ostensibly **Piazza Napoleone**, a huge expanse carved out by the Bourbons to house their administration. From here, **Via Fillungo** – the "long thread" – heads north through the heart of the medieval city to the Piazza Anfiteatro, built over the old Roman arena. To the west of Via Fillungo is Lucca's real social heart, **Piazza San Michele**, with its sensational church, while to the east, fronting a rather anonymous square, is the

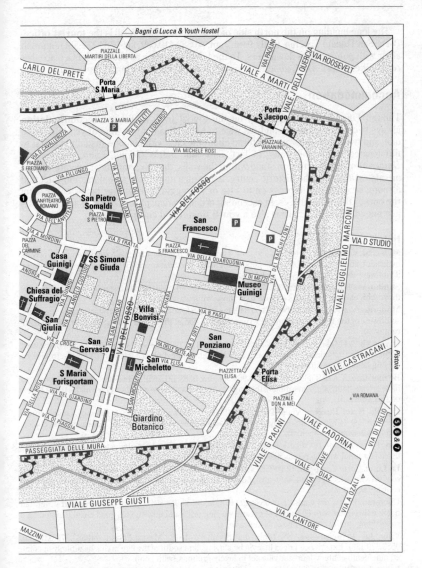

duomo. Farther east still, the Fosso ("ditch") cuts off the quarter around **San Francesco.** Everything is within a few minutes' walking distance of Piazza Napoleone.

Arriving by **bus**, regardless of the company you're travelling with, you'll find yourself just inside the western stretch of walls, in Piazzale Giuseppe Verdi. The **train station** is a short way outside the walls to the south, a very easy walk to the centre – come out of the station, walk up to the main road and turn left: about 200m down cross the street right and follow the road ahead through the walls. The station has foreign exchange facilities. **City buses** leave from Corso Garibaldi and Piazzale G. Verdi.

The lone building on the north side of Piazzale Giuseppe Verdi is the **tourist office**, Porta San Donato Vecchia (daily 9am–7pm; ☎0583.419.689, fax 0583.312.581), a swish affair with public toilets downstairs. To the left of the office as you face it is a place that rents **bikes** (April–Oct), good for a circuit of the walls or getting to the outlying villas.

Accommodation

Though Lucca isn't a major stop on the tourist trail, its limited **accommodation** always seems in demand – and it's wise to book ahead at any time of year. Six or so one- and two-star **hotels** are scattered about the city, with just one (usually the first to fill) located inside the walls. In fact, only four hotels (*Diana, Luna, Puccini* and *Universo*) of any description stand within the walls, though a variety of **private rooms** are also available in the historic centre. If you turn up without a booking and can't find a room, be prepared to press on to Pisa or Viareggio. The listings below cover all of the one- to three-star places, in ascending order of price, plus a couple of special treats just outside the city. There is also a **youth hostel** and **campsite**.

Hotels

Melecchi, Via Romana 37 (☎0583.950.234). Lucca's only one-star has nine rooms, none with private bathroom, and is a couple of blocks outside the walls: the *Stipino* and *Bernardino* are very close by if you want more comfort (see below). ②.

Stipino, Via Romana 95 (☎0583.495.077, fax 0583.490.309). Adequate two-star hotel with 21 rooms; those with en-suite are L40,000 more than those without. ②–③.

Moderno, Via V. Civitali 38 (☎0583.55.840, fax 0583.53.830). A 12-room two-star outside the walls, southwest of the train station on the wrong (south) side of the tracks. All rooms have private bathrooms. ③.

Diana, Via del Molinetto 11 (☎0583.492.202, fax 0583.47.795). Located within the walls a block west of the duomo, this nine-room two-star would be a fine budget choice if it weren't for the frequency of complaints about surly staff. ③.

Bernardino, Via di Tiglio 109 (☎0583.953.356, fax 0583.491.765). A two-star whose 26 rooms all have private bathrooms: marginally the most expensive and closest to the centre of the three hotels on this street. ③.

Piccolo Hotel Puccini, Via di Poggio 9 (☎0583.55.421, fax 0583.53.487). Friendly, central three-star with just 14 rooms: almost right next to San Michele, so it's an obvious mid-range first choice, and thus essential to book. ④.

Rex, Piazza Ricasoli 19 (☎0583.955.443, fax 0583.954.348). A modern, characterless but comfortable three-star hotel with 25 rooms just east of the train station. ⑤.

La Luna, Corte Compagni 12 (☎0583.493.634, fax 0583.490.021). A nicely located three-star with 30 rooms to the west of Piazza Anfiteatro, but you are paying a full L75,000 more here than at the more central *Puccini*. ⑥.

Universo, Piazza del Giglio 1 (☎0583.493.678, fax 0583.954.854). Lucca's not-so-grand grand old hotel: a three-star with 60 rooms of greatly varying price and quality, so a good chance of finding a room: bang on the central Piazza Napoleone. ⑥.

Villa La Principessa, SS 12bis del Brennero 1616, Massa Pisana (☎0583.370.037, fax 0583.379.136). Experience Lucca in style by staying 3km south of the city in this beautifully appointed nineteenth-century four-star villa set in lovely grounds (with pool). ⑨.

Locanda L'Elisa, SS 12bis del Brenner 1952, Massa Pisana (☎0583.379.737, fax 0583.379.019). A luxury five-star and one of Tuscany's top hotels. The L500,000-a-night price tag buys you one of ten beautiful suites and all the pampering and elegance you'd expect for this sort of money. ⑨.

Private rooms

Casa Alba, Via Fillungo 142, second floor (☎0583.495.361). Four clean, pleasant rooms (doubles and singles) on Lucca's main street just north of Piazza Anfiteatro, all sharing two bathrooms; discounts for stays of two nights or more in low season only. ②.

Centro Storico, Corte Portici 16 (☎0583.490.748). Five doubles sharing two bathrooms, located on a courtyard off Via Calderia just northwest of Piazza San Michele. ②.

San Frediano, Via degli Angeli (☎0583.469.630). Six rooms, including singles and doubles with a choice of private and shared bathrooms: situated on a street between Via Fillungo and Via C. Battisti just southeast of San Frediano. ②.

La Torre, Via del Carmine 11 (☎0583.957.044). Five nice double rooms sharing just one bathroom; located off Piazza del Carmine south of Piazza Anfiteatro. ②.

L'Arancio 1, Via Romano 57 (☎0583.496.517). Five rooms outside the walls, but recommended, especially the spacious, wood-beamed doubles with private bath. *L'Arancio 2* (same details) nearby has another five rooms with two shared bathrooms. ②.

Sainte Joustine, Via San Giustina 30 (☎0583.587.964 or 0347.312.7405). Seven rooms, singles and doubles, sharing three bathrooms on the street that runs to the Palazzo Mansi. ③.

Villa Romantica, Via N. Barbantini 246 (☎ & fax 0583.496.872). Six rooms near Piazza del Carmine, all with private bathrooms. ④.

Hostel and campsite

Ostello Il Serchio, Via del Brennero 673 (☎0583.341.811). Located 3km out of town: to get there take bus #1/1a, #6 or #7, or leave the city at Porta Santa Maria, turn right at the roundabout onto Viale Batoni, then first left up Viale Civitali, which leads into Via del Brennero – the hostel is on the left, next to a service station. Twelve rooms with sixty-two beds. Reception 4.30–11pm, midnight curfew. Food available, but not good (full pension L47,000). It's rarely full, and you can camp at the back for the same price. Open March 1–Nov 2. L19,000.

The City

Lucca is a delightful place simply to wander at random. It's one of the few places in Tuscany, even Italy, where the locals are happy to ride bikes rather than drive cars, and as a result much of the old centre is refreshingly free of traffic. However you arrive in the city, you're most likely to gravitate first to **Piazza San Michele**, home to the church of San Michele, the apotheosis of the Pisan-Romanesque style. Lucca is reputed to have once had seventy churches to service its spiritual needs, and even today you can hardly walk for five minutes without coming on a small piazza and marble-fronted facade. Most were built obliquely to the grid of streets, so you rarely confront a church head on, but rather as a sudden apparition as you enter a square.

After San Michele you might want to potter around the streets to the west, or push straight on to the **duomo**, another Romanesque gem, with one of Italy's most sublime funerary sculptures. Thereafter you could clamber up to the **walls** – a trip to the city is not complete without strolling part of the panoramic and tree-lined promenade atop the bastions. You can access the circuit from almost any part of the city, however, and from the duomo you could just as easily head back north to take in **Piazza Anfiteatro** and **San Frediano**, the third of the city's trio of outstanding churches.

San Michele

Head to the long-time historical heart of Lucca and you come to the site of the Roman forum, now the square surrounding **San Michele in Foro** (daily 7.30am–12.30pm & 3–6pm, closed during services), a church with one of Tuscany's most exquisite **facades**. The church is first mentioned in 795, but most of the present structure dates from between 1070 and the middle of the twelfth century (you can see the date 1143 marked on a pillar on the left side of the main portal's triumphal arch). The building is unfinished, however, money having been diverted to the facade, begun in the thirteenth century; funds ran out before the body of the church could be raised to the standard of the facade.

The effect is wonderful, the upper loggias and the windows fronting air, like the figure of the archangel at their summit. Its Pisan-inspired intricacy is a triumph of eccentricity, mirrored in many of Lucca's churches. Each of its myriad columns is different – some twisted, others sculpted or candy-striped. The impressive twelfth-century **campanile** is the city's tallest.

It would be hard to match the facade's bravura architectural display, and the **interior** barely tries. On the rear wall is a statue of the *Madonna and Child* by local sculptor Matteo Civitali, previously on the facade. Italians flock for spiritual regeneration to the second altar on the left, the so-called *Rifugio dei Peccatori* – "The Refuge of Sinners". On the opposite altar there's a modest terracotta *Madonna and Child* by Andrea della Robbia; the best work of art is a beautifully framed painting of *SS. Jerome, Sebastian, Roch and Helena* by **Filippino Lippi**, at the end of the right-hand nave. Look out also for the **organ**, marvellously painted with intricate fleurs-de-lys.

The western quarter

The birthplace and family home of Puccini, the **Casa Natale di Giacomo Puccini** (July–Sept Tues–Sun 10am–6pm; Oct–Dec & March–Jun Tues–Sun 10am–1pm & 3–6pm; Jan–Feb Tues–Sun 10am–1pm; L5000), is in Corte San Lorenzo 9, off Via di Poggio, very close to San Michele – where the composer's father and grandfather both played the organ. Today the house is a school of music, and maintains a small museum containing the Steinway on which he wrote *Turandot*, scores, photographs, even his overcoat.

Just a couple of blocks to the west of San Michele is **San Paolino**, where Puccini cut his teeth as organist. A dull Baroque church (begun in 1522), it was built over a vast Roman edifice, possibly a temple, and founded in honour of Lucca's first bishop and patron saint, St Paulinus, whose remains are kept behind the high altar. Some third-rate eighteenth-century frescoes are his only memorial. South of San Paolino, tucked behind the Palazzo Ducale, is **San Romano**, a big, blunt Romanesque hall, probably founded in the eighth century and adapted and enlarged after 1281 in a bizarre hotch-potch of styles; it would be one of the city's more interesting churches if the restoration started in 1987 had actually shown any real progress. At the moment the whole place is sadly dilapidated.

North of San Paolino, at Via Galli Tassi 43, is the **Museo Nazionale di Palazzo Mansi**. This seventeenth-century building houses the four-room **Pinacoteca Nazionale** (Tues–Sat 9am–7pm, Sun 2–6.30pm; L8000), an eclectic grouping of pictures whose real highlights are a Pontormo portrait – possibly of Alessandro de' Medici (see p.116 for the dirt on this sensitive youth); Bronzino's portrait of Cosimo I (the artist painted several versions of this portrait); two male portraits by Tintoretto; and works by the Sienese Mannerists Beccafumi and Rutilio Manetti. If anything, the palace itself is more worth seeing than the paintings inside: all magnificently over-the-top Rococo, reaching its zenith in a spectacularly gilded bridal suite. Also worth seeing is the section of the museum that traces the development of Lucca's important **textile** industry, and its silks and damasks in particular.

Duomo di San Martino

It needs a double-take before you realize why the **Duomo di San Martino** (daily: summer 7am–7pm; winter 7am–5pm; free except for the sacristy) looks odd. The city's cathedral is fronted by a severely asymmetric **facade** – its right-hand arch and loggias squeezed by the bell tower, which was already in place from an earlier building. Nonetheless, the building sets the tone for Lucca's other Romanesque churches and little detracts from its overall grandeur, created by the repetition of tiny columns and loggias and by the stunning **atrium**, whose bas-reliefs are some of the finest sculptures in the city.

It's well worth looking closely at these **carvings**, some dated as early as the fifth century, and executed by a variety of mainly Lombard artists, most of whom are unknown.

Part of the sculpture, however, is attributed to **Nicola Pisano**, and may well be his first work after arriving in Tuscany from Apulia. His are probably the offerings around the left-hand door – the *Deposition* (in the lunette), *Annunciation, Nativity* and the *Adoration of the Magi*. Other panels display a compendium of subjects: a symbolic labyrinth, a Tree of Life (with Adam and Eve at the bottom and Christ at the top), dragons, bears, a bestiary of grotesques, and the months of the year with their associated activities – December has a particularly graphic pig-sticking. The panels of the *Life of St Martin* (1204–10), between the doors, are the masterpiece of the architect, **Guidetto da Como,** responsible for the upper facade's three tiers of arcades. Walk along the flanks of the building to take in the ornate apse and transepts, as well as the extraordinary patterns of arches and marbles in the bricked-up side walls. One of the greatest of the exterior sculptures, a group depicting *St Martin on Horseback with the Beggar* by an unknown early fourteenth-century Lombard sculptor, has been removed inside the church, and stands at the rear right against the west wall.

The **interior** is best known for the contribution of **Matteo Civitali** (1435–1501), who only gave up his daytime job as a barber to become a sculptor in his mid-thirties. He's represented here by a couple of water stoups near the entrance, the pulpits and several tombs and altars – notably the tomb of Pietro da Noceto, secretary to Pope Niccolo V (right wall of the south transept); the tomb of Domenico Bertini, to the left of the preceding tomb on the transept's adjoining wall; and the altar of San Regolo, on the chancel wall immediately right of the apse.

His most famous work, however, is the **Tempietto,** the gilt and marble octagon encountered halfway down the church. Some fanatically intense acts of devotion are performed in front of it, directed at the **Volto Santo** (Holy Face), Lucca's most famous relic. A cedarwood Crucifix with bulging eyes, it's said to be a true effigy of Christ carved by Nicodemus, an eyewitness to the Crucifixion, but is probably a thirteenth-century copy of an eleventh-century copy of an eighth-century original.

Legend has it that the *Volto Santo* came to Lucca of its own volition in 782, first journeying by boat from the Holy Land, and then brought by oxen guided by divine will – a story similar to the ecclesiastical sham of St James's bones at Santiago di Compostela in Spain. As at Santiago, the icon brought considerable power to the local church: it may be no coincidence that it appeared during the bishopric of Anselmo di Baggio, who was later elevated to the papacy. The effigy attracted pilgrims from all over Europe and inspired devotion in all who heard of it: King William Rufus in England used to swear by it (*per sanctum vultum de Lucca*), London merchants kept a copy of it, and in France a certain St Vaudeluc was conjured into existence from a corruption of the French for the icon's name – St Vault de Lucques.

Elsewhere in the church the works of art are of less disputed origin. The finest of them is the **Tomb of Ilaria del Carretto** (1407–10), housed in the **sacristy** entered midway down the south (right) nave (April–Oct Mon–Sat 10am–6pm; Nov–March Mon–Fri 10am–4.45pm, Sat 9.30am–6.45pm; year-round Sun 9–10am, 11.30am–noon & 1–5pm; L3000 or L7000 combined ticket with the Museo della Cattedrale and San Giovanni). Considered the masterpiece of Sienese sculptor Jacopo della Quercia, it consists of a raised dais and the sculpted body of Ilaria, second wife of Paolo Guinigi, one of Lucca's medieval big shots. In a touching, almost sentimental gesture, the artist has carved the family dog at Ilaria's feet – a symbol of fidelity. Restoration of the work in the mid-1990s led to accusations that the restorer's cleaning techniques were overenthusiastic, and had robbed the stone of its variegated textures. The craftsman concerned sued his chief critic, Professor James Beck, the world's leading authority on Jacopo della Quercia, for defamation. Also within the sacristy is a superb *Madonna Enthroned with Saints* by Domenico **Ghirlandaio.**

Other pictorial highlights of the cathedral include a *Madonna and Child*, painted in 1509 by Bartolommeo della Porta, or **Fra Bartolommeo** (in the enclosed chapel to the left of the high altar in the north transept). In the main part of the duomo, the first chapel on the left has a *Presentation of the Virgin* by Alessandro Allori (1598), and the third altar on the right a *Last Supper* (1592) by **Tintoretto**.

Museo della Cattedrale and San Giovanni

Occupying a converted twelfth-century building across Via Arcivescovato from the cathedral, is the **Museo della Cattedrale** (April–Oct Mon–Sat 10am–6pm; Nov–March Mon–Sat 10am–2pm; Sun year-round 10am–5pm; L5000, L7000 with the cathedral sacristy and San Giovanni). The Carretto tomb is destined one day to be displayed here, but at present the museum's four floors are home to a collection of ecclesiastical and other ephemera interspersed with the occasional artistic gem. Room I has a collection of illustrated miniatures, while Room II on the floor above houses a reliquary from Limoges decorated with stories from the Life of St Thomas à Becket; an ivory diptych from Constantinople dated 506; and – one of the highlights – the so-called Croce dei Pisani, an ornate crucifix probably commissioned by Paolo Guinigi after 1408. Room VII contains sculpture from the cathedral, most notably a large statue of St John the Evangelist by Jacopo della Quercia.

On the north side of the square stands the large basilica of **SS. Giovanni e Reparata** (same hours as Museo della Cattedrale; L2000 or L7000 with cathedral sacristy and museum), Lucca's original cathedral until 715. Rebuilt many times, it preserves a lion-flanked carved Romanesque portal, saved during restructuring of the facade in 1589. Inside, excavations have uncovered a tangle of architectural remains, embracing a wide range of much earlier buildings on the site. Earliest fragments include first-century Roman villa mosaics (columns in the present nave are mostly Roman in origin), parts of the original fourth-century church pavement, an eighth-century baptistery with fine 1393 ceiling, and traces of a ninth-century Carolingian church and crypt of San Pantaleone.

North to San Frediano

North of the duomo, **Via Fillungo** cuts through Lucca's luxury shopping district, a tight huddle of streets and alleys where medieval fragments and bricked-up loggias compete with Liberty-style shop fronts and lunchtime and early-evening throngs. Amid the crowds it's easy to miss the gorgeous facade of **San Cristoforo**, the deconsecrated church at the southern end; inside, the left-hand wall is completely covered in writing – the names of Lucca's dead in the two world wars. Farther on is the **Torre delle Ore**, the city's clock tower since 1471; then at no. 58 there's the famous *Caffè di Simo*, a bar worth the price of a drink just for the early twentieth-century ambience. Beyond, the street branches into a warren of lanes that lead to Piazza San Frediano.

San Frediano is again Pisan-Romanesque, and was built between 1112 and 1147 on the site of a sixth-century basilica of San Vincenzo but orientated back to front (west-facing), probably because the old entrance would have been blocked by the new set of medieval city walls nearby. In place of the characteristic multiple loggias of Lucca's other great facades is a magnificent thirteenth-century mosaic of *The Ascension* with the apostles gathered below.

The **interior** (Mon–Sat 7.30am–12.30pm & 3–6pm; Sun 9am–1pm & 3–6pm except during services; free) lives up to the facade's promise – a delicately lit, hall-like basilica, with subtly varied columns and capitals and some fine treasures. Immediately facing the door is one of the best, the **Fonte Lustrale**, a huge twelfth-century piece executed by three different craftsmen. The first, an unknown Lombard, carved the stories of Moses on the outer slabs of the basin – including a superb *Crossing of the Red Sea*, with the Egyptian soldiers depicted as medieval knights. The second, one Maestro Roberto, added the Good Shepherd and six prophets on the other two basin slabs, their enframing arches showing a clear Byzantine influence. To the third sculptor, an unknown Tuscan, is owed the decoration of the Apostles and the Months on the cup above the basin and the beautiful fantasy masks from which the water is disgorged. Set behind the font is an *Annunciation* attributed to Matteo della Robbia, festooned with trailing garlands of ceramic fruit.

A figure of St Bartholomew by Andrea della Robbia, is to be found lower down to the left, close to the left-hand of the two chapels behind the font, the Cappella Fatinelli, which houses the incorrupt body of **St Zita** (died 1278). A Lucchese maidservant, Zita achieved sainthood from a fortuitous white lie: she used to give bread from her household to the poor and when challenged one day by her boss as to the contents of her apron, replied "only roses and flowers" – into which the bread was duly transformed. She is commemorated on April 27 by a flower market outside the church and by the Lucchesi freeing her of her finery and bringing her out to touch.

Moving to the top of the church, note the wonderful twelfth-century Cosmati marble **pavement** of the presbytery, while on the left are fragments of San Frediano's original tomb. Frediano, an Irish monk, is said to have brought Christianity to Lucca in the sixth century. Moving back down the left (north) nave from the high altar, the first chapel, the **Cappella Trenta** contains a superb carved altarpiece with niche statues of the Madonna, Child and Saints by Jacopo della Quercia; the worn pavement tombs of the chapel's donors, Lorenzo Trenat and his wife, are also by della Quercia.

The best frescoes in the city, meanwhile, are to be found in the Cappella di Sant'Agostino, the next chapel but one: **Amico Aspertini**'s *The Arrival of the Volto Santo* (see p.207) and *The Baptism of St Augustine* on the left wall, and *The Miracle of St Frediano* on the right, the last depicting the River Serchio in flood being diverted by the saint's crib. Dating from the early sixteenth century, the murals are painted in a style that is much influenced by the realism of Flemish and German painters. The large fresco of the Madonna and Child on the right of the entrance door is also by Aspertini, while the nearby statue *Virgin Annunciate* is by Matteo Civitali.

Close by San Frediano, at Via degli Asili 33, is the **Palazzo Pfanner**, whose interesting rear loggia and statued gardens are due to reopen after a major repair job. They are also visible from the city walls, as is another fine church, **Sant'Agostino**, in the throes of what looks like long-term restoration.

Piazza Anfiteatro and around

East of San Frediano you reach the remarkable **Piazza Anfiteatro**, aerial shots of which are featured in just about all of Lucca's tourist literature. A ramshackle circuit of medieval buildings, as yet unprettified, it incorporates elements of the Roman amphitheatre that once stood here. Much of the original stone was carted off in the twelfth century to build the city's churches, while parts of the old structure were used as a medieval prison and salt warehouse, but arches and columns can still be seen embedded in some of the houses, particularly on the north side of the outer walls. Medieval slums used to occupy the centre of the arena, but these were cleared in 1830 on the orders of the Bourbon ruler, Marie Louise.

A couple of blocks east is **San Pietro Somaldi**, its delicate facade dating from 1248, this time stone on the lower levels, topped with two tiers of Pisan marbling and tiny columns. Above the lovely **portal** is a good carved frieze executed by Guido da Como in 1203, *Jesus Giving the Keys to St Peter*, and the customary pair of lions, common symbols for the Resurrection in medieval art – after the belief that cubs when born lay dead for three days until a male lion brought them to life by breathing in their faces. The church's interior is whitewashed and blank, save for a sumptuous detached fresco of the *Assumption* on the right wall, and an uncredited fifteenth-century work above the first left-hand altar.

The **Torre Guinigi**, south of San Pietro in Via Sant'Andrea, is the strangest sight in Lucca's cityscape. This battlemented tower, attached to the fifteenth-century town house of Lucca's leading family, is surmounted by an ancient **holm oak** whose roots have grown into the room below. You can climb the 44-metre tower, entering on Via Sant'Andrea, for a close-up of the tree and easily the best view over the city (daily: March–Sept 9am–7.30pm; Oct 10am–6pm; Nov–Feb 10am–4.30pm; L4500). The adjacent fortress, which has some wonderful austere medieval details, fronts a startling number of streets.

Continue south along Via Guinigi and you come to the twelfth-century **Santa Maria Forisportam** ("outside the gate"), signalling the limit of the Roman and medieval city until 1260. Ruskin claimed that it was this church that sparked his interest in medieval architecture. The facade in fact sports just two unfinished tiers and none of its relatives' decorative columns, but it's appealing for all that, with a few carvings above the doors and the usual jutting animals high on the front. The interior has the angular simplicity of the other churches, though no particular works of art.

San Francesco and the Museo Nazionale

The city's canal and parallel road, the **Via del Fosso**, mark the entry to Lucca's more lacklustre eastern margins. The most attractive part of this quarter is the **Giardino Botanico** (April–Sept Tues–Sat 9am–1pm, Sun 9am–1pm & 3.30–6.30pm; Oct–March Mon–Sat 9am–1pm; L5000) at the southern end of Via del Fosso, an extensive patch of green laid out in 1820 which neatly complements the ramparts. Green-fingered visitors should enjoy some of the rarer exhibits, especially the medicinal plants, the sequoia, ginko tree, camphor tree and a cedar of Lebanon planted at the garden's opening.

Otherwise, the only significant sights are in the north of this quarter, around the church of **San Francesco**, fronted by a relatively simple facade and adjoining a crumbling brick convent. The inside of the church is a vast empty barn, relieved only by a delicate rose window, some lovely inlaid choir stalls and fine but damaged Florentine fresco fragments to the right of the high altar depicting the Marriage and Presentation of the Virgin.

Across the street is the much-restored **Villa Guinigi**, built to supplement the family's medieval town house. This is now home to the city's major museum, the **Museo Nazionale di Villa Guinigi** (Tues–Sat 9am–7pm, Sun 9am–2pm; L4000), an extremely varied collection of painting, sculpture, furniture and applied arts. The lower floor is mainly sculpture and archeological finds, with numerous Romanesque pieces and works by della Quercia and Matteo Civitali. Upstairs, the gallery moves onto paintings, with lots of big sixteenth-century canvases, and more impressive works by early Lucchese and Sienese masters, as well as fine Renaissance offerings from such as Fra' Bartolommeo.

Around the walls

Climbing up at one of the bastions, you can follow the four-kilometre circuit of the city **walls**, either on bike or on foot. It's worth taking time to savour them, the mid-afternoon shutdown being perhaps the best time to walk their broad promenade, which is lined successively with plane, lime, ilex and chestnut.

Construction of the walls started around 1500, prompted by the need to replace medieval ramparts rendered inadequate by advances in weapon technology. By 1650 the work was completed, with eleven bastions to fortify walls that were thirty metres wide at the base, twelve metres high and surrounded by moats thirty-five metres across. There were originally just three gates. Perhaps the best feature, from the present-day perspective, was the destruction of all trees and buildings within a couple of hundred metres of the walls, creating a green belt of lawns that has shielded the old town from the ugliness that's sprouted on the outside.

Ironically, having produced a perfect set of walls, Lucca was never called on to defend them. The only siege was against the floodwaters of the River Serchio in 1812, when the gates were sealed against the deluge that had flooded the countryside. Napoleon's sister and city governor, Elisa Baciocchi, one of the last people allowed in, had to be winched over the ramparts by crane. Marie Louise of Bourbon, her successor, had the walls transformed to their present garden aspect, arranging them, as the local tourist handout puts it, "with unparalleled good taste and moderation".

Eating

As a wealthy, gastronomic centre, Lucca has some high-quality restaurants. Local specialities often feature *zuppa di farro*, a thick soup using an ancient variety of grain grown in the Garfagnana (and parts of Umbria), roast mountain goat (*capretto*) and puddings based on chestnut flour, such as *castagnaccio*. For something to add to a picnic lunch, or to take home, try the excellent *Caniparoli* in Via San Paolina, a wonderful chocolate shop, and *La Cacioteca*, Via Fillungo 242, which sells a wide variety of cheeses. For sixty types of bread, rolls or delicious *focaccia* (freshly baked every two hours) head for *Forno Amedeo Giusti*, Via Santa Lucia 18–20. Two places on Piazza San Michele are worth a call: *Pizzeria Pellegrini* (at no. 25), for excellent pizza by the slice; and *Pasticceria Taddeucci*, partly for its cakes (the aniseed and raisin *buccellato* is the traditional favourite), partly for its 1881 wood-panelled and mosaic-tiled interior.

Restaurants

Buca di Sant'Antonio, Via della Cervia 1 (☎0583.55.881). Lucca's finest restaurant has been around for 200 years. For pudding, try the house special – *semifreddo Buccellato*, an ice-cream-like confection. L40,000–65,000; booking essential. Closed Sun evening, Mon and 3 weeks in July.

Canuleia, Via Canuleia 14 (☎0583.47.470). Excellent cooking, with odd desserts like *salami di cioccolata*. Good value, given the quality, at L30,000–45,000: located close to Piazza Anfiteatro. Closed Sat, Sun & 10 days in Aug.

Da Giulio, Via delle Conce 47 (☎0583.55.948). The city's best-known local trattoria, just north of the Palazzo Mansi towards Porta San Donato. It's always packed, so get there before 8pm if you don't want to queue. Food is not exceptional – you come here for the lively atmosphere. Around L35,000–45,000. Closed Sun, Mon & Aug.

Da Guido, Via Cesare Battisti 28 (☎0583.47.219). One of the cheapest places in town at around L20,000. Closed Sun.

Da Leo, Via Tegrimi 1, near Piazza del Salvatore (☎0583.492.236). Another good-value, family-run place near Piazza San Michele which still preserves the authentic look and feel of an old-fashioned trattoria. From about L25,000. Closed Sun.

La Mora, Via Sesto di Moriano 1748, Località Ponte Moriano (☎0583.406.402). The best place locally, but it's 9km out of town: the sublime regional cooking currently enjoys a Michelin star, and the wine list is good, too. Around L80,000. Closed Wed, plus 10 days in Jan & June.

Listings

Banks and exchange At the train station (daily 6am–9pm), most city banks, and also at Lucca Change, Piazza Napoleone 23 (March–Nov daily 9am–7.30pm, Dec–Feb Mon–Sat 9am–1pm & 3–7pm; ☎0583.495.726) and Catarsi Change, Via San Paolino 97 (Mid-March to Oct daily 9am–7pm; ☎0583.56.332).

Bike rental Try the stand by the tourist office, or Barbetti Cicli, Via dell'Anfiteatro 23 (☎0583.954.444); Cicli Bizzarri, by the walls in Piazza Santa Maria 32 (☎0583.496.031); or Antonio Poli, Piazza Santa Maria 42 (☎0583.493.787).

Buses Lazzi (☎0583.584.876) and CLAP (☎0583.587.897) both operate out of Piazzale G. Verdi. Most CLAP services are to towns and villages north of the city (including Bagni di Lucca, Barga, Castelnuovo di Garfagnana), but they also run to Florence, Viareggio, Forte dei Marmi and other places. Lazzi concentrates more on long-distance routes; destinations include Rome, Florence, Siena, Abetone, La Spezia, Prato, Pisa, Pistoia, Empoli, Massa, Lerici, Torre del Lago, Livorno and Viareggio.

Hospital The Campo di Marte, in Via dell'Ospedale (☎0583.9701).

Lost property At the *Comune*, Ufficio Economato, Via Cesare Battisti 10 (☎0583.442.388).

Police The *Questura*, at Via Cavour 38 (☎0583.4551).

Post office Via Vallisneri 2 (Mon–Sat 8.15am–7pm; ☎0583.496.669).

Taxis Ranks at the station (☎0583.494.989), Piazzale G. Verdi (☎0583.581.305) and Piazza Napoleone (☎0583.492.691).

Trains Considerably less frequent than buses for connections to Pisa (and Pisa airport – twice a day), Pistoia, Prato, Florence and Viareggio, but often a touch quicker and more comfortable. The station is on Piazza Ricasoli (☎147.888.088).

East of Lucca: the villas, Collodi and Pescia

As with Florence's hinterland, Lucca's surroundings are dotted with outstanding **villas**, built by wealthy merchants as retreats from the rigours of city life, or simply as an indulgence on the part of aristocratic landowners. Some of these started life as simple country houses, others had grandiose ambitions from the word go; most have been repeatedly altered since their inception. Many involved the leading architects of their day, either in the construction of the villas themselves, or in the design of the magnificent **gardens** that accompanied them.

Three of the villas – **Villa Reale**, **Villa Mansi**, **Villa Torrigiani** (also known as the Villa di Camigliano) – lie within a ten-kilometre radius of the city to the northeast, so if you rent a bike from Lucca's tourist office they can all be reached in a hour or so. Slightly farther afield is the **Villa Garzoni** at **Collodi**, which competes for attention with the **Parco di Pinocchio** – an attraction advertised on roadside hoardings all over Tuscany.

The Villa Reale at Marlia

By general consent, the **Villa Reale** at Marlia is the most beautiful of the villas close to Lucca. **Access** is via the SS445 from Lucca to Barga, turning off to Marlia after eight kilometres; a less direct but better-signposted route takes the SS435 for Montecatini Terme, with a left turn after seven kilometres, also signed for the Villa Reale.

The Villa Reale's life as a country house started with the destruction of a fortress on this site in the fourteenth century, its first gardens being laid out a century later. The present Neoclassical look dates from 1806, when Napoleon's sister, Elisa Baciocchi, compelled the Orsetti family to sell up. Having ousted the owners she and her personal architect, Morel, set about a radical remoulding of the villa and garden, completely refurbishing the interior and planning an English park complete with huge monumental lake.

Some of the garden's most important earlier fixtures were respected, though Napoleon's downfall and Elisa's subsequent eviction undoubtedly saved some earlier components due for destruction. Sadly, the vigour of court life at the Villa Reale also vanished with Elisa. The violinist Paganini had been employed as resident composer – he was later known to claim his playing had caused his patroness to swoon with ecstasy.

The **garden** only is open to the public (guided tours March–Nov Tues–Sun 10am, 11am, 3pm, 4pm, 5pm; tour bookings for other times ☎0583.30.108, fax 0583.30.000; L9000). Its most striking aspect is the sweeping lawn that runs from the house down to the lake, a feature of the original layout that was enlarged under the Baciocchi regime. To its left, set deep in the woods, is the **Grotto of Pan**, an elaborate two-storey hideaway with mosaic floor, much trailing greenery and a ceiling of stone plants and flowers. The hidden fountains which once sprayed the unwary are regrettably no longer working.

To one side of the lawn, an avenue of ilex trees leads to the heart of the original garden, centred on a trio of so-called **garden rooms**, which become progressively more confined. The first has a collection of lemon trees and a pool on which swans drift; the second features a high-spouting fountain; the third is a tiny and intimate "green theatre", its orchestra pit and seats all made of box and yew hedges, and edged with a variety of exotic flora.

The Villa Mansi

Arguably the least interesting of the villa quartet is the **Villa Mansi** at Segromigno, 5km east of Marlia. Originally a plain sixteenth-century country house, the villa was enlarged in 1635 by Muzio Oddi and expanded many times in subsequent centuries. The harmonious late-Renaissance facade remains, much adorned with statuary, and flanked by two pavilions joining the three-arched portico.

The **garden** (summer Tues–Sun 10am–12.30pm & 3–7pm; winter same days 10am–12.30pm & 3–5pm; L9000 garden & villa, L6000 garden only; ☎0583.920.234) has suffered more brutal treatment. The few early sections that remain intact are the best: the French-inspired eastern part, with its star-shaped avenues and irregular arrangement of fountains and basins; and the western part, laid out between 1725 and 1732 by the Sicilian architect Filippo Juvarra – the man who refashioned Turin. At the beginning of the nineteenth century much of Juvarra's geometric work was replaced by haphazard borrowings from English garden design. Innovations by the present owners have continued the garden's dubious development.

The Villa Torrigiani

Situated just two kilometres from the Villa Mansi, the **Villa Torrigiani**, or Villa di Camigliano, at Camigliano (March to 1st week of Nov daily except Tues 10am–12.30pm & 3pm–dusk; closes 7pm in summer; L15,000 garden & villa, L10,000 garden only, under 10 free) was built for the Buonvisi family in the sixteenth century, and transformed almost entirely by Alfonso Torrigiani in the eighteenth century to conform with the prevailing taste for villas and gardens in the English manner. Though little from the original survives, the present ensemble is a fine example of less formal garden design. From Lucca, the **approach** to Camigliano village is to take the SS435 for Montecatini Terme, and fork left at Borgonuovo (11km) on the signed road to the village. The villa is clearly marked from the village centre.

A magnificent avenue of cypresses leads to the villa's stately Baroque facade, adorned with a similar surfeit of statuary to the Villa Mansi's – Oddi was probably the architect here, too. The **interior** has been slightly diminished by a spate of thefts, but there's still a wealth of furniture and some odd points of passing interest. The extravagantly decorated central hall and the elliptical staircase are outstanding, both products of the eighteenth-century modifications.

The **gardens**, and larger park alongside, are complex and beautiful affairs, noted above all for their *giochi d'acqua* (water games). Intended to drench unsuspecting visitors with hidden sprays and fountains activated by the owner, or by the pressure of footsteps on levered flagstones, these tricks were especially popular with Mannerist gardeners, but in fact were first used in Roman times.

The games here, initiated by the fun-loving Marquis Niccolò Santini – Lucca's ambassador to the court of Louis XIV – are among the finest examples still functioning. They're all contained in the so-called **Garden of Flora**, a sunken garden to the east of the villa – all that has survived the garden's eighteenth-century anglicization. The Marquis would first herd his guests into the garden from an upper terrace, whereupon they would find their path blocked by a wall of spray. Attempting to retreat back down the beautiful pebble-mosaic path, they would discover that this too was now awash with water. Seeking sanctuary on the roof of the Temple of Flora, a small cupola-topped grotto, they would blunder into the biggest soaking of all, as water gushed from the domed roof, from the four statues set in the walls (representing the four winds), and, as if this weren't enough, shot up from the floor as well. In 1985, frosts damaged some of the underground piping, but the gardeners occasionally provide impromptu demonstrations of the temple's aquatic surprises.

Collodi and around

When Carlo Lorenzini published the children's book that was to make him famous, he changed his surname to the name of his birthplace, **COLLODI**, a little town 15km east of Lucca. Thus, whereas other Tuscan towns adopt the Baptist or the Mother of Christ as their patron, Collodi has dedicated itself to a puppet with an erectile nose – **Pinocchio**. To English-speakers reared on the glutinous Disney version, it's difficult to appreciate the reverence accorded Pinocchio in his homeland, but the tale's moral simplicity and exemplary Tuscan prose ensures it a massive following. The saintly Pope John Paul I used to address missives to the novel's hero, and Italian newspaper polls have seen *Pinocchio* shortlisted as a contender for Greatest Novel of All Time.

Parco di Pinocchio

Created in the 1950s, the **Parco di Pinocchio** (daily: summer 8.20am–8pm; winter 7am–5.30pm; L12,000, under-14s L7000) honours the famous book with statues of its characters, a sequence of mosaics depicting moments from Pinocchio's life, and various tableaux scattered around the paths that wind through the park.

The monsters and mazes are fun without any background knowledge, but you'll need to have read the book in order to get the most from the park – and to field questions should you be visiting the park with infatuated children. Pinocchio's importance to the nation can be gauged from the fact that Michelucci – architect of Florence's train station and several prestigious churches – was commissioned to design the **restaurant and museum** near the entrance, which usually contains a display of drawings for a special edition. Be warned that you'll be lucky to get out of the park having forked out only for the tickets – there's a very inviting toy shop ready to hook the kids as you leave.

The Villa Garzoni

Overshadowing the Pinocchio park, the vast **Villa Garzoni** evolved from a castle that stood here in the days before Lucca surrendered this region to Florence. The house took on its present form in the second half of the seventeenth century, but it was towards the end of the following century that it acquired the magnificent formal **garden** (9am–sunset; L10,000) that makes this one of Italy's finest villas.

Access is usually through a gate on the main road, but the garden was designed to be entered through the wood adjoining the villa, so that the visitor would emerge from the wilderness into this precisely orchestrated landscape. Maximizing the theatrical possibilities of the steep slope, the Garzoni deploys the full resources of the Baroque garden: circular fountains, topiary animals, patterns of flowers and coloured stones, a water staircase, a zigzagging cascade of steps and terraces, and terracotta figures cropping up in every corner.

Villa Basilica

One of the most dramatically sited Romanesque churches in Tuscany is a short distance north from Collodi at **VILLA BASILICA**, a tiny village clinging to a ridge below Monte Pietra Pertusa. To get to it just follow the main road out of Collodi for 3km, then keep an eye out for an acute turn to the left. It's a sternly unadorned building, made attractive by the backdrop of woods and terraces on the other side of the valley; to get the best view of all, you could clamber up to the ruins of the fortress above the village.

Pescia – and Castelvecchio

In summer, every second person on the streets of **PESCIA** is a florist: this medium-sized town, 8km west of Montecatini Terme (see p.189), is Italy's top producer of cut flowers, boxing around three million lilies, carnations, gladioli and other blooms per day at the height of the season. Each September of even-numbered years it hosts the technicolour **Biennale del Fiore**, held in the gargantuan market hall on the outskirts.

Split by the Pescia river, the town has two distinct zones: the left bank forms the ecclesiastical quarter, the right is the secular and commercial district. The **duomo**, rebuilt Baroque but with a fourteenth-century campanile, takes second slot to **San Francesco** in Via Battisti – reached by walking towards the river from the cathedral and turning right before the bridge. Here Bonaventura Berlinghieri's panel of *Six Scenes from the Life of St Francis* (third altar on the right), painted nine years after Francis's death, provides what's publicized as the most accurate surviving portrait of him, but is in fact a routinely stylized image of the saint. On the other side of the nave, the Cappella Cardini was added to the Gothic church by the architect known simply as Buggiano, employing the style of his adoptive father, Brunelleschi. The nearby oratory of **Sant'Antonio Abbate**, just before San Francesco, has a *Deposition* that's an outstanding specimen of thirteenth-century woodcarving.

Over on the right bank, at one end of the elongated **Piazza Mazzini**, the church of **Madonna di Piè di Piazza** is another worthy creation by Buggiano. At the other end of the square stands the bemedalled **Palazzo dei Vicari**, Romanesque home of the local council. For admission to the **Museo Civico**, in the Palazzo Galeotti on Piazza Santo Stefano (follow the signs from the Palazzo dei Vicari), you normally have to ask at the library on the ground floor. Inside there's an endearingly shambolic assembly of Tuscan paintings, illuminated manuscripts and prints, as well as a section dedicated to the Sicilian-born opera composer Giovanni Pacini; one of the most successful musicians of his time, he is now held in such low regard that his manuscripts are just strewn round the room like out-of-date theatre programmes.

There's no reason to hang around in Pescia unless it's to sample the town's edible specialities – asparagus and a questionable stew known as *cioncia*, made from ox's muzzle. For L35,000–55,000 you can get an excellent **meal** at *Cecco*, Via Forti 84 (☎0572.477.955; closed Mon and periods in Jan & June) – try the *pollastrino*, chicken cooked in a terracotta vessel with lemon and garlic. A slightly more routine and more expensive experience is to be had at *La Buca*, at Piazza Mazzini 4 in the old centre (☎0572.477.339; closed Tues and periods in Aug & Nov).

Castelvecchio

Thirteen kilometres upstream from Pescia – past the paper mills that keep Pescia's second industry going – stands the strange **Pieve San Tommaso** in the village of **CASTELVECCHIO**. Founded in the eleventh century, it bears a frieze of ghoulish faces on the facade and apse, suggesting a strong pagan undertow to the Christian piety of this area. Inside are some wonderfully carved capitals and a gloomy crypt that intensifies the threatening aura of the grimacing heads.

The Versilia Coast

The northern coast of Tuscany is known, somewhat hyperbolically, as **the Riviera della Versilia**. **Carrara** and **Massa** are its main towns, known above all else as the marble capitals of Italy – huge blocks of stone, fine white dust and mine-scarred rockfaces are the memories likeliest to endure from a visit. The beach resorts that run unbroken between **Viareggio** and **Forte dei Marmi** offer Italian beach culture in all its glory. Much of the sand is leased to the virtually indistinguishable *stabilimenti*, who in turn charge admission to their strips and rent out chairs and umbrellas; if you blanch at paying, there are public beaches (*spiaggia pubblica*) at regular intervals. For a swim and some sun in cheerfully crowded conditions, this coast is not as black as it's usually painted: the water may be cleaner elsewhere but it's not filthy, and the sand is immaculately groomed. And **bus** and **train** links to all points are excellent, especially in the summer, when you can move up and down the coast with more ease than anywhere else in Tuscany.

Viareggio and Torre del Lago

The best town on the coast, **VIAREGGIO** is also Tuscany's biggest seaside resort, the so-called Biarritz of the Riviera della Versilia. Less pretentious than its supposed model, it nonetheless shares its air of elegance, thanks mainly to the long avenue of palms that runs the length of its seafront promenade. A modest collection of Liberty-style frontages – designed by the father of the Italian Art Nouveau, Galileo Chini – adds to the sense of refinement, though for the most part the buildings are the old-style hotels you'd find in British seaside towns.

In the early part of last century, the town's reputation for exclusivity was well deserved; these days all that's left is the high prices. The excellent **beaches** are all private, charging L25,000 and upwards for admission – except for the free stretch between Viareggio and Torre del Lago – and in summer the few hotels that aren't full usually hold out for *pensiona completa*. You may well prefer to join the majority and cram into the train for a day trip. This is certainly what Florentines do: in summer, special early morning trains from the city are packed with raucous *ragazzi* and at least a dozen ghetto-blasters per carriage.

The town

Arriving at the **train station**, ten minutes' walk back from the seafront, you can pick up details from the summer-only **tourist office**, or else from the main office (daily 9am–1pm plus summer 4–7pm; ☎0584.962.233) one block back from the beachside boardwalk at Viale Carducci 10. **Buses** stop near the centre at Piazza d'Azeglio and Piazza Mazzini; tickets and information are available from CLAP (☎0584.53.704) and Lazzi (☎0584.46.234) offices, both in Piazza d'Azeglio.

Lacking any real centre, Viareggio's main focus is its promenade, the **Passeggiata Margherita**, a broad thoroughfare that runs along the seafront for three kilometres. Most of the Art Nouveau fronts are crowded together around the town's best-known

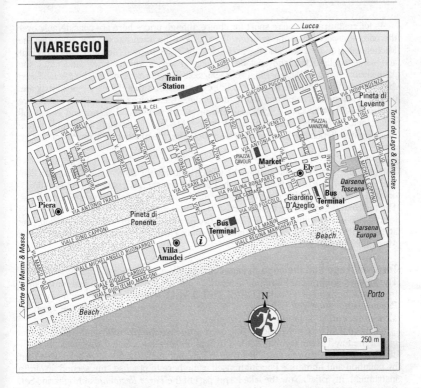

spot, the *Gran Caffè Margherita*, seemingly inspired by a pastry chef rather than an architect, close to the start of the Passeggiata near the marina. Across the marina and distinct from the town, the **Viale dei Tigli**, is a beautiful six-kilometre avenue of lime trees that stretches to the south. Along its length there's access to various beaches, and to the bulk of the town's campsites.

The town has over one hundred one-star **hotels**, with the biggest concentrations near the tourist office on Viale Carducci, and along Via Vespucci and Via Leonardo da Vinci. More upmarket options are equally numerous, so if you fail to strike it lucky at one place, the next hotel is rarely more than a few seconds' walk away. There's almost nothing to choose between hotels, but among the cheaper options you might try first are the *Piera*, Via Antonio Fratti 684 (☎0584.50.737; ②) with garden and all rooms with private bathrooms; *Villa Amadei*, Via F. Gioia 23 (☎0584.45.517; ②) and the more pricey and central two-star *Ely*, Via Carrara 16 (☎0584.50.758, fax 0584.407.387).

If you're **camping**, head out along Viale dei Tigli. There are several sites off this avenue on the edge of the Parco Regionale: the first is the *Viareggio*, Via Comparini 1 (☎0584.391.012, fax 0584.395.462; April–Sept) on the left after about a kilometre, followed by the larger *Paradiso*, Via dei Lecci (☎0584.392.005, fax 0584.387.206; April–Sept) and half a dozen others. To **hire a bike** head for the **Pineta di Ponente** (see map). Mopeds and Vespas are available at Noleggio, Galleria d'Azeglio (☎0584.46.410), from L35,000 per day.

As for **restaurants**, you're spoilt for choice, though prices here are considerably over the odds – especially on the seafront. For the best the town has to offer, make for the Michelin-starred *Romano*, Via Mazzini 120 (☎0584.31.382; closed Mon and 3 weeks in Jan) and some sublime fish and seafood cooking. Lower down the price ladder, try the *Margherita*, Piazzale Margherita (☎0584.962.553; closed Wed) or the long-established *Montecatini*, Viale Manin 8 (☎0584.962.129; closed Mon), with its Liberty-style nineteenth-century villa and garden. On a still tighter budget, the choices are *Da Dino*, Via Cesare Battisti 35–37 (☎0584.962.053; closed Thurs), which does good pizzas and cheap full meals, and *La Darsena*, Via Virgilio 154 (☎0584.392.785; closed Sun). Otherwise you're more likely to depend on pizzas or takeaway food from the **market**, held on Piazza Cavour.

CARNEVALE

The only time Viareggio hits national headlines is during the three-week **Carnevale** (late Jan/early Feb), one of the liveliest in Italy. Each Sunday there's a parade of colossal floats, or *carri*, carrying lavishly designed papier-mâché models of politicians and celebrities. The top *carri* designers are feted as artists, and their imaginative creations are displayed for the rest of the summer in the **Hanger-Carnevale** at the top of Via Marco Polo. Ask at the tourist office for opening times or contact the Fondazione Carnevale, Piazza Mazzini 22 (☎0584.962.568).

Torre del Lago and the Lago di Massaciuccoli

The journey south from Viareggio along the Viale dei Tigli is worth it just for the lime trees; whether you press onto **TORRE DEL LAGO** depends on how much you value Puccini, who spent the later part of his life in a villa on the edge of the **Lago di Massaciuccoli** (bus from Piazza d'Azeglio).

No more than two metres deep, yet covering an area the size of Pisa, the **lake** itself is one of the few Tuscan lagoons not lost to land reclamation. Once it supported virtually all the aquatic birds it was possible to see in Italy, but many species have been wiped out by pollution and hunters – Puccini himself came here to practise "my second favourite instrument, my rifle". Now the lake forms part of the *Parco Regionale* of Migliarino-San Rossore, and is also a protected bird sanctuary; as a result there are some 80 breeding and another 65 occasional species on the lake. You can take **boat trips** on it; L10,000 for a trip around the lake, or sign up for an hour's bird-watching – ask in the *Ristorante Antonio* or ring ☎0584.350.424.

In the hamlet itself, it's easy to miss the **Villa Puccini**, set back from the shore and surrounded by bars, trees and high iron railings. Visits are in guided groups of no more than 25 people for around thirty minutes (Tues–Sun half-hourly: April–July 10am–12.30pm & 3.30–5.30pm; July–Aug 10am–12.30pm & 4–7pm; Oct–March 10am–12.30pm & 2.30–5pm; L5000); the rooms feature original furnishings, mementos and the piano on which Puccini bashed out many of his operas.

In late July and August the **Festival Pucciniano** presents the master's works in Torre del Lago's outdoor theatre and various other venues (information from the festival office, Viale Puccini 25a; ☎0584.359.322). It's an extremely popular show, as are the international regattas held on the lake through the summer.

Torre del Lago has a huge **campsite**, the *Bosco Verde*, Viale Kennedy 5 (☎0584.359.343, fax 0584.341.981; April–Sept) – and eight **hotels**, all one-star, mostly along the main Viale Marconi, except for: *Butterfly*, Via Belvedere Puccini 24 (☎ & fax 0584.341.024; ②), right by the lake; the *Albergo Antonio*, Via Puccini 260 (☎0584.341.053; ②), near the Villa Puccini; and *Le Grazie*, Viale Kennedy 27 (☎0584.341.025; ②), on the way to the sea. Along the *lungomare* there are plenty of good restaurants and *pizzerie*; also a couple of **clubs** that draw people of all persuasions from as far afield as Florence.

Pietrasanta to Forte dei Marmi

North of Viareggio, the resorts of Lido di Camaiore and Marina di Pietrasanta are merely continuations of the Versilia's ribbon development, distinguishable only by a gradual shift downmarket as you move towards Forte dei Marmi.

The town of **PIETRASANTA**, 2km back from the beach (Marina di Pietrasanta), passes for an interesting place in these parts, but is no more than a busy marble centre with one or two old buildings. However, there are useful buses into the mountains from Piazza Matteotti in the town centre, with several services daily to Seravezza, where you can change for connections to Levigliani and Stazzema, and one to Castelnuovo di Garfagnana. The bus stop is by the two-star **hotel** *Stipino*, Via Provinciale 50 (☎0584.71.448, fax 0584.72.421; ③), and the three-star *Palagi*, Piazza Carducci 23 (☎0584.70.249, fax 0584.71.198; ⑤), which has full details of departures. The town's summer-only **tourist office** is at Piazza del Duomo (☎0584.795.260).

Another inland town, **CAMAIORE**, has a couple of Romanesque churches and the eighth-century **Badia dei Santi Benedetti**, but it's an ugly semi-industrial spot, worth passing through only if you're taking the minor road back to Lucca.

Forte dei Marmi

As these places go, **FORTE DEI MARMI** is a pleasant resort, with lush, tree-lined streets and a good beach. It's a good place for a swim and stroll, but there's nothing here to justify its reputation as the trendiest spot on the coast, nor the high prices in its top hotels and restaurants. Once a major port for marble from the Apuane, it's now one of the second-home capitals of Tuscany, and a retreat for writers and artists who hole up in its more isolated, tree-surrounded villas.

The town, however, is again a good point of access to the mountains, with **buses** to Seravezza, Levigliani, Stazzema and Farnocchia (see below). CLAP services run to the interior and to Lucca, Viareggio and Pietrasanta from the **train station** (at Querceta, 3km inland) and from Via Matteotti in the town itself. Lazzi services run from nearby Via Pascoli to La Spezia, Pisa, Lucca and Florence. The **tourist office** at Via Achille Franceschi 8b (☎0584.80.091) can provide full lists of the hundred-odd hotels if you get the urge to stay. **Restaurants** largely cater to the well-heeled, though there are the usual seafront *pizzerie*. For about L100,000-plus you can have one of the region's finest culinary experiences at the Michelin-starred *Lorenzo*, Via Carducci 61 (☎0584.84.030; closed Mon and lunchtime July–Aug). Fish at its freshest is the choice: "a fish has 24 virtues", says owner Lorenzo Viani, "but loses one with each hour that passes."

For a few hundred metres to the north of Forte di Marmi there's actually a stretch of **dunes** with no development at all; it looks a tempting camping option, but local police will shift you within minutes if you try to pitch a tent. Beyond the dunes, nondescript Cinquale and Ronchi resume the corridor of beachfront commercialism.

The Alpi Apuane

Tuscany's Versilian coast is dominated by the mountains of the **Alpi Apuane**, a forty-kilometre spread of genuinely alpine spectacle. Now a protected *Parco Naturale* (and earmarked for promotion to *Parco Nazionale* status), they are crisscrossed by well-marked **footpaths**, and offer huge rewards for the walker and naturalist. If you want to do more than admire the jagged knife-edge ridge of the mountains from afar, there are numerous **marked trails** starting from roadheads deep in the mountains, and the biggest concentration of these tracks is in the peaks east of Forte dei Marmi and Pietrasanta, centred on Pania della Croce (1859m) and Monte Forato (1223m).

Thanks to their position and height, the Apuane are a perfect combination of different ecological habitats, from tundra through Alpine meadow to Mediterranean grassland. An extraordinary variety of **wild flowers** makes this one of the country's richest botanic enclaves, but the most noticeable vegetation is the immense forests of **chestnut and beech** which cover virtually all the lower slopes. These shelter some of the mountains' three hundred species of **birds**; sadly, protection came too late to preserve many larger mammals from hunters, though you may see marmots – rare in the Apennines – on the higher, sunnier slopes.

The Apuane are also the Italian **speleology** capital, riddled with some of the greatest challenges in European caving. An estimated 400km of galleries run through the mountains, the deepest – the *Antro del Corchia* – touching minus 1120m. For information on this and other activities contact the **tourist office** and **park visitor centre** in Seravezza, at Via Corrado del Greco 11 (Tues–Sun: summer 9am–1pm & 4–8pm; winter 9am–1pm & 2.30–6.30pm; ☎0584.757.325).

Walking in the Apuane

Detailed *Multigraphic-Wanderkarte* 1:25,000 **maps** of the Apuane (widely available in the area) mark all the main trails with the international convention of red and white stripes and black number, though some short diversions to the summits are marked in blue without numbers. On maps and on the ground you'll also find paths marked "A", a reference to **Apuane Trekking**, an eight-day path along the ridge, following a route roughly north to south.

The main approach to the northern group of peaks, round **Pania della Croce**, is from **LEVIGLIANI**, reached by bus from Forte dei Marmi and Pietrasanta, from where a mining road runs towards Monte Corchia (1677m) – about half of which has been removed by quarrying. You can sometimes get lifts up this far from mining lorries, although going up it on the mine's working days is officially prohibited. Then from the top of the mining road you can pick up trail #9 to the 32-bed **Rifugio Giuseppe del Freo** (2hr 30min walk from Levigliani; open daily June 15–Sept 15; rest of the year, weekends only; ☎0584.778.007; L52,000 for bed, dinner and breakfast). From the refuge you can climb Pania della Croce (trail #126; 2hr 30min from the refuge), one of the best walks locally, or choose from seven other paths. If you'd prefer **hotel** comfort to the rigours of the refuge, Levigliani has a couple of two-star options: the *Vallechiara*, Via Lambora 12 (☎ & fax 0584.778.054; ③) and the *Raffaello*, Via Nord 11 (☎ & fax 0584.778.063; ③).

For the southern peaks, round **Monte Forato**, the best access point is **STAZZEMA**, a lovely village in its own right, with **hotel** accommodation at the one-star *Procinto*, Via IV Novembre 21 (☎0584.78.004; ②). The bus from Forte dei Marmi and Pietrasanta goes to Farnocchia – itself the starting point for some easy paths through the trees – and then to Stazzema. The classic walk from Stazzema (trail #5) is a gentle climb through chestnut woods to the **Procinto**, a huge table-top crag mentioned by Dante. Below the crag at 865m is the 52-bed **Rifugio Forte dei Marmi** (open daily June 5–Sept 5; rest of the year, weekends only; ☎0584.777.051; bed only L20,000), a perfect base for walks along the main ridge – to the *Rifugio del Freo* (see above), for example, in a couple of hours. The Procinto walk is a comfortable day's outing, with time to walk up to Monte Nona (1279m), drop back to the refuge for a snack, and then return to Stazzema by trails #121/126.

Massa

It might have a castle and cathedral, but the character of busy, modern **MASSA** is encapsulated more by its bland broad streets and Fascist civic architecture. The town's most distinctive sight is on the main street, a **fountain** consisting of a big marble ball and fat babies – easily seen from a passing bus or car. If you do stop off, the **Castello Malaspina** (Tues–Sun 8.30am–12.30pm & 3–6pm; L3000) is worth an hour if you've time to spare, with its loggia and spread of Renaissance rooms clustered around the eleventh-century kernel. The castle was the base of the Malaspina family, lords of Massa from the sixteenth to the eighteenth century. Otherwise there's only the two-tiered **duomo** – in local marble, of course – and the **Piazza degli Aranci**, hub of what remains of the old town.

Practicalities

Buses come and go from Massa's **train station**: if you want to take a trip down the Versilia's beach strip, take the bus to Marina di Massa, and then transfer to one of the Lazzi services that run up and down the coast at two-hourly intervals (more frequent in July–Aug) – they stop every few hundred metres.

Most of the **hotels** – and there are lots of them – are in Marina di Massa. A good one is the *Miramonte* at Via Monte Grappa 7 (☎0585.241.067; ④). There's also a **youth hostel**, the *Ostello della Gioventà* (☎0585.780.034; open April–Sept; curfew 11.30pm; L14,000), on the seafront between Marina di Carrara and Marina di Massa, at Via delle Pinete 237, Partaccia; you can take a direct bus from Carrara train station, or from Marina di Massa for a northbound coast bus. There's a free beach nearby, but the sand's poor; you're better off heading south to stretch out.

The best-known **restaurant** in Marina di Massa is the *Da Riccà*, Lungomare di Ponente (☎0585.241.070; closed Mon), which is good but expensive (from L60,000). Also worth trying is the cheaper *Trattoria Baria*, Via San Leonardo (☎0585.240.278; closed Tues). Alternatively, cheap snack and pizza outlets abound. If you're in Massa itself, the best bet is the wonderfully old-fashioned *Il Passeggero*, run by the same family for over 50 years, just off the main Piazza degli Aranci at Via Alberica 1 (☎0585.489.651; closed Sun and evenings Mon–Thurs; from L30,000). For **picnic** and other food supplies in Massa, visit Gli Svizzeri, Via Cairoli 53, for wonderful and often exotic foods in a shop that's been around since the 1850s.

Into the mountains

Behind Massa, a road climbs up into the Alpi Apuane **to Castelnuovo di Garfagnana** (see p.228), a scrappy ride, with new villas and ramshackle *pizzerie* taking the edge off the views. Two kilometres above the village of Antona there's a council-owned refuge, the **Rifugio-Albergo di Massa** (April 15–Sept 30; ☎0585.319.923). It's not in the best part of the Apuane, and not a place to stay, but if you go through the road tunnel just beyond it, Club Alpino Italiano trails #41/188 lead up to Monte Altissimo (1589m) and a couple of low ridge walks. Just before the refuge, at Pian della Fioba, there's a small **botanical garden** with some of the Alps' many hundreds of different wild flowers.

Carrara

You can't get away from marble in **CARRARA**, a town whose very name is said to derive from *kar*, the Indo-European word for stone. However, the town itself is a surprisingly attractive place, once you get away from the sprawling factories around the station. Set in the hills above this mess, central Carrara has a rural hill-town feel, with peeling pastel stucco on its houses, elegant side streets lined with rows of green shutters and a couple of piazzas and a **duomo** that would do credit to any Tuscan town. By contrast, the town's "resort", **Marina di Carrara**, is grim – more a container port than a beach. If you want the sea, it's best to drive inland to Massa, and then drop down to the coast there.

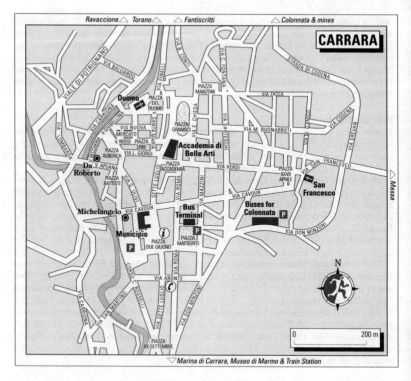

Carrara feels like a self-sufficient town, and its people have always had a reputation as a breed apart – something they preserved even under the long-term domination of the Malaspina nobles, the local medieval big shots. Before their rule, the town had developed as a trading centre poised between Tuscany, the mountains and the Ligurian coast. Roman exploitation of the marble made trade with the nearby colony of Luni particularly brisk, and something of its scale can be seen in the ruins of the colony currently being excavated over the Ligurian border.

The Town

The old town, connected to the train station by a regular bus service, centres on **Piazza Alberica**, a gracious square whose beauty owes much to the hills which come down on two sides, and to the elegant colours and tone more often associated with Liguria than Tuscany. Stray blocks of marble sit at its centre, a legacy of the annual *Scolpire all'Aperto*, a festival in which sculptors from around the world are invited to the town, given a block of marble, and left to work in the middle of the square. If you're here between late July and early October, you may get to watch them chipping away.

A short walk brings you to the eleventh-century **duomo**, rather squashed into its piazza, but graced with a huge tower and a lovely facade built to the inevitable Pisan-Romanesque pattern. Only the intricate rose window, a superb fourteenth-century addition, departs from the norm. The interior has a severe simplicity but contains some beautiful works – a fifteenth-century **pulpit** and five appealing statues by the fourteenth-century sculptor Bergamini. The piazza's fountain, known locally as *Il*

CARRARA MARBLE

Ever-present on the Versilia coast, whether as blocks waiting shipment or as huge snow-like scars on the mountains, **marble** has been the lifeblood of the region for over two thousand years. Over two hundred working concerns extract 700,000 tonnes of stone annually, making this still the world's single largest producer of marble. Huge wire saws slice into the mountains at a rate of about 8cm an hour, their twenty-four-hour whine the bane of local residents. Environmentalists oppose the speed of extraction, and the industry is threatened by government plans to give national park status to the Apuane, but the quarry owners will fight all the way to preserve the two thousand jobs that remain, in an industry which employed as many as fourteen thousand men barely one hundred years ago. With an estimated thousand jobs directly dependent on each job in the quarries, the Carrara employers have no lack of supporters elsewhere in Italy.

Marble is a metamorphic form of limestone, hardened by colossal heat and pressure. Though it takes many forms, **Carrara stone** is usually white-grey and is prized for its flawless lustre. The many other types you'll see are mostly blocks which have been imported – from as far away as Russia – to be worked by the highly reputed local factories.

The Romans were the first to extract this stone commercially, driving pegs of fig-wood into natural faults and then soaking them until the swollen wood split the stone. In time they used scored lines and iron chisels to produce uniform blocks about two metres square – still the basic measure.

Practices remained little changed until the Renaissance, when **Michelangelo** began to visit the area. His wet nurse was from this part of Tuscany, and he claimed he became a sculptor by ingesting the marble dust in her milk; he also claimed to have introduced the art of quarrying to Carrara, a process he considered as important as sculpting itself. The *David* is sculpted from Carrara marble, and local folklore is full of Michelangelo's pilgrimages to distant corners of the mountains in search of perfect stone.

Gigante (The Giant), is an incomplete work by the lacklustre Florentine Bandinelli. Also in the square is the house where Michelangelo put up while checking out his marble supplies, while nearby are Petrarch's digs at Casa Repetti in Via Santa Maria. The castle on Piazza Gramsci was once a Malaspina fortress and is now the **Accademia delle Belle Arti**. It looks much as a castle should and has a few Roman fragments and plaster casts around its courtyard.

In Via XX Settembre, 2km out of town on the road down towards Marina di Carrara, is the **Museo Civico di Marmo** (April–Sept Mon–Fri 10am–1pm & 4–7pm; Oct–March same days 10am–1pm & 2–5pm; L5000). Run as a promotional exercise by the local Chamber of Commerce, it's an impressive display that looks at the history and production of the stone – lots of photographs, examples of different types of marble, and a room devoted to rather dubious examples of marble art. A bus runs there from Piazza Matteotti.

The Quarries

Any short trip into the interior brings you across the huge scars of the marble **quarries**, some of the most startling sights in Tuscany. A particularly accessible site is at **Colonnata** (taking its name from a column of Roman slaves brought in to work the mines), just 8km from Carrara and served by hourly CAT **buses** from Via Don Minzoni, five minutes from the main terminus in Piazza Matteotti. Don't go all the way to Colonnata village, but get off at the *Visita Cave* signs by the mine; if you're driving, follow the yellow *Cava di Marmo* signs from the town up the twisting road. You'll see a huge, blindingly white marble basin, its floor and sides perfectly squared by the enormous wire saws used to cut the blocks that litter the surroundings. There are even bigger quarries farther south, notably at Monte Corchia.

Walking

Colonnata village also marks an entrance point for **walks** in the Alpi Apuane, the CAI trail #38 behind the village leading to a dense web of paths around **Monte Rasore** (1422m) and **Monte Grondice** (1805m); the 1:25,000 *Multigraphic-Wanderkarte* **map** #101/102 is useful for making sense of this. As an alternative, take the SS446 north from Carrara to Campo Cecina (18km), where the all-year **Rifugio Carrara** (1320m; ☎0585.841.972; L23,000) offers accommodation (book ahead) and a rather more gentle selection of paths.

Carrara practicalities

Carrara's **tourist office** is at the Marina, Piazza Menconi 6b. The Telecom Italia **telephone** office is on the corner of Via Roma and Via Aronte (Mon–Sat 9am–12.30pm & 3–7.30pm); the **post office** is in Via Mazzini, on the corner with Via Aronte.

Accommodation is tight in the old town and is more or less limited to the potentially noisy two-star *Da Roberto* on Via Apuana 5 (☎0585.70.634; ②) and the more salubrious three-star *Michelangelo*, Corso Carlo Roselli 3 (☎0585.777.161, fax 0585.74.545; ③). Other than that, head down to the coast and Marina di Carrara, where the **youth hostel** (see "Massa" p.221) and most of the hotels are to be found, or you could opt for halfway between, near the station, and try the one-star *Da Maurin*, Via Fiorino 2 (☎0585.859.385; ②) or the two-star *Da Sergio*, Via Provinciale 180 (☎ & fax 0585.857.695; ③).

Restaurants are numerous, few of them tourist-orientated. For L30,000–60,000 you can eat at the *Osteria della Contrada*, Via Ulivi 2 (☎0585.776.961; closed Mon); best mid-price option is the *Roma di Prioreschi*, Piazza Cesare Battisti 1 (☎0585.70.632; closed Sat). An excellent little spot for a drink is the *Bar Garibaldi*, Piazza Battisti 1 (closed Sun), filled with old photos of performers from the neighbouring Animosi theatre, and for wine with snacks and light meals the *Enoteca Ninan*, Via Bartolini 3 (☎0585.74.741; closed Sun). For **picnic** supplies, tuck into Ricci, Via Rosselli 1 (closed Wed afternoon and Sun), which still preserves a wonderful Art Nouveau interior. For a treat, head out to Colonnata, where the *Venanzo*, Piazza Palestro 3 (☎0585.750.062; closed Thurs and also Sun evening, booking essential) has attracted even the president of Italy, though success has not yet caused prices to rise: reckon on around L50,000 upwards for what should be a sensational meal.

The **train station** is close to the sea, with a regular bus service to the old town (Piazza Matteotti – which is also the terminal for local buses to Massa, Marina di Massa and the youth hostel). Frequent trains run to La Spezia, Viareggio, all points on the coast and Pisa. Lazzi bus connections for La Spezia and Florence leave from Piazza Menconi, in the Marina. Finally, for detailed **walking** and **climbing** information contact CAI, who also organize a series of free excursions into the Parco delle Alpi Apuane in July and August (office at Via L. Giorgi 1; ☎0585.776.782).

The Garfagnana

The **Garfagnana** is the general name for the area encompassing the Serchio valley north of Lucca, one of Tuscany's least-explored yet most spectacular corners. The paucity of visitors is accounted for by the lack of any great sights – medieval **Barga** and the spa town of Bagni di Lucca are the only historic towns – but for anyone with an interest in **hiking** or fine scenery, there are rewards aplenty. Much of the Garfagnana is protected as a regional **nature reserve**, whose excellent on-the-ground organization has mapped and signposted a good range of walks. The best of these are on the east of the Serchio valley, up in the mountainous **Orecchiella** range. The Serchio's western flanks are the equally spectacular mountains of the **Alpi Apuane**, but as the main ridge here is better reached from the coastal side, it is covered in an earlier section (see p.219).

If you don't have a car, the best way to see the Garfagnana is on the **train** line which runs the entire length of the Serchio, past Barga and the region's rather lacklustre major centre, **Castelnuovo di Garfagnana** – the handiest place to stay as a base for exploring – and then cuts through the head of the valley to **Aulla**, centre of the Lunigiana (see p.232). From there you can drop down by train to La Spezia, and complete a loop back to Lucca via Massa and Viareggio. For Bagni di Lucca, it's easiest to travel by bus from Lucca, as the Bagni di Lucca train station is about 4km out of town. Other buses from Lucca run up and down the valley, with stops in Barga, Castelnuovo di Garfagnana and elsewhere.

The Lower Serchio valley

Although the road north up the Serchio soon leaves Lucca behind, there's something laborious about the first part of the journey along the **Serchio valley**, with dusty hills and snatches of light industry dotting the way to Barga, 50km north. Buses from Lucca call at all the peripheral villages but you're unlikely to want to stop at any of them if you don't have your own transport.

A first possible detour for the mobile is the **Pieve di Brancoli**, a twelfth-century abbey, reached by a twisting hillside road on the east bank of the valley, 10km out of Lucca. More easily visited, with its own rail stop, is **DIECIMO**, over on the west bank. Its Latin name is explained by a past as a Roman outpost, positioned ten Roman miles (17km) from Lucca. No more than a hamlet, it is dominated by a large, white **Romanesque campanile** – clearly visible from the river.

Four kilometres on, road and rail line bypass **BORGO A MOZZANO**, which basically comprises a single cobbled street of medieval houses and the famous **Ponte della Maddalena** (or Ponte del Diavolo). Narrow, steep and elegant, this strange five-arched bridge was constructed in the eleventh century. According to legend it was built by the Devil in exchange for the soul of the first person to cross it; here, as in every European village where a version of this tale survives, the villagers outfoxed the Devil by sending across an unsuspecting animal – in this case a dog. If you need to stay, **accommodation** in Borgo includes the one-star *Gallo d'Oro*, Via del Brennero 3 (☎0583.88.380; ②), whose nine rooms share a single bathroom, and two-star *Il Pescatore*, Via Maggio 2, Ponte Pari (☎0583.88.071; ②), all eight doubles with private bath.

Bagni di Lucca and the Lima valley

Though it had been a spa for centuries, **BAGNI DI LUCCA**, 25km from Lucca, hit the social big time only in the early nineteenth century, when the patronage of Elisa Baciocchi brought in Europe's fashionable elite. The town boasted one of Europe's first official casinos – roulette was invented here – and was graced by the presence of such romantic luminaries as Byron, Shelley, Browning and Heine.

Today, Bagni di Lucca retains its elegance and pretty surroundings and the atmosphere is fairly subdued. If you want to spend a day or two soaking in the salty or sulphurous waters, there are a dozen **hotels** spread out along the valley – most of them reasonably priced, despite claims to famous past guests. Try the two-star *Svizzero*, Via C. Casalini 30 (☎ & fax 0583.805.31; ②), for some old-world charm; the one-star *Roma*, Via Umberto I 110 (☎ & fax 0583.87.278; ②); or the only slightly more expensive three-star *Bridge*, a couple of kilometres away in the square at Ponte a Serraglio (☎ & fax 0583.805.324; ③).

The best place to **eat** is *Circolo Dei Forestieri*, Piazza Varraud 10 (☎0583.86.038; closed Mon and Tues lunch), which serves food both exquisite and inexpensive, in a beautiful building with a columned terrace; best to book in advance. Or visit the busy pizzeria *Da Vinicio*, a block downstream from Bagni's bridge (closed Mon).

The pace of the town may quicken in the summer, since Bagni di Lucca became host to an **opera festival** (late July to early Aug), in which musicians who have recently finished their training appear in productions under the direction of established professionals. As well as reviving works that have fallen out of the standard repertory, the festival also commissions new pieces. You can get information about the festival from the **tourist office** at Via Umberto I (Mon–Sat 9am–2pm; ☎0583.805.508, fax 0583.807.877). **Bus** tickets and information are available from the Bar Centro Commerciale, Via Roma 9 (☎0583.87.343).

The Lima valley

East of Bagni, the **Lima valley**, a tributary of the Serchio, rises towards the border with Emilia-Romagna. Two **buses** daily (morning and afternoon) make the run over the hills to San Marcello Pistoiese, the afternoon service continuing to the skiing and walking centre of Abetone.

In the valley itself, there are several possible rough road diversions to villages with **ancient churches** and spectacular mountain surroundings. Pieve di Controne, just 3km northeast of Bagni, has a strange old church in red stone, fronted by a facade covered with odd diagonal motifs. San Cassiano, 10km from Bagni, has a twelfth-century church of the same name, with a wonderful carved facade, three tiers of very shallow arches, and a much older and dirtier tower that cuts off half the marble-faced front. Just south of the valley, Lucchio (18km from Bagni), cascading down the mountainside, is crowned by a castle ruin.

Past Lucchio, you enter the province of Pistoia, as **SAN MARCELLO PISTOIESE** proclaims. The business centre of the Pistoian mountains, San Marcello observes one of the quirkier Tuscan rituals: the releasing of a hot-air balloon on September 8 as a valediction to summer. Buses follow the main road north of here – a continuation of the N66 from Pistoia – to **ABETONE** (18km from San Marcello) which is the nearest winter-sports resort to Florence. Its six chair lifts can cope with an hourly capacity of fourteen thousand people and at the height of the skiing season the system is tested to the fullest; even in summer there's often not too much space in the town's thirty-odd hotels, as thousands come up from the sweltering lowlands to revive themselves in the mountain air. As a package-tour destination it's not too bad, but Abetone isn't a place to go out of your way to see.

With your own transport, you could make a more exciting **approach to Abetone from Bagni di Lucca** by taking the high mountain road to Montefegatesi, and then over the main ridge of the Orecchiella (impassable in bad weather), passing down through the mountains to the dramatic gorge called the **Orrido di Botri** before climbing up to the pass of **Foce a Giovo** (1674m).

Barga

The ancient hill town of **BARGA** – poised 3.5km to the east of its train station on the Serchio – marks the start of the valley's best scenery. The old village itself is quiet and pretty, with a long tradition of independence and a strong economic base founded first on silk and later wool: felt hats became a speciality in the nineteenth century. It grew up originally around a Lombard castle, and was besieged by Lucca and Pisa before falling to Florence, under whose influence it remained until 1859. Where it differed from other Lucchesi strongholds was in its rule by elected council, a system it retained even under the Florentines.

Definitely worth a visit if you're up this way, Barga's surroundings also repay attention, dominated by hills and an incredibly lush vegetation. If you have transport of your own and fancy some mountain driving, a couple of tempting minor roads lead into the wild country of the Orecchiella, offering stunning views over steep wooded slopes and across to the jagged profiles of the Alpi Apuane.

Neptune Fountain, Piazza della Signoria, Florence

Panorama of Florence from Piazzale Michelangelo

San Gimignano

The Gates of Paradise, Florence

Ponte Vecchio, Florence

A flock on the move in the Crete

The road to Pienza

The Rocca Nuova, Volterra

Cloister fresco, Monte Oliveto Maggiore

The abbey of San Galgano

GREG EVANS

The bay at Lacona, Elba

IMAGISSIMO/GIORGIO MAJNO

Marble quarry, Carrara

GREG EVANS

Torre Guinigi, Lucca

IMAGISSIMO/GIANLUIGI SOSIO

Santa Maria della Spina, beside the Arno, Pisa

Among those in the know, Barga is also becoming increasingly celebrated for two small but high-quality summer music festivals: **Barga Jazz** and **Opera Barga**; for information contact Concorso Barga Jazz, Ufficio Cultura del Comune di Barga, Vicolo Giannetti (☎0583.724.770, fax 0583.724.759) and the Associazione Culturale Teatro e Musica Opera Barga, Via della Fornacetta 11 (☎ & fax 0583.723.250).

The Duomo

Barga's **duomo**, San Cristofano, was founded in the ninth century and expanded over the next four hundred years, with remedial work in 1920 after a severe earthquake. It stands at the village's highest point, fronted by a terrace that provides a huge panorama of rooftops, mountains and villa-spotted hills. Built in a honey-blonde stone known as *albarese di Barga*, the **facade**, probably adapted from part of the earliest church, is decorated in a shallow pattern of Lombard Romanesque-influenced reliefs and tiny arches, a delicate contrast to the **campanile**, which seems to have erupted from the tiled roof. Left of the door is a wonderful little relief of an obviously convivial feast, sculpted in 1200; on the architrave is an equally rustic harvest scene and twin lions.

Inside, the naves are beautifully divided by low walls of inlaid marble and overlooked by a superlative and idiosyncratic **pulpit**, widely considered one of the finest such creations prior to the pulpits of Nicola and Giovanni Pisano in Pisa, Siena and elsewhere. Probably created by the thirteenth-century sculptor Guido Bigarelli da Como (or a pupil), it consists of a huge rectangular stand, lavishly carved with scenes from the Scriptures and supported by four red marble pillars, the front pair of which are propped up by another pair of lions. One, with an inane smirk, surmounts a dragon (a symbol of evil), while the other stands on a man (a symbol of heresy) who is simultaneously stroking and stabbing the animal. The rear left pillar is supported by a grotesque dwarf, snub-nosed symbol of the pagan world. The church's other unmissable artefact is a tenth- or twelfth-century **statue of St Christopher**, looking rather like a huge wooden puppet. Continuing the building's eccentric streak, the saint carries a child on one shoulder and a club the size of a small tree on the other. There are many less unconventional touches around the church: a cluster of **della Robbia terracottas** in the right chapel, **frescoes** on several pillars, a carved choir screen and two Giottesque **Crucifixes** – the overpoweringly framed example above the altar is particularly good.

Just below the duomo to the left, the *centro storico* signs point the way to the Baroque chapel of **Santissimo Crocifisso dei Bianchi**, an oddly attractive extravagance, with a blue-gilt altar and four diversely excessive side chapels. Also worth a quick look up by the cathedral is the **Museo Civico del Territorio di Barga**, Palazzo Pretorio, Arringo del Duomo (hours vary: call ☎0583.711.100; L3000), a collection of geological and paleological exhibits tracing the area's prehistoric background.

Practicalities

It's a long haul up from Barga's **train** station to the town and coming from Lucca it's easier to use the regular CLAP **bus**, which takes an hour and a quarter. Moving on, there are eight buses daily to Castelnuovo di Garfagnana and four to Bagni di Lucca; all buses depart from the Porta Reale, alongside the big car park where the road stops outside the walls (bus information Via Canipaglia 2; ☎0583.723.050).

Barga's small **tourist office** is at Piazza Angelio 3 (hours vary, generally daily 10am–noon; ☎0583.723.499), a straight walk down from Santissimo Crocifisso. Several **hotels** and **restaurants** are ranged along the road north down to the Serchio at **ALBIANO**, a rather scrappy neighbourhood in comparison with the town itself, but with good views. Aim to stay in the three-star *Villa Libano*, Via del Sasso 6 (☎0583.723.059, fax 0583.724.185; ③), next to the town park and linked to a nice restaurant with a garden terrace; or at the slightly pricier three-star *Alpino*, Via

Mordini 16 (☎0583.723.336, fax 0583.723.792; ③). Just to the south of Barga, in Fornaci di Barga, is the two-star *Gorizia*, Viale Cesare Battisti (☎ & fax 0583.75.074; ②), near the train station, with a garden and restaurant.

The Grotta del Vento

From Gallicano, across the river from Barga train station, you can drive west for 9km, following the bottom of the Turrite valley, to what is rated as Tuscany's best cave, the rather commercialized **Grotta del Vento** in Fornovo Lasso. From April to September the cave guides put on three different tours daily, through the caverns and lakes of this bizarre subterranean landscape; one-hour tours (on the hour 10am–noon & 2–6pm; L10,000), two hours (11am, 3pm, 4pm & 5pm; L18,000), or three hours (10am & 2pm; L25,000). For the rest of the year the cave is open only on Sundays and public holidays for the one-hour visits. Whenever you go, get there in the morning to miss the crowds.

Castelnuovo di Garfagnana

Despite its mountain-ringed location, Garfagnana's main town, **CASTELNUOVO DI GARFAGNANA**, is a disappointment – a rather featureless sprawl, with a daytime market bustle to its centre but virtually no life after 5pm except on balmy summer evenings. The only thing to see is the fourteenth-century **Rocca**, built by the Este dukes of Ferrara and best known for its former commander, the poet Ariosto, author of *Orlando Furioso*. By all accounts he didn't much enjoy his tour of duty in the 1520s, and mournful evocations of the area's landscape were to colour much of his later poetry. The rest of the town was badly damaged by bombing in the last war (it formed part of the retreating Nazis' defensive "Gothic Line"), though a lovely **terracotta** of *St Joseph and the Angels*, attributed to Verrocchio or the della Robbia, survived in the duomo (north wall).

However, if you intend to explore the Orecchiella to the east, Castelnuovo is the obvious base. Some of the mountain roads that radiate east and west offer astounding views for car drivers, and the villages around are highly attractive. For serious hiking, it's also well worth a stop in order to pick up maps and information.

Practicalities

There are two **tourist offices** just beyond the arch of the town's main square, **Piazza Umberto I**. The first, a Pro Loco at Loggiata Porta 10 (☎0583.641.007), keeps irregular hours and is mainly concerned with the town itself, while the other, at Piazza delle Erbe 1 (April–Sept daily 9am–1pm & 3.30–6.30pm, plus Jun–Sept until 7.30pm; Oct–March Tues–Sun 9am–1pm & 3.30–5.30pm; ☎0583.65.169 or 0583.644.242), is a **park visitor centre** which offers a wealth of information on **trekking** and other activities in the Garfagnana and Parco delle Alpi Apuane. The office is crammed with maps and pamphlets, and the staff can book you into mountain refuges, advise on accommodation and on where to hire a **mountain bike**. Note that besides the town's campsite (see below) the only official camping area in the Garfagnana is the *Monte Argegna* (☎0583.611.182; July 15–Sept 15), near Giuncugnano (876m) in the north of the valley above Piazza al Serchio. For specialized **climbing** information contact the Club Alpino office below the parking lot in Via Vittorio Emanuele (☎0583.74.352).

There are several **hotels** in Castelnuovo, the most central being the one-star *Aquila d'Oro*, Vicolo al Serchio 6 (☎0583.62.259; ①), jammed in an alley above a squalid-looking bar. Most people stay in the three-star *Da Carlino*, Via Garibaldi 15 (☎0583.644.270, fax 0583.65.575; ③), up the steep street out of Piazza Umberto I, a modernish place with a rather over-priced **restaurant** (from L45,000). For good, home-made food, at a better price (L25,000–30,000), try the excellent *Vecchio Mulino*, Via Vittorio Emanuele 12

(☎0583.62.192; closed Sun), a century-old *enoteca* with snacks (great *panini*) and simple meals: it also sells a good range of wines by the bottle or glass. *Caffè Ariosto* at Piazza Umberto I 2 does wicked cocktails, including some fruit-based concotions of barman Walter Borelli's own invention. Out of town in Le Monarche is the three-star *La Laterna* (☎ & fax 0583.62.272; ④).

There's a **campsite** in a wooded setting close to the train station at Piella, the *Parco di Piella* (☎0583.62.916; open all year). To get there, walk down from Piazza delle Erbe to the river, cross the bridge, take Via XX Settembre left into Via G. Marconi, and then walk up the narrow alley straight ahead, Via dei Cappuccini. From the **train station**, which is ten minutes from the centre, turn right and first left up Viale della Rimembranza.

Bus services run from Piazza della Repubblica (information ☎0583.62.039) to a variety of destinations. There are eleven daily connections to Lucca; nine to Barga; two to Florence; two to Massa; three to Corfino (for the Orecchiella park centre – see next page); eight to Castiglione; two to Passo delle Radici (for San Pellegrino); and six to Piazza al Serchio.

The Orecchiella

Though higher than the spectacular Apuane on the other side of the valley, the **Orecchiella mountains** are a generally tamer – but no less beautiful – terrain, rounded and thickly wooded, with steep lateral valleys and gentle grassy slopes above the tree line. The headquarters of the park which protects these uplands is a **park centre** 7km beyond the village of **Corfino**. The one monument of note is the monastery at **San Pellegrino**, now home to a museum of Garfagnana traditions. If you have transport, and whether you intend to hike or not, it's well worth following some of the minor roads into the mountains for a glimpse at one of the prettiest and least known of Tuscany's scenic enclaves.

San Pellegrino in Alpe

The sixteen-kilometre drive up the minor road northeast from Castelnuovo to **SAN PELLEGRINO IN ALPE** (1524m) offers stunning views over the steep valleys and ridges of the Orecchiella. If you don't have a car, there's the option of the two daily summer **buses** from Castelnuovo, which take the parallel and almost equally impressive major road via Castiglione.

San Pellegrino's magnificently sited **monastery** is partly given over to an excellent **Museo della Campagna**, Via del Voltone 14 (June–Sept Tues–Sun 9.30am–1pm & 2.30–7pm; Oct–May Tues–Sun 9am–noon & 2–5pm; L3000). Similar museums chronicling the art and culture of rural life can be pretty dire but this is a huge and fascinating display of the Garfagnana's peasant traditions. The exhibits cover four floors, and range over every imaginable aspect of country life: whole rooms are devoted to single themes – one contains dozens of different spinning wheels. Elsewhere are tiny objects of mind-boggling ingenuity, for things like bilberry-picking, all displayed with great clarity.

The adjacent hamlet has a bar, a couple of run-down **pensioni**, and reasonably priced shops where you can buy local honey, oil, mushrooms, grappa and sweet chestnut flour, once the area's staple diet.

Other **accommodation** is to be found on the pass at the top of the road – the **Foce delle Radici** – where there's a high (1525m), bleak and isolated hotel, the two-star *Lunardi* (☎ & fax 0583.649.071; ③). Down the parallel road towards Castiglione and Castelnuovo there's a hotel in a great location about 6km from the pass (ask the bus driver to drop you off): *Il Casone* (☎0583.649.090, fax 0583.649.048; ③), perched at over 1300m.

If you are using the green TCI *Toscana* map, note that the apparent short cut between Castiglione and the Castelnuovo–Corfino road does not in fact exist.

Corfino and the park centre

Reached from Castelnuovo by a beautiful road past meadows, thatched barns and views over the Apuane and Orecchiella, **CORFINO** is a small hill village (850m) which provides walkers with a choice of three **hotels**: the *Panoramico*, Via Fondo la Terra 9 (☎0583.660.161, fax 0583.660.159; ③) and *California*, Via Bagno 1 (☎0583.660.173; ②), both three-stars, and the similarly priced two-star, *La Baita*, Via Prato all'Aia (☎0583.660.084; mid-July to Sept; ③). Of these, the last is definitely the best – it's run by a pleasant family, with *mamma* in inspired charge of the kitchen.

Whatever standard of walk you want, or if you just fancy a drive in the area, it's worth visiting the excellent **park centre** (July–Aug daily 9am–7pm; May, June & Sept Sat & Sun 9am–5pm; ☎0583.619.098), a chalet-type development in wild countryside 7km to the north. It has a small bar, telephones, information and exhibition centre, a lake with nicely sited picnic spots, and an excellent **botanical garden**. There's nowhere to stay at the centre itself but in the park is the all-year *Rifugio Orecchiella* (☎0583.619.010; L30,000, with dinner and breakfast L65,000), and nearby, the *Rifugio Isera* (☎0583.660.203; April–Oct; L23,000). Both these refuges offer snacks and simple meals.

Walks from the centre

If you're going in for serious **walking**, you should pick up one of the widely available *Multigraphic-Wanderkarte* 1:25,000 maps (sheet #15 or #18), which show all the marked trails in the area. However, there are three **marked circular walks** pioneered by *Airone*, the leading Italian natural history magazine, and laid out by the centre which you can tackle without too much planning.

Walk 1 (5hr) takes in the summit of the craggy limestone Cima Pania (1602m) and the nature reserve of the Pania di Corfino, the most important of the three special reserves in the park and a noted area for nesting birds of prey, including peregrine falcons. **Walk 2** (4hr) passes through oak and beech forest and a stretch of grassy meadow. **Walk 3** needs two days, with a choice of overnight stops: *Rifugio C. Battisti,* or, in an emergency, *Rifugio La Bargetana* or *Rifugio di Monte Prado*.

In addition to these walks, there are also seven **Club Alpino paths** (2–3hr). The centre's board-plan or staff will make sense of the paths if you need help.

Long-distance paths

If you want a real challenge, there's also a long-distance marked path known as **Garfagnana Trekking**, which starts and finishes at **Castelnuovo** and is designed to take about ten days. The Castelnuovo *Centro Accoglienza* has full details, and it's marked as a separate route on the *Wanderkarte* maps. As well as taking in the best of the Orecchiella, five of the stages of this walk go through the Alpi Apuane.

An even more ambitious long-distance route, the linear **Grande Escursione Appenninica**, runs through the Orecchiella on its 24-stage trail from Sansepolcro across the roof of Tuscany to the Passo dei due Santi above La Spezia.

The Eastern Apuane

North of Castelnuovo di Garfagnana the Serchio valley floor is itself not very memorable but if you have transport – or can fit in with very sparse bus services – there are several possible diversions into the **Apuane mountains** to the west.

Over the ridge to Massa

The most obvious of these Apuane forays is the road which climbs **over the main ridge to Massa** – a route covered by a morning and afternoon bus from Castelnuovo. The road is not quite the scenic backwater it appears on the map, but the early stretch, up the **Turrite valley**, is verdant and tree-lined, with good views of the vast crags of the Pania della Croce (1859m). Much of the road was widened following the opening of the hydroelectric station at Torrite, but it degenerates immediately beyond the tunnel into Massa province.

The one hamlet of consequence is **ISOLA SANTA**, with a rustic **restaurant**, *Da Giacco*, especially good during the mushroom season (Sept–Oct), overlooking the river and a small lake, and *La Ceragetta* at nearby Capanne di Careggine (☎0583.667.065; L35,000; closed Mon). A section of the long-distance *Garfagnana Trekking* (GT) passes a hundred metres west of the hamlet, and you can follow it north towards Lago di Vagli (about 5hr walking; see below) or south for a couple of hours to the above-average bar and accommodation of *Rifugio Freo*. The best circular walk from Isola Santa is north on the GT.CAI-marked trail #145 to Monte Sumbra (1764m), and back the same way, a stiff climb but only about 8km in total.

Back on the main road, 6km beyond Isola, and shortly before the tunnel, a road leads off north to Arni (2km).

Lago di Vagli and some walks

North of Castelnuovo, the best diversion comes at Poggio (8km), where there's a choice of two roads. One runs to the high village of **CAREGGINE** (882m), notable for little except its views over the valley and the mountains to the rear. The other leads to **Lago di Vagli**, an artificial creation that submerged the village of Fabbriche (whose church tower is still visible above the water), but left three others intact – Roggio, Vagli Sotto and Vagli Sopra.

ROGGIO is immersed in chestnut trees, and boasts the biggest single specimen in Italy, 10m round and 26m high. It has a small one-star **hotel**, *La Guardia*, Piazza La Guardia (☎0583.649.121; ②), or you may be able to rent one of four rooms for around L60,000 (all with private bathroom) at *Coletti Pietro*, Via del Fiore (☎0583.649.179).

Equally enticing, **VAGLI DI SOTTO** sits on an arm of the lake, hires out boats for messing around on the water, and has a popular three-star **hotel**, *Le Alpi*, Via Vandelli 8 (☎0583.664.057, fax 0583.664.347; ③). A cheaper option is to rent one of four rooms (all shared bath) from Toni Elda, Via Europa 1 at nearby Bivio (☎0583.664.052; ①). The village also provides the starting point for a couple of excellent **walks** onto the highest ridges of the Apuane – for which the *Multigraphic-Wanderkarte* map (#101/102) is invaluable. Vagli di Sopra, above the lake, has a few **rooms** for rent. All of these villages have *trattorie* which, though small, offer excellent cooking.

The **first path** from Vagli di Sotto follows the road southwest up the Tambura valley, before linking with the CAI-marked trail #35; you can then follow this west to **Monte Focoletta** (1620m), or, more interestingly, east to CAI #144, which takes you to the top of **Monte Sumbra** (1764m) and then in a wide circle via the Tassetora valley back to Vagli di Sotto – a fantastic and varied day's walk (16km).

The **second path**, CAI #177, climbs to the Passo della Focolaccia (1650m), a meeting point of several other trails. The pass offers excellent views to the Apuane's highest point, **Monte Pisanino** (1947m), just to the north, and access to a superb ridge (trail #179.186) that takes you to the top of **Monte Grondilice** (1805m). From the summit you can carry on to Carrara, or north (on the GT) to the 40-bed *Rifugio Donegani* (☎0583.610.085; May–Nov; L18,000), the starting point for many trails. The refuge is also accessible by road from the Serchio valley to the north via Piazza al Serchio and Gramolazzo.

The Lunigiana

Few people make it to Tuscany's northernmost tip, the **Lunigiana**. A land of rocky, forested landscape, with just two sizeable towns – **Aulla** and **Pontrémoli** – this is one of the most insular regions in Tuscany. Its isolation was ensured over centuries by its mountainous approaches – only broken last century by the carving out of a rail tunnel and twisting mountain road at Piazza al Serchio.

The Lunigiana's name derives from the **Luni**, an ancient tribe who proved a tough lot for the Romans to crack and were equally impervious for some centuries to Christianity. In later centuries numerous would-be rulers built castles to exact tolls from anyone passing through the valley – hence the tourist-board name for the Lunigiana, "Land of the Hundred Castles".

Many of the touted **castles** are now in private hands and numerous others were left in ruins by the last war, but the region still repays a visit for the scenery and self-contained feel. If you want to do more than scoot through on the train, there's an extensive **bus network**, with Aulla the hub of a system that connects within the region itself and with Massa and Carrara farther afield. **Train** connections are frequent to Parma, La Spezia, Massa, Lucca and Pisa.

Equi Terme, Fosdinovo and Fivizzano

The train from the Garfagnana emerges from its long tunnel at **EQUI TERME**, which advertises itself for guided tours of **La Buca**, its cave once inhabited by lions, leopards and Neolithic man (daily 3pm; L10,000). The tiny village enjoys a superb scenic backdrop of crags and knife-edge peaks, sitting at the foot of the towering **Il Solio** canyon, and boasts a large **outdoor swimming pool** (June–Oct daily 2.30–6.30pm). If you need **accommodation**, there's the central *La Posta*, Via Provinciale 15 (☎0585.97.937; ③), with a fine **restaurant** and garden, and the three-star *Hotel Terme*, Via Noceverde (☎0585.97.830, fax 0585.97.831; ④).

Heading towards the coast from here by road, the most interesting route is via **FOSDINOVO**, a beautifully situated village that sits along a spur overlooking steep, wooded valleys. Host to Dante in 1306, the **Castello della Malaspina** here is certainly the best of the region's fortresses, and houses a museum of arms, armour and bric-a-brac from local tombs (guided tours usually Tues–Sun 10am–1pm & 3–6pm, but call ☎0585.68.891 to confirm; L5000). If you want to break for a **meal**, head for the long-established and family-run *Il Cucco*, Via Cucco 26 (☎0585.68.907; closed Thurs; from L25,000).

FIVIZZANO – to the north, on the N63 road into Emilia – is a more substantial place, with its medieval **Piazza Medicea**, dominated by a Medici fountain and a retinue of Florentine palazzi. The village also has a fine thirteenth-century church, **SS. Jacopo e Antonio**, with a handful of Renaissance paintings. If you want a **room** or **meal**, the obvious choice is the central two-star *Hotel-Ristorante Giardinetto* in Via Roma 151 (☎0585.92.060; ③; restaurant closed Mon). You might pass this way heading for the **Passo di Cerreto** (1261m), a walking and skiing centre on the Emilia-Romagna border. En route, 6km out of Fivizzano, look for the hamlet of Vendaso on the right, home to the Romanesque church of **San Paolo**.

Aulla and around

AULLA, squeezed onto a green strip at the confluence of two rivers, was almost totally destroyed in the last war and has virtually nothing of note except for the **Fortezza della Brunella**, a sixteenth-century Genoese castle that testifies to the town's early strategic importance and contains a small natural history museum (daily: summer 9am–noon & 2–6pm; winter 9am–noon & 3–5pm; L3000). With time on your hands, you might look into the parish church, built within the ruins of the eighth-century **San Caprasio**, an abbey that long dominated the hinterland.

Your best bet for really getting to grips with the Lunigiana is to head for some of the surrounding villages, most of which were fortified by the Malaspina nobles. Try Licciana Nardi, named after an early freedom fighter shot in 1844 while leading an uprising in southern Italy (his remains are in the big sarcophagus in the village's Piazza del Municipio), Caprigliola (6km south on the border with Liguria), Bibola or Ponzanello.

A more well-defined target is **VILLAFRANCA IN LUNIGIANA**, halfway from Aulla to Pontrémoli, again with the ruins of a Malaspina castle, but of more interest for its **Museo Ethnografico** (summer Tues–Sat 9am–noon & 2–7pm; winter same days 3–6pm; L5000). Occupying an old mill in Via Borgo, this documents the area's rural traditions, with a special nod to the omnipresent sweet chestnut. From **BAGNONE**, 5km east, there are opportunities for walks into the remote chestnut-covered ridges of Monte Sillara (1867m) and Monte Marmagna (1851m).

If you're in the Aulla area overnight, the best place for **food** and **accommodation** is the one-star *Alpi Apuane* (☎0187.418.045; ②), 3km east of the town at Pallerone on the train line from Lucca to Aula. The food, in particular, is splendid (restaurant closed Mon), as it is in Pontremoli's restaurants (see below), so you may wish to wait.

Pontremoli

PONTREMOLI is the Lunigiana's biggest centre, and the northernmost town in Tuscany. Part is still evocatively medieval, especially the area rambling north of the **Torre del Campanone**. The tower, now the duomo's campanile, originally formed part of a fortress built by Lucca's Castruccio Castracani in 1322 to keep the town's warring factions apart: hence its nickname, *Cacciaguerra* – "chaser-away-of-war". The **duomo** itself is an extraordinary Baroque affair.

The most captivating things in the town, however, are the twenty or so prehistoric **stele** housed in the **Museo del Comune** – whose home is the **Castello del Piagnaro**, a bleak fourteenth-century castle (Tues–Sun: June–Sept 9am–noon & 4–7pm; Oct–May 9am–noon & 2–5pm; L3000). These highly stylized statues fall into three groups. The oldest date from 3000–2000 BC, and are crude rectangular blocks with just a "U" for a face, and only the suggestion of arms and trunk. The second group (2000–800 BC) have more angular heads and more detail; the last pieces (700–200 BC) are more sophisticated still, and usually have a weapon in each hand. Most stele were funerary headstones, but here it's thought they represented a pagan communion between heaven (the head), earth (the arms and their weapons) and the underworld (the buried bottom third). Those with heads missing perhaps suffered at the hands of Christians intent on doing away with idolatry.

Fifteen minutes' walk south of the town, the small church of **Santissima Annunziata** was built to celebrate an appearance of the Virgin in 1471; it contains a trio of treasures, the most important an octagonal marble **tempietto** by Jacopo Sansovino, the others a fifteenth-century *Annunciation* and a Florentine altarpiece by an unknown artist.

Pontremoli has the only **tourist office** in the Lunigiana (☎0187.831.180), in the central Piazza Municipio. Enquire here about the plentiful **accommodation** possibilities, or call at the three-star *Napoleon*, Piazza Italia 2 (☎0187.830.544; ③) which has its own **restaurant**. The local culinary speciality is a type of large pancake-like pasta, *testaroli*, available in any one of the town's top *trattorie*: *Da Bussè*, Piazza Duomo (☎0187.831.371; closed Fri & evenings Mon–Thurs; around L35,000) is best – a lovely, snug place that's been in the same family for generations. Another traditional place, and just about as good, is the *Trattoria del Giardino da Bacciottini*, Via Ricci Armani 13 (☎0187.830.120; closed Sun evening and Mon), which is just a few thousand lire more expensive: next door is a co-owned shop selling local Lunigiana products. For drinks and wonderful cakes, head for the historic *Caffè degli Svizzeri* at Piazza della Repubblica 21.

travel details

TRAINS

Lucca to: Pisa (hourly; 30min); Pisa airport (2 daily; 45min); Florence, via Pescia, Montecatini, Pistoia and Prato (hourly; 1hr 5min–1hr 50min); Viareggio (hourly; 35min); Aulla, via Barga and Castelnuovo di Garfagnana (7 daily; 2hr).

Massa to: Viareggio, Pisa, Livorno, Rome (6 daily; 15min, 30min, 40min, 4hr 30min).

Aulla to: Lucca via Castelnuovo di Garfagnana and Barga (7 daily; 2hr).

BUSES

Barga to: Bagni di Lucca (4 daily; 40min); Castelnuovo di Garfagnana (8 daily; 30min); Lucca (8 daily; 1hr 15min).

Lucca to: (**Lazzi**) Bagni di Lucca (7 daily; 50min); Camaiore (6 daily; 1hr); Florence (24 daily; 1hr 15min); Forte dei Marmi (14 daily; 1hr 15min); La Spezia (4 daily; 2hr 50min); Lerici (1 daily; 2hr 20min); Livorno (1 daily; 1hr 20min); Marina di Carrara (8 daily; 1hr 40min); Marina di Massa (8 daily; 1hr 30min); Pisa (22 daily; 40min); Prato, changing at Florence (5 daily; 2hr 15min); Viareggio (14 daily; 45min); (**CLAP**) Barga (11 daily; 1hr 15min); Castelnuovo di Garfagnana (9 daily; 1hr 30min); Forte dei Marmi, changing at Viareggio (hourly; 1hr 15min); Massa, changing at Viareggio (7 daily; 1hr 35min); Pescia (12 daily; 45min); Pietrasanta, changing at Viareggio (10 daily; 1hr); Viareggio (12 daily; 50min).

CHAPTER FOUR

PISA, THE CENTRAL COAST AND ELBA

Flying to Tuscany you'll most likely arrive at **Pisa**, a city which – thanks to its tower – is known, at least in name, to almost every visitor to the province. Like Lucca, a little way to the north, Pisa bears the architectural stamp of the Middle Ages, the Torre Pendente being just one element of Italy's most refined medieval ensemble, the Campo dei Miracoli, or Field of Miracles. Since before the time of Galileo it has had one of Italy's major universities, and student life remains an important aspect of Pisa's strong sense of identity. It's an underrated place, seen by most outsiders on a whistle-stop trip – which means that finding accommodation here is often less troublesome than in Tuscany's more overtly enticing towns. Furthermore, its excellent road and rail connections to Florence and to the north and south make it a good base for wider exploration.

The chief city of the central Tuscan coast is the no-nonsense port of **Livorno**, which is worth a call more for its food than for its sights. To the south, the so-called **Etruscan Riviera** is one of the least attractive areas of Tuscany, with its dingy resorts and drab hinterland of low hills and reclaimed swampland – known often as the Pisan Maremma. When this coastal strip becomes clogged with huge numbers of Italian holidaymakers who spend their summers here, the temptation to press on south by rail or car along the fast, new *superstrada* can be overwhelming. However, it is not all unremittingly bad. There are pockets of unspoilt sand around **Baratti**, and some beautiful areas of pine woodland (*pineta*) have been preserved at the important **nature reserve** at **Bólgheri**.

Close to Baratti, at the southern tip of the flatlands, **Piombino** provides the main point of embarkation for the biggest island of the Tuscan archipelago – **Elba**. Though peak-season crowds fill every hotel room on the island, Elba can be a seductive place

---

ACCOMMODATION PRICES

Throughout this guide, **hotel** accommodation is graded on a scale from ① to ⑨, indicating the cost of the **cheapest double room** in each establishment in high season (for **hostels**, rates per person are given in lire). The price bands to which these codes refer are as follows:

① up to L60,000	④ L120,000–150,000	⑦ L250,000–300,000
② L60,000–90,000	⑤ L150,000–200,000	⑧ L300,000–350,000
③ L90,000–120,000	⑥ L200,000–250,000	⑨ over L350,000

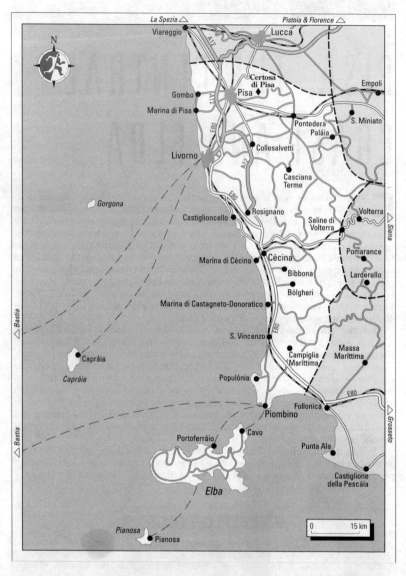

in spring or early autumn, when it almost rivals the charm of outlying **Capraia**, a spot still remarkably untouched by tourism. Capraia was once a prison island, a function still performed by Gorgona, the tiny island to the north. The jail on nearby Pianosa is now closed, and each year from January to April, up to one hundred people at a time are allowed to visit, though there are plans to convert the island into a nature reserve like the tiny Montecristo, which is now accessible only to research scientists.

Pisa

Since the beginning of the age of the tourist brochure, **PISA** has been known for just one thing – the **Leaning Tower**, the favourite shorthand image for invoking Italy. It is indeed a freakishly beautiful building, a sight whose impact no amount of prior knowledge can blunt. Yet it's just a single component of the city's amazing religious core – the **Campo dei Miracoli** – where the duomo, baptistery and Camposanto complete an unrivalled quartet of medieval masterpieces. These, and a dozen or so churches and palazzi scattered about the town, belong to Pisa's "Golden Age", from the eleventh to the thirteenth century, when the city, then still a port, was one of the maritime powers of the Mediterranean. The Pisa-Romanesque architecture of this period, distinguished by its white and black marble facades, is complemented by some of the finest medieval sculpture in Italy, much of it from the workshops of Nicola and Giovanni Pisano.

The city's political zenith came in the second half of the eleventh century with a series of victories over the Saracens, whom the Pisans drove out from Corsica, Sardinia and the Balearic islands, and harassed even in Sicily. Decline set in early, however, with defeat at sea by the Genoese in 1284 followed by the silting up of the harbour. From 1406 the city was governed by Florence, whose Medici rulers re-established the University of Pisa, one of the intellectual forcing houses of the Renaissance; **Galileo**, Pisa's most famous native, was one of the teachers there. Subsequent centuries saw the city fade into provinciality – its state when the Shelleys and Byron took palazzi here, forging what Shelley termed their "paradise of exiles". The modern city has been revitalized by its airport and industrial suburbs and, of course, money from tourism.

Arrival, information and accommodation

Coming in by **train** you arrive at the Piazza della Stazione on the south bank of the Arno; by **bus** at the nearby Piazza Vittorio Emanuele II or adjacent Piazza San Antonio. From here, the **Campo dei Miracoli** is about twenty minutes' walk, across the Ponte di Mezzo,

---

PISA AIRPORT

Pisa city centre is just a five-minute **train** ride from **Galileo Galilei airport**, most visitors' point of entry to Tuscany. Trains leave the airport station hourly until 8.25pm for Florence, calling at **Pisa Centrale** on the way. There is also a bus service to downtown Pisa that's more frequent, though no quicker or cheaper, which runs until 10.15pm – after which it's a taxi, or a 20-minute slog on foot, bearing in mind the last train to Florence leaves Pisa Centrale at 11pm. If your destination is Siena, you'll have to change at Empoli, 35 minutes' ride away.

The airport concourse boasts a pair of 24-hour automatic **exchange** machines for banknotes. There's also an impressive turnout of **car-rental** firms, though on-the-spot deals are more expensive than those arranged in advance. If you've pre-booked a car and your flight is delayed, the rental desk will remain open until your arrival (at least up until midnight), so don't panic. All the firms will demand a deposit to cover the full fuel tank, either off your credit card or in cash – expect to leave L100,000–150,000. The deposit is returned if you bring the car back with a full tank; always refuel before getting to the airport, as petrol is pricier here than elsewhere, and the airport petrol station takes a long lunch break.

The drive from the airport to Florence is straightforward, but **the road into Pisa** is so confusing that you'll end up driving four times the necessary distance if you don't get detailed directions from the car-rental desk.

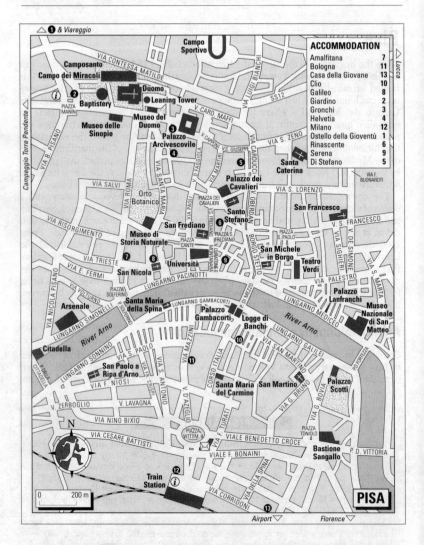

or a five-minute bus ride (#1) from outside the train station; local bus tickets are sold at a kiosk to the right of the station as you leave. If you arrive by **car**, follow the signs to the official car park outside the Porta Nuova, just west of the Campo dei Miracoli.

To pick up a **map** – and full hotel lists for the city and province – look in at one of the **tourist offices**: to the left (as you leave) of the train station (summer Mon–Sat 9am–6pm, Sun 9am–1pm; winter Mon–Sat 9.30am–1pm & 3–5.30pm), or next to the Campo dei Miracoli, in Via Cammeo 2 (summer Mon–Sat 9am–noon & 3–6pm, Sun 10.30am–4.30pm; winter Mon–Sat 9am–1pm & 3–5.30pm).

There are **currency exchange** bureaux at the station, the airport, and in the middle of the row of stalls at the Campo dei Miracoli. The station also has a **telephone office** (daily 7.30am–10.45pm) and a **left luggage office**, while the main post office is a hundred metres away in Piazza Vittorio Emanuele II.

Accommodation

People tend to cover Pisa as a day trip, or stay just a night, so **accommodation** is usually not too hard to find. In summer, however, it's still best to phone ahead or arrive early in the day. Prospects for budget travellers are good, with a youth hostel, a fairly central campsite, and a women-only hostel; if these are full, campers and hostellers may have to head elsewhere, keeping in mind that the nearby coast is liable to be even more packed.

The most attractive of Pisa's budget **hotels** are grouped around the Campo dei Miracoli, and these are obviously the ones that are quickest to fill, after which try the similar-cost places in the centre of the city, around Piazza Dante and Piazza dei Cavalieri. As usual the hotels near the station tend to be tattier and cheaper.

HOTELS

Amalfitana, Via Roma 44 (☎050.29.000, fax 050.25.218). Pleasant two-star, a couple of minutes south of the Campo dei Miracoli. ③.

Bologna, Via Mazzini 57 (☎050.502.120, fax 050.43.070). Another two-star, on the station side of the river, parallel to Corso Italia. ②.

Clio, Via San Lorenzino 3 (☎050.28.446). Clean and welcoming place at the river end of Corso Italia. ②.

Di Stefano, Via Sant'Apollonia 35 (☎050.553.559, fax 050.556.038). Tidy if characterless hotel, in a quiet street just off the northeast side of Piazza dei Cavalieri. ②.

Galileo, Via Santa Maria 12 (☎ & fax 050.40.621). Nine big, nicely decorated rooms; not the quietest hotel in town, but central and good value. ②.

Giardino, Piazza Manin 1 (☎050.562.101). Tucked behind a self-service restaurant just west of the baptistery. ②.

Gronchi, Piazza Arcivescovado 1 (☎050.561.823). Just east of the Campo; elegant in a run-down sort of way, and a definite first choice, despite the midnight curfew. ①.

Helvetia, Via Don G. Boschi 31 (☎050.553.084). Spotless and friendly place off Piazza Arcivescovado; midnight curfew. ②.

Milano, Via Mascagni 14 (☎050.23.162, fax 050.44.237). In side street leading into Piazza della Stazione; one of the better hotels in the station area. ②.

Rinascente, Via del Castelletto 28 (☎050.580.460). Occupies an old palazzo south of Piazza dei Cavalieri; very popular. ②.

Serena, Via D. Cavalca 45 (☎ & fax 050.580.809). Off the east side of Piazza Dante; a favourite with students. ②.

HOSTELS

Casa della Giovane, Via Corridoni 29 (☎050.43.061). Women's hostel, five minutes' walk, turning right out of the station. L30,000.

Ostello della Gioventù, Via Pietrasantina 15 (☎ & fax 050.890.622). Take bus #3 from the station or the city centre – signs close to the Campo dei Miracoli suggest that it's a brief walk away, but it's a 40-min slog. Make sure you have mosquito repellent in summer, as the hostel is right by a swamp. Nearby supermarket, and very friendly staff. Reception opens 6pm. L22,000.

CAMPSITES

Campeggio Torre Pendente (☎050.561.704). Large, well-maintained site, with a laundry, bar, restaurant and shop; 1km west of the Campo dei Miracoli at Viale delle Cascine 86 (signposted from Piazza Manin). Open April to mid-Oct.

Internazionale, Via Litoranea 7, Marina di Pisa (☎050.36.553, fax 050.35.211). Largish beach site, 10km from central Pisa. Open May–Sept.

Mare e Sole, Viale del Tirreno, Pisa Calambrone (☎050.32.757, fax 050.30.488). Another beach campsite, 15km from Pisa, near Tirrenia; bus #7. Open April–Sept.

The Campo dei Miracoli

Since it was first laid out, Pisa's ecclesiastical centre has been known as the **Campo dei Miracoli** (Field of Miracles), and the sight of it is as stunning today as it must have been to medieval travellers. Nowhere in Italy are the key buildings of a city – the cathedral, baptistery and bell tower – arrayed with such precision, and nowhere is there so beautiful a contrast of stonework and surrounding meadow. Underneath the pavements and the turf lies a mix of sand and silt, whose instability accounts for the crazy tilt of the Leaning Tower, and of its companions. Take a close look at the baptistery and you'll see that it's inclined some way out of the vertical, while the facade of the duomo is a few degrees out of true as well. The weird angles aren't the only oddity – the tapering domes of the baptistery and duomo, with the precarious top storey of the Tower behind them, comprise the strangest skyline in Tuscany.

The souvenir stalls around the edge of the Campo are in themselves quite a sight, offering an inexhaustible range of kitsch delights, such as as a silver-plated plastic replica of the Leaning Tower with a mermaid wrapped round its base – presumably an arcane reference to Pisa's maritime history.

The Leaning Tower

The two strangest facts about the **Leaning Tower** (the Torre Pendente) are that it has always tilted, and that no one put their name to it – as though the masons involved somehow knew it was doomed. Begun in 1173, it started to subside when it had reached just three of its eight storeys, but it leaned in the opposite direction to the present one. Odd-shaped stones were inserted to correct this deficiency, whereupon the tower lurched the other way. Over the next 180 years a succession of architects continued to extend the thing upwards, each one endeavouring to compensate for the angle, the end result being that the main part of the tower is slightly banana-shaped. Around 1350, Tomasso di Andrea da Pontedera completed the magnificent stack of marble and granite arcades by crowning it with a bell-chamber, set closer to the perpendicular than the storeys below it, so that it looks like a hat set at a rakish angle. Galileo exploited the overhang in one of his celebrated experiments, dropping metal balls of different mass to demonstrate his theory of the constancy of gravity.

Eight centuries on, the tower leans 4.5 metres from the upright and is nearing its limits. In 1989 the Ministry of Public Works in Rome suggested its closure to visitors; facing the loss of over two million pounds a year in tourism revenue, the Pisans disagreed. However, the collapse of a church tower in Pavia, killing four people, concentrated minds on the risks keeping the tower open and in January 1990 it was finally shut. Since then the situation has worsened: having moved annually by about one millimetre over the last couple of decades, the tower shifted that much on one night in 1995, following an ill-conceived attempt to halt the incline.

Soon after the closure, ten steel bands were wrapped round the lowest section of the tower, to prevent the base from buckling under the weight of the 15,000 tonnes of marble above. Various schemes aimed at arresting the effects of gravity were then discussed. A

TICKETS FOR THE CAMPO DEI MIRACOLI SIGHTS

For L18,000 you can buy a **combined ticket** which gives entry into the duomo, the baptistery, the Camposanto, the Museo dell'Opera del Duomo and Museo delle Sinopie. Otherwise you can buy an entrance ticket for just the duomo (L3000); a ticket for just two monuments (L10,000); for three monuments (L13,000); or for four (L15,000). The tickets are available at each of these sights.

Japanese consortium – rather missing the scenographic importance of the tower – submitted a plan for encasing it in a structure that would double as a viewing platform and a prop, while from the US came the idea of installing a vast underground refrigerator that would grip the foundations in a block of permafrost. In the end it was decided to shore up the northern side of the tower by placing over 800 tonnes of lead ingots at its base to counterbalance the force of the leaning stonework, but even this straightforward plan ran into problems, with the discovery of a subterranean Etruscan site during the early stages of the work. But work continued regardless, and after nine months the weights at the base had managed to stabilize the movement. The project entered its second phase in 1998 when a delicate drilling operation began, to remove water and silt from beneath the tower's northern foundations. The resulting subsidence has already begun to bring it back from the brink, and experts have calculated that correcting the building's tilt by ten percent will add three hundred years to its life. The plastic-coated braces attached to unsightly steel cables that stretch across the piazza will remain in place for some time, however, to catch the tower if things go wrong. It seems unlikely that it will reopen to the public in the foreseeable future.

The Duomo

The **Duomo** (summer Mon–Sat 10am–7.40pm, Sun 1–7.40pm; winter Mon–Sat 10am–12.45pm, Sun 3–4.45pm; L3000) was begun a century before the campanile, in 1064. With its four levels of variegated colonnades and its subtle interplay of dark grey marble and white stone, it's the archetype of the Pisan-Romanesque style, a model often imitated but never surpassed. Squares and discs of coloured marble are set into the magnificent facade, but the soberly graceful effect of the primary grey and white is such that you notice these strong tones only when you look closely.

The original bronze doorway, the **Portale di San Ranieri**, stands opposite the Leaning Tower. Its scenes from the life of Christ, cast around 1180 by Bonnano Pisano, first architect of the Leaning Tower, are powerfully diagrammatic; the Massacre of the Innocents, for example, is represented by the smallest possible cast – Herod, one mother and one soldier. The Portale's place on the main facade has been taken by massive doors from the workshop of Giambologna, a panoply of Renaissance detail.

Inside the duomo, the impact of the crisp black and white marble of the long arcades – recalling the Moorish architecture of Córdoba – is slightly diminished by the incongruous gilded ceiling, the fresco in the squashed circle of the dome, and the massive air vents bunged through the upper arches. Much of the interior was redecorated, and some of the chapels remodelled, after a fire in 1595, so most of the paintings and sculpture are Renaissance or later.

A notable survivor from the medieval building is the apse mosaic of *Christ in Majesty*, completed by Cimabue in 1302, but the acknowledged highlight is the **pulpit** sculpted by **Giovanni Pisano**. This was packed away after the fire, sixteenth-century Pisans evidently no longer concurring with the Latin inscription around the base, which records that Giovanni had "the art of pure sculpture . . . and would not know how to carve ugly or base things, even if he wished to". Only in 1926 was it rediscovered and put back together in the nave.

The last of the great series of pulpits created in Tuscany by Giovanni and his father Nicola (the others are in Siena and Pistoia), it is a work of amazing virtuosity, the whole surface animated with figures almost wholly freed from the block. Its narrative density rewards close attention – the story of the Passion, from Judas's betrayal to the scourging of Christ, for instance, is condensed into a single panel. Unfortunately the most tumultuous panel of all – the *Last Judgement* – can't be seen properly because a column gets in the way.

In the right transept you'll find the mummified body of Pisa's patron saint, Ranieri, and (set into the east wall) the tomb of the Holy Roman emperor **Henry VII**, who died near Siena, allegedly from eating a poisoned wafer at Mass. Having laid Siena to waste, the Ghibelline (ie pro-imperial) Pisans bore the body of their hero back to the Camposanto, where Tino da Camaino carved the effigy in 1315. In photographs the sculpture looks wonderful, but it's now mounted so high on the wall that you can see little more than its delicate profile.

Lastly, the cathedral has a piece of scientific legend. It is said that the forerunner of the huge bronze incense lamp, swung to fumigate the central aisle, provided the inspiration for Galileo's theory of the movement of the pendulum.

The Baptistery

The third building of the Miracoli ensemble, the circular **Baptistery** (daily: summer 8am–7.40pm; spring & autumn 9am–5.40pm; winter 9am–4.40pm; L10,000), is a slightly bizarre mix, with three storeys of Romanesque arcades peaking in a crest of Gothic pinnacles and a dome shaped like the stalk end of a lemon. It was begun in the mid-twelfth century by a certain Deotisalvi ("God save you"), who left his name on the column to the left of the door. Lack of money – caused mainly by Genoa's incursions into the Pisan trade network – prevented its completion in the style in which it had been started. In the latter half of the thirteenth century the Gothic top storeys and attendant flourishes were applied by Nicola and Giovanni Pisano, who rounded off the job with a glorious gallery of statues – the originals of which are now displayed in the Museo dell'Opera del Duomo (see opposite).

This is the largest baptistery in Italy, and the plainness of the vast interior is immediately striking, with its unadorned arcades and bare dome. The acoustics are astonishing too – as demonstrated at intervals by the custodian. At the centre, continuing the exotic strain of Pisan-Romanesque, is a mosaic-inlaid **font** by Guido da Como (1246), raised on stone steps for ease of immersion.

Overlooking it is Nicola Pisano's **pulpit**, sculpted in 1260, half a century before his son's work in the cathedral. This was the sculptor's first major commission and manifests a classical spirit in part attributable to the influence of the court of Emperor Frederick II, whose Italian power base was in Nicola's native Apulia. Thus the seated Virgin in the *Adoration of the Magi* is almost a literal copy of a figure of Phaedra on a Roman sarcophagus now housed in the Museo dell'Opera del Duomo, while the nude figure of Daniel (underneath the *Adoration*) is evidently Hercules under an alias. The complexity of the cultural make-up of fourteenth-century Pisa is shown by the Gothic sharp-angled drapery and by the architectural elements of the pulpit – the decoration of the arches and the foliage of the capitals recalling the stonework of French Gothic cathedrals.

The Camposanto

The screen of sepulchral white marble running along the north edge of the Campo dei Miracoli is the perimeter wall of what has been called the most beautiful cemetery in the world – the **Camposanto** (daily: summer 8am–7.40pm; spring & autumn 9am–5.40pm; winter 9am–4.40pm). According to Pisan legend, at the end of the twelfth century the city's archbishop brought back from the Crusades a cargo of soil from Golgotha, in order that eminent Pisans might be buried in holy earth. The building enclosing this sanctified site was completed almost a century later.

The Camposanto basically takes the form of an enormous Gothic cloister, each of whose long sides is as big as a cathedral nave. A few **tombs** are set into the rectangle of lawn at its centre, but most are housed under the shelter of the arcades. Some of the memorials, such as the Egyptian examples, are installed here as museum pieces, but most are for people who were actually buried in the Camposanto. Together they constitute a virtual encyclopedia of the ways in which death has been accommodated, from the terse classical style – recording the occupant's name, status and nothing else – to the opposite extreme, where the focus of interest is not on the deceased but on those left behind – as in the romantic tomb surmounted by a woman identified as "The Inconsolable".

However, when Ruskin described the Camposanto as one of the three most precious buildings in Italy, along with the Sistine Chapel and the Scuola di San Rocco in Venice, it was not its tombs but rather its **frescoes** that he was praising. Paintings once covered over two thousand square metres of cloister wall, but now the brickwork is mostly bare. Incendiary bombs dropped by Allied planes on July 27, 1944 set the roofing on fire and drenched the frescoes in a river of molten lead; the masterpieces of **Benozzo Gozzoli** were all but destroyed – just a few patches of his Old Testament scenes remain, to the left of the entrance. Close by there's another picture that came through the bombing: a fascinating fourteenth-century **Theological Cosmograph**, showing the concentric spheres of the universe and the tripartite division of the Earth into Europe, Asia and Africa.

The most important surviving frescoes are the remarkable fourteenth-century cycle by the painter known as the *Maestro del Trionfo della Morte*, the **Master of the Triumph of Death**. These have been detached from the wall and put on show in a room opposite the entrance, beyond a photographic display of the Camposanto before the bombing. Painted within a few months of the Black Death of 1348 – a pestilence which hit Tuscany so badly that it was known throughout Europe as the Florentine Plague – the *Triumph* shows a trio of aristocratic huntsmen stopped in their tracks by a trio of coffins, the contents of which are so putrescent that one of the riders has to pinch his nose. Over to the right, squadrons of angels and demons bear away the souls of the dead, whose final resting place is determined in the terrifying *Last Judgement* at the far end of the room. There's no more ruthless catalogue of horrors in Western art than this.

The Museo dell'Opera del Duomo

A vast array of statuary from the duomo and baptistery, plus ecclesiastical finery, paintings and other miscellaneous pieces are displayed in the **Museo dell'Opera del Duomo** (daily: summer 8am–7.20pm; spring & autumn 9am–5.20pm; winter 9am–4.20pm), at the southeast corner of the Campo.

The collection kicks off with pieces dating from the period of the duomo's construction, showing how Islamic influences, filtered through the intermediary of Byzantium, came to be expressed in the city's art – notably in the marble inlays from the duomo facade. The large bronze griffon is a more direct borrowing from Islam, having been thieved from the Middle East by a Pisan war party in the eleventh century. The other main cultural input shown here is from Burgundy, source of the strange painted wooden Crucifix, a gigantic figure with a tiny head and mantis-thin arms.

Sculptures by the various Pisanos are the high points of the museum, but the first pieces you encounter – Nicola and Giovanni's figures from the baptistery – are too eroded and pitted to give much of an idea of their power. Room 5, however, which is given over to works by **Giovanni Pisano**, contains the most affecting statue in Pisa, the *Madonna del Colloquio*, so called because of the intensity of the gazes exchanged by the Madonna and Child. Giovanni's great contemporary, **Tino da Camaino**, monopolizes the next room, where fragments from the tomb of Emperor Henry VII are assembled; the magnificent figures of the emperor and his counsellors may have come from the tomb as well.

Nino Pisano – no relation to Nicola and Giovanni – is the subject of room 7, where his creamy marble monuments to archbishops Giovanni Scherlatti and Francesco Moricotti show the increasing suavity of Pisan sculpture in the late fourteenth century. Giovanni Pisano returns in the **treasury**, his ivory *Madonna and Child* showing a remarkable ingenuity in the way it exploits the natural curve of the tusk from which it's carved. The other priceless object here is the *Pisan Cross*, which was carried by the Pisan contingent on the First Crusade.

Upstairs, big and witless altarpiece paintings take up a lot of room, as do cases of ecclesiastical clothing and lavish examples of intarsia, the art of inlaid wood, much practised here in the fifteenth and sixteenth centuries. Strangest objects on view are the two ancient parchment rolls known as **Exultets**, from the opening word of the chant on the eve of Holy Saturday. It was during this service that the cantor would unfurl these scrolls from the pulpit, so that the congregation could follow his words through the pictures painted on them.

A fine collection of engravings by **Carlo Lasinio** comes near the end of the museum; it was mainly thanks to his efforts that the Camposanto was rescued from ruin at the beginning of the nineteenth century, and his fastidious record of the cloister frescoes is one of the most poignant things in the city. Finally, the museum has a large collection of **Roman and Etruscan** pieces, many of which were slotted into odd corners of Pisa's churches to brighten them up a bit. The most famous image is a thin-lipped bust of Julius Caesar, featured on a dozen editions of his writings.

The Museo delle Sinopie

On the south side of the Campo, the only gap in the souvenir stalls is the entrance to the **Museo delle Sinopie** (daily: summer 8am–7.40pm; spring & autumn 9am–5.40pm; winter 9am–12.40pm & 3–4.40pm). After the catastrophic damage wreaked on the Camposanto by the bombers, the building's restorers removed its *sinopie*, the monochrome sketches for the frescoes. These great plates of plaster are now hung from the walls of this hi-tech museum, where gantries and galleries give you the chance to inspect the painters' preliminary ideas at close range, but it's a rather scholastic enterprise.

The rest of the city

Away from the Campo dei Miracoli, Pisa takes on a very different character. Few tourists penetrate far into its squares and arcaded streets, with their Romanesque churches and – especially along the banks of the Arno – ranks of fine palazzi. With the large student population it can be quite a lively place, particularly during the summer festivals and the monthly market, when the main streets on each side of the river become one continuous bazaar.

There is currently great excitement over the discovery, in the marshy ground by the San Rossore railway station, of a number of **Roman ships**, almost perfectly preserved in Pisan mud for two millennia. Eight vessels have thus far been recovered, including what experts believe could be the first Roman warship ever found. When all the ships are recovered and conservation work has finished, this "nautical Pompeii" may be put on public display – check with the tourist office for latest information.

Piazza dei Cavalieri and the eastern districts

The **Piazza dei Cavalieri** is an obvious first stop from the Campo, a large square that opens unexpectedly from the narrow backstreets. Perhaps the site of the Roman forum, it was the central civic square of medieval Pisa, before being remodelled by Vasari as the headquarters of the Knights of St Stephen. This order was established by Cosimo I, ostensibly for crusading, though in reality they amounted to nothing more than a gang of licensed pirates, given state sanction to plunder Turkish shipping. Their palace, the curving **Palazzo dei Cavalieri** (now a school), covered in *sgraffiti* and topped with busts of the Medici, faces a statue of Cosimo and adjoins the order's church of **Santo Stefano**, designed by Vasari and housing banners captured from the Turks.

On the other side of the square is the Renaissance-adapted **Palazzo dell'Orologio**, with its archway and clock tower. This was a medieval palace, in whose tower the military leader Ugolino della Gherardesca was starved to death in 1208, along with his sons and grandsons, as punishment for his alleged duplicity with the Genoese enemy – an episode described in Dante's *Inferno* and Shelley's *Tower of Famine*.

Northeast from here, across the wide Piazza dei Martiri della Libertà, stands the Dominican church of **Santa Caterina**, whose Romanesque lower facade dates from the year of its foundation, 1251. Inside, there's an *Annunciation* and a tomb by Nicola Pisano, and a fourteenth-century painting of the *Triumph of Thomas Aquinas*, the ideological figurehead of the Dominicans. Nearby, in front of the **Porta Lucca** – the main northern gate of medieval Pisa – you can see the unimpressive remnants of the city's Roman baths, while tucked into the northeast corner of the city walls is the church of **San Zeno**, parts of which go back to the fifth century.

From Via San Zeno, Via Buonarotti runs south to the plain Gothic **San Francesco**, whose well-preserved frescoes include work by Taddeo Gaddi and Niccolò di Pietro Gerini. Count Ugolino and his offspring are buried in the second chapel on the right. If you continue down Via di Simone from the back of the church, you'll come out at the Museo Nazionale.

Borgo Stretto to the Museo Nazionale

Heading from Piazza dei Cavalieri towards the Arno, Via Dini swings into the arcaded **Borgo Stretto**, Pisa's smart street, its windows glistening with Laura Biagiotti jewellery, Romeo Gigli shades and other desirables that seem slightly out of tune with the city's unshowy style. More typically Pisan is the **market** just off Via Dini (weekday mornings and all day Saturday), its fruit, vegetable, fish, meat and clothing stalls spilling onto the lanes around Piazza Vettovaglie.

Past the Romanesque-Gothic facade of **San Michele** – built on the site of the Roman temple to Mars – the Borgo meets the river at the traffic-knotted Piazza Garibaldi and **Ponte di Mezzo**, the city's central bridge. A left turn along Lungarno Mediceo takes you past the **Palazzo Toscanelli** (now the city archives), which was rented by Byron in 1821–22, after his expulsion from Ravenna for seditious activities. The poet's lunatic reputation, already well established thanks to his menagerie of horses, cats and dogs, was given a further boost when he got into a scrap with a bunch of Pisan soldiers, a contretemps that brought his brothers in exile – Shelley, Leigh Hunt, and Walter Savage Landor – out onto the streets. This display of hot-blooded solidarity prompted the writer Guerrazzi to muse that he at last understood "why the English are a great people, and the Italians a clump of rags in the shop of a second-hand dealer".

A couple of doors farther along the *lungarno* is the **Museo Nazionale di San Matteo** (Tues–Sat 9am–7pm, Sun 9am–2pm; L8000), where most of the major works of art from Pisa's churches are now gathered. Supposedly for reasons of security, the Pisan authorities have decided that visitors to this and certain other museums under their jurisdiction must present some form of ID before going into the gallery; for foreigners this basically means that if you don't have your passport with you, you don't get in. Quite why they should make so much fuss about one of Tuscany's minor galleries, while letting anyone get within felt-pen range of the Camposanto frescoes, is a mystery.

Fourteenth-century religious paintings make up the meat of the collection, with a Simone Martini polyptych and work by Antonio Veneziano outstanding in the early sections. Later on, there's a stash of Middle Eastern ceramics pilfered by Pisan adventurers, a panel of *St Paul* by Masaccio, Gozzoli's strangely festive *Crucifixion* and Donatello's reliquary bust of the introspective *St Rossore*. Also housed in the museum are the antique armour and wooden shields used in the annual *Gioco del Ponte* pageant (see p.247).

West of Ponte di Mezzo

The faculty buildings of Pisa's **university** – still one of the most important in the country – are scattered all over the city, but the main concentration is to the west of the Ponte di Mezzo, around **Piazza Dante**. The general tone of the streets – especially the *osterie* and bars – is the attraction of this quarter, though it does have a couple of sights worth singling out.

Immediately to the north of the piazza, the bare stone nave of the eleventh-century **San Frediano** preserves some capitals from that period. To the west, at the end of Via Santa Maria, rises Pisa's second **leaning tower**, the thirteenth-century campanile of **San Nicola**. Cylindrical at its base, mutating into an octagon then a hexagon, it contains a majestic spiral staircase that was Bramante's inspiration for his grand Belvedere staircase in the Vatican. Inside the church, the Crucifix in the first chapel on the left is attributed to Giovanni Pisano, while Nino Pisano is credited with the wooden *Madonna and Child* in the fourth chapel on this side. In the chapels on the other side of the nave, there's a *Madonna* by Francesco Traini and a painting showing Pisa around 1400, being protected from the plague by St Nicholas of Tolentino.

Across the river

The more down-at-heel districts south of the Arno are popularly known as the **Mezzogiorno**, the name disparagingly used by northern Italians when referring to the semi-developed south of the country. On the second Sunday and the preceding Saturday of each month the opposite banks are linked by a big **street market**, with hippy earrings, candles and other craft stuff filling the lower reaches of Borgo Stretto, and furniture and general bric-a-brac around the south-bank **Logge di Banchi**. Formerly the city's silk and wool market, this vast and usually deserted loggia stands at the top of the main shopping street of the *mezzogiorno*, Corso Italia, which starts off classy and gets progressively shabbier as it nears the train station.

East along the **Lungarno Galilei**, the only real sight is the octagonal San Sepolcro, built for the Knights Templar by Diotisalvi, first architect of the baptistery. A short way past here is the ruined **Palazzo Scotti**, Shelley's home during the period when Byron was in residence on the other side of the river.

Along the *lungarni* to the **west** of the Ponte di Mezzo, the rather monotonous line of palazzi – mirroring those on the facing bank – is suddenly enlivened by the spry turreted oratory of **Santa Maria della Spina**. Rebuilt in 1323 by a merchant who had acquired one of the thorns (*spine*) of Christ's crown, it's the finest flourish of Pisan-Gothic. Originally built closer to the river, it was moved here for fear of floods in 1871. The interior is a disappointment that visitors are usually spared by extremely erratic opening hours.

Farther west again, **San Paolo a Ripa d'Arno** probably occupies the site of Pisa's very first cathedral. The arcaded facade was built in imitation of the present cathedral in the twelfth century; the interior, badly damaged in the last war, has a handsome Roman sarcophagus and a finely carved capital (second on left), but nothing else to detain you. Behind the church is the octagonal **Cappella di Sant'Agata**, also built in the twelfth century.

San Michele

A couple of kilometres east of the centre, secreted in a residential area, stands Pisa's third leaning tower, the campanile of **San Michele dei Scalzi** – you get to it by walking along the riverbank upstream from Ponte di Mezzo. Everything in this building is severely askew: the columns in the nave lurch this way and that, the windows in the apse are all over the place, and the walls set up a drunken counterpoint to the tilt of the tower.

Eating, drinking and entertainment

Pisa's proximity to the coast means that seafood is the staple of its **restaurant** menus. As for the atmosphere in the city's eating places, the university is as strong an influence as the tourist trade, supporting places that cater for a regular clientele of impecunious students at one end of the range, and for their less inhibited teachers at the other. There's the usual scattering of city centre bars, but at night Pisa can be an eerily quiet place, as the majority of its students are Pisan natives who still live at home. In term time, though, there's usually a fair number of one-off events going on – the walls around Piazza Dante are the place to look for posters.

Restaurants

The restaurants in the environs of the Leaning Tower are generally not good value, though any of the numerous *pizzerie* down Via Santa Maria will do for a quick refuel if that's all you need. Head a few blocks south, to the areas **around Piazza dei Cavalieri and Piazza Dante**, and you'll find predominantly local places, many with prices reflecting student custom. The restaurants below are listed in ascending order of cost.

Mensa Universitaria, Via Martiri. Housed in the modern university building off Piazza dei Cavalieri, the student refectory does meals from L8000. Open mid–Sept to mid–July Mon–Fri noon–2.30pm & 7–9pm, Sat & Sun noon–2.30pm.

Cassio, Piazza Cavallotti 14. Just off Via Santa Maria, this excellent *tavola calda* and pizzeria is the place to come for a midday pit-stop. Closed Sat & Sun.

Antista, Piazza Guerrazzi 4, by the Fortezza Nuova. A long-established family-run trattoria, serving fine *ragù toscana*, plus a good choice of pizzas from a wood-fired oven. Closed Thurs & Sun.

Il Vecchio Dado, Lungarno Pacinotti 21. Next to the *Royal Victoria Hotel*, on the waterfront; classy pizzas, excellent fish and lively atmosphere. Closed Wed.

La Mescita, Via Cavalca 2. Patronized by students and professors in equal numbers, this small restaurant is virtually an academic institution. Vegetarian fixed menu L35,000; other fixed menus L40,000. Closed Sun.

Il Paiolo, Via Curtatone e Montanara 9. Lively place with outside seats and English beer, half a block north of the river. Open until 2am. Closed Sat lunch, Sun and Aug.

La Cereria, Via Pietro Gori 33. Popular unpretentious restaurant tucked away to the north of Via Benedetto Croce, not far from the train station. Excellent seafood and pasta dishes, and a pleasant garden. Closed Tues.

Il Viale, Viale Bonaini 78. Excellent seafood restaurant, five minutes' walk from the train station. Closed Fri.

Bruno, Via L. Bianchi 12. To the east of the Campo dei Miracoli, this place specializes in simple Pisan dishes such as the local *baccalà*. From L50,000 per person. Closed Mon dinner and Tues.

Il Cucciolo, Via S. Bernardo. Always reliable, offering unfussy, delicious meals from around L30,000 without wine. Closed Sun dinner & Mon.

Taverna Kostas, Via del Borghetto 39. Long-standing local favourite, offering a mix of Greek and Mediterranean cooking as well as Pisan seafood. Closed Sun lunch, Mon & Aug.

Lo Schiaccianoci, Via Vespucci 104 (☎050.21.024). Wonderful fish restaurant, but a tiny place – so it's almost essential to book ahead. Around L50,000 per person. Closed Sun.

OUT OF TOWN

La Gattaiola, Via San Lorenzo 2–4, Fauglia (☎050.650.852). High-class trattoria, installed in an old cellar in the village of Fauglia, 20km from central Pisa off the main road to Rome – so only feasible if you have a car. Excellent meals for around L50,000. A lot of Pisans make the trip at weekends, when it's best to ring ahead. Closed Mon.

Festivals and events

The city's big traditional event is the **Gioco del Ponte**, held on the last Sunday of June, when twelve teams from the north and south banks of the city stage a series of "push-of-war" battles, shoving a seven-tonne carriage over the Ponte di Mezzo. The event has taken place since Medici times and continues in Renaissance costume. Other celebrations – concerts, regattas, art events – are held around the same time, and the city has a festive feel for most of the month, with banners and pavement drawings brightening the streets. Most spectacular of the ancillary shows is the **Luminara di San Ranieri**, when buildings along both river banks are lit by 70,000 fairy lights in honour of Pisa's patron saint. Among **regular events**, look out for concerts at the Teatro Comunale Verdi in Via Palestro, and for more offbeat and contemporary shows (even the odd rock concert) held in a former church at the end of Via San Zeno. The city also has an adventurous **art-house cinema**, Cinema Nuovo, in Piazza della Stazione.

On from Pisa

Moving on from Pisa, the easiest destinations are **Lucca**, half an hour by train or bus, or **Florence**, an hour up the Arno by train. Along the Arno, the most interesting diversions come east of San Miniato and are covered on pp.191–3; on the Pisan side, the only compelling detour is to the **Certosa di Pisa**, a marvellous Baroque charterhouse, which you could take in on a brief loop from the main road. Beyond, there is little to be said for **Cáscina**, whose medieval core is firmly entrenched in industrial sprawl, and even less for **Pontedera**, home of the Piaggio factory, producer of the ubiquitous Vespa.

Heading for **Siena**, the simplest approach by public transport is to take the Florence train, changing for the journey south at Empoli. Driving, you have more choice. You could roam through the Pisan hills to **Volterra**, via Casciano Terme, or – faster but less scenic – via Cáscina, or follow a stretch of the coast, turning inland to Volterra at Cécina.

For just a quick taste of the coast, **Marina di Pisa** and **Tirrenia** are the city's local resorts. Neither is very inspiring but the area just inland has the intermittently open San Rossore park and the ancient church of **San Piero a Grado**.

The Certosa di Pisa

Of the thirty Carthusian monasteries left intact in Italy, none makes a more diverting excursion than the fourteenth-century **Certosa di Pisa**, set at the foot of the forested Monte Pisano, close by the village of Calci, 10km east of Pisa. A regular CPT bus service runs to the village (from 100m west of Piazza Vittorio Emanuele II); if you're in a car, just get to the amazing Medici aqueduct – immediately visible on the eastern outskirts of the city – and follow it all the way. The guided tour of the monastery (Tues–Sat 9am–6pm, Sun 9am–noon; L8000) gives a remarkable sense of how the building related to the lives of this order. As with the Museo Nazionale in Pisa, you may need your passport to get in.

The size of the Certosa is startling. From the frescoed central **church**, where a freestanding marble angel does service as a lectern, the tour passes through eleven other **chapels** in which Sunday Mass was apparently conducted simultaneously. Looking as fresh as the day they were decorated (they have not been restored), these are strangely sybaritic interiors – all powder blue, baby pink, pale violet and pallid green, with stucco details and trompe l'oeil pillars and balustrades to perk things up. Floors are covered with tiles that are only paint-deep, and there's a rectangular chapel tricked out to look like an oval room with a dome.

This ballroom decor contrasts with the more conventional monasticism of the **cloister** and its cells. Each of the monks had a suite of three sparse rooms – a bedroom, a study and a workroom – as the order placed great emphasis on the importance of manual occupation. Attached to every suite is a self-contained garden, walled so that the monks could maintain their soul-redeeming isolation. Except on a Sunday – the one day when conversation was permitted and all the monks ate together – their meals were served through hatches, positioned to minimize the possibility of coming face to face.

From the cloister the tour progresses to the **refectory**, where frescoes of seminal moments in the history of the monastery are interspersed with images of the months and their associated crops – a reminder of the order's agricultural self-sufficiency. Nearby are the luxuriously appointed **guest rooms**, where high-born VIPs – various Medici among them – would stay for a bout of not-too-rigorous scourging of the spirit. Their private cloister features yet more trompe l'oeil, its windows "opening" onto the dining room and monks' cloister.

The visit is made especially absorbing by little details that the guide points out – like the panel with sliding wooden paddles to designate the day's duties (eg head-shaving), or, at the end of the tour, the measuring machines in the **pharmacy**. Above the gate as you leave, an inscription reads "Egredere sed non omnis" (Leave, but not entirely) – once addressed to any monk who had to go out on some mission in the wider world.

Parts of the Certosa complex are owned by the University of Pisa, who have installed their **natural history** collections here –"of great interest for the material on reptiles' respiratory apparatus", according to the official guide. To ascertain the truth of this, you'll have to visit when the collections are open (summer Tues–Sat 9am–6pm, Sun 9am–noon; winter Tues–Sat 9am–4pm, Sun 9am–noon; L8000).

Over Monte Serra

If you're in a car, you could make a loop down to the Arno from the Certosa by following the scenic mountain pass over **Monte Serra** – where the *Rosa dei Venti* bar-restaurant provides an opportunity for a quick bite. Beyond the summit, the road meanders down to the village of **BUTI**, its Gothic-windowed castle looking down on the main square and over the Arno valley.

The descent has flattened out by the time you get to **VICOPISANO**, a couple of kilometres north of Cáscina (see below). Built on a plump little hummock of a hill, the core of the village retains four towers of its fortifications, one of which was built by Brunelleschi after the Florentines had conquered Pisa. In the lower part of the village there's a handsome Romanesque church, fronted by a green piazza and backed by hills that have been blackened by forest fires.

Along the Arno and over the Pisan hills

The Arno valley commences with a glum stretch of unrelievedly industrialized development. **CÁSCINA**, a town you wouldn't know you'd entered if there weren't road signs to tell you so, might have been well known if Michelangelo's ill-fated fresco for Florence's Palazzo Vecchio had survived – this was the site of the battle depicted in it. As for its own monuments, a clutch of **churches** within the medieval walls might justify a car stop: the frescoed San Giovanni Evangelista, built by the Knights of St John, and the Romanesque San Casciano and San Benedetto a Settimo, the latter with a fourteenth-century alabaster altarpiece carved in Ireland. Otherwise the dominant sights are the workshops which turn out the low-grade furniture that's the town's economic mainstay.

Into the hills
From Cáscina or Pontedera, the road south goes through Ponsacco and then past the **Medici villa** at **CAMUGLIANO**. Built by Alessandro de' Medici and continued by his successor, Cosimo I, it's one of the less scintillating of the family homes and anyway closed to the public.

Over to the west, **CASCIANO TERME** is a pleasant, workaday spa town, and the little town of Rivalto, 6km south, an attractively medieval settlement. The road southwest from Casciano, emerging on the N68 near Cécina, takes in the best of the Pisan hills, though with little to suggest any great rewards for more prolonged exploration.

To the east of the main N439 road to Volterra, there's a fine thirteenth-century church at **PALAIA**, though only devout admirers of the Romanesque will want to drive the 10km from Capánnoli to see it. Past Capánnoli you're into a rather more humdrum swathe of hills, until Volterra and its eroded cliffs rear up ahead (see p.350).

West of Pisa: San Piero, San Rossore and the coast

Six kilometres west of Pisa, on the road to the coast, the monastic complex of **San Piero a Grado** was allegedly founded by St Peter himself, on his way to Rome and martyrdom. The site is now in ruins except for the glorious eleventh-century **basilica**, a double-apsed church built from lustrous local yellow sandstone. St Peter's story is detailed in a sequence of pale fourteenth-century frescoes inside the basilica (daily 9am–noon & 3–6pm), where the whiff of the sea conjures a uniquely evocative atmosphere. At one end of the basilica a section of a fourth-century oratory has been excavated, the most ancient Christian site in this part of Tuscany.

Marina di Pisa and Tirrenia

MARINA DI PISA is an unobjectionable little town cursed with water made grubby by industrial waste. The view out to sea is impaired by a long breakwater parallel to the shore, a sight frequently worsened by passing tankers. These factors, combined with the usual private beach strips, don't exactly entice.

TIRRENIA, 5km south, is a better bet – with finer sand, separated from the road by pines and parkland. It has a good spread of hotels and a couple of campsites. **Buses**, taking thirty minutes, run from Pisa to both resorts every fifteen minutes in summer, every thirty minutes in winter; they are best avoided on a Sunday, when hundreds of locals nip down to the sea.

Parco Naturale di San Rossore

The **Parco Naturale di San Rossore** spreads over much of the coastal hinterland between Lucca and Livorno. Its pine woods are among the densest in Tuscany, supporting populations of deer, goats and wild boar, and until World War II were also home to a herd of dromedaries, descendants of the animals placed here by Grand Duke Ferdinando II in the 1620s, then bred for their load-carrying capacities. There are plans to grant the Rossore area national park status, but at the moment general access is restricted to Sundays and national holidays (park information ☎050.525.211; mornings only).

At the park's centre is the village of **GOMBO**, scene of the most celebrated cremation of the nineteenth century. In 1822 Percy Bysshe Shelley, drowned while sailing from Livorno, was here reduced to ashes in front of his friends Edward Trelawny and Lord Byron. Trelawny recorded the suitably extraordinary culmination – "the brains literally seethed, bubbled and boiled as in a cauldron . . . what surprised us all was that the heart remained entire. In snatching this relic from the fiery furnace, my hand was severely burnt; and had anyone seen me do the act I should have been put into quarantine."

Livorno and around

As Tuscany's third largest city – after Florence and Prato – and Italy's second biggest port – after Genoa – **LIVORNO** should really have more going for it than it does. Unfortunately Henry James's observation still holds true: "It has neither a church worth one's attention, nor a municipal palace, nor a museum, and it may claim the distinction, unique in Italy, of being the city of no pictures." Livorno's principal appeal – apart from its **ferry connections** – is the excellent seafood.

Livorno's poor showing has a lot to do with the last war, when its port facilities invited blanket bombing. In fact, its origins go back to Roman times, though the port was only developed under Cosimo I as an alternative to Pisa, whose harbour was silting up. Later Medici dukes declared it a **free port** and instituted a liberal constitution, an extraordinarily enlightened move which prompted an influx of Jews, Greeks, Spanish Muslims, English Catholics and a cosmopolitan throng of other refugees, turning it into the Tangier of its day. As one of the few Italian harbours safe from the Spanish, it flourished on the back of trade with England and Holland, and attracted a community of British expatriates (such as Shelley), whose anglicization of the city's name – **Leghorn** – is still used in the tourist brochures.

Greater freedom of European trade brought some decline, though the city retained a reputation for enterprise that was especially manifest after World War II, when it was amongst the first to realize the importance of container traffic – the basis of its current prosperity.

The City

The Livorno **train station** is 2km east of the centre; local bus services (#1, #2, #7 or #18) run from here to **Piazza Grande**, the heart of what's left of the old town. Out of town buses, except those from Florence, terminate in Piazza Grande; Lazzi buses to and from Florence (currently only one service per day) are at Piazza Manin, a three-minute walk from Piazza Cavour towards the sea.

The **Porto Mediceo** is the town's most picturesque corner, still conforming to the pentagonal canal-enclosed plan devised for the Medici by Buontalenti in 1557. The **duomo** in Piazza Grande – now a postwar reconstruction – is its focal point, of interest mainly for its doorway by Inigo Jones, whose subsequent plan for London's Covent Garden was a direct copy of the square. More absorbing is the bustle of the port itself, with fishing boats spilling back into the canals of the so-called "Little Venice", a liner often blocking the view out to sea, and Sangallo's **Fortezza Vecchia** flanking the harbour on the right.

Farther down the quay, at the centre of Piazza Micheli, is Livorno's only art work of note, the famous *Quattro Mori* (1623) by the Carraran sculptor Pietro Tacca. Though Ferdinando I is the centrepiece, the key figures are the four Moors, alternatively considered to be slaves, or memorials to the success of Tuscan raids against North African shipping.

The bulky **Fortezza Nuova** (daily 8am–7pm; free), a moated, semi-derelict recreation area, is where Livorno's citizens turn out for their Sunday walk. Of more general interest on this northern side of the inner pentagon is the **Mercato Americano** (Mon 2–7pm, Tues–Sat 9am–7pm), across Piazza Repubblica in Piazza XX Settembre. So called because of the amount of GI surplus on sale here after the war, it still deals in military gear (there's a big US naval base near the city) and the usual flea-market paraphernalia. The streets around Piazza XX Settembre – **Via Oberdan** in particular – are good territory for cafés, *pizzerie* and *trattorie*.

Around Livorno

For good views over Livorno and the hillside villas which were home to expatriates like Byron, Shelley and Napoleon III, you could take a bus out to hill-top **MONTENERO**, 5km to the southeast – or take the bus to the outskirts then hop onto the funicular. The sanctuary here has been a place of pilgrimage since an apparition of the Virgin in the fourteenth century; the present church is less interesting than the panorama.

If all you want is a quick dip before leaving town, **ARDENZA** is Livorno's nearest rocky beach, a one-time village but now a suburb, just ten minutes on bus #5 from Piazza della Repubblica, or #1 from Piazza Grande. It's all very urban and tacky, with

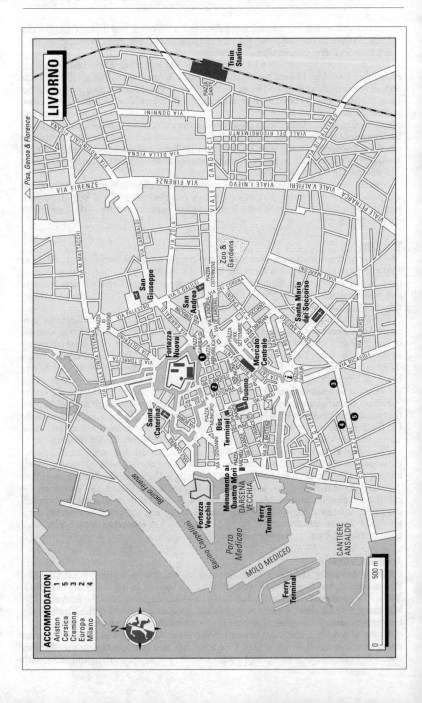

MODIGLIANI

There's a nice irony to the fact that the most famous son of this sensible mercantile city was the archetypal bohemian – hard-drinking, womanizing **Amedeo Modigliani**. By the time Modigliani reached his mid-twenties he was renowned as the most dissolute figure in Montparnasse, but his family background in Livorno could not have been more respectable. His mother, Eugenia Garsin, was from a prosperous and highly intellectual family, brought up speaking French, Italian, English and Hebrew. His father's ancestors, also Sephardic Jews, were equally grand – Amedeo's great-grandfather, for example, had been an adviser to Napoleon.

Amedeo was born in Via Roma in 1884, the year that his father's wood and coal company was declared bankrupt. The Modiglianis were obliged to move from their villa to a more humble property in Via delle Ville, and it was there that Amedeo was living when he began his studies at the Livorno art school. By 1900, aged 16, he had become bored with the academicism of his training, and soon embarked on a travelling apprenticeship that was to take him to Naples, Florence and Venice. In 1906 he arrived in Paris, where he was to spend most of the rest of his life. He returned to Livorno briefly in 1909 for a vacation by the sea, and came back again four years later, antagonizing most people he met with his arrogance and wild behaviour. A friend tried to persuade him to take a studio near the Carrara marble quarries, but he missed the big city too much, and was on his way after a few months. He lived for just one more decade. "I am going to drink myself dead," he declared, and in effect he did, dying of meningitis at the age of 35 – and leaving the latest of his innumerable mistresses nine months pregnant. She committed suicide on the afternoon of his death.

Before leaving Livorno for the last time, he had asked some students at his former art school if they knew of somewhere he could store a group of sculptures he had carved. "Throw them in the canal," they are alleged to have replied. In 1984 the city authorities decided to follow up the lead by dredging the canal round the old town, and duly discovered three stone heads. They turned out to be fakes – the three schoolboys responsible for the hoax appeared on TV to demonstrate how they used Black & Decker power tools to create the sculptures that nearly sold for millions.

crowded swimming off a paved promenade, or – for a small fee – from a couple of concrete *bagni*. A better alternative is to head north to **Tirrenia** (25min by bus from Piazza Grande; see p.250).

Practicalities

Livorno's **tourist office** is on the second floor at Piazza Cavour 6 (Mon–Fri 9am–1pm, plus Tues & Thurs 3–5pm); in summer there's also a small booth on the Molo Mediceo, the dock for ferries. Being a port, the city has a rash of basic **hotels**, some of which – around the harbour and station – are grim dives, to be avoided by all but the desperate. It's best to head for the centre of the old town, especially around Corso Mazzini or the Fortezza Nuova, where you should have no problems finding a reasonable room. One of the best two-star choices is the *Milano*, Via degli Asili 48 (☎0586.219.155, fax 0586.219.129; ②) which offers quiet, clean rooms and a garden. Other options include the *Corsica*, Corso Mazzini 148 (☎0586.882.280, fax 0586.882.103; ②); the *Cremona*, Corso Mazzini 24 (☎0586.889.157; ③); the *Ariston*, Piazza della Repubblica 11 (☎ & fax 0586.880.149; ④); and the *Europa*, Via dell'Angiolo 23 (☎0586.888.581, fax 0586.880.085; ③).

Livorno's **youth hostel** is the *Villa Morazzana*, Via di Collinet 68 (☎0586.500.076, fax 0586.502.426; L25,000) The nearest **campsite** is *Camping Miramare* (☎0586.580.402; mid-April to Sept), on the Via Aurelia past Antignano, a short distance to the south; there's another, the *Collina 1*, Via di Quercianella 269 (☎ & fax 0586.579.573), on the road to Castellaccio.

LIVORNO FERRIES

There are regular car and passenger ferry services from Livorno to Capraia, Sardinia and Corsica, with less frequent departures for Sicily. Ferries to Capraia leave from Porto Mediceo; ferries to Sardinia and Corsica leave from Calato Carrara, near the Stazione Marittima. Boats are often fully booked – for cars at least – through July and August.

Corsica Ferries, Stazione Marittima (☎0586.881.380). To Corsica (Bastia) and Sardinia (Golfo Aranci); daily April–Sept.

Moby Lines, Via Veneto 24 (☎0586.826.823, fax 0586.826.824). To Sardinia (Olbia); three times a week, daily in high season.

Sardinia Ferries, Stazione Marittima (☎0586.881.380, fax 0586.896.103). To Corsica (Bastia); daily from the end of March to early November.

TO.RE.MAR, Porto Mediceo (☎0586.896.113, fax 0586.887.263). To Capraia; one daily most of the year, twice daily on Thurs & Sat June–Sept.

Note: US citizens travelling to Corsica will need to obtain a **visa** from the French consulate at Via Mazzini 70 (☎0586.882.348)

For **meals** the great temptation is the seafood. The local speciality is *cacciucco*, a spicy fish stew, traditionally made from scraps the boats couldn't sell. There are dozens of good **trattorie**, the more esteemed being the *Aragosta* at Piazza Arsenale 6 (closed Sun), *Le Volte*, Via Calafati 4 (☎0586.896.868; closed Sun) and the big, busy *La Barcarola*, Viale Carducci 63 (☎0586.402.367; closed Sun). These are relatively upmarket at around L60,000–70,000 per person, but you'll have no problem digging out a regular neighbourhood choice such as the excellent family-run fish restaurant *La Parmigiana*, Piazza Orlando (closed Mon) or *Trattoria Galileo* in Via della Campana 20. For pizza, try *Pizzeria Umbra*, Via E. Mayer 1, or the *Rustic Inn*, Via Bosi 16.

The Etruscan Riviera

There's little to distinguish the resorts that cling to the road south from Livorno along the absurdly titled **Etruscan Riviera**. Most are remorselessly developed and edged with stony or scrubby beaches, and have an appeal only if you want to share the Italian cheek-by-jowl seaside experience. All points on the coast as far south as Follonica can be reached by **bus** or **train** from Livorno; the faster Rome–Pisa expresses often stop only at Cécina, which has inland connections for Volterra.

Quercianella to Vada

Thirteen kilometres south of Livorno, **QUERCIANELLA** is a relatively small resort which has clung onto a hinterland of scrub-covered hills and rocky headlands. The beach is pebbly, but nevertheless popular and well developed. If you want to **stay**, the one-star *Pensione Sottocosta*, Via G. Pascoli 32 (☎ & fax 0586.491.027; ③), overlooking the sea, is a reasonable bet.

Next stop is **CASTIGLIONCELLO**, the biggest of the resorts, sprawled over several small bays, some with sand, most with pebbles, and all crammed with boats and beach huts. Probably the best beach is the fee-charging Quercetano; the bay at Caletta is one to avoid, as is Rosignano (1km south), graced as it is with a vast chemical works with outlets into the sea. Castiglioncello has a summer **tourist office** at Via Aurelia 967; in addition to accommodation lists, they hand out details of a small July **dance festival** and September **literary festival**.

Smaller **VADA**, 5km south of Rosignano, has a featureless modern centre but is preferable to Castiglioncello, with a good beach and a long flat stretch of sand and pines to the south. These shade a couple of large **campsites**, the better being the *Tripesce*, Via Cavallaggeri 88 (☎0586.788.167; April to mid-Oct).

Cécina

The town of **CÉCINA**, 3km inland, marks the start of the Maremma's coastal plains. It has a small **museum**, in Via Guerrazzi (Tues–Sat 4.30–7.30pm, Sun 9.30am–1.30pm; L3000), with a few Etruscan and Roman remains, and a summer-only **tourist office** in Viale Galliano, Marina di Cécina, a source of information on the town's back-to-back **festivals** – antiques in July, arts and music in September and a miscellaneous "October Fair". Essentially, though, it is a place to pick up **bus** and **train** connections for Saline di Volterra (see p.351). If these leave you stranded in town, you will find the cheapest **rooms** at the *Hotel Il Ponte*, Largo 1 Maggio 3 (☎0586.680.795; ②); for a meal at around L35,000, try the *Antica Cécina* at Via Cavour 17.

At **MARINA DI CÉCINA**, a quite pleasant coastal strip, there are fair sections of beach, most freely accessible save for a patch cordoned off by the local military academy. A range of **hotels** is to be found on Viale della Vittoria, among them the two-star *Miramare* (☎0586.620.295; ③) and *Azzurra* (☎0586.620.595; ②). To the north there's also a number of huge **campsites**. For cheapish food, there's *La Triglia*, a good *rosticceria* in Viale Galliano 5 (April–Sept).

The Bólgheri reserve and Bibbona

South of Cécina the main road pulls back from the coast, leaving a few tracts relatively unspoilt. If you take any of the minor turnings to the sea you'll find pine forest and beaches only slightly touched by development, but the best stretch is the exquisite **Rifugio Faunistico di Bólgheri** (visits need to be pre-booked ☎0586.778.111; Nov to mid-April, Fri & first and third Sat of the month 9am–noon & 2–4.30pm; L10,000), a nature reserve run by the World Wide Fund for Nature. The entrance is off the main SS1, just south of the glorious avenue of trees that runs to Bólgheri village; take the lane that runs over the railway towards the sea.

Founded in 1962, this was the first private nature reserve in Italy, and is now recognized as a wildlife centre of international importance. The reserve is a microcosm of the various habitats associated with the ancient Maremma: seashore, dunes (full of rare plants), marsh and lakeland, pine groves, tracts of juniper and mixed scrub forest, *macchia*, grassland and some of the most ancient stands of cypress in Italy. Such is the tranquillity of the area that even in daylight you can expect to see **boar**, **roe-buck**, **martens**, black and white **porcupines**, even **otters** – an extremely rare species in Italy. Thousands of **birds** also settle here: it's the southern limit of the lapwing and a spot for rarities like bluethroats, Blyth reed warblers (their first sighting in Italy), grey herons, cranes, black storks and hunters like the osprey and lesser-spotted eagle.

The nearby resort of **MARINA DI BIBBONA** has an immensely broad stretch of sand running for miles south from the village along a pinewood backdrop: all it takes for privacy is the patience to walk beyond the beach umbrellas. For a cheap **beach hotel**, bear left on the approach road to Forte di Bibbona and try the two-star *Paradiso Verde*, Via del Forte 9 (☎ & fax 0565.600.022; ③) with a garden, or for an extra star, the *Flora*, Via del Mare 26 (☎ & fax 0565.600.015; ④).

SAN VINCENZO is the fast-growing resort of the moment, though again there's a good beach with plenty of quieter spots out on the fringes. Summer **accommodation**, however, is at a premium, and if you arrive on a whim and want to stay, you'll probably have to camp at the only **campsite**, the *Park Albatross*, one mile from the sea at Pineta di Torre Nuova (☎0565.701.018). Otherwise try the **tourist office** at Via B. Alliata.

Inland – Castagneto Carducci to Campiglia

If you're driving along the sluggish Via Aurelia from Pisa, you could take time out from the plain-induced monotony by turning off at Donaratico – 8km before San Vincenzo – for a 35-kilometre loop into the hills and a handful of scarcely visited **medieval villages**. Also, the wines from these parts produced under the newly created DOCs, Montescudaio, Bolgheri and Val di Cornia, are well worth seeking out, especially the refreshing Vermentinos and the Cabernet- and Merlot-based reds.

CASTAGNETO CARDUCCI, 6km on from Donaratico, is renowned for two things: it was the birthplace of the poet Carducci, winner of the Nobel Prize in 1906; and it produces what is widely considered the best **olive oil** in Italy. The village is riddled with little alleyways and has a parish church filled with faded frescoes and painted terracotta saints.

Beyond, the road is a rollercoaster of sea views and woods, with a single **hotel**, the two-star *La Selva*, Via delle Fornaci 32 (☎0565.794.239; ③), just before the road touches the little village of **SASSETTA**, a car-free maze of minute streets. For the first three Sundays of October, the alleys are filled with tables laden with seasonal dishes and chestnuts for the annual *Festa della Tordata*, or thrush, which was traditionally eaten in times less PC. The road then twists down to **SUVERETO**, whose thin shield of modern outskirts hides another old centre, with its thirteenth-century **Palazzo Comunale** and the church of **San Giusto**, built in Pisan-Romanesque mode. The village's December festival addresses itself to the local wild boar.

A slight detour on the return to the coast takes in **CAMPIGLIA MARÍTTIMA**, another little gem, partly spoilt by new houses and holiday homes, but with a perfect central piazza, composed of civic palazzi and a fine Romanesque church. For something to **eat**, the trattoria opposite the train station is very popular, with good local food for around L20,000; or else, the slightly more expensive *Il Canovaccio*, Via Vecchio Asilo 1. There's also a reasonable two-star hotel, *Il Piave*, Piazza Nicciolini 18 (☎ & fax 0565.226.050; ②), near the Campiglia station.

Populonia and the Golfo di Baratti

Perched on a high rocky headland 5km off the main coast road, **POPULONIA** was once a centre of Etruscan and Roman iron production, using ore from Elba. Now it's a tiny place looking down on the broad, half-moon bay of the **Golfo di Baratti**, with some of the nicest beaches for miles around. There's an impressive-looking fortress at the edge of the village, disappointing inside except for the fine views across the hills of southern Tuscany and as far as Livorno on a clear day. The enterprising inhabitants in Via S. Giovanni di Sotto (off the main street) have opened a small private **museum** of Etruscan odds and ends (open daily, 9am–12.30pm & 2–7pm ☎0565.294.360; L2500). The same street has a **restaurant**, the *Populonia*, with very good meals but expect to pay about L40,000.

On the bay below, once Populonia's port, there's a cluster of houses glorified with the name of **BARATTI**, a colourful base for fishing boats, whose Etruscan roots are celebrated in a new, 80-hectare archeological park (July & Aug daily 9am–8pm; June & Sept Wed–Mon 9am–8pm; Oct–Feb Tues–Fri 9am–2pm, Sat & Sun 9am–5pm; March–May Tues–Sun 9am–sunset; L12,000 includes access to one tomb, L20,000 for access to both). A multimedia presentation provides background detail, followed by tours of the caves and a necropolis or two. There's scope for some freelance **camping** locally, or try the campsite *Sant'Albinia*, Via della Principessa (☎0565.29.389; open May to mid-Sept); if you want a **hotel** try the seafront *Alba* (☎0565.29.521; ②) with a garden.

Piombino

PIOMBINO, the nearest port to Elba, is not a place to linger, being dominated by a massive steelworks to the south that was rebuilt after wartime bombing and is likely

---

PIOMBINO FERRIES

Tickets to Elba are sold at the port and at the town's various travel agents, costing about L11,000 per person and from L40,000 per car, one-way, rising to about L100,000 in July and August.

Moby Lines, Piazzale Premuda 8 (☎0565.221.212). Daily ferries to Portoferraio, en route to Bastia (Corsica) July–Sept.

TO.RE.MAR, Piazzale Premuda 13 (☎0565.311.100). Ferries several times daily (almost hourly in summer) to Cavo and Portoferraio (50min); less often to Rio Marina (50min) and Porto Azzurro (1hr 30min).

Also a summer-only hydrofoil (*aliscafo*) to Portoferraio (25–35min) – half the journey time, but almost double the per person price at L18,000.

---

soon to be closed. The only point in passing through is to take the **ferry to Elba**. If you come down the coast by train, get out at Campiglia Maríttima, from where there's a connecting train to Piombino port (don't get out at Piombino town).

In the event that you have to spend a night here, try the two-star *Roma* in Via San Francesco 43 (☎0565.34341; ③), a relatively peaceful side street, or the hotel in Campiglia (see above). There are also three vast **campsites** on the road to Follónica; for emergencies only. The main **tourist office** is at Via Ferruccio (☎0565.225.639).

Elba

Nearly thirty kilometres long and twenty across, **ELBA** is the third largest Italian island after Sicily and Sardinia, yet until thirty years ago it was known only for its mineral resources and as Napoleon's place of exile. Now, however, it's suffering the fate of many a Mediterranean idyll, devoured by tourism in the summer and all but deserted in the long closed season. If you come here in August, when an estimated one million visitors flood onto Elba, you'll have trouble finding a room or even space to camp. To get the most out of the island, visit in spring or late summer.

Elba's enduring appeal comes from its exceptionally clear water, fine white beaches and a mountainous interior ideally suited to easy summer strolls. Development is spread over a series of fairly restrained resorts and the towns and villages retain their distinct characters. **Portoferraio** is very much the capital, and centre of the road and transport network that makes the island an easy place to explore; **Marina di Campo**, over on the south coast, has the best beach. The least visited and loveliest part of the island centres on **Monte Capanne** (1018m) and the western coast from **Marciana** to **Fetovaia**. The flatter **southern coast** from Marina di Campo to Capoliveri has the island's main concentration of **campsites**, though there are sites in or near most centres. **Poggio** and the central **interior villages** are sheltered by lush woods and give access to hikes in the hills. In the island's eastern segment – the old mining district – **Porto Azzurro**, and the more pleasant **Capoliveri**, give access to a string of smaller but much visited villages.

The island has been inhabited since about 3000 BC due to its **mineral** wealth. The Greeks named it Aethalia (Sparks) after its many forges, and it was Elban iron in the Roman swords that conquered an empire. The last iron ore mine closed in 1984, but it's still a geologist's dream, with an estimated thousand different minerals running the A to Z from andalusite to zircon.

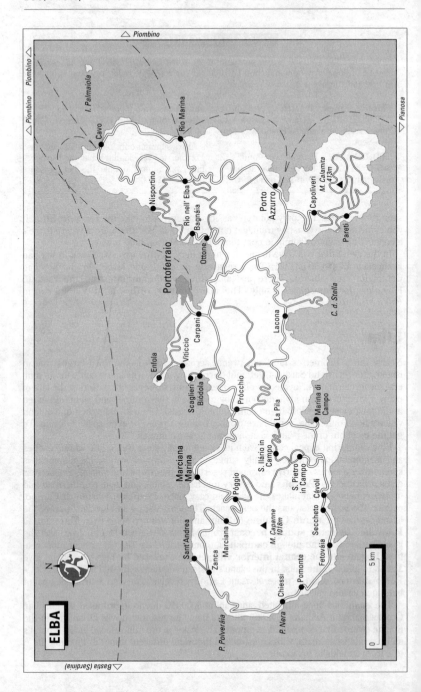

Getting around the island

Buses run to just about everywhere on the island, whether or not they're main tourist centres. The key services **from Portoferraio**, the main terminal, are to **Procchio** (14 daily), **Marina di Campo** (10 daily) and **Porto Azzurro** (12 daily), all a lot less frequent in low season; other services are more sporadic, and there are none going anywhere after 8pm. For general information on Elba bus services, contact ATL at Viale Elba 20, Portoferraio (☎0565.914.392); they also do an eight-hour tour of the island in July and August. **Boats** are much used to reach out-of-the-way beaches, and they're well advertised at all the ports.

Bike or **moped rental** is a good option for exploring the island. Both are available from TWN, Viale Elba 32 (☎0565.914.666), right by the bus station; mopeds cost L35,000–60,000 for 24 hours, bikes L20,000.

There are also several **car-rental** agencies in Portoferraio: in the port area try Rent Chiappi, Calata Italia 30 (☎0565.916.779), or Tesi Viaggi, in the same street (☎0565.930.222); in town, try Happy Rent, Viale Elba (☎0565.914.665), or Rent Mondo, Via Renata Fucini 6 (☎0565.917.276). Reckon on at least L100,000 a day – although some places offer small cars for slightly less – and be ready for considerable summer congestion, especially anywhere near a decent beach.

Portoferraio and around

PORTOFERRAIO is most people's first port of call, and unless you're interested solely in beach life it's a place you'll come back to: it's probably the island's liveliest town – closely followed by Capoliveri – and has the widest range of accommodation. Beyond the busy port area, it also retains an **old town** which might be low on sights but has more than a little charm, and a few kilometres inland there's one of the crucial sights on the Napoleonic trail, the villa at **San Martino**.

Information and accommodation

The **tourist office** (summer Mon–Sat 8am–8pm; winter Mon–Sat 8am–7pm) is up the steps at Calata Italia 26. It provides a map and a list of the island's hotels, apartments and campsites, and will often phone around to try and find space. So too, will the **Associazione Albergatori** at Calata Italia 21 (daily 9am–12.30pm & 3.30–7pm).

If these fail to turn up something – as is all too likely in August – tour the bars and ask about **private rooms**; in season prices are on a par with hotels. If you can get a group together, an **apartment** may work out cheaper. Bookable through the tourist office, most have two double rooms with cooking facilities, and can be rented by the day except during July and August, when you'll get weekly rental only.

Portoferraio's better **hotel** options are: the *Villa Ombrosa*, Via de Gasperi 3 (☎0565.914.363, fax 0565.915.672; ⑤), near the beach at Le Ghiaie; *L'Ape Elbana*, Salita Cosimo de' Medici 2 (☎ & fax 0565.914.245; ④), just off Piazza della Repubblica in the oldest part of town; and *Il Touring*, Via Roma 13 (☎0565.915.851; ⑤). If you are really stuck for a bed, the *Massimo*, Calata Italia 23 (☎0565.914.766, fax 0565.970.177; ⑤), with sixty-nine rooms, should have some chance of space. The plushest place is the *Crystal*, Via Cairoli (☎ & fax 0565.917.971; ⑦), virtually on Le Ghiaie beach.

The nearest **campsites** are *La Sorgente* (☎0565.917.139), the nearby *Acquaviva* (☎0565.915.592) and *La Enfola* (☎0565.939.001); all between 5km and 6km along the road west to Viticcio and quite accessible by bus.

If you fail to find accommodation you can get by for a few days sleeping on beaches, though this is officially prohibited. Leave your bags at the **left luggage** at the bus terminal, Viale Elba 20 (L2500 a day), rent a moped if you can afford it, and set out in search of a secluded spot.

The Town

Portoferraio consists of a modern sector – where the ferries arrive – and the old Medicean port with its fortifications and fishing harbour. To get to the latter, turn right off the ferry along Calata Italia, past all the car parks, to the harbourside Calata Mazzini, the town's *passeggiata* parade. Midway round Calata Mazzini is the entrance to the old town, the **Porta a Mare**, from where an ampitheatre of streets rises towards the walls on the high cliffs.

The town's most obvious features are the **fortifications**, built – like Livorno's – by the Medici; you can pass an hour or so wandering around them, even though many of the main bastions are now in private hands. Most visitors walk up Via Garibaldi and make straight for Napoleon's home in exile, the **Villa dei Mulini** (Mon–Sat 9am–7pm, Sun & hols 9am–1pm; L8000, includes same-day entry to San Martino). Built specifically for the ex-emperor on a site chosen for its fine views of the bay, the villa features a stunning Baroque bedroom, a library sent over from Fontainebleau, and various pieces of memorabilia – including the Napoleonic Elban flag (see box below).

A small, rock-enclosed **beach** called Le Viste is signposted from the Palazzina, but otherwise there's little else to see, unless you're determined to check out every Napoleon-related scrap. In that case you could drop into the small Napoleonic museum in Via Garibaldi's **Chiesa della Misericordia** (Mon & Thurs–Sat 10am–1pm & 4–6pm; L1000) and the similar place lower down in **Santissimo Sacramento** – both contain death masks of the emperor and not a lot more. There's a **Museo Archeologico** in the fort (April–June Mon–Wed & Fri–Sat 9.30am–12.30pm & 4–7pm; July & Aug same days 9.30am–12.30pm & 6pm–midnight; L4000) which houses mainly Roman remains found in the sea around Elba and pieces from pre-Roman sites on the island.

NAPOLEON AND ELBA

Elba is indissolubly linked with Napoleon, even though he was exiled here for little more than nine months – from May 4, 1814 to February 26, 1815. According to island tradition, after renouncing the thrones of France and Italy by the Treaty of Fontainebleau, Napoleon chose Elba as his place of exile for the "gentleness of its climates and its inhabitants". In fact, he had no choice – the allies packed him off here, sweetening the pill by ordaining that Elba would be "a separate principality for his lifetime, held by him in complete sovereignty". The dethroned emperor spent the journey south doodling a new flag for his pocket-sized domain: a red diagonal on a white background – echoing the Medici banner – plus the bees of his own imperial emblem.

After a confusing episode in which his ship was shelled from Portoferraio, Napoleon came ashore to a rousing welcome, and soon set about reorganizing the island's economy and infrastructure. Some of this work might have been motivated by altruism or an inability to forgo politics, but much of what he achieved was for his own ends. The iron ore mines were revamped to supplement his income, his promised salary from Louis XVII having never materialized; the public works were to occupy and pay for the five-hundred-strong Napoleonic Guard that stuck by him. Portoferraio was given drains because the stench offended the imperial nostrils.

Some of the longer-term planning, however, undoubtedly paid dividends to the islanders – education and the legal system were overhauled, roads were built, agriculture was modernized, land was cleared, defences were repaired. These multifarious schemes suggested that Napoleon had resigned himself to his life sentence, but intrigue, rumour and unrest in France persuaded him to have another go. The day after Sir Neil Campbell, his British keeper, left for Livorno, he returned to France and the "Hundred Days" that were to culminate in Waterloo.

San Martino

Napoleon's sister Elisa bought the **Villa Napoleonica di San Martino** (Mon–Sat 9am–7pm, Sun & public holidays 9am–1pm; L8000 including same-day entry to Villa dei Mulini) as a summer residence just before the emperor – who had built it as a summer retreat – left the island for good. It's located 6km from Portoferraio on the #1 bus route, which passes the **Museo delle Ceramiche** (Mon–Sat 10am–12.30pm & 4–7.30pm; closed winter; free), where artist Italo Bolano has landscaped huge walls of ceramic tiles into the countryside.

Engulfed by a vast car park and trolleys flogging Napoleonic souvenirs, the villa is a rather chilly affair, but its drab Neoclassical facade is at least sprinkled with exuberant "N" motifs. The monograms were the idea of Prince Demidoff, husband of Napoleon's niece – and it was he who bought up the villa to create a Napoleonic museum. By all accounts, the great man himself hardly spent any time here, and the permanent exhibits are no great shakes, though special annual exhibitions are held on a Napoleonic theme. Highlight of the house is the **Sala Egizia**, with friezes outlining Napoleon's Egyptian campaign, one of his more successful. At the back of the palazzo is Napoleon's own modest summer retreat – in some respects he had simple tastes – which was home to the famous graffito "Ubicunque felix Napoleon" (Napoleon is happy anywhere) until 1993, when it was discovered to be a fake and consequently removed.

Food and other practicalities

Portoferraio's **restaurants** are expensive and few have food to merit the prices. The well-patronized *Pizzeria Il Castagnacciaio* in Via del Mercato Vecchio (parallel to Piazza della Repubblica) sells the cheapest – and smallest – pizzas; a better bet is the *Albatros*, Via Roma 10 (on the steps above Piazza della Repubblica). *L'Ape Elbana* hotel restaurant has a choice of six tourist menus from L15,000, and *Trattoria Granchio*, Via Dietro la Pieve 13, has reasonable prices and good food. Best known of the more upmarket choices are *La Ferrigna*, Piazza della Repubblica (☎0565.914.129; closed Tues), and the *Trattoria La Barca* in Via Guerazzi (☎0565.918.036; closed Wed except in summer), both at around L60,000 per head.

For **bars**, pick from any of the places around Piazza della Repubblica in the heart of the old town, or Piazza Cavour – particularly *Bar Roma*, which is the most popular bar with locals, with music in the summer and upmarket prices; or try *Bar Kursaal* in the same square.

The town **post office** is in Piazza Hutre, off Piazza della Repubblica. If you plan on **hiking**, the Comunità Montana, Via Manzoni 11 (☎0565.938.111), should provide a contour map of the Monte Capanne area, and helpful advice.

Eastern Elba

Eastern Elba is a distinct geographical area, basically comprising two tongues of land, each dominated by mountain ridges. Away from the main seaside centres of **Rio Marina** and **Porto Azzurro** the beaches are comparatively quiet, but much of the southern isthmus – **Monte Calamita** – was the heart of the mining industry, and is still owned by the quarrying companies. Close by, on the southern coast, **Lacona** boasts one of the island's main concentrations of **campsites**; **Barbarossa** is another popular camping spot, with some particularly fine beaches.

Portoferraio to Rio nell'Elba

South of Portoferraio the main road divides, one spur heading west, the other east towards Porto Azzurro. Following the latter, the first stop is the spa of **SAN GIOVAN-NI**, where Germans and Italians pay through the nose for the privilege of wallowing in its sulphurous marine mud. A few kilometres on at **LE GROTTE** are the ruins of a **Roman villa**, little more than a few stones and mosaic fragments among the gorse, but worth a stop for a great view over the sea, into which most of the building has tumbled.

Soon after comes a left turn for Rio nell'Elba and **MAGGAZZINI**, a little place with a sand and shingle beach and a couple of hotels: the three-star *Mare* (☎0565.933.069, fax 0565.933.408; ⑨) and two-star *Tirrena* (☎0565.933.002, fax 0565.933.452; ④). Moving on to **OTTONE**, there's the one-star *Villa Gaia* (☎0565.933.160; ③), and the *Rosselba le Palme* **campsite** (☎0565.933.101; mid-April to Sept), rated by many the island's best.

West-facing **BAGNAIA**, just beyond Ottone (off the direct road to Rio nell'Elba), is famous for its sunsets. There are two **hotels** here, the *Punta Pina* (☎0565.961.077; ⑨) and *La Feluca* (☎0565.961.084, fax 0565.961.085; ⑨), and a bar, the *Kikuty Snac*. If you have the patience to drive the twisting road beyond, the twin tiny hamlets of Nisporto and Nisportino mark the beginning of the most unspoilt beaches and coastline on Elba's north shore. You can walk into the hills behind, or take boats out to the beaches beyond the end of the road. The only **accommodation** in the immediate vicinity is the *Camping-Villaggio Sole e Mare* at Nisporto (☎0565.934.907, fax 0565.961.180; open all year) or the neighbouring campsite *Ut Cala di Nisportino* (☎0565.934.908; May–Sept). There's a **hotel** 2km from the sea at La Ginestra – the three-star *La Ginestra* (☎0565.943.181; ④).

A narrow, scenic road climbs from Nisportino to Rio nell'Elba through La Ginestra; if you've taken the more direct route from Maggazzino you'll pass the old castle at **VOLTERRAIO**, once the strongest in Elba and now a silent and evocative ruin, with a great view over its desolate surroundings. It's a stiff climb from the road.

RIO NELL'ELBA itself is a graceless place, though old enough in parts and almost unique in having apparently resisted Elba's tourist boom. From its high vantage it surveys a wild countryside devastated by repeated forest fires. There's nowhere to stay, and just one place to **eat**, *Manganini*, Piazza del Popolo.

Cavo and Rio Marina

CAVO, on the northern extremity of Elba, is a shabby, isolated and polluted place, its beach a very un-Elban grey; car ferries from Piombino to Portoferraio stop off here, but there's little to invite a stay.

The main town on Elba's east coast is **RIO MARINA**, a ferry terminal for connections to Piombino, Portoferraio and Porto Azzurro. Tourism and a busy harbour have replaced once ore as the source of revenue, but this again isn't one of the better Elban towns. Its only sight is the **Museo dei Minerali Elbani** next to the Palazzo Comunale, a display of some two hundred Elban minerals (March–Oct Mon–Sat 9am–noon & 3–6pm, Sun 9am–noon; L3500). There's just one **hotel**, the *Rio* at Via Palestro 31 (☎0565.924.255; ⑦), next to the scrubby public gardens overlooking the port. Close by is one of the island's best **restaurants**, *La Canocchia*, Via Palestro 3 (closed Mon in winter), where a fine meal comes to around L70,000. Marginally cheaper options for eating out abound in the lower port, where there's also an excellent fish restaurant, *Da Oreste la Strega*, in Piazza V. Emanuele.

For a **beach**, head south to the hamlet of **ORTANO**, dominated by a big tourist complex, but with public sand too; there's an on-beach **campsite**, the *Canapai* (☎0564.939.165; May–Sept) and a **hotel**, *Easytime*, Via Pan Porticciolo (☎ & fax 0565.962.531; ⑤). You get to it by a turning 1500 metres back along the road to Rio nell'Elba.

Porto Azzurro

The resort of **PORTO AZZURRO** was heavily fortified by Philip III of Spain in 1603 as protection against continual raids by the French and the Austrians; today his fortress is the island's prison. The town's small old quarter, closed to cars, centres on **Via d'Alarcon**, a bustle of bars, shops and restaurants, with traditional open-front shops and balconied houses in the cobbled area near Piazza Matteotti. The best place to swim is from the rocks east of the harbour.

Porto Azzurro's **accommodation** is limited and lacklustre: best bets are the *Belmare*, Banchina IV Novembre 25 (☎0565.95.012, fax 0565.958.245; ④), the *Arrighi*, Via V. Veneto 18 (☎0565.95.315; ③), and the *Villa Italia*, Viale Italia 41 (☎ & fax 0565.951.19; ③). The best of the **campsites** are at the small nearby resort of Barbarossa – the *Da Mario* (☎0565.958.032; mid-April to mid-Oct) and *Arrighi* (☎0565.95.568; April–Nov) both give straight onto the beach. There's a one-star hotel here too, the *Barbarossa* (☎0565.95.087; ②).

For **food** there are plenty of identikit joints, the best known being the *Delfino Verde* in Lungomare Vitaliani (☎0565.95.197); *Da Floriano*, Via Ricasoli 35 (☎0565.950.92) is good for fish. Of the town centre **bars**, try *Il Sottoscala* at Via Ricasoli 11, or *Lo Scoglio*, Via Cavour 17. Other local nightspots include the *Rock Bar* at Banchina IV Novembre, a restaurant which fails to live up to its name, usually playing waltzes, and the *Sugar-Reef Nightclub*, 10km along the coast at Capoliveri.

Out of town, **boat trips** run along the coast to the south twice daily in summer, costing around L40,000 for a stretch of coast, or L70,000 to go around the island; you can buy tickets direct from the boats or from one of the travel agents along the seafront.

Off the Rio Marina road to the north, at **TERRANERE**, there's a bizarre sulphurous pond, its half-stagnant waters a violent yellow contrast to the sea; the beach here is scattered with mine debris. Nearby, up an unsignposted left turn off the same road, is the **Santuario della Madonna di Monserrato**, about 1km beyond the so-called Piccolo Miniera, a tourist-trap mine reconstruction. The short walk at the end of the road brings you to the church whose chief claim to fame is its replica of the Black Madonna of Montserrat; chapel and Madonna were both commissioned in 1606 by the island's Spanish governor, who claimed this site reminded him of the holy mountain outside his native Barcelona.

Naregno

East of the road between Porto Azzurro and Capoliveri, **NAREGNO** is a small resort with a good beach, though not as good as the less accessible sand to the south at Côte Piane, Liscolino and Buzzancone. None can match the village's **accommodation** possibilities, however, which include the seafront *Villa Rodriguez* (☎0565.968.423; ④), *Frank's Hotel* (☎0565.968.144, fax 0565.968.405; ⑥) and *La Voce del Mare* (☎ & fax 0565.968.455; ④).

Capoliveri

CAPOLIVERI, 3.5km south of Porto Azzurro, is the best of the towns on Elba's eastern fringe, a prosperous centre whose close-knit streets have made few concessions to tourism. Occupying a naturally fortified spot, it's amongst the oldest settlements on the island – in Roman times its name was Caput Liberi. Its hinterland remains undeveloped, as the mining companies have not sold their disused plots to the hoteliers – though much of the area is thus out of bounds.

There's nothing specific to see, but **old streets** such as Via Roma, Via Cavour and Vicolo Lungo are pleasant places to roam, and there are numerous half-hidden bars in the alleyways, as well as a sprawl of outside tables in the central piazza. The town is at its busiest on Thursdays, when locals and tourists flood in for the weekly **street market**; it is also very lively in the evenings, with a reputation for being the place to go for a night out.

Capoliveri makes an ideal base for visits to the fine **beaches** at Naregno, Morcone and Innamorata (see below). However, the town has become very upmarket and it is practically impossible to stay there cheaply: it only has **apartments**, rented out by numerous private agencies, which are very expensive with few high-season vacancies; try the *Agenzia della Lucia*, Via Melline 9. Amongst the **restaurants**, *Il Chiasso*, Via Sauro (☎0565.968.709; closed Tues), is outstanding at around L80,000 a head. Its more reasonable rivals include *Summertime*, Via Roma 56, with friendly service and excellent food, and the rustic and informal *Porto Franco* in Via da Brescia off the main piazza. To sample local **wines** make for the *Enoteca Elba* in Piazza Matteotti or *La Buca dei Vini* at Via Roma 34; and for delicious homemade ice cream drop in at *Patelli Gelateria* in Via Roma. As for **nightlife**, Capoliveri brims with life well into the small hours: *Ophir* disco, 2km away at La Trappola, is the prime dancing spot, with *Sugar-Reef*, a friendly late night jazz bar, just below it.

South of Capoliveri

The much touted local church at **Madonna delle Grazie** – another place of pilgrimage – has a school-of-Raphael altarpiece but is otherwise more or less a waste of time, as is the overbuilt area around.

It's better to continue to the trio of resorts at **MORCONE**, **PARETI** and **INNAMORATA**. The last is the quietest and has a fine sand and shingle beach; the other hamlets have large beaches, the one at Morcone being more regimented than its neighbour. Parking is difficult, as is **accommodation**. Morcone has no hotels, though there are some **rooms** to rent and Residency la Scogliera will put people up on a nightly basis in mini-apartments (☎0565.968.424; ④). Pareti offers the *Pensione Villa Miramare* (☎0565.968.673; ③) and *Dino* (☎0565.939.103, fax 0565.968.172; ⑤). There's nowhere to stay in Innamorata except a tourist village, but it's worth visiting for the **restaurant** *I Gemini da Pietro*, with its friendly owner, well-cooked fish and a terrace overlooking the sea – perfect for sunsets.

Roads continue south into the hills of **Monte Calámita**, and to the stretch of unspoilt coast known as the **Costa dei Gabbiani**, both areas with mine-restricted access and with some of the beaches reserved for the newly emerging tourist villages. The area's name (Calamity) is a pun referring to the magnetic properties of the rocks, which allegedly attract boats towards them – *calamita*, without the accent, means "magnet".

Lacona

LACONA, well round the coast to the west of Porto Azzurro, is one of the island's main camping centres, and its flat foreshore is crowded with **bars and discos** designed to cater to the beach crowd once the sun's gone down. The **campsites** to head for are *Il Lacona* (☎0565.964.161) or the nearby *Lacona Pineta* (☎0565.964.322), both set in the pine woods on the eastern arm of the Golfo di Lacona. *Stella Mare* (☎0565.964.007) is on the beach a bit farther out along the headland, also amidst plenty of greenery – all three are open all year. The best-value **hotel** is the *Pensione Giardino* (☎0565.964.059, fax 0565.964.353; ④).

Western Elba

Western Elba's road system allows for a circular tour of the area, but many people make immediately for specific targets – usually **Marina di Campo**, with its huge beach and the island's largest concentration of hotels after Portoferraio. Upmarket alternatives are offered by the north-coast resorts of **Procchio** and **Marciana Marina**, while backpackers favour the relatively less commercialized **Énfola** area. Fewer visitors go inland to **Marciana**, one of Elba's nicest villages, or to the long sweep of the **western coast**, whose hamlets and beaches are amongst the island's most tranquil. Though the western zone tends to be rockier than the east, it's better for **walking**, the highlights being **Monte Capanne** and its surrounding ridges.

Énfola

If you want a spread of beach and a choice of **campsites** near Portoferraio, follow the scenic road below Monte Poppe to the headland at **Capo d'Énfola**. You pass through the busy but pretty hamlets of Sorgente and Punta Acquaviva (both with a campsite), and a rare bargain for accommodation in Acquaviva, the one-star *Stella Del Mare* (☎0565.916.352; ②), before reaching **ÉNFOLA**, where the land narrows to a 75-metre-wide isthmus with beaches on both sides. The road ends at a small car park next to the *Bar Emanuel* (closed winter), where you can get down to either strip of sand. Two hundred metres back from the bar, a road strikes off left to **VITICCIO**, another small spot with a dead-end road, parking area, and sand and shingle beach.

There are numerous **hotels** in the area, pick of the bunch being the three-star *Paradiso* at Viticcio (☎0565.939.034, fax 0565.939.041; ⑥) or two-star *Scoglio Bianco* (☎0565.939.036, fax 0565.939.048; ⑤). **ÉNFOLA** has a shady **campsite**, *Énfola Camping* (☎0565.939.001; April to mid-Oct). On the bus route between Énfola and Viticcio is the recommended, but not yet too popular, Sansone **beach**; ask the driver for the stop.

Biodola and Scaglieri

From Viticcio a footpath runs a couple of kilometres round the coast to Scaglieri and Biodola, otherwise reached by a side road from the main highway out of Portoferraio. **BIODOLA** consists simply of a road, two big hotels and a superb **beach**, which inevitably gets a summer blitz of visitors. Parking is difficult, but there are no buses. Biodola's two **hotels** are very expensive, though there's a cheaper and beautifully situated place two minutes from the beach, the *Casa Rosa* (☎0565.969.931, fax 0565.969.857; full pension ⑦).

SCAGLIERI is a similar sort of place but a touch livelier and more picturesque, fronted by a shop, two bars and a couple of places to **eat**: *I due Pini* is the better of the two *pizzerie*. You can **stay** at the *Albergo-Ristorante Danila* (☎0565.969.915, fax 0565.969.865; ⑤) or there's a **campsite**, the *Scaglieri* (☎0565.969.940; April to mid-Oct), on the hillside.

Procchio

PROCCHIO suffers from being at the junction of main roads south and west, the greenery of its surroundings offset by an incessant stream of summer traffic. With its buzzing bars and shops it's not a place to get away from it all, but the sea is good and the white beach excellent – access to much of the sand is free and it's large enough not to seem overcrowded. However, this is a relatively expensive town. The cheaper **hotels** are the *Da Renzo* (☎0565.907.505; ③); *Hotel di Procchio* (☎0565.907.477, fax 0565.907.350; ④); *Delfino* (☎0565.907.455, fax 0565.907.252; ④); and *Monna Lisa* (☎0565.907.519; ④). More expensive, but not unreasonable, are the *Fontalleccio* (☎0565.907.431, fax 0565.907.547; ⑥) and *Edera* (☎ & fax 0565.907.525; ⑥). Campsites don't exist. **Restaurants** along the roadside strip are much of a muchness; the *Orso Bianco* does good ice cream.

Marciana Marina and Poggio

Farther round the north coast, **MARCIANA MARINA** has the minor distinction of being the smallest *comune* in Tuscany, a status it's proud of, allowing few hotels and aiming to preserve an air of residential order away from the seafront. The traffic-filled promenade of bars, restaurants and trinket shops does nothing to lure you into staying. Even the beach, overlooked by a Pisan watchtower, is shingly and forgettable. There are no camp-sites and accommodation is largely restricted to private houses and apartments.

Situated 5km inland from Marciana Marina, **POGGIO** is renowned for its **spring water**, from the *Fonte di Napoleone*. It also has a tight medieval centre whose decorat-ed doorways and patchwork of cheerful gardens make this an attractive place to **stay**. Best overnight option is the *Albergo-Ristorante Monte Capanne*, Via Pini 1 (☎0565.99.083; ②), in a lovely, peaceful setting. **Food** here is good and the village claims one of the island's leading restaurants, the *Publius*, Loc. Poggio, Via XX Settembre 13 (☎0565.99.208) – great views, classic Tuscan cooking and steep prices.

Poggio is a good base for a **walk** to the summit of **Monte Capanne** (1018m), Elba's highest point. Before setting off, pick up the local *Sentieri del Parco* **map** which covers forty percent of the island, or a less detailed equivalent on sale in Poggio and Marciana. A marked trail climbs the spur to the south of the village, the quickest of the many paths that radiate from villages around the west coast. Allow about two hours at a leisurely pace, and be prepared for the bar and crowded terrace at the summit.

Marciana

The high and isolated village of **MARCIANA**, the oldest settlement on Elba, is perfectly placed between great beaches (Promonte and Sant'Andrea), mountainous interior (Monte Capanne) and a modern centre for supplies (Procchio). Its **old quarter** is a delight, too, its narrow alleys, arches, belvederes and stone stairs festooned with flowers and climbing plants. There's virtually no traffic or commercial development, and with the skeletal out-line of its old fortifications it feels very distinct from the rest of the island's towns.

Marciana's history is encapsulated in the small **Museo Archeologico** in Via del Pretorio (April–Sept daily 9am–12.30pm & 3.30–7.30pm; Oct–March open on request; L3000), in the **Fortezza Pisana** above the village in Via del Pretoria (Mon–Sat 10am–1pm & 3–6pm, Sun 10am–1pm; L3000), and in the palaces of the Appiani, Elba's leading fifteenth-century family, who made Marciana their home base.

Outside the village there's a trio of interesting **churches**, the oldest of which is the twelfth-century Pisan-influenced **San Lorenzo**; now largely in ruins, it's on a track off the road to Poggio. More intriguing is the **Santuario della Madonna del Monte**, about half an hour's walk along the road curving uphill west of the village. Though it dates from the eleventh century – and was probably a pagan temple well before that – its appearance is largely sixteenth-century, the Renaissance church serving to house a stone painted by a heavenly hand with the image of the Virgin. The island's most impor-tant shrine, it's also featured on the Napoleonic trail, as the ex-emperor came here to seek spiritual solace from the monks; by all accounts he received solace of a different kind when he was joined by his Polish mistress, Maria Walewska.

The third church, the **Santuario di San Cerbone**, is passed on the **walk** to Monte Capanne (trail #1; 3hr). The track starts from the southern tip of the village, the church appearing after an hour at the junction with trail #6. San Cerbone was buried here, dur-ing a miraculous cloudburst that hid the ceremony from Lombards who had the saint's valuable remains in their sights.

If you don't want to walk up Monte Capanne, there's a popular **cable car** to the top (daily: April–Oct 10am–12.15pm & 2.45–5.15pm, plus July–Aug until 6.15pm; L20,000 return, L12,000 single); most people choose to walk down either to Marciana or Poggio, though if you're trekking with your gear you could drop down to the coast via one of the numerous marked trails.

Marciana's only drawback is its shortage of **accommodation**, restricted to rented rooms and apartments available through the *Birreria La Porta*, Piazza Umberto I (☎0565.904.253) at the entrance to the village, which also serves good sandwiches and salads; the other decent place to eat is the reasonably priced *Ristorante Bellavista* which is in the same piazza.

Sant'Andrea and around

The dispersed village of **SANT'ANDREA**, 6km west of Marciana, just off the coast road, is currently one of Elba's trendiest retreats, with villas and hotels creeping farther into the wooded hinterland each year. It's popular with divers, drawn here by what is reputedly some of the clearest sea water around Elba. **Accommodation** is at a premium, but it's not necessarily expensive, and most is discreetly set amid almost tropical vegetation. On the beach itself there's the small *Bambu* (☎0565.908.012; ③); the pleasant *La Cernia* (☎0565.908.194; ⑤) is midway between the coast and the main road. Or try *L'Oleandro* (☎0565.908.088; ③), *Piccola Pineta* (☎0565.908.022, fax 0565.908.036; ③) or *Bella Vista* (☎0565.908.015, fax 0565.908.079; ③).There are also plenty of apartments to rent.

Immediately south are the linked hamlets of **PATRESI**, **MORTAIO** and **LA GUARDIA**, rated as having the island's finest seas and still fairly unspoilt into the bargain. Cliffs drop to the sea, as they do all round this section of coast, with plenty of rock pillars and stacks for underwater enthusiasts. Most local **accommodation** is in apartments, though there are two **hotels**, the eleven-room *Villa Rita* (☎0565.908.095; ④) and the two-star *Belmare* (☎0565.908.067; ④), at Patresi. For pizza and full **meals**, try *Il Faro*, on the road near Patresi, with a veranda and sea view.

Chiessi to Cavoli

Further round the coast road **CHIESSI** and **POMONTE**, each have a small stony beach, beautifully clear water, rocky hinterland and little commercialism. By **FETOVAIA** you're back to beach development, but the sand is superb – and a big car park prevents some of the chaos of other Elban resorts. There's lots of apartment accommodation and several top-whack hotels. Try the central *Lo Scirocco* (☎0565.988.033, fax 0565.988.067; ⑤), the *Pensione Montemerlo* (☎ & fax 0565.988.051; ⑤), out of town on the hill, *Anna* (☎0565.988.032, fax 0565.988.073; ⑤) or *Da Alma* (☎0565.988.040, fax 0565.988.074; ④).

Farther on, **SECCHETO** is good for a swim from the rocks at the western end of town, or for tanning on the largely nudist stretch beyond – *le piscine* – where the water forms deep pools in the hollows of a Roman granite mine. Two **hotels** with average-priced rooms are *La Stella* (☎0565.987.013, fax 0565.987.215; ⑤), at the end of the road to the sea, and the nearby *Da Fine* (☎0565.987.017, fax 0565.987.250; ⑤). Better than either, if you don't mind being away from the coast, is the *Locanda dell'Amicizia* (☎0565.987.051, fax 0565.987.277; ③), set in a peaceful spot at **Vallebuia**, in the little valley north of Seccheto. The **bar** on the main road, which can sometimes direct you to available apartments, is popular, fairly cheap and does excellent pizzas. As on much of this section of coast there is no campsite, and no shelter if you want to pitch a tent on the quiet.

Nearby **CAVOLI** is more upmarket, though the beach is good if you don't mind the crowds. There are two similar beachside *pensioni*: the *Lorenza* (☎0565.987.054, fax 0565.987.080; ④) and the *Conchiglia* (☎0565.987.010, fax 0565.987.257; ④).

Marina di Campo

Set in one of the island's few areas of plain, **MARINA DI CAMPO** was the first and is now the largest resort on Elba. The huge white **beach** is what makes the place popular: the water's clean, and there's space on land if you walk to the east end or out to the rockier west. There's also all the tourist frippery and **nightlife** you'd expect in any major seaside centre, with key discos and clubs changing by the month.

Pick of the numerous **hotels** are: *Lido*, Via Mascagni 29 (☎0565.976.040; ④); *Pensione Elba*, Via Mascagni 43 (☎0565.976.224, fax 0565.977.280; ④, plus two- or four-bed apartments); *Santa Caterina*, Viale Elba (☎0565.976.452, fax 0565.976.745; ⑤); *Barracuda*, Viale Elba 2 (☎0565.976.893, fax 0565.977.254; ⑤); and *Thomas*, Viale degli Etruschi 32 (☎0565.977.732; ⑤). If you arrive early in the day you might find space at one of the three **campsites**. Best deals for a **meal** are *Rosticceria Mazzarri*, at Via Roma 19, *Il Golfo* situated at the eastern end of the beach, *Kontiki* in the port (for fish), and *La Triglia* at Via Roma 58, the town's best-known restaurant (L30,000–50,000 per person).

You can **hire bicycles** and **boats** from Residency Montauti, Via Pisa 3 (☎0565.976.194). For a break from the crowds you might take a bus trip out to two smaller **hill-villages** close by: the very pretty Sant'Ilario in Campo and San Piero in Campo, whose parish church has a hotchpotch of frescoes.

Capraia

CAPRAIA, 30km northwest of Elba, is a Mediterranean island in the old sense: unspoilt, with just a couple of hotels and one road that links the small port to the old town on the hill. Its former use as a penal colony ensured that the terrain remained largely untouched, and now – despite considerable pressure from potential hoteliers – the local council have held back on commercial development, instead promoting the formation of a *Parco Naturale* to protect the island's natural heritage. This makes it difficult to visit, and the two hotels and single campsite come close to saturation point in summer; again, it's best to come slightly out of season.

Getting to Capraia is no problem, with a daily **ferry** from Livorno throughout the year – twice daily on Thursdays and Saturdays in summer.

Capraia Isola

From the tiny harbour to the town of **CAPRAIA ISOLA** – the only inhabited part of the island except the port – is a gentle walk of about a kilometre; there's a bus if you're feeling lazy. The island's long periods of desolation – mainly due to pirate raids – have done little for its monuments. Capraia Isola's Baroque church and convent of **Sant'Antonio** is largely ruined, and the big castle, the privately owned **Fortezza di San Giorgio**, has seen considerably better days.

For information on wildlife, walking, accommodation and boat trips, contact the **park Cooperativa** (☎ & fax 0586.905.071) or the summer-only **tourist office** (☎0586.905.138); the two share an office in Via Assunzione.

For **hotels**, there's the three-star *Da Beppone*, Via Assunzione 78 (☎ & fax 0586.905.001; ④) or the four-star *Il Saracino* (☎0586.905.018, fax 0586.905.062; ⑧) in the upper part of town at Via L. Cibo 40; you'll probably have to pay at least half-pension in peak periods. There are, however, numerous private **rooms** and **apartments** for rent; the tourist office will ring around for you, or you can just wander round town and look for the signs – virtually everyone can point towards a room.

There's a single **campsite**, *Le Sughere* (☎0586.905.066; May–Sept), behind the town's small church of the Assumption. **Free camping** is feasible, but the terrain is rocky, and there's little cover or fresh water.

The best **restaurant** is *La Garitta*, Via Genova 14, up in the top of the town near the castle; run as a bar during the day, it's an informal place, dedicated to simple seafood. Still in the upper town, the *Cala Rossa*, in Via V. Emanuele, is a homely trattoria. There are a couple of other basic places down on the harbour: *Da Beppone*, Via Assunzione, is the best of these.

The interior and the beaches

From Capraia Isola you can easily strike off into the interior, which is dominated by a spine of steep hills, largely rocky and covered in scrub. Tracks crisscross the whole island, but there are four distinct and fairly obvious **walks**: to the **Torre dello Zenobito**, a Genoese watchtower on the island's southernmost tip; to **Il Piano** and the

Pisan church of **Santo Stefano**, using the rough road south of the town; to the light-house on the west coast, farther down the same track; and to the **Laghetto**, a tiny lake in the hills and the focus of the *Parco Naturale*.

Isolation has favoured the development of various indigenous animal and vegetable species, several of them similar to species otherwise confined to Corsica and Sardinia. These include subspecies of buzzard, sparrow, large finch and La Marmora's warbler amongst the birds, and campion, toadflax and blue button amongst the plants. Birds are the main natural interest, with numerous itinerant visitors, and forty resident species including peregrines, shearwaters and up to a hundred pairs of the rare Corsican gull.

Unfortunately, winter storms in 1998 stripped the island's only real beach, the **Cala della Mortola**, of all its sand. However, there are plenty of rocky coves and the water's clean and clear everywhere – even in the port area. There is a range of small boats available for hire, from canoes at L15,000 an hour to powered rubber dinghies at L140,000 for the day. Try the park Cooperativa (☎0586.905.071) or the Agenzia Della Rosa Emme (☎0586.905.266); both outfits also run a trip **round the entire island** (twice daily in season; about L20,000 per person for groups of eight and up). For **subaqua** enthusiasts there are a couple of clubs based in the port – contact the Capraia Diving Club on the harbour (☎0586.905.137) for help and equipment hire.

travel details

TRAINS

Pisa to: Florence (hourly; 1hr), via Empoli (35min; change for Volterra and Siena); Lucca (hourly; 30min); Viareggio (every 30min; 20min); Livorno (every 30min; 15min).

Livorno to: Rome (every 30min; 3–4hr); La Spezia (5 daily; 1hr 20min); Pisa (every 20min; 15–30min); Florence (12 daily; 1hr 30min).

BUSES

Pisa to: Viareggio, Florence, Livorno and La Spezia.

Livorno to: Piombino and Pisa.

FERRIES

Livorno to: Capraia, Bastia (Corsica) and Olbia (Sardinia).

Piombino to: Portoferraio, Rio Marina, Porto Azzurro and Cavo (all on Elba).

CHAPTER FIVE

THE MAREMMA

The **Maremma** – the coastal plain that runs south from the Piombino headland – was the northern heartland of the **Etruscans**, whose drainage and irrigation canals turned it into an area of huge agricultural potential. Their good work, however, was largely lost under the Romans, who abandoned much of the land and left it to revert to marsh – a decline that continued through the Middle Ages, when war and further dereliction turned the region into a malarial swamp. For years, virtually the only inhabitants were migrant charcoal burners and shepherds (who in summer abandoned the infested lowlands for the hill-villages of Amiata – and the famous *butteri*, the cowboys who tend the region's oxen and horses.

Modern attempts to revive the Maremma were started in 1828 by Grand Duke Leopoldo of Tuscany, who instigated new drainage schemes and introduced a crude health service, with free quinine for malaria sufferers. At the turn of last century, though, Grosseto's regional council still had to move its offices annually to the healthier surroundings of Scansano, and real progress only began under Mussolini. The malarial mosquito was finally banished in 1950, and something of the Maremma's grim legacy lives on in its common Italian nickname, *La Miseria*.

Drainage has returned a measure of prosperity to the Maremma, but at the cost of destroying its ancient landscapes and prompting the expansion of **Grosseto**, one of Tuscany's more miserable towns. A few efforts have been made to preserve the old world, mainly in the **Monti dell'Uccellina** but also in the **nature reserves** at **Burano** and **Orbetello**, two of the finest **birdwatching** spots in the country. You'll also stand a chance of seeing wild boar; a hoary-skinned sub-species (*Sus scropha majori*) of which has developed in isolated, swamp-encircled habitats.

There are plenty of seaside diversions here as well, with glorious **beaches** at **Marina di Alberese** and in the Uccellina, and moderately upmarket resorts at **Punta Ala** and around **Monte Argentario**. Increasingly well known are the idyllic island of **Giglio**, visited from the Argentario, and the area around the Lazio border, both suffering slow colonization by Rome's bourgeoisie. **Massa Maríttima** is the area's most historically interesting town, its medieval centre a fine example of Romanesque architecture.

Almost everything you'll want to see clings to the coast, which is served by the main Rome–Pisa **rail line** and the old Roman road, the Via Aurelia (SS1). To cut across country, there's a rail link from Grosse to Siena, and a few **buses** that run inland from Grosseto, Orbetello and Massa Maríttima.

ACCOMMODATION PRICES

Throughout this guide, **hotel** accommodation is graded on a scale from ① to ⑨, indicating the cost of the **cheapest double room** in each establishment in high season (for **hostels**, rates per person are given in lire). The price bands to which these codes refer are as follows:

① up to L60,000	④ L120,000–150,000	⑦ L250,000–300,000
② L60,000–90,000	⑤ L150,000–200,000	⑧ L300,000–350,000
③ L90,000–120,000	⑥ L200,000–250,000	⑨ over L350,000

THE BUTTERI

The *butteri*, the Maremma's very own cowboys, have for centuries taken care of the region's half-feral horses and its celebrated white cattle, a special breed imported from Asia for their resilience to the rigours of the Maremma climate and terrain. For most of the year the *butteri* ride with the herds on the Maremma's grasslands, the key event of the year being the so-called *merca* in April, when the one-year-old calves and foals are rounded up, counted and branded. You stand most chance of seeing them on the Ombrone estuary, particularly on the road to Marina di Alberese.

From time to time the *butteri* make an appearance in local festivals and special events. Such performances are nothing new: in 1911 Buffalo Bill brought a travelling troupe of cowboys to Rome, where they were trounced by the *butteri* in a series of rodeo events in the Piazza del Popolo. Today the best known of their tourist shows is the August rodeo in Alberese, and they also prove their skills in perhaps the most demanding equestrian arena in the world – as the riders in the Siena Palio.

Massa Maríttima

Once the second city of the Sienese Republic and still graced with some of Siena's civic style, **MASSA MARÍTTIMA** is the finest historic town of the Maremma. Named "Massa" by the Romans – their word for a large country estate – it gained its maritime suffix in the Middle Ages, when it became the pre-eminent town of this coastal region. The sea has receded somewhat since that time, and is now twenty kilometres distant across a silt-filled plain, and scarcely visible from the town's hill-top.

Massa, like Volterra to the north, has long been a **mining** town, its silver, copper and other mineral reserves generating wealth since Neolithic times. Designation as a bishopric in the ninth century – in place of declining Populonia – gave it additional impetus, leading to the formation of an independent republic in 1225; in 1310 it produced Europe's first charter for the protection of miners, the *Codice Mineraio*.

Sadly for Massa, its mineral riches attracted the rival attentions of Pisa and Siena, the latter finally absorbing the town in 1335. Those one hundred years of glory, however, funded the building of its monuments – notably the exquisite duomo – and saw the doubling of the population (a trend reversed after absorption into the Grand Duchy of Tuscany in 1555). Subsequent visitations of plague and malaria, together with a downturn in mining activity, left Massa a virtual ghost town by 1737, its population reduced to just 537 inhabitants. Like other Maremma towns, its recovery only began with the reopening of mines and the draining of coastal marshes in the 1830s.

The Town

A small industrial estate mars the approach to Massa – and blocks of new buildings do little to improve the effect. All this is overshadowed, however, by the medieval splendour of Piazza Garibaldi in the lower, mainly Romanesque, **Città Vecchia**. The upper town, **Città Nuova**, is more Gothic in appearance and was built largely as a residential centre. An immensely steep and picturesque lane, **Via Moncini**, connects the two. (For most of the Middle Ages, the lower town was inhabited by a Pisan clan, the Todini; the upper by their Sienese rivals, the Pannochieschi.)

Most of the upper town's interest centres on **Piazza Garibaldi**, a small, eccentric but exquisite example of Tuscan town planning. Its thirteenth-century duomo is set on broad steps, at a dramatically oblique angle to the square.

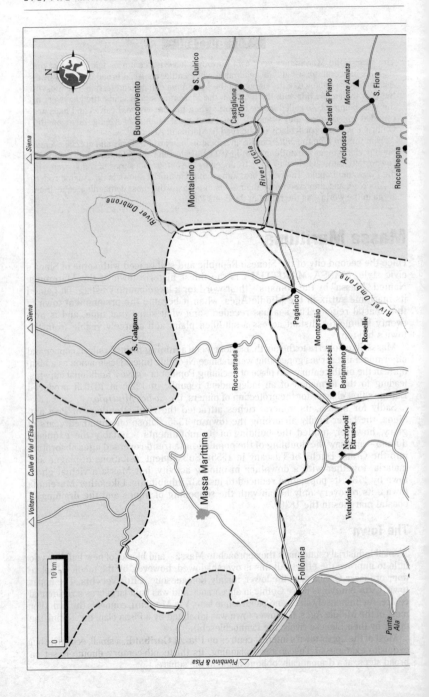

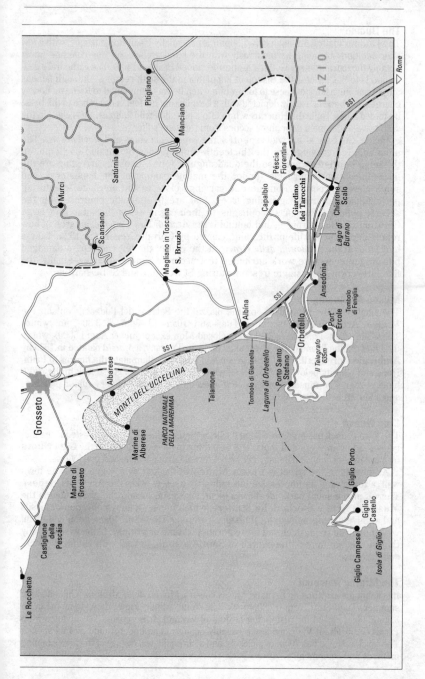

The Duomo

The **Duomo** (daily 8am–noon & 3–7.30pm) is essentially Pisan Romanesque, with a few later additions blending harmoniously with the blind arches and tiny columns (most notably the extraordinary Gothic **campanile**, added in about 1400). The cathedral's dedication is to St Cerbone, the Bishop of Populonia in the sixth century. Although famous for persuading a flock of geese to follow him when he was summoned to Rome on heresy charges, Cerbone is usually depicted with a bear licking his feet, a reference to the beast he tamed when Totila the Hun threw him into a pit full of wild animals. Bas-reliefs in the architrave of the main door show scenes from the saint's life.

Inside, the bare stone walls set off some superb carvings and works of art. The most admired carvings are the thirteenth-century ones by Giraldo da Como, on the huge **baptistery** and also the quadrangular **font**. Almost as arresting are the fifteenth-century tabernacle (under the marble canopy of the baptistery), and some eleventh-century Romanesque carvings close to the entrance – featuring powerful and primitive grinning faces, that are in dramatic contrast with the severe, polished Roman sarcophagus to their right. Over the altar is a large Giovanni Pisano altarpiece, and behind it the *Arca di San Cerbone*, an arch of bas-reliefs depicting the life of the saint, carved by Gori di Gregorio in 1324. Take a look, too, at the *Madonna delle Grazie* at the end of the left transept, a damaged but gorgeous Sienese work attributed to Duccio or Simone Martini. Finally, the fine little crypt has a single fresco featuring St Cerbone and St Bernardino.

Museo Archeologico

The smaller of the two palaces on the piazza, the Palazzo del Podestà, contains the **Museo Archeologico** (summer Tues–Sun 10am–12.30pm & 3.30–7pm; winter Tues–Sun 10am–12.30pm & 3.30–5pm; closed Mon except July & Aug; L5000), where the chief exhibit is one of the finest altarpieces in Tuscany, a *Maestà* painted in 1335 by **Ambrogio Lorenzetti**. Vivid pink, green and tangerine illuminate the figures of Faith, Hope and Charity below the Madonna, while Cerbone and his geese lurk in the right-hand corner. The museum otherwise houses only a handful of very minor paintings and a few archeological finds.

Città Nuova

The town council has organized what it calls a "tourist itinerary", a signposted route that takes you to some very dull spots. The best thing to do is wander up to the **Città Nuova** by Via Moncini, whose tributary alleyways reveal small gardens and good views.

At the end of the street is **Piazza Matteotti**, flanked by a segment of the town wall, a tower, and an impressive but militarily useless arch, the **Arco dei Senesi**. There's also a small park, ideal for a picnic or siesta. Across the piazza stands the **Museo di Arte e Storia delle Miniere**, which houses a puny collection of fossils and archive photographs of local history (summer Tues–Sun 10am–noon & 4–7pm; winter open on request; closed for restoration at time of writing). Otherwise the only thing to see up here is the church of **Sant'Agostino**, graced with simple cloisters and little else.

The Mining Museum

Inevitably, given its mining heritage, Massa boasts a **Museo della Miniera** (Guided tours: summer Tues–Sun 10am–12.30pm & 3.30–7pm; winter same days 10am–noon & 3.30–4.30pm; closed for restoration at time of writing). It is situated five minutes from Piazza Garibaldi off Via Corridoni – suitably enough in an underground air-raid shelter. The mock-up mine has 700m of galleries, and a chronological display of the area's mining methods and equipment.

East of the town – Roccatederighi

Situated 15km east of Massa, **ROCCATEDERIGHI** is difficult to fit into any logical itinerary, but with transport is well worth the twenty-minute diversion. Perched on a needle of rock, the village has been literally carved from stone, and offers one of the finest **views** of the Maremma. Gird yourself for the haul up one of the impossibly steep alleys, to the rock pillars that command the area.

Practicalities

Most **buses** stop on Via Corridoni close to Piazza Garibaldi – get off when you see the campanile of the duomo. There are three or four services daily between Massa and Volterra (changing at Monterotondo) plus one to Grosseto and several to Florence and Siena. The nearest train **station** is Massa-Follónica, 19km away on the main Pisa–Rome rail line; a bus shuttle meets the incoming trains. The **tourist office** is just off Piazza Garibaldi in Via Parenti 22 (☎0566.902.756).

Despite Massa's popularity – notably with Germans – there are surprisingly few places to stay. The only central accommodation is the three-star *Il Sole*, Via della Libertà 43 (☎0566.901.971, fax 0566.901.959; ③). If that's full, there are two modern hotels on the approaches to Massa: the two-star *Duca del Mare*, Piazza Dante Aligheri 1–2 (☎0566.902.284, fax 0566.901.905; ③), and the two-star *Girifalco*, Via Massetana Nord 25 (☎ & fax 0566.902.177; ③). The nearest **campsites** are on the coast at Follónica (see below). There are plenty of wooded spots on the road north, if you fancy pitching a tent on your own; however, unofficial campers are not welcomed and may be moved on.

Piazza Garibaldi has some pleasant **bars** (particularly the one under the arches in the corner by Via Moncini), though its restaurants are geared for the tourist trade. Better **restaurant** options include the *Cris*, Via degli Albizzeschi (☎0566.903.830; closed Sat); the excellent value *Vecchio Borgo*, just behind Piazza Garibaldi at Via Parenti 12 (☎0566.903.950; closed Mon); or the nearby *Ricordi Reflessi Trattoria* (☎0566.902.644; closed Wed) at Via Parenti 19, something of a tourist trap but with good food and a strange local wine from Monte Regio. For **pizza**, served at outside tables, try the *Pizzeria Barbalu*, Piazza Matteotti 5; or the no-nonsense *pizza al taglio* at Vigolo Giambellano 14, off Via della Libertà.

Follónica to Marina di Grosseto

The popular, downmarket resort of **Follónica** marks something of a watershed on the Maremma coast. To the north, the flatlands drag up towards Cécina, but to the south lies a tract of relatively unspoilt, hilly countryside, a landscape similar to that of the Tuscan heartland. Pick of the mixed bag of small resorts along this stretch is **Castiglione della Pescaia**, beyond which lies a magnificent belt of classic Maremma pine forest.

Follónica and its gulf

FOLLÓNICA, the rail access point for Massa Maríttima, is a large and scruffy town, its untidy beach spoilt by high-rise buildings and, at the far southern end, by factory-outlet pipes. It's very much a family resort, packed out in summer; its big, colourful Friday **market** is about the only real attraction.

The **train station** is at the top of Via Matteotti, which leads straight down to the sea. If you're passing through and want an hour's sun and sea, the best part of the **beach** lies along the stands of pines to the south, before the pipes: follow the main road for about a kilometre from the centre, then strike off through the trees at the garage on the left – you'll find cars parked on the roadside.

The **tourist office** is one street back from the beach, about two hundred metres west of the central Piazza XXV Aprile, on the intersection of Viale Italia and Via Matteotti; they produce a detailed map, and offer help with accommodation.

Of the numerous **hotels** – most on or near the seafront – good choices are the two-star *Miramare*, Lungomare Italia 84/86 (☎ & fax 0566.41.521; April–Oct; ③), and *Orchidea*, Via Italia 41/43 (☎0566.40.334; ④). There are also two **campsites** along the seafront: *Campsite Tahiti*, Viale Italia 320, Pratoranieri (☎ & fax 0566.60.255; mid-May to Sept), is not as nicely situated as the *Pineta del Golfo*, at Via delle Collachie 3 (☎0566.53.369, fax 0566.844.381; open all year), which is at the southern edge of town, off the main SS322.

For **food** there are plenty of modest restaurants. If you want to splash out on the Follónica's finest gastronomic experience, head for the *Leonardo Capelli*, Piazza XXV Aprile 33 (☎0566.57.360; closed Mon).

Scarlino and Tirli

Nine kilometres east of Follónica, **SCARLINO** is invitingly situated on a steep, wooded hillside – beyond a huge, red-striped chimney that does its best to wreck the view. The village itself is medieval in an attractive if unexceptional sort of way, while the hills behind are dotted with fragments of castles and monasteries.

Farther south, and accessible by minor roads through the hills, is **TIRLI**, where – as in other local villages – they venerate the hermit St Guglielmo. He is renowned for slaying a dragon, a "rib" of which is contained in the village church. There are walks into the woods behind the village, one to the ruins of **Malavalle monastery** – scene of the slaying – and to the miraculous **spring of Sant' Anna**, a point of pilgrimage on July 24. Guglielmo's feast day is the first Sunday in May, an excuse for a *festa* which involves the saint's old drum and some so-called "miracle herbs".

Punta Ala and Le Rocchette

Unless you're feeling particularly flush, there's not a lot of point in making the detour to **PUNTA ALA**, a ritzy, purpose-built resort on the southern spur of the Gulf of Follónica (buses from Follónica and Castiglione della Pescaia). Beautifully situated below a castle-topped headland, Punta Ala is dominated by its millionaires' marina. All but a couple of the **hotels** are four-star jobs, as are the **campsites**, most of which are at Capo Civinini, north of the resort where the lane from the main road meets the coast. The cheapest place to stay is the three-star *Punta Ala,* Via del Pozzino 5 (☎0564.922.646, fax 0564.922.636; ⑨): prices drop considerably out of season. The most acclaimed restaurant is in the very pricey *Gallia Palace Hotel,* Via delle Sughere (☎0564.922.022, fax 0564.920.229; mid-May to Sept; ⑨).

The minor road marked on the TCI road map, between Punta Ala and **LE ROCCHETTE** to the south, is little more than a footpath: car access is from the main SS322. There's a handful of bars close to a good beach, whose tiny approach lane is chaotic in high summer. With transport, it could be a convenient point to camp, though the **campsites** have little free space in August. Try the 150-pitch *Rocchette* (☎ & fax 0564.941.213; May to mid-Sept), the similarly-sized *Baia delle Rocchette* (☎0564.941.092, fax 0564.941.242; April–Oct) or the 350-pitch *Santa Pomata* (☎0564.941.037, fax 0564.941.221; April–Oct).

Castiglione della Pescaia

Set among low, wooded hills that are a welcome break from the flat around Grosseto, **CASTIGLIONE DELLA PESCAIA** still affects the air of a fishing village. It does admittedly have a marina and tourist centre, but lacks Punta Ala's exclusivity, and of all the Maremma resorts, this is where you're most likely to have a good time. The bars are fun, the beach is okay, and the walled **old town** on the hill – believed to have been an Etruscan port – is a charming spot to wander, and offers great views from its castle.

The best-sited **hotels** are on the main road north, an area still blessed with stands of umbrella pines. The modern three-star *Miramare* overlooks the sea at Via Vittorio Veneto 35 (☎0564.933.524, fax 0564.933.695, *miramare@tin.it;* ③), while the two-star *Iris,* Via Moni 5 (☎0564.933.639, fax 0564.934.531; ③), is near the water at the foot of the old town. The best of the seven local **campsites** are on the road towards Grosseto – the pick of these is the *Etruria* (☎0564.933.483, fax 0564.938.247; April 25–Sept 30), about 1km south.

There are a lot of cheap **restaurants** and **pizzerie**, but for a splurge go to the *Miramare,* which is renowned for its innovative fish restaurant; expect to pay up to L75,000 per person, including wine. Also excellent but pricey is *Il Corallo,* Via Nazario Sauro 1 (☎0564.933.668; closed Tues except in summer, and Nov–Jan).

There is a **tourist office** at Piazza Garibaldi 78 (☎0564.933.678). The fish **market** at the harbour, in the morning and late afternoon, is worth checking out if you're self-catering.

South to Marina di Grosseto

The road south from Castiglione runs through a stunning woodland of **umbrella pines** (*pineta*), a small section of which is administered as a nature reserve by the World Wide Fund for Nature (entry is restricted; for details contact the Comune di Castiglione ☎0564.927.411). The rest of the woodland – about twelve square kilometres in all – is accessible on foot, and the thing to do is to leave your car on the roadside, and walk down to the superb beaches via one of the many tracks through the trees. A **bus** service between Grosseto and Castiglione stops en route if you're without transport.

Marina di Grosseto

At first glance **MARINA DI GROSSETO** looks a dreadful place, with its gridiron streets and scattering of big, brand-new houses. As Maremma resorts go, however, it's surprisingly upbeat, and the clean, broad **beach** is backed by low-key bars and restaurants. Trees shade the open-plan residential district, giving it a touch of style.

You could bus out here from Grosseto for the day, though with a car or bike you'd be better off heading to the superior beaches at Marina di Alberese (see p.281). There is at least no shortage of **accommodation** in Marina's purpose-built modern hotels, ranging from the *Tre Stelle*, Via dei Platani 15 (☎ & fax 0564.34.538, *trestelle@strservice.it*; ②), to the three-star *Lola Piccolo*, Via XXIV Maggio (☎0564.34.402, fax 0564.34.011; ⑤). For assistance in finding a room, try the small summer **tourist office** at Via Piave 10 (☎0564.34.449).

Campsites are plentiful in and around Marina; the more enticing are strung out on the main road north through the *pineta*. Most convenient is the *Rosmarina* site in Via delle Colonie 37 (☎0564.36.319, fax 0564.34.758; April–Sept), 1km north; it also has hotel accommodation (⑤). A couple of kilometres south at Principina a Mare there's a huge campsite, the *Principina* (☎0564.31.424, fax 0564.31.414; April–Oct).

Grosseto

Travelling by train, the chances are that you'll pass the provincial capital, **GROSSETO**, with no more than a glance (by and large all it deserves), but by bus or car, you'll be forced into the heart of its unappealing centre. Ringed by a factory-ridden plain, and composed mainly of characterless condominiums, this commercial metropolis was raised from the ruins of heavy bombing. Urban dreariness may explain the city's high incidence of drug addiction – apparently the highest in Italy – and maybe even its penchant for American football; the local team is the Grosseto 61'ers.

Most **trains** on the main Rome–Genoa line stop at Grosseto, where you can change for Siena, or for *locale* connections to Orbetello, Cécina (for Volterra) and Follónica (for Massa Maríttima). Timetabling often leaves about an hour or so between connections – which is about all the time you need for the **old centre**, contained within a largely intact hexagon of walls commissioned by Cosimo I, after the Florentines wrested control of the city from the Sienese.

The Town

To reach the old centre, walk up from the station to join Via Roma, a road interrupted by an over-the-top post office and bleak piazza, both monuments to Fascist architectural endeavour. The best of what survives in Grosseto is on **Piazza Dante**, where a quirky statue shows Leopoldo II protecting Mother Maremma and crushing the serpent malaria under his foot. The **duomo** was started in 1294, but there is virtually nothing left to suggest antiquity: the white and pink marble facade is a product of the nineteenth century, while the interior has suffered repeated and ill-advised modifications.

The best pieces from the duomo have been transferred to the **Museo Archeologico** at nearby Piazza Baccarini (☎0564.455.132; closed for restoration at time of writing). The second-floor **Pinacoteca** has a handful of good Sienese paintings, notably Sassetta's *Madonna of the Cherries*, and a *Madonna and Child* attributed to Simone Martini. Most of the archeological finds are from the Etruscan settlements at Vetulonia and Rusellae (see opposite), neatly arranged and well-labelled, but not likely to set the pulse racing. The **Museo Civico**, Via Mazzini 61 (Tues–Sat 9am–12.30pm & 3–7.30pm), is worth a visit, to gain an outline of the social and natural history of the entire Maremma region.

The town's only other significant work is an early Crucifix by Duccio in **San Francesco**, just north of the museum, also home to a few patches of fresco. Look out for the cloisters alongside the church (distinguished by a well called the *Pozzo della Bufala* – Well of the Buffalo).

From San Francesco you can walk round the **walls** (a trip of about forty minutes), one of the more rewarding things the place has to offer. Public gardens – some well kept, others virtually jungle – fill the spaces in the corner turrets, apart from one which retains some Florentine fortifications.

Practicalities

The city's **tourist office** is near the train station at Via Fucini 43 (Mon–Fri 9am–1pm & 2.30–5.30pm, Sat 9am–1pm & 2.30–4.30pm; ☎0564.454.510).

You'd have to be desperate to stay overnight, but in emergencies there are plenty of bottom-range **hotels**. Central options include the one-star *Appennino*, Viale Mameli 1 (☎0564.23.009, fax 0564.416.134; ②), and the *Mulinacci*, Via Mazzini 78 (☎0564.28.419, fax 0564.22.452; ④). The nearest **campsites** are at Marina di Grosseto (bus from the station).

If you have money to burn, there are several reputable **restaurants** to choose from, including the *Buca di San Lorenzo*, Via Manetti 1 (☎0564.25.142; closed Mon; L60,000–80,000), *Il Canto del Gallo*, Via Mazzini 29 (☎0564.414.589; closed Sun), and *La Locanda*, Via Vinzaglio 11 (☎0564.22.239; closed Sun). On a more earthy scale, there are many basic **pizzerie**, such as the homely *Maremma* in Via F. Calboli and the *Italiana* in Via Mazzini.

The **market** is on Thursday and draws people from all over the province. The liveliest day in Grosseto's year is August 10, when the local **festa** features a group of *butteri* leading an ox-drawn cart that bears a statue of St Lawrence.

Rusellae and Vetulonia

Etruscan enthusiasts might want to visit **Rusellae** and **Vetulonia**, two ancient sites north of Grosseto. To reach either, you really need your own transport.

Rusellae

For **RUSELLAE**, the nearer of the sites, take the SS223 Siena road for 10km and watch for the signpost to the ruins on the plateau above – DON'T take the turn for modern **Roselle** about a kilometre earlier. The track leads to a small car park, with the site about five minutes away on foot (daily 8am–dusk; L4000). One of the twelve towns of the Etruscan federation, Rusellae rose above the lake and marshy ground now occupied by Grosseto, and survived the arrival of the Romans. By the fifth century, however, it had all but been abandoned, eclipsed by the rise of Grosseto. Most of the finds are in Grosseto's museum, and all that's visible are the foundations of some buildings, scattered necropolises, and the outlines of a Roman amphitheatre. The tombs at Rusellae are perhaps more interesting than those at Vetulonia, but unfortunately are closed.

Vetulonia

Twenty kilometres north of Grosseto off the Follónica road (the SS1), **VETULONIA** is a more rewarding destination. This ancient city was another member of the Etruscan federation and survived through to the Middle Ages, though Massa Maríttima had long taken over its pivotal function. It was probably destroyed during a revolt against the Pisans in the fourteenth century: blocks from its buildings are now incorporated into the village above the ruins, which stand at the road junction for Buriano to the south.

Little of genuine Etruscan vintage remains apart from a couple of big **tombs** – the Tomba della Pietrera and the Tomba del Diavolino – though scholars claim to have unearthed an Etruscan brothel, complete with lewd graffiti apparently left by the women who staffed it. Much of the area is still being excavated (daily 8am–dusk; L4000 entrance to main site; tombs free).

Perhaps the best reason for a visit to the area, though, is the fine **restaurant** in the main square of modern Vetulonia, the *Taverna Etrusca* (☎0564.949.802; closed Thurs). It looks like an ordinary bar (the dining room is at the back through a beaded curtain), but the regional specialities – including wild boar – and the views, are superb. It also has a handful of rooms – the only **accommodation** in town if you decide to stay overnight. The pizzeria, in front of the now closed museum, does the best pizzas in the area plus delicious desserts; there's a garden and stables at the back.

Monti dell'Uccellina

Currently designated a *Parco Naturale*, the hills and coastline of the **MONTI DELL'UCCELLINA** are set to become a fully-fledged *Parco Nazionale*, recognition for an area claimed to be the last virgin coastal landscape on the Italian peninsula.

The heart of the park is a hump of hills that rises suddenly from the plain, about a dozen kilometres south of Grosseto. A breathtaking piece of countryside that combines cliffs, coastal marsh, *macchia*, forest-covered hills, pristine beaches and some of the most beautiful stands of umbrella pines in the country, it is a microcosm of all that's best in the Maremma – devoid of the bars, marinas, hotels, roads and half-finished houses that have destroyed much of the Italian littoral. Kept remote for centuries by malaria and impassable swamp, it's now preserved through the determination of its owners to keep the region sacrosanct. The result is an area that rewards the casual walker, birdwatcher, botanist, or anyone simply in search of a stretch of unspoilt sand.

The park

There is no public road access into the park – all drivers should park near the reserve headquarters in the main square at **ALBERESE**. Without a car it is difficult to get here from Grosseto. Irregular buses run from the station every day except Sunday; otherwise it's a choice between taking a taxi from the station (L30,000) or one of the two daily **trains** to the Stazione di Alberese, a four-kilometre walk from the village. Alberese's **park headquarters**, in Via del Fante (☎0564.407.098), has details of a range of guided and unguided tours – we've detailed the pick of the marked trails below.

Admission to the park (see box opposite) secures you a basic **map**, and a place on an hourly **bus** which runs 10km into the hills, drops you at Pratini (really just a field) and leaves you to your own devices. It's about a twenty-minute stroll from there to the beach. Really energetic types might walk all the way from Alberese; if you want to see the wildlife at dusk (the best time) you'll have to walk back anyway, as the last bus from Pratini departs at 5.30pm in summer. It'll usually take you back to Grosseto.

Walking in the Uccellina

Once off the bus at Pratini you've the choice of **walking** either to the beach (follow the *Strada degli Olivi*), or along one of the seven **marked trails** which crisscross within the park. Most people rush headlong for the **beach**, an idyllic curving bay backed by cliffs and wooded hills. The obvious stretch is to the left, though you can trudge the beach for miles to the right, round the huge *pineta* towards the mouth of the Ombrone, Tuscany's second longest river.

The best of the marked trails is **Trail 1** (*San Rabano*; 6km; 5hr), which starts from the drop-off point. The track climbs quickly to Uccellina's main ridge (417m), with views to the coast and to Monte Amiata in the interior, reaching the abbey of **San Rabano** after about ninety minutes. Built in the eleventh century and abandoned five hundred years later, the church is now an ivy-covered ruin, with stone carvings littering the grass. The path then drops right, returning below the ridge to the *Strada degli Olivi* through evergreen woods.

Trail 2 (*Le Torri*; 5km; 3hr) starts nearer the beach and connects some of the medieval **watchtowers** built by the Spanish, who, with the Sienese, were the only people to bother with the area, using it as a source of cork and charcoal. Taking in several coastal habitats, it offers an extraordinary view over the **umbrella pines** (*Pinus pinea*) on the sand bar and dunes below. These are the park's crowning glory and one of the most memorable natural sights in Tuscany – a vast, unique canopy of emerald green that stretches almost as far as the eye can see. It's well worth dropping down from the tower to explore the woods, where you could roam for hours, restricted only by the areas of marsh at their fringes. Many of these pines were planted (the domestic variety to be harvested for their pine nuts, the maritime ones to consolidate the dunes on the estuary).

The level **Trail 3** (*Le Grotte*; 8km; 4hr) takes in a long stretch of the woods, and the canals that divide the park, but is one of the less rewarding walks. It starts near no. 2 and its ultimate destination is a group of caves, one of which (*La Grotta della Fabbrica*) has yielded some of the oldest human remains found in Italy. The trail is quite remote, however, and does offer good chances to see wildlife.

Trail 4 (*Cala di Forno*; 12km; 6hr) is the longest, most varied, and least used of the trails, taking in hill, coast and cliff scenery, and reaching the large headland (the Cala di Forno) that dominates the bay to the south. The return takes you along the dunes and a superb stretch of beach at Portovecchio.

There are several other, shorter trails if you are just looking for a quick stroll.

Marina di Alberese

Although part of the park, its stringent entry restrictions do not apply to the **MARINA DI ALBERESE**, whose **beach** – though not as superb as that in the park proper – rates as one of the best in Tuscany. It's open all year, but there's a barrier at Spergolaia, which is closed when pressure of numbers becomes too great. Campers, caravans and trailers are excluded in theory, but in practice no one seems to take much notice. There's nowhere to stay here and camping is prohibited, though people likely do get away with it.

FLORA AND FAUNA IN THE UCCELLINA

Even if you're not looking out for it, you'd have to be extremely unlucky not to see any interesting wildlife in the protected environment of the Uccellina. An extraordinary range of species thrive here, in what is effectively a compendium of Mediterranean coastal **habitats** – wooded hills, olive groves, pastures, marshland, *pineta*, primary and secondary *macchia*, dunes, retro-dunal areas, estuary and mudflats.

The Monti dell'Uccellina (mountains of the little bird) take their name from the number of **birds** that use the hills as a stepping stone between Europe and North Africa. The **Ombrone estuary** is the key target of serious birdwatchers during the spring and autumn migratory cycles, when a varied assortment of waders, ducks, herons and egrets can be seen. Rarities like ospreys, bee-eaters, flamingoes, and even falcons and short-toed eagles, can be spotted in the rockier hinterland, and you're almost guaranteed the sight of herons wheeling away from the canals, perhaps with hoopoes, shrikes, kingfishers, and the rare, brightly coloured Knight of Italy.

Other species are most likely to be encountered towards dusk, with roe-deer prevalent in the hills, and the famous **wild boar** an often audible (if not visible) inhabitant of the scrub and pine forest. An indigenous Maremma breed, it's a smaller specimen than other Italian boar, most of which are descended from bulky, Eastern European stock. The crested **porcupine**, introduced by the Romans, is also fairly common (Italy is the only place it's found outside Africa), as are badgers and foxes; it is hoped that the increasingly rare otter will flourish here too. In the cultivated land to the north and on the flat fringes of the estuary you'll see the semi-wild **horses** for which the Maremma is famous.

Tracking down **flora** is more a job for the specialist, though the pines and cork oaks are unmissable, as are the huge banks of rosemary bushes, purple with flowers in the late summer. The dwarf pine, Italy's only indigenous pine, has its northernmost natural limit in the park, and numerous floral rarities pepper the park's dunes, *macchia* and marshes.

The World Wide Fund for Nature's main branch in Florence runs summer **work camps** in the park; for details contact WWFN, Via Canto dei Nelli 8 (☎055.230.2675). Grosseto's local birdwatching group also runs summer work camps, and provides information on the park's birds (☎0564.454.527).

The arrow-straight access road is a pleasure in itself, shaded by an avenue of pines, and flanked by hills, corrals of horses and fields of white oxen. Towards the sea it enters a dense *pineta*, and ends with a car park (L2000) laid out under the trees. Except for a mobile bar and pleasant picnic area, there's no other development. The pines come right down to the beach, and in places into the sea itself, their smooth, bleached trunks creating the feel of a tropical island. The Italians, gregarious as ever, stick to the area at the end of the road, so you don't have to walk far to find solitude. The sand is clean, the sea shallow and perfect for swimming – and it's all rounded off by beautiful views to the Argentario, Giglio and the tree-covered backdrop of the Uccellina.

At the southern tip of the Uccellina, and just outside the park's confines, **TALAMONE** is a fishing village and discreet summer resort. Save for a yacht-filled marina, most of its old charm is still, so far, intact. The Sienese – who never had a proper outlet to the sea – once planned to turn its hole-in-the-wall harbour into a port to rival Pisa, but clogging weed doomed the project to failure. (In his *Inferno*, Dante used it as a metaphor for pointless enterprise.) The town's greatest moment came in 1860, when Garibaldi and the Thousand stopped here for three days on their way to Sicily.

The town's sixteenth-century Spanish **castle** was once home to the Museo della Maremma (transferred to Grosseto's Museo Civico; see p.279), but is now closed to the public.

Three trails lead off into the hills from Talamone, making it a good base for exploring the southern edge of the park. There are three **hotels** here: the central *Telamonio*, Piazza Garibaldi (☎0564.887.008, fax 0564.887.380; closed Oct–March; ⑦), room with breakfast included; the *Capo d'Uomo*, Via Cala di Forno 7 (☎0564.887.077, fax 0564.887.298; closed Nov–March; ⑤), with sea views; and the *Baia di Talamone*, Via della Marina 8 (☎0564.887.310, fax 0564.887.389; closed Nov–Jan; ⑥). There's also a **campsite**, the *Talamone International Camping* (☎0564.887.026, fax 0564.887.170; April–Sept). Among the **restaurants**, try the central *La Buca di Nonno Ghigo*, Via Garibaldi (☎0564.887.067; closed Mon), which is small, rustic and pricey, or the *Da Flavia*, Piazza IV Novembre (☎0564.887.091; closed Tues), known for its fish and seafood.

Scansano and Magliano

The settlements of **Magliano** and **Scansano** offer one of the Maremma's few reward-ing inland diversions. If you're spending any time in the region, Scansano is worth con-sidering as an alternative base to Grosseto, and even if you're just passing through, the enclosing walls of Magliano are a sight not to be missed. The landscape here is more inviting than most of the coast, with vineyards and woods of sweet chestnut reminiscent of Chianti – as well as excellent vistas of the Uccellina.

Both villages are somewhat off the beaten track: just four buses a day run to them from Grosseto, plus a couple from Orbetello on school days. A car is thus a distinct advantage, allowing you to combine the two in a cross-country route from the coast or Grosseto to Monte Amiata, via Roccalbegna.

Scansano

Twenty-five kilometres southeast of Grosseto (on the SS322), **SCANSANO** is a cramped little hill-village with fine clear views to the ridges of the Uccellina. It is sited 500m above sea level, on a spur that pushes into an impressive wooded gorge; the end of the spur is capped in picturesque style by the bulk of the parish church. The main road climbs into the **Piazza Garibaldi**, occupied by a stern statue of the eponymous hero, several tiny **trattorie** and the one-star **hotel**, *La Posta*, Piazza Garibaldi (☎0564.507.189; ①).

There's quieter but more upmarket accommodation in the **old town**, entered through the arch off Piazza Garibaldi, and little more than a single street that runs the length of the spur. The mid-price option here is the two-star *Magini*, Via XX Settembre 64 (☎0564.507.181, fax 0564.507.893; ③). Alternatively, 3km out of town at Castagneta, on the SS322 to Manciano, there's the *Antico Casale* (☎0564.507.219, fax 0564.507.805; ⑦) which also has a **restaurant** with a good reputation. The **tourist office** (summer only) is on Via XX Settembre.

The Scansano area produces a fine DOC wine, **Morellino di Scansano**, which, like the better-known Brunello di Montalcino, is made entirely from Sangiovese grapes. It's noted by experts as one of the Tuscan wines to watch, and should be on offer in all the local restaurants.

Magliano in Toscana

South of Scansano the road passes through the hamlet of Pereta – where a single huge tower crowns a fortified *borgo* and a couple of streets – before reaching **MAGLIANO IN TOSCANA**, descendant of the Etruscan town of Heba. The place today is essentially a village, its most remarkable feature an almost completely intact circle of **walls**; those on the south side dating from the thirteenth century, the rest a fifteenth-century legacy of the Sienese. The bastions are so impressive from a distance that they draw you towards the town, through the ugly estate that suddenly appears round a bend in the road. Close up, the village itself is a strange crumbling mixture of old and new, with concrete hous-es squeezed in alongside medieval dwellings.

The main **church**, in Corso Garibaldi, is a Baroque mess, but retains some well-preserved frescoes from the original building. Close by are the tiny Piazza del Popolo and the abandoned **Palazzo dei Priori**, built by the Sienese. The ghost-town atmosphere doesn't invite further exploration, but you should carry on to the end of the main street, where an arch in the walls frames a view over classic Tuscan countryside.

A short hike away are the ruins of **San Bruzio**, 2km south of the village on the road to Marsiliana. A single, bleached white stump of a tower is all that remains of this twelfth-century abbey, but it's a pleasant place, set in a large olive grove. Local legend suggests it was built on the site of a pagan temple and, more salaciously, that it was connected by a tunnel to the now-vanished nunnery of Sant'Anna.

There's a single one-star **hotel** in Magliano, *I Butteri*, Via Provinciale 8 (☎0564.589.824; ②), and a good little **restaurant-pizzeria**, the *Sandra*, Corso Garibaldi 20 (closed Mon). For more upmarket cuisine, try the *Antica Aurora*, Chiasso Lavagnini 12–14 (☎0564.592.030; closed Wed), or *Ristorante Da Guido*, Via Roma, 18 (☎0564.592.447; closed Tues).

Orbetello and its lagoon

ORBETELLO is principally distinguished by its strange location on a narrow isthmus in the middle of the **Laguna di Orbetello**. Little in the place excites real attention, but it has become something of a resort, thanks to its being the gateway to the dramatic rocky outcrop of **Monte Argentario**. On summer weekends, it becomes a bottleneck, as cars full of tourists pile in to Porto Ercole and Porto San Stefano, the Argentario's supposedly chic resorts. As well as seafront attractions, the Orbetello area offers much to naturalists, its lagoon boasting a **nature reserve** known as the Italian birdwatchers' El Dorado.

The **train station** is 4km away at Orbetello Scalo, on the mainland edge of the lagoon, a prominent stop for trains on the Rome–Pisa line. There are connections for Siena and slow trains to smaller stations to the north and south. Connecting buses run from the station to the **bus terminal** just off Piazza della Repubblica; from here there are regular services to Grosseto, Porto Ercole and Porto San Stefano, as well as daily buses to Capálbio and Pitigliano.

The Town

Orbetello is an unassuming and pleasant place, graced with palm trees, the pastel-coloured remnants of Spanish walls, and a main street – the Corso Italia – thronged each evening with a particularly vigorous *passeggiata*. It was probably Etruria's leading port, though little evidence of its ancient past remains except for a few blocks of Etruscan wall underwater near the causeway. The Byzantines took advantage of its easily defended position, holding out longer here than anywhere else on the Tyrrhenian coast. Thereafter the papacy gained control, and did not relinquish it until 1559, when the Spanish established a military *Presidio* with Orbetello as its capital. The town's last claim to fame was as the headquarters of Mussolini's seaplane squadrons; the surviving **aircraft hangar** is one of Tuscany's more bizarre architectural attractions.

The **Spanish fortifications** are the town's conspicuous feature, and a fine example of military architecture. The elegant arsenal, the **Polveriera de Guzman**, houses a small archeological museum. Nearby, the **duomo** in Piazza della Repubblica appears promising with its lovely Gothic facade, only to disappoint with a grim Baroque interior. Orbetello's lively **street market** is held on Saturdays.

The nature reserve

Orbetello's **lagoon** was formed when Monte Argentario became joined to the mainland by two narrow sand spits (or *tomboli*): one to the north – Tombolo di Giannella – and one to the south – Tombolo di Feniglia. In the lagoon's northernmost corner, near the hamlet of Albinia, the World Wide Fund for Nature has established an eight-square-kilometre **nature reserve** (guided tours Sept–April Sun & Thurs at 10am & 2.30pm; L10,000, WWFN members free; ☎0564.820.297). The entrance to the reserve is off the main road 2km east of Albinia, marked by a small panda sign; the warden can be contacted at the building at the end of the track.

The reserve, and the lagoon in general, offer exceptional **birdwatching**, with confirmed sightings of 200 of Italy's estimated 450 species. Even rare species are frequently sighted, and many of them are known to breed in the area. Notable are the stone curlew, osprey, black-winged stilt, bee-eater, Montagu's harrier, and – most importantly – the Knight of Italy, otherwise known to breed only in Sardinia and the Po delta. Little egrets, terns, storks and herons arrive in large numbers, glossy ibis and cranes are regular visitors, and it's not unknown for flamingoes to stay for the summer.

One reason for the variety is the relative lack of avian refuge on Italy's west coast. Another is the lagoon's modest depth (one-metre), which means an accessible mulch of fish and assorted food; there's also a variety of marsh, *macchia*, dune and reed habitats for nest-building. Evening is the best time around the lagoon: not only is the wildlife most visible then, but the **sunsets** over the water and the mountains of the Argentario are fabulous.

The tomboli

It's possible to see wildlife from almost any point on the lagoon, and if time is tight, exploring the southern *tombolo* is a good substitute for a tour of the reserve – the campsites and driveable road detract from the appeal of the northern Tombolo di Giannella. The **Tombolo di Feniglia** has one of Italy's most beautiful *pinete*, a long sandy dune covered in parasol pines, and is protected by a small nature reserve where roe deer can often be seen. The road along it is off-limits for cars, though you can walk its whole course, dropping down to the lagoon side for great views, or to the other side for a fine beach. You could continue this walk to the **Lago di Burano** (see p.289), if you carry on through Ansedonia, and then along the beach south for about an hour.

Practicalities

The Orbetello **tourist office** (Mon–Sat 9am–noon & 5–7pm; ☎0564.861.226) in Piazza della Repubblica is a useful source of information on the *tomboli*, and also on **accommodation** in Orbetello and the mainland hamlets of Albinia and Ansedonia (both served by local buses).

Orbetello is the nicest option, and has two one-star **hotels**, *La Perla*, Via Volontari del Sangue 10 (☎0564.863.546, fax 0564.865.210; ③); and the *Piccolo Parigi*, Corso Italia 159 (☎0564.867.233, fax 0564.867.211; ②). The town's best budget **restaurant** is the *Pizzeria Gennaro* in Corso Italia (closed Mon). For something ritzier – though they do pizzas too – try *La Goletta* in Via del Pino, towards the Tombolo di Giannella (☎0564.820.034; closed Wed).

Most of the area's fourteen **campsites** are on and around the lagoon and along the main SS1 Via Aurelia. The most attractive is the all-year *Feniglia* (☎0564.831.090, fax 0564.867.175), the only site on the Tombolo di Feniglia. Two more are to be found out on the Tombolo di Giannella: the three-star *Il Veliero* (☎0564.820.201, fax 0564.821.198; April 15–Sept 15) is a vast site; the *Comunale Giannella* (☎ & fax 0564.820.049; March–Dec) is perhaps the better, if tattier choice. Albinia also has a couple of sites, and there are four more within 6km, on the SS1 to the west. *Campo Regio* (☎0564.870.163, fax 0564.871.572), 4km west, is the only one of these open all year.

Monte Argentario

The high, rocky terrain of **Monte Argentario** is as close to wilderness as southern Tuscany comes. The interior is mountainous, reaching 635m at its highest point – **Il Telegrafo** – and the coast is sectioned dramatically into headlands, bays and shingle beaches. Away from the villas of rich Romans, much of the area is still uninhabited scrub and woodland, badly prone to forest fires but still superb **walking** country. The main centres of **Porto Santo Stefano** and **Porto Ercole** once had a reputation for exclusivity, but these days they're too well known to pander solely to the top end of the market. Prices are manageable, as are the crowds, though you'll probably need to book ahead for peak periods.

With your own transport you might follow the touted **scenic drive** (*gita panoramica*) around the entire island, a tortuous trip of about 24km, not all of it on paved roads; you will need a four-wheel drive for the stretch near Porto Ercole which is otherwise impassable. There is a **car-rental** outlet in Porto Santo Stefano – Fanciulli, Via Campone 96 (☎0564.817.291).

Porto Santo Stefano

PORTO SANTO STEFANO is the more developed of the Argentario resorts, and also the more fashionable – which in Italy is a lot worse than just being popular. Something of the charm which first brought people here still shines through, however, despite the hotels and villas that have all but obliterated the original village. A few fishing boats still cluster in the town's smaller harbour, having relinquished the main port to the marina and its mega-yachts.

If you're on a budget, you'll probably stay only as long as it takes to get a **ferry** to the island of Giglio (see opposite). Information and sailing times are available from the quayside TO.RE.MAR office (☎0564.810.803), or the neighbouring Maregiglio (☎0564.812.920), or the **tourist office** at Corso Umberto 55a (daily: summer 8am–2pm & 4–6.30pm; winter 8am–2pm). Boats make the one-hour trip three times daily year-round, five times daily in summer (one-way tickets L10,000 for foot passengers, L50,000–75,000 for cars). **Buses** run to the port from the train station at Orbetello Scalo, so you can avoid almost any contact with the place at all.

Affordable **accommodation** does exist, though mainly in private rooms, for which the tourist office supplies lists. You'll need to book well ahead to secure a place at either of the town's cheaper **hotels**: the central *Da Alfiero*, Via Cuniberti 14 (☎0564.814.067, fax 0564.813.094; ④), and less convenient *Week End*, Via Martiri d'Ungheria 3 (☎ & fax 0564.812.580; ③). If money is no object, try Porto Santo Stefano's finest, the three-star *Belvedere* (☎0564.812.634; ⑤), near the beaches at Poggio Calvella, a short way west. The nearest campsites are those listed in the Orbetello entry, on previous page.

Restaurants are generally swanky and overpriced; back-street *pizzerie* and bar snacks are the best options. If you're going for a blowout, *Da Siro*, Corso Umberto I 102 (☎0564.812.538; closed Mon & Nov), has quite a reputation. *La Bussola*, Piazzale Facchinetti (☎0564.814.225; closed Mon) is good for fish, or try *La Formica*, one of the more popular and reasonable fish restaurants, at Pozzerella, 1500m east of the village (☎0564.814.205).

Porto Ercole

PORTO ERCOLE is more intimate than Santo Stefano, with an attractive old quarter and a fishing-village atmosphere. Though founded by the Romans, its chief historical monuments are two **Spanish fortresses** facing each other on opposing sides of the harbour, and a third one above the new town. At the entrance to the old town, a plaque on the stone gate commemorates the painter **Caravaggio**, who in 1610 keeled over with sunstroke on a beach nearby (taken to a local tavern, he soon died of a fever, and was buried in the parish church of Sant'Erasmo).

A couple of good **walks** suggest themselves from the village, the most obvious being along the Tombolo di Feniglia (see p.285). The other is to the top of **Il Telegrafo**, accessible either by road and track from the ridge that runs up from the lighthouse to the south, or on a rough road that leaves the port to the north and then runs west under the main ridge. The way is fairly open, and superb views make the haul worthwhile.

Reasonably priced **hotels** in Porto Ercole are limited to the one-star *Conchiglia* in Via della Marina (☎0564.833.134; ③), and the *Albergo-Gelateria Stella Marina* in Lungomare A. Doria (☎0564.833.055, fax 0564.836.057; ⑤). For information about **rooms**, ask in *Bar Centrale*, on the main road opposite the bus stop. The nearest **campsite** is on the Tombolo di Feniglia (see p.285). For a **meal**, try the excellent *La Lampara*, Lungomare A. Doria 67 (☎0564.833.024), which serves Neapolitan specialities, pizza included.

The island of Giglio

The largest of the Tuscan islands after Elba, **GIGLIO** is visited by an ever-increasing number of foreign tourists and is so popular with Romans that in high season there's standing room only on the boats. Yet it's well worth making the effort to stay on this fabulous island. The rush is fairly short-lived, most visitors are day-trippers, and few of them explore the tracks across the unspoilt interior, a mix of barren rock and reforested upland. The island is rich in **fauna** such as peregrine falcons, mouflon, kestrels and buzzards, and in **wild flowers** too – this is the only place outside North Africa to shelter wild mustard, and the sole spot in Tuscany to support the yellow flowers of artemisia.

The island derives its name not from *giglio* (lily), but from the Roman colony **Aegilium**, in its day a resort for the rich and famous, a function it continued to fulfil throughout most of the Middle Ages. Granite quarries kept the economy buoyant, and Giglio stone was used to construct many medieval churches. Later, pirate incursions took the edge off its appeal, despite the miraculous defensive power of St Mamiliano's right arm, a relic hacked from a sixth-century Sicilian bishop exiled on the island of Montecristo. The limb proved effective when waved at Tunisian pirates in 1799, but less so on other occasions – notably in 1534, when Barbarossa carried off most of the island's population.

Transport
There are five **ferry** connections daily in summer from Porto Santo Stefano to **Giglio Porto** (see below); the rest of the year daily sailings drop to three. (Porto Santo Stefano is also the embarkation point for the tiny island of **Giannutri**, dealt with at the end of this section.)

From Giglio Porto there's an excellent **bus** service to Giglio's two main villages, **Giglio Castello** and **Campese** (L2000). It's best not to come by car – it's expensive at any time of the year, and in summer you need a permit to bring a car onto the island.

Around the island

Small, rock-girdled **GIGLIO PORTO** is the place you're most likely to stay on Giglio, as it boasts eight of the island's twelve hotels. It has no particular sights, but the scene is wonderful, with pale-coloured houses offset by a backdrop of terraced vineyards. As much of the land around rises sheer from the sea, the **beaches** are modest: you'll find one to the north of the port at Punta Aranella, and a couple to the south at Cala delle Canelle and Cala delle Caldane. The port's big day is August 10, when locals vie with one another to retrieve a flag tied to the end of a greasy pole over the harbour (the *Cuccagna a Mare*). Further frolics ensue later in the day during the *Palio Marinaro*, a competition at sea between the port's three districts.

There's a **tourist office** opposite the ferry ramp at Via Umberto I 48, which can provide details of accommodation options – including a fair number of houses around the port which have **rooms to let** (most also place advertisements in their windows). The **hotels** generally offer only full board in high season, and most are open only from June to September. If you can spare the amount for full board, the one to go for is the three-star *Pardini's Hermitage Hotel* in the Cala degli Alberi cove, accessible by boat or on foot (**☎**0564.809.034; ⑦); it has just ten rooms, so book ahead – for boat access, enquire at the Giglio Sub shop in the port. A more modest choice is *La Pergola,* in the port's Via Thaon de Revel (**☎**0564.809.051; ④), or the two-star *Da Ruggero*, in Via del Saraceno 86 (**☎**0564.809.121; ④).

Giglio Castello

GIGLIO CASTELLO, hidden away in the hills, just under six hairpin kilometres from the port, was for a long time the island's only settlement and the sole spot safe from pirate attack. Surprisingly well preserved, its maze of arches and medieval alleyways is still surrounded by thick walls. Buses from the port stop near a vine-covered patio **bar** in the large main square, also the entrance to the granite fortress and medieval quarter.

Begun by the Pisans, the **castle** was completed by the Grand Duchy of Tuscany; rough paths around the walls enable you to clamber over the rocks for superb views over the island and ruins far below. For a look at St Mamiliano's miraculous arm, check out the Baroque **church**; to explore Giglio's interior, take the road that runs south from the village towards the island's main ridge.

Accommodation is limited to private rooms; *Affittacamere Mario Landini*, Via Contrada Santa Maria, is one possibility (**☎**0564.806.074; ③). *Da Maria* in Via Casamatta is the island's best **restaurant** (**☎**0564.806.062), though the seafood doesn't come cheap. In summer an open-air **disco** opens up near the square.

Giglio Campese

Sited at the western end of the island road, **GIGLIO CAMPESE** is a growing resort. It has Giglio's best **beach** – a fine stretch of sand, overlooked by a Medici tower and curving for two kilometres from a huge phallic rock which the tourist brochures are too modest to photograph. Around the base of the tower is a modern, turreted apartment complex with a couple of restaurants, tennis courts and all manner of water-sports facilities – including diving gear for hire and lessons in how to use it.

The resort has four **hotels**, cheapest of which is *La Lampara*, Via Provinciale 66 (**☎**0564.804.022; ④). Better value is the *Giardino delle Palme*, Via della Torre (**☎** & fax 0564.804.037; ④), for its garden and tennis facilities. Otherwise try the *Da Giovanni*, Via di Mezzo Franco 10 (**☎**0564.804.010; June–Sept; ⑤); while top of the range with private beach is the three-star *Campese*, Via della Torre 18 (**☎**0564.804.003, fax 0564.804.093; ⑤). There's also a **campsite**, the *Baia del Sole* (**☎**0564.804.036, fax 0564.804.101; May–Sept).

Giannutri

The southernmost Tuscan island, **GIANNUTRI**, is privately owned, and overnight stays are impossible unless you're a friend of the inhabitants. The few people who come over for the day do so to visit the ruins of a **Roman villa** at Cala Maestra. The island policeman asks travellers to remove backpacks before stepping ashore, and checks for tents and drugs.

Given this sort of attitude, and the island's physical make-up – flat, dull and walkable end-to-end in two hours – it's a place for island obsessives only. If you're curious, the tiny **boat** *M/S Gabbiano II* leaves Porto Santo Stefano daily from May 1 to September 15 at 10am, returning at 5pm; out of season it runs only Wednesday, Saturday and Sunday (☎0564.812.920).

South from Orbetello

South of Orbetello most of the terrain is a drab foretaste of the expanses of Lazio, but there are several worthwhile diversions if you're headed this way. At **Ansedonia** you can inspect one of Tuscany's few ancient Roman sites, before moving on to the important **nature reserve** at **Lago di Burano**. Inland **Capálbio** rates as one of the area's loveliest villages, while near **Chiarone**, which has fine beaches, there's the **Giardino dei Tarocchi**, a series of monumental sculptures that's quickly becoming both a tourist attraction and artistic talking point.

Ansedonia and Lago di Burano

ANSEDONIA crouches under a rocky crag at the end of the Tombolo di Feniglia. Peppered with holiday villas, it has a long beach and, on the hill-top above the village, the remains of **Cosa**, founded by the Romans in 273 BC as a frontier post against the Etruscans. It was one of their most important commercial centres in the area until its population – according to the historian Rutilius – was driven out by an army of mice. Most of the old *municipium* was devastated by the Visigoths in the fourth century, and what survived was sacked by the Sienese in 1330. Recent excavations have exposed enough of the Roman colony to suggest some idea of its former layout.

To reach **the site**, leave Ansedonia on the road east, passing a couple of medieval towers (converted into houses) and the so-called **Tagliata Etrusca**, a none-too-exciting series of cuts into the rock, believed to have been part of a system to drain the marshland. After about a kilometre, where the road bends sharp right, there's a signed track to Cosa off to the left. You'll find a ring of **walls** eight metres high in places, the remains of a defensive cordon of eighteen towers. There's also the outline of the gridiron **street plan**, a **forum** (with basilica and senate discernible nearby), two **temples** and some recently uncovered **mosaics** and **wall paintings**. It's worth climbing to the top of the hill, not only to see the remains of the **acropolis**, but also for fine views across to Giannutri and Monte Argentario.

If you need a local place to stay, there's a **hotel** near the Tagliata, the two-star *Vinicio*, Via delle Mimose 86 (☎0564.881.220, fax 0564.881.604; ③). The best of Ansedonia's **restaurants** is the quiet *Il Pescatore*, Via della Tagliata (☎0564.881.201; closed Tues).

Lago di Burano

You can walk to the **Lago di Burano** along the beach from Ansedonia, or catch a slow train from Orbetello to Capálbio Scalo, less than 100m from the water. Technically a lagoon rather than a lake, Burano is a placid stretch of water, shielded from the sea by vegetation-covered dunes. Completing the scenic picture – which is captivating at dusk with the sun behind Monte Argentario – is a superb and mysterious-looking tower, the **Torre di Burinaccio**.

Though you can just walk onto the enclosing beach, access to the lagoon itself is restricted, as the WWFN runs Burano as a **nature reserve**. Recognized as a wetland habitat of international significance, this and the Orbetello lagoon are together rated as the most important area for **birds** on Italy's west coast. The lagoon shares many of the species found in Orbetello, and for similar reasons (the lagoon here is also only a metre deep). Notable species include the bluethroat, great spotted cuckoo, great white heron and velvet scoter.

The entrance to the reserve is on the perimeter road 500m east of the station. Warden Fabio Cianchi conducts visits (☎0564.898.829; Sept–April Thurs & Sun 10am & 2.30pm; L10,000, WWFN members free), picking out observation points and explaining the **nature trail** that takes in the dune, woodland and scrub habitats around the lake. With prior arrangement, it's possible to stay overnight in the twelve-bed forestry hut on site. **Camping** nearby is prohibited, but the **beach** here stretches for miles and is perfect for pitching a tent on the quiet. The *Agrialbergo Capalbio*, Strada della Sugherella 3 (☎ & fax 0564.898.763; ③), a one-star **hotel**, is near the Capálbio Scalo train station.

Chiarone, the Tarot Garden and Capálbio

CHIARONE is nothing more than a station and a couple of bars, though its **beaches** – fifteen minutes' walk away – are some of the best and quietest on this part of the coast. The virgin coastal stretch is commonly regarded as enjoying the first unpolluted water north of Rome. Fifteen kilometres of unbroken sand stretch away towards Monte Argentario, with plenty of opportunities for **camping** in the dunes. Things get grubby on-shore as the summer wears on, but the gentle, shelving seabed makes for good swimming, and all it takes for solitude on the sand is a few minutes' walk.

A handful of **trains** to and from Grosseto stop at Chiarone station. There's one **hotel**, *La Palma*, Via Stazione 5 (☎ & fax 0564.890.341; ⑤), and a beach **bar** and **campsite** – the *Chiarone* (☎0564.890.101, fax 0564.898.351; May–Sept) – at the end of the road to the dunes.

Il Giardino dei Tarocchi

By car from Chiarone it's possible to visit one of Italy's oddest and increasingly well-known works of modern art: **Il Giardino dei Tarocchi** (The Tarot Garden), a huge set of sculptures by Niki di Saint Phalle, most famous for the *Fontaine Stravinsky*, created with her then husband Jean Tinguely outside the Pompidou Centre in Paris. The brightly coloured pieces are clearly visible from the Via Aurelia: to reach them it's a five-kilometre drive on the road from Chiarone to Pescia Fiorentina.

Using land donated by friends, the work has been more than ten years in the making, and is still some way from completion (summer Mon–Fri 2.30–7.30pm; winter first Sat of month 9am–1pm; L20,000). Nonetheless it's already a staggering sight – a whimsical mix of Gaudí, arcane symbolism and sheer fun that children love, and which inspires bewildered admiration in adults. The bigger pieces will each represent one of the Tarot's twenty-two major arcana. Amongst those already finished are **The Tower** – three storeys of glittering broken mirrors – and **The Goddess**, a sphinx-like creation with the head of Queen Victoria, in which the artist lives. Plants and fountains form an integral part of the scheme.

Capálbio

Stranded in empty country, the hill-village of **CAPÁLBIO** is virtually unknown to outsiders, though not to Rome's cultural and political elite, many of whom have homes in the locality. Most are attracted by the almost perfectly medieval interior, which at night is a deathly quiet maze of streets straight out of the Middle Ages. Views are superb, and though there's little to see apart from a few frescoes and the Aldobrandeschi fortifications, it definitely warrants a look if you're touring by car.

(There are also two **buses** daily from Orbetello). There are several **restaurants** to choose from, including the superb *Trattoria la Torre da Carla*, Via V. Emmanuele 33 (☎0564.896.070; closed Thurs), in the heart of the old town. There are two **hotels**: the two-star *La Mimosa*, Via Torino (☎ & fax 0564.890.220; ③), several kilometres out of Capálbio towards the Via Aurelia, and the central but rather more pricey *Valle del Buttero*, Via Silone 21 (☎0564.896.097, fax 564.896.518; ⑤).

travel details

TRAINS

Grosseto to: Orbetello (10 daily; 30min), going on to Tarquinia (50min), Civitavecchia (1hr 5min) and Rome (1hr 30min); Piombino, changing at Campiglia Maríttima (10 daily; 20min); Follónica (13 daily; 35min); San Vincenzo (10 daily; 45min); Cécina (10 daily; 1hr); Livorno (21 daily; 1hr 15min), going on to Pisa (1hr 40min; connections for Lucca, Pistoia, Prato and Florence); Siena (6 daily; 1hr 20min); Florence (7 daily via Siena and Buonconvento; 3–4hr depending on train).

Orbetello to: Tarquinia (10 daily; 35min), going on to Civitavecchia (35min) and Rome (1hr); Grosseto (14 daily; 30min); Piombino, changing at Campiglia Maríttima (10 daily; 50min); Follónica (8 daily; 30min); San Vincenzo (4 daily; 50min); Cécina (7 daily; 1hr 10min); Livorno (8 daily; 1hr 45min), going on to Pisa (8 daily; 2hr); Siena (3 daily; 1hr 50min); Florence (3 daily direct; 2hr 50min).

BUSES

Massa Maríttima to: Follónica (every 45min; 10min); Piombino (2 daily; 25min); Siena (2 daily; 1hr 40min); San Galgano (2 daily; 1hr).

Grosseto: frequent buses to all main towns in Grosseto province, especially Castiglione della Pescaia (via Marina di Grosseto), Orbetello, Alberese (for the Monti dell'Uccellina), Magliano in Toscana and Scansano. Also frequent services to Arcidosso, Pitigliano and villages en route. Less frequent connections to Siena and Rome.

Orbetello to: Porto Santo Stefano, Porto Ercole, Grosseto, Capálbio and Pitigliano and villages en route.

FERRIES

Porto Santo Stefano to: Giglio Porto (5 daily in summer, 3 for rest of year); Giannutri (1 daily in summer, 3 weekly for rest of year).

CHAPTER SIX

SIENA

SIENA is the perfect counterpoint to Florence. Self-contained and still partly rural behind its medieval walls, its attraction lies in its cityscape: a majestic Gothic whole that could be enjoyed without venturing into a single museum. In its great scallop-shaped piazza, **Il Campo**, it has the loveliest of all Italian public squares; in its zebra-striped **duomo**, a religious focus to match; and the city's whole construction, on three ridges, presents a succession of beautiful vistas over medieval cityscapes to the bucolic Tuscan countryside on all sides. It is also a place of immediate charm: airy, easy-going and pedestrianized – where Florence is cramped, busy and traffic-ridden – and it is startlingly untouristed away from the few centres of day-trip sightseeing. Perhaps most important of all, the city is host to the undisputed giant of Italian festivals, the **Palio**, a bareback horse race around the Campo, whose sheer excitement and unique importance to the life of the community is reason enough to plan your holiday around one of the two race dates – July 2 and August 16.

The contrasts with Florence are extended in Siena's **monumental** and **artistic** highlights. The city's duomo and **Palazzo Pubblico** are two of the purest buildings of Italian Gothic, and the finest of the city's paintings – of which many are collected in the Palazzo's **Museo Civico** and the separate **Pinacoteca Nazionale** – are in the same tradition. Other outstanding Sienese painting remained stamped with Byzantine, Romanesque and Gothic influences long after classical humanism had transformed Florence. It is a style characterized by brilliance of colour and decorative detail and an almost exclusive devotion to religious subjects – principally the city's patroness, the Virgin. Its traditions were shaped by a group of artists working in the last half of the thirteenth century and the first half of the fourteenth: **Duccio di Buoninsegna**, **Simone Martini** and the brothers **Ambrogio and Pietro Lorenzetti**. Arguably the greatest of all Siena's paintings belongs to the first of these, a magnificent *Maestà* housed in another of Siena's outstanding galleries, the **Museo dell'Opera del Duomo**. Another supreme work, the fresco cycle of Domenico di Bartolo, an artist working on the cusp of the Renaissance, fills part of the **Ospedale di Santa Maria della Scala**, the city's hospital for some 800 years, now one of the city's premier exhibition spaces.

In its **sculpture**, Siena drew mainly on foreign artists: the Florentines Donatello and Ghiberti worked on the font in the baptistery, while Michelangelo and Nicola and Giovanni Pisano left their mark on the duomo.

ACCOMMODATION PRICES

Throughout this guide, **hotel** accommodation is graded on a scale from ① to ⑨, indicating the cost of the **cheapest double room** in each establishment in high season (for **hostels**, rates per person are given in lire). The price bands to which these codes refer are as follows:

① up to L60,000	④ L120,000–150,000	⑦ L250,000–300,000
② L60,000–90,000	⑤ L150,000–200,000	⑧ L300,000–350,000
③ L90,000–120,000	⑥ L200,000–250,000	⑨ over L350,000

As a provincial capital, Siena has good transport links with some of the finest sights and countryside of Tuscany. The city makes a good base for much of the territory covered in the following two chapters, while to the north is the wine heartland of Chianti (see p.168).

History

Though myth attributes its origins to Senius and Acius, sons of Remus (hence the she-wolf emblem of the city), **Siena** was in fact founded by the Etruscans and refounded as a Roman colony – Saena Julia – by Augustus. Over the course of the next millennium it grew to be an independent republic, and in the thirteenth and fourteenth centuries was one of the major cities of Europe. It was almost the size of Paris, controlled most of southern Tuscany and its flourishing wool industry, dominated the trade routes from France to Rome, and maintained Italy's richest banks. The city also developed a highly sophisticated civic life, with its own written constitution and a quasi-democratic council – the *comune*. It was in this great period that the city was shaped, and in which most of its art and monuments are rooted.

This golden era, when the Republic of Siena controlled a great area of central and southern Tuscany, reached an apotheosis with the defeat of a much superior Florentine army at the **Battle of Montaperti** in 1260. Although the result was reversed nine years later, shifting the fulcrum of political power towards Florence, Siena's merchants and middle classes – the so-called *Popolo Grasso* – embarked on an unrivalled urban development; from 1287 to 1355, under the rule of the **Council of Nine**, the city underwrote first the completion of the **Duomo** and then the extraordinary **Campo**, with its exuberant **Palazzo Pubblico**. Sienese bankers, meanwhile, had spread their operations throughout Europe, and with Duccio, Martini and the Lorenzettis, the city was at the forefront of Italian art.

Prosperity and innovation came to an abrupt halt with the **Black Death**, which reached Siena in May 1348. By October, when the disease had run its course, the population had dropped from 100,000 to 30,000. The city was never fully to recover (the population today is around 60,000) and its politics, always factional, moved into a period of intrigue and chaos. Its art, too, became highly conservative, as patrons looked back to the old hierarchical religious images. The chief figures in these war-ridden and anarchic years were the city's two nationally renowned saints, **Caterina** (1347–80) and **Bernardino** (1380–1444), who both exercised enormous influence, amid two further outbreaks of the plague.

As the sixteenth century opened, a period of autocratic rule under the tyrannical Pandolfo Petrucci (the self-styled Il Magnifico) brought a further military victory over Florence, but ended with the city embroiled in ever-expanding intrigues involving the Borgias, the Florentines, the papacy, the French and the empire of **Charles V**. The last proved too big to handle for the Sienese; imperial troops imposed a fortress and garrison, and then, after the Sienese had turned to the French for help to expel them, the imperials laid siege to the city and the surrounding countryside. The effects of the siege (1554–55) proved more terrible even than the Black Death, with the population plummeting from 40,000 to as few as 8000. The republic was over, although a band of loyalists – comprising around 700 families – took refuge at Montalcino and prolonged it there for a while, at least in name.

Two years after the siege, Philip II, Charles's successor, gave up Siena to **Cosimo I**, Florence's Medici overlord, in payment for war services, the city subsequently becoming part of Cosimo's Grand Duchy of Tuscany. This was the death knell. For sixty years the Sienese were forbidden even to operate banks, while control of what was by now an increasingly minor provincial town reverted, under Medici patronage, to the nobles.

Siena's swift decline from republican capital to little more than a market centre explains the city's astonishing state of medieval preservation. Little was built and still

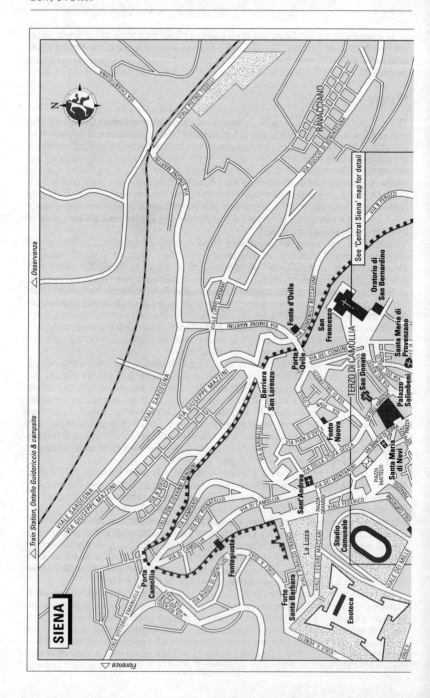

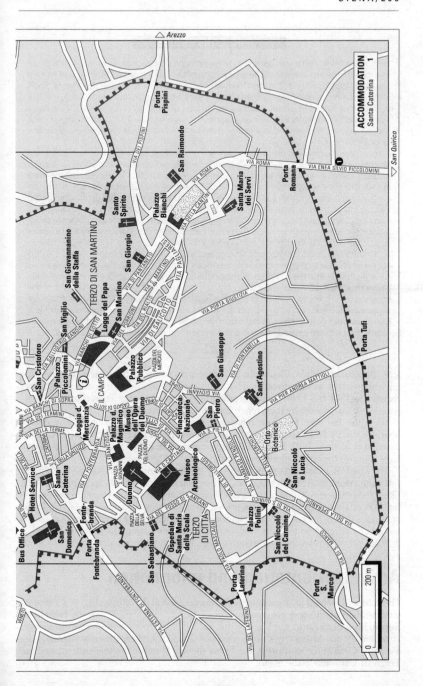

THE CONTRADE

Within the fabric of the medieval city, Siena preserves its ancient division into wards, or *contrade*. These are integral to the competition of the Palio (see pp.302–303) and sustain a unique neighbourhood identity, clearly visible as you wander around the streets. Each of the seventeen *contrade* has its own **church**, **social centre** and **museum**. Each, too, has its individual **flag** and a heraldic **animal motif**, after which most of them take their names. The animals – giraffe, snail, goose, porcupine, etc – can be seen all around the city on wall plaques and are represented in a series of modern fountains near the *contrada* churches or headquarters.

There were once social distinctions between the *contrade* and although these today are blurred to the point of extinction, **allegiance to one's contrada** – conferred by birth – remains a strong element of social life. After a conventional church baptism, anyone born in a ward division is baptized for a second time in their *contrada* fountain. Subsequently, the *contrada* plays a central role in activities: for kids, in the flag-twirling and drumming for the Palio and local *contrada* festivals, for adults in the social clubs – a mix of bar and dining club – and in the attendance of a herald at marriages and funerals. *Contrade* also dispense social assistance to needy members, and the respect accorded to the institution is said to have a significant effect on the city's social cohesion. Certainly, for a city of its size, Siena has remarkably low levels of crime and drug usage. Indeed, the only violence tolerated is during the Palio, when *contrada* members may well get into fights with their ancient rivals.

For an insight into the workings of the *contrade*, it is worth paying a visit to one of their **museums**, each of which gives pride of place to its displays of Palio trophies. All of the museums are open to visitors during the build-up to the Palio and at other times by appointment; if you're interested, ask the tourist office to phone. Each *contrada* also has its own **annual celebration**, accompanied by parades and feasts. And at almost any time of year, you will see groups practising flag-waving and drum-rolling in the streets.

---

less demolished, while allotments and vineyards occupied the spaces between the ancient quarters, as they do today. This near-pristine state also reflects its escaping war damage in 1944 and 1945 (unlike nearby Poggibonsi and other Tuscan towns); Siena was taken, unopposed, by the French Expeditionary Force on July 3, 1944.

Since the last war, however, Siena has again become prosperous, partly due to **tourism**, partly to the resurgence of the **Monte dei Paschi di Siena**. This bank, founded in Siena in 1472, is one of the major players in Italian finance and in its home base is one of the city's largest employers.

The Monte dei Paschi coexists, apparently easily enough, with one of Italy's strongest **left-wing councils**. Though this quiet, rather bourgeois provincial capital may not look like a red city, some 35,000 of the 250,000 population of Siena province are card-carrying PDS or Communist Party members – a loyalty won by the communists' role in the resistance during the last war. In Siena itself, the council perceives its major problem as too great a reliance on tourism. Building on the existing strengths of the university, it now has plans for rejuvenation through a biotechnology park and other hi-tech projects.

Arrival, orientation and information

The centre of Siena is its great square, **Il Campo**, built at the intersection of a Y-shaped configuration of hills and the convergence of the city's principal roads, the **Banchi di Sopra**, **Banchi di Sotto** and **Via di Città**. Each of these roads leads out across a ridge, straddled by one of the city's three medieval districts, or *terzi* (literally "thirds"): the **Terzo di Città** to the southwest, the **Terzo di San Martino** to the southeast, and the **Terzo di Camollia** to the north.

This central core – almost entirely medieval in plan and appearance – is initially a little disorientating, though with the Campo as a point of reference you won't go far wrong. Movement around is also made easier by the fact that the city centre has been effectively pedestrianized since the 1960s. Everywhere of use or interest in the city is within easy walking distance, with the exception of St Bernardino's monastic retreat, L'Osservanza, and the youth hostel and campsite.

Arrival

Many people head to Siena **from Florence**. There are two ways of getting here from the Tuscan capital: by SITA bus from the bus station on Via di Caterina da Siena just west of Santa Maria Novella railway station – be sure to jump on an express (journey time is a little over an hour), as some buses are excruciatingly slow; or by train from Santa Maria Novella – some services are direct, but most connections involve a change at Empoli (journey time is about 80 minutes). If you're driving, the two cities are 78km apart and linked by a fast four-line highway, which starts from the Firenze Certosa junction of the A1 autostrada 6km south of Florence – head for Porta Romana in the Oltrarno and follow signs.

Arriving in central Siena by local **bus from the station**, you are generally dropped in Piazza Matteotti; **buses from Florence** and elsewhere stop at one of a series of numbered bays along Viale Curtatone, by the church of San Domenico, from where you can see the city – dominated by the duomo and town hall bell towers – spread out below. When **departing**, note that the bus information board at the end of Viale Curtatone – which lists bus departures – may not correspond to the latest timings, though the bay numbers it directs you to for various destinations are correct. To double-check go to the TRA-IN ticket and information office for out-of-town buses in nearby Piazza San Domenico (☎0577.204.245). For information on bus services within the city, visit or call the information office in Sottopassaggio La Lizza, Piazza Gramsci (☎0577.204.246).

The **train station** (☎0577.280.115) is less convenient, sited in Piazza Fratelli Rosselli, 2km to the northeast in the valley below the city. Its main foyer has a small train **information office**, exchange facilities and a *Digiplan* machine which provides basic tourist information. Connecting buses (#15 is the most direct) shuttle between the station and Piazza Matteotti, at the top end of Viale Curtatone (other services drop in slightly different central locations). The bus stop is the one across the road outside the station, *not* the one on the station side of the forecourt. Alternatively, local **city taxis** are to be found at ranks by the train station (☎0577.44.504) and on Piazza Matteotti (☎0577.289.350), or can be called elsewhere between 7am and 9pm by phone (☎0577.49.222). Note, however, that in Siena it's virtually impossible to book taxis in advance and you should allow plenty of time for cabs to reach you through the city's labyrinthine one-way system.

Parking in Siena can be a problem. If you are **driving into the city**, follow signs to the *centro* and try to find a parking space at one of the following: around **Piazza Gramsci** or the large triangle of **La Lizza**, just north of Piazza Matteotti; opposite San Domenico in the car park **alongside the stadium**; or **off the Viale Manzoni**, which loops around the northeast wall of the city. Coming up from the south, the **area around the Porta Romana** is a good bet. Viale Manzoni is free parking; at the others a machine or an attendant issues tickets, usually by the hour: rates are reasonable. Note that you cannot park around La Lizza on **Wednesday mornings** (8am–2pm), when the market takes place; offending cars are towed away.

Information

Siena's main listed **tourist office** is at Via di Città 43 (Mon–Fri 9am–2.30pm & 3.30–7pm; ☎0577.42.209), though you'll get little joy here as it's largely an administrative office. Head instead to the office on the northeast side of Campo, at no. 56 (March 22 to mid-Nov

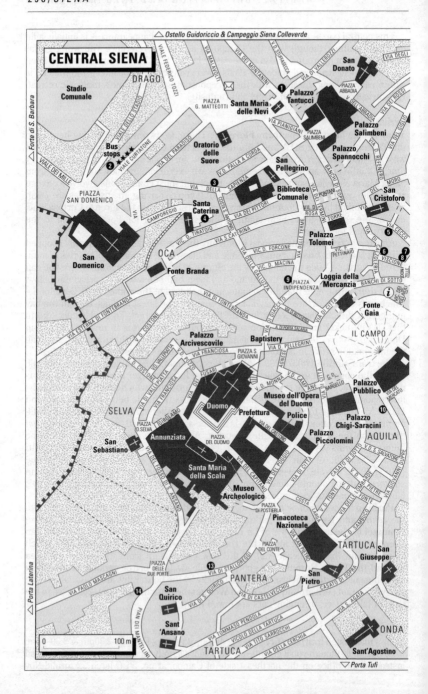

△ *Ostello Guidoriccio & Campeggio Siena Colleverde*

CENTRAL SIENA

△ Forte di S. Barbara

DRAGO

Stadio
Comunale

PIAZZA
G. MATTEOTTI

Santa Maria
delle Nevi

❶ Palazzo
Tantucci

San
Donato

PIAZZA
ABBADIA

Palazzo
Salimbeni

Palazzo
Spannocchi

Bus
stops ❷

Oratorio
delle
Suore

❸

San
Pellegrino

Biblioteca
Comunale

San
Cristoforo

PIAZZA
SAN DOMENICO

Santa
Caterina
❹

OCA

San
Domenico

Fonte Branda

Palazzo
Tolomei

❺
❻ ❼
❽

❾ PIAZZA
INDIPENDENZA

Loggia della
Mercanzia

BANCHI DI SOTTO

ℹ

Fonte
Gaia

IL CAMPO

Palazzo
Arcivescovile

Baptistery

PIAZZA S.
GIOVANNI

SELVA

Palazzo
Pubblico

Duomo

Prefettura

Museo dell'Opera
del Duomo

Police

❿

San
Sebastiano

Annunziata

PIAZZA
D.SELVA

PIAZZA
DEL DUOMO

Palazzo
Chigi-Saracini

Palazzo
Piccolomini

AQUILA

Santa Maria
della Scala

Museo
Archeologico

PIAZZA
DI POSTIERLA

Pinacoteca
Nazionale

△ Porta Laterina

PIAZZA
DELLE
DUE PORTE

❸

PANTERA

TARTUCA
San
Giuseppe

San
Pietro

❹

San
Quirico

Sant
'Ansano

TARTUCA

ONDA

Sant'Agostino

0   100 m

▽ Porta Tufi

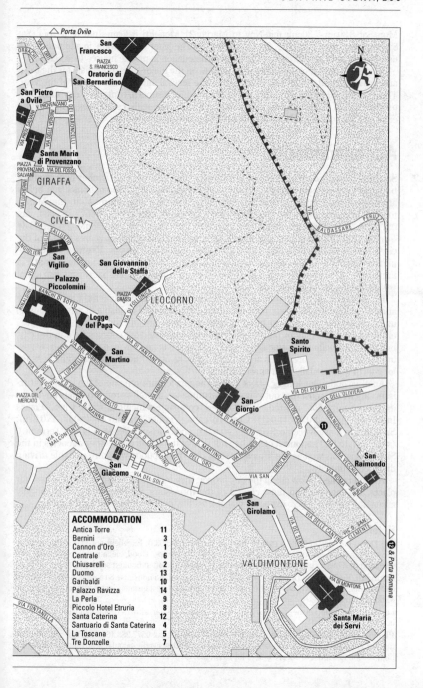

Mon–Sat 8.30am–7.30pm; mid-Nov to March 21 Mon–Fri 8.30am–1pm & 3–7pm, Sat 8.30am–1pm; ☎0577.280.551, fax 0577.270.676). The latter can provide, in addition to the usual maps, a list of addresses offering accommodation in private houses (see below).

The offices provide a wide range of leaflets on the major sites, hotel lists for the town and province, and a handy booklet listing the festival and cultural events of the year. The most useful freebie, though, is the tourist office's superb, contoured **city map**; better than any of those on commercial sale, it is complete with a street key, a map of the environs, and details of hotel locations inside and outside the city.

Accommodation

Securing a hotel room in Siena for any time between Easter and October now requires booking six months in advance. If you haven't done so, and all the options listed below are booked solid, make your way to the **Siena Hotels Promotion** booth (mid-March to Oct Mon–Sat 9am–8pm; rest of year Mon–Sat 9am–7pm; ☎0577.288.084, fax 0577.280.290; *shpnet@novamedia.it*), opposite the church of San Domenico on Viale Curtatone. The staff here are generally very helpful and will book rooms in any of the city's hotels. Alternatively, try the city's second specialist agency, **Protur**, less conveniently situated – unless you're coming in by car – on the south side of the city at Via Fontanella 4, Parcheggio Il Campo (Mon–Fri 9am–1pm & 3–7pm, Sat & Sun 9am–1pm; ☎0577.45.900, fax 0577.283.145).

For budget accommodation, call in at the **tourist office** at Piazza del Campo 56 (see above), which provides daily lists of **rooms** (*affittacamere*) available in private houses, usually totalling around two hundred places. These are offered mainly to students, either at the university or on the numerous language and art courses held in the city, but some are willing to offer shorter lets. They're certainly worth a try if you're staying for a week or more; rates are around L40,000–50,000 per person a night (less for long-term lets), usually for a shared room.

Another option for **longer stays** is to arrange a let through one of the local **agriturismo agencies**; most rent out villas and farmhouses, as well as rooms or flats on farms, in the countryside around. Siena-based companies include: Casa Club, Piazza Indipendenza 2 (☎0577.44.041); Casa Toscana, Via dei Termini 85 (☎0577.270.279); Sudcar, Via Castelvecchio 3 (☎0577.40.522); and Turismo Verde, Via dei Termini 6 (☎0577.47.157). The tourist office has full lists of the dozen or so other agencies in the Siena region, as well as the fifteen or so *agriturismo* options within reasonable driving distance of the city.

All hotels listed below are in the city proper: they include most of the one- and two-star places and the best and most central of the three-stars, and are arranged in roughly ascending order of price; expect to pay at least fifty percent more during the Palio.

Hotels

Tre Donzelle, Via Donzelle 5 (☎0577.280.358, fax 0577.223.933). Excellent one-star option right in the heart of town, just off Banchi di Sotto, north of the Campo. Good, clean rooms, some with private bath, but has a curfew of 12.30am and its 27 rooms are often booked solid. ②.

Garibaldi, Via Giovanni Dupré 18 (☎0577.284.204). A good, no-nonsense 8-room one-star (4 shared bathrooms), sited above one of the city's better low-cost restaurants, just south of the Campo. Midnight curfew. ②.

La Perla, Via delle Terme 25 (☎0577.47.144). Regular one-star with 13 rooms (all with bathroom), in a very central location, two blocks north of the Campo. Curfew 1am. ②.

Piccolo Hotel Etruria, Via Donzelle 1–3 (☎0577.288.088, fax 0577.288.461). Almost next door to the *Tre Donzelle* (see above). A very neat two-star, and deservedly popular – advance booking for high season is a must to secure one of its 13 rooms. ③.

Bernini, Via della Sapienza 15 (☎0577.289.047). Nine inexpensive but rather pokey one-star rooms, most with private bathrooms. ③.

Centrale, Via Cecco Angiolieri 26 (☎0577.280.379, fax 0577.42.152). As the name suggests – a block north of the Campo; just 7 large rooms on the third floor in a quiet street. ③.

La Toscana, Via Cecco Angiolieri 12 (☎0577.46.097, fax 0577.270.634). Big, well-priced 42-room three-star in an atmospheric and central location, on an alley behind Piazza Tolomei. Rooms with and without bathrooms, unusual in this category. ④.

Cannon d'Oro, Via Montanini 28 (☎0577.44.321, fax 0577.280.868). A stylish 30-room two-star hotel tucked down an alleyway just beyond where Banchi di Sopra becomes Via Montanini. Friendly and well maintained, this is the best choice among the central mid-price hotels. ④.

Chiusarelli, Viale Curtatone 15 (☎0577.280.562, fax 0577.271.177). A nice old three-star villa hotel with 50 rooms and a garden at the back, but it's on a busy street near the bus stops, so this is probably not a first choice for light sleepers. ④.

Antica Torre, Via Fiera Vecchia 32–40 (☎ & fax 0577.222.255). By far the nicest and most intimate of the three-stars: just 8 (smallish) rooms squeezed into a old medieval tower. Top rooms have views. Booking essential. ⑤.

Santa Caterina, Via Enea Silvio Piccolomini 7 (☎0577.221.105, fax 0577.271.087). A 19-room three-star ten minutes' walk from the Campo, on the street that leads out of town from Porta Romana. Has the advantages of air-conditioning and parking. ⑥.

Duomo, Via Stalloreggi 34 (☎0577.289.088, fax 0577.43.043). Rooms – apart from those with views of the duomo – are reliable but unexceptional, but this is the best-located of the city's three-star hotels. ⑥.

Palazzo Ravizza, Pian dei Mantellini 34 (☎0577.280.462, fax 0577.221.597). An elegant 36-room three-star hotel in a pleasant and convenient backwater of town, near San Niccolò al Carmine. Ask for a rear room as those at the front suffer from traffic noise. ⑥.

Hostels

Ostello della Gioventù "Guidoriccio", Via Fiorentina 89, Lo Stellino (☎0577.52.212, fax 0577.56.172). The hostel (111 beds) is located 2km northwest of the centre. Take bus #3, #10 or #15 from Piazza Gramsci and ask for "Ostello"; or, if you're coming from Florence, ask to be let off at "Lo Stellino", just after the Siena city sign. Dorm beds and also several double rooms, restaurant (meals L14,000) and bar. HI card required. Curfew 11pm. L23,000 includes breakfast.

Santuario di Santa Caterina, Via Camporegio 31 (☎0577.44.177). This old pilgrim hostel behind San Domenico offers single (L80,000), double (L100,000), triple (L125,000) and quad (L150,000) rooms. The only couples they'll accept are married ones. Try to get a room in the annexe on Vicolo del Tiratoio, where there's no curfew as they just give you the door key. Bookings taken only Mon–Sat 1–3pm.

Campsite

Campeggio Siena Colleverde, Strada di Scacciapensieri 47 (☎0577.280.044, fax 0577.333.298). Secure, well-maintained campsite, 2km out to the north; take bus #8 from Piazza del Sale or #3 from Piazza Gramsci. Shop, bar and swimming pool. Open late March to mid-Nov. L20,000 per person, plus L3000 extra to use the swimming pool.

The Campo

The Campo is the centre of Siena in every sense: the main streets lead into it, the Palio takes place around its perimeter, and in the evenings it is the natural place to gravitate towards, for visitors and residents alike. Four hundred years ago, Montaigne described it as the most beautiful square in the world – an assessment that still seems pretty fair.

With its amphitheatre curve, the Campo appears an almost organic piece of city planning. In fact, when the Council of Nine began buying up land in 1293, they were adopting the only possible site – the old marketplace, which lay at the convergence of the city quarters but was a part of none (the old Roman forum probably also occupied the site). To build on it, it was necessary to construct an enormous buttress beneath

THE SIENA PALIO

"The Palio helps Siena to survive in its own mind. It is a metaphor for the continuity of the life of the people.."

Roberto Barzanti, former Siena MEP and mayor.

The **Siena Palio** is the most exciting and spectacular festival event in Italy, a twice-yearly bareback horse race around the Campo, supported by days of preparation, pageantry and intrigue. It has been held since at least the thirteenth century, in honour – like almost everything in Siena – of the Virgin, and it remains a living tradition, felt and performed with an intensity that comes as a shock in these days of cosily preserved folklore. For days around the festivals the air of rivalry is palpable, quite often breaking into violence amid the bragging celebration of victory by one or other of the *contrade*.

Except at times of war, the Palio has virtually always taken place. In 1798, for example, when the city was in chaos after an earthquake, the July Palio was cancelled but the August race took place. The following year, however, the Palio was again cancelled, due to political unrest: Sienese counter-revolutionaries took the opportunity to rise against the French-held fortress and sacked the ghetto area of the city. In 1919, when half of Italy was in the throes of strikes and rioting, Siena's factions of the left and right agreed to defer such politics until after the Palio.

THE RACE
Originally the Palio followed a circuit through the town, but since the sixteenth century it has consisted of three laps of the **Campo**, around a track covered with sand and padded with mattresses in an attempt to minimize injury to horses and riders. Despite all probabilities no jockey has ever been killed.

Even before the race, fortune plays the pre-eminent part: as there is only room for ten riders, each year the *contrade* have to draw lots to take part. The participants also draw lots both for the horses and for starting positions in the race itself – the jockeys are paid "mercenaries", and employed according to an unreliable and shifting combination of loyalties reinforced by large cash payments and bonuses, and sometimes the threat of violence if they are treacherous. The result of all this is that in any one year perhaps three or four *contrade* have a serious chance of victory; for those disadvantaged by poor horses or riders, and the seven *contrade* who aren't even taking part, the race becomes a vehicle for schemes, plots and general mayhem. Each *contrada* has its traditional rival, and ensuring that one's rival loses is as important as winning for oneself. The only rule of the race is that the jockeys cannot interfere with the others' reins; everything else is accepted and practised. The jockeys are professional outsiders, traditionally the *butteri*, or cowboys, of the Maremma area, who during the Palio live in fear of the threats of rival *contrade* and under the suspicions of their own. They may be bribed to throw the race, or to whip a rival or his horse; *contrade* have been known to drug horses, and even to mount an ambush on a jockey making his way to the race. And it's the horse that wins – it doesn't matter if the jockey has been thrown en route to victory.

THE CALENDAR
There are two annual Palios, held on **July 2** (formerly the Feast of the Visitation) and **August 16** (the day after the Feast of the Assumption), each of which is preceded by a fascinating sequence of events.

June 29/August 13. The year's horses are presented in the morning at the town hall and drawn by lot. At 7.15pm the first trial race is held in the Campo.

June 30/August 14. Further trial races at 9am and 7.45pm. The evening race is usually followed by a concert in the Campo.

July 1/August 15. Two more trial races at 9am and 7.45pm, followed by a street banquet and pretty much all-night revelry in each of the *contrade*. Restaurants also move their tables outside for these Palio nights.

July 2/August 16. The **day of the Palio** begins with a final **trial race** at 9am, then in the early afternoon each of the ten chosen *contrade* takes its horse to be blessed in its church – "Go little horse and return a winner" are the priest's words. It's worth trying to see one of these **horse blessings**, which are often preceded by an extraordinary struggle to get the animal up or down the entrance steps; if the horse defecates in church, it's taken as a good omen.

At around 5pm the town hall bell begins to ring and the *corteo storico*, a pageant of horses, riders and medieval-costumed officials, processes through the city to the Campo. The *corteo* includes *comparse* – symbolic groups of equerries, ensigns, pages and drummers – from each of the *contrade*, who perform various *sbandierata* (flag-twirling) and athletic feats in the square. They are preceded by officials of the *comune* of Siena and representatives from all the ancient towns and villages of the Sienese Republic, led by the standard-bearer of Montalcino, which offered refuge to the last republicans.

The **race itself** begins at 7.45pm in July, 7pm in August, lasts for little more than ninety seconds and there's no PA system to tell you what's going on. At the start (in the northwest corner of the Campo) all the horses except one are penned between two ropes; the free one charges the group from behind, when his rivals least expect it, and the race is on. It's a hectic, violent and bizarre spectacle, and the jockeys don't even stop at the finishing line, but gallop at top speed out of the Campo, followed by the frenzied mass of supporters. Losers can be in danger of assault, especially if there are rumours of the race being "fixed" flying about.

The **palio** – a silk banner – is subsequently presented to the winning *contrada*, who then make their way to the church of **Provenanzo** (in July) or the **duomo** (in August) to give thanks. The younger *contrada* members spend the rest of the night and much of the subsequent week swaggering around the town celebrating their victory, even handing out celebratory sonnets. In the evening all members of the *contrada* hold a jubilant street banquet.

PALIO PRACTICALITIES

It's not hard to get a view of any of the practice races or ceremonies, but for the Palio proper you need a little planning. Most ordinary spectators crowd for free into the centre of the Campo. For the **best view** you need to have found a position on the inner rail by 2pm (ideally at the start and finish line), and to keep it for the next six hours. If you haven't done so, there's really no rush, as you'll be able to see a certain amount from anywhere within the throng. Toilet and refreshment facilities are minimal, which is perhaps why so little drinking goes on – for at least two hours you won't be able to leave the centre of the square. If you arrive **late in the day**, you might try making your way to Via Giovanni Dupré, behind the Palazzo Pubblico. From here, the police usually allow people into the centre of the square an hour or so before the race.

Tickets for grandstand/balcony seats cost L280,000–600,000 or more and are sold out months before the race. If you're interested in a seat for next year's event, contact Palio Viaggi, Piazza Gramsci 7 (☎0577.280.828).

Inevitably, **rooms** are extremely difficult to find at Palio time, and if you haven't booked, either reckon on staying up all night, or commuting from a neighbouring town. If you're in Italy during Palio time, but can't reach Siena, get to a bar with a TV – the races are shown live and generally repeated on the evening news.

the lower half of the square, where the Palazzo Pubblico was to be raised. The piazza itself was completed in 1349, when the council laid its nine segments of paving to commemorate their highly civic rule, and to pay homage to the Virgin – the folds of whose cloak it was intended to symbolize.

The stage-like Campo was from the start a focus of city life. As well as its continuing role as the city's marketplace – for livestock as well as produce – it was the scene of executions, bullfights, communal boxing matches, and, of course, the Palio. St Bernardino preached here, too, holding before him the monogram of Christ's name in Greek – IHS – which he urged the nobles to adopt in place of their own vainglorious coats of arms. A few did so (the monogram is to be seen on various palazzi), and it was adopted by the council on the facade of the Palazzo Pubblico, alongside the city's she-wolf symbol, which is itself a reference to Siena's legendary foundation by the sons of Remus.

Making no bones about its expression of civic pride, the **Palazzo Pubblico**, with its 97-metre bell tower, the **Torre del Mangia**, occupies virtually the entire south side of the Campo. Built largely in the first decade of the fourteenth century, the palace's lower level of arcading is characteristic of Sienese Gothic, as are the columns separating the windows. The council were so pleased with this aspect of the design that they ordered its emulation on all other buildings on the square – and it was indeed gracefully adapted on the twelfth-century **Palazzo Sansedoni** across on the north side.

The other main exterior feature of the Palazzo Pubblico is the **Cappella di Piazza**, a stone loggia set at the base of the tower, which the council vowed to build at the end of the Black Death in 1348. Funds were slow to materialize, however, and by 1376, when the chief mason at the cathedral turned his hand to its design, new Florentine ideas were already making their influence felt. The final stage of construction, a century later, when the chapel was heightened and a canopy added, was wholly Renaissance in concept.

At the highest point of the Campo, the Renaissance again makes an appearance in the **Fonte Gaia** (Gay Fountain), designed and carved by Jacopo della Quercia in the early fifteenth century. Its panels are poor, nineteenth-century reproductions – the badly eroded originals can be seen on the rear loggia of the Palazzo Pubblico – but they give an idea of what was considered one of the city's masterpieces. Its conception – the Virgin at the centre, flanked by the Virtues – was a conscious emulation of the Lorenzetti frescoes on *Good and Bad Government* in the Palazzo Pubblico (see p.307). The fountain's name comes from festivities celebrating its inauguration, the climax of a long process that began in the 1340s, when masons managed to channel water into the square; it was completed some seventy years later, following the restoration of the republic.

The Museo Civico

In the days of the *comune*, the lower floors of the Palazzo Pubblico housed the city accounts, and the upper storeys, as today, the council. Nowadays, the principal rooms have been converted into the **Museo Civico** (Mon–Sat from 10am, closing at 1pm Nov, Jan & Feb, 4pm March, 5pm April & Oct, 6pm May–June & Sept, between 7.30 and 11pm July–Aug; Sun 9.30am–1.30pm; closed Dec; L8000 or L16,000 for combined ticket with Ospedale di Santa Maria della Scala), entered through the courtyard to the right of the Cappella di Piazza.

The museum starts on the first floor of the Palazzo. At the top of the stairs you're directed through a disappointingly miscellaneous five-room picture gallery, whose nineteenth-century hunting scenes are enough to put you off *cinghiale* (wild boar) for the rest of the visit. (You could go against the indicated route and head straight into the medieval highlights: see below.) You then wind round into the **Sala del Risorgimento** (1878–90), painted with scenes commemorating Vittorio Emanuele, first king of Italy. These depict various battle campaigns, the king's coronation and his earlier meeting with Garibaldi and his army on the road to Capua, where he refused Garibaldi governorship of the Neapolitan provinces – instead inflicting a decade of martial rule.

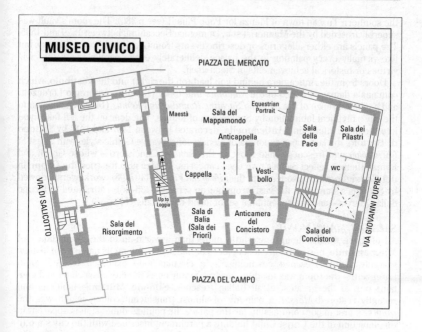

MUSEO CIVICO

PIAZZA DEL MERCATO

Maestà

Sala del Mappamondo

Equestrian Portrait

Anticappella

Sala della Pace

Sala dei Pilastri

VIA DI SALICOTTO

Up to Loggia

Cappella

Vestibollo

wc

VIA GIOVANNI DUPRE

Sala del Risorgimento

Sala di Balia (Sala dei Priori)

Anticamera del Concistoro

Sala del Concistoro

PIAZZA DEL CAMPO

SALA DI BALIA

The real medieval interest begins as you reach the **Sala di Balia** (or dei Priori), frescoed by Spinello Aretino and his son, Parri, in 1407 with episodes from the life of Siena-born Pope Alexander III – in particular his conflict with Frederick Barbarossa, the German Holy Roman Emperor. The story is a complex one. The pope and emperor came into dispute following Barbarossa's destruction of Milan in 1162 – an event that caused the formation of a Lombard League of Italian states, supported by the Vatican and the Venetians. Barbarossa entered Rome in 1166, whereupon the pope fled to Venice (where he is depicted, disguised as a monk, but recognized by a French pilgrim). The scenes include a superbly realized naval conflict – in which the Venetians are shown capturing the emperor's son and the Germans desperately trying to rescue him – and the pope's eventual reconciliation with Barbarossa, in a procession led by the doge of Venice. For a fresco-by-fresco explanation, it's worth investing in the crackly telephone commentary.

Beyond, you progress through the **Sala dei Cardinali** (or Anticamera del Concistoro), graced by a detached fresco (by the entrance door) depicting *Three Saints and Donor* attributed to **Ambrogio Lorenzetti**, transferred here in the nineteenth century, and probably once part of a much larger work depicting the *Madonna and Child* : in such pictures the donor – the individual responsble for commissioning the picture – would have been shown kneeling at the feet of the Madonna. On the centre of the left wall is a beautiful *Madonna and Child* attributed to Matteo di Giovanni, whose Madonna has the unquiet look of a painter whose propensity for the unsettling found expression in several grisly depictions of the *Massacre of the Innocents*: one of them is to be found later on in the museum.

SALA DEL CONCISTORO

Beyond lies the **Sala del Concistoro**, entered via an ornate marble doorway (1448) by Bernardo Rossellino, the sculptor and architect responsible for redesigning much of the southern Tuscan town of Pienza for Pope Pius II (see p.380). The room's vault was superbly frescoed by the Mannerist star, Domenico Beccafumi, between 1529 and 1535. The panels are either allegories or describe events from Greek and Roman history, but like virtually every painting in the palace deliberately evoke parallels with the civic virtues or historical achievements of Siena itself.

Doors from the Anticamera behind you lead (on the right) into the **Vestibolo**, which contains a damaged fresco of the *Madonna and Child* (1340) by Ambrogio Lorenzetti and a gilded bronze of the *She-Wolf Suckling Romulus and Remus* (1429), an allusion to the city's mythical foundation by Senius, son of Remus. The door on the left takes you into the more interesting **Anticappella**, decorated between 1407 and 1414 by **Taddeo di Bartolo**, the last major exponent of Siena's conservative Gothic style, with a vast *St Christopher* and frescoes – like those in the Sala del Concistoro – whose Greek and Roman themes reflect Siena's own civic concerns. Taddeo also frescoed the **Cappella del Consiglio** with episodes from the *Life of the Virgin* (1407–08), work overshadowed by Sodoma's altarpiece, the vast wrought-iron screen (1435–45) – attributed to Jacopo della Quercia – and the exceptional set of inlaid choir stalls (1415–28).

SALA DEL MAPPAMONDO

All of these works, though, are little more than a warm-up to the great **Sala del Mappamondo**, one of the great set pieces of Italian art. Taking its name from its now scarcely visible frescoed cosmology – a circular map executed by Ambrogio Lorenzetti – the room was used for several centuries as the city's law court and contains one of the greatest of all Italian frescoes, **Simone Martini**'s fabulous and recently restored *Maestà*, a painting of almost translucent colour, which was the *comune*'s first major commission for the palace. Its political dimension is apparent in the depiction of the Christ Child holding a parchment inscribed with the city's motto of justice, and the inscription of two stanzas from Dante on the steps below the throne, warning that the Virgin will not intercede for those who betray her or oppress the poor. It is one of Martini's earliest known works, painted at the age of thirty in 1315 – before this extraordinary debut not a thing is known of him – though he touched up parts of the picture, following damage from damp, six years later. The richly decorative style is archetypal Sienese Gothic and its arrangement makes a fascinating comparison with the *Maestà* by Duccio (with whom Martini perhaps trained) in the cathedral museum. Martini's great innovation was the use of a canopy and a frieze of medallions which frame and organize the figures – a sense of space and hint of perspective that suggest a knowledge of Giotto's work. Martini was to experiment further in this direction, in his great cycle of the *Life of St Martin* in Assisi, painted a couple of years later.

The fresco on the opposite wall, the marvellous *Equestrian Portrait of Guidoriccio da Fogliano*, is a motif for medieval chivalric Siena, and was, until recently, also credited to Martini. Depicting the knight setting forth from his battle camp to besiege a walled hill town (thought to be Montemassi, a village southwest of Siena, near Roccastrada), it would, if it were by Simone, be accounted one of the earliest Italian portrait paintings. Art historians, however, have long puzzled over the apparently anachronistic castles – according to some they are of a much later style than the painting's supposed date of 1328. The work would also seem to be painted over a fresco to the right by Lippo Vanni, which is dated 1364 (see below). In the mid-1980s the waters were further muddied when, during restoration, another apparently anachronistic fresco was found – the painting you now see beneath the Martini showing two men in front of a castle, believed to be the one at Arcidosso in southern Tuscany; it has been variously attributed to Martini, Duccio, Pietro Lorenzetti or Memmi di Filippuccio.

The current state of the debate is confused, with a number of historians – led by the

American Gordon Moran (whom the council for a while banned from the Palazzo Pubblico and accused of belonging to the CIA – interpreting the *Guidoriccio* as a sixteenth-century fake, and others – including an Italian commission of experts – maintaining that it is a genuine Martini overpainted by subsequent restorers. Things reached such a pitch that a neutral referee – an Englishman, Professor Andrew Martindale – was called in to arbitrate; his findings, however, proved inconclusive. Tempers recently boiled over when the Americans accused the Sienese of deliberately destroying evidence that would support their case during a "routine" restoration. Much rests on a scrupulous analysis of Siena's vast archives in the Palazzo Piccolomini: details contained in the records of payments for various paintings of the period may well help solve the mystery. The only other option – often suggested but not yet countenanced – is to strip away all the frescoes concerned to study exactly what overlays what.

At least there's no problem with the coffered figures to the right and left of the uncovered fresco – these are a pair of saints by Sodoma dating from 1529. The other large frescoes in the room also depict Sienese military victories, namely the *Victory at the Val di Chiana* (1364) by Lippo Vanni (on the long wall) and the *Victory at Poggio Imperiale* (1480) by Christoforo Ghini and Francesco d'Andrea. Don't miss the figures on the pilasters below the latter, which from left to right are Sodoma's *Blessed Tolomei* (1533), founder of the abbey at Monte Oliveto Maggiore; *St Bernardino* (1450) by Sano di Pietro; and *St Catherine of Siena* (1461) by Vecchietta.

SALA DELLA PACE

The Palazzo Pubblico's most important and interesting frescoes are to be seen in the **Sala della Pace** (Room of Peace): Ambrogio Lorenzetti's *Allegories of Good and Bad Government*, commissioned in 1338 to remind the councillors of the effects of their duties, and widely considered one of Europe's most important surviving cycles of secular paintings. The walled city they depict is clearly Siena, along with its countryside and domains, and the paintings are full of details of medieval life: agriculture, craftwork, trade and building, even hawking and dancing. They form the first-known panorama in Western art and show an innovative approach to the human figure – the beautiful, reclining Peace (Pax) in the *Good Government* hierarchy is based on a Roman sarcophagus still on display in the Palazzo Pubblico. An odd detail is that the "dancing maidens" in *Good Government* are probably young men – women dancing in public, according to the historian Jane Bridgeman, would have been too shocking in medieval Siena, and the figures' short hair and slit skirts were characteristic of professional male entertainers.

The moral theme of the frescoes is expressed in a complex iconography of allegorical virtues and figures. *Good Government*, painted on the more brightly lit walls and better preserved, is dominated by a throned figure representing the *comune* (he is dressed in Siena's colours), flanked by the Virtues (Peace – from which the room takes its name – is the nonchalantly reclining figure in white) and with Faith, Hope and Charity buzzing about his head. To the left, on a throne, Justice (with Wisdom in the air above) dispenses rewards and punishments, while below her throne Concordia advises the republic's councillors on their duties. All hold ropes, symbol of agreement. *Bad Government* is ruled by the figure of Fear (or the Devil), whose scroll reads: "Because he looks for his own good in the world, he places justice beneath tyranny. So nobody walks this road without Fear: robbery thrives inside and outside the city gates." Fear is surrounded by figures symbolizing the Vices. Ironically, within a decade of the frescoes' completion, Siena was engulfed by the Black Death – in which Lorenzetti and his family were among the victims – and the city was under tyrannical government. However, the paintings retained an impact on the citizenry – St Bernardino preached sermons on their themes.

SALA DEI PILASTRI AND LOGGIA

The room adjoining the Sala della Pace, the **Sala dei Pilastri** (or delle Colonne), displays panel paintings from the thirteenth to the fifteenth century, whose conservatism and strict formulaic composition points up the scale of Lorenzetti's achievement. Notable among them is one of the earliest Sienese masterpieces, Guido da Siena's gripping *Maestà* (1221/1260), for which Duccio repainted the Virgin's face; a fascinating picture of *St Bernardino Preaching in the Campo* by Neroccio di Bartolomeo (note how the men and women in the crowd are separated by a white cloth); and a graphically violent *Massacre of the Innocents* (removed from Sant'Agostino) painted by Matteo di Giovanni – one of four he completed in the city. The stained-glass figure of St Michael in one of the windows is attributed to Ambrogio Lorenzetti.

Backtracking through the museum, it is worth climbing the stairs between the Sala del Risorgimento and Sala di Balia to the rear **loggia**, where you can enjoy a view over the city, crane your neck to see the current council chambers and examine the original panels of the **Fonte Gaia** (1409–19). Their state of erosion makes it hard to appreciate that Jacopo della Quercia was rated by Vasari on a par with Donatello and Ghiberti, with whom he competed for the commission of the Florence baptistery doors. Michelangelo, too, was an admirer, struck perhaps by the physicality evident here in the much-damaged *Expulsion of Adam and Eve*.

Torre del Mangia

Off to the left of the Palazzo Pubblico's courtyard, opposite the entrance to the Museo, there is separate access to the **Torre del Mangia** (same hours as Museo Civico; L7000); climb up the 503 steps and you have fabulous and vertigo-inducing views across town and countryside. Built between 1338 and 1348 – the cresting was designed by Lippo Memmi – the tower takes its name from its first watchman – a spendthrift (*mangiaguadagni*) called Giovanni di Balduccio, who is commemorated by a statue in the courtyard. It was the last great project of the *comune* before the Black Death and exercised a highly civic function – its bell being rung to order the opening of the city gates at dawn, the break for lunch, the end of work at sunset and finally the closing of the city gates three hours later.

The Duomo

Few buildings reveal so much of a city's history and aspirations as Siena's cathedral, or **Duomo** (daily mid-March to Oct 9am–7.30pm; Jan to mid-March and Nov–Dec 7.30am–1pm & 2.30–5pm; free), the magnet to which most visitors gravitate after taking in the Campo. Complete to virtually its present size around 1215, it was subjected to constant plans for expansion throughout the city's years of medieval prosperity. A project at the beginning of the fourteenth century attempted to double its extent by building a baptistery on the slope below and using this as a foundation for a rebuilt nave, but the work ground to a halt as the walls gaped under the pressure.

For a while, the chapter pondered knocking down the whole building and starting from scratch to the principles of the day, but eventually they hit on a new scheme to re-orientate the cathedral instead, using the existing nave as a transept and building a **new nave** out towards the Campo. Again cracks appeared, and then in 1348 came the Black Death. With the population halved and funds suddenly cut off, the plan was abandoned once and for all. The extension still stands at the north end of the square – a vast structure that would have created the largest church in Italy outside Rome.

The exterior

Despite all the grand abandoned plans, the duomo, as it stands, is a delight. Its style is an amazing conglomeration of Romanesque and Gothic, delineated by bands of black

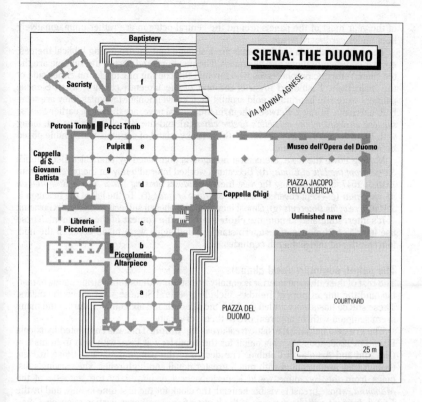

and white marble, an idea adapted from Pisa and Lucca – though here with much bolder and more extravagant effect. The lower part of the **facade** was in fact designed by the Pisan sculptor Giovanni Pisano, who from 1284 to 1296 created, with his workshop, much of its statuary – the philosophers, patriarchs and prophets, now removed to the cathedral museum and replaced by copies.

In the next century the **Campanile** was added, its windows multiplying at each level, as was the Gothic **rose window** above the doors. Thereafter work came to a complete halt, with the **mosaics** designed for the gables having to wait until the nineteenth century, when money was found to employ Venetian artists. Immediately above the central door, note St Bernardino's bronze monogram of Christ's name (see p.304).

The pavement

The facade's use of black and white decoration is echoed by the duomo's great marble **pavement**, which begins with geometric patterns and a few scenes outside the church and takes off into a startling sequence of 56 figurative panels within. These were completed between 1349 and 1547, with virtually every artist who worked in the city trying his hand on a design. The earliest employed a simple *sgraffito* technique, which involved chiselling holes and lines in the marble and then filling them in with pitch; later tableaux are considerably more ambitious, worked in multicoloured marble. Unfortunately, the whole effect can only be seen from August 7 to August 22; the rest of the year most of the panels around the central octagon are rather unimaginatively kept under cardboard wraps.

The subjects chosen for the panels are a strange mix, incorporating biblical themes, secular commemorations and allegories. The most ordered part of the scheme are the ten *Sibyls* – mythic prophetesses who foretold the coming of Christ – on either side of the main aisle. Fashioned towards the end of the fifteenth century, when Sienese painters were still imprinting gold around their conventional Madonnas, they are totally Renaissance in spirit. Between them, in the central nave, are the much earlier *Sienese she-wolf enclosed by the republic's twelve cities* (a) and the *Wheel of Fortune* (c), along with Pinturicchio's *Allegory of Virtue* (b), a rocky island of serpents with a nude posed between a boat and the land.

Moving down the nave, the central hexagon is dominated by Domenico Beccafumi's *Stories from the Life of Elijah* (d). Beccafumi worked intermittently on the pavement from 1518 to 1547, also designing the vast friezes of *Moses Striking Water from a Rock and on Mount Sinai* (e – kept covered) and the *Sacrifice of Isaac* (f). To the left of the hexagon is a *Massacre of the Innocents* (g), almost inevitably the chosen subject of Matteo di Giovanni.

It's interesting also to note the **choir stalls**, in the context of the pavement. These use intarsia techniques of a superb standard and again were made between the mid-fourteenth and mid-sixteenth centuries.

The pulpit, sculptures and chapels

The rest of the cathedral interior is equally arresting, with its zebra-stripe bands of marble, and the line of **popes' heads** – including several Sienese – set above the pillars. These stucco busts were added through the fifteenth and sixteenth centuries and many seem sculpted with an apparent eye to their perversity.

The greatest individual artistic treasure is the **pulpit**. This was completed by Nicola Pisano in 1268, soon after his pulpit for the baptistery at Pisa, with help from his son Giovanni and Arnolfo di Cambio. The design of the panels duplicates those in Pisa, though they are executed with much greater detail and high relief. The carving's distance from the Byzantine world is perhaps best displayed by the statuette of the *Madonna*, whose breast is visible beneath the cloak for the first time in Italy, and by the *Last Judgement*, with its mastery of the human figure and organization of space. Come equipped with plenty of coins for lighting.

Almost all the cathedral sculpture is of an exceptional standard. Close by the pulpit in the north transept are Tino di Camaino's **Tomb of Cardinal Petroni** (1318), a prototype for Italian tomb architecture over the next century, and, in front, **Donatello's** bronze pavement **Tomb of Bishop Pecci** (1426). The Renaissance **High Altar** is flanked by superb candelabra-carrying angels by Beccafumi. In the **Piccolomini Altarpiece**, the young **Michelangelo** also makes an appearance. He was commissioned to carve the whole series of fifteen statues here, but after completing saints Peter, Paul, Pius and Gregory in the lower niches he left for a more tempting contract in Florence – the *David*.

Further Renaissance sculptural highlights are to be seen in the two circular transept chapels. The **Cappella di San Giovanni Battista**, on the left, focuses on a bronze statue of the *Baptist* by Donatello, cast in 1457, a couple of years after his expressionist *Mary Magdalene* in Florence, whom the Baptist's stretched and emaciated face recalls. The **frescoes** in this chapel, with their delightful landscape detailing, are by **Pinturicchio**, of whom more below.

The **Cappella Chigi**, or Cappella del Voto, was the last major addition to the duomo, the behest of Pope Alexander VII, another local boy, in 1659. It was designed by **Bernini** as a new setting for the *Madonna del Voto*, a thirteenth-century painting which commemorated the Sienese dedication of their city to the Virgin on the eve of the Battle of Montaperti. The style is pure Roman Baroque, with wild, semi-clad figures of Mary Magdalene and St Jerome, the latter holding a cross in ecstasy like some 1970s rock guitarist. Outside the chapel, the walls are covered in a mass of devotional objects – silver limbs and hearts, *contrada* scarves, even the odd Palio costume and crash helmet.

Libreria Piccolomini

Midway along the nave, on the left, the entrance to the **Libreria Piccolomini** is signalled by Pinturicchio's brilliantly coloured fresco of the *Coronation of Pius II*. The library (daily Jan to mid-March & Nov–Dec 10am–1pm & 2.30–5pm; mid-March to Oct 9am–7.30pm; L2000 or L8500 combined ticket with Museo dell'Opera and baptistery) is well worth a visit for the beautiful fresco cycle within.

The frescoes and library were commissioned by Francesco Piccolomini (who for ten days was Pius III) to house the books of his uncle, **Aeneas Sylvius Piccolomini, Pope Pius II**. They do justice to the man whom Jacob Burckhardt adopted almost as a hero in his classic *The Civilization of the Renaissance in Italy*. Pius, born at nearby Pienza in 1405, was the archetypal Renaissance man, writing poetry, a geography and the *Commentaries* – a deeply humanist work in which he enthuses over landscape, antiquity and architecture, and describes the languages, customs and industries encountered on his travels.

Pinturicchio's frescoes, painted with an equal love of nature and classical decor as well as a keen sense of drama, commemorate the whole gamut of Pius's career. The cycle begins to the right of the window, with Aeneas's secular career as a diplomat: attending the Council of Basle as secretary to an Italian bishop (panel 1); presenting himself as an envoy to James II of Scotland (panel 2); being crowned poet laureate by the Holy Roman Emperor, Frederick III (panel 3); and then representing Frederick on a visit to Pope Eugenius IV (panel 4). Aeneas subsequently returned to Italy and took orders, becoming first Bishop of Trieste and then of Siena, in which role he is depicted presiding over the meeting of Frederick III and his bride-to-be, Eleonora of Portugal, outside the city's Porta Camollia (panel 5).

In 1456 Aeneas was made a cardinal (panel 6) and just two years later was elected pope (panel 7), taking the title Pius II. In political terms, his eight-year rule was not a great papacy, despite his undoubted humanism and diplomatic skill, with much of the time wasted in crushing the barons of Romagna and the Marche. The crusade he called in 1456 at Mantua (panel 8) to regain Constantinople from the Turks – who took the city in 1453 – came to nothing, and the last picture of the series (panel 10) shows his death at Ancona, where he had gone to encourage the troops. It was said that his death was brought on by grief for the failure to get the crusade off the ground, or possibly by poisoning by the troops, eager to terminate their pledge. Between these two panels is the event for which Siena most remembers him – the canonization of St Catherine.

In art history terms, Pinturicchio stands as a relatively minor figure. Originally from Perugia, he worked with Perugino in the Sistine Chapel before beginning this, his acknowledged masterpiece, in 1502. His skills lie in the brilliant colouring, the naturalistic detail – the storm scene in Aeneas's departure for Basle is one of the first in Western art – and in an easy disposition of crowds, ideal for the pageants here, and enhanced by their illusionistic placing within a series of loggias.

The library is now used to display the cathedral's **choirbooks**, illuminated by Sano di Pietro and other Sienese Gothics. At the centre of the room is displayed a Roman statue of the **Three Graces**, supposedly copied from a lost Greek work by Praxiteles. It was bought by the Piccolomini nephew and was used as a model by Pinturicchio and Raphael.

The Baptistery

The cathedral **Baptistery** (daily: Jan to mid-March & Nov–Dec 10am–1pm & 2.30–5pm; mid-March to Sept 9am–7.30pm; Oct 9am–6pm; L3000, L8500 with combined ticket for Museo dell'Opera and Libreria Piccolomini or L9500 with addition of Oratorio di San Bernardino) is unusual in being placed beneath the main body of the church. It is an essential visit, containing one of the city's great Renaissance works – a hexagonal font with scenes illustrating the Baptist's life. To reach it, turn left out of the duomo, walk left down the side of the walls and follow the flight of steps down behind the cathedral; en route you'll pass the Cripta delle Statue museum – not worth the opportunistic entrance charge.

The cathedral chapter responsible for the baptistery **font** (1417–30) must have had a good sense of what was happening in Florence at the time, for they managed to commission panels by **Ghiberti** (*Baptism of Christ* and *John in Prison*) and **Donatello** (*Herod's Feast*), as well as by the local sculptor **Jacopo della Quercia** (*The Angel Announcing the Baptist's Birth*). Jacopo also executed the marble tabernacle above, and the summit statue of *John the Baptist* and the five niche statues of the Prophets. Of the main panels, Donatello's scene, in particular, is a superb piece of drama, with Herod and his cronies recoiling at the appearance of the Baptist's head. Donatello was also responsible for two of the corner angels (*Faith* and *Hope*) and (with Giovanni di Turino) for the miniature angels on the tabernacle above.

The lavishly **frescoed walls** almost overshadow the font, their nineteenth-century overpainting having been removed after a vigorous assault by the restorers. With your back to the entrance the best include (on the left arched vault lunette) a fresco of scenes from the life of St Anthony (1460) by Benvenuto di Giovanni, a pupil of Vecchietta; scenes from the life of Christ by Vecchietta himself (inside left wall of the central stepped chapel); and the same artist's *Prophets*, *Sibyls* and *Articles of the Creed* (the main vaults), the last a repeat of a theme he would use in the Ospedale di Santa Maria della Scala (see p.315).

Piazza del Duomo

The southwest side of the cathedral square, **Piazza del Duomo**, is occupied by the medieval **Ospedale di Santa Maria della Scala** (facing the cathedral facade), whose 850-year period as Siena's main hospital has recently come to an end, allowing free public access for the first time to some of the most staggering medieval Italian frescoes to have seen the light of day. To its left is the **Museo Archeologico**, a modest but well-presented collection, and part of a scheme that will see the former hospital turned into Siena's principal exhibition space. The other sides of the square continue the history of Sienese power, with the **Archbishop's Palace**, the **Palazzo del Magnifico** built for Petrucci in 1508, and the **Palazzo Granducale**, built later in the century for the Medici. More interesting than any of these, however, is the **Museo dell'Opera del Duomo**, home to Siena's single greatest work of art – Duccio's *Maestà* – and a range of other significant sculptures and paintings.

Ospedale di Santa Maria della Scala

The **Ospedale di Santa Maria della Scala** (daily: summer 10am–6.30pm; winter 10.30am–4.30pm; L8000 or L16,000 combined ticket with Museo Civico) has seen hospital use for over eight hundred years, listing among its charitable workers saints Catherine and Bernardino. Its recent closure arouses mixed feelings, for the functioning building gave a sense of purpose to the cathedral square, which won't be matched by its intended use as Siena's principal cultural and museum space. At the same time, the *comune*'s grandiose plans for the enormous building – which include a new home for the Pinacoteca Nazionale – mean that some quite extraordinary works, long hidden from all but the most determined visitors, are now on public view for the first time in centuries. More will be revealed as time goes by, but already you can view a **frescoed chapel** by Vecchietta (considered his masterpiece); the **Oratorio di Santa Caterina della Notte**, a finely decorated subterranean chapel used by, among others, St Catherine; an **entire church** – Santissima Annunziata; and – best of all – a vast **secular fresco cycle** by Domenico di Bartolo, a work now talked of as third only to the frescoes in the duomo and Palazzo Pubblico in Siena's artistic pantheon.

A history of the hospital

According to legend the hospital was founded by **Beato Sorore**, a ninth-century cobbler-turned-monk who worked among orphans, a story given credence by the reputed discovery of his "tomb" in 1492. In fact Sorore was almost certainly mythical, his name a corruption of *suore*, or nuns, who for centuries tended the sick as a part of their vocation. The hospital was probably founded by the cathedral's canons, the first written record of its existence appearing in 1090. Its development was prompted by the proximity of the **Via Francigena**, a vital trade and pilgrimage route between Rome and northern Europe, which in the early Middle Ages replaced the deteriorating Roman consular roads used previously. Its route passed below Siena's walls, giving rise to the growth of numerous rest-places (*ospedali*) where travellers and pilgrims could seek shelter and succour. Some forty of these grew up in Sienese territory alone, the most important of which was Santa Maria della Scala. Initially pilgrims were the main concern: hospital work, in the modern sense, came later: "hospitality rather than hospitalization" was the credo.

The foundation was one of the first European examples of the **Xenodochium**, literally an "abode", a hospital that not only looked after the sick but could also be used as a refuge and food kitchen for an entire town in times of famine and plague. This role made the hospital a vital part of the city's social fabric, its importance leading to a long-running and ill-mannered tussle between lay and secular authorities. In time it passed from the cathedral canons into the hands of hospital friars, and in 1404, after an intense dispute, into the care of the *comune*, who appointed its rectors and governing body. Alms and bequests of money over the centuries kept it richly endowed, the Sienese taking to heart St Paul's stricture that Charity was the most important of the three Cardinal Virtues.

Some of the donated funds were diverted away from humanitarian concerns, and into artistic and architectural commissions – as early as 1252 Siena's bishop gave permission for Santa Maria's abbot to build a **church**, the precursor of the present Santissima Annunziata (see below). In 1335 the hospital commissioned Simone Martini and Pietro and Ambrogio Lorenzetti, the city's three leading painters, to fresco the building's exterior facade (works now lost to the elements). In 1359 it paid an exorbitant sum to acquire from Constantinople a nail used during the Passion, a piece of the True Cross, and a part of the Virgin's girdle, along with a miscellany of **saints' relics**. In 1378 it financed the setting of a **stone bench** along the length of the hospital's exterior, still much used by visitors as a shady spot to view the duomo. Its original purpose was to provide the hospital's dignitaries with somewhere to sit during the city's interminable religious and civic ceremonies.

Cappello del Manto and Sala del Pellegrinaio

Turning right beyond the ticket office, you enter a small vestibule known as the **Cappello del Manto**, which contains an arresting and beautifully restored fresco of *St Anne and St Joachim* (1512), the earliest major work in Siena by the Mannerist Domenico Beccafumi. The protagonists depicted are the parents of the Virgin, whose story – popular in Tuscan painting – is told in the apocryphal gospels, biblical adjuncts reintroduced to the medieval world in the *Golden Legend* by Jacopo da Voragine (see also *The Legend of the True Cross* in Arezzo, p.415). Having failed to conceive during twenty years of marriage, the pair are each told by an angel to meet at Jerusalem's Golden Gate. Here they kiss – the scene depicted in the fresco – a moment which symbolizes the Immaculate Conception of their daughter.

Uplifted by contemplation of this event, you turn left into a vast room (partly used as a bookshop), a majestic whitewashed space typical of the "longitudinal" architectural elements introduced into Italy by French Cistercians travelling the Via Francigena. Turning immediately left (rooms off to the right are used for temporary exhibitions) brings you into another similarly elongated space, the **Sala del Pellegrinaio**, its walls completely covered in a fresco cycle of episodes from the history of Santa Maria della Scala by Domenico di Bartolo and Vecchietta. Incredibly, this astounding area was used as a hospital ward until recently.

The ward was built around 1380 and the frescoes begun in 1440, their aim being to not only record scenes from the hospital's history, but also to promote the notion of charity towards the sick and – in particular – the orphaned, whose care had been a large part of the hospital's early function. Their almost entirely **secular content** was extraordinary at the time they were painted, still some years short of the time when Renaissance ideas would allow for other than religious narratives. It's well worth taking the trouble to study the eight major panels in detail – each is full of insights into the Sienese daily life of the time – along with the three-part sequence on the end wall by the window. The cycle starts at the left end of the left wall and moves clockwise.

THE LEFT WALL AND END WALL

The **first panel**, *The Dream of the Mother of Beato Sorore*, is by **Vecchietta**, his only contribution to the cycle. It depicts in part a dream in which the mother of Sorore, the hospital's mythical founder (see previous page), foresees her son's destiny. Her vision focuses on the abandoned children of the hospital, the *gettatelli* (from *gettare*, to throw away), who are shown ascending to Paradise and the waiting arms of the Madonna. Sorore is shown twice: on the right of the painting with upraised hand receiving the first *gettatello*, and kneeling at the foot of the child-filled ladder.

The ladder (*scala*) is the key to the Santa Maria della Scala, which may take its name from this part of the legend. Another version of the story suggests that a three-runged ladder, a symbol of the Trinity, was found during the hospital's construction. The more likely explanation is that the hospital was simply built opposite the steps, or *scala*, of the duomo. Whatever the origins, a three-runged ladder surmounted by a cross is the symbol you now see plastered all over the museum's literature and slick displays.

The **second panel**, *The Building of the Hospital*, depicts a mounted bishop of Siena at the head of a procession passing the hospital, which is in the process of being built, and almost running down a stonemason in the process. Note the buildings, a strange mixture of Gothic and Renaissance which bear little relation to anything in Siena, and the rector of the hospital, portrayed behind the ladder on the right doffing his hat to the visiting dignitaries. The **third panel**, the weakest of the cycle, is by **Priamo della Quercia**, brother of the more famous Jacopo, and shows the *Investiture of the Hospital Rector by the Blessed Agostino Novello*, the latter traditionally, but erroneously, credited as being the author of the hospital's first statute. The decorous figure on the left is thought to be a portrait of Emperor Sigismondo (who passed through Siena in 1432), or, more probably, a representation of the Byzantine emperor Paleologus III, who took part in the Council of Florence in 1439. The **fourth panel** shows one of Santa Maria's defining moments, when in 1193 Pope Celestine III gave the hospital the right to elect its own rector, thus transferring power from the religious to lay authorities. For the rest, the fresco is an excuse to portray day-to-day life in Siena – note, for example, the preponderance of oriental merchants.

The paintings on **either side of the end wall** are late sixteenth-century works, but illustrate two fascinating aspects of the hospital's work. The vast number of orphans taken in meant that an equally large number of wet nurses, or *baliatici*, were needed to feed the infants. At one time their numbers were such that feeding took place in the vast room now occupied by the bookshop. The pictures here show the nurses in action, and the payment for their services: in grain (on the left wall) and hard cash (on the right).

THE RIGHT WALL

Moving across to the long right wall, the **fifth panel**, the most famous in the cycle, shows *The Tending of the Sick*, a picture crammed with incident, notably the close scrutiny being given to a urine sample by two doctors on the left, the youth with a leg wound being washed, and the rather ominous scene on the right of a monk confessing a patient prior to surgery. Alongside, the **sixth panel** shows *The Distribution of Charity*, one of the hospital's main tasks, an event which takes place in the old hospital church (now replaced by Santissima Annunziata) with the central door of the duomo just visible in the background. Bread is distributed to beggars, pilgrims and children (one of whom passes it on to his mother); at the centre an orphan puts on clothes which it has been given. In one strange vignette a child is shown trying to express milk from its mother's breast. On the left, meanwhile, the hospital's rector is shown doffing his hat, possibly to Sigismondo.

The **seventh panel** illustrates further work of the hospital, underlining the vital part it played in maintaining the social fabric of the city. It shows the reception, education and marriage of one of the female orphans, who were provided with a small grant designed to enable them to marry, stay on in the hospital or join a convent. Also included are details which suggest how the hospital not only took in children, but committed itself to caring for them over a long period. Thus the wet nurses are shown in action on the table to the left, along with scenes to suggest weaning, education and play. Bartolo also shows off his exotic learning and Renaissance credentials in the panel, not only by including an array of extraneous detail, but also by painting a carpet under the feet of the married couple whose dragon and phoenix symbols belong to the period of the Ming dynasty. The final **eighth panel**, which details the feeding of the poor and the elderly, is less engaging than the rest, partly because of the awkwardly sited window, reputedly built by a nineteenth-century superintendent so that he could survey the sick below from his first-floor office without the bother of having to go into the ward.

The rest of the hospital

More of Santa Maria is being opened up year by year. At present the big draws after the Bartolo frescoes are **Santissima Annunziata** and the **Sagrestia Vecchia**. For the first, exit the Sala del Pellegrinaio away from the bookshop and turn left. Remodelled in the fifteenth century, the **church** is disappointingly bland, but worth a look for the high altar's marvellous bronze statue of the *Risen Christ* by **Vecchietta**, its features so gaunt the veins show through the skin. Vecchietta clearly understood and absorbed the new approach of Donatello, and several art historians consider this the finest Renaissance sculpture in the city. Before the church's remodelling, frescoes by Vecchietta had entirely covered its walls, a loss as tantalizing as the missing Martini and Lorenzetti frescoes on the hospital's exterior.

Some idea of what was lost can be grasped in Vecchietta's **fresco cycle** (1446–49) in the **Sagrestia Vecchia**, also known as the Cappella del Sacro Chiodo – it once housed the nail (*chiodo*) from the Passion and others of the hospital's precious relics (to reach it exit the church and turn left and left again). Art critics pay this more attention than the Bartolo fresco, ranking it as one of the **masterpieces** of fifteenth-century Sienese art, but for the casual viewer it makes less easy viewing, largely because its subject – an illustration of the *Articles of the Creed* – involves some theological knowledge. If you can manage the Italian, however, the various panels and vaults are well described. Each lunette illustrates one or more articles, the figure of one of the Apostles to the right holding the text of the article in question, the scenes below or to the left depicting an episode from the Old Testament which embodies the article's meaning.

The frescoes are extremely unusual, partly in that they illustrate a **written text** – something that remained rare until much later in the Renaissance – and partly in that they revolve around the figure of Christ (depicted twice in the main vaults). The latter was a strange choice in a city dedicated to the Madonna, a city in which virtually every work of note either eulogizes Siena itself or includes Christ only as an adjunct to the Virgin (usually as a *Madonna and Child*). It's thought the choice was suggested by the "nail from the Cross" contained in the chapel, a relic with obvious relevance to the story of Christ.

Domenico di Bartolo's high altarpiece, the *Madonna della Misericordia* (1444), is more intelligible than much of the cycle, and shows the Madonna casting a protective cloak over various of Siena's inhabitants. This theme, a common one in Sienese and other central Italian works, derives from a vision of the Madonna experienced by a ninth-century Cistercian monk. At first painters depicted only members of the religious orders beneath the protective cloak, monks to one side, nuns to the other. At the beginning of the twelfth century members of religious confraternities were allowed protection, and a few decades later the privilege was extended to all inhabitants of a town or city. Men and women usually remained segregated, however, which makes this version – in which they're mixed – unusual. The fresco once graced the Cappella di Manto at the entrance of the Ospedale (see above), the Virgin's cloak (*manto*) having given the chapel its name. It was detached and fixed here in 1610, its side parts torn away to fit the dimensions of the new altar; in 1969, however, the discarded fragments were found and reattached.

Finally, descend to the **Oratorio di Santa Caterina della Notte**, an oratory that belonged to one of a number of the medieval confraternities who maintained oratories in the basement vaults of the hospital. It's a dark and strangely spooky place, despite the plethora of decoration – one can easily imagine St Catherine passing nocturnal vigils down here. Even if you prove immune to the atmosphere, it's worth coming down here for Taddeo di Bartolo's sumptuous triptych of the *Madonna and Child with SS. Andrew and John the Baptist* (1400).

Museo Archeologico

The **Museo Archeologico** (summer Mon–Sat 9am–2pm, Sun 9am–1pm; winter Mon–Sat 9am–1.30pm, Sun 9am–12.30pm; closed 1st & 3rd Sun of the month; L4000) occupies part of the former Ospedale, entered from the southern end of Piazza del Duomo (the left corner if you have your back to the duomo). The frescoes in the slickly turned out ticket hall augur well, but though the museum is superbly presented, there's little here to excite anyone who's seen the larger Roman and Etruscan collections of Volterra, Chiusi and elsewhere. The eight rooms are arranged according to the various private and other collections which make up the museum's patrimony, which means they are also grouped roughly by provenance. Thus there are local finds from Chiusi and Volterra, as well as smaller centres such as Casole d'Elsa, Pienza and Sarteano, these latter exhibits suggesting the often overlooked ubiquity of Etruscan culture across southern Tuscany. The finds from in and around Siena in **rooms 8 and 9** are interesting for the same reason, in particular the jewellery and small bronzes from the Poggiolo burial chamber near Monteriggioni. A small free leaflet (in English) is usually available at the door if you want more background.

Museo dell'Opera del Duomo

After the Museo Civico and Ospedale, the best art in Siena is probably to be seen in the **Museo dell'Opera del Duomo** (daily: Jan to mid-March & Nov–Dec 9am–1.30pm; mid-March to Sept 9am–7.30pm; Oct 9am–6pm; L6000, L8500 with combined ticket for baptistery and Libreria Piccolomini or L9500 with addition of Oratorio di San Bernardino), which occupies the projected reorientated nave. An additional bonus is the chance to climb to the top of the **"new nave"**, an arguably better vantage point than the Torre di Mangia for a view over Siena.

Downstairs, in the Galleria delle Statue, the statuary by **Giovanni Pisano** (1250–1314) seems a little bizarre when displayed at eye level: the huge, elongated, twisting figures are obviously adjusted to take account of the original viewing position, which was ranged across the duomo's facade. They are totally Gothic in conception, and for all their subject matter – philosophers from antiquity are represented alongside Old Testament prophets and other characters – show little of his father Nicola's experiment with classical forms on the cathedral pulpit. In marked contrast is Donatello's ochre-coloured *Madonna and Child*, a delicate piece in the centre of the room (removed from the door of the duomo's south transept), alongside a bas-relief by Jacopo della Quercia of *St Anthony Abbot and Cardinal Antonio Casini*.

On the first floor a curator admits you to the **Sala di Duccio**, curtained and carefully lit to display the artist's vast and justly celebrated **Maestà**. Originally painted on both sides, it depicts the *Madonna and Child Enthroned* (or *Maestà*) and the *Story of the Passion*. The four saints in the front rank of the main painting, the *Maestà*, are Siena's patron saints at the time, Ansano, Savino, Crescenzio and Vittore, while the ten smaller figures at the rear of the massed ranks represent ten of the Apostles. (Peter and Paul are in the second rank, accompanied by John the Baptist and other saints.) On its completion in 1311 the work was, as far as scholars can ascertain, the **most expensive painting ever commissioned**, and had occupied Duccio for almost four years. It was taken in a ceremonial procession from Duccio's studio around the Campo and then to a special Mass in the duomo; everything in the city was closed and virtually the entire population attended. It then remained on the duomo's high altar until 1505. This is one of the superlative works of Sienese art – its iconic, Byzantine spirituality accentuated by Duccio's flowing composition and a new attention to narrative detail in the panels of the predella and the reverse of the altarpiece, both now displayed to its side.

The *Maestà* – the Virgin as Queen of Heaven surrounded by her "court" of saints – was a Sienese invention, designed as a "sacrifice" to the Virgin, the city's patroness (the consecration took place in 1260), a quality emphasized by the lavish use of gold. Duccio's rendering of the theme was essentially the prototype for the next three centuries of Sienese painters; his achievement, as Bernard Berenson put it, was to add "the drama of light to that of movement and expression" and a realization of the space in which action takes place.

This quality is best observed in the narrative panels, most of which have been gathered here, after the altarpiece's dismemberment in 1771 and its removal to the museum in 1887. Only a handful of panels are missing and – to quite understandable local disgust – will not be released by their owners to the city: two are in Washington, three in London's National Gallery and three in the Frick and Rockefeller collections in New York. One of the most effective of the surviving panels is the *Betrayal of Judas*, where trees relieve the main group of figures – Christ is "pointed" by the central tree – and rows of lances break the golden sky. The *Descent from the Cross*, too, is a marvellously composed image.

Also in the room is a *Madonna di Crevole*, also by Duccio (an early work), and Pietro Lorenzetti's triptych of the *Nativity of the Virgin*, the latter remarkable for breaking with the tradition of triptych painting by running a single scene across two of the painting's three panels. The gilded statues in the room off to the right of the *Madonna and Child with Four Saints* are attributed to Jacopo della Quercia, as is the separate statue of *St John the Baptist*.

In the room behind the Sala is a fascinating nineteenth-century drawing of the cathedral pavement, providing a unified view impossible on the spot. But for the art that followed

Duccio, and some that preceded, you need to make your way upstairs. Here you enter the **Sala di Tesoro**, featuring amid its reliquaries the head of St Galgano and a startling *Christ on the Cross* (1280), an important early work in wood by Giovanni Pisano in which Christ is shown on a Y-shaped tree growing out of the skull of Adam. The latter symbolizes the Tree of Life, or Tree of Knowledge, which grew from a sprig planted in the dead Adam's mouth and would – in the apocryphal story – eventually yield the wood used to crucify Christ (Piero della Francesca tells this story in Arezzo's fresco cycle depicting the *Story of the True Cross*; for the full story see p.415).

Beyond the Sala di Tesoro you reach the **Sala della Madonna dagli Occhi Grossi**. The work that gives its name to this room is the cathedral's original, pre-Duccio altarpiece – a stark, haunting Byzantine icon (literally the "Madonna of the Big Eyes") in the centre of the room. It occupies a special place in Sienese history, for it was before this painting that Siena's entire population came to pray before their famous victory over the Florentines at Montaperti in 1260. It was also a promise made in front of the painting prior to the battle that saw Siena dedicated to the Madonna in the aftermath of victory. Around it are grouped a fine array of panels, including works by Simone Martini, Pietro Lorenzetti and Sano di Pietro. Note the panels flanking Sano's *Madonna and Child*: one shows St Bernardino preaching in the Campo and Piazza San Francesco (the latter now home to the saint's oratory; see p.327); the other shows St Apollonia, patron saint of dentists, martyred in Alexandria in the fourth century for refusing to make sacrifices to pagan gods.

The **stairs to the new nave** – known as the **Scala del Falciatore** – are reached through a small door in the room beyond signed *Ingress al Panorama*. Beyond, a balcony offers sensational views over the city and surrounding hills: clamber the stairs of the narrow staircase halfway up for still more angles on the panorama.

South of the Campo

Back in the Campo, the streets behind the Palazzo Pubblico descend several levels to the **Piazza del Mercato**, now mainly a car park with a belvedere-like platform and a pleasant café-pizzeria and restaurant. It is here you realize how abruptly the town ends: buildings rise to the right and left for a few hundred metres along the ridges of the **Terzo di San Martino** and **Terzo di Città**, but in the centre the land drops away to a rural valley. These two southern ridges reveal a neighbourhood Siena surprisingly unbothered by tourism and terminate in churches founded by the medieval orders – the **Servites** in San Martino, the **Carmelites** and **Augustinians** in Città. Each has an important museum too, respectively the state archives of the **Palazzo Piccolomini**, and the **Pinacoteca Nazionale**, Siena's main art gallery.

Terzo di San Martino

Marking the start of Banchi di Sotto, the main thoroughfare through Terzo di San Martino, is the **Loggia di Mercanzia**, designed as a tribune house for the merchants to do their deals. The structure was the result of extraordinary architectural indecision by the city authorities, the chronicles recording that "on one day they build in a certain way and on the following destroy and rebuild in a different manner." It was completed in 1421 in accordingly hesitant style, with Gothic niches for the saints carved by Vecchietta and Antonio Federighi, two of the city's leading Renaissance sculptors.

Palazzo Piccolomini

Following the Banchi di Sotto from here, you pass the more committed Renaissance buildings of the **Palazzo Piccolomini** (at Banchi di Sotto 52) and **Logge del Papa**, commissioned in the 1460s by Pope Pius II, the Pienza-born Aeneas Sylvius Piccolomini.

Pius, whose life is depicted in the duomo, was the city's great Renaissance patron and an indefatigable builder. The Logge was built in 1462 by Federighi. The palace – one of three the pope built for his family in the city – was designed by Bernardo Rossellino, architect of Piccolomini's famous "new town" of Pienza (see p.380). Note the half-moon symbols, Pius's coat of arms, insinuated across much of the facade.

The Palazzo Piccolomini now houses the **Archivio di Stato** (Mon–Fri 9am–1pm; free), an absolutely unmissable detour, but probably made by one visitor in five hundred to the city. Most people are put off by the notion that you have to be conducted by an employee through the building. In fact, staff are more than willing to assist; enter the courtyard and take the stairs on the left to the reception, where someone will be summoned. You're then taken through corridors of archives – great bundles of vellum and leather-bound **documents** for each of the towns and villages in Siena's domain, each one labelled in ancient medieval script with the year in question: 1351, 1352, 1353 – a quite overwhelming amount of information for any budding historian, and most of it still unread. If you're lucky you'll also be able to pop out onto the palace's **terrace**, which offers a rarely seen view of the Campo.

Eventually you're left to your own devices among the *Tavolette di Biccherna* (the city's account books), the tax records (the *Gabelle*) and hallowed **manuscripts** dating back to the earliest days of Siena's recorded history. The *Tavolette* are fascinating painted wooden panels designed as covers for civic records and accounts: what makes them more interesting still is the fact that the *comune* commissioned some of the leading painters of the day to execute the beautifully detailed **vignettes**. Among those employed were Sano di Pietro and Ambrogio Lorenzetti, who painted the 1344 *Gabella* with a version of his *Good Government* fresco in the Palazzo Pubblico.

The paintings began with religious themes, but soon moved towards secular images of city life, providing a record of six centuries of Sienese history. Later panels were designed to be hung as pictures in the council offices, rather than mounted on the books. The city is depicted frequently in the background, protected by the Virgin and mushrooming with towers – much like San Gimignano today. Early panels include several pictures of the *camerlingo* (a duty always filled by a Cistercian monk from San Galgano) doing the audits. Later ones move into specific events: victories over the Florentines; Pius's coronation as pope (1458); entrusting the city keys to the Virgin in the duomo (1483); the demolition of the Spanish fortress (1552); the fall of Montalcino, the Sienese Republic's last stand, (1559) and the entry into Siena of Cosimo I (1560); war with the Turks (1570); and subsequent Medicean events.

San Martino

From the Palazzo Piccolomini and the Logge, Via di Pantaneto, Via del Porrione or Via di Salicotto take you quickly away from the bustle around the Campo towards the Porta Romana. Before setting off, however, Mannerist fans should spend a couple of minutes in the church of **San Martino**, founded in the eighth century or earlier, but now a pale Baroque shadow of its former self. The third altar on the left (north) wall features an outstanding *Nativity* (1522–24) by Domenico Beccafumi, a work painted at the same time as the artist was working on the duomo's pavement, and one which encapsulates his passion for bizarre structures and peculiar light effects. The Virgin's strange gesture, in which she covers the Infant Jesus with a veil, prefigures the Crucifixion, at which she also covers Christ's naked body.

In **Via di Salicotto** – which runs directly behind the Torre del Mangia, a couple of blocks from the Logge del Papa – you find yourself in the territory of the *Torre* (tower) *contrada*. They maintain a museum at no. 76 (daily except Thurs 10am–12.30pm; call custodian in advance ☎0577.222.555) and a fountain-square a few houses beyond. A famous sign on this street, posted in 1641, informs the citizens that the Florentine governor forbids prostitutes to practise in the neighbourhood.

Santa Maria dei Servi

Via di Salicotto, or Via San Martino, will bring you into the *Valdimontone* (ram) *contra-da*, whose museum (☎0577.222.590), fountain and parish church are in Via di Valdimontone, alongside the massive brick church and campanile of **Santa Maria dei Servi**, the Servites' monastic base. The church (closed 12.30–3pm), which is well worth the walk, is set in a quiet piazza, approached by a row of cypresses and shaded by a couple of spreading trees – good for a midday picnic or siesta; it also offers tremendous views across the city.

The Renaissance-remodelled **interior** is remarkable for a variety of top-notch paintings. The first, above the first main altar on the right (south) wall, is the so-called *Madonna di Bordone* (1261) by **Coppo di Marcovaldo**, a Florentine artist captured by the Sienese at the Battle of Montaperti and forced to paint this picture as part of his ransom for release. The next altar to the left features the *Nativity of the Virgin* (1625) by Rutilio Manetti, Siena's leading follower of Caravaggio. Two altars down, in the last altar of the left aisle, is Matteo di Giovanni's *Massacre of the Innocents* (1491), one of two versions of this episode in the church, and one of four in the city by the infanticide-obsessed Matteo. The popularity of this subject in the late fifteenth century may have been due to the much publicized massacre of Christian children by the Saracens at Otranto in 1480. Matteo's rendition is a touch less blood-crazed than his Sant'Agostino version (moved to the Palazzo Pubblico since its restoration; see p.308), but only just – certain features are common to both, including the powerful sense of claustrophobia and several unnecessarily perverse details, of which the most disturbing are the woman scratching the face of the soldier about to dispatch her child and the two smiling children watching the massacre from the balcony on the right.

Cheek-by-jowl violence also characterizes Pietro Lorenzetti's much earlier version of the *Massacre*, which is found on the right wall of the second chapel to the right of the high altar. (Note Herod watching the carnage from a balcony on the left.) The serene *Madonna and Child* to the right is by Segna di Bonaventura, nephew of the great Duccio. Lorenzetti is further represented by damaged frescoes of the *Banquet of Herod* and the *Death of John the Baptist*, located on the right wall of the second chapel to the left of the high altar. A fine *Adoration of the Shepherds* (1404) by one of Lorenzetti's followers, Taddeo di Bartolo, hangs in the same chapel.

Moving to the **left transept** involves a progression along a line of Sienese art history, for it contains a *Madonna della Misericordia* (1431) by one of Taddeo's pupils, Giovanni di Paolo. The painting shows the Virgin sheltering a group of nuns on one side and a group of monks on the other, the latter led by Filippo Benizzi (1235–85), a Florentine general of the Servite order. To its left usually hangs another of the church's outstanding paintings, the beautifully serene *Madonna del Popolo* (1340) by Lippo Memmi, widely considered one of the masterpieces of this painter (removed to the Pinacoteca at the time of writing). Down the north aisle towards the entrance, the last altar before the rear wall contains the eye-catching *Madonna del Belvedere* (1363), one of only a handful of works attributed to Jacopo di Mino, a pupil of Lippo Memmi.

Porta Romana

From Santa Maria dei Servi, you're just a hundred metres from the **Porta Romana**, the massively bastioned south gate of the city. The outer arch of this gate has a fragmentary fresco of the *Coronation of the Virgin*, begun by Taddeo di Bartolo and completed by Sano di Pietro. If you leave the city here, and turn left along the Via Girolamo Gigli, you could follow the walls north to the **Porta Pispini**, another impressive example of defensive architecture and again flanked by a fresco of the Virgin, this time a Renaissance effort by Sodoma.

On the city side of the Porta Romana, the huge ex-convent of San Niccolò now houses the city's psychiatric hospital. Opposite is the little church of **Santuccio**, worth looking into for its seventeenth-century frescoes depicting the life of St Galgano (see p.359). In the adjacent sacristy, at Via Roma 71, are the premises of the **Società Esecutori di Pie Disposizioni** – the Society of Benevolent Works, formerly the Society of Flagellants. This medieval order, suppressed in the eighteenth century, and later refounded along more secular lines, maintains a small collection of art works (Mon & Wed–Fri 9am–noon, Tues 3–7pm; ring for admission). It includes a triptych of the *Crucifixion, Flagellation and Burial of Christ* attributed to Duccio, and a semicircular tablet, with wonderful Renaissance landscape, of *St Catherine of Siena Leading the Pope Back to Rome*.

Terzo di Città

Via di Città, one of Siena's key streets, cuts across the top of the Campo through the oldest quarter of the city, the area around the cathedral. The street and its continuation, Via San Pietro, is fronted by some of Siena's finest private palazzi, including the Buonsignori, home to the **Pinacoteca Nazionale**, the city's main picture gallery. The district is also worth exploring for its own sake, with a variety of options taking you in loops past churches such as Sant'Agostino and some of the city's tucked-away corners.

Walking to the Pinacoteca you pass the **Palazzo Chigi-Saracini** at Via di Città 82, a Gothic beauty, with its curved facade and back courtyard, though the palace itself is normally closed to the public. It houses the **Accademia Chigiana**, who sponsor music programmes throughout the year and mantain a small art collection (open Mon–Fri by appointment, ☎0577.46.152), including exceptional works by Sassetta, Botticelli and Donatello. It was from this palace that the Sienese victory over the Florentines at Montaperti was announced, the town herald having watched the battle from the tower. Almost opposite is a second **Palazzo Piccolomini**, this one built in 1460 by Bernardo Rossellino as a residence for Pius II's sister, Caterina. Known as the Piccolomini delle Papesse (of the she-popes), it is now headquarters of the Banca d'Italia.

Pinacoteca Nazionale

The **Pinacoteca Nazionale** (summer Tues–Sat 9am–7pm, Sun 8.30am–1.30pm; winter Tues–Sat 8.30am–1.30pm & 2.30–4/5.30pm, Sun 8am–6pm; L8000), housed at Via San Pietro 29 in another fourteenth-century palace, is a roll of honour of Sienese Gothic painting, and if your interest has been spurred by the works by Martini in the Palazzo Pubblico or Duccio in the cathedral museum, a visit is the obvious next step. The collection offers an unrivalled chance to assess the development of art in the city from the twelfth century through to late Renaissance Mannerism.

The main rooms are arranged in chronological order, starting on the second floor. On the **ground floor** are a handful of Renaissance works, best of which are Sodoma's frescoes from Sant'Agostino and panel of the *Deposition*, displaying his characteristic drama and delight in costume and landscape, and **Beccafumi's** *St Michael and the Fallen Angels* and *St Catherine Receiving the Stigmata*. Currently installed on the **first floor** is a reconstruction of the strange *Santuario del Romituzzo* – a chapel removed from Colle di Val d'Elsa, crowded with anatomical ex-voto objects placed to appeal for the relevant divine intercession.

Up on the **second floor, room 1** begins with the earliest known Sienese work, an altar frontal dated 1215 of *Christ Flanked by Angels*, with side panels depicting the discovery of the True Cross (see p.415 for this story). The figures are clearly Romanesque; the gold background – intricately patterned – was to be a standard motif of Sienese art over the next two centuries. The first identified Sienese painter, **Guido da Siena**, makes an appearance with the same subject in **room 2**, though the influences on his work – dated around 1280 – are distinctively Byzantine rather than Romanesque, incorporating studded jewels amid the gold. In some of his narrative panels – *Christ Entering Jerusalem, The Life of St Peter* and *St Clare Repelling a Saracen Attack* – his hand seems rather freer, though the colouring is limited to a few delicate shades.

Duccio di Buoninsegna (1260–1319), the dominant figure in early Sienese art, is represented along with his school in **rooms 3 and 4**. Bernard Berenson considered Duccio the last great painter of antiquity, in contrast to Giotto, the first of the moderns. The painter's advances in composition are best assessed in his *Maestà*, in the Museo dell'Opera del Duomo. Here Duccio simply shows that he "fulfilled all that the medieval mind demanded of a painter", in the words of Berenson: his dual purpose being to demonstrate Christianity to an illiterate audience and make an offering (the painting) to God. A rather more Gothic and expressive character is suggested by **Ugolino di Nerio**'s *Crucifixion* and *Madonna* in room 3.

Sienese art over the next century has its departures from Duccio – Lorenzetti's mastery of landscape and life in the *Good and Bad Government*, for example – but the patrons responsible for commissioning works generally wanted more of the same: decorative paintings, whose gold backgrounds made their subjects stand out in the gloom of medieval chapels. As well as specifying the required materials and composition, the Sienese patrons – bankers, guilds, religious orders – would often nominate a particular painting as the model for the style they wanted.

The innovations of **Simone Martini** – the attention to framing and the introduction of a political dimension – are best seen in the Palazzo Pubblico. Here, he has just a single, highly conventional and beautiful *Madonna* in **room 6**. The works by the **Lorenzetti brothers**, Pietro and Ambrogio, in **rooms 7 and 8**, are, however, more rewarding. Pietro's include a marvellous *Risen Christ*, which could almost hold company with Masaccio, and the *Carmine Altarpiece*, whose predella has five skilful narrative scenes of the founding of the Carmelite order. Attributed to Ambrogio are two tiny panels, *City by the Sea* and *Castles by a Lake*, which the art historian Enzo Carli claims are the first ever "pure landscapes", without any religious purpose. They are thought to have been painted on a door, one above the other.

Moving through the fourteenth century, in **rooms 9 to 11** the major Sienese artists are **Bartolo di Fredi** (1353–1410) and his pupil **Taddeo di Bartolo** (1362–1422). Bartolo is best known for the New Testament frescoes in San Gimignano, whose mastery of narrative is reflected in his *Adoration of the Magi*. Taddeo, painter of the chapel in the Palazzo Pubblico, has archaic elements – reinserting huge areas of gold around a sketch of landscape – but makes strides in portraiture and renders one of the first pieces of dynamic action in the museum in his *Stoning of SS. Cosmas and Damian*.

These advances are taken a stage further in **Sassetta**'s *St Anthony Beaten by Devils* (no. 166), where Siena seems at last to be entering the mainstream of European Gothic art, and taking note of Florentine perspective. The influence of the patrons, however, is still prevalent in the mass of stereotyped images – gold again very much to the fore – by **Giovanni di Paolo** (1403–82), which fill most of **rooms 12 and 13**, and the exquisite Madonnas by **Sano di Pietro** (1406–81) and **Matteo di Giovanni** (1435–95) in **rooms 14 to 18**. It is astonishing to think that their Florentine contemporaries included Uccello and Leonardo.

The **third floor** of the museum – not always open – presents the self-contained **Collezione Spannocchi**, a miscellany of Italian, German and Flemish works, including a Dürer, a fine Lorenzo Lotto *Nativity*, Paris Bordone's perfect Renaissance *Annunciation*, and Sofonisba Anguissola's *Bernardo Campi Painting Sofonisba's Portrait* – the only painting in the museum by a woman artist. Anguissola, who is mentioned by Vasari as a child prodigy, painted at the height of Mannerism; this work is a neat little joke, the artist excelling in her portrait of Campi, but depicting his portrait of her as a flat, stereotyped image.

Sant'Agostino and a loop to the duomo

Keeping south from the Pinacoteca, you come to **Sant'Agostino** (daily mid-March to Oct 10.30am–5.30pm; L3000), where you should take the opportunity to admire the previously long-closed church's outstanding paintings, among them a *Crucifixion* (1506) by Perugino (second altar of the south aisle), an *Adoration of the Magi* (1518) by Sodoma and a lunette fresco of the *Madonna and Child with Saints* by Ambrogio Lorenzetti (both in the Cappella Piccolomini), and two monochrome lunette medallions by Luca Signorelli (Cappella Bichi, south transept). The church **piazza** is quite a pleasant space, with a kids' playground and usually a few football games in progress. Along with the Campo, this square was the site of violent medieval football matches – *ballone*, as they called it – which were eventually displaced in the festival calendar by the Palio.

At no. 4 in the church piazza is the **Accademia dei Fisiocritici** (Mon–Wed 9am–1pm & 3–6pm, Thurs 9am–1pm; free), housing museums of zoology, geology and mineralogy: all a bit pedestrian, though with a few oddities – like terracotta models of *funghi* – to entertain botanists. Continuing the theme, you could make your way across the piazza to the **Orto Botanico** (Mon–Fri 8am–5pm, Sat 8am–noon; free) at Via Pier Andrea Mattioli 4, whose herbarium is stocked with every Tuscan species.

An interesting walk from Sant'Agostino is to loop along the **Via della Cerchia**, a route that takes you past some good neighbourhood restaurants (see p.327) to the Carmelite convent and church of **San Niccolò al Carmine** (or Santa Maria del Carmine) in a predominantly student-populated section of the town. The church, a Renaissance rebuilding, contains a sensational *St Michael* by Domenico Beccafumi (midway down the south wall), painted following the monks' rejection of his more intense Mannerist version of the subject in the Pinacoteca (deemed to contain too many nudes for comfort). An hermaphrodite St Michael is shown at the centre of the crowded painting, looked down on by God, who has ordered the saint to earth to dispatch the Devil, whose extraordinary face can be seen at the base of the picture. To the painting's left is a fragment of an *Annunciation* attributed to Ambrogio Lorenzetti.

If you follow the **Via del Fosso di San Ansano**, north of the Carmine square, you find yourself on a country lane, above terraced vineyards and allotments, before emerging at the *Selva* (wood) *contrada*'s square and church of **San Sebastiano**. Climb up the stepped Vicolo di San Girolamo from here and you come out at the duomo. Alternatively from Sant'Agostino, you could cut back to the Campo along **Via Giovanni Dupré**, where the *Onda* (wave or dolphin) *contrada* has its base at no. 111; to visit the **museum** you need to make an appointment at least three days in advance (☎0577.48.384). The *Onda* church is San Giuseppe, at the Sant'Agostino end of the street.

Terzo di Camollia

The northern **Terzo di Camollia** is flanked, to west and east, by the churches of the most important medieval orders, the **Dominicans** and **Franciscans**, vast brick piles which rear above the city's outer ridges. Each has an important association with Siena's major saints, the former with **Catherine**, the latter with **Bernardino**. Bernardino's pilgrim trail also leads out of the city to the north, to the **Osservanza** monastery, his principal retreat.

The central part of the Camollia takes in the main thoroughfare of **Banchi di Sopra**, the base of the **Monte dei Paschi** – long the city's financial power. North from here, you move into a quiet residential quarter, all the more pleasant for its lack of specific sights or visitors. To the west, interestingly detached from the old city, is the **Fortress**.

San Domenico

The Dominicans founded their monastery in the city in 1125. Its church, **San Domenico** (begun 1226), is a vast, largely Gothic building, typical of the austerity of this militaristic order. The Catherine association is immediately asserted. On the right of the entrance is a kind of raised chapel, the **Cappella delle Volte**, with a contemporary portrait of her by her friend and disciple Andrea Vanni, who according to tradition captured her likeness from life during one of her ecstasies in 1414; below are steps and a niche, where she received the stigmata, took on the Dominican habit, and performed several of her miracles. The saint's own chapel, the **Cappella di Santa Caterina** (erected in 1488), is located midway down the right (south) side of the church. Its entrance arch has images of saints Luke and Jerome by Sodoma, while the marble tabernacle on the high altar (1466) encloses a reliquary containing Catherine's head (other parts of her body lie dotted across Italy). The church's highlights, however – frescoes by Sodoma (1526) – occupy the walls to the left and right of the altar and, respectively, depict her swooning and in ecstasy. Just to the left of the chapel, above the steps to the crypt, is a detached fresco of the *Madonna and Child, John the Baptist and Knight* by Pietro Lorenzetti.

Other **notable paintings** are found in some of the other chapels, especially the first to the right of the high altar, which contains a Matteo di Giovanni triptych of the *Madonna and Child with SS. Jerome and John the Baptist* and fragments of detached frescoes by Lippo Memmi and Andrea Vanni. The high altar boasts a fine marble tabernacle and two sculpted angels (1465) by the sculptor and architect Benedetto da Maiano, best known for the Palazzo Strozzi in Florence and several fine works in San Gimignano (see p.344). The second chapel to the left of the high altar houses *St Barbara, Angels and SS. Catherine and Mary Magdalene* surmounted by an *Epiphany*, considered the masterpiece of Matteo di Giovanni, though its effect is somewhat undermined by the odd eighteenth-century frescoes around it. The more appealing *Madonna and Child with Saints* (1483) opposite is by the Florentine-influenced Benvenuto di Giovanni.

St Catherine's house

St Catherine's **family home**, where she lived as a Dominican tertiary – of the order but not resident – is a short distance away to the south of San Domenico. Known as the **Casa e Santuario di Santa Caterina** (daily: summer 9am–12.30pm & 3.30–6pm; winter 9am–12.30pm & 2.30–6pm; free), its entrance is on Via Benincasa, behind Via Santa Caterina. The building has been much adapted, with a Renaissance loggia and a series of oratories – one on the site of her cell. The paintings here are mostly unexceptional Baroque canvases but it is the life that is important: an extraordinary career that made her Italy's patron saint and among the earliest women to be canonized.

Born Caterina Benincasa, the daughter of a dyer, on March 25, 1347 – Annunciation Day – she had her first visions aged five and took the veil at age eight (sixteen in some versions), against strong family opposition. She spent three years in silent contemplation, before experiencing a mystical "Night Obscure". Thereafter she went out into the turbulent, post-Black Death city, devoting herself to the poor and sick, and finally turning her hand to politics. She prevented Siena and Pisa joining Florence in rising against Pope Urban V (then absent in Avignon), and proceeded to bring him back to Rome. It was a fulfilment of the ultimate Dominican ideal – a union of the practical and mystical life. Catherine returned to Siena to a life of contemplation, visions and stigmata, retaining a political role in her attempts to reconcile the later schism between the popes and anti-popes. She died in Rome in 1380 and was canonized by Pius II (as depicted in the cathedral) in 1460. She joined St Francis as a patron saint of Italy in 1939.

Close by the Santuario are the church of **Santa Caterina**, home of the *Oca* (goose) *contrada* – known as "the infamous ones" after their record number of Palio victories – and the best preserved of Siena's several fountains, the **Fonte Branda**. Aided by the fountain's reliable water supply, this part of the city was an area for tanneries into the twentieth century. The fountain also features in Sienese folklore as the haunt of werewolves, who would throw themselves into the water at dawn to return to human form.

Monte dei Paschi di Siena

Between the two monastic churches lies the heart of business Siena, the **Piazza Salimbeni**, whose three interlocking palazzi have formed, since the fifteenth century, the head office of the **Monte dei Paschi di Siena**.

Banking was at the heart of medieval Sienese wealth, the town capitalizing on its position on the Via Francigena, the "French road" between Rome and northwest Europe, and the main road between Rome and Florence and Bologna. Sienese banking families go back to the twelfth century and by the end of the thirteenth they were trading widely in France, Germany, Flanders, England and along the Danube, where they maintained networks of corresponding dealers. Activity declined after the Black Death but in the fifteenth century the Republic set up the *Monte* as a lending and charitable institution, to combat the abuses of usury. It consolidated its role under Medici rule and slowly moved into more strictly banking activities. In the twentieth century it merged with other Tuscan and Umbrian banks to become one of the key financial institutions in Italy.

There is some historical interest in the exteriors of the bank's palazzi: the **Spannocchi**, on the right, was the first great Renaissance palace built in Siena (1473) and the prototype for the Palazzo Strozzi in Florence, while the **Salimbeni**, in the centre, was a last flourish of Gothicism. However, to appreciate the role of the *Monte* in Siena you need to tour the building. In 1972, Pierluigi Spadolino undertook a **radical restructuring**, encasing the building's interior medieval and Renaissance features within an ultra-modern and hi-tech framework. This is a sight in itself, but it also provides a wonderful showcase for the bank's **art collection** – the bulk of which is housed in the deconsecrated church of San Donato, linked by an underground passage with the main palazzi. The paintings here include some of the finest Gothic works in Siena, among them an exquisitely coloured *Madonna* by Giovanni di Paolo, a *Deposition* by Sano di Pietro and a *Crucifixion* by Pietro Lorenzetti. Also displayed are a series of paintings depicting the Palio and its sixteenth-century bull-fighting precursor in the Campo.

At certain times of year, the bank publicly exhibits its art collections; however, they are not strictly considered a tourist attraction, and you definitely need to make an **appointment** as far in advance as possible – don't just turn up or call the day before (☎0577.234.595 or 0577.294.758). Better still, write to the Ufficio Segreteria Generale, Piazza Salimbeni 3, Siena. With any luck, you will be shown the archives and major halls of the bank, as well as the paintings, and the visit ends with a trip up to the tower for a view over the Campo.

To Porta Camollia

Heading north from the Piazza Salimbeni, Banchi di Sopra changes name to **Via Montanini** and then **Via di Camollia**, which run through the less monumental parts of the Terzo di Camollia, good for regular shopping and largely untouristed bars and restaurants.

Two churches are worth a brief look on this street. **Santa Maria delle Nevi** contains a famous altarpiece – *Our Lady of the Snows* (1477) – by Matteo di Giovanni, while **San Bartolomeo** fronts one of the nicest *contrada* squares in the city, home of the *Istrici* (porcupine); the *contrada* has its museum at Via Camollia 87 (Sat afternoon & Sun morning; ring for appointments Mon–Fri between 5 and 7pm, ☎0577.48.495). At the end of the street is the Renaissance **Porta Camollia**, inscribed on its outer arch "Siena opens her heart to you wider than this gate." It was here that a vastly superior Florentine force was put to flight in 1526, following the traditional Sienese appeal to the Virgin.

A short distance east of Banchi di Sopra – reached by a circuitous network of alleys – is another of the city's fountains, the **Fonte Nuova**. A further, highly picturesque fountain, the **Fonte Ovile**, is to be seen outside the Porta Ovile, a hundred metres or so beyond. Both were built at the end of the twelfth century. Near Fonte Nuova, in Via Vallerozzi, is the church of **San Rocco**, home of the *Lupa* (she-wolf) *contrada*; its museum is at nos. 71–73 (visits by appointment; ☎0577.270.777).

Away to the west, behind the church of Santo Stefano, the gardens of **La Lizza** – taken over on Wednesdays by the town's large market – lead up to the walls of the **Forte di Santa Barbara** (free access). The fortress was built initially by Charles V after the siege of 1554–55, but subsequently torn down by the people, and had to be rebuilt by Cosimo I, who then moved his troops into the garrison. Its Medicean walls resemble the walls of Lucca, designed by the same architect. Occasional summer concerts are held within the fort, which is also a permanent home to the wine collections and bar of the *Enoteca Italiana* (see p.328).

San Francesco

St Bernardino, born in the year of Catherine's death, began his preaching life at the chill monastic church of **San Francesco**, across the city to the east. A huge, hall-like structure, like that of the Dominicans, it has been heavily restored after damage by fire in 1655 and subsequent use as a barracks. Its remaining artworks include fragmentary frescoes by Pietro and Ambrogio Lorenzetti: a *Crucifixion* (1331) by Pietro in the first chapel to the left of the high altar and two collaborative frescoes in the third chapel to the left of the high altar (the latter depicting *St Louis of Toulouse becoming a Franciscan* and the graphic *Martyrdom of Six Franciscans at Ceuta in Morocco*). There is also a glittering polyptych by Lippo Vanni of the *Madonna and Child with Four Saints* (1370) in the sacristy (entered from the right of the south transept). It's also worth hunting down the detached fresco right of the entrance door, its choir of angels part of a *Coronation of the Virgin* (1447) by Sassetta that once decorated the city's original Porta Romana. It was completed by Sano di Pietro, a pupil of Sassetta, after the master contracted a fatal chill while working outdoors on the fresco.

Also walk to the end of the right (south) aisle, where you'll find the fourteenth-century **Tomb of the Tolomei**, the best of the church's many funerary monuments. It houses various scions of the Tolomei, one of Siena's grandest medieval families. The clan provided numerous of the city's bankers, as well as some of its leading churchmen, among them Bernardo Tolomei, founder of the abbey at Monte Oliveto Maggiore (see p.364). Also buried here is Pia de' Tolomei, first wife of Baldo Tolomei who came to live in Siena after his marriage to his second wife. Pia died, consumed with jealousy, in a castle in the Maremma, prompting Dante's famous reference to her in the *Purgatorio*: "Siena me fé, disfecemi Maremma" (Siena made me, the Maremma unmade me).

Oratorio di San Bernardino and Museo Diocesano

In the piazza to the right of San Francesco as you face the church, adjoining the cloisters, is the **Oratorio di San Bernardino and Museo Diocesano** (mid-March to Nov Mon–Sat 10.30am–1.30pm & 3–5.30pm; L4000 or L9500 combined ticket with baptistery, Libreria Piccolomini and Museo dell'Opera). The best art works here are in the beautifully wood-panelled upper chapel: fourteen large frescoes by Sodoma, Beccafumi and Girolamo del Pacchia on the *Life of the Virgin*, painted between 1496 and 1518 when the former pair were Siena's leading painters. In the lower chapel are seventeenth-century scenes of the **saint's life**, which was taken up by incessant travel throughout Italy, preaching against usury, denouncing the political strife between the Italian city states and urging his audience to look for inspiration to the monogram of Christ. Sermons in the Campo, it is said, frequently went on for the best part of a day. His actual political influence was fairly marginal but he was canonized within six years of his death in 1444, and remains one of the most famous of all Italian preachers. His dictum on rhetoric – "make it clear, short and to the point" – was rewarded in the 1980s with his adoption as the patron saint of advertising. The attached diocesan museum contains an array of devotional art from the thirteenth to the seventeenth century; the pieces are beautifully displayed, but as a collection it ranks well below the Museo dell'Opera del Duomo.

If your interest in Bernardino extends to a short pilgrimage, take bus #12 from Piazza Matteotti to Madonnina Rossa (10–15min), from where it's a short walk uphill to the monastery of **L'Osservanza** (daily 9am–1pm & 4–7pm). This was founded by Bernardino in 1423 in an attempt to restore the original Franciscan rule, by then corrupted in the cities. Much rebuilt since, the monastery has a small museum and a largely Renaissance church, whose features include an Andrea della Robbia *Annunciation* and a triptych by Sano di Pietro.

Eating, drinking, nightlife and events

Siena feels distinctly provincial after Florence. The main action of an evening is the **passeggiata** from Piazza Matteotti along Banchi di Sopra to the Campo – and there's not much in the way of nightlife to follow. For most visitors, though, the Campo, the city's universal gathering place, provides diversion enough, while the presence of the university ensures a bit of life in the bars, as well as a cluster of cheaper *trattorie* alongside the restaurants.

Restaurants

Siena used to have a poor reputation for **restaurants** but over the last few years things have looked up, with a range of imaginative *osterie* opening up and a general hike in standards. The only place you need surrender gastronomic ideals is for a meal out in the Campo: the posh restaurant here, *Il Campo*, isn't worth the money – though it's the one to go for if you want to eat in style in the square – which leaves a choice of routine but reasonably priced *pizzerie*. For cheaper meals, you'll generally do best walking out a little from the centre, west towards San Niccolò al Carmine, or north towards the Porta Camollia.

Local specialities include *pici* (noodle-like pasta with toasted breadcrumbs), *salsicce secche* (dried sausages), *finocchiona* (minced pork flavoured with fennel), *capolocci* (spiced loin of pork), *pappa col pomodoro* (bread and tomato soup), *tortino di carciofi* (artichoke omelette) and *fagioli all'uccelletto* (bean and sausage stew). The city is also famous for a whole range of **cakes and biscuits**, including the ubiquitous *panforte*, a dense and delicious wedge of nuts, fruit and honey that originated with pilgrimage journeys, *cavallucci* (aniseed, nut and spice biscuits), *copate* (nougat wafers) and rich, almond *ricciarelli* biscuits. Restaurants are listed in roughly ascending order of price.

Mensa Universitaria, Via Sant'Agata 1 (daily noon–2pm & 6.45–9pm). The university canteen has full meals for around L15,000, pasta dishes for a lot less. It's a bit hidden away, on the continuation of Via Giovanni Dupré, below the church of Sant'Agostino. Closed Aug.

Ristorante Garibaldi, Via Giovanni Dupré 18. A cheap and filling restaurant sited below a *locanda*, just south of the Campo. Full meals from L20,000. Closed Sat.

Osteria del Ficomezzo, Via dei Termini 71 (☎0577.222.384). A small, simple osteria a touch off the tourist track with a cool, pastel interior: good value set-price menus at lunch, with innovative Tuscan food (menus change weekly): more expensive à la carte in the evening. From L25,000. Closed Sun & July.

Osteria Castelvecchio, 65 Via di Castelvecchio (☎0577.49.586). Adventurous, first-rate and nicely informal *osteria* and a good bet for vegetarians (plus plenty of meat and home-made pasta too). Menus change daily. Sited off Via San Pietro, near the Pinacoteca Nazionale. From L35,000. Closed Tues & periods in Jan and July.

Osteria Il Carroccio, Via del Casato di Sotto 32 (☎0577.41.165). Just 50m from the Campo, and not many tables – room for 40 inside and 20 outside, so book: Tuscan food, and an informal atmosphere. Menus change weekly, but there's a *degustazione* menu at L45,000, slightly more than the L30,000–40,000 you pay off the normal menu. Closed Wed & Feb.

Antica Osteria Da Divo, Via Franciosa 29 (☎0577.286.054). Runs *Osteria Le Logge* (see below) a close second for ambience, thanks to its extraordinary subterranean cellar dining rooms. Upstairs is pretty, too, and the food, on its day, is well above average. One drawback is that the air-conditioning doesn't reach into the furthest recesses of the lowest vault – so be sure to get a table in the upper levels. Around L45,000. Closed Sun in winter.

La Taverna del Capitano, Via del Capitano 8 (☎0577.288.094). One of Siena's newest restaurants, this is a serene dining room with medieval vaulted ceiling and straight-down-the-line Tuscan cooking – *panzanella* (bread salad), *pici, pappardelle, bistecche* and the like. Around L45,000. Closed Tues & the second half of Nov.

Nello, Via del Porrione 28-30 (☎0577.289.043). Good-quality Tuscan food and exceptionally friendly service: the place has been in the same family for three generations. Around L45,000 per head. Closed Sun & Jan.

Ai Marsili, Via del Castoro 3 (☎0577.47.154). One of the best places to splurge in Siena. Quite formal, and service can be shaky, but food is generally excellent; expect to pay around L50,000 – and be sure to book.

Osteria Le Logge, Via del Porrione 33 (☎0577.48.013). The best-looking restaurant in central Siena, in an old cabinet-lined *farmacia* off the Campo by the Logge del Papa. Good pasta and some unusual *secondi*, but the quality of food – once exceptional – can these days be rather uneven. L60,000 for a full meal. Closed Sun.

Cane e Gatto, Via Pagliaresi 6 (☎0577.220.751). Don't be put off by the lack of any menu: this friendly restaurant serves superb Tuscan *cucina nuova*, among seven courses on its *menù degustazione*. This will cost you L80,000 (excluding wine), but if you'd rather pay less, ask for just a selection of dishes. Located southeast of the Campo, off Via di Pantaneto. Closed Thurs.

Picnics, snacks and ice cream

It's an easy matter to put together your own picnic, allowing a very cheap meal in the Campo or other squares – Piazza Santa Maria dei Servi is a nice spot. Slices of **pizza by weight** can be bought from many small hole-in-the wall places around the city, while the best picnic supplies – or treats to take home – come from the Pizzicheria Morbidi, Banchi di Sotto 27, and Manganelli 1879, Via di Città 71–73, two sensational and extravagantly stocked **food stores**. The market building south of the Campo in Piazza del Mercato is also good for picnic provisions, while Wednesday mornings see a full-scale open-air **market** – with food and clothing stalls – sprawl across La Lizza, below the fortress.

Among the best **bars for snacks** is the main branch of *Nannini* at Banchi di Sopra 22–24, a constant call for locals with perhaps the largest range of sweet and savoury snacks. **Ice cream** is bought by most Sienese at one or other end of the *passeggiata* – either at the *Nannini Gelateria*, at the Piazza Matteotti end of Banchi di Sopra, or at *Gelateria Artigiani*, just off the Campo at the corner of Via di Città and Via dei Pellegrini. **Panforte** is best bought fresh by the *etto* (100g) in any of the bakeries or the *pasticcerie* along Banchi di Sopra; the gift-packaged slabs aren't so good. A good place to start is La Nuova Pasticceria in Via Giovanni Dupré 37.

Bars

For a drink, there are pleasant, **neighbourhood bars** in most *contrade* – Via del Porrione, southeast of the Campo, has several, as does Via Camollia, north of Piazza Matteotti. In the **Campo**, *Bar Fonte Gaia* stays open later than most. On a more sedate note, the *Enoteca Italiana* (Tues–Sat noon–1am; Mon noon–8pm; free) inside the Forte di Santa Barbara (or Fortezza Medicea) has a cellar exhibiting every single Italian wine, and a bar – at its best in early evening – where you can order a glass of any of the cheaper wines, or buy any bottle from the range. Another good place for **wines** and spirits is the *Enoteca San Domenico*, Via del Paradiso 56. At various times of year the Enoteca organizes special *incontri* with particular wine regions. It also hosts occasional weekend **discos**.

For **live music**, there's *L'Officina* at Piazza del Sale 3a (☎0577.286.301), at the north end of the Terzo di Camollia, which offers around a hundred bottled beers and many on tap, along with *crostini* and *foccaccine* snacks. There are live bands on occasion, too, at the **disco-bar** *Al Cambio* (☎0577.43.183), south of the Campo at Via di Pantaneto 48.

Events

Posters for **city events** are to be seen around Piazza Matteotti or on the stepped alley leading out of Piazza del Mercato to Via di Salicotto. The day's **concerts, films and activities** are also advertised in the Siena supplement of *La Nazione* newspaper, and major cultural events are also detailed in the tourist office's free pamphlet. There are five in-town **clubs** and dance floors: *Al Cambio*, Via di Pantaneto 48; *Barone Rosso*, Via dei Termini 9; *Caffè 115*, Via dei Rossi 115; *Gallery*, Via di Pantaneto 13; and *L'Officina*, Piazza del Sale 3.

Classical music tastes are the most likely to be rewarded, as the Monte dei Paschi and Accademia Chigiana sponsor impressive concerts throughout the year. The most prestigious – often featuring a major opera production – are held in the period around the Settimana Musicale Senese (third week of Aug). Details can be obtained from the tourist office or the Accademia Chigiana at Via di Città 89 (☎0577.46.152); tickets costing from L15,000 to L45,000 are available from Viagi SETI, at Piazza del Campo 56.

Other cultural events include **Siena Jazz**, a tuition fortnight in the last week of July and first week of August, which usually includes a few public sessions, and a range of concerts – mostly rock and jazz – in the PDS-Communist Party summer **Festa dell'Unità**.

Listings

ACI (Automobile Club of Italy), Viale Vittorio Veneto 47 (☎0577.49.001).

Banks and exchange Banks are concentrated along Banchi di Sopra, north of the Campo, and there's an automatic exchange machine in the window of the Monte dei Paschi at no. 92. The *Hotel Coop* opposite San Domenico and the train station ticket office will also change cash and travellers' cheques, but the most central option is the Exact in Via di Città, which charges a hefty commission but is open daily 8.30am–11pm.

Bike and scooter rental Rent bikes at DF Bike, Via Massetana Romana 54 (☎0577.271.905); scooters and bikes at DF Motoricambi, Via dei Gazzani 16–18 (☎0577.288.387) or Automotocicli Perozzi, Via del Romitorio 5 (☎0577.223.157).

Books and newspapers English-language books – novels plus a fair selection of books on Siena and Tuscany – are to be found at the Libreria Senese, Via di Città 94; two virtually adjacent branches of Feltrinelli, Banchi di Sopra 66; and Bassi, Via di Città 6–8. Bassi also stocks British and American newspapers (the *Guardian* European edition and *International Herald Tribune* arrive in the afternoon) and magazines.

Bus enquiries TRA-IN, Piazza Gramsci (☎0577.204.246), or at Piazza San Domenico (☎0577.204.245) for out-of-town services.

Car rental Try Avis, Via Simone Martini 36 (☎0577.270.305 or 0577.49.275); Hertz, Viale Sardegna 27 (☎0577.45.085); General Cars, Viale Toselli 20/26 (☎0577.40.518).

Language courses The Sienese are reputed to speak some of the "purest" Italian in the country. To study here, contact the Italian Language and Culture School for Foreigners, Piazzetta Grassi 46 (☎0577.280.695).

Left luggage 24-hr locker service at the railway station.

Lost property *Comune di Siena*, Casato di Sotto 23 (Mon–Sat 9am–12.30pm plus Tues 3–5pm).

Market Siena's market takes place at La Lizza on Wed (8am–1pm).

Police *Questura*, Via del Castoro (immediately east of the duomo); special *Ufficio Stranieri* (Foreigners' Office) in Piazza Jacopo della Quercia (Mon–Tues 8.30am–10.30am; Wed 8.30am–10.30am & 3.30–5.30pm).

Post office The main post office is on Piazza Matteotti (Mon–Fri 8.15am–7pm, Sat 8.15am–noon).

Swimming pool There's a *Piscina Comunale* on Piazza G. Amendola, to the north of the city, off Viale Vittorio Emanuele; take bus #5 from Piazza Matteotti.

Telephones International calls can be made from the main Telecom Italia office at Via dei Termini 40 (Mon–Sat 8am–8.30pm, Sun 9am–12.45pm & 3–7.45pm). Alternatively, try *Bar Centrale* (open till midnight) at Via Cecco Angiolieri 37, a block north of the Campo; you pay at the bar after making your call. Other special Telecom Italia phone booths at Via di Città 113, Via Pantaneto 44, Via dei Rossi 86 and Viale Vittorio Emanuele II 15.

Train enquiries ☎0577.280.115 (daily 7am–8.30pm).

travel details

Leaving Siena is easiest by bus. From the station by San Domenico, Lazzi and TRA-IN have connections throughout the province – half-hourly to Poggibonsi (for connections to San Gimignano buy a through ticket), and half a dozen times daily to Montalcino and Montepulciano. Lazzi and SITA services also run throughout the day to Florence, and regularly to Massa Maríttima, Volterra and Rome; for Rome buy tickets well in advance. For Florence, take a *diretto*, which arrives in an hour; those marked "Via Strove" take nearly three hours. There's no shortage of information: you can make use of a computer display (with print-outs) in the bus office and there's a board by the church, detailing times and departure bays, though its departure times are sometimes a touch out of date, so double check with the information office.

Trains are generally less convenient as they're slower – around an hour and forty minutes to Florence – and getting to the station involves a connecting bus. However, Siena is linked with the Florence to Pisa line via Empoli – there are plenty of through trains to Florence, but not to Pisa – and

is connected to Grosseto (and thence Rome) to the southwest. There's also a very pretty minor line southeast through Asciano and San Giovanni d'Asso – useful if you fancy a hike to the monastery of Monte Oliveto Maggiore (see p.364).

TRAINS

Siena to: Asciano (12 daily; 35min); Buonconvento (6 daily; 25min); Chiusi (12 daily; 1hr 35min); Empoli (hourly; 50min–1hr 20min; change for Pisa, 30min); Florence (9 daily; 1hr 40min); Grosseto (6 daily; 1hr 20min).

BUSES

Siena to: Arezzo, Asciano, Buonconvento, Certaldo, Chianciano Terme, Chiusi, Colle di Val d'Elsa, Florence, Gaiole, Greve, Grosseto, Lucca, Massa Maríttima, Montalcino, Monte Amiata, Monte San Savino, Montepulciano, Monteriggioni, Pienza, Poggibonsi, Radda, Rome, San Gimignano (via Poggibonsi), San Quírico d'Orcia, Sinalunga, Vescovado and Volterra.

CHAPTER SEVEN

THE SIENESE HILL TOWNS

J ust as Siena provides a perfect antidote to Florence, so the rural **hill-towns** that cluster around the old capital of the Sienese Republic provide an intimate counterpoint to the larger towns that crowd in on the Tuscan capital. Most of Siena's satellites are more appealing than their Florentine equivalents, and benefit from surroundings that exemplify the timeless pastoral quality for which the region is renowned. **San Gimignano** is the pick of the bunch, thanks mainly to its famous crop of towers, a vision of medieval perfection now somewhat compromised by the huge numbers of day-trippers who crowd its warren of streets. That said, the fresco-lined Collegiata and its clutch of minor churches, not to mention an excellent civic museum, are all unmissable attractions, and well worth building an overnight stay around. **Monteriggioni**, a less well-known and thus less spoilt medieval village, is another must-see, and can easily be incorporated into a visit to **Colle di Val d'Elsa**, another centuries-old enclave but one that is often overlooked by visitors who are deterred by its unlovely outskirts. You should also try to fit **Volterra** into your itinerary: slightly cut off from the other Sienese hill towns, it's a dramatically situated, brooding sort of town whose Etruscan origins are never far from the surface. Known primarily for its archeological museum, it also has a fascinating art gallery and a captivating cathedral square that's as attractive as almost any in Italy.

From Siena to San Gimignano

Heading west from Siena, most people have San Gimignano firmly in their sights. If you have time, the best route to follow is the N2 as far as the turreted fortress-hamlet of **Monteriggioni**, then turn west to **Colle di Val d'Elsa**, whose striking medieval upper town extends along a narrow ridge. From Colle, a scenic and minor road, which walkers might try paralleling across country, runs on via Bibbiano to San Gimignano.

On **public transport**, you can stop easily enough at Colle, before catching another bus to the industrial town of Poggibonsi – and a connection from there to San Gimignano; for Monteriggioni, you can catch a bus to the turning up to the village (and

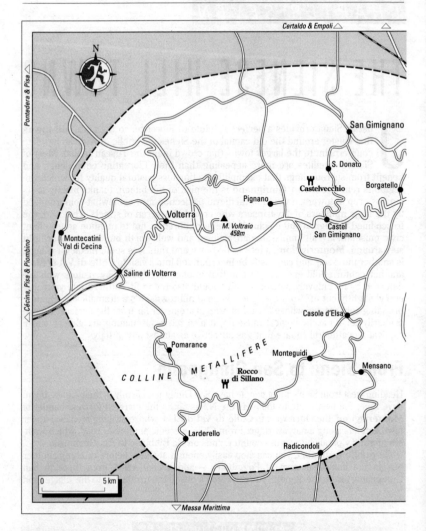

hail another one on from there to Colle or back to Siena). Most buses from Siena (or Florence) to San Gimignano involve a Poggibonsi connection, though there's a direct TRA-IN service in summer.

Note that the route north from Poggibonsi to Empoli – via Certaldo and Castelfiorentino – is covered on pp.194-197.

Monteriggioni

The perfectly preserved walls of **MONTERIGGIONI** declare their presence for miles ahead from the N2 or the Siena-Florence motorway. The citadel, begun by the Sienese in 1213, was a strategic target for any troops marching on Siena from the north and is

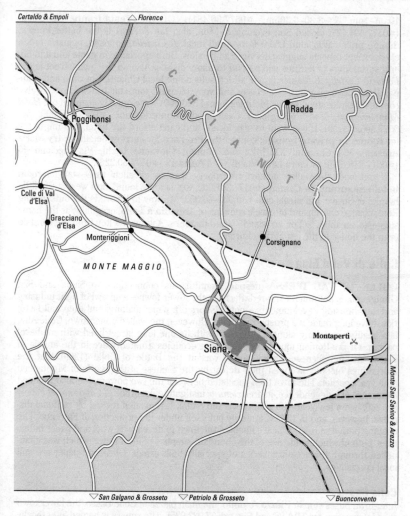

immortalized in Dante's *Inferno*, in which he compares the towers – added during reconstruction in 1260 after the Sienese victory at Montaperti – to giants in an abyss. The verse greets you as you enter the village, which consists of just a couple of dozen houses, two restaurants, and the odd bar. The houses give way to gardens as they near the ramparts, and an athlete could probably run the main street, from south to north gates, in about ten seconds.

All of which, of course, accounts for the charm of the place. The walls apart, there are no sights bar a pretty Romanesque church – just long views out over the Tuscan countryside. You don't necessarily need a car or bike to reach the place – the train station is 2km distant at Castellina Scalo (about 20 minutes' walk). There is a small seasonal Pro Loco, or **tourist office**, at Largo Fontebranda 5 (April–Oct daily except Wed

10am–1pm & 3.30–6.30pm; ☎0577.30.481). Of the **restaurants**, *Il Pozzo* (☎0577.304.127; closed Sun evening & Mon, also Jan & Aug) is the better known, though pricey at around L50,000 for a full meal. *Il Castello*, opposite, is just a touch cheaper, but reports suggest service can be slow. Both specialize in game and add liberal sprinklings of truffles and *porcini* to many dishes. Also on the main street is the *Fattoria Castello di Monteriggioni*, which sells a fine local Chianti, Vinsanto and grappa. The village also boasts a classy and very pleasant four-star **hotel** whose twelve rooms – despite steep prices (doubles from L340,000) – are quickly snapped up: *Hotel Monterrigioni*, Via I Maggio, 4 Castello di Monteriggioni (☎0577.305.009, fax 0577.305.011; ⑨). If you want to stay locally and can't afford the hotel, you might try for **rooms in private houses**: contact the Pro Loco for current details, or try Maria Arezzini, Via Giovanni XXIII 22 (no phone); Giovanna Lachi, Via Ricciano 46 (☎0577.318.570); or Piera Lelli, Via di Val d'Aosta 19 (☎0577.50.220).

If you fancy the walk – or have transport – a really excellent three-star, ten-room **hotel-restaurant**, *La Casalta* (☎0577.301.002; ④), is to be found 4km west at the little hamlet of Strove; full meals cost L30,000–40,000. Midway to Strove is the outstanding Romanesque church and monastic remains of **Abbadia a Isola**, originally, as the name suggests, an abbey set on an island – amid marshes. Ask for the key from the caretaker in the house to the left of the church.

Colle di Val d'Elsa

COLLE DI VAL D'ELSA, despite plentiful bus connections to Siena and San Gimignano, is not much explored. Perhaps the lower town – a sprawl of light industry and new housing developments – puts visitors off: paper-making, and then nail factories, have long made it a prosperous place. However, the walled upper town, Colle Alta, is a beauty, stretching along a ridge and with its one long street lined with medieval palazzi. Of pre-Roman foundation, the town occupies a noted place in the annals of Florentine and Sienese rivalry, for it was at the Battle of Colle (1269) that the Florentines bloodily avenged their defeat by the Sienese at the Battle of Montaperti nine years earlier. The town then vacillated between the two powers, but also retained a measure of independence, its free *comune* instigating the office of *Capitano del Popolo* in 1286, just a few years after Florence and Siena. It remained racked by factional disputes, however, and in 1333 voluntarily put itself under the protection of Florence. The ensuing period of relative peace enabled the town to develop its wool and paper industries, both of which made use of the abundant supplies of local water, which was channelled through the area in a series of specially built canals. Glass and paper are still local specialities.

Colle Basso

Inter-town buses stop in **Piazza Arnolfo**, the main piazza of Colle Basso, the lower town (bus information for TRA-IN and Sita ☎0577.923.925). The square is named after locally raised Arnolfo di Cambio – architect of the duomo and Palazzo Vecchio in Florence – who was born here around 1232. A block north is the town's major piece of modern architecture, a regional headquarters of the Monte dei Paschi bank, designed by **Giovanni Michelucci**; mixing Portakabin-like offices with open girders, it's not one of his most captivating efforts. En route for the upper town (see opposite page) drop into Colle Basso's only other worthwhile sight, the thirteenth-century church of **Sant'Agostino**, largely rebuilt by Antonio da Sangallo the Elder in 1521, three years after embarking on his masterpiece, the church of San Biagio in Montepulciano (see p.391). The second altar on the right contains a glorious *Madonna and Child with Saints* by Taddeo di Bartolo, probably a surviving panel of a triptych. The eye-catching marble tabernacle in the north aisle, the *Madonna del Piano*, is attributed to Baccio da Montelupo (1469–1535).

Colle Alta

From Piazza Arnolfo, it's a pretty steep ten-minute climb up to **Colle Alta**. If you want to skip the exercise and take a **taxi** there's a rank in Piazza Arnolfo, or you can call ☎0577.923.610 or 0577.921.379. Otherwise follow Via San Sebastiano and then the brick-paved **costa**, which brings you out at the eastern tip of the town. If you drive or take a bus up to Colle Alta, you're directed around a circuitous route to the west end of the ridge, by the Porta Nuova.

At the top of the *costa*, you've little choice but to follow **Via del Castello**, the centre of a three-street grid, past a scattering of tower-houses; Arnolfo di Cambio was born in the one at no. 63, the so-called Torre di Arnolfo, on the left at the beginning of the street. Just a little farther down is the small Romanesque church of **Santa Maria in Canonica**, built in the twelfth or thirteenth century, but thought to have far older origins. Its interior is notable for a stupendous late fourteenth-century tabernacle of the *Madonna and Child with Saints* by Pier Francesco Fiorentino; the frame, which is almost as impressive as the painting, is the original.

Midway along the street, the **Piazza del Duomo** opens out, flanked by the cathedral and three museums. The **duomo**, its Romanesque origins all but obliterated by later remodelling (1603–1815), features a marble pulpit (1465) by Giuliano da Maiano, who used four pillars and capitals from a much older work to frame his bas-reliefs. His brother, Benedetto, was responsible for the font (1468), the two having worked together during the same period in nearby San Gimignano. The fourth chapel on the right has a famous *Nativity* (1635), the masterpiece of Rutilio Manetti, the leading Sienese follower of Caravaggio. In the depths of the right transept stands the **Cappella del Santo Chiodo**, commissioned by the Piccolomini pope, Pius II, to house a nail (*chiodo*) from the Cross, the relic providing the inspiration for the beautiful tabernacle attributed to Mino da Fiesole. The nearby bronze lectern, palm branch and eagle are by Pietro Tacca, a pupil of Giambologna, whose eccentric work will be familiar to anyone who's seen his strange fountains in Florence's Piazza Santissima Annunziata. Tacca also probably cast the impressive bronze Crucifix above the high altar, the work having been designed by Giambologna.

The **Museo Archeologico** (May–Sept Tues–Sat 10am–noon & 5–7pm, Sat & Sun 10am–noon & 4–7pm; Oct–April Tues–Fri 3.30–5.30pm, Sat & Sun 10am–noon & 3.30–6.30pm; L3000), housed in the former Palazzo Pretorio (1335) to the left of the duomo, is of passing interest only, save for the finds from the local *Tomba dei Calisna Sepu*, one of Tuscany's most important Etruscan tombs: key treasures from it are scattered in museums as far afield as Berlin. Just out of the piazza on the right, the three-room **Museo Civico e d'Arte Sacra** in the old Palazzo dei Priori at Via del Castello 31 (April–Oct Tues–Fri 4–6pm, Sat & Sun 10am–noon & 4–7pm; Nov–March Sat & Sun 10am–noon & 3–6pm; L5000) is the more interesting of the town's two museums, housed in the old bishop's palace, which retains frescoes of hunting scenes by Bartolo di Fredi. It also has a fair collection of Sienese paintings gathered from local churches; more works from around town are due to be installed here. The most interesting canvas is a *Maestà* from Abbadia Isola, once attributed to Duccio, but now given to the anonymous Maestro di Badia a Isola.

About a hundred metres beyond Piazza del Duomo, stands the covetable **Palazzo Campana**, a Mannerist *tour de force* built in 1539 by Baccio d'Agnolo, the architect responsible for the rather less amenable Palazzo Bartolini in Florence. From here a bridge connects the town's medieval core to its fifteenth- and sixteenth-century expansions. Off to the north stands an imposing Franciscan monastery, whose church, **San Francesco**, claims a high altarpiece (occasionally removed) of the *Madonna and Child with Four Saints* (1479) by Sano di Pietro, a painting that's more than worth the walk (ring the bell of the seminary if the church is shut). Pay particular attention to the scenes in the predella, which illustrate episodes from the lives of the saints depicted in the main painting (Benedict, Cyrinus, Donatus and Justina). The second panel from the left depicts Cyrinus, a Croatian saint, preaching to the crowd who have come to watch his martyrdom: he's shown miraculously floating on the stone which had been tied round his neck in an attempt to drown him. Donatus, patron saint of Arezzo (his birthplace), was martyred in the fourth century, and is remembered primarily for frightening off a dragon which had been poisoning local wells: Sano shows him with his mule, bravely marching to meet the dragon emerging from its cave. The right-hand scene shows the third-century Justina, a royal princess, patron of Padua but much venerated in Pisa, being martyred on the orders of her father.

Remaining with the main road through this quarter you come to the *Hotel Arnolfo* in Piazza Santa Caterina. Off to the left of this square is an alleyway called **Vicolo della Fontanella**, with a **glass workshop** – Colle makes much of its money from glass factories in the lower town – and the *Enoteca della Fortuna*, a wine shop with a tiny restaurant upstairs (see below). At the end of the main road is the hugely bastioned **Porta Nuova**, attributed to Giuliano da Sangallo.

Practicalities

Colle's **tourist office** is at Via Campana 43 (Mon–Sat: April–Oct 9.30am–1.30pm & 3.30–7pm; Nov–March 10am–1pm & 3.30–5.30pm; ☎0577.922.791). There's also a small, summer-only Pro Loco at Piazza Arnolfo 5 (☎0577.920.389): this main lower-town piazza is also home to the **police station** (☎0577.920.003; lost property section ☎0577.920.831). Car, bike and scooter **rentals** are available from Mario Antichi, Via Livini 1 (☎0577.923.366). **Walking tours** of the area (On Foot in Tuscany; ☎ & fax 0577.960.035; *sammonti@iol.it*), led by an experienced, locally based English guide, are a recent innovation, designed for independent travellers keen to explore the countryside; suitable for all ages, trips include picnic lunch of local produce and wine from the Chianti region.

If the town's artistic attractions seem on the slight side, **food** provides a major spur to a couple of hours' exploration. In **Colle Alta**, the *Enoteca della Fortuna*, mentioned above, is a great little Tuscan restaurant – very reasonably priced at around L35,000 (☎0577.923.102). If money is no object, in **Colle Basso** there is the highly recommended and Michelin-starred *Arnolfo*, Via XX Settembre 50 (☎0577.920.549), worth the L90,000 or so for a wonderful meal. It also has five rooms (⑥). To round things off, call in at the main café in Piazza Arnolfo for an **ice cream**, reckoned by not a few Tuscans as the finest in the province.

The town has three main **hotels**. On a budget, the choice is limited to the 24-room two-star *Hotel Il Nazionale* at Via Garibaldi 20, in Colle Basso just west of the square (☎0577.920.039, fax 0577.920.168; ③). More upmarket are the big 38-room *La Vecchia Cartiera*, a three-star in Via Oberdan 5–9, again just off Piazza Arnolfo (☎0577.921.107, fax 0577.923.688; ⑤), and the very central 32-room three-star *Arnolfo*, Via F. Campana 8, the only hotel in Colle Alta (☎0577.922.020, fax 0577.922.324; ④) – it's some L40,000 cheaper and preferable to the *Carteria*. An alternative choice is the 15-room three-star *Hotel Villa Belvedere* (☎0577.920.966, fax 0577.924.128; ⑥), an eighteenth-century villa on Via Senese, 3km south of town on the Monteriggioni road, with tennis and riding facilities and a pool.

Colle has all the facilities you'd expect of a moderate-sized town, but **nightlife** is restricted to a single club, *H2O*, a pub-disco at Via Savalgna 20 (☎0577.920.460), together with a self-styled "pub": the *Bistro Bel Ami*, Via Pozzo Tondo 7; and the *Sapia Tea Room*, Via del Castello 6. Market day is Friday.

Casole d'Elsa

The roads south of Colle lead into the **Colline Metallifere** (Metal Hills), dotted with geothermal energy plants (the largest are out towards Larderello, see p.357) and their snaking pipelines. Other sights are few, though the countryside, as ever, is liberally sprinkled with Romanesque churches and inspiringly placed farmhouses and cypress groves.

Heading for the abbey church of San Galgano (see p.359), or merely as part of a scenic loop back to Siena, if you are driving, you might consider the very pretty rural route through **CASOLE D'ELSA**, a village which looks inviting from a distance, but yields relatively little of substantial interest. TRA-IN buses also pass this way from Siena. Casole's fortress, the village's most imposing sight, is now employed as council offices. An **Etruscan tomb** discovered nearby, reputedly one of the richest ever found, may add to Casole's quiet appeal, though few of its treasures have thus far reached the **Museo Archeologico e della Collegiata** at Piazza della Libertà 1 (mid-March to mid-Nov Tues–Sat 10am–noon & 4–7pm, Sun 10am–noon & 3–6pm; Jan to mid-March & mid-Nov to Dec Tues–Sat 3–6pm; L3000).The Museo stands alongside the fifteenth-century Gothic **Collegiata** church (restored after war bomb damage), highlights of which are an important *Madonna and Child* and *Massacre of the Innocents* by Andrea di Niccolò, and a *Madonna and Child* attributed to Segna di Buonaventura. The church is also worth a look for the tomb of Bishop Tommaso Andrei (died 1303) by Gano da Siena.

The village's **tourist office** is in the same square at Piazza della Libertà 1 (opening hours as for museum above; ☎0577.948.705). Markets are held in the piazza on the first and third Mondays of the month. **Bikes** can rented from Sophie Guilleminot, Località Molino La Senna (☎0577.948.709).

Casole has a stunning **hotel**, the very smart *Relais La Suvera* (☎0577.960.300, fax 0577.960.220; ⑨), a four-star located in the hamlet of **Pievescola**. Originally a Sienese castle, it was converted into a villa by Baldassare Peruzzi during the Renaissance. The hotel incorporates the villa, along with a converted church and mill. What with its loggia, extensive grounds, stepped terraces, antique furniture, priceless works of art, ritzy suites and beautiful rooms, it's no wonder it's ranked by many as **Tuscany's finest hotel** of its type. It should be – rooms in various annexes start at L500,000 for a double room: stay in the Villa proper and you'll drop a cool million lire a night.

At a more realistic level, both Casole and **Radicondoli**, another pretty though insubstantial village 15km to the south, have useful run-of-the-mill hotels: the big four-star, 42-room *Gemini* with swimming pool, at Strada Provinciale 4 outside Casole (☎0577.948.622, fax 0577.948.241; ⑤); the three-star, 13-room *Verde Oasis* at Via Guido Rossa 18 in Radicóndoli (☎0577.790.760, fax 0577.790.570; ④); and the three-star *La Sorgente* in Bagni delle Galleraie, a hamlet of Radicóndoli (☎0577.793.150; ⑤). Casole also has *agriturismo* rooms to let, just north of the village, and a **restaurant**, *Il Merlo* (closed Tues), that serves reasonable traditional Tuscan food. Radicóndoli has the panoramically sited *Caffè-Bar-Trattoria-Pizzeria La Pergola*.

Another possible lunch stop is the hill-top hamlet of **Mensano**, on an especially scenic stretch of road between the two villages, which has a tiny, family-run trattoria up by the children's playground at the summit.

Poggibonsi

POGGIBONSI has little more than its transport links and its politics to recommend it. A serious industrial town, conspicuously ugly alongside its Tuscan neighbours, it is reputed to be the home to Italy's reddest council. Prior to the last war it might have looked more like Colle, but bombing left little trace of its past other than the **Castello della Magione**, a little Romanesque complex, possibly with Templar origins, consisting of a chapel and pilgrim hospice. The unfinished **Medici fort** at the top of the town isn't worth the slog. The superb four-star **hotel** up here, however, most certainly is: the *Villa San Lucchese*, Località San Lucchese 5 (☎0577.934.231, fax 0577.934.729; ⑧) is a lovely villa hotel with swimming pool, tennis courts and a rural setting that seems a world away from the tatty town down in the valley.

If transport connections aren't working in your favour, there are bars and cafés to pass the time, and – if things are desperate – a moderately priced hotel if you have to stay over, the two-star *Italia* at Via Trento 36 (☎0577.936.142; ③). For **eating**, try the pizzeria *Piero*, Via della Libertà 62 (☎0577.938.871; closed Wed), for great thin-crust pizzas and reliable pastas. Another good restaurant is *Il Sole* at Via Trento 5 (☎0577.936.283; closed Mon & July–Aug). Note that in addition to its **bus** connections, Poggibonsi has a station on the Siena–Empoli **train line**.

San Gimignano

SAN GIMIGNANO – "delle Belle Torri" – is perhaps the best-known village in Italy. Its stunning skyline of towers, built in aristocratic rivalry by the feuding nobles of the twelfth and thirteenth centuries, evokes the appearance of medieval Tuscany more than any other sight. And its image as a "Medieval Manhattan" has for decades caught the tourist imagination, helped along by its convenience as a day trip from Florence or Siena.

The town is all that it's cracked up to be: quietly monumental, very well preserved, enticingly rural and with a fine array of religious and secular frescoes. However, from May through to October, San Gimignano has very little life of its own – and a lot of daytrippers, with a preponderance of high-spending Germans. If you want to get any feel for the place, beyond the level of art treasures or quaintness, you really need to come well out of season. If you can't, then aim to spend the night here – in the evenings the town takes on a very different pace and atmosphere.

Some history

San Gimignano was probably founded by the Etruscans – tombs in the surrounding countryside bear witness to their presence locally – and later inhabited by the Romans. It reputedly took its present name in 450 from San Gimignano, a bishop of Modena, whose intervention is supposed to have saved the settlement from the attacks of Attila the Hun (see below for more on the saint). During the tenth century a feudal castle was built on the site – a stronghold which was soon surrounded by a cluster of houses, and which by the twelfth century had become a free *comune*. A second (surviving) set of walls was added in the middle of the thirteenth century, about the time that the town's predominantly wooden houses began to be replaced by stone structures and the first of the famous **towers**.

Wealth increased during the Middle Ages, and San Gimignano's population of 15,000 (twice the present number) prospered as a result of agricultural holdings and a position close to the Via Francigena, the ancient trade and pilgrimage route between Rome and northern Europe. At its heyday, in the fourteenth century, the town's walls enclosed five monasteries, four hospitals, public baths and a brothel.

A force to be reckoned with, the town was mostly controlled by two great families – the Ardinghelli and the Salvucci – heads of the **Guelph** and **Ghibelline** factions respectively. Inter-family **feuds**, however, had long wreaked havoc. The first Ardinghelli versus Salvucci conflict erupted in 1246, and for the following century there were few years of peace. Guelph and Ghibelline loyalties provided further fuel, and whenever the town itself was united there were wars with Volterra, Poggibonsi and other nearby towns. The vendettas came to a halt only after the Black Death of 1348. It had a devastating effect both on the population and – as the pilgrim trade collapsed – on the economy. The Ardinghelli family, despite opposition from the Salvucci, applied to Florence for the town to become a part of that city's *comune*: a request that was approved by only one vote – a reflection on San Gimignano's fractious reputation.

Subjection to Florence in 1353 broke the power of the nobles, leaving San Gimignano unaffected by the struggles between aristocracy and local council which racked other Tuscan towns. The tower houses, symbolic of real control elsewhere, posed little threat

– and so were not torn down; today, fifteen (of an original seventy-two) survive. The town itself, further hit by plague in 1464 and 1631, passed into a rural backwater existence.

At the turn of the nineteenth century, travellers spoke of San Gimignano as "miserably poor"; it was hardly romanticized by E.M. Forster, who took the town (he calls it Monteriano) as the setting for his novel *Where Angels Fear to Tread*. San Gimignano's postwar history has been one of ever-increasing affluence, through tourism and the production of an old-established, but recently rejuvenated, white wine, *Vernaccia di San Gimignano*. Its *comune* has since found itself in crisis once more, however, with the discovery that ancient, leaking drains have been undermining the foundations of several towers, causing large cracks to appear.

Arrival, orientation and information

Most people visit San Gimignano as a **day trip** from Siena. Using public transport you'll need to take a **train** or SITA **bus** to Poggibonsi (40min) and then pick up one of the roughly hourly TRA-IN buses for the 20-minute journey to San Gimignano. At Poggibonsi exit the station, head straight across the square ahead of you and turn right down the street at the top. The TRA-IN **bus stop and office** is a couple of hundred metres down on the left. Alternatively, walk left down the length of platform 1, exit through the gates at the end and the office is just across the road. There are also around four buses daily between San Gimignano and Volterra, though it's a tortuous route that's not feasible as a one-day return.

Once up at the walled town, orientation is straightforward. Arriving by **bus**, you can get out either at **Piazzale Martiri di Monte Maggio**, just outside Porta San Giovanni, the south gate, or by **Porta San Matteo**, the northern gate. **Bus timetables** in San Gimignano are displayed in the Piazza del Duomo and **tickets** can be bought from the tourist office; virtually all major destinations (Florence, Siena, Volterra, Colle di Val d'Elsa) involve connections at Poggibonsi, which is also the nearest **train station**. Last buses back to Florence or Siena are usually around 8.30–9pm. Buses pick up passengers at the north gate, San Matteo, and by the southern gate, San Giovanni, in Piazzale Martiri di Monte Maggio.

If you're **driving**, follow the road clockwise around the walls and you pass three pay **car parks** – the simplest option for a short stay. The most convenient – but also the busiest – is that on Via dei Fossi just west of Porta San Giovanni (see map). Free parking is possible on the outskirts of town (on the approach from the south close to Piazzale Martiri di Monte Maggio), but not really worth the effort in summer, unless you need a space for several days or find the pay car parks full. To drive within the walls – not necessary unless you're dropping off luggage at your hotel – you need to be issued with a permit from one of the hotels; the way in is through **Porta San Jacopo** at the northeast corner.

The **tourist office** (daily: March–Oct 9am–1pm & 3–7pm; Nov–Feb 9am–1pm & 2–6pm; ☎0577.940.008), on the south side of Piazza del Duomo, is helpful, supplying lists of hotels, rooms and apartments: it also sells **bus tickets** and does foreign exchange, though San Gimignano is full of *cambio* kiosks and cash/exchange machines.

Accommodation

A crucial factor to enjoying the town is to get a room inside the walls – which from May to October means booking ahead and/or arriving early in the day. The town's four main **hotels** are all expensive three-star joints but budget alternatives are to be found in a **youth hostel**, a convent, and a dozen or so privately let rooms. To help in the search, try the immensely helpful **booking agency**, Co-op Hotels Promotion, just inside the Porta San Giovanni at Via S. Giovanni 125 (summer Mon–Sat 9.30–7pm; winter

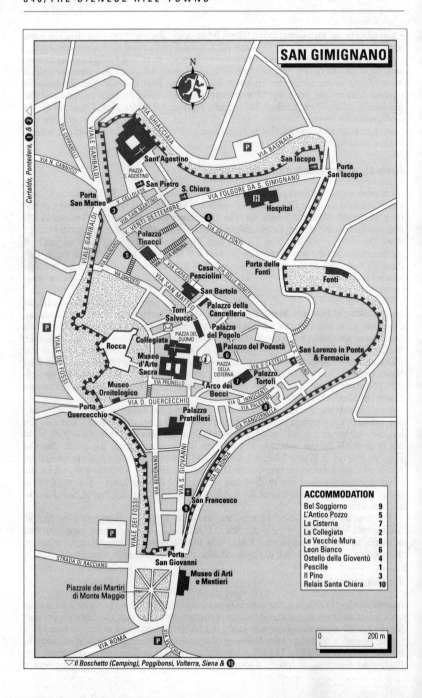

SAN GIMIGNANO

N

Certaldo, Pontedera, **1** & **2**

VIA CEPPARELLI
VIA N. CANNICCI
VIALE GARIBALDI
VIA GHIACCIAIA
VIA BAGNAIA

Sant'Agostino
San Iacopo
Porta
San Iacopo

PIAZZA
S. AGOSTINO
San Pietro
V. CELLOLESE
S. Chiara

Porta
San Matteo
VIA SAN MARTINO
VIA FOLGORE DA S. GIMIGNANO
Hospital

VIALE GARIBALDI
V. VENTI SETTEMBRE
VIA DELLE FONTI

Palazzo
Tinacci
VIA DELLA VERGINA
Porta delle
Fonti

VIA MAINARDI
VIA CAPASSI
VIA DELLE ROMITE
Fonti

VIA DIACCETO
Casa
Pesciolini

San Bartolo

Torri
Salvucci
Palazzo della
Cancelleria

VIA SAN MATTEO
Palazzo
del Popolo

Collegiata
PIAZZA DEL
DUOMO
Palazzo del Podestà

Rocca
Museo
d'Arte
Sacra
PIAZZA
DELLA
CISTERNA
San Lorenzo in Ponte
& Farmacia

VIA D. CASTELLO
Palazzo
Tortoli

Museo
Ornitologico
VIA PRUNELLO
Arco dei
Becci

Porta
Quercecchio
VIA D. QUERCECCHIO
VIA D. INNOCENTI
VIA PALESTRO

Palazzo
Pratellesi
VIA PIANDORNELLA

VIA BERIGNANO
VIA S. GIOVANNI
VIA DI RONDA

San Francesco

STRADA DI RACCIANO
VIALE DEI FOSSI

Porta
San Giovanni

Piazzale dei Martiri
di Monte Maggio
Museo di Arti
e Mestieri

VIA ROMA
VIA VECCHIA

Il Boschetto (Camping), Poggibonsi, Volterra, Siena & **10**

ACCOMMODATION

Bel Soggiorno	9
L'Antico Pozzo	5
La Cisterna	7
La Collegiata	2
Le Vecchie Mura	8
Leon Bianco	6
Ostello della Gioventù	4
Pescille	1
Il Pino	3
Relais Santa Chiara	10

0   200 m

Mon–Sat 9.30am–12.30pm & 3–6pm; ☎0577.940.809), which arranges rooms in hotels and private houses, apartments and *agriturismo* lets. Note too that the up-scale hotels do offer parking facilities, but charge in the region of L20,000 nightly for the privilege. The accommodation list below runs in roughly ascending order of price.

Hotels and guesthouses

Il Pino, Via San Matteo–Via Cellolese 4 (☎0577.942.225, fax 0577.940.415). A lovely, small guest-house above a restaurant, just inside the Porta San Matteo; 2 doubles and 3 singles. ②.

Le Vecchie Mura, Via Piandornella 15 (☎0577.940.270). A couple of double rooms above a restaurant, but more appealing than it sounds, with welcoming owners and superb views. ②.

La Cisterna, Piazza della Cisterna 24 (☎0577.940.328, fax 0577.942.080). One of the oldest-established (1919) and most elegant town hotels, built into a medieval ensemble at the base of some of the piazza's fourteenth-century towers. It's worth paying more for a room with either a (potentially noisy) piazza outlook, or (more restful) country view. ⑤.

Leon Bianco, Piazza della Cisterna 13 (☎0577.941.294, fax 0577.942.123). Tasteful 17-room three-star hotel with air-con, in a fourteenth-century mansion in the main square. Like the *Cisterna*, the better rooms, which have medieval features such as vaulted ceilings, look out over the square or the Elsa valley. The roof terrace for breakfast, drinks or lounging is a bonus. ⑥.

Bel Soggiorno, Via San Giovanni 91 (☎ & fax 0577.940.375). Similar quality, price and facilities to the *Leon Bianco*, though beware of having to take full pension in summer. The hotel restaurant rates quite highly, but you pay extra for breakfast, unlike the *Cisterna* and *Leon Bianco*. The 22 rooms are smallish but beautifully done: only eight have air-con. ⑦.

Pescille, Località Pescille, Strada Castel San Gimignano (☎0577.940.186, fax 0577.943.169). A three-star, 50-room hotel, the *Pescille* is 4km north of San Gimignano, has a pool and tennis courts, and is ringed by vineyards and olive groves. Rooms are restrained and suitably rustic: the best is the panoramic and eyrie-like Tower Room. Breakfast available, but no restaurant. ⑥.

L'Antico Pozzo, Via San Matteo 87 (☎0577.942.014, fax 0577.942.117; closed Nov to mid-March). An 18-room three-star. Very swish decor, reflected in the price. ⑦.

Relais Santa Chiara, Via G. Matteotti 1 (☎0577.940.701, fax 0577.942.096). Located in a panoramic position on the Poggibonsi road half a kilometre out of town. A smart 41-room, four-star with swimming pool and spacious grounds, but now challenged in the upmarket stakes by the much more expensive and intimate *La Collegiata*. Breakfast and lunch are served, but there is no restaurant. ⑨.

La Collegiata, Località Strada 27 (☎0577.943.201, fax 0577.940.566). One of Tuscany's new breed of super-expensive hotels. For honeymoons and very special occasions only, given that doubles come in at around L800,000. Located 2km out of town off the Certaldo road. ⑨.

Hostel and campsite

Ostello della Gioventù, Via delle Fonti 1 (☎0577.941.991). A 75-bed HI hostel, well positioned in the north of town: reports suggest it could be better run, and the breakfast – as ever – is poor. Reception open 7.30–9.30am and 5–11.30pm. Beds in shared dorms, or, for a couple of thousand lire more, in 3-bed rooms. L24,000 (meals L16,000).

Camping Il Boschetto (☎0577.940.352, fax 0577.941.982; April to mid-Nov). The nearest campsite is 3km downhill from Piazzale Martiri di Monte Maggio at Santa Lucia, off the Volterra road. It has a bar and shop.

Private rooms

Within the walls, San Gimignano's **private rooms** are scattered around a dozen or so houses. They charge from around L60,000 for a double, a little less – reluctantly – for a single. Most have shared bathrooms. It is also possible to rent **apartments** with cooking facilities by the day – a cheap way of staying if you are in a group, but be sure to book ahead.

Cesarina Benucci, Via Diacceto 23 (no phone). Two singles with shared bathroom.

Aladina Bettini, Via Berignano 51 (☎0577.940.431 or 0577.907.080). One double, two singles and an apartment with bathroom and kitchen from about L100,000 a day.

Pietro Boldrini, Via San Matteo 95 (☎0577.940.908). Two doubles with shared bathroom.

Carla Rossi Busini, Via degli Innocenti (☎0577.955.041, fax 0577.941.268). One triple, plus a 3-bed apartment with kitchen, bathroom and living rooms from L120,000–150,000 a day depending on season. Busini also rents one double with private bathroom, and a 4-bed, two-bathroom apartment at Via Santo Stefano 11 from L120,000–190,000 daily.

Dina Conforti Totti, Via Mainardi 6 (☎0577.940.478). Two doubles with shared bathroom.

Maurizio Frosali, "Alla Casa de' Potenti", Piazza delle Erbe (☎0577.942.194 or 0577.943.190). Four doubles with private bathroom superbly located near the Collegiata: also two doubles (shared bathroom), and a 4-bed apartment with kitchen, living room and dining room at Via delle Vergini 6 from L70,000 daily (2 people sharing) or L140,000 (4 people).

Lida Gonnelli, Via Quercecchio 5 (☎0577.941.228). Two doubles with private bathrooms.

Ivosca Marri Gattolin, Via San Piero 1 (☎0577.940.433 or 0577.940.258). One double with private bathroom, two more with shared facilities.

Graziano Nacci, Via Santo Stefano 6 (☎0577.940.730). Three doubles with bathrooms. Address postal bookings c/o Piazza della Cisterna 15.

Nello Nencioni, Via Piandornella 20 (☎0577.940.546). Two doubles, one with private bathroom.

Rino Nencioni, Via Mainardi 6 (☎0577.940.137). One double, one single, with shared bathroom.

Mauro Pescini, Via San Matteo 44 (☎0577.941.011). One double room with private bathroom, plus a double-room apartment with bathroom, kitchen and living room from L135,000 a day.

Bruno Rosi, Via Santo Stefano 13 (☎0577.940.932). One double, one single, with shared bathroom.

The Town

San Gimignano is not much more than a village: you could walk from one end to the other in fifteen minutes, or around the walls in an hour. It deserves at least a day, however, both for the frescoes in the churches and museums, and for the surrounding countryside – some of the loveliest in Tuscany. From the fine south gate, **Porta San Giovanni** (1262) – the best place to start a tour – the palazzo-lined **Via San Giovanni** leads to the town's interlocking main squares, the Piazza della Cisterna and Piazza del Duomo. On the right of the street, about a hundred metres up, is the former church of **San Francesco** – a Pisan-style Romanesque building converted now, like many of the palazzi, to a shop selling *Vernaccia* and other local wines. Ignore the scrum around the tasting table and walk through to the lovely garden at the rear, where before tackling the town you can enjoy an incomparable view across the Tuscan hills.

You enter the **Piazza della Cisterna** through another majestic gateway, the **Arco dei Becci**, part of the original fortifications built before the town expanded and acquired its second set of thirteenth-century walls. The square is flanked by an anarchic cluster of towers and palazzi, and is named after the public cistern (1273) – still functioning – at its centre. The well was extended in 1346 on the orders of the then *Podestà*, Guccio de' Malvoli, whose coat of arms adorns one of the faces: note the rope-cut grooves, witness to centuries of use. It was in this square, and in other streets within the older inner walls, that most of the leading families had their houses.

To the left (northwest) of the square, beside an arch leading through to the Piazza del Duomo, are the twin Ardinghelli towers and palace; a Salvucci rival rears up close by. The tower on the square's northeast flank, topping the Palazzo Cortesi, is known as the Torre del Diavolo, so named, according to legend, because its owner returned after a long journey convinced that it had grown taller, the only explanation for the phenomenon, he alleged, being that a DIY-inclined devil had been busy during his absence. At its foot lies the little **Vicolo dell'Oro**, so named because it probably once housed the workshops of the town's goldsmiths (*orefici*).

The more austere **Piazza del Duomo**, off to the left of Piazza della Cisterna, introduces further towers and civic palazzi. Facing the duomo (more properly the **Collegiata**, as San Gimignano no longer has a bishop), the crenellated **Palazzo del Popolo** (or Palazzo Comunale), the town hall and home to the Museo Civico, stands to your left, the older **Palazzo del Podestà** (1239) behind you.

The Palazzo del Popolo was begun in 1270, probably to a plan by Arnolfo di Cambio, born in nearby Colle di Val d'Elsa, also responsible for Florence's duomo and Palazzo Vecchio. Oddly, the lower, older half, shows a Sienese influence, while the upper sections have a decidedly more Florentine flavour. The palace's Torre Grossa (see below) was completed in 1311, some time after a 1255 ordinance in which the *comune* decided that the town's tower-building frenzy had run its course. The Torre della Rognosa of the Palazzo del Podestà, which survives, was set as the maximum height (54m) for any subsequent private tower, the idea being that none should exceed the towers of the civic authorities. Looking around the skyline, it would seem that the rule was not much respected. The Salvucci clan, for example, responded at one point by building two towers in Via San Matteo, the Torri Salvucci, each shorter than the maximum, but arranged so close together as to make it clear that their combined height would be higher than anything conjured up by the *comune*.

The Collegiata

The first church on the site of the **Collegiata** was begun in the tenth century. Work on the present building, which is orientated back to front in respect of the earlier structure, began in the early twelfth century. The church was consecrated by Pope Eugenius III in 1148 and enlarged and altered by Giuliano da Maiano between 1466 and 1468. The plain facade (1239) could hardly provide a greater contrast with the **interior**, one of the most comprehensively frescoed churches in Tuscany. You need a good pocketful of L100 or L200 coins to do justice to the cycles, which fill just about every available space, their brilliant colours set off by Pisan-Romanesque arcades of black and white striped marble. The church is open in summer from 9am to 12.30pm and 3 to 6pm, and in winter from 9.30am to 12.30pm and 3 to 5.30pm. Admission is free, except for access to the small Cappella di Santa Fina (see below).

The three principal **fresco** cycles fill the right and left walls, plus two short side walls which protrude from the inside (entrance) wall of the facade. Beginning on this rear entrance wall you'll find a large central fresco of *St Sebastian* (1465) by Benozzo Gozzoli, painted five or six years after the artist's sumptuous fresco cycle in the Palazzo Medici-Riccardi in Florence (see p.114). Sebastian was often invoked during plague epidemics – one had struck San Gimignano in 1464, which was the reason for Gozzoli's commission – thanks largely to his powers of recovery: he actually survived an assault with arrows – though rather oddly remains the patron saint of archers – and was eventually martyred by being pummelled to death. The inscription below the heavily arrowed saint, who appears blithely unaffected by the casual and courtly display of archery, reads "in praise of the most glorious athlete, Sebastian".

Either side of Sebastian, on pedestals, are two wooden **statues** of the *Archangel Gabriel* and the *Madonna Annunciate*, carved by the Sienese sculptor Jacopo della Quercia in 1421 and given their slightly garish painted finish by Martino di Bartolomeo five years later. In front of each statue are pillars painted with frescoes by Gozzoli of the *Annunciation* and saints Anthony, Augustine and Bernardino. These pillars anchor the side walls containing the first of the church's fresco cycles, Taddeo di Bartolo's *Last Judgement* (1410), with *Paradiso* depicted to the right, *L'Inferno* to the left. One of the most gruesome depictions of a customarily lurid subject, the latter offers a no-holds-barred illustration of the Seven Deadly Sins, including Bosch-like fantasies on lust and gluttony, each wonderfully grisly detail now bright and clear after a recent restoration.

The church's other cycles depict scenes from the Old Testament (two tiers on the left wall) and the New Testament (two tiers on the right); in the lunettes above, scenes of the Creation above the Old Testament episodes are paralleled across the church by episodes from the Nativity. Somewhat surprisingly, the **Old Testament** and **Creation** scenes (26 in all), whose vision seems entirely medieval, were painted later, between 1356 and 1367. Created by Bartolo di Fredi, they reflect the influence of Lorenzetti's *Good and Bad Government* in Siena in their delight in genre detail, forming an essentially human narrative: *Abraham and Lot leading their flock towards Canaan*, for example, is a Tuscan farming scene, with appropriate landscape. They are also quirkily naturalistic – there are few odder frescoes than that of the *Drunkenness of Noah*, exposing a prominent penis in his stupor: Noah is traditionally considered to have been the first to promote agriculture and viticulture, and – more to the point – the first to have abused the products of the vine.

If your biblical knowledge is a bit ragged, the cycle (which is read left to right, top to bottom) follows the story of the *Flood* with those of *Abraham and Lot* (their trip to Canaan), *Joseph* (his dream; being let down the well; having his brothers arrested and being recognized by them), *Moses* (changing a stick into a serpent before the Pharoah; the Red Sea; Mount Sinai) and *Job* (temptation; the devil killing his herds and destroying his house; thanking God; and being consoled by friends). Above, note the fresco, perhaps the most beautiful of the entire cycle, depicting the *Creation of Eve* (fourth lunette from the left), in which Eve emerges from the rib of the sleeping Adam.

The authorship of the **New Testament** scenes (begun 1333) is disputed, with some historians now attributing them to Lippo Memmi, collaborator and brother-in-law of Simone Martini, or to a member of Memmi's workshop. Traditionally, the attribution is to Barna di Siena, another follower of Martini, possibly a pupil, who is supposed to have died in a fall from the scaffolding while at work here in the 1350s. Whatever, the scenes of Christ's Life and the Passion mark a distinct departure from Martini's style, with their interest in emotional expression. In *The Kiss of Judas* the focus of eyes is startlingly immediate, as is the absorption of all the figures in the action – St Peter thrusting into the foreground with his assault on the Roman soldier, while the other disciples gather their cloaks and flee. The same dramatic vision comes through in *Christ Carrying the Cross* and the dark dealings of *Judas Accepting the Pieces of Silver.* One of the most dramatic scenes of all is the *Resurrection of Lazarus*, in which a dumbstruck crowd witnesses the removal of a door to reveal the living Lazarus in the winding bandages of burial.

THE CAPPELLA DI SANTA FINA

Many of the chapels of the cathedral were remodelled between 1468 and 1475 as part of Giuliano da Maiano's renovation of the church, work which brought San Gimignano more fully into the Florentine Renaissance orbit. The **Cappella di San Gimignano**, to the left of the high altar, features an altar by Giuliano's brother, Benedetto da Maiano, partly constructed from fragments of an earlier work. The ciborium atop the high altar is also by Benedetto, though both brothers reserved their best work for the **Cappella di Santa Fina**, a Renaissance masterpiece located at the top of the right (south) aisle (April–Oct Mon–Sat 9.30am–7.30pm, Sat 9.30am–5pm; Nov–Dec Mon–Sat 9.30am–5pm; Jan–March Mon–Sat 9.30am–12.30pm & 3–5pm; Sun & public holidays 1–5pm; L6000 or with the single museum ticket: see box on p.343).

Giuliano designed the chapel (1468–75), while Benedetto designed its altar, marble shrine and bas-reliefs (1475), though the most eye-catching part of the ensemble, which is dedicated to San Gimignano's patron saint, is a pair of frescoes in opposing lunettes by Domenico Ghirlandaio (1475).

St Fina, the subject of the frescoes and the frieze of the shrine, was born in San Gimignano in 1238 and struck by a dreadful and incurable disease at the age of ten. She gave herself immediately to God, repented her sins (the worst seems to have been accepting an orange from a boy), and insisted on spending the agonized five years until her death lying on a plank on the floor (the idea being that she would be brought closer to Christ through increased suffering). As a result of her position, and her complete paralysis during her final days, she was tormented, among other things, by mice, which she was unable to scare away. The board, on her death, was found to be covered in flowers.

Both details appear in the fresco of the right lunette, which depicts the *Announcement of Death*, the time of Fina's demise having been vouchsafed to her by St Gregory in a vision (notice the flower-covered board and the wonderfully ugly mouse in the semi-darkness to the rear of the composition). The fresco in the opposite (left) lunette, the *Funeral of St Fina*, is more accomplished – it is said to have greatly impressed Raphael – and shows the saint on her deathbed with the towers of San Gimignano in the background. Also depicted are three miracles associated with Fina: the restoration of a blind choirboy's sight; the curing of her nurse's paralysed hand; and the ringing of San Gimignano's bells by angels on the saint's death.

Ghirlandaio left a self-portrait (in the figure behind the bishop saying Mass), as well as portraits (in the figures to either side) of Davide, his brother, and Sebastiano Mainardi, his brother-in-law. Both probably assisted Ghirlandaio with the frescoes, as they did with his masterpiece, the fresco cycle in the sanctuary of Santa Maria Novella in Florence (see p.108). The fresco's composition, with the dead saint surrounded by onlookers, owes much to Benozzo Gozzoli's almost identical scene painted ten years earlier in Sant'Agostino (see below), which in turn was influenced by Giotto's iconoclastic treatment of the *Funeral of St Francis* in Santa Croce in Florence (see p.126).

The Baptistery and Museo d'Arte Sacra

To the left of the Collegiata, an arch surmounted by a statue of St Gimignano (1342) leads into a courtyard. Straight ahead is the loggia to the **Baptistery**, frescoed with an *Annunciation* by Ghirlandaio and Sebastiano Mainardi (1482). Rather anonymous **Sacred Art** and **Etruscan museums** are housed in the old Rector's Palace off to the left of the court in Piazza Pecori, which is a favourite for busking musicians in summer (both museums daily: April–Oct 9.30am–7.30pm; Nov–Dec & Feb–March 9.30am–5pm; closed Jan; L7000). If you do bother with the museums, the better of the two is the **Museo d'Arte Sacra**, whose highlights include a *Madonna and Child* by Bartolo di Fredi; a superb wooden Crucifix, perhaps from as early as the eleventh century; several glorious illuminated choir books; and a marble bust of *Onofrio di Pietro* (1493) by Benedetto da Maiano, a work commissioned by San Gimignano's *comune* to honour Di Pietro, an eminent local scholar.

The Museo Civico

The **Palazzo del Popolo**, the other key component of the Piazza del Duomo, is partly given over to council offices, but most of the building is devoted to the **Museo Civico**. This is home to an outstanding miscellany of paintings, and to the **Torre Grossa**, the only one of San Gimignano's towers which you can climb (museum and tower March–Oct daily 9.30am–7.20pm; Nov–Feb Tues–Sun 9.30am–12.50pm & 2.30–4.50pm; museum L7000, tower L8000; combined ticket L12,000, available only April–Sept 12.30–3pm & 6–7.20pm, March & Oct 12.30–2.30pm).

On entering the palazzo from the square you find yourself within a courtyard, built in 1323 during extension work on the palace. Its well (1360) incorporates fragments removed from local Etruscan tombs, while the stone crests around the walls represent the coats of arms of various medieval magistrates. A loggia opens on the right, from which justice and public decrees were occasionally proclaimed, hence the subject matter of its three frescoes, all of which make an allusion to justice: the left wall features an allegory (1513) by Sodoma depicting a throned magistrate flanked by the figures of Dishonesty, Prudence and Truth; in front is a *Madonna and Child* by Taddeo di Bartolo (the artist responsible for the Collegiata's *Last Judgement*) in which the Madonna is flanked by saints Gimignano and Gregory – the Child meanwhile holds a biblical inscription recommending sagacity in the administration of justice; the right wall features a chiaroscuro by Sodoma depicting St Ivo, a Breton lawyer whose *pro bono* legal work among the poor, widowed and orphaned saw him canonized in 1366 and made patron saint of lawyers, jurists and magistrates.

From the courtyard, stairs lead to a picturesque little balcony and the cramped ticket office, where there are often queues of people dumbstruck by the prices and bewildered by the various permutations of tickets available (see above). While the museum is well worth the admission, the price for the Torre Grossa, the highest surviving and best preserved of the town's towers, is a touch excessive, notwithstanding the spectacular panoramic views.

The first of the museum's rooms and the palazzo's public chambers, frescoed with hunting and tournament scenes, is known as the **Sala del Consiglio**, or Sala di Dante – the poet visited as Florence's ambassador to the town in 1300, making a plea here for Guelph unity. Most of the paintings displayed are fourteenth-century works, Sienese in origin or inspiration, and executed in the years before San Gimignano passed under Florentine control and influence. The room's highlight is Lippo Memmi's *Maestà* (1317), his finest work, closely modelled on Simone Martini's painting on an identical theme, completed two years previously, in Siena's Palazzo Pubblico (see p.306). San Gimignano's *Podestà* at the time, Mino de' Tolomei, is shown kneeling at the Madonna's feet, looked down on by a multitude of saints arranged in distinct rows. The fresco was enlarged at a later date, Benozzo Gozzoli having added the two saints at the extreme right and left in 1466. The fresco on the end wall shows San Gimignano's population swearing allegiance to Charles of Anjou.

Four smaller rooms on this floor are often given over to temporary exhibitions, usually easily ignored in favour of the main **Pinacoteca**, or art gallery, on the next floor. Arranged in four rooms, the **finest pictures** are in the large salon immediately on the right at the top of the stairs. On the wall on the right as you enter is a superb painted Crucifix (1260–65) by Coppo di Marcovaldo, a Florentine artist – believed to have been the teacher of Cimabue – captured by the Sienese at the Battle of Montaperti in 1260. This work, reckoned one of the masterpieces of early Tuscan painting, was probably also painted while the artist was in "captivity". It's a far more complex painting than it first appears, its apex being crowned by panels of the *Assumption of the Virgin* and *Christ Pantocrator*. (The similar – but eight-metre high – *Christ* on Florence's baptistery ceiling is attributed to Marcovaldo.) Panels next to each of Christ's hands depict the Madonna and St John, and the three Marys. Christ's body is flanked by six scenes from the Passion: the *Kiss of Judas*, *Flagellation*, *Crucifixion*, *Christ and Pilate*, the *Crown of Thorns* and the *Deposition*.

Other outstanding pictures in the room include two early tondi of the *Annunciation* (1482–83) by Filippino Lippi on the opposite end wall, with the Madonna portrayed separately in one, the Archangel Gabriel in the other; both are beautifully offset by their vast original frames. Between them is Pinturicchio's *Madonna Enthroned with SS. Gregory and Benedict* (1512), commissioned by the abbey of Monte Oliveto Maggiore (see p.364), one of the last works and masterpieces of this artist. Equally arresting are two contrasting paintings of the *Madonna and Child with Saints* by Benozzo Gozzoli, both painted in 1466. The more interesting of the two shows the Madonna with John the Baptist, Mary Magdalene, St Augustine and St Martha, the last (the sister of Lazarus) being particularly venerated in Tuscany, as she is the patron saint of builders and – even more significantly – of cooks.

The larger of the two rooms off to the right contains lesser but no less interesting paintings. Look out in particular for the triptych by Taddeo di Bartolo depicting *Scenes from the Life of St Gimignano* (1393), the first of three panel paintings in this and the adjoining room devoted to the lives of the saints. It was painted when Taddeo was working on the *Last Judgement* frescoes in the Collegiata, where the painting was originally installed above the high altar. The large central panel, which shows the saint with San Gimignano on his lap, is flanked on each side with vignettes from his life. The most extraordinary is one of the four scenes on the right, in which the saint is disturbed while praying by what is euphemistically described as an urgent "*bisogno*" or need – in other words, a desperate call of nature. In answering the call he finds himself met by the Devil, whom he causes to vanish by making the sign of the Cross. The other panels on the right, which describe the saint's exorcism of the Byzantine emperor's daughter, show Gimignano being borne to Constantinople, his calming of a storm during the voyage and the eventual exorcism of the princess. The four panels on the left depict St Severus officiating at Gimignano's burial; saving San Gimignano from Attila the Hun (the saint is seen remonstrating vigorously with Attila); and preventing a downpour of rain soaking his followers in a leaky church.

Also of interest are *Scenes from the Life of St Bartholomew* (1401) by Lorenzo di Niccolò, whose panels include the attempt to martyr the saint by flaying him alive (top right) – the operation is shown in graphic detail – and his subsequent beheading, in which bloody strips of skin hanging from the saint's body hamper the work of the exasperated executioners. The same artist was responsible for the double-sided **reliquary tabernacle** showing *St Fina* and *St Gregory* and *Eight Scenes from the Life of St Fina* (1402), San Gimignano's patron saint (see p.344). Fina is shown holding San Gimignano in one hand, and a bunch of violets – a symbol of humility – in the other. The scenes on one face show the mother of St Fina looking after her daughter (with a relative desperately trying to beat off hordes of mice) and the Devil casting Fina's mother down some stairs (to no ill effect); San Gimignano's citizens in procession paying homage to the dead saint (note Fina's flower-covered board); and the funeral procession during which Fina's nurse, Beldia, miraculously recovered the use of her paralysed hand. The panels on the other face show Fina miraculously extinguishing a fire; saving a boat in a storm; saving a builder falling from a building; and exorcising a man possessed by the Devil.

Perhaps the gallery's most fascinating and enjoyable paintings, though, are the **frescoes of wedding scenes** hidden away in a small room off the stairs (straight ahead on exiting the main salon). Unique in their subject matter, they show a tournament where the wife rides on her husband's back, followed by the lovers taking a shared bath and climbing into bed: the man, remarkably, manages to keep on the same red hat through all three operations. Some commentators, however, have seen the pictures in a less jolly light, describing them as allegorical scenes designed to warn men of the wiles of women. They were completed in the 1320s by Memmo di Filippuccio, the father of Lippo Memmi, who since 1303 had been working as a more or less official painter for the *comune*.

The Rocca

Just behind the Piazza del Duomo, a signposted lane leads to the **Rocca**, the old fortress, with its one surviving tower. It was built in 1353, to Florentine orders but at local expense, "in order to remove every cause of evil thinking from the inhabitants". A couple of centuries later, its purpose presumably fulfilled, it was dismantled by Cosimo I. Nowadays its 283-metre perimeter encloses an orchard-like public garden, with figs, olives and a well in the middle. From the ramparts, there are superb views over the countryside.

A block south of the Rocca in Via Quercecchio, a **Museo Ornitologico** (Tues–Sun: March–Oct 9.30am–12.30pm & 3–6pm; Nov–Feb 9.30am–1pm & 2.30–5pm; L4000) has been created from the stuffed bird collections of some local worthy in the deconsecrated church near the Porta Quercecchio.

San Lorenzo in Ponte

Heading away from the central squares and Via San Giovanni, the crowds quickly thin away. Following the Via di Castello east of Piazza della Cisterna leads past the Romanesque **San Lorenzo in Ponte** (1240), one of the few other churches kept open, whose brick-built interior is almost completely covered by dramatic frescoes (1413) by the little-known but accomplished Florentine, Cenni di Francesco. The dramatic fragments include a *Last Judgement* on the left wall and (in the presbytery) the figures of the *Apostles, Christ and the Virgin with Angels*, and *Scenes from the Life of St Benedict*. Cenni was also responsible for the restored frescoes in the adjoining oratory, notably the entrance wall's *St Lawrence and Saints* and *Madonna and Child with Angels*, in which the Madonna's head – an earlier work – has been attributed to Simone Martini.

The attached **Farmacia Preindustriale** was part of a medieval hospital, supported by the town council, and has an interesting display of medicines and equipment, as well as the story of San Gimignano under plague, and its role on the pilgrims' road to Rome. At the end of the street a rural lane winds down to the walls, a public well-house – the **Fonti** – and open countryside. The little Pisan-Romanesque church here, **San Iacopo**, has a painting of *St James* by Pier Francesco Fiorentino. North from Piazza del Duomo, **Via San Matteo** is one of the grandest and best preserved of the city streets, with quiet little alleyways again running down to the walls. Passing a couple of mighty tower houses, the street ends at the **Porta San Matteo**, just inside of which, in a corner of the walls, is the **Convento di Sant'Agostino**.

Sant'Agostino

After the Collegiata, **Sant'Agostino** (daily May–Sept 7.30am–noon & 3–7pm; Nov–March 7.30am–noon & 3–6pm) is the most important church in San Gimignano, a large, hall-like thirteenth-century structure with several fine paintings, an impressive Renaissance altar, and an outstanding restored fresco cycle by Benozzo Gozzoli on the *Life of St Augustine*.

On the rear wall, immediately on the left as you enter by the church's side door, is the **Cappella di San Bartolo**. Framed by a draped marble curtain, it houses the remains of St Bartolo (1228–1300), yet another of San Gimignano's patron saints. Born near Pisa, he became a lay Franciscan, but at 52 contracted leprosy and was forced to retire to a leper colony, where he died twenty years later. According to legend, while he was in the colony several of his leprous toes came off in the hands of a nun who was washing his feet. Mortified with embarrassment, he took the loose toes and miraculously reattached them to his foot. This is one of three miracles depicted in the predella reliefs on the magnificent altar by Benedetto da Maiano (1495). The three figures above are the *Theological Virtues*, while the frescoes to the left, by Sebastiano Mainardi depict saints Lucy, Nicholas of Bari and Gimignano, who holds the town of San Gimignano in his arms.

On the right (south) wall are several striking frescoes, among them a *Madonna and Child with Eight Saints* (1494) by Pier Francesco Fiorentino and a figure of *Christ with the Symbols of the Passion* by Bartolo di Fredi (author of the Collegiata's Old Testament cycle), who was also responsible for the frescoes on the *Life of the Virgin* (1356) on the side walls of the chapel to the right of the high altar. The chapel's striking altarpiece, the *Nativity of the Virgin* (1523), is by Vincenzo Tamengi (1492–1530), an otherwise little-known local artist.

All paintings in the church, however, pale beside those on the walls around the high altar, a seventeen-panel fresco cycle on the **Life of St Augustine** (1463–67) by Benozzo Gozzoli, pictures which provide a superb record of life in Renaissance Italy, particularly the city life of Florence, which forms a backdrop to many of the scenes. Read from low down on the left, the first panels depict the saint – who was born in 354 in what is now Tunisia – being taken to school by his parents and flogged by his teacher, studying grammar at Carthage university and crossing the sea to Italy. The next recount his academic career: teaching philosophy and rhetoric in Rome and Milan – Gozzoli depicts the journey between the cities as a marvellously rich procession – and being received by the Emperor Theodosius. Then comes the turning point in his life, when he listens to the preaching of St Ambrose, and then, while reading St Paul's Epistle to the Romans, hears a child's voice extolling him *"Tolle, lege"* (take and read). After this, Augustine was baptized, returned to Tunisia to form a monastic community and was subsequently made bishop of Hippo. He was one of the fathers of the early Christian Church, producing two of its fundamental great theological works – the *Commentaries* and the *City of God*. Gozzoli depicts just a few crucial scenes: Augustine meeting the child whose voice he had heard (and who now rebuked him for trying to penetrate the mysteries of the Trinity); the death of his mother, St Monica; blessing the people, as bishop; confuting a heretic; having a vision of St Jerome in Paradise; and his death, a scene which almost exactly prefigures Ghirlandaio's depiction of the death of St Fina in the Collegiata.

Gozzoli started out with considerable promise, working as assistant to Fra' Angelico at the Vatican, then landing the contract for the Palazzo Medici chapel in Florence. These frescoes were painted late in life, after a frustrating career spent on minor commissions around the Tuscan countryside. The wonderful narrative freshness of the cycle prompted Bernard Berenson to characterize him as "a Fra' Angelico who had forgotten heaven and become enamoured of the earth and the spring time".

Given the richness of the cycle, it's remarkable that the high altar's *Coronation of the Virgin* (1483) manages to hold its own. It's by Piero del Pollaiuolo, brother and collaborator of the more famous Antonio del Pollaiuolo. Moving back down the left (north) wall you come to a door leading to the **sacristy** and Renaissance **cloister** and another fresco by Sebastiano Mainardi of *San Gimignano Blessing Three Dignitaries* (1487). The effigy above is of *Fra Domenico Strambi*, the patron who commissioned the Gozzoli frescoes and Pollaiuolo altarpiece. The marble reliefs (1318) beyond, showing four half-figures of bishops, are believed to be part of the original shrine to St Bartolo, and are attributed to Tino da Camaino. The fresco fragment beyond, a *Madonna* by Lippo Memmi, is overshadowed by a large fresco of *St Sebastian*, painted by Gozzoli in 1464, the year in which plague ravaged San Gimignano.

SAN GIMIGNANO FESTIVAL

San Gimignano's first **festival** here was held at the end of the 1920s, and except for a break during World War II has run just about every year since: 2000 sees its 66th outing. Some of the great (and many of the not-so-great) names of **Italian opera** have passed through over the years – Galliano Masini, Mario Del Monaco, Gino Bechi, Giovacchino Forzano and Iris Adami Corradetti – not that this has given the town false airs. Where else could you find *Tosca* on the same bill as Enrico Morricone's soundtrack for *A Fistful of Dollars*? Not to mention a series of Italian popular songs – offered by the Filarmonica "G. Puccini" no less – which includes such novelties as *La Canzone del Grappa* (a paean to Italian hooch).

These days the festival's quiet provincial air is increasingly compromised by snooty outsiders, particularly at the highlights of the event – the outdoor opera performances in Piazza del Duomo. The atmosphere remains cheerfully informal, however, with the steps of the Collegiata set aside as terracing for the town's kids. Even the official blurb exhorts you to "mettere il vestito della festa" and "cantare con la compagnia" (put on your party clothes and sing along). **Details** and **tickets** are available from the tourist office.

Eating and drinking

San Gimignano isn't especially famous for its **food** – there are too many tourists and too few locals to ensure high standards. However, the tables set out in summer on the carless streets and squares and the local wines still make for a beguiling evening. At lunchtime, you might prefer to pick up supplies from the bars or delicatessens and head out to the countryside – a matter of walking out from just about any of the gates. As an after-meal treat, drop in on the award-winning *Gelateria di Piazza*, on Piazza della Cisterna – the jovial owner creates some of the best ice cream in Tuscany. At night, San Gimignano is very much on the quiet side, with little entertainment beyond the evening *passeggiata* along Via San Giovanni and Via San Matteo. The one "club-disco", the *Bar Toscana*, is out of the village in Canonica at Via del Pino 1 (☎0577.944.907).

Le Vecchie Mura, Via Piandornella 15 (☎0577.940.270). Housed in an old vaulted stable within the structure of the city walls; follow sign off Via San Giovanni. Good atmosphere, fair-value pizzas and good set meals. Be sure to book. Closed Tues.

Ristorante Il Pino, Via San Matteo 102 (☎0577.942.225). San Gimignano's first-choice restaurant. Lovely interior, specializes in *antipasti* and dishes sprinkled with truffle. L20,000–30,000. Closed Thurs.

Osteria del Carcere, Via del Castello 13 (☎0577.941.905). A relatively new and informal *osteria* with young owners, a few steps from Piazza del Duomo. Excellent hams and salami, plus Tuscan cooking with an innovative edge. Just 30 covers, so book. L30,000–40,000, excluding wine. Closed Wed & Jan–Feb.

Ristorante La Stella, Via San Matteo 75. Often an extremely touristy spot, but still good value; well-reputed restaurant that serves produce from its own farm. From L30,000. Closed Wed.

Osteria delle Catene, Via Mainardi 18 (☎0577.941.966). A thoroughly reliable place for straightforward Tuscan food. The wine list – over 100 choices – is good, too. Just 38 covers, so booking ahead's a good idea. L35,000–40,000. Closed Wed, Jan & part of Dec.

Ristorante Dorandò, Vicolo dell'Oro 2 (☎0577.941.862). Advertises itself as re-creating Etruscan and Renaissance dishes – "each dish we present is a fragment of Tuscan history, an archeological fragment". Don't be put off: the dishes are classic Tuscan cooking and the chefs generally know their business. L50,000–70,000. Closed Mon & parts of Jan and Feb.

Birreria di Pietrafitta, 4km from San Gimignano on the road to Poggibonsi. This popular pub with its large shady beer garden provides welcome relief from the crowds of San Gimignano. Wide selection of beers, wines and cocktails. Good *panini* and snacks available all day. Daily 11am–2am.

Listings

Car rental Hertz (☎0577.942.220).

Festivals These include Carnevale (February), with floats and parades through town, and a summer cultural festival (July–Aug), featuring a series of classical concerts, theatre and films held in an open-air theatre in the Rocca (see box on previous page).

Lost property The *Vigili Urbani* (civil police) at Via Santo Stefano 23 (☎0577.940.346).

Markets Thursday morning in Piazza del Duomo, Piazza delle Erbe and Piazza della Cisterna (8am–1pm). Clothes, crafts and a variety of food – including rolls with *cinghiale* filling – are on sale; there is also a much smaller market on Saturday.

Police Piazza Martiri di Montemaggio (☎0577.940.313).

Taxis Ring ☎0577.940.499 or 0577.940.049 (mobile ☎0338.743.0163); otherwise ☎0577.941.572 (mobile ☎0335.618.7312); car with driver also available.

Volterra

Built on a high plateau enclosed by yellowy-grey volcanic hills, lofty **VOLTERRA** has a bleak, isolated appearance – a surprise after the pastoralism of the region around. D.H. Lawrence wrote, accurately, that "it gets all the wind and sees all the world . . . a sort of inland island, still curiously isolated and grim". However, its small, walled medieval core certainly merits a stop, with its cobbled and austere stone streets, dark stone palazzi and

WALKS FROM SAN GIMIGNANO

San Gimignano's position, with the best of Tuscan countryside spread below, may well inspire the idea of walking. If you plan anything more than a ramble, it's worth calling in at the *Ufficio Tecnico* in the town hall to buy copies of the local IGM contour maps.

A good **circular walk**, which would take most of the day, is to strike directly west into the hills to Poggio Attendi, follow the ridge south to San Donato, and loop back to San Gimignano via Montauto and Santa Lucia. Another possibility is to walk to **Colle di Val d'Elsa** (about 5hr): follow the Volterra road out of town, turn immediately left to Monteoliveto and Santa Lucia, and then make for the villages of Monti and Borgatello. With an early start, you could also walk to **Volterra** (6–7hr): make initially for San Donato, then cut across country past Castelvécchio (now a farm), the villa of Pignano and Monte Voltráio.

walled gateways. There are great views from the windswept heights, enjoyable walking, and one of the country's most important Etruscan museums.

The town lies at the heart of a mining region which yields alabaster (every other shop sells artefacts), as well as a variety of minerals. The mines – and the easily defended site – made it one of the largest Etruscan settlements, Velathri, and ensured its survival through the Roman era as Volaterrae. During the Dark Ages it became an important Lombard centre, and even sheltered the Lombard kings for a time. In the Middle Ages, however, the mines proved Volterra's downfall as the Florentines began to cast a covetous eye over their wealth. Florence took control of the town from 1360, and in 1472 – anxious to secure the town's alum deposits, vital for Florence's dyeing industry – crushed all pretensions to independence with a terrible siege and pillage by Lorenzo de' Medici and the Duke of Urbino – one of the three principal crimes Lorenzo confessed to Savonarola on his deathbed.

Subsequently, Volterra was a Florentine fief, unable to keep pace with changing and expanding patterns of trade and sliding into provincial obscurity. It was to remain part of the Grand Duchy of Tuscany until Italian unification in 1860. Physically, the town also began to subside, its walls and houses slipping away to the west over the *Balze* (cliffs), which form a dramatic prospect from the Pisa road. Today, Volterra occupies less than a third of its ancient extent.

Arrival, information and accommodation

There is little more to Volterra than its old, walled centre, so orientation is straightforward. **Buses** arrive on the south side of the town at **Piazza Martiri della Libertà**, from where it's a five-minute walk to the central **Piazza dei Priori**, with the **duomo** and **tourist office** at Via G. Turazza 2 (☎0588.87.257 or 0588.86.150) just around the corner. You can buy bus tickets and check the TRA-IN schedules at the tourist office. For bus information ring ☎0588.86.150.

Cars are best parked outside the north circuit of walls, by the Porta San Francesco or Porta Fiorentina, though if you're in luck you might find a space at the Piazza Martiri della Libertà. Best of all, if you can find a spot, is the underground "Dogana" parking, convenient for the duomo. The nearest **train station** is 9km west at Saline di Volterra (connecting bus); the rail line links to the busy coastal route between Pisa and Rome. For train information ring ☎0588.44.116. If you need a **taxi**, try Longarini (☎0588.87.517).

Volterra looks thin on **accommodation** if you judge by official hotel lists, but there's a youth hostel, campsite and a couple of villa accommodations just outside the town. Apartments and *agriturismo* stays in and around Volterra are also on offer – ask at the tourist office, which has a free accommodation service, or Viaggi ATUV, Piazza Martiri della Libertà (☎0588.85.019). As at San Gimignano you can stay in private rooms at a convent, too.

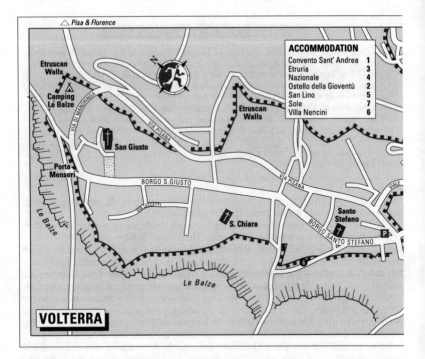

Hotels

Etruria, Via Matteotti 32 (☎0588.87.377). Best value of the hotels proper – and located on the main street, right in the centre. ④.

Nazionale, Via dei Marchesi 11 (☎0588.86.284, fax 0588.84.097). In the heart of town, this three-star hotel is the inn D.H. Lawrence stayed at when researching *Etruscan Places* – the medieval *palazzo* was transformed into a hotel in 1860. Now much modernized, with 36 mostly tiny rooms, all with bath. ③.

San Lino, Via San Lino 26 (☎0588.85.250, fax 0588.80.620). Volterra's grandest – a four-star hotel with 43 rooms and pool on the street leading in from Porta San Francesco. ⑤.

Sole, Via dei Cappuccini 10 (☎ & fax 0588.84.000). A modern three-star in a quiet location outside the town walls, near the church of San Alessandro. Again, all ten rooms with bath. ③.

Villa Nencini, Borgo Santo Stefano 55 (☎0588.86.386, fax 0588.80.601). Attractive three-star hotel insinuated into a seventeenth-century building, with a pool and garden, sited just outside Porta San Francesco on the town's northwest edge. ④.

Convent, hostel and campsite

Convento Sant' Andrea, (☎0588.86.028). On the northeast outskirts of the town; follow the road out of Porta Marcoli. There are beautiful views from the old cells, now let as private rooms with old painted brass beds – to both women and men, and couples. L27,000 per person (L34,000 with private bath).

Ostello della Gioventù, Via Don Minzoni (☎0588.85.577). Housed in a converted mansion beyond the Etruscan museum, close to the Porta a Selci; open from 6pm, HI membership is not required, and the 11.30pm curfew is unlikely to prove a problem given Volterra nightlife. Very helpful staff. L20,000.

Camping Le Balze, Via Mandringa (☎0588.87.880). Well-equipped and nicely positioned site, 1km west from the centre, outside Borgo San Giusto (follow signs for the *Balze*). Has a pool and tennis courts; riding can also be arranged. Open April–Sept.

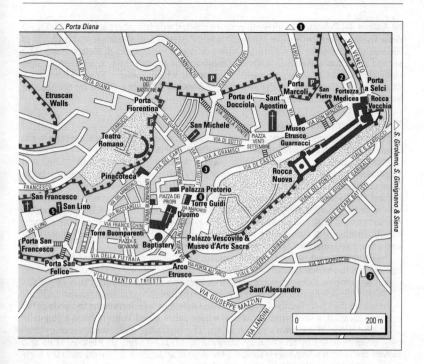

Map legend and labels:
△ Porta Diana · **❶**
VIALE D'ANNUNZIO · VIALE DEI FOSSI · PORTA · VIA VENETO
PIAZZA DEL BASTIONE · **P**
Etruscan Walls · VIA DI PORTA DIANA · Porta Fiorentina · Porta di Docciola · Sant' Agostino · Porta Marcoli · San Pietro · Fortezza Medicea · **❷** · Porta a Selci · Rocca Vecchia
FERRUCCI · **P** · VIA GUARNACCI · San Michele · Museo Etrusco Guarnacci · VIA DON MINZONI
Teatro Romano · VIA DI SOTTO · PIAZZA VENTI SETTEMBRE · VIA A. GRAMSCI · VIA DE CASTELLO
VIA DEI SARTI · VIA DELLE PRIGIONI · **❸** · Rocca Nuova · VIALE DEI PONTI · VIALE G. CARDUCCI
Pinacoteca · VIA DI MANDRINGA · PIAZZA DEI PRIORI · Palazzo Pretorio · **❹** · Torre Guidi · VIALE GIUSEPPE GARIBALDI · VIALE GIUSEPPE BATTISTI · S. Girolamo, S. Gimignano & Siena
FRANCESCO · San Francesco · **❺** · San Lino · VIA RICCIARELLI · Duomo · VIA DEI MARCHESI · VIALE CESARE BATTISTI
VIA SdLINO · VIA FRANCESCHINI · Torre Buomparenti · VIA ROMA · Palazzo Vescovile & Museo d'Arte Sacra
Porta San Francesco · VIA DELLA PIETRAIA · PIAZZA S. GIOVANNI · Baptistery · VIA PORTA ALL'ARCO
Porta San Felice · VIALE TRENTO E TRIESTE · Arco Etrusco · VIALE GIUSEPPE GARIBALDI · VIA DEI CAPPUCCINI · **❼**
VIA GIUSEPPE MAZZINI · Sant'Alessandro · VIA LANDINI
0 ____ 200 m

The Town

The **Piazza dei Priori** is the heart of Volterra, enclosed by an almost totally medieval group of buildings. The battlemented town hall, or **Palazzo dei Priori**, is the eye-catcher. Built in between 1208 and 1257, and said to be the oldest such palace in Italy, it may have served as the model for Florence's Palazzo Vecchio – though the influences are largely reversed on its facade, which is studded with Florentine medallions. The tower has been closed on and off for the last few years – though if you find it open (weekdays 9am–1pm are the best bet), pay and enter for spectacular views of the area. In the main building, you can take a look at the first-floor **Sala del Consiglio Comunale**, used as the town's council chamber without interruption since 1257. Its end wall is frescoed with a huge *Annunciation* (1383) attributed to Jacopo di Cione.

Opposite the town hall is the **Palazzo Pretorio**, surmounted by the **Torre del Porcellino** (Piglet's Tower), named after the much-worn carved boar on a bracket to the right of the top window; completing the ensemble are the **Palazzo Vescovile**, or Bishop's Palace (formerly the town's granary), and a pair of tower houses, the **Buomparenti**, at the junction of Via Roma and Via Ricciarelli. Modest relatives of those of San Gimignano, the towers are linked by a passageway above the street.

The Bishop's Palace houses the rich little three-room **Museo di Arte Sacra** (daily: mid-March to Oct 9.30am–1pm & 3–6:30pm; Nov to mid-March 9am–1pm; L12,000 combined ticket with Pinacoteca and Museo Etrusco Guarnacci), entered at Via Roma 1, whose displays in the first room include an Andrea della Robbia bust of *St Linus* – a Volterran who was St Peter's successor as pope; a silver reliquary bust of *St Ottaviano* by Andrea del Pollaiuolo; a fifteenth-century painted wooden tabernacle by Bartolomeo della Gatta, better known for his work around Arezzo and Cortona; and a clutch of Sienese altarpieces by Neri di Bici, Taddeo di Bartolo and Segna di Bonaventura. The second room has a gilded Crucifix by Giambologna, though the real highlights, especially for fans of Mannerism, reside in room 3, which features Rosso Fiorentino's *Madonna di Villamagna* (1521) and the *Madonna di Ulignano* (1545) by the leading local artist Daniele da Volterra.

The Duomo and its square

Backing directly onto the civic power centre, Volterra's cathedral square seems a touch down-at-heel, with its partial facades and crumbling masonry.

The **Duomo**, or Basilica di Santa Maria Assunta (consecrated in 1120), and **Baptistery** (second half of the thirteenth century) are essentially Romanesque, clad in bands of black and white marble – the style popularized in the twelfth century by Pisa. Behind the baptistery, della Robbia plaques of swaddled babies signal a building that was once a foundlings' hospital. On the baptistery's exterior note the main portal, whose rounded arch contains the carved heads of *Christ*, the *Madonna* and the *Apostles* (1283). Inside are a water stoup fashioned from an old Etruscan funerary monument and a fine baptismal font (1502) by Andrea Sansovino.

Inside the duomo, striped marble Romanesque aisles and a coffered Renaissance ceiling lend the building a rather makeshift appearance. Moving down the right (south) aisle you come to a chapel in the right transept with an outstanding Pisan *Deposition* (1228), its life-size figures disarmingly repainted in their original bright colours. On the right side of the choir lies the Cappella di San Ottaviano, which contains the body of the eponymous saint, a sixth-century hermit whose relics saved Volterra from a plague in 1522 – he is one of the town's patron saints. The high altar, a nineteenth-century travesty, is surmounted by an exquisite tabernacle (1471) by Mino da Fiesole. Mino also carved the two kneeling angels flanking the high altar. In the left (north) aisle the highlights are two fifteenth-century terracotta figures in the oratory near the entrance: they depict the *Nativity* and *Adoration of the Magi*, the former graced with a painted background by Benozzo Gozzoli. Farther down is a thirteenth-century Pisan pulpit, assembled in 1584 from a variety of earlier fragments. On the altar alongside is a beautiful *Annunciation* (1497), generally attributed to Fra' Bartolommeo.

The Pinacoteca

Paintings and sculpture gathered from Volterra's churches, including one that was swallowed up by the *Balze*, are displayed at the **Pinacoteca Comunale**, installed in the Palazzo Minucci-Solaini at Via dei Sarti 1, just off the Piazza dei Priori (daily: mid-March to Oct 9am–7pm; Nov to mid-March 9am–2pm; L12,000 joint ticket with Museo di Arte Sacra and Museo Etrusco Guarnacci).

The mansion is an interesting building in its own right, part frescoed and with a multi-level cloister; its designer may have been Antonio da Sangallo. The collections are arranged chronologically, and begin with a group of **statuary** from the lost church of San Giusto al Bostro, including a wonderful Romanesque capital carved from local alabaster, its mix of pagan and Christian emblems including a double-tailed mermaid and Daniel in the lions' den. The **painting** displays begin with largely Sienese works, notably Taddeo di Bartolo's polyptych of the *Madonna and Child with Saints* (1411) and the same artist's *Madonna della Rosa*, part of a dismembered polyptych, and panel of *SS. Nicola da Totentino and Peter* (all room III). But by the fifteenth century Florence dominates the art scene – as it did the politics. Major Renaissance paintings from this period include a *Christ in Glory* (1492) with a marvellous imaginary landscape by Ghirlandaio in room X, and a *Madonna and Saints* (1491) and *Annunciation* by Luca Signorelli, the latter reckoned one of the artist's masterpieces (room XI).

The museum's best work, however, is **Rosso Fiorentino**'s extraordinary *Descent from the Cross*, painted for the church of San Francesco in 1521. This is one of the masterpieces of Mannerism, its figures, without any central focus, creating an agitated, circular tension from sharp lines and blocks of discordant colour. The art historian Frederick Hartt sees in the painting "the dilemma of a lost generation" – it was painted in the decade that culminated in the Sack of Rome – and virtual blasphemy in the vision of a smiling Christ and gibbering Joseph of Arimathea (at the top).

The Rocca, Arco Etrusco and archeological remains

South of Piazza dei Priori, **Via Marchesi** leads to a lush area of grass, trees and shade known as the **Parco Archeologico** (daily 10am–noon & 4–7pm; free). There's not much archeology about the place – a few odd lumps of rock, said to be part of a Roman bathhouse – but it's a beautiful part of the town to lie around for a few hours, and there is a good-value café-bar in one corner. Overlooking the park to the east is the **Rocca** – built by the Medici after their sacking of the town – and, with its rounded bastions and central tower, one of the great examples of Italian military architecture. For the last century and a half it has been a prison, for lifers and hard cases.

The first turning left off Via Marchesi, **Via Porta dell'Arco**, runs downhill to the **Arco Etrusco**, an Etruscan gateway, third-century BC in origin, built in Cyclopean blocks of stone, with Roman and medieval surrounds; the three blackened and eroded lumps on its outer face are probably images of Etruscan gods. The gate was narrowly saved from German destruction in the last war, during the course of a ten-day battle between the partisans (Volterra was a stronghold) and Germans. A memorial commemorates the partisan losses.

If you turn north instead off Via Marchesi, and follow Via Matteotti and its continuation, Via Guarnacci, you reach the Porta Fiorentina. Just to the west of the gate, below the road, is an area of excavations including a **Roman theatre** (now restored for use in the summer theatre festival) and a **bath complex** with mosaic floors. Following the **Via Diana**, straight ahead from the gate, makes for a pleasant walk, leading past the cemetery to remains of the Etruscan Porta Diana. Out beyond here tracks lead through farmland that was once a vast **Etruscan necropolis** – wandering through, you'll spot various unmarked, underground tombs.

Museo Etrusco Guarnacci

Volterra's Etruscan legacy is represented most importantly at the **Museo Etrusco Guarnacci**, Via Don Minzoni 15 (daily: mid-March to Oct 9am–7pm; Nov to mid-March 9am–2pm; L12,000 with Pinacoteca and Museo di Arte Sacra). One of Italy's major archeological museums, it consists entirely of local finds, including some six hundred funerary urns.

Made of alabaster, tufa and terracotta, the **urns** date from the fourth to first centuries BC – earlier tombs were lost as the cliffs fell to nothing. On their sides, bas-reliefs depict domestic events (often boar hunting) or Greek myths (usually a trip to the underworld); on the lid is a bust of the subject and symbolic flowers – one for a young person, two for middle-aged, three for elderly.

Unfortunately the display, grouped according to subject, is stultifyingly old-fashioned and uninstructive, and only a few pieces manage to stand out from the mass-produced ware. Most of the best are arranged on the top floor and date from the "golden age" of the third and second centuries BC. Among them is the much-reproduced **Gli Sposi**, a disturbing portrait scene of a supposed husband and wife – all piercing eyes and dreadful looks. On this floor, too, are a number of small bronze sculptures, including the extraordinary **Ombra della Sera** (Shadow of the Evening), an elongated nude which provided inspiration for Giacometti. The farmer who unearthed it displayed rather less reverence – he used it as a poker for a few years.

To the Balze

To reach the *Balze* – the famous eroded cliffs – follow the Via di San Lino northwest from the Piazza dei Priori. This passes the church of **San Francesco**, whose adjoining Cappella della Croce di Giorno, built in 1315, contains fascinating and very early narrative frescoes (1410) of the *Legend of the True Cross* (see p.415) by Cenni di Francesco, a little-known but accomplished local artist. Rosso Fiorentino's famous *Descent from the Cross*, now in the Pinacoteca (see p.354), once stood above the high altar. From the nearby **Porta San Francesco** follow Borgo Santo Stefano and its continuation, Borgo San Giusto, past the Baroque church and former abbey of **San Giusto** – its dilapidated but striking facade framed by an avenue of cypress trees.

At the **Balze** you gain a real sense of the extent of Etruscan Volterra, whose old town walls drop away into the chasms. Gashes in the slopes and the natural erosion of sand and clay are made more dramatic by alabaster mines, ancient and modern. Below are buried great tracts of the Etruscan and Roman city, and landslips continue – as evidenced by the locked and ruined monastery ebbing away over the precipice.

Food and festivals

As a hunting centre, Volterra's gastronomic efforts are dominated by wild boar (*cinghiale*). You see stuffed heads of the unfortunate beasts throughout town, and the meat is packaged as salamis or hams, as well as roasted in the restaurants, along with *lepre* (hare) and *coniglio* (rabbit).

Restaurants listed below cover the best of a similarly priced bunch. Cheaper options include a self-service at Via Matteotti 19 and a few *pizzerie* – there's a good one opposite the *Ristorante da Beppino* in Via delle Prigioni. Buying your own food, there's a good choice of shops on Via Matteotti and a **Saturday market** in the Piazza dei Priori. For great cakes and pastries visit Migliorini, Via Gramsci 24 (closed Sun afternoon). If all you want is a light meal or a glass of wine, the best bet is the *Enoteca Sacco Fiorentino* in the central Piazza XX Settembre at no. 18 (closed Fri & Nov–March): the menu has dozens of snacks, good puddings and an extensive wine list.

Restaurants

Da Badò, Borgo San Lazzaro 9 (☎0588.86.477). Excellent local trattoria which has made a name for itself in national foodie guides, so booking might be an idea – it opens only for lunch. Serves up delicious *crostini*, and Volterran game staples such as *pappardelle alla lepre*. On the SS68 Florence to Siena road. From L35,000. Closed Wed & two weeks in July and Sept.

Da Beppino, Via delle Prigioni 13–21 (☎0588.86.051). Reliable, established restaurant with lots of space (180 covers) and in the heart of the old town; only a tad pricier than lesser places on this street. Outside tables and lots of hunting dishes, plus an emphasis on truffles and mushrooms. From L27,000. Closed Wed.

Etruria, Piazza dei Priori 6 (☎0588.86.064). Best of the more expensive places: located on the main square in an old *palazzo*, with period furniture and frescoes: booking ahead is a good idea. Closed Thurs and periods in Jan, Feb & Nov.

La Pace, Via Don Minzoni 55. Welcoming neighbourhood restaurant located near the hostel – excellent pasta dishes and no pressure to have full meals. If you do, count on around L20,000.

Osteria dei Poeti, Via Matteotti 55–57 (☎0588.86.029). One of the most popular and welcoming restaurants in town – and they don't stint on portions. A central location, with a rustic appearance that retains many features of the original medieval building. From L25,000. Closed Thurs.

Festivals

The major Volterran festival is a **crossbow contest** – a colourful spectacle held in the Piazza dei Priori in July or August. In July, too, there's a small **theatre festival**, and the last Monday of September sees the Piazza dei Priori play host to a **bird fair**.

South to Massa Maríttima

Most travellers take in Volterra from the Florence–San Gimignano–Siena route, heading back east, or striking north to Pisa. The road south (N439), **over to Massa Maríttima** (covered by APT buses), is much less explored – a very wild, mountainous route that is given an added surreal quality by the presence of *soffioni*, hot steam geysers from which boric acid is extracted. To the east of the road are the **Colline Metallifere** – the metal hills – mined by the Etruscans and still inhabited by wolves (an odd thought), just fifty miles from Rome.

Pomarance, Larderello and Castelnuovo

Leaving Volterra, it's a highly scenic drive down to **POMARANCE**, itself a dull and largely modern centre – the area was badly bombed in 1945 – noteworthy only for a handful of paintings in the parish church of **San Giovanni Battista**. Just east is the great ruined bastion of the **Rocca di Silano** – a landmark for almost the whole extent of this route.

Billing itself as the "World Centre of Geothermal Energy", **LARDERELLO** signals the heart of *soffioni* country and takes its name from a nineteenth-century Frenchman, François De Larderel, who introduced the system for harnessing energy from the vapours. ENEL, the electricity company, have set up a small **Museo Storico** (Mon–Sat 8am–5pm, but call first; ☎0588.673.712) on the subject. Modernist buffs might also take a look at the church by **Giovanni Michelucci**, near the centre of town.

All around Larderello huge silver pipes run across the fields, with steam and smoke rising intermittently from chimneys amid the dark foliage. There are fourteen power stations and some sixty kilometres of piping. Settlements are few, presumably due to the strong whiffs of sulphur, and the only sizeable village past Larderello is **Castelnuovo di Val di Cecina**, a neat little *borgo medioveale*. Beyond here, the road is hemmed in by woods and there's scarcely a farmhouse to be seen. With transport, you could cut east along a tiny, winding road, south of Castelnuovo, through **Montieri** and on to San Galgano (see p.359).

travel details

TRAINS

Saline di Volterra to: Cécina (8 daily; 35min; connections to Pisa and Rome).

Poggibonsi to: Empoli (hourly; 45min); Florence (9 daily; 1hr 5min).

BUSES

Poggibonsi to: San Gimignano and Colle di Val d'Elsa, also to Volterra and Massa Maríttima.

San Gimignano to: Poggibonsi, whence connections to Florence, Siena and Volterra.

Siena to: Colle di Val d'Elsa, Monteriggioni, Poggibonsi and Volterra.

Volterra to: San Gimignano (via Poggibonsi), Siena, Florence, Massa Maríttima and Livorno.

CHAPTER EIGHT

SOUTHERN TUSCANY

T he region **south of Siena** is Tuscany at its best: an infinite gradation of hills, trees and cultivation that encompasses the *Crete Senese*, the vineyards of Montepulciano and Montalcino, the Monte Amiata uplands and finally a landscape of sulphurous springs and castle-topped outcrops of tufa. The *crete*, especially, is fabulous: a sparsely populated region of pale clay hillsides, dotted with sheep, cypresses and the odd monumental-looking farmhouse.

The towns on the whole live up to this environment. **Montepulciano** is the most elegant and makes a superb base, with its independent hill-town life, acclaimed Vino Nobile wine and backdrop of Renaissance buildings. **Montalcino** too has appealing wines (its Brunello is regarded as Tuscany's finest vintage) and classic hill-town looks, while **Pienza** is a unique Renaissance monument, a town created by the great humanist pope, Pius II. In the south of the region, the urban highlights are **Pitigliano**, isolated on an extraordinary crag, and nearby the forgotten, half-abandoned medieval town of **Sovana.**

Monasteries are a major attraction of the area, and feature some of the greatest houses of the medieval Italian orders: Cistercian **San Galgano** and **Abbadia San Salvatore**, Benedictine **Monte Oliveto Maggiore** and **Sant'Antimo**, and Vallambrosan **Torri**. All are tremendous buildings, encompassing the best Romanesque and Gothic church architecture in Tuscany.

Equally memorable are the extraordinary **sulphur springs** that erupt from the rocks, or are channelled into geothermal energy, punctuating the landscape with pillars of white smoke. Several of the springs have for centuries formed the nucleus of **spas**. The most interesting is **Bagno Vignoni**, still with its Medicean basin in the village square. Here, and at **Bagni di Petriolo**, **Bagni San Filippo** and – most spectacularly – **Saturnia**, you can immerse yourself in open-air rock pools below warm cascades.

San Galgano and the western crete

If you have transport, the route past the abbeys of **Torri** and **San Galgano**, the sulphur spring of **Petriolo**, and the villages of the western *crete* makes one of the best trips out from Siena. It could be done in a day, or alternatively with a night's stop at Buonconvento, Montalcino or one of the Murlo villages.

ACCOMMODATION PRICES

Throughout this guide, **hotel** accommodation is graded on a scale from ① to ⑨, indicating the cost of the **cheapest double room** in each establishment in high season (for **hostels**, rates per person are given in lire). The price bands to which these codes refer are as follows:

① up to L60,000	④ L120,000–150,000	⑦ L250,000–300,000
② L60,000–90,000	⑤ L150,000–200,000	⑧ L300,000–350,000
③ L90,000–120,000	⑥ L200,000–250,000	⑨ over L350,000

If you are dependent on public transport, it's perhaps best to content yourself with San Galgano, which lies just off the N73 Siena–Massa Maríttima road, covered by three daily buses. You could get back to Siena in the day, continue on to Massa Maríttima, or stop near the abbey at the village of **Palazzetto**.

Torri

Driving south from Siena, it's best to follow the N223 Grosseto road as far as the junction signposted to Brenna, Stigliano and Torri. Taking this very minor road, you find yourself in the **Rosia valley**, a belt of ancient farmland strung with patches of vineyard, and overlooked by a series of cream-stone villages set along the wooded ridge to the south. All these villages are pastoral beauties, approached from the valley floor along cobbled roads and avenues of cypress trees, with farmyards backing onto many of the houses.

To give a point of focus to the trip, come on a Monday or Friday morning, when you can visit the **Monastero dei Santi Trinità e Mustiola** at **TORRI**, the last of the villages, just 2km east of the Siena–Grosseto road. The monastery, founded in the eleventh century, was an important power base for the Vallombrosan order, until difficulties with the papacy led to its suppression by Pius II in 1464. It retains its Romanesque church and a magnificent three-tiered cloister, executed in panels of black and white marble. The capitals of the lower tier, in particular, are outstanding; their style and subject matter (fantastic animals and Old Testament stories) recalling the French-influenced work at Sant'Antimo (see p.375). Abandoned in the sixteenth century, the complex was bought privately in 1966. It is scarcely ever visited – but note that opening hours are Mondays and Fridays 9am to noon; at other times it's kept firmly locked and nobody local has a key.

San Galgano

The **Abbazia di San Galgano**, midway between Massa and Siena, is among the greatest Gothic buildings in Italy. It is certainly the most romantic – roofless, with a grass field for a nave, patches of fresco amidst the vegetation, and panoramas of the sky, clouds and hills through a rose window. (If you have ever seen Andrei Tarkovsky's film *Nostalgia*, it will be immediately familiar from the finale, in which the director transformed the nave into a Russian landscape complete with a *dacha*.)

The Abbey

In the twelfth and thirteenth centuries, San Galgano – which was one of the Cistercians' two largest foundations in Italy – was the leading monastic power in Tuscany. Its abbots ruled over disputes between the cities, and at Siena its monks supervised the building of the duomo, and held posts as *casalinghi*, or accountants, for the *comune*. The monks were a mix of Italians and French, and through them the ideas of Gothic building were imported to Italy, along with sophisticated schemes for land drainage and agriculture. As at all Cistercian houses, the monastic population included large numbers of lay brothers, who dedicated themselves to manual labour while the "choir monks" looked after the prayer and study.

The order built the **church** and **abbey** here between 1218 and 1288, at which time the complex must have looked like a small town, with its numerous workshops, dormitories and guest quarters. However, at the end of the century, during the wars between the Tuscan cities, the English *condottiere* Sir John Hawkwood and his mercenary troops sacked the abbey, and by 1397 the abbot was San Galgano's sole occupant. During the fifteenth century it was repopulated for a while, until the papacy handed its income to a particularly profligate cardinal. The monks left and the building gradually decayed – the campanile actually collapsed during a Mass attended by villagers.

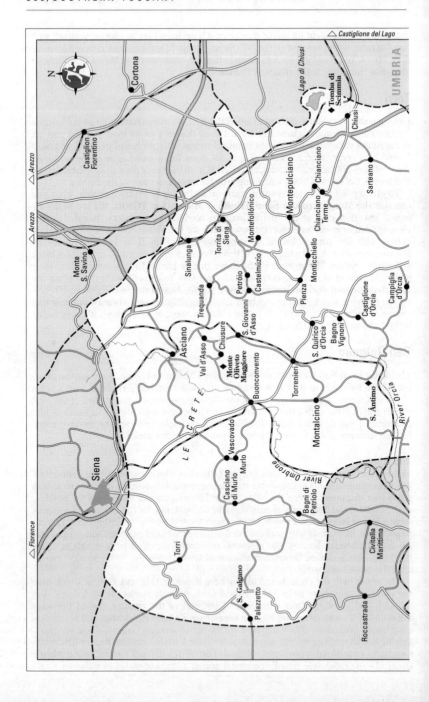

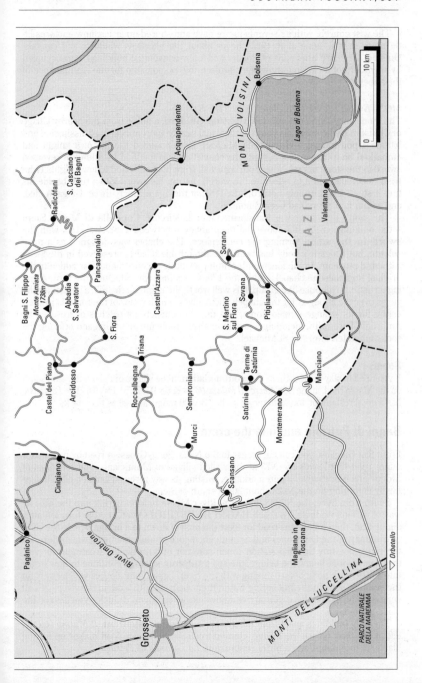

The vast church, with its seventy-metre nave and shored-up aisles, now encloses little more than a stone altar. Birds hover about the glassless windows and capitals. Outside, there are brief runs of cloister and a few conventual buildings, part-occupied by members of a community welfare project now responsible for the maintenance of the abbey and its surrounds.

MONTE SIEPI AND THE SWORD IN THE STONE

The monastery commemorates **St Galgano Guidotti**, a noble from the nearby village of Chiusdino, who spent his youth in the usual saintly apprenticeship of dissipation and battles. Upon having a vision of St Michael, he renounced the life of a knight and embarked on a career as a hermit. His conviction was fortified by a kind of reversed sword-in-the-stone miracle when, during a visit from his family and fellow knights (who tried to persuade him to return to the world), he ran his sword into a rock beside his hut: it stuck fast, forming a crucifix. In 1181, at the age of thirty-three, Galgano died, and within four years had been canonized.

The saint's hermitage was transformed into the circular **Cappella di Monte Siepi** – the building on the hill above the main abbey – between 1182 and 1185, with the **sword in the stone** forming the centrepiece. The chapel was designed as a mausoleum, but Galgano's body has been lost, though his head is preserved in the Siena cathedral museum. In the fourteenth century a Gothic second chapel was added to the original Romanesque chapel, and in the 1700s a rectory was attached, the three forming a rustic, farmhouse-like group. It is well worth the climb up the hill, as much for the views over the abbey as for the chapels themselves. The interior of the rotunda is interesting for its strange striped dome, and the side chapel has patches of frescoes by Ambrogio Lorenzetti, including a just-about-discernible image of Galgano offering the rock-embedded sword to St Michael.

Rooms

If you need to stay nearby, there is **accommodation** in the village of Palazzetto, 4km south on the Massa road, at the *Bar-Albergo Il Palazzetto* (☎ & fax 0577.751.160; ②). The *Palazzetto* has a good restaurant, too, with meals in the L30,000 range, as well as bar snacks.

Bagni di Petriolo and into the crete

From San Galgano, you can cut across to the N223 Siena–Grosseto road by means of a minor road that leaves the N73 at the walled village of Monticiano. The road east of Monticiano is attractive, if unremarkable, twisting its way through wooded hills, before finally emerging on the N223 about 20km south of Siena.

South from here, the N223 follows the River Merse before rearing into the hills by way of various viaducts. To reach **BAGNI DI PETRIOLO** you need to turn left after about 4km, then follow this road for 9km (no buses) down to a bridge beside the river (a tributary of the Ombrone) and a rough enclosure of huge medieval walls. Here, on the right, is a tiny thermal station (open summer only), offering treatment for visitors. On the left, below the bridge, the spa's **sulphur springs** continue to flow freely into a little rock pool, before mixing with the river. Leave your clothes well away from the sulphur, soak in the hot spring water, then wash off with a dip in the river – it's all very moody, especially if you arrive midweek, when if you're lucky you'll have the place to yourself.

The only buildings apart from the spa are a **pizzeria-restaurant**, *Il Mulino* (on the left of the road before the bridge, coming from Siena), whose food makes up for the bland surroundings, and a **hotel-restaurant**, *La Locanda di Petriolo*.

The Murlo villages

With transport, you can follow a paved track off the Petriolo road, through the hills to **CASCIANO DI MURLO**; the track runs alongside a formidable estate that is fenced off to protect its woodland and shooting. Scarcely more than a hamlet, Casciano has a 29-room, three-star **hotel**, the *Mirella* (☎0577.817.667, fax 0577.817.575, *mirella@sienanet.it*; ④), a **riding centre**, and a **campsite**, *Le Soline* (☎0577.817.410), open year-round, located at nearby Casafranci. A fine place to break your journey, or base yourself for a few days, Casciano is also easily reached from the N223 (it's 6km from the turning).

East from Casciano, a very high and beautiful road leads into the beginnings of the *crete*, with hills punctuated by the occasional lake and farmhouse on the approach to **VESCOVADO DI MURLO**. Vescovado, a largely modern village, is worth a stop for its **bar-restaurant**, the *Osteria Deo* (closed Tues), a thoroughly unpretentious place off the square which serves up vast portions of pasta, fish and big roasts; it's frequented by the local priests, which is always a good sign. Vescovado also has a **hotel**, the three-star *Murlo*, Via Martiri di Rigosecco (March–Oct; ☎0577.814.033, fax 0577.814.243; ④), roadside signs for which you'll have seen dotted across half of southern Tuscany. It has the added bonus of a swimming pool, but beware of Saturday nights in summer, when the local disco means you'll have a hard job catching a wink of sleep until the small hours. There's also *agriturismo* accommodation at Palazzina (☎0577.817.776; ③), a farmhouse between Casciano and Vescovado.

Just a couple of kilometres south of Vescovado is **MURLO** – a tiny medieval *borgo* whose ring of houses forms defensive walls, enclosing the town hall and church. The oldest settlement in the area, Murlo's Etruscan past is commemorated in the **Museo Etrusco**, housed in the Castello di Murlo (April–Sept Tues–Sun 9.30am–12.45pm & 3–7pm plus July & Aug 9–11pm; March & Oct Tues–Sun 9.30am–12.30pm & 3–5pm; Nov–Feb Tues–Sat 10am–noon, Sun 10am–noon & 2–5pm; L5000). Exhibits include sphinx statues, a large terracotta tomb frieze depicting hunting scenes, and some odd bowls, decorated with warriors holding women whose legs form the handles. To the south of Murlo, a track leads to an even smaller *borgo*, the ten-house La Befa, which has a renowned **osteria** (closed Wed), set in rich mushroom territory; meals are around L25,000.

At Vescovado or Murlo you're within easy striking distance of Buonconvento, and near enough to Asciano, Montalcino or Siena. The **Montalcino route** is lovely, as is the **Asciano road**, a superb scenic route, taking you into the heart of the *crete*, across sparsely populated countryside. Just off the N2, which you need to join for a few kilometres before heading east to Asciano, there are **rooms** at the *Pensione Vicoletto* (☎ & fax 0577.374.688; ③) in the medieval hamlet of Lucignano d'Arbia.

Monte Oliveto and the central crete

The heartland of the *crete* is the area southeast of Siena, around the Benedictine monastery of **Monte Oliveto Maggiore** – arguably Tuscany's finest. The region is studded with lonely cypresses on sun-baked clay hills, and contains all the other classic Tuscan images. The abbey is reached easily enough by car via **Asciano** or **Buonconvento**, 9km distant to the north and west, respectively; **Montalcino**, too, is only 24km distant to the south and makes an excellent base for the whole district. You can get to Asciano or Buonconvento by train or bus from Siena, though you'll have to hitch (more promising from Buonconvento) or hike (prettier from Asciano) the rest of the way.

Buonconvento

BUONCONVENTO is the most obvious base if you are visiting Monte Oliveto Maggiore and travelling on south. The small town looks unremittingly industrial as you approach, but once through the suburbs you come upon a perfect, walled medieval village. In its day, this was one of Siena's key outer defences, and it was here, in 1313, that Emperor Henry VII of Luxembourg, en route to besiege Siena, famously died of malaria, exhaustion or – in some versions – being fed a poisoned Host during Mass. This was a man whom Dante, among others, had seen as the saviour of Italy (Dante particularly wished the emperor to attack Florence, from which he was then exiled – he rather loquaciously equated the emperor's arrival with that of the "lamb of God, who removes the sins of the world").

The old centre is characteristically Sienese, with its brick bastions, town hall and its works of art – most of which have been removed from the churches to the excellent and little-known **Museo d'Arte Sacra**, in the main street of the old quarter at Via Soccini 18 (summer 10.30am–1pm & 2.30–8pm, closed Wed; winter Sat & Sun 10am–1pm & 2–5pm; L6000).

Pride of place in the charming two-room museum – which on its own is worth the trouble of pulling into town – goes to a small *Madonna and Child with Angels* by Matteo di Giovanni, whose knowing Mary must surely be a portrait. Other works include a *Madonna and Child* attributed to Duccio; a *Madonna and Saints* (1470–82) and *Coronation of the Virgin* by Sano di Pietro; a lovely four-panelled *Annunciation* (1397) by Andrea di Bartolo; the curious *Madonna del Latte* by Luca di Tommè showing a breast-feeding *Madonna*; and an *Annunciation* (1490–1500) by Benvenuto di Giovanni, a Florentine-influenced work which strikes an anomalous note among the surrounding Sienese treasures.

Art attractions aside, Buonconvento makes an enjoyable stop. You can get here easily by **train** or **bus** from Siena, Montalcino and elsewhere: there are also a couple of fast through-trains to Florence and Grosseto daily, this being one of the key stations for southern Tuscany (for train information ring ☎0577.806.104). **Tourist information** can be obtained at the Museo d'Arte Sacra (☎0577.807.181).

If you need to **stay** – and there are worse overnight stops if you're travelling far and don't want to get tangled up in Siena – the town has a single **hotel-restaurant**, the *Albergo Roma*, Via Soccini, 14 (☎0577.806.021, fax 0577.807.284; ②), inside the walls. The hotel is a bit basic but its food is fine, the restaurant representing a perfect piece of old-fashioned 1950s Italiana. Up the street from the hotel, in the Palazzo del Popolo in Piazza Gramsci, there are regular weekend **dance** evenings – a great experience, with all the local farmers coming in for a waltz. The lively weekly **market** (Sat 8am–1pm) is also held in Piazza Gramsci.

Alternative **accommodation** near Buonconvento is offered by the Pieve a Salti farm (☎0577.807.244; ④) at Pieve a Salti (signed from Buonconvento), part of the *agriturismo* scheme. Up in the hills, just 4km east of town, it's comfortable and welcoming, and the beautifully situated swimming pool has views over what seems like half of southern Tuscany. You can rent rooms for the night, or simple self-contained apartments in the rustic houses dotted across the estate. Meals are available in the cosy central house.

Monte Oliveto Maggiore

The **Abbazia di Monte Oliveto Maggiore** is sited in one of the most beautiful tracts of Sienese countryside. Approaching from Buonconvento, you climb through forests of pine, oak and cypress, and then into the olive groves that enclose the monastery. From the east, coming through Asciano or San Giovanni d'Asso, the road passes through perhaps the wildest section of all the *crete*. It all appears much as it would have to Pope Pius

II, who in 1463 eulogized the woods and gardens that the monks had created from the chalk hills, and the way the russet-coloured brick buildings merged with their setting. Also preserved here is one of the most absorbing Renaissance fresco cycles that you'll find anywhere, a *Life of St Benedict* painted by Sodoma and Luca Signorelli.

The monastery had been founded a century and a half before Pius's visit by one Giovanni Tolomei. A Sienese noble, Giovanni was a major political force in Siena, who renounced all worldly goods after being struck blind and experiencing visions of the Virgin. Adopting the name Bernardo, he came with two companions to the *crete* and lived the life of a hermit. They soon drew a following in this heyday of monasticism, and within six years the pope recognized them as an order – the **Olivetans**, or White Benedictines. Attempting to recapture the simplicity of the original Benedictine rule, these first Olivetans were a remarkable group, going out in pairs during the Black Death to nurse the sick and minister to the dying in all the Sienese towns. During the Feast of the Assumption in 1348, they all met up in Siena – miraculously with no casualties – after their months of perilous work, though Bernardo died later in the year as did many of the brothers.

The remaining monks rebuilt the order, and over the following two centuries Monte Oliveto Maggiore was transformed into one of the most powerful monasteries in the land. (Pius II had a personal reason to visit, as his relative Ambrogio Piccolomini was one of Bernardo's original companions, and in 1536, Emperor Charles V paid a call, together with a two-thousand-strong army).

The monastery only really fell from influence with the nineteenth-century suppression of the Italian orders, and after the last war, the Italian government allowed Olivetan monks to repopulate it. They have largely restored the buildings and gardens, which they continue to maintain as a monument, supplementing their state income with a highly advanced workshop in restoring ancient books. They also produce wine, honey, olive oil and a cure-all herb liquor, *Flora di Monte Oliveto*, for sale at the monastery shop.

The Monastery

Monte Oliveto is **open to visits** daily 9.15am–noon and 3.15–5.45pm (5pm in winter). At the gatehouse there is a good **café-restaurant**, and also a **hostel** (closed for refurbishment at time of writing), as is the Benedictine custom. This, however, has a minimum stay of ten days (most guests stay two to three months) and summer places are almost always taken; if you want to try your luck, phone ahead (☎0577.707.611).

From the **gateway**, surmounted by a square watchtower and niches containing della Robbia terracottas, an avenue of cypresses leads to the abbey. Off to the right, signs direct you along a walk to the **Blessed Bernardo's grotto** – a chapel built on the site where Tolomei settled as a hermit. The **abbey** itself is a huge complex, though much of it remains off limits to visitors. The entrance leads past the gift shop to the **Chiostro Grande**, covered by frescoes of the *Life of St Benedict*, the man traditionally regarded as the founder of Christian monasticism.

SODOMA AND SIGNORELLI'S LIFE OF ST BENEDICT

The St Benedict fresco cycle was begun by **Luca Signorelli**, a painter from Cortona who trained under Piero della Francesca before working for the papacy on the Sistine Chapel. He worked at Monte Oliveto in 1497, completing nine panels (in the middle of the series) before abandoning the work for a more stimulating commission at Orvieto Cathedral. Like much of his work elsewhere, the scenes show a passionate interest in human anatomy, with figures positioned to show off their muscularity to maximum effect.

A few years after Signorelli's departure, Antonio Bazzi (known as **Il Sodoma**), took over, painting the remaining 27 scenes between 1505 and 1508. Sodoma was from Milan and familiar with Leonardo's work, which he often emulated. How he took his nickname is unclear: Vasari suggests it was apt since "he was always surrounded by young men, in whose company he took great pleasure", though letters by Sodoma himself speak of three wives and thirty children. Whatever, the artist was a colourful figure, keeping an extraordinary menagerie of pets: "Badgers, apes, cat-a-mountains, dwarf asses, horses and barbs to run races, magpies, dwarf chickens, tortoises, Indian doves . . . .".

Sodoma brought a sizeable contingent of these pets to Monte Oliveto, including a raven which imitated his voice, and they make odd appearances throughout his colourful, sensual frescoes – a badger is depicted at his feet in a self-portrait in the third panel. There's a notable eroticism, too, in many of the secular figures: the young men coming to join Benedict as monks, and the "evil women", seen tempting the monks in a panel towards the end of the series – these were originally nudes, before protests from the abbot. If the panels strike you as of differing quality, you might give credence to Vasari's anecdote that Sodoma complained about the money he was being paid, which the abbot subsequently raised on condition that he took more care over the remaining work, the first three historical panels of the sequence.

The **cycle** begins on the east wall, on the right of the door into the church. St Benedict, who was born in Norcia in 480, is depicted in events recorded in Gregory the Great's *Dialogues*. In the early panels he is shown leaving home to study in Rome, before withdrawing to the life of a hermit, where he experiences various tribulations and temptations before agreeing to become abbot to a group of disciples. He was an indefatigable builder of monasteries, and the next panels focus on this activity: the foundation of the twelve houses, which formed the basis of the Benedictine order, as well as depictions of various miracles to help in their construction.

The mid-sequence of the cycle depicts various attempts by an evil priest, Florentius, to disrupt the saint's work: he tries first to poison Benedict and then sends in the temptresses, before God steps in and flattens his house (the first of Signorelli's panels). The following eight scenes painted by Signorelli depict aspects of monastic life, and Benedict's trial by – and reception of – Totila, king of the Goths, before Sodoma takes over again, with the saint foretelling the destruction of Monte Cassino, the chief Benedictine house, by the Lombards. More scenes of monastic life follow, including the burial of a monk whom the earth would not accept, another monk's attempted escape (Benedict intercepts him with a serpent) and the release of a peasant persecuted by a Goth.

THE CHURCH, LIBRARY AND REFECTORY

The rest of the monastery is inevitably overshadowed by the frescoes. The main **church** – entered off the Chiostro Grande – was given a Baroque remodelling in the eighteenth century and some superb stained glass in the twentieth. Its main treasure is the **choir stalls**, inlaid by Giovanni di Verona and others, from 1500 to 1520, with architectural, landscape and domestic scenes (including a nod to Sodoma's pets with a depiction of a cat in a window).

Back in the cloister, stairs lead up, past a Sodoma fresco of the Virgin, to the **library**, a fine Renaissance arcade lavished with carvings by Giovanni and associates. Sadly, it has had to be viewed from the door since the theft of sixteen codices in 1975. Also on view is the **refectory**, a vast room frescoed with allegorical and Old Testament figures, which gives some idea of Monte Oliveto's heyday.

Asciano

ASCIANO lies on a tiny branch rail line between Siena and Grosseto that takes you through marvellous *crete* countryside. The railway station, Asciano Centro (there is also an Asciano Scalo) is in Via Roma: for **train information** ring ☎0577.718.873. The road approach, the N438 from Siena, is still more scenic, with scarcely a hamlet amid the hills; this route is covered by bus just once daily (the same departure as for Chiusi).

Of Etruscan foundation, the town is first mentioned in records in 715. In the ninth century it was ruled by the powerful Scialenghi counts, but in 1169 passed to Siena, which promptly ordered the destruction of the town's fortress. In 1234 it fell briefly to Florence, but was soon recaptured by the Sienese. Its most famous son is **Domenico di Bartolo** (1400–45), the painter responsible for the fresco cycle in Siena's Ospedale di Santa Maria della Scala (see p.312).

The town itself is partially walled and shelters a trio of tiny provincial museums. In an oratory adjoining the thirteenth-century Collegiata di Sant'Agata (in Piazza Fratelli Bandiera) stands the **Museo d'Arte Sacra** (for admission contact the tourist office ☎0577.719.510), a beautiful and unusual Romanesque-Gothic building, which, like the museum in Buonconvento, contains an unexpected wealth of Sienese paintings. It has a dozen or so works by major Sienese painters (among them Ambrogio Lorenzetti, Sano di Pietro, Taddeo di Bartolo and Matteo di Giovanni).

To the left of the Collegiata, at Via Mameli 36, the **Museo Cassioli** (mid-June to mid-Sept Tues–Sun 10am–12.30pm & 4.30–6.30pm; rest of year Tues–Sun 10am–12.30pm; L4000) displays paintings by local artist Amos Cassioli (1832–91). Close by, at Corso Matteotti 46, is a **Museo Etrusco** (same hours and fee as Museo Cassioli), formerly the church of San Bernardino, whose exhibits are mainly finds from the Etruscan tombs at Poggio Pinci, 5km east of Asciano. A combined ticket (L6000) is available for these last two museums.

For **information** visit the summer-only tourist office in Corso Matteotti (☎0577.719.510); out of season try the small Pro-Loco in Via Amos Cassioli 2 (no phone). The town has one reasonably priced, three-star **hotel**, *Il Bersagliere*, Via Roma 39–41 (☎ & fax 0577.718.629; ②). Local bars provide basic food, though the best **restaurant** in the vicinity is *La Pievina* (☎0577.718.368; closed Mon & Tues), 5.5km north along the Siena road at the hamlet of the same name.

San Giovanni d'Asso and east to Sinalunga

Continuing on the train line from Asciano, the next stop – and another possible starting point to hike to Monte Oliveto – is **SAN GIOVANNI D'ASSO**, a quiet, rustic place, whose medieval past is hinted at by the presence of half a dozen churches. (Romanesque San Pietro, an eleventh-century gem, is the most interesting, and there's an imposing, if extremely blunt thirteenth-century **castle**. Only ever a Sienese fiefdom, the fortress was inhabited at various times by the Buonsignori, whose Sienese palace now houses the city's Pinacoteca, and by the Salimbeni, whose dynastic seat in the city is now the headquarters of the Monte dei Paschi bank. Later it became a granary, and in time was given to Siena's Ospedale di Santa Maria della Scala (see p.312).

East from San Giovanni, a fine though bus-less road meanders towards Sinalunga. The attraction here is primarily the landscape – classic Tuscan miniatures – though the road is marked out by a series of hill-top villages, most of them endowed with a castle and a smattering of medieval churches. **CASTELMUZIO** was a favourite preaching ground for Bernardino of Siena, whose confraternity houses a small **Museo d'Arte Sacra**; the saint is also depicted in panels by Giovanni di Paolo, his close friend, and Giovanni's pupil Matteo di Giovanni, in the church of SS. Trinità e Bernardino. Close by is one of Tuscany's oldest churches – the eighth-century **Pieve di Santo Stefano** in **CENNANO** – while at neighbouring **PETROIO**, built on a curious circular plan, is the best **castle** in the district, a thirteenth-century brick affair where Siena's magistrates were obliged to live for a period in the thirteenth century. A few kilometres to the northeast is the **Abbadia a Sicille**, built by the Templars as a hospice on the pilgrim road to Rome. **TREQUANDA**, a slightly larger village with a couple of restaurants and bars, also preserves a good section of its castle. In the central square, the simple Romanesque parish church of **SS. Pietro e Andrea**, fronted by a brown-and-white chequered stone facade, has a fresco by Sodoma of the *Transfiguration*, and a high altarpiece of the *Madonna and Saints* by Giovanni di Paolo. The inlaid wooden urn contains the body of Bonizella Piccolomini (1235–1300), a mere beatific, who never reached the heights of more illustrious family descendants such as Aeneas Piccolomini (Pope Pius II).

East of Trequanda you reach **SINALUNGA**, a modern, thriving centre with rail connections to Siena, Arezzo and Chiusi. It has one notable painting – an *Annunciation* by Benvenuto di Giovanni – in the church of **San Francesco**, sited beside the Franciscan convent at the top of an avenue of cypresses. The church should have another fine picture – a *Madonna* by Sano di Pietro – but that went missing in 1972 and has been replaced by a sad facsimile. Just out of town in the hamlet-suburb of Pieve is a pleasant **hotel**, the *Santorotto* (☎ & fax 0577.679.012; ②). In Sinalunga itself, at Viale Matteotti 5, there's a friendly and idiosyncratic **restaurant** called *Kris* (☎0577.631.225; closed Mon), which specializes in fish dishes but becomes an Indian restaurant on Wednesday nights.

Other good-value **hotels** in these parts are to be found 7km south at the next rail stop, Torrita di Siena: the *Belvedere* (☎0577.686.442; ②) and *La Stazione* (☎ & fax 0577.685.158; ②). There is further accommodation at the **spas** of Rapolano Terme and Terme San Giovanni, north of Sinalunga on the Siena road. Both are modern, upmarket places of little interest to anyone not visiting "to take the cure".

Montalcino

MONTALCINO is a classic Tuscan hill-town, set within a full circuit of walls and watched over by a castle of almost fairy-tale perfection. A quiet, immediately likeable place, affluent in an unshowy way, it is scarcely changed in appearance since the sixteenth century. It looks wonderful from below, its walls barely sullied by any modern building, and once up in the town the rolling hills, vineyards, orchards, olive groves and ancient oaks look equally lovely in turn. While there are few specific sights, the town makes an excellent base for much of southern Tuscany, lying within easy striking distance of the abbeys of Monte Oliveto and Sant'Antimo, and close to the towns of Pienza and Montepulciano.

A brief history

Montalcino's origins are unknown, though it has probably been inhabited since Paleolithic or Etruscan times. No one is quite sure where its name comes from, though its coat of arms – a holm oak atop six hills – suggests that it derives from the Latin *Mons Ilcinus* – the Mount of the Holm Oak. The first reference to the town appears in 814, when it is mentioned in a list of territories ceded to the abbey of Sant'Antimo by Louis the Pious, the son of Charlemagne (see p.375). It was probably only permanently settled around the year 1000, colonized by fugitives fleeing Saracen attacks on the Maremma coast. The exiles' four family groups – the Borghetto, Pianello, Ruca and Travaglio – defined the four quarters or *contrade* of the town; the rival flags still hang outside the houses and they compete against each other in twice-yearly archery tournaments.

Though independent for much of its early medieval history, the town succumbed to Sienese rule in 1260 after the Battle of Montaperti, having previously looked to Florence for protection. Having been forced to change sides, the town eventually took its new rulers to heart. In 1526 it took just two days for its citizens to fight off a besieging army dispatched by Pope Clement VII. In 1553, over a period of four months, it withstood the attack of a combined Spanish and Medici army. The town's finest hour, however, came in 1555, when on April 21 the venerable Sienese Republic was forced, once and for all, to capitulate to the Medici. A group of Sienese exiles, supported by the French, then formed a last bastion of Sienese power in Montalcino, flying the flag of the

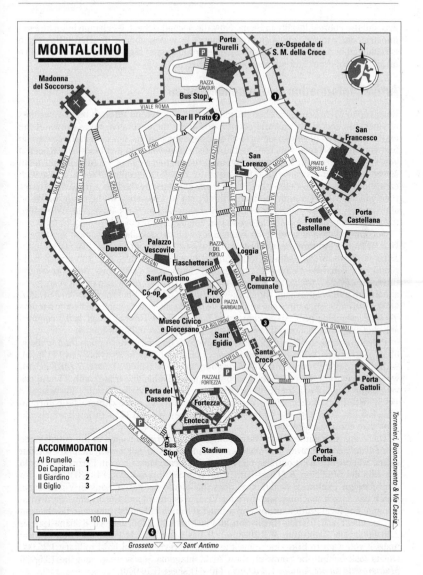

Map of Montalcino showing:

MONTALCINO

Porta Burelli, ex-Ospedale di S. M. della Croce, Madonna del Soccorso, PIAZZA CAVOUR, Bus Stop, Bar Il Prato, VIALE ROMA, San Francesco, VIA DEL PINO, San Lorenzo, VIA MAZZINI, VIA CIALDINI, VIA DELLA LIBERTA, VIA P STROZZI, VIA SPAGNI, PRATO OSPEDALE, VIA DEL MISTERO, VIA RASTRELLARA, Porta Castellana, COSTA SPAGNI, Fonte Castellane, Duomo, Palazzo Vescovile, PIAZZA DEL POPOLO, Loggia, VIA MOGLIO, Fiaschetteria, VIA SPAGNI, Sant'Agostino, Co-op, VIA RICASOLI, Pro Loco, PIAZZA GARIBALDI, Palazzo Comunale, VIA MATTEOTTI, Museo Civico e Diocesano, VIA BOLDRINI, Sant'Egidio, VIA S SALONI, VIA DONNOLI, Santa Croce, VIA PANFILO DELL'OCA, PIAZZALE FORTEZZA, Porta del Cassero, Fortezza, Enoteca, VIA A MORO, Bus Stop, Stadium, Porta Gattoli, Porta Cerbaia, Grosseto, Sant'Antimo, Torrenieri, Buonconvento & Via Cassia, 0 100 m

ACCOMMODATION

Al Brunello	4
Dei Capitani	1
Il Giardino	2
Il Giglio	3

old Republic for four years in the face of almost constant attack. Surrender was only countenanced following the treaty of Cateau Cambrésis (1559) between France and Spain. This heroic interlude is acknowledged at the Siena Palio, where the Montalcino contingent, under their medieval banner proclaiming "The Republic of Siena in Montalcino", still takes place of honour.

In the following centuries, the town declined to a poor, malaria-stricken village. Although the malaria was sorted out in the nineteenth century, in the 1960s Montalcino was still the poorest locality in Siena. Now the second richest, its change in fortunes is due principally to the revival and marketing of its wines, notably the **Brunello**, which is reckoned by many the finest in Italy. The production of high-quality honey and olive oil and income from tourism also play a part.

Arrival, information and accommodation

Roads up to Montalcino, perched 567m above sea level, wind through bucolic swathes of vineyards and pretty pastoral countryside (note the decorative roses grown at the end of many rows of vines): views to all sides are stupendous. Once up at the town, you find yourself on a road which rings the walls. Buses will stop just below the **Rocca** if you wish, but terminate in **Piazza Cavour** at the northern end of Via Mazzini, the main street: either point is convenient for Piazza del Popolo, the centre of town. Those with cars should aim to park either in the small pay **car park** by the Rocca (take the narrow road which strikes through the arch – the **Porta al Cassero** – in the castle walls) or, alternatively, use the large, free car park below the fortress (take Via Aldo Moro towards the ugly estate at the five-road junction by the Rocca).

Accommodation is severely limited and it's wise to book ahead at almost any time of year. There are just three central **hotels**: the two-star *Albergo Il Giardino*, Piazza Cavour (☎ & fax 0577.848.257; ②), with its rather mixed bag of ten doubles (six with private bathroom), of which those facing onto the piazza are likely to be a little noisy; the more central three-star *Albergo Il Giglio*, Via S. Saloni 49 (☎ & fax 0577.848.167; ④), in recent years given a thorough internal overhaul; and the new *Hotel dei Capitani*, Via Lapini 6 (☎0577.847.227, fax 0577.847.239; ⑤), a three-star place whose slick facilities are complemented by a tempting little swimming pool. About 2km out at Belaria, on the Grosseto road, is the comfortable, but soullessly modern *Al Brunello* (☎0577.849.304, fax 0577.849.430; ⑦).

Private rooms are less expensive and likely to be a far better option than in many other places. Try *Affitacamere Mariuccia*, Piazza del Popolo 28 (☎0577.849.113; ②), with three double rooms; *Anna Affitacamare* at Via S. Saloni 31 (☎0577.848.666; ②), where there are three comfortable rooms (single, double and triple) with TV and private bathrooms, plus a four-bed apartment; or Maria Locatelli, *"Casali"*, Via Spagni 3 (☎0577.847.150; ②), who offers two doubles and a triple, each with private bathroom (this last has links with the *Grappolo Blu* restaurant – see p.373 – through which you can make enquiries directly).

There are also numerous private rooms and *agriturismo* rooms in the countryside immediately around town. The small – and, it must be said, not terribly helpful – **tourist office** will provide a list of these on request: it's located just up from Piazza del Popolo at Costa del Municipio 8 (Tues–Sun 10am–1pm & 2–6pm; ☎0577.849.331). They also offer **foreign exchange** facilities, as does the Monte dei Paschi bank in Via Mazzini, which has a cash machine next door for Visa, Mastercard and Eurocheque card withdrawals. For local **guides**, **maps** and a small selection of English-language **books** visit the excellent and friendly bookshop at Via Matteotti 22 (Tues–Sat 8.30am–1pm & 2.30–8pm; Sun 10am–1pm & 2.30–8pm). It has a particularly good selection of local maps if you want to **hike**, including the recently revised local IGM military 1:25,000 sheets (ask behind the counter); the CAI Montagnola Senese map; and the 1:25,000 *Multigraphic Monte Amiata-Val d'Órcia* (40–41) sheet (L10,000).

The Town

Wherever you end up, the triangular **Piazza del Popolo** lies only a few minutes' walk away. An odd little square, it is set beneath the elongated medieval tower of the **Palazzo dei Priori**, or Palazzo Comunale (1292), apparently modelled on Siena's Palazzo Pubblico. Crests of long-forgotten dignitaries dot the walls, while the statue (1564) beneath the portico, surprisingly, represents the reviled Medici ruler, Cosimo I – it was sculpted just five years after Montalcino had surrendered to the Florentines. Inside the town hall there is an exhibition on the history and making of Brunello: shops the length and breadth of the town sell the stuff, most at ridiculously elevated prices (see next page).

Occupying other sides of the square are an elegant Renaissance double **loggia**, almost a reprimand in proportional architecture, and a wonderful nineteenth-century **café**, the *Fiaschetteria Italiana*. The café is the heart of town life and the focus, inevitably, of the *passeggiata* along Via Mazzini. On busy summer afternoons, however, service can be slow – not a problem if all you want to do is watch the world go by. If you've worked up a thirst, however, the **bar** to the right of the loggia, which also has outside tables, is usually quicker with liquid refreshment.

The Rocca

Following Via Mazzini's continuation, Via Matteotti, or Via Ricasoli, and curving up to the right, you emerge at the south end of town by the **Rocca** (April–Oct daily 9am–8pm; Nov–March Tues–Sun 9am–1pm & 2–6pm; free). It was begun in 1361 on the orders of the Sienese, but by the end of the fifteenth century the advent of artillery had left the castle all but redundant – not that this discouraged those who defended it during the 1526, 1553 and 1555 sieges. The ramparts were added by Cosimo I in 1571, together with the large Medici crest (a shield with six balls), whose present peripheral position – tucked away at the back above the road junction – is surely no accident.

Impressively intact, the walls enclose a public park and in-house **enoteca** – a reasonable place to sample some of the famed Brunello along with bread, cheese and salami (though at times it becomes hectic and uncomfortably clogged with tourists). The *enoteca* also sells tickets for access to the ramparts (L3500) and a glimpse of the famous banner. The castle view is said to have inspired Leonardo's drawing of a bird's-eye view of the earth; the Val d'Órcia is easily made out and on a clear day you can even see Siena.

Museo Civico

Heading north down Via Ricasoli brings you to the **Museo Civico** (April–Dec Tues–Sun 10am–6pm; Jan–March Tues–Sun 10am–1pm & 2–5pm; L8000), built with a grant of almost £500,000 from the EU and a more modest £100,000 from the *comune*. Here the old civic and diocesan collections are featured under one roof for the first time. Like many galleries in the region, the quality of the paintings on show is out of all proportion to the size of the town. Montalcino's begins with a superb *Crucifixion* dating from the end of the twelfth century – one of the **oldest pieces** of Sienese art in existence. An anonymous work, it was originally hung in the abbey at Sant'Antimo. It is followed by a more mannered *Madonna and Child with Two Angels*, a lovely anonymous late thirteenth-century work. Bartolo di Fredi has two works on show: an oddly narrow *Deposition* and a more conventional *Coronation of the Virgin*. There's also a *Madonna and Child* by Bartolo's collaborator, Luca di Tommè.

One of the gallery's most interesting works is the *Madonna dell'Umiltà* (Madonna of Humility) by Sano di Pietro, a comparatively rare subject, in which the Virgin is shown sitting or kneeling on a simple cushion rather than poised on a throne or chair. Its appearance dates from the beginning of the fourteenth century, and coincided with the ideas promulgated by the more radical wing of the Franciscan order, which advocated a return to the more rigorous and humble outlook of the first Franciscans. Two paintings by Girolamo di Benvenuto (1470–1524) also merit a close look: an *Adoration of the Shepherds* (with ugly shepherd and fractious Child) and the more spectacular and unusual *Madonna della Cintola*. The latter concerns the Apostle Thomas, who according to legend cast doubt on the Assumption into Heaven of the Virgin (hence "doubting Thomas"). To assuage his worries he opened her tomb, which he found covered in flowers – beautifully depicted in this painting. Casting his eyes upwards, he then saw the Virgin, who removed her belt, or girdle (*cintola*), and let it fall into the hands of the kneeling Thomas. The subject was particularly popular in Tuscany – Agnolo Gaddi, for example, devoted an entire fresco cycle to the theme in Prato, which claims to have the girdle in question (see p.181).

Among the gallery's **sculptures** and miscellaneous **artefacts**, make a special point of looking for the pair of illuminated twelfth-century Bibles and the rare polychrome wooden statue *St Peter*, one of the few documented works of the sculptor Francesco di Valdambrino: it was commissioned in 1425 and given by Pius III to the town's Confraternity of St Peter. You'll also notice an almost comical *Annunciation*, an early fifteenth-century Umbro-Sienese work, in which the puppet-like Gabriel and the Virgin sport impossibly rosy cheeks and beautifully mannered hairstyles.

Churches

Walking a few paces up Via Ricasoli from the museum brings you to the church of **Sant'Agostino**, a severe Gothic-Romanesque affair begun in 1360 whose barn-like single nave is dotted with patches of fresco. The most extensive of these – and with a wide variety of themes – cover the arched presbytery, and are probably the work of Bartolo di Fredi. The most interesting pictures, however, are two anonymous panels of *Scenes from the Passion*. One, on the left wall, also shows St Anthony Abbot sharing bread with a curiously attired St Augustine; the second, to the right of the side entrance, is an extraordinary and almost surreal collection of disembodied heads and symbols. Note the moon and sun, which in paintings of the Passion or Crucifixion serve, among other things, to symbolize the anguish of all creation at the death of Christ.

To the north, Via Spagni takes you past the **Duomo**, or San Salvatore, an eleventh-century Romanesque church, horrendously remodelled in Neoclassical style between 1818 and 1832 by an architect aptly called Fantastici; its interior is unarresting, however, save for an impressive little pyramid of reliefs in the baptistery chapel salvaged from the original church. Via Spagni continues to emerge in front of the distinctive Renaissance **Santuario della Madonna del Soccorso**, a seventeenth-century sanctuary built over an ancient chapel; its chief appeal is the sensational view from the adjoining park. Drop down Viale Roma to Piazza Cavour and pop into **Santa Maria della Croce**, a hospital founded in the thirteenth century, more recently appropriated by the local council. Just inside the main entrance is the former pharmacy, still covered in a pretty little array of original frescoes. Nearby, facing the Porta Castellana, is a medieval washhouse, the **Fonte Castellane**, and beyond it the deconsecrated church of **San Francesco**, graced with pleasant cloisters, della Robbia school terracottas and an annexe that was once a medieval hospital.

Wine, food, festivals and transport

Sampling **Montalcino's wines** is easily done. Apart from the *enoteca* in the Rocca and the *Fiaschetteria Italiana* – which has a superb *cantina* at the back – there are half a dozen cheaper café-bars with good stocks. The *Caffè Cacciatore*, opposite the *Fiaschetteria*, is plain but doesn't impose too much surcharge on sitting outside under the loggia. Farther along Via Matteotti, there's the friendly *Bar Mariuccia*, the locals' bar – where the football is watched – with a breathtaking view from the vast windowed terrace at the back (and the town's only pay-after-the-call phone). For bottles to take away, try the *Enoteca Ars Bibendi* on Piazza del Popolo, which has a knowledgeable, English-speaking owner. In addition to the classic Brunello and the more briefly barrel-aged Rosso di Montalcino table wine, it's worth trying some of the white Moscadelletto di Montalcino, a dessert wine produced in small quantity and at its best chilled.

Eating

Montalcino is remarkably blessed with good **restaurants**, and you'll be hard-pushed to have a bad meal in any of them. The following places are listed in roughly ascending order of price. In summer it's worth booking a table at just about all of them.

Pizzeria San Giorgio, Via S. Saloni (☎0577.848.507). Far and away the best of the town's clutch of *pizzerie*. Crispy pizzas and full meals from as little as L20,000. Closed Mon.

Il Moro, Via Mazzini 44 (☎0577.849.384). A consistently reliable and no-nonsense modern trattoria with the best budget meals in town. L30,000–35,000. Closed Thurs.

Taverna Grappolo Blu, Via Scale di Moglio 1 (☎0577.847.150). Located in a little alley off Via Mazzini. The old stone-walled interior is cool and appealing, and the unusual pastas are excellent. A shame about the piped classical music. L25,000–35,000. Closed Fri.

Trattoria Sciame, Via Ricasoli (☎0577.848.017). This informal and vaguely trendy little bar-trattoria just down from the Rocca has its devotees, but it's not the restaurant you'd choose first in Montalcino. L35,000. Closed Tues.

Il Giardino d'Alberto, Piazza Cavour 1 (☎0577.849.076). Pleasant interior, with good local cooking: the chef is the owner. L30,000–35,000. Closed Wed.

La Cucina di Edgardo, Via S. Saloni 21 (☎0577.848.232). Montalcino's swankiest restaurant. While the food is usually excellent, its sometimes pretentious *cucina nuova* leanings may not be to all tastes. L35,000–45,000. Closed Wed.

Il Poggio Antico, I Poggi, 2km from town on the Grosseto road (☎0577.849.200). This restaurant has a *Michelin* star, so the prices, service – exaggerated and zealous – and food are predictably elevated. The reverential air and the grand approach, however, seems to put people off, for the place often appears almost empty. L70,000 plus. Closed Mon.

Festivals

Festa della Madonna del Soccorso (May 8). A small palio – featuring the same horses that will appear later in the year at Siena – is held on the sports field below the fort.

Montalcino Teatro (third and fourth weeks of July). An international theatre festival, presenting works in progress in the churches, Rocca, eighteenth-century *Teatro degli Astrusi*, and sometimes in the *crete* around the town.

Torneo della Apertura della Caccia (second Sun in Aug). Tournament marking the start of the hunting season that is said to have fourteenth-century origins – inspiring some of the tales in the *Decameron*. Half the town dresses up in medieval costume for parades and archery competitions (on the sports field) between the *contrade*. Street banquets complete the day.

Festa dell'Unità (mid-Aug). Ten-day festival organized by the former communist party in the pine wood above the town. Live music most nights, cheap food and wine – and usually a lot of fun.

Sagra del Tordo (last Sun in Oct). Similar events to the *Caccia* festival, but if anything even more widely touted.

Market Montalcino's weekly market is held on Fridays (7am–1pm) in Viale della Libertà.

MONTALCINO'S DISCO: CAMIGLIANO

One of the stranger features of life in northern Italy is the distance people are prepared to drive to a party, restaurant or disco. Montalcino is no exception, offering zilch in the way of nightlife of its own. On Saturday nights in summer, locals drive 14km southwest to an **open-air disco** at the village of Camigliano. It's quite an occasion, patronized by just about everyone from the surrounding farms and villages, as well as a fair selection of foreign residents – identifiable by their eccentric dancing. Recently the event has lost a little of its earthy old-world flavour, but it's still fun and offers plenty of local colour. Music ranges from the latest Europop to traditional Italian songs, and with an entrance fee of L10,000, it won't break the bank. The only problem is that you need to drive: there's no local accommodation or transport.

Transport

TRA-IN **buses** (☎0577.204.111) run more or less hourly from Piazza Cavour and Viale P. Strozzi to Buonconvento and Siena, most of them via Torrenieri, and five times daily (Mon–Sat) to Monte Amiata, passing Sant'Antimo (see opposite page). At Torrenieri you can also pick up one of six daily buses south to Arcidosso, or five east to San Quírico and Montepulciano. There's also a daily SIRA bus (☎0641.730.083) to and from Rome (it departs for Rome mid-afternoon from Piazza Cavour), useful as a direct way of getting to Pienza and Montepulciano, which it passes en route to the A1 motorway. Bus tickets are available from tobacconists around town, and from the *Bar Il Prato* on the corner of Viale Roma and Piazza Cavour.

For **rail connections** to Siena or Grosseto, head to Buonconvento, Torrenieri or to Sant'Angelo, 9km south of Montalcino and connected by three buses daily. Most services are slow, stopping numbers, but buried in the timetable are a couple of fast through trains daily to Florence (via Siena) and Grosseto (for connections to Rome and Pisa).

There's no official taxi in Montalcino, but if you miss a bus or need an early getaway it's sometimes possible to **hire a car** with driver through Maurizio Tornesi at the *Bar Il Prato* in Piazza Cavour (☎0577.848.121).

Vineyards and villages around Montalcino

As Brunello is Italy's premier wine, it seems a shame not to get out to at least one of the **vineyards**. As well as those detailed below, you can visit most others if you ask at the winegrowers' headquarters in Montalcino's Palazzo Comunale; the only period when visitors might not be welcome is at harvest time (Sept–Oct).

Fattoria dei Barbi

The **Fattoria dei Barbi** (☎0577.849.421) is 7km southeast of Montalcino, signposted off to the left just after the hamlet of La Croce on the Sant'Antimo road. Its *cantina* (Mon–Sat 9.30am–noon & 2–5.30pm, Sun 3–6pm) offers tasting facilities and a superb stock of vintages. Attached is a very fine **restaurant**, the *Taverna dei Barbi* (☎0577.849.357; closed Wed), run by an Englishwoman but serving up strictly local recipes – lots of *porcini, pici, papardelle* and delicious grilled pork, the *brasato al Brunello*, washed down, of course, with the Barbi's own wine. Figure on around L50,000 for an extensive meal.

Villa Banfi, Castello di Poggio alle Mura and Sant'Angelo in Colle

With a third of its three thousand hectares devoted to vineyards, the **Villa Banfi** is Montalcino's largest and most modern wine producer. It was taken over in the 1970s by an Italian-American wine-importing family, the Mariani, and has English-speaking guides available to show you round. The villa is located just outside the village of Sant'Angelo Scala, 18km southwest of Montalcino; it's served by occasional weekday buses from Montalcino and is on the Siena–Asciano–Grosseto rail line. By the station are a couple of **restaurants**: *Trattoria Casini*, which serves basic food at basic prices, and *Il Marrucheto*, which is fancy and expensive.

Five kilometres to the west of the station, inside the Banfi estate, is the **Castello di Poggio alle Mura**, a thirteenth-century castle built for the Salimbeni clan of Siena, though subsequently added to in a mishmash of styles. Recently renovated, it has a small **Museo del Vetro** (daily: summer 10am–7pm; winter 10am–6pm; L3000) with Roman and Etruscan artefacts, and a display of traditional implements for wine-making. There is a new hotel-*Agriturismo* establishment here, *La Pieve* (☎0577.816.026; ③). If the main gate is closed, ask at the *enoteca* alongside, or at the nearby post office.

At the halfway point on the road from Montalcino to Villa Banfi is the tiny walled village of **SANT'ANGELO IN COLLE**, set on a low hill (it can also be reached on a beautiful but partly gravel-surfaced road from Sant'Antimo). The Sienese used it as a military base against Montalcino in the mid-thirteenth century and as part of their frontier thereafter. It has some interesting frescoes inside the Romanesque church, **San Michele**, on the piazza (check out the lovely views from behind the church) and a couple of **bar-restaurants**. The one on the piazza, *Il Pozzo* (☎0577.864.015; closed Tues), is recommended for its roasts – about L30,000 for two courses without wine: the food is good, but the attitude of the owners can be a little dismissive. If you can't get a table here you could do a lot worse than have a snack and a glass of wine at the friendly little *enoteca* in the small main square.

Sant'Antimo

It's a moot point which of Tuscany's many abbeys is the most beautiful, has the most fascinating history, or boasts the loveliest setting, but many would put the **Abbazia di Sant'Antimo** (Mon–Sat 10.30am–12.30pm & 3–6.30pm, Sun 9.15–10.45am & 3–6pm; free) near the top of their list. It's a glorious, isolated Benedictine monastery which stands comparison with the nearby foundations of San Galgano, Monte Oliveto and San Salvatore. Located a short distance from the hamlet of Castelnuovo dell'Abate, 10km south of Montalcino, and splendidly isolated in a timeless landscape of fields, olive groves and wooded hills, the abbey stood empty for some five hundred years, and is today maintained by a small group of French monks – a Cistercian offshoot known as the Premonstratensians, who celebrate Mass several times daily in haunting Gregorian chant.

Mythology and history of the abbey

Tradition ascribes the foundation of the abbey to **Charlemagne**, who, while returning with his army from Rome in 781, halted in the nearby Starcia valley. Here he prayed to God, asking for relief from the disease which was crippling his army, and offering to found a church if his prayers were answered. An angel appeared, showing the emperor a herb (called *Carolina* in Italian) which he was instructed to dry and give to his men as a powder with wine. The cure worked as promised, and Charlemagne duly founded Sant'Antimo.

If this story sounds too good to be true, it is known that the abbey existed in 814, when Charlemagne's son, **Louis the Pious**, enriched it with vast tracts of land and privileges in a charter dated December 29 of that year. Other scholars suggest it may have been founded on the site of a Roman villa, or possibly by the last of the area's Lombards in about 760, the date of the foundation of the Abbadia di San Salvatore (see p.395). In fact St Antimo (feast day May 11) was probably a bishop martyred in Rome during the persecutions of Diocletian and Maximian (304–5 AD). Certainly it's known that in 781, the year of the abbey's supposed foundation, St Antimo's relics, along with those of St Sebastian, were given to Charlemagne by Pope Hadrian I.

Whatever the truth of Sant'Antimo's origins, the decidedly **pre-Romanesque** style of the primitive church (see next page), together with documentary evidence, confirms a late eighth- or early ninth-century foundation. Over the two centuries that followed, the abbey's importance grew, thanks in part to its location close to the intersection of several of central Italy's most important medieval **trade and pilgrimage routes**. Oldest of these was a former Etruscan road linking Chiusi with Rusellae on the coast, a route which passed directly in front of the abbey (traces of the sunken lane can still be seen). This was crossed by the old Roman consular road, Via Clodia, again right in front of the abbey. The most important of the ancient roads, however, was the

Via Francigena, which for centuries was the most important pilgrimage route between Rome and northern Europe. Countless towns and villages grew up along the route, together with numerous hospices for pilgrims: Siena – whose Santa Maria della Scala was one of the most important of these (see p.312) – and San Gimignano are just two local towns which owe their early medieval prosperity to the Via Francigena.

Sant'Antimo's heyday dates from 1118, when an enormous **bequest** allowed work to begin on the main body of the present church and a complex of monastic buildings (now largely lost). The grant's original deed – a document many hundreds of words long – was engraved in the steps of the altar, where it survives to this day. With new-found funds, the abbey authorities now had access to expertise and ideas from elsewhere in Europe, and looked for inspiration to the great Benedictine mother house at Cluny, in Burgundy, and to **French architects**, whose plans for the new church appear to have been based on the abbey church of Vignory (begun in 1050) in the Haute-Marne.

Over the years funds began to run low – hence the unfinished facade – as religious bequests increasingly found their way to new orders such as the Camaldolese and Cistercians. Worse, the rising power of Siena began to strip away the abbey's privileges and lands; in 1212, following Siena's sacking of Montalcino (then under the abbey's ownership), Sant'Antimo's abbot was forced to cede a quarter of the territory of Montalcino to the Sienese Republic. By 1293 it retained only a fifth of its original possessions, which had once made it the second richest abbey in Tuscany. **Financial problems** were soon followed by moral and spiritual decline. In 1439 Pope Eugenius IV had the abbot imprisoned for "villainy"; then in 1462, Pius II **suppressed the abbey** for good, convinced that it was beyond spiritual or financial salvation.

The abbey soldiered on for a few years under the auspices of the bishops of Siena and the newly created diocese of Montalcino, but after 1492 – when Montalcino's bishops opted to live instead in the town – it was largely **abandoned**, its buildings ransacked for stone for use in Castelnuovo and Montalcino. What remained was bought by the state in 1867.

The church

The monks' quarters aside, little remains of the plundered monastic buildings – a ruined refectory and chapterhouse are now used as barns, and accommodation for recently arrived monks. But the twelfth-century **church** itself is in excellent repair and is one of the most outstanding examples of Italian Romanesque, built in a soft, creamy stone and perfectly proportioned.

EXTERIOR

The **facade** was the last part of the church to be built, and so suffered most from the shortfall of funds. The traces of arches in the stones, and the pilasters with attached columns, suggest that a portico once provided a grander entrance: the lions which supported the portico, and symbolized the power of Satan waiting to devour the faithful, are now inside the abbey. Recent studies suggest the portal on the church of Santa Maria in nearby San Quírico d'Órcia (see p.378) was one of two portals intended for the abbey, and was perhaps given away in the light of the abbey's subsequent decline. The surviving **portal** contains a twelfth-century lintel whose Latin text alludes to one Azzo, a monk who may have been one of the original architects of the church. Otherwise the capitals, frieze and recessed, fluted arch are all lifted directly from French (Languedoc) models. Around the corner, on the left (north) wall, the little filled-in doorway and lintels survive from the earlier ninth-century church.

INTERIOR

The French flavour becomes more marked in the lovely **interior**, whose basilican plan – with an ambulatory, and radiating chapels – is unique in Tuscany, and found elsewhere in Italy in only a handful of churches. Its presence here allowed pilgrims to walk around the apse and pray before the martyrium, the spot under the high altar which contained the relics of the saint being venerated. The **high altar** features a polychrome statue of the crucified Christ, an outstanding Romanesque work dating from the end of the twelfth century. Note the inscription on the altar steps (see opposite page).

The **capitals** on the pillars of the ambulatory display some exquisite carving, a feature for which the abbey is particularly celebrated. Many are carved in lustrous alabaster, a stone which features elsewhere in the building, lending a beautifully subtle tone to the walls and sculpture. Here the carving is more Lombard than French, leading to the theory that two separate workshops – one from France (the Auvergne) and one from Lombardy (Pavia) may have worked alongside one another. Equally plausible is the idea that many of the capitals derive from the earlier Carolingian church, built before the French-inspired church of 1118.

The abbey's finest capital sits atop the second column on the right of the nave. It depicts *Daniel in the Lions' Den*, the protagonist – arms raised in prayer – a study of calm while his fellow prisoners are crushed and eaten by rampant beasts. Clearly superior to anything else in the abbey, it is the work of the so-called **Master of Cabestany**, a sculptor of French or Spanish origin whose distinctive hand has been identified in abbeys across France, Catalonia and Italy – he seems always to have worked for the Benedictines. By way of comparison, wander across to study the capital on the second column on the left, which depicts a shepherd and sheep in a far more mundane style.

Increasingly, the rest of the church is often closed to visitors. Areas affected include the **sacristy**, which occupies part of the ninth-century Carolingian church, entered (when open), from a door in the right aisle. It features an array of primitive black-and-white frescoes with such details as a rat looking up attentively at St Benedict, and a pair of copulating pigs. Note the stoup with Pius's Piccolomini crest at each corner. Further frescoes are to be found in some of the rooms built around the **women's gallery**, fitted out in the fifteenth century by the bishops of Montalcino: it's approached from the nave by a circular stairway, though here, too, access is often restricted.

Practicalities

There are occasional **buses** along the Sant'Antimo road, leaving Montalcino from Monday to Friday at 6am and 1.40pm (returning at 7.50am and 3.35pm), Saturday at 4.35pm, (returning at 4.50pm). Alternatively, it's a pleasant country walk or feasible hitch. Additional rewards are at the *Bar-Trattoria Bassomondo* (closed Mon) across the road, which does wonderful *crostini*, *ribollita* and *pici*. Around L25,000 a head.

The Val d'Órcia and Bagno Vignoni

The **Val d'Órcia** stretches from San Quírico d'Órcia down towards the border with Lazio and the lake of Bolsena. A gorgeous stretch of country, it is marked at intervals by fortresses built from the eighth century on, when the road through the valley, the **Via Francigena**, was a vital corridor north from Rome (see p.313).

The major attraction along the initial section of the valley is the remarkable Medicean sulphur baths of **Bagno Vignoni**. With transport – or enthusiasm for walking – you might strike off south from here to the region's medieval power base, the monastery of San Salvatore (see p.395). **Walkers** might also consider approaching Bagno Vignoni across country from Montalcino (a five-hour hike which would entail staying in Bagno Vignoni), or going on from Bagno Vignoni along the old gravel road to Pienza; note that some local tourist offices will provide photocopies of detailed walking maps.

San Quírico d'Órcia

A rambling, part-walled village, **SAN QUÍRICO D'ÓRCIA** stands at a crossroads on the Siena to Bolsena road overlooking the Órcia and Asso valleys. It's quiet and rather decayed – an odd mix of modern and medieval – overlooked by the precarious ruins of a seventeenth-century palazzo, whose Baroque exterior frescoes are fading before your eyes. Its name comes from San Quírico a Osenna, an ancient church on the Via Francigena, though of the eponymous saint little is known except that he was martyred, probably in the fourth century. Hospitals and hospices sprang up here to accommodate pilgrims in the early Middle Ages, as they did in Siena and other settlements along the Via Francigena.

The main – and highly worthwhile – reason for stopping in the town is to look around the exceptionally pretty Romanesque **Collegiata**, with its three portals sculpted with lions and other beasts; the south door may be the work of Giovanni Pisano (or his school), while the main portal is rightly considered the finest piece of Lombard work in the region. The church was built in the twelfth century, probably on the ruins of a still older church. Inside is a delicate triptych of the *Virgin and Saints* by Sano di Pietro in the north transept, as well as a marvellous set of nine Renaissance choir stalls, whose figures and trompe l'oeil may have been executed to designs by Luca Signorelli. The stalls originally formed part of a larger nineteen-stall set in the Cappella del Battistero in Siena cathedral.

There's a **tourist office** at Via Dante Alighieri 33 (April–Oct & mid-Dec to Jan daily 10am–1pm & 3.30–7pm; ☎0577.897.211), or try the Pro-Loco at Piazza della Libertà 2 or Comune at Via Dante Alighieri 65 (☎0577.898.247) when the main office is shut.

San Quírico is a regular stop on the Siena–Buonconvento–Pienza–Montepulciano TRA-IN **bus** route, as well as a stop on the once-daily SIRA Montalcino–Rome service. It has a small two-star **hotel**, *Il Garibaldi* (☎0577.898.315; ②) on the Via Cassia, the main road.

If you want an isolated and peaceful place to stay, Ripa d'Órcia, about five kilometres southwest of San Quírico at the end of a minor but perfectly passable gravelled road, has an absolutely stunning hotel-restaurant, *Castello Ripa d'Órcia* (☎0577.897.376, fax 0577.898.038, *info@castelloripadorcia.com*; ⑤), located in an isolated and ancient castle which is visible for miles around. Views from the castle are sensational, and there are lovely strolls and marked trails down to the Órcia valley and Sant'Antimo from right outside the walls.

Bagno Vignoni

Six kilometres south of San Quírico, **BAGNO VIGNONI** is scarcely even a hamlet – just a handful of buildings around a central square. The square, however, is one of Tuscany's most memorable sights, occupied by an arcaded Renaissance *piscina*. This was built by the Medici, who, like St Catherine of Siena, took the sulphur cure here. The hot springs still bubble away in the bath (they formed an amazing set in Tarkovsky's film *Nostalgia*), though they are currently out of bounds for bathing; plans to restore the *piscina* and develop the spa as a resort have so far been thwarted – thankfully – by the Siena council.

You can, however, bathe in the sulphur pools at the foot of the hillside below the village, or use the sulphur pool at the four-star *Posta Marcucci* **hotel**, a fifteenth-century summer house erected by Pius II on the side of the piazza. The *Posta Marcucci* (☎0577.887.112, fax 0577.887.119, *info@hotelpostamarcucci.it*; ⑥) allows non-residents use of the pool for L18,000 a day. The village's other hotel, the three-star *Le Terme* (☎0577.887.150, fax 0577.887.497; ④), which overlooks the *piscina*, has a marginally better restaurant. The best place to **eat**, however, is the *Antica Osteria del Leone*, Via dei Mulini 3 (☎0577.887.300; closed Mon). Food here is Tuscan with twist – try the rabbit (*coniglio*) with pine nuts. You can **rent bikes** from Club Mountain Bike in Piazza del Moretto.

Rocca, Castiglione and Vivo d'Órcia

The **Rocca d'Órcia** (summer 9.30am–1pm & 3–7pm; winter 10am–12.30pm & 3–6pm; L3000), three kilometres south of Bagno Vignoni, is visible almost the whole way from San Quírico: from the eleventh to the fourteenth century this dramatic pile of a castle belonged, like almost every castle along this stretch of the Via Francigena, to the **Aldobrandeschi** family. Although Santa Fiora (see p.399) was the clan base, this was their most important fortress, a strategic site allowing them to rob or extract tolls from any traffic along the route. After a change of ownership to the Salimbeni family, who built most of the present structure, the castle was only properly incorporated into the Sienese Republic in 1418.

CASTIGLIONE D'ÓRCIA, the village below the *rocca*, is a fine-looking place, built almost entirely of stone, with an elaborately cobbled piazza and a trio of medieval churches. In the Romanesque church of **SS. Stefano e Degna** are panels (temporarily removed to Montalcino – due to return in 2000) by Pietro Lorenzetti, Vecchietta and one attributed to Simone Martini – a hint of the wealth Castiglione must once have enjoyed. Vecchietta, incidentally, was born in the village in 1412.

Moving south towards Monte Amiata, the hamlet of **VIVO D'ÓRCIA** is another medieval treat, with beautiful walks along the river and in the woods, where you come upon the Romanesque **Cappella dell'Ermicciolo**, part of a twelfth-century Camaldolese monastery, the Eremo del Vivo, altered in 1536, reputedly by Antonio da Sangallo the Younger. There are **hotels** in both villages, all of which double as **restaurants**: *Le Rocche*, Via Senese 10 (☎0577.887.031; ②; restaurant closed Wed), in Castiglione; the *Amiata*, Via Amiata 212 (☎0577.873.790; ③; restaurant closed Fri) and *La Flora*, Via IV Novembre 18 (☎0577.873.724; ②; restaurant closed Wed), both in Vivo. For *agriturismo* accommodation try *I Lecci*, Loc. Lecci, Castiglione (☎0577.887.287; ②), which offers rooms, meals and pony-trekking.

Bagni San Filippo and Radicófani

East of Vivo d'Orcia, just a few hundred metres off the N2, is the tiny spa of **BAGNI SAN FILIPPO**. Like Vignoni, this has an outdoor hot sulphur spring cascading from the rocks, as well as an unostentatious modern spa building and pool. There is also a tiny chapel, **La Grotta del Santo**, commemorating the village saint, who took refuge here after being offered the papacy. Otherwise, San Filippo consists of just a handful of houses, a bar and a three-star **hotel-restaurant**, *Le Terme* (☎0577.872.982, fax 0577.872.684; ⑤; restaurant closed Thurs).

On the other side of the N2 from San Filippo, a road veers east into the hills to the majestically situated **Rocca** of **RADICÓFANI** (783m), which vies with the Rocca d'Órcia for the title of most imposing fortress in southern Tuscany. Clamped to a basalt outcrop, it commands the strategic heights between the Paglia and Órcia valleys. The castle is identified with one Ghino di Tacco, a fourteenth-century bandit who features in the writings of both Dante and Boccaccio (the *Decameron* tells of Tacco's imprisoning the abbot of Cluny in this fortress, then curing him of indigestion.) Views from the walls are stunning. Below the castle, which was devastated by an explosion in the eighteenth century, is a handsome little village, with an old Capuchin convent, a cluster of churches and the sadly dilapidated **Palazzo La Posta** – the "Great Duke's Inn", where centuries of grand tourists – including Montaigne and Charles Dickens – put up on their way to Rome. The best of the churches, the Romanesque **San Pietro**, features several good glazed terra-cotta works from the school of Andrea della Robbia, together with a polychrome wooden *Madonna* (second pillar on the left) by Francesco di Valdambrino. A rare sculptor, Valdambrino (1375–1435) often collaborated with the great Sienese sculptor Jacopo della Quercia, having worked with him on the panels for the Fonte Gaia, now displayed in Siena's Palazzo Pubblico. He is best known for his *St Peter* in Montalcino (see p.372).

The village remains a handy place to stay, with two modest **hotels** – the *Eni*, Via dell'Orcia 16, Loc. Contignano (☎0578.52.025; ②) and *La Torre*, Via Matteotti 7 (☎0578.55.943; ②).

Pienza

PIENZA is as complete a Renaissance creation as any in Italy, conceived as a Utopian "New Town" by **Pope Pius II**, Aeneas Sylvius Piccolomini (see p.311). The site Pius chose was the village of Corsignano where he was born in 1405, the first of eighteen children of a noble family exiled from Siena in 1385 (the village, at least in part, formed part of the Piccolominis' traditional feudal domain). Archeological evidence suggests it was inhabited as early as the Bronze Age. In Roman times it was a hill-top fort of some renown, and by the thirteenth century it had a reputation as an anarchic border town: Boccaccio spoke of "Corsignan de' Ladri" ("Corsignano of the thieves") in his novel *Cecco di Fotarrigo*. Today there's little to see beyond Pius's central Renaissance piazza – the pope's death marked the end of his beloved project – though few places in Tuscany have as much immediate charm. There are also some extraordinary **views** from the walls, a scattering of good **bars and restaurants**, and a range of **accommodation** – from rooms to a *Relais* hotel – if you want to stay.

A brief history – Pius and Rossellino

The **construction of Pienza** began in 1459, less than a year after Pius's election to the papacy in August 1458. History rather harshly suggests the new pope wished to avenge himself on Siena – which had unjustly exiled his family – by building a city that would be both Siena's antithesis and its superior. It's also claimed Pius could not live with the shame of having come from a village as humble as Corsignano. His architect on the project was **Bernardo Rossellino**, who worked on all the major buildings here under the guidance of Leon Battista Alberti, the great theorist of Renaissance art, building and town planning.

Rossellino's commission was to build a cathedral, papal palace and town hall, but Pius instructed the various cardinals who followed his court to build their own residences too, turning the project into nothing less than a Vatican in miniature (see

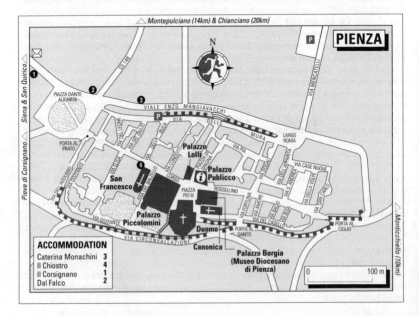

"Palazzo Vescovile" p.383). Astonishingly, the cathedral, the papal and bishop's palaces, and the core of the town were completed in just three years. Limited though it was, it constituted the first "Ideal City" of the Renaissance to become a reality.

After consecration of the cathedral, Pius issued a papal bull rechristening the "city" Pienza, in his own honour, and stipulating that no detail of the cathedral or palaces should be changed. The wish was fulfilled rather more easily than he could have expected, for he died within two years, and of his successors only Pius III, his nephew, paid Pienza any regard. The city, intended to spread across the hill, never grew beyond a couple of blocks to either side of the main Corso, and its population remained scarcely that of a village. Today, with a population of 2500, it still has an air of emptiness and folly: a natural stage set, which was used by Zeffirelli for his film of *Romeo and Juliet*.

The Town

There is no difficulty finding your way about Pienza. Roads, buses and cars converge on the **Piazza Dante**, just outside the Porta al Murello, main entrance gate to the papal town. From here the **Corso** leads to Rossellino's centrepiece, **Piazza Pio II**, enclosed by the duomo, Palazzo Piccolomini, Bishop's Palace, Palazzo Pubblico and a palace built by one of Pius's more ambitious Vatican followers – Cardinal Borgia, the future Pope Alexander VI.

Piazza Pio II

The juxtaposition of civic and religious buildings in the **Piazza Pio II** was deliberate, and aimed to underline the balance between Church and town through architectural harmony. If it all seems a little cramped, it's partly because Rossellino wished to retain the existing east–west axis of Corsignano's main street. It's also because Pius's insistence that his palace loggia should command a view, and that the duomo should be flooded with light, meant that the piazza's two key buildings had to be orientated towards the valley to the rear. For the duomo, in particular, this was to have near-disastrous consequences (see below). Apart from the town hall, based on the medieval Palazzo Vecchio in Florence, the ensemble is entirely Renaissance in conception. The piazza's small well, the **Pozzo dei Cani**, sets the tone, its twin columns and classical frieze a perfect miniature of Renaissance ambitions.

THE DUOMO

The **Duomo**, or Santa Maria Assunta (closed 1–2.30pm), has one of the earliest Renaissance **facades** in Tuscany, its three-tiered veneer of Istrian marble surmounted by a vast garland of fruit enclosing Pius's papal coat of arms. The **campanile**, rocked to its foundations by an earthquake in 1545, was virtually rebuilt in 1570.

On Pius's orders, the **interior** took inspiration from Franciscan Gothic churches and the German *Hallenkirchen*, or hall-churches, which he had seen on his pre-papal travels as a member of the Curia. The hall-churches, as here, were distinguished by naves and aisles of equal height. The tall **windows** were also a papal whim, designed to produce a *domus vitrea* (hall of glass), whose flood of light was intended to symbolize the age's humanist enlightenment. Pius's *Commentaries* also talk of the strangely elongated **capitals** of the nave's columns as *felici errori*, or "happy errors". Legend claims the pope found the church's earlier columns too short and insisted that Rossellino find some way of lengthening them. In fact the capitals were deliberately introduced by Rossellino, partly to accentuate the nave's soaring Gothic effect, and partly to evoke parallels with similar capitals in Siena's Loggia di Mercanzia, and the duomo, Loggia dei Lanzi, and church of San Lorenzo in Florence.

To satisfy Pius's whims, and to fit the cramped site, Rossellino had to build on sandstone with a substratum of clay. Before completion a crack appeared, and following an earthquake last century it has required progressively more buttressing and ties. The nave dips crazily towards the back of the church – still shifting at an estimated rate of 1mm per year – and alarming cracks are still all too obvious, tagged by small glass ties designed to reveal further movement. At last report, however, authorities say there is no imminent danger of collapse and no need for further buttressing.

Several outstanding and contrasting **altarpieces** – the church's highlights – still fill the principal chapels, each commissioned by the pope and his architect from some of the major painters of the age. Pius's choice of artists was deliberate: each was Sienese, as was he (at least by family origin) – Rossellino, it's worth noting, was from Settignano, just outside Florence. This partisan choice, however, rather undermined Pius's Renaissance credentials, for Florentine painters by this time were far ahead of their more backward-looking Sienese counterparts. Pius's choice of each subject – the Madonna, to whom the church was dedicated – was equally considered, as was the choice of saints included in each painting. Thus St Sabina in Giovanni di Paolo's work was featured because Pius was titular head of the Basilica di Santa Sabina in Rome; St Peter appeared because he was the first pope; and saints Catherine and Bernardino achieved prominence through their Sienese connections.

The first painting, midway down the right (south) wall, is Giovanni di Paolo's *Madonna and Child with SS. Bernardino, Anthony Abbot, Francis and Sabina* with a *Pietà* above – note the Piccolomini arms at the bottom left and right of the frame. The first apse chapel features Matteo di Giovanni's *Madonna and Child with SS. Catherine of Alexandria, Matthew, Bartholomew and Lucy* with the *Flagellation* above: here, too, there's a nod to Pius in the shape of more coats of arms. The next apse contains a travertine tabernacle attributed to Rossellino, behind whose little central door is a **reliquary** containing bones alleged to be from the head of St Andrew, Pienza's patron saint. Another work by Rossellino, a vast **font**, can be seen in the crypt, along with Romanesque fragments recovered from Santa Maria, the former church near the site. The central apse – normally containing the high altar – is empty, Pius having stipulated that nothing should block the light coming from the central windows. Instead he commissioned the choir (1462), the tell-tale papal shield again appearing at the top of the central bishop's throne.

The **fourth chapel** houses a triptych of the *Assumption with SS. Agatha, Callistus, Pius I and Catherine of Siena* by **Vecchietta**, born in nearby Castiglione dell'Orcia: it's considered one of his masterpieces and is by far the finest of the church's altarpieces. The fifth chapel features Sano di Pietro's *Madonna and Child with SS. Philip, James, Anne and Mary Magdalene.*

Pius, realizing his Sienese painters lagged behind Florentine thinking, made specific requests in an attempt to bring a little Renaissance flavour to what were essentially Gothic works. Thus Sano was asked to replace the niches traditionally used in the predella (panels in the lower part of altarpieces) with a more classical frame of small pillars. The "V" arrangement of the saints around the Virgin was also new – at least in the works of Sano. Vecchietta similarly staked a claim for modernity by enclosing his *Assumption* triptych – very much a Gothic conceit – in a fixed frame that effectively made the painting a single, rather than hinged, tripartite work. Similar efforts towards a more Renaissance effect are found in the last painting, Matteo di Giovanni's *Madonna and Child with SS. Nicholas, Martin, Augustine and Jerome*, midway down the north wall. The saints here, for example, are set on different levels – compare the same artist's painting across the nave (where they are on one level) – while the Virgin's upper throne is decorated with heads whose classical inspiration is unmistakable.

PALAZZO PICCOLOMINI

Pius's residence, the **Palazzo Piccolomini**, to the right of the duomo, was modelled on Alberti's Palazzo Rucellai in Florence, and built by Rossellino over the demolished remains of the Piccolomini's former feudal holding in the village. All three main facades are identical, novelty being provided by the imaginative addition of a triple-tiered loggia at the back, making it the first Italian building to be designed specifically to afford views over a swathe of countryside. Its cost was astronomical, Rossellino spending five times his allotted budget (50,000 as opposed to 10,000 gold florins) – a charge that he was liable to repay. Pius, however, accepted the expense, delighted at the building and its views:

> *From the three porticoes which face the sun at midday the view extends to Amiata, that towering and densely wooded mountain. Thence the eye travels down into Val d'Orcia, passing over green pasturelands and hills clothed with long grass or rich corn in season, and many vineyards, and so up again to castles and villages set on precipitous rocks, and to the right as far as a place called Bagno di Vignoni, and leftwards to Monte Cetona, which is higher than Radicófani and is the portal of the winter sun.*

For this vista, you can walk into the superb courtyard at any time of day and through (on the left) to the original "hanging garden" behind; it has remained unchanged over the centuries and is the perfect embodiment of the Renaissance concept that gardens form an intermediary between nature and architecture. The triple-tiered loggia, with its three orders of Classical columns (Ionic, Doric and Corinthian), owes a clear debt to the great imperial buildings of ancient Rome.

For a glimpse of the splendour envisaged for Pius, however, you need to climb the steps in the courtyard to the first-floor **papal apartments** (Tues–Sun 10am–12.30pm & 3–6pm; L5000), occupied until 1962 by the Piccolomini family. **Guided tours** conduct you to Pius II's dining room, library and music room, each filled with furniture, books, carpets and manuscripts. The highlights, though, are the papal bedroom – complete with a gloriously vulgar canopied bed – and the cavernous **Sala d'Armi**, filled with rows of fearsome pikes and other weapons.

PALAZZO VESCOVILE

The **Palazzo Vescovile**, or Palazzo Borgia, to the left of the duomo, began as a single-storey Gothic palace, but was given to Roderigo Borgia by Pius on condition that he demolish it and rebuild in a more modern manner. Borgia, then a cardinal, would later become the infamous Pope Alexander VI and father four children, among them the notorious Lucrezia and Cesare Borgia. Showing the astuteness, if not the meanness, that would characterize his papacy, Borgia refrained from knocking down the palace, but saved money by altering a few superficial details and adding an extra storey. Thus on the ground floor – clearly of different vintage – you can still see the outlines of the old Gothic windows, bricked in to form tiny square windows more in keeping with Renaissance ideas. Still more visible are the holes which pockmark the upper part of the building, the legacy of a **mortar bombardment** during World War II that also knocked chunks out of the cathedral's apse. The highest marks have an even earlier vintage, having been inflicted by the artillery of Charles V and the Medici during their assault on the Sienese Republic between 1552 and 1559. How much time Borgia spent in the palace is uncertain – though the Borgia arms are clearly visible on the shield on the corner of the building. In any event, it appears he made a gift of the building in 1468, when it became the Palazzo Vescovile, or Bishop's Palace.

MUSEO DIOCESANO

Like many small southern Tuscan museums, the **Museo Diocesano**, Corso il Rossellino, 30 (10am–1pm & 2–6pm; closed Tues; L8000), deserves more attention than it receives. Its star attraction is a superb thirteenth- or fourteenth-century *piviale*, or **cope**, an English work (signed *Opus Anglicanum*) of fantastically embroidered silk embellished with scenes from the life of the Virgin and St Catherine of Alexandria, together with various saints and apostles (originally the cope would also have been studded with pearls and precious stones). Tradition claims it was given to Pius by Thomas Paleologus, prince of the Peloponnese and brother of the Byzantine emperor. However, it's more likely to derive from a papal wardrobe dating from the papacy's sojourn in Avignon, where it appears in an inventory dated 1369.

The museum also contains superb tapestries, crosiers, miniatures, illuminated manuscripts, choir books with miniatures by Sano di Pietro and others – produced for Orvieto cathedral but bought by Pius – and a whole slew of topnotch **paintings**. Look out in particular for the *Madonna dell'Umiltà and SS. Elizabeth of Hungary and John the Baptist*, an anonymous work (by the "Maestro dell'Osservanza"), so-called because its Madonna is shown seated on a simple oriental carpet rather than the more usual ornate throne. Also outstanding are a famous *Madonna della Misericordia* (c. 1364) by Bartolo di Fredi, his first signed and dated work. Among the figures sheltered by the vermilion-robed Madonna are the Emperor Charles IV (in red cloak and crown on the right), who visited Siena in 1355 en route for Rome, together with the pope (alongside) and Charles's queen (to the left, crowned, in pink). It seems likely Siena's Council of Twelve, then in thrall to the emperor, commissioned the work to commemorate the visit.

More eye-catching still is a magnificent 48-panel painting whose tiny anonymous miniatures depict scenes from the life of Christ. It was one of only a handful of surviving "portable" paintings once used by mendicant monks as a preaching aid, during their perambulations around the countryside. The picture was brought here from the castle of Spedaletto in the Val d'Orcia, together with a painting often regarded as the first Renaissance Sienese painting: Vecchietta's seminal polyptych of the *Madonna and Child with SS. Blaise, Florian, John the Baptist and Nicholas* (1462). The lunette, clearly Florentine in flavour, depicts the *Annunciation*, whose receding classical columns and three naves of equal height deliberately recall the "hall-church" design of the duomo. The predella, by contrast, depicts three scenes with a more Sienese touch: the *Crucifixion*, with Siena's bare-hilled *crete* as background; the *Miracles of St Nicholas*; and the *Martyrdom of St Blaise*. Blaise (*Biagio* in Italian) was martyred with a tool used for carding wool (he is always depicted with the tool in his hand), and is thus the patron saint of carders and textile workers – hence his widespread popularity in Florence and Tuscany, whose medieval prosperity largely derived from the wool trade (for more on St Blaise see p.392).

The palaces

Pienza has little to show in the way of the **palaces** Pius envisaged being built by his retinue of cardinals. Twelve houses for the "people" were built, however, and at Pius's own expense, so keen was he to see his perfect city realized. Both carrot and stick were employed to encourage the reluctant hangers-on to comply with papal wishes, most notably in the case of the hapless Francesco Gonzaga, who was informed in no uncertain terms that the promised bishopric of Mantua would not be forthcoming unless a palace appeared in Pienza with his name on it (whether the palace was ever built is still a case for debate). Apart from the Borgia travesty (see previous page), virtually the only palace to see the light of day was the **Palazzo Ammannati** (across the street from the Palazzo Piccolomini), built by the eponymous cardinal, a close friend of Pius; sadly it was still unfinished at the pope's death. To its left is the smaller **Palazzo dei Cardinali**, and to the right the larger **Palazzo Comunale**, the latter probably also designed by Rossellino, despite its appearance, which is more medieval than Renaissance.

The rest of the town

A short way down the main street from Piazza Pio II stands the church of **San Francesco**, one of two churches to survive from the original Corsignano, and the only significant medieval building remaining in Pienza. Its walls were once entirely covered in fourteenth-century frescoes, only a few of which (scenes from the life of St Francis) survive in the apse. More remains of the large Crucifix on the right, a fourteenth-century work by a follower of Duccio, and the arresting *Madonna della Misericordia* on the left, attributed to Luca Signorelli.

Be certain to take the alley to the left of the church – or those to either side of the duomo – to gain access to Pienza's **walls**, rebuilt after being razed to the ground by the armies of the Medici and Charles V of Spain in 1559. You can see why Pius wanted his loggia, for the views from here are some of the finest from any town in Tuscany. Head east past the duomo and you come to a lovely series of little **lanes** leading back into the village, each with impossibly twee names – notably Via dell'Amore (street of love) and Via del Bacio (street of the kiss): the names were altered from more warlike ones in the nineteenth century so as to be more in keeping with the village's Renaissance idea of itself. In the other direction a more rural lane runs out of Piazza Dante along a level ridge past public gardens.

Not to be missed is the ten-minute downhill walk from Piazza Dante (signed off the south side) to the **Pieve di Corsignano** (or San Vito), the village's original parish church, and the place where Pius was baptized. Extremely ancient, it probably dates from the tenth century, and is one of the best Romanesque churches for miles around. The cylindrical tower – used to shelter the townspeople during bandit raids – is highly unusual, as are the carvings above the main and side doors. You can get the key from the farmhouse just behind the church – leave a small tip.

Practicalities

Pienza is a pleasant place to stay, but there's not much life after dark, so it might also be considered a day trip from Montepulciano. TRA-IN **buses** cover the routes to Buonconvento and Siena (7 daily) and Montepulciano (9 daily); for details of times, call in at the helpful **tourist office** (daily 9.30am–1pm & 3–6.30pm; ☎0578.749.071) inside the Palazzo Comunale on Piazza Pio II. It's also worth checking on the daily departures to and from Rome, which provide a fast additional link to Montalcino or Montepulciano. If you're stranded and need a **taxi** ring ☎0578.748.699.

Accommodation is limited if you want to stay: the *Ristorante dal Falco* at Piazza Dante 8 (☎0578.748.551; ③) has six rooms, each with bathroom, but they're quickly snapped up, as are the three private doubles c/o Caterina Monachini, Via E. Mangiavacchi 9 (☎0578.748.121; ④). Much more expensive is the modern but very pleasant three-star *Hotel Il Corsignano*, Via della Madonnina 11, about 150m west of the piazza on the left (☎0578.748.501, fax 0578.748.166; ⑥): rooms at the back have little terraces and something of a view. If you're doing Tuscany in style, or fancy a treat, the obvious choice is the three-star *Il Chiostro di Pienza Relais*, Corso Il Rossellino 26 (☎0578.748.400, fax 0578.748.440; ⑦). The only in-town hotel, it's an extremely chi-chi conversion – complete with frescoes, vaults and other medieval trappings – which has been infiltrated into the old cloister and buildings of a Franciscan monastery.

Among **restaurants**, the best are the *Falco* in Piazza Dante (closed Fri), a simple trattoria which offers superb *gnocchi* and a filling *pecorino alla griglia* (hot cheese wrapped in prosciutto) – around L30,000 for a full meal; and the excellent and friendly *Latte di Luna*, Via San Carlo 2–4 (☎0578.748.606; closed Tues) at the eastern end of the main street; the latter is blessed with a small terrace for outdoor eating and an ancient well incorporated into the old interior: reckon on L30,000–40,000 for the works. Alternatively, you can get good-value beers and *crostini* at the *Birreria Sperone Nudo*, a great old-world place in the middle of the town; you're further spoilt for choice of picnic food as the town, centre of a region producing *pecorino* sheep's cheese, seems to have gone overboard on *alimentari* and "natural food" shops.

Festivals include a **"Meeting with a Master of Art"** (Aug–Sept), when a contemporary Italian artist is featured in the Palazzo Civico, and the **Fiera del Calcio** (first Sun in Sept), which celebrates the local *pecorino* with a medieval market and fair in the main square.

East to Montepulciano: Monticchiello

The area around Pienza is enticing walking country. The track west to Bagno Vignoni is a fine two-hour walk. To the east, it's around 11km along the old road through Monticchiello to Montepulciano. If you are dependent on buses, which have a lull in the morning along this route, it's certainly worth hiking at least one of these stretches.

MONTICCHIELLO is a minor attraction in itself: a walled village with a leaning watchtower, lovely views of Pienza and a great **church** (if locked, you can collect a key from the house next door), which houses numerous fourteenth-century Sienese frescoes – look out for the gargantuan *St Christopher* – and a *Madonna* by Pietro Lorenzetti. Outside the church, in the corner on the right as you stand with your back to the facade, is a tiny old-fashioned shop selling some of the most beautiful **fabrics** imaginable. They're all made by hand locally, and are exported – quietly – to all corners of the globe. As an added bonus the hamlet has a more-than-decent **restaurant**, the *Taverna di Moranda*, Via di Mezzo 17 (☎0578.755.050; closed Mon), run by an Italo-French couple who offer superb local food and an extensive selection of big-name local wines.

During the last week of July and the first week of August, the village puts on a now-renowned **Teatro Povero**, featuring a play written and performed by the villagers to evoke the local folk and farming traditions – a kind of Tuscan *Archers*. It's a pleasantly informal occasion, enjoyed equally for the food at the *taverna* set up for the duration of the festival.

Montepulciano

The highest of the Tuscan hill towns, **MONTEPULCIANO** (665m) is built along a narrow tufa ridge, with a long main street and alleys that drop away to the walls. It's a stunningly good-looking town, full of vistas, odd squares and corners, and endowed with dozens of Renaissance palazzi and churches, which embody the state of architecture fifty years after Bernardo Rossellino's pioneering work at Pienza. Largely forgotten in subsequent centuries, the town today makes most of its money from its wine industry, based on the famed **Vino Nobile**, though its tourist profile becomes higher with each passing year. Along with Montalcino it's perhaps the best base in southern Tuscany, with Pienza, Chiusi and Bagno Vignoni all within easy reach by car or public transport.

Arrival and orientation

Montepulciano is on the main **bus** routes between Siena and Chiusi, and is also served by a couple of buses from Florence daily. Its **train station** is on the Siena–Chiusi line too, but only the *locali* stop and you'll need a (not always connecting) bus for the 10km trip into town. Regular buses also link with more frequent main-line trains at Chiusi, not much farther away. The buses stop in town at both the north and south gates, the **Porta al Prato** and **Porta al Farine**; buses arrive at the latter first – climb the steps above the bus stop to get into town – though Porta al Prato at the lower end of town is the main "bus station". If you're **driving**, follow the road around below the east circuit of walls and look for a parking space; don't be tempted by the area around the Porta al Prato or you'll be ticketed. Up around the **Fortezza** is also a good place to start looking.

The Prato and Farine gates are equally convenient for exploring the town, though our account assumes a starting point at the Porta al Prato. Between the two gates runs the town's main street, the **Corso**, whose name is appended in turn to **Via Gracciano, Via di Voltaia** and **Via dell'Opio**. The town's main focus is the **Piazza Grande**, home to the **duomo** and an ensemble of palaces. Note that it's a long and unrelenting uphill climb from Porta al Prato to the piazza. To see the town's other big sight, the Renaissance church of **San Biagio**, requires a pleasant ten-minute stroll (downhill) to the west of town.

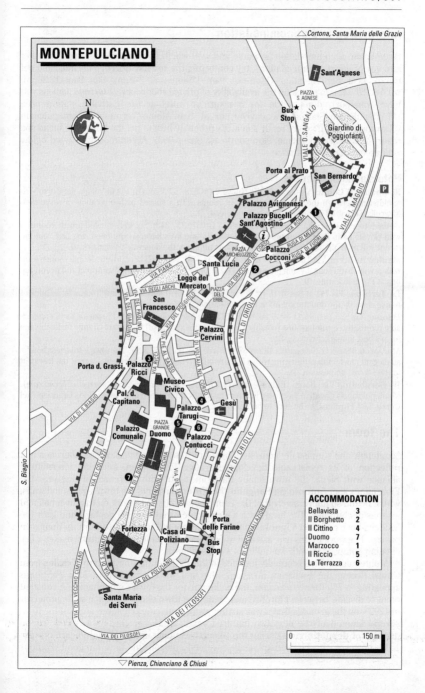

△ *Cortona, Santa Maria delle Grazie*

MONTEPULCIANO

N

Sant'Agnese

PIAZZA
S. AGNESE

Bus
Stop ★

VIALE D. SANGALLO

Giardino di
Poggiofanti

Porta al Prato

San Bernardo

VIALE I. MAGGIO

P

Palazzo Avignonesi

Palazzo Bucelli
Sant'Agostino

VIA ROMA

❶

ⓘ

RUGA DI MEZZO

Palazzo
Cocconi

RUGA DI FUORI

PIAZZA
MICHELOZZO

Santa Lucia

CORSO

VIA BRACCIOLINI

VIA PIANA

Logge del
Mercato

PIAZZA
D.ERBE

❷

VIA DEGLI ARCHI

VIA DEL POGGIOLO

VIA DEL GIARDINO

San
Francesco

VIA DI ORIOLO

VIA DEL PAOLINO

Palazzo
Cervini

VIA DI VOLTAIA NEL CORSO

Porta d. Grassi

Palazzo
Ricci

VIA RICCI

❸

Pal. d.
Capitano

Museo
Civico

VIA DI S. BIAGIO

Palazzo
Comunale

PIAZZA
GRANDE

Duomo

❺

Palazzo
Taruggi

❹

❻

Gesù

Palazzo
Contucci

S. Biagio ◁

VIA DI COLLAZZI

❼

VIA DI ORIOLO

VIA DI S. DONATO

VIA FIORENZUOLA VECCHIA

VIA DEL TEATRO

VIA DI CIRCONVALLAZIONE

Porta
delle Farine

Fortezza

Casa di
Poliziano

Bus
Stop ★

VIA DEL VECCHIO CIMITERO

VIA DEL POLIZIANO

Santa Maria
dei Servi

VIA DEI FILOSOFI

VIA DEI FILOSOFI

ACCOMMODATION

Bellavista	**3**
Il Borghetto	**2**
Il Cittino	**4**
Duomo	**7**
Marzocco	**1**
Il Riccio	**5**
La Terrazza	**6**

0   150 m

▽ *Pienza, Chianciano & Chiusi*

Information and accommodation

Once again, accommodation is sparse and well worth booking ahead. If you can't get into any of our recommendations, try contacting the **tourist office,** Via Gracciano nel Corso, near Sant'Agostino (Mon–Sat 9am–12.30pm & 3–8pm, Sun 9am–12.30pm; ☎0578.757.341), to check on the availability of private rooms or *agriturismo*. Unless you have transport, don't settle for a room or hotel at the outlying station area (Montepulciano–Stazione/Acquaviva), or at Sant'Albino/Terme di Montepulciano (5km southeast). If you're really stuck, it's probably best to get the bus to the bland spa resort of Chianciano Terme, 9km southeast (see p.393). Accommodation listed below is in ascending order of price.

Hotels and guesthouses

Ristorante Il Cittino, Vicolo della Via Nuova 2 (☎0578.757.335). Off Via di Voltaia nel Corso – so equidistant between the gates. Three decent rooms with a shared bathroom above a restaurant. Marcella Trabalzini is the contact name you need. ①.

Bellavista, c/o Gabriella Massoni, Via Ricci 25 (☎0578.757.348). Six well-situated private rooms, 5 with private bath. Four have stupendous views. No one lives here, so you must ring first, and the owner will drive up to let you in: there's a public phone in the doorway downstairs. ②.

Meublè Il Riccio, Via Talosa 21 (☎ & fax 0578.757.713). Five well-kept private double rooms, each with private bathroom, TV and phones, off Piazza Grande; contact Ivana Migliorucci and get off the bus at Porta di Farine. ③.

La Terrazza, Via Piè al Sasso 16 (☎ & fax 0578.757.440). Pleasant two-star rooms in an ancient house close by the duomo; get off at Porta di Farine. ③.

Duomo, Via San Donato 14 (☎ & fax 0578.757.473). A friendly welcome, 13 spacious and comfortable rooms, three-star facilities (notably TVs) and a nice setting off the Piazza Grande make this the town's best upmarket choice. ⑤.

Marzocco, Piazza G. Savonarola 18 (☎0578.757.262, fax 0578.757.530). The town's smartest hotel – an elegant nineteenth-century inn with a full-size billiard table. Very courteous owners, but loses out to the *Duomo* on position. ⑤.

Il Borghetto, Via Borgo Buio 7 (☎0578.757.535, fax 0578.757.354, *scarpelli@bccmt.com*). Montepulciano's grandest three-star, in a very tastefully refurbished old house off Via Gracciano nel Corso. Just 11 rooms, so be sure to book. ⑤.

The Town

Montepulciano's unusually consistent array of Renaissance palazzi and churches is a reflection of its remarkable development after 1511, when, following intermittent alliance with Siena, the town finally threw in its lot with Florence. In that year the Florentines sent **Antonio da Sangallo the Elder** to rebuild the town's gates and walls, which he did so impressively that the council took him on to work on the town hall and a series of churches. The local nobles meanwhile hired him, his nephew, and later the Modena-born architect **Vignola** – a founding figure of Baroque – to work on their own palazzi. The work of this trio, assured in both its conception and execution, makes a fascinating comparison with Rossellino's work at Pienza.

Montepulciano was reputedly founded in the sixth century by a group of **exiles** from Chiusi fleeing the barbarian invasions, the first written allusion to *Mon Politianus* appearing in 715 (hence *poliziani*, the nickname for the town's inhabitants). A constant point of dispute between Florence and Siena, the town chose Florence as its protector in 1202 – on the grounds that it was farther away. Both cities captured and lost the town several times over the next two hundred years, while her citizens suffered several decades of **despotic rule** during the fifteenth century under the del Pecora clan. In 1511, however, the Florentines again assumed control, this time for good. Famous names from Montepulciano include the great classical scholar Angelo Ambrogini (1454–94), better known by his adopted name of **Poliziano**, which he took in honour of his home town. **Marcellus II** (1501–55), a pope who had the misfortune to die just three weeks after being elected pontiff, was also born here.

The Corso: Porta al Prato to the Fortress

Sangallo's first commission was Montepulciano's main gate, the **Porta al Prato**, at the north end of town. Before embarking on the climb up, you should visit the church of **Sant'Agnese**, named in honour of a local Dominican abbess, Agnese Segni (1268–1317), who was canonized in 1726 and is buried in the church. The first chapel on the right contains the *Madonna di Zoccoli*, attributed to Simone Martini (or his school), while the second altar on the left features a fourteenth-century Sienese fresco of the *Madonna del Latte*. This subject, which shows a breast-feeding Madonna, is a common feature of Sienese (and Tuscan) painting of the period, the Virgin's milk, in Christian iconography, symbolizing the font of Eternal Life (many a Tuscan church in the Middle Ages claimed to have genuine drops of the Madonna's milk). The subject vanished entirely following the Council of Trent, which in a fit of Counter–Reformationary zeal banned any use of "unnecessary" nudity in the portrayal of religious characters.

Inside the Porta al Prato the **Corso** begins, the palazzi immediately making clear the town's allegiance to Florence. In the first square, beside the *Albergo Marzocco*, is the **Colonna del Marzocco**, a stone column bearing the heraldic lion (*marzocco*) of Florence. The original lion, now in the museum (this is an 1856 copy), was fixed to its column in 1511, when it replaced a statue of the she-wolf suckling Romulus and Remus, the symbol of Siena (according to legend the city was founded by Senius, son of Remus). Across the street further lion heads decorate the **Palazzo Avignonesi** (no. 91), probably the work of Vignola. Sangallo makes a second appearance with the **Palazzo Cocconi** (no. 70), virtually opposite the **Palazzo Bucelli** (no. 73), whose base is strikingly inset with Roman and Etruscan reliefs. These were lovingly collected in 1648 by the palace's erstwhile owner, Pietro Bucelli, whose extensive Etruscan collection – an unusual one given the classically obsessed era in which it was amassed – now resides in Florence's Museo Archeologico.

Just beyond this crop of palazzi is the eye-catching church of **Sant'Agostino**, designed around 1427 by the earlier Medici protégé, Michelozzo – who also carved the terracotta relief of the *Madonna and Child* above the door; within are a *Crucifixion* on the third altar on the left wall by Lorenzo di Credi and an equally good *St Bernardino* by Giovanni di Paolo on the right wall. Pride of place goes to a polychrome Crucifix on the high altar attributed to Donatello. Across the street a medieval **tower house**, a rare survival in Montepulciano, is surmounted by a *commedia dell'arte* figure of a clown, the **Pulcinella**, who strikes out the hours on the town clock; most un-Tuscan, it is said to have been put up by an exiled bishop from Naples.

About a hundred metres farther along you reach the Renaissance **Loggia di Mercato** and a fork in the roads: turn right here if you want to make straight for the Piazza Grande (see below). The Corso continues to the left past further palazzi, including the **Palazzo Cervini**, attributed to Sangallo. Begun for the doomed Marcellus II before he became pope, it is now occupied by a bank, and has the grand civic gesture of an external courtyard. Beyond this, you pass the church of **Gesù**, remodelled in Baroque style by Andrea Pozzo (as are many other churches in the town and region), before the road turns the corner and rambles outside the town walls. Just prior to the turn – at no. 5 – is the **Casa di Poliziano**, birthplace of the Renaissance humanist and poet Angelo Ambrogini (Poliziano), who translated many of the Greek classics under the patronage of Lorenzo de' Medici, as well as teaching the Medici children.

Via di Poliziano loops outside the walls to the Gothic-fronted **Santa Maria dei Servi**, another Baroque interior job by Pozzo. Inside it's visited by devout locals eager to prostrate themselves before the much venerated *Madonna della Santoreggia*, a fifteenth-century fresco (second altar on the left). The only other attention-grabbing work is a *Madonna and Child*, oddly inserted into a larger painting (third altar on the right) by a follower of Duccio. Via di Poliziano then re-enters town by the old **Fortezza**, now partly occupied by houses. At the end of Via di San Donato, the last quiet stretch back into town, you'll find yourself in the cathedral and town hall square, Piazza Grande.

Santa Lucia, Via del Poggio and the Museo Civico

A quicker approach to Piazza Grande at the Loggia di Mercato (see above) would be to head right. A block to the north of here, a beautiful little piazza fronts the church of **Santa Lucia**, built in 1633, which has a fabulous, if damaged, *Madonna* by Luca Signorelli in a chapel on the right, though the church is rarely open. Turning instead to the south, Via del Poggio runs down to the church of **San Francesco**: note the ruined pulpit to the side of the facade, from which St Bernardino of Siena is supposed to have preached. The imposing Via Ricci takes over for the last stretch to the Piazza Grande; it is flanked on one side by the Renaissance **Palazzo Ricci**, on the other by the Sienese-Gothic **Palazzo Neri-Orselli**.

The latter is home to the town's **Museo Civico** (closed for restoration at time of writing), an extensive collection of small-town Gothic and Renaissance works. The courtyard contains the original Florentine *marzocco* lion removed from the Corso (see above), while the first-floor room opens with a series of glazed terracottas by Andrea della Robbia. The most important panel is a *St Francis*, painted by the saint's near-contemporary, Margaritone da Arezzo; the most enjoyable is Jacopo de Mino's lush *Coronation of the Virgin*.

The Piazza Grande

The **Piazza Grande**, Montepulciano's theatrical flourish of a main square, is built on the highest point of the ridge, providing the obvious site for the town's duomo (see below). Its most distinctive building, however, is the **Palazzo Comunale**, a thirteenth-century Gothic palace to which Michelozzo added a tower and rustication in imitation of the Palazzo Vecchio in Florence. You can climb the tower for free (closed Sun), and on those fabled clear days the view supposedly stretches to Siena, 65km northwest.

Two of the palazzi on the square were designed by Sangallo. The **Palazzo Nobili-Tarugi**, by the lion and griffon fountain, is a highly innovative building, with a public loggia cut through one corner; it originally had an extension on the top floor, though this has been bricked in. More tangible pleasures await at the **Palazzo Cantucci**, one of many buildings scattered about the town that serve as *cantine* for the **wine trade**, offering *degustazione* and sale of the Vino Nobile. The lower part is by Sangallo, the upper by Baldassare Peruzzi, who was Siena's leading sixteenth-century architect.

THE DUOMO

Sangallo and his contemporaries never got around to building a facade for the **Duomo** (closed 1–3.30pm), whose plain brick pales against the neighbouring *palazzi*. Begun in 1680 by Ippolito Scalzi, the building was raised over an earlier church, of which the ugly fourteenth-century campanile is virtually the only reminder.

The **interior** boasts an elegant Renaissance design, and has several outstanding works of art dotted around its rather foreboding walls. The first of these are fragments of the **tomb of Bartolomeo Aragazzi** (1427–36) by the multi-talented Michelozzo, a monument which was criminally dismembered in the nineteenth century. Aragazzi was born in Montepulciano, and achieved prominence as the secretary to Pope Martin V (pontiff from 1417 to 1431), the first pope to occupy the Holy See in Rome after the Grand Schism (1378–1417) divided the papacy between Rome and Avignon. He is often described as the first "Renaissance" pope, his election coinciding with the competition to design the baptistery doors in Florence. Pope Martin was assisted in his adopted role by Aragazzi, who scoured French and German monasteries for manuscripts and oversaw the publication of classical texts by Vitruvius and others. Bas-reliefs from the tomb can now be seen at the base of the first two columns on either side of the nave (right and left), and the effigy of Aragazzi himself is mounted on the rear (west) wall to the right of the door. At the other end of the church, two of the tomb's statues surmount the high altar – which is also garlanded by putti and festoons from the tomb: two sculpted angels from the piece can be found even farther away, in London's British Museum.

Aragazzi also commissioned a painting that would be a highlight of this or any other church: **Taddeo di Bartolo**'s iridescent high altarpiece of the *Assumption*, perhaps the supreme rendition of a subject that was a favourite among Siena's leading artists. The date of the painting's commission (1401) is noteworthy, for it came at a time when Montepulciano – which oscillated constantly between Florentine and Sienese domination – found itself free of Florentine rule for a brief period (1390–1404); Aragazzi's choice of a Sienese artist, and a subject dear to the Sienese, is thus revealed as an act of political as well as artistic significance. The main panels of the triptych, its predella and its gilt-turreted upper panels are crammed with detail and incident. Note, in particular, the apostles gathered around the Virgin's tomb in the main painting: Doubting Thomas is shown receiving the Madonna's girdle (see p.181), while a grief-stricken St John views her flower-decked sepulchre. Behind the latter to the right is the Apostle Thaddeus, Taddeo's namesake; the face is probably a self-portrait, an extremely unusual feature in a painting executed on the cusp of the Renaissance, when such self-advertisement would later become quite common.

Elsewhere in the church hunt out a work by Vecchietta, best known as a painter but here represented by an excellent piece of sculpture: the marble **ciborium** in the chapel to the right of the high altar. On the left (north) wall of the church, opposite the pillar of the third nave, is a poetic *Madonna del Pilastro* (Madonna of the Pillar) by Sano di Pietro. At the bottom of the north aisle, close to the main remnants of Aragazzi's tomb, the first chapel – the **Baptistery** – contains a wealth of eye-catching big-name art: the font and its six bas-reliefs (1340) are by Giovanni d'Agostino; the riot of glazed terracotta on the wall, the so-called **Altare dei Gigli** (Altar of the Lilies), is by Andrea della Robbia – it frames a relief of the *Madonna and Child* attributed to Benedetto da Maiano; and the niche statues of St Peter and John the Baptist are attributed to Mino da Camaino.

San Biagio

Antonio da Sangallo's greatest commission came in 1518, when he was invited by the town's Ricci nobles to design the pilgrimage church of **San Biagio** (daily 9am–noon & 3–6pm) on the hillside below the town. The model for this was his brother Giuliano's design for the facade of San Lorenzo in Florence, which was never built. The Montepulciano project was more ambitious – the only bigger church project of its time was St Peter's in Rome – and occupied Antonio until his death in 1534. He lived to see its inauguration, however (in 1529), the ceremony performed by the Medici pope Clement VII. To reach the church, follow Via San Biagio out from the Porta di Grassi; it's about fifteen minutes' walk.

The church, built over an earlier chapel to San Biagio, or St Blaise (see box on next page), is one of the most harmonious Renaissance creations in Italy, constructed inside and out from a porous travertine, whose soft honey-coloured stone blends perfectly with its niche in the landscape. A deeply intellectualized building, its major architectural novelty was the use of freestanding towers (only one was completed, in 1545) to flank the

---

SAINT BLAISE

San Biagio (**St Blaise**) was an Armenian doctor who became a bishop before being called by God to abandon his worldly affairs in favour of a contemplative life in the mountains. There he lived in a cave, surrounded by wild animals who brought him food and drink, and in return were healed by him when they became sick (he is often shown, St Francis-like, talking to the birds). He was eventually imprisoned on a charge of practising magic, and tortured by having his body scraped with a sharp-pronged instrument used to card wool (paintings of him always show him holding such an instrument). Thus he became the patron saint of carders, which is why he appears so frequently in Florentine and Tuscan paintings, the textile industry having been the bedrock of the region's medieval prosperity. In a more homely vein, he is also invoked by Italians against sore throats, having saved a child who caught a fish bone in her throat.

---

facade (note the tower's three orders of Classical columns – Doric, Ionic and Corinthian). Within, it is spoilt a little by extraneous decoration – a Baroque trompe l'oeil covers the barrel vault – but is equally harmonious. It also has superb acoustics.

Nearby, scarcely less perfect a building, is the **Canonica** (rectory), endowed by Sangallo with a graceful portico and double-tiered loggia.

Food, festivals and transport

The town has a fair spread of **restaurants**, all of them offering local wines. For superb home-made pasta try the *Trattoria Diva* (☎0578.716.951; closed Tues), just inside the Porta al Prato on Via Gracciano nel Corso, an old-world fossil of a type rarely found these days, with meals for around L35,000 – unless you go for a vintage Vino Nobile from the co-owned *enoteca* next door. Alternatives include the next-door *Pulcino*, which has an excellent wine list and does a fine *ribollita*; the smart *Ristorante Il Cantuccio*, in an alley to the right of Via Gracciano nel Corso 67; and the *Rosticceria di Voltaia* at Via di Voltaia nel Corso 86 (closed Fri), with full meals around L25,000 and cheaper take-aways. The *Caffè Poliziano*, Via di Voltaia nel Corso 27–9, has a lovely Art Nouveau interior, serves wonderful cakes and snacks, and has live music on a Sunday night.

There's an open-air **market** (with especially good *porchetta*), held in the gardens outside the Porta al Prato on Thursday mornings; this is also the site of the local **youth bar**, with table football and a jukebox through to midnight.

Festivals
Cantiere Internazionale d'Arte (July–Aug). A major international performing arts festival (especially music), founded by composer Hans Werner Henze in the 1970s. The festival makes a point of supporting young musicians, with artists and stagehands alike slumming it in the local co-operative mess rooms. Look out for opera performed in the intimate Teatro Poliziano, Via del Teatro 6. For further details contact the theatre box office (☎0578.757.281) or the festival headquarters at Via del Teatro 4 (☎0578.758.307 or 0578.757.089).

Bruscello (Aug 14–16). The Festival of Assumption is celebrated with a sequence of masked plays and light opera in the town squares.

Bravío delle Botti (last Sun in Aug). A barrel race through the streets from Sant'Agnese to the Piazza Grande, between teams from each of the town's eight *contrade*. Costume processions precede the race and a street banquet follows.

Transport

The main **transport** links are with Chiusi. LFI **buses** run more or less every half-hour to Chianciano Terme, Chiusi and Chiusi station. To the west, TRA-IN has seven buses daily on the circuit through Pienza, San Quírico d'Órcia, Torrenieri (change for Montalcino) and Buonconvento, with three continuing to Siena. All buses leave from outside Porta al Prato and Porta di Farine; buy tickets from bars or shops in town, not on the bus.

If you're making a **train** connection, take a bus to Chiusi; Montepulciano's own station, 10km northeast, is a stop only for *locali*. **Bikes** can be rented at Cicloposse, Via Matteotti 45 (☎0578.716.392); local **car rental** can be arranged through Bernardini (☎0578.716.293) or Paolo Cencini (☎0578.716.532).

East to Chianciano Terme and Chiusi

CHIANCIANO TERME, midway between Montepulciano and Chiusi, is one of Tuscany's major spas, as evidenced by the presence of some two hundred-odd hotels. Its particular specialities are liver and bladder complaints, handy if you've overworked the Vino Nobile, though the clinic-like spa buildings aren't the usual image of a Tuscan holiday.

If you find yourself staying here, with Montepulciano full, you might want to wander up to the old hill town, **Chianciano Vecchio**, though there's little specific to see, save a Romanesque Collegiata and middling sacred art museum. The local tourist handouts fastidiously trace a series of "Medically Recommended Walks" in its *"Chianciano . . . What a healthy liver!"* pamphlet. Perhaps the most compelling is to the huge outdoor **municipal pool**.

Through Sarteano

If you have transport, a more enjoyable route to Chiusi is the minor road that runs south just before Montepulciano's own little spa at Sant'Albino. This follows a fine, scarcely populated stretch of the Val d'Órcia down through the estates of Castellúccio and La Foce – the latter the home for many years of the American writer Iris Origo, author of the classic *Merchant of Prato*. It was at La Foce that she hid partisans and Allied troops during the German occupation of Italy after Mussolini's fall in 1943, events recorded in her autobiography *War in Val d'Órcia*. You turn north to reach Chiusi at **SARTEANO**, a pleasant village set below a castle and within patches of Etruscan wall; it has an *Annunciation* by Domenico Beccafumi in the church of San Martino, and an excellent restaurant, *La Giara*, at Viale Europa 1.

Chiusi

CHIUSI, 14km southeast of Montepulciano, is a useful transport hub, with trains and buses west to Siena, south to Orvieto and Rome, and north to Montepulciano, Castiglione del Lago, Cortona and Arezzo. As a target in its own right, it is only really worth a special detour for Etruscan enthusiasts: the town – known to the Etruscans as Camars – has a reasonable archeological museum and a half-dozen ancient tombs on its periphery, out towards Lago di Chiusi.

The museum and the duomo, Chiusi's other worthwhile site, are close by each other on Via Porsenna, a short walk up from the **bus stop** on the Viale Garibaldi; there's a **tourist office** at Via Porsenna 61 (Mon–Fri 9.30am–12.30pm & 3–7pm, Sat & Sun 9.30am–12.30pm; ☎0578.227.667), and a small kiosk at the **train station** which is 3km east at Chiusi Scalo, a regular stop for all the inter-town buses.

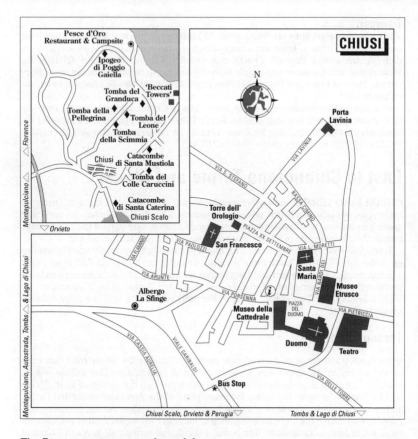

The Etruscan museum, tombs and duomo

Chiusi's **Museo Etrusco** (Tues–Thurs 9am–2pm, Sat & Sun 9am–1pm; L4000) ought to be pretty good, for the region is littered with tombs. Many of the best exhibits, however, have been spirited away to Florence and Rome and what remains is a modest collection: numerous sarcophagi, a few terracottas with traces of ancient paint, cabinets of pots (one with erotic dancing scenes), and the odd treasure – notably the *Gualandi Urn*. If you are interested in seeing the tombs themselves, ask one of the museum guards if they'll take you to the *Tomba della Pellegrina e Leone* (3km north), for which they hold the keys. Other local tombs (including the more famous frescoed *Scimmia* and *Colle*) have thus far remained locked away from public view.

At the Romanesque **duomo** there is further evidence of Chiusi's ancient past. The building itself consists almost entirely of Etruscan and Roman blocks, while the museum (L3000) gives access to **catacombs** (guided visits at 11am; L6000) which were used by early Christians in the fifth century. The cathedral interior is a mass of what appears at first sight to be mosaic work, but is in reality mock-Byzantine paintwork, created in 1915.

Lago di Chiusi

Chiusi's **lake** lies 5km north of the town, reached along the road past the Etruscan tombs. The route is served only sporadically by bus (4 daily Mon–Fri) but for anyone driving or planning to camp for a few days, it makes a fine detour. The buses run to the **restaurant-bar-campsite** *Pesce d'Oro* (☎0578.21.403), set amid trees by a small quay for rowing boats; the swimming is warm in summer. For food alone, you're best off at the lake's other signposted restaurant, *Da Gino* (closed Wed); they serve fine fish meals at around L30,000.

Practicalities

With time to kill in Chiusi, the best thing to do is **eat**. The *Osteria dei Bonci* on Via dei Bonci (an alley off Via Porsenna) is a pleasant bar-pizzeria, and there are excellent pizzas at **Il Capannino** in the same street, while the *Ristorante Zaira*, just up the road at Piazza Graviano, serves "Etruscan dishes" – boar, pigeon and the like – for L25,000 and up.

Should you want to stay, Chiusi has just one hotel, *Albergo La Sfinge* at Via Marconi 2 (☎0578.20.157, fax 0578.222.153; ③). Less expensive hotels are clustered down at Chiusi Scalo, an unattractive modern suburb that makes its living care of a large slaughterhouse and meat storage plant.

Monte Amiata

At 1738m, Monte Amiata is the highest point in southern Tuscany, a broad-based mountain whose hazy outline forms the backdrop to many a town and landscape in the region. A circle of towns rings its lower slopes – some historical spots, others more modern, most having been plumped up over the last few years in an attempt to attract tourism to a traditionally impoverished area. None, with one exception, are worth a trip for their own sake, but the effect of all the villages together, plus pretty streets, old castles and plenty of bucolic countryside makes this a good area to tour by car or bike for a day or so. It's also delightful walking country, refreshingly cool in summer – and there's skiing in winter.

The main centre and transport hub is **Abbadia San Salvatore**, worth a visit for its great abbey, whether you intend to venture onto the mountain or not. The town is accessible by bus from Siena (2 daily), Buonconvento (6 daily), Chiusi (3 daily), Arcidosso and Santa Fiora (6 daily), Grosseto (6 daily) and Montepulciano (1 daily).

Abbadia San Salvatore

There's been a settlement on the site of **ABBADIA SAN SALVATORE**, Monte Amiata's main town, since prehistoric times, though its real significance dates from the eighth century when its great abbey became the controlling centre of the Via Francigena. Its importance only waned with the rise of the Aldobrandeschi in the eleventh century. Thereafter it was contested by Orvieto and Siena, but in 1559 – along with most of southern Tuscany – fell within the orbit of the Medici's Grand Duchy of Tuscany.

Today the town is an initially disorientating modern sprawl that hides a perfect and largely self-contained **medieval quarter**. Buses will drop you on the **Viale Roma**, immediately outside the old walls; if you arrive by car you'll have to negotiate a maze of tree-lined streets. The abbey itself is actually in the modern part of the town, and best reached with Viale Roma as the starting point. From the north end of the street, walk down Via Cavour, passing Via Mentana on the left, and take the next right, Via del Monastero.

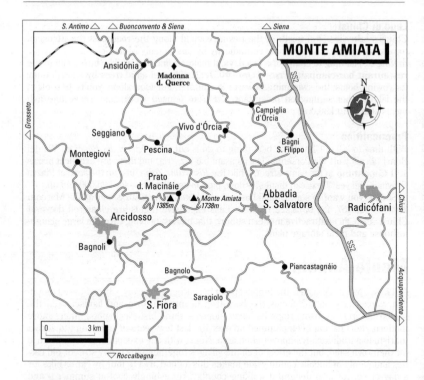

The Abbey

Church tradition dates the **Abbadia San Salvatore** to 743, making it one of the oldest abbeys in Tuscany, and ascribes its foundation to King Rachis, a Lombard king who is supposed to have converted to Christianity while contemplating a Crucifix now affixed to the abbey's south wall. He was subsequently visited by an apparition of Christ as he went to do battle with the Perugians, a revelation which prompted him to take up a monastic life and found the abbey at the site of the vision. The actual story of the abbey's birth is slightly different. For a start, the Crucifix element is anachronistic, as the work dates from the twelfth century, some 400 years after Rachis's death. Rachis himself, however, was involved in the foundation, though it appears his withdrawal into monastic isolation was forced on him, principally by leading Lombard nobles who opposed his ever-increasing leanings towards Rome. Forced to abdicate, the king symbolically awarded his crown to the pope and was succeeded by his brother, Astolfo.

The present Romanesque **church**, built in Amiata's distinctive brown trachite, was consecrated in 1036, a rebuilding programme having been instigated a year before when the abbey was at the height of its wealth and power. The present crypt (see below) dates from this period, though other parts of the building were altered during the brief tenure of the Camaldolese and later the Cistercians, who took over the abbey from the Benedictines in 1228.

Among the Cistercian additions was the triform window in the **facade**, though critics are unable to agree on the age of the two distinctive towers (one clearly unfinished), features found in very few other churches in Italy. The narrow frontage, squeezed between the towers, prepares you for a thin and immensely long **interior**, whose Latin-cross plan is generally considered the first of any Romanesque church in Tuscany. The single-naved basilica culminates in a raised chancel, framed by a series of broad and beautifully decorated arches.

Little survives in the way of art, much having been removed to Florence when the abbey was owned by the Medici – a period when it remained monkless for 157 years. The best of what remains is the wooden **Crucifix** involved in the Rachis legend (at the beginning of the right-hand wall), though it's a disquietingly modern-looking piece, and easily passed by. Many of the paintings are by the Nasini clan, a three-generation dynasty of painters born in nearby Castel del Piano (see p.400). The south transept features **frescoes** on the *Legend of King Rachis* by Giuseppe Nasini (1657–1736), the north transept panels on the *Life of the Virgin*; none is terribly accomplished, but they have a faintly ridiculous charm all the same.

The **crypt**, by contrast, is outstanding: one of the most monumental in Tuscany, it is an astounding space of bare, crude stone supported by thirty-five strange fluted columns. Atop each pillar is a superbly carved lintel, whose motifs and figures show a Lombard and in some cases Byzantine hand, the latter – distinguished by a more rectangular approach – typical of northern Italian work of the period. Note, too, how each pillar is worked in a wide variety of styles.

If you're lucky enough to get into the **monastery** alongside the abbey (it's rarely open), try to see the **treasury**, which has a minute eighth-century Irish reliquary, a fine reliquary bust of *Pope St Mark* (1381) and an extremely rare and beautiful red silk Persian cope dating from the eighth century.

Practicalities

Abbadia's **tourist office** is near the cinema at Via Adua 25 (Mon–Sat 9am–1pm & 4–6pm; ☎0577.775.811). As tourism headquarters for the Amiata region, the office is well worth a visit. For more information on **walking**, plus details of some innovative and cheap tours, contact Amiata Trekking, Piazza Fratelli Cervi 21 (☎0577.777.751).

There are numerous **hotels** in the modern town. The cheapest choice is the *Cesaretti*, Via Trento 37 (☎0577.778.198; ①); the *San Marco*, Via Matteotti 13 (☎ & fax 0577.778.089; ③) is centrally located, or there's the slightly more upmarket *Italia*, Viale Roma 34 (☎ & fax 0577.778.007; ③). The *San Marco* has a reasonable **restaurant**, and there are any number of cheap, if rather characterless, *pizzerie*.

The **bus terminal** is in front of the *Bar Centrale* in Viale Roma; there's a timetable fixed to the Agenzia VAII, Viale Roma 45, which is also the place to buy **tickets**. In addition to the two through services to Siena, there are six buses daily to Buonconvento (for train connections to Siena and Grosseto), three daily to Chiusi (trains to Rome, Florence and Siena), six daily to Arcidosso and Santa Fiora, four daily to Grosseto, one to Montepulciano (school days only) and two daily to Rome (via Orvieto).

The summit and slopes

The summit of **Monte Amiata** is accessible by road and in summer is packed out with vehicle-delivered parties, many ill-shod for the last few steps to the highest point. In July and August it has a thrice-daily bus from Abbadia San Salvatore; at other times, hitching should be possible. A number of the tatty bars at the summit rent out mountain bikes to explore the lower slopes.

At the car park is what amounts to an alpine hamlet, with bars, a handful of hotels and a short ski run – all in the shadow of a peculiar Eiffel Tower structure adapted in the form of a cross, erected in 1946 by Pope Pius XII. Alongside are a crop of radio masts, and huts selling some of the trashiest trinkets conceivable. None of this detracts from the **views**, which stretch southeast to Bolsena and west to the sea, with the nearer towns neatly delineated in a circle below. The best viewpoint is from the so-called *Madonna delle Scout*, a statue littered with the pendants of innumerable scout troops.

Amiata walking: the Anello della Montagna

Away from the summit, the woods and pathways of Amiata's **lower slopes** make up one of the region's most beautiful natural enclaves, huge forests of beech and chestnut blanketing the area and providing refuge for deer and wild boar. The mountain's extravagant greenery, so at odds with much of the surrounding countryside, derives from its volcanic origins, eruptions having formed ridges of trachite, which is fertile when broken down and also porous, allowing surface water to filter away. When the water hits the impervious volcanic rock below, it flows out in a series of **springs**, a striking feature of Amiata, whose slopes frequently echo to the sound of running water.

The combination of Amiata's lush vegetation and crisp mountain air makes it superb **walking** territory. The appearance of a new, detailed Multigraphic map has made hiking in the region a far more straightforward undertaking (*Carta dei Sentieri e Rifiugi Masiccio del Monte Amiata*; L10,000), and considerable effort has gone into marking the **Anello della Montagna**, a path which circles the mountain between about 900 and 1300 metres. With a car you can join the path from virtually any of the roads which climb from the surrounding towns; large boards mark the departure points from the road, and detail the route to either side. It's also possible, however, to walk up from the towns on paths which radiate from the main circuit: the best departure point for this approach is Abbadia San Salvatore.

The Anello's total circuit is 29km, in theory walkable in a day, though the local council have broken it into ten basic sections. It's fairly practical to walk half the route, and then take a **bus** back from Santa Fiora or Arcidosso (each have six connections daily with Abbadia San Salvatore). The trail markings are clearly indicated on concrete posts in red, yellow and green, though they coincide with the older CAI markings of red and white stripes; either way, it's fairly hard to go wrong. It's also possible to walk at will from the road, though if you venture too far, the chances are you'll wind up lost.

Staying on the mountain

If you want to **stay** on the mountain, the best base is **Prato Macinie** (1385m), a tree-enclosed patch of meadow and the site of one of Amiata's ski lifts (there are fourteen in all, along with twelve pistes). It's not far from the summit, but far enough to be unspoilt and away from the commercialism. The hotel, *Le Macinaie* (☎0564.955.001, fax 0564.959.013; ④) fills up, so book ahead.

In a similarly pretty setting, the **Prato della Contessa** (1500m), two kilometres south on the summit road, has the three-star *Hotel Contessa* (☎0564.959.000, fax 0564.959.002; ④), while nearby there's *Lo Scoiattolo* (☎0564.959.003; ③). All of these hotels function as **restaurants**. The nearest **campsite** is at Castel del Piano (see p.400).

Villages around Monte Amiata

If you have transport, the ring of towns around Monte Amiata is worth a little exploration. None has outstanding features but all claim a rural setting and more or less medieval centres – usually built around an Aldobrandeschi castle. Most also have a good sprinkling of hotels.

Piancastagnaio

Five kilometres south of Abbadia San Salvatore, **PIANCASTAGNAIO**, at 772m, spreads across the slopes of a mountain plateau, capped by one of the area's most impressive fortresses, a fourteenth-century Aldobrandeschi number. It has a maze of pretty streets, plus a fine Romanesque church – the twelfth-century Santa Maria Assunta. On the road outside the village, left of the main gate, the church of **Santa Maria delle Grazie** has a recently uncovered fifteenth-century fresco cycle by Nanni

DAVIDE LAZZERETTI OF MONTE LABBRO

Arcidosso-born **Davide Lazzeretti** (1834–78) is the most extraordinary figure Monte Amiata – a region renowned for its mystics and seers – has thrown up: either a visionary prophet, or a crazed communist born before his time, according to greatly divergent Italian points of view. As early as the age of fourteen, a Franciscan monk had foreseen great and strange things for the boy, the first of which – a vision vouchsafed him twenty years later – prompted Lazzeretti to travel to Rome, to try and interest the pope in his revelation. Scorned, he retired to a contemplative life on Monte Subiaco, in a deliberate imitation of St Benedict, who had retired to the same mountain slopes southeast of Rome 1400 years earlier.

Returning to Amiata between 1870 and 1871, Lazzeretti achieved notoriety as the founder of an ill-defined socio-religious sect, the **Jurisdavidic Church**, which as well as preaching Christianity under the banner "Long live the Republic, God and Liberty" agitated for justice and social reform amongst the peasant community which made up his following. In 1873 he was arrested, the authorities unhappy with his persuasive republican preaching – not to mention his new title – the "Messiah of Monte Amiata". In 1876 he was excommunicated, but continued to preach both in Italy and abroad, calling for a society based on co-operative principles and republican government. In time, his five thousand followers organized themselves into Italy's first co-operative, sharing land and animals, and building a huge temple to the movement on top of Monte Labbro, south of Arcidosso. In 1877 the Church refused to allow him to continue using the temple, and in 1878 Lazzeretti met the violent end of a radical; shot – with the connivance of local landowners – by the *carabinieri* as he led an unauthorized religious procession through Arcidosso.

Repression soon dispersed the movement, which was in any case being undermined by a drift away from the land to Amiata's mercury mines. Nonetheless, Lazzeretti is remembered today as a pre-emptor of socialist and land reform movements still twenty years away at the time of his death. He is commemorated on the night of August 14, the anniversary of his death, with a huge bonfire at the largely ruined temple on Monte Labbro. (Whether or not you want to pay your respects, the trip to the summit makes a fine walk or drive – a rough road takes you virtually to the top).

di Pietro. Another recently discovered cycle resides in **San Bartolommeo**, a humble Franciscan church on the Abbadia road restructured in the eighteenth century. The pictures, which depict the *Life of the Virgin*, are in the chapterhouse, off the cloister.

The village's **hotels** are all grouped along Viale Gramsci and Via Grossetana – the *Del Bosco*, Via Grossetana (☎ & fax 0577.786.090; ③), has pleasant doubles. A rural, and slightly cheaper alternative, is the *Piccolo Mondo* (☎0577.785.100; ②), 4km east on the minor road to Quaranta.

Santa Fiora

SANTA FIORA's craggy position drew an admiring observation from Dante as to its impregnability; its castle – of which only a tower remains – provided the feudal seat of one of the major branches of the **Aldobrandeschi**. This clan, which ruled much of southern Tuscany and the Maremma from the ninth century, had its roots in a Lombard dynasty from Lucca – the family name is an Italian corruption of "Hildebrand", testament to the family's northern German origins. In 1274 the clan divided into two main branches, one of which was installed in Santa Fiora, ruling Monte Amiata and the northern Maremma, the other in nearby Sovana, from where they controlled the coast and the southern Maremma (see p.406). Santa Fiora then passed through the family's female line, and was eventually ceded by marriage to the Sforza Cesarini family, whose **palazzo**, built from the old fortress, lies alongside the Aldobrandeschi **tower**, now a clock tower overlooking a picturesque little square.

The village has a couple of fine churches. The **Pieve di Santa Fiora e Lucilla**, reached on Via Carolina from the square, has its walls, altar and pulpit adorned with a wide variety of topnotch terracottas (1480–90) by Andrea della Robbia and his workshop. The beautiful church, incidentally, was named after two local saints whose relics, brought here in the eleventh century, reside in the nearby priest's house. A steep, partly stepped lane leads to **Sant'Agostino**, which possesses a fine painted wooden image of the Madonna and Child attributed (dubiously) to Jacopo della Quercia, though it's been claimed for the time being by the small museum in Pitigliano's Palazzo Orsini (see p.404).

Down the road you come to gardens and the oratory of **Madonna delle Nevi** – the della Robbia figures above the entrance are the local saints Fiora and Lucilla – and then to the village's nicest feature, the **Peschiera** (Sat & Sun 10am–12.30pm & 3.30–dusk; L2500), a spring-fed lake and eighteenth-century garden surrounded by woodland and gurgling brooks. The road beyond passes evidence of Amiata's industrial side, tall chimneys signalling the thermal power plants and mercury mines that have kept the area's economic head above water.

The village **tourist office** is in Piazza Garibaldi (☎0564.971.124) and there are a couple of **hotels**. The best option is the *Fiora*, Via Roma 8 (☎0564.977.043; ②); the *Eden* (☎ & fax 0564.977.033; ②), Via Roma 1, is slightly more expensive.

Arcidosso and Castel del Piano

To the north of the summit, **ARCIDOSSO** is one of the larger Amiata towns, dominated by a blunt Sienese tower, but of little other interest. It was, however, the birthplace of **Davide Lazzeretti** (see box on previous page), and also features in one of the most heated artistic debates ever to embroil Tuscany; it's thought to be Arcidosso's skyline that is depicted in the painting uncovered in Siena's Palazzo Pubblico, a discovery that has thrown into doubt the attribution of Simone Martini's *Guidoriccio da Fogliano* (see p.306 for more on this controversy).

Walkers might find the local *Comunità Montana dell'Amiata* office of use, and there are three small **hotels** if you find yourself stuck: the *Gatto d'Oro*, Via dei Venti (☎ & fax 0564.967.074; ③); *Dayana*, Via Risorgimento (☎ & fax 0564.966.406; ③); and the *Toscana*, Via Lazzaretti 47 (☎0564.967.486, fax 0564.967.000; ④).

More tempting on the horizon is **CASTEL DEL PIANO**, the main commercial town of this area. It doesn't really live up to the promise, though the **old centre** warrants a quick wander, with its covered market, Palazzo Pretorio and Romanesque San Leonardo. Many of its churches are lumbered with the seventeenth-century works of the Nasini, a three-generation dynasty of second-rate painters, all of whom were born in the town: their work is also found in the abbey at Abbadia San Salvatore.

There is a **tourist office** at Via Marconi 9 (☎0564.955.284) and a broad range of **hotel** choices, the best value being the *Poli*, Piazza Garibaldi (☎0564.955.287; ②). There is also a **campsite**, the *Amiata*, Via Roma 15 (☎0564.955.107; open all year). The town is also the biggest centre in the region for shopping and provisions.

Seggiano and Pescina

SEGGIANO is an old Etruscan centre, today distinguished principally by its Renaissance church of the **Madonna della Carità**, set in an olive grove just outside the village. It was built as a votive offering by the town's inhabitants in 1603 as thanks for deliverance from famine. They wouldn't be too impressed to see what's become of their labour of love, for the church has managed to have every one of its altarpieces stolen: grim modern paintings have taken their place. Better-educated thieves might have made for the nicely situated **Oratorio di San Rocco**, also on the village's outskirts, whose *Madonna Enthroned* (1493) by Girolamo di Domenico is by far the best of the paintings in the immediate vicinity. Nearby, also in a beautiful setting, is a tiny fortified hamlet, Potentino.

Five very winding kilometres east of Seggiano is **PESCINA**, which deserves mention for its superlative **restaurant**, *Le Silene*, which doubles as a modest hotel. It is visited by people from miles around so book ahead to secure a table, especially for Sunday lunch (☎ & fax 0564.950.805; ③). If you don't fancy eating, allow a couple of minutes for the little **parish church**, which has a *Madonna and Child* by Lucca di Tommè, an underrated fourteenth-century Sienese painter with works scattered across southern Tuscany.

South to Saturnia and Manciano

Around 14km from Arcidosso, **TRIANA** stands on the junction of the roads west to Grosseto and south to Saturnia and Pitigliano. A perfect little fortified hamlet, it commands huge views from its castle. If you have a car, a rewarding detour off the road south is to follow the new highway to Grosseto as far as Roccalbegna. Relying on buses, however, this only really makes sense if you're making for Grosseto: two buses cover the route daily.

Roccalbegna

ROCCALBEGNA is one of the finest villages in southern Tuscany: aerial pictures of its perfect medieval streets decorate many local tourist offices, but barely hint at the rugged grandeur of its position, perched 522m up the slopes of Monte Labbro above the Albegna valley. Although the place is not on any obvious route, and visitors are few, the detour here is more than worthwhile, and there's a single **hotel** if you want to stay – the *Albergo-Ristorante La Pietra*, Via XXIV Maggio (☎0564.989.019; ②).

The **Rocca** of the town's name is obvious from afar, poised on a crag that rises almost to a pyramid above the village. Like so many in the region, it formed a defensive retreat for the Aldobrandeschi, overlords of the Maremma for several centuries. A superb walk to the top starts from the Piazza IV Novembre at the far end of the village: turn left up Salita Sasso (a yellow sign), go past the *Bar-Tabacchi* and it's then ten minutes up the winding lane and a final scramble to the fortifications. The views over the wild and rocky countryside are tremendous, though outdone by the famed vista over the village's grid of streets. The local saying "se il sasso scrocca, addio la Rocca" (If the rock crumbles, it's goodbye to the village) seems incontrovertible from this point.

In the village, be sure to look in on the Romanesque church of **SS. Apostoli Pietro e Paolo**, noted for its medieval interior and patches of fresco, but more for a tremendous triptych of the *Madonna and Child with SS. Peter and Paul* (1340) by Ambrogio Lorenzetti. It's astonishing to find a painting here, in the middle of nowhere, by one of Siena's finest – the artist was responsible for the frescoes of *Good and Bad Government* in Siena's Palazzo Pubblico. In a touching detail, Lorenzetti has painted the Madonna affectionately clasping the Child's foot. Note too, the cherries held in the Infant's hands, symbols of Heaven, eternal life and the rewards of a righteous life. Next door to the church, up some steps in Via Campana, is the small **Oratorio del Crocifisso**, now a small museum (open on request). Its high altar contains a fourteenth-century painted Crucifix (1360) by Luca di Tommè, whose presence in Roccalbegna is no accident – Lorenzetti was his main influence.

South to Saturnia

Moving south to Saturnia, there are a couple of minor places of note. **PETRICCI**, 5km south of Triana, has a **hotel**, the *Ristorante-Albergo La Cerinella* (☎ & fax 0564.984.015; ②). Another 5km on you reach **SEMPRONIANO**, a crumbling half-forgotten village centred on another Aldobrandeschi castle. Its Romanesque church, **SS. Vincenzo e**

Anastasio, has a painting of a dragon supposedly slain nearby and placed in the castle for public edification. By contrast, neighbouring Romanesque **Santa Croce** has a noted wooden medieval Crucifix. On a minor road 5km to the east is the virtually abandoned hamlet of **ROCCHETTE**, sited below a castle on a spur overlooking the Albegna valley. If you make the detour you'll find one of the prettiest places for miles, along with some cracking views.

Saturnia: Le Cascatelle

Word is spreading about the sulphurous hot springs at **SATURNIA**, as the almost year-round convoys of battered Volkswagen campers and crowds of noisy Italians testify. Nonetheless, they're not that easy to find. If all you want is a dip you should initially ignore the hill-town and follow the road south towards Montemerano. A large **spa complex** – with fierce admission charges, a vast pool and a five-star hotel – is signposted to the left, and about 200m on (as the road takes a sharp curve) a dirt track heads off straight, unsignposted but usually signalled by a cluster of cars and vans. Two minutes' walk from here brings you to the **cascatelle**, sulphur streams and springs which burst from the ground, forming natural rock-pool jacuzzis of warm water, in which you can lie around for hours submerged up to your neck. Entrance is unrestricted and free, and even on cold days there are invariably a few people ready to indulge. The heavy pedestrian traffic means there's a bit of litter, but apart from a small café, there's no commercialism at all.

The bubbling main pool is a bizarre sight, the water an intense turquoise, and all the more surreal if the weather is overcast and the steam rising overhead. The place also has something of a cult aspect, and it's not unusual for parties to come up at night from Rome. Rumour has it, however, that the water here has already been channelled through the resort's treatment centre: not a very nice thought, and perhaps enough to discourage bathing in the April to October spa season.

ACCESS AND ACCOMMODATION

There are two daily **buses** along the road between Santa Fiora and Manciano: be sure to get out at the springs (*Le Terme*) and not at Saturnia village; hitching should be reasonably easy, as there's usually someone heading for the springs.

If you intend to **stay** near the springs, you'll need a shower to wash off the sulphur smell, which is not too noticeable when bathing, but can linger for days. The nearest **hotel** is the excellent two-star *Albergo-Ristorante Stellata* (☎0564.602.978; ⑤), in an isolated spot 1km down from the falls on the road to Manciano (it's signposted left on a dirt road). The nearest **campsite**, *La Ciabatta*, is 4km down the same road at Montemerano.

All the other accommodation possibilities are in Saturnia proper, a fairly unassuming place. Camper vans are allowed to park overnight in the more modern of the main squares, and there are a couple of **hotels** – the *Saturnia*, Via Mazzini 4 (☎ & fax 0564.601.007; ④), and *Villa Clodia*, Via Italia 43 (☎0564.601.212, fax 0564.601.1305; ④), which is tucked away in one of the village's nicer quarters. When all's said and done, perhaps the best reason to come here is a **restaurant**, the appealing *Bacco e Cerere*, Via Mazzini 4 (☎0564.601.235; closed Tues). The service is friendly, the atmosphere intimate (room for just thirty diners) and the food – puddings especially – worth every one of the L55,000 it'll cost to do the job properly.

Montemerano and Manciano

Midway between Saturnia and Manciano lies **MONTEMERANO**, a medieval hill-village (with modern component below) cannily fortified on two levels, its balconies and interlocked alleys decked with a more than usual abundance of geraniums and

The Duomo, Siena

The Palio, Siena

Orvieto

Cappella Nuova, the Duomo, Orvieto

San Michele, Bevagna

Ponte delle Torri, Spoleto

In the Monte Sibillini, overlooking the Piano Grande

Lago Trasimeno

Olive oil production

Assisi

other hanging greenery. A fascinating church and exceptional restaurant are gradually bringing the tourists in, but for the time being it remains a pretty and all-but-undocumented little gem. Come in August and you can partake in the annual tripe festival.

Once you have pottered around the streets – which will take only a few minutes – head for **San Giorgio**, a prettily frescoed little church full of artistic treasures. The first is a wooden bas-relief of the *Assumption* (1455–65) by Vecchietta, a painter who also successfully turned his hand to sculpture: it's located a short way down the nave on the right (south) wall. Beyond it, by the door at the end of this wall, is a faded fresco of *St Orsola*. Ahead, at the bottom of the arch to the right of the high altar, is the winsome and wonderfully titled *Madonna della Gattaiola*, literally the "Madonna of the Cat-flap", painted around 1450 by an anonymous follower of Sassetta known as the "Master of Montemerano". Originally one half of an *Annunciation* (note the Virgin's Bible, a feature of such paintings), the picture probably formed part of an organ or double-doored tabernacle (the archangel Gabriel would have occupied the second panel). It was then used as the door to a granary, probably the point at which it received the hole in the bottom right of the Virgin's cloak which led to its nickname. All this is simply a light-hearted prelude to the church's real highlights, namely a polychrome wooden statue of *St Peter* (1455–60), another work by Vecchietta (left of the high altar steps), and a glorious fifteenth-century polyptych by Sano di Pietro of the *Madonna and Child with SS. Peter, George, Lawrence and Anthony of Padua*.

If you want to **stay** in or around the village, the smart three-star *Oliveto* (☎0564.602.849, fax 0564.602.639; ⑤) is the upmarket choice, located on the outskirts of the village, near the turn-off for Saturnia. A cheaper alternative is the one-star *Laudomia* (☎0564.620.062, fax 0564.620.013; ②) at Poderi di Montemerano, midway between Montemerano and Manciano. For centuries a coaching inn, it has an attractive, antiques-crammed **restaurant** to go with its handful of rooms. About 2km north of Montemerano is the pastorally situated *Acqua Viva* (☎0564.602.890, fax 0564.602.895, *acquaviva@laltramaremma.it*; ⑥), a definite – if expensive – first-choice treat, with rooms in two attractively converted buildings, surrounded by the hotel's own wine estate. You might be better off, however, saving money on accommodation and splashing out on a meal at the Michelin-starred restaurant *Da Caino*, Via Canonica 3 (☎0564.602.817; closed all day Wed & lunchtime Thurs except in summer). The coveted Michelin rosette is not the recommendation in Tuscany it might be elsewhere, but here it reflects absolutely first-class cooking. There are just 24 covers, so booking is essential, and you're looking at around L80,000 if you're going to stretch the chef. For about half this you can eat at the *Enoteca dell'Antico Frantoio*, Piazza Solferino 7 (☎0564.602.615; closed Tues except in summer), which, if it weren't for its exalted neighbour, would be considered excellent in its own right. Much the same goes for the *Osteria Passaparola*, Via del Bivio 16 (☎0564.602.827; closed Thurs), which also offers a handful of rooms (②).

Manciano

MANCIANO, though hardly somewhere you'd make a special journey for, is an attractive market town, with a medieval quarter grouped around a Sienese fortress, and a plentiful supply of bars in which to soak up its small-town atmosphere.

As well as a supplies stop, Manciano is an important hub of the southern Tuscan **bus** network. RAMA buses leave from the bottom of Via Marsala, the street that leads from the roundabout up to the old town; you can get tickets from the tobacconist's at no. 57. Services include four daily to Grosseto (via Orbetello and Albinia), three to Saturnia, one to Scansano and five to Pitigliano. It's unlikely you'll want to stay in the town, but if stranded there are four **hotels**, most central of which is the *Rossi*, Via Gramsci 2 (☎ & fax 0564.629.248, *hotelrossi@laltramaremma.it*; ④).

Pitigliano and around

PITIGLIANO, the largest town in Tuscany's deep south, is best approached along the road from Manciano, to the west. As you approach, it soars above on a spectacular outcrop of tufa, with medieval buildings perched above the valley floor, and its quarters linked by the arches of an immense aqueduct. **Etruscan tombs** – some converted to storage cellars for wine – honeycomb the cliffs, a feature repeated all over the surrounding area.

Neolithic remains suggest a settlement on the site from earliest times, though it first rose to prominence as an Etruscan and later Roman town. In the early Middle Ages the town belonged to the ubiquitous Aldobrandeschi, who ruled it from nearby Sovana, then one of the clan's two principal southern Tuscan power bases. In 1293 it passed by marriage to the counts of Orsini, a major Roman family who produced three popes and countless cardinals, bishops and minor papal dignitaries. Under the clan the town became more important than Sovana, from which the bishopric was eventually transferred. Its ultimate fate (in 1608), like much of the region, was to become a part of the Grand Duchy of Tuscany. Pitigliano was also known for its thriving **Jewish community**, which flourished from around the fifteenth century until its annihilation in the last war.

It has today a slightly grim, occasionally sinister sort of grandeur, the result partly of its mighty fortress – dividing the upper town from the more modern lower suburb – and partly because of the tall alleys of the ghetto area. Seen on a sunny day, though, it is a gem of small-town Italy, seemingly populated entirely by old women knitting or lacemaking. Together with the villages of **Sorano** and **Sovana** it constitutes one of the most worthwhile and neglected spots in the province.

The Town

The major entry point to the medieval town is through **Piazza Petruccioli** – host to a car park, hotel and the main bus stop, and to a small belvedere that looks along the houses and cliffs on the town's southern edge. Immediately through the gate is the high-walled and rather claustrophobic Piazza Garibaldi, and beyond it the massive **aqueduct** (1543) and **fortress**, contemporary building projects completed in the sixteenth century under Giuliano da Sangallo, along with a complex string of fortifications. Within the fortress is the Renaissance **Palazzo Orsini**, home to the recently refurbished and well-designed **Museo Etrusco** (10am–1pm & 2.30–5.30pm; closed Wed; L5000), which houses an interesting collection of vases, jewellery and trinkets unearthed in the nearby Etruscan site of Poggio Buco. The palace (Tues–Sun 10am–1pm & 3–5.30pm; L5000) itself – which requires a separate admission – is also worthwhile. Begun in the thirteenth century, it was extended by Niccolò Orsini two centuries later. The ramp leading to the main entrance arch has a small pillar decorated with a text lauding Gian Francesco Orsini, responsible for instigating the nearby aqueduct: it also contains a crest bearing the Orsini's family arms, which consists of the head of a lion and a bear, the latter a pun on the clan's name (*orso* means bear in Italian); the same arms appear on the fine well in the courtyard. Inside, much of the palace has been restored, bringing new lustre to a succession of lovely Tuscan ceilings and interiors. All manner of jewellery, vestments and other ecclesiastical ephemera litter the rooms, with just valuable works of art as distraction: a wooden *Madonna and Child* attributed to Jacopo della Quercia and a painting of the *Madonna Enthroned* (1494) by Guidoccio Cozzarelli. There are also two works by **Francesco Zuccarelli** (1702–88), who was born in the town but worked mainly in Venice and London.

More absorbing exhibits are on show in the new **Museo della Civaltà Giubonnai**, located in a series of cellars beneath the fortress which were discovered by accident during a clean-up. Some of the labyrinth had remained unseen and untouched for three hundred years; other parts had been filled with rubble during Sangallo's work on the foundations. The collection, growing all the time, centres on folk, domestic and agricultural ephemera of the Maremma. At present you need to make an appointment (☎0564.615.243) with the curator, but the hope is to fix regular hours and admission.

The fortress backs onto **Piazza della Repubblica**, the town's elongated and beautiful main square, its symmetry accentuated by a pair of fountains and immaculately pollarded ilex trees. Wander over to the balcony for a panorama taking in the river, trees, waterfalls and the faint outline of Monte Amiata away to the north.

Beyond lies the old town proper, a tight huddle of arches, alleys and medieval streets. It consists of three main streets, merging into one at the end of the town. Taking the left fork out of the square, Via Zuccarelli brings you to the ruins of the **synagogue** – its rusted gates are the only identifying sign, despite the claims of the local tourist pamphlet that restoration is under way. The Jewish community moved here in 1649, from nearby Castro, which Pope Innocent X had ordered to be destroyed. A couple of minutes' walk beyond, the road comes to an end by the Renaissance church of **Santa Maria**, its door flanked by the arms of the Orsini family. To the left of the main door under the tower, note the twelfth-century bas-relief depicting a human figure and two winged dragons. Inside, the church preserves a few patches of fresco, less interesting than the building's peculiar trapezoidal plan. Nearby, immediately outside the Porto Capisotto and the medieval ramparts, is a stretch of **Etruscan wall**.

Heading back to Piazza della Repubblica, Via G. Orsini brings you to Piazza Gregorio VII and the Baroque **Duomo**, with its butter-coloured stucco facade and giant campanile, the latter a surviving portion of a much earlier Romanesque church on the site. The western end of the square features a prominent travertine pillar (1490) with another text praising the Orsini. The third street of the grid, **Via Roma**, best encapsulates the town's provincial feel, a collection of odd, half-empty shops giving off a smell of mothballs; here, as elsewhere, the main pleasure is exploring the arches and alleys that lead off the main street.

Pitigliano practicalities

Pitigliano has a summer **tourist office** on Via Roma (10am–1pm & 2.30–6pm). The town doesn't exactly buzz with visitors, though, and with luck you should find room at its single **hotel**, the *Albergo Guastini* on Piazza Petruccioli (☎0564.616.065, fax 0564.616.652, *htlguastini@laltramaremma.it*; ②); the hotel is happier doing full-board deals, which is no problem as the rates are reasonable and the food fair. An out-of-town alternative is the *Albergo Corano* (☎0564.616.112, fax 0564.614.191; ③), a modern place with a pool; it's located just beyond the village of Madonna delle Grazie on the road to Manciano.

The best **restaurant**, if you don't eat at the *Guastini*, is a tiny wooden-beamed trattoria, *Del Orso*, on Via Roma. The town's one stab at **nightlife** is the *Birreria dell'Orso*, Piazza Gregorio VII, good for beer and snacks, and with outside tables next to the duomo. The local **wine**, Bianco di Pitigliano, hard to find elsewhere, is sold at two good-value outlets on Via Santa Chiara (off Piazza Petruccioli) and celebrated in a September **wine festival**.

There's a reasonable **bus** service (pick-up and drop-off in Piazza Petruccioli), with three departures daily to Grosseto via Manciano, three to Orbetello (weekdays only), four to San Quírico. A school bus serves Sovana and Sorano at 1.30pm from Monday to Saturday.

Sovana

Fine Etruscan tombs and pristine Romanesque architecture would place **SOVANA** firmly on the tour circuit, if only it were closer to Siena or Florence. As it is, you can explore this breathtaking, part-abandoned medieval centre in virtual solitude – save at weekends, when Romans and, increasingly, northern Europeans flock to the place.

The town dates to at least the seventh century BC, when the Etruscans took up residence. It fell to the Romans in the third century BC, later becoming a Lombard fiefdom. The town's principal monuments, though, derive from its time as the capital of the **Aldobrandeschi**, a noble clan whose domain extended over much of southern Tuscany and northern Lazio; they were said to have a castle for every day of the year. Their golden age came with the birth in Sovana in 1020 of a scion, Hildebrand, who in 1073 was to become Pope Gregory VII, a great reformer who also kept a favourable eye on family business. Decline set in during the fourteenth century, when Sovana's low-lying position made it vulnerable both to malaria and Sienese attacks, and its population and power drifted to nearby Pitigliano. Siena took control of the town in 1410, ceding power to the Grand Duchy of Tuscany in 1557. Today, Sovana's residents number just 123.

The village

Sovana's main street, **Via di Mezzo**, is almost the sum of the place, a broad expanse of fishbone-patterned brick paving, laid in 1580 by Ferdinand I de' Medici and recently restored to impressive effect. Guarding its start are the ruins of the Aldobrandeschi castle, built in the eleventh century on Etruscan foundations: it fell into greater disrepair with each of its subsequent owners – the Sienese, Orsini and Medici, who tried to repopulate the place in the seventeenth century by importing 58 families from Albania.

At its end, the street swells slightly to form the **Piazza del Pretorio**, a perfect medieval ensemble dominated on the left by **Santa Maria**, one of the most beautiful churches in southern Tuscany. Built in the thirteenth century to a Romanesque-Gothic plan, it has a simple stone interior dominated by an exquisite **ciborium**, a unique piece of pre-Romanesque paleo-Christian sculpture from the eighth or ninth century. Such canopies disappeared from churches in about the thirteenth century, confirming the work's far earlier provenance. Superbly preserved early frescoes around the walls set the seal on a marvellous building.

Opposite the church is the low-arched **Loggia del Capitano**, whose stone coats of arms proclaim Medici possession, and whose arches conceal a nice bar with a handful of outdoor tables. Next to it is the thirteenth-century **Palazzo Pretorio**, home to a small **museum and gallery** (Tues–Sat 10am–1pm & 2.30–5.30pm; L3000) which traces the area's history, paying particular attention to local Etruscan tombs and discoveries. Particularly illuminating are the reconstructions of how tombs might originally have looked, well worth seeing if you intend to head out and explore the necropolis (see below). The nine stone banners here are those of the town's Sienese and Medici governors. The little pillar to the right of the main door was used to pin up public declarations.

From the square a back lane to the left leads through gardens and olive groves to the huge **Duomo**, or Cattedrale di SS. Pietro e Paolo (closed 1–3pm), whose exterior wall and superb portal bear some of the finest Lombard-Romanesque carvings in Tuscany. The church's nucleus went up in the eighth century (the date of many of the carvings) or possibly earlier – it's known the town was a centre of a diocese in the sixth century – and was augmented in the tenth with the addition of an apse and crypt. The bare, triple-naved **interior** features some twelfth-century carved capitals, reminiscent of the Benedictine work in Sant'Antimo: the finest is that on the second pillar in the left aisle, a work which suggests the hand of Lombard masons. There are also traces of fresco, a fine Gothic font and a wonderful **crypt**, divided into five tiny naves by ancient columns. Sadly, the crypt has been closed off to the public and you can now only peer in rather than wander around. The **urn** in the main church contains the remains of St Mamiliano, a sixth-century saint who evangelized much of the region.

Beyond the duomo you can walk down to an old town **gateway** and traces of Etruscan wall, or turn back to Piazza Pretorio along the village's modest residential street, which sports a couple of shops and little more.

The Etruscan tombs

All round Sovana, but especially on the road to Saturnia, **Etruscan tombs** riddle the countryside, many approached by original "sunken" Etruscan roads. Why these roads should be sunken still puzzles scholars: some believe the purpose was defensive, in that they would enable people to move unseen from town to town; others posit that they were used for moving livestock, and were cut below ground level to prevent the animals from straying. The larger graves are well marked off the road by yellow signs. The necropolis as a whole, of which the marked tombs form a tiny part, extends for miles and rates in archeological (if not tourist) terms with the graves at Tarquinia and Cerveteri. Most of the tombs date from the seventh century BC and just about every type of Etruscan grave is present, including *colombari*, small niches cut into the rock to take cinerary urns. What the tombs lack in paintings they often make up for with elaborate carvings.

The key tombs are the **Tomba Ildebranda** (10am–dusk; L5000), considered the best single tomb in Tuscany, its fame causing it to be fenced off and an admission fee for viewing it applied. If you take the road to Saturnia, however, tombs start to appear after the tunnel, all of which can be visited free. Among others, you pass the **Poggio Pesca** and the **Pola**, a couple of minutes' uphill scramble from the road.

Sovana practicalities

Sovana presents some genuine medieval charm, and though a bit twee and touristy does offer two good **hotels**. Opposite Santa Maria is the *Albergo-Ristorante Etrusca* (☎0564.616.183, fax 0564.614.193; ④), a tiny place that's worth booking to be sure of a room. The *Etrusca*'s **restaurant** is absolutely first-rate, its beautifully elegant interior scattered with covetable antique furniture; expect to part with L40,000–45,000. Just off the piazza is the recently refurbished *Hotel Scilla* (☎0564.616.531, fax 0564.614.329; ④), whose restaurant also has a beautiful setting, with a pergola draped in flowers and greenery. There's also a pizzeria, *La Tavernetta*, midway down Via di Mezzo (closed Thurs).

Sorano

All the approaches to **SORANO** are extraordinary: from the south the route is lined with caves and tombs cut into the hillside; from the west, the road is cut into walls of tufa. The village, visible for miles on either approach, has a decidedly weird feel, with only a fraction of the old houses still lived in. Parts of the tangled streets suggest a faded grandeur, others are desolate and derelict. Landslips are the main problem, several streets having been declared terminally uninhabitable after one big slide. Attempts to keep Sorano alive have included a policy of sponsoring ceramic workshops and various other arts and crafts businesses. The small **tourist office**, Piazza Busati, makes a point of promoting these, and will also help if you want guidance around the wealth of Etruscan remnants in the valley.

The village itself is full of intriguing medieval corners, but has little in the way of specific sights. The old castle, the **Masso Leopoldino**, dominates the centre but offers no more than views from its aerial-ringed battlements. The more impressive fortress as you enter the town is the **Fortezza Orsini**, a blunt and perfectly preserved piece of Renaissance military engineering. Built over an old Aldobrandeschi fort in 1552, it was often besieged but never captured.

Nearby Sovana is perhaps a better overnight option, but if you need to stay Sorano has a couple of **hotels**, the one-star *La Botte* (☎0564.638.633, fax 0564.638.535; ③) or the smarter *Della Fortezza* (☎0564.632.010, fax 0564.633.209; ⑤), situated inside the fortress.

San Quírico

From Sorano there are constant views over the wooded gorge of the River Lente, whose rushing waters echo through the streets. Down on the valley floor, tantalizing ancient tracks crisscross the countryside, linking clearly visible rock tombs, Roman wells and old watermill workings.

Five kilometres east of Sorano is the hamlet of **SAN QUÍRICO**, to the north of which you can explore the **Rupestre di Vitozza**, a series of two hundred tombs, grottoes and paleo-Christian remains, and the remnants of Vitozza, San Quírico's medieval antecedent. The village has a salubrious two-star **hotel**, the *Agnelli* (☎ & fax 0564.619.015; ②); the hotel **restaurant** has a great village atmosphere and serves up surprisingly good fish and seafood (bought in fresh daily). Prices are keen, making it extremely popular with locals, and there are pizzas too.

travel details

TRAINS

Siena–Chiusi (10 daily; 1hr 30min) via Asciano (35min) and Sinalunga (1hr).

Siena–Asciano–Sant'Angelo–Grosseto (3 daily).

Siena–Buonconvento–Grosseto (3 daily).

Sinalunga to: Arezzo (12 daily; 1hr); Monte San Savino (12 daily; 35min).

Chiusi to: Arezzo (hourly; 1hr); Cortona (hourly; 20min).

BUSES

Abbadia San Salvatore to: Arcidosso (6 daily); Buonconvento (6 daily); Chiusi (3 daily); Grosseto (6 daily); Montepulciano (1 daily); Santa Fiora (6 daily); Siena (2 daily).

Chiusi to: Chianciano (14 daily; 30min); Montepulciano (14 daily; 45min).

Montalcino to: Buonconvento (hourly).

Montepulciano to: Buonconvento (7 daily; 1 hr); Chianciano (every 30min; 25min); Chiusi (every 30min; 50min); Pienza (7 daily; 20min); San Quírico d'Órcia (7 daily; 40min); Torrenieri (7 daily; 50min).

Pitigliano to: Grosseto via Manciano (3 daily); Orbetello (3 daily – weekdays only); San Quírico (4 daily); Sovana and Sorano (1 daily Mon–Sat); Viterbo (1 daily).

Torrenieri to: Arcidosso (6 daily; 40min); Buonconvento (6 daily; 25min); Grosseto (2 daily; 1hr 20min); Montalcino (15 daily; 20min).

CHAPTER NINE

AREZZO PROVINCE

Upstream from Florence, the Arno valley – the **Valdarno** – is a solidly industrialized district, with warehouses and manufacturing plants enclosing many of the small towns strung along the train line. Some of the villages up on the valley sides retain an appealing medieval square or a cluster of attractive buildings but there's no very compelling stop before you reach the provincial capital of the upper Arno region, **Arezzo**, one hour's train ride from Florence. This solidly bourgeois city has its share of architectural delights – including one of the most photogenic squares in central Italy – though the droves of foreign visitors who travel to Arezzo come to see one thing: the fresco cycle by **Piero della Francesca** in the church of San Francesco. These are not the only crowds to fill Arezzo's hotels, for Italians flock here in even greater numbers for antiques, traded each month on the Piazza Grande in quantities scarcely matched anywhere else in the country.

For visitors on the trail of the masterpieces of Tuscan art, there are two essential calls in the vicinity of Arezzo. The first is the modest hill-town of **Monterchi**, where della Francesca painted one of the most powerful images of the Renaissance, the pregnant *Madonna del Parto*. Two other magnificent works by the same artist are to be seen in his birthplace, **Sansepolcro**, almost on the Umbrian border to the east and one of the pleasantest Tuscan backwaters.

Art is far from being this province's sole attraction. In the **Casentino**, the stretch of the Arno valley between Arezzo and the source of the river to the north, small hill-towns such as **Poppi** and **Bibbiena** stand above a terrain of vineyards and pastures, cradled by thickly wooded upland. The secluded peaks of the Casentino also harbour two of Italy's most influential monasteries, **Camaldoli** and the Franciscan sanctuary of **La Verna**, Tuscany's holiest pilgrimage site. The ancient woodlands cradling these sanctuaries have been protected within the new **Parco Nazionale delle Foreste Casentinesi**, an area that extends across the surprisingly high, wild and forested border country of northern Tuscany into Emilia-Romagna. The park is being actively promoted, and there are good maps, park centres and marked (and unmarked) trails if you want to explore on the ground.

To the south of Arezzo stretches the agricultural plain of the **Valdichiana**, where the ancient hill-town of **Cortona** is the major attraction – and a nicer overnight stop than Arezzo – its steep streets forming a distinctive urban landscape and giving an unforgettable view over Lago Trasimeno and the hills to the west. It's also home to a

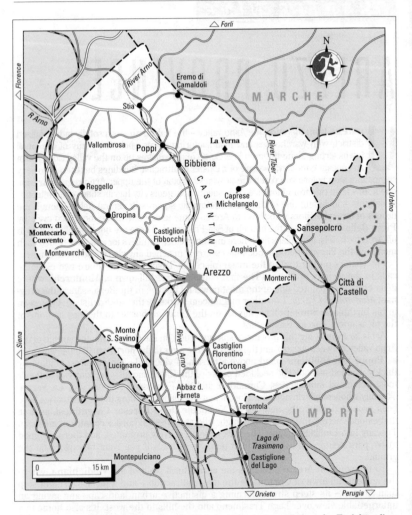

pair of excellent little galleries, one of which features major paintings by Fra' Angelico and locally-born Luca Signorelli.

Trains on the Florence–Rome rail line run up the Arno valley, through Arezzo and on down the Valdichiana: for Cortona the nearest station on this line is Camuccia, though more services stop at the more distant Terontola. For the Casentino, there's a private rail line which runs to the head of the valley from the main FS station at Arezzo. Otherwise, Arezzo and Cortona are the centres of overlapping **bus** networks, which between them cover most of Arezzo province – including major points on the Piero della Francesca trail. Note that if you bus to Sansepolcro, then the private FCU railway from here to Perugia by way of Città di Castello gives you another way into Umbria. Generally, though, a car is essential if you want to get to some of the region's remoter sights and back on the same day, or to get the most out of the wilder reaches.

Florence to Arezzo

If you're travelling by public transport from Florence to Arezzo there's no choice of route, as buses and trains all follow the **Valdarno**, just about the most unattractive stretch of waterway in Tuscany. Moving around by car, the obvious choice is between the two major roads that run roughly parallel to the river: the Autostrada del Sole and the SS69. If you want to cover the kilometres quickly, take the former; if you want to see the few sights of Valdarno, go for the latter, but be warned that the tarmac is perpetually clogged with lorries rumbling in and out of the industrial estates that pepper this part of the region. There is a third alternative, in the shape of the road that skirts the upland region known as the **Pratomagno**. It's a fairly tiring drive, with a gear-change required every couple of hundred metres, but at least the passengers have the benefit of the view across to Chianti, and there's the odd Romanesque church along the way if the blind corners get a bit too much.

The Valdarno route

River, rail line and autostrada come together at the bottleneck known as Incisa Valdarno, 25km out of central Florence. Petrarch grew up here and some vestiges of the old town are preserved – but insufficient to make the place appealing. **FIGLINE VALDARNO**, 5km south, was the birthplace of another eminent Tuscan, Marsilio Ficino, court philosopher to Lorenzo il Magnifico. The old quarter around Piazza Ficino has a few handsome buildings and one interesting interior – the frescoed **Collegiata di Santa Maria**, which contains a fourteenth-century *Madonna* by the so-called Maestro di Figline.

   SAN GIOVANNI VALDARNO, midway between Florence and Arezzo, is the most heavily industrialized but also the most rewarding town in the valley. The arcaded **Palazzo Comunale** is yet another design from Arnolfo di Cambio, who in the thirteenth century was put in charge of fortifying this Florentine town against the Aretines – the citizens of Arezzo. At the back of the palazzo, next to the church of Santa Maria della Grazia, the **Museo della Basilica di Santa Maria della Grazia** (Tues–Sat 10am–12.30pm & 4–7pm, Sun 4–7pm; free) in Piazza Masaccio houses a Fra' Angelico *Annunciation* painted for the Convento di Montecarlo, plus a lovely version of the same subject by his obscure contemporary, Jacopo del Sellaio. Also on show is a *Madonna and Child with Four Saints*, attributed to Masaccio, who was born at San Giovanni in 1401. His house, the **Museo Casa Masaccio** at Corso Italia 83, is open for temporary exhibitions only (for details ring ☎055.912.421). The Gothic church of San Francesco, at right angles to Santa Maria, is blotched with frescoes as well.

   In the Pliocene era the Valdarno was a vast lake, its shores patrolled by troops of prehistoric elephants. Fossil remnants of these colossal beasts are the pride of **MONTE-VARCHI**, where they are installed at Via Poggio Bracciolini 36–38 in the **Museo Paleontologico** (Tues–Sat 9am–12.30pm & 4–6pm, Sun 10am–noon; L5000); around 1500 other exhibits keep them company. In the centre of town in Via Isidoro del Lungo, the sacristy of the **Collegiata di San Lorenzo** has been converted into a small Museo di Arte Sacra (Tues, Thurs & Sat 10am–noon, otherwise opened by appointment with the sacristan; ☎055.980.468; L3000), which has a little chapel covered in ceramics by Andrea della Robbia. In the church there's a reliquary containing one of Tuscany's more desperate holy mementos – water from a spring in a cave where the Holy Family are said to have rested on the flight into Egypt.

   This might not seem reason enough to stop on the way to Arezzo; beyond Montevarchi, there's no reason at all, unless, that is, you have time to take a meandering diversion off the SS69 into the southeastern corner of the Chianti hills. If you do, you should arm yourself with a large-scale road map and follow the road to Mercatale, then take the turning for Bucine; from this road you can reach the fortified hill-top eyrie of **SAN LEOLINO**, which gives fabulous views. From there, head to **CENNINA**, where the castle ruins stare across the Arno towards the Pratomagno, then strike west for the highlight of this diversion, the completely unspoiled medieval village of **CIVITELLA**, with its magnificent ruined thirteenth-century castle. From here, it's just 8km to the autostrada, to the southwest of Arezzo.

The Pratomagno route

To maximize the pleasure of the wooded road above the east bank of the Arno, drive to Pontassieve and get onto the N70 towards the Passo della Consuma (see p.176). The first turning to the right rises to **VALLOMBROSA**, whose **abbey** is the mother foundation of the Vallombrosan order, established in 1038 by the Florentine Giovanni Gualberto (see p.106). When Giovanni was canonized in 1193 this abbey became extremely influential, and by the fifteenth century it was administering wide tracts of Tuscan territory. Much rebuilt since those days, it now resembles a fortified villa with its high perimeter wall and corner towers and impresses mainly by its location, pillowed against the fir-covered hills. Part of the complex is still occupied by monks, part by a forestry school; neither contingent welcomes visitors.

Milton stayed at Vallombrosa and in *Paradise Lost* he compared the throng of demons in hell to the "autumn leaves that strow the brooks/In Vallombrosa". Though the forests have dwindled in the intervening centuries, they are still extensive, as you'll appreciate if you drive over the Pratomagno ridge to Poppi (see p.424) through **MONTEMIGNAIO** – a beautiful route round the flank of Monte Secchieta. For a **walk** through the forests, as good a starting point as any is the tiny resort of Saltino, the next village after Vallombrosa along the road to Arezzo. From here paths lead up to the peak of Monte Secchieta, a winter ski resort (also accessible by road from the junction 5km east of Vallombrosa on the road to Montemignaio); the view from the summit is amazing.

Beyond Saltino the terrain opens out, with terraces bordering the road as it snakes down to Reggello, a diffused and characterless place much praised by connoisseurs of Tuscan olive oil. A kilometre to the south, the church of **San Pietro a Cascia** has some columns that might appeal to Romanesque cognoscenti. More Romanesque architecture appears at **PIAN DI SCÒ**, 10km on, where there's an eleventh-century *pieve*, as well as superb *agriturismo* **accommodation** at *Fattoria Casa Mora* (☎055.960.696; May–Sept; ④). Otherwise the only local accommodation is in Montemignaio, or more precisely the adjoining hamlet of Castello, namely the one-star *Il Castello*, Via Roma 56 (☎0575.542.012; ②) or the nearby two-star *Da Corrado*, Via Roma 2 (☎ & fax 0575.542.166; ②). More remote, mountain accommodation exists at over 1000m on the nearby Passo della Consuma – either the two-star *Miramonti*, Via Consumma 45 (☎0575.830.6566, fax 0575.830.6469; ②), which has rooms with and without private bathrooms, or two-star *Sbaragli*, Via Consuma 3 (☎0575.830.6651; ③).

CASTELFRANCO DI SOPRA, 2km farther, was yet another town fortified by Arnolfo di Cambio but the street plan and one gate are virtually the only traces of his handiwork; its most attractive feature is a much restored thirteenth-century *badia* on the main road. There's one hotel, the two-star *Colombo*, Via Europa 5 (☎055.914.9026; ②). Another 10km brings you to **LORO CIUFFENNA**, where ranks of new apartments form an unflattering prelude to a small medieval quarter down by the Ciuffenna river; a Romanesque tower and bridge form the core. A short distance south of Loro Ciuffenna, tucked into the hills at Penna Alta, you'll find the best **restaurant** along this route, the family-run *Il Canto di Maggio* (☎055.970.5147); the splendid Tuscan menu works out at around L50,000 per head.

The most substantial cultural site comes a couple of kilometres on, in the hamlet of **GROPINA**, which is reached by taking a steep and sharp left turn just outside Loro.

Here the parish church of **San Pietro** (daily 8am–noon & 4–7pm) has some of the finest Romanesque carving in Tuscany, dating from the early thirteenth century. The capitals depict knights, fighting animals and various standard motifs, but you'll have to travel a long way to find anything quite like the **pulpit**, with its knotted columns and rows of alarmed-looking figures with upraised arms.

The last place of any interest before Arezzo is **CASTIGLION FIBOCCHI**, whose central patch – now enclosed by light industry – is little changed since the Middle Ages; you'll get the measure of the place by driving through in low gear.

Arezzo

Maecenas, the wealthy patron of Horace and Virgil, was born in **AREZZO** and it's still a place with the moneyed touch. The economy rests on its jewellers and goldsmiths, a clan so numerous that the city has the world's largest gold manufacturing plant. Topping up the coffers are the proceeds of Arezzo's antiques industry: in the vicinity of the Piazza Grande there are shops filled with the sort of furniture you put in a vault rather than in your house, and every month the **Fiera Antiquaria** (see box p.419) turns the piazza into a vast showroom.

ACCOMMODATION	
Astoria	3
Ceccio	4
Continentale	5
La Toscana	2
Milano	6
Ostello Villa Severi	1

Occupying a site that controls the major passes of the central Apennines, Arezzo was one of the most important settlements of the Etruscan federation. It maintained its pre-eminence under Roman rule, and was a prosperous independent republic in the Middle Ages until, in 1289, its Ghibelline allegiances brought about a catastrophic clash with the Guelph Florentines at Campaldino. Arezzo temporarily recovered from this reversal under the leadership of Bishop Guido Tarlati, whose bellicosity earned him eventual excommunication. However, subjugation came about in 1384, when Florence paid the ransom demanded of Arezzo by the conquering army of Louis d'Anjou. When the French departed, the city's paymaster was left in power.

Even as a mortgaged political power, Arezzo continued to be a major cultural force – as it had been since Guido d'Arezzo, the first theorist of musical notation, was born here in the tenth century. Petrarch (1304–74) later brought further prestige to the city, and in the sixteenth century Pietro Aretino and Giorgio Vasari, both Aretines, further bolstered its reputation. Yet it was an outsider who gave Arezzo its greatest monument – **Piero della Francesca**, whose frescoes for the church of San Francesco belong in company with Masaccio's cycle in Florence and Michelangelo's in Rome.

Information and accommodation

The main **tourist office** is on the edge of the train station forecourt, on the right as you come out of the station (summer Mon–Sat 9am–1pm & 3–7pm, Sun 9am–1pm; winter Mon–Sat 9am–1pm & 3–6pm, plus first Sun of month 9am–1pm; ☎0575.377.678); the helpful staff speak English and have masses of information on Arezzo and its province. The **police station** is at Via Leone Leoni 15 (☎0575.21.351), the **post office** at Via Guido Monaco 34, and the **hospital** Via Pietro Nenni 17 (☎0575.3051). If you need a **taxi** try the rank in Piazza della Repubblica or call ☎0575.382.626.

Rooms are scarce at any time of year in Arezzo, and are almost impossible to come by on the first weekend of every month, owing to the antiques fair; in addition the town is booked solid at the end of August and beginning of September, when the *Concorso Polifonico Guido d'Arezzo* and the *Giostra del Saracino* follow in quick succession. Assured of regular bookings throughout the year, Arezzo's hoteliers seem to try that little bit less hard than many in the region.

Hotels

Astoria, Via Guido Monaco 54 (☎0575.24.361, fax 0575.24.362). A 32-room two-star right by the main post office; has been known to negotiate its prices during slack periods. Rooms with private baths L25,000 extra. ②.

Cecco, Corso Italia 215 (☎0575.20.986, fax 0575.356.730). Very central 42-room two-star: spacious if slightly institutional in feel. Rooms with private baths cost L20,000 more. ②.

La Toscana, Via M. Perennio 56 (☎0575.21.692). One-star with 11 rooms (plus five more in a *dipendenza*, or annexe) on the main road coming in from the west; cheaper and has more single rooms than any other one-star in town, and is far more salubrious. A private bathroom adds L15,000 to the price. ②.

Continentale, Piazza Guido Monaco 7 (☎0575.20.251, fax 0575.350.485). Large old three-star with restaurant right on the hub of the lower town. Excellent views from the roof terrace, but inferior overall to the nearby and marginally cheaper *Milano*. ⑤.

Milano, Via della Madonna del Prato 83 (☎0575.26.836, fax 0575.21.925). Centrally situated hotel, which has been upgraded from one to three stars but still offers good value for money. ⑤.

Hostel

Ostello Villa Severi, Via Francesco Redi 13 (☎ & fax 0575.299.047). In an old villa some way north of the town – a 15-min walk from the duomo past the old cemetery, or take bus #4 from Piazza Guido Monaco by the station. Reception open 8am–2pm & 5pm–midnight. Open June–Sept, plus Easter weekend, Christmas & New Year; L23,000 (half-board L41,000, full board L56,000).

The Town

There are two distinct parts to Arezzo: the **older quarter**, at the top of the hill, and the businesslike **lower town**. Most of the lower town remains hidden from day-trippers, as it spreads behind the **train station** and the adjacent **bus terminal**. From the station forecourt you go straight ahead for Via Guido Monaco, the traffic axis between the upper and lower town and a street that nobody walks along except to shop or to call at the main post office. The parallel **Corso Italia**, now pedestrianized, is the route to take up the hill, and the stretch immediately north of Via Francesco Crispi is also the place to hang out in the evenings; the *passeggiata* crowds – and the bars – thin out towards the top of the climb.

San Francesco – Piero della Francesca's church

Off to the left of the Corso, on Via Cavour, not far from its summit, stands the building everyone comes to Arezzo to see: the basilica of **San Francesco** (daily 8.30am–noon & 2.30–6.30pm). Built after 1322, the shabby brick basilica earned its renown in the early 1450s, when the Bacci family commissioned **Piero della Francesca** to continue the decoration of the choir. The project had been started by Bicci di Lorenzo, who had got no further than scenes of Heaven, Purgatory and Hell in the vault before he died. For the wall paintings, Piero's patrons nominated a subject with rather fewer dramatic possibilities, but which suited the contemplative personality of the artist perfectly: it inspired a work that carries an emotional charge unsurpassed by any other fresco cycle.

The theme chosen was **The Legend of the True Cross**, a story in which the physical material of the Cross forms the link in the cycle of redemption that begins with humanity's original sin. Starting with the right wall, Piero painted the series in narrative sequence, working continuously until about 1457 – the precise chronology isn't known. However, the episodes are not arranged in narrative sequence, the artist preferring to arrange them according to the precepts of symmetry: thus the two battle scenes face each other across the chapel, rather than coming where the story dictates. As is always the case with this mystical rationalist painter, smaller-scale symmetries are present in every part of the work: the retinue of the Queen of Sheba appears twice, in mirror-image arrangement, and the face of the queen is exactly the same as the face of the Empress Helena. This orderliness, combined with the pale light and the statuesque quality of the figures, create an atmosphere that's unique to Piero, a sense of each incident as a part of a greater plan.

Damp has badly damaged areas of the chapel and some bits have peeled away as a result of Piero's notoriously slow method of working. Most of the rest, however, has emerged in magnificent condition from the massive restoration that was planned for completion in 1992, the five-hundredth anniversary of Piero's death and was fully unveiled in February 2000. At present there is a **charge of L10,000** to view the paintings in guided groups, although this arrangement is subject to change. Contact the tourist office or call ☎0575.355.668 to check latest details and to avoid disappointment.

The literary source for the cycle, the medieval *Golden Legend* by Jacopo de Voragine, is a very convoluted story; the basilica plan on the following page is a basic guide to the events depicted. The *Annunciation* and two *Prophets* on the window wall are not explicitly related to the legend, but the former is pictorially linked to the narrative by its cruciform plan and by the visual allusion of the beam above the Virgin's head.

The Pieve di Santa Maria and Piazza Grande

A short distance to the west of San Francesco in Piazza di Badia, a huge Baroque tower signals the presence of the hulking **Badia**, otherwise known as the church of SS. Flora and Lucilla (Mon–Sat 8am–noon & 4–7pm; Sun 10.15am–12.30pm; & 7–9pm

THE LEGEND OF THE TRUE CROSS

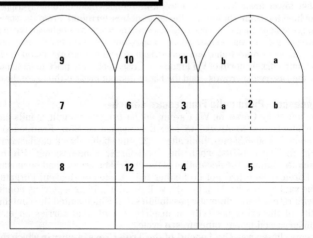

1a. Adam announces his death and implores Seth, his son, to seek the "oil of mercy" from the Angel of Eden.

1b. Instead the Angel gives Seth a sprig from the Tree of Knowledge, which is planted in the dead Adam's mouth.

2a. Solomon orders a bridge to be built from a beam fashioned from the tree that grew from Adam's grave. The Queen of Sheba, visiting Solomon, kneels in prayer before the bridge, sensing the holiness of the wood.

2b. The Queen of Sheba foresees that the beam will later be used to crucify a man, and that the death will bring disgrace to the Jews; she tells Solomon of her prophecy.

3. Solomon orders the beam to be buried.

4. The Emperor Constantine has a vision of the Cross, hearing a voice that declares "Under this sign shall you be victorious".

5. Constantine defeats the rival emperor Maxentius, and then is baptized.
An interesting historical note is that the figure of Constantine – the first emperor to rule the Byzantium – is a portrait of the Byzantine emperor John Paleologus, the last but one Byzantine emperor, who had been in Florence in 1439.

6. The Levite Judas, under torture, reveals to the servants of St Helena – mother of Constantine – the burial place of the three crosses from Golgotha.

7. The crosses are excavated; the true Cross is recognized when it brings about a man's resurrection. Arezzo – serving as Jerusalem – is shown in the background.

8. The Persian king Chosroes, who had stolen the Cross, is defeated by the Emperor Heraclius. On the right he kneels awaiting execution; behind him is visible the throne into which he had incorporated the Cross.

9. Heraclius returns the Cross to Jerusalem.   10. A prophet (by an assistant).

11. A prophet.   12. The Annunciation.

free). Inside, the main altarpiece by Giorgio Vasari is encased in a marble frame that looks like a monstrous sideboard. The generally inaccessible cloister refectory has a similarly heavy-footed example of Giorgio's output.

Farther up the Corso from San Francesco stands one of the finest Romanesque structures in Tuscany, the twelfth-century **Pieve di Santa Maria** (daily 8am–1pm & 3–6.30pm; free). Its arcaded facade, elaborate yet severe, belongs to a type associated more with Pisa and western Tuscany, and is doubly unusual in presenting its front to a fairly narrow street rather than to the town's main square. Dating from the 1210s, the carvings of the months over the portal are an especially lively group. The campanile, known locally as "the tower of the hundred holes", was added in the fourteenth century.

The oldest section of the chalky grey **interior** is the raised sanctuary, where the altarpiece is Pietro Lorenzetti's *Madonna and Saints* polyptych, painted in 1320 and horribly restored. The unfamiliar saint on the far left, accompanying Matthew, the Baptist and John the Evangelist, is St Donatus, bishop of Arezzo in the fifth century and martyred in the pagan backlash following the Goths' invasion. His relics are contained in a beautiful fourteenth-century gold and silver bust (1346), by an unknown local goldsmith, in the crypt.

The **Piazza Grande**, on the other side of the church, is a handsome if somewhat impractical public square, slanting down towards its fountain at a sweeping gradient. The *passeggiata* runs out of steam before reaching this altitude, and the piazza really comes alive for the *Fiera Antiquaria* and – more raucously – for September's *Giostra del Saraceno* (see p.419). A diverting assortment of buildings encloses the space, the wooden balconied apartments on the east side facing the apse of Santa Maria, the Baroque Palazzo dei Tribunali and the **Palazzetto della Fraternità dei Laici**, known for its outstanding **portal**, and in particular for the relief *Madonna della Misericordia* (1434) and its neighbouring niche statues. These are the work of Bernardo Rossellino, and were added to the earlier Gothic work below, which includes a lunette fresco of the *Pietà* by Spinello Aretino. The lovely arched loggia and cornice across the top of the palace are from yet another era – they date from 1460 and are the work of Giuliano da Settignano. The piazza's northern edge is formed by the arcades of the **Loggia di Vasari**, occupied by shops that in some instances still retain their original stone counters.

The Duomo and around

At the highest point of the town rises the large and unfussy **Duomo** (daily 7am–12.30pm & 3–6.30pm; free), whose harmonious appearance belies the protracted process of its construction. Begun in 1278, it was virtually finished by the start of the sixteenth century, but the campanile dates from 1859 and the facade from 1914.

The church's stained-glass windows, a rarity in Italy, were made around 1520 by Guillaume de Marcillat, an Arezzo-based Frenchman; they let in so little light that his other contributions to the interior – the paintings on the first three bays of the nave – are virtually impossible to see. Off the left aisle, separated from the nave by a huge screen, the Cappella della Madonna del Conforto has terracottas by the della Robbia family, but the best of the building's art works lie farther down the aisle. Just beyond the organ is the **tomb of Bishop Guido Tarlati** (died 1327), head of the *comune* of Arezzo during its resurgence in the early fourteenth century; the monument, plated with marble reliefs showing scenes from the militaristic bishop's career, was possibly designed by Giotto. The tiny fresco nestled against the right side of the tomb is **Piero della Francesca's** restored *Magdalene*, his only work in Arezzo outside San Francesco. The small Museo Diocesano (Thurs–Sat 9am–noon; L5000), alongside the duomo, won't make anyone's day.

Arezzo's public park, the **Passeggio del Prato**, extends from the east end of the duomo; the **Fortezza Medicea**, at its far end, is a good place to take a picnic and gaze down over the town or across the vineyards towards the Casentino. Cosimo I's fortress here was demolished in the eighteenth century, leaving only the ramparts.

Just south of the park and the duomo, at Vicolo dell'Orto 28, is the supposed birthplace of the poet Petrarch (1304–74), the **Casa Petrarca** (Mon–Sat 10am–noon & 3–5pm; free), rebuilt after its destruction during the war. It's for literary pilgrims only: all that's open to visitors is the library containing manuscripts and a letter signed by the poet.

San Domenico, Vasari's house and the art museum

A short distance in the opposite direction from the duomo is the church of **San Domenico** (daily 8am–noon & 3.30–5.30pm; free), constructed mostly in the late thirteenth century but with a Gothic campanile. It's more striking inside: the high altar has a dolorous Crucifix by **Cimabue** (1260), painted when the artist would have been about twenty, while tatters of fifteenth- and sixteenth-century frescoes all round the church create the effect of a gigantic picture album.

From here signs point the way to the **Casa di Giorgio Vasari** (Mon & Wed–Sat 9am–7pm, Sun 9am–12.30pm, closed Tues; free) at Via XX Settembre 55, designed by the biographer-architect-painter. Born in Arezzo in 1511, Vasari was taught to paint by his distant relative Luca Signorelli, and went on to become court painter, architect and general artistic supremo to Cosimo I. His major contribution to Western culture, however, is his *Lives of the Most Excellent Italian Architects, Painters and Sculptors*, the first attempt to relate artists' work to their social context, and a primary source for all histories of the Renaissance. Taking greater pleasure from the products of his imagination than later generations have managed to extract, Vasari frescoed much of his house with portraits and mythological characters, a decorative scheme that makes this one of the brashest domestic interiors in Tuscany. Portraits include his wife as the muse of conjugal love (in the "Chamber of Apollo") and Michelangelo and Andrea del Sarto (in the "Chamber of Fame"). Minor paintings are strewn all over the place, proof that Giorgio was far from the most inept painter of his day.

At the foot of the hill, at Via San Lorentino 8, the fifteenth-century Palazzo Bruni-Ciocchi houses the **Museo Statale d'Arte Medioevale e Moderna** (Tues–Sat 9am–7pm, Sun 9am–12.30pm; L8000), containing a collection of paintings by local artists and majolica pieces from the thirteenth to the eighteenth centuries, generously spread over three floors. Highlights are the first floor's medieval and Renaissance paintings by the likes of Spinello Aretino, Luca Signorelli, Vasari, Bartolomeo della Gatta, and – most beautifully – a *Madonna della Misericordia* by Spinello's son, Pari; devotees of ceramics will revel in the five rooms containing works from Deruta, Gubbio, Faenza and other traditional major Italian centres of production.

The Museo Archeologico

All the principal sights are in the upper part of Arezzo, with the exception of the **Museo Archeologico** (Mon–Sat 9am–2pm, Sun 9am–1pm; L8000), which occupies part of an abandoned monastery built into the wall of the town's Roman amphitheatre, to the right of the station at Via Margaritone 10. The desultory remains of the amphitheatre are part of the museum, but more impressive are the marvellously coloured **coralline vases**, produced here in the first century BC; they show why Arezzo's glassblowers achieved their reputation as consummate craftsmen throughout the Roman world. If you're here out of high season you may not be able to see them, though – the erratic opening hours of this museum reflect the low consumer demand, and it's often shut for days at a time in winter.

Eating and drinking

Though there's no cut-price gourmet experience to be had in Arezzo, the town's **restaurants** more than atone for its hotels, offering menus to suit every budget, at a generally reliable standard. The eateries below are listed in roughly ascending order of price. Nightlife goes on in **bars** around piazzas Guido Monaco, Grande and San Domenico. For a particularly good cup of **coffee**, visit the *Caffè Donatello*, Via Vittorio Veneto 125, where owner Maurizio Sestini roasts his own beans on the premises. If you're after picnic supplies, buy your **bread** at Pane e Salute, a 100-year-old bakery at Corso Italia 11. For **ice cream** the first choice is *Il Gelato*, off Corso Italia near the centre of town at Via de' Cenci 24.

Penny's Pub, Piazza Sant'Agostino 13. Good selection of sandwiches and snacks; open till 1am. Closed Mon.

La Torre di Gnicche, Piaggia San Martino. This fine little *enoteca* is just the place for a glass of wine, with its selection of local Colli Aretini and other Italian wines, plus snacks, cheeses, hams, and a handful of hot dishes. From L15,000–30,000; closed at lunch, all day Wed, one week in Aug and two weeks in Jan.

Otello, Piazza Risorgimento 16 (☎0575.22.648). Opposite the regional tourist office, close to the *Milano* hotel. Bright and trendy joint, with generally good if unambitious food. Closed Mon.

Il Saraceno, Via Mazzini 6 (☎0575.27.644). Family-run trattoria with a good wine cellar and menus of traditional Aretine specialities from around L30,000; pizzas too. Closed Wed and periods in Jan & July.

Antica Osteria L'Agania, Via Mazzini 10 (☎0575.25.381) A central, informal trattoria with welcoming atmosphere and local dishes (special emphasis on truffles and mushrooms in season), at around L30,000 per head – draws much of its clientele from the antiques dealers. Closed Mon & a period in June.

Le Tastevin, Via de' Cenci (☎0575.28.304). Highly recommended by Aretines for local, home-made food at about L30,000–45,000. Music in the central piano bar might not be to all tastes. Closed Sun except during market weekends, plus a period in Aug.

La Buca di San Francesco, Via San Francesco 1 (☎0575.23.271). Tourist-orientated place next to San Francesco, but not at all bad: it's been in business since 1929, and the interior preserves parts of the old Etruscan-Roman pavement and medieval frescoes. Food is reliable and Tuscan in inspiration, at around L45,000–60,000 per head. Closed Mon evening, Tues & July.

FESTIVALS

Arezzo's premier folkloric event is the **Giostra del Saraceno**, held in the Piazza Grande on the first Sunday in September. The day starts off with various costumed processions; in the afternoon the action switches to the jousting arena in the piazza. The piazza is the junction of the four quarters of the city and the sides of the square are decked with flags to mark their affiliations. Each quarter is represented by a pair of knights on horseback, who do battle with a wooden effigy of a Saracen king. In one hand it holds a shield marked with point scores, a bit like a darts-board; in the other it has a cat-of-three-tails which swings round when the shield is hit, necessitating nifty evasive action from the rider. A golden lance is awarded to the highest-scoring rider. In recent years this event has become so popular that reduced versions of the show have been staged in the summer; check at the tourist office for the latest information on dates and ticket availability.

The musical tradition that began with Guido d'Arezzo is kept alive chiefly through the international choral competition that bears his name: the **Concorso Polifonico Guido d'Arezzo**, held in the last week of August. The less ambitious **Pomeriggi Musicali** is a season of free concerts held in various churches, museums and libraries; on average there's one concert a week from mid-January to June. In late June and July the **Arezzo Wave** rock festival hits the Fortezza Medicea.

The **Fiera Antiquaria** takes over the Piazza Grande on the Saturday before the first Sunday of each month. The most expensive stuff is laid out by the Vasari loggia, with cheaper pieces lower down the square and in the side streets. The Roman numberplates in the car parks give you a clue as to what league this is; nothing – not even the old postcards – could be described as a bargain.

To Sansepolcro – the Piero trail

Arezzo is the springboard for one of Tuscany's most rewarding art itineraries – the Piero della Francesca trail, whose other stops lie east of the city at **Monterchi** and **Sansepolcro** (the artist's birthplace), and which continues in Perugia, where you'll find a stunning Piero altarpiece in the main art gallery (see p.449). There's no train link between Arezzo and Sansepolcro, the rail approach to Sansepolcro being the private FCU Terni–Perugia line. The SITA **bus** company runs seventeen services a day to Sansepolcro, nearly all of which continue to Città di Castello (see p.464) for train connections to Perugia; five departures stop at Monterchi at convenient times for a visit. Otherwise, the nearest regular stop to the village is Le Ville, 2km to the west, from where the buses veer away through Anghiari – a pleasant enough place, but best seen by car. If you don't have your own transport, hitching is a viable alternative, as this is a busy stretch of road.

Monterchi – the Madonna del Parto

The farming village of **MONTERCHI** is 25km east of Arezzo, and for the last few kilometres of the journey the roadsides bear signs for the **Madonna del Parto** – surely the only painting in Tuscany to be signposted as if it were a town. The sole representation of the pregnant Madonna in Renaissance art, the fresco was painted for a cemetery chapel that stands on the outskirts of Monterchi, and remained hidden under plaster for centuries before its rediscovery in 1889 – by which time the *St Lucy* and the *Pietà* that Piero also painted here had both been lost. The Madonna was removed to Sansepolcro after an earthquake damaged the chapel in 1917 but at the insistence of the local *comune* it was brought back here within five years. During World War II they became so worried that some misfortune might befall the fresco that a false wall was constructed to protect it, and since then the Madonna has received the attentions of a number of restorers.

Several years ago the fresco was moved from the cemetery chapel to an ex-primary school on Via della Reglia, there to undergo major restoration. Security was the reason given for the switch, but local feeling is that it's more to do with the restoration's sponsors, who are well served by the publicity which goes with the painting – publicity which might be unseemly around a cemetery chapel. It's best to park below the village just off the main road, and walk up the lane and steps to and straight through the village proper: the former school, an undistinguished building if ever there was one, lies on the far side just outside the old village walls. The painting looks likely to remain in its utilitarian box, despite the mutterings of many who feel its former home is more appropriate. It is the focal point of a permanent exhibition (Tues–Sun 9am–1pm & 2–7pm; L5000) recounting the technical details of the fresco's restoration, and also that of the San Francesco cycle in Arezzo. The picture is still an object of pilgrimage, and the museum is cleared when local pregnant women come to pray to the Virgin.

Despite the restoration, the colours of the *Madonna del Parto* lack the freshness of the Arezzo cycle, but even bleached to black and white this would be an overwhelming picture. Two attendant angels draw back the flap of a small pavilion to reveal the pregnant Virgin, who places her hand on the upper curve of her belly, her eyes downcast as if preoccupied with a foreknowledge of the course of the child's life. No other artist of the Renaissance produced anything comparable to its beautiful gravity.

Anghiari – and Michelangelo's birthplace

Most buses from Arezzo to Sansepolcro call at **ANGHIARI**, an agricultural hill-town set amid fields of sunflowers and tobacco plants, all thriving thanks to EU subsidies. The battle here between Florence and the Milanese army of Filippo Maria Visconti in 1440 was the subject of perhaps the most famous lost art work of the Renaissance, Leonardo da Vinci's fresco in Florence's Palazzo Vecchio. Anghiari's diminutive historic centre of narrow streets, stepped alleyways and tunnels commands a fine view across the upper Tiber towards Sansepolcro.

Michelangelo, effectively Leonardo's competitor in the decoration of the Palazzo Vecchio, was born 17km north of Anghiari in the place that now carries the name **CAPRESE MICHELANGELO** – it was just plain Caprese before the town's chief magistrate and his wife produced their precocious son. The ancient village is perched high on a cliff overlooking the car park, bus stop (regular services from Anghiari) and one of its two **hotels**, the *Buca di Michelangelo* (☎0575.793.921, fax 0575.793.941; ②). A stepped path rises from here through cypresses and allotments to the arched gateway. The castle and Michelangelo's supposed birthplace, the Casa del Podestà, have been converted into a **Museo Michelangelo** (Tues–Fri 10am–5pm, Sat & Sun 10am–6pm; L4000) in Via Capoluogo, where a few bits of Renaissance furniture and a load of plaster casts create the undernourishing experience that's typical of these shrines to the legendary. Sustenance of a different kind is to be found nearby at Alpe Faggeta, where the *Fonte della Galletta* restaurant offers excellent Tuscan food from L35,000 a head (closed Mon–Thur from Jan to March, Tues rest of year except July–Aug, when it is open daily). It forms part of the three-star *Il Faggetto* hotel, Località Alpe Faggetta (☎0575.793.925, fax 0575.793.652; ③). A cheaper accommodation option is the **hostel** in the nearby hamlet of *Fragaiolo*, *Ostello Michelangelo* (☎0575.792.092, fax 0575.793.994; L12,000; May–Sept).

There are some excellent **walks** in the surrounding hills. The best starts a short distance to the north of Caprese: follow the plunging road to Lama (2km), then take the turning for nearby *Fragaiolo*; from here a waymarked trail rises to La Verna (see p.424), a solid half-day's trek.

Sansepolcro

The SITA bus from Arezzo takes an hour to get to **SANSEPOLCRO**, an unassuming place which makes its way in the world as a manufacturer of lace and, more lucratively, pasta. If the historic district within the industrialized zones were a bit more substantial it could make a lot more money out of tourism; as it is, thousands of people come here each year to see **Piero della Francesca**'s *Madonna della Misericordia* and *Resurrection*, then leave a couple of hours later. There really isn't much more to the place than these pictures, but it's a relaxing, friendly town, and has a couple of fine restaurants to complete the day.

Born here at some time around 1420, Piero spent much of his life in the isolation of what was then the village of Borgo San Sepolcro; a three-year sojourn in Florence was probably his longest continuous absence. Patrons in Ferrara, Rome and Urbino called upon his services, even though his creative process was so painstaking that on one occasion his father had to apologize to a client for Piero's slowness. He returned to Sansepolcro in the 1470s, having abandoned painting as his eyesight failed. Most of his last twenty years were devoted to working on his treatises *On Perspective in Painting* and *On the Five Regular Bodies*, in which he propounded the geometrical rules that determine all accurate representation of the world, and extolled the human form as the exemplar of perfect proportion.

The Museo Civico

The **Museo Civico** is at Via Niccolò Aggiunti 65 (daily 9.30am–1pm & 2.30–6pm; L10,000), in the road that emerges from the town walls right by the bus station. The museum entrance is on the main square. Minor works include two panels by Matteo di Giovanni that used to flank della Francesca's *Baptism* (now in London's National Gallery), a good *Annunciation* by Santi di Tito and a painted standard by Signorelli, who was one of his pupils.

A couple of minor della Francesca paintings are hung by the entrance to the main room, but the eye immediately latches onto the **Madonna della Misericordia**, Piero's earliest known painting and the epitome of his graceful solemnity. It was created in the 1440s, soon after he had been made a member of Sansepolcro's governing council, a position he was to hold for the rest of his life. Tiny panels surround the central image of the Madonna, a conventional and antiquated format that was specified by his patrons, the charitable Compagnia della Misericordia. There's no conventional fragility about this Madonna, though: compassionate and all-capable, she protects her worshippers with a cape as solid as a wall. The hooded man at her feet is wearing the uniform of the Misericordia, a sinister garb still worn by members of the modern Misericordia when bearing a body to a funeral.

The **Resurrection**, opposite, was painted for the adjoining town hall, probably in the early 1450s, and moved here in the sixteenth century. Aldous Huxley once dubbed this "the greatest painting in the world", a piece of hyperbole that may well have saved the painting from obliteration. In 1944 the British Eighth Army was ordered to bombard Sansepolcro, but an officer recalled Huxley's article and delayed the attack in the hope that the Germans would withdraw – which they did.

Much of the picture's power comes from its unique emphasis on the Resurrection as a physical event: muscular and implacable, Christ steps onto the edge of the tomb – banner in hand – as if it were the rampart of a conquered city. One of the soldiers in the foreground places his hand on his eyes, a gesture that might be read as simple weariness or the despair of the vanquished heathen. The strange landscape in the background – with leafless trees on one side and reborn foliage on the other – was the starting point for Kenneth Clark's description, which pinpoints a pre-Christian strand to the painting's significance: "This country god, who rises in the grey light while humanity is asleep, has been worshipped ever since man first knew that the seed is not dead in the winter earth, but will force its way upwards through an iron crust."

After this, everything else in the gallery seems trivial, though it's difficult not to get hooked by Pontormo's sadistic *Martyrdom of St Quentin*, which gives special meaning to the word "fingernails". In the basement there's a tedious collection of carved bits from old Sansepolcro houses, and on the top floor an equally dull fresco show.

The rest of the town

Lesser art treasures are to be found round the corner from the Museo Civico in the Romanesque-Gothic **duomo**, where the chapel to the left of the chancel houses a mighty tenth-century *Volto Santo*, depicting Christ as a robed patriarch. (The crown and gown with which this Crucifix is dressed for November's Feast of the Redeemer are usually on show in the Museo Civico.) Also displayed in the duomo is an *Ascension* by Perugino, restored in 1997.

The church of **San Lorenzo** (9am–1pm & 3–7pm; shorter hours in winter), down in the southwest corner of the *centro storico*, can be seen with the same ticket as the Museo Civico. It has a *Deposition* by the Mannerist Rosso Fiorentino, painted within half a century of della Francesca's last works but seeming to belong to another world.

Sansepolcro practicalities

The last **bus** back to Arezzo leaves at 7.24pm, the last to Città di Castello at 9.28pm (arriving 9.52pm). If you decide to stay, there is usually space in at least one of the town's half-dozen **hotels**. One of the cheapest is the *Orfeo*, just outside the walls near the bus terminal at Viale A. Diaz 12 (☎0575.742.061; ②). First recommendation, though, is the three-star *Fiorentino*, Via Luca Pacioli 60 (☎ & fax 0575.740.350; ③), a hotel with what is usually a very good **restaurant** (closed Fri & three weeks in July) – meals here are excellent value at around L40,000, and the proprietors are most welcoming. Note too that doubles without private bathroom cost a full L30,000 less. Another excellent restaurant is the family-run *Ventura*, Via Niccolò Aggiunti 30 (☎0575.742.560; closed Sat, Aug & two weeks in Jan; ②), renowned for its old stone and wood-beamed ceiling, its *antipasti*, and curious trolley-serving methods: full meals at around L45,000 a head. It also has the seven cheapest rooms in town. *Pizzerie* and bars are clustered in Viale A. Diaz, while the best **food shop** is the Enogastronomia in Via Pacioli 44, a treasure trove of mushrooms, truffles, cheeses and wines.

Just about the only time you'll have difficulty in finding a room is the second Sunday in September, the date of the **Palio della Balestra**, the return leg of the crossbow competition against the archers of Gubbio. The shoot-out is preceded by some very flashy flag-hurling, whose practitioners – clad in costumes inspired by Piero's paintings – show off their skills at various other times of the year as well. For details call in at the **tourist office** in Via della Fonte (daily: April–Oct 10.30am–1pm & 4–7pm; Nov–March 10am–1pm & 4–6pm; ☎0575.730.231), two minutes' walk from the museum.

North of Arezzo: the Casentino

North of Arezzo, beyond the city's textile factories, lies the lush upper valley of the Arno, a thoroughly agricultural area known as the **Casentino**, whose unshowy little towns see few tourists. From Bibbiena to Pratovecchio the valley is a broad green dish, ruffled by low hills and bracketed by the peaks of the Pratomagno on one side and on the other by the ridge between the Arno and the Tiber. Thick woodland of oak, beech and pine covers much of the upper slopes, the remnant of the forest that used to coat much of the Casentino. During the Medici centuries the timber from here supplied the shipyards of Pisa, Livorno and Genoa, as well as the building sites of Tuscany.

Florence did not always have territorial rights in this region. From the eleventh century the northern part of the Casentino was ruled by the **Guidi** dynasty of Poppi, who kept control from a string of castles whose ruins still litter the hills. In the Middle Ages Arezzo, landlord of the southern Casentino, brawled constantly with Florence for possession of this lucrative valley. After Florence bested him at Campaldino (see p.425), the traditionally Ghibelline Guidi counts recognized the authority of the Guelph city, and were in return allowed to maintain their power base here, though within a century or so the Florentines had ousted them completely. The seclusion of the higher ground fostered a strong **monastic** tradition as well, and the communities at **Camaldoli** and at **La Verna** continue to be important centres for their respective orders.

By **public transport**, the best target for a day trip from Arezzo is **Poppi**, which is connected to the city by bus and by the private LFI **train** line which shares the state FS station in Arezzo. There are fourteen trains daily (five on Sun, when services may be replaced by a bus): journey time is 55 minutes. To strike into the hills, to the monasteries of La Verna and Camaldoli, really requires a car; buses do run from Bibbiena train station (see below) to La Verna, Badia Prataglia and Camaldoli, but they are too infrequent to make a round trip feasible. You could, however, overnight in these places.

Bibbiena

The chief commercial town of the Casentino is **BIBBIENA**, a place swathed in straggling development, much of it connected with tobacco production. In the fairly attractive innermost quarter, the main sight is the church of **San Lorenzo**, a fifteenth-century building that contains a fair quantity of terracotta from the della Robbia workshops. Up the top end of town, close to Piazza Tarlati – its name a sign of its links with Arezzo (see p.414) – the oddly shaped church of **SS. Ippolito e Donato** has a fine altarpiece by Bicci di Lorenzo. Once you've seen these, there's no reason to hang around.

The town does have a use, however, if you're determined to head by public transport to Camaldoli and Badia Pataglia for the national park (see below). There are eight **buses** daily (Mon–Sat only) from outside the train station to the latter, and four daily (Mon–Sat only) to the former. Three buses daily (Mon–Sat) also run to Chiusi Verna, passing the road (4km) for La Verna (see below).

La Verna

In 1213 a pious member of the Guidi clan, Count Orlando, donated to **St Francis** a plot of land at **LA VERNA**, 23km east of Bibbiena and just inside the national park (see below), but included here as it lies at the park's most peripheral and southeasterly point. It was at this hermitage, on September 14, 1224, that Francis received the **stigmata** from a vision of the crucified Christ, a badge of sanctity never previously bestowed.

Francis's mountain-top sanctuary grew into a monastic village, whose ten chapels are connected by a network of corridors, cloisters, dormitories and stone pathways. Thousands of pilgrims come here annually, some of them staying in the guesthouse adjoining the monks' quarters, most coming to pay an hour's homage at the site of the miracle. If you want **accommodation** in historic and peaceful surroundings in spectacular countryside, this is the place (☎0575.5341; ④; L25,000 extra for all meals). A few visitors make the climb to see the magnificent ceramics by **Andrea della Robbia**, but unlike at the basilica at Assisi, secular sightseers don't obscure the purpose of the place. The sanctuary is open every day from 6am to 8.30pm, though in winter the road can be heavy going.

Relics of the saint – his walking stick, belt, drinking glass – are displayed in the fifteenth-century **basilica**, where there's a glorious *Ascension* by della Robbia – whose other masterpieces are the focal points of the **Chiesa delle Stimmate** and the **Cappella di Santa Maria degli Angeli**. Halfway along the corridor leading to the Stimmate (stigmata) chapel – a walkway painted with modern scenes of the story of St Francis – a small door opens into a gash in the crag, where he used to sleep. According to Franciscan orthodoxy, the rocks at La Verna were split apart at the moment of Christ's death. The route also passes the marginally more comfortable cell in which St Anthony of Padua stayed in 1230. The **Sasso Spicco**, reached by a flight of steps near the corridor, was Francis's place of meditation.

A path through the forest above the sanctuary leads to the summit of **La Penna** (1283m), from where there's a panorama of the Casentino meadows in one direction and the savage serrations of the Apennines in the other. The drive from La Verna to Sansepolcro is a fabulous descent into the upper Tiber valley; the valley itself, however, is a mess of light industry and quarries.

Poppi

POPPI, 6km to the north of Bibbiena and plainly visible from there, is sited high above the bus and train terminals. If you emerge at these, in the modern lower suburb of Ponte a Poppi, follow Via Dante Alighieri, a cobbled short cut which leads to the upper town in ten minutes' walk.

The old town is not much more than a couple of squares and an arcaded main street, Via Cavour, but it is lent a monumental aspect by the Casentino's chief landmark, the **Castello dei Conti Guidi** (daily 9.30am–12.30pm & 3–6pm; L5000). Built for the Guidi lords in the thirteenth century, its design is based closely on Florence's Palazzo Vecchio and it's likely that Arnolfo di Cambio was the architect here as well. The courtyard, with its wooden landings and beautiful staircases, is the most attractive bit of architecture in the Casentino; much of the interior is occupied by a massive library but the parts that are open to the public contain a superb array of arms and some well-preserved medieval frescoes. At its lower end, Via Cavour climaxes at the magnificent twelfth-century **Badia di San Fedele**; its very dark interior – locked most of the time – contains a beguiling thirteenth-century painting of the Madonna and Child. Opposite the *castello* at Piazza della Repubblica 6 is the town's lone **hotel**, the small but fine two-star *Casentino* (☎0575.529.090, fax 0575.529.067; ③), with a good location opposite the castle, a nice courtyard garden, and a bar and cavernous **restaurant** popular with locals.

A short distance north of Poppi, where the road splits, is the site of the **Battle of Campaldino**, where in 1289 the Florentine Guelphs defeated the Arezzo Ghibellines to establish Florence's pre-eminence in the power struggles of Tuscany. Nearly two thousand men died in the battle – one who survived was Dante, then twenty-four years old. A column right on the junction marks the battle site.

Parco Nazionale delle Foreste Casentinesi

The **Parco Nazionale delle Foreste Casentinesi** is one of Italy's newest national parks, a vast area spanning Tuscany and Emilia-Romagna which is designed to protect the region's centuries-old forests, its hills and wild mountains – wolves still roam these parts and the Apennine peaks touch 1658m – as well as various monasteries and other sanctuaries such as La Verna and Camaldoli. Much money and effort is being put into promoting the park, so there's plenty of good literature, maps and pamphlets available from a wide range of sources. Of particular help is the *Servizi Turistico Alberghieri* pamphlet, which lists all accommodation options, including many cheap *agriturismo* possibilities off the beaten track.

The main tourist office in Arezzo (see p.414) makes a good place to start if you want to plan a trip, but the park has its **headquarters** in the town of Pratovecchio, at Via G. Brocchi 7 (Mon–Thurs 8am–1pm & 3–5pm, Fri 8am–1pm; ☎0575.50.301), and an information centre in Bibbiena at Via Berni 25 (☎0575.593.098). There are also visitor reception points at other Tuscan centres, each dealing with a different theme (the environment, religion, nature and so on): these are found at Chiusi della Verna (near La Verna) at Parco Martiri della Libertà 21 (☎0575.532.098); Badia Prataglia (10km east of Camaldoli) at Via Nazionale 14a (☎0575.559.477); and Serravella (between Camaldoli and Badia Prataglia) at Via Coleschi (☎0575.539.174).

Roads between the villages and over the border into Emilia-Romagna provide a window on the considerable wilderness of the area, but to get to grips with the scenery properly you need to **walk**. You could follow one of nine specially marked **short trails**, the *Sentiera Natura*, three of which start in Tuscany: Badia Prataglia (**Trail 2**, *La Faggetta*), a path up a pretty valley through an ancient beech wood; Camaldoli (**Trail 5**, *Alberi e Bosco*), a track that starts near the monastery and wends through the surrounding woods; and Chiusi della Verna (**Trail 6**, *Natura, Storia* and *Spiritualità sul monte di San Francesco*), a path on Monte della Verna which traces "nature, history and spirituality in the mountains of St Francis". If you want to be a little more ambitious, the forests are crisscrossed by numerous other ancient tracks and lanes, most marked on the SELCA 1:25,000 map of the park, the *Carta Escursionistica-Parco Nazionale delle Foreste Casentinesi, Monte Falterona, Campigna*, available from most park centres and local book shops.

Badia Prataglia

Moving from east to west, the first of the Parco Nazionale's best centres for walking and touring is **BADIA PRATAGLIA**, 12km northeast of Bibbiena, and 10km east of Camaldoli, the park's other principal Tuscan base. There's not an awful lot to do or see in a cultural sense, but the village marks the starting point of several walks, and has several accommodation possibilities. The cheapest **hotel** is the *Mimosa*, Via Nazionale 7 (☎ & fax 0575.559.061; ②), one of four two-star places on this street. Just a touch more expensive are the *Bellavista*, Via Nazionale 34 (☎0575.559.011, fax 0575.559.440; July–Sept; ②), and *La Torre*, Via Sassopiano 41 (☎0575.559.005; ②). Most comfortable option is the three-star *Bosco Verde*, Via Nazionale 8 (☎0575.559.017, fax 0575.559.430; ③), open mid-March to mid-Oct. There is also a **hostel**, the *Casanova* (☎0575.559.320, fax 0575.299.047; L35,000, full pension from L55,000; July–Oct). Campers should make for the *Il Capanno* **campsite** (☎0575.518.015; mid-June to mid-Sept). If you need a pre- or post-hike **snack**, duck into the Pasticceria Anna, Via Nazionale 35.

Camaldoli

One of the best bases for the park is **CAMALDOLI**, just over 15km northeast of Poppi, where in 1012 St Romauldo (aka Rumbold) founded an especially ascetic order of the Benedictines. Notwithstanding the severity of its order, this sylvan retreat became a favourite with non-monastic penitents, so much so that a second site was opened up to accommodate visitors and to administer the woodlands that Romauldo had been granted. This lower complex has been much rebuilt and the only point of interest is its sixteenth-century pharmacy, which now sells herbal products. Accommodation is available at three **hotels**. The two one-stars, *Camaldoli*, Via Camaldoli 13 (☎ & fax 0575.556.019; ②) and *La Foresta*, Via Camaldoli 5 (☎ & fax 0575.556.015; ②) are identically priced, although the latter has some rooms without private bathroom at a saving of L10,000. For more comfort, and another L40,000, there's the three-star *Il Rustichello*, Via del Corniolo 14 (☎0575.556.020, fax 0575.556.046; ③). There are also two **campsites**, the *Fonte del Menchino* (☎ & fax 0575.556.157; June–Sept), on the Strada dell'Eremo, and the *Parco Pucini* (☎0575.556.006, fax 0575.556.157; June–Sept) in the nearby hamlet of Pucini.

On summer weekends lots of people come out here for a postprandial shop followed by a stroll through the forest up to the **Eremo**, the more fundamentalist wing of the monastery – which is around 3km higher up the mountain. These days both men and women can visit, but no one is allowed near the actual living quarters. More strenuous walking options high into the forested hills all around are numerous, either from the Eremo (where the country to the north is very wild), or from Camaldoli village itself: from the latter two, paths worth considering are those to Badia Prataglia to the east (about 6km) and an eight-kilometre round trip up Poggio Muschioso (1158m – Camaldoli sits at 812m) to the west.

Pratovecchio and Stia

PRATOVECCHIO, the birthplace of Paolo Uccello, retains some old arcaded streets, but the major attractions are outside the town, up a narrow little road to the southwest. **Pieve di Romena**, though patched up a few times since its foundation in the twelfth century, is a wonderfully preserved Romanesque church, with splendid capitals and a beehive-shaped sacristy. An inscription on the first column to the right identifies the sculptor as the parish priest, Albericus; on the second pillar on the left another states that the work was completed during a famine in 1152. Close by are the still intimidating ruins of the **Castello di Romena** (generally open Mon–Sat 9am–noon & 3–6pm; free), built by the Guidi counts and once the mightiest castle in the Casentino. Dante was a guest here and in the *Inferno* he mentions one of its former tenants, Adamo da Brescia, whose counterfeit coins wreaked such havoc with the local economy that the enraged Florentines roasted him alive. If you're in town, be certain to drop into *L'Osteria di Giovanni*, Via Roma 57 (closed Tues), either for a drink or his speciality, a sandwich made from delicious local ham smoked over a fire of juniper wood.

The LFI rail line finishes 2km on at the wool-producing town of **STIA**, the nearest town to the source of the Arno, which rises to the north on Monte Falterona. Winters can be arduous here, and the steep roofs give Stia an alpine feel. The porticoed Piazza Tanucci is the heart (and summit) of the medieval town, where the Romanesque interior of **Santa Maria della Assunta** features a *Madonna* by Andrea della Robbia and a triptych by Lorenzo di Bicci. Stia has a reasonably priced two-star **hotel and restaurant**, *La Foresta*, Via Roma 27 (☎0575.58.481; ③), with some rooms without private bathrooms at a L25,000 discount. There's also a good restaurant on the piazza, the *Filetto* (closed Sat, June & Oct) – meats are especially good, roasted over the kitchen's open fire: around L35,000 per head.

At Stia the road divides: to the west of Monte Falterona one branch passes another Guidi fortress and the frescoed church of Santa Maria delle Grazie on its way to the Sieve valley (see p.176); the other, to the east, crosses the Passo la Calla then drops down into Emilia-Romagna.

South of Arezzo: the Valdichiana

Travelling south from Arezzo you enter the **Valdichiana**, prosperous cattle country that produces the much prized Florentine *bistecca*. As with the Maremma, this former swampland was first drained by the Etruscans, whose work was allowed to unravel in medieval times, when the encroaching marshes drove the farmers of the region back up to the hill-towns. Only in the nineteenth century, with the reclamation schemes of the Lorraine dukes of Tuscany, did the Valdichiana become fertile again. It's an underwhelming landscape but its flatness does at least mean that the towns on its flanks – of which **Cortona** is the most inspiring – have very long sight-lines.

Castiglion Fiorentino

Looming high above the road and railway 17km south of Arezzo are the walls and massive tower of **CASTIGLION FIORENTINO** – known as Castiglion Aretino until Arezzo became a Florentine holding in 1384. The fortified old town is so far above the train station that it makes more sense to visit by bus; the half-hourly bus from Arezzo to Cortona bowls through here thirty minutes into its one-hour journey, stopping right outside the walls in Piazza Matteotti.

From here the Corso Italia rises to the navel of the *centro storico*, the elegant Piazza del Municipio. There's a modest art gallery, the **Pinacoteca Comunale**, a short distance up the hill from the Municipio (Tues–Sun 10am–12.30pm & 3.30–6pm; L5000) at Piazza del Municipio 12, whose pride and joy – Signorelli's *Virgin with St Anne* – has gone to the Museo Diocesano in Cortona: it retains works by Taddeo Gaddi and two fine fourteenth-century paintings by Bartolomeo della Gatta. Opposite the palazzo is Castiglion's distinguishing feature, a **loggia** – supposedly by Vasari – which forms a picture-frame for the hills to the east. Look down to the right through the loggia and you'll see the rooftops of the two churches worth a call – the **Collegiata**, for a *Holy Family* by Lorenzo di Credi, and the adjoining **Pieve**, for Signorelli's fresco of the *Deposition*.

Cortona

From the valley floor a five-kilometre road winds up through terraces of vines and olives to the hill-town of **CORTONA**, whose heights survey a vast domain: the Valdichiana stretching westward, with Lago Trasimeno visible over the low hills to the south. A scattering of Etruscan tombs aside, it is the medieval period that dominates the steep streets of Cortona – limitations of space have confined almost all later

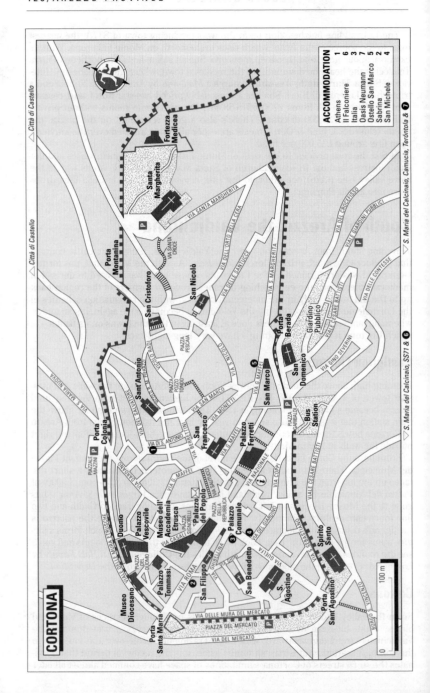

CORTONA

development to the lower suburb of Camucia, which is where the approach road begins. Even without its art treasures, this would be a good place to rest up, with pleasant hotels, excellent restaurants and an amazing view at night, with the villages of southern Tuscany twinkling like ships' lights on a dark sea.

According to folklore, Cortona was founded by Dardanus, later to establish the city of Troy and to give his name to the Dardanelles. Whatever its precise origins, there was already a sizeable Umbrian settlement here when the **Etruscans** took over in the eighth century BC. About four hundred years later it passed to the Romans and remained a significant Roman centre until its destruction by the Goths. By the eleventh century it had become a free *comune*, constantly at loggerheads with Perugia and Arezzo; in 1258 the Aretines destroyed Cortona, but the town soon revived under the patronage of Siena. It changed hands yet again at the start of the fifteenth century, when it was appropriated by the Kingdom of Naples and then sold off to the Florentines, who never let go.

Arrival and information

Cortona is easily visited as a day trip from Arezzo, although in most ways it's the more pleasing of the two towns in which to spend the night. There are hourly LFI **buses** between the two towns, and stopping **trains** from Arezzo call at Camucia-Cortona station (6km), from where a shuttle (roughly every half an hour) takes ten minutes to run up to the centre of the old town. Buy tickets at the station bar. The fast Florence–Rome trains stop at Terontola, 10km south, which is also served by a shuttle roughly every hour (25 minutes to Cortona's Piazza Garibaldi); Terontola is the station to get off at if you are approaching from Umbria. If you're **driving**, the centre is closed to traffic. Good parking options include Piazza del Mercato to the west, Piazza Mazzini by Porta Colonia, Piazza Garibaldi (the most convenient and therefore busiest) and in front of Santa Margherita below the Fortezza, though this leaves quite a walk back uphill from the centre of town.

The **tourist office** at Via Nazionale 42 (Mon–Sat 8.30am–12.30pm & 3–6pm; ☎0575.630.352, fax 0575.630.656) can provide leaflets and help out with accommodation. A Saturday **market** is held in the Piazza della Repubblica, and on Mondays a huge agricultural fair and general market takes place in Camucia.

Accommodation

There are half a dozen **hotels** in the town proper, only three of which could be described as inexpensive options: the one-star, 22-room *Athens*, Via S. Antonio 12 (☎0575.630.508, fax 0575.604.457; ②); the comfortable three-star *Italia*, Via Ghibellina 5 (☎0575.630.254, fax 0575.630.564; ④); and the tiny three-star, eight-room *Sabrina*, Via Roma 37 (☎0575.630.397, fax 0575.604.627; ③. There are a few one- and two-star places down at Camucia and Terontola, but there is little point coming to Cortona and then spending the night down in the valley. However, Cortona does have an HI **youth hostel**, the *Ostello San Marco*, situated in the heart of the town at Via G. Maffei 57 (☎0575.601.392; L19,000; doubles and family rooms available; open mid-March to mid-Oct). It's a clean and spacious hostel in an old monastery, with fantastic views from the dormitories and friendly management – but, as ever, don't expect much of the breakfast.

If you have more money to spare, then Cortona has some very pleasant hotels indeed. Nicest in-town option is the *San Michele*, Via Guelfa 15 (☎0575.604.348, fax 0575.630.147; ⑥), a central four-star converted from a patrician medieval town house – try for rooms in the tower. About twenty minutes' walk south from Via Garibaldi, and ideal if you have transport, is the *Oasi Neumann*, Via delle Contesse 1 (☎ & fax 0575.630.354; ④), a three-star high on a hillside with splendid views. Converted from a monastery, it retains traces of its original character, and makes a more atmospheric place to stay than the hotels in town. For a financially reckless treat, drive 3km on the

SS71 towards Arezzo and *Il Falconiere*, Località San Martino (☎0575.612.679, fax 0575.612.927; ⑨), an intimate four-star with a well-regarded restaurant, lovely garden with pool, and beautifully presented rooms with antiques, old frescoes (in some cases) and tasteful linen and fittings.

The town
The bus terminus is in **Piazza Garibaldi**, from where the only level street in town, **Via Nazionale**, leads into **Piazza della Repubblica**, the first of three interconnected squares. This one is the most sociable – the town's best restaurants are all within seconds of the piazza, and the tall staircase of the squat, castellated **Palazzo del Comune** is the grandstand from which the *ragazzi* appraise the world as it goes by. It is also close to two of the town's main sights, an Etruscan museum and Diocesan museum, essential ports of call before heading through the **upper town** towards the Fortezza Medicea, preferably by way of Via Berrettini. From the fortress you can drop down and explore lesser churches such as San Nicolò and San Domenico.

MUSEO DELL'ACCADEMIA ETRUSCA
One flank of Piazza della Repubblica's Palazzo del Comune forms a side of **Piazza Signorelli**, named after the artist Luca Signorelli, Cortona's most famous son – as is the decorously peeling nineteenth-century theatre. Opposite the theatre the crudely powerful Palazzo Casali, its facade like a rockface with windows, houses the **Museo dell'Accademia Etrusca** (Tues–Sun 10am–7pm; L8000). There are six rooms given over to the Etruscans, one an enormous hall with unengrossing paintings round the walls and Etruscan stuff in smart new cabinets in the middle. The major exhibit – honoured with its own bijou temple – is an Etruscan bronze lamp from the fifth century BC, its circumference decorated with alternating male and female squatting figures. A further three rooms contain Etruscan finds excavated in 1990–92 from nearby Sodo; a model shows the layout of the tumulus and tombs. However, the main attraction is the fabulous gold, turquoise and crystal **jewellery**, dating from the fifth and sixth centuries BC. Beads shaped like acorns and berry clusters are set in sophisticated filigree and hammered gold settings, wonderful examples of the finesse of Etruscan jewellers.

Elsewhere there are ranks of Etruscan figurines and masses of domestic odds and ends which evidently don't interest even the curators, as they can't be bothered labelling anything. The painter **Gino Severini**, another native of Cortona, gets a room to himself at the end. An acolyte of the Futurist firebrand Filippo Marinetti, Severini seems to have lacked any convictions of his own, being content to jog along through semi-Cubist prints, conventional portraits and collages.

THE MUSEO DIOCESANO
Piazza Signorelli links with Piazza del Duomo, where you might not realize that the cathedral is in front of you, as all you see on entering the square is the well-scrubbed arcade along its flank. Built in the sixteenth century, the **Duomo** is now in such a state that its facade has been buttressed with brick; the interior is fresh but rather vacant.

The couple of churches that used to face the duomo have been knocked together to house the **Museo Diocesano** (Tues–Sun 9.30am–1pm & 3.30–7pm; L8000), a tiny but high-quality collection of Renaissance art plus a fine Roman sarcophagus, carved with fighting centaurs. Predictably Luca Signorelli features strongly, his anatomical drawing and perspective slightly out of kilter in a way that's endearing or irritating according to taste. Only two works, however – *The Dead Christ* (1502) and *Apostles* (1512) – are unequivocally his: seven others are attributed to him and his school. Outstanding paintings from Sassetta (a triptych of the *Madonna dell'Umilità with Saints* from 1435) and Pietro Lorenzetti (a *Crucifix* from 1315–20) are also on show, but neither measures up to **Fra' Angelico**, represented by a *Madonna, Child and Saints* and an exquisite *Annunciation*. Painted during Fra' Angelico's ten years at Cortona's monastery of San Domenico, the latter has a courtly Adam and Eve being expelled from Eden in the background, the bruised sky contrasting with the dazzle of the angel's wings. Also worthy of note is Bartolomeo della Gatta's *Assumption*.

THE UPPER TOWN

To get the full taste of Cortona take Via Santucci from Piazza della Repubblica and then clamber along Via Berrettini, at the near end of which stands the Gothic-Baroque hybrid of **San Francesco**. Crusty outside and dusty within, it has a Byzantine ivory reliquary for a piece of the True Cross on the high altar. Above the third altar on the left hangs an *Annunciation* by the man the street is named after, Pietro Berrettini, otherwise known as Pietro da Cortona. This is his last work, left unfinished; the best of him is in Rome.

A further work by Signorelli is to be found in the church of **San Nicolò**, reached by veering right across Piazza della Pescaia then going up the stepped Via San Nicolò. It's an unassuming little church with a gravel forecourt like a country hotel, and has to be opened by the caretaker – ring the bell on the left-hand side wall. Signorelli's high altarpiece is a standard which he painted on both sides: a characteristically awkward *Entombment* on the front and a *Madonna and Saints* on the back – revealed by a neat hydraulic system that swivels the picture away from the wall.

From Piazza della Pescaia, a steep path leads to the mock-Romanesque **Santa Margherita**. Rebuilt in the nineteenth century, it contains the tomb of **Margaret of Cortona**, the town's patron saint. The daughter of a local farmer, she spent her long years of widowhood helping the poor and sick of Cortona, founding a hospital that stood close to the site of this church. So intense was her relationship with the Almighty that the townspeople would pack into the Franciscan church at Mass to observe her delirious behaviour: "she became ashen pale, her pulse ceased, she froze, her throat was so affected by hoarseness that she could scarcely be understood when she returned to her senses". Her Gothic tomb (1362), with marble angels lifting the lid of her sarcophagus, is now mounted on the wall to the left of the chancel.

The **Fortezza Medicea**, at the summit of the town, is often shut, but the area around is good ground for a picnic, and offers superb **views** over ruined Etruscan and Roman walls towards Trasimeno. You could descend to Piazza Garibaldi by the stepped Via Crucis, where the Stations of the Cross are marked with booths sheltering unsubtle mosaics by Severini.

SAN DOMENICO AND SANTA MARIA DEL CALCINAIO

A last church to check out is **San Domenico**, completed in 1438, a minute's walk from Piazza Garibaldi, where the high altar's *Coronation of the Virgin* polyptych by Lorenzo di Niccolò Gerini is proudly spotlit even during daylight hours.

Below the piazza, the middle distance is occupied by the perfectly proportioned though crumbling Renaissance church of **Santa Maria del Calcinaio**. The masterpiece of Giorgio di Martini, it was begun in 1484 to enshrine a miraculous image of the Virgin that a lime burner had unearthed here. Another Tuscan church of this vintage – Santa Maria delle Carceri in Prato – was built for similar reasons, but the number of pilgrims who flocked to Cortona made it impossible for the architect to employ the fashionable central-plan design used in Prato. Hence this highly refined compromise – classical detailing on a Gothic-sized cruciform church.

Just past Santa Maria, signs direct you farther down the hill to the Etruscan **Tanella di Pitagora** – a well-preserved fourth-century BC chamber tomb, fancifully identified with the Greek mathematician.

Eating and drinking

For meals, Cortona is a town where you can treat yourself without ruining your finances. One of the nicer-looking **restaurants** is *La Loggetta* (closed Mon), which also occupies the best site in town overlooking Piazza della Repubblica at Piazza Pescheria 3; a meal will cost around L45,000, but the food can be uneven and the service sullen. Cheaper and perhaps better, is the *Osteria dell'Teatro*, Via Maffei 5 (☎0575.630.556; closed Wed & two weeks in Nov), a small, rustic-looking place close to the central Teatro Signorelli: go for soups, the *antipasti dell'osteria* for starters and any of the home-made fresh pastas (dinner bookings advisable; L35,000–40,000 per person). The *Tonino* in Piazza Garibaldi (☎0575.630.500; closed Mon lunch & all Tues) specializes in *antipasti*: a large selection plus a pasta dish costs around L40,000 – accompanied by a panoramic view from the terrace. Another great view is from the popular and reasonably priced pizzeria *La Casina dei Tigli*, in the public gardens below Piazza Garibaldi.

Monte San Savino and around

On the opposite side of the Valdichiana from Cortona stands **MONTE SAN SAVINO**, now a market town, once a contentious border post between the territories of Florence, Siena and Arezzo – it was completely razed in 1325 on the orders of Bishop Tarlati of Arezzo. The town retains a slightly decrepit mix of medieval and Renaissance monuments, but it is not one of Tuscany's more seductive hill-towns. Should you be determined to explore it, however, there are regular trains from Arezzo to the station in the lower town, from where there's the usual bus shuttle; buses from Cortona also periodically cross the valley.

The town was the birthplace of **Andrea Sansovino**, now best remembered as the mentor of Jacopo Sansovino, a crucial figure in Venice's artistic history. Terracotta was one of his preferred media – the town remains a major producer of majolica – and some of Andrea's best ceramic work is in the church of **Santa Chiara**, which stands in the northern Piazza Gamurrini, the square nearest the place where the buses stop. The altarpiece of *SS. Lawrence, Roch and Sebastian* was his first major work, while the tabernacle to the left of the high altar was a collaboration with Andrea della Robbia.

Virtually next to the church stands the fourteenth-century Sienese castle known as the **Cassero**, which houses a small tourist office and stages the occasional art exhibition; it also has a modest three-room **ceramics museum** (Tues–Sun 9.30am–12.30pm & 4–7pm; L3000). Also on the square is a monument to Monte San Savino's one-time governor, Mattias de' Medici; it allegedly cost so much that Mattias forbade any more such potentially ruinous projects.

Continuing down the narrow main street from Piazza Gamurrini you'll pass the **Loggia dei Mercanti**, a collaboration between Sansovino and Antonio da Sangallo the Elder – architect of the Palazzo Comunale across the way. Beyond the Palazzo Pretorio lies the small central square, Piazza di Monte, on both of whose churches Sansovino left his mark. He designed the now disintegrating portal of **San Giovanni**, and added the cloister to the fourteenth-century Sant'Agostino. Inside are some fifteenth-century frescoes and a typically unrestrained altarpiece from Vasari, who, it seems, ferreted his way into every cranny of the region.

Lucignano

Eight kilometres south of Monte San Savino and served by six buses a day is the trim little town of **LUCIGNANO**. It is laid out as a concentric pattern of four ellipses, though the density of the centre and its gradients make it difficult to discern the arrangement on the ground. Nucleus of the pattern is the **Collegiata**, an unexceptional church given a touch of panache by the circular staircase leading to its door – like a terrace for a diminutive amphitheatre.

Round the back, the **Museo Comunale** (Tues–Sun: summer 10am–1pm & 4–7pm; winter 10am–12.30pm & 3.30–5.30pm; L5000) contains the most arresting artefact on this side of the Valdichiana, an amazing fourteenth-century reliquary made in Arezzo. It's known as the *Albero*, or "tree", for its tree-like shape, with gold and silver adornments and branches of coral leafed with crystal, enamels and miniatures. Thirteenth- and fourteenth-century frescoes, some of them by Bartolo di Fredi, decorate the adjacent striped church of **San Francesco**. And that's about it, apart from the inevitable Medici fortress on the hill to the north, with its smart new dovecote.

Accommodation is at the one-star *Il Monte*, Via Aldo Moro 5 (☎0575.844.444; ③) or three-star *San Gallo*, Piazza Vittorio Veneto 16 (☎0575.810.049, fax 0575.810.220; ④).

Farneta

If you're driving back to Cortona, the quickest route takes you past the ancient Benedictine **Abbazia di Farneta**, which stands close to the Valdichiana exit from the autostrada. Built largely with stone plundered from a nearby Roman temple dedicated to Bacchus, this beautiful building has been restored virtually single-handedly by the local priest, who since the late 1930s has stripped the abbey of its eighteenth-century accretions. He also excavated the remarkable **crypt**, dating from the ninth and tenth centuries – an operation which yielded numerous archeological discoveries. A few minor finds are on show in the priest's house, but repeated robbery attempts have necessitated transfer of the more precious pieces – such as an eighth-century Lombard carving of the Crucifixion – to the museum in Cortona.

travel details

TRAINS

Arezzo to: Assisi (12 daily; 1hr 35min); Bibbiena (hourly; 50min); Bolzano (5 daily; 7hr 30min); Camucia-Cortona (hourly; 20min); Chiusi (hourly; 1hr); Florence (hourly; 1hr); Foligno (every 2hr; 1hr 50min); Monte San Savino (12 daily; 25min); Orvieto (7 daily; 1hr 20min); Perugia (every 2hr; 1hr 15min); Poppi (hourly; 57min); Rome (hourly; 1hr 40min); Terni (1 direct daily; 2hr 35min); Terontola (hourly; 25min); Trento (5 daily; 7hr); Udine (5 daily; 7hr); Venice (5 daily; 5hr 10min); Verona (5 daily; 5hr 15min).

BUSES

Arezzo to: Bibbiena & La Verna (1 daily – change at Bibbiena for Poppi & Camaldoli); Città di Castello (at least 12 daily; 1hr 30min); Cortona (hourly; 1hr); Sansepolcro (17 daily; 1hr), some via Monterchi, most via Anghiari; Siena (5 daily Mon–Fri).

Bibbiena to: Badia Prataglia (8 daily Mon–Sat; 40min); Camaldoli (4 daily Mon–Sat 40min); Chiusi Verna (3 daily Mon–Sat; 50min).

Cortona to: Arezzo (hourly; 50min); Castiglione del Lago (7 daily; 1hr); Chianciano (4 daily; 1hr), changing for Montepulciano.

PART THREE

UMBRIA

Città di Castello

Gubbio

CHAPTER 10
**PERUGIA AND
NORTHERN UMBRIA**

Lago Trasimeno

Perugia

Assisi

CHAPTER 11
**ASSISI AND
THE VALE
OF SPOLETO**

Città di Pieve

CHAPTER 13
**ORVIETO AND
SOUTHERN UMBRIA**

Todi

Norcia

Spoleto CHAPTER 12
**SPOLETO AND
THE VALNERINA**

Orvieto

Terni

N

CHAPTER TEN

PERUGIA AND NORTHERN UMBRIA

Perugia, many people's first taste of Umbria, makes for a distinctly uncharacteristic introduction to the region. The home of Buitoni pasta and Perugino chocolate, it's a place whose historic core is hidden within a ring of initially off-putting industrialized suburbs, and whose big-city feel, universities and famous summer **jazz festival** make it wholly different from its bucolic, hill-town neighbours. If you've come to Umbria for the rural experience, you may in fact be tempted to by-pass Perugia altogether. Its medieval heart, however, demands at least a day's exploration, two sights alone making the trip more than worthwhile: the **Palazzo dei Priori**, justifiably hyped as one of the greatest public palaces in Italy, and the **Galleria Nazionale**, which boasts the region's best collection of Umbrian art. And if actually staying in the city doesn't appeal, its highlights can easily be taken in on day trips from Assisi or Spoleto.

West of Perugia lies the placid **Lago Trasimeno**, not so spectacular scenically, but an ever popular magnet for campers and one of the few places in the region where you can put your feet up on a beach. The nicest town, if you want to save a long trawl round its shores, is **Castiglione del Lago**, with the more brash **Passignano** the main camping and after-hours resort.

Head north from Perugia and you'll find a relatively undistinguished region centred on the upper reaches of the **Tiber valley**. Routes follow the river's lacklustre course, useful mainly for onward forays into Tuscany and the Marche – in particular to Sansepolcro or Urbino for the paintings of Piero della Francesca. Unheralded **Città di Castello** is the only worthwhile Umbrian port of call, a plain-bound town whose art gallery contains the region's only painting by Raphael, an artist apprenticed to Perugino, Umbria's pre-eminent Renaissance painter.

East of the Tiber, potholed minor roads climb through swathes of attractively barren country to **Gubbio**, one of Italy's medieval gems, a place that's been saddled with the label of the Umbrian Siena. Much in the town merits the comparison, however, not least its overbearing civic palace, the **Palazzo dei Consoli**, a piece of medieval bluster up there with Perugia's Palazzo dei Priori. Churches and galleries abound, and the honeycomb of old

---

ACCOMMODATION PRICES

Throughout this guide, **hotel** accommodation is graded on a scale from ① to ⑨, indicating the cost of the **cheapest double room** in each establishment in high season (for **hostels**, rates per person are given in lire). The price bands to which these codes refer are as follows:

① up to L60,000	④ L120,000–150,000	⑦ L250,000–300,000
② L60,000–90,000	⑤ L150,000–200,000	⑧ L300,000–350,000
③ L90,000–120,000	⑥ L200,000–250,000	⑨ over L350,000

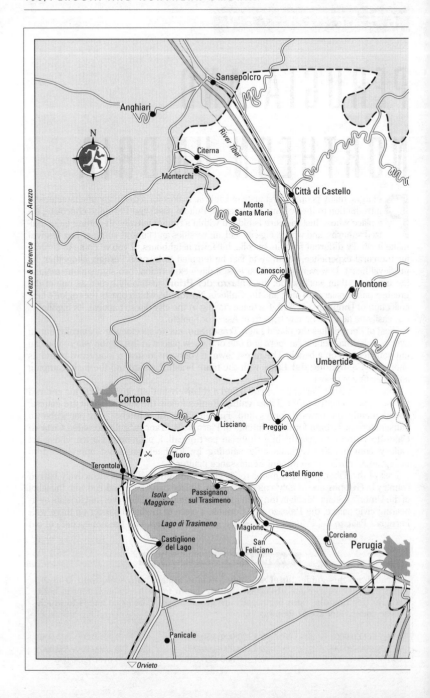

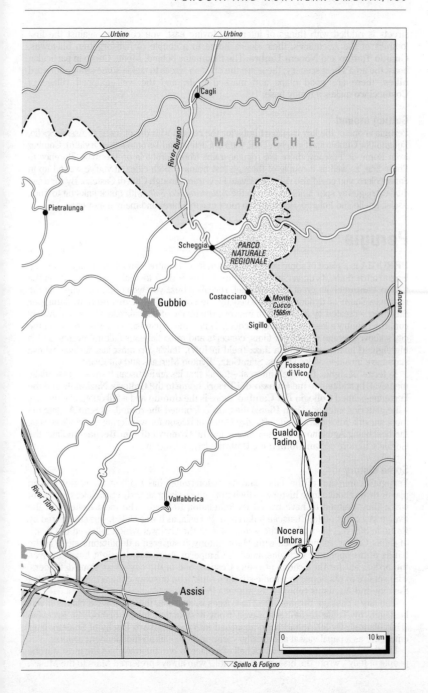

streets is riddled with things of interest. Moving east, you come up against the first foothills of the Apennines, their slopes home to a couple of half-forgotten hill-towns, **Gualdo Tadino** and **Nocera Umbra**. The mountains behind, Monte Cucco in particular, boast the area's best scenery; these are the obvious places to tackle some straightforward **hikes**: there are good maps and marked trails, and the well-equipped village of **Costacciaro** makes a handy base.

Getting around

Perugia is one of the key transport hubs for the region, with direct trains to Assisi, Spello, Foligno (for Gubbio and Spoleto), Todi, Città di Castello and Teróntola (for Orvieto). Coming from Rome or Tuscany, there are regular trains from Teróntola on the main Florence to Rome line, as well as a couple of through fast trains to both cities. If you've wound up in Sansepolcro, you could also ride the private FCU train through Città di Castello. By car a fast dual-carriageway spur links the city to the *Autostrada del Sole*, with quick links on to Todi, Assisi, Spello and Foligno. Buses run to most major centres and many minor ones.

Perugia

PERUGIA is a place of some style – at least in its old centre – and a city proud of its big-league attractions, its universities, its sights and its Serie A football team. A drink on the **Corso Vannucci**, its great central street, reveals a buzz you won't find elsewhere in the region, a sense of dynamism embodied by the cosmopolitan **Università Italiana per Stranieri** – created by Mussolini to improve the image of Italy abroad and now, privately run, the country's largest language school. This same dynamism remains evident in the city's above-average number of films, concerts and miscellaneous cultural events, and is highlighted further at **Umbria Jazz** (held in July), Italy's foremost jazz festival, whose stars have included Miles Davies, Stan Getz, Wynton Marsalis and Gil Evans.

In terms of sights, Perugia's interest – for all that it's an Etruscan town – is essentially medieval. In addition to the **Palazzo dei Priori**, home to the **Galleria Nazionale** and the Perugino-painted **Collegio del Cambio**, there is the **duomo** and a full quota of churches – the glittering interior of **San Pietro** the most celebrated, the rotunda of **Sant'Angelo** the most ancient. Idiosyncratic one-offs give plenty of reason for wandering the city's streets, the best being Agostino di Duccio's facade for the **Oratorio di San Bernardino** and the Gothic sculpture of **San Domenico**, Umbria's largest church.

Some history

Perugia's command of the Tiber and its major routes has made it the region's main player throughout a long history – albeit not quite as long as early chroniclers made out when they claimed to have traced its foundation to Noah. The most easterly of the twelve key cities of the Etruscan federation, Perusia, as it was called, was conquered by Rome in 309 BC, later taking the wrong side in the civil war which followed the death of Julius Caesar. Allying itself with Mark Antony, it suffered a debilitating siege at the hands of his opponent Octavius, later the Emperor Augustus. It might have survived the ordeal but for the actions of Gaius Cestius, one of the city's less stout defenders, who set fire to his house in a panic-stricken funk. The ensuing conflagration destroyed the city, and Augustus rebuilt it as Augusta Perusia.

The city's passage through the Dark Ages is obscure, though legend claims it was besieged by Totila in 547 and saved from destruction by its bishop, St Ercolano (Herculanus). By 592 it had been absorbed into the Lombard Duchy of Spoleto, later emerging as a papal vassal and finally – around 1140 – as an independent *comune*.

Medieval Perugia was evidently a hell of a place to be: "the town had the most warlike people of Italy", wrote the historian Sismondi, "who always preferred Mars to the Muse".

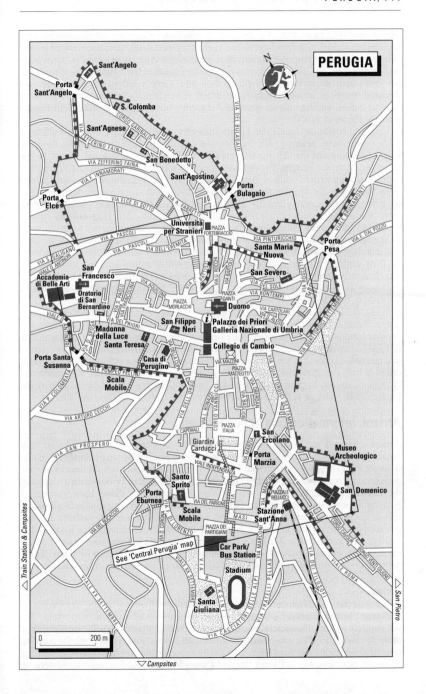

PERUGIA

Sant'Angelo
Porta Sant'Angelo
S. Colomba
CORSO GARIBALDI
Sant'Agnese
VIA ZEFFERINO FAINA
VIA ZEFFERINO FAINA
San Benedetto
VIA F. INNAMORATI
Sant'Agostino
Porta Bulagaio
VIA A. FABRETTI
Porta Elce
VIA ELCE DI SOTTO
VIA DEL BULAGAIO
Università per Stranieri
PIAZZA FORTEBRACCIO
VIA PINTURICCHIO
Porta Pesa
VIA E. DAL POZZO
VIA S. GALIGANO
VIA A. PASCOLI
VIA A. PASCOLI
VIA DELL'EREMITA
Santa Maria Nuova
VIA U. ROCCHI
VIA BARTOLO
San Severo
VIA DEL SOLE
VIA R. ROSCETTO
VIALE Z. FAINA
VIALE DI ANTINORI
San Francesco
Accademia di Belle Arti
VIA DEI PRIORI
VIA AQUILONE
VIA DELLA LUCE
PIAZZA MORLACCHI
PIAZZA DANTI
VIA BONTEMPI
VIA CARTOLARI
Oratorio di San Bernardino
Duomo
VIA DEL VERZARO
VIA DEI PRIORI
San Filippo Neri
Palazzo dei Priori
Galleria Nazionale di Umbria
VIA ALESS
VIA MAESTA DELLE VOLTE
Madonna della Luce
Santa Teresa
Casa di Perugino
Collegio di Cambio
VIA MAZZINI
PIAZZA MATTEOTTI
Porta Santa Susanna
VIALE POMPEO PELLINI
Scala Mobile
VIA DELL'ORSO
VIA BONAZZI
CORSO VANNUCCI
VIA BAGLIONI
VIA QUATTRO NOVEMBRE
VIA P. COLOMBATA
VIA ARTURO CECCHI
V. CAPORALI
PIAZZA ITALIA
San Ercolano
VIA SAN PROSPERO
Giardini Carducci
Porta Marzia
Museo Archeologico
VIALE INDIPENDENZA
San Domenico
Santo Sprito
VIA DEL PARIONE
Porta Eburnea
VIA DEL PASCOLO
Scala Mobile
MASI
VIA MARCONI
PIAZZALE BELLUCCI
Stazione Sant'Anna
VIA DELLA CUPA
VIA D. OFRENA
VIA D. LORENZO
PIAZZA DEI PARTIGIANI
See 'Central Perugia' map
Car Park/ Bus Station
CORSO CAVOUR
BORGO VENTI GIUGNO
VIALE ROMA
Stadium
VIALE XX SETTEMBRE
Santa Giuliana
VIA B. ORSINI
VIA CACCIATORI DELLE ALPI
VIA FRATELLI PELLAS
VIA DEI FILOSOFI

◁ Train Station & Campsites

▷ San Pietro

▽ Campsites

0   200 m

Male citizens played a game – for pleasure – in which two teams, wearing beaked helmets and clothes stuffed with deer hair, stoned each other mercilessly until the majority on one side were dead or wounded. Children were encouraged to join in to promote "application and aggression". In 1265 Perugia was also the birthplace of the **Flagellants**, who within ten years had half of Europe whipping itself into a frenzy before the movement was declared heretical. In addition to some hearty scourging, they took to the streets on moonlit nights, wailing, singing dirges and clattering human bones together – all as expiation for the wrongs of the world.

Using its economic muscle and numerous short-lived alliances, the city built up a huge power base, peaking with its conquest of Siena in 1358. Around this time the *Priori* (members of the ten leading guilds), noble families, and papal agents began vying for control, plunging Perugia into a period when, according to one chronicler, "perfect pandemonium reigned in and about the city". Individual *condottieri* rose briefly from the chaos, the key figures being Biondo Michelotti – stabbed to death in 1398, after five years in power – and the oddly named Braccio Fortebraccio (Arm the Strong Arm), whose eight years of rule brought short-lived stability. The Oddi nobility ran the town until 1488, when the colourful but demented **Baglioni** took over.

The story of the Baglioni is the stuff of soap opera – complicated vendettas, incestuous marriages, hearts torn from bodies and eaten, and any number of people murdered on their wedding nights. After one episode was settled with a hundred murders, the bloodied cathedral had to be washed down with wine and reconsecrated. One Baglioni, Malatesta IV, assigned the defence of Florence in 1530, famously sold his services to the enemy, earning the title "world's greatest traitor".

When the last Baglioni, the wimpish Ridolpho, bungled an assassination of the papal legate, it was a cue for the papacy to step in. Pope Paul III, one of the more powerful and peculiar pontiffs, razed the Baglioni palaces in 1538, then entered the city demanding that all its nuns line up and kiss his feet. Thus refreshed, he built the Rocca Paolina, a huge fortress that guaranteed church supremacy for three centuries. During the nineteenth-century unification of Italy, Perugia's liberation from the papacy was particularly violent, with numerous citizens massacred by Swiss Guards sent to bolster Church control. Liberation from the Nazis in 1944, courtesy of the British Eighth Army, was considerably less bloodthirsty.

Arrival, information and accommodation

Arrival in Perugia can be a dispiriting business, its approaches a confusing and off-putting medley of suburbs, busy roads and hard-to-find parking places. Once in the medieval centre, however, things improve considerably. The old city revolves around **Corso Vannucci**, a broad pedestrian thoroughfare capped at its northern end by the **Piazza IV Novembre** – home to the duomo and Palazzo dei Priori – and at its southern extreme by **Piazza Italia**, jumping-off point for the city's southern quarters. Once off the Corso, the **twisting medieval alleys** are initially disorientating, but by dividing the city into western, northern and southern sections you soon get to grips with the layout. You can walk everywhere, although you'll cover a fair bit of ground in the course of a day's sightseeing – particularly if you take in sights at the extreme northern and southern ends of town. You should also be prepared for **steep climbs** between Perugia's many levels. Hi-tech lifts and escalators help out only occasionally.

Arrival

Arriving on the state **train** network you'll find yourself well away from the historic centre at **Piazza Vittorio Veneto**: it's too far to walk from here – it's all uphill on busy roads – but the centre's an easy ten-minute ride on bus #11, #12, or #15, though the numbering is prone to change: look for something going to Piazza Italia or Piazza Matteotti; the bus stop lists the destinations. Services leave from the forecourt outside the station and, depending on the service, drop you in **Piazza Italia** or **Piazza Matteotti**, both equally convenient for

Corso Vannucci. City bus tickets (L1200, valid for 20min from validation on the bus) are available from a small booth in the forecourt or a machine by the entrance.

If you're coming on the private FCU rail lines from Todi or Terni to the south, or from Città di Castello or Sansepolcro to the north, you'll arrive at the more central **Stazione Sant'Anna**, in the southern part of town near the **bus terminal** at **Piazza dei Partigiani**. If you're arriving by **car**, the historic centre is closed to traffic. The best bet is to follow the signs for Piazza dei Partigiani in the south, where there's a large and convenient two-storey covered car park (hourly tariff). From here you can jump on one of the signed *scala mobile* (escalators) through the weird subterranean Via Baglioni Sotterranea to Piazza Italia. Another good option, in the west, is the parking in **Viale Pellini** (hourly tariff), again connected by escalators, this time to Via dei Priori. If you're driving in from the north, however, you may find the car park in **Via Sant'Antonio** more convenient.

Perugia also has a small **airport**, Sant'Egidio, 18km east of the city centre. It handles domestic flights to and from Milan and Bologna (not Rome); as yet there's no connecting bus to the centre, leaving taxis as the only alternative.

Information

The **tourist office** is at Sala San Severo, Piazza IV Novembre 3 (Mon–Sat 8.30am–1.30pm & 3.30–6.30pm, Sun 9am–1pm; ☎075.573.6458 or 075.572.3327, fax 075.573.6828). It's good for advice on city events and helpful in finding accommodation. The regional office is at Via Mazzini 21 (Mon–Fri 9am–1pm; ☎075.572.5341), and there's a small summer-only office at the train station (daily 8.30am–1.30pm). On the eastern edge of Piazza dei Partigiani there is also a privately run **Infotourist Point**, Largo Cacciatori delle Alpi 3 (Mon–Sat 8.30am–1.30pm & 3.30–7.30pm; also summer Sun 9am–1pm; ☎075.573.6336, fax 075.572.7235). This offers a fair amount of tourist information, and also operates as an outlet of Box Office, a ticket agency which can make bookings for all manner of events across the region, including Umbria Jazz. A young person's help line, **Informa Giovanni** (Mon–Fri 10am–1.30pm, also Mon & Wed 3.30–5pm; ☎075.572.0646 or 075 572.8724) offers guidance on the latest bars, clubs and cheap pizzerias.

At the station and in Piazza Italia you'll see some hi-tech *Digiplan* machines, primed to provide tourist information (in Italian) on computer print-out – great in theory but often either broken or out of paper.

Accommodation

Perugia has plenty of **accommodation** in all price ranges, though reservations are in order as some of the cheapest places may be taken up by long-stay students: book, too, during the July jazz festival, when room rates will likely be raised. Unlike some Tuscan cities, **prices** are otherwise pretty standard year-round, with no real "low season". More than in most Umbrian towns, it pays to be in or very near the historic centre; you don't want to be out in the suburbs at any price. Recommendations below are the most central (bar one out of town splurge); private bathrooms where available put about L20,000 on the price. If you're **camping** you have no choice but to be out of town. It's worth considering the nicer campsites around Lago Trasimeno, and then using them as bases for day trips to the city.

HOTELS

Piccolo, Via Bonazzi 25 (☎075.572.2987). Despite its name, not as small as some of the one-stars below: it has 10 rooms, with and without private bathrooms, and is as central as can be. ②.
Anna, Via dei Priori 48 (☎ & fax 075.573.6304). Central one-star with 13 rooms and a choice of private or shared bathrooms. ②.
Paola, Via della Canapina 5 (☎075.572.3816). A popular if slightly peripheral one-star place, but only 8 rooms (4 shared bathrooms), so be sure to call in advance. It's tricky to find: follow signs for the *Umbria* from the Corso (see below), go down the steps in the passageway, turn right and follow the second set of steps towards the car park. ②.

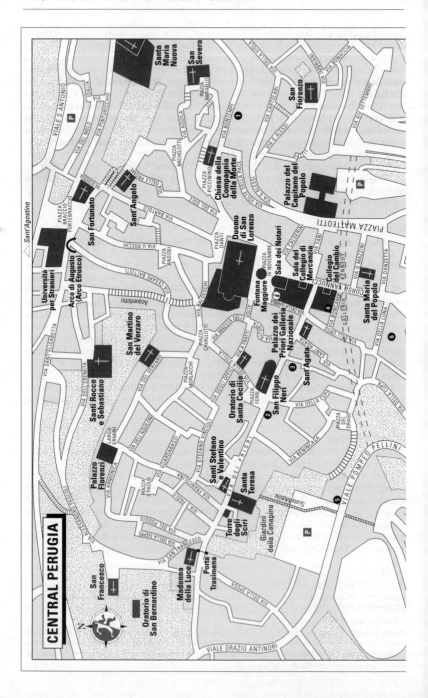

CENTRAL PERUGIA

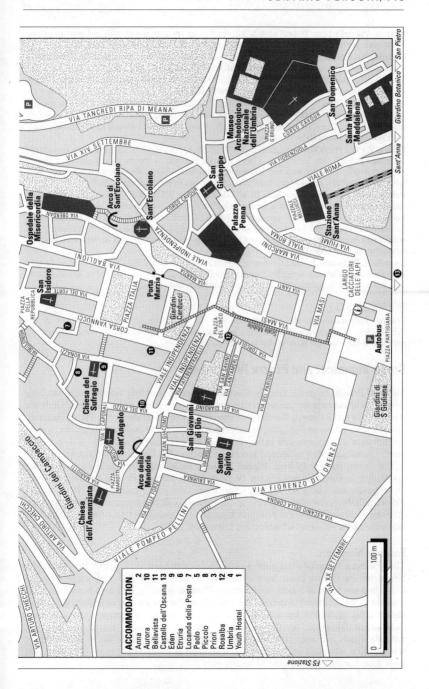

ACCOMMODATION

Anna	2
Aurora	10
Bellavista	11
Castello dell'Oscana	13
Eden	9
Erruria	6
Locanda della Poste	7
Paolo	5
Piccolo	8
Priori	3
Rosalba	12
Umbria	4
Youth Hostel	1

Etruria, Via della Luna 21 (☎075.572.3730). An 8-room one-star, rooms with and without private bathrooms, perfectly positioned just west of Piazza della Repubblica and the Corso. ②.

Umbria, Via Boncambi 37 (☎075.572.1203). Comfortable 18-room two-star with prices only a whisker above the one-stars above; rooms with and without private bath. ②.

Eden, Via C Caporali 9 (☎075.572.8102, fax 075.720.342). An 18-room two-star (all rooms with private bath) in an alley just a few paces west of the Corso. ③.

Aurora, Viale Indipendenza 21 (☎075.572.4819 or 075.572.4453, fax 075.572.4819). A 14-room two-star immediately south of Piazza Italia. Basic and clean, with very helpful staff, but on a very busy road. ③.

Rosalba, Via del Circo 7 (☎ & fax 075.572.0626). A two-star with 11 rooms, all with private bathrooms, south of Piazza Italia. ③.

Priori, Via dei Priori-Via Vermiglioli 3 (☎075.572.3378, fax 075.572.3213). Perugia's first-choice mid-range hotel, if only because it's a large 49-room two-star, so there's a good chance of finding space; tastefully fitted out and well located in the historic centre. Also has a great terrace overlooking the rooftops. Rooms vary hugely in price, so ask to see a selection. ③–④.

Palace Hotel Bellavista, Piazza Italia 12 (☎075.572.0741, fax 075.572.9092). A quiet three-star with 74 rooms; the most reasonably priced of the up-market hotels at the southern end of Corso Vannucci. ④–⑤.

Locanda della Posta, Corso Vannucci 97 (☎075.572.8925, fax 075.573.2562). Central 39-room four-star, and though the five-star *Brufani* just to the south is smarter (and more expensive), this is the first choice in Perugia if you want a treat. Goethe and Hans Christian Andersen are just two luminaries to have stayed here. ⑥.

Castello dell'Oscano, Località Cenerente, Strada Forcella 37 (☎075.690.125). For when credit-card madness takes hold: this converted four-star hotel has just 22 rooms, all part of an amazing castle with full medieval trappings set in acres of parkland 5km from Perugia. ⑧.

YOUTH HOSTEL

Centro Internazionale di Accoglienza per la Gioventù, Via Bontempi 13 (☎ & fax 075.572.2880). The position of this hostel – just 2 minutes from the duomo – is ideal, but there's a midnight curfew and the place is shut 9.30am–4pm; L16,000.

Corso Vannucci and Piazza IV Novembre

Medieval Perugia hinges around the **Corso Vannucci**, one of Italy's great people-watching streets, its broad expanse packed from dawn to the early hours with a parade of Umbria's style-makers and followers. Named after the city's most celebrated artist, Pietro Vannucci, better known simply as Perugino, the street has several of the city's key sights, not to mention the most atmospheric café in the city – the *Pasticceria Sandri* at no. 32 – and one of the better central places for coffee and lunchtime snacks – the *Café del Cambio* at no. 29.

The Corso strikes off from **Piazza Italia**, a largely nineteenth-century ensemble, concluding in the medieval **Piazza IV Novembre**, former site of a Roman reservoir. On opposite sides of it are the city's two traditional power centres: the **Palazzo dei Priori**, still the home of the council, and the **duomo**. At the centre is perhaps the most graceful fountain in Italy, the **Fontana Maggiore**, stunningly restored to as near a pristine state as its 700-year-old sculptures allow.

Fontana Maggiore

The **Fontana Maggiore** has quite a pedigree: designed in 1277 by Fra' Bevignate, the Silvestrine monk who had a hand in shaping Orvieto's cathedral, and sculpted by the father-and-son team of Nicola and Giovanni **Pisano**, possibly with help from Arnolfo di Cambio. It was installed to receive the water from the town's new aqueduct, a five-kilometre affair designed by a leading hydraulic engineer of the age, the Venetian Boninsegna. However, as the chronicler Bonazzi observed, "beasts, barrels and unwashed pots and unclean hands were forbidden the use of the water, and indeed it was guarded with such jealous care that it seemed as though the people of Perugia had built their fountain for the sake of beauty only".

The **sculptures** and **bas-reliefs** on the two polygonal basins were part of a carefully conceived decorative scheme designed to illustrate the city's glory and achievements. By some canny calculation none of them line up directly, encouraging you to walk around the fountain chasing a point of repose that never comes. The lower basin has 25 double reliefs, twelve showing the *Labours of the Months*, together with the appropriate sign of the zodiac – December's pig-sticking is particularly graphic. The remaining reliefs include a lion and griffon, Perugia's medieval symbols; four double panels depicting the Liberal Arts; scenes from the Old Testament – note the relief of the large lion and smaller lion being beaten, an allegory expounding the virtues of punishment; and reliefs portraying Roman scenes and two of Aesop's fables. Most of the 24 upper basin statues are by Giovanni Pisano and depict a wide range of characters, among them saints, Old Testament heroes and a variety of allegorical figures representing Victory, Theology and the like. Giovanni also completed the three figures in the basin, believed to represent the three Cardinal Virtues – Faith, Hope and Charity.

The Palazzo dei Priori

The far end of the Corso is dominated by the gaunt bulk of the **Palazzo dei Priori**, with its majestic Gothic doorway, rows of trefoil windows (from which convicted criminals were thrown to their deaths) and businesslike Guelph crenellations. Often cited as Italy's most impressive civic palace (it's certainly one of the country's largest), it was begun in 1293 by two local architects and completed in 1443, its impressive effect deriving as much from its sheer bulk as the harmonious beauty created by the buildings around it. Four separate sights are hidden within its precincts: the **Sala dei Notari**, **Sala del Collegio della Mercanzia**, **Collegio del Cambio** and – the star turn – the **Galleria Nazionale dell'Umbria**. All are worthwhile, but orientation within the palazzo can be a little confusing – it's easiest to tackle them in the order given below.

THE SALA DEI NOTARI

The **Sala dei Notari** (Mon–Sat 9am–1pm & 3–7pm; same hours Sun July–Sept only; free), the medieval lawyers' former meeting hall, is entered via the fan-shaped steps opposite the duomo. It's an obvious point of reference, its doorway topped by copies of a bronze Guelph lion and Perugian griffon (the originals are in the Galleria Nazionale; see below). Once thought to be Roman, the figures were probably made in 1274 or 1281, making them among the first pieces of large-scale casting in medieval Italy. Latest research, however, suggests the body of the griffon, at least, may be Etruscan, the wings having been added during the thirteenth-century casting. The chains below, according to tradition, were snatched from the gate and gallows of Siena during a raid in 1358. The triple-arched **loggia** is thought to be a remnant of San Severo, a church demolished to make way for the palace in the thirteenth century.

The Sala is one of the oldest parts of the palazzo, dating from the late 1290s – about the same time as the civic palaces in Florence and Siena were being raised. It's a tremendous space, overarched by superb vaulting. Before the lawyers got their hands on it, it was used as a meeting place for the townspeople in times of crisis and decision. Its celebrated **frescoes**, however, were substantially repainted in the last century, the net result being little more than flashes of colour, fancy flags and swirls. They represent the arms of various *podestà*, or magistrates of the city, from 1297 to 1424, infinitely duller than the hard-to-see thirteenth-century frescoes of scenes from the Old Testament which adorn the upper arches.

THE SALA DEL COLLEGIO DELLA MERCANZIA

The **Sala del Collegio della Mercanzia** (March–Oct Mon–Fri 9am–1pm & 2.30–5.30pm, Sat 9am–1pm & 2.30–6.30pm, Sun 9am–1pm; Nov–Feb Tues & Thurs–Fri 8am–2pm, Wed & Sat 8am–5pm, Sun 9am–1pm, closed Mon; L2000, or L6000 with

Collegio del Cambio) is hidden behind an inconspicuous door at no. 15 farther down the Corso side of the palazzo (to the right of the palace's main portal). Since 1390 it has been the seat of the merchants' guild – the city's most important, and a body that survives as a charitable institution to this day. At first glance it amounts to little, but at close quarters the room reveals intricately inlaid wooden panelling, breathtaking fifteenth-century work, considered some of Italy's finest.

THE COLLEGIO DEL CAMBIO

The **Collegio del Cambio**, which lies a few doors down at Corso Vannucci 25 (March–Oct Mon–Sat 9am–12.30pm & 2.30–5.30pm, Sun 9am–12.30pm; Nov–Feb Tues–Sat 8am–2pm, Sun 9am–12.30pm; L5000, or L6000 with the Mercanzia), was the guild home of the town's moneychangers, a body (founded in 1259), like the merchants' guild, which survives as a charitable body to this day. Its walls are covered with frescoes by **Perugino** – these are not only considered his masterpieces, but also reckoned one of the best-preserved Renaissance schemes in the country. The commission was awarded by the bankers' guild in 1496, about the same time as Perugino was approached to fresco part of the duomo in Orvieto, an undertaking eventually executed by Luca Signorelli. The city's bankers were determined to have paintings commensurate with their own sense of self-importance, and to this end probably paid Perugino – then at the peak of his powers – more than was on offer in Orvieto. This probably explains the painter's mysterious disappearance from Orvieto, where he spent just five desultory days working in the cathedral.

Having paid their money, the bankers were determined to impose upon the painter their theme of choice; Francesco Maturanzio, a leading humanist theorist, was brought in as consultant, and proposed the fusion of classical and Christian culture, painting Christian icons alongside figures of classical myth. Though not an unusual Renaissance conceit, the vigour and uncompromising way in which the themes are yoked together created a distinctly curious juxtaposition. The thesis intended to suggest that there was unity in variety, and that human perfection, expressed by classical art, was obtainable through Christ's example.

Whatever the metaphysical intent, the frescoes certainly succeed aesthetically, unified by Perugino's melancholy tone, idealized and soft-focus figures and mellow landscapes. The paintings cover virtually all the walls and ceiling vaults of the single room, part of which – probably the prophets and sibyls on the right-hand wall (behind the ticket desk) – was painted by Perugino's pupil **Raphael**, then only about thirteen years old. Up on the door-side wall there's a famous but unremarkable self-portrait of the master, looking on with sour-faced disapproval – ironically the only element to disturb the frescoes' beautiful evenness of tone.

The ceiling vaults illustrate the main gods of the classical world: Apollo on his chariot at the centre; Saturn, Jupiter and Mars above the Corso wall; Mercury, Venus and Diana towards the window. Right of the window are portraits of famous Greeks and Romans, real and mythical, with the allegorical figures of Prudence and Justice joined by Cato (symbol of Wisdom), and with Socrates and Trajan, among others, below. The end wall, farthest from the entrance, introduces the Christian strand, with a *Nativity* and the *Transfiguration*, cleaned after having been blackened by smoke from the room's former oil lamps. The right-hand wall shows God amongst the angels, with sibyls to the right and men to the left: Isaac, Moses, Daniel (possibly a portrait of Raphael), David, Jeremiah and Solomon. The lovely little chapel to the rear, the **Cappella di San Giovanni Battista**, is smothered in frescoes on the *Life of John the Baptist* (1513–18) by Giovanni di Paolo – like Raphael, a former pupil of Perugino.

THE GALLERIA NAZIONALE

The **Galleria Nazionale dell'Umbria** (Mon–Sat 9am–7pm, Sun 9am–1pm; closed first Mon of every month; L8000), on the fourth floor of the palace complex, is the region's main repository of Umbrian art. Its entrance is through the opulent doorway on the Corso; having pushed past harassed Perugians on their way to do battle with council bureaucracy, you might well find the small lift isn't working, in which case you have to clamber up the stairs, a route once taken by nobles on horseback. Dust has now settled on a long restoration project, which has turned the gallery into one of central Italy's best: the result is a 16-room romp through both the history of Umbrian painting and the schools which influenced it. Be certain to follow the gallery's proscribed itinerary – after passing though the ticket office rotonda the order is a little confusing: make for room 2 straight ahead and left (room 1 is that in which you're standing). Free guides in several languages are usually available just beyond the ticket office.

The entire chronology of the **Umbrian art** canon is traced, from its Byzantine-influenced roots, its parallel development with the Sienese in the thirteenth and fourteenth centuries, through to its late fifteenth-century golden age when Perugia became the main focus of endeavour. The region's premier painters, Perugino and Pinturicchio, are predictably well covered, as are their imitators, or artists who worked in a late-Renaissance vein and fall outside the confines of the Umbrian school.

Some of the gallery's finest moments, however, have nothing to do with indigenous painters. This is particularly true of early rooms, where the **Sienese** largely hold sway. Amongst a welter of anonymous works, the early highlight is **room 2**'s large *Crucifixion* by the so-called **Maestro di San Francesco**, one of the gallery's earliest pieces, and painted by the anonymous hand believed to be responsible for some of the superlative frescoes in the nave of the Lower Church in Assisi's Basilica di San Francesco. Also look out for an outstanding *Madonna and Angels* by **Duccio** (1304–8), its static beauty the obvious model for many of the Umbrian works that follow. Other named Sienese masters include Bartolomeo da Siena, Domenico di Bartolo and Taddeo di Bartolo, the last named responsible here for three altarpieces (Room 5), including a *Pentecost* which displays a radical approach to composition, at odds with the more conservative Umbrians to come.

In acknowledging the increasing influence of Tuscan painters on Umbrians as the fifteenth century progressed, the gallery almost allows a pair of paintings by outsiders to steal the show. One is an astounding triptych by **Fra' Angelico**, the *Madonna and Child with Angels and Saints*. Radiant with the painter's gorgeous swathes of blue, it was painted in 1437 for Perugia's church of San Domenico (at time of writing displayed on its own in the Sala Podiani at the end of the gallery). The other is more extraordinary still: **Piero della Francesca**'s sensational polyptych in room 4 of the *Madonna and Child and SS. Anthony of Padua and John the Baptist with SS. Francis and Elizabeth of Hungary*, executed for Perugia's Sant'Antonio monastery between around 1459 and 1468, about the time of his Arezzo cycle. It's full of eccentric compositional nuances, particularly in the small *Annunciation* hinged to the top of the main painting, in which a mannered succession of arches around the Virgin recedes into a blank wall. The predella depicts miracles performed by the saints in the main painting.

Dozens of anonymous **early fifteenth-century Umbrian works** follow, amounting in many cases to no more than a surfeit of the religious iconography that fills Umbrian paintings without the redeeming dulcet qualities of the Sienese. The better of the Umbrians are Matteo da Gualdo and Nicolò Alunno, the latter represented by a *gonfalone*, or painted banner (room 10), a genre later to become the special preserve of Perugian painters. Alunno's banner hangs next to a similar work by **Benedetto Bonfigli**, an important mid-period Umbrian painter, who also has works in room 7 (a superb *Annunciation and St Luca*) and – more significantly – in room 13. The latter was the palazzo's **chapel**, decorated between 1454 and 1480 by Bonfigli with surviving fragmentary episodes from the life of Saints Ercolano and Louis of Toulouse (Perugia's patron saints). The frescoes provide a detailed picture of aspects of fifteenth-century Perugia – walls, towers and monuments – that have now largely vanished.

Heralded by a bevy of Perugian contemporaries, **Perugino** marks the apotheosis of the Umbrian school. His immense output is encapsulated here by about a dozen works, mostly in room 15, the large foyer-type area of the ticket hall. This is not the most intimate setting for some sublime pictures, but little can detract from the art of a painter talked of by his contemporaries in the same breath as Michelangelo and Leonardo da Vinci. The loveliest painting is probably the *Madonna della Consolazione* (1496–8), a work whose imagery and bravura technique underline just how much Raphael, Perugino's pupil, would take from his master. Almost equally fine are two earlier pieces painted around 1475, a *Pietà* and *Adoration of the Magi*.

The second-ranked Umbrian, and Perugino's occasional collaborator, **Pinturicchio**, is not so well represented, save for the gargantuan *Pala di Santa Maria dei Fossi* (1495), also in room 15, widely considered one of the masterpices of the Umbrian canon. This aside, however, there is little here to compare with the artist's frescoes of Spello's Santa Maria Maggiore (see p.504) or the works in Siena's Piccolomini library (see p.311). Other rooms contain perfectly good works by followers of Perugino; names to look out for are Sinibaldo Ibi, Giannicola di Paolo and Eusebio di San Giorgio, all fluent interpreters of Perugino's merging of Umbrian and Florentine traditions.

The rest of the gallery ploughs a remorseless course through seventeenth- to nineteenth-century Umbrian offerings, most of them large gloomy canvases.

The Duomo

Piazza IV Novembre is backed by the plain-faced **Duomo**, or San Lorenzo. There's been a church on this site for a thousand years, but the cornerstone for the present building was laid in 1345m, though subsequent construction was almost immediately interrupted by the Black Death (1348). Most of the building was completed late in the following century and even then the facade, which is in the lovely pink stone of most local towns, was left unfinished. Taking a pragmatic approach to the problem, the Perugians pinched the marble facing intended for Arezzo's cathedral, though a subsequent hammering from Arezzo brought about its shame-faced return.

The most interesting face of the cathedral is the one fronting the piazza. To the right of the portal is a bronze statue (1555) of Pope Julius III by Vincenzo Danti, and to the left an unfinished **pulpit** built for the roving St Bernardino of Siena, who was something of a hit with the Perugians. It was here that he preached the original Bonfire of the Vanities, urging women to burn their wigs and everyone else to give up books, fine clothes and general good times. To the left are remains of the Loggia Fortebraccio (1423), taken from the house of the city's one-time strong-armed ruler.

The Baroque **interior** is imposing enough, though short on art works. Its pride and joy is the Virgin's "wedding ring", a novel relic, housed in the Cappella del Sant'Anello (first chapel on the left). An unwieldy piece of agate, said to change colour according to the character of the person wearing it, it was stolen by the Perugians from Chiusi in 1473 and encased in a series of fifteen boxes, fitted like Russian dolls; it's brought out for public edification once a year on July 30. Embedded in the wall nearby are fragments of an altar by Agostino di Duccio (1473); next to them is a lovely painting by Berto di Giovanni showing 1520s Perugia in the background, with a small lunette above by Giannicola di Paolo.

In the right aisle, the first chapel, closed by an iron screen, contains a widely admired *Deposition* painted in 1569 by Barocci, apparently under the influence of poison administered by a jealous rival. More toxin-related mementos are contained in the transepts, where urns hold the ashes of Pope Martin IV, who died in the city after eating too many eels, and Urban IV, who was reputedly poisoned with *aquetta*, an imaginative little brew made by rubbing arsenic into pork fat and distilling the resultant ooze.

The most conspicuous piece of art, though, is the *Madonna delle Grazie* attributed to Giannicola di Paolo, on the third pillar of the right nave. Easily recognized by its tinselly votive offerings, it's supposed to have miraculous powers, and mothers still bring their newly baptized children to kneel before it.

MUSEO DELL'OPERA DEL DUOMO

Through the cathedral sacristy (or if it's closed, through a courtyard to the left of the entrance) are the cloisters and **Museo dell'Opera del Duomo**, or Museo Capitolare (daily 8am–noon & 3.30–6pm; free, but closed at time of writing), a rich little treasury with some fine examples of the miniatures for which medieval Perugia was renowned; a *Madonna and Saints* (1484) by Luca Signorelli, and works by Umbrian and Sienese masters such as Meo da Siena, Andrea Vanni and Bartolomeo Caporali.

West and east of the Corso

For a feel of medieval Perugia, the most rewarding streets are to the west of the Corso, in particular **Via dei Priori**, entered through the archway in the Palazzo dei Priori. This curves downhill through a slice of the old city, taking in a succession of little churches and culminating in the **Oratorio di San Bernardino**, one of Perugia's prime pieces of sculpture. From here it makes sense to walk east on Via A. Pascoli, a street which leads neatly to Piazza Fortebraccio, key to the sights in the city's northern quarters (see below). East of the Corso there are a couple of extra diversions in the fine medieval quarter around **Piazza Danti**, the small square behind the duomo. From here, too, you could continue – though slightly less rewardingly – to **Piazza Fortebraccio** by way of Santa Maria Nuova.

West: Via dei Priori to San Francesco

The steeply sloping **Via dei Priori**, if you're to believe the medieval chroniclers, was a conduit for almost constantly flowing rivers of blood. The side streets, too, have associations with Perugia's gory past, notably **Via della Gabbia**, part way down, where there once hung a large iron cage used to imprison thieves and wayward clergymen. A journal written in 1492 records the fate of one priest, Angelo di Ferolo, who wound up behind its bars – "it was very cold and there was much snow, and he remained there until the first day of February both night and day and that same day he was brought out dead". You can still make out long spikes on some of the lower walls of the street, used as hooks for the heads of executed criminals.

Just beyond, on the left, is the little church of **Sant'Agata** (1219–1314), scattered with fourteenth-century fragments of Umbrian school frescoes. **San Filippo Neri**, farther down on the right, is a Baroque church worth a look only for its high altarpiece, a painting by Pietro da Cortona, a local star who would make his name in Rome and Florence. Dropping down farther still you come to **Santi Stefano e Valentino** on the right, a lovely little church with fragments of frescoes which puts the ugly **Santa Teresa** opposite to shame. Nearby is the unmissable 46-metre **Torre degli Sciri**, one of the few medieval towers (they reputedly numbered seven hundred) to have survived Perugia's violent historical passage. Off to the right near here, Via della Cupa leads off towards Via Deliziosa and signs for the **Casa di Perugino** at no. 17 – not really worth the detour.

Towards the end of Via dei Priori comes **Madonna della Luce**, dominated by a fresco by G. B. Caporali and an altarpiece by Tiberio d'Assisi, both accomplished followers of Perugino. The tiny chapel takes its name – Madonna of the Light – from an incident in 1513, when a young barber swore so profusely on losing at cards that a Madonna in a wayside shrine closed her eyes in horror, and kept them closed for four days. The miracle inspired celebrations, processions and the building of this new church. Immediately to the left, the **Arco di San Luca**, or Porta Trasimena, has been one of the principal entrances to the city since Etruscan times.

Bearing right beyond the Madonna della Luce brings you to a welcoming patch of grass, frequented by students from the art school next door, and conveniently placed for admiring Agostino di Duccio's colourful **Oratorio di San Bernardino**. Its richly embellished facade is far and away the best piece of sculpture in the city – an odd but appealing mix of bas-reliefs and coloured marble, commissioned in 1457 by the city's magistrates in gratitude to St Bernardino for trying to bring peace to Perugia. The detail of the carving warrants a close look, especially the lower frieze depicting the Bonfire of the Vanities – a pile of Perugian wigs, books and hosiery elicited by the saint's preaching. The church interior is rarely open, but contains the tomb of Fra' Angelo, who ordered the oratory's construction, and a high altar fashioned from a fourth-century Christian sarcophagus.

To the right of the Oratorio is what's left of **San Francesco**, Bernardino's lodging in the city, and in its time Perugia's most sumptuous church. Started just four years after Francis's death in 1226, it's been laid low by earthquakes and landslips, though the curiously jumbled facade is still just about standing and the interior is often used as a concert hall.

East: around Piazza Danti

Piazza Danti is a pleasant little square, the scene of a weekend flower and terracotta market and site of a third-century BC **Pozzo Etrusco**, or Etruscan well, entered at no. 18 (April–Sept daily 10.30am–1.30pm & 2.30–6.30pm; Oct–March Mon–Sat 10.30am–1.30pm & 2.30–4.30pm/Sat until 5.30pm, Sun 10.30am–1.30pm & 2.30–5.30pm; L3500 includes admission to San Severo). Its 430,000-litre capacity was sufficient to supply the entire city. Close by, and the chief sight of this district, is the church of **San Severo** (same hours as Pozzo Etrusco; L3500 joint ticket). It's a little difficult to find: take Via Bontempi off the square, then the tiny Via Raffaello curving left, and the church is straight ahead in Piazza Raffaello. Legend claims it was built on the site of a pagan temple to the sun – the spot is east-facing and the town's highest point – which gave its name to the Porta Sole district of the Etruscan city. There would once have been five such districts, spreading down from the temple to five corresponding gates in the outer wall. Most of the church is a Baroque rehash, grafted onto a building that dates from 1007, though one chapel was spared – the one that contains one of **Raphael**'s first complete works, a *Holy Trinity and Saints*, painted shortly before he settled in Florence in 1505. The lower panels, depicting *Six Saints*, were painted in 1521 by Perugino, then in his dotage, a year after the death of his erstwhile pupil.

Return to Via Bontempi, turn left downhill, and you'll come to **Santa Maria Nuova**, a sprawling and much knocked-about church recently restored more or less to its original Gothic appearance. Its main point of interest is the *gonfalone* in the second chapel on the right; created in 1472 by Bonfigli, it features a view of Perugia under attack from divine thunderbolts.

In the area above here, the **Porta Sole** proper, there once stood the palace of Cardinal Montemaggiore of Cluny, the city's papal governor from 1372. Though his residence was described by contemporaries as the most beautiful in Italy, he was hated by the locals as "that French Vandal, that most iniquitous Nero" – perhaps because he removed bits of the duomo to aid its construction. Within three years a revolt and siege had sent him scurrying; the palace was reduced to rubble by a vast catapult, the so-called *cacciaprete* – the priest-hunter.

The northern quarters

The **northern quarters** of the *centro storico* focus on **Piazza Fortebraccio**, ten minutes' walk downhill from Piazza IV Novembre, or a similar distance from San Francesco along Via A. Pascoli or Santa Maria Nuova on Via Pinturicchio. The first route follows Perugia's oldest street, the 2500-year-old **Via Ulisse Rocchi**; the latter passes the modern university buildings and goes under the famous raised walkway, the **Via del Aquedotto**, pictures of which dominate Perugia's tourist handouts. Sights up here are not the most captivating in the city, but the church of **Sant'Angelo**, at least, is worth the walk, if only to have a picnic or take a snooze in its grounds.

Piazza Fortebraccio and Sant'Agostino

Unlovely **Piazza Fortebraccio** is dominated by the **Arco di Augusto**, or Arco Etrusco, a massive gateway whose lowest section represents one of the few remaining monuments to Etruscan Perugia. It dates from the second century BC, when it was the main entrance to the city. The upper arch and bulwarks were added by the Romans when they recaptured the city in 40 BC; under the arch you can still see the letters spelling out its new name, Augusta Perusia – the first part immodestly large, the latter considerably smaller. The top-storey loggia is a sixteenth-century addition.

On the western side of the square, housed in the Palazzo Gallenga, is the **Università Italiana per Stranieri**, founded in 1925 and now a favourite of foreign students keen to bone up on Italian art, language and culture. The bar downstairs here is a friendly, cosmopolitan meeting ground, but don't expect much joy from the ironically titled information desk in the foyer. Posters around the place give details of concerts and English language films, especially frequent in the April to December term times.

A short walk north from Piazza Fortebraccio, along Corso Garibaldi, brings you out to the half-defunct church of **Sant'Agostino**, originally Romanesque, now botched Baroque, and filled with wistful signs explaining what paintings used to hang in the church before they were spirited to France by light-fingered Napoleonic troops. The missing pictures have been replaced with what someone presumably considers "modern art". The church, however, is not entirely ruined: there's a beautiful **choir** (1502), probably based on drawings by Perugino, and a couple of patches of fresco on the left-hand wall, giving a tantalizing idea of what the place must once have been. Adjoining is the fifteenth-century **Oratorio di Sant'Agostino**, its ludicrously ornate ceiling looking as if it's about to erupt in an explosion of gilt, stucco and chubby plaster cherubs. It's entered from the piazza – Sant'Agostino's sacristan, if he's around, should open up if you ask nicely.

Sant'Angelo

At the end of Corso Garibaldi, tucked into the northern corner of the walls, is the circular **Sant'Angelo** (Tues–Sun 9.30am–noon & 3.30–dusk; free), founded in the fifth century as a temple to St Michael the Archangel (hence Angelo). One of the oldest churches in Umbria – Spoleto's San Salvatore just pips it for antiquity – it was probably built on the site of a Roman temple, its two rings of pillars deriving from an earlier building (there was once a third set, removed to build the church of San Pietro; see opposite page). Further evidence of a pagan predecessor lurks in the high altar, which is cobbled together from Roman fragments.

In a touch of decorative subtlety, all the columns of the inner ring are made from a different type of stone, but otherwise the church is beautifully plain, its Baroque additions having been stripped away. The setting, too, is delightful, a grassy and tranquil retreat, the shade of the walls and cypresses outside providing a favourite siesta spot.

Piazza Italia and south along Corso Cavour

Perugia's other highlights are grouped together on the southern side of town along **Corso Cavour**, the busy main road out of town towards Assisi, which leads off from the nineteenth-century **Piazza Italia**.

The piazza itself has a couple of curiosities nearby. Just to the east is the strange octagonal church of **Sant'Ercolano** (now a war memorial and rarely open), raised between 1297 and 1326 on the spot where the head of Perugia's first bishop miraculously reattached itself after the Goths had chopped it off. A little to the south of this is the **Porta Marzia** (Tues–Sun 8am–2pm), a superb Etruscan archway above an entrance to **Via Baglioni Sotteranea**, a submerged medieval street that is one of the city's most extraordinary sights. Its houses, built over Etruscan ruins, now form part of the foundations for the piazza, but were once part of the **Rocca Paolina**, a colossal sixteenth-century papal fortress designed by Sangallo, the remains of which can perhaps best be seen coming up on the escalators from Piazza dei

Partigiani. Taking in ten churches and four hundred houses, the Rocca was connected by tunnels to strategic points throughout the city. At Unification the fort was pulled down, using dynamite and bare hands, by what appears to have been every man, woman and child in the city – and even then the process took thirty years. Trollope, watching the demolition, wrote that "few buildings have been laden with a heavier amount of long-accumulated hatred".

San Domenico

The unmissable landmark on Corso Cavour is **San Domenico**, which at 122m in length is Umbria's biggest church. Its unfinished exterior has an attractively melancholy air, with pigeons nesting and grass growing on the pinkish marble, but the interior (begun in 1305) collapsed in the sixteenth century and the vast, cold Baroque replacement (1632) looks like an EU warehouse waiting for a food mountain.

Like Sant'Agostino, however, it's full of hints of past beauties. In the fourth chapel on the right is a superb **carved arch** by Agostino di Duccio (1459), a fragment of the original church spoilt only by nineteenth-century frescoes and a doll-like Madonna. To the right of the altar is the **tomb of Benedict XI**, another pope who died in Perugia – this time from eating poisoned figs – after ruling just eight months in 1304. He left to posterity one of the greatest Gothic carvings of its kind in Italy, an elegant and well-preserved piece by one of the period's leading sculptors – Giovanni Pisano, Lorenzo Maitani or Arnolfo di Cambio – nobody knows which. Certainly it's modelled on the tomb of Cardinal de Braye in Orvieto, one of Arnolfo's most influential works (see p.589). Some of the marble work is missing, picked out by troops when a Napoleonic cavalry regiment was billeted in the church. Nearby are extensive patches of fresco, another good choir, and – a welcome splash of colour – some impressive stained-glass windows (1411), the largest in Italy after those of Milan cathedral.

Housed in the church's unfinished cloisters is the **Museo Archeologico Nazionale dell'Umbria** (Mon–Sat 9am–7pm, Sun 9am–1pm; L4000). Before being wrecked by Augustus, Perugia was a big player in the Etruscan federation, which is why this museum has one of the most extensive Etruscan collections around. Years of reorganization, however (still ongoing), have left everything a tad confused and poorly labelled. Some of the best bits of the museum are not Etruscan at all, but are to be found in the rooms devoted to the **Prehistoric Collection**, notably the Bronze Age weapons and artefacts displayed in the main *Salone*. The site that produced the bulk of the Etruscan exhibits is the small but very fine **Ipogeo dei Volumni**, 7km east of the city in Via Assisana at Ponte San Giovanni (July–Aug Mon–Sat 9.30am–12.30pm & 4.30–6.30pm, Sun 9.30am–12.30pm; Sept–June Mon–Sat 9.30am–12.30pm & 3–5pm, Sun 9.30am–12.30pm; L4000; thrice-daily bus from Piazza Garibaldi or train to Ponte San Giovanni) – a trip that probably only the keenest Etruscophiles will find rewarding.

San Pietro

Farther down Corso Cavour, through the double-arched **Porta San Pietro** (1147), is the tenth-century basilica of **San Pietro**, the city's first cathedral and still the most beautiful and idiosyncratic of its churches. Advertised by a rocket-shaped bell tower visible for miles around (rebuilt in 1463), it's tangled up in a group of buildings belonging to the university's agricultural department; the none-too-obvious entrance is through a doorway in the far left-hand corner of the first courtyard off the road.

The interior comes as a shock. Few churches, even in Italy, are so sumptuously decorated, every inch of space being covered in gilt, paint or marble. Surprisingly the effect is appealing, and in the candle-lit gloom the church actually feels like a sacred place. That so much of the Romanesque building survives is due to events at Unification, when the church's Benedictine monks sided with the townspeople in their revolt against papal control. Loyalty to the cause of liberation was not forgotten, and when the religious houses were broken up a year later, San Pietro was allowed to keep its patrimony.

The interior's finest single component is the extraordinary **choir** (1526), which has been called the greatest in Italy; in fact, all the woodwork here is superb – look out also for the intricately gilded side-pulpits. As for the **paintings**, there's a *Pietà* by Perugino between the first and second altars on the left, three works by Vasari in the Cappella del Sacramento, and a much-praised painting of *Christ on the Mount* by Guido Reni (located on the left wall of the Cappella Ranieri); the eleven eye-catching frescoes around the upper walls are by a disciple of Veronese. The baffling fresco on the rear wall is a genealogical tree of the Benedictines, collecting together the most eminent members of the order. The best pictures of all are five saints by Perugino and a possible Raphael, gathered in the **sacristy**; you'll probably have to get the sacristan to let you in.

If you've walked this far, incidentally, you might want to push on a touch further down the road beyond San Pietro and rest up in Perugia's shady **Orto Botanico**, founded in 1768, at Borgo XX Giugno 74 (March–Sept Mon–Fri 8am–5pm, Sat 8am–1pm; free). The gardens divide into two: the medieval section on the left immediately beyond the church, and the larger botanical section on the right through the Porta San Costanzo.

Eating, drinking and entertainment

Perugia is strong on events, with films, theatre and concerts packing a page or so each day in the listings of the local *Corriere dell'Umbria* newspaper. It's also, for the time being, the possessor of a Serie A football team, Perugia having been reinstated to the top league in 1999. It's a bit less rewarding, though, in its cuisine. While a plethora of fast-food and snack bars cater for the student market, good **restaurants** are surprisingly thin on the ground. Selections below cover just about everything of quality, and are ranged in order of price. There are also plenty of places to **drink**, including a rash of Irish pubs, plus a slew of ersatz Australian and Scottish bars.

Restaurants

Falchetto, Via Bartolo 20. Central, reliable restaurant in a simple medieval setting just off Piazza Danti; reasonably priced if you stick to the basics. L25,000–30,000. Closed Mon.

Dal Mi' Cucco, Corso Garibaldi 12 (☎075.573.2511). A variety of set-price menus are available here: the restaurant, as the old local dialect name suggests, presents traditional Perugian dishes. Good value at around L25,000. Closed Mon.

Osteria Il Gufo, Via della Viola, at the junction with Via Alessi (☎075.573.4126). The best sort of new osteria: relaxed atmosphere, old marble tables, kitchen open to view, traditional regional cooking with the odd dash of innovation – just 35 covers with a few tables on the tiny piazza outside in summer. From L25,000. Closed Sun, Mon & a period in Aug and Sept.

Giancarlo, Via dei Priori 36 (☎075.572.4314). Simple but perfectly cooked Umbrian staples, a central location and low prices means you'll have to book or join the queues to eat at this no-nonsense trattoria. L25,000–40,000. Closed Fri & 20 days during Aug–Sept.

Cesarino, Piazza IV Novembre 4–5 (☎075.572.8974). *Cesarino* is a very central old trattoria-pizzeria that has been around for over 30 years; sadly it's been modernized a touch recently. Booking is essential, as it's the sort of place that appeals to students, locals, Perugia's first-team footballers and politicians alike. Around L35,000, less for pizzas. Closed Wed.

Aladino, Via delle Prome 11, near the Porta Sole (☎075.572.0938). A fine and very welcoming restaurant whose varied food combines the Umbrian cooking of the owner's wife with the Sardinian influences provided by his mother. Wines are particularly interesting. L45,000. Open for dinner only. Closed Mon & two weeks in July or Aug.

La Taverna, Via delle Streghe 8 (☎075.572.4128). A serious restaurant which claims the highest rating – with the *Aladino* – in the Italian foodie guides which count. A mixture of regional and one-off inventive dishes – and heavyweight desserts. Wines are overpriced, though, and when the place is full service and food can occasionally suffer. L45,000. Closed Mon & July 15–31.

Cafés and bars

Australian Pub, Via del Verazo 39. Oz comes to Italy: an Aussie-style pub on two levels (terrace with views) near Piazza Morlacchi which also sells pizzas and snacks. Evenings only. Closed Wed.

Caffè Morlacchi, Piazza Morlacchi 8. Smart but student-orientated bar; get to it along Via delle Volte from Piazza IV Novembre.

Café del Cambio, Corso Vannucci 29. One of the smarter Corso cafés, with reasonable snacks and an efficient lunchtime service; there's a snappy restaurant downstairs.

Contrappunto, Via Scortici 4a. A combination of pub, restaurant and pizzeria close to the University For Foreigners, with live music usually Thurs and Fri – anything from Irish, jazz, Latin to pop covers. Closed Mon.

Enoteca Provinciale, Via Ulisse Rocchi 16–18. Close to the duomo, this wineshop-cum-bar is the best place to indulge in the local wines; also does excellent snacks. Mon 4.30–8.30pm, Tues–Sat 10.30am–2.30pm & 4.30–10pm. Closed Sun.

Pasticceria Sandri, Corso Vannucci 32. The most atmospheric café in Perugia – turn-of-the-century Viennese style with lots of brass, wood panels and frescoed ceilings. Worth at least one cake and cappuccino just for the interior. Closed Mon.

Sullivan's, Via Bovaro 2 (near Sant'Ercolano). If you must visit an Irish pub, come here – it's also a restaurant and has live music a few nights a week (currently Mon, Wed & Fri). Closed Tues.

Markets

There is a permanent **covered food market** – the Mercato Coperto – off Piazza Matteotti (Mon–Sat 7.30am–1pm). An open-air general market operates on the **Scala di Sant'Ercolano**, near the church of the same name, on Tuesdays and Saturdays (8am–1pm). Other picnic supplies can be obtained from the Salumeria Temperini, Corso Cavour 30, which sells excellent hams and salami, and Ceccarini, Piazza Matteotti 16, probably Perugia's best bakery.

Listings

Airport enquiries ☎075.692.9947. Tickets ☎075.592.8017.

Bicycle rental Ciclismo Sport, Via Cicioni, Settevalli (☎075.505.2531).

Books and newspapers Libreria Filosofi, Via dei Filosofi 18–20, has the best selection of English-language titles. For English newspapers, try the stands along the Corso.

Bus enquiries ASP, Piazza dei Partigiani (☎075.573.1707) or Pian di Massiano (☎075.751.145); SIT (☎0743.212.211); ATC (☎0744.402.900); Sulga (☎075.500.9641).

Car rental Avis (Perugia airport ☎075.692.9346; train station ☎075.500.0395); Hertz, train station–Piazza Vittorio Veneto 4 (☎075.500.2439 or 0337.650.837).

Exchange facilities Foreign exchange is handled by most of the banks on Corso Vannucci.

First aid ☎075.578.3422.

Hospital Via Bonacci Brunamonti (☎075.60.81 or 075.57.81).

Lost property ☎075.577.5373.

Maps Eliografica, Via delle Streghe, can supply hiking maps for the province.

Post office The main branch is on Piazza Matteotti (Mon–Fri 10am–5.30pm, Sat 10am–2pm).

Student travel CTGS Student Centre, Via del Roscetto 21 (☎075.572.0284 or 075.572.7050).

Study courses For details and prospectuses contact the Università Italiana per Stranieri, Palazzo Gallenga, Piazza Fortebraccio 4 (☎075.64.344). Summer painting and sculpture courses are run by the Accademia di Belle Arti, Piazza San Francesco al Prato 5 (☎075.29.106).

Taxis ☎075.500.4888.

Telephones Booths at the post office are open until 11.45pm; the Telecom Italia offices in Via Marconi, Corso Cavour and Corso Vannucci are open 8.30am–10pm.

Tourist information Piazza IV Novembre 3 (☎075.573.6458).

Train enquiries FS state line, Piazza Vittorio Veneto (information ☎147.888.088; bookings ☎075.500.7467 or 075.500.188); FCU private line, Stazione Sant'Anna (☎075.572.9121).

Lago Trasimeno

The most tempting option near Perugia – whose surroundings are generally pretty bleak – is the reed-fringed **Lago Trasimeno**. An ideal spot to hole up for a few days and do some swimming (if you don't mind murky water), it is the biggest stretch of water on the Italian peninsula and the fourth largest in Italy overall – after Garda, Maggiore and Como – though at times in danger of drying up completely. With modern demands on water from agriculture and increased silting, the lake's greatest depth now reaches no more than seven metres (average 4.9m) – hence the bath-warm water in the summer. It's mostly clean, however, largely because the tourist and fishing industries are the area's economic bread and butter. Large banks of weed occasionally drift in during the summer, but they're peremptorily taken care of by the council and dumped on the shore.

People have lived on or close to its shores since Paleolithic times, though its greatest historical fame dates from 217 BC, when the Romans suffered one of the worst defeats in their history at the hands of **Hannibal** (see p.458). Its strategic postion, close to Perugia and main lines of communication, meant that numerous castles and fortified villages grew up on its shores and in the hills around, predecessors of present-day towns such as Castiglione del Lago. Attempts to regulate the fluctuating water level date back to Roman times, and a number of serious proposals have been put forward to drain the lake altogether. These remained largely in abeyance for much of the late Middle Ages, when the (then) wooded shores were exploited for hunting, and again in the nineteenth century, when the marshy surrounds became a breeding ground for malarial mosquitoes.

These days the main drawback to Trasimeno is its popularity. In high season the lake is covered with speed boats, yachts and windsurfers. If you're after relative seclusion, steer clear of the northern shore – recently opened up by Perugia's motorway spur – and head instead for the stretches south of Magione and Castiglione, though even here the foreign number plates are in ever greater evidence. Be warned, also, that **unofficial camping** is not as easy as it looks, because the best spots have been grabbed by commercial sites and much of the remaining shoreline is marshy. If you're just passing through, probably the nicest thing to do is settle down for a long **fish lunch** at one of the lakefront restaurants in Castiglione, or take a **boat trip** from Passignano, Tuoro or Castiglione to the Isola Maggiore, one of the three islands in the lake.

Passignano

The lake's most accessible point is **PASSIGNANO**, a newish and reasonably attractive resort strung out along the northern shore and served by hourly trains from Perugia and Teróntola (near Cortona). Popular with Italians whose idea of a day out is to spend most of it in a car, the town in summer is often one big traffic jam, Sundays being especially bad. In the evenings, though, it's an enjoyable place as people come flooding in from the surrounding campsites, livening up the bars, discos and fish restaurants. The waterfront strip is the chief focus, and there's plenty going on in the web of streets behind as well. Bar two dull Renaissance churches and a bit of a castle, there's nothing much to see in the old centre – so you can skip the town in the daytime unless it's to catch a boat or mingle with posturing teenagers.

Passignano's **tourist office** is at Via Roma 36 (June–Sept Mon–Sat 9am–noon & 4–7pm, Sun 9am–noon; Oct–May Mon–Fri 9am–noon & 3–6pm, Sat 9am–noon; ☎075.827.635). There are around a dozen **hotels**, most in the upper bracket – the best value are the one-star *Del Pescatore*, Via San Bernardino 5 (☎075.829.6063, fax 075.829.201; ③), and *Florida*, Via II Giugno 2 (☎075.827.228; ③) – all rooms in both have private bathrooms – or the more up-market three-star *Trasimeno*, Via Roma 16a (☎075.829.355, fax 075.829.267; ④). You can also find **rooms** for rent at Via A. Costi 1 (☎075.827.503; ③) and Via Fratelli Rossi 18

HANNIBAL AND THE BATTLE OF LAGO TRASIMENO

On the coast west of Passignano, between Sanguineto (the Place of Blood) and Ossaia (the Place of Bones), is the spot where the Romans suffered the most traumatic defeat in their history at the hands of **Hannibal** on June 24, 217 BC. The Carthaginian leader was headed for Rome, having already crossed the Alps and won a sweeping victory at Placentia – though by this stage only one of the famous elephants was still alive. He was accompanied, however, by a battle-hardened army of around 40,000. He was met by a Roman force of some 25,000 men under the Consul **Flaminius** (builder of the Via Flamina) close to an amphitheatre of hills above the lake – a location, said the historian Livy, that was "formed by Nature for an ambush".

Things might have gone better for Flaminius if he'd heeded the omens that piled up on the morning of battle. First he fell off his horse, next the legionary standards had to be dug from the mud, then – and this should have been the clincher – the sacred chickens refused their breakfast. Poultry accompanied all Roman armies in the field, their behaviour or the look of their innards at moments of crisis being interpreted as communications of the will of the gods. With the chickens against him Flaminius didn't stand a chance.

Hannibal lured him into a masterful ambush, ranging his men in the hills above the amphitheatre under the cover of early morning mist. Meanwhile he sent a small detachment over the hills to the rear of the amphitheatre, allowing Flaminius to see them, thus tricking the Roman commander into thinking he had seen the tail end of Hannibal's army vacating the basin. Thus duped, Flaminius abandoned his marshy position on the lake shore in favour of the amphitheatre's drier ground. As he marched into the trap Hannibal's men poured down the surrounding slopes, creating havoc among the Roman soldiers – who were marching in a non-battle formation – many of whom barely had time to draw their swords. The only escape lay in a muddy retreat back to the lake shore, where they were mercilessly pursued and hacked down by Hannibal's men. Sixteen thousand Romans – two entire legions – were killed, including the hapless commander, run through with a lance. The slaughter lasted for three hours. Hannibal, for his part, is thought to have lost just 1500 men. The Roman prisoners were killed to a man, but not members of other Italic tribes, whom Hannibal released as part of a propaganda exercise designed to win over the tribes to his cause.

Hannibal's sappers had orders to bury the dead where they fell, and recently 113 mass graves, or *ustrina* – deep stone-lined pits with lids – have been discovered. Scientific dating of the remains tallies exactly with the date of the battle. A (poorly) way-marked **tour** can be made of the battlefield area off the minor lakeside road about a kilometre west of Tuoro (see below).

(☎075.827.504; ③). The two main **campsites** are the expensive three-star *Kursaal*, Via Europa 24 (☎075.828.085, fax 075.827.182; April–Sept), and the cheaper two-star *Europa* (☎075.827.405, fax 075.829.200; April–Sept), both in the nearby hamlet of San Donato.

There are plenty of simple **pizzerie** and cheap **restaurants** in town, but the best is *La Darsena*, Via Perugina 52 (☎075.829.331; closed Tues), a place that gets away from the area's obsession with fish (though fish is still available) and lays on a full meal for around L40,000. For double that – if you want to eat lots of fish – make for the equally good *Cacciatori da Luciano*, Via Nazionale 11 (☎075.827.210; closed Wed – except during summer – & Nov).

Boats run roughly nine times daily throughout the year to the Isola Maggiore via Tuoro (see below) from the landing stage in front of Piazza Garibaldi. For more information contact APM-Navigazione (☎075.827.157). The journey takes around thirty minutes one way. **Bikes** can rented in town from Brunello Ragnoni, Via II Giugno 32 (☎075.829.6064).

Tuoro sul Trasimeno

The rambling hill-village of **TUORO**, 4km west of Passignano and a three-kilometre walk from the Trasimeno battlefield, is a quiet but decidedly dull little place giving road access into the desolate, beautiful mountains north of the lake – the best of the scenery within easy reach of Perugia. In summer you can also take boats across to Isola

Maggiore (see p.461) and to main towns on the lake's shore – details are available from SPNT, on the waterfront at Pontile di Tuoro, Punta Navaccia.

The office is also home to a seasonal **tourist office** (June–Aug daily 9am–1pm & 4–7pm; ☎075.827.157), which has information on two itineraries around the battlefield: the *Interno* (8km) takes you through the Valle della Battaglia itself, while the *Esterno* (16km) concentrates more on the area's scenery. The former, it has to be said, is not terribly exciting, even when you've managed to find its start, which is vaguely signed a kilometre from Tuoro on the right as you drive west from the village on the minor road towards Cortona (look for the long, straight tree-lined road). This said, the various cost-ly-looking **observation platforms** give an excellent idea of the lie of the land, though it's hard to reconcile the tranquil farm country in front of you with a scene of mass slaughter. A permanent memorial to the carnage exists in the place names of two local hamlets, Sanguineto (the "place of blood"), which you pass on the battlefield tour, and Ossaia (the "place of bones"), which lies to the northwest just below Cortona.

Tuoro has a single two-star **hotel**, the eight-roomed *Volante Inn*, Via Sette Martiri 52 (☎075.826.107, fax 075.825.088; ②). A couple of places rent **rooms**: at Via Roma 47 (☎075.826.191; ③), and Via A. Gramsci 18 (☎075.826.670; ③). Otherwise there is a three-star **campsite**, the *Punta Navacci*a, Via Navaccia 4, Punta Navaccia (☎ & fax 075.826.357; April–Sept), or you could head north to **Lisciano Niccone**, 11km from the lake, where from October to May there's good American-run B&B accommodation at the *Casa San Martino* (☎075.844.288; ⑤); in high season this beautifully converted farmhouse is rented out as one unit. **Bikes** can be rented (May–Sept) at Tuoro's bathing area (Balneazione Tuoro) at Punta Navaccia (☎0330.646.281).

Castel Rigone

CASTEL RIGONE, 8km east of Passignano, is the outstanding – virtually the only – village in the mountains above the lake. If you have time you can make a neat little car tour of the area by taking the road north out of Tuoro to Lisciano (13km), then cutting back southeast to Castel Rigone via Pian di Marte and Trecine (20km). Castel Rigone itself is a faintly odd little village with superb views and a small, geranium-strewn medieval centre. Most of its incumbents are pensioners, here for the bracing climate and fresh air. There are two smart, rather staid **hotels**, the better of which is the *Relais La Fattoria*, Via Rigone 1 (☎075.845.322, fax 075.845.197; ④–⑧), occasionally cited for its **restaurant**, which in reality isn't up to much. Cheaper and more rustic is the four-room, six-apartment **agriturismo** *Locanda del Galluzzo* (☎ & fax 075.845.352; ③) with swimming pool, back in the hamlet of Trecine, 2km west of Castel Rigone. A little outside Castel Rigone village is the Renaissance church of **Madonna dei Miracoli**, much lauded, but not worth a special visit and somewhat out of place in the overall medieval context.

Castiglione del Lago

CASTIGLIONE DEL LAGO cuts a fine silhouette from other points on the lake, jutting into the water on a fortified promontory. In the event it doesn't quite live up to its distant promise, but is a friendly, unpretentious place that can hold anyone's attention for a couple of days – longer if all you want to do is crash out on one of its modest but pleasant beaches. It's easy to reach by road and rail, though as a lot of the fast trains on the Rome–Florence line no longer stop here, you'll probably end up taking a *locale* either from Chiusi or Teróntola.

There's little in the town to make a point of seeing, despite its Etruscan and Roman origins, though the largely sixteenth-century **castle**, or Rocca del Leone (April–Oct daily 10am–1pm & 3–7pm; Nov–March Sat–Sun 10am–4pm; L3000) is well preserved, partic-ularly its strange fortified passageway, part of a defensive scheme that in the thirteenth century made it one of Europe's impregnable fortresses. Its design has been attributed to **Frate Elias**, the controversial Franciscan monk (see p.490) who may also have been responsible for the Basilica di San Francesco in Assisi. A combined ticket of L3000 lets you into the castle and ducal palace, the Palazzo della Corgna, the latter full of large rooms with ceilings covered in frescoes of Classical subjects. Machiavelli once stayed over here, as did Leonardo da Vinci (in 1503), who made a drawing of the town's fortifications. The castle ramparts offer good views of the lake, and there's a central stage for outdoor summer events. You might also hunt down the church of **Santa Maria Maddalena** at the western end of the main Via Vittorio Emanuele, where the main left altar has a fine *Madonna and Child* by Eusebio di San Giorgio, a follower of Perugino.

Small **beaches** are dotted around the promontory, with the best swimming at the modest public beach on its southern side. All become extremely busy in summer.

Practicalities

The main **tourist office** for the Trasimeno region is in Castiglione's main square, at Piazza Mazzini 10 (June–Sept Mon–Sat 8.30am–1.30pm & 3–7.30pm, Sun 8am–1pm; Oct–May Mon–Fri 8.30am–1.30pm & 3–7pm, Sat 8am–1.30pm; ☎075.965.2484 or 075.965.2738, fax 075.965.2763); they have on their books around fifteen *agriturismo* choices in the surrounding countryside, a lot of reasonable if characterless **rooms** in private houses, and apartments to rent on a weekly basis, usually a cheaper option if you can get a party together.

Amongst the **hotels**, prices have shot up to capitalize on the town's increasingly high profile as a "resort": the top-priced places are the pleasant family-run three-star, 16-room *Duca della Corgna*, Via Bruno Buozzi 143 (☎075.953.238, fax 075.962.2446; ④), close to the centre and boasting many rooms with nice views; the eight-room *La Torre*, Via Vittorio Emanuele 50 (☎ & fax 075.951.666; ④); and – perhaps the best overall choice – the 19-room, three-star *Miralago*, Piazza Mazzini 6 (☎075.953.063 or 075.951.157, fax 075.951.924; ④), a more atmospheric establishment, chiefly because it commands good views of the lake. Slightly less expensive than these are the three-star *Trasimeno*, Via Roma 174 (☎075.965.2494, fax 075.952.5258; ③), and the modern two-star *Fazzouli*, Piazza Marconi 11 (☎075.951.119, fax 075.951.112; ②) and one-star *Santa Lucia*, Via Bruno Buozzi 84 (☎ & fax 075.965.2492; ②), the town's two cheapest hotels.

Most of the **campsites** are off the main road some way south of the town. The *Lido Trasimeno* (☎ & fax 075.965.9350; April–Sept) on the shore north of the castle has good facilities (swimming, windsurfing school, sailing) but it's next to a training school for police Alsatians. Best **eating**, apart from the string of easy-going summer-only restaurants on the promenade, is the long-established *La Cantina*, Via Vittorio Emanuele II 89a (☎075.965.2463; closed Mon except in summer), and the newer and slightly more expensive *L'Acquario*, Via Vittorio Emanuele II 69 (☎075.965.2432; closed Fri, also Tues in winter), which concentrates more on fish; from about L40,000. Another nice, moderately priced place is the *La Fontana* restaurant in the *Miralago* hotel (see above), which in summer has tables in a garden at the rear with pleasant views of the lake. The town's lively **market** is on Wednesdays.

Isola Maggiore

In summer, regular boats from the lakeshore jetty make the trip out to **Isola Maggiore**, one of the lake's three islands, a fun ride if you don't mind the crowds. The crossing takes twenty minutes, and there are connecting boats to Tuoro and Passignano, as well as to lesser resorts on the lake's southern and eastern shores. (For sailing times call ☎075.827.157.)

Once over, there's a single village of about one hundred people – traditionally known for its lacemaking – and a pretty **walk** round the island's two-kilometre perimeter. Follow the quaint brick-paved street from the landing stage to the twelfth-century church of **San Salvatore** at the top and the path continues beyond. The island is famed for a visit by St Francis in 1211, a forty-day sojourn during which he consumed just half a loaf of bread; a chapel marks the point of his disembarkation, and there's a small Franciscan monastery on the southeast shore. The best outing, though – and another lovely walk – is through the olive groves to the church of **San Michele Arcangelo**; sited at the island's highest point, the twelfth-century building is decorated with frescoes and has a *Crucifixion* painted by Bartolomeo Caporali in 1460.

The island's single two-star **hotel** is *Da Sauro*, located at the village's northern limit at Via G. Guglielmi 1 (☎075.826.168; ④); be sure to book ahead, whether it's for a room or for a table in the adjoining and equally popular **fish restaurant** (open daily March–Oct; closed Nov–Feb; from L30,000). Alternatively, once everyone's gone home you might discreetly pitch a tent.

South of the lake: Panicale

The low hills to the south of Trasimeno make a good scenic backdrop. If you have a car you might take a detour to **PANICALE**, 5km south of the shore, a village of Etruscan origins which gave birth to the pioneering painter Tommaso Fini, better known as Masolino da Panicale (1383–1440), the master of Masaccio. The streets offer picture-postcard views of the lake, plus two easily missed Perugino paintings in the church of **San Sebastiano**, outside the walls off Piazza Vittoria (the custodian lives at Piazza del Mercato 13). Apart from a tiny medieval core, there's little else to the place, though during the April *festa* some miraculous plumbing fills the fountains with wine – well worth investigation. The village is a quiet place for lunch or a stopover, and also breaks your journey if you're walking some of Trasimeno's marked trails. There are just two **hotels**, the one-star *Masolino,* Via Roma 7 (☎075.837.180, fax 075.837.151; ②) and the fine three-star *Le Grotte di Boldrino,* Via Virgilio Ceppari 43 (☎075.837.161, fax 075.837.166; ③): the latter is built into part of the old medieval walls and surrounded by a garden; rooms are spacious and nicely furnished with antiques. The hotel **restaurant** offers both pizzas and full meals, though reports suggest the quality can be erratic.

On the map, the **main road** below Panicale from Perugia to Città della Pieve (the SS220) looks a good touring proposition; in fact it's a laborious route, spotted by light industry and the odd factory chimney. The only point of interest is the **Santuario di Mongiovino**, a Renaissance temple high above the road, 7km south of Panicale, and roughly equidistant from Perugia and Città della Pieve. It looks a good deal more impressive from afar than it does close up.

WALKS AROUND THE TRASIMENO

There's some good **walking** locally, with treks possible up Monte Castiglione on the mule track from the Passo di Gosparani (7km north of Tuoro); up Monte Acuto from Galera or Monteacuto (15km northeast on the Umbértide road); or up Monte Murlo from Preggio, a hill-village 6km north of Castel Rigone, and worth a visit in its own right. If you feel less adventurous, twelve new **walking trails** have been marked around the lake from centres such as Magione, Panicale, Passignano and Castiglione del Lago. Ask at tourist offices for the map-brochure *Itinerari Turistici del Trasimeno* (free). Trail 3, for example, links Castel Rigone to Tuoro (30km; 9–10hr or two days) via Passignano, mostly via the high ridges above the lake. Trail 2 (26km; 8–9hr or two days) follows a lower route between Tuoro and Passignano, continuing east to Magione. Trail 4 is an easy 18km (6hrs) from Tuoro to Castiglione del Lago. You could, in theory, link several trails and effect a full circuit of the lake. Paths are mainly cross-country and have been designed to take in historic churches and buildings en route; longer routes, of course, can easily be split into manageable one-day walks.

The Upper Tiber

Rome's great river, the **Tiber** (Tevere), actually spends most of its life in Umbria, rising just to the north of the province. In its relatively unexciting upper reaches, north of Perugia, you're faced with the problem that the fine countryside and walking territory above the valley are out of reach without a car, bike or lucky hitch.

The Ferrovie Centrale Umbra (Central Umbrian Rail Line) and fast SS3, however, connect Perugia with **Umbértide** and **Città di Castello**, the area's only sizeable towns. At Umbertide there's the option of striking east across the mountains to Gubbio, while at Città di Castello you have the choice of moving east to Urbino (in the Marche) – a magnificent drive – or following the Tiber along the trail of Piero della Francesca's unsettling masterpieces at Sansepolcro, Arezzo and Monterchi (all covered in Chapter Nine).

Santa Maria di Valdiponte

Highlight of the area immediately north of Perugia is the abbey of **Santa Maria di Valdiponte** at Montelabate, on the east side of the valley 16km from Perugia. This monastic foundation once controlled twenty castles in the area, and similar abbeys administered great swathes of the land between Gubbio and the Tiber. Built between the twelfth and fourteenth centuries, the church itself is of rather less interest than the **cloisters**, which are medieval perfection, and the various artistic treasures scattered around the complex – including frescoes by such as Fiorenzo di Lorenzo and Bartolomeo Caporali.

Umbértide and around

Bombed to the edge of oblivion in the last war, **UMBÉRTIDE** is now a light-industrial town relieved by a tiny and captivating medieval centre. Artistic attractions are limited to the **Palazzo Comunale** – the best Baroque conversion in Umbria – and a *Deposition* by Luca Signorelli in the church of **Santa Croce**.

You'd only want to use this place as a way-station. There are a couple of **hotels** on the main road, the cheaper being the two-star *Moderno*, Via Nazionale 186 (☎ & fax 075.941.3759; ②); rather better if only because it's more central, is the two-star *Capponi*, Piazza XXV Aprile 19 (☎075.941.2662, fax 075.941.3803; ②), whose **restaurant** is the standard place to eat.

The castle of **Civitella Ranieri** rises invitingly just to the northeast of Umbértide, but it's privately owned, so don't bother with the steep climb for a closer look. More worthwhile is the hill-village of **MONTONE**, 6km north, which harbours a collection of minor Umbrian paintings in the nicely executed **Museo Civico** (April–Sept Fri–Sun 10.30am–1pm & 3.30–6pm; Oct–March Sat–Sun 10.30am–1pm & 3–5.30pm; L6000), housed in the former church and convent of San Francesco. The church has some beguiling frescoes from as early as the eleventh century, the best of which are in the apse and depict *Scenes from the Life of St Francis* (1422–23) by Antonio Alberti. The most interesting painting is a *gonfalone*, or banner, by Bartolomeo Caporali, portraying the *Madonna del Soccorso* (1481), with a view of fifteenth-century Montone in the foreground. The village also has a couple of **hotels**, the two-star *Fortebraccio*, Via dei Magistrati 11 (☎ & fax 075.930.6215; ②), and the slightly more expensive *Locanda del Capitano*, Via Roma 5–7 (☎075.903.6521, fax 075.930.6455; ③); there's another, the one-star *Adamo* (☎ & fax 075.930.6146; ②), in the hamlet of Corlo, midway along the road from Umbértide. If you're heading east to Gubbio – the most likely reason to be passing through – you might stop off at **CAMPO REGGIANO**, 11km east of Umbértide, for a look at its tiny eleventh-century church and crypt of San Bartolomeo.

Monte Corona (693m), 6km south of Umbértide, is topped by the **Badia di San Salvatore**, a twelfth-century monastery – which again looks good from the outside, but was ravaged by a sixteenth-century interior conversion.

Walking in the Upper Tiber

With thousands of hectares of natural woodland and abandoned pasture, the desolate countryside on each flank of the Upper Tiber teems with protected wildlife, including many rare species of birds, deer, wild boar and even wolves – now pushing farther up the Italian peninsula every year. Freelance exploration is easy, especially if you have transport, but for detailed information on **walking** in the region, contact the CAI branch in Città di Castello, at Via della Tina 14 (☎075.855.6788).

The area's only **hotel** is the three-star *Candeleto* (☎ & fax 075.936.183; ②) in the village of Candeleto close to Pietralunga; there's a **campsite** nearby, *La Pineta* (☎075.946.0080, fax 075.946.0646; June–Sept). Cheaper than the *Candeleto*, and more in keeping with the region's rural tone, are the **agriturismo** bed and breakfasts near Pietralunga – the three-room *I Fornelli*, c/o Claudio Capaccioni, Via Fornelli 6, Castelguelfo (☎075.933.061; ②) or *La Cerqua* in the hamlet of San Salvatore (☎075.946.0283, fax 075.946.2033; ③): the latter has a range of rooms and apartments at varying prices.

Città di Castello

Umbria's northernmost town, **CITTÀ DI CASTELLO**, is a plain-bound and still little-visited spot whose more than passable *centro storico* is a touch spoilt by the industry on its outskirts – mainly tobacco-processing plants, the town being one of Italy's leading producers. On either side of the valley bottom, green wooded hills provide a pleasant backdrop, and harbour one of Umbria's larger concentrations of rented summer houses and farmhouses. At the town's southern edge lies the **Pinacoteca Comunale**, the main artistic reason for visiting the town. The old centre is also a pleasant enough place to spend a night, particularly if you devote an evening to sampling the local Colli Altotiberini wines, or happen to catch the town during one of its burgeoning number of festivals (see below).

In the Pleistocene Age the Tiber valley at this point was submerged beneath an immense lake similar to Lago Trasimeno and the narrow sheet of water that once covered the Vale of Spoleto. Archeological remains suggest a human presence in the region dating back to the Stone Age. An Umbrian town, Tifernum, later developed on the site, giving way in time to a Roman trading centre, **Tifernum Tiberinum**, whose gridiron of streets remains imprinted on the town centre to this day. A bishopric by the sixth century – the Church's seventh-century nickname for the place was *castrum felicitas* (Castle of Happiness) – the town reached its peak around 1500, when the enlightened despotism of the Vitelli nobles brought leading artists here, the young Raphael and Signorelli among them. Nemesis arrived in the form of Cesare Borgia, who invited the head of the Vitellis to a banquet, had him strangled and then absorbed the town into the papal domain.

Access is by direct **train** on the private FCU line from Perugia or Terni to the south, or from Sansepolcro to the north; the station is just outside the walls to the southeast, just five minutes' walk from the centre. You could alternatively take a main line FS train to Arezzo and pick up an ACT bus to Città di Castello, whose **bus station** is in Piazza Garibaldi, on the east edge of the *centro storico*. If you're coming in by **car** there are car parks around the city walls, one of the most convenient being that on Viale Nazario Sauro in the west, which is linked by a path through the walls and a pair of escalators to the public gardens in front of the duomo.

Pinacoteca Comunale

The **Pinacoteca Comunale**, towards the south of the walled town at Via della Cannoniera 22 (April–Oct Tues–Sun 10am–noon & 2.30–6.30pm; Nov–March Tues–Sun 10am–12.30pm & 3–5.30pm; L8000), is housed in the Palazzo Vitelli alla Cannoniera, one of four surviving palaces in Città di Castello formerly owned by the Vitelli, the town's erstwhile overlords. One of the region's more prepossessing buildings, the palazzo was built

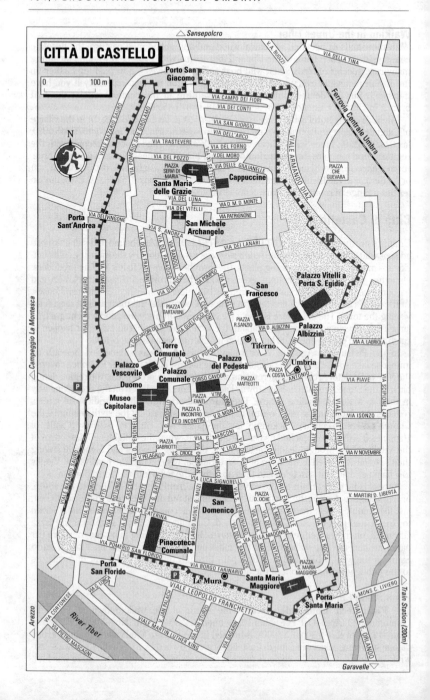

for Alessandro Vitelli between 1521 and 1532 by Sangallo the Younger and Pier Francesco da Viterbo, and decorated with some extraordinary and beautiful *sgraffito* by Vasari on the garden facade. Inside, the painted stairwells and period furniture complement the paintings, recently restored sixteenth-century frescoes by Cola dell'Amatrice on the stairs and in the first-floor *Salone* being some of the most striking. Not all the palazzo's former guests, however, had time to appreciate the high-class fittings; Laura, one of the Vitelli women, was wont to throw her rejected lovers to their deaths from the windows.

The gallery spreads over two floors. Most of the rooms, while hardly bursting with paintings, have something of interest. Highlights include *The Martyrdom of St Sebastian* (1497–8) by Luca Signorelli, and a damaged but still ravishing standard by Raphael depicting the *Creation of Eve* and *SS. Roch and Sebastian*. Raphael spent about five years in Umbria and the region once had many works by him, several of them in Città di Castello. Today the only pieces in Umbria entirely by him are the standard here and the panel in the church of San Severo in Perugia – many of the others were removed to France by Napoleon. A marvellous thirteenth-century *Maestà* by the anonymous Maestro di Città di Castello is also finally ensconced in the gallery, having been backwards and forwards to Florence for restoration since 1969.

Other works include Sienese and later Venetian paintings, among them outstanding pieces by Antonio Vivarini and his brother-in-law Giovanni d'Alemagna (the two often worked in collaboration), as well as versions of the *Madonna and Child* by Spinello Aretino, Neri di Bicci and Andrea di Bartolo. The sculptural high spot is provided by the *Reliquary of St Andrew* (1420), which is graced with two gilded bronze statuettes by the workshop of Lorenzo Ghiberti. There are also ceramics from the della Robbias, a lovely sacristy cupboard (1501) in poplar and walnut, and a miscellaneous sculpture collection distinguished by a fourteenth-century marble relief of the *Baptism of Christ*.

The Duomo

Many of Città di Castello's buildings have lost their medieval aspect to later facades, most notably the rather odd-looking **Duomo**, whose half-finished Baroque frontage was begun in 1632 and abandoned some fifteen years later. The church was founded at some early but unknown date, and by 580 had already been rebuilt at least once. Further versions followed in the eleventh and fourteenth centuries, and again in 1458, when the building had to be reconstructed virtually from the ground up after an earthquake. Something of its chequered construction history can be seen in the wonderful round **campanile**, which combines an eleventh-century base with a newer Gothic upper level, and in the Gothic lines of the **north portal**, whose carvings include two fine panels (1339–59) depicting *Mercy* and *Justice*.

At first glance the heavily reworked **interior** promises little, though for Mannerist fans there is a treat in the shape of an age-darkened altarpiece by Rosso Fiorentino. Located on the fourth altar on the right (south) side, it shows figures representing the town's inhabitants sheltering beneath Christ in Glory with the Madonna and SS. Anne, Mary Magdalene and Mary the Egyptian. If you're lucky enough to find the **sacristy** open (door on the right), its small annexe contains a much-damaged fresco of *Christ and Four Saints* by the school of Luca Signorelli, uncovered in 1968.

MUSEO CAPITOLARE

Perhaps the most interesting visit in town after the Pinacoteca is the **Museo Capitolare**, or Museo del Duomo, which is entered immediately to the right of the cathedral's dog's-dinner facade at Piazza Gabriotti 3a (Tues–Sun: April–Sept 10.30am–1pm & 3–6.30pm; Oct–March 10am–12.30pm & 3–5.30pm; L5000). Pride of place in the beautifully vaulted fifteenth-century rooms goes to the *Tesoro di Canoscio*, displayed at the right-hand end of the main hall, or *Salone*. A hoard of paleo-Christian silverware, the nine plates, eleven spoons and five miscellaneous pieces – some of them beautifully engraved – were probably made in Constantinople and date from the sixth century. Probably used to celebrate the Eucharist, they were turned up in the nearby hamlet of Canoscio in 1935 by a farmer ploughing his fields. The rest of the main hall is littered with displays of religious ephemera such as reliquaries, chalices, crosses and the like – spanning some six hundred years – most of which can be overlooked in favour of a painting of the *Madonna and Child with St John* by Pinturicchio.

Subsequent rooms house further religious artefacts arranged in chronological order, the next noteworthy exhibit (in a room off the corridor beyond the *Salone*) a gilded altar-relief – reputedly presented to Città di Castello by Pope Celestine II in 1142 – showing Christ surrounded by the symbols of the Evangelists and scenes from his life. Other worthwhile pieces to look out for include a magnificent crozier (1324) and several naive but appealing paintings: an *Annunciation* by the local painter Francesco da Tiferno (active 1490–1510), a *Madonna* (1492) by the school of Luca Signorelli, and a picture of *St Floridus* (1412), the sixth-century bishop of Città di Castello who rebuilt the duomo in 580 (see above).

Palaces

Just east of the duomo, in Piazza Gabriotti, lies Città di Castello's old civic heart, dominated by the **Palazzo Comunale** (or Palazzo dei Priori), whose unfinished sandstone bulk was begun in 1322 by Angelo da Orvieto, the architect partly responsible for Gubbio's more impressive Palazzo dei Consoli (see p.473). Immediately opposite rises the **Torre Comunale**, or Torre Civica, seat of the town's medieval prison, which can be climbed for some nice views over the rooftops (Tues–Sun 10am–12.30pm & 3–5.30pm; L2000). A graceful fourteenth-century loggia leads out of the square to the **Palazzo del Podestà** (finished 1368), again by Angelo da Orvieto, though much of the medieval work has been obscured by seventeenth-century additions.

You can extend your knowledge of the town's palace architecture by visiting Piazza Garibaldi and the **Palazzo Vitelli a Porta Sant'Egidio**, built in 1540 for Paolo Vitelli, possibly to a design by Vasari, the attribution appearing likely in view of Vasari's involvement with the Palazzo Vitelli alla Cannoniera (see p.464). Its garden frontage provides its best aspect, an outlook which would be improved if the grotto, garden and statues in front of it were tidied up. The palace now belongs to a bank, but you'll catch a glimpse of the interior if you attend one of the many concerts held here during the summer season. The fifteenth-century **Palazzo Albizzini** (Tues–Sat 10am–12.30pm & 2.30–6pm, Sun 9am–1pm; L8000), on the same piazza, is more easily seen, as it houses a public collection of paintings donated to the town by the local artist Alberto Burri (1915–95).

Churches

None of Città di Castello's churches can be said to set pulses racing, but taken together they offer a worthwhile medley of miscellaneous treasures. **San Domenico**, a gloomy Gothic affair built between 1271 and 1424, might once have been more tempting, but its Signorelli *Madonna* has been snapped up by the Pinacoteca, while the Raphael *Crucifixion* which once adorned its east nave now resides in London's National Gallery. In their place you must make do with a set of lovely inlaid choir stalls (1435) and several fifteenth-century patches of local and Sienese fresco. **Santa Maria delle Grazie** (rebuilt in 1587) is almost equally tantalizing, for its main treasure, a painting of the *Madonna delle Grazie* (1456) – the only documented work of Giovanni di Piamonte, also known as a collaborator of Piero della Francesca – is kept hidden in a cupboard on the church's north side and only exhibited on February 2 and August 26. Worthy of interest, though, is a fresco of *The Dormition of the Virgin*, attributed to the Gubbian master Ottaviano Nelli. **San Francesco**, situated on Piazza Raffaello Sanzio, dates from 1273, though its interior bears the all too obvious marks of an eighteenth-century restoration. It, too, once boasted a Raphael (which is now in Milan's Brera gallery) but now has to make do with an altarpiece by Vasari, located in the Cappella Vitelli (also by Vasari) off the north aisle. Finally, **San Giovanni Decollato**, in Via Sant'Andrea, has frescoes which show the influence of Luca Signorelli, while the nearby **San Michele Archangelo** (Via Sant'Angelo) contains a high altarpiece by Raffaellino del Colle (1480–1566), an accomplished artist active locally in Citerna, Gubbio and elsewhere.

Practicalities

Città di Castello's **tourist office** is in the Palazzo del Podestà in Piazza Fanti (daily 9am–1pm & 4–7pm; ☎075.855.4922). There is also an APT at Via Sant'Antonio 1 (☎075.855.4817, fax 075.855.2100) which deals with the whole Upper Tiber region and so is a useful stop if you're thinking of spending any time locally. The town's top-of-the-range **hotel** is the very pleasant central four-star *Tiferno*, Piazza Raffaello Sanzio 13 (☎075.855.0331, fax 075.852.1196; ⑤). Two other central and cheaper alternatives are the pleasant three-star *Le Mura*, Via Borgo Farinario 24 (☎075.852.1070, fax 075.852.1350; ④), a renovated rural house virtually next door to the Pinacoteca – bathrooms are a little small for the price, but there's an appealing and curious little garden with fountain; the recommended two-star *Umbria*, Via dei Galanti 4 (☎075.855.4925, fax 075.852.0911; ③), tucked away in a convenient alley off Via Sant'Antonio. There's also a quite inexpensive three-star **campsite** at La Montesca, 1km west of town on the minor road to Monte San Marina – the *Montesca* (☎075.852.0808, fax 075.852.0786; May–Sept).

The best **restaurant** by quite a distance is *Il Postale di Marco e Barbara*, Via De Cesari 8 (☎075.850.1356; closed Mon & also Sun evening Oct–March) – reckon on around L50,000 upwards for a memorable meal. Next best central choice is the *Amici Miei*, Via del Monte 2 (☎075.855.9904; closed Wed), nicely located off Piazza Matteotti in a vaulted cellar; cooking is simple and straightforward, and you pay a set price (currently an immensely good-value L30,000) for a four-course menu with wine. *Il Bersaglio*, Via V. E. Orlando 14 (☎075.855.5534; closed Wed & two weeks in July) is also good, but it's out of the old centre, 200m southeast of Porta Santa Maria; it's cosy inside, and meals cost around L45,000, with the option of two *degustazione* menus. Cheaper places include the pizzeria *Adriano Due*, Piazza Che Guevara (closed Wed) and the *Trattoria Lea*, Via San Florido 28 (closed Mon).

The tourist office can provide details of the town's internationally renowned **Festival of Chamber Music** (held late Aug–early Sept). An equally well-known **Mercato del Tartufo** – a truffle show and market – is held every November. A **market** takes place in Piazza Gabriotti on Thursday and Saturday, and on the third weekend of every month there's also a **flea market**, the *Fiera del Rigattiere*, held in Piazza Matteotti.

Around Città di Castello

Beyond Città di Castello you have a choice of three routes: striking east towards Urbino and the Marche or pressing on into Tuscany, either by heading north towards Sansepolcro or west towards Arezzo. All are accessible by train or bus from Città di Castello, though only drivers are likely to want to stop en route. One of the nicest drives for its own sake is to the village of **Monte Santa Maria Tiberina**, atop a hill about 8km west of Città di Castello.

Garavelle

A couple of kilometres south of Città di Castello, in the hamlet of **GARAVELLE**, is one of Umbria's best **folk museums** (Tues–Sun: May–Sept 9am–12.30pm & 3–7pm; Oct–April 9am–noon & 2–6pm; L5000). Situated in Via Marchese Cappelletti, this is basically an eighteenth-century farmhouse, preserved with all the accoutrements of daily life – pots, pans, furniture and so forth, plus a range of exhibits covering wine-making, weaving and carpentry, and there's even a blacksmith's forge.

The Sansepolcro route

North along the Sansepolcro road, a kilometre east of **LAMA**, you can see faint remains believed to have been a villa owned by Pliny. Five kilometres beyond, **SAN GIUSTINO** is a more or less modern settlement, save for the **Castello Bufalani**, a thirteenth-century castle partly converted by Vasari into a splendid villa. Visits are at the discretion of the owners; enquire at the tourist office in Città di Castello. By a quirk of fate, **COSPAIA**, a huddle of houses on the hill outside, was a tiny independent republic until 1826, though there are no visible reminders of its past glories.

Citerna

Head west on the SS221 out of Città di Castello and you hit **CITERNA**, a perfect fortified hill-top village whose powerful wooded position attracted attention as late as 1944, when the Germans destroyed its strategically important castle (leaving only the present little tower). The town dates from Roman times, was rebuilt after barbarian depredations in the seventh and eighth centuries, and achieved high renown in 1849 when Giuseppe Garibaldi, hero of Italian Unification, spent three days here after the unsuccessful Roman uprising of 1848. Today its neat brick houses are spick and span, despite a massive earth-quake in 1917 and damage inflicted during both world wars. The fine local church, **San Francesco**, built in 1316 and revamped in 1508, has a grand assortment of gilded wooden altars; a faded niche fresco by Luca Signorelli and assistants, a late work (1522–23) depicting the *Madonna and Child with SS. Francis and Michael* (second altar on the right); and an outstanding and extravagantly framed sixteenth-century painting of the *Madonna and St John the Evangelist* by Raffaellino del Colle (left transept). The busy and recently restored *Deposition* (1568) in the choir is by the otherwise obscure Alessandro Forzorio from Arezzo.

The village also has a **hotel**, the 25-room, three-star *Sabaria*, Via della Pineta 2 (☎075.859.2118, fax 075.859.3410; ④). As a rustic alternative, there are two **agriturismo** options in farms in the countryside nearby: Fernando Parigi, Via Monte Santa Maria Tiberina, Petralta (☎ & fax 075.857.0228; horse-riding available; ③), and Giancarlo Signorelli, Marcignano, Rovereto (☎075.857.0276; ②).

From Citerna it's an extremely short hop into Tuscany to see Piero della Francesca's *Madonna del Parto* at Monterchi (see p.420).

Gubbio

High, remote **GUBBIO** has the most beautiful medieval appearance of the northern Umbrian towns – indeed it is so well preserved that guides and the local tourist blurb promote it as the Umbrian Siena. It's not quite that, but the streets are all rosy-pink stone, the monuments worthwhile, and the medieval nooks and crannies as endearing as any in Italy. Better still, the countryside around is gorgeous – the forest-covered mountains of the Apennines rearing up behind and the waters of the Camignano gorge tumbling through the town itself. A broad and largely unspoilt plain stretches out in front of the town, the whole natural ensemble – especially on grey, windswept days – maintaining the image of Gubbio as a resolute mountain outpost. Its charms are not surprisingly attracting ever greater numbers of visitors, and on a summer morning the streets can be heaving. Come off-season, however, or stay the night, and you'll see the town in a different light.

Some history

Local folklore insists that Gubbio was one of the first five towns built after the Great Flood. It was actually founded by the Umbrians around the third century BC, later passing to the Etruscans, for whom it marked the easternmost limit of their territorial ambitions. Several

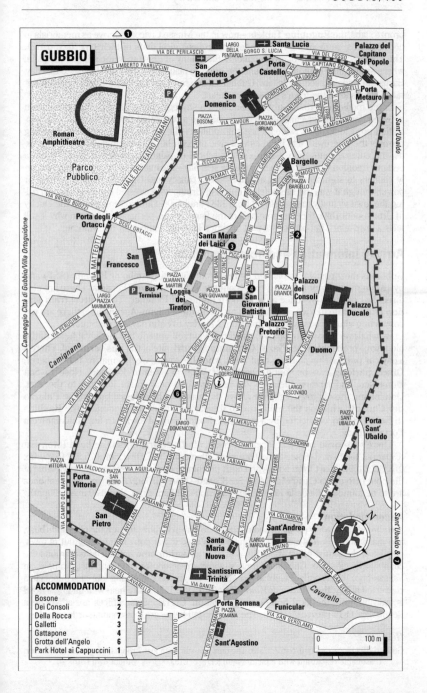

GUBBIO

Roman Amphitheatre

Parco Pubblico

San Benedetto

Santa Lucia

Porta Castello

Palazzo del Capitano del Popolo

Porta Metauro

San Domenico

Bargello

Porta degli Ortacci

Santa Maria dei Laici

San Francesco

Bus Terminal

Loggia dei Tiratori

San Giovanni Battista

Palazzo dei Consoli

Palazzo Ducale

Palazzo Pretorio

Duomo

Porta Sant'Ubaldo

Porta Vittoria

San Pietro

Sant'Andrea

Santa Maria Nuova

Santissima Trinità

Porta Romana

Funicular

Sant'Agostino

ACCOMMODATION

Bosone	5
Dei Consoli	2
Della Rocca	7
Galletti	3
Gattapone	4
Grotta dell'Angelo	6
Park Hotel ai Cappuccini	1

Camignano

Cavarello

0   100 m

bronze slabs, the **Eugubine Tablets** – now in the Museo Civico – survive as memorials to both cultures, some of the most important archeological finds of their type (see p.473). The Romans, inevitably, followed, building the colony of Iguvium at the edge of the plain, where a sprinkling of monuments and the gridiron plan of their streets survive to this day. Barbarian raids subsequently saw Gubbio's focus move up the hillside, whose steep terraced slopes form the town's present-day heart.

In the medieval period, Gubbio maintained a strategic importance as the pivotal town between Rome and Ravenna, its *comune* achieving a status that rivalled Perugia. The population grew to 50,000 – twice its present number – the town's wealth and size providing not only the wherewithal to build its vast civic palaces, but also the impulse towards artistic and cultural innovation. Umbria's first school of painting developed here, as did a ceramic tradition which continues to the present day – the market in pricey ceramics largely panders to sightseers. From about 1350 the papacy and Gabrielli nobility jostled for power, though it was the Montefeltro dukes of Urbino who wrested eventual control, ruling the town virtually unchallenged from 1383 until 1508. Gubbio remained in the Duchy of Urbino until 1624, then became part of the Papal States, perhaps one reason why it still feels a town apart, not properly a part of either Tuscany, Umbria or the Marche.

Arrival, information and accommodation

Gubbio is most easily approached by **bus** from Città di Castello or Perugia (ASP) and by **car** on the very meandering cross-country SS298 road from Perugia. There are also direct bus connections once a day to both Rome and Florence. The nearest **train station** is at Fossato di Vico, 19km south on the Rome–Foligno–Ancona line; there are ten connecting shuttle buses to Gubbio from Monday to Saturday, six on Sundays.

By whatever means you arrive, you'll find yourself outside the medieval heart of the old town – probably in the **Piazza Quaranta Martiri**, site of the **bus terminal**. There's a pay **car park** at this point (except Tues, when the town's weekly market is held here). Other **parking** can be found nearby off Viale del Teatro Romano, close to San Domenico, and farther afield in Via del Cavarello near Porta Romana to the east. Dominating the old town's skyline above the piazza is the colossal bulk of the **Palazzo dei Consoli**, while on the hill above to the east sits a second landmark, the **Basilica di Sant'Ubaldo**, connected by a steep lane from the top of town or a fun funicular from Porta Romana.

There's a **tourist office** at Piazza Odersi 6, off the central Corso Garibaldi (Mon–Sat 8.30am–1.30pm & 3–6pm, Sun 9.30am–12.30pm; ☎075.922.0693 or 075.922.0790, fax 075.927.3409). Apart from banks and cash machines, **currency exchange** is available at the **post office**, Via Carioli 11 (Mon–Sat 8.30am–6pm; ☎075.927.3925), while telephones are to be found at Via della Repubblica 13 (Mon–Sat 8am–9pm, Sun 9.30am–12.30pm).

Accommodation

You shouldn't have any problem finding a place to stay in Gubbio, though the place gets busy, and many of the **hotels** cater to well-heeled Italians. If you don't mind being out of town, enquire at the tourist office about the twenty or so **agriturismo** options dotted around the countryside close to Gubbio – there's some great accommodation, for example, in Vallingegno, 14km south of Gubbio just off the Perugia road, including four apartments in a converted abbey, the *Abbazia di Vallingegno* (☎075.920.158). Extra help with finding a hotel is available from the local **hoteliers' association**, GOTE, whose offices are at Via della Repubblica 11-13 (☎075.922.0066). The places listed below are in ascending order of price.

HOTELS

Galletti, Via Piccardi 1 (☎075.927.7753). The only one-star, with just 7 rooms; overlooking the river; has a reasonable restaurant with a picturesque terrace. L15,000 less without own bath. ②.

Grotta dell'Angelo, Via Gioia 47 (☎075.927.1747, fax 075.927.3438). Reliable 18-room two-star, with a passable restaurant; all rooms with private bath at identical prices to the *Galletti*. ②.

Dei Consoli, Via dei Consoli 59 (☎075.927.3335). One of the best locations – in an atmospheric street – but only 9 rather plain two-star rooms (all with private bathroom), so try to book ahead. Best are the quieter rooms away from the street. Closed Jan & Feb. ②.

Della Rocca, Monte Ingino (☎ & fax 075.922.1222). A little out-of-town three-star hotel; to get there from the centre, take the funicular or walk up to Monte Ingino and follow the signs from the Basilica. ④.

Gattapone, Via G. Ansidei 6 (☎075.927.2489, fax 075.927.2417). First choice among the slightly pricier places; renovated central three-star hotel in a quiet medieval building off Via della Repubblica, with 18 spacious rooms (small bathrooms) and a peaceful garden. ④.

Bosone, Via XX Settembre 22 (☎075.922.0668, fax 075.922.0552). This sizeable old-world three-star, full of frescoes, medieval vaults and antiques, offers a touch of luxury. ⑤.

Park Hotel ai Cappuccini, Via Tifernate (☎075.9234, fax 075.922.0323). Major-league hedonism (swimming pool, sauna, garden, gym), in an elegantly converted fourteenth-century monastery. Set in parkland just outside town. ⑦–⑨.

CAMPSITES

Città di Gubbio (☎ & fax 075.927.2037). Large 100-pitch site with swimming pool in a good setting, in Ortoguidone, 1.5km south of town, off the Perugia road. Open April–Sept.

Villa Ortoguidone (☎075.927.2037). The only four-star campsite in Umbria, it's expensive, and with only 12 pitches you will be lucky to get a space. Close to, and part of, the *Città di Gubbio* site. Open April–Sept.

The Town

Piazza Quaranta Martiri makes an obvious place to start a tour of the town; it was named after forty citizens shot by the Nazis in 1944 as a reprisal for partisan attacks in the surrounding hills. After taking in **San Francesco** and its fresco cycles you should head into the medieval town proper, where the vast **Palazzo dei Consoli** houses the town's museum and picture gallery, and then wander the short distance to the adjoining **duomo** and **Palazzo Ducale**, the latter based on the Montefeltros' famous palace in Urbino. A lane behind the duomo leads up to **Monte Ingino** – the route taken by competitors during the famous **Corsa dei Ceri** (see box on p.475) – a hill-top eyrie which offers lovely views and plenty of picnic and strolling opportunities. Alternatively, take in the streets around **San Domenico** and then head east to Porta Romana, where a funicular also runs up Monte Ingino.

San Francesco and around

In Piazza Quaranta Martiri, slightly stranded from the medieval heart of town, is the town's finest church, Gothic **San Francesco**, possibly designed by Fra' Bevignate, the brains behind Perugia's Fontana Maggiore. Within the newly restored interior is an engaging if faded cycle of **frescoes** painted around 1410 by Ottaviano Nelli (c.1375–c.1444), leading light of the Gubbian school. Ranged around the chapel to the left of the apse, the seventeen panels show *Scenes from the Life of the Virgin Mary*. High up in the apse you can just make out early thirteenth-century frescoes showing *Christ Enthroned with Saints*, while the chapel to the right of the apse has still more frescoes, this time fourteenth-century *Scenes from the Life of St Francis*. A small chapel in the sacristy is reputedly the room in which St Francis slept when he visited Gubbio, a sojourn that included his famous taming of a wolf which had been terrorizing the town. The structure is known to have been part of a medieval house belonging to the Spadalonga, family friends of the saint. Take a look, too, at the simple cloisters beyond, still clinging to a few fourteenth-century frescoes.

Opposite the church is the distinctive fourteenth-century **Loggia dei Tiratori**, or weavers' loggia, Italy's best surviving example of this now rare type of building. Wool was stretched out in the shade of its arches to dry and shrink evenly away from the heat of the sun. The little church to its left is **Santa Maria dei Laici**, built in the fourteenth century but altered to dull effect three centuries later. Behind the loggia Via Piccardi leads past the church of **San Giovanni Battista**, restored to its thirteenth-century state, and distinguished by an enormous door and oddly elongated campanile. Just off to the west Via Baldassini contains the **Casa di Sant'Ubaldo**, the former home of one of Gubbio's patron saints. Ubaldo, born in Gubbio in 1100, became a bishop and earned his saintly spurs by helping defend the town from Barbarossa in 1155: he's buried up in the basilica bearing his name on Monte Ingino.

The Palazzo dei Consoli

Bearing east into the medieval town, along Via della Repubblica, centre-stage is taken by the austere **Palazzo dei Consoli**, a superb building whose crenellated outline and campanile dominate the countryside for miles around. Its western face is particularly impressive, vast buttressing supporting a building that rises almost 100m from the base of the foundations to the tip of the campanile. The plain **facade** is disturbed only by a triple-paired window motif that's unique to Gubbio and repeated elsewhere in the town, by a lovely doorway, and by a hole at the top right-hand corner – made to hold the cage, or *gogna* (from *vergogna* or "shame"), in which criminals were incarcerated. Take in the little **lunette** above the door, which features a *Madonna and Child with John the Baptist and Ubaldo*, Gubbio's patron saints.

An overbearing gesture of civic pride, the palace took the place of the previous civic headquarters in Via Ducale, embarrassingly overshadowed by a symbol of religious power – the duomo – a building subsequently lost beneath the foundations of Montefeltro's Palazzo Ducale (see box on next page). Work began in 1321, probably to the plans of the eminent Gubbian architect Matteo Gattapone. Angelo da Orvieto (active 1334–52), fresh from civic palaces in Città di Castello, may have designed the doorway and its flanking Gothic windows. Building took a couple of hundred years to finish, during which time vast tracts of the medieval town were levelled, most of the space going to accommodate the huge **Piazza Grande** (or Piazza della Signoria), a windswept belvedere with excellent views, and a suitable setting for this colossal building and for the lesser (and unfinished) **Palazzo Pretorio** opposite, built to the same Gattapone design.

THE MUSEO CIVICO

The cavernous barrel-vaulted **Salone dell'Arengo**, where the council officers discussed their business, now accommodates a **Museo Civico** (Tues–Sun: April–Sept 10am–1pm & 3–6pm; Oct–March 10am–1pm & 2–5pm; L7000). Much of this consists of coins and sculptures, scattered like a medieval jumble sale in the main hall, but one of its adjoining rooms off to the left also contains Umbria's most important archeological find, the **Eugubine Tablets**.

Discovered in 1444 by an illiterate shepherd – who twelve years later was conned by the *comune* into swapping the priceless treasure for a worthless piece of land – the tablets consist of seven bronze slabs, four of which probably date from about 200 BC, and three from around 100 BC. They are the most significant extant record of the **Umbrian language**, believed to have been a vernacular tongue without standard written characters. The bastardized Latin and Etruscan of their texts aimed at producing a phonetic transliteration of the dialect, using the main languages of the day. Gubbio was close to the shrine of the so-called Apennine Jove, a major pagan deity visited by pilgrims from all over Italy, and it's thought the tablets were the work of Roman and Etruscan priests taking advantage of the established order to impose new religious cults in a region where their languages weren't understood. The ritual text – the most important to have survived from antiquity – comprises a prayer divided into stanzas, a list of Gubbio's enemies, and a series of instructions for conducting services and the art of divination from sacrificed animals and the flight of birds. Most importantly, they suggest Romans, Etruscans and Umbrians achieved some sort of coexistence, refuting a long-held belief that succeeding civilizations wiped out their predecessors.

THE PINACOTECA

The museum ticket also gets you into the **Pinacoteca**, housed in five wonderful medieval rooms at the top of a steep flight of steps on the second floor of the palace. Though the paintings aren't anything special, they trace the development of the Gubbian School, one of central Italy's earliest, names to look out for being Guido Palmerucci and Mello da Eugubio. Sienese artists are also represented, notably by Rutilio Manetti, the city's leading follower of Caravaggio, and there's a lovely Crucifix by the Maestro di San Francesco (best known for his work in the Basilica di San Francesco in Assisi). The gallery's star painting, the *Madonna del Melograno* (Madonna of the Pomegranate) by Pier Francesco Fiorentino, was stolen in 1979 and must now surely be considered lost for good.

The Duomo

A couple of streets north of the Palazzo dei Consoli, the town's rather plain thirteenth-century Gothic **Duomo** is redeemed by a fine **interior**. Immediately noticeable is the strange arched ceiling, a Gubbian speciality known as "wagon vaulting", in which the ten arches are gracefully curved, apparently to emulate the meeting of hands in prayer. There are some fine twelfth-century stained-glass windows, a glitzy Baroque chapel and a wealth of frescoes and panel paintings, some good, some indifferent. Look for the works by Eusebio di San Giorgio (sixth niche on the left), the altarpiece by Timoteo Vito (seventh niche on the left) and the work by Sinibaldo Ibi next door.

The small **Museo Capitolare** adjoining the church is closed indefinitely following recent thefts, but if you get the chance it's worth a look, if only for a Guido Palmerucci fresco and the florid Flemish **cope** – parts of which were pinched in 1990 – presented to the cathedral by Pope Marcellus II: extravagantly embroidered, it portrays scenes from the Passion.

The Palazzo Ducale

Opposite the duomo – and overshadowing it – is the **Palazzo Ducale** (Mon–Sat 9am–7pm, Sun 9am–1.30pm; closed first Mon of the month; L4000), built in 1470 over an earlier Lombard palace and the town's twelfth-century Palazzo Comunale by Federigo da Montefeltro, the renowned Duke of Urbino, and designed as a scaled-down copy of his palace in Urbino. The architect of the two buildings was probably the same man, Dalmatian-born Luciano Laurana, selected by Federigo after he'd failed to find a suitably bold Florentine designer. The interior is now open after years of restoration, the tone for the building being set by the calming Renaissance **courtyard**, close to which a stone staircase leads down to a series of vaulted storerooms and excavations which have revealed the remains of four earlier buildings on the site. Among them are fragments from the tenth century and remnants of the town's former twelfth-century Palazzo Comunale, the building superseded by the Palazzo dei Consoli.

As in Urbino, many of the **rooms of the main palace** appeal as much for their measured architectural calm as for any surfeit of paintings or furniture. Most are virtually empty, but works from the cathedral museum (see above) and others from local churches in storage since an earthquake in 1984 are gradually being exhibited here. One room, the duke's former study (off room 2), was left bare after its intarsia wood panelling was stripped in the last century (it found its way to the Metropolitan Museum in New York). All the stone-carved windows and doorways are superb, however, as are the fireplaces and cool terracotta floors. The large central **Salone** offers some cracking views of the Palazzo dei Consoli and contains a fireplace that must have worked wonders during Gubbio's mountain-cold winters. **Room 5** has a couple of Madonnas by Mello da Eugubio, a local fourteenth-century painter whose work also features in the Pinacoteca.

Outside the palace, around the corner into Via Ducale, is one of Umbria's oddest novelties, the **Botte dei Canoncini**, a house-sized wine barrel with a 40,000-litre capacity, made in the sixteenth century.

Via dei Consoli and the Anfiteatro

Wandering around this area of the old town you'll soon come across Gubbio's **Porte della Morte**, the "doors of death" – narrow, bricked-up doorways wedged into the facades of medieval town houses. A historical conundrum found only in Gubbio, Assisi and southern France, the party line has it they were cut to carry a coffin out of the house and then, having been tainted by death, sealed up. A nice theory, and very Italian, but to judge by the constricted stairways behind the doors, their purpose was probably defensive – the main door could be barricaded, leaving the more easily defended passageway as the only entrance. Gubbio's best examples are in **Via dei Consoli**.

There are dozens of similar picturesque odds and ends around Gubbio's streets, which lend themselves to a slow ramble. The **Bargello** – built in 1302 as the medieval police station – in Via dei Consoli is worth tracking down and gives you a chance to survey the adjoining **Fontana dei Matti** (Fountain of the Mad), undistinguished but for the tradition that anyone walking round it three times will wind up deranged. There is usually someone about wondering whether to give it a go. Another take on the madness angle is that you qualify for a *patente da matto*, a licence of madness, if you make the run and are simultaneously soaked with water by three locals.

From here you can head east towards the funicular (see below) or drop down to look into the nearby church of **San Domenico**, distinguished by a fine intarsia lectern, and take in two other impressive medieval buildings – the fifteenth-century **Palazzo Beni** and the **Palazzo del Capitano del Popolo**, the latter home to an odd little private museum of modern sculpture and medieval torture instruments.

Following the walls back round, anticlockwise, to the Piazza Quaranta Martiri, you might make a detour to the **Anfiteatro Romano** (daily 9am–1pm; free). Built in the first century, it's tame by Colosseum standards, though at 112 metres in diameter still one of the largest in the Roman world. It retains its seats and much of the lower arcades – the setting for a summer festival of Shakespeare and classical drama. Current excavations are uncovering more remains. Close by is a Roman **mausoleum**, easily reached from Piazza del Mercato; a blockhouse affair nine metres high, no one is really sure for whom it was intended.

The funicular and Basilica di Sant'Ubaldo

A path near the duomo zigzags uphill to the **Basilica di Sant'Ubaldo**, but the fun and panoramic way up (providing you're not nervy about heights) is to take the six-minute **funicular** – which has open ski-lift type "cages" for two people – from Porta Romana over on the east side of town (daily: June & Sept 10am–1.15pm & 2.30–5pm; July–Aug 8.30am–7.30pm; Oct–May 10am–1.15pm & 2.30–5pm except Wed; L6000 one-way, L8000 return).

En route to the Porta, you can take in Ottaviano Nelli's masterpiece, the winsome *Madonna del Belvedere* (1413) at **Santa Maria Nuova**, together with patches of fresco left by his pupils (if the church is shut, try the custodian at Via Dante 66). Little **Sant'Andrea** nearby, probably of eleventh-century foundation and recently restored, is also worth a passing look. Porta Romana itself has a little private museum, the **Museo Torre Mediovale** (April–Sept daily 8.30am–8pm; Oct–March Tues–Sun 9am–1pm & 3–6.30pm; L3500) devoted to local ceramics and displays on the mechanics of defending

---

CORSA DEI CERI

Held each year on May 15, the vigil of the feast day of Gubbio's patron saint, Ubaldo, the **Corsa dei Ceri** is little known outside Italy, but in Tuscany and Umbria ranks second only to Siena's Palio in its exuberance and bizarre pageantry. The rules and rigmarole of the nine-hundred-year-old ceremony are mind-boggling, but in essence begin with an **early morning Mass** and a procession through the packed streets of the vast wooden *ceri*, or "candles", removed from Ubaldo's Monte Ingino basilica. Each is dedicated to a particular saint – Ubaldo, Anthony and George. At 10.30am another procession makes its way to the Piazza Grande, where an hour later the four-metre-high *ceri* are raised by members of the town's three traditional confraternities: the builders, represented by St Ubaldo, the artisans (St George) and the peasants (St Anthony); a statue of the relevant saint tops each column.

There follows yet another procession through the streets to show the *ceri* to the townspeople (and also TV crews from across Italy). The pillars are then dumped until 4.30pm while all concerned adjoin for a gut-busting fish lunch in the Palazzo dei Consoli. Yet another procession ensues, during which the clergy are finally allowed to participate, a journey which takes the *ceri* through just about every last corner of the town. Back in the Piazza Grande at 6pm the mayor brandishes a white banner to signal the beginning of a **race**, the climax of the day, which involves the carrying of the *ceri* to the Basilica di Sant'Ubaldo.

No sooner has the race begun, than there's a stop at the Porta del Monte. It then resumes up the steep path to the basilica, each confraternity being allowed ten official carriers who have to be replaced every ten minutes – but without stopping. "Race" is something of a misnomer, however, for the *cero* of Ubaldo always "wins", the other teams having to ensure they're in the basilica before the doors are shut by the leaders. The *ceri* are then abandoned in the basilica, and the saints brought down in a candlelit procession. Thereafter there's more celebration and a good deal of drinking.

A scholarly debate rages over the origins, which are generally cited as either a secular feast commemorating the day in 1155 when Ubaldo talked Barbarossa out of flattening Gubbio, or a hangover from some pagan fertility rite. These days the Church claims it as its own, though judging by the very phallic *ceri* and the roar that goes up when they're raised to the vertical in Piazza Grande, there's something more than Christian jubilation going on.

---

a medieval gateway. Just outside the walls, the thirteenth-century **Sant'Agostino** contains an apse smothered in 26 Nelli frescoes of *Scenes from the Life of St Augustine* (1420) and panel paintings by him on the second and fifth altars.

Once atop Monte Ingino (827m), the **views** and a bar are the main attractions. Even better vistas are at hand if you climb up to the **Rocca**. The **Basilica** itself, five minutes from the funicular station, is not of great interest, though it's revered for the body of the town's patron saint, Ubaldo, whose missing three fingers were hacked off by his manservant as a religious keepsake. Amid the interior, you can't miss the big wooden pillars, or *ceri* (candles), featured in Gubbio's annual *Corsa dei Ceri* (see above).

Eating

Gubbio offers some good small-town cooking. A workaday **restaurant** is the *Bargello*, Via dei Consoli 37 (closed Mon), a friendly pizzeria in a pleasant street. Similarly good is the *San Francesco e il Lupo*, Via Carioli 24, for pizzas or full meals. The *Grotta dell'Angelo* (closed Tues), annexed to the hotel, has a wonderful cave of a dining room (the *grotta* of its name), with excellent basic meals for L20,000 and upwards.

Well known and more pricey – with meals around L60,000 and up – are the *Taverna del Lupo*, Via Ansidei 21 (☎075.927.4368; closed Mon & two weeks in Jan or Feb), a more traditional place with medieval interior, and probably a touch better than its smaller up-market

rival, the vaguely modish *La Fornace di Maestro Giorgio*, Via M. Giorgio 2 (☎075.927.5740;
closed Sun evening, Mon & Feb); it's sited in the converted workshop of one of Gubbio's
medieval master ceramists. The *Bosone Garden* restaurant, attached to the *Bosone* hotel,
opposite the *Maestro Giorgio*, has an interesting menu (around L40,000), and is perhaps the
nicest spot for outdoors eating in Gubbio (closed Wed).

Gualdo Tadino

The main centre to the east of Gubbio is **GUALDO TADINO**, a hill-town which takes its
name from the German *wald* (wood), a throwback to the days of the Holy Roman Empire
and Italy's northern European rulers ("Tadino" was tagged on to its name as late as
1833). It occupies the site of ancient **Tadinum**, a Roman staging post on the Via Flaminia,
and lies close to the site of the battlefield at which Narses, a eunuch and renowned
Byzantine general, killed Totila and won a famous victory over the Goths in 552. Later it
was the birthplace of **Matteo da Gualdo** (1435–1513), an accomplished but little-known
painter (at least outside Umbria) whose works crop up in Assisi, Trevi and Spoleto, as
well as in his home town. Today, the town, which sprawls over the lower slopes of the
Apennines, has the remote outpost feel of other eastern Umbrian towns – notably Norcia
and Gubbio. But while the medieval centre is a touch bleak, with little of substance to see,
it's quiet and atmospheric, and makes a good base for exploring the beautiful **Monte
Cucco** region (see opposite page). Economic well-being flows from the town's renowned
ceramics, best seen during a big summer exhibition devoted to the craft.

The town was badly hit by the 1997 earthquake and some buildings were razed
entirely; accessibility and opening times of all sites remain subject to change for the
foreseeable future.

The Town

The Gothic **Duomo** (1256), also known as San Benedetto, is located in the central Piazza
Martiri della Libertà, and boasts a facade similar to the one in Todi – the three-tiered
arrangement being a recurrent Umbrian design – and a fine carved doorway and rose window: the interior, though, was done to death in the last century. The little **fountain** on the
Corso Italia flank of the building is attributed to Antonio da Sangallo the Elder. The building opposite the cathedral is the **Palazzo Comunale**, of eighteenth-century vintage, and
close by is the nicely restored **Palazzo del Podestà**. Secreted away somewhere are various precious works of art left to the cathedral over the years, but currently hidden from
public view owing to lack of funds and the high probability they'll be lifted by thieves.

Similar worries prevail in the small **Pinacoteca Comunale**, which is closed indefinitely,
though there are plans to reopen it in a building in the nearby Piazza del Sopramura. Most
of the exhibits are by **Matteo da Gualdo** (see above), mercilessly lampooned by nineteenth-century critics for his "incorrect drawing", though his brilliant colouring has since
restored him to critical favour. However, Matteo's paintings, together with a Sienese
Coronation of the Virgin by Sano di Pietro, are eclipsed by a sublime polyptych (1471) by
Nicolò Alunno, whom Berenson described as "the first painter in whom the emotional,
now passionate and violent, now mystic and ecstatic temperament of St Francis's country-
men were revealed". You might enquire at the Pro Loco in Via Calai 39 about the possibility
of having the gallery opened, though the chances of success may be slim.

The church of **San Francesco** is likely to be more rewarding. Deconsecrated, its
airy interior is used for temporary exhibitions, and features frescoes on the *Life of St
Julian* by the school of Ottaviano Nelli (above the west door), a lunette with a damaged
Madonna (high on the south wall), and a large painted Crucifix by a follower of the
Maestro di San Francesco (see p.491). On the north side of the church also look out for

part of a Roman sarcophagus flanked by two winged figures representing Victory, and the unmissable raised fourteenth-century pulpit. Among the apse frescoes is a *Crucifixion* by Matteo da Gualdo. There's another bright Matteo triptych in the recently restored church of **Santa Maria**, in Piazza XX Settembre, close by. And if the paintings of Matteo really appeal, it's worth driving to the hill-village of San Pellegrino, 6km to the northwest just off the Gubbio road (SS219), where the church has several of his works and a triptych (1465) by Giovanni di Camerino, recovered after its recent theft.

Practicalities

Gualdo is an easy trip by **bus** from both Gubbio and Città di Castello, and there are three connections daily from Foligno (Mon–Sat); **trains** from Assisi, Foligno or Spoleto are frequent, and there's a **shuttle bus** from the train station to the old centre.

The cheapest **hotel** is the large 59-room one-star *Centro Sociale Verde Soggiorno*, Via Don Bosco 50 (☎075.916.263, fax 075.914.2951; ②), with a choice of rooms with and without private bathroom. Otherwise try the two-star *Dal Bottaio*, Via Casimiri 17 (☎075.913.230; ②) or *Gigiotto*, Via Morone 5 (☎075.912.283, fax 075.910.0263; ②); the latter also has the town's most venerable **restaurant** (closed Wed & Nov). The nearest **campsite** is in the mountains at Valsorda (see below).

Parco Regionale del Monte Cucco

Some of Umbria's best upland scenery is to be found in the mountains east and north of Gualdo on the border with the Marche, much of it protected by the **Parco Regionale del Monte Cucco**. Where this area really scores is in its organized trails and backup for outdoor activities of every kind; if you want to don walking boots without too much fuss, this is the area to do it. Most importantly, and unusually for Italy, good **maps** are also available: it's worth investing in the 1:50,000 *Kompass* sheet "Assisi-Camerino" (#665), which covers the area around Gualdo, and in the special trail map issued in Costacciaro, the main centre inside the park. **Access** is easy, with buses from Gualdo to Valsorda and from Perugia, Gualdo, Gubbio and Assisi to Costacciaro.

Valsorda

The southernmost base for exploration of the park is the resort of **VALSORDA** (1000m), 8km northeast of Gualdo on the southern extremity of the park. Regular buses run from Gualdo to the village, which is a launching pad for easy hill walks and a reasonably scenic, if developed, spot in its own right.

You can tackle the straightforward trek up **Serra Santa** (1421m), on a track of motorway proportions carved out by pilgrims over the years. From the summit you could then drop into the spectacular **Valle del Fonno** gorge and follow it down to Gualdo. Paths follow the main ridge from Valsorda north and south, and it's feasible to walk all the way to Nocera Umbra (described on next page. In the past Valsorda boasted a couple of **hotels**, but these have closed. There is, though, a one-star **campsite**, the forty-pitch *Valsorda* (☎075.913.261; June–Sept), perched at 1010m.

Costacciaro

To get closer to the heart of the mountains you head north from Gualdo past Fossato di Vico, a hill-town whose eleventh-century Romanesque gem, **San Pietro**, contains some fine Nelli frescoes. Beyond Fossato the road passes through Sigillo and then **COSTAC-CIARO**, the centre for all the park's outdoor pursuits and access point for the **Grotta di Monte Cucco**, at 922m the fifth-deepest cave system in the world. The cave was explored as early as 1889, but has only recently been opened up by the hundreds of cavers that flock here from all over Europe; over 40km of galleries have now been charted. Above, the huge, bare-sloped Monte Cucco (1566m) is the main playground for **walkers**.

Costacciaro activities

The best place to go if you want to get seriously wet or muddy, or just tag along with a tour party, is the **Centro Nazionale di Speleologia**, Corso Mazzini 9 (call ☎075.917.0236 for details of tours). One of the country's most energetic and organized outdoor centres, it offers sorties for enthusiasts and guidance for visiting experts – public access is restricted to a metal ladder that runs 40m down into a large cavern.

For **walkers**, the centre's main offering is a good 1:16,000 **map** which charts the area's thirty **marked trails**. The straightforward ascent of Monte Cucco (4-hr round trip) begins from the **Val di Ranco**, a valley which cuts east into the mountains from Costacciaro: follow trail 1 to the summit, via Pian delle Macinare, and trail 2 for the descent (both with yellow and red trail markings).

As well as the lowdown on caving, the centre also supplies information and gear to **hang-gliders**, Monte Cucco being one of Italy's leading centres for the sport. The centre **hires equipment** for other activities too – the area has modest ski runs and a few limestone walls for climbers at Le Lecce and the Fossa Secca.

Park accommodation

There are a few **accommodation** possibilities in and around Costacciaro, the best of them the *Monte Cucco da Tobia* in the Val di Ranco (☎ & fax 075.917.7194; ②), a fabled mountaineers' and cavers' hangout. Also convenient for walkers is the one-star *Cappelloni*, Val di Ranco (☎075.917.7131; open May–Sept; ②). The caving centre (see above) has limited **hostel** accommodation (June–Sept daily; Oct–May Sat & Sun; L22,000), but be certain to book ahead as it's often full of school parties. In the same street is a one-star hotel with just five rooms, *Il Torrione*, Corso Mazzini (☎075.917.0740, fax 075.917.0741; ②). There's another hostel, the *Ostello Centro di Volo Libero* (☎075.917.0761; L22,000), which is mainly a hang-gliders' hang-out, at Villa Scirca, 3km north of Sigillo. The nearest **campsite** is at Fornace, 3km north of Costacciaro – *Rio Verde* (☎075.917.0138; Easter–Sept). Freelance camping is prohibited within the *parco regionale*, but elsewhere you'll have few problems finding a discreet pitch for a tent.

Nocera Umbra

Sitting on a spur above the Topino valley 15km south of Gualdo, **NOCERA UMBRA** is in some ways a carbon copy of its neighbours, with wooded hills as a backdrop and a grim new town on the valley floor detracting from what was a passable medieval quarter above – sadly, much of the town will be under scaffolding for years to come, following the devastation wreaked by the 1997 earthquake. Nocera is otherwise best known for its bottled **mineral waters**, processed in a large plant by the station.

As in Gualdo, the town's main attraction is a small **art gallery**, housed in the church of San Francesco on Piazza Caprera. St Francis was probably in Nocera as early as 1215 and by 1221 had been asked to form a convent here; it was ransacked by Frederick II in 1248 and replaced by the present church in 1336. Before the earthquake it housed several pieces by Matteo da Gualdo, a *Madonna and Child* by the Sienese Segna di Bonaventura, a large thirteenth-century Crucifix and – the high spot – another polyptych by Alunno, encased in a glorious frame. Until renovations are completed, however, no one knows when or where these treasures will be exhibited (call ☎0742.81.246 for the latest information). The **duomo** in Via San Rinaldo is the only other thing to see – and there's not much to it, the interior having been gutted in the eighteenth century.

Practicalities

Highly accessible from Gualdo, Nocera could just as easily be seen from Assisi or from Foligno, 20km to the southwest, both with good **bus** and **train** links to the town. The train station, however, is a long way from the town it's meant to serve, though there are regular connecting buses to the old centre: for so humble a place, it's hardly worth the hassle of a public transport expedition. All five hotels in and around the town are temporarily closed: two – the *Flaminio* and *Centrale* – have functioning restaurants.

Bagni di Nocera and the hills

To sample the spa life, take the road to **BAGNI DI NOCERA**, 4km east, where the Sorgente Angelica spring (open June–Oct) has been famous since the seventeenth century. People came from as far away as Portugal and the Middle East to enjoy its supposedly miraculous cures; these days the spa is a modern and characterless complex, partly redeemed by its natural surroundings.

If you have transport, the villages and hilly countryside to the east repay aimless exploration. The main local outing is to **Monte Pennino** (1571m), a minor winter resort, accessible on a road that reaches virtually to the summit.

To the west is a quieter pocket of countryside, a good way to meander towards Assisi, with the well-preserved castle at **Rocca di Posignano** a spot to head for if you want a focus to your itinerary.

travel details

TRAINS

Città di Castello to: Perugia (hourly; 50min); Sansepolcro (hourly; 50min).

Fossato di Vico (for Gubbio) to: Foligno (10 daily; 50min); Gualdo Tadino (5 daily; 10min); Nocera Umbra (10 daily; 20min); Orte (10 daily; 1hr 55min); Rome (10 daily; 2hr 40min); Spoleto (10 daily; 1hr 15min); Terni (10 daily; 1hr 30min).

Perugia to: Assisi (hourly; 25min); Città di Castello (hourly; 50min); Deruta (hourly; 30min); Florence (6 daily; 2hr 15min); Foligno (hourly; 40min – for connections to Spoleto, Fossato di Vico, Terni, Narni and Orte); Passignano (hourly; 30min); Sansepolcro (hourly; 1hr 40min); Spello (hourly; 35min); Terni (hourly; 1hr 50min); Teróntola (hourly; 40min – for 6 connections daily to Rome and also Siena); Todi (hourly; 50min).

BUSES

Perugia to: Ascoli Piceno (1–4 daily; 3hr); Assisi (3–12 daily; 30min); Castiglione del Lago (7–9 daily Mon–Sat; 1hr 15min); Chiusi (5 daily Mon–Sat; 1hr 45min); Città della Pieve (5 daily Mon–Sat; 1hr 30min); Florence (1 daily; 2hr); Gualdo Tadino (6 daily Mon–Sat, 2 daily Sun; 1hr 25min); Gubbio (10 daily Mon–Sat, 4 daily Sun; 1hr 10min); Todi via Deruta (3–7 daily Mon–Sat; 1hr 15min); Nocera Umbra (1 daily Mon–Sat; 1hr 20min); Norcia (1 direct daily; 2hr 50min); Orvieto (1 daily; 2hr 25min); Passignano (7 daily Mon–Sat; 1hr 10min); Rome (2–6 daily; 2hr 30min); Rome Fiumicino airport (1–3 daily; 3hr); Siena (3–7 daily; 1hr 30min); Spello (4 daily Mon–Sat; 55min); Spoleto (1 daily direct Mon–Sat; 1hr 20min); Torgiano (7 daily Mon–Sat; 30min).

Gubbio to: Fossato di Vico (to connect with trains), continuing to Gualdo Tadino and Nocera Umbra (10 daily; 30min); Perugia (10 daily Mon–Sat, 4 daily Sun; 1hr 10min); Rome (1 daily; 2 hr 40min); also services to Città di Castello, Umbértide, Arezzo and Florence.

Città di Castello to: Rome Tiburtina (1 daily; 3hr 15min); Rome Fiumicino airport (1 daily Mon–Sat; 3hr 50min); Todi (1 direct daily Mon–Sat; 2hr).

CHAPTER ELEVEN

ASSISI AND THE VALE OF SPOLETO

The **Vale of Spoleto**, the broad plain between Perugia and Spoleto, is Umbria's historic and spiritual heartland: a beautiful sweep of countryside that has a majestic focus in **Assisi**. Birthplace of St Francis, Italy's premier saint, this hill-town has been an object of pilgrimage for over seven hundred years, now attracting a staggering five million visitors annually. Most of these millions come as an act of faith, but a substantial number visit simply to see the sublime paintings in the **Basilica di San Francesco**, where frescoes by **Giotto** and **Pietro Lorenzetti** comprise one of the greatest monuments of Italian art. Yet for all the coach parties of pilgrims, both religious and secular, Assisi remains a town with an uncompromised identity – as an overnight stay, after the car parks have cleared, will reveal. It has also emerged from the trauma of the 1997 earthquake, which brought Assisi to worldwide prominence when part of the Basilica collapsed, destroying some of its more minor frescoes.

Quieter hill-towns are just around the corner. **Spello**, the most accessible, remains one step ahead of the tourist boom and features more art treasures in the shape of Pinturicchio's frescoes in the church of Santa Maria Maggiore. Nearby **Bevagna**, like Spello an outpost on the Roman Via Flaminia, is a tiny, wall-enclosed village locked around a central square that's without equal in Umbria. Lording it over the vale is **Montefalco**, a windblown hive of medieval streets that is home to yet another superb fresco cycle – this one by Benozzo Gozzoli – and one of the province's strangest attractions, a quartet of mummified holy corpses. Across the valley is **Trevi**, hardly ever visited, but perhaps the most perfectly situated of all Italian hill-towns. **Foligno**, the regional capital, has a sprawling, provincial appeal and a handsome duomo, and provides a good standby for accommodation.

Foligno is also the centre of the network of transport links throughout the region. The main **rail** link from Rome to Ancona passes through Foligno, whence there are

---

ACCOMMODATION PRICES

Throughout this guide, **hotel** accommodation is graded on a scale from ① to ⑨, indicating the cost of the **cheapest double room** in each establishment in high season (for **hostels**, rates per person are given in lire). The price bands to which these codes refer are as follows:

① up to L60,000	④ L120,000–150,000	⑦ L250,000–300,000
② L60,000–90,000	⑤ L150,000–200,000	⑧ L300,000–350,000
③ L90,000–120,000	⑥ L200,000–250,000	⑨ over L350,000

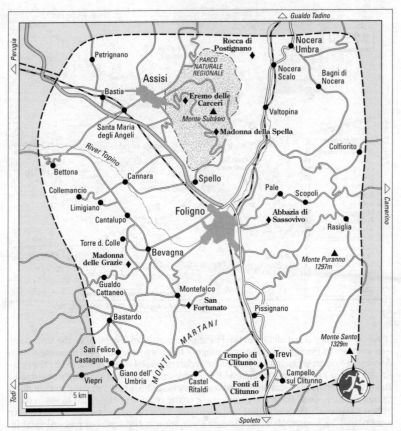

connections to Spoleto, Terni and Narni to the south, Nocera and Gualdo Tadino to the north, and a branch line spur that runs to Teróntola via Spello, Assisi and Perugia. **Buses** radiate from Foligno to the local villages, and there are frequent connections between Perugia, Assisi and points to the south. **Road** journeys are quick thanks to the dual carriageway (SS3) between Perugia and Foligno.

Assisi

ASSISI would be an irresistible target even without its great Basilica and Franciscan sideshow. Visible for miles around, it nestles enticingly beneath the whaleback slopes of Monte Subasio, its prominent castle and pink-stoned medieval houses lording it over the Vale of Spoleto. At close quarters the tacky tourist paraphernalia and mountains of religious kitsch are offset by tranquil backstreets, geranium-filled window boxes and buildings in the muted, pinkish stone that distinguishes all the vale's towns. With sufficient enthusiasm you can see almost all the sights in a day, but the town changes for the better come evening, and it's worth trying to stay at least one night.

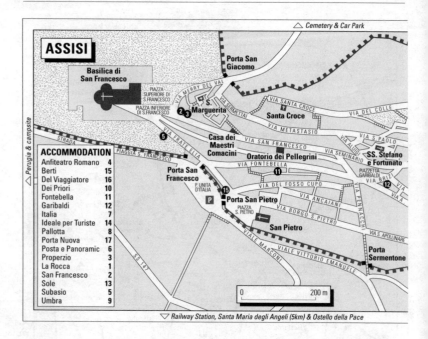

▽ *Railway Station, Santa Maria degli Angeli (5km) & Ostello della Pace*

Assisi's history is not all tied to the Franciscan masthead. Founded by the Umbrians – in contrast to Perugia's Etruscan heritage – the town later achieved prominence as Asisium, a Roman *municipium*. Thereafter invaders passed it over, attracted by the richer pickings of Perugia, but in the end it fell under the control of that city's monstrous Baglioni family. These were men, said one Franciscan historian, "who did not shudder to murder men, cook their flesh, and give it to the relations of the slain to eat in their prison dungeons". Plague, famine and eventually Church control turned the town into a moribund backwater. However, Francis's elevation to the status of national saint in 1939 managed to reverse its economic decline, and it is now one of Europe's major pilgrimage centres.

Arrival, information and accommodation

Getting in and out of Assisi is easy. There are hourly **trains** from Foligno (via Spello) and from Teróntola (via Perugia) to Assisi station (☎075.804.0272), located in the modern suburb of Santa Maria degli Angeli, 5km from the old town. Half-hourly buses (tickets from the station kiosk) run from the station to **Piazza Matteotti** (20min), some by way of Largo Properzio, east of the Basilica di Santa Chiara – from where there's an unreliable escalator to the gateway at Porta Nuova. Both spots are less than five minutes' walk from the heart of the medieval town, **Piazza del Comune**. From Piazza del Comune, the main street leads west along the ridge of the town to the Basilica di San Francesco.

The main **bus terminal** and a massive underground **car park** are in **Piazza Matteotti**, in the east of the town above the duomo. A board in the piazza's northwest corner, on the junction of Via del Comune Vecchio, has a full schedule for bus departures, and there's a flashy electronic display next to the ticket and information office, ASP Agenzia (daily 7.30am–9.30pm). Twice-daily long-distance SULGA (☎075.500.9641) buses to Rome's

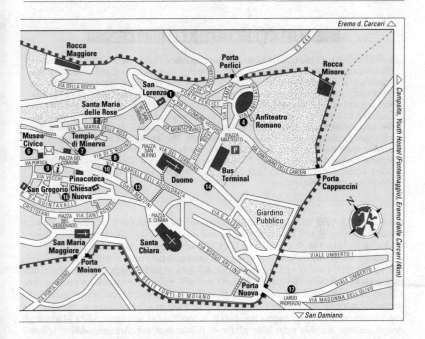

Tiburtina station (1.45pm & 4.45pm) and Florence's Piazza Adua (6.45am) leave from Piazza San Pietro, at the other end of town. Tickets for these services are available on the bus or from the Stoppini travel agent at Corso Mazzini 31 (☎075.812.597).

Parking in central Assisi is virtually impossible, traffic being restricted chiefly to service vehicles. It's best to leave cars in Piazza Matteotti or in Piazza Unità d'Italia (the latter is closer to the Basilica); if you don't mind a long walk to the Basilica, park up by the Rocca, where there are hundreds of free spaces. Other free parking is available by the cemetery off Viale Albornoz on the road from Porta San Giacomo. Orange **minibuses** provide connecting services around the town, though in practice you'll find distances are short and that it's easiest to walk. Minibus tickets are sold at shops and newsagents with an ASP or *Comune di Assisi* ticket flash on display.

Information

The **tourist office** is usually at Piazza del Comune 12 (Mon–Sat 8.30am–1pm & 3.30–6.30pm, Sun 9am–1pm; ☎075.812.534 or 075.812.450), but since the earthquake has moved between several temporary homes around the piazza while its premises are checked. The staff do their best to help with finding accommodation and they also provide some useful maps and pamphlets. The tourist office sometimes has a range of individual duplicated sheets with details of trains, buses, private rooms and *agriturismo* options – but you have to ask. There are usually seasonal **summer information offices** in Largo Properzio, Porta Nuova (☎075.816.766), Santa Maria degli Angeli (☎075.812.479), and at the train station (☎075.813.499).

Accommodation

There are getting on for a hundred **hotels** in Assisi, along with a large stock of **private rooms** and extraordinarily cheap **pilgrim hostels** (*Case Religiose di Ospitalità*). At

ASSISI AND THE 1997 EARTHQUAKES

Assisi has been a little quieter since the **earthquakes** of September 1997 – two major tremors and many aftershocks – which killed four people in the Basilica di San Francesco and destroyed some of the building's less significant frescoes. While the event made world headlines, the damage to Assisi, the Basilica and the rest of Umbria was somewhat overdramatized: the earthquake epicentres were well to the east in Colfiorito and the Marche, and nearby towns Spoleto and Orvieto suffered virtually no ill-effects. Some precautionary scaffolding and buttressing aside, there are now few tangible signs in Assisi that anything happened at all. The important Lower Church of the Basilica has remained open, and the Upper Church – where the partial ceiling collapse occurred – was formally reopened by a representative of the Pope in November 1999. Other sights are opening as checks are completed, and the town's intrinsic medieval charm remains undiminished.

most times of year this is just about adequate for the number of visitors, though advance booking is still highly advisable, and essential if you plan to visit over Easter or during the *Festa di San Francesco* (Oct 3–4) or *Calendimaggio* (May 21–22).

Listings below detail a selection of the best (and generally most central) hotels, hostels and rooms. The **tourist office** can provide full lists of all lodgings, including over fifty rooms for rent (ask for the *Extralberghieri*), and will make reservations for you, too. For a list of rooms ask for the leaflet *Esercizi Extralberghieri*: note that you can get good deals on weekly rates for most private lodgings. Try to insist on a central location, avoiding the concentrations of cheaper rooms and hotels in San Pietro Campagna, Santa Maria degli Angeli and the horribly grim little village of Bastia, 4km out. Accommodation is listed below in ascending order of price.

HOTELS

Italia, Vicolo della Fortezza 2 (☎075.812.625, fax 075.804.3749). The most central one-star hotel; 13 rooms, 11 with bathroom, in an alley off the north side of Piazza del Comune. Highly recommended – if they've got space. Open March–Oct. ②.

Anfiteatro Romano, Via Anfiteatro Romano 4 (☎075.813.025, fax 075.815.110). Good-value one-star hotel, in one of the most pleasant parts of town. Seven rooms and a choice with and without bathrooms. ②.

La Rocca, Via di Porta Perlici 27 (☎ & fax 075.812.284). A 15-room one-star beyond the duomo at the very end of Via di P. Perlici. Quiet and with fine views from some rooms; most with own bath. ②.

Berti, Piazza San Pietro 29 (☎075.813.466, fax 075.816.870). Two-star located in a quiet piazza, and handy for the Basilica. ③.

Garibaldi, Piazzetta Garibaldi 1 (☎075.812.624). Restored two-star hotel with 12 rooms in an imposing palazzo – just downhill from Piazza del Comune in one of Assisi's quieter corners. ③.

Ideale per Turisti, Piazza Matteotti 1 (☎075.813.570, fax 075.813.020). Follow signs south from Piazza Matteotti a short way outside the walls to reach this very slightly outlying but very reasonable 11-room two-star hotel: all rooms with private bathroom. ③.

Pallotta, Via San Rufino 6 (☎ & fax 075.812.307). Seven-room two-star in a good location between the duomo and Piazza del Comune: all rooms with private bathroom. ③.

Posta e Panoramic, Via San Paolo 17–19 (☎075.816.202, fax 075.812.558). Centrally located two-star with 14 rooms west of the duomo – on the street parallel to Via San Francesco. ③.

Sole, Corso Mazzini 35 (☎075.812.373, fax 075.813.706). Functional two-star hotel with 19 rooms in a convenient position one minute's walk from the Basilica di Santa Chiara. Also has an 18-room annexe at Corso Mazzini 20, so a good chance of finding space when others are full. ③.

Del Viaggiatore, Via Sant'Antonio 14 (☎075.816.297 or 075.812.424, fax 075.813.051). Small, personal, 16-room two-star above a decent restaurant in the web of streets between Santa Maria Maggiore and Piazza del Comune. ③.

Properzio, Via San Francesco 38b (☎075.813.188, fax 075.815.201). Simple, 9-room two-star handily placed on the main street right by the Basilica. ③.

Porta Nuova, Viale Umberto I 21 (☎075.812.405, fax 075.816.539). Basic 20-room three-star standby south of Piazza Matteotti in a quiet area above Basilica di Santa Chiara. ④.

Dei Priori, Corso Mazzini 15 (☎075.812.237, fax 075.816.804). Three-star, 34-room hotel, slightly east of Piazza del Comune: rates vary considerably between rooms. ④–⑤.

San Francesco, Via San Francesco 48 (☎075.812.281, fax 075.816.237). Reliable and conveniently situated three-star hotel just a minute's walk from the Basilica; 45 rooms – some with views – so there's a good chance of finding space. ④.

San Pietro, Piazza San Pietro 5 (☎075.812.452, fax 075.816.332). Large but rather perfunctory three-star hotel with 46 rooms by the gate south of the Basilica. ④.

Umbra, Vicolo degli Archi 6 (☎075.812.240, fax 075.813.653). An excellent and very popular up-market choice, with 25 three-star rooms almost immediately off the southern edge of Piazza del Comune. ⑤.

Subasio, Via Frate Elia 2 (☎075.812.206, fax 075.816.691). Full of old-world style, the four-star *Subasio* is Assisi's traditional hotel of choice if you're feeling flush: past guests include Marlene Dietrich, Charlie Chaplin and Elizabeth Taylor. Surprisingly unstuffy for all that; the 61 rooms vary considerably, but most have views. ⑥.

Fontebella, Via Fontebella 25 (☎075.812.456, fax 075.812.941). By far the most elegant and intimate of Assisi's smart hotels, despite its three-star rating and the fact that it is less high profile than the Subasio: try for a room on one of the top two floors for views over the roof tops and the Vale of Spoleto. ⑧.

PILGRIM HOSTELS

All the *Case Religiose di Ospitalità* below are open to both women and men and are located in the town proper. Costs are from around L25,000 per person, depending on whether rooms have private bathrooms and how many people are sharing a room; none charges more than L60,000. Most offer singles and doubles and sometimes a couple of dormitory rooms. Virtually all provide breakfast for an extra L5000 (not worth it) and very reasonable half- and full-board options, though don't expect anything fancy by way of food. Pilgrims know about and use these places, so try to book in advance.

Casa del Terzario, Piazza del Vescovado 5 (☎075.812.366, fax 075.816.377). A definite first choice for location and rooms, though not all rooms have private bathrooms.

Suore dell'Atonement, Via G. Alessi 10 (☎075.812.542, fax 075.813.723). All 20 rooms offered by the American nuns here have private bathrooms. Breakfast is included.

Istituto Beata Angelina, Via Merry del Val 4 (☎ & fax 075.812.511). Most of the 16 rooms have private bathrooms; located very close to the Basilica.

Monastero Sant'Andrea, Vicolo Sant'Andrea (☎075.812.274, fax 075.815.130). Located in a hard-to-find but excellently situated alley just south of Via San Giacomo and Porta San Giacomo. Take the turn uphill off Via San Francesco by the Casa dei Maestri Comacini.

Monastero San Coletta, Borgo San Pietro 3 (☎075.812.345, fax 075.816.489). Handy for the Basilica: located just west of the church of San Pietro. Breakfast included, but no half-board or full-board deals.

Monastero San Giuseppe, Via Sant'Apollinare 1 (☎ & fax 075.812.332). Located in the southeast corner of town just west of Santa Maria Maggiore.

Monastero Santo Quirico, Via Giovanni di Borino (☎075.812.688). Has 14 rooms, 12 of which have private bathrooms.

ROOMS IN PRIVATE HOUSES

Giustina Lanfaloni, Borgo San Pietro 13 (☎075.813.356). Five singles with one shared bathroom 100m up from San Pietro on the right. Out of the way and so a good chance of space. ②.

Maria Alunni, Via dell'Acquario 3 (☎075.813.182). Charming proprietress; 4 spotless, airy rooms and lots of greenery. ③.

Marco Gambacorta, Via Sermei 9 (☎075.815.206). Six double rooms (3 bathrooms) in the small lane immediately north of the Basilica di Santa Chiara off Via Santa Chiara. ③.

ST FRANCIS OF ASSISI

St Francis is the most extraordinary figure that the Italian Church has produced, a revolutionary spirit who redefined and reinvigorated medieval Christianity. His impact upon the evolution of the Catholic Church stands without parallel, and all that he accomplished in his 44 years was achieved simply through the power of preaching and personal example. Dante placed him alongside another Messianic figure, John the Baptist, while Mussolini, of all people, called him "il più santo dei santi" ("the most saintly of the saints"); his appeal today remains undiminished.

The events of his life, though encrusted with myth, are well chronicled. He was born in Assisi in 1182, the son of a wealthy merchant and a Provençal woman – which is why he replaced his baptismal name, Giovanni, with Francesco (Little Frenchman). The Occitan literature of Provence, with its troubadour songs and courtly love poems, was later to be the making of Francis as a poet and speaker. One of the earliest writers in the vernacular, Francis laid the foundation of a great Franciscan literary tradition – his *Fioretti* and famous *Canticle of the Sun* ("brother sun . . . sister moon") stand comparison with the best of medieval verse.

In company with many other saints, his formative years were full of drinking and womanizing; he was, says one chronicler, "the first instigator of evil, and behind none in foolishness". Illness and imprisonment in a Perugian jail instilled the first seeds of contemplation; abstinence and solitary wanderings soon followed. The culmination of several visions came in Assisi in 1209, when the crucifix in San Damiano bowed to him and told him to repair God's Church. Francis took the injunction literally, sold his father's stock of cloth and gave the money to Damiano's priest, who refused it.

Francis subsequently renounced his inheritance in the Piazza del Comune: before a large crowd and his outraged father, he stripped naked in a symbolic rejection of wealth and worldly shackles. Adopting the peasant's grey sackcloth (the brown Franciscan habit came later) he became a beggar, and began to preach and to mix with lepers, in obeyance of Christ's invocation to the Apostles: "to heal the sick, and carry neither purse, nor scrip [money], nor shoes". His message was disarmingly simple – throw out the materialistic trappings of daily life, and return to a love of God rooted in poverty, chastity and obedience. Furthermore, learn to see, in the beauty and profusion of the natural world, the all-pervasive hand of the Divine – a keystone of humanist thought, and a departure from the doom-laden strictures of the Dark Ages.

Annalisa Martini, Via San Gregorio 6 (☎075.813.536). Six rooms in the second alley on the left off Via Portica after leaving Piazza del Comune. ③.

Palma Ceccarini, Via Arco dei Priori 4 (☎075.812.895). A single and double, each with private bathroom. ③.

Cristina Lombardi, Via del Comune Vecchio 20 (☎075.816.419). Four singles (2 bathrooms) in the pretty street between Piazza Matteotti and Via Porta Perlici. ③.

Bernardo Pampanini, Piazza Matteotti 2 (☎075.813.020). Three doubles in one of the less medieval corners of Assisi, but still convenient for all the sights. ③.

Maria Fortini, Via Villamena 19 (☎075.812.715). Three rooms off Piazza Matteotti on a street leading to Porta Perlici. ④.

Il Duomo, Vicolo San Lorenzo 2 (☎075.812.742). The best private lodgings in town, located in a tiny flower-decked medieval alley; walk up Via di Porta Perlici from the duomo and Vicolo San Lorenzo is second on the left. ④.

Leonello Orbi, Via Sant'Antonio (☎075.815.220). Five doubles, each with bathroom, in a superbly situated alley just south of Piazza del Comune by Sant'Antonio and the Chiesa Nuova. ④.

YOUTH HOSTELS

Ostello di Fontemaggio, Strada Eremo delle Carceri 8, at the hamlet of Fontemaggio, 2km down the road to the Eremo delle Carceri (☎075.813.636 or 075.812.317, fax 075.813.749). Clean, 10-bed, single-sex dorms at L17,000 per person; or a choice of 15 one-star hotel rooms (②).

In time he gathered his own twelve apostles and, after some difficulty, obtained permission from Pope Innocent III to found an order that espoused no dogma and maintained no rule. Francis himself never became a priest. In 1212 he created a second order for women, the Poor Clares, and continued the ambitious peregrinations that took him as far as the Holy Land with the armies of the Crusades. (The Italian equivalent of "shanks's pony" is *il cavallo di San Francesco* – St Francis's horse.) In Egypt he confronted the Sultan, Melek el-Kamel, offering to undergo a trial by fire to prove his faith. On another occasion, in the Lazio village of Greccio, he produced the first ever Christmas crib: a real-life tableau, complete with cows and sheep, it was perhaps the most striking example of the earthy Franciscan style.

In 1224 Francis received the stigmata on the mountaintop at La Verna (see p.424). Two years later, nursing his exhausted body, he died on the mud floor of his hovel in Assisi, having scorned the offer of the bishop's palace. His canonization followed swiftly, in 1228 in a service conducted by Pope Gregory. His eulogistic tribute, delivered in a mournful and booming voice, was broken intermittently by uncontrollable sobs, as he compared the saint to "a full moon, a rising sun . . . the morning star hovering above dawn mists". A subdeacon read an extended list of Francis's miracles, while a learned cardinal – "not without copious weeping" – provided a commentary on his deeds, the pope listening, with "rivers of tears punctuated by deep-drawn wails". Priests and the attendant entourage wept so piteously that "their vestments were in great part wet and the ground was drenched with their tears".

Almost immediately after his death the first schism arose in the Franciscan order over the building of the grandiose Basilica for the saint's mausoleum (see main text). Francis's movement had few sympathizers in the wealthy and morally bankrupt papacy of the time, and while his popularity had obliged the Vatican to applaud while he was alive, the papacy quickly moved in to quash the purist elements and encourage the more "moderate" wings. Gradually it shaped the movement to its own designs, institutionalizing and diluting Francis's message in the process.

For all the subsequent history, however, Francis's achievement as the first man to subvert the rigid orthodoxy of the hierarchical Church is beyond question. Moreover, the Franciscans have not lost their ideological edge, and their views on the primacy of poverty are thought by many to be out of favour with the current pope.

Ostello della Pace, Via di Valecchie 177 (☎075.816.767). Located on the road that leads west out of town from Porta San Pietro and Viale G. Marconi, ten minutes' walk from Piazza unità d'Italia. Coming from the station by bus, try to be dropped at "Villa Guardi": the hostel is signposted from here. Dorm beds at L22,000 or two small doubles at L27,000 per person.

CAMPSITES

Fontemaggio, Strada Eremo delle Carceri 8 (☎075.813.636, fax 075.813.749). A 244-pitch two-star site alongside the youth hostel at Fontemaggio and under the same management (see above). Open all year, with full services and adjoining supermarket.

Internazionale Assisi, Via S. Giovanni Campiglione 110 (☎075.813.710). Not such a pleasant setting but a three-star rating, 3km west of Assisi on the SS147 to Bastia. Open April to mid-Oct.

The Basilica di San Francesco

The **Basilica di San Francesco** ranks second only to St Peter's in Rome as a point of Catholic pilgrimage, and its cycle of paintings by Giotto has long been considered one of the turning points in Western art, moving from the Byzantine world of iconic saints and Madonnas to one of humanist narrative.

The building also has an extraordinary history. It was conceived, shortly after Francis's death, by the man who had taken over the running of the order a decade or

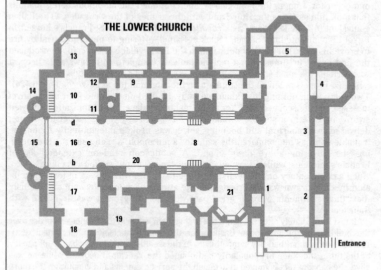

BASILICA DI SAN FRANCESCO, ASSISI

THE LOWER CHURCH

1 Cappella di San Sebastiano
2 Pulpit (1459)
3 Tomb of Filippo di Courtenay
4 Tomb of Blascio Fernandez
5 Tomb of Cardinal Albornoz (by Gattapone)
   Frescoes (1368) by Andrea da Bologna
6 Life of St Stephen by Dono Doni (1575)
7 Cappella di San Antonio di Padova.
   Frescoes (1610) by Cesare Sermei da Orvieto
8 Stairway to the crypt and the Tomb of St Francis
9 Frescoes by Giotto or school of Giotto
10 Right Transept: frescoes by Giotto, Cimabue and followers
11 Portrait of St Francis (Cimabue?)
12 Five Saints (Martini?) incl. Portrait of St Clare (fourth left)
13 Cappella di San Nicola: scenes from the Life of St Nicola
   by followers of Giotto
14 Entrance to cloisters, Tesoro and the Upper Church
15 Choir (1471)
16 Vaults of the High Altar by Giotto and/or followers of Giotto:
   a St Francis Enthroned
   b Allegory of Obedience
   c Allegory of Poverty
   d Allegory of Chastity
17 Left transept: frescoes by Pietro Lorenzetti
   (assisted by Ambrogio Lorenzetti)
18 Cappella di S.G. Battista (1288). Madonna and
   Child with SS. Francis and John by Pietro Lorenzetti
19 Sacristy. Relics of St Francis and Madonna
   and Child (Umbrian anon.)
20 Coronation of the Virgin by Puccio Capanna d'Assisi
21 Cappella di San Martino. Scenes from the Life of
   St Martin (1322) by Simone Martini

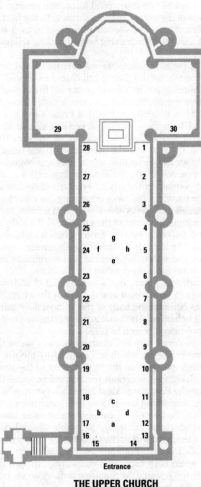

1 Homage in Piazza del Comune
2 Francis offers cloak to poor man
3 The dream of the weapons
4 Francis's calling in San Damiano
5 Francis renounces his worldly goods
6 Francis appears to Innocent III in a dream
7 Innocent III approves the Franciscan Order
8 Francis appears to his companions in a flaming chariot
9 Brother Leone sees the celestial throne destined for St Francis
10 Francis chases the Devils from Arezzo
11 Francis proposes trial by fire before the Sultan
12 The ecstasy of Francis
13 The Christmas crib at Greccio
14 Francis causes a fountain to flow
15 The sermon to the birds
16 Francis predicts the death of a knight
17 Francis preaches before Pope Honorius III
18 Francis appears to the Franciscan friars at Arles
19 Francis receives the stigmata
20 The death and funeral of Francis
21 Francis appears to Brother Augustin and the Bishop of Assisi
22 The truth of the stigmata confirmed
23 St Clare mourns at San Damiano
24 The canonization of St Francis
25 Francis appears to Pope Gregory IX
26 The recovery of a man from a mortal wound
27 The triumph of a woman after confession
28 Pietro d'Alife, accused of heresy, released from prison
29 Crucifixion by Cimabue (1277), and Five Apocalyptic Scenes
30 Crucifixion and Life of St Peter by Cimabue

Entrance

THE UPPER CHURCH

a St Jerome
b St Ambrose
c St Gregory
d St Augustine
⎱ by Filippo Resuti?

e St Francis
f Virgin Mary
g Christ
h John the Baptist
⎱ by Jacopo Torriti (1290)

so earlier, one **Elias of Cortona**. Elias, one of the saint's earliest disciples, served as vicar-general of the Franciscans through to 1239, presiding over a series of bitter disputes and schisms, until being deposed and excommunicated. In the early years of the post-Francis order, however, he ran things very much his way, capitalizing on the saint's popular appeal to build the Franciscans into a powerful force, and raising the money to make the founder's Basilica one of the great Christian shrines. To the horror of the more ascetic and zealous followers of the saint – to whom Francis himself was allied in his final years – Elias set about a massive fundraising project, selling religious indulgences across Europe.

The "fundamentalist" wing argued that the indulgences were a corruption and their proposed magnificence at odds with Francis's maxim that "small churches should be built, for they ought not to raise great churches for the sake of preaching to the people or for any other reason, for they will show greater humility and give a better example by going to preach in other churches". They pointed out, too, that Francis's choice of burial site was intended as a gesture of humility – he had picked one of the most despised spots of medieval Assisi, known as the Colle del Inferno, or Infernal Hill, where criminals were taken for execution. It was to no avail. The burial site was rechristened "Hill of Paradise" and a building more ambitious than any in Italy was begun.

While construction of the Basilica proceeded, the political background became increasingly murky, the strangest twist coming on the day of Francis's canonization. Elias by this time had fallen out with the papacy, which was organizing the ceremony, and as the saint's hearse proceeded through the streets of Assisi, he and a posse burst onto the scene and seized the body. Ignoring the anger of the crowd and the indignation of the papal entourage, they hurried the coffin into the Lower Church and bolted the doors behind them. Prompted perhaps by the fear that his master's remains would be stolen or desecrated (medieval relics had enormous financial and spiritual value), Elias had decided to bury Francis in a secret tomb deep within the Basilica.

The episode gave rise to a myth, retailed by Vasari, that a vast hidden church had been built below the Basilica, far greater in beauty and grandeur than the churches above. Inside this sealed chamber it was believed the body of the "almost alive saint" hovered above the altar awaiting his call to heaven. The tomb actually remained undiscovered, or at least unreached, until a two-month search in 1818.

The construction of the Basilica is in two tiers, with one church placed on top of the other. This posed enormous engineering problems, which were solved by the use of massive arched buttressing that effectively propped up the western end of the town. One of the wonders of early medieval architecture, its creator remains unknown; all the original drawings were burnt in a raid by the Perugians. Most historians presume it to have been the work of Lombard masons, who would have drawn their inspiration from the Gothic churches of southern France. As one of the earliest examples of Italian Gothic, the Basilica exerted great architectural influence, its single-naved Upper Church becoming a model for countless Franciscan churches around the country.

Admission to both parts of the Basilica is free. Both are usually open daily from 6.30am to 7.30pm (except Nov–March when both may close noon–2pm), though the Upper Church may close or have restricted opening on Sundays; both close on holy days. If possible, visit early or late in the day: the crowds at other times make it hard to get a view of the frescoes, especially in the Lower Church. It's also worth taking a couple of minutes to wander the **cloisters**, entered from the Lower Church. One final point – the custodians of the Basilica enforce their dress code extremely vigorously, so don't turn up with arms and legs exposed.

The Lower Church

The sombre **Lower Church** – down the steps to the left – is the place to begin if you want to follow the architectural and artistic chronology of the shrine. Its convoluted floor plan and low-lit vaults were intended to create a mood of calm and meditative intro-spection. The low-level natural light has been augmented by fairly discreet spotlighting, a concession that has altered somewhat the atmosphere of the chapel, but also makes it possible to study the frescoes and intricate decoration that cover every surface so densely that they really need several visits to take it all in.

The highlights span a century of continuous artistic development. Important but somewhat stilted early works by Byzantine-influenced artists line the walls of the main nave, many of them credited to the mysterious **Maestro di San Francesco**, the anony-mous hand which crops up elsewhere in Umbria. The oldest frescoes in the Basilica (1253), they depict *Scenes from the Passion* (right wall) and *Episodes from the Life of St Francis* (left wall). Faded in places, they have also been partly obliterated by the sub-sequent opening up of the side chapels, a necessity forced on the Franciscans by the need to accommodate the rising number of pilgrims visiting Assisi. Alongside these painters are Roman artists like **Pietro Cavallini**, who with **Cimabue** pioneered the development of fresco. After them came **Giotto**, and after him the masters of the Sienese School, **Simone Martini** and **Pietro Lorenzetti**.

Don't overlook the church's minor works, notably the little *Madonna Enthroned* (1422) by the Gubbian artist Ottaviano Nelli (on the left as you enter just right of the Cappella di San Sebastiano), or the **Tomb of Cardinal Albornoz**, built as a temporary resting place for the Spanish firebrand responsible for reinforcing papal power in Umbria. He rebuilt and regarrisoned the castles of Assisi, Narni and Spoleto, among others, and was rewarded for his pains with a tomb in the Basilica (his remains were later removed to Toledo, his home town). The tomb, remarkably, is the work of Matteo di Gattapone, the architect responsible for Spoleto's Ponte delle Torri and Gubbio's Palazzo dei Consoli, projects conceived on a far vaster scale.

SIMONE MARTINI

Simone Martini's frescoes in the **Cappella di San Martino**, the first chapel on the left as you enter the nave (21 on the plan), are among the Lower Church's highlights. He worked here in the mid-1310s, shortly after painting the great *Maestà* in Siena, and was given completely free rein – every detail, even the floor and stained glass, came under his control.

The panels on the underside of the arch as you enter the chapel were probably paint-ed in 1317. They show eight saints, and were painted to honour St Louis of Toulouse, who had just been sanctified – he is the red-robed figure in the upper left panel, flanked by saints Francis, Anthony and Clare.

In the interior chapel, a far more distinct and insular space than much of the Lower Church, is a complete fresco cycle of the life of **St Martin of Tours**. The father of monasticism in France, Martin was venerated as far afield as Ireland and Africa; here, however, he is featured partly as a sop to the Franciscan friar who commissioned the chapel, who had been made cardinal with the title of San Martino ai Monti. The ten-panel cycle starts on the left-hand wall and moves clockwise around the chapel, the lowest four panels representing scenes from the secular part of Martin's life up to and including his conversion, the remaining four wall frescoes and two painted ceiling vaults treating the period after his conversion.

Martin was born in 315 in what is now Hungary and brought up in Italy at Pavia. The key event of his conversion – and the first depicted in the cycle – came as a young offi-cer at Amiens, when he gave half his cloak to a beggar, a figure he was later led to rec-ognize as Christ. To the right is the *Dream of St Martin*, in which Christ and angels appear to the saint, a panel which mingles secular and sacred iconography amid a panoply of courtly emblems. This trait is continued in the next panel on the right-hand wall, *St Martin is Knighted*, which is an out-and-out evocation of life at court without religious iconography of any kind. To its right is the scene where *St Martin Renounces his Weapons* – "I am Christ's soldier; I am not allowed to fight." Here too, Martini seems to reserve his finest painting for the background: the tents, spears, lances and costumes of the Roman camp and the Emperor Julian.

The narrative moves to the second tier back on the left-hand wall, starting with the *Miracle of the Resurrected Child*, another episode never before depicted in Italian art, in which Martin, transported presumably by artistic licence to Siena (the city's Palazzo Pubblico is in the background) raises a child from the dead before its mother and an expectant crowd. Alongside is the *Meditation*, with the saint moved to distraction by contemplation of the Divine, and unmoved by the acolytes trying to direct his attention to the Mass. Moving round to its right is the *Miraculous Mass*, an unusual subject portrayed here for the first time. Martin has again given a cloak to a beggar, and is about to celebrate Mass when angels appear to present him with a beautifully embroidered piece of material. The next fresco, the *Miracle of Fire*, is damaged, though the sense of the scene is clear – a tongue of flame is forced down the throat of the Emperor Valentinian for refusing to give Martin an audience.

The uppermost level depicts two self-explanatory scenes, the saint's death and burial, both distinguished by the exquisite detail of the saint's robes, and by the architectural details which correspond to the moods of the episodes: severe, bare-walled and geometrical around the scene of death, and more ornate in the Gothic chapel that hosts the funeral.

GIOTTO

The question of **Giotto**'s involvement in the Basilica has been at the centre of one of Italy's greatest art history controversies. Twentieth-century historians opined that Giotto had never painted in Assisi at all. Some still hold this view, though the modern consensus is that Giotto was indeed responsible for the bulk of the paintings in the Upper Church, executed from about 1295.

Authorship in the Lower Church is more dubious, and credit for the allegorical frescoes in the **vaults over the altar** – some of the church's most beautiful and complex – has been taken from Giotto and given to nameless assistants. The same goes for the *Life of Mary Magdalene* cycle (c. 1309) in the **Cappella della Maddalena**, the third chapel on the right, as well as the right transept's *Childhood of Christ* (see below). In the hothouse atmosphere of the Basilica during its decoration, however, co-operative efforts must have been commonplace – so definitive attributions are all but impossible.

CIMABUE

Cenno di Pepo, popularly known as **Cimabue** (c. 1240–1302), was the first great named artist to work on the Basilica. Vasari's *Lives of the Artists* opens with an account of him, in which he is described as the father of Italian painting, and an obsessive perfectionist, often destroying work with which he was not completely happy. He probably painted in the transepts of the Upper Church between 1270 and 1280, and was active in the Lower Church some time later.

His major painting in the Lower Church – where much of his work was later overpainted – is in the **right transept** (right wall), the over-restored *Madonna, Child and Angels with St Francis*, a work which survives from the church's earlier decorative scheme (1280). Ruskin described this painting as the noblest depiction of the Virgin in Christendom. It includes the famous portrait of St Francis, which you'll already have seen plastered all over the town. Next to it, the *Crucifixion* has been attributed to Giotto, as have – though with less certainty – the scenes on the end wall and vaults depicting the *Childhood of Christ*. To the left are a half-length *Madonna and Child* and pair of saints, while on the side wall is a set of five saints – all the work of Simone Martini. One of the figures – an image much duplicated around town – is believed to be St Clare, founder of the women's chapter of the Franciscans (see p.498). The painting shows a clear attempt at the depiction of emotion, the use of light and shade to add verisimilitude to figures, and the creation of a coherent three-dimensional sense of space – all steps on the path trodden with equal certainty by Giotto and Martini's Sienese compatriot, Pietro Lorenzetti.

PIETRO LORENZETTI

Martini's Sienese contemporary, **Pietro Lorenzetti**, is represented by a beautiful series of works in the **transept** and **chapel left of the main altar**. Recent criticism sees the *Six Scenes of the Passion*, on the ceiling of the left-hand transept, as his earliest surviving works, probably painted on a visit to Assisi in about 1314. Restrained, static pieces, they betray the influence of Duccio, an impulse shrugged off when the artist returned to the Basilica in the years 1324–25 and 1327–28. By this time he had absorbed the lessons of Giotto, bringing them to bear on the *Passion of Christ* in the left transept, a cycle he had probably started on his visit ten years earlier.

The frescoes portraying scenes leading up to Christ's Crucifixion are comparatively weak. The *Last Supper*, however, in which Christ and the Apostles are crowded into a curious hexagonal loggia, reveals a treatment of light and shadow hardly matched during the trecento. The moon and stars light the sky, while to the left is a kitchen illuminated by light from a fire, in which servants unconcernedly scrape food into a dog's bowl – a fine incidental detail paralleled by the two chattering servants to the left of Christ, who are quite oblivious to events before them. The only illumination at the table is from the haloes of Christ and the apostles, a deliberate juxtaposition of material and spiritual light.

Three other panels stand out in the cycle: the *Entombment*, *Crucifixion* and *Deposition*. Dominating almost an entire wall, the *Crucifixion* shows an amazing sense of drama, with Christ raised high above a crowd of onlookers, and closer study reveals carefully observed nuances of character in the crowd. These natural touches recur in the faces of the *Deposition*, less immediately striking but still amongst Lorenzetti's masterpieces for its bold and simple composition. The upper portion of the Cross is completely missing, leaving just the broad horizontal and huge amounts of vacant space, all focusing on the figure of Christ, his limbs bent with rigor mortis.

Lorenzetti also painted in the chapel beyond, the **Cappella di San Giovanni Battista** (18 on the plan), where he left the frescoed triptych of the *Madonna and Child with SS. Francis and John the Baptist*. The central panel of stained glass here is attributed to Jacopo Torriti, one of the largely unsung but important Roman artists to have frescoed parts of the Upper Church.

THE TOMB

Before leaving the Lower Church, drop down to the **crypt** and the **tomb of St Francis**, a spot that remained hidden until 1818. The present tomb, rebuilt in the 1920s, honours Francis's desire for a humble burial, replacing a more elaborate tabernacle raised in the excitement of discovery. Above the main altar is the simple stone coffin that contains the body; at the four corners of the central canopy are the bodies of Francis's earliest key companions, the beatific Leone, Rufino, Masseo and Angelo.

There's a short account of the tomb's fascinating history and discovery (in English) tacked to the bare stone walls.

THE TREASURY MUSEUM

The well-presented **Tesoro Basilica di San Francesco e Collezione Perkins** (closed for restoration at time of writing, but usually open April–Oct Mon–Sat 9.30am–noon & 2–6pm; L3000) is entered from doors in the transept behind the main altar. It contains a rich collection of paintings, including 55 masterpieces from the Frederick Mason Perkins Collection, a bequest from an American philanthropist which includes work by Fra' Angelico, Pier Francesco Fiorentino, Luca Signorelli and Masolino. It's also particularly strong on the Sienese, with paintings by Pietro Lorenzetti, Segno di Bonaventura, Bartolo di Fredi and Taddeo di Bartolo. The museum's own original collection contains paintings by Benozzo Gozzoli and little-known Umbrians like Lo Spagna, Bonfigli and Dono Doni. The remainder of the gallery is crammed with copes, vestments, silverware, reliquaries and the like, given to the Franciscans over the centuries. Pride of place goes to a **tapestry** (1479) of St Francis and an **altar front** (1478), both presented by Pope Sixtus IV, the latter with figures by Antonio del Pollaiuolo, together with a series of thirteenth-century Tuscan and Umbrian crucifixes.

The Upper Church

After the Lower Church the **Upper Church** is a completely different architectural, aesthetic and emotional experience, its airy Gothic plan intended to inspire celebration rather than contemplation. In fact it feels less a church than a gallery for **Giotto**'s dazzling frescoes on the **Life of St Francis**, rightly regarded – notwithstanding the odd doubt as to its attribution – as one of the greatest of all Italian fresco cycles.

GIOTTO'S LIFE OF ST FRANCIS

Giotto's cycle starts from the **far right-hand side of the nave**. Although a consensus has not been achieved by critics over the date of the frescoes, most believe they are early works, painted with assistants some time around 1296, when he was aged just 29. The style and peripheral narrative content of the last four frescoes of the 28 has led to their being attributed to the so-called **Maestro di Santa Cecilia**, who may also have overpainted parts of the first panel.

Giotto was by far the most important artist to work in the Basilica. Dante immediately recognized his supremacy and in a famous passage (actually intended to illustrate the hollowness of earthly glory) wrote: "Cimabue thought to lord it over painting's field. And now his fame is obscured and the cry is Giotto." It seems that he actually got the commission on the prompting of Cimabue, and that some test pieces in the Lower Church persuaded the friars that Giotto was equal to the task of decorating the upper part of the Basilica.

Like many writers and artists of the age, Giotto was a member of the Franciscan Tertiaries – a lay order which had occupied much of the saint's last years. His frescoes reveal a profound sympathy for the spirit of St Francis and show an almost total rejection of the artistic language of the Byzantines, whose remote icons were highly inappropriate for Francis's very human message. The cycles are full of the natural beauty that moved the saint to profound joy, and the figures are mobile and expressive – aspects of Giotto's art typified by the famous panel showing *The Sermon to the Birds*. More than any other, this fresco crystallizes the essence of Franciscan humility, with the flock addressed as an indivisible part of God's creation and attending to the saint as distinct from them solely by virtue of the power of speech.

Giotto's narrative genius cuts straight to the heart of the matter, as seen in the very first panel, *The Homage in Piazza del Comune*, in which the universality of Francis's appeal is evoked in a single act of tribute. Moreover, the frescoes display a wealth of everyday detail that made them accessible to the ordinary people of his age. Thus the first people to look at *Francis Offering his Cloak to a Poor Man* would have recognized the world in which it is set as the one they themselves inhabited – the backdrop includes a detailed view of Assisi from the Porta Nuova, along with the Benedictine abbey on Monte Subasio, now vanished. This attention to the tone and substance of the real world, to its textures and solidity, makes the art of Giotto as revolutionary as Francis's message to the medieval Church.

THE CHOIR AND THE OTHER FRESCOES

The **choir** is a second focal point after the Giotto frescoes. Its 105 inlaid stalls – completed in the fifteenth century – are of immense intricacy and delicacy, most of them depicting famous Franciscans or episodes from their lives. The central throne is a papal seat, the only one in the country outside St Peter's in Rome.

Behind the throne, and in the **left transept**, are frescoes by Giotto's probable master, **Cimabue**. These suffered during the ceiling collapse, but were already almost ruined from the oxidation of badly chosen pigments, though the transept's *Crucifixion* remains an impressive composition, its dynamism an obvious departure from static Byzantine order. Giotto and Duccio may have helped on the painting as pupils.

Running around the church immediately above Giotto's Franciscan panels is another much damaged though virtually complete cycle depicting *Scenes from the Old and New Testaments*. Vasari believed these scenes were by Cimabue, though today they are attributed to artists of the Roman school – **Torriti**, **Rusuti** and **Pietro Cavallini** – who were working in the church around the same time. Before coming to Assisi all three had worked primarily in mosaic, a traditional Byzantine medium, but in the Basilica they turned to fresco, moving, like Cimabue, with cautious innovation towards a freer interpretation of old themes. The *Four Doctors of the Church* (in the vaults), especially, shows a narrative sense absent in earlier art: cloaks are left thrown over chairs, books lie open as if half-read. The Doctors, moreover, are depicted as characters in their own right, distinct individuals rather than the symbolic representatives of artistic convention.

To the Piazza del Comune

East from the Basilica, the trinket-lined **Via San Francesco** heads off along the ridge of medieval Assisi towards the **Piazza del Comune**. To each side steep and often stepped alleyways lead down to city gates and peripheral churches, of which **San Pietro** most rewards the diversion. If all you want to do is head back towards the centre of town at a gallop, the lanes to the north of Via San Francesco – in particular **Via Metastasio** – make a far more peaceful and attractive way of doing so. Secreted away in these alleys east of the Basilica are a medley of little **churches** – Santa Margherita, Sant'Andrea, Santa Croce: none are any great shakes artistically, but all make pretty enough diversions.

San Pietro

Wonderfully restored to its Romanesque-Gothic state, **San Pietro** is a peaceful antidote to the crowds of the Basilica above it. Grass and benches outside offer fine views over the Vale of Spoleto and of the fine, two-tiered facade – pink below, creamy-white above – with its three huge rose windows.

Originally Benedictine, the church dates from the thirteenth century, though it may have been founded as long ago as the second century. The bare interior, mainly Romanesque, also shows the first hints of Gothic in its gently pointed arches and in the ceiling, supported by strange curved vaulting.

Via San Francesco

Along **Via San Francesco** itself there are several minor sights. The first of them, on the left at no. 14, is Assisi's finest medieval town house, the headquarters of the masons' guild, known as the **Casa dei Maestri Comacini**, as a disproportionate number of the Basilica's builders hailed from Como. At no. 11 is the **Oratorio dei Pellegrini** (daily 9am–noon & 3–8pm; free), an exquisite fifteenth-century building that served as part of a hospice for visiting pilgrims. The interior is covered in fetching frescoes, some by the local sixteenth-century artist Matteo da Gualdo, beginning with a faded sample outside under the wooden-eaved exterior. Inside he was responsible for the murals on the altar wall, the vault and side walls being the work of another local artist, Pierantonio Mezzastris. Painted in 1477, the pictures depict *Scenes from the Life of St James*, including the comical *Miracle of the Two Hens*, an episode in which the saint restored two dead chickens to life so they could testify to the innocence of a falsely accused pilgrim. Another shows the *Miracle of the Hanged Man*, in which the saint supports an apparently dead man until he is found alive by his parents. Two scenes on the left wall represent episodes from the life of St Anthony Abbot: distributing alms and receiving camels which have brought him and his fellow monks food; the *Three Saints* on the inner face are attributed to Perugino or L'Ingegno, one of his followers. If people are at prayer here – and they often are – you may have to content yourself with a glimpse of the paintings through the glass door.

A short way beyond the hospice on the right is the arched portico of **Monte Frumentario**, a thirteenth-century hospital – one of the first in Italy. It adjoins the **Fontano di Corletta**, whose inscription warns that the penalty for washing your smalls in the water was one *scudo* and the surrender of your laundry.

The **Museo e Foro Romano** (daily: mid-March to mid-Oct 10am–1pm & 3–7pm; mid-Oct to mid-March 10am–1pm & 2–5pm; L4000, or L10,000 with Pinacoteca and Rocca Maggiore; see box opposite), almost at the end of the street, is a nondescript affair, housed in the crypt of the defunct church of San Nicolò. A passage from the museum runs under the Piazza del Comune, where excavations are in progress to uncover the Roman remains here without disrupting the piazza above; at present it's hard to make any sense of the underground maze, which scholars now believe is not the old Roman forum (as was long believed), but a religious sanctuary linked to the surviving Tempio di Minerva (see below). The Roman forum, it's now thought, may have occupied the present-day site of the duomo.

Piazza del Comune

The **Piazza del Comune** was built over either the site of the Roman forum or an important sacred area – theories differ. Today, in any event, it's a stunning medieval square, lined with plenty of pricey bars from which to watch your fellow pilgrims. The **tourist office** is here, as are the impressive Neo-Gothic **post office** and the Telecom Italia telephones (daily 8am–midnight), housed in a frescoed medieval hall complete with vaulted ceilings.

The piazza is dominated by the **Tempio di Minerva**, six Corinthian columns and a pediment from a Roman temple – a perfectly preserved and now dazzlingly restored facade from the first century. It was the only thing Goethe wanted to see in Assisi, and he went a bit overboard – "the first complete classical monument I have seen . . . so perfect in design . . . I cannot describe the sensations which this work aroused in me, but I know they are going to bear fruit for ever." He didn't bother with the Basilica, calling it a "Babylonian pile". While the temple is great from the outside, the church behind is a seventeenth-century conversion whose slight lack of interest has been redeemed by a fine recent restoration of its Baroque interior.

On the other side of the piazza, the much-restored **Palazzo Comunale** contains the town's **Pinacoteca Comunale** (closed for restoration at time of writing, but usually open daily: mid-March to mid-Oct 10am–1pm & 3–7pm; rest of year 10am–1pm & 2–5pm; L5000, or L10,000 with Rocca & Museo e Foro Romano), whose collection seems very small beer in the light of the riches in the churches. If you're not sated, however, the small four-room collection is well worth a few minutes. Most of the exhibits are frescoes detached from local churches and palaces, together with a handful of characteristically interesting paintings from otherwise little-known Umbrians. The best pictures are in **room 2**, where there are frescoes by Tiberio d'Assisi, a lunette by L'Ingegno and a *Madonna della Misericordia* and *St Blaise* by Nicolò Alunno. Also

---

COMBINED TICKETS

Two different **combined tickets** are generally available for some of Assisi's smaller museums, though both are subject to the reopening of the duomo and two of the museums concerned. A L10,000 ticket allows entry to the Pinacoteca Comunale, the Rocca Maggiore and the Museo e Foro Romano. Another L4000 ticket enables you to see the two small museums connected with the duomo, the Museo Capitolare and the Cripta della Cattedrale.

---

here is a remarkable picture showing *St Julian Murdering his Parents*, the saint having returned home one day and mistaken them for his wife and her lover. Other artists represented – mainly Umbrian – include followers of Giotto, Ottaviano Nelli, Pace di Bartolo and the anonymous L'Ingegno (The Genius).

The Duomo, Santa Chiara and the Rocca

Just east of the Piazza del Comune, the Franciscan trail continues, with important stops at the **duomo** and **Santa Chiara**, while to the south you might pay quick homage to the **saint's birthplace**, a spot commemorated by the unremarkable Chiesa Nuova and a piazza boasting two prominent bronze statues (1984) of Francis's parents. Up in the northeast corner of the walls a sweep of park leads to the **Rocca** – the best-preserved castle in Umbria, with fine views over the city and across the Vale of Spoleto to Montefalco and the Monti Martani.

The Duomo

The typically three-tiered Umbrian facade of the **duomo**, or San Rufino (daily 7am–noon & 2.30pm–dusk; free), is a captivating sight as you emerge from the narrow streets. Its Romanesque **portal**, though dirty and worn, is a superb piece of carving, guarded by two red marble lions and framed by lilies, leaves, faces, birds, winged crocodiles and a pair of griffons. Look in the lunette for the child being suckled, and its two dour, stony-faced parents. Alongside is a huge, stolid **campanile**, managing somehow to fit into the overall scheme of the church.

According to tradition the first church on the site was built around 412, ostensibly to house the bones of St Rufinus, Assisi's first bishop, martyred some 170 years earlier. Another, better-documented building was raised around 1029 by Bishop Ugone, from which the crypt and present campanile survive. Yet another church – more or less the one you see today – was begun in 1140 and consecrated in 1253. A small museum, the **Cripta della Cattedrale** or Basilica Ugoniana (March–Oct daily 10am–noon & 2–6pm; L2500, or L4000 with Museo Capitolare), reached down steps to the right of the facade, contains fragments from these earlier churches. The area was not discovered until 1895, and features remnants of very early frescoes, parts of a Roman wall and conduit and a third-century Roman sarcophagus used as Rufinus's original tomb.

Inside, the main point of interest is the **font** used to baptize St Francis, St Clare and (possibly) the future Emperor Frederick II, apparently born prematurely in a nearby village. It's at the near end of the church on the right, fronted by Romanesque statues of a lion and winged ox. Opposite, the beginning of the left aisle contains a little door which leads to an impressive Roman cistern, recent research having led scholars to believe that the cathedral square – rather than the Piazza del Comune – was the site of the town's original Roman forum. The church also has a couple of offbeat sights: a terracotta Virgin (left of the altar) which burst into tears in 1494, and a stone knelt on by an angel attending Francis's baptism – he left the imprint of his knee on it. St Rufinus's remains, incidentally, still lie beneath the altar. The **Museo Capitolare della Cattedrale** (March–Oct Mon–Sat 10am–noon & 2–6pm; L2500, or L4000 with Cripta della Cattedrale), off a corridor midway down the right aisle, has a passable little collection of paintings, the admittance fee worth spending for a fine triptych by Nicolò Alunno showing scenes from the life of St Rufinus.

The Basilica di Santa Chiara

South of the duomo, though most easily reached from the Piazza del Comune, is the **Basilica di Santa Chiara** (daily 7am–noon & 2pm–dusk; free), the burial place of St Clare, St Francis's devoted follower. The church was begun in 1257 and consecrated in 1265, twelve years after her death. It is on the site formerly occupied by the church of San Giorgio, where St Francis went to school, where his canonization took place, and where his body lay during construction of the Basilica. Clare, too, was buried in the church until her own resting place was completed.

The church is a virtual facsimile of the Basilica di San Francesco, with its simple facade and opulent rose window. Its engineering, however, wasn't up to the same standards, and the strange buttresses were added in 1351 to prevent its collapse.

The **interior** is dark and bare, the result, sadly, of some zealous early censorship. A seventeenth-century German bishop called Spader, afraid that the nuns might be corrupted by contact with worldly tourists, had its cycle of frescoes obliterated. Only a few patches of earlier Sienese frescoes from the original San Giorgio have survived, mostly in the transepts and cross vaults above the high altar. High in the south transept are *Scenes from the Apocalypse and Life of Christ*, and under them *The Death and Funeral of St Clare*, all the work of a close collaborator of Giotto. The scenes above the high altar, above which hangs a large thirteenth-century Crucifix, show *Scenes from the Life of St Clare*, while the two registers way up in the north transept depict *Episodes from Genesis*. The altar's *Madonna and Child* (c.1265) is probably the work of the Giottesque artist of the south transept. One of the two chapels off the right aisle, the **Oratorio del**

SAINT CLARE

Santa Chiara – **St Clare** – was a close early companion of St Francis and the founder of the **Poor Clares**, the Franciscan nuns. Born in 1182 into a noble family, she had a deeply religious upbringing from her mother, an education which backfired when at seventeen – enraptured by the preaching of Francis – she rejected her family and two offers of marriage to live with the saint. In an act of symbolic removal from the world he cut off her blonde hair, the locks of which are still visible in her basilica, and replaced her finery with a rough cassock. A year after her conversion she took her leave of Francis, and – but for the occasional vision – never saw him again until his death.

After initial opposition from the family, Clare's sister, St Agnes, joined her in spiritual retreat, and was later joined by her widowed mother. Other young girls from Assisi, similarly inspired by Francis's example, added to the growing community of women, which was soon installed by Francis in the church of San Damiano. In 1215 Clare obtained the "privilege of poverty" from Pope Innocent III – this was permission for the creation of an order of nuns to live solely on alms and without property of any kind. Over the years the Poor Clares' right to exist was frequently challenged, yet Clare – like Francis – managed to disseminate the movement throughout Europe.

The saint died on August 12, 1253, outliving Francis by twenty-seven years. She was canonized two years later, and by undignified quirk is now the patron saint of television, awarded the honour in 1958 by Pope Pius XII in recognition of her televisual powers – although bedridden, she was able to see and hear the rites of a Christmas service performed by Francis a kilometre away.

Crocifisso, contains the Byzantine **Crucifix** that bowed its head and spoke to Francis in San Damiano. Alongside are various clothes and oddments that belonged to Clare and Francis. The **body of Clare** herself, back from a session with a Roman saint-restorer, rests in the Baroque horror of the **crypt**.

The Rocca

The seductive medieval **streets** leading up from the duomo to the Rocca are the quietest in Assisi, partly because of their distance from tourist targets, but perhaps as much due to their fierce gradients. They have another attraction, too, in that this is where you'll find the cheapest bars and snacks.

Rising above the town, the **Rocca Maggiore** (daily 10am–dusk; L5000, or L10,000 with Museo e Foro Romano & Pinacoteca) dates back to Charlemagne, who is supposed to have raised the first defensive walls here after sacking the town. The structure you see today, though, owes most to Cardinal Albornoz, who arrived to assert papal authority in 1367, repairing an earlier castle that had been ravaged by repeated skirmishes with Perugia. Church governors reputedly dispensed justice by hanging criminals from the battlements or by throwing them out of a castle window into the ravine. The fortress is well worth the climb, with its looming towers, turrets and parapets, and the green surrounds provide ideal picnic territory. You'll also be rewarded with all-embracing views taking in Assisi, Perugia and the Vale of Spoleto across to Montefalco and the Monti Martani.

Outside the walls: San Damiano and the monasteries

After a visit to Santa Chiara, the Franciscan trail leads south to **San Damiano** and, for the energetic, to a couple of sites farther outside town – the **Eremo delle Carceri** (4km east) and **Santa Maria degli Angeli** in the new town around the station (5km).

San Damiano

To reach **San Damiano** (daily 10am–6pm; free), walk down the Borgo Aretino from Santa Chiara and then follow the signs through the car park and olive grove – a very steep downhill walk of about fifteen minutes.

It was in this church in 1205 that Francis received his calling to make repairs, and where he brought St Clare and her followers, "pouring the sweetness of Christ into her ears". Clare herself remained here to her death, though the nuns left seven years after their mistress's departure. After installing the Poor Clares, Francis came here just once, towards the end of his life, when – sick and half-blind – he composed the *Canticle of the Sun*. His body, however, rested here briefly after death, fulfilling a promise to Clare that she might see him once more.

Owned by Lord Lothian until 1983, the church now belongs to the Friars Minor, who have kept it in much the same state as it was centuries ago – a condition laid down by Lothian when he made his bequest. Alone amongst the spots in Assisi with Franciscan associations, this one preserves something of an ideal that is recognizably Franciscan – rural and peaceful in its groves of olives, cypresses and wild flowers, with the pastoral Vale of Spoleto stretching away below.

Signs point the way round the complex, starting outside with a fresco depicting St Roch – the saint invoked against infectious diseases – proudly displaying a plague sore. The little **balcony** above the main entrance is the point from which Clare, holding aloft the Sacrament, turned back an entire Saracen army that was pursuing Assisi's Guelphs.

Inside, the nave of the church – which was a Benedictine foundation at least as early as 1030 – is simple and smoke-darkened, with a beautifully decrepit wooden choir and lectern. On the right-hand side is the small window where San Damiano's priest threw the money that Francis offered him to repair the church. Nearby you can see the tiny hole where the saint hid "for a month" from the wrath of his father. Beyond some stairs leading to a terrace and small garden is a vestibule with a woodwormed choir and two frescoes, one a lovely *Madonna and Child* by an unknown Giottesque artist.

Up the stairs you reach the **oratory**, and then a small **dormitory**, with a cross and flowers marking the spot where Clare died. A door to the right leads to the **cloisters**, where you may catch a glimpse of the refectory, still equipped with its original table and oak benches.

The Eremo delle Carceri

All over Assisi you'll see pictures of the **Eremo delle Carceri** (daily 6.30am–dusk; free), an active monastery situated in oak woods about 6km east of the town. It can be easily reached by road but the best approach is to walk: a footpath, a *very* steep climb for the first kilometre or so, runs all the way from the Porta Cappuccini (outside the gate turn left along the track of cypresses, and then follow the marked path up and to the right behind the Rocca Minore (at the major fork a little way beyond turn right – it should be signposted but sometimes the sign's missing); once at the top of the climb keep going level and straight until you hit the road just above the monastery). Allow at least an hour, less coming back. The monastery is only closed for religious festivals; admission is free, but a gratuity is expected as the monks – who sometimes act as guides – live only off the alms they receive.

The hermitage was an early place of retreat for Francis and his followers: the saint caused the well in the courtyard to flow (as depicted by Giotto) and a cell known as the **Oratorio Primitivo** has been identified as that occupied by Francis. There's also a chapel containing various unlikely relics – Francis's pillow and a piece of the Golden Gate through which Jesus passed into Jerusalem. The hermitage once owned a lock of the Virgin's hair, too, and some earth from the mound which God used to create Adam, though these treasures have sadly disappeared. A word of warning – there are some very low doors and tight corners, so the interior is not for claustrophobics.

On the other side of the church is a dry riverbed, once a torrent until Francis told it to hush because it was spoiling his prayers. It fills up today only when some public calamity is at hand. One of the walls here was built over the so-called *buco del diavolo*, a crevice into which Francis cast a devil by the power of prayer. The old holm oak, kept upright by iron stakes, is said to have shaded the saint, and to have been a spot where birds collected to hear his sermons. Beyond this point a lovely **path** ambles into the woods, with plenty of nooks and side tracks to escape for a siesta or a spot of Franciscan or wine-inspired meditation.

Santa Maria degli Angeli

Difficult to miss from almost any point in the Vale of Spoleto, the huge domed basilica of **Santa Maria degli Angeli** rises from the new town clustered around Assisi station – an area to which it has given its name. A majestically uninspiring pile, it was built between 1569 and 1684, then rebuilt after an earthquake in 1832.

The basilica's function is to shelter the **Porzuincola** (Little Portion), the hut-cum-chapel that Francis made the centre of the earliest Franciscan movement. Stranded like a doll's house in the church's austere Baroque bowels, it has been embellished with dreadful nineteenth-century frescoes on the outside, but inside there are features claimed to be those of Francis's rough-stone hovel, as well as good fourteenth-century frescoes on the life of the saint.

Bits of the old monastery have been excavated under the main altar, site of the saint's death and of Clare's abrupt conversion. Buried in the chapel is Brother Cataneii, one of the earliest Franciscans. He performed so many miracles from beyond the grave, and attracted so many expectant crowds as a result, that Francis implored him in prayer, "now that we are infected with all these people of the world, I enjoin thee by obedience to make an end of thy miracles and allow us to recover in peace"; the miracles stopped.

In the garden you can see descendants of the **rose bushes** into which Francis threw himself while grappling with some immense nocturnal temptation. The thorns obligingly dropped off after contact with his saintly flesh. They now bloom, thornless, every May, their leaves stained with the blood shed that night.

Pilgrims flock to the basilica on August 1–2 for the **Pardon of St Francis**, a visit which guarantees automatic absolution. The pardon recalls a vision of Christ that Francis experienced, when he was asked what might be best for the human soul. Francis replied: forgiveness for all who crossed the threshold of his chapel. The already vast numbers of pilgrims were swelled in the 1920s by the supposed movement of the eight-metre-high bronze Madonna on the facade.

Eating

Multilingual tourist menus proliferate in the town's **restaurants** and prices can be steep; for cheaper and more authentic outlets make for peripheral districts away from the Basilica and Piazza del Comune. Listings below are in ascending order of price.

Restaurants

I Monaci, Scaletta del Metastasio, Via Fontebella. Entrance in a stepped alley off the north side of Via Fontebella, a few steps down from Piazzetta Garibaldi. Large, friendly place for pastas and pizzas from a wood-fired oven; one of the few places where pizzas are available at lunchtime. Closed Wed.

Pallotta, Via San Rufino 4 (☎075.812.649 or 075.812.307). Near some sticky tourist traps, but a very reasonable, unpretentious and welcoming old-style trattoria; book, or arrive before 12.30pm to be sure of getting a place for lunch. Closed Tues.

Ristorante La Rocca, Via di Porta Perlici 27. Annexed to the hotel, this is a big, cheap, high-quality locals' place with reasonable food and no frills. About L30,000. Closed Wed.

La Fortezza, Vicolo della Fortezza 2 (☎075.812.418). Invariably busy but friendly restaurant, with a high reputation, great food, medieval setting and reasonable prices. However, service can be very slow at busy times. Essential to reserve in summer; L35,000. Closed Thurs & Feb.

Buca di San Francesco, Via Brizi 1 (☎075.812.204). The reputation as the best in town is now belied by erratic quality, though when it delivers the cooking can be outstanding. As a bonus there's a half-covered outside terrace for summer eating. From about L40,000. Closed Mon & two weeks in July.

ASSISI FESTIVAL CALENDAR

Easter week. Processions and festivities thoughout the week.

Calendimaggio (week after first Tues in May). Procession to celebrate St Francis's vision of Lady Poverty.

Festa della Voto (June 22). Procession in medieval costume to celebrate the town's salvation.

Perdono (Aug 1–2). Pilgrimage to the church of Santa Maria degli Angeli.

Palio della Balestra (Aug 11). Medieval tournament.

Francis's return to Assisi (first Sun of Sept). Festival held most years to celebrate the saint's final return home.

Festa di San Francesco (Oct 3–4). The big event – a major pilgrimage that draws crowds of pilgrims and ecclesiastics from all over Italy and beyond.

Festa del Corpus Domini (Nov). Another major procession, through flower-strewn streets.

Medioevo, Via dell'Arco dei Priori 4b (☎075.813.068). Just south off the Piazza del Comune, this extremely tasteful medieval vaulted dining room is recommended if you want to dress up and splurge, though the excellent cooking has a vaguely "international" flavour; L50,000. Closed Wed, Jan & July 1–21.

San Francesco, Via San Francesco 52 (☎075.813.302). Generally good and original cooking that takes Umbrian basics as its starting point; around L70,000 for a complete blow-out. Closed Wed & two weeks in July and Nov.

Listings

Bike rental Bruno Bartolucci, train station, Santa Maria degli Angeli (☎0368.431.758; mobile 0330.088.2762).

Bus enquiries Assisi and around ASP (☎075.573.1707); Rome, Florence SULGA (☎075.500.9641); Siena and Ascoli Piceno AMADIO (☎0736.341.838); Foligno, Montefalco and Bevagna SPOLETINA (☎0742.670.746).

Car rental Assisorganizza, Via Borgo Aretino 11a (☎075.815.280); Valentini, Via Patrono d'Italia 11–13, Santa Maria degli Angeli (☎075.801.9063); or Nicola Corridoni on Via Frate Elia (☎075.812.983), who rents cars with or without a driver.

Discotheque Pilgrim-bound Assisi has just one in-town disco, the *Hermitage*, located under the *Hermitage* hotel at Via degli Aromatari 1 (☎075.816.671).

Exchange Slickest facilities at the automatic machines outside the Cassa di Risparmio branches in Piazza del Comune and Piazza Unità d'Italia; Banca Popolare at Piazza Santa Chiara 19; and Banca Toscana at Piazza San Pietro 6. You can also change money at Interchange, Via San Francesco 20d (daily 9am–8pm; ☎075.816.220); Exact Change, Corso Mazzini 25a (☎075.812.706; daily 9am–7.30pm); the post office in Piazza del Comune (Mon–Fri 8.10am–5.25pm; Sat 8.10am–12.50pm), and at the train station ticket office (☎075.804.0272; daily 8am–9pm).

First aid *Pronto Soccorso*, Ospedale di Assisi (☎075.812.824 or 075.813.9227).

Lost property At *Vigili Urbani*, Vicolo Volta Pinta (Mon–Sat 9am–noon; ☎075.812.820).

Markets Assisi's main market is held Saturday mornings in Via Alessi and Via San Gabriele dell'Addolorata. An antiques market is held at the weekend of the second week of every month in Piazza Chiesa Nuova.

Police Piazza Matteotti 3b (☎075.812.239 or 075.812.376) or Piazza del Comune (☎075.812.215).

Post office Piazza del Comune 10 (Mon–Sat 8am–6.30pm; Sun 8am–1pm).

Taxis Train station (☎075.804.0275); Piazza San Francesco (☎075.812.606); Piazza Unità d'Italia (☎075.812.378); Piazza del Comune (☎075.813.193); Piazza Santa Chiara (☎075.812.600).

Telephones Telecom Italia, Piazza del Comune 11 (daily 8am–midnight), for international phone calls. For *scatti* calls (where you pay after your call), *Bar Mazzini*, Corso Mazzini, and *Bar Bibiano*, Piazza Unità d'Italia.

Train enquiries ☎075.804.0272.

Travel agent Stoppini, Corso Mazzini 31 (☎075.812.597), sells train and bus tickets, as well as ferry tickets to Sardinia. Very busy, so arrive in good time.

Spello

Ranged on broad walled terraces above the Vale of Spoleto, **SPELLO** offers an easily accessible taste of small-town Umbria and a major art attraction in its superlative frescoes by **Pinturicchio** in the church of Santa Maria Maggiore. It also boasts a few reminders of its Roman past, when as **Hispellum** it served as a retirement home for pensioned-off legionaries and an important staging post on the Via Flaminia. Later it fell to the Lombards – who destroyed it – then became part of the Duchy of Spoleto. In 1238 it fell to Frederick II – who also destroyed it – and then passed under the yoke of Perugia. Despite the repeated hammering, the main core of the town is, as ever, beautifully medieval – at least once you're off the main street – evoking a typically Umbrian later career: racked by internal rivalry, pestered by other cities – usually Assisi – and

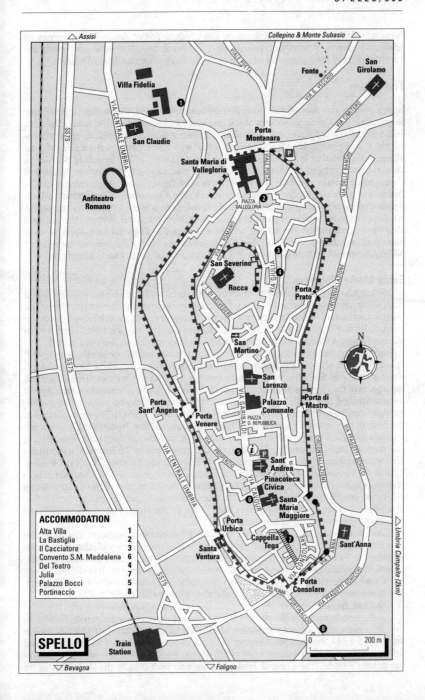

Fonte

San Girolamo

VIA S. VECCHIO

Villa Fidelia

1

VIA CENTRALE UMBRIA

SS75

San Claudio

Porta Montanara

VIALE POETA

VIA DELLE BANCE

Santa Maria di Vallegloria

Anfiteatro Romano

PIAZZA VALLEGLORIA

2

3

VIA GIULIA

4

VIA A. ROMANO

San Severino

Rocca

VIA DI BELVEDERE

Porta Prato

CIRCONVALLAZIONE

N

San Martino

San Lorenzo

Porta Sant' Angelo

Porta Venere

VIA GARIBALDI

Palazzo Comunale

PIAZZA D. REPUBBLICA

Porta di Mastro

VIA PIAGOTTI SCHICCI

VIA CENTRALE UMBRIA

SS75

VIA F. PROPERZIO

5

i

Sant' Andrea

Pinacoteca Civica

VIA CAVOUR

CIRCONVALLAZIONE

△ Umbria Campsite (2km)

6

Santa Maria Maggiore

Porta Urbica

Santa Ventura

Cappella Tega

7

VIA CONSOLARE

VIA S. ANNA

Sant'Anna

Porta Consolare

VIA ROMA

PORTINACCIO

VIA PIAGOTTI SCHICCI

8

ACCOMMODATION

Alta Villa	1
La Bastiglia	2
Il Cacciatore	3
Convento S.M. Maddalena	6
Del Teatro	4
Julia	7
Palazzo Bocci	5
Portinaccio	8

SPELLO

Train Station

0   200 m

eventually dragged into near oblivion by the Church. Today, despite its proximity to Assisi and Spoleto, it remains relatively quiet and rural, though several new hotels and a rash of chintzy food shops are testament to the increasing numbers of tourists.

The Town

Buses stop at the foot of the town just outside the **Porta Consolare**, one of five Roman gates in the Augustan-era walls that more or less enclose the town. The gate is in a slightly sorry state, with a small tree growing from its crumbling upper reaches, but it still gives some idea of the glory that was Rome, and retains three original **statues**, figures that local folklore claims depict a family killed by eating poisonous mushrooms. Parts of the old Roman road are also exposed here, while to the left range some of the best-preserved stretches of the original Augustan-era walls. Inside the gate begins the single main street, **Via Consolare-Via Cavour**, which bends and climbs steeply – without pavements, so beware – to the town proper. A couple of minutes' walk – you might take the rubber-surfaced alley on the left as a short cut – will bring you to the odd little **Cappella Tega** (always open to view behind glass), half-covered in fifteenth-century frescoes by the leading local artist Nicolò Alunno. A minute or so beyond is the church of Santa Maria Maggiore.

Santa Maria Maggiore

In 1600 Spello had some 2000 inhabitants (compared with around 8000 today) and a staggering one hundred churches, of which 22 were dedicated to the Virgin. One of the most important of these was **Santa Maria Maggiore**, which celebrated both the Virgin's Birth (September 8) and the Assumption (August 15), the latter alluded to in the inscription *Assumpta Est* below the *Madonna* in the niche on the main portal.

Begun in the twelfth century, the church was remodelled five centuries later to dull effect, the most obvious alterations being the **facade**, which was shifted forward a full nine metres, and the mundane Baroque botch visited on the interior. The facade did keep parts of the original Romanesque portal, however, some of whose fine carving has been attributed to Binello and Ridolfo, the mysterious craftsmen responsible for the strange sculptures on the churches of nearby Bevagna (see p.511) The two columns at the base of the campanile are from an earlier Roman building, Spello's main street following exactly the course of the old Roman road (a Roman aqueduct runs beneath it to this day). Another outstanding Roman fragment greets you in the **interior**, a **stoup** for holy water fashioned from the altar tomb (60 AD) of Gaius Titienus Flaccus, a leading light of the Lemonian clan, Hispellum's most important Roman family. The dead man is shown on horseback above an inscription, while in the lower part of the stoup you can still make out a little hollow once used to store his ashes. Another similar tomb – that of a young woman – was moved from the church in the eighteenth century and now supports the cross on top of the campanile.

More fascinating inside, however, are the **Pinturicchio** paintings covering the Cappella Baglioni, on the left as you enter, vast frescoes which rank with the artist's masterpieces in Siena's Libreria Piccolomini and Rome's Sistine Chapel and Borgia apartments. The paintings were executed in 1501 and are now glowing from restoration work in 1978 which brought out Pinturicchio's colourfully decorative detail to stunning effect. The three panels are read from left to right; the ceiling vaults depict the *Four Sibyls*.

The **first fresco** features the *Annunciation*, with the Virgin having just read the prophetic text from the Bible open in front of her. Midway down the ornate column to the right you can make out an allusion to the date of the painting (*MCCCCCI*). Below and to the right the obvious hanging painting is a self-portrait of Pinturicchio, and under it a plaque with his name from which dangle brushes, styluses and other tools of the painter's trade. The **central fresco** on the rear wall depicts the *Adoration of the*

Child, with the shepherds shown left of Christ and the Magi behind them to the left. Behind the Magi one of the group of armed men amidst the rocks bears an anachronistic detail – a shield with the Baglioni coat of arms. The painting is also remarkable for its preponderance of symbols, in particular the cross (a prefiguration of Christ's Crucifixion), the peacock (symbolizing eternal life and the incorruptibility of the flesh) and the flask of wine and bread in the bottom right-hand corner (an allusion to the Eucharist). The **final fresco**, the *Disputation in the Temple*, has fewer symbols, but rather more points of incidental narrative and decorative interest. Thus there is a portrait of Troilo Baglioni, the man who commissioned the paintings, who is shown in his black prioral habit at the extreme left of the painting. Alongside him stands his treasurer, easily identified by his bag of money (another pictorial reminder of who paid for the frescoes). Over on the extreme right the grisly-featured old woman is an allusion to the "Old Woman of the Cross", the central character in one of Spello's seminal medieval legends. The harridan is said to have tried to fan the mutual hatred of the inhabitants of the upper and lower town, disputes which have plenty of grounding in historical fact. Before any bloody encounter could take place, however, she was vaporized by the miraculous apparition of a cross above the town hall in 1346. Pinturicchio also makes an appearance, his name being picked out on the note being held by the character in the prominent white headgear in the group to the right of Christ. The artist's hand can also be seen in the disturbing details in the background: the disabled beggars in front of the temple and, more macabre, the tiny figure dangling from a gibbet on the hill-top to the right of the large palm tree. Sadly the paintings are behind glass, and you need L1000 notes to illuminate the spectacle. The barrier also means you can't get a proper look at the chapel's **ceramic pavement** (1566), a faded testimony to the skill of Deruta's medieval craftsmen (see p.578).

Elsewhere in the church are a couple of further paintings by Pinturicchio: in the **Cappella del Sacramento**, the chapel to the left of the apse, is a faintly etched angel holding a plaque above a little lavabo; the inscription – *Lavamini et mundi, estote* - means "Wash yourself and be pure." Beyond that, in the canon's room, is an overpainted but beautifully lyrical *Madonna and Child*. Two good late paintings by Perugino adorn the two pillars flanking the apse. One is a *Pietà*, the other a *Madonna and Child with SS. Blaise and Catherine*. The only other worthwhile painting is a single tantalizing fresco of the *Agony in the Garden* (1391) to the left of the large window at the rear of the apse. It's the work of Cola Petruccioli, an accomplished early Umbrian painter, and represents all that remains of a complete cycle sacrificed to the apse's blanket of whitewash in the seventeenth century.

Pinacoteca Civica

For years Santa Maria Maggiore housed Spello's civic art collection. Then various pieces were stolen and the whole lot was hidden away for a couple of decades. Now everything's on show again in the new **Pinacoteca Civica** (Tues–Sun: July–Sept 10am–1pm & 4–7pm; Oct & March–June 10am–1pm & 3.30–6.30pm; Nov–Feb 10am–1pm & 3–6pm; L5000), situated in the old Palazzo dei Canoncini almost immediately to the left of the church. Most of the best pieces are in the first four of the eight rooms, each of which is arranged chronologically. These are heralded by the lobby's wonderful polychrome wooden statue of the Madonna and Child, an Umbrian work dating from the end of the twelfth century. Close by is an extraordinary statue of the crucified Christ, its arms hinged to resemble a crude marionette. Such statues, now extremely rare, were used by religious confraternities during Holy Week celebrations: its hinged arms would be opened or folded according to the particular religious celebration.

The gallery's vaguely open-plan arrangement makes it hard to figure out which room is which, but everything is well labelled, making it easy to track down **room 1**'s superb enamelled cross (1398). The central figure depicts the Virgin, invariably included in works destined for a church dedicated to the Madonna. Nearby, the little diptych (1391) by Cola Petruccioli, designed as a portable preaching aid for itinerant monks, shows the *Crucifixion* on one panel and the *Coronation of the Virgin* on the other. **Room 2** has two of the gallery's highlights, a pair of early fifteenth-century panels of a triptych by the anonymous Maestro dell'Assunta di Amelia: one shows *St John and the Prophet Isaiah*, the other *John the Baptist and Nicholas of Bari*. The original triptych was stolen in 1970, and the main central panel – a *Madonna and Child* – has never been recovered.

In the rear to the left, **room 3** has a still better work, the superbly restored *Crucifixion, Virgin and Saints* by Nicolò Alunno. Nearby is a double-sided *gonfalone*, or banner, probably painted by one of Alunno's assistants. One side depicts the *Madonna della Misericordia* shielding Spello's citizens beneath her cloak, the other the *Miracle of the Cross of Spello*, the event alluded to in Pinturicchio's fresco of the *Disputation in the Temple* in Santa Maria Maggiore (see previous page).

None of the other rooms has anything to match these paintings, but they're still well worth a wander. Look out, in particular, for the double-sided *gonfalone* (1576) in **room 4** (across the entrance corridor) by Lorenzo Doni, depicting a particularly graphic *Martyrdom of St Barbara* on one side, and the members of Spello's Confraternity of St Barbara on the other. Also pause in front of the five canvases by Marcantonio Grecchi in **room 6**, especially the painting of the *Madonna and Child with St Felix and Andrea Caccioli*; St Felix, an early bishop of Spello, is one of the town's patron saints. The painting's charm lies in the perfectly realized little portrait of Spello held by the two protagonists, the town looking much the same as it does today.

Sant'Andrea

A short distance uphill from the gallery lies **Sant'Andrea**, Spello's other main church, a simple thirteenth-century facade hiding a darkly atmospheric interior. Most surfaces are inexpertly painted, though the overall effect is superb, and there is another outstanding **Pinturicchio** – a *Madonna and Child with Saints* in the right transept, executed with Eusebio di San Giorgio. On the extreme right is the figure of St Lawrence, who is shown holding the black griddle on which he was roasted to death. A panel depicting this martyrdom in detail is shown as a luminous square picture rather oddly stitched into the lower half of his robes. The vast eye-catching hanging Crucifix above the altar is by an unknown fourteenth-century Umbrian follower of Giotto.

The spread of impressive-looking decoration in the apse and elsewhere dates from the last century and may, it's thought, conceal all sorts of hidden treasures. Certain of these recently came to light when the large altar in the left transept was removed for cleaning. Behind it were revealed areas of important early fresco, much of which, it appears, had been whitewashed over following some long-forgotten plague epidemic. Shortage of funds has as yet prevented any further investigation. What you can usually see in the left transept, though, is another in Umbria's long line of eerily preserved mummies (see pp.515–516 for more on these). This time it's the body of the Spello-born beatific **Andrea Caccioli** (1194–1254), one of the earliest followers of St Francis, whom Caccioli met in the nearby abbey of Vallegloria in 1219. Four years later he joined the Franciscans, preaching widely throughout Italy, France and Spain, becoming known in the last as the "saint of the water" for his oft-demonstrated ability to induce a deluge in areas where it hadn't rained for months. In 1253 he returned to Spello, which offered him and the Franciscan Friars Minor the church of Sant'Andrea, making this the town's first Franciscan foothold.

A diversion from Sant'Andrea along nearby Via Torri di Properzio (left off Via Cavour) brings you to the best remnant of Roman Spello, the perfectly preserved if slightly forlorn **Porta Venere**, named after a long-vanished temple to Venus. Spello was a major religious centre, and Constantine is said to have built one of Umbria's largest shrines to the goddess in the vicinity. The imposing twin towers flanking the gate might be Roman or medieval – no one's sure.

The rest of the town

Farther up Via Cavour beyond Sant'Andrea, the main **Piazza della Repubblica** is part grotesque twentieth-century, part medieval, with its arched **Palazzo Comunale** boasting a couple of fourteenth-century frescoes by local painters. A few doors beyond, still on the main street, **San Lorenzo** rates as one of Umbria's more successful Baroque conversions. A mongrel of a church, its succession of architects left a variety of decorative effects, some laughable, like the obviously fake marbles, others more persuasive – as with the *baldacchino*, a bronze canopy copied from Bernini's piece for St Peter's in Rome. The most arresting sight is the minutely realistic statue of St Peter the Martyr, midway down the west wall, complete with trickle of blood from the cleaver delicately planted in his head.

At the top of Spello's main street you'll probably be heartily sick of having to dodge cars, but here you can start to explore the alleys and backstreets that provide the town's far more typically Umbrian hill-town charm. Views from the east side of town are especially good, with lovely panoramas over the bucolic countryside below Monte Subasio: the *Bar Giardino* sign on the right before San Lorenzo guides you into a bar with a huge grassy terrace and tables to the rear, a wonderful spot to soak up the scenery. If you're after streetlife, however, the smart bar with terrace just opposite San Lorenzo is the best bet. The arch to its right leads to the highest point of the town, occupied by the **belvedere** and **Rocca** – the latter giving the only view you need of the paltry and overgrown remains of the first-century AD Roman **amphitheatre** to the west. Once it could hold 15,000 people; these days you'd be hard pushed to squeeze in a hundred.

If you do trek out to the amphitheatre, you could make the trip more worthwhile by continuing on to the half-collapsed twelfth-century church of **San Claudio**, which has a strange Romanesque asymmetry inside and out. It was raised from the ashes of an old Roman building on the same site. A ten-minute walk beyond the church is the hugely prominent but little-known **Villa Fidelia** with a beautiful **garden** and the miscellaneous **Straka-Coppa private collection** of paintings, sculptures, old furniture and costumes, together with displays on the Futurists (July–Aug daily 10.30am–1pm & 4–7pm; April–May & Sept Thurs, Sat & Sun 10.30am–1pm & 3–6pm; Oct–March Sat & Sun 10.30am–1pm & 2.30–5pm; L5000). A nicer way to get here, ignoring the amphitheatre, is to follow the country lane which drops down from the northwestern corner of Piazza Vallegloria at the northern end of town.

Over Monte Subasio

A stiffer but wonderful **walk** starts beyond the Rocca at the Porta Montanara. This route is worth climbing just for twenty minutes or so for superb views of Spello and the Vale of Spoleto, though if you follow it the whole way you can reach Assisi (allow a full day for this) via the top of Monte Subasio and or the Eremo delle Carceri.

To get onto the route, take the second right turn after the gate (signposted for Collepino), walk past the olive oil works on the right, and after 100m take the (initially surfaced) track left at the fountain. The path is marked by the *Club Alpino Italiano* – look for trail no. 50 and red spot markings which run all the way to Assisi. Detailed walking **maps** of the area – and it's advisable to have them – are usually available from the newsagents to the right of San Lorenzo near the top of Spello's Via Garibaldi. If you're **driving**, be sure to follow the well-signed part-gravel road from the same northern end of town over Monte Subasio to Assisi (signed "Monte Subasio" and *La Baita*, the latter a panoramic bar-restaurant on a side road halfway up): be certain not to miss the left turn after a couple of kilometres and go sailing on to Collepino and Armenzano. The **views** are superlative and there are sensational spreads of **orchids** and **narcissi** in late May and early June. Once on the top above the trees, you can walk pretty much at will.

Practicalities

Spello is an alternative base for Assisi, with a good range of accommodation, several good restaurants and a small **tourist office** at Piazza Matteotti 3 (Mon–Sat 9.30am–1pm & 3–6pm; ☎0742.301.009 or 0742.651.408). Reasonably regular stopping **trains** serve the town from Foligno and Perugia – check that they really do stop – and up to nine **buses** (Mon–Sat) stop off here on the Assisi–Foligno run. If you're in a car the most central **parking** is in a car park on the right immediately after the church of Sant'Andrea. The tortuous main street is one-way along its entire length (uphill), so only approach this parking area from Porta Consolare. Alternatively you can leave a car around Porta Consolare and walk up, or walk down from the big empty car park off Via Cimitero by Porta Montanara (approached on Via Circonvallazione on the east side of the town).

Accommodation

Convento Santa Maria Maddalena, Via Cavour 1 (☎0742.651.156). Very pleasant and low-cost rooms almost immediately opposite Santa Maria Maggiore. Ring the bell on the rather anonymous door on the side of the building facing back down the hill. ②.

Portinaccio, Via Centrale Umbra 46 (☎0742.651.313, fax 0742.301.615). If you baulk at the prices in Spello's central hotels and don't mind being outside the walls, make for this big place on the main road roundabout 100m south of Porta Consolare. ③.

Il Cacciatore, Via Giulia 42 (☎0742.651.141, fax 0742.301.603). Good-value and friendly 16-room two-star hotel, with fine views from some rooms: roadside rooms are noisy. It's worth staying here, though, just for the superlative panoramic terrace. ③.

Julia, Via S. Angelo 22 (☎0742.651.174, fax 0742.301.081). Two-star in an alley in the lower half of town. Rather overpriced for what it offers, but sited close by Santa Maria Maggiore. ④.

Alta Villa, Via Mancinelli 2 (☎ & fax 0742.301.315). Very comfortable, if rather gaudily luxurious three-star hotel, several minutes' walk from the old town (follow the signs from the corner of Piazza Vallegloria). ④.

La Bastiglia, Via dei Mollini 17 (☎0742.651.277, fax 0742.301.159). Smallish but smart three-star rooms, many of which command a fine view. Also has a panoramic terrace. ⑤.

Del Teatro, Via Giulia 24 (☎075.301.140, fax 0742.230.1612). Stung by competition from the *Alta Villa* and *Bocci*, the owners of the *Cacciatore* opened this superbly appointed intimate three-star hotel down the road. ⑤.

Palazzo Bocci, Via Cavour 17 (☎0742.301.021, fax 0742.230.1464). Tasteful and immensely smart hotel in a converted, frescoed palazzo just up from Santa Maria Maggiore. A definite first choice if you're doing Umbria in style. ⑥.

CAMPING

Camping Umbria, Via Rapacchiano (☎0742.651.772). The nearest campsite, 2km east of town at Chiona. Open April to early Oct.

Eating

Spello's best **restaurant**, set in a vaulted medieval town house, is *La Cantina*, Via Cavour 2 (☎0742.651.775; closed Wed), a friendly local place serving plenty of regional specialities – and wonderful fresh pasta. *Il Molino* at Piazza Matteotti 6–7 (☎0742.651.305; closed Tues) is flashier and more expensive, with an equally pleasing medieval setting and some good food if you avoid the occasional unfortunate pretension to Italian *nouvelle cuisine*. *Il Cacciatore*, Via Giulia 42 (☎0742.651.141; closed Mon), has middling food and service, but one of the great Umbrian terraces for summer eating. The cheaper *Pinturicchio*, on the left at the top of the main street just past San Lorenzo, is a first-rate trattoria stand-by. You should be able to have a full meal in any of the three top spots for around L40,000.

Another important gastronomic stop is the *Bar-Gelateria* on Via Roma just opposite the Porta Santa Maria Maggiore, which serves up **ice cream** and sorbets just a wafer away from perfection.

Foligno and around

Sooner or later you're almost bound to find yourself in **FOLIGNO**, one of the largest Umbrian towns and a nodal point for trains and buses. A largely modern place, ringed with factories and concrete sprawl, its star turns were bombed out of existence during the war. What remains is a not unpleasant provincial town, though with nothing that would merit a special visit. However, the residue of its medieval heritage is conveniently concentrated in the central **Piazza della Repubblica**, so a quick look is feasible as you're passing through or changing trains. The town is also a good **accommodation** stand-by if surrounding towns are fully booked.

The Town

The **duomo** is the main eye-catcher on Piazza della Repubblica, the twelfth-century Palazzo Comunale opposite having been ruined by a Neoclassical facade at the beginning of the last century. Unusually, the church boasts two facades, the south frontage containing one of the most impressive **portals** in the region – a riot of carving full of zodiac signs, intricate patterning and enough bizarre animals to fill a zoo. Check out two curious details – a likeness of Frederick II on the left (one of only two in Italy) and a Muslim star and crescent near the apex of the arch. The other facade is only a little less appealing, though its mosaics are a nineteenth-century afterthought. The interior holds little joy; a panel by Nicolò Alunno in the sacristy is the only feature worth seeking out.

To the duomo's right, at the western end of the piazza, is the **Palazzo Trinci**, the much-altered home of the Trinci, Foligno's medieval big shots. Between 1305 and 1339 their influence spread over broad swathes of Umbria. Before this the town had suffered repeated thumpings from Saracens, Goths and Barbarossa, eventually becoming a bastion of imperial power – an allegiance which put it in almost constant conflict with Perugia. When the family's power waned the town continued to thrive; it was in Foligno that the first book was printed in Italian – three hundred copies of Dante's *Divine Comedy*. The palazzo itself is in the last throes of a restoration project that has been under way for donkey's years. Now visible are a fine courtyard and frescoed staircase, though opening dates for the **Pinacoteca Comunale** on the second floor are still not fixed. Its high points are a frescoed chapel by Ottaviano Nelli, an *Annunciation* attributed to Benozzo Gozzoli and a painted passageway known as the *Hall of the Planets and Liberal Arts*.

The only other monument which hints at Foligno's former glory is **Santa Maria Infraportas**, a church of pagan origins in which St Peter is said to have celebrated Mass. The oldest part of the current eighth-century church is the **Cappella dell'Assunta** off the left nave; the Byzantine mural behind its altar is the town's most precious piece of art.

Practicalities

If Assisi's and Spello's hotels are full, you may have cause to try Foligno's accommodation options. None is especially cheap, though they are more likely to have space. The **train and bus stations** are both just outside the Viale, which follow the circuit of the old walls. From either station it's a ten-minute walk into the Piazza della Repubblica. The **tourist office** is across the square from the bus station at Porta Romana 126 (Mon–Sat 9am–1pm & 3–6pm; ☎0742.354.4459 or 0742.349.9854, fax 0742.340.545). If

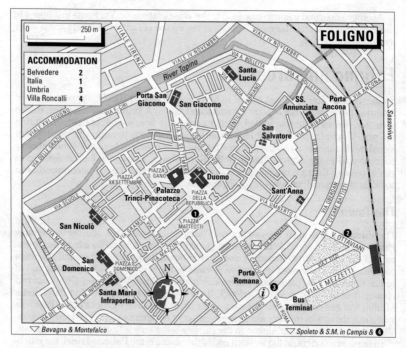

you are headed to Montefalco (see p.514), there are infrequent buses, or you could try hitching from the Porta Todi, round Via N. Sauro from Piazzale Alunno.

Accommodation

Belvedere, Via F. Ottaviani 23 (☎0742.353.990, fax 0742.356.243). A 20-room two-star just north of the train station. ③.

Italia, Piazza Matteotti 12 (☎0742.350.412, fax 0742.352.258). A large (35 rooms) and functional three-star place, but very centrally located immediately south of Piazza della Repubblica. ③.

Umbria, Viale Cesare Battisti 1 (☎ & fax 0742.352.821). Similar three-star, but right on busy junction with Piazzale Alunno and thus convenient for the train station; has 48 rooms, so there's usually something available. ④.

Villa Roncalli, Viale Roma 25 (☎0742.391.091, fax 0742.391.001). Best of the upmarket three-star places. ④.

Eating

Cheap **pizzerie** are numerous, and any walk around the streets will uncover one to suit. If you want to treat yourself, the local favourite is the highly acclaimed **restaurant** of the *Villa Roncalli* hotel (closed Mon & Aug 1–10); expect to pay about L50,000 a head. For light meals and a glass of wine at around half this price, head for the *Il Bacco Felice*, Via Garibaldi 73–5 (closed Mon).

East of Foligno

Visible from afar from the Vale of Spoleto, the Benedictine **Abbazia di Sassovivo**, 6km east of Foligno, is one of the oldest monasteries in Umbria, dating from 1070. Set in wooded countryside, it also claims the region's finest medieval **cloisters**, with 128 variegated columns and 58 arches all decorated with mosaics and coloured marbles. The church is dull, however, save for its eleventh-century crypt.

To the north of the abbey, the SS77 road to Camerino threads through the beautiful **Menotre valley**, a region of small, lost villages and virgin hill country. To explore properly, you'll need transport or the will to hike. With the latter in mind, the *Kompass* "Assisi-Camerino" **map** (#665) is invaluable.

PALE, 8km east of Foligno, is the first village you'll come to in the Menotre. It has a castle and a stalactite-crammed cave, the **Grotta di Pale**. Paths from the village cover the 4km to the summit of the craggy **Sasso di Pale** (958m), also accessible from Santa Lucia, 1km on from Pale.

The only place of any real size in the valley is **COLFIORITO**, 25km from Foligno. Once an important Iron Age site, controlling one of the lowest Apennine passes into the Marche, it sits at the heart of some extraordinary countryside, mostly marsh and upland plain – rather like the Valnerina – surrounded by fields of grass and mountain peaks. Green and cool in summer, the town has become something of a vacation retreat and is well served by **hotels**, though it has to be said that none is especially prepossessing. The best bet is the two-star *Lieta Sosta*, Via Adriatica 230 (☎0742.681.321, fax 0742.681.322; ③), which also has a smaller but similarly priced one-star annexe. A cheaper option is the *Valico*, Via Casette di Cupigliolo (☎ & fax 0742.681.385; ②).

Bevagna and around

BEVAGNA, 8km southwest of Foligno, is even more serene and handsome a backwater than Spello, with a windswept central piazza of austere perfection and two of Umbria's finest Romanesque churches. An Umbrian and then an Etruscan settlement, it became Mevania under the Romans, a staging post on the Via Flaminia (built in 220 BC) – now the Corso Matteotti, which bisects the town from end to end. Its decline dates from the building of a new spur to the Flaminia five centuries later, a road which was routed through Terni and Spoleto rather than Bevagna. After the Roman era it was sacked by just about everybody – Barbarossa, Frederick II, Foligno's Trinci family and, inevitably, by Perugia's Baglioni. Today it has scarcely spread beyond its medieval walls, remaining miraculously unscarred by the urban blight of most nearby hill-towns.

The Town

On whatever bearing you start to wander the village, the backstreets sooner or later converge on the pedestrianized main square, **Piazza Silvestri**, vast and open after the shadowed streets of its surroundings. Every member of this unimprovable arrangement is thoroughly medieval, with the sole exception of the nineteenth-century fountain, and even that blends in perfectly.

Two churches face each other across the square, both untouched and creaking with age. The smaller, deconsecrated **San Silvestro**, is a magnificent squat example of early Umbrian-Romanesque; its exterior bears a plaque with the date of construction – 1195 – and the name of the builder, Binello, who was also responsible for San Michele opposite, but of whom nothing else is known except for his work on Spello's Santa Maria Maggiore (see p.504). Pieces of Roman remains are woven into the facade, whose upper half is faced in pink Subasio stone and boasts the stump of an unfinished tower. The **interior** – which tends to be open when the rest of the town is shut – is superbly ancient in look and feel, with a raised presbytery and sunken crypt. Look out for the capitals of the blunt columns in the nave, which are of an Egyptian order (rather than Doric, Ionic or Corinthian) and were perhaps copied from a Roman temple to distant deities.

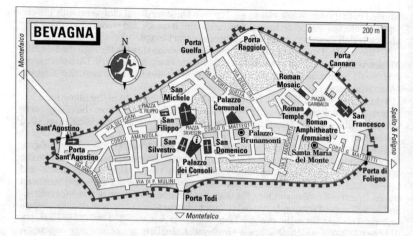

The second church, **San Michele**, appears and feels more recent, perhaps due to its rose window, punched through in the eighteenth century. It is in fact San Silvestro's contemporary and is built to a similar interior plan; its capitals are similarly eccentric, as are the magnificently surreal **gargoyles** over the main doorway. The square's third component is the twelfth-century **Palazzo dei Consoli**, distinguished by a broad stone staircase below which sits the small **tourist office**. To its left is **SS. Domenico e Giacomo**, rectangular and workaday, its Baroque interior relieved only by fragments of fresco and two early wooden sculptures. The church's prime position was a gift from the *comune* to the Dominicans for help in rebuilding the town after one of its sackings. Be sure to have a look at the small cloister, reached through the church.

One other surprise lurks in the square, the delightful and recently restored nineteenth-century **Teatro Torti**, infiltrated into the Gothic shell of the former Palazzo dei Consoli. It may not sound terribly enticing, but the theatre, full of minuscule boxes and balconies, is a gem, one of only a few surviving examples of the tiny provincial theatres that once flourished across Italy. Enquire at the tourist office for admittance: the key is usually kept by a local professor who likes nothing better than to be summoned out to show off what is obviously his pride and joy.

If you really want to exhaust Bevagna's tourist offerings, the church of **San Francesco** at the town's highest point claims to have the stone from which St Francis preached his famous sermon to the birds, a discourse that according to the local claim occurred on the road between Bevagna and Cannara (perhaps Francis spoke to several flocks of Umbrian birds, for the spot is commemorated too at Assisi's Eremo delle Carceri).

Roman Bevagna

Of equally modest interest is the small **Museo Comunale** (June–Aug Mon–Sat 10.30am–1pm & 2–5.30pm; April, May & Sept Mon–Sat 10.30am–1pm & 2.30–5pm; Oct & March Sat–Sun 10am–1pm & 2.30–5pm; Nov & Feb Sat–Sun 10.30am–1pm & 2–4pm; L5000) at Corso G. Matteotti, located on the stairs of the council headquarters at Corso Matteotti 72. The paintings are eminently forgettable, but the medley of Roman remains – all found locally – are worth a few minutes. None, though, compares with the genuinely impressive black-and-white **Roman mosaic** on the north side of Via Porta Guelfa (ring the bell at no. 2 next door to the left for the custodian; free). Laid down in the second century, it formed part of a bath complex – hence the associations of its dolphins, lobsters and other sea creatures. To the south, the pillars and half-columns of the **Roman temple** date from roughly the same period. Just to the north, **Porta Cannara**, best preserved of the town's gates, offers access to a nice stretch of the medieval walls.

Farther east on Corso Matteotti be sure to explore **Via dell'Anfiteatro**, whose little houses follow the line of the former Roman amphitheatre, and which gives access to a series of little tunnels that burrow mysteriously into the old under-stage area.

Practicalities

Three **buses** run to Bevagna from Foligno and on to Montefalco (four from Montefalco), terminating in the little square immediately behind and to the south of San Silvestro. **Tickets** for onward journeys can be bought in the bar secreted away in the medieval loggia on the square's eastern edge. The small **tourist office** (☎0742.361.667; irregular hours) in Piazza Silvestri provides a good map and leaflet on the town, with English translations. For years Bevagna had no **hotel**; now there's the central three-star *Palazzo Brunamonti*, Corso G. Matteotti 79 (☎0742.361.932, fax 0742.361.948; ⑤). It is also possible to stay at the Benedictine Santa Maria del Monte **convent** at Corso Matteotti 15 (☎0742.360.133; ③) – the food is excellent, but the nuns warm to you more readily if you attend Mass.

Restaurant choice is otherwise limited to the cheap and cheerful *Da Nina*, Piazza Garibaldi 6 (☎0742.360.161; closed Tues), or the excellent *Ottavius*, located off the same square in which the buses stop at Via del Gonfalone 4 (☎0742.360.555; closed Mon & first two weeks of July; full meals around L40,000). It's wonderfully situated in an old single-vaulted medieval room, and the food – great *gnocchi al Sagrantino* and succulent *filetto* – is pure Umbrian. The **bar** just off the central piazza is good for ice cream and snacks and has perhaps Umbria's most miserable service and most oddball clientele.

Around Bevagna

The rich agricultural plain surrounding Bevagna is only worth exploration if you have a car. In the hills above the town, clearly delineated on the skyline, is the Renaissance church of **Santa Maria delle Grazie** (rarely open), admirable from below, but by no means worth the journey for a closer look.

The most rewarding trip is to take the minor road northwest towards Cannara. Two kilometres out is the restored but very pretty **Convento dell'Annunziata**, followed by the one-horse hamlet of **CANTALUPO** and the tiny stone chapel of Madonna della Pia. Take a minor left turn 1km beyond and you hit **LIMIGIANO**, a classic fortified hamlet centred on a thirteenth-century church, San Michele. At the crossroads for Cannara, a left turn leads to **COLLEMANCIO**, where 500m north of the village's public gardens are the unexcavated ruins of Urbinum Hortense, a Roman or possibly Etruscan settlement destroyed by Totila in 545. The odds and ends – traces of a temple, pavement and mosaics – merit a wander, while the views over the Vale of Spoleto are superb. In the village, the *Pensione Il Rientro* (☎075.72.420; ⑤) has a handful of **rooms**.

CANNARA itself, stranded mid-plain but sheltered by trees, has three churches, each with significant paintings by major Umbrian artists: San Giovanni has frescoes by Lo Spagna, while San Matteo and San Francesco have works by Nicolò Alunno. The Palazzo Comunale in Piazza Umberto houses a small gallery with frescoes detached from local churches and archeological finds from Urbinium. If you do come here, or are nearby in the evening, make a point of **eating** at *Perbacco*, Via Umberto I 14 (☎0742.720.492; open evenings only; closed Mon & 4 weeks during July–Aug), a fine osteria at the centre of the village (around L35,000).

Montefalco

As you'd expect from its name – the Falcon's Mount – **MONTEFALCO** commands the Vale of Spoleto. The local tag of "la ringhiera dell'Umbria" (the balcony of Umbria) may be a touch hyperbolic but the views are nonetheless majestic and once past the modern suburbs you enter one of the finest hill-towns in the area, a maze of tiny, cobbled streets, with an artistic heritage – including pictures by Perugino and a stunning Gozzoli fresco cycle – out of all proportion to its size.

The town was the birthplace of eight saints, good going even by Italian standards, and began life as a small independent medieval *comune* known as Coccorone. It was destroyed by Frederick II in 1249, his only legacy a gate named in his honour, whereafter Montefalco took its new name. Its chief historical interest lies in a brief interlude in the fourteenth century, when the town became a refuge to Spoleto's papal governors, left vulnerable by the defection of the popes to Avignon. Their munificent presence resulted in the rich decoration of local churches and the commissioning of Lorenzo Maitani, who was later to work on the duomo in Orvieto, to strengthen the town **walls** (still impressively intact) and to build a fortress for the exiled rulers. Power thereafter devolved to Foligno's Trinci family, to the rapacious Baglioni and eventually to the Church – cue for several centuries of quiet decline.

The Town

The five **buses** daily from Foligno's Porta Romana (Mon–Sat), and one daily from Perugia (Mon–Sat) drop you at the foot of Via Umberto I, the main offshoot of **Piazza del Comune**, the town's main square. The chief attraction, the ex-church of **San Francesco** and its museum, is a stone's throw away from the square, while the rest of the town is little more than five minutes' walk from end to end. The only outlying site, **San Fortunato**, is about fifteen minutes' walk away, the slightly dull stroll relieved by the comprehensively frescoed church of **Sant'Illuminata** en route.

San Francesco

The cavernous fourteenth-century church of **San Francesco** (daily: June–July 10am–1pm & 3–7pm; Aug 10.30am–1pm & 3–7.30pm; March–May & Sept–Oct 10.30am–1pm & 2–6pm; Nov–Feb 10.30am–1pm & 2.30–5pm; L7000) hosts one of the great Renaissance fresco cycles, a series of panels on the *Life of St Francis* (1452) by **Benozzo Gozzoli**. Gozzoli, a pupil of Fra' Angelico, has a comparatively lowly place in the pantheon of Florentine artists, but this delightful cycle – which duplicates in its subjects many of Giotto's panels in Assisi – is marvellously bold in its colouring and utterly assured of its narrative. It is also of great social interest for its closely observed townscapes: Arezzo is depicted, as is Montefalco – visited by St Francis after his sermon to the birds outside Bevagna. The panels completely fill the apse, with twenty medallions around them depicting famous Franciscans; underneath the main window appear Petrarch, Dante and Giotto, members of the lay tertiary order. Further work by Gozzoli fills the walls and vaults to the right, as well as the first chapel on the left (south) side of the church. The striking but obviously cruder frescoes in the fourth, fifth and sixth chapels on this side are the work of the fifteenth-century Foligno artist Giovanni di Corraduccio.

Elsewhere are displayed paintings by many of the leading lights of the Umbrian Renaissance – **Perugino**, **Nicolò Alunno**, **Tiberio d'Assisi** – and some fascinating little-known characters. Perugino's *Nativity* (1503) on the west wall, in particular, is worth looking out for, as Lago Trasimeno is featured in the background. Works originally commissioned for San Francesco remain in situ, with others housed in the excellent **Museo Civico di San Francesco** up the stairs (same hours & ticket as church). In the gallery

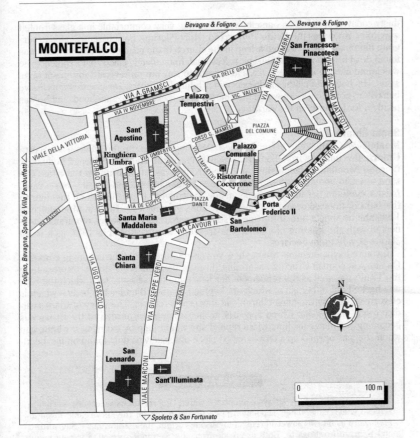

look for Francesco Melanzio's *Madonna Enthroned with Six Saints*, the work of a leading local Renaissance painter, and for the two panels – one by Melanzio – showing the *Madonna del Soccorso*. The story – common in Umbria though rarely painted elsewhere – concerns a young mother who, tired of her whingeing child, cries "would that the Devil might take you away"; the Devil duly appears, prompting the mother to invoke the Virgin to save her infant. The museum also operates as a **tourist information point** with town maps and walking tours, as well as a wide selection of art books and magazines.

Sant'Agostino

The Augustinians' monastery and church of **Sant'Agostino** is 200m away from the Franciscans' power base, across the Piazza del Comune. A simple Gothic hall, begun in 1275, it is typical of the order, designed with a view to minimize the fripperies and maximize the preaching space. It has a few excellent frescoes that have survived the damp – including a *Coronation of the Virgin* by Caporali (1522) – but its main interest, lending a distinctly spooky air, lies in its collection of **mummies**.

Midway down the right nave are the first of these – the tiny bodies of **Beata Illuminata** and **Beata Chiarella**, clad in dusty muslin which only half hides their bones, skin and yellow faces. At the top of the left-hand side of the church is another dusty cadaver, propped on one elbow and looking very comfortable in a glass-fronted wardrobe. Known as the **Beato Pellegrino** (Holy Pilgrim), he apparently came to venerate Illuminata and Beata, fell asleep in the church in the position he's in now, and was found dead next morning against a confessional. Immediately placed in a sepulchre, he was found outside it the next day, and refused to stay put on several subsequent occasions. His body and clothes didn't decay for a hundred years. Despite this impressive behaviour, nothing was known of the character, so there was no sainthood, and he was plonked for posterity in his wardrobe.

Santa Chiara

Montefalco's collection of mummified flesh continues in the church of **Santa Chiara**, five minutes from San Francesco in Via Verdi. Here the wizened body of St Clare of Montefalco languishes in a see-through casket high up on the altar. The saint – not to be confused with her more famous namesake at Assisi – has a small **fresco cycle** on her life in a chapel inside the convent (ring the bell on the door to the right of the casket and ask one of the nuns to unlock it). Born in Montefalco in 1290, she became a nun at the age of six and embarked on a series of miracles connected with the Passion of Christ. The frescoes were restored in 1932, as a small plaque beside them declares.

If you're lucky, the nuns might show you around the rest of the adjoining **convent**. On show is a small Crucifix enshrining three of the saint's gallstones (representing the Trinity) as well as the remains of her heart and the scissors with which the relic was hacked out of her, all of which are kept in a cupboard under her body – which is cleverly shared by the main church and this private chapel. The story of Clare's cardiac organ relates that Christ appeared to her, saying the burden of the Cross was becoming too heavy for him; Clare replied she would help by carrying it within, and when she was opened up a cross-shaped piece of tissue was duly found on her heart.

SAGRANTINO

Montefalco's **wines** have always been prized within Umbria but have recently started to achieve wider fame. Their reputation rests not so much on the serviceable *Rosso di Montefalco* as on two powerful reds of mysterious origin, the extraordinary **Sagrantino** and **Sagrantino Passito**. Both are made from the Sagrantino grape, a variety found nowhere else in Europe. Why it should be unique to a tiny area of central Italy is a mystery: it appears in records in the nineteenth century, but experts claim a far more ancient pedigree, some saying it was imported by the Saracens, others that it was introduced by Syrian monks in the seventh century, or perhaps came from Piedmont or Catalonia. Its name may derive from its sacramental use by Franciscan communities who used to cultivate this grape.

Sagrantino is a dry red, usually made with up to five percent of the common Trebbiano Toscano. Sagrantino Passito is similar, with the important difference that it uses semi-dried or *passito* grapes to produce that rarest of drinks – a sweet red dessert wine. Both varieties, in the words of Italian wine guru Burton Anderson, have a remarkable "dark purple-garnet colour, rich, berry-like scent, and warm, rich full flavour". The Sagrantino, he adds, has "voluptuous body" and "staggering strength", qualities to which even the least educated palate will be able to attest after a couple of glasses. **Adanti** are the leading producers of both varieties, their singular *Rosso d'Arquata*, in Anderson's words, "one of central Italy's most original and enjoyable red wines". Any of the many producers in the tiny DOC area, however, should come up trumps, especially Antonelli, Benincasa, Caprai, Rocca di Fabbri and Paolo Bea – the last are producers of what Anderson describes as a "titanic" Sagrantino Passito. The *alimentari* or smart bar-*enoteca* in Montefalco's main Piazza del Comune contain a superb selection of all the area's wines.

Other sights include a miraculous tree that grew from a staff planted by Christ, who appeared again to Clare in the shrubbery. The nuns think it's the sole wild specimen of its species in all of Europe; the berries are used to make rosaries, and are said to have powerful medicinal properties.

Sant'Illuminata and San Fortunato

Down the street from Santa Chiara's seat of miracles is the tiny church of **Sant'Illuminata**, worth a visit for its triple-arched Renaissance **portico** and comprehensively frescoed **interior**. The standard of painting isn't always terribly high – most are by the obscure local man Melanzio – but the overall effect is captivating.

Keep heading out of town from here, down the avenue of horse chestnuts, then turn left at the T-junction, and a ten-minute trudge brings you out at the **Monastero di San Fortunato** (closed daily noon to 4pm), set amongst ilex woods, the site home to a church since the fifth century. It has noted frescoes on the *Life of St Francis* (1512) by Tiberio d'Assisi – one of Perugino's leading disciples – in its Cappella delle Rose, to the left of the main courtyard. Gozzoli painted the very faded *Madonna and Child with Angels* over the door of the main church (the *St Sebastian* is by Tiberio), the dark fresco of St Fortunatus inside on the left altar, and the three worn tondi on the sarcophagus of St Severus in the little chapel off the right aisle. The St Fortunatus fresco once sat above the remains of Fortunatus himself, whose bones were laid out in a macabre skull-and-crossbones arrangement; at the time of writing they have been temporarily removed. The saint died in 390, and in rotting away proved rather more corruptible than Sant'Agostino's holy personages.

Practicalities

Practicalities are straightforward in Montefalco, everything being within a few minutes' walk of everything else. There is no proper **tourist office**, though the ticket desk at the San Francesco museum, Via Ringhiera Umbra (☎0742.379.598), does the job, with information on the town, as well as a detailed resumé of the gallery's contents. **Buses** drop off and pick up just outside the walls at the bottom of Via Umberto I in Viale della Vittoria. The **post office** (☎0742.377.978) is at the top of Corso G. Mameli virtually on the main square, as is the main bank for **exchange**, the Istituto di Credito (☎0742.33.746). There is a **hospital** in Via Ringhiera Umbra below the museum (☎0742.339.020). The **police station** is in Via A. Gramsci (☎0742.379.148).

There's just one two-star **hotel** within the town walls, the small, cosy but fairly basic *Ringhiera Umbra*, Via Umberto 1 (☎ & fax 0742.379.166; ③), which also has a relaxed little restaurant in the medieval vaulted room downstairs. The *Villa Pambuffetti*, Via Vittoria 3 (☎0742.378.823; ⑦), is a fantastic four-star villa-hotel with park and pool, 100m out of town on the road west towards Foligno. Prices are high, but if you're honeymooning, or want a night of credit card madness in Umbria, this is the place – though make sure you're in the main villa, not the gatehouse. The room to get, if you can, is the one in the old tower with a 360° view.

For something grander than the *Ringhiera*'s **restaurant**, try the outstanding *Coccorone*, set in a medieval building on the corner of Largo Tempestivi and Via Fabbri (☎0742.79.535; closed Wed), where the chances are you'll have one of Umbria's better meals – great pastas and *crespelli* (rolled pancakes), and superlative *tiramisù*. To find it, follow the off-putting yellow signs for the "Tipical Ristorant". The restaurant in the *Pambuffetti* is also good, though more formal; the dining room is a lovely glass-enclosed space with views onto the garden. This makes it great in summer, but no match in winter for the roaring wood-fire cosiness of the *Coccorone* (the fire burns in summer as well – it's used to grill all the meats). Prices, too, are higher in the *Pambuffetti* – you're paying for elegance rather than better food.

There's not much else in the way of life, though you might while away an hour in the **bar-enoteca** in the main square, part of a chic but rather self-conscious little development of craft and food shops; in the cool cellar downstairs from the bar you can drink wine and eat light meals. Otherwise, try the little *Bar Giardino*, signed off the western end of Corso Umberto I. Perhaps the best place to buy food and wine is the old shop on Piazza del Comune, which has a well-priced stock of truffles, local oils and leading **wines** (see box on p.516). Prices might be a touch higher than in Montefalco's supermarkets, but the choice is unbeatable.

Trevi

Heading south from Foligno across the plain of Spoleto, few people give **TREVI** more than an admiring glance from the train or highway. From across the valley, the town looks merely enticing, but at closer range Trevi has the most stupendous appearance of any town in Umbria – its medieval houses perched on a pyramidal hill and encircled by miles and miles of olive groves. Because so few bother to make the steep detour, the town's atmosphere is that of a pleasant, ordinary, provincial town still apparently stuck somewhere in the 1950s.

If you are coming by **train**, from Foligno or Spoleto, make sure you don't catch an express, which won't stop at Trevi station. From the station, jump on the connecting bus for the four-kilometre haul into town. The buses will drop you near Piazza Mazzini, where you'll find the **tourist office** at no. 6 (Mon–Sat 9.30am–1pm & 3.30–6pm; ☎0742.781.150). Cars can be parked in Piazza Garibaldi, outside the town walls to the east.

The Town

As with most Umbrian hill-towns, the pleasure of Trevi lies in tramping the medieval streets, which are obsessively well kept and characterized by complicated patterns of cobblestones and more than the usual profusion of summer geraniums. Pieces of Roman Trevi are embedded in the inner of two sets of medieval **walls**, raised when Trevi paraded as a minor independent *comune*.

The main sight is the **Pinacoteca Comunale**, also known as the Museo della Città, housed on the northern edge of the village (take Via Dan Francesco from Piazza

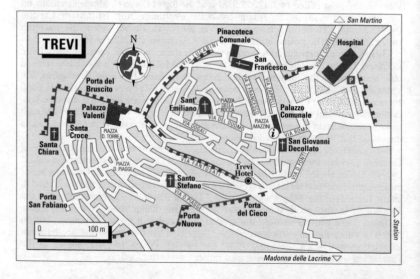

Mazzini) in the former Convento di San Francesco in Largo Don Bosco (June–July Tues–Sun 10.30am–1pm & 3.30–7pm; Aug daily 10.30am–1pm & 3–7.30pm; April–May & Sept Tues–Sun 10.30am–1pm & 2.30–6pm; Oct–March Thurs–Sun 10.30am–1pm & 2.30–5pm; L5000). It offers artistic diversions in the form of a *Madonna and Child* attributed to Pinturicchio, a triptych and polyptych with *Scenes from the Life of Christ* by Giovanni di Coraduccio, a fifteenth-century artist from Foligno who also painted in Montefalco's church of San Francesco; and – the most important painting – Lo Spagna's superb *Coronation of the Virgin with St Francis, Saints and Angels* (1522). The same artist was also responsible, with assistants, for the works nearby: *Santa Cecilia* (1520) and *SS. Caterina and Alessandria* (1522).

The highest point of the town is **Sant'Emiliano**, comely twelfth-century Romanesque on the outside, Baroque horror-show within. Another of Umbria's many martyrs and saints, Emilianus was an Armenian missionary cut off in his prime in 302. The only early survivors of the butchery of the building are a captivating *Altar of the Sacrament* (1522) and frescoes by Melanzio, who was active in many villages hereabouts (notably Montefalco) at the start of the sixteenth century. The Palazzo Lucarini next door has a small museum of modern art, the **Trevi Flash Museum** (Wed–Sun 10am–1pm & 3–6.30pm; L5000) – one for devotees of the genre only.

Most noteworthy of the peripheral churches is the **Madonna delle Lacrime**, one kilometre from the centre on the approach road from the station, home to a fine *Epiphany with St Peter and St Paul* from 1521 (second altar on the right) by Perugino and a sweep of frescoes (1520) by Lo Spagna in the chapel of the left transept.

Finally, be sure to take a stroll north from Piazza Garibaldi, following the tree-lined Via Ciufelli left of the hospital complex. This offers a superb view of the valley and after ten minutes brings you to the conventual church of **San Martino**, site of Trevi's original parish church. It has a lunette above the door by Tiberio d'Assisi plus two pictures in the tabernacles on either side of the presbytery, one of *St Martin Dividing his Cloak with Beggar* by Tiberio, the other a fifteenth-century *Madonna and Child with St Francis and St Antony of Padua* by Mezzastris, a local painter. In the separate Cappella di San Giralmo, in a chapel to the left of the church, is an important *Assumption and Saints* (1512) by Lo Spagna, another Spoletan artist, and *St Emilianus* by Tiberio d'Assisi.

Practicalities

Trevi has just one **hotel**, the 12-room, three-star *Trevi*, Via Fantosati 2 (☎0742.780.922, fax 0742.780.772; ⑤). A couple of good places to **eat** in town are the *Osteria La Vecchia Posta*, Piazza Mazzini 14 (☎0742.381.690; closed Thurs except in July & Aug), with a handful of tables outside in the summer, and *Maggiolini*, Via San Francesco 20 (☎0742.381.534; closed Tues). Four kilometres south, in the hamlet of Pigge, the *Pescatore*, Via Chiesa Tonda 5 (☎0742.780.483; ④), has rooms and one of the very best restaurants in the whole area, the *Taverna del Pescatore* (☎0742.780.290; closed Wed except in summer; L45,000–55,000).

South of Trevi

Moving south from Trevi, the Vale of Spoleto becomes increasingly pockmarked with new houses and small factories. This makes its main sight, the **Fonti di Clitunno** – a series of springs revered since Roman times – all the more unexpected. It is located by the main road below the fortified hamlet of **Campello**, an out-of-the-way accommodation possibility.

The Fonti di Clitunno

The sacred **Fonti di Clitunno** (daily: April to mid-June 9am–1pm & 2–7pm; mid-June to mid-Sept 9am–8pm; mid-Sept to Oct 9am–12.30pm & 2–5pm; L2000; Nov–March visits by arrangement; ☎0743.521.141; L1500) has provided inspiration to poets from Virgil to Byron. Originally dedicated to the oracular god **Clitunnus**, the springs were often used as a party venue by the likes of Caligula and Claudius, even though their major curative effect is allegedly that of removing any appetite for alcohol. Earthquakes over the years have upset many of the underground sources, so the waters aren't as plentiful as they once were, but they still flow as limpid as they did when Byron extolled "the sweetest wave of the most living crystal . . . the purest god of gentle waters".

There's a certain amount of commercial fuss around the entrance but the springs, streams and willow-shaded lake beyond are languidly romantic, with faint traffic noise and the occasional coach party the only intrusions on weekdays – at weekends the racket is more intense.

The Tempietto di Clitunno

A few hundred metres north of the Fonti, and easily missed, is the so-called **Tempietto di Clitunno** (daily: April–Oct 9am–8pm; Nov–March 9am–2pm; free), accessible from the road only (not directly from the Fonti). It looks like a miniature classical temple, but is actually an eighth-century Christian church cobbled together with columns from the ruins of Roman temples and villas, all long vanished. Scholars until recently were fooled into thinking it a genuine piece of Roman antiquity, though Goethe was one notable dissenter from the party line. The track which runs below the facade is the remains of the original Via Flaminia.

The entrance is to the side; if it's shut, try ringing the bell on the gate. Inside are some faded frescoes, said to be the oldest in Umbria; dated to the eighth century, these Byzantine fragments represent Christ, St Peter and St Paul.

Campello and around

Though its position above the Fonti di Clitunno is impressive enough, the main attraction of the small fortified hamlet of **CAMPELLO** is the fact that it offers accommodation. For **hotel** rooms try either the two-star *Fontanelle*, Via d'Elci 1 (☎0743.521.091, fax 0743.275.052; ③) in the hamlet of Fontanelle, or the two-star *Ravale*, Ravale Campello, close to the Fonti (☎0743.521.320, fax 0743.520.861; ③); both have **restaurants** and reasonable rooms.

Equipped with a car or bike, there are superb **mountain excursions** on the roads northeast of Campello. Minor roads follow deep-cut valleys via **PETTINO** and Spina into marvellous countryside, the hills on either side rising to over 1400m at Monte Maggiore and Monte Brunnette.

travel details

TRAINS

Assisi to: Foligno (hourly; 15min – for connections south to Spoleto, Terni and Rome, and north to Fossato di Vico (for Gubbio) and the Marche); Perugia (hourly; 25min); Spello (hourly; 10min); Teróntola (hourly; 1hr 25min – for connections to Rome, Florence and Arezzo).

Foligno to: Ancona (10 daily; 15min) via Nocera Umbra; Fossato di Vico (40min) and Fabriano, Jesi and Falconara; Teróntola (hourly) via Spello, Assisi, Perugia and halts en route; Rome (10 daily) via Spoleto, Terni, Narni and Orte.

BUSES

Assisi to: Bastia and Capodacqua (7 daily); Cannara (4 daily); Foligno, via Spello (10 daily); Florence (1 daily); Gualdo Tadino (1 daily); Gubbio (2 weekly); Norcia, Cascia and the Valnerina (1 daily Mon–Sat from Santa Maria degli Angeli); Perugia (10 daily); Rome (1 daily); Santa Maria degli Angeli (every 30min); Todi and Orvieto (1 weekly–Fri).

Bevagna to: Foligno (5 daily); Montefalco (3 daily).

Foligno to: Bevagna (3 daily Mon–Fri); Gualdo Tadino (1 daily Mon–Sat); Montefalco (5 daily); Spello (7 daily Mon–Sat); Urbino (1 daily Mon–Sat). Also to Assisi, Spoleto (via the Fonti di Clitunno and Trevi) and Nocera Umbra.

Montefalco to: Bevagna (4 daily Mon–Sat); Foligno (5 daily Mon–Sat).

CHAPTER TWELVE

SPOLETO AND THE VALNERINA

astern Umbria is in many ways the most enjoyable part of the region. The area offers superb walking and car or cycle touring amid some of the wildest scenery in central Italy, and in its main city and transport hub, **Spoleto**, you have the most stimulating base in Umbria. The walking and scenery are at their best in the extreme east, where the spectacular **Monti Sibillini** look down over the **Piano Grande**, a vast highland plain which in spring becomes a breathtaking expanse of wild flowers. There is sporadic public transport access to these areas from both Spoleto and **Norcia**, the earthquake-prone birthplace of St Benedict, founder of Western monasticism. Equally beautiful, and a little easier to reach, are the villages of the **Valnerina**, an upland valley enclosed by high mountain walls immediately east of Spoleto.

Spoleto should feature on any Umbrian itinerary – particularly if you have the opportunity to catch its summer **Festival dei Due Mondi**, a contemporary arts jamboree with considerable international kudos. The festival has had a trickle-down effect on the rest of Spoleto's year, too, inspiring a full programme of exhibitions and concerts. This is a hill-town which, for all its medieval and Roman sights, is not over-whelmed by its past.

Access to Spoleto is straightforward, as the town lies on the Rome–Ancona rail line, with links to Terni and Narni to the south, and to Foligno, Assisi and Perugia to the north. Buses provide feasible links for the main villages of the Valnerina, and for the trailheads of the Monti Sibillini and Piano Grande, though to get the most from the countryside really requires transport of your own – or, better still, some determined hiking. If you're driving, note there's a quick new road tunnel (not yet marked on most maps) just east of Spoleto off the old minor road over the mountains to Vallo di Nera. The tunnel picks up the Valnerina road a little south of the old Vallo di Nera junction close to Sant' Anatolia di Narco.

ACCOMMODATION PRICES

Throughout this guide, **hotel** accommodation is graded on a scale from ① to ⑨, indicating the cost of the **cheapest double room** in each establishment in high season (for **hostels**, rates per person are given in lire). The price bands to which these codes refer are as follows:

① up to L60,000	④ L120,000–150,000	⑦ L250,000–300,000
② L60,000–90,000	⑤ L150,000–200,000	⑧ L300,000–350,000
③ L90,000–120,000	⑥ L200,000–250,000	⑨ over L350,000

Spoleto

"The most romantic city I ever saw", said Percy Bysshe Shelley of **SPOLETO**, a place which would demand a visit with or without its famous summer festival. One of the most graceful of all Italian hill-towns, it maintains a bustling life of its own, a seductively medieval appearance and a superb assembly of museums and Romanesque monuments. Its road and transport links make it the natural base for exploring eastern Umbria, and it's a possible base for visits farther afield – Assisi, for example, is an easy day trip. The one drawback to the place is its ever-increasing popularity. Hotels are relatively thin on the ground, and during the height of the summer festival, accommodation is tight and prices inflated.

Of Bronze Age origin, the city was an important Umbrian centre, the vast gorge-surrounded crag at its heart an obvious point of strategic importance. The city's ancient grandeur is attested to by a series of well-preserved **Roman walls**. Cicero described Spoletium, founded in 241 BC, as Rome's most renowned colony, and it was strong enough to turn away Hannibal in 217 BC after his victory at Lago Trasimeno (see p.459). Strategically sited between Rome and Ravenna, the town prospered as the focus of the Western Empire shifted from one to the other, though its real prominence was to come after AD 576 when it was established first as a Lombard and later as a Frankish dukedom. The autonomous Duchy of Spoleto eventually stretched to Benevento near Naples, dominating the greater part of central Italy.

During the emergence of the city states it became "the magnificent city, defended by a hundred towers". Its fall from grace came in the shape of Barbarossa, who flattened the city in 1155 during an Italian sojourn to restore his imperial authority. Ironically this cleared the way for rebuilding, rapid growth and the powerful re-emergence of a quasi-democratic regime (already in existence before 1155) which saw Spoleto at the height of its powers during much of the thirteenth century. Decline and deliverance into the hands of the Church followed a century later, the humdrum years that ensued being relieved in 1499 when the nineteen-year-old Lucrezia Borgia was appointed governor by her father, Pope Alexander VI. Thereafter it was downhill towards obscurity until the arrival of the festival almost forty years ago.

Arrival, orientation and information

Transport to Spoleto is straightforward. Regular fast **trains** on the Rome–Ancona line stop at the town, and there are regular local links with Terni, Orte and Foligno; city buses connect from the train station (✆0743.48.516 or 147.888.088) to Piazza della Libertà in the old Upper Town: tickets are available from the station bar and newspaper stall. Note that this service closes down around 8pm. Most **inter-town buses**, notably from Montefalco and Perugia, are run by Spolentina (✆0743.212.211 or 0743.47.807) and terminate in Piazza Carducci, a square in the upper town immediately south of Piazza della Libertà: a few off-load in the Lower Town in Piazza Garibaldi; Norcia and Valnerina buses operate from outside the train station (tickets from the bar or newsagent inside the station).

If you're arriving by **car** it's difficult to park in the Upper Town. The likeliest slots are those on Via della Rocca, best approached from the south on Via Monterone and the perilously narrow Via Brignone. An easier option is to use the larger **car parks** on Via Don P. Bonilli and Viale Cappuccini just west and south of the Giardino Pubblico off Viale Martiri della Resistenza.

The town's major architectural attractions are to be found in the medieval **Upper Town**, though the largely modern **Lower Town** also boasts three major Romanesque churches. The whole is a relatively compact area and getting around is easy enough on foot – though in summer you don't want to be walking up and down between the Upper and Lower towns too often.

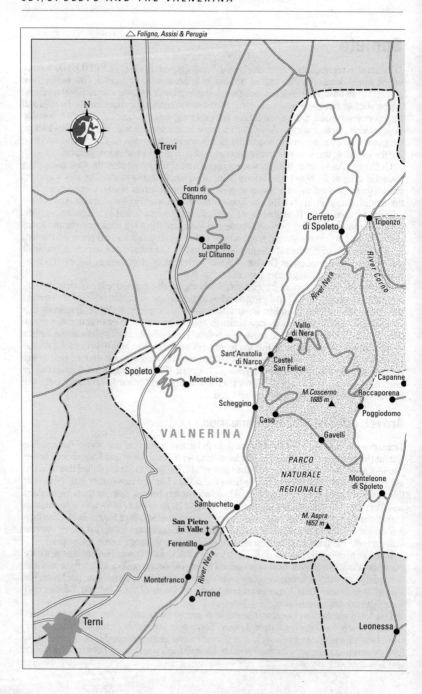

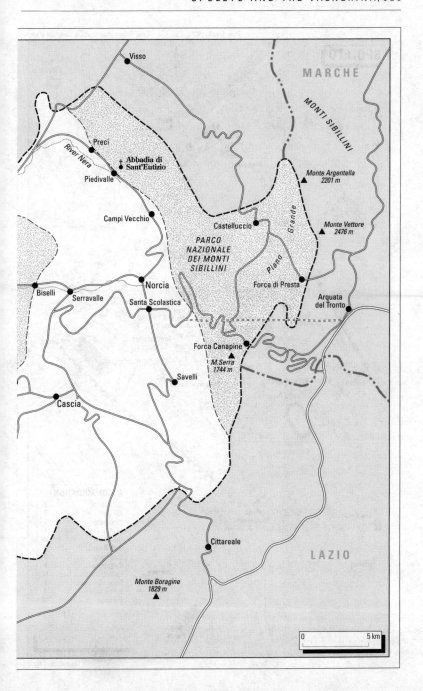

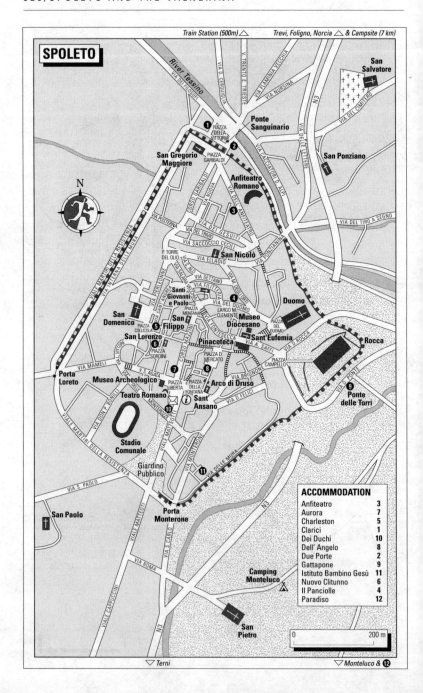

SPOLETO

River Tessino

V. TRENTO E TRIESTE
VIA DEI MOLISI
VIA D. CERQUIGLIA
VIA FLAMINIA VECCHIA
VIA DI NURSINA
N3

San Salvatore

VIA DEL CIMITERO
VIA DELLE LETTERE

Ponte Sanguinario

① PIAZZA DELLA VITTORIA
②
San Ponziano

San Gregorio Maggiore

PIAZZA GARIBALDI
CORSO GARIBALDI
VIA NUOVA

Anfiteatro Romano
③
VIA DELL'ANFITEATRO
VIA CACCIATORI D. ALPI

VIA DEL TIRO A SEGNO

VIA POSTERNA
VIA DEI GESUITI
VIA DEL TRIVIO
VIA SACCOCCIO CECILI

P. TORRE DEL OLIO
San Nicolò
VIA ELLADIO

VIA DI VISIALE
VIA M. DE'TODI
VIA SETTANO
VIA FILITTERIA
VIA PORLEONE

Santi Giovanni e Paolo
PIAZZA MENTANA
VIA DEL DUOMO
④
Duomo
VIA PONZIANINA

San Domenico
PIAZZA COLLICOLA
⑤ San Filippo
LARGO M. CLEMENTE
Museo Diocesano
PIAZZA DEL DUOMO

San Lorenzo
⑥
PIAZZA SORDINI
Pinacoteca
VIA FONTESECCA
Sant'Eufemia
VIA A. SAFFI
VIA D. ROCCA

Rocca

Porta Loreto
VIA MAMELI
VIA VITTORIO
⑦
PIAZZA DEL MERCATO
PIAZZA CAMPELLO
VIA BRIGNONE

Museo Archeologico
V. S. AGATA
⑧
Arco di Druso
VIA D. PONTE

Teatro Romano
PIAZZA LIBERTA
PIAZZA DELLA FONTANA
⑨ Ponte delle Torri

VIALE DON P. BONILLI
VIA DON P. BONILLI
① Sant'Ansano
VIA D. FELICI
VIALE MATTEOTTI

⑩
Stadio Comunale
VIA MONTERONE

Giardino Pubblico
⑪
VIA DELLE MURA

VIA S. PAOLO
San Paolo

Porta Monterone
VIALE MARTIRI DELLA RESISTENZA
VIALE MATTEOTTI
VIA S. CARLO

VIA ROMA
N3

Camping Monteluco
⌂

ACCOMMODATION

Anfiteatro	3
Aurora	7
Charleston	5
Clarici	1
Dei Duchi	10
Dell' Angelo	8
Due Porte	2
Gattapone	9
Istituto Bambino Gesù	11
Nuovo Clitunno	6
Il Panciolle	4
Paradiso	12

0 ————— 200 m

San Pietro

VIALE CAPPUCCINI

The **post office** (☎0743.43.752,), at Piazza della Libertà 12, has a foreign exchange facility; similar facilities can be found in the clutch of **banks** at the northern end of Via Mazzini. *Scatti* **telephones**, where you pay after making your call, can be found in the tourist office; *Bar Vincenzo*, Corso Mazzini 43; *Bar Italia*, Corso Garibaldi 48; and *Caffè Collicola*, Piazza Collicola. There is an unstaffed Telecom Italia office with pay phones and Italian phone directories at the western end of Via A. Saffi.

For help on accommodation – and to pick up details of cultural events and a handy pamphlet on walking in the region – the large **tourist office** at Piazza della Libertà 7 (daily 9/10am–1pm & 4.30–7.30pm; ☎0743.220.311, fax 0743.46.241) is a useful first stop. If you need **car rental** or a car with driver contact the reliable Armando Alcidi (☎0743.40.221) or Hertz, c/o Via Cerquiglia 36 (☎0743.47.217). **Bikes** can be rented from Scocchetti Cicli, Via Marconi 82 (☎0743.44.728). **Market day** is Friday, when stalls are set up in Piazza Garibaldi and Piazza del Mercato, though the latter has a handful of fruit and vegetable stalls most days of the week.

Accommodation

Rooms are hard to come by when the festival's in full swing – turning up without a booking, the best you can hope for is a room in the Lower Town, very much a second choice, but more likely to have space. If there's absolutely nothing going, your best bet is to head for Foligno, or to ask for the tourist office's *Affitacamere* list of fifteen or so private rooms. For some reason Spoleto's hotels seem to charge vastly different prices for different rooms within a single establishment, so it's worth asking if there's anything cheaper if the one you're offered seems too expensive. Hotels are listed below in ascending order of price.

Hotels

Anfiteatro, Via dell'Anfiteatro 14 (☎0743.49.853). A Lower Town two-star hotel with 9 slightly dingy rooms: prices vary enormously between rooms, so ask to see a selection. ②.

Dell'Angelo, Via Arco del Druso 25 (☎0743.222.385). Pleasant *pensione* in a very central Upper Town location; the composer Gioacchino Rossini stayed here in its smarter days. It has only 7 double rooms (no singles), so reservations are essential. ②–③.

Due Porte, Piazza della Vittoria 5 (☎0743.223.666). A modern 15-room two-star in a big, busy and potentially noisy Lower Town piazza close to the *Clarici* (see below) and just down the road from the train station. ②–③.

Aurora, Via dell'Apollinare 3 (☎0743.220.315 or 0743.223.004, fax 0743.221.885). Excellent and very popular mid-range two-star place, in a courtyard just off Piazza della Libertà; 15 rooms, all with private bathrooms. ③.

Il Panciolle, Via del Duomo 4 (☎0743.45.677). Seven rooms, each with private bathroom, above a nice restaurant in a quietish but convenient part of the Upper Town. A very good two-star option. ③.

Clarici, Piazza Garibaldi-Piazza della Vittoria 32 (☎0743.223.311, fax 0743.220.010). Reasonable, but rather basic, modern three-star hotel set just outside the walls of the Upper Town. ④.

Charleston, Piazza Collicola 10 (☎0743.220.052, fax 0743.221.244). Slightly fancier 18-room three-star: another fine Upper Town location, by the church of San Domenico. ④.

Nuovo Clitunno, Piazza Sordini 6 (☎0743.223.340, fax 0743.222.663). The best-value mid-range three-star in the Upper Town, just west of Piazza della Libertà. There's an L80,000 price differential among its 35 rooms, the cheapest of which are without private bathrooms. ④.

Paradiso, Monteluco 19 (☎0743.223.427, fax 0743.223.082). A faded modern three-star with 21 rooms, in the wooded hills above Spoleto – fine if you don't fancy in-town options or their alternatives on the main road to Terni. It's a long twisting drive up here, however, so not that convenient for sightseeing. ⑤.

Gattapone, Via del Ponte (☎0743.223.447, fax 0743.223.448). Umbrian hotels do not come much better than this. Splash out to enjoy views over the gorge and Ponte delle Torri in one of central Italy's nicest and most intimate four-star hotels. ⑧.

Dei Duchi, Viale G. Matteotti (☎0473.44.541, fax 0743.44.543). The upmarket four-star alternative to the *Gattapone*: nowhere near as nice (though rooms are at times a touch cheaper), but 49 comfortable modern rooms just off Piazza della Libertà. ⑨.

Private rooms

Iole Tommassoni, Via Cavallotti 9 (☎0743.220.441). One single and 2 doubles with bathrooms. Weekly rates of around L350,000 are available. ②.

Istituto Bambino Gesù, Via Monterone 4 (☎0743.40.232). Nine single and 6 double rooms, all with bathrooms, at a religious institution that's a simple hotel in all but name. ①–③.

La Tirallesca, Via Focaroli (☎0743.47.407). Five doubles, all with private bathrooms. Weekly rates (L400,000–550,000) are available. ②.

Campsite

Camping Monteluco (☎ & fax 0743.220.358). The closest campsite to town, just behind the church of San Pietro; very pleasant but tiny (just 35 pitches). Open April–Sept.

The Lower Town

Spoleto's art-festival credentials are immediately established by a grotesque monumental sculpture by Alexander Calder outside the train station. A relic of the 1962 festival, it serves as a gateway to the Lower Town, a quarter much rebuilt after Allies-inflicted bomb damage in the last war. The area does offer a trio of outstanding Romanesque churches, however, as well as a handful of Roman fragments. If these don't appeal, catch the city bus or take a taxi from the station to Piazza della Libertà, heart of the old town, tempting from this vantage with its skyline of spires and tiled roofs and splashes of craggy countryside; the fifteen-minute walk is enjoyable too, once beyond the concrete of Viale Trento e Trieste. Head up Corso Garibaldi from Piazza Garibaldi for the most direct approach on foot.

San Salvatore and San Ponziano

One of Italy's oldest churches, **San Salvatore** lies on the edge of the Lower Town, half-hidden in the cemetery, whose glimpse of the Italian way of death provides a faintly bizarre attraction in itself. Little has changed in the church since it was built by monks from the eastern Mediterranean in the fourth or fifth century, on a site probably chosen for its proximity to Christian and Neolithic catacombs. Most of the decoration and building materials are Roman. Conceived when the only models for religious buildings were Roman temples, the end result has a distinctly pagan feel, its dusty, gloomy interior (daily: May–Aug 7am–7pm; March–April & Sept–Oct 7am–6pm; Nov–Feb 7am–5pm; free) evoking an almost eerie antiquity, an atmosphere best enjoyed at dusk. The walls are bare, the floors covered in fallen stone, the crumbling Corinthian columns are wedged awkwardly alongside one another and the arches in the nave have been filled in to prevent total collapse. The apse, ringed round with Roman friezes and capitals, is a later addition that gives the church's upper half a crowded and lopsided appearance.

By contrast with San Salvatore's shattered facade, just a couple of minutes away is twelfth-century **San Ponziano**, dedicated to Spoleto's patron saint, with a Romanesque frontage which promises much but delivers little inside. A walk past and admiring glance are all the place merits, unless you can tempt the enthusiastic and voluble caretaker out of his house (on the left) to show you the **tenth-century crypt**, a fascinating structure of odd, triangular columns believed to be *metae* (turning posts) from a Roman *circo* (race-track), backed by well-preserved patches of Byzantine fresco.

San Gregorio and the Anfiteatro Romano

Across the river in Piazza Garibaldi, **San Gregorio** (summer Mon–Sat 7.30am–6.30pm; winter same days 7.30am–5.30pm; closed Sun 12.30–2.30pm; free) dates from 1069 at

THE FESTIVAL DEI DUE MONDI

Firmly established as Italy's leading international arts festival, the **Festival dei Due Mondi** – the Festival of the Two Worlds – came to Spoleto in 1958 when composer Giancarlo Menotti and his advisers chose the town over thirty other contenders on account of its small venues, outstanding scenery and an artistic, historical and cultural heritage almost without equal.

Menotti's original dream was to combine the best of young Italian and American talent, hence the "Two Worlds" tag, an idea which eventually saw the cloning of a sister festival in Charleston, South Carolina. Melbourne in Australia also came on board, albeit in a half-hearted way, to make it an unofficial Festival of the Three Worlds.

Spoleto has a problem, however – namely, what happens when its guru is gone. Menotti is now in his mid-eighties, though the advancing years have done little to mellow his autocratic style. Relations between Spoleto's town authorities and Menotti have also recently become strained, the maestro's avowedly independent approach having led the council to withhold many of the funds they have traditionally ploughed into the festival. Matters weren't helped when Menotti decided to find a niche for his adopted son, Francis ("Chip"), suggesting he should serve as his successor at the head of both festivals, thus compounding his musical and managerial autocracy with dynastic grandeur. Chip is now president of the Spoleto festival, and Menotti its artistic director. It's perhaps no coincidence that several of Menotti's works at recent festivals have been greeted by whistles, catcalls and walkouts.

The festival is staged annually for around **three weeks** from late June, encompassing music, dance and theatre, performed by top Italian and international companies. Tickets for the premier events can be expensive and elusive, but the festival generates an Edinburgh-type fringe – one of the few Italian festivals to do so – and the organizers have recently looked to more avant-garde acts to recover the edge of the festival's early days, so count on seeing some wacky shows on the programme. Cultural ripples continue to spread outside the main season: organ and classical music recitals in local churches precede the festival from April to June, and an opera season – mixing classics and the weird and wonderful – runs from August to September.

Tickets and information are issued from the **tourist office** in Piazza della Libertà and the **festival box office** at Piazza del Duomo 8–9 (☎0743.28.120 or 167.565.600; *www.spoletofestival.net*); tickets can also be obtained from travel agents in many larger Italian cities – prices range from L15,000 to L250,000. Details of future line-ups are available from the Festival Information Office (☎0743.40.396) or the Festival Press Office (☎0743.222.611 or 0743.223.041). All the larger Italian newspapers print reviews and timetables during and in the run-up to the festival.

Be warned that the festival attracts big crowds and hiked-up hotel and restaurant prices. If at all possible, it's best to book **rooms** well ahead.

the latest, but parts look as if they were built yesterday, a result of restoration after years of fire, flood and earthquake damage. Its narrow, porticoed **facade** incorporates a patchwork of fragments filched from Roman remains. The pragmatic mix of materials is most obvious in the tower, its lower half built of massive Roman blocks, the upper of more refined fifteenth-century workmanship. The similarly patchworked portico was a sixteenth-century afterthought, added when the church was heightened to imitate the duomo in the Upper Town. The **interior** commands most interest, its walls stripped back to their Romanesque state, with substantial frescoes interrupted by a series of intimidating stone confessionals. The frescoes are local fourteenth-century efforts, the best of them in the presbytery, which is raised several metres above the nave, allowing for a **crypt** supported by dozens of tiny, mismatched pillars.

Tradition has it that somewhere under the church are the bones of ten thousand Christian martyrs killed by the Romans in the amphitheatre close by; the chapel alongside the portico, the Cappella degli Innocenti, is the favoured candidate for their resting place. Parts of the **amphitheatre** itself are still visible in the barracks up the road, on Via dell'Anfiteatro. No one seems to mind if you walk straight into the complex, which was formerly a monastery; bear right from the main gateway for the most substantial remains. When the Romans passed on, the huge arena was cannibalized for its stone, first by Totila and then by Cardinal Albornoz for the castle in the Upper Town. What remained was adapted as a medieval shopping arcade, and later bricked up in the courtyard you see today.

The ever-ingenious Romans constructed special gutters to drain blood from the arena into the Tessino river, which ran crimson as a result. The liberal flow of Christian blood is said to have inspired the name for the Roman bridge under nearby Piazza Garibaldi – the **Ponte Sanguinaria**. It formed part of the improvements to the Via Flaminia ordered by the Emperor Augustus, remaining in use until the fourteenth century: it was rediscovered in 1817. Much remains intact below the piazza, and travel guides unfailingly suggest you can see its surprisingly substantial remains by climbing down the steps from the piazza, but it has actually been shut for years. Spoleto's council has tried to open the site on a regular basis (daily 10am–1pm & 3–5pm), though don't be surprised to find that all you can see is a glimpse of a single arch through closed railings.

The Upper Town

There's really no single, central piazza in Spoleto, but the place to head first in the Upper Town is **Piazza della Libertà**, terminus for a local and inter-town bus service and home to the large tourist office and post office. Orientation is difficult in the town's jumble of levels and twisting, narrow streets around, though distances are short and everything worthwhile is a short walk from the square. Shops, banks and services are mostly concentrated in **Corso Mazzini**, which runs north from Piazza della Libertà (the main cluster of banks is in Piazza Mentana at its northern end), and in **Corso Garibaldi**, which drops down to Piazza Garibaldi. Corso Mazzini is the scene of a rumbustious *passeggiata*, Sunday's walk being a particularly fine spectacle, but for the day-to-day social heart of the town you need to make for **Piazza del Mercato**, site of the old Roman forum.

Piazza della Libertà

For an introduction to Spoleto's much-touted Roman heritage, you only have to cross Piazza della Libertà from the tourist office. Here you can look through the railings at the much-restored first-century **Roman theatre**, excavated in 1891 and now used for festival and other performances throughout the summer. Its past includes a grisly episode in 1319 when four hundred Guelph supporters were rounded up by the Spoletans and dumped on the stage with their throats cut; the corpses were then pushed into a pile and burnt. Today it's a trifle overshadowed by the gaudily painted buildings on all sides. The worst of these offenders, the church and convent of Sant'Agata, absorbed much of the stage area in the Middle Ages, the theatre having been damaged and half-buried over the centuries by landslips.

The conventual buildings now house a restoration centre and modest **Museo Archeologico** (Mon–Sat 9am–7pm; Sun 9am–1pm; L4000), entered a few metres down nearby Via Sant'Agata beyond the attractive little medieval loggia on the street's left. The ticket includes admission to the **theatre**, which is worth wandering around in for a couple of minutes, the extraordinary vaulted tunnel beneath the tiered seats being particularly interesting. You then climb the steps to the first-floor museum, which opens with two small rooms whose displays include a superb shield, rings and other fragments from a Bronze Age tomb discovered in Piazza d'Armi during the building of Spoleto's municipal swimming pool. Next door to the right is a longer room, graced with a fine fresco of the *Last Supper* and a well-presented gallery of Roman portrait busts and miscellaneous statuary. A small annexe at the end is devoted to the remarkable **Lex Spoletina**, a pair of tawny-brown Roman stone inscriptions which forbade the chopping down of trees in the sacred woods of Monteluco. The translation, given below, states that cutting of wood was only allowed on a single day of sacrifice a year, the penalty for transgressors being the gift of an ox to Jove, to whom the woods were dedicated.

The injunction must have worked, since the forests, home to second-century hermits and later to saints Francis and Bernardino, are still there, cloaking the hills above the castle gorge and stretching unbroken some 8km east of the town. If you want to **roam through the woods**, take bus #9 from Piazza della Libertà or, if you're feeling extremely strong, walk from the Ponte delle Torri; **maps** of the route are available from the tourist office. The drive is long and winding, with intermittent views and a somewhat tatty collection of bars at the top: walk a little, however, and you're soon away from civilization.

Piazza del Mercato

The **Arco di Druso**, straddling the entrance to the Piazza del Mercato – the old forum – is the only one of innumerable arches scattered around town not embedded in a wall. It was raised in 23 AD by the Spoletan senate to commemorate victories in Germany by Drusus, son of Tiberius and heir to the empire until his early death, courtesy of Caligula. The **walls** hereabouts, and in Via dei Felici, are the city's oldest, built in the sixth century BC by the mysterious Umbrians.

To the right of the arch is what's described as a Roman **temple and shop**, though you'll need a vivid imagination to see it as anything other than a ditch. However, it's well worth popping into the church of **Sant'Ansano** (daily: summer 7.30am–noon & 3–6.30pm; winter 7.30am–noon & 3–5.30pm; free), to the right of the arch, for the **crypt of St Isaac**, entered by the glass door on the left of the high altar (where fragments of the temple have been uncovered). As well as containing more persuasive chunks of the temple than lie outside, the crude stone walls are decorated with recently restored frescoes that may date from the sixth century, a time when the spot was home to refugee Christian monks. The main structure dates from the twelfth century.

Nowhere do you get a better sense of Spoleto's market-town roots than in the homely **Piazza del Mercato**, which again is often host to temporary festival sculptures. In the square, old women wash fruit and vegetables in the striking 1746 fountain (its crown embellished with an attractive clock), the men drink in the bars and swap stall-holders' gossip, and tourists make barely a dent in the overall proceedings. Note the coat of arms atop the fountain monument, built by Carlo Maderno in 1626 for Pope Urban VIII: the left-hand crest features three bees, symbols of the Barberini, the Roman family from which Urban hailed. The *alimentari* on all sides of the square are a cornucopia of picnic provisions, with a bias towards truffles, oils and sticky liqueurs. Spoleto is at the heart of renowned **olive oil** country, the oils of its top producer, Monini, used in kitchens across Italy. These can be bought just about anywhere, but for an excellent selection of **local wines** and other rarer foodstuffs visit the little shop immediately on the left as you exit the square to the north. Its wines include Montefalco's excellent Sagrantino Passito (see p.516), together with truffle paste, dried *porcini* mushrooms and other more rarified products. Another good shop, at the opposite end of the square, is the old-fashioned Salumeria Padrichelli, Via Arco del Druso 22. The piazza's little open **market** runs from Monday to Saturday, 8.30am to 1pm, but there's almost more going on late in the evening when the outdoor tables of the main bar on the western side of the square are the best place for in-town summer drinking.

The Duomo

It's a short walk from Piazza del Mercato to the **Duomo**, or Santa Maria Assunta (daily: March–Oct 8am–1pm & 3–6.30pm; Nov–Feb 8am–1pm & 3–5.30pm; free), whose restrained and elegant facade is one of the loveliest in Umbria. The careful balance of Romanesque and Renaissance elements is framed by a gently sloping piazza and hanging gardens, with the broad background of sky and open countryside setting the seal on the beautifully unified whole. The lovely carving-swathed **portico**, an obvious addition, dates from 1491 and is flanked by two little external pulpits, one of which was used by the wandering St Bernardino of Siena to preach to the notoriously wayward Spoletans.

The building was consecrated in 1198, having been commissioned by Pope Innocent III to replace a seventh-century church flattened by Barbarossa. The twelfth-century **campanile** (with fifteenth- and sixteenth-century additions) borrowed much of its stone from Roman ruins, a hotchpotch technique continued in the rest of the building. Architectural details unusual in Italy add interest for the technically minded, most notably the **flying buttresses** tucked out of sight on the side walls – climb to Piazza F. Campello to the right for the best view. Strange, too, are the eight rose windows, clustered around a restored thirteenth-century mosaic of *Christ, the Virgin and St John*.

Less successful transformations were commissioned for the **interior**, where Pope Urban VIII's architect, Luigi Arrigucci, applied great dollops of Baroque midway through the seventeenth century. On the first altar on the left, behind glass, stands a brightly restored Crucifix (1187) by Alberto Sotio, the earliest documented Umbrian painter. Walking across to the right-hand side of the church, look in on the **Cappella Eroli** (1497), named after the Spoletan Bishop Costantino Eroli, located off the beginning of the right nave: it's adorned by Pinturicchio's faded but beautifully lyrical *Madonna and Child with the Baptist and St Stephen*, with a depiction of Lago Trasimeno in the background. In the adjoining and larger **Cappella dell'Assunta** (or Eroli) to its right are cruder but nonetheless striking frescoes by the Sicilian Jacopo Santori: that on the left wall shows another Eroli bishop, Francesco, who commissioned the chapel at the beginning of the sixteenth century, kneeling before a separate inset painting of the *Madonna*. The wall to its right has frescoes of saints *Michael the Archangel* (with sword) and *Lucy*, a popular Spoletan saint (see "Museo Diocesano" below): the wall to *its* right is adorned with the Eroli family shields.

Back across the church, do not miss the **Cappella delle Reliquie**, entered at the top of the left aisle. Restored in 1993, it features impressive intarsia work, vivid painted panels which depict characters from the Old Testament, and some beautifully frescoed ceiling vaults. The vaults and panels are the work of Francesco Nardini, an otherwise little-known sixteenth-century painter. On the right is an outstanding fourteenth-century polychrome wooden statue of the *Madonna and Child*, and to its right, behind glass, a fragmentary **letter** clasped in a gaudy blue-columned frame. The letter, in Latin, was written by St Francis to Fra' Leone, one of the saint's earliest and most besotted followers (he hoarded virtually every scrap and relic associated with Francis). It is one of only two letters written by the saint to have survived and was written after Francis received the stigmata at La Verna (see p.424), by which time he was virtually blind – hence the shaky handwriting. It salutes Leone and wishes him peace (the word *pacem* is clearly visible near the beginning), urging him to follow his own conscience in matters of faith rather than constantly coming to Francis for advice. It was originally kept in a Spoletan church, but vanished for centuries after its first publication in 1623, mysteriously reappearing in the Vatican archives during the reign of Pope Leo XIII. It was restored to the city in 1904.

All other works of art in the cathedral, however, are eclipsed by the building's original **marble floor**, and by magnificent **frescoes** on the *Life of the Virgin*, painted in 1467 by Filippo Lippi and his assistants Fra' Diamanti and Pier Matteo. The newly restored cycle fills the domed apse, starting from the left wall with the *Annunciation* and *The Dormition of the Virgin*, the latter with portraits of the three painters to the right: Lippi is the figure with the white monk's habit over a black tunic; the figures to either side are his assistants. The cycle concludes with the *Nativity* (mostly by Matteo and Diamanti), while above spreads the most glittering scene of all, the *Coronation of the Virgin*. Note the columns and classical motifs separating the panels, many of which Lippi copied directly from old buildings around Spoleto, notably the church of San Salvatore in the Lower Town.

Lippi died shortly after the cycle's completion, the rumour being that he was poisoned for seducing the daughter of a local noble family. The Spoletan cathedral authorities, not too bothered by such moral laxity, were delighted to have someone famous to put in their cathedral, being, as Vasari put it, "poorly provided with . . . distinguished men". Thus they refused to send the dead artist back to Lorenzo de' Medici, his patron, who had loaned Filippo to Spoleto, reputedly to stop his Florentine philandering. Interred in a **tomb** designed by his son Filippino Lippi, the corpse disappeared during restoration two centuries later, according to local legend spirited away by descendants of the compromised girl – a sort of vendetta beyond the grave. The empty tomb is on the left wall of the right transept.

Minor titbits elsewhere in the cathedral include a bronze of Urban VIII by Bernini, too high above the main door to get a good look at, and an icon from Constantinople presented by Barbarossa in 1185 to make amends for having wrecked the town thirty years earlier: it's housed in the chapel below the organ loft to the rear and right of the high altar. If you manage to chat up the sacristan, you might also, if lucky, be able to see the ninth-century **crypt** of San Primiano, part of the earlier church on the site destroyed by Barbarossa.

Sant'Eufemia

The town's most celebrated **church** is twelfth-century **Sant'Eufemia** (daily: summer 10am–12.30pm & 3.30–7pm; winter 10am–12.30pm & 2.30–6pm; L3000, or L5000 with Museo Diocesano), above and to the left of the piazza in Via Aurelio Saffi. You'll have seen the outside of the apse if you walked down the steps to the square, but the entrance is easily missed, as the church lies inside a courtyard complex off the street (look out for yellow signs on the wall outside).

The church was built in honour of a local bishop, St Giovanni, martyred by the Goths and reputedly buried here in 980, on a site within both the precincts of the old Benedictine monastery and the archbishop's palace. Excavations have revealed that it also lies over the Lombards' eighth-century ducal palace, and Roman remains have been found, too. Good use was obviously made of materials from these previous buildings, one of the mismatched columns being carved with distinctive Lombard motifs (that separating the first and second arches on the right). Many of the mismatched capitals, too, are also clearly from an earlier building. The church is also unique in Umbria for its *matroneum*, a high-arched gallery above the aisles which served the purpose of segregating the women of the congregation (reached from a tiny door at the beginning of the left aisle).

Like San Salvatore in the Lower Town, Sant'Eufemia is redolent with age and dank solemnity, its walls bare but for the odd patch of fresco, notably another *St Lucy* (something of a hit with Spoletans), complete with eyes in a bowl (see next page); it adorns the second column on the right. The only other frills are a stone chair and simple but stunning **altar**, both brought from the duomo in the thirteenth century. Recently, exhibitions of modern art have begun to be installed in Sant'Eufemia, and you now have to pay to enter the church, the only saving grace being that proceeds go to worthy causes.

Museo Diocesano

An excellent museum occupies the same courtyard as Sant'Eufemia, the **Museo Diocesano d'Arte Sacra** (daily: summer 10am–12.30pm & 3.30–7pm; winter 10am–12.30pm & 2.30–6pm; L4000, or L5000 with Sant'Eufemia; note that the museum occasionally closes without warning – contact the tourist office or call ☎0743.231.041 for current details), reached through the arch and up the stairs to the left of Sant'Eufemia's facade. Its rooms trace faith and history in the Spoletan diocese from Roman times to the nineteenth century, and contain a wealth of fascinating paintings and other artefacts culled from churches as far afield as the Val Castoriana in the mountains to the east. Most of these works – many removed after the 1979 earthquake which ravaged the Valnerina – are theoretically due to be returned to their respective churches, though the prevailing view is that they have been in Spoleto for so long that they will probably remain in the museum indefinitely.

The big entrance room augurs well, its walls covered in 113 colourful **portraits** of the various bishops and archbishops (and two popes) connected with the Spoletan diocese over the years. The wooden ceiling, as in many of the rooms which follow, is also outstanding. **Room 1** has some of the most interesting of the museum's pictures, beginning with three paintings on the wall to your left as you enter. The first, a thirteenth-century triptych of the *Madonna and Child* juxtaposes three scenes from the *Life of Christ* with a panel (bottom left) showing St Martin dividing his cloak and giving one half to a beggar (later revealed to be Christ). The strange *Madonna and Child* to its right shows the Child in the brown habit and triple-knotted belt of the Franciscans. The third work on this wall, a thirteenth-century dossal, was once used as the rear wall of a confessional, hence its faded appearance and the clear evidence of it having been sawn into pieces at some point.

Moving to the next wall, the first of three paintings is a triptych with St Lucy depicted to the right of the central panel's *Crucifixion*. The saint, a fourth-century martyr from Syracuse in Sicily, was much venerated in Spoleto and the Valnerina and is invariably depicted holding a dish containing a pair of eyes. She was killed for refusing to marry a high-ranking pagan Roman magistrate, the spurned official having her dragged behind two oxen and then boiled alive – on hearing that the magistrate had been captivated by the beauty of her eyes, Lucy is reputed to have torn them out and sent them to her tormentor (hence the eye motif in paintings of her). Lucy appears again in the next painting, also a triptych. Three episodes from Lucy's life make up the predella: giving to the poor; her denuniciation in front of the governor of Syracuse; and her ordeal by oxen. The third painting on this wall, a triptych with saints Sebastian and Catherine of Alexandria, is attributed to the same painter as the previous work, Bartolomeo da Miranda, active locally in the mid-fifteenth century. Sebastian was often invoked against plague, this painting having probably been a votive offering during an epidemic, a theory reinforced by the green of the Virgin's cloak (as opposed to the more usual blue). The colour is symbolic of rebirth and new life, as well as being the colour associated with Hope, one of the three Theological Virtues.

In **room 2** the first painting on the left wall is the *Adoration of the Child* by the Sienese Mannerist **Domenico Beccafumi.** A door in the room leads to a side room with a loom and modest displays on Spoleto's weaving and textile traditions. To the right of the door is a vast painting, bowed with age, of the *Assumption*, a popular theme with Spoletan artists as the town's cathedral is dedicated to the Assumption of the Virgin. To the right, on the next wall, is a *Madonna and Child with SS. Sebastian and Leonard.* St Sebastian, unusually, is shown holding a clutch of arrows, as opposed to being shot through with them, an allusion to the fact that he recovered from his ordeal by archery (he was martyred by being pummelled to death). St Leonard, on the other hand, is only rarely portrayed in central Italian art. Little is known of this sixth-century figure, other than that his faith persuaded King Clovis to grant him the right to release any prisoner he met. As a result he is the patron saint of prisoners, who would traditionally have made a votive offering of a shackle to the saint on their release – which is why he is shown in this painting holding a vast leg iron.

Room 3 has a series of contrasting wooden statues of the Madonna and Child, as well as an unusual statue of Christ with movable arms: like the similar statue in Spello's Pinacoteca it was used in Easter Week ceremonies, when the arms were extended during processions on Good Friday to mark the Crucifixion: on Easter Sunday the arms were lowered during ceremonies to celebrate the Resurrection. **Room 4** has two excellent polyptychs by members of the Sparapane family, a leading local fifteenth-century dynasty of painters (facing each other on opposite walls), though both are inferior to the exquisite smaller *Madonna and Child* on the table to the left, an anonymous Florentine work. Above are detached frescoes, notably a St Michael to the right, the Devil just visible at the bottom trying to tilt the scales in which Michael is weighing the souls of sinners and the saved.

Room 5 features the gallery's single greatest painting, a sublime freestanding *Madonna and Child with SS. Montano and Bartholomew* (1485) by **Filippino Lippi**. It's strange enough that Lippi, a Florentine, should have painted in Umbria, and stranger still that the painting should have been commissioned for Todiano, a now almost deserted village lost in the depths of the Valnerina (see p.542). The theory is that it was commissioned by a merchant who left the village and grew wealthy as a result of trade. Bartholomew and Montano are Todiano's patron saints, the latter an obscure saint best known for having tamed a bear and commanded it to take the place of an ox it had devoured. The little scene in the predella shows the bear alongside an ox pulling the plough of the deceased ox's owner. The parallel predella scene to the right shows St Bartholomew with his skin slung over his shoulder (the saint was martyred by being flayed alive). Another good freestanding Tuscan work, Neri di Bicci's *Madonna della Neve* (1464), stands midway down the room on the right. It's an excellent example of a relatively common theme, the *neve* (snow) referring to the miraculous fall of snow in August in Rome which is traditionally said to have marked out the site of the city's ancient Basilica di Santa Maria Maggiore. The snow can seen in the painting falling from the Virgin's cloak, the outline of a basilica and high altar clearly visible below. Its presence in Spoleto is explained by the strong medieval trading links between Spoleto and Rome.

On the room's left wall be sure to look for the two groups of decorated **wooden tiles**, a series of ex-votos painted with often amusing cartoon-like depictions of sick-bed scenes and escapes from perilous (and not so perilous) episodes for which the tiles give thanks. The left-hand group shows women being gored by bulls and a man hanging upside down from a tree and losing his hat, while the right group's highlights are a depiction of a precipitous fall from a hayrick (the Virgin, as in other tiles, looks down from a cloud in the top left) and a cart falling from a bridge and hurling its inhabitants into a river.

The Pinacoteca

Spoleto's **Pinacoteca** is stuck away in the farthest reaches of the Palazzo del Municipio, usually accessed off the east side of Piazza del Mercato on Via del Municipio (10am–1pm & 3–6pm; closed Mon). However, restoration work may mean you have to enter by climbing the stairs of the council offices themselves, signed off Via Aurelio Saffi almost opposite the courtyard entrance to Sant'Eufemia. The L5000 ticket for the gallery also gives entry to the remains of a Roman house in nearby Via Visiale (same hours; usually seen with the gallery's guide), the missable Galleria Comunale d'Arte Moderna on Corso Mazzini and, in theory (it's often closed), the chapel of SS. Giovanni e Paolo (see p.537).

After buying your ticket from a very officious office to the right of the Via del Municipio entrance, you then have to wait for someone to show you around the gallery on the upper floor. The process may change when the collection is moved to the Rocca; timing of the move depends on completion of the castle's restoration. The gallery's three main rooms are sumptuously decorated (hence the guide), and worth seeing in their own right. The highlights of **Room 1** are a triptych of the *Madonna delle Grazie* by Nicolò Alunno; a polyptych from the abbey of Sant'Eutizio (with its central panel missing) by

Nicola of Siena; a beautifully framed *Madonna and Child* by Antonello da Saliba, the Sicilian nephew of the more famous Antonello da Messina; and a fifteenth-century *Nativity* by Giacomo di Giovannofrio. **Room 2** features several impressive wooden Crucifixes, detached frescoes by Lo Spagna and two elongated panels depicting various saints, the last distinguished by the small collection of bones and relics along the top of each panel. The third principal room contains mostly forgettable seventeenth-century paintings and artefacts.

The Rocca

If you do nothing else in Spoleto, take the short walk out to the Ponte delle Torri, the town's picture-postcard favourite. It's best taken in as part of a circular walk around the base of the Rocca, or on the longer trek to San Pietro (see below). The **Rocca** itself is a perfectly endowed castle, with an impressive tally of towers, neatly delineated crenellations and sheer walls. It was built as one of a chain of fortresses with which the tireless Cardinal Albornoz tried to re-establish Church authority in central Italy in the years preceding the Great Schism. Later it became part fortress, part holiday home, with several popes staying over, most notably Julius II, sometimes accompanied by Michelangelo. The fort's main latter-day function has been as a high-security prison, testimony to the skill of its medieval builders; Slavic and Italian political prisoners were held here during the war, while more recent inmates included members of the Red Brigades and Pope John Paul II's would-be assassin, Ali Agca. Since its demise as a prison, a decade of restoration has kept the Rocca closed, partly as a result of the scale of the operation, partly through sheer mismanagement. Some £4 million of EU money has been sunk in the project, a condition of the funding (and subsequent grants) being that it should have been open to the public by 1998, when, among other things, a public park and National Museum of the Duchy of Spoleto were due to open (but didn't). When the builders do move out the entrance will be from Piazza F. Campello at the top of Via Aurelio Saffi, just to the left of the large fountain, whose massive stone face marks the end of a Roman and medieval aqueduct.

Highlights of the **interior** are the Camera Pinta within one of the main towers, which was almost entirely frescoed between 1392 and 1416 by local painters with a variety of courtly scenes; notice in particular the scene on the right wall, which depicts the town's Roman ampitheatre before it was completely ransacked of stone and built over. Frescoes from a variety of later epochs adorn many other parts of the complex, most notably the loggia of the main courtyard, the Cortile d'Onore. Rooms facing onto this courtyard on the ground and first floor contain the lion's share of the museum's collection, which as well as works transferred here from elsewhere also includes a series of frescoes detached from the walls of San Paolo inter Vineas (see below).

The Ponte delle Torri

Within minutes of leaving the shady gardens of Piazza F. Campello you suddenly find yourself in open countryside, with a dramatic view across the Tessino gorge and south to the mountains of Castelmonte. There's an informal little bar, often blaring crackly opera favourites from tinny speakers, about 100m before the Ponte to help you enjoy the view.

This is also a good point to look down on a fine stretch of the town's **walls** and the **Ponte delle Torri**, an astonishing piece of medieval engineering with a 240-metre span supported by ten vast arches, the most central ones some 76 metres high. The site is a notorious lovers' leap. Probably designed by the Gubbian architect Gattapone – the man responsible for Gubbio's Palazzo dei Consoli – it was planned initially as an aqueduct to bring water from Monteluco, replacing a Roman causeway whose design Gattapone borrowed and enlarged upon. In time it became part of the town's defences, providing an escape from the castle when Spoleto was under siege. The remains of what used to be a covered passageway connecting the two are still visible straggling down the hillside. It's possible to walk across the bridge, a highly recommended stroll, with obvious paths on the other side (wind up the stone steps to the right) leading left into lovely ilex woods with superb belvederes overlooking the bridge and gorge. Follow the level path for a kilometre or so and you bend round an arm of the gorge to emerge in peaceful olive groves.

San Pietro and San Paolo inter Vineas

If the idea of a walk doesn't appeal, you can easily double back to town from here on the circular Via della Rocca. Views back to the bridge are best on this loop, and you could scramble part of the way down into the gorge for time out from the crowds. Come here in the evening in June and July and the area is filled with thousands of fire-flies.

Taking the right fork on the far side of the bridge leads in a couple of kilometres to the church of **San Pietro** – a pleasant, shaded walk that again offers good glimpses of Spoleto (it's on tarmac, however, and without pavements, so watch out for traffic). The church's facade is visible from the bridge, and as you draw close reveals a series of twelfth-century **sculptures** that – with Maitani's bas-reliefs in Orvieto – constitute the finest Romanesque carving in Umbria. Partly Lombard in their inspiration, they draw variously on the Gospels and medieval legend for their complicated narrative and symbolic purpose. Much of the allegory is elusive, but reasonably self-explanatory panels include a *Wolf Disguised as a Friar* before a fleeing ram – a dig at dodgy monastic morals – and, particularly juicy, the *Death of a Sinner* (left series, second from the top). Here the Archangel Michael abandons the sinner to a couple of demons who bind and torture the unfortunate before bringing in the burning oil to finish him off. Compare this with the panel above, the *Death of a Just Man*, where St Peter frees the man of his chains while Michael holds his soul in his scales; the Devil, lashed by the keys of St Peter, tries to tip the scales in his favour and holds a scroll that laments *doleo quia ante erat meus* ("I mourn because he was mine before").

Best combined with a San Pietro excursion is a visit to the least visited of all Spoleto's churches, **San Paolo inter Vineas**, stranded south of the town centre off Viale Giacomo Matteotti. Mentioned as early as the sixth century by St Gregory the Great, it was rebuilt in the tenth century and has now been restored to its beautifully simple twelfth-century state. It preserves frescoes of the *Creation* and *Prophets* painted before the consecration of the present structure, which makes them among the oldest in the region: some are destined for the museum in the Rocca. If the church is shut ring for admission at the old people's home next door (daily 9am–2pm).

San Domenico to San Nicolò

Among Spoleto's lesser churches, the massive monastic **San Domenico**, on the town's western margins, warrants a diversion for its colourful pink and white marble banding. Inside – in an interior of stripped-down Baroque – there are some fragments of fresco fossilized in new yellow plaster, the outstanding picture being a large, early fifteenth-century fresco on the southern right-hand wall, *The Triumph of St Thomas Aquinas*. At the back of the church to the right of the presbytery is a small room filled with crude but eye-catching early frescoes; the Cappella dei Montevecchio in the left transept enshrines the umpteenth Nail of the Cross.

Close by in Via Filitteria is the tiny chapel of **SS. Giovanni e Paolo**, consecrated in 1174, which has an impressive thirteenth-century fresco outside, and has an interior covered in superb **frescoes** dating from the twelfth century onwards (daily 10am–1pm & 3–5pm; combined ticket – see p.535).

During even half-hearted wandering you'll probably come across **San Nicolò**, a couple of minutes north of SS. Giovanni e Paolo, impressively Gothic from the outside, but long deconsecrated and now a setting for third-rate exhibitions and jumble sales. In previous incarnations it was also a truffle market and workshop for repairing steam engines. Alongside is what must have been a beautiful **cloister**, now restored to a bare semblance of its original state.

Eating and drinking

As you'd expect from its festival and cultural aspirations, Spoleto is a town that takes its food pretty seriously. **Restaurants** below are in ascending order of price. For a **picnic**, stock up at the market and food shops in the Piazza del Mercato. The best **bar** in town is the *Vincenzo*, on Corso Mazzini – you'll see the big names there during the festival – but for late evenings out of doors make for the bar in Piazza del Mercato. On Sunday, late in the afternoon, the region's most extraordinary *passeggiata* takes place from the bar in Piazza della Libertà, surging down Corso Mazzini.

Restaurants

Del Mercato, Piazza del Mercato (☎0743.45.325). One of a couple of very old-fashioned and cheap eating places on the square, both catering mainly to Spoleto's workmen and market traders. L15,000. Closed Thurs.

Al Druso, Via Arco del Druso 25 (☎0743.221695). Busy trattoria-pizzeria downstairs from the hotel. Around L25,000 for meals; pizzas for much less. Closed Mon.

La Barcaccia, Piazza Fratelli Bandiera, off Via Fontesecca (☎0743.221.171). Located in a nook behind the Piazza del Mercato fountain, this little trattoria does a roaring trade during the festival, when it stays open all day to feed the hungry musicians. Closed Tues.

Il Panciolle, Largo Muzio Clemente-Via del Duomo 3 (☎0743.45.677). Has a great outside terrace at the back and remains an excellent choice for a reliable and reasonably priced, if never over-exciting, meal of Umbrian specialities like *strangozzi* and fire-grilled meats. Also known for its selection of cheeses. From L30,000. Closed Wed.

Pecchiarda, Vicolo San Giovanni 1, between Via Posterna and San Gregorio Maggiore (☎0743.221.009). A friendly, family-run atmosphere, outdoor summer pergola and fair prices have made this one of the town's most popular little *trattorie*. House red is a cheap and cheerful Sangiovese made by the owner. Closed Thurs except in summer.

Pentagramma, Via Martani 4 (☎0743.223.141). Owned by relatives of *Sabatini*'s chef-patron, this medieval vaulted dining room with its out-of-place red-chequered tablecloths specializes in traditional Spoletan staples. Middle to upper price bracket, with a relaxed and rather un-Italian bistro atmosphere. Located immediately off Piazza della Libertà. L40,000. Closed Mon.

Apollinare, Via Sant'Agata 14 (☎0743.223.256). Pushes *Sabatini* for the title of Spoleto's best Upper Town restaurant. The blue and gold upholstery is initially off-putting, but the medieval setting is good and the welcome friendly: the menu is tiny, and the *menù degustazione* excellent value. Don't miss the sublime *caramello* starter – a cheese and truffle delight. L50,000 up. Closed Tues.

Sabatini, Corso Mazzini 54 (☎0743.221.831) Best-known top choice in the Upper Town, though the *Apollinare* perhaps just pips it for quality of cooking; simple elegant interior and small garden for summer eating; interesting, if occasionally over-elaborate variations of local dishes: just avoid cheese risotto, the house speciality. L50,000 and up. Closed Mon.

Il Tartufo, Piazza Garibaldi 24 (☎0743.40.236). Regarded, rightly, as the best restaurant in Spoleto, and particularly renowned for its superlative truffle and Umbrian dishes. Piped music, Lower Town location and high prices work against it, however, though the medieval interior is wonderful; you can eat outdoors in summer, and pick from a couple of *degustazione* menus. L60,000 upwards. Closed Wed.

The Valnerina

The **Valnerina** has a stark, wild sort of beauty, all the more dramatic after the pastoral hill country to the west. The "little valley of the Nera", it constitutes a self-contained area of high mountains, steep wooded valleys, upland villages and vast stretches of barren nothingness. Deserted farms bear witness to a century of continuous emigration, and wolves still roam the summit ridges, half-heartedly protected by a *Parco Regionale*. Few parts of Tuscany or Umbria are so genuine a "forgotten corner".

Access to the heart of the region can be tricky without your own transport but there are six **bus** services daily from Spoleto to Norcia, with stops at most villages along the way. In many cases you'll find a bus waiting at key junctions to connect with more distant towns and villages. **Piedipaterno** and **Borgo Cerreto** are the main intersections, where you can pick up connections south towards Terni. Because access to the Valnerina's lower reaches is more straightforward from the south, that region is dealt with in Chapter Thirteen. However, you may well wish to detour south from Scheggino to include the Valnerina's principal highlight – the tremendous abbey of **San Pietro in Valle** (see p.561).

Spoleto to San Felice

Just before the Norcia road drops to the valley – there are tremendous **views** from this point – and the junction with the main SS209, the beautiful and tortuous **SS395** meets the minor road north to Geppa and Montefiorello, a superb switchback that rejoins the main road at Borgo Cerreto, 15km on. If you have time for a leisurely exploration of the Valnerina, this is perhaps a diversion to go for.

A kilometre south of Piedipaterno and the junction of the SS395 and SS209 lies a turn-off left to the village of **VALLO DI NERA**, a self-contained medieval ensemble perched on a hill, the type of fortified village you'll see all the way up and down the valley. If you're going to visit just one of these before Norcia, Vallo is probably the one to choose, not least because of the minor but beautiful fourteenth-century apse frescoes in the church of **Santa Maria** in the lower part of the village (the house at no. 4 has the key if the building is shut). Later, but no less arresting frescoes (1536) adorn the church of **San Giovanni Battista** at the top of the village (try the priest's house next door for access if the church is shut). They're the work of the Sicilian artist Jacopo Santori (or Siculo), who frescoed one of the Eroli chapels in Spoleto's duomo (see p.532).

A couple of kilometres south on the main road you pass **Castel San Felice**, another picture-perfect fortified village, and a couple of kilometres farther arrive at a turn-off to the more lacklustre **Sant'Anatolia di Narco**, continually inhabited since the eighth century BC. Take the turn left just before the village (visible on the hill above) at the roadside **hotel**, the *Tre Valli*, Via della Stazione 10 (☎0743.613.118; ②), cross the river and look for the small yellow sign 100m or so beyond on the left directing you to the little twelfth-century church of **San Felice**. Its facade bears only the bare essentials – arched doorway, rose window and two pairs of narrow windows. Lumpen red and white marble slabs floor the lovely interior, which is distinguished by a raised sanctuary, an ancient sarcophagus in the crypt, and fifteenth-century frescoes of Christ (in the apse) and the *Adoration of the Magi* (on the left wall of the nave).

From Sant'Anatolia a sensational minor **road**, to Monteleone di Spoleto, strikes southeast, offering great **views** and cutting across the main mountain ridge. You pass the somnolent little villages of Caso and Gavelli (1127m), both looking across a vast tree-covered **gorge** whose scale and appearance make it look like something in South America rather than central Italy. Around a kilometre past Caso look out on the left for the little bell tower of **Santa Cristina** (signed), a Romanesque church with a scattering of frescoes. Off-road **walks** from higher up to nearby summits are straightforward, the best target being **Monte Coscerno** (1685m) – the peak on your left as you drive up – reputedly home to Umbria's two pairs of **golden eagles**. To pick up the track drive about a kilometre past Gavelli, looking out for a yellow-signed lane back to Gavelli on the right. Opposite this, on the left, a stony track kicks off obliquely uphill. Simply follow this clear, broad path-cum-gravel road up and up (a gentle climb), looking out for the one single diversion – an obvious left turn at the pass after about 45 minutes –

THE SURGEONS OF PRECI

Preci was once famous for its thirty families of **surgeons**, who from the twelfth to the mid-eighteenth century handed down their medical knowledge and hearsay from generation to generation. Over the years their patients included such luminaries as Pope Sixtus V, Sultan Mehmed the Conqueror and Elizabeth I of England. Their most notorious sideline was the castration of young boys foolish enough to show operatic potential, a spin-off that developed from the technique of using castration to prevent death from hernia – an area of expertise that the Preci surgeons picked up from their work on pigs.

The methods employed by the surgeons were entirely empirical: if something didn't work and the patient died, another approach was tried the next time. Their only classroom was the operating table, more often than not the kitchen table of the patient concerned. Crude anaesthetic in the shape of a jug of rum or strong wine would be administered, with boiling vinegar used as a post-operative antiseptic. Though some of Preci's surgeons gained a reputation for their skill in extracting kidney stones, most of the doctors were quacks, and when the papacy introduced more stringent licensing of medical practitioners the end of the tradition was swift. Not one of Preci's sawbones was granted a licence.

---

which will take you on to the breezy open ridge to the **summit** (continue right for a few metres on the track that begins to go down and you'll have fine **views** as far as Monte Vettore and the Sibillini). Views from Coscerno, according to extremely improbable local lore, on a clear day embrace the dome of St Peter's in Rome.

Scheggino, Triponzo and the Corno valley
Three kilometres south of Sant'Anatolia and again laid out below a castle, **SCHEGGINO** is one of the more appealing spots in the region. Much of its charm derives from a couple of canals below the tiny and much-tidied medieval streets. A further fine incentive for stopping is an excellent **hotel-restaurant**, the *Albergo-Trattoria del Ponte*, Via di Borgo 17 (☎075.61.131, fax 0743.61.131; ③; restaurant closed Mon & Sept 1–15). Make a point of sampling one of the local specialities – trout and truffles, the first plucked from the ice-clear river, the last harvested by the local Urbani family, the top operators in the Italian truffle world (their factory is the yellow building on the left about a kilometre distant heading north from the village on the main road). The only **campsite** for miles around is the *Valnerina* at nearby Valcasana (☎0743.61.115; open June–Sept), reached by taking the road east for a kilometre past the trout farm just outside Scheggino. There's a great outdoor public swimming pool on the left, midway between the village and campsite (late June–Aug only).

You can continue south from Scheggino to Terni, but a better itinerary would be to return to Sant'Anatolia and head north to **TRIPONZO** (Three Bridges), an ancient hamlet whose prominent marking on the map belies its size – just a shop and a couple of houses. Nonetheless, it was mentioned by Virgil, who talked of the Nera's creamy waters, an allusion to the **sulphurous springs** that feed into the river here.

Forsaking the Nera valley just before Triponzo, the SS396 heads off north through a tunnel along the deep **Corno valley to Norcia**, the scenery becoming increasingly wild amid steep mountains cut by tempting deserted side valleys. On the road, there are **hotels** at the hamlet of Biselli – the two-star *Dei Cacciatori* (☎ & fax 0743.822.347; ③) – and a couple of kilometres farther on at the larger village of Serravalle, which has a good two-star, the *Italia* (☎ & fax 0743.822.320; ③).

Preci, the Abbazia di Sant'Eutizio and on to Norcia
If you stay with the **Nera valley**, the next point beyond Triponzo is the fortified village of **PRECI** – 12km north – which has a **hotel** with occasionally unreliable plumbing and

a swimming pool, the *Agli Scacchi* (☎0743.99.221; ②). Nearby at Castelvecchio is a beautifully sited and top-grade rural **hotel** and **campsite**, the *Collaccio* (☎0743.99.430; April–Oct), with friendly, English-speaking owner, swimming pool and a chance to indulge in horse-riding, cycling, tennis and hang-gliding. There are wooden chalets for rent which sleep four to six people (③), bunk rooms (①) and farmhouse with hotel rooms (③), as well as a cheap **restaurant** (huge portions).

Two kilometres south, signposted off the Norcia road at Piedivalle, is the **Abbazia di Sant'Eutizio**, a rambling monastic complex which was one of the cradles of the Benedictine movement. Initially the site of a Roman building, then a cemetery for hermits who had lived in the hills, it became a community that eventually controlled over one hundred churches and local castles, its domain extending as far as the Adriatic. After years of neglect and near ruin the complex has been extensively restored, thanks largely to the efforts of a single Benedictine monk based in Norcia. The effect is perhaps a little too polished and tidy, but there's no denying the beauty and tranquillity of the place, nor its seminal place in the history of the Benedictines.

Its Romanesque **church**, built in 1190, has a fourteenth-century apse and gallery and, inside, a *Crucifixion* by Nicola da Siena (1461) above the high altar. The altar houses the sepulchre of St Eutizio, one of the early hermits, who was known for his missionary zeal and for his ability to induce rain; when there is a drought, locals still parade his tunic round the fields. Crawling through the specially constructed tunnel below the altar is also supposed to guarantee relief from all manner of back ailments. Down in the **crypt** are a couple of vast sandstone columns, perhaps remnants of the original Roman building on the site. Steps behind the abbey church, to the right of the fountain, lead to the caves of the earliest monks. According to Gregory the Great, it was in these grottoes that Benedict – in conversation with Eutizio and a fellow hermit, Spes – discovered his religious vocation. From these unspoiled caves was to emerge the great **Benedictine order**, whose monks, beavering away in half-lost monasteries such as Sant'Eutizio, would help preserve much of Western learning though the depredations of the Dark Ages.

The fifteen-kilometre stretch of road south from the Abbazia runs through delightful and pastoral country, the Castoriana and Nida valleys, which once made up one of the most important north-to-south trading routes in this part of the Apennines. The road passes little medieval hamlets such as Piedivalle and Campi. Just before the latter, on the roadside to the left, is the church of **San Salvatore**, a double-fronted Romanesque beauty gleaming from restoration work necessitated by the 1979 earthquake that ravaged the Valnerina (the fault line runs along this valley, more or less in front of the church). It's rarely open, but the interior is smothered with frescoes by Giovanni and Antonio Sparapane, a fifteenth-century dynasty of painters active around Spoleto and the Valnerina: if it's shut you can gain a tantalizing glimpse of the interior through the grille of the left-hand door.

Above you can see the village of **Campi Vecchi**, arched across the wooded hillside to the north; to reach it drive through Campi and keep your eyes open for the yellow sign directing you to "**Sant'Andrea**", the church clearly visible at the right-hand side of the village. Once up and parked outside the arch entrance, you'll find the church's portico frames one of the loveliest views in the area. The key to the church is kept by a woman in the village – with your back to the church, walk down the steps and take the lane right in the little piazza: the house is about four down on the right. With a little prompting she should regale you with stories of the cholera pit beneath the church, and the evil princess buried under the inverted Roman inscription on the facade, as well as show you the beautifully kept interior – leave a generous tip. There's another unexpected treat, too, in the same little street as the custodian's house which strikes off right at the bottom of the church's steps. About 50m down on the right is the chapel of **Santa Maria di Piazza**, so broken and well disguised you could walk past it. You can look through the open windows at the interior, but should be able to gain entry by ringing the bell of the same custodian's house – she has the key for this little treasure as well. The vaults are covered in several superbly well-preserved and accomplished frescoes on the *Life of the Virgin*, the work of the Sparapane. Other areas of frescoes have been revealed on the whitewashed walls, but there's no money at present to pay for their restoration.

Across the valley two villages, **Abeto** and **Todiano**, appear invitingly over the woods and hilly ridges. Don't be tempted to drive up to see them, for though they were once stuffed with paintings and other works of art (now in Spoleto's Museo Diocesano), they're weirdly and almost completely deserted.

Beyond Sant'Angelo, 4km south of Piedivalle, the road climbs to 1008m at Forca d'Ancarano, a pass which affords spectacular views over surrounding mountains before the precipitous drop down to Norcia. From Preci **an alternative route** to Norcia runs through Visso (in the Marche), then onwards by the desolate and stunning road over the Passo di Gualdo (1496m) and through Castelluccio (see p.548).

Norcia

Noted on the one hand as the birthplace of St Benedict – founder of Western monasticism – and on the other as one of the country's great culinary capitals, small, walled and stolid **NORCIA** is the only place of substance in eastern Umbria. Its air of faint desolation and low, sturdy houses are a world away, though, from the bucolic towns to the west, a contrast explained by the constant threat of earthquakes. Thick-walled and heavily buttressed, Norcia's buildings have been compulsorily stunted since 1859, when a law forbade the raising of houses over 12.5m high. The last tremor, a particularly violent one, was in 1979 (the 1997 quake had little effect here) – outside the town you'll see ranks of temporary housing, ready for the next big one. At the same time it's a prosperous and likeable place, the sort of town where everything works and everybody knows everyone else. If it seems a touch dour at first acquaintance, its streets are relieved by glimpses of the mountains to the rear, views of which unfold unexpectedly at many a corner.

Norcia has been inhabited since prehistoric times, thanks to its abundant springs, fine agricultural land and – more to the point – a vital position commanding one of the lowest east-to-west routes across the Apennines. Ancient Norcia was the northernmost town of the Sabines, contemporaries of the Umbrians, before becoming Nursia, a minor Roman *municipio* (290 BC). After the attentions of sixth-century barbarians, recovery took a long time to come – and when it did, **earthquakes** periodically discouraged long-term development. For five centuries before Italian Unification, though, the town was effectively a frontier post between the Papal States and the Kingdom of Naples, making it a safe haven for bandits and refugees from opposing sides. Papal reaction was to build the **Castellina** in 1554, a huge, blunt fortress that dominates the town centre. Thereafter Norcia and the surrounding countryside was drained by emigration, a trend that continues today, but whose effects have been tempered by the success of its small food-processing concerns.

The Town

Buses drop you at the **Porta Romana**, from where it's a straight walk on Corso Sertorio to the central **Piazza San Benedetto**, a large, open area with something of a *High Noon* atmosphere in mid-afternoon, but at other times the lively focus of the town's evening *passeggiata* and its comings and goings. It's presided over by a statue of a suitably severe and disapproving Benedict, erected in 1880 on the 1400th anniversary

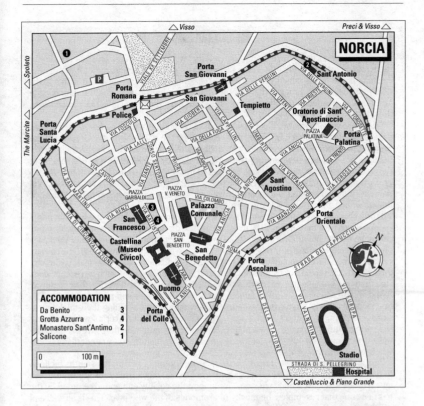

NORCIA

ACCOMMODATION

Da Benito	3
Grotta Azzurra	4
Monastero Sant'Antimo	2
Salicone	1

of his birth. Following victories by the *Azzurri*, or Milan or Juve in soccer matches, the saint is liberally adorned with the flags, hats and scarves of the team in question. In earlier centuries the square was the site of a bullring and a place of execution for witches, traitors, adulterers and necromancers (the last common in the area: see p.549).

San Benedetto

The piazza's most arresting sight is the church of **San Benedetto**, built, according to legend, over the house where Benedict and his sister, St Scholastica, were born; it's more likely to have been the site of a Roman temple, as the square itself was the site of the forum. Despite repeated post-earthquake reconstructions, the facade – sole survivor from the 1389 original – remains an attractive, two-tiered affair, its design typical of several churches in the region (notably San Francesco and Sant'Agostino in Norcia itself). It features a lovely Gothic portal, rose window, niche statues of Benedict and Scholastica and a fourteenth-century campanile to the rear. During Norcia's blast-furnace summers the newer arched gallery (1570) to the right provides welcome shade, and it has a drinking fountain too. Notice also the unusual old stone measures, used for selling or distributing wine and olive oil when the gallery was used as a market.

Within there's a good restored niche **fresco** on the left as you enter (next to the font). Possibly the work of Francesco Sparapane, one of a dynasty of local fifteenth-century painters, it shows *SS. Barbara and Michael*, with a *Madonna and Child* above. The only other worthwhile painting is Filippo Napoletano's *St Benedict and Totila*

TRUFFLES

Though disconcertingly turd-like in appearance, weight for weight **truffles** are one of the world's costliest foodstuffs – only saffron costs more. Norcia is one of Italy's truffle capitals, home to the fabled black truffle – *tuber melanosporum* – pursued with a great deal more fanfare in France. (Italy's other mushrooming heartland is the countryside around Alba, nestled in the Piedmontese hills, but here the prize is the *tuber magnatum*, the white truffle.)

Truffles have been known, if not understood, since ancient times. The first written record dates from the 5th century BC. They were enjoyed by the Babylonians, the Greeks and the Romans, who consumed them as much for their reputed aphrodisiac qualities as their gastronomic allure. Plutarch believed they were mud cooked by lightning; Juvenal that they were the product of thunder and rain. Pliny, bewildered by their origins, considered them Nature's greatest miracle. In the Middle Ages they were considered a manifestation of the Devil. And no wonder, for here was a plant apparently without root, branch, or stem; without leaf, fruit or flower; lacking, in fact, all visible means of growth.

Truffles are actually subterranean fungi of the class *Ascomycetes*, part of the *Tuber* genus, a species which over the course of 100 million years has disappeared underground, probably as part of an evolutionary defence against the weather. Their underground existence precludes photosynthesis, meaning they rely for nutrients on a symbiotic relationship with the roots of certain trees, most commonly the oak, hazel, beech and lime. Unlike a normal mushroom, their spores are spread not by the wind, but by truffle-eating animals such as rodents, deer, slugs and wild boar – and to ensure they're snuffled up, they need to advertise their presence.

And this is where the truffle's famous perfume – and dogs and pigs – come in. The fungi mature slowly, often over the course of several months, attaining their final dimensions – anything from the size of a pea to the size of a football – over a few days during the spring. Only when ripe – from about November onwards – do they give off their distinctive perfume, and only then for about ten days, thus ensuring they're snaffled up only when laden with viable spores. Thereafter they become poisonous and rot.

Pigs and truffles once went together, pigs being foremost among the sleuths inclined to nose them out (goats, foxes, ferrets and – in Russia – even bear cubs are used). Pigs love truffles – at least female ones do – for among the volatile compounds exuded by the truffle is one that resembles the musky pheromones of the wild boar. This is all well and good, but not only are sows huge and difficult to manage, they're also prone to attacks of sexual frenzy when close to a truffle. Dogs are therefore now preferred, and can be worth anything up to £250 when trained.

There are countless **types of truffle**. Nine are edible, though only six are well known and commercialized. Four are considered a delicacy, and of these two are found in quantity around Norcia and Spoleto. Varieties mature at different depths and at different times of the year, so that April and May are the only times of the year when fresh truffles are not available. Umbria's most common type is the **tartufo nero**, gathered from a few centimetres below the ground between mid-November and mid-March.

(1621), located in the left arm of the left transept. It's well worth going down into the **crypt**, excavated as recently as 1910, where the little apse at the head of the left aisle is traditionally held to be the place where Benedict and Scholastica were born. It's half covered in faded frescoes depicting the *Annunciation*, *Nativity* and other scenes. Stone fragments of a late Roman edifice are clearly visible closed off nearby, making this by far the most evocative part of the church.

La Castellina

Across the square from San Benedetto is the unmissable **Castellina**, an extraordinarily gaunt affair with no concessions to architectural subtlety. The superb granite lions outside came originally from the crypt of San Benedetto. It was built on the site of a Benedictine

More prized is the **tartufo pregiato**, available over the same period. Rarer are the two summer and autumn **scorzone** varieties.

But why all the fuss? These poo-like fungi's perfume has been compared to leaf mould, over-ripe cheese, garlic, methane and armpits. But for enthusiasts, the appeal lies in the truffle's unique and subtle flavour. Elizabeth David, in her classic cookbook, *Italian Food*, called them the "most delicious of all foods anywhere". Brillat-Saverin, the famous 19th-century French gastronome, went right over the top, stating that "without truffles there can be no truly gastronomic meal".

The truffle's mystery, its seemingly spontaneous appearance and ethereal existence, is also important. So, too, is the rarity and thrill of the hunt – it's the only gourmet food, indeed one of the only foods of any description, that can't be grown to order. The truffle is gloriously unpredictable, a fact which has made commercial cultivation something of an agricultural Holy Grail. One tree will yield truffles while its apparently identical neighbour will not – and nobody knows why.

Money also plays its part. Many a *cavatore*, or truffle-hunter, sells either directly to a restaurant, or, more likely than not, to an agent working for Signor Urbani, king of the truffle world, whose small company, based in Scheggino (see p.540), a village a few kilometres from Norcia, controls 65 percent of the world's truffle trade. Truffles, after all, are big business: a kilo of white Alban truffles could be yours for £1990; an equivalent quantity of Beluga caviar costs around £1750. Black truffles, of the type found in France and Umbria, retail at around £300 a kilo. So valuable are the finds that it's not unusual for people to hunt at night equipped with a torch and trowel, searching a spot where dogs have sniffed out their prey earlier in the day.

Every aspect of truffle exploitation is **controlled by law**, from hunting and final sale to the ownership of land rights and the precise definition of varieties, but in practice most people moonlight (literally), with only those working for large producers being obliged to obey the bureaucratic niceties. Old-timers say this free-for-all, a relatively recent phenomenon, is ruining the business as newcomers ravage old beds for short-term gain, thereby destroying yields not only for a season, but for years to come.

You'll find shops all over Norcia selling truffle paste, truffles under oil (to preserve them), and truffle-flavoured oils, cheeses, liqueurs, pâtés – even truffle chocolate. For the real thing, however, head for the *Grotta Azzurra*'s tremendous restaurant, a temple to Umbrian cuisine, and treat yourself to either *risotto al tartufo* or *tagliolini al tartufo*, the latter the classic way to tackle a truffle. If finances allow, indulge in their award-winning marriage of truffle and steak, *Filetto del Cavatore* ("Fillet of the Truffle-Hunter").

If you enjoy truffles you'll be in exalted company – Louis XVIII, Napoleon, Churchill and Rita Hayworth were all passionate devotees of the mysterious tuber. So, too, however, was the unfortunate Duke of Clarence. In 1368, so the story goes, the hapless duke, approaching his wedding night and a frisky Italian wife with some trepidation, so gorged on white truffles – anxious to enlist their aphrodisiac support – that he collapsed and died before he could test their amatory powers. Where the truffle is concerned, therefore, the watchwords are *caveat* eater – eater beware.

---

priory and Norcia's old parish church for Pope Julius III by the usually sophisticated Vignola and now houses the town's **Museo Civico**. The whole complex was shut for decades until the summer of 1996, when it was tentatively reopened, superb restoration work on the castle and its interior having at last been completed. Regular hours for the museum have not been fixed, however, and it's not known whether there are the finances to repeat the 1996 experiment and other periodic openings since. If it is open, both the building and the handful of top-quality exhibits are well worth the admission (provisionally L5000). Most of the rooms, which look down prettily onto the square, are taken up with **sculptures**, the highlights being a rare thirteenth-century *Deposition* – five figures in all – a *St Sebastian* (minus arrows) and a poignant life-size glazed terracotta *Madonna* by Andrea della Robbia. Among the **paintings** look out for a bizarre *Risen Christ* (1460) by

Nicola da Siena, in which a near-naked but curiously sexless Christ is shown stepping forcefully from his marble sepulchre. There is also a lovely picture attached to a casket lid of Benedict and Scholastica, the former shown holding a painted church, as well as a beautifully restored *Madonna and Child with Saints* by Giacomo di Giovannofrio, the Virgin sitting atop a gloriously decorated throne beneath a coffered Renaissance vault.

Duomo and Palazzo Comunale

Almost adjacent to the Castellina to the left is the largely uninteresting sixteenth-century **Duomo**, its less than dominating position a result of comparative modernity, its forlorn interior the legacy of countless earthquakes. It does have one outstanding work, however, the **Cappella della Madonna della Misericordia**, located at the end of the north aisle. It consists of an ornate altar (1640–41) of inlaid marble whose appearance, so at odds with central Italian work of the period, has led experts to attribute it to Francesco Duquesnoy, a noted sculptor in the employ of the Neapolitan court. At the heart of the altar is an early sixteenth-century painting, probably by Francesco Sparapane, the *Madonna and Child with SS. Benedict and Scholastica*. Benedict is shown pointing to a painted miniature of Norcia, whose prominent Gothic campanile no longer exists, having collapsed in the eighteenth century.

Completing Piazza San Benedetto's ensemble is the now superbly restored **Palazzo Comunale**, oddly but beautifully multicoloured, and based around a 1492 portico and later additions which blend delightfully to create the town's most distinctive building. Norcia has no **tourist office** at the time of writing (it's hoped to open one in the Castellina), so if you want a **map** and **pamphlets** on the town you need to visit the offices of the *Vigili Urbani*, located under the palace's arches.

Food shops

The piazza's other main component is its **food shops**, no small consideration in a town renowned for its culinary delights. Anything that can be done to a pig, food-wise, the Norcians apparently do, and better than anyone else – which is why you'll see butchers in other parts of Italy are called *Un Norcino*. Sausages, salami, hams and wild boar, reputedly the country's best, are all in abundance, as are less appetizing non-porcine delicacies such as mountain ram and sausage-filled sacs claiming to be mules' testicles. On this theme it's worth noting that Norcian butchers in the past claimed a notorious sideline, namely the castration of young boys, a skill passed down by the surgeons of Preci (see p.540) and honed by their work on similarly luckless pigs. A leg-crossing contemporary account survives which describes the procedure: [the boy] would be "drugged with opium or some other narcotic, placed in a very hot bath, until he was in a state of virtual insensibility. Then the ducts leading to the testicles were severed, so that the latter in the course of time shrivelled and disappeared."

Local mountain **cheeses** are excellent too – two years old and never in a fridge – and if finances permit you could indulge in the area's rare **black truffle**. The season runs from January to April, but all year you can sample the foul truffle *digestif* called *Amaro di Tartufo*, truffle *grappa*, and even truffle chocolates. The *Bar Vignola*, with outside tables, between San Benedetto and the Castellina, is a good place to indulge in these or more standard refreshments. The shop to the left, one of the town's more pungent, offers a good selection of genuine products (don't be put off by the cheerful sales patter of the owner), as does Moscatelli, midway down Corso Sertorio on the left as you head towards the walls.

The rest of the town

Away from the square, head northeast to the **Tempietto**, or **Edicola** (literally the "kiosk"), one of the town's more unusual buildings. Built in 1354 by Vanni Tuzi, it's a small arched structure, decorated with bas-reliefs and open to the street on all sides.

Its purpose is unknown, but it may have been commissioned in honour of San Felicianus, who evangelized Norcia, as a shrine to be used in Holy Week processions – hence the signs of the Passion which figure among its decoration; possibly it was used as a *contra pestum*, a votive offering against the plague (an epidemic ravaged much of Italy at the time the work was built).

Beyond the Tempietto is a quarter of town that fell into disrepair during the Middle Ages and was taken over by shepherds from Castelluccio (see next page). Adopting it as their own, they built small houses – complete with stalls for their sheep – amidst a jumble of streets that contrasts with the central grid. Look out for the church of **Sant'Antonio Abate** – the shepherds' saint, invoked to protect their flocks – and the nearby **San Giovanni**, known for its wooden ceiling and magnificent Renaissance altar of the *Madonna della Palla*. Located on the right wall, the arched and gilt marble surround frames a painting of the eponymous Madonna (1469), so-called because someone is supposed to have kicked a ball (*palla*) against the painting, causing the Virgin's expression to change miraculously at an act of such wanton sacrilege. Among the town's other churches be sure to see **Sant'Agostino**, half filled with surprisingly accomplished and well-preserved frescoes, those on the entrance wall depicting, among other things, the grisly martyrdoms of several saints (located in Via Anicia, two blocks east of the Edicola). Also make time for the tremendous wooden ceiling of the **Oratorio di Sant'Agostinuccio** just behind Piazza Palatina.

Practicalities

Norcia is well served by **buses** from Spoleto, Terni, Perugia, Foligno and Assisi, and can be the base for some good trips into the Piano Grande (see next page) and north to the Castoriana valley and abbey of Sant'Eutizio. A new road through the mountains into the Marche (emerging just above Arquarta del Tronto) also looks set to open up the area; it's now open after squabbles between regional councils over who was to pay for drainage of the major tunnel – which lies under the Umbria–Marche border – had kept the multi-billion lire project closed for a decade after its virtual completion. In the southeast corner of Piazza San Benedetto and just outside the Porta Ascolana there are *tabacchi* that sell **walking maps** and **guides** – handy if you're going on into the Sibillini.

You should have few problems with **hotel** rooms, first choice on a budget being the 37-room one-star *Monastero Sant'Antonio*, Via delle Vergini 13 (✆0743.828.208; ②), located just east of Porta San Giovanni (call to confirm it is still open). Of the slightly more upmarket options, the eight rooms of one-star *Da Benito*, Via Marconi 5 (✆0743.816.670; ③), are pleasant enough, but if you can afford the extra get a room at the livelier *Grotta Azzurra*, Via Alfieri 12 (✆0743.816.513, fax 0743.817.342; ④), the best, busiest and friendliest hotel in the town itself (it's also extremely central, immediately off the main square – and right alongside *Da Benito*). Under the same management as the *Grotta Azzurra* is the *Salicone* (✆0743.828.076, fax 0743.828.081; ⑥), just outside the town walls at Porta Romana, a very smart three-star hotel – with some of the best sports facilities in central Italy. All sorts of leading soccer, volleyball, basketball and other sports teams from across Europe have come to train here. If you have no joy with these places there is a clutch of three or four modern hotels outside the Porta Romana. The nearest **campsite** is a long way away just outside the hamlet of Scheggino (see p.540), though a short walk out of town to the east offers scope for freelance pitching.

You'd be foolish not to try local specialities in the **restaurants**, the most lauded of which – in most Italian foodie guides – is the *Trattoria del Francese*, Via Riguardati 16 (✆0743.816.290; closed Fri), which in the event turns out to have a rather tatty trattoria atmosphere. Far better is to make for the medieval dining halls of the *Grotta Azzurra*, complete with huge fire, suits of armour and tapestries, where you can sample Castelluccio lentils, truffles, mountain mushrooms, cheeses and hams, and probably enjoy one of the best meals you'll eat in Umbria. If you're here for a couple of days and want a change, try the *Taverna de' Massari* (☎0743.816.218) at Via Roma 13 just east of San Benedetto on the way to the Porta Ascolana. If you're watching the budget there are plenty of *pizzerie* in the back streets, plus a couple set into the walls just south of the Porta Ascolana.

The Piano Grande and the Monti Sibillini

The mountainous landscape east of Norcia is one of the most distinctive in all Italy, with its centrepiece the eerie **Piano Grande** – an upland prairie devoid of any feature save sheep, hang-gliders and the odd bedraggled haystack. Surrounded on all sides by the sheer and barren mountains of the **Monti Sibillini**, the Piano Grande forms a colossal amphitheatre that's often swathed in a dense, early morning mist. Gazing down on this wilderness from the remote hamlet of **Castelluccio**, it's easy to imagine the hazards for the unsuspecting traveller in past centuries. Papal rulers actually forbade crossing the plain during winter, and even today the bells of Castelluccio toll on gloomy days to guide shepherds across its desolation. If it looks familiar, you've probably seen Zeffirelli's glutinous Franciscan epic, *Brother Sun, Sister Moon*, for which it was a key set. The plain is also famous for being – reputedly – the world's largest football pitch, having hosted a match between two teams of a hundred players each; the home side went down by twelve goals to one.

Spring is the best period to visit the *piano*, when it blazes with an extraordinary profusion of **wild flowers**, one month radiant with buttercups, the next with poppies and narcissi. Woven into the floral carpet are rare Alpine flora, including the *Carex buxbaumi*, an Ice-Age relic discovered in 1971 and believed to be unique. On the mountains around you find tulips, fritillaries and peonies as well as further rarities like Apennine edelweiss (found elsewhere only in parts of the Abruzzo), the martagon lily, bear's grape, Apennine potentilla and the Alpine buckthorn – but you don't need to be an expert to enjoy the startling spectacle.

Castelluccio

At 1452m, **CASTELLUCCIO** is one of Italy's highest continually inhabited settlements, and the only habitation for many kilometres around. An isolated farming settlement, it is served by bus twice a day for only half the week, from Norcia's Porta Ascolana (currently Mon–Thurs 6.25am & 1.30pm). As well as its appeal as a belvedere onto the grasslands and a trailhead for mountain walks, the village attracts rabid attention from hang-gliders, drawn by the Sibillini's treeless slopes. There are now likely to be several campervans parked in the windblown square. A couple of bars have smartened themselves up, as has the long-established hang-gliding school, signs of change that benefit the locals little – most of the hang-gliding jocks camp and spend little money locally.

So far, though, the place has made few other concessions to tourism and the feel is of an uncompromising and bleak working village. The almost incestuously interrelated population has dropped from 700 in 1951 to around 150 today; most of the remaining inhabitants are migrant shepherds, many of them Sardinians or former Yugoslavs, who spend the winter months down in Norcia. The most immediately noticeable thing in the village is its **graffiti**, daubed in thick white paint on huge walls; this forms a kind of social document for the community, the pieces – often malicious and some going back generations – recording stories and myths about local people. Wander up to the parish church, just restored, which has a marvellous fresco cycle on the left wall describing the life of St Anthony Abbot, patron saint of shepherds and their flocks. On the arch outside the church to the right as you look down to the Piano Grande notice also the Fascist plaque, of a type long ago removed from other, less remote towns and villages in Italy, which salutes the Duce, "refounder of the Italian Empire".

Practicalities

It's well worth calling ahead for a room. There is only one **hotel** as such, the two-star, *Sibilla* (☎0743.870.113; ③), an Alpine-looking building in the village centre with just eleven double rooms (ask for one with views over the Piano Grande – half of them look onto the scrappy car park piazza). The only alternative is the rooms offered in a rather chilly modern annexe behind the *Taverna di Castelluccio* (☎0743.870.158; ②). The *Taverna* itself is a friendly place, with good **food**; it's well worth trying the tiny lentils for which the village is famous. The *Sibilla*, though, has a **restaurant**, which, while less appealingly rustic, serves up remarkably good food. Castelluccio's shops, such as they are, have only the most basic supplies, though fruit and bread vans visit regularly – except in winter, when the place is frequently cut off by snow.

Camping anywhere in the hills around is no problem, there being plenty of grassy flat ground a stone's throw from the village. Farther afield, be sure to take huge amounts of water, as the limestone hills have no surface source. You could also stay at the smartly refurbished *Forca Canapine* (☎0743.823.007; ③), a huge pink building on the Norcia to Arquata road on the pass at the southern edge of the Piano Grande (8km from Castelluccio) – also an excellent base for walks in all directions. A similar distance north of the village on the Visso road, and similarly well sited for hiking, is the lonely and more humble *La Fiorita* (☎0737.98.148; ②).

For **hang-gliding** information contact the *Scuola di Volo* just north of the village. For **walking information** – and maps and books on the area – the bar of the *Sibilla* and *Bar del Capitano*, on the southern edge of the village with a great belvedere over the Piano Grande, are both handy.

Walking in the Sibillini

The **Monti Sibillini** are the only really wild mountains of Tuscany and Umbria, and the most precious natural environment for many hundreds of miles. The most northerly of the big Apennine massifs, they run north to south for about forty kilometres, their summit ridge marking both the Umbrian border and the watershed between the Adriatic and Tyrrhenian seas. In **Monte Vettore** (2476m) they have the third highest point on the peninsula, a massive, barren mountain that rises above the Piano Grande with majestic grandeur. The Sibillini have recently been designated a **national park**, a status that sadly exists more on paper than on the ground, with no binding laws to stop hunting or building.

According to local tradition, the mountains were home to one of the three ancient **sibyls** – the wise women with oracular powers who were supposed to have foretold the coming of Christ. Later misogynist versions of the sibyl myth transformed them into temptresses possessed by the Devil – those lured to the sibyls' caves were doomed to remain trapped there until the Day of Judgement – which perhaps explains why these mountains have a reputation for necromancy and Devil worship. By happy coincidence the code for the *Kompass* map to the area is 666, the Devil's number.

Hiking in the Sibillini is superb, whether you fancy casual day hikes or more demanding backpack ventures. Unlike the Alps or Abruzzo there are few marked paths – these are not yet well-known mountains – and you're unlikely to meet many people other than shepherds. However, the Club Alpino Italiano (CAI) has discreetly tagged a few trails, with a view ultimately to creating a continuous path on the summit ridge.

Among **maps**, the 1:50,000 *Kompass: Sibillini* is adequate and widely available, though locally you should be able to pick up the better 1:25,000 *Montevettore* produced by *Universo* and the *Unione Italiana Sport Popolare* or the similiar CAI map. **Paths** marked on maps do generally exist – not always the case with *Kompass* maps – but in good weather the hills are so open (bar a few glorious beech woods) that you can wander pretty much at will, at least on the western, Umbrian side of the mountains. This is less true on the eastern flanks (in the Marche) which are dotted with dangerous crags and screes. However, around Castelluccio and the western ramparts the worst you'll have to contend with are some of the steepest grass slopes you'll ever come across.

For enthusiasts or emergencies there are several mountain huts (marked on maps), none with services, and often in a poor state.

The hikes

Castelluccio is undoubtedly the best base for **day hikes**, with trails leaving from the village in all directions. **Monte Vettore** via Forca di Presta (8km east of Castelluccio on the road to the Marche) is the obvious big target, returning along the ridge via Quarto San Lorenzo and Forca Viola. This is a pretty tough full day's outing, which you could take at a more leisurely pace by starting at the summer-only **refuge** at *Forca di Presta* (☎0743.99.278 or 0743.99.165; always call in advance). Sited at 1500m, the *rifugio* is a source of basic food, maps and information.

Another good walk from Forca di Presta or Castelluccio, mainly downhill through woods, takes you to **ARQUATA DEL TRONTO**, in the Marche, a smallish place with two **hotels**, the better of which is *Ca' Martina* (☎0743.99.261; ②), on a little side road just north of the village well placed for the paths on and off the hills. A third rewarding hike is to strike across country from Castelluccio to Norcia, a route comfortably accomplished in a day, though the route-finding here requires a little more diligence: paths to the ridge (around 1800m) are straightforward, but the drop from the ridge can be a bit of scramble if you miss the path. Trails lower down, which you'll easily pick up, are much better.

For a quick and easy glimpse of the scenery north of Castelluccio follow the *strada bianca* (gravel road), for about twenty minutes, past the *Scuola di Volo*, round the corner into the Valle Canatra and on to the Fonte Valle Canatra. It's an all but level stroll which you could prolong by following the obvious cart track to the head of the lovely pastoral valley and the open plains under Monte delle Rose (1881m). This is also good camping territory. Another excellent, straightforward and not overly demanding walk is to leave Castelluccio on the upper *strada bianca* west and then follow the rough road and clear path along the ridges of the Piano Grande's western rim (Colle Tosto, Monte Vetica etc), and overnight at Forca Canapine.

A more ambitious and longer hiking route is to cross over the ridge east of Castelluccio into the Marche, where the best-known walk runs to the **Lago di Pilato**, an idyllic spot under Monte Vettore. This is supposedly the burial place of Pontius Pilate, the story being that Pilate's body was dispatched from Rome on a cart pulled by two oxen, who traipsed through wild country and then plunged into the lake, disappearing without trace. The legend has made the lake the heart of the mountains' supposed necromantic practices; Norcians used to sacrifice animals here, and humans too, so it is said, to placate the demons and protect themselves from storms and bad weather. When the area was part of the Papal States a wall was built by the Church to prevent access to the lake, and stones inscribed with occult symbols have been found on the shores. In many recent summers the lake has all but dried up, putting in danger an endemic crustacean (*chirecephalus marchesonii*) which used to stain the water red, a colouring anciently attributed to the blood of Pilate.

From Lago di Pilato, another superb trail runs under the main ridge along the Valle del Aso to the hamlet of **FOCE**, where there are **beds** at the *Rifugio della Montagna* (☎0743.960.327; L25,000). The combined trek from Castelluccio to the lake and then to Foce makes a perfect day's walk. The only problem is you'll have to haul yourself back over the mountains if you're returning to Castelluccio the next day, so this is a route for seasoned hikers.

East of Foce, **MONTEMONACO** in the Marche makes another good Sibillini walking base. A nice medieval village in itself, it provides a starting point for walks up Monte Sibilla (2173m) and the spectacular yet easy hike in the **Gola del Infernaccio** (Hell's Canyon).

This is a huge gorge complete with cliffs and crashing river, which opens out into a broader upland where an upper track takes you to the **Eremo di San Leonardo**, sometime home to the Capuchin hermit Pietro Lavini (who has become something of a tourist attraction). Cheapest of the village's **hotels** is the *Orsa Maggiore*, Via Roma (☎0736.960.128; ②); the *Rifugio Monte Sibilla*, handier for the mountains, is 8km from the village.

Cascia and around

CASCIA, 18km south of Norcia, figures large on the map but is disappointing in actuality, only recommendable to pilgrims in search of **St Rita**. Her presence – and the stupendously ugly twentieth-century **Basilica** – dominate both the new and the earthquake-damaged hill-town, which was abandoned for a time in the eighteenth century. Little known elsewhere, Rita has a massive cult following in Italy, especially amongst women, for whom she is a semi-official patron saint. Thousands come annually to venerate her shrine.

The Basilica di Santa Rita and the town

Rita's Basilica in the old town is a monument to religious vulgarity probably without equal – a piece of Fascist architectural brutalism that attempts to place Byzantine and Romanesque elements in a modern context, and in doing so produces a fantasy in white marble that probably belongs in Disneyland. Rita's exhumed and mummified body lies behind grilles on the left, northern side of the basilica, surrounded in the half-gloom by flickering candles and votive offerings, whose appeals for the saint's salvaging of impossible situations include the pennants of several Italian football teams.

The interior is smothered in extravagant stonework – all bearing the robust, strong-lined bludgeoning of Fascist masonry – and the vaulted ceiling and cupola glow with garish painting-by-numbers frescoes. The altar is surrounded by what appears to be gold barbed wire and is surmounted by a large golden egg. Visitors are taken in groups to Rita's original

---

SAINT RITA

Rita experienced – and survived – the kind of hardships borne by women throughout history, which is the main reason for her appeal, and also why she's sometimes known as the "saint of the impossible". Born in 1381, a poor child of aged parents, she was forced to marry at fifteen and endured eighteen years of mistreatment from an alcoholic husband. Having weaned himself from the bottle and repented his past, the husband died in a brawl a few weeks later. Rita's children, for the most part wretched wasters, both died attempting to avenge their father.

Beaten, widowed and childless, Rita sensibly thought it about time she became a nun. Her knowledge of the marital bed, however, made this impossible; only a relaxation of convent rules allowed her to become an Augustinian, a development held up as one of her "impossible" miracles. No sooner had she joined than she developed a sore in the middle of her forehead, an excrescence so foul-smelling that none of the nuns would come near her. This supposedly developed when a thorn fell from a crown of thorns as she was praying to a statue of Christ, and so was regarded by her companions as a kind of stigmata. The smell abated only once – to allow her to join her companions in a week's visit to Rome to meet the pope; on their return the odour returned as virulent as ever.

Rita died in 1457, but the process of her beatification was laborious, hampered by doubts as to the veracity of her miracles, by the fact that she was a woman (and one with a past), and doubtless by the size of her grassroots support, a groundswell the papacy feared beyond their control. The proclamation of her beatification finally came in 1628, and her elevation to sainthood as late as 1900, and then only in the wake of a huge public campaign.

Augustinian monastery, which is now annexed to the building, for a view of the cell in which she died, a vine which grew from her walking stick and a rose – which Rita coaxed into life out of season – transplanted from her garden in Roccaporena (see below).

Cascia's other remaining sights are few, and many are still under restoration following a catastrophic earthquake in 1979. The most important is the church of **Sant'Antonio Abate**, which contains fifteenth-century Umbrian frescoes on the *Life of St Anthony* and a depiction of *The Passion* by Nicola da Siena. A new gallery, collecting together the best of the town's paintings, is due to open in the Palazzo Santi above Piazza Garibaldi. In the Upper Town, **San Francesco**, begun in 1425 but rebuilt almost completely in 1925, houses a fourteenth-century Gothic choir, a fresco of the *Madonna and Child* by a fifteenth-century Umbrian artist – on the west entrance wall – and more early local frescoes around the pulpit. Nearby **Santa Maria** is the town's oldest church (founded in 825), a large airy space, still with a medieval atmosphere of sorts, and the place where Rita was baptized (the font is at the top of the left nave in a special chapel left of the choir). On the west wall are frescoes of the *Deposition* by Nicola da Siena and *St Michael Weighing the Souls of Sinners and the Saved*. At the beginning of the right nave is a *Nativity* in which the Madonna seems to be sleeping on a large air-bed.

Practicalities

The **tourist offices**, in the central square at Piazza Garibaldi 1 (Mon–Sat 9am–1pm & 4–6pm; ☎0743.71.147) and Via G. Da Chiavano 2 (Mon–Fri same hours; ☎0743.71.401, fax 0743.76.630), are the main offices for eastern Umbria, including the Valnerina, Norcia and the Piano Grande, and so can be worth a visit for maps and pamphlets.

Amongst the huge, pilgrim-orientated **hotels**, the best for general purposes is the two-star *Centrale*, Piazza Garibaldi 36 (☎0743.76.736; ②); a little more up-market is the three-star *Cursula*, Via Cavour 3 (☎0743.76.206, fax 0743.76.262; ③), which has Cascia's best **restaurant**, its food being perhaps the single best reason for a visit to the town if you have no particular bent for Rita.

Roccaporena and the Corno valley

Cascia's countryside is considerably more rewarding than the town. If you want a quick taste – and to stay on the St Rita trail – the trip to **ROCCAPORENA**, the saint's birthplace, admirably fits the bill. The best way to get here is to take the marked and well-worn **Sentiero-Passeggiata di Santa Rita**, a perfectly level path that contours above the Corno gorge for 6km between Cascia and the village. The track can be picked up in the centre of town through the forecourt of the *Delle Rose* hotel: drop down into the underground car park, walk through it and take the gate 100m beyond, slightly to the left when you emerge. After 4km – you simply follow the same track all the way, with no diversions left or right – cut down to cross the river on a track that branches off right just after a ruined house and the point where a large pipe crosses the river: you'll know if you've gone too far as the track, which has been following an underground aqueduct, becomes too narrow to walk on. The last kilometre is on the road.

The surreal little village of Roccaporena, 6km west of Cascia, sits at the bend of a deep-sided, heavily wooded valley, dominated by a soaring vegetation-shrouded crag, the **Scoglio di Santa Rita**. Perched on the needle-point summit is a tiny chapel, a touch tiring to reach but with magnificent views. In the village, a small but often pilgrim-thronged place devoted almost entirely to Rita in some shape or form, the parish church of **San Montano** has the graves of Rita's family, and is the spot where she concluded her unfortunate marriage.

More people make the pilgrimage to the site of the saint's now rather tatty garden, an unlikely spot for horticulture, given its barren, cliff-edge location. It's easily found by following signs for the **Orto di Santa Rita** towards the cross on the valley side opposite the Scoglio. The spot is marked by a modern bronze statue of the saint, on and around which are often dozens of invocations, scrawled on scraps of paper. There's just one place to **stay**, the three-star *Roccaporena-Casa del Pellegrino* (☎ & fax 0743.776.348; ③), an institutional but spotless and comfortable pilgrims' hotel. It also has a cheap, Fifties-era canteen-like restaurant, more or less the only place in the village to eat.

The Corno valley and Monteleone

There are plenty of opportunities for **walks** into the hills from Roccaporena, and particularly along the wooded arm of the **Corno valley** that makes a dog's-leg turn to the south. To pick up paths simply follow the gravel road beyond the *Casa del Pellegrino*, which climbs quickly, becoming a cart track after a couple of kilometres. One kilometre east into the valley, it's worth making a brief detour to the hamlet of Capanne, for its views and small fifteenth-century church. An hour's walk north-west from there, over upland, leads to the lonely **Madonna delle Stelle**, a restored monastery which you can also reach – more easily – from the Borgo Cerreto to Monteleone road.

　　MONTELEONE itself, on the only road south into Lazio, is the only place of any size for miles around. Surrounded by grand hill country, it's a fine, if in parts earthquake-battered, medieval village, noted for woodcarving and delicacies such as olives, wine and truffles. The main sight is the church of **San Francesco**, graced with an exceptional Gothic door, and scattered with artistic and archeological fragments excavated from a massive Neolithic necropolis nearby. The village is best known, however, for *farro*, a crude grain which finds its way into soups – *zuppa di farro* – across the Valnerina. It's reputedly what wheat would have been like if it hadn't been improved over the centuries: the Romans and Etruscans used it as a staple grain, and allegedly fed it to their soldiers before they went into battle. It's an odds-on favourite to succeed polenta – it's almost as dull and tasteless – as the next "peasant" food to hit the trendy restaurants outside Italy.

travel details

TRAINS

Spoleto to: Arezzo (8 daily; 2hr 10min); Florence direct (8 daily; 2hr 30min–3hr); Foligno via Trevi (15 daily; 20min; connections for Spello, Assisi, Perugia and Teróntola); Fossato di Vico (12 daily; 1hr); Narni (10 daily; 40min); Nocera Umbra (8 daily; 40min); Orte (9 daily; 55min; additional connections to Rome and Florence); Perugia direct (15–20 daily; 45min); Rome (12 daily; 1hr 30min); Terni (15 daily; 30min).

BUSES

Spoleto to: Foligno via Trevi and Fonti di Clitunno (7 daily); Gavelli, Usingi and Poggiodomo (1 daily Mon–Sat, early morning); Montefalco (2–3 daily Mon–Sat); Norcia (5 daily Mon–Sat, 1 Sun); Perugia (5 daily; change at Foligno); Rome (1 daily); Urbino (1 daily); the Valnerina (5 daily Mon–Sat; change at Piedipaterno for San Anatolia, Scheggino and Ceselli).

Norcia to: Cascia (frequent services daily); Castelluccio (2 daily Mon–Thurs); Spoleto (5 daily Mon–Sat, 1 Sun); also one direct daily service to Foligno, Perugia, Rome, Terni, San Benedetto del Tronto and Ascoli Piceno.

Cascia to: Ascoli Piceno, Foligno, Monteleone, Norcia, Perugia, Rieti, Roccaporena, Rome, San Benedetto del Tronto, Spoleto and Terni.

CHAPTER THIRTEEN

ORVIETO AND SOUTHERN UMBRIA

S outhern Umbria features two of the province's most illustrious hill-towns – Orvieto and Todi. Each has become a little too popular for its own good, but they are essential visits, the former for Italy's richest Gothic cathedral, the latter for its atmosphere and stunning high-altitude location. Often bypassed in the rush to these star attractions are a number of smaller but perhaps more enjoyable centres, notably Narni – occupying a promontory above the River Nera – and Amelia, whose encircling walls are among the most redoubtable in the country.

Terni, a transport hub and the province's largest supply centre after Perugia, is the area's low spot, a grim industrial city whose most valuable role is as the southern gateway to the Valnerina. Buses up to the valley's historical highlight, the Abbazia di San Pietro in Valle, pass close to the most celebrated landscape attraction in this part of Umbria, the Cascate delle Marmore – a partly artificial waterfall that nonetheless provides an impressive spectacle.

Umbria's main rail line goes through Terni, from where northbound trains head through Spoleto and southbound services via Narni to connect with the Rome–Florence route at Orte; northbound services from here will take you to Orvieto. The most enjoyable ride is provided by the Ferrovia Centrale Umbra (FCU), a private single-track line that runs from Terni to Perugia, and then on to Città di Castello and Sansepolcro. Using spartan two-carriage trains, this fills the gaps left by the state network, rattling through lovely countryside to provide access to Todi, and to minor halts like Deruta, heart of the region's ceramic tradition. Good road links follow almost identical routes, and if you're hitching, the big junction with the A1 at Orte – an obvious gateway in and out of the region – offers options in all directions.

ACCOMMODATION PRICES

Throughout this guide, hotel accommodation is graded on a scale from ① to ⑨, indicating the cost of the cheapest double room in each establishment in high season (for hostels, rates per person are given in lire). The price bands to which these codes refer are as follows:

① up to L60,000	④ L120,000–150,000	⑦ L250,000–300,000
② L60,000–90,000	⑤ L150,000–200,000	⑧ L300,000–350,000
③ L90,000–120,000	⑥ L200,000–250,000	⑨ over L350,000

Terni

TERNI, the southernmost major town in Umbria, was the unlikely birthplace of one of the world's most famous saints, St Valentine, patron of lovers and bishop of the town until his martyrdom in 273. A less romantic city, however, would be hard to imagine. Prewar Terni formed the cradle of Italy's industrial revolution, claiming the country's first steel mill and producing the world's first viable plastic, and its armaments and steel industries made it a target for Allied bombing in 1944. During over a hundred air raids, most of the town – including the best part of its Roman and medieval heritage – was reduced to rubble. These days Terni is no longer the manufacturing powerhouse that earned it its nineteenth-century tag of the "Manchester of Italy", though postwar rebuilding has put the arms and chemical industries back on their feet – the gun which allegedly shot Kennedy was made here.

Arrival and accommodation

Terni's ugliness and its function as a communications centre means that it's likely to have the barest walk-on part in most Umbrian itineraries, but relying on public transport you may find yourself having to stay here. You can **change money** at the station ticket office and at the post office in Via del Plebiscito. For the usual range of maps and pamphlets, look in at the **tourist office** at Viale C. Battisti 7a (Mon–Sat 9am–1pm & 4–7pm; ☎0744.423.047); coming from the train station, take Viale della Stazione – Viale C. Battisti is 300m up, seventh on the right. The regional tourist office covering the Lower Valnerina, Narni and Otricoli is nearby at Viale C. Battisti 5 (☎0744.423.047, fax 0744.427.259).

HOTELS
Brenta, Viale Brenta 12 (☎0744.283.007). Central 23-room one-star hotel. ②.
Brenta II, Via Montegrappa 51 (☎ & fax 0744.273.957). A middling two-star hotel with 23 rooms, each with bathroom, in a quiet, backwater neighbourhood, across the river to the east. ②.
De Paris, Viale Stazione 52 (☎ & fax 0744.58.047). Large 63-room three-star joint – a bit soulless but convenient for the station. ④.
Garden, Viale Bramante 4 (☎0744.300.041, fax 0744.300.414). Top-of-the-range luxury, with swimming pool, flower-filled balconies and all the frills. ⑤.

SAINT VALENTINE

Terni's tourist literature treads carefully around the subject of **St Valentine**, talking of his "delicate tradition" – delicate, that is, because there are doubts about whether he ever existed and exactly whose body it is that pilgrims venerate in the Basilica di San Valentino, 2km south of Terni. The uncertain identity of the corpse, however, didn't stop someone stealing the saint's head as a love-token in 1986; it was found three years later, wrapped in newspaper, under a park bench.

According to the delicate tradition, Valentine was elected first bishop of Terni in the year 197 and attempted to bring converts to Christianity – then still outlawed – by encouraging the religious marriage of young people. It's also said that star-crossed lovers would turn to him for advice, drawn by his open-mindedness and his custom of giving them flowers from his garden. His most famous success was the union of Sabinus and Serapia, two lovers – he pagan, she Christian – barred from marriage by their lack of a shared faith. Valentine comforted them with the assurance that their souls would never be separated and, when the young Serapia died, converted Sabinus and thus achieved the reunion of the lovers when Sabinus died soon after.

Evidence of Valentine's other qualifications for sainthood is scarce, though after his martyrdom in Rome, his head is said to have rolled 93km from its place of execution. Oddly enough, his following in Italy is considerably less than in the unromantic Anglo-Saxon countries.

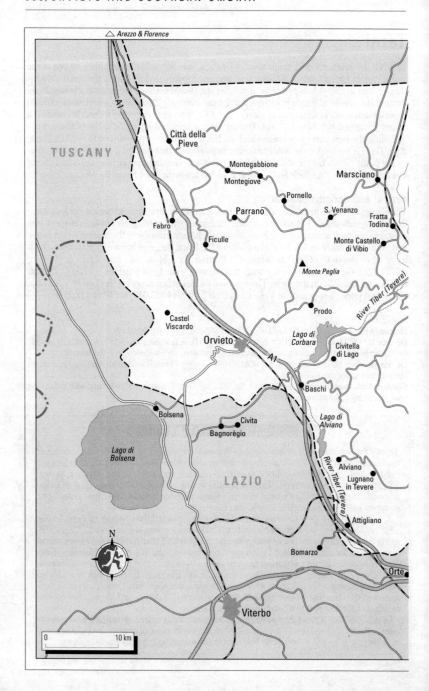

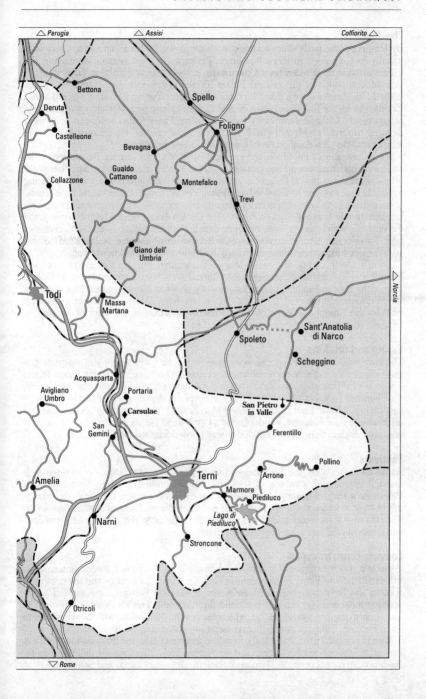

△ Perugia   △ Assisi   Colfiorito △

Bettona
Deruta
Castelleone
Bevagna
Gualdo Cattaneo
Collazzone
Montefalco
Spello
Foligno
Trevi
Giano dell' Umbria
Todi
Massa Martana
Spoleto
Sant'Anatolia di Narco
Scheggino
Acquasparta
Portaria
Carsulae
Avigliano Umbro
San Pietro in Valle
Ferentillo
San Gemini
Pollino
Amelia
Arrone
Terni
Marmore
Piediluco
Narni
Lago di Piediluco
Stroncone
Otricoli

△ Norcia

▽ Rome

The Town

By Umbrian standards there's almost nothing to see in Terni, and what there is is usually lost amongst modern buildings. Perhaps the best reason for leaving the train station is the **Pinacoteca Comunale**, in the Palazzo Fabrizi at Via Fratini 55, four blocks south of the central Piazza Tacito (Tues–Sun 10am–1pm & 4–7pm; L3000). Its star turns are *The Marriage of St Catherine* by Benozzo Gozzoli and a *Crucifixion* by the Folignese artist Nicolò Alunno, along with works by a triumvirate of moderns – Chagall, Kandinsky and Joan Miró. There's also a two-room showing devoted to Orneore Metelli (1872–1938), an impoverished shoemaker from Terni who chronicled his daily life in colourful and naive paintings.

If you have more time to kill, the greenest parts of a grey city are the gardens of its southwest quadrant around San Salvatore and the Roman amphitheatre. **San Salvatore**, off the shapeless sprawl of Piazza Europa, is the town's most interesting church, featuring a rotunda that was long believed to have been a Roman temple to the sun, but has recently been dated to the eleventh century. Nonetheless, excavations have revealed extensive remains from Roman buildings on the site. The portico dates from the twelfth century, and the chapel – which has frescoes by an unknown Umbrian painter – from two centuries later. Two blocks west are the remains of the **Roman amphitheatre**, built in 32 AD to hold 10,000 spectators; comprehensively ruined, it's home to the town's bowls club.

Terni's other sights are minor-league attractions, led by the church of **San Francesco**, just north of San Salvatore. Started on a Romanesque plan in 1265, it is defined by its campanile, a fourteenth-century addition picked out on its corners in vivid ceramics. In the centre, off Via Cavour, are **Sant'Alò**, a twelfth-century church built by the Knights of Malta, and the **Palazzo Spada**, the last work of Antonio da Sangallo the Younger, who died in Terni in 1546.

Eating and drinking

The town puts on a rather better showing in its restaurants, with a couple of top-grade gastronomic venues and numerous serviceable *trattorie*. The *Tacito*, Piazza Tacito, is a good local trattoria on the square south of the station (closed Fri), and the *Da Carlino*, Via Piemonte 1 (✆0744.420.163) is another of Terni's better ones: it's located in the northeast corner of town; from L45,000 (closed Mon & Aug). For something between the two price-wise, try *La Piazzetta*, Via del Leone 34 (✆0744.58.188), a small place with reliable regional cooking, from around L30,000 a head (closed Sun and two weeks in Aug).

Festivals

As far as festivals go, the best times to be in Terni are **May Day** – celebrated with unusual vigour and a parade of floats by this committed left-wing town – and **St Valentine's Day**, February 14, marked by a festival and market. Classical music buffs might want to know about the June **International Piano Festival**, a high-class event that was won some years back by Ivo Pogorelich, then just about the most glamorous and controversial figure on the concert circuit.

Leaving Terni: transport

Terni is a major **rail** junction, with trains running on the state network (information ✆0744.401.283) to Rome (connections at Orte for Orvieto, Florence and the north), to Spoleto and Foligno (connections for Assisi, Spello and Perugia), and to Rieti in the south (connections for the east coast and the Abruzzo). There's also the private FCU line (information ✆0744.415.2970), which shares the FS station, with hourly trains to Todi, Perugia, Città di Castello, Sansepolcro and stations en route.

Buses are run by ACT and leave from the forecourt near the train station. Services run to numerous local villages, and to Narni, Todi, the Cascate delle Marmore, Piediluco, Arrone, Ferentillo, Triponzo, Spoleto, Orvieto, Viterbo and Scheggino.

The Lower Valnerina

Terni is the ideal point of entry for the **Lower Valnerina** and on to Norcia and the
Sibillini, driving or taking a bus along the SS209, which follows the valley into its upper
reaches (see p.538). Buses from Terni go as far as Triponzo (see p.540), via
Piedipaterno, where you could link up with bus connections on to Norcia or Spoleto.
The lower valley's highlight is undoubtedly the **Abbazia di San Pietro in Valle**, 18km
north of the city, but on the way you'll pass a number of fine natural diversions, like the
Marmore waterfalls and **Lago di Piediluco**. Scenery is generally scrappy until
Ferentillo, however – when the hills start to rise in impressive fashion – so there's an
argument for simply ignoring the valley's lower reaches until you hit San Pietro.

The Cascate delle Marmore

The first stop of interest in the valley comes just 6km southeast of Terni at the **Cascate
delle Marmore** (access by train or buses from Terni's Piazza Dante), which at 165m
are among the highest waterfalls in Europe. They were created by the Romans in 271
BC, when they diverted the River Velino into the Nera during drainage of marshlands
to the south. Further channels were cut in 1400 and 1785, both with the intention of
draining Rieti's plain without flooding Terni, though the falls' major boost came with
the damming of Lago di Piediluco in the 1930s to satisfy industrial demand for hydroelectric power. Terni's power-station complex is the largest hydroelectric plant in Italy.

Pictures of the falls in full spate adorn most Umbrian tourist offices, but what they don't
tell you is that the water can be diverted through turbines at the flick of a switch, leaving
a none-too-spectacular trickle. The times when the water flows are notoriously variable,
but evenings are usually likeliest, especially during July and August when there's an
impressive *son et lumière*. (Flow times most years are: May–Aug Sat 5–9pm, Sun
10am–1pm & 3–11pm, plus July 15–Aug 11 Mon–Fri 5–6.30pm; Sept–Oct & mid-March
to April Sat 6–9pm and Sun 10am–noon & 3–9pm; Nov to mid-March Sun 3–6pm).

There are two **observation points**: the belvedere in Marmore village, and the SS209
road down below. A steep and frequently muddy path connects the two, starting 100m
downstream of the falls, and there are swimming pools at the bottom of the cascade when
the water's turned off. The green and luxuriant setting, tumbling water and acres of gleaming marble add up to a spectacular show – shame about the factories around the corner.

Marmore has a **campsite**, the *Marmore*, at the nearby hamlet of Campacci
(☎0744.67.198, fax 0744.368.425; April–Sept).

Lago di Piediluco and Piediluco village

Surrounded by steep, thickly wooded hills, **Lago di Piediluco** is rather like a miniature
alpine lake: its waters are dark and deep, a bit on the cold side for swimming and in places
unsafe, though the fringes are edged with beaches. Piediluco **train station** is sited on the
southwest edge of the lake, 3km from Marmore and a kilometre or so from Piediluco village on the north shore. The station is a perfect access point if you want to put up a tent
on the southern, less-visited shore or to walk the scenic minor road (no vehicle access)
to Monte Caperno – reached by walking through the quarry by the station.

At **Monte Caperno** there's a quay for boats to and from Piediluco village, and a famous
echo that's constantly being tried out. It reproduces with perfect clarity phrases up to
four seconds in length – the stock Italian test phrase being lines from the mystic poet
Jacopone da Todi (see p.574): "Per te, amor, conumone languendo e vo stridendo, per te
abbracciare" (I'm pining for you my darling, and I'm looking forward to embracing you).

PIEDILUCO village is a major sailing and canoeing centre, always crowded at weekends with people escaping from Terni. **Accommodation** can be tight. Head first for the
two-star *Lido*, Piazza Bonanni 2 (☎0744.368.354, fax 0744.368.292; ③), and if this is full,

try the smart three-star *Casalago*, Mazzalvetta 3 (☎0744.368.421, fax 0744.368.425; ③), overlooking the lake. The *Casa dell'Amicizia*, Strada Panoramica 7 (☎0744.368.088, fax 0744.368.099; ③), is a twelve-room three-star hotel. The **campsite** at nearby Ara Marina, *Il Lago* (☎ & fax 0744.369.199; April–Sept), is large and often busy. Note that nearby Labro, whose medieval houses look attractive from a distance, is owned lock, stock and barrel by Belgians and operates only as a holiday village. For **food**, try the small family-run *Tavoletta*, Via Forca 4 (☎0744.368.196; from L30,000; closed Wed and periods in June and Oct).

Arrone and Montefranco

Desolate and sparsely populated these days, the Valnerina was once the hub of communications between the Kingdom of Naples and the Dukedom of Spoleto, and later a bone of contention between the Church and the Holy Roman Empire – which explains the liberal sprinkling of castles.

Moving north up the valley, **ARRONE** and **MONTEFRANCO** are the first of several fortress villages. Montefranco has the better of the views, but portions of its medieval centre are in ruins, and there's little cheer either in the shape of food and drink, or from its inhabitants. Across the valley Arrone sits atop a rocky pinnacle, crowned by an inviting little tower. The village's alleys again lack the sparkle of their distant promise, though the church of **Santa Maria Assunta** in the central Piazza Garibaldi contains recently uncovered sixteenth-century frescoes.

With transport you could make the scenic drive from Arrone to **POLINO**, a twelve-kilometre succession of hairpins through dense forest to Umbria's smallest *comune* – just a couple of hundred people, a tiny castle and one nameless trattoria. Press on and you reach **COLLE BERTONE** (1232m), a minor winter resort in good walking country. There's a small **hotel** here, perched idyllically at 1241m, *La Baita* (☎0744.789.132; ②).

Other local **accommodation** is scarce. Near Arrone on the main road, look for the two-star *Rossi*, Isola 7, Castel del Lago (☎0744.388.372, fax 0744.388.305; ②); its **restaurant** (closed Fri) is one of the better around. At Racognano, on the SS209 near Montefranco, there's the ritzier three-star *Fonteghia* (☎0744.388.621, fax 0744.388.598; ④), also with a restaurant. A cheaper place to eat is the *Rema* on the Polino road from Arrone.

Ferentillo and its mummies

FERENTILLO is rapidly becoming the **free-climbing** capital of Italy, its crags swarming at weekends as new and more difficult routes are pioneered. The village itself sprawls across two rocky hillsides, guarded by twin fourteenth-century towers, and merits a stop for one of Umbria's more grotesque ménages – the Ferentillo **mummies**.

These are to be found propped up in **Museo delle Mummie** in the crypt of San Stefano (daily: April–Oct 9am–12.30pm & 2.30–7.30pm; March & Nov 10am–12.30pm & 2.30–6pm; Dec–Feb 10am–12.30pm & 2–5pm; L4000) in the Precetto quarter, on the east side of the Nera. Now behind glass and viewed on guided tours – a precaution taken in the wake of the theft of a head – the corpses were simply dumped in the crypt and preserved by accident, apparently dried by their bed of sandy soil and a desiccating wind from the south-facing windows. The characters are a curious mix: two French soldiers hanged during the Napoleonic wars; a bearded dwarf; a mother who died in childbirth (the child displayed alongside her); a papal soldier, bolt upright with his gun, housed in the case of a grandfather clock; a lawyer shot in a local feud over a farm; a farmer whose gun backfired in the same feud and blasted a hole in his stomach; and a hapless Chinese couple who came to Italy in 1880 for their honeymoon and died of cholera. To round things off there's a pile of leering skulls with a mummified owl perched in their midst.

You wouldn't necessarily want to stay locally, but there's a good **restaurant**, the *Piermarini*, Via della Vittoria 53a (☎0744.780.714; closed Mon & three weeks Aug–Sept), whose interesting cooking ventures beyond the more usual Umbrian standards.

San Pietro in Valle

Six kilometres up the valley from Ferentillo, at an abrupt turn to the left, is a more highbrow distraction, the **Abbazia di San Pietro in Valle** (daily summer 10am–noon & 2–5pm; free; if closed ring at the custodian's house, signed on the left midway up the 2km approach road), set high on the hillside near a thickly wooded cleft. Privy to some sublime views, it is one of central Italy's finest abbeys and one of Umbria's few memorials to the Lombards' Dukedom of Spoleto. At the time of writing considerable restoration work is under way: more ominously, the abbey buildings, which have been in private hands since 1860 (the abbey church is a state-owned national monument) have been part-converted into a hotel, a development that can only be to the long-term detriment of this perfect medieval ensemble.

In Roman times there was probably a pagan temple on the site, later replaced by a series of small hermitic communities. Meanwhile, in Spoleto, the sixth Lombard Duke of Spoleto, **Faroaldo II**, who reigned between 703 and 720, experienced a vision in which St Peter told him to found a monastery in his honour at a place in which he would discover a lone and disconsolate monk. While hunting some time later he came across a recently bereaved monk, and so duly founded an abbey, but also abdicated his throne in favour of the monastic life. At his death eight years later he was buried in the abbey, his tomb a magnificent Roman **sarcophagus** which survives to this day to the right of the high altar. The abbey became a mausoleum for many of the Spoletan Lombard dukes, the last to be buried here being Franco Vinigisio, who abdicated in 822.

The abbey was sacked by a Saracen raiding party in 881 and restored in 991, when a series of fortresses were built to lend it added protection. One of these, **Umbriano**, can still be seen on the opposite side of the valley; fanciful legend has it that it was the first settlement ever founded in Umbria. Thereafter the abbey became one of the most powerful religious houses in the region, controlling vast tracts of land and dominating the lives of thousands of people. In 1234 it passed from the Benedictines to the Cistercians, but by 1300 had become so corrupt that Boniface VIII was forced to transfer responsibility for its operation to Rome. In 1484 Innocent VIII sold its land and feudal rights to Franceschetto Cybo and his descendants, who took the title of Count of Ferentillo: it remained in their domain until 1730, passing through other minor aristocratic hands until 1860, when the church was appropriated by the newly formed Italian state and the buildings sold to the local Costanzi family (which owns them still).

THE CHURCH

The highlight of the complex is the **church**, much of which survives from two separate periods of building – in the eighth and twelfth centuries – the earlier date probably having yielded the transept, the three apses and parts of the rough mosaic pavement behind the main altar. Immediately as you enter via the main rear door there is a small conical **stone altar** on your right, a pagan altar dating back to the first century BC. On the left is a series of medieval and Roman fragments from the earliest buildings on the site. The rear wall has two accomplished sixteenth-century **frescoes**, *The Madonna of Loreto* and *The Madonna and Child with St Sebastian*. Out of the door immediately off the right side of the church is a faultless two-tiered **cloister**, usually decked out with a profusion of flower-filled pots; the custodian should open the door for you to see two exquisite ninth-century statues of saints Peter and Paul, one to either side of the portal.

Moving down the church you cross a **stone division** set into the floor, flanked by two small pillars: this marked the point beyond which those who had not been baptized were forbidden to progress. Up above, covering most of the side walls, are two breathtaking, if badly faded, **fresco cycles**. Painted in 1190, they are considered some of the most important paintings of their period in Italy, being amongst the first attempts to move away from the stylized influence of Byzantine painting. Most of these precocious pictures are biblical scenes, those on the left-hand wall from the Old Testament, those on the right-hand from the New. Most show a startling sense of invention and composition, full of narrative detail and attempts at light and shade unique for their time: the artist is unknown.

The **Old Testament** scenes are better preserved, and are worth studying, the narrative wonderfully vivid once you know the scene depicted. They are arranged in three tiers, and progress left to right from the top tier down. The **first tier** shows the *Creation of the World*; *Creation of Adam*; *Creation of Eve* (who is shown emerging from Adam's rib, with the four Rivers of Paradise – looking like fish – at Adam's side); *Adam Naming the Animals*; *Original Sin*; *God's Warning*; and *The Expulsion from Paradise*. The **second tier** depicts the *Sacrifice of Cain and Abel*; *Cain Slaying Abel*; *God's Warning to Noah*; *The Construction of the Ark*; *Noah Giving Thanks to God*; *Abraham and the Three Angels*; *The Sacrifice of Isaac*; and *Isaac and Jacob*. Only one fresco survives of the lowest tier, its theme unclear. The **New Testament** on the opposite wall depicts, in the badly faded **upper tier**, angels and Old Testament characters. The **second tier** has seven better-preserved panels, which from left to right are: *The Shepherds being told of Christ's Birth*; *Journey of the Magi*; *Epiphany*; *Departure of the Magi*; *Massacre of the Innocents*; *Baptism of Christ*; and the *Wedding at Cana*. The **lowest tier** has four panels that can be clearly made out: *Christ's Entry into Jerusalem*; *The Last Supper*; *The Washing of the Feet*; and *Calvary*.

The church's magnificently preserved **altar** is a still more significant artefact, being one of only a tiny handful of dated works of art anywhere in Italy of Lombard vintage – its age is obvious even from a cursory glance at the almost Celtic figures and motifs that decorate its two main faces. It was carved by Ursus, the left of the two crude figures depicted in the lower front section (his signature is still clearly visible): the other figure is Ilderico, Duke of Spoleto between 739 and 742, who commissioned the piece.

To each side are well-preserved Roman **sarcophagi**, the right-hand specimen – Faroaldo's tomb – especially appealing, backed by some of the gloriously coloured Giottesque frescoes (c. 1320) that dot much of the apse and shallow transepts. In the **left transept**, look for the tiny fresco on the side wall which depicts Faroaldo's vision of St Peter: the duke is shown lying in a canopied bed while his companions play dice to the right. The capitals in the apse, incidentally, are probably from the original Roman building on the site, likely crowning fluted columns that are now concealed under the plaster work of subsequent centuries. Three other carved sarcophagi lie elsewhere in the church, along with odd stone fragments around the walls, including a bas-relief of a monk, brought from Syria by refugee Christians in the seventh century.

On your way out of the abbey (the route currently lies around the back of the church rather than through the cloister) look at the twelfth-century **campanile**, similar to the Lombard-influenced towers common in Rome and Lazio, and distinguished by fragments and reliefs salvaged from the eighth-century church.

Accommodation is available in the abbey hotel (☎0744.780.129, fax 0744.435.522; ③), a lovely place to stay for all that its presence seems almost sacrilegious. You can also stay in Sambucheto, the hamlet at the foot of the approach road, where the nine-room *Ninfa del Nera* sits on the busy main road at Via del Monastero 3 (☎0744.780.172; ②); it also has a **restaurant**.

Narni

Half an hour by train either from Terni or from Orte (including a spectacular trip through a tree-filled gorge), **NARNI** is an intimate and unspoilt hill-town, jutting into the Nera valley on a majestic spur crowned by another of Cardinal Albornoz's formidable citadels. The fortress draws an admiring glance before you see the welter of chemical works around Narni Scalo, the new town that's grown up around the station – thankfully almost

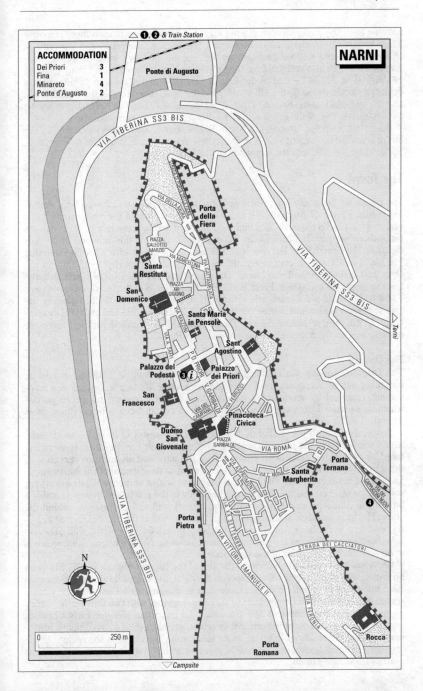

NARNI

ACCOMMODATION

Dei Priori	3
Fina	1
Minareto	4
Ponte d'Augusto	2

invisible from the medieval core. Narni's stage-set medievalism is even more complete than Perugia's or Assisi's, its quiet piazzas, Romanesque churches and labyrinth of ancient streets and stepped passageways forming one of Italy's most congenial town-scapes. There are also vestiges from the time when Narni was a Roman colony (Narnia) established in 299 BC – one of the first in Umbria – and a linchpin in the capital's defences, standing close to the Tiber valley and the undefended road to the capital. It was also the birthplace of the Roman emperor Nerva, and of Erasmo da Narni, better known as Gattamelata, one of the greatest of all medieval *condottieri*, or mercenaries.

Buses run from the forecourt at **Narni Scalo station**, with tickets available on the bus or from the newsagent's kiosk in the station. You may have to wait for a connection, but don't be tempted into the long and very tedious walk.

The Town

The circuitous bus route from Narni Scalo to the medieval town allows a brief view of the Roman **Ponte di Augusto**, a solitary arch in the middle of the river, remnant of a bridge which in its day was 30m high and spanned 160m, a product of Augustan-era renovations to the Via Flaminia. In the eighteenth century this was one of the key sights on the Grand Tour, but now is so lost among the lower town's development that you could easily miss it completely: the best viewpoint is provided by the train from Orte, just before you pull into Narni. The buses terminate at **Piazza Garibaldi**, the town's rather odd social hub. From here, Via Mazzini leads to the heart of the old town – still built on the old Roman grid – through an arch in the city walls, following the course of the Via Flaminia, whose construction in 220 BC set the seal on Narni's importance. If you're approaching by **car** Piazza Garibaldi has limited parking; there are more spaces on the approach to the square in Via Roma.

The Duomo

The **Duomo**, fronting Via Garibaldi's first bend, was rebuilt in 1145 and is now an intriguing mix of accretions from most centuries since. Its facade is small and unassuming, cramped by surrounding buildings and by the Lombard-influenced portico which dates from 1492 (with later additions). The portal, laced with carvings, dates from the twelfth century.

Inside, the church has a slightly lopsided feel, the result of its outer south aisle, which was added in the fifteenth century. The extravagant Baroque altar is overshadowed by gold-leafed **pulpits** on either side of the nave and an intricate **screen** – all three mainly late fifteenth-century works, but incorporating fragments of Romanesque and paleo-Christian reliefs. The Cosmati pavement is also attractive, while elsewhere parts of the original church show through, chiefly in the patches of fresco – notably a little niche *Madonna and Child* on the west (rear) wall and in the apse behind the choir. The little **wooden statue** (1475) near the rear wall at the start of the left aisle – representing St Anthony Abbot – is by the Sienese master Vecchietta, who may also have been responsible for the painting of *San Giovenale*, Narni's patron saint, which is to be seen on the last pillar of the right aisle.

Giovenale was reputedly buried on the site of the present church in 376, his tomb finding its way into the cellar-like chapel on the right, the **Cappella di San Giovenale** (also known as the Oratorio di San Cassio). It is shielded by a Cosmatesque marble screen and relief of *Two Lambs adoring the Cross*, together with two thirteenth-century niche statues of the *Pietà* and *San Giovenale*. An important piece of early Christian architecture, the chapel dates from 558; its crude, age-blackened walls contain a **ninth-century mosaic** of Christ (high up on an inner wall), the oldest in the region. Inside are more Cosmati fragments and reliefs, together with the sixth-century sarcophagus used as Giovenale's tomb.

Giovenale is the focus of the town's main **festival**, during which a fortnight of festivities lead up to the Corsa dell'Anello, held on the second Sunday in May. On the Saturday evening of that weekend a torchlight procession takes place. The next day contestants from the town's three medieval quarters compete to thrust a lance through a ring (*anello*) suspended in Via Maggiore.

Pinacoteca Civica

The Palazzo Vescovile alongside the duomo, a seventeenth-century former bishop's palace, is probably destined to house the town's **Pinacoteca Civica**, or civic art museum. It will collect work currently held in the Palazzo del Podestà and various churches around the town; there will also be a section devoted to the gold and silverware from the cathedral treasury. The influence of Tuscan artists in the region will be acknowledged in Benozzo Gozzoli's *Annunciation* (1451-2) and a tabernacle attributed to the school of Agostino di Duccio. One section will be devoted to San Girolamo, an important former Franciscan convent 13km southeast of the Narni. Formerly it was home to the town's best painting, Domenico Ghirlandaio's *Coronation of the Virgin* (see below), commissioned for the convent in 1486 by Cardinal Eroli, a cleric who was also busy in Spoleto (see p.532). Other works from the convent displayed include detached fifteenth-century frescoes, a painted terracotta bust of St Bernardino of Siena attributed to the Sienese artist Vecchietta, and a lunette attributed to Pier Matteo d'Amelia frescoed with a *Madonna and Child and Saints Francis and Giralomo*. The best of the cathedral treasury's exhibits are six bronze chandeliers and a pair of eighteenth-century reliquaries.

Piazza dei Priori

Via Garibaldi continues through a vibrant residential centre, following the line of the old Roman *Cardo Maximus* past Via del Campanile on the left, which provides a glimpse of the cathedral's fifteenth-century campanile (built on a Roman base). It soon emerges into the **Piazza dei Priori**, a perfect little civic square where pride of place goes to the fourteenth-century **Palazzo dei Priori** and its loggia, designed by the Gubbian Matteo Gattapone, the architect responsible for Gubbio's Palazzo dei Consoli and Spoleto's vast Ponte delle Torri. Next to its high arches and Roman inscription is a little exterior pulpit, built for the peripatetic St Bernardino. The striking town house alongside, covered in medieval reliefs, is the Palazzo Sacripante.

The somewhat eccentric building opposite the Palazzo dei Priori is the **Palazzo del Podestà**, or Palazzo Comunale, cobbled together by amalgamating three town houses and adding some token decoration. The thirteenth-century Romanesque sculptures above the main door are worth a glance, as are the numerous Roman fragments of the courtyard, and if you can get into the Sala di Consiglio (admission on request downstairs in the tourist office) you'll see a majestic *Coronation of the Virgin* by the Florentine **Domenico Ghirlandaio** (destined to be the centrepice of the new art gallery). The last is the town's pride and joy, and it was so admired by the authorities of Todi and Trevi that they commissioned cheaper copies by the local artist Lo Spagna. Another small room nearby contains paintings removed from San Domenico, the town's former picture gallery, among them an *Annunciation* by another Florentine, Benozzo Gozzoli, and a double-sided standard dated 1409 by the anonymous Maestro di Narni showing the *Dormition* and *Coronation of the Virgin*. All the town's paintings, however, are currently being shuffled around several locations, with the Palazzo Vescovile designated as their final home.

The rest of the town

Beyond the piazza, Via Mazzini passes the inconspicuous but lovely church of **Santa Maria in Pensole**, on the right after 50m. An utterly simple basilica, unchanged since it was built in 1175, it has an enchanting triple-arched Romanesque portico and a beautiful carved frieze around the square doorways. Inside, the church is plain save for a few simple carvings and capitals, though interesting rooms below the nave with Roman remains are occasionally open.

The ex-church of **San Domenico**, a slightly forlorn building a short way farther down Via Mazzini, is now home to Narni's archives and public library (Mon–Thurs 9am–1pm & 3.15–6pm, Fri 9am–1pm; closed Sat–Sun; free). It's worth dropping by for the wealth of medieval fresco fragments around the walls and the funerary wall monument (1494) to Gabriele Massei, crafted by followers of Agostino di Duccio. You could also try asking in the library to view the Roman **aqueduct** which lies below the building. Behind the church to the left, at the beginning of Via Aurelio Saffi, a small **garden** with fragments of an old tower offers great views down into the Nera gorge: the distinctive building way down below is the recently restored twelfth-century Benedictine **Abbazia di San Cassiano** (generally open to the public on Sun).

The northern tip of the town is graced by further gardens and more good views, together with steep little streets which you can follow down to Via Gattamelata, where no. 70 is reputedly the birthplace of the eponymous *condottiere*. Towards the street's southern end lies the tatty, water-stained church of **Sant'Agostino**, its large bare portal concealing an interior with a redoubtable fourteenth-century stone altar and a few medieval faded frescoes amidst half-hearted Baroque. The best fresco, to the right of the main door, is a *Madonna Enthroned with SS Lucy and Apollonia* (1482) by the accomplished local artist Pier Matteo d'Amelia, best known as one of Fra' Filippo Lippi's two assistants on the apse frescoes in Spoleto cathedral. Also spare a moment for the fresco fragments in the apse, which depict a variety of saints.

Returning to Piazza Garibaldi and heading south takes you into a warren of little streets, none with much by way of sights, but worth wandering for their own sake: at the top of this quarter lies the **Rocca**, a massive affair lording it over the town and surrounding country. It's reached by Via del Monte, a street that threads through the *terziere di Mezule*, one of the three areas into which the medieval town was divided. The castle was commissioned by Cardinal Albornoz in the 1370s and is attributed to Gattapone, responsible for the town's Loggia dei Priori; it formed a link in the chain of fortresses by which Albornoz sought to reassert papal authority across Umbria. If you do come up here bring a picnic – the park around the castle is a perfect spot for a snack and siesta.

Practicalities

The **tourist office** is at Piazza dei Priori 3 (Mon–Sat 9am–1pm & 4–6pm; ☎0744.715.362). Narni shows refreshingly little interest in tourism but if you can find a room it makes a nice spot to go to ground for a couple of days. The cheaper of the two town **hotels** is the three-star *Minareto*, Via dei Cappuccini Nuovi 32 (☎0744.726.343, fax 0744.726.284; ③), situated outside the walls just southeast of the Porta Ternana; but if you're prepared to pay the extra you're better off plumping for the old-world finery of the very central three-star *Dei Priori*, Vicolo del Comune 4 (☎0744.726.843, fax 0744.726.844; ④). The alternatives – for emergencies only – are three hotels in Narni Scalo, the best two being in Via Tuderete, the road which winds up to the old town from Narni Scalo: the three-star *Fina*, at no. 419; (☎0744.733.648, fax 0744.750.326; ④); and the cheaper two-star *Ponte d'Augusto* at no. 303 (☎0744.750.635, fax 0744.750.974; ②). There's an out-of-town **campsite** at Monte del Sole, on the road to Borgaria 5km south of Narni (☎ & fax 0744.796.336; April–Sept).

Virtually the only proper **restaurant** in the heart of the old town is the classy *La Loggia*, Vicolo del Comune (☎0744.722.744; closed Mon and second half of July). **Pizzerie** and bars are gathered on Piazza Garibaldi, and there are good snacks at *Il*

Forno bakery off Piazza del Popolo. If you have a car, then the best restaurant around, the *Monte del Grano* (☎0744.749.143; closed Mon) lies 15km south of Narni in the hill-top hamlet of San Vito, at Strada Guadamello 128 (from Narni take the SS3bis south along the Nera). It's small and has a fine reputation, so booking is usually essential: note that it's closed Mon and from mid-January to mid-March, and that it's only open in the evening on weekdays. Service, food and ambience all justify the L65,000-a-head price tag, though not all the often innovative dishes are a complete success. If this is too much, or too far to travel, then there are two cheaper top-rate places closer to town: *Il Cavallino* Via Flaminia Romana 220 (☎0744.761.020) lies in Testaccio, 2km out from Narni on the old Rome road; it's a popular place that's been run by the same family for three generations (around L35,000; closed Tues & two weeks in July). *Da Sara*, Strada Calvese 55–7 (☎0744.796.138), is in wooded, hilly country 8km from town near the hamlet of Moricone; it's a typical rural trattoria, with a small bar-*osteria* alongside (around L35,000; closed Wed). Both places have outside tables in the summer.

Buses for the train station (☎0744.737.707) and out-of-town destinations like Terni, Amelia and Orvieto leave from Piazza Garibaldi; the ATC office for information and tickets is at no. 27. **Train** links are frequent to both Terni and Orte (where you can pick up connections to Orvieto on the Rome–Florence line). The **post office** is at Via Vittorio Emanuele 40 and has a foreign exchange facility.

Amelia and around

AMELIA, 11km east of Narni Scalo, sits perched on top of a sugarloaf hill, its position and surrounding countryside the nicest for some distance around. The town is as delightful as its setting, enclosed by some of the oldest and mightiest **walls** in Italy. Formed from vast polygonal blocks joined without mortar, they are up to four metres wide and eight high. Parts are known to have belonged to an Umbrian acropolis of the fifth century BC, though the Roman historian Pliny claimed the town was formed in the eleventh century BC, three centuries before Rome. The Romans took advantage of the fortifications in 90 BC when they used the town, then named Amerina, as a staging post on the Via Amerina, one of nine military roads linking Etruria to the Via Flaminia. Thereafter the town within the walls was all but destroyed by Totila, and later history followed a predictable course through rule by the nobility and slow decline.

The Town

Access to the town is through one of its four original gates: the main entry is the **Porta Romana**, with the **tourist office**, Via Orvieto 1 (Mon–Fri 9am–1pm & 4–6pm; ☎0744.981.453), located to its left. A minibus shuttle runs between here and the centre. There's also a lift from a lower car park to the upper town, letting you out near the post office. More of the walls can be seen from a small park to the left of Porta Romana, and from the pleasant two-kilometre path which starts here and encircles the town.

Immediately inside the gate stands the church of **San Francesco**, also known as SS. Filippo e Giacomo, its typically plain-faced facade relieved by a rose window of 1401. Off the right-hand side of the church's interior the Cappella di Sant'Antonio contains six **tombs** belonging to members of the Geraldini family, the clan that held sway over Amelia for long periods during the Middle Ages. One family member, Alessandro (1455–1525), achieved fame outside his native town as one of the key advocates in the Spanish court of Columbus's 1492 expedition to the New World. The monuments (1477) on the top right, to Matteo and Elisabetta Geraldini, are the work of Agostino di Duccio. It's also worth nipping next door to the church to look at the **cloister** of the ex-Collegio Boccarini.

From San Francesco, the spiralling Via della Repubblica draws you to **Piazza Marconi**, a lovely old square, from which the stepped Via del Duomo leads steeply to the town's summit, site of a panoramic cathedral square. A small park here offers the best views. The most striking feature of the **Duomo**, a Romanesque church ruined by Baroque superfluities and nineteenth-century frescoes, is a twelve-sided **tower**, dated 1050 and claimed by some to symbolize the Apostles, by others to represent the signs of the zodiac. It's studded with Roman fragments and originally served as the town's principal civic tower. Inside, the church boasts two standards reputedly won from the Turks at the Battle of Lepanto (either side of the entrance to the second chapel on the right), the *Tomb of Giovanni Geraldini* (1476) by Agostino di Duccio (first chapel in the north aisle) and a column against which St Fermina, the local patron saint, is said to have been martyred (first on the right). The distinctive **octagonal chapel** is attributed to Antonio da Sangallo, its two funerary monuments to Ippolito Scalza, the latter artist having played a key role during the construction of Orvieto's duomo.

Art is otherwise thin on the ground – a collection of Roman statuary in the courtyard to the left of the **Palazzo Comunale** in Via Garibaldi is one diversion, together with the same palace's fine fifteenth-century *Madonna and Child with Saints* by Pier Matteo d'Amelia, housed in the Sala Consigliare (admission on request). You might also investigate the recently uncovered frescoes and *sinopie* in **Sant'Agostino**'s sacristy in Via Cavour, thought to date back to the year 1000, showing four saints, red star motifs and floral decoration. Amelia's attraction otherwise is the typically Umbrian mix of views, medieval streets and close-at-hand countryside. You could walk the short distance to **Monte San Salvatore**, worthwhile for its views and a tiny ninth-century chapel, or head for the nearby rural church of **Madonna delle Cinque Fonti**, supposed site of a St Francis sermon.

Practicalities

Buses run from the village to Terni and Orvieto, together with the lesser centres of Lugnano in Teverina, Attigliano and Avigliano. There are also services from the two nearest train stations, Narni Scalo and Orte. On the main approach road to the town, close to the tourist office, is one of two local **hotels**, the three-star *Scoglio dell'Aquilone*, Via Orvieto 23 (☎0744.982.445, fax 0744.983.025; ③). The other is the three-star *Anita*, Via Roma 31 on the Narni road (☎0744.982.146, fax 0744.983.079; ③). Another option is the one-star, ten-room *Amerino*, Via Amerina 54 (☎0744.989.667; ②), at Fornole, midway to Narni.

For **food** try the excellent *Il Carleni*, hidden in the alleys of the upper town at Via P. Carleni 21 (☎0744.983.925; closed Mon & Tues), where a full meal of smoked quail, *filetto al gorgonzola* and other such treats will set you back around L50,000. In summer there's the chance to eat outside. You might also try the restaurant in the *Anita* or *La Tavernetta* pizzeria in the old centre on Via della Repubblica. If you have transport, *La Gabelletta*, Via Tuderte (☎0744.982.159; closed Mon & July 15–30) at Gabelletta, 3.5km northeast on the Foce road, is a large, courteous and highly rated restaurant where you can expect to pay L40,000 for the works. Finally, be sure to indulge in Amelia's **local speciality**, a teeth-rotting combination of white figs, chopped nuts and chocolate.

Lugnano in Teverina

The run along the back roads to Orvieto from Amelia (possible by bus) is a treat, offering plenty of oak forests and the chance to catch one of southern Umbria's Romanesque highlights, the twelfth-century **Santa Maria Assunta** in LUGNANO IN TEVERINA. Fronted by an exotic and recently restored portico (1230), the church has finely carved twin pulpits and has somehow hung onto a triptych by Nicolò Alunno in the apse; the interior also has plenty of lovely carved capitals, a reconstructed *cantoria* and a Cosmatesque floor and the beautifully pillared crypt features a fine sculpted screen and further Cosmati marble work.

The village has a single **hotel**, the central 10-room, two-star *La Rocca*, Via Cavour 60 (☎0744.902.129; ②); food in the attached **restaurant** is also okay. Additionally, there's fairly cheap nine-room **agriturismo** farm accommodation in Giove, a crumbling hamlet to the south; contact Signore Cardillo, Le Fossate 121 (☎0744.992.606; ②).

From Lugnano it's well worth crossing the Lazian border to **BOMARZO**, just 17km south. Ten minutes' walk from the village is the **Parco dei Mostri** (daily dawn–dusk; L15,000), a sixteenth-century theme park of fantasy and horror devised by the hunch-backed Duke of Orsino. It has become one of the area's primary tourist attractions.

Otricoli

OTRICOLI, 15km south of Narni, is almost the last town in Umbria and a reasonable enough representative of its hill-towns. However, its medieval streets and the fresco-dotted church of Santa Maria are eclipsed by the remains of **Otriculum**, a collection of Roman ruins within easy walking distance. To reach them, get on the main road that bypasses the village, head downhill for 200m, and take the signposted track that strikes off right towards the Tiber.

Unusually the settlement has no walls, having served more as a pleasure garden than a defensive site; it was built as a sort of holiday village for Rome's hoi polloi, who cruised in by boat on the Tiber. The colony is still largely unexcavated and draped in clinging undergrowth; the best of the visible remains are a partly buried amphitheatre, a succession of twin-level arches and the rambling ruins of some small villas, cisterns and bathhouses.

Turner stopped off here to paint the scene (a work now in the Tate Gallery) and in the sixteenth century Montaigne described the spot as "infinitely pleasant". It may not stay that way for much longer. So far no more than a trickle of tourists visit but plans to make this an archeological park mean it may be headed for the big time. In the meantime you can find rooms up in Otricoli at the one-star, seven-room *Umbria*, Via Roma 72 (☎0744.709.013; ②).

Towards Todi – Carsulae and around

Moving north from Narni on the SS3bis dual carriageway, or on the parallel FCU rail line or road from Terni, the principal attraction is **Carsulae**, the largest **Roman site** in Umbria.

The hills east and west of these routes contain a number of typical Umbrian villages, of which the most substantial is **CESI**, 12km northwest of Terni and known as *la ringhiera della valle Ternana* (the balcony of the Terni valley). In addition to a handful of churches and a ruined fort, it offers a fine walk to the church of Sant'Erasmo and on to the summit of Monte Torre Maggiore.

Carsulae

The building of the Via Flaminia from Rome to Ancona confirmed this region's importance as the crossroads of Italy, and colonies along its route were to evolve into modern-day Narni, Terni, Spoleto and Spello. Some settlements, however, such as **CARSULAE**, 15km from Terni, were abandoned after earthquakes and civil war. In its day, this particular pile of stones was known as the Pompeii of central Italy, and its beauty praised by both Tacitus and Pliny the Younger. To get there, take the first junction for San Gemini Fonte on the main Todi to Terni road (ie before the tunnel heading south), and then just before that village (not before plain San Gemini) take the dusty signposted track to the ruins.

The unenclosed site is today dominated by a church, **San Damiano**, made from materials filched from the ruins; other precious marbles went to build local houses. Behind the church you can follow a long stretch of the original **Via Flaminia** (complete with grooves made by chariots) to a substantial arched gateway, built by Trajan; beyond the arch, on the left, is a large square Roman tomb.

Walking back on the Flaminia, the site of the **Basilica Forense**, the law courts, is off to the left; behind it (across the modern lane) rise the remnants of the **amphitheatre**, built in the hollow of a natural depression. Behind the arena is a **theatre**, its orchestra still impressively intact, and to its rear a spread of ruins still awaiting excavation. Back across the site, behind San Damiano and the Flaminia, is the **forum**, composed of numerous low walls and the vague outlines of baths, well and two temples.

North to Todi

PORTARIA, 3km north of Carsulae, is an inviting-looking village, clearly visible from the SS3bis, straggling along the cliffs on the eastern side of the valley. If you have your own transport it's worth driving up for bird's-eye views over the valley.

To the west, **SAN GEMINI** and **ACQUASPARTA** are both spa towns, each with passable medieval centres but plenty of modern building. In San Gemini, there's accommodation, in the unlikely event you're stranded here, at the two-star *Duomo*, Via del Duomo 4 (☎0744.630.015, fax 0744.630.336; ③).

The high, wooded hills west of Acquasparta shelter a handful of windblown hamlets. All are within about 15km of Acquasparta, and only readily seen in a car. Montenero has the best of the many **castles** in the area, and virtually every other village boasts a **Romanesque church**; the best are Santa Maria at Quadrelli, and San Martino and Santa Vittoriana in Dunrobba. In Avigliano, 3km southwest of Dunrobba, there's a **hotel**, the one-star *Meridiana*, Via Matteotti 31 (☎ & fax 0744.933.104; ②). Driving round the hills, though rewarding, is a slow business; if you're going west there's no petrol almost until you reach Orvieto.

Todi

TODI is one of the emerging Umbrian hill-towns, still at heart an agricultural centre but an increasingly favoured retreat for foreign ex-pats and Rome's arts and media types. Gentrification is manifest in a scattering of estate agents, shuttered holiday homes and the revamped and decidedly high-profile **Todi Festival** – ten days of music, ballet and other arts at the beginning of September. The town has its sights, too, with an impressive **Piazza del Popolo** and the churches of **San Fortunato** and **Santa Maria della Consolazione**, though perhaps what lingers most in the memory is its position, a stunning and daunting prospect from below.

Todi's history is one of the region's longest, Iron Age remains suggesting some three thousand years of continual habitation. Tradition has it the Umbrian town was built where an eagle dropped a tablecloth snatched from a local family – hence the eagle and cloth in the town's insignia. More certain is the Etruscan heritage, and coins bearing the name **Tutare** suggest a town of some independence during pre-Roman rule. The name means "border", and Tutare was probably one of several outposts used by the Etruscans to defend their frontier along the Tiber. Necropolises all round Todi have yielded some of the finest Etruscan treasures, most of them – including a famous bronze statue of Mars – shipped off to Rome. Ancient Roman rule came – in 42 BC – and went, leaving little except a second set of walls and indistinct ruins to add to those of the Etruscans.

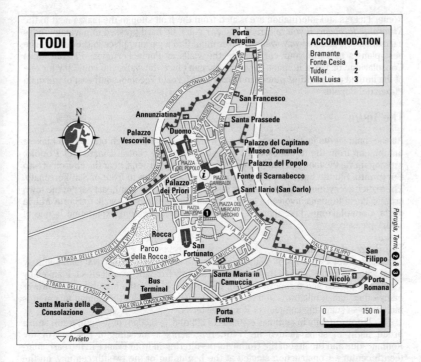

The town's heyday was the thirteenth century, when as a free *comune* – one of Umbria's first – it managed to annex Amelia and Terni, and to build a third set of walls and a crop of civic palaces. The Atti were the leading noble family, overseeing – in tandem with the Church's representatives – a period of decline interrupted only by a flicker of six-teenth-century prosperity that produced more palaces and Todi's great Renaissance church of Santa Maria della Consolazione.

Arrival and transport

Access to Todi by public transport can be a headache. By **train** you can approach from Terni or Perugia on the FCU line, but the town's two **stations** are both in the middle of nowhere and connecting buses can involve a longish wait. **Ponte Naia**, 5km distant, is marginally closer, and has a more reliable bus shuttle to the old town; the other station is **Ponte Rio**, 6km northeast of the town.

A more convenient way to visit the town is by **bus** from Perugia – there are six daily, the last bus back leaving at 5pm. They stop at the **terminus** for long-haul buses in Piazzale della Consolazione next to Santa Maria della Consolazione; orange **minibuses** run from the terminus up to the centre; if you fancy the walk follow the marked foot-path that strikes off Viale della Consolazione, 20m beyond the corner on the right. Buy tickets for the minibuses and long-haul buses from the unlikely-looking stall that sells nuts and miscellaneous nibbles.

Buses **back to Ponte Naia** station leave from Piazza Jacopone – between Piazza del Popolo and San Fortunato – fifteen minutes before each train departure. Some inter-town buses also leave from Piazza Jacopone, together with a once-daily service to

Rome. Tickets and information are issued from the fruit shop in the piazza next to the *Ristorante Jacopone*. If you're arriving by **car** you'll be hard pressed to navigate Todi's narrow streets and one-way system, never mind find a parking place in the centre. The best plan is to leave your car outside the walls at Porta Perugina, Piazzale della Consolazione or Porta Romana. If you really can't face the walk, you could try for one of the limited pay **parking places** in Piazza del Mercato Vecchio, southeast of the main Piazza del Popolo.

The Town

All the main sights in Todi are within a few minutes' walk of each other. If you take a minibus up from the terminus you'll find yourself at the central **Piazza del Popolo**; walking up via the footpath leaves you in the municipal gardens, near the church of **San Fortunato**. Shuttle buses from the station drop passengers in front of San Fortunato. Thereafter everything's within walking distance, though the southeast part of the town around Porta Romana involves a long downhill hike, as does the walk to **Santa Maria della Consolazione**. Like many a hill-town, however, random exploration is one of Todi's pleasures.

The Piazza del Popolo

The **Piazza del Popolo** is often described as the most perfect medieval piazza in Italy – and with full justice, even if the cars detract slightly from the overall effect. Flanked by a range of palazzi and a superb duomo, it's enough to take the breath away, however many other Italian hill-towns you've seen. Originally the site of the Roman forum, it is built above a surviving complex of Roman cisterns.

The **Duomo** (daily in summer 8.30am–12.30pm & 2–5.30pm or 3–7pm; free), atop a broad flight of steps (added in 1740), represents a merging of the last of the Romanesque and the first of the Gothic forms filtering in from France in the early fourteenth century. Construction started at the beginning of the twelfth century, on the site of a Roman temple to Apollo, and continued intermittently until the seventeenth. The square, three-tiered **facade**, recently restored, is inspired simplicity, with just a sumptuous rose window and ornately carved composite doorway (1513 and 1639) to embellish the pink weathered marble – the classic example of a form found all over Umbria and the Abruzzo. The exterior sides of the church are more complicated and it's worth walking down adjoining side streets for glimpses of arches, windows and bulging buttresses.

In the **interior** there's some impressive nineteenth-century stained glass in the arched right-hand aisle, a lovely font (1507), an exquisite fourteenth-century *Madonna and Child* and, at the end of the aisle, a fetching altarpiece by Perugino's follower Giannicolo di Paolo. Nothing, however, matches the **choir**, carved with incredible delicacy and precision by a local father-and-son team between 1521 and 1530; a nice touch are the panels at floor level near the front which depict the tools used to carve the piece – though you may have to run the gauntlet of church attendants to get a close look. On the rear west wall, a dreadful sixteenth-century *Last Judgement* (derived from Michelangelo's Sistine Chapel fresco) defaces the back wall. Underground, there's a mildly interesting crypt-cum-passageway, entered from the top of the north aisle, scattered with Roman and possibly Etruscan fragments.

The piazza's other key buildings are a trio of thirteenth-century public palaces, squared off near the duomo in provocative fashion – the *comune*'s aim being to put one over on the Church. The **Palazzo del Capitano**, built around 1290, and the adjoining **Palazzo del Popolo**, dating from 1213 (one of Italy's earliest civic palaces), are the most prominent, thanks mainly to their external staircase, which looks like the set of a thousand B-movie swordfights. Several films have in fact been shot in Todi, which offers the twin attractions of scenographic authenticity and proximity to Cinecittà, Italy's major film studios across the border in Lazio. Most notable was the ill-fated *Cleopatra* – which explains the yellowing photographs of a pouting Elizabeth Taylor in many of the local bars.

The upper floors of Palazzo del Capitano house the small but superbly presented **Museo Comunale**, or Museo della Città (Tues–Sun: April–Aug 10.30am–1pm & 2.30–6pm; March & Sept 10.30am–1pm & 2–5pm; Oct–Feb 10.30am–1pm & 2–4.30pm; L6000), beautifully restored after having been closed for "reordering" since 1977. It's hard to know why things took so long, because the art gallery section only has a couple of dozen paintings, chief among which is a Lo Spagna copy of Ghirlandaio's *Coronation of the Virgin* (1507–11). Other parts of the museum are divided into sections devoted to the history of Todi, to local and Derutan ceramics, to textiles, coins, and to a variety of archeological displays on the town's Etruscan and Roman heritage. Changing exhibitions elsewhere give you a chance to see some of the palaces' interior spaces. The restored **Palazzo dei Priori**, built between 1293 and 1337, was the seat of Todi's various rulers and is now the town hall – note the eagle coat of arms, complete with tablecloth; if you can look like you're on council business you should be able to look inside.

The best place to enjoy the piazza's streetlife is from the **bar** down on its southwest corner, a locals' local in contrast to the smarter place midway down the piazza's western side – though the latter does a good line in sandwiches and enjoys more sunshine. Finally, for some wonderful **views** of the surrounding countryside, wander to **Piazza Garibaldi** just alongside the square. The statue here (1890) is of Giuseppe Garibaldi, while the scenically perfect cypress is supposed to have been planted to celebrate Garibaldi's visit to Todi in 1849.

San Fortunato

The single most celebrated site after the piazza is the enormous **San Fortunato** (daily 9.30am–12.30pm & 3–5pm), set above some half-hearted gardens a minute's walk away to the south. Its disproportionate size is testimony to Todi's medieval wealth, and the messy-looking and squat facade – an amalgam of Romanesque and Gothic – reflects the time it took to build the church (1292–1462). Lorenzo Maitani was commissioned to decorate the facade as he did Orvieto's duomo, and the story goes that the burghers of that town, unable to stomach the prospect of a rival church, took out a contract on him. If true, it was money spent too late, because his florid **doorway** stands good comparison with that in Orvieto, all arched swirls and carved craziness. The angel in the niche to the left of the portico is outstanding, and has been attributed to Sienese sculptor Jacopo della Quercia.

The light, airy **interior**, recently highlighted by cleaning and several controversial coats of whitewash, marks the pinnacle of the Umbrian Gothic tradition of large vaulted churches. The style was based on the smaller German-influenced "barn" churches common in Tuscany, distinguished – as here – by a single, low-pitched roof with naves and aisles of equal height. (San Domenico in Perugia is another, less successful example.) Note the grey stone brackets, added to correct the increasingly alarming lean of the supporting pilasters. The two battered stoups may date from an earlier church on the site. At the rear sits an excellent **choir** (1590), heavier and with more hints of the Baroque than the one in the duomo, as well as a few scant patches of fresco – the *Madonna* by **Masolino di Panicale** (1432) in the fourth chapel on the right is a good if somewhat battered example of this painter's rare work. Finally, take a look at the last chapel on the right, the **Cappella del Sacramento** (an amazing concentration of lovers' graffiti), at the tomb of Jacopone in the crypt (see next page) and at the **cloisters**, outside and to the right of the church. A quiet lane leads from the right of the church into the public gardens.

JACOPONE DI TODI

Fra' Jacomo dei Benedetti, known to all as **Jacopone**, was among Italy's leading medieval poets, a trenchant critic of the papacy, and the author of what was to become one of Christendom's most famous carols, the *Stabat Mater Dolorosa*. For much of his life, however, he displayed an eccentricity perhaps unequalled by any of Italy's crazed medieval mystics. Born in Todi in 1228, he pursued the life of decadence that seems the birthright of those ultimately destined for sainthood. He gambled, feasted, cavorted in fine clothes and rarely levered himself from bed before midday. After training as a lawyer in Bologna, however, he returned to Todi a respectable attorney. Aged about 38 he married **Vanna**, a young, rich and deeply devout member of the Umbrian aristocracy. A year after the marriage, however, Vanna was attending a local public festival when the platform on which she was sitting gave way. Injured, she was carried from the scene by Jacopone, who, tearing away her fine clothes, found she had been wearing a hair shirt beneath her *haute couture*. Seconds later she died in his arms.

Jacopone was inconsolable, shocked at both Vanna's death and his ignorance of her deep devotion. The experience became the catalyst for his own conversion. He sold his house, gave his wealth to the poor, distanced himself from family and friends and tramped Todi's streets dressed in rags, often spending days on all fours. He appeared at a niece's wedding dressed in tar and feathers. He added soil and wormwood to his food, to make it repugnant, and demanded to be given the most menial tasks. Applying to join the Franciscans, who had recently been established in Todi by Francis himself, he was rejected because his behaviour was deemed too extreme even by the Franciscans' exacting standards – it was to be many years before they allowed him into their community.

Spurned, he wandered Umbria's countryside for a decade, deliberately remaining cold, hungry, thirsty and dirty to atone for his sins. He also began to compose the poems and *laude* (hymns) for which he was to become famous, writing 211 in all and becoming, in the words of one modern authority, "the most popular and the most inspired of the poets of the Franciscan tradition".

He also achieved considerable fame for his outspoken criticism of the papacy. Boniface VIII, one of the most vice-ridden of popes, was a regular visitor to Todi, where he had a reserved stall in the cathedral. One of his favourite tricks was to have the tongues of heretics nailed to doors. Jacopone bravely – if tactlessly – said of him: "Blasphemous tongue, that has poisoned the world,/There is no kind of ugly sin/In which you have not become infamous." He was imprisoned for his eloquence, lucky to escape with his life, and remained incarcerated for five years in the papal dungeons of Palestrina, near Rome. Only the election of Pope Benedict XI in 1303 secured his release. Returning to Todi he joined a Franciscan convent at Collazzone, north of Todi, where he contrived to die on Christmas Day, 1306. Todi remembers him with a piazza and the vast mausoleum in the crypt of San Fortunato.

Santa Maria della Consolazione

If you've not already seen Santa Maria della Consolazione before coming up into town, the nicest way to approach the church is after San Fortunato by way of the **public gardens**. An enjoyable spot for a siesta or picnic, the gardens are full of shady nooks and narrow pathways, and a cut above the normal town plot. On this western edge of town, there's also a kids' playground and a very small **Rocca** – of Albornoz vintage – both far less noteworthy than the views, which are extensive, if often obscured by haze. At the gardens' western end a zigzag path cuts down to Viale della Consolazione for the church.

Many architectural cognoscenti rate **Santa Maria della Consolazione** (closed daily 1–3pm) as one of the best Renaissance churches in Italy. Completed in 1607, the project was initiated a century earlier by Cola da Caprarola, possibly using one of Bramante's drafts from St Peter's in Rome. The church's use of alternating types of window in the cupola – "rhythmic bays" – are a Bramante trademark. Over the years, virtually every leading architect of the day had his say, including Sangallo, Peruzzi and Vignola. Eventually it came to conform to most of the precepts articulated by Alberti, the great theoretician of Renaissance architecture: a Greek-cross floor plan (purity of form and proportion), isolation in an open piazza, a white or near-white finish (purity again), high windows (cutting off from earthly contact) and a preference for statuary over painting (again of greater "purity" than painting).

The rest of the town

For a reminder of ancient Todi, take a look at the so-called **nicchioni** (niches) in Piazza del Mercato Vecchio; sited just below the Piazza del Popolo, they constitute more or less all that's left of the Roman colony. The town's proud of them, but they don't amount to much: four slightly overgrown arches, which perhaps formed the wall of an Augustan basilica.

Two minutes' walk down the lane from the lowest corner of the piazza brings you to **San Ilario** (also known as San Carlo), an ancient Lombard chapel well off the beaten track, and all too often locked to protect a fresco of the *Madonna della Misericordia* by Lo Spagna. Just beyond the church, adjoining a crumbling, flower-strewn arbour, is the **Fonte Scarnabecco** (1241), an unusual arched fountain that was Todi's lifeblood and social meeting place before piped water.

Last-call churches include **San Filippo**, dull except for frescoed panels on the right-hand wall, and the more interesting **San Nicolò**, distinguished by a striking wooden ceiling, three imposing Gothic arches and two small Umbrian frescoes on the left-hand wall. Both are immediately inside the medieval walls at Porta Romana. You might also drop in on thirteenth-century **Santa Maria in Camuccia**, two minutes off Via Roma, recently robbed of – but later reunited with – a priceless twelfth-century wooden Madonna. Two beautifully fluted Roman columns flanking the entrance are the most substantial parts of a large collection of Roman pieces dug up from under the church; for a look at the minor pieces, chat up the resident priest – the stuff is in his quarters.

Practicalities

Todi's **tourist office** (daily 9am–1pm & 4–7pm; closed Sun afternoon in winter; ☎075.894.2686 or 075.894.3395, fax 075.894.2406) is located under the arcade of the Palazzo del Popolo at Piazza del Popolo 38. The **post office** is in Piazza Garibaldi (Mon–Fri 8.30am–6.30pm, Sat 8am–noon); for currency **exchange** there's a convenient bank opposite the tourist office.

Accommodation

All but one of Todi's **hotels** are outside the walls, the only central option being the pricey but very pleasant four-star *Fonte Cesia* (☎075.894.3737, fax 075.894.4677; ⑥), just south of Piazza del Popolo at Via Lorenzo Leoni 3. This relatively new arrival has slightly dented the custom of the town's other four-star, the *Bramante*, Via Orvietana 48 (☎075.894.8381, fax 075.894.8074; ⑤), a converted convent with swimming pool and tennis courts. Other hotels are in modern and therefore uninspiring parts of town. Ten minutes' walk down the main road from Porta Romana brings you to the three-star *Tuder*, Via Maestà dei Lombardi 13 (☎075.894.2184, fax 075.894.3952; ③), a functional place if ever there was one. A short distance beyond it is the relatively posh three-star *Villa Luisa*, Via Angelo Cortesi 147 (☎075.894.8571, fax 075.894.8472; ④). Todi also has three sets of **rooms** for rent within the walls: Elisa Mariotti, Via del Forno 12 (☎075.894.2809; ③); Serenella Proietti, Via del Monte 17 (☎075.894.3231; ③); and the luxurious *San Lorenzo*, San Lorenzo 3 (☎075.894.4555; ⑤). The monastery of Santissima Annunziata, Via San Biagio 2 (☎075.894.2268; ②), will also take women, families and couples, and the Convento di Montesanto, Viale Montesanto (☎075.894.8886; ②), occasionally accepts guests, but in both cases be certain to confirm availability.

With a car or bike you might use the **agriturismo** accommodation in nearby hamlets. Bed and breakfast, swimming and horse riding are offered at the idyllically situated *La Palazzetta*, c/o Patrizia Caracciolo, in Aspoli, 8km west of Todi in the hills (☎075.885.3219, fax 075.885.3358; March to mid-Dec; ④). Equally delightful is the *Tenuta di Canonica*, Canonica 75 (☎075.894.545, fax 075.894.581; ④), situated on a hilltop 5km from Todi; you get magnificent views, rooms with beamed ceilings and four-posters and a swimming pool. To reach it, take the road for Orvieto and Lago di Corbara, turn right at the Prodo-Titignano junction, then left at the Cordigliano turning. In the other direction, try the three-room *Agricola Todini* in Collevalenza (☎075.887.231; ⑤), 11km southeast of Todi on the Massa Martana road, where the high rates buy you swimming, riding, archery and other diversions.

Restaurants

The town's most enjoyable **restaurant** for lunch is the *Umbria*, behind the tourist office; prices are high – up to L50,000 – and service can be slow and offhand, but the panorama from the outside terrace makes it all worthwhile; in season arrive early or book to be sure of an outside table (☎075.894.390; closed Wed). Cheaper alternatives include the friendly, old-fashioned *Cavour* at Corso Cavour 21 (closed Wed), with outside dining on a fine panoramic terrace, and the basic *Pizzeria-Rosticceria* off Corso Cavour in Piazza B. d'Alviano, 100m from Piazza del Popolo (closed Mon after 8pm).

Along the Tiber valley

North of Todi, the **Tiber valley** broadens out to a plain, edged with low hills and dotted with light industry. It's not an area where you'll want to spend a lot of time – and most people tear through on the new dual carriageway or crawl along on the FCU train. A few of the castles, villages and Romanesque churches, however, are worthwhile if you're in no hurry to get to Perugia.

The west bank

Off to the west of the valley, the spectacularly sited **MONTE CASTELLO DI VIBIO** is a possible first halt, 12km from Todi, off the N397. This eagle's nest of a village dominates the countryside almost more than Todi, and its castle was one of a reputed 365 fortresses that formed a defensive screen around the town. There's little to see, save extraordinary views and the usual maze of medieval alleyways. It does, however, make an excellent base if Todi's hotels are full or you wish to be away from the crowds, thanks to a 20-room three-star hotel, *Il Castello* (☎075.878.0560, fax 075.868.0561; ④), superbly converted from a sixteenth-century patrician town house.

Below Monte Castello the walled village of **FRATTA TODINA** is guarded by another castle, strengthened in the fifteenth century by the local warlord Braccio Fortebraccio as a garrison for his troops. Near the centre of the village is a Franciscan monastery, which features in many of the stories and legends of the order. Moving north, **MARSCIANO** is the region's main town – modern and without interest. **CERQUETO** has Perugino frescoes of *St Sebastian* in its parish church – and there are other damaged works attributed to the artist at the edge of the village in the Maestà di Santa Lucia. Impressive castle remains are to be seen a kilometre away at Sant'Elena.

The east bank

GIANO DELL'UMBRIA is the most substantial village on the east flank of the valley, 23km from Todi along a looping detour off the N316. Two buses daily (Mon–Sat) come here from Foligno, one more on school days. A perfect fortified hamlet, it is ringed by olive groves and pastoral countryside. Take the road south of the village, fork left at the junction after about a kilometre and you'll come to the only hotel for a long way, the two-star *Park Hotel* (☎0742.90.551; ③), with just seven rooms but a cavernous dining room. The only **campsite**, the *Pineta di Giano*, is opposite the hotel at Colle del Gallo, Montecerreto (☎0742.90.178; April–Sept); it has a swimming pool and a beautiful site, backed by the tree-covered slopes of the Monti Martani. Several paths run up to the summit ridge, which in May and June has exceptional carpets of wild flowers, and magnificent views as far as Todi all year. There's an excellent little-known **restaurant**, *Il Buongustaio* (closed Wed), immediately within Giano's walls at the village's southern entrance.

North of Giano, the unfortunately named Bastardo is a modern mess with nothing to recommend it. **GUALDO CATTANEO**, just beyond, is by contrast an enticing medieval hill-village. Virtually every hamlet within a ten-kilometre radius of here has a **castle**, those at Barattano, Cisterna, Pozzo and Sargano being particularly outstanding. Some hamlets have a castle and Romanesque church, as at Marcellano, with its frescoed twelfth-century church of **Sant'Angelo**, and Grutti, whose name derives from the nearby grottoes of early Christians.

Slightly north are two more short-stop villages. **COLLAZZONE** has the usual hill-town tally – good views and medieval streets – with scenic roads around through olives and oak forest. The parish church in **CASTELLEONE**, over towards Deruta, has frescoes by Matteo da Gualdo, a fifteenth-century Umbrian more usually active farther north.

Madonna dei Bagni

The church of **Madonna dei Bagni**, 2km south of Deruta, is the one sight on the main SS3bis that's definitely worth a detour. Its walls are covered with hundreds of votive tiles left by pilgrims over the last three centuries, yielding a unique insight into the peculiarities of religious belief and the changes in daily life. The most entertaining are those offered as thanks for escapes from dangerous and not so dangerous corners – fire, flood, famine, a fall from a cow, a bite from a donkey. They also represent an off-beat record of the area's thriving ceramic tradition. Sadly, a hundred tiles were stolen in 1980, so opening times are curtailed as a result. The best time to try is on Saturday morning, when it's not unknown for coach parties to show up; otherwise ask at the tourist office in Deruta.

ROMANESQUE CHURCHES EAST OF THE TIBER

With a car you might try to take in some of the hill-villages east of the Tiber – almost any you choose will be quiet and boast a **Romanesque church**. Most of these are built over the graves of early monks and martyrs, the Tiber and Naia valleys having been amongst the earliest to be colonized by Christians fleeing Roman persecution.

This area and the region south towards Terni thus formed the springboard of Umbria's monastic tradition. Perhaps the most rewarding churches are those you come on by accident, in crumbling hamlets or in the midst of the ilex woods that blanket surrounding hills. If you prefer to plan a visit, the following are outstanding: Viepri, Villa di San Faustino, Santa Maria in Partano, San Teranzano and the Abbazia di San Fidenzio.

Deruta

DERUTA is best known for its **ceramics** and seems to be devoted entirely to the craft. Some of the stuff is mass-produced trash and some so big that you'd need a trailer to get it home – much, though, is handmade, hand-painted, portable and by general consent among Italy's best. The Romans worked the local clay, but it was the discovery of distinctive blue and yellow glazes in the fifteenth century, allied with the Moorish-influenced designs of southern Spain, that put the town firmly on the map. Some fifty workshops traded as far afield as Britain, and pieces from Deruta's sixteenth-century heyday have found their way into the world's major museums. Designs these days are mainly copies, with little original work; if you're serious about this sort of thing, avoid the roadside stalls and head for the workshops of the new town for the best selection and prices.

The **old town** on the hill isn't particularly compelling, apart from the **Museo Regionale della Ceramica** (daily: April–June 10.30am–1pm & 3–6pm; July–Sept 10am–1pm & 3.30–7pm; Oct–March 10am–1pm & 2.30–5pm but closed Tues; L5000), alongside the tourist office on the main Piazza dei Consoli. The museum features a varied ceramic collection, with a few works by contemporary craftspeople, and a sixteenth-century **tiled floor** lifted wholesale from the church of San Francesco. It also contains a tiny art gallery whose high spots are a detached, damaged but rare fresco (1478) by Fiorenzo di Lorenzo and a *Madonna and Child* and *gonfalone* by Nicolò Alunno. **San Francesco** itself is the only other mild distraction in the town, largely ruined in the eighteenth century and distinguished only by the tiniest fragments of fourteenth-century fresco.

Torgiano

TORGIANO, 8km north of Deruta, is the last worthwhile stop before Perugia. Though a fairly dull town, it is home to Umbria's finest wines, all of them produced by **Giorgio Lungarotti**, one of the new breed of Italian producers. A self-made man and now something of a national celebrity, he's put together an unexpectedly interesting and extensive 20-room **wine museum** in a fine palazzo on Via Garibaldi (daily: May–Sept 9am–1pm & 3–7pm; Oct–April 9am–1pm & 3–6pm; L5000). A varied and comprehensive look at every aspect of viticulture, the collection, which has explanations in English, includes oddments of medieval machinery, documents, waffle irons (to make the traditional *cialde* biscuits eaten with Vinsanto) and archeological fragments connected with wine-making.

You can buy the cheaper Torgiano wines in most Italian supermarkets, but the **Rubesco Riserva**, which rates as one of Italy's very finest, is rather more elusive. Also look out for Torre di Giano, Chardonnay and Castel Grifone, all widely available in the town and elsewhere.

Orvieto

ORVIETO sits on a spectacular table-top of volcanic tufa whose sheer sides fall 325m to the vine-covered valley floor – a cliff-edged remnant of the four volcanoes whose eruptions also bequeathed the soils that produce Orvieto's fine wines. Out on a limb from the rest of Umbria, the town is perfectly placed between Rome and Florence to serve as a historical picnic for tour operators, and tourists flood here in their millions, drawn by the **duomo** – one of the greatest Gothic buildings in Italy and home of some amazing frescoes by Luca Signorelli, recently unveiled after years of painstaking restoration. Once these have been admired, Orvieto is not especially exhilarating, though the *centro storico*, the views and the renowned white **wine** are enough to justify a night's stop.

The city is one of the most ancient in Italy, thanks to its irresistible site. Bronze and Iron Age tribes were present before it became **Volsinii Veteres**, or Velzna, a leading member of the twelve-strong Etruscan federation. In 264 BC the Romans displaced the Etruscans to present-day Bolsena, or Volsinii Novi – the place they abandoned becoming known as

Urbs Vetus (the old city), thus Orvieto. Its medieval influence was considerable, the independent *comune* challenging Florence and eventually claiming land as far as Monte Amiata in the north to the coast at Orbetello. Power and prestige remained high until the usual internecine squabbling, the Black Death of 1348 sounding the town's effective death knell. It passed to the Church for good a hundred years later and became something of a papal home from home – 32 popes in all were to stay in the city.

Arrival, information and accommodation

Fast **trains** on the Rome to Florence run tend to bypass Orvieto, so you may well have to change to a slower connecting service at Orte or Chiusi. Orvieto's **station**, also the terminal for some out-of-town **buses**, is in the grim new town of Orvieto Scalo, a twisting three-kilometre drive from the old centre. The local #1 bus makes the trip every fifteen minutes via Piazzale Cahen to Piazza XXIX Marzo, a short way north of the duomo; the #2 and #3 run by marginally longer routes to the slightly more central Piazza della Repubblica: tickets for all three buses are on sale from the station bar – buy one for the return trip, too, as outlets are few. As a fun alternative, you could take the restored nineteenth-century **funicular** from the far side of the station forecourt. After rising through the trees and burrowing through the remains of the town's medieval fortress its end point is Piazzale Cahen; from here minibus A (every 15min) shuttles backwards and forwards to Piazza del Duomo – though it's an easy walk – while minibus B (every 20min) makes a circuit of the old town, touching Piazza XXIX Marzo and Piazza della Repubblica; bus tickets are valid for the funicular ride. Be sure to hang on to your bus or funicular tickets, as they earn you a reduction on admittance to the town's best museum, part of an enlightened policy to try and keep cars out of the centre.

This said, **cars** aren't prohibited in the old town, but finding a parking space is a tall order. There are car parks in Piazzale Cahen and off Via Roma just to the west, but you may be best off parking in the big free car park on the east side of the station and taking the bus or funicular to the old town. Another alternative is to park at Campo della Fiera, below the southwest corner of the old town, where you can pick up local buses #2 or #3 on their run from the station to Piazza della Repubblica; **pedestrian escalators** up to the centre also run from this point.

The excellent and very helpful **tourist office** at Piazza del Duomo 24 (Mon–Fri 8am–2pm & 4–7pm, Sat & Sun 10am–1pm & 3.30–6.30pm; ☎0763.341.772 or 0763.342.562) operates a free **accommodation service**; in addition to the hotels, it has details of a few private rooms and a dozen or so bed and breakfast **agriturismo** options in hamlets scattered around the town. Usually, hotels are pretty easy to find in the centre of town. If you run into problems there are a dozen or so cheap, modern but characterless places in Orvieto Scalo. All but one of the local **campsites** are some way out. The *Benvenuti a Orvieto/Welcome to Orvieto* pamphlet has just about all the extra practical information you'll need.

Hotels

Istituto SS. Salvatore, Via del Popolo 1 (☎0763.342.910). You can stay cheaply with the nuns in this central Dominican convent, but the minimum stay is two nights and there is a 10pm curfew (9pm autumn and winter); 14 rooms with and without bathrooms. ②.

Duomo, Vicolo di Maurizio 7 (☎0763.341.887). An excellent central 17-room two-star option in the first alley to the left of the duomo: some cheaper rooms without private bathroom. ③.

Posta, Via Luca Signorelli 18 (☎0763.341.909). First choice amongst the cheaper central hotels, 2-min from the duomo, with a garden and 20 cool, quiet and pleasant rooms with and without private bathrooms. ③.

Filippeschi, Via Filippeschi 19 (☎ & fax 0763.343.275). Moderately priced 15-room three-star located just west of Piazza della Repubblica. ④.

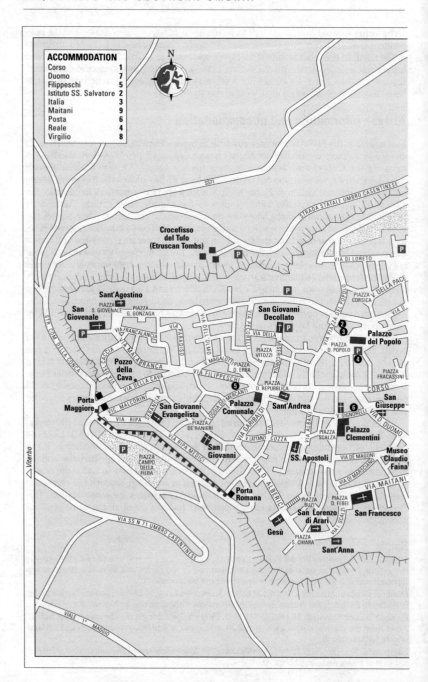

ACCOMMODATION

Corso	1
Duomo	7
Filippeschi	5
Istituto SS. Salvatore	2
Italia	3
Maitani	9
Posta	6
Reale	4
Virgilio	8

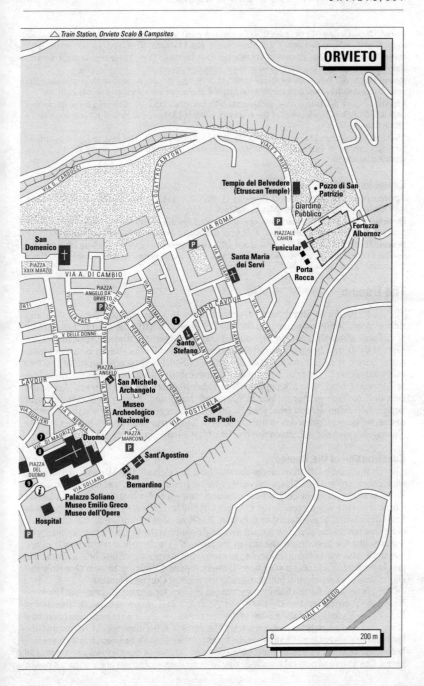

ORVIETO

Tempio del Belvedere
(Etruscan Temple)

Pozzo di San
Patrizio

VIALE E. CRISPI

Giardino
Pubblico

VIA QUATTROCANTONI

VIA G. CARDUCCI

VIA ROMA

PIAZZALE
CAHEN

Fortezza
Albornoz

San
Domenico

Funicular

PIAZZA
XXIX MARZO

Santa Maria
dei Servi

VIA BELISARIO

Porta
Rocca

VIA A. DI CAMBIO

VIA DI MONTEMARTE

PIAZZA
ANGELO DA
ORVIETO

VIA U. ILARIO

VIA CAVALLOTTI

VICO. DELLA PACE

CORSO CAVOUR

VIA ANGELO DA ORVIETO

VIA FARNESE

V. DELLE DONNE

VIA DI BERTICHE

Santo
Stefano

VIA SANTO STEFANO

CAVOUR

PIAZZA
S. ANGELO

San Michele
Archangelo

VIA S. PORCARI

VIA GUALIERI

VIA C. NEBBIA

VIA SANT'ANGELO

Museo
Archeologico
Nazionale

VIA POSTIERLA

San Paolo

VIC. DI MAURIZIO

PIAZZA
MARCONI

Duomo

Sant'Agostino

PIAZZA
DEL
DUOMO

San
Bernardino

VIA SOLIANA

Palazzo Soliano
Museo Emilio Greco
Museo dell'Opera

Hospital

VIALE 1° MAGGIO

0   200 m

Corso, Corso Cavour 343 (☎ & fax 0763.342.020). A good but slightly pricey three-star hotel close to the Corso's intersection with Via di Montemarte: just 12 rooms, all with private bathroom. ④.

Italia, Piazza del Popolo 13 (☎0763.342.065, fax 0763.342.066). The biggest central hotel, with 45 three-star rooms, and thus likely to have space in an emergency. ④.

Reale, Piazza del Popolo 25 (☎ & fax 0763.341.247). Slightly less expensive three-star than the neighbouring *Italia* if you go for one of the handful of cheaper rooms without private bath. ④.

Virgilio, Piazza del Duomo 5–6 (☎0763.341.882, fax 0763.343.797). Celebrated for its perfect position, though only a handful of the relatively modest 13 three-star rooms actually have views of the duomo. ⑤.

Maitani, Via Lorenzo Maitani 5 (☎0763.342.012, fax 0763.342.011). The best and most central of Orvieto's quartet of four-star hotels if you're splashing out – and with 40 rooms there's a good chance of space. ⑥.

Campsites

Agricampeggio Sossogna, Rocca Ripasena 61 (☎0763.343.141). Small site 7km west of Orvieto, with limited tenting space. Open May to mid-Oct.

Orvieto (☎0744.950.240). Smart three-star site on the Lago di Corbara shore, reached by the SS448 Todi road; it's a couple of kilometres' walk from the *Scacco Matto* (see below). Open all year.

Scacco Matto (☎0744.950.163, fax 0763.950.373). Basic one-star site by the Corbara lake; take the bus for Civitella del Lago (two daily) or Narni (six daily; alight at Baschi). Open April–Sept. Has a few rooms to rent as well. (②).

The Duomo

The historian Jacob Burckhardt described Orvieto's **Duomo** as "the greatest and richest polychrome monument in the world"; Pope Leo XIII called it the "Golden Lily of Italian cathedrals", adding that on the Day of Judgement it would float to Heaven carried by its own beauty. Though the cathedral's overall effect might be a bit rich for some tastes, it rates – with Assisi's Basilica di San Francesco – as one of the two essential sights in Umbria. The interior is **open daily** throughout the year from 7am to 1pm and from 2.30 to 5.30pm from November to February; to 6.30pm in March and October; to 7pm in April; 8pm in May and June; and 7.30pm between July and September. Admission is **free**, though there is a charge of L3000 to see the superbly restored Signorelli frescoes in the Cappella di San Brizio (also known as the Cappella Nuova). Tickets are sold from the tourist office outside in Piazza del Duomo.

Construction of the Duomo

Church tradition holds that the duomo was built to celebrate the **Miracle of Bolsena**, which occurred in 1263. The protagonist, a young Bavarian priest, was on a pilgrimage to Rome to shake off his disbelief in transubstantiation – the idea that the body and blood of Christ are physically present in the Eucharist. While he celebrated Mass in a church near Lago di Bolsena, blood started to drip from the Host onto the *corporale*, the white linen cloth that covers the altar, "each stain severally assuming the form of a human head with features like the Volto Santo, the face of the Saviour". The linen was whisked off to Pope Urban IV, who was holed up in Orvieto to escape the literal and political heat in Rome. He proclaimed a miracle and a year later Thomas Aquinas, then teaching in Orvieto's San Domenico, drew up a papal bull instigating the feast of **Corpus Domini**.

The cornerstone for the building was not put in place for another 25 years (laid by Pope Nicholas IV on November 13, 1290) and Aquinas's bull makes no specific mention of Bolsena, so it's likely that the raising of the duomo was as much a shrewd piece of political pragmatism as a celebration of a miracle. The papacy at the time was in retreat and the Umbrian towns – not least Orvieto – at the height of their civic expansion. Thus it seems likely that the building of this awe-inspiring cathedral, in one of the region's most powerful towns, was a piece of political muscle-flexing to remind errant citizens of the papacy's power.

It was in fact miraculous that the duomo was built at all. Medieval Orvieto was so violent that at times the population considered abandoning the city altogether. Dante wrote that its family feuds were worse than those between Verona's Montecchi and Cappelli, inspiration for Shakespeare's murderous Montagues and Capulets in *Romeo and Juliet*. In addition to civic strife, the building was also dogged by a committee approach to design, the plans being modified continually to accommodate changes in architectural taste. At least the site posed no problems: the city's highest point was previously home to an Etruscan temple and Orvieto's first cathedral, Santa Maria Prisca. Even today the cathedral continues to dominate the skyline for miles around.

The architect of the building is unknown, though it seems possible that it was Arnolfo di Cambio, designer of Florence's duomo. At Orvieto the plan initially was for a simple and orthodox Romanesque church, but in the early years of work a local architect's extravagant departures into the Gothic brought the structure close to collapse, leading to the call-up in 1310 of the Sienese master, **Lorenzo Maitani**. In the course of three decades he guided the construction at its most crucial stage and produced the magnificent carvings on the facade. Though building dragged on for over three hundred years, exhausting 33 architects, 152 sculptors, 68 painters and 90 mosaicists, the final product is a surprisingly unified example of the transitional Romanesque-Gothic style.

The facade

The monumental facade is just the right side of overkill: a riot of columns, spires, bas-reliefs, sculptures, dazzling colour, colossal doorways and hundreds of capricious details held together by four enormous fluted pillars. Many have compared it to a painted triptych in an elaborate frame. Fifty-two metres high and recently cleaned and overhauled, it is a stunning spectacle from the piazza, particularly at sunset or under floodlights. Most of the basic work was accomplished by Maitani, but such illustrious names as Andrea Pisano and Andrea Orcagna – responsible for much of the rose window – also had a hand in design and construction.

The four pillars at the base are among the highlights of fourteenth-century Italian **sculpture**. The work of Maitani and his pupils, they depict episodes from the **Old and New Testaments** in staggering detail: lashings of plague, famine, martyrdom, mutilation and murder – Cain slaying Abel is especially powerful. They were created partly to point an accusing finger at Orvieto's moral slackers, as the extraordinary final panel makes clear, with the damned packed off to eternal fire, brimstone and the company of an awful lot of snakes.

Maitani was also responsible for the four large bronzes of the symbols of the Evangelists across the first tier, and for the angels over the beautiful central **doorway**. These, however, together with the *Madonna* in the lunette, have been removed for restoration and will probably be replaced by copies: the originals are lined up for display in the Museo dell'Opera. The **mosaics**, the facade's showiest aspect, are mostly eighteenth- and nineteenth-century additions, replacements for originals nabbed by Rome. Only the four examples in the corners of Orcagna's huge **rose window** (1359), have any vintage, completed around 1388. The central bronze doors, by Emilio Greco, were made as recently as 1965, and in the best traditions of the duomo were added after much talk and controversy.

Cappella di San Brizio

At first little grabs your attention in the duomo interior, save a few snatches of fresco in the scalloped side niches and the work immediately on your left as you enter, a heavily restored *Madonna and Child* (1425) by Gentile da Fabriano, with a very sickly-looking Jesus. However, in the right transept – the **Cappella di San Brizio** – are **Luca Signorelli**'s superlative paintings of the **Last Judgement** (1499–1504), one of Italy's great fresco cycles and one that had a profound influence on Michelangelo's version in the Sistine Chapel, painted forty years later. The frescoes are now open to public view, having been under restorers' wraps for several years (April–Oct Mon–Sat 10am–12.45pm & 2.30–7.15pm, Sun 2.30–6.45pm; Nov–March Mon–Sat 10am–12.45pm & 2.30–5.15pm, Sun 2.30–5.45pm; L3000).

Several painters tackled the chapel before Signorelli. **Fra' Angelico** made a start in 1447, completing two of the ceiling's eight vaults, **Christ in Glory with Angels (1)** and **The Prophets (3)**, with the assistance of Benozzo Gozzoli, whose hand can be seen in the angels of the latter panel. Angelico, it appears, suggested the frescoes' central theme, the Last Judgement, but was then called to Rome to work in the Vatican, never to return. The murder of a local grandee involved in financing the project, Arigo Monaldeschi, then brought work on the duomo to one of its periodic halts. Perugino popped up forty years later and for reasons unknown disappeared – never to return – after working for just five days. Signorelli saved the day, graciously restoring Fra' Angelico's work and completing the vaults according to the original plan.

Work then started in earnest on the walls, all but the lowest of which are crowded with passionate and beautifully observed muscular figures, creating an effect that's both realistic and almost grotesquely fantastic at the same time. Seven main episodes are painted in the eight panels of the vaults and the twelve floor-level groups of frescoes. The first is the **End of the World (9)** on the entrance wall, the last of the major episodes painted (1503–4). In the lower right foreground are depicted Eritrea, a sibyl, shown holding a book of prophecies, while alongside is the Prophet David, who is shown asserting the veracity of the prophecies. Behind them an earthquake brings down a temple and three youths fall prey to brigands; in the background ships are tossed on a sea convulsed by a tidal wave brought on by the earthquake. High up on the left you see the fall of the rebel angels, many of whom unleash thunderbolts of fire which fall on a terrified crowd below. A putto in the panel's centre holds a sign with the mark of the Opera del Duomo (O.P.S.M), a reminder of the cathedral works committee responsible for commissioning and overseeing the project.

The first lunette panel on the wall left of the entrance depicts one of the cycle's most powerful works, the **Preaching of the Antichrist (10)**, the iconography of which is unique (the subject itself is very rare in Italian painting). It derives from a text whose precise authorship is unknown, but which unites elements from ancient millennial texts – the world was widely expected to end in the year 1000 – and the *Golden Legend* of Jacopo da Varagine (also the inspiration for Piero della Francesca's Arezzo cycle: see p.415). The Antichrist is shown preaching and bears the image of Christ, albeit one that displays a demonic demeanour, with a devil whispering in his ear. Various historical figures stand amidst the crowd, designed to represent all colours, creeds and conditions of the human family: Signorelli has portrayed himself with Fra'Angelico (in the black of a Dominican monk) in the left foreground, both apparently unperturbed by the garroting taking place in front of them. Also present are Dante, Cesare Borgia (on the extreme left of the group with beard, blond hair and red hat) and Pius II (see p.311), the corpulent fellow behind the figure with hands on hips alongside the Antichrist. Groups of Franciscan and Dominican monks can be seen trying to calculate the precise date of the end of the world – one counts off three and a half years with his fingers, the 1290 days the reign of the Antichrist was expected to endure.

The sequence then moves to the first lunette on the right wall with the **Resurrection of the Dead (11)**, summoned by the trumpets of the angels depicted on high. Signorelli here departs from convention, painting the figures emerging dramatically from the bare earth rather than from tombs, the traditional iconography employed in depictions of this scene. Note the small scratched figures at the centre of the panel, probably drawn by Signorelli to illustrate some point to the cathedral committee. The adjoining lunette on the right wall depicts **Inferno (12)**, probably Signorelli's first completed fresco in the chapel.

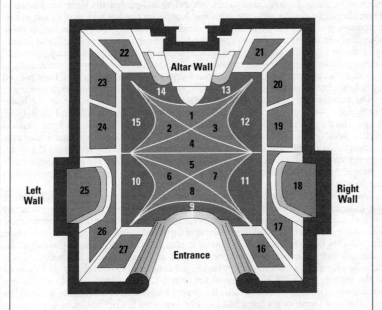

CAPPELLA DI SAN BRIZIO

1. Christ in Glory with Angels
2. The Apostles
3. The Prophets
4. Portents of the Last Judgement
5. The Martyrs
6. The Patriarchs
7. The Doctor of the Church
8. The Virgins
9. The End of the World
10. The Preaching of the Antichrist
11. The Resurrection of the Dead
12. Inferno
13. Purgatory
14. The Calling of the Saved
15. Paradiso
16. Monument to Cardinal Ferdinando Nuzzi (d. 1717)
17. Portrait of Tibullus
18. Pietà, SS. Faustino and Pietro Parenzo, and Martyrdom of the Saints by Luca Signorelli
19. Ovid and four tondo scenes from Metamorphases
20. Portrait of Claudian
21. Scenes from Ovid's Metamorphases
22. Scenes from Dante's Purgatorio
23. Portrait of Statius
24. Portrait of Dante: Medallions here and around and joining panels show scenes from Cantos 1 - 11 of Purgatorio
25. Cappella Gualtieri (1736); painting of Saints (1724) by Ludovico Muratori
26. Portrait of Sallust: Medallions - Classical scenes and grape harvest
27. Empedodes (?) and The End of The World

On the altar wall right of the window is **Purgatory (13)**, which in its portrayal of the damned inevitably draws on Dante's *The Divine Comedy*, but also utilizes the iconography of pagan works such as the battle scenes carved on the reliefs on Trajan's Column in Rome. The panel left of the window shows the **Calling of the Saved (14)**, a portrayal that includes two of Orvieto's saintly protectors, Costanzo and Brizio, at its centre; St Michael weighing the souls; and angels serenading and guiding the elected to **Paradiso (15)**, the scene portrayed in the adjoining lunette on the left wall. In this last mural, Paradise's peace and harmony are symbolized by a heavenly choir of nine angel musicians and – in the centre – by two angels who scatter roses and camellias. These flowers were painted onto dry plaster, a less durable technique than the more usual practice of adding paint to wet plaster – hence their faded appearance. The altarpiece, incidentally, is the *Madonna di San Brizio*, an anonymous work held by tradition to have been painted by St Luke, but in truth probably executed towards the end of the fourteenth century.

The outstanding **frescoes and medallions** (numbered **16** to **26**) on the lower parts of the walls are also by Signorelli and include portraits of Homer, Dante, Ovid, Virgil, Horace, Lucan, Empedocles and others, together with episodes from classical myth – notably Ovid's *Metamorphoses* and Dante's *Divine Comedy*. Of particular note is the *Pietà with SS. Faustino and Pietro Parenzo* (**18**) in the recess on the right. Vasari claimed that the figure of the dead Christ was a close portrait of Signorelli's own son, Antonio, who died from the plague in 1502 while the artist was employed on the frescoes.

Everything here has a didactic purpose, further illustrating or drawing allusions to the main theme of the frescoes above. Dante's *Divine Comedy* – which is frequently evoked – forms an obvious corollary, with its themes of salvation and damnation. Elsewhere, however, Signorelli uses Classical myth and literary figures to his own ends; Empedocles (**27**), for example, is shown in shocked contemplation of the end of the world, though he in fact never prophesied such an event. Some critics believe this is actually a figure of a common man who has not converted to Christianity, and looks on at the horrors that await him as one of the damned. The portrait of Stazio is used in a similar way. The figure looks towards the chapel's high altar as if receiving spiritual illumination, but Dante writes that while the poet converted to Christianity, he kept his conversion and subsequent faith a secret. Throughout the Middle Ages the figure was therefore a symbol of salvation and also of only partial redemption – just the sort of character who would have been compromised, to say the least, come the Day of Judgement.

Cappella del Corporale and the apse

The artistic pyrotechnics of the Cappella di San Brizio rather overshadow the opposite transept's **Cappella del Corporale**, which contains the sacred *corporale* of the Miracle of Bolsena, locked away in a massive, jewel-encrusted casket designed in 1358 as a copy of the facade. On the chapel walls are extensive **frescoes** (1357–64) by a local artist, Ugolino di Prete Ilario, depicting episodes from the *Miracle of Bolsena* (right-hand wall) and various *Miracles of the Sacrament* (opposite). The chapel also houses (on the right) the glorious freestanding *Madonna dei Raccomandati* (1339) by the Sienese painter Lippo Memmi.

The entire **apse** is covered in frescoes (1370–84) by Ugolino with scenes from the *Life of the Virgin*, many of which were touched up by Pinturicchio, who was eventually kicked off the job for "consuming too much gold, too much azure, and too much wine".

The rest of the town

Nothing in Orvieto can quite live up to the duomo, though the piazza has a tremendous **Etruscan museum** and a couple of other worthwhile sights. The dark tufa used as building stone around town can make parts seem a little dour during aimless exploration, particularly in poor weather, but some of the town's peripheral corners provide attractions that more than justify the walk – **San Giovenale** and the strange **Pozzo di San Patrizio** in particular. Trying to arrange a logical itinerary is difficult, but as distances are modest the walking's not too onerous.

Piazza del Duomo

On the right of the duomo lies the **Palazzo Soliano**, or Palazzo dei Papi, begun for Pope Boniface VIII in 1297. For years it has been home to the **Museo dell'Opera del Duomo** (closed for long-term restoration), previously one of the most chaotic museums in Italy though the restoration will probably tidy things up. Doubt and controversy surround the project, however, as a museum of modern sculpture (see below) has been installed in part of the building, suggesting that a new home may have to be found for all or part of the collection. Amidst a meaningless assembly of stone fragments, moth-eaten vestments, pottery and woodwormy sculptures, however, several fine items manage to stand out. They include some topnotch paintings, notably a self-portrait by Signorelli, a *Madonna and Child* (1268) by the influential early Tuscan painter Coppo di Marcovaldo, and five parts of a polyptych from San Domenico by the Sienese master Simone Martini. Among the sculptures are wooden and marble Madonnas by Nino, Giovanni and Andrea Pisano, a lovely font filled with Escher-like fishes, and unfinished but important pieces by Arnolfo di Cambio.

The same building contains the **Museo Emilio Greco**, a collection of bronzes and other work by the contemporary sculptor – well known in Italy, less so abroad – responsible for the duomo's doors (Tues–Sun: April–Sept 10.30am–1pm & 3–7pm; Oct–March 10.30am–1pm & 2–6pm; L4000, or L8000 for the *Biglietto Cumulativo* which includes entry to Pozzo di San Patrizio).

With the Palazzo Soliano on your right, the **Palazzo Papale** ahead of you, beyond the cathedral's east end, houses the **Museo Archeologico Nazionale** (Mon–Sat 9am–7pm, Sun 9am–1pm; L4000), as yet largely empty, save for four vast vaulted rooms which contain Greek vases (fourth century BC), two reconstructed painted tombs with their original murals, and other Etruscan artefacts excavated during recent digs from Orvieto's own Cannicella and Crocifisso del Tufo tombs (see below).

If the Etruscans appeal, however – and even if they don't – you are better off spending your money on the **Museo Claudio Faina** (Tues–Sun: April–Sept 9am–1pm & 3–6pm; Oct–March 10am–1pm & 2.30–5pm; L8000, or L5000 if you hold a funicular or ATC bus ticket), reopened after a renovation project which has turned a previously dull museum into a wonderful showcase for one of Italy's leading private archeological collections. It's worth the admission price simply for a **view** of the duomo from the upper floor. The germ of the collection is 34 vases given in the nineteenth century to Mauro Faina, a Perugian count, by Princess Maria Bonaparte, Napoleon's grandniece (the count had been a regular "visitor" to the princess's home). Over the years Faina, together with his nephew, added obsessively to the collection, which was left to the city in 1954. The exhibits spread over 22 rooms on two upper floors of the Palazzo Faina (plus a small ground-floor civic collection), arranged in a modern museum setting that would be the envy of far grander galleries. Highlights include three vast Attic **amphorae** (room 6) attributed to Exekias (sixth century BC), one of antiquity's finest vase painters – their presence in Orvieto testimony to the town's prosperity at the time. Also famous is the so-called **Vanth group** (rooms 11, 18 and 22), the name given to a collection of pots made locally in the last two decades of the fourth century BC. Vanth was an important female divinity associated with the Etruscan underworld, often portrayed with two serpents around each arm and, in the manner of medieval saints, with symbols such as keys, taper, mantle and scroll, the last partially unrolled to reveal the name of the goddess. As here, she was often portrayed greeting the recently deceased on their arrival in the underworld.

There are also many black *bucchero* **vases** (rooms 10, 11 and 14), so-called because at the time of their discovery they were thought to resemble vases from South America known to the Spanish as *bucaro*. The black colour was imparted in the kiln, where the firing process oxidized iron compounds in specially chosen clay. Quality declined around the fifth century BC, the result of insufficiently pure clays, a shortfall which resulted in *bucchero grigio*, or grey ware (gradually replaced by simple black-glazed pottery). A similar falling-off of quality occurred with the familiar black-figure Attic vases (rooms 11, 13 and 16), invented in Corinth around 700 BC, and made by painting a figure in black silhouette before incising detail so that the lighter-coloured clay beneath showed through. Such pottery was wildly popular throughout the Mediterranean, but no market was as large as Tyrrhenian Etruria. It was eventually replaced by Attic red-figure pottery (rooms 11, 14, 17 and 18), invented in Athens around 530 BC, in which figures and decorative details were composed in the clay and the rest of the pot painted black. If the pots begin to pall, the museum also has a large collection of coins, bronzes and miscellaneous funerary objects.

Underground Orvieto

If Etruscan remains appeal, their sixth-century BC tombs, the **Crocifisso del Tufo**, are well worth a look (daily: summer 9am–7pm; winter 9am–one hour before dusk; L4000); walk down the town's approach road from Piazza Cahen to the small car park on the left and follow the signs. There are rows of massive and sombre stone graves (more are being excavated), though none have the grandeur or the paintings of the more famous necropolises in Tarquinia or Cerveteri. Still visible, however, are Etruscan inscriptions above the tomb entrances – thought to refer to the names of the erstwhile occupants. Far more fascinating still are guided tours (in English, German or Italian) which visit the **Grotte della Rupe**, the extraordinary honeycomb of caves, wine cellars, aqueducts, quarries and tunnels cut into the crag below the town, used – and added to – since Etruscan times. A staggering 1200 separate caves have been found beneath Orvieto, around a third of the entire area under the town having been excavated at one time or another. Two separate organized **tours** can be made, the better of the pair being the tours run by *Speleotecnica* (☎0347.383.1472) on behalf of the *comune* (daily at 11am & 4pm; L10,000; at other times on request, including tours in English). Tours last an hour or so and depart from outside the tourist office at Piazza del Duomo 24, which is also where you buy tickets. Slightly more commercialized trips to different sections of the labyrinth – notably under the *Italia* hotel – are run by *Le Grotte di Orvieto* (☎0763.343.882) and usually depart from Via del Popolo next to the Banco Nazionale (daily 10am–1pm & 3–5/7pm; L9000).

If you want a glimpse of the sort of thing you'll see on the tours make for the **Pozzo della Cava** (summer daily except Tues 9am–9pm; winter 8am–8pm; L2500) at Via della Cava 26, a large smooth-sided Etruscan-era well (some forty such wells have been found around the town). It's a slightly cynical money making exercise – it used to be free – but striking enough if you haven't time for the full tours.

The churches

The tiny Romanesque **San Lorenzo di Arari** (or dell'Ara), a short walk west of the duomo, was built in 1291 on the site of a church destroyed by monks from nearby San Francesco because the sound of its bells got on their nerves. Four restored frescoes (1330) on the left of the nave depict traumatic scenes from the *Life of St Lawrence*, including execution by roasting, and there's a Byzantine-influenced *Christ Enthroned with Four Saints* in the apse. An Etruscan sacrificial slab rather oddly serves as the altar from which the church derives its name, *arari* meaning "altar".

From nearby Piazzale Cacciatore there's a good **walk** around the city's southern **walls** along Via Ripa Medici, with views over to a prominent outcrop of rock in the mid-distance, part of the old volcanic crater.

Ten minutes or so brings you to the ancient **San Giovenale**, set amid rustic surroundings on the western tip of Orvieto's plateau. New studies have established the previously accepted date of its foundation – 1004 – as the date of its first restoration. It's not much to look at from outside, but the musty **interior** is a distinctive hybrid of a church, the thirteenth-century Gothic transept, with its two pointed arches, standing rather oddly a metre above the rounded Romanesque nave. Beautiful thirteenth- and fifteenth-century **frescoes** cover all available surfaces; they include a *Tree of Life* to the right of the main door and the macabre *Calendar of Funeral Anniversaries* partly covered by the side entrance.

From the church back to the centre of town, Via Malabranca and Via Filippeschi are the best preserved of the medieval streets. En route, **San Andrea**, in Piazza della Repubblica, is worth a look for its twelve-sided campanile, odd patches of fresco and pieces of Roman and Etruscan city in the crypt: you may need to apply to the sacristan in Via Cipriano Manente 17 for access to the crypt excavations.

San Domenico, a convenient stop before taking the bus back to the station, stands next to the town's Fascist-era barracks – far and away the ugliest building in the town. Half of the church, built between 1233 and 1264 – making it Italy's first church to be dedicated to St Dominic – was sliced off during the construction of the barracks. The principal art work is the *Tomb of Cardinal de Braye* (died 1281) a pioneering work by Arnolfo di Cambio in the **Cappella Petrucci**, entered via a door on the south (right) wall. This defined the format of wall tombs for the next century, showing the deceased lying on a coffin below the Madonna and Child, within an elaborate architectural framework.

The Pozzo di San Patrizio and Rocca

Orvieto's novelty act is the huge cylindrical well known as the **Pozzo di San Patrizio**, signposted to the left of the funicular terminus in Piazza Cahen (daily: April–Sept 10am–7pm; Oct–March 10am–6pm; L6000, or L8000 with Museo Emilio Greco). Pope Clement VII commissioned it, from Antonio da Sangallo the Younger, two years after the Sack of Rome, which he'd been forced to flee disguised as a greengrocer. An attack on Orvieto was expected from the imperial troops, and the well was designed to guarantee the town's water supply during siege; the attack never materialized, which was fortunate, as it took ten years of digging to hit water. Incidentally, while in Orvieto Clement took the fateful decision not to annul Henry VIII's marriage to Catherine of Aragon.

The well is a virtuosic piece of engineering, thirteen metres wide and sixty-two deep, and takes its name from a supposed resemblance to the Irish cave where St Patrick died at the ripe old age of 133. Water was brought to the surface by donkeys on two broad 248-step staircases, cannily designed in a double helix so that they never intersect. Half the well is carved from solid tufa, half is brick-lined, and the whole thing is lit by 72 strange windows cut from the spirals into the central shaft. Skinflints in Italy are said to have pockets as deep as the Pozzo di San Patrizio.

The direct recipient of the water from the *pozzo* was the nearby **Rocca**, built in 1364 by Cardinal Albornoz, the papal fireband recruited to restore Church authority across central Italy. Views from the ruins are wonderful, and they are close to the small **public gardens**, one of Orvieto's few patches of green and home to the prominent remains of an Etruscan temple, the Tempio del Belvedere. The castle itself was built over the only stratum of travertine in the town, a robust piece of rock that escapes the landslips which strike the tufa with increasing regularity. Defoliation, the collapse of ancient sewers, the lowering of the water table and the intensification of traffic culminated in disastrous slips during 1977 and 1979, finally prompting the injection of vast funds from the European Union. Miles of tunnels and caves dating back to the Etruscans still honeycomb the rock, a labyrinth once used for quarrying, burials and the fermenting of wine. The subterranean conditions were said to be responsible for the excellence of Orvieto's wine; modern methods now make a drier product, better selling but less exalted than the traditional semi-sweet *abboccato*.

Eating and drinking

Orvieto's tourist traffic once inflated prices in the town's many **restaurants**, and for years it has had fewer genuine culinary high spots than neighbouring towns. Recently, however, a crop of good small **trattorie** has opened, together with a selection of excellent more upmarket places. Prices in the former should keep you under budget; the cheaper **pizzerie** are mostly clustered together at the bottom of Corso Cavour. Recommendations below are in roughly ascending order of price.

CRAMST or *Al San Francesco*, Via Lorenzo Maitani 15 Via B. Cerretti 10 (☎0763.343.302). Walk 50m up Via L. Maitani from Piazza del Duomo, take the first left, and follow the big signs to the tree-shaded piazza. Very popular with locals, this is a co-operatively run 400-seat canteen affair, offering a choice between a restaurant (evenings) and self-service trattoria; L17,000 and under; L35,000 in the restaurant. Closed Sun.

La Bottega del Buon Vino, Via della Cava 26. An *enoteca*/bar annexed for cheap and reliable snacks under L15,000 and meals at around L30,000. It boasts a few outside tables on a steep street, and an Etruscan well of which the owner is immensely proud (see p.588). This is also a better place to sample Orvieto wine than the expensive bars around the duomo. Closed Tues.

La Grotta, Via Signorelli 5 (☎0763.341.348). Just off Via del Duomo and opposite the hotel *Posta*, this is a good-value and friendly trattoria, offering reliable Italian staples for around L35,000. Closed Mon.

Osteria dell'Angelo, Corso Cavour 166 (☎0763.341.805). Arguably the best of Orvieto's top three restaurants, this simple and tiny (30-cover) place began life as an *enoteca*, so the wine list is as good as the often adventurous cooking. L35,000. Closed Mon.

Trattoria dell'Orso, Via della Misericordia 16–18 (☎0763.341.642). Friendly two-roomed place with simple wooden walls and a handful of tables. Excellent local cooking, and good value for money. Located in an alley just north of Piazza della Repubblica. L35,000. Closed Mon evening & Tues.

Maurizio, Via del Duomo 78 (☎0763.341.114). The smart-looking, modern interior may be off-putting, but the food here is good if you're prepared to pay more than just the basics. Well known, but somewhat overtaken by newer and cheaper rivals. L40,000. Closed Tues.

Trattoria Etrusca, Via Lorenzo Maitani 10 (☎0763.44.016). A serious restaurant – and the best in town for a treat – but with surprisingly fair prices; a nice medieval vaulted dining room, plus topnotch Umbrian specialities and good service. Be sure to go downstairs to see the wine cellars, carved out of solid tufa. Full meals run up to L40,000. Closed Mon & Jan 20–Feb 20.

La Volpe e L'Uva, Via Ripa Corsica 1 (☎0763.341.612). Another good and popular restaurant offering traditional cooking – the menu, if anything, is almost too long – and great value for money. A touch bigger and cheaper than *I Sette Consoli*. L45,000. Closed Mon & March.

I Sette Consoli, Piazza Sant'Angelo 1a (☎0763.343.911). Popular, just 35 covers and more than usually reasonable food, but the dining room is a trifle austere. Located just off Corso Cavour northeast of the duomo. Treat yourself to the *degustazione* menu, with three wines and five courses: otherwise about L50,000. Closed Wed & a period in Feb or March.

Gigli d'Oro, Piazza del Duomo (☎0763.341.903). Cooking here is hardly original, but the quality's always high: what you're paying for, though, are elegant surroundings and the pleasure of dining in the shadow of the duomo. L70,000. Closed Wed.

Listings

Bike rental Renato Testa, Via di Montemarte 47 (Mon–Sat 8.30am–8pm, also Sun same hours in summer; ☎0763.344.303). In Orvieto Scalo, bikes can be rented from Star Bike, Via Monte Nibbio 35–37 (☎0763.301.649).

Car rental Hertz, c/o Fiat Garbini, Strada dell'Arcone, Orvieto Scalo (☎0763.301.303); Carpinelli, Via Di Loreto 20 (☎0763.344.139); Mangiavacchi, Via del Caccia 19 (☎0763.341.492).

Exchange facilities Multiservice, Via Largo Barzini 7 (May–Sept Mon–Fri 9.30am–1pm & 2.30–7pm, Sat–Sun 10am–1pm & 3.30–7pm; Oct–April daily 10am–1pm & 4–7pm; ☎0763.342.297) is far quicker than the banks. There is also foreign exchange at the main post office.

Post office (☎0763.344.528) in Via Cesare Nebbia, off Corso Cavour.

Telephones In the station bar and in *Bar Valentino*, Corso Cavour 127–9.

Around Orvieto

The environs of Orvieto are not the most compelling in Umbria. However, if you have transport and time to spare, **Monte Peglia** might make you dally en route to Todi or Perugia, as might the **Lago di Corbara** on the way to Todi, and **Città della Pieve** if you're heading to Montepulciano.

West of Orvieto: Civita

The road to Lago di Bolsena – which lies across the border in Lazio – gives some of the best **views** of Orvieto: it's where the postcard shots are taken from and where Turner set up his easel for a landscape now in the Tate Gallery. In itself, the wooded pocket of countryside around Castel Giorgio is pretty enough, but only worth bothering with if you're in a car. Farther afield, however, straddling the Lazio border, lies an almost lunar landscape, scarred with deeply eroded canyons, some wooded but most just bare, wasted slopes.

At the heart of this district lies the tiny, crag-top **CIVITA**, known as "la città che muore" – the city which is dying – due to the crumbling of the rock below it. People have been emigrating from these disintegrating dwellings since the sixteenth century, leaving a population today of around seven – though apparently an Italian computer company have just bought up the place wholesale. The only access is via a precarious bridge from the nearby village of Bagnoregio, 15km southwest of Orvieto.

Monte Peglia

Monte Peglia is the name for the triangular expanse of wild, sparse land that rises between the Chiani valley and the Tiber, to the northeast of Orvieto. With its hill-top hamlets, olive groves, vines, herds of white oxen and miles of deserted roads and tracks, this is the archetype of pastoral lowland Umbria. Villages marked on the maps often turn out to be no more than scattered farms, many of them abandoned.

The only realistic way of tackling this remoteness is with your own transport, and you'll get the best quick taste of the area on the circuitous and beautifully deserted SS79bis from Orvieto Scalo to Todi. Superb initial views peter out as the road climbs through hairpins into densely wooded hill country – though, haze allowing, there are occasional glimpses as far as Perugia. The picturesque castle at Prodo is perhaps the best vantage point. The best of the scenery is north of this road and something of a **wildlife** haven, its high point the summit of **Monte Peglia** itself (837m).

Lago di Corbara

The SS448 to Todi is almost as scenic a route as that through Monte Péglia, passing medieval Baschi and running along the flattish southern shore of **Lago di Corbara**, before taking off into an unexpectedly dramatic **gorge** for the rest of the route on to Todi. Close to the lake's southern tip, enclosed on three sides by water, there's the *Villa Bellago* (☎0744.950.521, fax 0744.950.524; ⑥), a beautiful hotel-resort set in a twenty-acre estate; it has just twelve rooms, occupying converted nineteenth-century farm buildings. Beyond, midway down the shore, is the *Vissani* **restaurant** (☎0744.950.206; closed Sun evening, Wed & Thurs lunch and four weeks during July–Aug), rated by virtually every Italian gastronomic guide as one of the finest in Italy (Michelin, though, give it just two stars); booking is obligatory and you'll need to be prepared to part with L270,000–300,000 per person.

Farther east, the lakeside scenery improves considerably, the strange purple-red rocks of the gorge contrasting with the forested slopes. The road's fairly quiet, with plenty of **camping** and picnic opportunities as the valley flattens out towards Todi.

Città della Pieve

CITTÀ DELLA PIEVE is the sort of place that can easily be seen in an hour, despite the vague enticement of the distant view. Travelling by rail, it's definitely not worth the long haul up from the train station, unless you're a committed fan of **Perugino**, the town's most illustrious son.

Straggling along its ridge, the town, founded by the Etruscans, consists of tiny, red-brick houses (there is no local building stone) and narrow streets, one of which, Via della Baciadonna, claims to be the narrowest in Italy – the width of a woman's kiss, the name suggests. The seventeenth-century **duomo**, in Piazza Plebiscito, has a couple of late works which show Perugino in his worst light, one the *Madonna Enthroned with Saints* (1514) in the apse, the other the *Baptism of Christ* (1510) on the first altar of the north (left) aisle. However, in the nearby **Oratorio di Santa Maria dei Bianchi** (May–Sept daily 10.30am–12.30pm & 4–7pm; Oct–April Fri–Sun 10.30am–12.30pm & 3.30–6.30pm; L3000), on Via Pietro Vannucci, the main street off Piazza Gramsci, is one of his masterpieces – *An Adoration of the Magi* (note Lago Trasimeno in the background), which was painted in just 29 days in 1504. If the building is shut you might try knocking at the custodian's house at Via Pietro Vannucci 42. Out in the piazza, on the corner with Via Vannucci, check out the small sandstone **obelisk** at the foot of the stairs leading to the big Palazzo Della Corgna (used as the Biblioteca Comunale): it's thought to be an Etruscan sundial from the sixth century BC. Other lesser pieces by Perugino are to be found in **Santa Maria dei Servi** on Via Roma – a *Deposition* (1517), an important late work: yellow tourist signs point the way. Unhappily for Città, Napoleon removed cartloads of the town's other Peruginos to the Louvre.

The town makes a peaceful enough stop and has one two-star **hotel**: the 33-room *Vannucci*, Via Icilio Vanni 1 (☎0578.299.572, fax 0578.298.063; ③). A **tourist office** at Piazza Matteotti 4 is only sporadically open.

travel details

TRAINS

Terni to: Foligno (40min; connections to Assisi and Perugia); Narni (12 daily; 15min) and Orte (40min; connections to Rome, Orvieto, Chiusi, Arezzo and Florence); Nocera Umbra (1hr) and towns in the Marche (Fabriano, Ancona) and Spoleto (12 daily; 20min). Frequent trains on the FCU line to Todi, Deruta and Perugia, with connections to Teróntola and Foligno (on the FS network) and Città di Castello and Sansepolcro (on the FCU line).

Orvieto to: Arezzo (7 daily; 1hr 20min); Chiusi (7 daily; 40min; connections to Siena, 1hr 30min); Florence (7 daily; 1hr 30min); Orte (12 daily; 40min; connections to Narni, Terni, Spoleto and Foligno); Rome (7 daily; 1hr 30min). Stopping trains to Orte for Attigliano (for Bomarzo), and to Chiusi for Città della Pieve and all stations en route.

BUSES

Terni to: Orte, Todi, Rieti (via Marmore, Piediluco and Colli sul Vellino), Narni, Amelia, Arrone, Pollino and Scheggino (via Ferentillo and Ceselli).

Narni: Frequent buses to Terni and Amelia. Fewer services to Orvieto, Calvi dell'Umbria, Moricone and Otrícoli.

Amelia to: Avigliano (connecting bus to Todi via Dunarobba), Narni, Terni, Lugnano in Teverina (and Attigliano).

Todi to: Deruta (3 daily); Marsciano (2 daily); Orvieto (1 daily, early morning); Perugia (3 daily); Pesciano (4 daily); Terni (8 daily).

Orvieto to: Amelia (6 daily); Narni (6 daily); Perugia (1 daily, early morning); Terni (6 daily); Todi (1 daily, 1.30pm).

THE HISTORICAL BACKGROUND: TUSCANY

A comprehensive history of Tuscany in its medieval and Renaissance heyday would consist in large part of a mosaic of more or less independent histories, as each of the region's cities has a complex story to tell. In an overview such as this, fidelity to the entanglements of central Italy's past is impossible. Instead, within a broad account of the main trends in the evolution of Tuscany, we have concentrated on the city that emerged as the dominant force – Florence. The brief reviews of the other major towns – Siena, Pisa, Arezzo, Prato, Pistoia and so on – are supplemented by background given in the appropriate sections of the guide. Similarly, crucial episodes in the history of Florence and its culture – for instance, the ascendancy of Savonarola – are covered in greater detail in the chapter on that city.

ETRUSCANS AND ROMANS

The name of the province of Tuscany derives from the **Etruscans**, the most powerful civilization of pre-Roman Italy. There's no scholarly consensus on the origins of this people, with some experts insisting that they migrated into Italy from Anatolia at the start of the ninth century

BC, and others maintaining that they were an indigenous tribe. All that's known for certain is that the Etruscans were spread thoughout central Italy from the eighth century BC, and that the centre of gravity of their domain was in the southern part of the modern province, roughly along a line drawn from Orbetello to Lago Trasimeno. Their principal settlements in Tuscany were Roselle, Vetulonia, Populonia, Volterra, Chiusi, Cortona, Arezzo and – most northerly of them all – Fiesole.

It seems that the Etruscans absorbed elements of those cultures with whom they came into contact – thus their trade with Greek settlements produced some classically influenced art that can be seen at its best in Florence's archeological museum and in Cortona. The Etruscan language has still not been fully deciphered (a massive translation programme is under way in Perugia), so at the moment their wall paintings and terracotta funerary sculptures are the main source of information about them, and this information is open to widely differing interpretations. Some people have inferred an almost neurotic fear of death from the evidence of their burial sites and monuments, while others – most notably D.H. Lawrence – have on the contrary intuited an irrepressible and uncomplicated vitality.

There may have been an Etruscan settlement where Florence now stands, but it would have been subservient to their base in the hill-town of Fiesole. The substantial development of Tuscany's chief city began with the **Roman** colony of **Florentia**, established by Julius Caesar in 59 BC as a settlement for army veterans – by which time Romans had either subsumed or exterminated most Etruscan towns. Expansion of Florentia was rapid, with a steady traffic of trading vessels along the Arno providing the basis of accelerated growth in the second and third centuries AD.

This rise under the empire was paralleled by the growth of **Siena**, **Pisa** and **Lucca**, establishing an economic primacy in the north of Tuscany that has endured to the present. According to legend Siena was founded by the sons of Remus, supposedly fleeing their uncle Romulus, while the port at Pisa was developed by the Romans in the second century BC. Lucca was even more important, and it was here that Julius Caesar, Crassus and Pompey established their triumvirate in 56 BC.

BARBARIANS AND MARGRAVES

Under the comparative tranquillity of the Roman colonial regime, **Christianity** began to spread through the region. Lucca claims to have been the first Christian city in Tuscany – evangelized by a disciple of St Peter – though Pisa's church of San Pietro a Grado is said to have been founded by Peter himself. In Florence, the church of San Lorenzo and the martyr's shrine at San Miniato were both established in the fourth century.

This period of calm was shattered in the fifth century by the invasions of the **Goths** from the north, though the scale of the destruction in this first barbarian wave was nothing compared to the havoc of the following century. After the fall of Rome, the empire had split in two, with the western half ruled from Ravenna and the eastern from Constantinople (Byzantium). By the 490s Ravenna was occupied by the Ostrogoths, and forty years later the Byzantine emperor Justinian launched a campaign to repossess the Italian peninsula.

The ensuing mayhem between the Byzantine armies of Belisarius and Narsus and the fast-moving Goths was probably the most destructive phase of central Italian history, with virtually all major settlements ravaged by one side or the other – and sometimes both. In 552 Florence fell to the hordes of the Gothic king **Totila**, whose depredations so weakened the province that less than twenty years later the **Lombards** were able to storm in, subjugating Florence to the duchy whose capital was in Pavia, though its dukes preferred to rule from Lucca.

By the end of the eighth century Charlemagne's **Franks** had taken control of much of Italy, with the administration being overseen by imperial **margraves**, again based in Lucca. These proxy rulers developed into some of the most powerful figures in the Holy Roman Empire and were instrumental in spreading Christianity even further, founding numerous religious houses. Willa, widow of the margrave Uberto, established the Badia in Florence in 978, the first monastic foundation in the centre of the city; her son Ugo, margrave in turn, is buried in the Badia's church.

The hold of the central authority of the Holy Roman Empire was often tenuous, with feudal grievances making the region all but ungovernable, and it was under the imperial margraves that the notion of an autonomous Tuscan entity began to emerge. In 1027 the position of margrave was passed to the **Canossa** family, who took the title of the Counts of Tuscia, as Tuscany was then called. The most influential figure produced by this dynasty was **Matilda**, daughter of the first Canossa margrave. When her father died she was abducted by the German emperor Henry III, and on her release and return to her home territory she began to take the side of the papacy in its protracted disputes with the empire. The culmination of her anti-imperialist policy came in 1077, when she obliged the emperor Henry IV to wait in the snow outside the gates of Canossa before making obeisance to Pope Gregory VII. Later friction between the papacy, empire and Tuscan cities was assured when Matilda bequeathed all her lands to the pope, with the crucial exceptions of Florence, Siena and Lucca.

GUELPHS AND GHIBELLINES

Though Lucca had been the titular base of the imperial margraves, Ugo and his successors had shown a degree of favouritism towards **Florence** and over the next three hundred years Florence gained pre-eminence among the cities of Tuscany, becoming especially important as a religious centre. In 1078 Countess Matilda supervised the construction of new fortifications for Florence, and in the year of her death – 1115 – granted it the status of an independent city. The new *comune* of Florence was essentially governed by a council of one hundred men, the great majority drawn from the rising merchant class. In 1125 the city's increasing dominance of the region was confirmed when it crushed the rival city of Fiesole. Fifty years later, as the population boomed with the rise of the textile industry, new walls were built around what was now one of the largest cities in Europe.

Not that the other mercantile centres of Tuscany were completely eclipsed, as their magnificent heritage of medieval buildings makes plain. **Pisa** in the tenth and eleventh centuries had become one of the peninsula's wealthiest ports and its shipping lines played a vital part in bringing the cultural influences of France, Byzantium and the Muslim world into Italy. Twelfth-century **Siena**, though racked by conflicts between the bishops and the secular authorities and between the nobility and the merchant class, was booming thanks to its cloth industries and its exploitation of a local silver mine – foundation of a banking empire that was to see the city rivalling the bankers of Venice and Florence on the international markets.

Throughout and beyond the thirteenth century Tuscany was torn by conflict between the **Ghibelline** faction and the **Guelphs**. The names of these two political alignments derive from **Welf** – the family name of the emperor Otto IV – and **Waiblingen** – the name of a castle owned by their implacable rivals, the Hohenstaufen. Though there's no clear documentation, it seems that the terms Guelph and Ghibelline entered the Italian vocabulary at the end of the twelfth century, when supporters of Otto IV battled for control of the central peninsula with the future Frederick II, nephew of Otto and grandson of the Hohenstaufen emperor Barbarossa (1152–90). Within the first few years of Frederick II's reign (1212–50), the labels Guelph and Ghibelline had changed their meaning – the latter still referred to the allies of the Hohenstaufen, but the Guelph party was defined chiefly by its loyalty to the papacy, thus reviving the battle lines drawn up during the reign of Matilda.

To muddy the waters yet further, when Charles of Anjou conquered Naples in 1266, alliance with the anti-imperial French became another component of Guelphism, and a loose Guelph alliance soon stretched from Paris to Naples, substantially funded by the bankers of Tuscany.

Ghibelline/Guelph divisions approximately corresponded to a split between the feudal **nobility** and the rising **business classes**, but this is only the broadest of generalizations. By the beginning of the thirteenth century the major cities of Tuscany were becoming increasingly self-sufficient and inter-city strife was soon a commonplace of medieval life. In this climate, affiliations with the empire and the papacy were often struck on the basis that "my enemy's enemy is my friend", and allegiances changed at baffling speed – if, for instance, the Guelphs gained the ascendancy in a particular town, its neighbours might switch to the Ghibelline camp to maintain their rivalry. Nonetheless, certain patterns did emerge from the confusion: Florence and Lucca were generally Guelph strongholds, while Pisa, Arezzo, Prato, Pistoia and Siena tended to side with the empire.

As a final complicating factor, this was also the great age of **mercenary** armies, whose loyalties changed even quicker than those of the towns that paid for their services. Thus **Sir John Hawkwood** – whose White Company was the most fearsome band of hoodlums on

the peninsula – is known today through the monument to him in Florence's Duomo, but early in his career was employed by Ghibelline Pisa to fight the Florentines. He was then taken on by Pope Gregory XI, whom he deserted on the grounds of underpayment, and in the end was granted a pension of 1200 florins a year by Florence, basically as a form of protection money. Even then he was often absent fighting for other cities whenever a fat purse was waved in his direction.

MEDIEVAL FLORENCE BEFORE THE MEDICI

In this period of superpower manoeuvring and shifting economic structures, city governments in Tuscany were volatile. The administration of Siena, for example, was carried out by various combinations of councils and governors and in 1368 its constitution was redrawn no fewer than four times. However, Florence provides perhaps the best illustration of the turbulence of Tuscan politics in the late Middle Ages.

In 1207 the city's governing council was replaced by the *podestà*, an executive official who was traditionally a non-Florentine, in a semi-autocratic form of government that was common throughout the region. It was around this time, too, that the first *arti* (guilds) were formed to promote the interests of the traders and bankers, a constituency of ever-increasing power. Then in 1215 Florence was riven by a feud that was typical of the internecine violence of central Italy at this period. On Easter Sunday one **Buondelmonte de' Buondelmonti**, on his way to his wedding, was stabbed to death at the foot of the Ponte Vecchio by a member of the Amidei clan, in revenge for breaking his engagement to a young woman of that family. The prosecution of the murderers and their allies polarized the city into those who supported the *comune* – which regarded itself as the protector of the commercial city against imperial ambitions – and the followers of the Amidei, who seem to have politicized their personal grievances by aligning themselves against the *comune* and with the emperor.

These Ghibellines eventually enlisted the help of Emperor Frederick II to oust the Guelphs in 1248, but within two years they had been displaced by the Guelph-backed regime of the *Primo Popolo*, a quasi-democratic government drawn from the mercantile class. The *Primo*

Popolo was in turn displaced in 1260, when the Florentine army marched on Siena to demand the surrender of some exiles who were hiding out in the city. Though greatly outnumbered, the Sienese army and its Ghibelline allies overwhelmed the aggressors at **Montaperti**, after which the Sienese were prevented from razing Florence only by the intervention of Farinata degli Uberti, head of the Ghibelline exiles.

By the 1280s the balance had again moved back in favour of Florence, where the Guelphs were back in control – after the intervention of Charles of Anjou – through the *Secondo Popolo*, a regime run by the *Arti Maggiori* (Great Guilds). It was this second bourgeois administration that definitively shifted the fulcrum of power in Florence towards its bankers, merchants and manufacturers – whereas in Siena, the second richest city in Tuscany, the feudal families retained a stranglehold for far longer. Agitation from the landed nobility of the countryside around Florence had been a constant fact of life until the *Secondo Popolo*, which in 1293 passed a programme of political reforms known as the *Ordinamenti della Giustizia*, excluding the nobility from government and investing power in the **Signoria**, a council drawn from the *Arti Maggiori*.

Strife between the virulently anti-imperial "Black" and more conciliatory "White" factions within the Guelph camp marked the start of the fourteenth century in Florence, with many of the Whites – Dante among them – being exiled in 1302. Worse disarray was to come. In 1325 the army of Lucca under **Castruccio Castracani** defeated the Florentines and was about to overwhelm the city when the death of their leader took the momentum out of the campaign. Then in 1339 the Bardi and Peruzzi banks – Florence's largest – both collapsed, mainly owing to the bad debts of Edward III of England. The ultimate catastrophe came in 1348, when the **Black Death** destroyed as many as half the city's population.

However, even though the epidemic hit Florence so badly that it was generally referred to as the Florentine Plague, its effects were equally devastating throughout the region, and did nothing to reverse the economic – and thus political – supremacy of the city. Florence had subsumed Pistoia in 1329 and gained Prato in the 1350s. In 1406 it took control of Pisa and thus gained a long-coveted sea port, and five years later Cortona became part of its territory. From this time on, despite the survival of Sienese independence into the sixteenth century, the history of Tuscany increasingly becomes the history of Florence.

THE EARLY MEDICI

A crucial episode in the liberation of Florence from the influence of the papacy was the so-called **War of the Eight Saints** in 1375–78, which brought Florence into direct territorial conflict with Pope Gregory XI. This not only signalled the dissolution of the old Guelph alliance, but had immense repercussions for the internal politics of Florence. The increased taxation and other economic hardships of the war provoked an uprising of the industrial day-labourers, the **Ciompi**, on whom the wool and cloth factories depended. Their short-lived revolt resulted in the formation of three new guilds and direct representation for the workers for the first time. However, the prospect of increased proletarian presence in the machinery of state provoked a consolidation of the city's oligarchs and in 1382 an alliance of the city's Guelph party and the **Popolo Grasso** (the wealthiest merchants) took control of the *Signoria* away from the guilds, a situation that lasted for four decades.

Not all of Florence's most prosperous citizens aligned themselves with the *Popolo Grasso*, and the foremost of the well-off mavericks were the **Medici**, a family from the agricultural Mugello region whose fortune had been made by the banking prowess of Giovanni Bicci de' Medici. The political rise of his son, **Cosimo de' Medici**, was to some extent due to his family's sympathies with the *Popolo Minuto*, as the members of the disenfranchised lesser guilds were known. With the increase in public discontent at the autocratic rule of the *Signoria* – where the Albizzi clan were the dominant force – Cosimo came to be seen as the figurehead of the more democratically inclined sector of the upper class. In 1431 the authorities imprisoned him in the tower of the Palazzo Vecchio and two years later, as Florence became embroiled in a futile and domestically unpopular war against Lucca, they sent him into exile. He was away for only a year. In 1434, after a session of the *Parlamento* – a general council called in times of emergency – it was decided to invite him to return. Having secured the military support of the Sforza family of Milan, Cosimo became the pre-eminent figure in the city's political life, a position he maintained for more than three decades.

Cosimo il Vecchio – as he came to be known – rarely held office himself, preferring to exercise power through backstage manipulation and adroit investment. His extreme generosity to charities and religious foundations in Florence was no doubt motivated in part by genuine piety, but clearly did no harm as a public relations exercise – even if it didn't impress the contemporary who recorded that his munificence was due to the fact that "he knew his money had not been over-well acquired".

Dante, Boccaccio and Giotto in the first half of the fourteenth century had established the **literary and artistic ascendancy** of Florence, laying the foundations of Italian humanism with their emphasis on the importance of the vernacular and the dignity of humanity. Florence's reputation as the most innovative cultural centre in Europe was strengthened during the fifteenth century, to a large extent through Medici patronage. Cosimo commissioned work from Donatello, Michelozzo and a host of other Florentine artists, and took advantage of the 1439 Council of Florence – a conference of the Catholic and Eastern churches – to foster scholars who were familiar with the literatures of the ancient world. His grandson **Lorenzo il Magnifico** (who succeeded Piero il Gottoso – the Gouty) continued this literary patronage, promoting the study of the classics in the Platonic academy that used to meet at the Medici villas. Other Medici were to fund projects by Botticelli, Michelangelo, Pontormo – in fact, most of the seminal figures of the Florentine Renaissance.

Lorenzo il Magnifico's status as the *de facto* ruler of Florence was even more secure than that of Cosimo il Vecchio, but it did meet one stiff challenge. While many of Florence's financial dynasties were content to advise and support the Medici, others – notably the mighty Strozzi clan – were resentful of the power now wielded by their fellow businessmen. In 1478 one of these disgruntled families, the Pazzi, conspired with Pope Sixtus IV, who had been riled by Lorenzo's attempt to break the papal monopoly of alum mining. This **Pazzi Conspiracy** resulted in an assault on Lorenzo and his brother Giuliano during Mass in the Duomo; Lorenzo was badly injured and Giuliano murdered, an outcome that only increased the esteem in which Lorenzo was held. Now that the plot had failed, Sixtus joined forces with the ferocious King Ferrante of Naples to launch a war on Florence, and excommunicated Lorenzo into the bargain.

Taking his life in his hands, Lorenzo left Florence to persuade Ferrante to leave the alliance, a mission he somehow accomplished successfully, to the jubilation of the city.

THE WARS OF ITALY

Before Lorenzo's death in 1492 the Medici bank failed, and in 1494 Lorenzo's son Piero was obliged to flee following his surrender to the invading French army of Charles VIII. This invasion was the commencement of a bloody half-century dominated by the so-called **Wars of Italy**.

After the departure of Charles's troops, Florence for a while was virtually under the control of the inspirational monk **Girolamo Savonarola**, but his career was brief. He was executed as a heretic in 1498, after which the city continued to function as a more democratic republic than that of the Medici. In 1512, however, following Florence's defeat by the Spanish and papal armies, the Medici returned, in the person of the vicious **Giuliano, Duke of Nemours**.

Giuliano's successors – his equally unattractive nephew **Lorenzo, Duke of Urbino**, and **Giulio**, illegitimate son of Lorenzo il Magnifico's brother – were in effect just the mouthpieces of Giovanni de' Medici (the Duke of Nemours' brother), who in 1519 became **Pope Leo X**. Similarly, when Giulio became **Pope Clement VII**, he was really the absentee ruler of Florence, where the family presence was maintained by the ghastly Ippolito (illegitimate son of the Duke of Nemours) and **Alessandro** (illegitimate son of the Duke of Urbino).

The Medici were again evicted from Florence in the wake of Charles V's pillage of Rome in 1527, Pope Clement's humiliation by the imperial army providing the spur to eject his deeply unpopular relatives. Three years later the pendulum swung the other way – after a siege by the combined papal and imperial forces, Florence capitulated and was obliged to receive Alessandro, who was proclaimed **Duke of Florence**, the first Medici to bear the title of ruler. Though the sadistic Alessandro lost no opportunity to exploit the immunity that came from his title, in the wider scheme of Italian politics he was a less powerful figure than his ancestors. Tuscany was becoming just one more piece in the vast jigsaw of the Habsburg empire, a superpower far more interventionist than the medieval empire of Frederick II could ever have been.

THE LATER MEDICI

After the assassination of Alessandro in 1537, power passed to another **Cosimo**, not a direct heir but rather a descendant of Cosimo il Vecchio's brother. The Emperor Charles V, now related to the Medici through the marriage of his daughter to Alessandro, gave his assent to the succession of this seemingly pliable young man – indeed, without Habsburg consent it would not have happened. Yet it turned out that Cosimo had the clear intention of maintaining Florence's role as the regional power-broker, and he proved immensely skilful at judging just how far he could push the city's autonomy without provoking the imperial policy-makers.

Having finally extinguished the subversive threat of the Strozzi faction at the battle of **Montemurlo**, Cosimo went on to buy the territory of Siena from the Habsburgs in 1557, giving Florence control of all of Tuscany with the solitary exception of Lucca. Two years later Florentine hegemony in Tuscany was confirmed in the Treaty of Cateau-Cambrésis, the final act in the Wars of Italy. Soon after, though, the new Habsburg emperor, Philip II, installed a military outpost in the Orbetello area to keep Tuscany under scrutiny.

Imperial and papal approval of Cosimo's rule was sealed in 1570, when he was allowed to take the title **Cosimo I, Grand Duke of Tuscany**. In European terms Tuscany was a second-rank power, but by comparison with other states on the peninsula it was in a very comfortable position, and during Cosimo's reign there would have been little perception that Florence was drifting inexorably towards the margins of European politics. It was Cosimo who built the Uffizi, extended and overhauled the Palazzo Vecchio, installed the Medici in the Palazzo Pitti, had the magnificent Ponte Santa Trìnita constructed across the Arno and commissioned much of the public sculpture around the Piazza della Signoria.

Cosimo's descendants were to remain in power until 1737, and aspects of their rule continued the city's intellectual tradition – the Medici were among Galileo's strongest supporters, for example. Yet it was a story of almost continual if initially gentle economic decline, as bad harvests and recurrent epidemics worsened the gloom created by the shift of European trading patterns in favour of northern Europe. The half-century reign of **Ferdinando II** had scarce-

ly begun when the market for Florence's woollen goods collapsed in the 1630s, and the city's banks simultaneously went into a terminal slump. The last two male Medici, the insanely pious **Cosimo III** and the drunken pederast **Gian Gastone** – who was seen in public only once, vomiting from the window of the state coach – were fitting symbols of the moribund Florentine state.

TO THE PRESENT

Under the terms of a treaty signed by Gian Gastone's sister, Anna Maria de' Medici, Florence passed in 1737 to the **House of Lorraine**, cousins of the Austrian Habsburgs. The first Lorraine prince, the future Francis I of Austria, was a more enlightened ruler than the last Medici had been and his successors presided over a placid and generally untroubled region, doing much to improve the condition of Tuscany's agricultural land and rationalize its production methods. Austrian rule lasted until the coming of the French in 1799, an interlude that ended with the fall of **Napoleon**, who had made his sister – Elisa Baciocchi – Grand Duchess of Tuscany.

After this, the Lorraine dynasty was brought back, remaining in residence until the last of the line, **Leopold II**, consented to his own deposition in 1859. Absorbed into the united Italian state in the following year, Florence became the **capital of the Kingdom of Italy** in 1861, a position it held until 1871.

Italy's unpopular entry into World War I cost thousands of Tuscan lives, and the economic disruption that followed was exploited by the regime of Benito **Mussolini**. The corporate Fascist state of the 1920s did effect various improvements in the infrastructure of the region, but Mussolini's alliance with Hitler's Germany was to prove a calamity. In 1943, as the Allied landing at Monte Cassino was followed by a campaign to sweep the occupying German forces out of the peninsula, Tuscany became a battleground between the Nazis and the **partisans**. The districts around Monte Amiata and the Val d'Órcia sheltered particularly strong partisan groups, and many of the province's hill-towns had their resistance cells, as numerous well-tended war memorials testify.

Yet, as elsewhere in Italy, the loyalties of Tuscany were split, as is well illustrated by the case of Florence, an ideological centre for the resistance but also home to some of Italy's most ardent Nazi collaborators. Wartime Florence in fact produced one of the strangest paradoxes of the time: a Fascist sympathizer in charge of the British Institute and a German consul who did so much to protect suspected partisans that he was granted the freedom of the city after the war.

Although most of the major monuments of Tuscany survived the war – sometimes as a result of pacts between the two sides – there was inevitably widespread destruction. Grosseto, Pisa and Livorno were badly damaged by Allied bombing raids, while Florence was wrecked by the retreating German army, who bombed all the bridges except the Ponte Vecchio and blew up much of the medieval city near the banks of the Arno.

POSTWAR TUSCANY

Tuscany is a prosperous, conservative region that tends to return **Christian Democrat** (DC) members of parliament. On a local level, however, **communist** support is high, the party's record in the war and subsequent work on land reform maintaining a loyal following. Excluded from national government by the machinations of the DC, the communist party has projected itself as the grassroots opposition to the centralization and corruption of Roman politics. It's a strategy that has been particularly successful in Tuscany, which has clung onto an image of itself as a state within the state. Since the 1970s the town halls of the region have been governed predominantly by communist-led coalitions, forming the heartland of the so-called "red belt" of central Italy.

Despite migration from the land in the 1950s and 1960s, the economy of Tuscany has been adroitly managed. The labour-intensive vineyards, olive groves and farms continue to provide a dependable source of income, boosted by industrial development in the Arno valley and around Livorno and Piombino. Production of textiles, leather goods and jewellery have brought money into Prato, Florence and Arezzo, but **tourism** plays an uncomfortably large and ever-increasing part in balancing the books of these and other historic centres.

The problem is worst in Florence, where the latest and most ambitious attempt to break the city's ever-increasing dependence on its visitors is the so-called **Firenze Nuova**, a development to the northwest of the city, on the way to Prato. Underwritten by Fiat and La Fondiaria (the insurance and property wing of the Montedison conglomerate), the scheme is touted as a fully viable city, where people will work, live and play, leaving Florence to develop as a cultural and small-scale commercial city. The doubters, however, see it as a cynical exercise by the two giant companies, one of which owns much of the land that Firenze Nuova is to be raised on, while the other plans to build a car plant out there. At the moment speculation about the impact of Firenze Nuove appears premature – the construction work seems to be progressing in fits and starts, and there is little chance of Florence's twin being completed within the fifteen-year timetable drawn up for it.

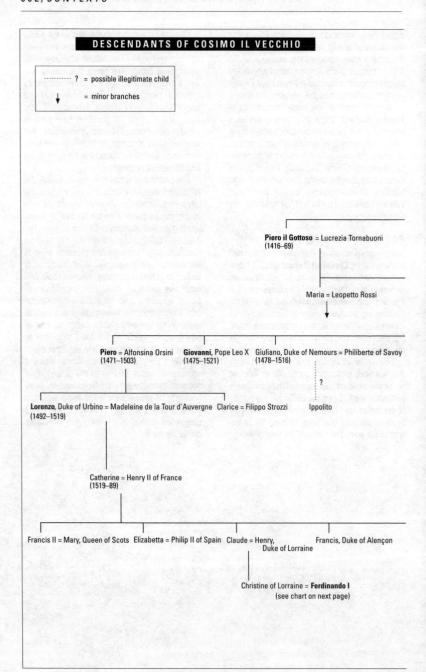

DESCENDANTS OF COSIMO IL VECCHIO

---------- ? = possible illegitimate child

↓ = minor branches

Piero il Gottoso = Lucrezia Tornabuoni
(1416–69)

Maria = Leopetto Rossi

Piero = Alfonsina Orsini   **Giovanni**, Pope Leo X   Giuliano, Duke of Nemours = Philiberte of Savoy
(1471–1503)   (1475–1521)   (1478–1516)

                                                                                    ?

Lorenzo, Duke of Urbino = Madeleine de la Tour d'Auvergne   Clarice = Filippo Strozzi   Ippolito
(1492–1519)

Catherine = Henry II of France
(1519–89)

Francis II = Mary, Queen of Scots   Elizabetta = Philip II of Spain   Claude = Henry,   Francis, Duke of Alençon
                                                                          Duke of Lorraine

Christine of Lorraine = **Ferdinando I**
(see chart on next page)

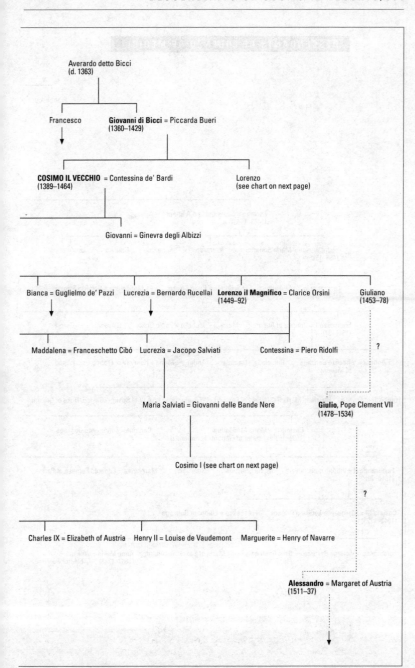

DESCENDANTS OF LORENZO DE'MEDICI

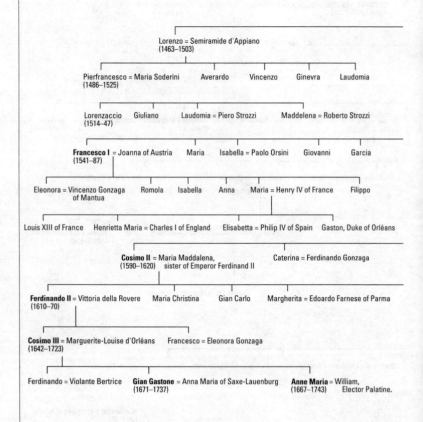

Francesco

Lorenzo = Semiramide d'Appiano
(1463–1503)

Pierfrancesco = Maria Soderini   Averardo   Vincenzo   Ginevra   Laudomia
(1486–1525)

Lorenzaccio   Giuliano   Laudomia = Piero Strozzi   Maddelena = Roberto Strozzi
(1514–47)

Francesco I = Joanna of Austria   Maria   Isabella = Paolo Orsini   Giovanni   Garcia
(1541–87)

Eleonora = Vincenzo Gonzaga   Romola   Isabella   Anna   Maria = Henry IV of France   Filippo
              of Mantua

Louis XIII of France   Henrietta Maria = Charles I of England   Elisabetta = Philip IV of Spain   Gaston, Duke of Orléans

Cosimo II = Maria Maddalena,   Caterina = Ferdinando Gonzaga
(1590–1620)   sister of Emperor Ferdinand II

Ferdinando II = Vittoria della Rovere   Maria Christina   Gian Carlo   Margherita = Edoardo Farnese of Parma
(1610–70)

Cosimo III = Marguerite-Louise d'Orléans   Francesco = Eleonora Gonzaga
(1642–1723)

Ferdinando = Violante Bertrice   **Gian Gastone** = Anna Maria of Saxe-Lauenburg   **Anne Maria** = William,
                                    (1671–1737)   (1667–1743)   Elector Palatine.

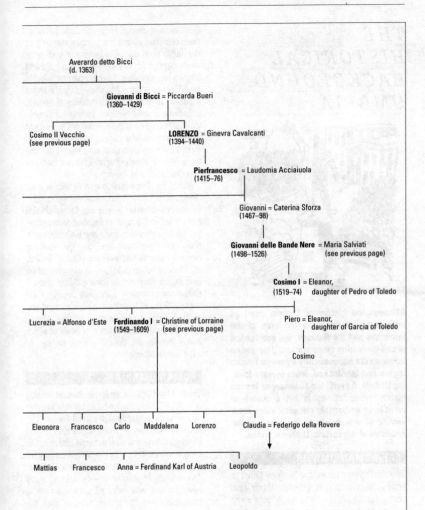

Averardo detto Bicci
(d. 1363)

Giovanni di Bicci = Piccarda Bueri
(1360–1429)

Cosimo II Vecchio
(see previous page)

LORENZO = Ginevra Cavalcanti
(1394–1440)

Pierfrancesco = Laudomia Acciaiuola
(1415–76)

Giovanni = Caterina Sforza
(1467–98)

Giovanni delle Bande Nere = Maria Salviati
(1498–1526)   (see previous page)

Cosimo I = Eleanor,
(1519–74)   daughter of Pedro of Toledo

Lucrezia = Alfonso d'Este   **Ferdinando I** = Christine of Lorraine
                             (1549–1609)   (see previous page)

Piero = Eleanor,
        daughter of Garcia of Toledo

Cosimo

Eleonora   Francesco   Carlo   Maddalena   Lorenzo   Claudia = Federigo della Rovere

Mattias   Francesco   Anna = Ferdinand Karl of Austria   Leopoldo

THE HISTORICAL BACKGROUND: UMBRIA

Although the history of Umbria overlaps with that of Tuscany in the eras of the Etruscans and the Romans, the emergence of self-governing cities marks a divergence between the economically dynamic Tuscan region and landlocked, more inward-looking Umbria. As with the summary of Tuscan history, what follows is but a sketch of what is an immensely complex story, more details of which are to be found in the accounts of the various Umbrian towns.

PRE-ROMAN UMBRIA

Over 1500 years before the birth of Christ, a large-scale migration of primitive tribes from central Europe and the east brought permanent settlers to the marshy lowlands around Terni and Perugia. As time went by, these tribes started to move away from the plains in favour of the uplands around Norcia, giving rise to the first of the **hill-towns** that were eventually to dominate the entire region.

By the eighth century BC these peoples were absorbed by the larger and more sophisticated tribes that followed them from the north. These gradually formed themselves into three distinct groups: the Samnites, the Latins (who later became the Romans), and the **Umbrians**. All three had common cultural roots, spoke dialects of a shared language, and between them occupied all but the southernmost tip of the Italian peninsula. The Umbrians' own territory extended far beyond the region's present boundaries, including the best part of what is now Tuscany and the Marche – a vast area for a people of whom almost nothing is known. Only the Eugubine Marbles found near Gubbio yield any clues as to the religion or language of what was clearly a cogent civilization. Other than these, the Umbrians' only memorials are the walls still standing, more or less intact, in a dozen-odd cities in the region.

When the **Etruscans** began to encroach on these cities, their predominantly agricultural inhabitants retreated quietly into the mountains and carried on life much as they had done before. In time they started to trade and intermarry with their new neighbours and the two cultures became more or less indistinguishable. By 700 BC Etruscan influence in Umbria extended as far east as the Tiber, and in some isolated cases – Gubbio for example – some way beyond it. All aspects of their life point to a sophisticated and ordered social set-up, with a political system formed around a confederation of cities, of which two – Perugia and Orvieto – were situated in what is now Umbria.

ROMAN UMBRIA

The first time Umbria appears in **Roman** records is in 309 BC, the occasion being Perugia's defeat at the hands of the Roman consul Fabius. The battle marked the beginning of the end for the Etruscan cities, and though some continued to cling to independence, by the second century BC most had become reluctant allies of the Romans. Any vestiges of autonomy were stripped away when Perugia was defeated a second time, a consequence of the power struggle that followed the murder of Julius Caesar in 44 BC. This effectively amounted to a confrontation between the consul Mark Antony, his brother Lucius, and **Octavius**, Caesar's great-nephew. In 40 BC the dispute reached crisis point, and while Antony was preoccupied with Cleopatra in Egypt, Octavius succeeded in harrying Lucius from Rome. Lucius, unhappily for the citizens of Perugia, decided to take refuge within their walls – an action that resulted in the city's destruction at the hands of Octavius.

Octavius went on to proclaim himself the **Emperor Augustus**, and with this proclamation the Imperial Age began. Under his rule, Umbria continued to enjoy a period of prosperity that had begun with the opening of the **Via Flaminia** in 220 BC. The new road linked Rome to the Adriatic coast and to the cities of the north, and gave Umbria immense strategic importance. It superseded the Tiber as the focal point of the region and brought in its wake a massive increase in trade and prosperity: colonies were built from scratch or on the sites of Umbrian and Etruscan settlements, land was drained and roads constructed. Umbria – named as such for the first time – became a unified and thriving province.

EARLY CHRISTIANITY AND THE BARBARIAN INVASIONS

Christianity spread quickly in Umbria, thanks mainly to Roman lines of communication. By the first century AD towns such as Spoleto and Foligno had become bishoprics, and within 200 years most towns had Christian communities. As religious practice increasingly adhered to the monastic pattern established in the eastern Mediterranean, it was in Umbria's remote countryside, however, rather than its cities, that Christianity found its most enduring home. The first recorded **monastery** was founded at Monteluco, near Spoleto, by Julian, a Syrian from Antioch. From such beginnings was born the extraordinary religious and monastic tradition in Umbria that was to culminate with St Francis, nearly a millennium later.

St Benedict, the most significant of Umbria's early saints, was born in Norcia in 480 AD, within a few years of the deposition of the last Roman Emperor, and at the very moment that the first Barbarian invaders from the north were turning towards Italy. The order he founded and the rule he drew up to guide its members were of incalculable importance in ensuring the survival of Western culture in the tumult that followed the fall of Rome. The rule aimed to move men to a perfect love of God through a combination of prayer, study and work, thus ensuring that countless monks were quietly working, studying and preserving aspects of learning that might otherwise have vanished for good.

As the **Goths** and **Huns** plundered the country, Umbria succumbed to the consequences of plague and famine. The only order in these desperate times came from the clergy, who began to take over the civic functions formerly carried out by the Roman state. Bishops took it upon themselves to become generals, frequently instigating resistance to the invaders. While on the face of things their achievements seemed negligible, in that virtually every Umbrian city was razed to the ground, they won increasing respect for themselves and the Church they represented.

After the death of their leader, **Totila**, at Gualdo Tadino, the Goths were replaced by the **Lombards**, who by 571 had established three principalities in Italy, the central one of which contained most of Umbria and had Spoleto as its capital. This **Dukedom of Spoleto** was to achieve great importance throughout central Italy, despite being cut off from the Lombard kingdom centred on Pavia to the north by a narrow corridor of territory controlled by the Byzantines – a ribbon of land running from the Adriatic to Rome, including Narni, Amelia, Terni and Perugia. This buffer-state remained a thorn in the Lombards' side for 300 years, though in Umbria it had the effect of guaranteeing the Dukedom of Spoleto considerable independence of action, a habit that in the coming years would be a hard one to break. The Lombards generally adopted the manners and customs of the local people, establishing an order which brought a short-lived increase in artistic and commercial initiative. Acknowledging the increasing growth of Christianity, they built monasteries alongside those of the Benedictines.

In 754 the growing power of the **papacy** as a force in Italian politics was illustrated by Pope Stephen III's appeal to the **Franks** to rid Italy of the Lombards. The Franks took up the invitation, first under Pepin the Short, and then under his more famous son, **Charlemagne**. By 800 the Lombards and Byzantines had both been driven out of the country.

BETWEEN THE EMPIRE AND THE PAPACY

The papacy received great tracts of land from Charlemagne, who in return demanded that Pope Leo III crown him emperor of the new **Holy Roman Empire**. Peace reigned while Charlemagne lived, but the harmony between papacy and empire disappeared within a few years of his death. The divisions amongst his successors and their preoccupations in northern Europe again left much of Italy prey to invasion and conflict. The papacy was no healthier, weakened by the rival claims of powerful families; with no central authority, it was not long before the whole country reverted once more to chaos.

The anarchy of the next few years set the tone of events for centuries to come. Many towns and old Roman centres, such as Carsulae (near Todi), unsuited to the rigours of constant invasion and siege, were either abandoned or destroyed, to be replaced by **fortified villas and castles**, for which the region's hilly terrain was ideal. Around these fortresses developed independent and self-sufficient communities, creating a pattern of isolated, independent and ambitious hill-towns, each with an eye on the territory of its neighbour.

Throughout this whole period Italy was the scene of a complicated, confused and constantly shifting conflict between the parties of the empire and the papacy, the **Guelphs** and **Ghibellines** (see p.596). As elsewhere, Umbrian towns frequently switched their allegiances, exacting new measures of independence from whomever ruled them at the time, in exchange for promises of loyalty. Yet of all its cities, only Perugia ever really came to merit attention on a national scale. It had become a free *comune* in 1139, owing its wealth to trade links with Rome and the burgeoning economic power of Florence, and was soon the prime mover in any machinations that affected the region as a whole.

Occasionally, however, the Umbrians were distracted from their squabbles by events taking place in the world at large. In 1152, for example, the truce between the empire and the papacy produced by the Concordat of Worms was shattered by the election of a new and ambitious emperor: Frederick Hohenstaufen. His determination to reassert the power of the empire in Italy spelt doom for the Umbrian cities, who soon had cause to fear the man better known by his Italian nickname of **Barbarossa**. As he marched south, some towns, such as Assisi, took his side while others, such as Perugia, tried to stand up to him; the majority – of which Spoleto was the most notable example – were partly or completely destroyed.

Like Charlemagne before him, Barbarossa was unable to ensure the survival of the authority he had imposed on the empire. After his death Pope Innocent III set about exploiting the anti-imperialist feeling aroused in Italy by the ferocity of his campaigns, and to ally it with the collective guilt at the capture of Jerusalem by the infidel Saladin in 1187, hoping thereby to resurrect papal fortunes. When he came to Umbria, however, he met with little success, cities such as Perugia and Spoleto being quite happy to accept new powers of autonomy, but turning obstructive when papal governors were sent to oversee them.

MEDIEVAL COMMUNES AND WAR LORDS

In 1308 the papacy moved to Avignon, and the outlook for the Church grew even more bleak from 1387 until 1417, when Europe was divided in its support for rival popes in Rome and France. The power vacuum which resulted from this **Great Schism** was the single most important factor in allowing the development of democratic communes in central Italy. At the same time, the influence of the older noble families was eclipsed by the emergence of a mercantile class, brought to prominence by the increase and diversification of trade. With the influx of new money and new men, secular building took place on an unprecedented scale, giving the rapidly expanding cities the appearances that they have largely retained to the present day.

Liberal and sophisticated **constitutions** were drawn up to administer the new towns, of which **Spoleto**'s, instituted at the end of the thirteenth century, serves as a typical example. Originally civic issues were decided by a show of hands in the *arringo*, a general assembly of all adult males convoked in the central piazza. By 1296, when a new constitution was drawn up, the size of the population had made such an arrangement impracticable, and the role of the *arringo* was reduced to a body that could express opinions, but no longer take decisions. The legislative function was taken over by a General Council elected from the twelve parishes that made up Spoleto's administrative districts. Final executive and judicial power lay with the **podestà**, a kind of troubleshooter elected for a year and often brought in from outside the city – as in Tuscany. He was answerable to the **capitano del popolo**, a police chief and appeals judge who was also responsible for the day-to-day running of the administration. Below him were a host of elected minor officials, all of whom were, in the manner of contemporary Italian bureaucracy, constrained by rigid job specifications.

The theory was reasonable, but the practice was often rather different. First, the cities spent so much time arguing with their neighbours that their administrations were obliged to be almost constantly prepared for war. Second, towns were plagued by continual dissent from within as Guelphs and Ghibellines fought each other, most of them citing their allegiances to distant authority merely as an excuse to wipe out local rivals and seize power. Citizens soon came to realize that a strong executive was the only means to combat such disorder, and began to accept the domination of forceful individuals, usually the heads of the strongest **noble families** of the moment, or the person who could muster the largest private army – in most cases one and the same man.

At about the same time, other powerful individuals began to figure in Umbria's affairs: the **condottieri**, or itinerant private soldiers hired to fight battles on behalf of their citizens. Most of them were English or French refugees from the Hundred Years' War, or German and Swiss stragglers from the imperial armies. Some were astute enough to form themselves into efficient bands and soon found in Umbria a healthy market for their services. The cities were losers in every way in these contracts, wasting money on unreliable allies while property was destroyed and land plundered. Added to this, there was the everyday chaos produced by warring noble families, whose disputes were often settled in bloodshed worthy of Jacobean tragedy. Taking into account the normal range of calamities, such as plague and famine, which could strike the medieval world at any time, life in Umbria should have been intolerable.

But against this background of violence and suffering, the artistic and intellectual life of the region went from strength to strength. The same subtle changes being wrought throughout northern Italy that were to culminate in the **Renaissance** were also taking place in Umbria. In religion, St Francis had almost single-handedly revitalized man's relations to the divine. In painting, Cimabue, Giotto and their followers had introduced a naturalism that left behind the stilted beauty of the Byzantines. A university was founded in Perugia as early as 1308, and the first edition of Dante's *Divine Comedy* was printed not in Florence, but in Foligno.

PAPAL CONSOLIDATION AND THE RISORGIMENTO

Gradually the infighting exhausted the cities, and the **papacy** – which out of choice or necessity had largely stood back from the centuries of bloody disorder – seized the opportunity to exert its power. One by one the cities fell: Spoleto in 1354 to the crusading Cardinal Albornoz; Foligno

in 1439, when the ruling Trinci family surrendered to soldiers of Pope Euginius V; Spello in 1535, after 150 years of despotic rule; and Gubbio in 1624, handed over to Urban VIII by the last of the ruling Montefeltro.

The old civic administrations were replaced by papal governors and for the two centuries before Unification Umbria slumbered under the **rule of the Church**. Although order was restored, peace and papal rule were no guarantee of prosperity. The isolation that had once served the region so well now began to tell against it. Absentee landlords – amongst whom the papacy figured large – collected rents but took little interest in land management, so that the soil deteriorated and with it the agriculture on which Umbria depended. Such industry as existed was agriculture-based and so shared in its stagnation, and in any case it was cut off from the prosperous markets to the north by poor communications. To anyone surveying the Umbrian scene at the end of the eighteenth century it would have seemed as if very little had changed in almost 500 years.

Matters improved somewhat in the upheaval that followed the French Revolution and the rule of **Napoleon**, when the French organized the region into two districts and tried to encourage economic growth. In the more liberal atmosphere of the times, a more freethinking class of merchants emerged, which the return of papal rule after Napoleon's death could do little to repress. By the time of the battle for the Unification of Italy, this spirit had found broader and more popular support, and Umbria welcomed Garibaldi's troops into Perugia on September 11, 1860.

Unfortunately, when trade barriers between the regions were abolished the Umbrian economy was subjected to the rigours of free competition, with which it was ill-equipped to deal. Traditional craft and agricultural industries crumbled in the face of industrialization in the north. Private wealth remained idle, or was invested in the north, while the state failed to make the improvements to the region's infrastructure that might have halted the agricultural decline.

UMBRIA IN THE TWENTIETH CENTURY

In the first years of the twentieth century the Italian economy as a whole was on an upswing, and for a while things began to look up for Umbria as well, with light industry appearing in the region for the first time. But this flicker of prosperity came to an abrupt end when the small **Banca di Perugia**, which had been largely responsible for funding the new investments, was swallowed by the Banca Commerciale, which preferred to invest in the more profitable and less risky ventures in the north.

Where the capital went, the people went too. Although in 1911 half the region's population was illiterate, they did not need education to know that their future lay outside Umbria. Thousands **emigrated** to America or to the new factories of Turin and Germany, leaving a population at home who increasingly saw socialism as the answer to the region's ills. By 1919, Umbria's scattered left-wing parties commanded 48 percent of the vote and had established control of many local and regional councils. Hopes of reform, however, were quickly dashed by the rise of Mussolini, even if the preparations for war did put some energy into the regional economy.

World War II left Umbria relatively unscathed until the German retreat up the peninsula, when the key strategic corridors – between Lago Trasimeno, Perugia and Orvieto – made it the seat of bitter fighting. Resistance groups were active in the hills above the main valleys, with the area around Gubbio seeing particularly intense partisan activity.

Postwar emigration rates were higher than ever. Only when central government devolved more power to the regions did Umbria begin to prosper. Political control by now was in the hands of the **Communist Party**, which carefully directed funds at co-operative ventures and projects appropriate to the region's special needs, with transport, agriculture and latterly tourism as the main priorities. Road and rail links at last provided an economic lifeline to Rome and the north.

Finally, and perhaps most importantly, the last twenty years have seen the birth of what can only be described as a new pride and enthusiasm in Umbria. There is still poverty and there are still problems but there is also a powerful sense of vigour and community which seems determined to overcome them. It is a spirit that even the most casual visitor cannot fail to notice, manifestly obvious in the region's extraordinary range of cultural events, the diversity and skill of its craftspeople, the Umbrians' own obvious pride in their countryside and their heritage, and a host of more minor signs that at last point to progress.

A DIRECTORY
OF ARTISTS
AND
ARCHITECTS

Agostino di Duccio (1418–81). Born in Florence, Agostino served as a mercenary before turning to sculpture. Having possibly studied with Jacopo della Quercia, he carved the altarpiece for Modena cathedral then returned to Florence in 1442. His masterpiece is the Tempio Malatestiano in Rimini, on which Alberti and Piero della Francesca also worked. The best example in this region of his marble relief work, with its emphasis on linear grace, is the Oratorio di San Bernardino in Perugia. He returned to Florence briefly in the 1460s, a period during which he spoiled the marble block that was to become Michelangelo's *David*.

Alberti, Leon Battista (1404–72). Born illegitimately to a Florentine exile, probably in Genoa, Alberti was educated in Padua and Bologna. One of the most complete personifications of the Renaissance ideal of universal genius, he was above all a writer and theorist: his *De Re Aedificatoria* (1452) was the first architectural treatise of the Renaissance, and he also wrote a tract on the art of painting, *Della Pittura*, dedicated to his friend Brunelleschi. His theory of harmonic proportions in musical and visual forms was first put into practice in the facade of Santa Maria Novella in Florence, while his archeological interest in classical architecture found expression in the same city's Palazzo Rucellai, his first independent project. Even more closely linked to his researches into the styles of antiquity is the miniature temple built for the Rucellai family in the church of San Pancrazio. His other buildings are in Mantua and Rimini.

Albertinelli, Mariotto (1474–1515). A colleague of Fra' Bartolommeo in the workshop in San Marco, Albertinelli abandoned painting to be an innkeeper. His best work is the Uffizi *Visitation*.

Alunno, Nicolò (1430–1502). The greatest of the purely Umbrian painters before Perugino, Alunno was probably the pupil of the Venetian Carlo Crivelli, whose bright colouring and precise contours are a feature of his work. Emotionally more intense than Perugino, he usually rejects the conventional dulcet pastoralism of Umbrian art for a bleaker landscape like that around Gubbio and Foligno.

Ammannati, Bartolomeo (1511–92). A Florentine sculptor-architect, much indebted to Michelangelo, Ammannati is best known for his additions and amendments to the Palazzo Pitti and for the graceful Ponte San Trìnita (though in all likelihood this was largely designed by Michelangelo). He created the fountain in the Piazza della Signoria, with some assistance from his pupil Giambologna, and the Bargello contains some of his pieces made for the Bóboli gardens.

Andrea del Sarto (1486–1530). The dominant artist in Florence at the time of Michelangelo and Raphael's ascendancy in Rome. His strengths are not those associated with Florentine draughtsmanship, being more Venetian in his emphasis on delicacy of colour and the primacy of light. He made his name with frescoes for two Florentine churches in the San Marco district – the Scalzo and Santissima Annunziata. For a period in the 1510s he was in France, and the received wisdom is that his talent did not develop after that. However, two of his other major works in Florence date from after his return – the *Last Supper* in San Salvi and the *Madonna del Sacco* in the cloister of the Annunziata. His major easel painting is the *Madonna of the Harpies* in the Uffizi.

Arnolfo di Cambio (c.1245–1302). Pupil of Nicola Pisano, with whom he worked on sculptural projects in Bologna, Siena and Perugia before going to Rome in 1277. The most important of his independent sculptures are the pieces in Florence's Museo dell'Opera del Duomo and the

Tomb of Cardinal de Braye in San Domenico in Orvieto. The latter defined the format of wall tombs for the next century, showing the deceased lying on a coffin below the Madonna and Child, set within an elaborate architectural framework. However, Arnolfo is best known as the architect of Florence's Duomo and Palazzo Vecchio, and various fortifications in central Tuscany, including the fortress at Poppi.

Bandinelli, Baccio (1493–1560). Born in Florence, Bandinelli trained as a goldsmith, sculptor and painter. He perceived himself as an equal talent to Michelangelo and to Cellini, his most vocal critic. Despite manifest shortcomings as a sculptor, he was given prestigious commissions by Cosimo I, the most conspicuous of which is the *Hercules and Cacus* outside the Palazzo Vecchio. Other pieces by him are in the Bargello.

Beccafumi, Domenico (1484/6–1551). The last great Sienese painter, Beccafumi was in Rome during the painting of the Sistine chapel ceiling and Raphael's *Stanze*. He returned to Siena in 1513, when his work showed tendencies that were to become prevalent in Mannerist art – contorted poses, strong lighting, vivid artificial coloration. His decorative skill is especially evident in his illusionist frescoes in the Palazzo Pubblico and the pavement of the Duomo.

Benedetto da Maiano (1442–97). Florentine sculptor, best known for his portrait busts in the Bargello and the pulpit in Santa Croce.

Botticelli, Sandro (c.1445–1510). Possibly a pupil of Filippo Lippi, Botticelli was certainly influenced by the Pollaiuolo brothers, whose paintings of the *Virtues* he completed. The mythological paintings for which he is celebrated – including the *Birth of Venus* and *Primavera* – are distinguished by their emphasis on line rather than mass, and by their complicated symbolic meaning, a reflection on his involvement with the Neo-Platonist philosophers whom the Medici gathered about them. In the last decade of his life his lucid, slightly archaic style suffered from comparison with the more radical paintings of Michelangelo and Leonardo da Vinci, and his devotional pictures became almost clumsily didactic – a result, perhaps, of his involvement with Savonarola and his followers.

Bronzino, Agnolo (1503–72). The adopted son of Pontormo, Bronzino became the court painter to Cosimo I. He frescoed parts of the Palazzo Vecchio for Eleanor of Toledo, but his reputation rests on his glacially elegant portraits, whose surface brilliance makes no discrimination between the faces of the subjects and their apparel.

Brunelleschi, Filippo (1377–1446). Trained as a sculptor and goldsmith, Brunelleschi abandoned this career after his failure in the competition for the Florence baptistery doors. The main product of this period is his contribution to the *St James* altarpiece in Pistoia. He then devoted himself to the study of the building techniques of the Classical era, travelling to Rome with Donatello in 1402. In 1417 he submitted his design for the dome of Florence's Duomo, and all his subsequent work was in that city – San Lorenzo, the Spedale degli Innocenti, Cappella Pazzi (Santa Croce) and Santa Spirito. Unlike the other great architect of this period, Alberti, his work is based on no theoretical premise, but rather on an empiricist's admiration for the buildings of Rome. And unlike Alberti he oversaw every stage of construction, even devising machinery that would permit the raising of the innovative structures he had planned.

Buontalenti, Bernardo (c.1536–1608). Florentine architect, who began as a military architect to the papacy. Much of his later output was for the court of the Medici – the grotto of the Bóboli gardens, the gardens of the villa at Pratolino and tableaux for court spectaculars. Less frivolous work included the Fortezza del Belvedere, the facade of Santa Trìnita, the villa Artimino and the fortifications at Livorno.

Castagno, Andrea (c.1421–57). The early years of Castagno's life are mysterious, and the exact year of his birth is not known. Around 1440 he painted the portraits of some executed rebels in the Bargello, a job that earned him the nickname "Andrea of the Hanged Men". In 1442 he was working in Venice, but a couple of years later he was back in Florence, creating stained glass for the Duomo and frescoes for Sant'Apollonia. His taut sinewy style is to a large extent derived from the sculpture of his contemporary Donatello, an affinity that is especially clear in his frescoes for Santissima Annunziata. Other major works in Florence include the series of *Famous Men and Women* in the Uffizi and the portrait of *Niccolò da Tolentino* in the Duomo – his last piece.

Cellini, Benvenuto (1500–71). Cellini began his career in Rome, where he fought in the siege of the city by the imperial army in 1527. His sculpture is greatly influenced by Michelangelo, as is evident in his most famous large-scale piece, the *Perseus* in the Loggia della Signoria. His other masterpiece in Florence is the heroic *Bust of Cosimo I* in the Bargello. Cellini was an even more accomplished goldsmith and jeweller, creating some exquisite pieces for Francis I, by whom he was employed in the 1530s and 1540s. He also wrote a racy *Autobiography*, a fascinating insight into the artistic world of sixteenth-century Italy and France.

Cimabue (c.1240–1302). Though celebrated by Dante as the foremost painter of the generation before Giotto, very little is known about Cimabue – in fact, the only work that is definitely by him is the mosaic in Pisa's Duomo. He is generally given credit for the softening of the hieratic Byzantine style of religious art, a tendency carried further by his putative pupil, Giotto. Some works can be attributed to him with more confidence than others – the shortlist would include *The Madonna of St Francis* in the lower church at Assisi, the *Passion* cycle in the upper church, the *Maestà* in the Uffizi and the crucifixes in Santa Croce (Florence) and San Domenico (Arezzo).

Civitali, Matteo (1436–1501). Probably self-taught sculptor from Lucca, where all his important work is to be found.

Daddi, Bernardo (c.1290–1349). A pupil of Giotto, Daddi combined the solidity of his master's style with the more decorative aspects of the Sienese style. His work can be seen in the Uffizi and Santa Croce in Florence.

Desiderio da Settignano (c.1428–64). Desiderio continued the low relief technique pioneered by Donatello in the panel for the Orsanmichele *St George*, and carved the tomb of Carlo Marsuppini in Santa Croce, Florence. Better known for his exquisite busts of women and children – a good selection of which are on show in the Bargello.

Donatello (c.1386–1466). A pupil of Ghiberti, Donatello assisted in the casting of the first set of Florence Baptistery doors in 1403, then worked for Nanni di Banco on the Duomo. His early marble *David* (Bargello) is still Gothic in its form, but a new departure is evident in his heroic *St Mark* for Orsanmichele (1411) – possibly produced after a study of the sculpture of ancient Rome. Four years later he began the intense series of prophets for the Campanile, and at the same time

produced the *St George* for Orsanmichele – the epitome of early Renaissance humanism, featuring a relief that is the very first application of rigorous perspective in Western art.

In the mid-1520s Donatello started a partnership with Michelozzo, with whom he created the tomb of Pope John XXIII in the Florence Baptistery, a refinement of the genre initiated by Arnolfo di Cambio. He went to Rome in 1431, possibly with Brunelleschi, and it was probably on his return that he made the classical bronze *David* (Bargello), one of the first nude statues of the Renaissance period. Also at this time he made the *cantoria* to be placed opposite the one already made by Luca della Robbia, the pulpit for Prato cathedral (with Michelozzo) and the decorations for the old sacristy in Florence's church of San Lorenzo – the parish church of his great patrons, the Medici.

After a period in Padua – where he created the first bronze equestrian statue since Roman times – he returned to Florence, where his last works show an extraordinary harshness and angularity. The main sculptures from this period are the *Judith and Holofernes* (Palazzo Vecchio), the *Magdalene* (Museo dell'Opera del Duomo) and the two bronze pulpits for San Lorenzo.

Duccio di Buoninsegna (c.1255–c.1318). Though occupying much the same pivotal position in the history of Sienese art as Giotto does in Florentine art, Duccio was a less revolutionary figure, refining the stately Byzantine tradition rather than subverting its conventions. One of his earliest works was ordered by Florence's church of Santa Maria Novella – the *Maestà* now in the Uffizi – but the bulk of his output is in his home city. Despite frequent ructions with the civic authorities, for refusing to do military service among other transgressions, in 1308 he received his most prestigious assignment, the painting of a *Maestà* for Siena's Duomo. The polyptych no longer exists in its original form, but most of the panels are now in Siena's Museo dell'Opera del Duomo. This iconic image of the Madonna, with its rich use of gold and decorative colour, was to profoundly influence such painters as the Lorenzettis and Simone Martini, while the small scenes on the back of the panels reveal a less frequently acknowledged mastery of narrative painting.

Fra' Angelico (1387/1400–55). Born in Vicchio, Fra' Angelico joined the Dominican order in Fiesole, near his home town and later entered their monasteries in Cortona and Foligno. His first authenticated painting dates from the mid-1420s, but the first one that can be definitely dated is a *Madonna* he produced for the linen guild of Florence in 1433. Three years later the Dominicans took over the San Marco monastery in Florence, and soon after he embarked on the series of frescoes and altarpieces now displayed in the museum there. In the mid-1440s he was called to Rome to work on the Vatican, after which he worked at Orvieto, served for three years as prior of the monastery in Fiesole, and returned to Rome around 1452, where he died. For all their sophistication of technique, Fra' Angelico's paintings, with their atmosphere of tranquil piety, seem to belong to a less complex world than that inhabited by Donatello, his contemporary. His altarpieces of the *Madonna and Saints* – a genre known as *sacre conversazione* – were, however, extremely influential compositions.

Fra' Bartolommeo (c.1474–1517). Fra' Bartolommeo's earliest known work is the Raphael-influenced *Last Judgement* painted for the San Marco monastery in Florence in 1499. The following year he became a monk there, then in 1504 became head of the workshop, a post previously occupied by Fra' Angelico. In 1514 he was in Rome, but according to Vasari was discouraged by Raphael's fame. The works he later produced in Florence had an influence on High Renaissance art, with their repression of elaborate backgrounds and anecdotal detail, concentrating instead on expression and gesture.

Francesco di Giorgio Martini (1439–1501/2). Sienese painter, sculptor and architect, whose treatise on architectural theory was circulated widely in manuscript form – Leonardo had a copy. Employed for a long period by Federico da Montefeltro – also a patron of Piero della Francesca – he probably designed the loggia for the Palazzo Ducale in Urbino and the church of San Bernardino. The church of Santa Maria degli Angeli in Siena and the Palazzo Ducale in Gubbio might be by him; the one Tuscan building that was certainly designed by him is Santa Maria del Calcinaio in Cortona, one of the finest early Renaissance structures in Italy.

Gaddi, Taddeo (d.1366). According to tradition, Taddeo Gaddi worked with Giotto for 24 years, and throughout his life barely wavered from the precepts of his master's style. His first major independent work is the cycle for the Cappella Baroncelli in Santa Croce, Florence. Other works by him are in Florence's Uffizi, Accademia, Bargello and Museo Horne.

Agnolo Gaddi (d.1396), Taddeo's son, continued his father's Giottesque style; his major projects were for Santa Croce in Florence and the duomo of Prato.

Gentile da Fabriano (c.1370–1427). Chief exponent of the International Gothic style in Italy, Gentile da Fabriano came to Florence in 1422, when he painted the gorgeous *Adoration of the Magi* now in the Uffizi. In 1425 he went on to Siena and Orvieto, where the intellectual climate was perhaps more conducive than that in the Florence of Masaccio; he finished his career in Rome.

Ghiberti, Lorenzo (1378–1455). Trained as a goldsmith, painter and sculptor, Ghiberti concentrated on the last discipline almost exclusively after winning the competition to design the doors for Florence's baptistery. His first set of doors are to a large extent derived from Andrea Pisano's earlier Gothic panels for the building, yet his workshop was a virtual academy for the seminal figures of the early Florentine Renaissance – Donatello and Uccello among them. The commission took around twenty years to complete, during which time he also worked on the Siena baptistery and the church of Orsanmichele in Florence, where his *Baptist and St Matthew* show the influence of classical statuary. This classicism reached its peak in the second set of doors for Florence's baptistery (the *Gates of Paradise*) – taking the innovations of Donatello's low relief carving to a new pitch of perfection. The panels occupied much of the rest of his life but in his final years he wrote his *Commentarii*, the main source of information on fourteenth-century art in Florence and Siena, and the first autobiography by an artist.

Ghirlandaio, Domenico (1449–94). The most accomplished fresco artist of his generation, Ghirlandaio was the teacher of Michelangelo. After a short period working on the Sistine Chapel with Botticelli, he came back to Florence, where his cycles in Santa Trìnita and Santa Maria Novella provide some of the most absorbing documentary images of the time, being filled with contemporary portraits and vivid anecdotal details.

Giambologna (1529–1608). Born in northern France, Giambologna – Jean de Boulogne – arrived in Italy in the mid-1550s, becoming the most influential Florentine sculptor after Michelangelo's death. Having helped Ammannati on the fountain for the Piazza della Signoria, he went on to produce a succession of pieces that typify the Mannerist predilection for sculptures with multiple viewpoints – such as the *Rape of the Sabines* (Loggia della Signoria) and the *Mercury* (Bargello). His workshop also turned out scores of reduced bronze copies of his larger works – the Bargello has an extensive collection.

Giotto di Bondone (1266–1337). It was with Giotto's great fresco cycles that religious art shifted from being a straightforward act of devotion to the dramatic presentation of incident. His unerring eye for the significant gesture, his ability to encapsulate moments of extreme emotion and his technical command of figure modelling and spatial depth brought him early recognition as the greatest artist of his generation – and even as late as the sixteenth century artists were studying his frescoes for their solutions to certain compositional problems. Yet, as with Cimabue, the precise attribution of work is problematic. In all probability his first major cycle was the *Life of St Francis* in the upper church at Assisi, though the extent to which his assistants carried out his designs is still disputed. The Arena chapel in Padua is certainly by him, as are large parts of the Bardi and Peruzzi chapels in Santa Croce in Florence. Of his attributed panel paintings, the Uffizi *Maestà* is the only one universally accepted.

Gozzoli, Benozzo (1421–97). Though a pupil of Fra' Angelico, Gozzoli was one of the more worldly artists of the fifteenth century, with a fondness for pageantry that is seen to most impressive effect in the frescoes in Florence's Palazzo Medici-Ricardi. His celebrated cycle in Pisa's Camposanto was all but destroyed in the last war; his other surviving fresco cycles include the *Life of St Francis* in Montefalco and the *Life of St Augustine* in San Gimignano.

Guido da Siena (active mid-thirteenth century). Guido was the founder of the Sienese school of painters, but his life is one of the most problematic areas of Siena's art history. A signed painting by him in the Palazzo Pubblico is dated 1221, but some experts think that the date may have been altered, and that the work

is from the 1260s or 1270s – a period when other pictures associated with him are known to have been painted.

Leonardo da Vinci (1452–1519). Leonardo trained as a painter under Verrocchio, and it is said that his precocious talent caused his master to abandon painting in favour of sculpture. Drawings of landscapes and drapery have survived from the 1470s, but the first completed picture is the *Annunciation* in the Uffizi. The sketch of the *Adoration of the Magi*, also in the Uffizi, dates from 1481, at which time there was no precedent for its fusion of geometric form and dynamic action. Two years later he was in the employment of Lodovico Sforza of Milan, remaining there for sixteen years. During this second phase of his career he produced the *Lady with the Ermine* (Kraków), the fresco of the *Last Supper* and – probably – the two versions of *The Virgin of the Rocks*, the fullest demonstrations to date of his so-called *sfumato*, a blurring of tones from light to dark. Innumerable scientific studies and military projects engaged him at this time, and he also made a massive clay model for an equestrian statue of Francesco Sforza – never completed, like so many of his schemes.

When the French took Milan in 1499 Leonardo returned to Florence, where he devoted much of his time to anatomical researches. It was during this second Florentine period that he was commissioned to paint a fresco of the *Battle of Anghiari* in the main hall of the Palazzo Ducale, where his detested rival Michelangelo was also set to work. Only a fragment of the fresco was completed, and the innovative technique that Leonardo had employed resulted in its speedy disintegration. His cartoons for the *Madonna and Child with St Anne* (Louvre and National Gallery, London) also date from this period, as does the most famous of all his paintings, the Louvre's *Mona Lisa*, the portrait of the wife of a Florentine merchant. In 1506 he went back to Milan, thence to Rome and finally, in 1517, to France. Again, military and scientific work occupied much of this last period – the only painting to have survived is the *St John*, also in the Louvre.

Lippi, Filippo (c.1406–69). In 1421 Filippo Lippi was placed in the monastery of the Carmine in Florence, just at the time Masaccio was beginning work on the Cappella Brancacci there. His early works all bear the stamp of Masaccio, but by the

1530s he was becoming interested in the representation of movement and a more luxuriant surface detail. The frescoes in the cathedral at Prato, executed in the 1550s, show his highly personal, almost hedonistic vision, as do his panel paintings of wistful Madonnas in patrician interiors or soft landscapes – many of them executed for the Medici. His last work, the *Life of the Virgin* fresco cycle in Spoleto, was probably largely executed by assistants.

Filippino Lippi (1457/8–1504) completed his father's work in Spoleto – aged about twelve – then travelled to Florence, where his first major commission was the completion of Masaccio's frescoes in Santa Maria del Carmine (c.1484). At around this time he also painted the *Vision of St Bernard* for the Badìa, which shows an affinity with Botticelli, with whom he is known to have worked. His later researches in Rome led him to develop a self-consciously antique style – seen at its most ambitious in Santa Maria Novella.

Lippo Memmi (d.1357). Brother-in-law of Simone Martini, Lippo Memmi was his assistant on the Uffizi Annunciation. His major work is the *Maestà* in the Palazzo Pubblico in San Gimignano, and he may also have been responsible for the dramatic New Testament frescoes in the Collegiata of the same town.

Lorenzetti, Ambrogio (active 1319–47). Though Sienese, Ambrogio spent part of the 1320s and 1330s in Florence, where he would have witnessed the decoration of Santa Croce by Giotto and his pupils. He's best known for the *Allegory of Good and Bad Government* in the Palazzo Pubblico, which shows painting being used for a secular, didactic purpose for the first time, and is one of the first instances of a landscape being used as an integral part of a composition rather than as a mere backdrop. The Uffizi *Presentation of the Virgin* highlights the difference between Ambrogio's inventive complexity and the comparative simplicity of his brother's style (see below). There's a fine altarpiece by him in Massa Maríttima as well.

Lorenzetti, Pietro (active 1306–48). Brother of Ambrogio, Pietro Lorenzetti was possibly a pupil of Duccio's in Siena. His first authenticated work is the altarpiece in Arezzo's Pieve di Santa Maria (1320); others include frescoes in Assisi's lower church, in which the impact of Giotto is particularly noticeable, and the *Birth of the Virgin* in Siena's Museo dell'Opera del Duomo, one of the best demonstrations of his skill as a narrative painter. It's probable that both the Lorenzettis died during the Black Death.

Lorenzo Monaco (1372–1425). A Sienese artist, Lorenzo Monaco joined the Camaldolese monastery in Florence, for which he painted the *Coronation of the Virgin*, now in the Uffizi. This and his other earlier works are fairly conventional Sienese-style altarpieces, with two-dimensional figures on gold backgrounds. However, his late *Adoration of the Magi* (Uffizi), with its fastidious detailing and landscape backdrop, anticipates the arrival of Gentile da Fabriano and fully fledged International Gothic.

Lo Spagna (1450–1528). Possibly of Spanish origin – hence the name – Lo Spagna spent much of his life in Umbria. Like many of his contemporaries he came under the influence of Raphael, who spent at least five of his formative years in the region.

Maitini, Lorenzo (c.1270–1330). Sienese architect and sculptor, Maitini was the only local artist to challenge the supremacy of the Pisani. In 1310 he was made supervisor of Orvieto's Duomo, for which he designed the biblical panels of the facade – though it's not certain how much of the carving was actually by Maitini. Virtually nothing else about him is known.

Martini, Simone (c.1284–1344). The most important Sienese painter, Simone Martini was a pupil of Duccio but equally influenced by Giovanni Pisano's sculpture and the carvings of French Gothic artists. He began his career by painting a fresco counterpart of Duccio's *Maestà* in the city's Palazzo Pubblico (1315). Soon after he was employed by Robert of Anjou, the King of Naples, and there developed a sinuous, graceful and courtly style. In the late 1320s he was back in Siena, where he probably produced the portrait of *Guidoriccio da Fogliano* – though some experts doubt its authenticity. At some point he went to Assisi, where he painted a cycle of *The Life of St Martin* in the lower church. In 1333 he produced a sumptuous *Annunciation* for the Siena duomo; now in the Uffizi, this is the quintessential fourteenth-century Sienese painting, with its immaculately crafted gold surfaces and emphasis on fluid outline and bright coloration. In 1340 Martini travelled to the papal court of Avignon, where he spent the rest of his life. It was at Avignon that he formed a friendship with Petrarch, for whom he illustrated a magnificent copy of Virgil's poetry.

Masaccio (1401–28). Born just outside Florence, Tomasso di se Giovanni di Mone Cassai – universally known as Masaccio – entered the city's painters' guild in 1422. His first large commission was an altarpiece for the Carmelites of Pisa (the central panel is now in the National Gallery in London), which shows a massive grandeur at odds with the International Gothic style then being promulgated in Florence by Gentile da Fabriano. His masterpieces – the *Trinity* fresco in Santa Maria Novella and the fresco cycle in Santa Maria del Carmine – were produced in the last three years of his life, the latter being painted in collaboration with Masolino. With the architecture of Brunelleschi and the sculpture of Donatello, the Carmine frescoes are the most important achievements of the early Renaissance.

Maso di Banco (active 1340s). Maso was perhaps the most inventive of Giotto's acolytes, and his reputation depends chiefly on the cycle of the *Life of St Sylvester* in Santa Croce, Florence.

Masolino da Panicale (1383–1447). Masolino was employed in Ghiberti's workshop for the production of the first set of baptistery doors, and the semi-Gothic early style of Ghiberti conditioned much of his subsequent work. His other great influence was the younger Masaccio, with whom he worked on the Brancacci chapel.

Michelangelo Buonarroti (1475–1564). Though a titanic figure of Renaissance Italy, Michelangelo was in many ways the antithesis of Renaissance aesthetics, which had previously emphasized order, proportion and the continuity of tradition. He was born in Caprese, in eastern Tuscany, but his family soon moved to Florence, where he became a pupil of Ghirlandaio. Through Ghirlandaio he came into contact with the Medici, making his first stone reliefs for Lorenzo de' Medici. After the expulsion of the Medici he went to Rome in 1496, where he carved the *Bacchus* now in the Bargello. At this time he also created the *Pietà* for St Peter's, a work that secured his reputation as the most skilled sculptor of his day. He came back to Florence for four years in 1501, during which period he carved the *David* and the *St Matthew* (both in the Accademia) and painted the *Doni Tondo*, one of his very few forays into what he regarded as the menial art of easel painting.

Shortly before leaving Florence again, he was employed to paint a fresco of the *Battle of Cáscina* in the Palazzo Vecchio. Only the cartoon was finished, but this became the single most influential work of art in the city, with its exclusive emphasis on the nude form and its use of twisting figures – a recurrent motif in later Mannerist art. Work was suspended in 1505 when Michelangelo was called to Rome by Pope Julius II, who wanted the artist to create his monumental tomb. The project was never finished, like many of Michelangelo's schemes, and cost him forty years of intermittent labour. *The Slaves* in the Accademia were intended for one version of the tomb.

In 1508 Michelangelo began his other superhuman project, the decoration of the Sistine Chapel ceiling. In 1516 he was back in Florence, when he began the new sacristy of San Lorenzo for the Medici pope, Leo X. Work was interrupted frequently, building really only beginning in 1523, when he was also asked to build a library alongside the church – the Biblioteca Laurenziana. In the San Lorenzo project, as in his designs for the Campidoglio and St Peter's in Rome, Michelangelo created a vocabulary that was to provide the basis of Mannerist design – employing paradoxical details like brackets that support nothing, and emphasizing the building as a dynamic rather than a static ensemble (eg tapering window frames, columns that shrink into the wall rather than stand out from it). The sacristy contains a large array of sculptures but again the work represents just a portion of that planned.

The Medici were again expelled from Florence in 1527, and Michelangelo stayed in the city to supervise the defences when it was besieged by the Medici and Charles V in 1530. He left Florence for ever four years later, and spent his last thirty years in Rome, the period that produced the *Last Judgement* in the Sistine Chapel. Florence has one work from this final, tortured phase of Michelangelo's long career, the *Pietà* (now in the Museo dell'Opera del Duomo) that he intended for his own tomb.

Michelozzo di Bartolommeo (1396–1472). Born in Florence, Michelozzo worked in Ghiberti's studio and collaborated with Donatello before turning exclusively to architecture. His main patrons were the Medici, for whom he altered the villa at Careggi and built the Palazzo Medici, which set a prototype for patrician mansions in the city, with its rusticated lower storey, smooth upper facade, overhanging cornice and inner courtyard. He later designed the Villa Medici at Fiesole for the family, and for Cosimo de' Medici he added the light and airy library to the monastery of San Marco. In the Alberti-influenced tribune for the church of Santissima Annunziata, Michelozzo produced the first centrally planned church design to be built in the Renaissance period.

Mino da Fiesole (1429–84). Florentine sculptor, perhaps a pupil of Desiderio da Settignano, Mino is known chiefly for his tombs and portrait busts; there are examples of the former in Fiesole's Duomo and the Badìa in Florence, and of the latter in the Bargello.

Nanni di Banco (c.1384–1421). A Florentine sculptor who began his career as an assistant to his father on the Florence Duomo, Nanni was an exact contemporary of Donatello, with whom he shared some early commissions – Donatello's first *David* was ordered at the same time as an Isaiah from Nanni. The finest works produced in his short life are his niche sculptures at Orsanmichele (especially the *Four Saints*) and the relief above the Duomo's Porta della Mandorla.

Nelli, Ottaviano (active 1400–44). The artist that brought the International Gothic style to Umbria; his intricate and glittering paintings can be seen in Foligno, Assisi and Gubbio.

Odersi, or Oderigi (1240–99). The founder of the Umbrian school, little is known of Odersi except that he was a friend of Giotto and worked mainly in Gubbio. A handful of his miniatures survive, though Dante called him "l'onor d'Agobbio" (the pride of Gubbio) and stuck him in Purgatory as punishment for an obsession with art that left him no time for anything else.

Orcagna, Andrea (c.1308–68). Architect-sculptor-painter, Orcagna was a dominant figure in the period following the death of Giotto, whose emphasis on spatial depth he rejected – as shown in his only authenticated panel painting, the Strozzi altarpiece in Santa Maria Novella. Damaged frescoes can be seen in Santa Croce and Santo Spirito, but Florence's principal work by Orcagna is the massive tabernacle in Orsanmichele. Orcagna's brothers, **Nardo** and **Jacopo di Cione** were the most influential painters in Florence at the close of the fourteenth century – the frescoes in the Strozzi chapel are by Nardo.

Perugino (1445/50–1523). Born Pietro di Cristoforo Vannucci in Città della Pieve, Perugino was the greatest Umbrian artist. Possibly a pupil of Piero della Francesca, he later trained in Florence in the workshop of Andrea Verrocchio, studying alongside Leonardo da Vinci. By 1480 his reputation was such that he was invited to paint in the Sistine Chapel, filling the east wall with his distinctive gently melancholic figures; today only one of Perugino's original three panels remains. In 1500 he executed his greatest work in Umbria, a fresco cycle commissioned by the bankers' guild of Perugia for their Collegio di Cambio. This was probably the first occasion on which he was assisted by his pupil Raphael – and the moment his own career began to wane. Vasari claimed that he was "a man of little or no religion, who could never bring himself to believe in the immortality of the soul" and the production-line altarpieces that his workshop later turned out were often lacking in genuine passion. Yet he was still amongst the most influential of the Renaissance painters, the catalyst for Raphael and mentor for a host of Umbrian artists. In Tuscany he is best seen in the Uffizi and in the church of Santa Maria Maddalena dei Pazzi.

Piero della Francesca (1410/20–92). Piero was born in Borgo Sansepolcro, on the border of Tuscany and Umbria. In the late 1430s he was in Florence, working with Domenico Veneziano, and his later work shows the influence of such Florentine contemporaries as Castagno and Uccello, as well as the impact of Masaccio's frescoes. The exact chronology of his career is contentious, but much of his working life was spent in his native town, for which he produced the *Madonna della Misericordia* and the *Resurrection*, both now in the local Museo Civico. Other patrons included Sigismondo Malatesta of Rimini and Federico da Montefeltro of Urbino – of whom there's a portrait by Piero in the Uffizi. In the 1450s he was in Arezzo, working on the fresco cycle in the church of San Francesco, the only frescoes in Tuscany that can bear comparison with the Masaccio cycle in Florence. He seems to have stopped painting completely in the early 1470s, perhaps to concentrate on his vastly influential treatises on perspective and geometry, but more likely because of failing eyesight.

Piero di Cosimo (c.1462–1521). One of the more enigmatic figures of the High

Renaissance, Piero di Cosimo shared Leonardo's scholarly interest in the natural world but turned his knowledge to the production of allusive mythological paintings. There are pictures by him in the Uffizi, Palazzo Pitti, Museo degli Innocenti and Museo Horne.

Pietro da Cortona (1596–1669). Painter-architect, born Pietro Berrettini, who with Bernini was the guiding force of Roman Baroque. The style was introduced to Florence by Pietro's ceiling frescoes in the Palazzo Pitti. His last painting is in his home town.

Pinturicchio (1454–1513). Born Bernardino di Betto in Perugia, Pinturicchio was taught by Perugino, with whom he collaborated on the painting of the Sistine Chapel. His rich palette earned him his nickname, as well as Vasari's condemnation for superficiality. Most of his work is in Rome but his last commission, one of his most ambitious projects, was his *Life of Pius II* for the Libreria Piccolimini in Siena.

Pisano, Andrea (c.1290–1348). Nothing is known of Andrea Pisano's life until 1330, when he was given the commission to make a new set of doors for the Florence baptistery. He then succeeded Giotto as master mason of the Campanile; the set of reliefs he produced for it are the only other works definitely by him (now in the Museo dell'Opera del Duomo). In 1347 he became the supervisor of Orvieto's Duomo, a job later held by his sculptor son, **Nino**.

Pisano, Nicola (c.1220–84). Born somewhere in the southern Italian kingdom of the emperor Frederick II, Nicola Pisano was the first great classicizing sculptor in pre-Renaissance Italy; the pulpit in Pisa's baptistery (1260), his first masterpiece, shows clearly the influence of Roman figures. Five years later he produced the pulpit for the Duomo in Siena, with the assistance of his son **Giovanni** (c.1248–1314) and Arnolfo di Cambio. Father and son again worked together on the Fonte Gaia in Perugia, which was Nicola's last major project. Giovanni's more turbulent Gothic-influenced style is seen in two other pulpits, for San Andrea in Pistoia and for the Pisa Duomo. The Museo dell'Opera del Duomo in Siena has some fine large-scale figures by Giovanni, while its counterpart in Pisa contains a large collection of work by both the Pisani.

Pollaiuolo, Antonio del (c.1432–98) and **Piero del** (c.1441–96). Though their Florence workshop turned out engravings, jewellery and embroideries, the Pollaiuolo brothers were known mainly for their advances in oil-painting technique and for their anatomical researches, which bore fruit in paintings and small-scale bronze sculptures. The influences of Donatello and Castagno (Piero's teacher) are evident in their dramatic, often violent work, which is especially well represented in the Bargello. The Uffizi's collection of paintings suggests that Antonio was by far the more skilled artist.

Pontormo, Jacopo (1494–1556). Born near Empoli, Pontormo studied under Andrea del Sarto in Florence in the early 1510s. His friendship with Rosso Fiorentino was crucial in the evolution of the hyper-refined Mannerist aesthetic. His early independent works include the frescoes in the atrium of Santissima Annunziata in Florence, where his work shows an edgy quality quite unlike that of his master, who also frescoed this part of the church. In the 1520s he was hired by the Medici to decorate part of their villa at Poggio a Caiano, after which he executed a *Passion* cycle for the Certosa, to the south of the city. His masterpiece in Florence is the *Deposition* in Santa Felìcita (1525) – unprecedented in its lurid colour scheme but showing some indebtedness to Michelangelo's figures. The major project of his later years, a fresco cycle in San Lorenzo, Florence, has been totally destroyed. Other pieces by him are to be seen in the Uffizi and at Carmignano and Sansepolcro.

Quercia, Jacopo della (1374–1438). A Sienese contemporary of Donatello and Ghiberti, della Quercia entered the competition for the Florence baptistery doors which Ghiberti won in 1401. The first known work by him is the tomb of Ilaria del Carretto in Lucca's Duomo. His next major commission was a fountain for Siena's main square, a piece now reassembled in the loggia of the Palazzo Pubblico; before that was finished (1419) he had begun work on a set of reliefs for Siena's baptistery, a project to which Ghiberti and Donatello also contributed. From 1425 he expended much of his energy on reliefs for San Petronio in Bologna – so much so, that the Sienese authorities ordered him to return some of the money he had been paid for the baptistery job.

Raphael (1483–1520). With Leonardo and Michelangelo, Raphael Sanzio forms the triumvirate whose works define the essence of the High Renaissance. Born in Urbino, he joined Perugino's workshop some time around 1494 and within five years was receiving commissions independently of his master. From 1505 to 1508 he was in Florence, where he absorbed the compositional and tonal innovations of Leonardo; many of the pictures he produced at that time are now in the Palazzo Pitti. From Florence he went to Rome, where Pope Julius II set him to work on the papal apartments (the *Stanze*). Michelangelo's Sistine ceiling was largely instrumental in modulating Raphael's style from its earlier lyrical grace into something more monumental, but all the works from this more rugged later period are in Rome.

Robbia, Luca della (1400–82). Luca began as a sculptor in conventional materials, his earliest achievement being the marble *cantoria* (choir gallery) now in the Museo dell'Opera del Duomo in Florence, typifying the cheerful tone of most of his work. Thirty years later he made the sacristy doors for this city's Duomo, but by then he had devised a technique for applying durable potter's glaze to clay sculpture and most of his energies were given to the art of glazed terracotta. His distinctive blue, white and yellow compositions are seen at their best in the Pazzi chapel in Santa Croce, the Bargello, and at Impruneta, just outside Florence.

Andrea della Robbia (1435–1525) continued the lucrative terracotta business started by his uncle, Luca. His best work is at the Spedale degli Innocenti in Florence and at the monastery of La Verna.

Giovanni della Robbia (1469–1529), son of Andrea, best known for the frieze of the Ceppo in Pistoia.

Rossellino, Bernardo (1409–64). An architect-sculptor, Rossellino worked with Alberti and carried out his plans for the Palazzo Rucellai in Florence. His major architectural commission was Pius II's new town of Pienza. As a sculptor he's best known for the monument to Leonardo Bruni in Santa Croce – a derivative of Donatello's tomb of John XXIII in the baptistery. His brother and pupil **Antonio** (1427–79) produced the tomb of the Cardinal of Portugal in Florence's San Miniato al Monte, and a number of excellent portrait busts (Bargello).

Rosso Fiorentino (1494–1540). Like Pontormo, Rosso Fiorentino was a pupil of Andrea del Sarto, but went on to develop a far more aggressive, acidic style than his colleague and friend. His early *Deposition* in Volterra (1521) and the roughly contemporaneous *Moses Defending the Daughters of Jethro* (Uffizi) are typical of his extreme foreshortening and tense deployment of figures. After a period in Rome and Venice, he eventually went to France, where with Primaticcio he developed the distinctive Mannerist art of the Fontainbleau school.

Sangallo, Antonio da, the Elder (1455–1534). A Florence-born architect, Antonio da Sangallo the Elder produced just one major building, but one of the most influential of his period – San Biagio in Montepulciano, based on Bramante's plan for St Peter's in Rome.

His nephew, **Antonio the Younger** (1485–1546), was also born in Florence but did most of his work in Rome, where he began his career as assistant first to Bramante then to Peruzzi. He went on to design the Palazzo Farnese, the most spectacular Roman palace of its time. In Tuscany his most important building is the Fortezza da Basso in Florence.

Giuliano da Sangallo (1445–1516), sculptor, architect and military engineer, was the brother of Antonio the Elder. A follower of Brunelleschi, he produced a number of buildings in and around Florence – the Villa Medici at Poggio a Caiano, Santa Maria delle Carceri in Prato (the first Renaissance church to have a Greek-cross plan) and the Palazzo Strozzi, the most ambitious palace of the century.

Sassetta (c.1392–1450). Sassetta was basically a conventional Sienese painter, though his work does show the influence of International Gothic. Works by him are on show in Siena, Assisi and the Uffizi.

Signorelli, Luca (1450–1523). Though a pupil of Piero della Francesca, Signorelli is more indebted to the muscular drama of the Pollaiuolo brothers and the gestural vocabulary developed by Donatello. In the early 1480s he was probably working on the Sistine Chapel with Perugino and Botticelli, but his most important commission came in 1499, when he was hired to complete the cycle begun by Fra' Angelico in Orvieto's Duomo. The emphasis on the nude figure in his *Last Judgement* was to greatly affect Michelangelo. Shortly after finishing this cycle he went to Rome but the competition from Raphael and Michelangelo drove him back to his native Cortona, where he set up a highly proficient workshop. Works are to be seen in Cortona, Arezzo, Monte Oliveto, Perugia, Sansepolcro and in the Uffizi and Museo Horne in Florence.

Sodoma (1477–1549). Born Giovanni Antonio Bazzi, Sodoma arrived in Siena in 1501, having become familiar with the work of Leonardo da Vinci during a four-year spell in Milan. His major work was begun four years later, a cycle of 31 frescoes at Monte Oliveto. He later won contracts to work in Rome, though the work he commenced in the Vatican was handed over to Raphael.

Spinello Aretino (active 1370s–1410). Probably born in Arezzo, Spinello studied in Florence, possibly under Agnolo Gaddi. He harks back to the monumental aspects of Giotto's style – thus, paradoxically paving the way for the most radical painter of the next generation, Masaccio. His main works are in Florence's church of San Miniato al Monte and Santa Caterina d'Antella, just to the south of the city.

Uccello, Paolo (1396–1475). After training in Ghiberti's workshop, Uccello went to Venice, where he worked on mosaics for the Basilica di San Marco. He returned to Florence in 1431 and five years later was contracted to paint the commemorative portrait of *Sir John Hawkwood* in the Duomo. This trompe l'oeil painting is the first evidence of his interest in the problems of perspective and foreshortening, a subject that was later to obsess him. After an interlude in Padua, he painted the frescoes for the cloister of Santa Maria Novella (c.1445), in which his systematic but non-naturalistic use of perspective is seen at its most extreme. In the following decade he painted the three-scene sequence of the *Battle of San Romano* (Louvre, London National Gallery and Uffizi) for the Medici – his most ambitious

non-fresco paintings, and similarly notable for their strange use of foreshortening.

Vasari, Giorgio (1511–74). Born in Arezzo, Vasari trained with Luca Signorelli and Andrea del Sarto. He became the leading artistic impresario of his day, working for the papacy in Rome and for the Medici in Florence, where he supervised (and partly executed) the redecoration of the Palazzo Vecchio. His own house in Arezzo is perhaps the most impressive display of his limited pictorial talents. He also designed the Uffizi gallery and oversaw a number of other architectural projects, including the completion of the massive Madonna dell'Umiltà in Pistoia. He is now chiefly famous for his Tuscan-biased *Lives of the Most Excellent Painters, Sculptors and Architects*, which charted the rebirth of the fine arts with Giotto and the process of refinement that culminated with Michelangelo.

Veneziano, Domenico (1404–61). Despite the name, Domenico Veneziano was probably born in Florence, though his preoccupation with the way in which colour alters in different light conditions is more of a Venetian concern. From 1439 to 1445 he was working on a fresco cycle in Florence with Piero della Francesca, a work that has now perished. Only a dozen surviving works can be attributed to him with any degree of certainty and only two signed pieces by him are left – one of them is the central panel of the so-called *St Lucy Altar* in the Uffizi.

Verrocchio, Andrea del (c.1435–88). A Florentine painter, sculptor and goldsmith, Verrocchio was possibly a pupil of Donatello and certainly his successor as the city's leading sculptor. A highly accomplished if sometimes over-facile craftsman, he ran one of Florence's busiest workshops, whose employees included the young Leonardo da Vinci. In Florence his work can be seen in the Uffizi, Bargello, San Lorenzo, Santo Spirito, Orsanmichele and Museo dell'Opera del Duomo.

BOOKS

Most of the books recommended below are currently in print, and those that aren't shouldn't be too difficult to track down in second-hand stores. Wherever a book is in print, the UK publisher is given first in each listing, followed by the publisher in the US, unless the title is available in one country only, in which case we have specified the country concerned. If the same publisher produces the book in the UK and US, the publisher is simply named once.

TRAVEL BOOKS AND JOURNALS

Michael Adams, *Umbria* (Bellew in UK). Account by a former Guardian correspondent, excellent on the Roman and medieval periods, but – reissued from the 1964 original – badly dated on more modern matters.

Hilaire Belloc, *The Path to Rome* (Penguin; Regnery Gateway o/p). Entertaining account of a turn-of-the-century walk from France to Rome, via Florence and a fair swathe of Tuscany.

Charles Dickens, *Pictures from Italy* (Penguin; Ecco). The classic mid-nineteenth-century Grand Tour, recording the sights of Emilia, Tuscany, Rome and Naples in measured and incisive prose.

Wolfgang Goethe, *Italian Journey* (Penguin). Revealing for what it says about the tastes of the time – Roman antiquities taking precedence over the Renaissance.

Edward Hutton, *Florence; Country Walks About Florence; The Valley of the Arno; A Wayfarer in Unknown Tuscany; Siena and Southern Tuscany; Cities of Umbria; Assisi and Umbria Revisited; The Cosmati* (all out of print). A Tuscan resident from the 1930s to 1960s, Hutton was nothing if not prolific. Some of his prose adds a new shade to purple, but his books, between them, cover almost every inch of Tuscany and Umbria and are packed with assiduous background on the art and history.

Henry James, *Italian Hours* (Ecco; Penguin). Urbane travel pieces from the young James; perceptive about particular monuments and works of art, superb on the different atmospheres of Italy.

Jonathan Keates, *Tuscany* (George Philip in UK o/p); *Umbria* (George Philip, in UK o/p). Keates's contemporary rambles around the provinces read at times as if he was writing in the same age as Hutton (whose purple prose he also rivals). Nonetheless, both books are strong on stories, reliable on art and beautifully illustrated – though the photos, remarkably, feature not a living soul amid the monuments.

D.H. Lawrence, *Etruscan Places* (Olive Press in UK o/p); also included in *D.H. Lawrence and Italy* (Penguin). Published posthumously, these are Lawrence's musings on Etruscan art and civilization – which he considered pretty ideal ("ripe with the phallic knowledge", etc).

Mary McCarthy, *The Stones of Florence* (Harcourt Brace). Written in the mid-1960s, *Stones* is a mix of high-class reporting on the contemporary city and anecdotal detail on its history – one of the few accounts that doesn't read as if it's been written in a library.

H.V. Morton, *A Traveller in Italy* (Methuen in UK o/p). Morton's leisurely and amiable books were written in the 1930s (long before modern tourism got into its stride), and their nostalgic charm has a lot to do with their enduring popularity. But they are also packed with learned details and marvellously evocative descriptions.

Iris Origo, *War in the Val d'Órcia* (Allison and Busby; Godine). A stirring account of Origo's activities in the last war, hiding partisans and Allied troops on her estate near Montepulciano. In her biography *Images and Shadows* (John Murray, out of print), Origo expands on her Tuscan residence, with some intriguing insights into peasant life in the 1930s.

Tobias Smollett, *Travels through France and Italy* (Oxford University Press in UK). One of the funniest travel journals ever written – the apotheosis of Little Englandism, calling on an unmatched vocabulary of disgust at all things foreign.

Matthew Spender, *Within Tuscany* (Penguin). Recollections of twenty years of living in Tuscany – on the whole, refreshingly free of the condescension that besets most "Brits abroad" memoirs.

HISTORY AND SOCIETY
GENERAL

Harry Hearder, *Italy: A Short History* (Cambridge University Press). The best one-volume survey of the country from prehistory to the present.

Giuliano Procacci, *History of the Italian People* (Penguin; Harper & Row o/p). A comprehensive if undigestibly dense history of the peninsula, charting the development of Italy as a nation state and giving a context for the story of Tuscany and Umbria.

MEDIEVAL

Iris Origo, *The Merchant of Prato* (Penguin; Godine). Based on the massive documentation of Datini's business empire, this is a wonderfully lively re-creation of domestic life in fourteenth-century Tuscany.

Daniel Waley, *The Italian City Republics* (Longman in UK). Excellent general account, which gives much prominence to Florence and its Tuscan rivals.

FLORENCE AND THE RENAISSANCE

Harold Acton, *The Last Medici* (Cardinal in UK o/p). Elegant biography of the least elegant member of the dynasty, the perpetually wine-sodden Gian Gastone.

Gene A. Brucker, *Renaissance Florence* (Univ of California). Concentrating on the years 1380–1450, this brilliant study of Florence at its cultural zenith uses masses of archival material to fill in the social, economic and political background to its artistic achievements.

Jacob Burckhardt, *The Civilization of the Renaissance in Italy* (Penguin). Nineteenth-century classic of Renaissance scholarship – a book that did more than any other to form our image of the period.

Eric Cochrane, *Florence in the Forgotten Centuries 1527–1800* (University of Chicago Press o/p). Massively erudite account of the twilight centuries of Florence; intimidating in its detail, it's unrivalled in its coverage of the years when the city's scientists were more famous than its painters.

J.R. Hale, *Florence and the Medici* (Thames & Hudson in UK o/p). Scholarly yet lively, this covers the full span of the Medici story from the foundation of the family fortune to the calamitous eighteenth century. Vivid in its re-creation of the various personalities involved, it also presents a fascinating picture of the evolution of the mechanics of power in the Florentine state.

Denys Hays, *The Italian Renaissance in its Historical Background* (Cambridge University Press). The best brief coverage of a formidably complex subject.

Christopher Hibbert, *The Rise and Fall of the Medici* (Penguin; Quill). More anecdotal than Hale's book, this is a gripping read, chock-full of heroic successes and squalid failures.

Christopher Hibbert, *Florence: The Biography of a City* (Viking in UK). Yet another excellent Hibbert production, packed with illuminating anecdotes and fascinating illustrations – unlike most books on the city, it's as interesting on the political history as on the artistic achievements, and doesn't grind to a standstill with the fall of the Medici.

Mary Hollingsworth, *Patronage in Renaissance Italy* (John Murray; Johns Hopkins Univ Press). The first comprehensive English-language study of the relationship between artist and patron in quattrocento Italy's city-states. A salutary corrective to the mythology of self-inspired Renaissance genius.

George Holmes, *Florence, Rome and the Origins of the Renaissance* (Oxford University Press o/p). Magnificent portrait of the world of Dante and Giotto, with especially compelling sections on the impact of St Francis and the role of the papacy in the political and cultural life of central Italy.

SIENA, ASSISI AND PERUGIA

Edmund G. Gardner, *The Story of Siena*; **Margaret Symonds & L. Duff Gordon**, *The Story of Perugia* and *The Story of Assisi* (published in Dent's "Medieval Towns" series in the 1920s – now staples of second-hand bookshops). Pocket encyclopedias with lots of anecdote and historical detail you won't find elsewhere.

Judith Hook, *Siena: A City and its History* (Hamish Hamilton, o/p – but available in Siena). This superb study of the city and its art concentrates on the medieval heyday but also takes the story through to the present, and includes a good analytical section on the Palio.

Daniel Waley, *Siena and the Sienese in the Thirteenth Century* (Cambridge University Press o/p). Thorough socio-economic study.

CONTEMPORARY ITALY

Luigi Barzini, *The Italians* (Penguin; Atheneum). Published in 1964, Barzini's study left no stone unturned in the quest to pinpoint what exactly makes Italians. Packed with historical excursions, much remains valid.

Peter Nichols, *Italia, Italia* (o/p). Excellent survey of Italian life, written in the 1970s by the long-term Times correspondent.

Frederic Spotts & Theodor Wieser, *Italy: A Difficult Democracy: A Survey of Italian Politics* (Cambridge University Press). Authoritative and highly readable account of religion, social history and economics in postwar Italy.

William Ward, *Getting it Right in Italy* (Bloomsbury). A "manual" for living in and understanding contemporary Italy, Ward's array of statistics and stories make a totally compelling read.

ART AND ARCHITECTURE

Harold Acton, *The Villas of Tuscany* (Thames & Hudson in UK o/p). Huge and lavishly illustrated tome, with good architectural and historical background on most of the major Tuscan villas – many of them the homes of Sir Harold and his chums.

Frederick Antal, *Florentine Painting and its Social Background* (Harvard University Press). Very authoritative – and often very dull – study of patronage in early Renaissance Florence.

Charles Avery, *Florentine Renaissance Sculpture* (John Murray). Serviceable introduction to the milieu of Donatello and Michelangelo.

Michael Baxandall, *Painting and Experience in Fifteenth-Century Italy* (Oxford University Press). Invaluable analysis, concentrating on the way in which the art of the period would have been perceived at the time.

Keith Christiansen, *Painting in Renaissance Siena* (Abrams; Metropolitan Museum o/p). Definitive study of the city's art.

Vincent Cronin, *The Florentine Renaissance* and *The Flowering of the Renaissance* (both Pimlico in UK). Concise and gripping narrative of Italian art's golden years – the first volume covers the fifteenth century, the second switches the focus to sixteenth-century Rome and Venice.

J.R. Hale (ed.), *Concise Encyclopaedia of the Italian Renaissance* (Thames & Hudson in UK). Exemplary reference book, many of whose summaries are as informative as essays twice their length; covers individual artists, movements, cities, philosophical concepts, the lot.

Frederick Hartt, *History of Italian Renaissance Art* (Thames & Hudson; Abrams). If one book on this vast subject can be said to be indispensable, this is it. The price might seem daunting, but in view of its comprehensiveness and the range of its illustrations, it's actually a bargain.

Michael Levey, *Early Renaissance* (Penguin). Precise and fluently written account from former director of the National Gallery, and well illustrated; probably the best introduction to the subject. Levey's *High Renaissance* (Penguin) continues the story in the same style.

Michael Levey, *Florence: A Portrait* (Pimlico). A weighty, highbrow and often illuminating analysis of the city's history, and its artistic history in particular, with snippets and details missed by other accounts.

Anthony McIntyre, *Medieval Tuscany and Umbria* (Viking; Chronicle). A sketchy, limited and often superficial survey of the architecture of the period, ranging from vernacular buildings to the great cathedrals.

Anna Maria Massinelli and Filippo Tuena, *Treasures of the Medici* (Thames & Hudson; Vendome o/p). Illustrated inventory of the Medici family's collection of jewellery, vases and other *objets d'art*, published to celebrate the five-hundredth anniversary of the death of Lorenzo il Magnifico, perhaps the clan's most compulsive collector. Not the first book to buy for your Florentine library, but definitive in its field.

Peter Murray, *The Architecture of the Italian Renaissance* (Thames & Hudson; Schocken). Begins with Romanesque buildings and finishes with Palladio – useful both as a gazetteer of the main monuments and as a synopsis of the underlying concepts.

John Shearman, *Mannerism* (Penguin). The self-conscious art of sixteenth-century Mannerism is one of the most complex topics of Renaissance studies; Shearman's brief discussion analyses the main currents, yet never oversimplifies nor becomes pedantic.

Giorgio Vasari, *Lives of the Artists* (Penguin, 2 vols). Abridgement of the sixteenth-century artist's classic work on his predecessors and contemporaries. Includes essays on Giotto, Brunelleschi, Leonardo and Michelangelo. The first real work of art history, and still among the most penetrating books you can read on Italian Renaissance art.

INDIVIDUAL ARTISTS

The Complete Paintings series: Botticelli, Leonardo da Vinci, Piero della Francesca (Penguin). Paperback picture books, reproducing every painting in black and white, plus several colour plates. Also gives detailed analysis of dates, authenticity and a host of other art-historical issues.

James A. Ackerman, *The Architecture of Michelangelo* (Penguin; Univ of Chicago). If you come out of the Sagrestia Nuova in Florence wondering why people make such a fuss about Michelangelo's buildings, Ackerman's book will make you see it with fresh eyes.

Umberto Baldini and Ornella Casazza, *The Brancacci Chapel* (Thames & Hudson; Abrams). Written by the chief restorers of the Brancacci cycle of frescoes by Masaccio, Masolino and Filippino Lippi, this luscious book is illustrated with magnificent life-size reproductions of the freshly cleaned masterpieces. One to request for your birthday.

Luciano Bellosi, *Duccio: The Maestà* (Thames and Hudson). Published in 1999, this superb production aims to present "a very direct experience of Duccio di Buoninsegna's masterpiece", and it does just that, with page after page of the highest quality details from the greatest of all Sienese paintings. The analytical essay that precedes the reproductions is a useful introduction to the work, but essentially this is a book to contemplate rather than to read.

Bonnie Bennett and David Wilkins, *Donatello* (Phaidon; Moyer Bell). Worthy homage to one of the most influential figures in the history of Western art.

Kenneth Clark, *Leonardo da Vinci* (Penguin). Rather old-fashioned in its reverential connoisseurship, but still highly recommended.

Bruce Cole, *Giotto and Florentine Painting 1280–1375* (Harper Row o/p; HarperCollins o/p). Excellent introduction to the art of Giotto and his immediate successors.

Carlo Ginzburg, *The Enigma of Piero* (Verso). Art history as detective story, on a quest to decipher Piero's *Baptism*, the Arezzo cycle and the *Flagellation*.

Ludwig Goldscheider, *Michelangelo: Paintings, Sculpture, Architecture* (Phaidon, o/p). Virtually all monochrome reproductions, but a good pictorial survey of Michelangelo's output, covering everything except the drawings.

William Hood, *Fra Angelico at San Marco* (Yale University Press). Maintaining this imprint's reputation for elegantly produced, scholarly yet accessible art books, Hood's socio-aesthetic study of the panel paintings and frescoes of Fra' Angelico is unsurpassed in its scope. A book to read after you've made your first acquaintance with the pictures.

Marilyn Aronberg Lavin, *Piero della Francesca* (Chicago Univ Press). Despite looking like a book for browsing, the commentaries on the paintings are immensely informative and astute. The best English-language introduction to this most elusive and demanding of artists.

John Pope-Hennessy, *The Piero della Francesca Trail* (Thames & Hudson). This is basically a brief chronological survey of the artist's career, serviceable as a beginner's guide but nowhere near as stimulating as the Lavin book (see above) and its patrician tone gets a bit wearing.

John White, *Duccio* (Thames & Hudson in UK o/p). The fullest study of the Sienese master available in English, concentrating on his art in the context of medieval workshop practices.

LITERATURE

Dante Alighieri, *The Divine Comedy* (Oxford University Press, 3 vols). No work in any other language bears comparison with Dante's poetic exegesis of the moral scheme of God's creation – in late medieval Italy it was venerated both as a book of almost scriptural authority and as the ultimate refinement of the vernacular Tuscan language. Numerous translations have been attempted – the Oxford University Press edition is clear, and has the original text facing the English version. One of the better translations, Laurence Binyon's, is printed in full in the *Portable Dante* (Viking).

Ludovico Ariosto, *Orlando Furioso* (Penguin, 2 vols). Italy's chivalric epic, set in Charlemagne's Europe; has its exciting moments, but most readers would be grateful for a rather more abridged version.

Giovanni Boccaccio, *The Decameron* (Penguin). Set in the plague-racked Florence of 1348, Boccaccio's assembly of one hundred short stories is a fascinating social record as well as a constantly diverting and often smutty comedy.

Benvenuto Cellini, *Autobiography* (Penguin). Shamelessly egocentric record of the travails and triumphs of the sculptor and goldsmith's career; one of the freshest literary productions of its time.

Giacomo Leopardi, *Selected Poems* (Princeton University Press). A good selection from the work of Italy's greatest lyric poet; Eamon Grennan's translations are serviceable rather than inspired, but the original text is presented alongside, and the introduction is excellent.

Niccolo Machiavelli, *The Prince* (Penguin). A treatise on statecraft which actually did less to form the political thought of Italy than it did to form foreigners' perceptions of the country; yet there was far more to Machiavelli than the *Realpolitik* of The Prince, as is shown by the selection of writings included in Penguin's anthology The Portable Machiavelli.

Petrarch (Francesco Petrarca), *Selections from the Canzoniere* (Oxford University Press). Often described as the first modern poet, by virtue of his preoccupation with worldly fame and secular love, Petrarch wrote some of the Italian language's greatest lyrics. This slim selection at least hints at what is lost in translation.

Leonardo da Vinci, *Notebooks* (Oxford University Press). Miscellany of speculation and observation from the universal genius of Renaissance Italy; essential to any understanding of the man.

TUSCANY AND UMBRIA IN ENGLISH FICTION

Michael Dibdin, *Rat King* (Faber; Bantam). Crime time in Perugia. Best of the Italy-set books of an author who often tries a little too hard to underline just how much he thinks he knows about the country.

Timothy Holme, *The Assisi Murders* (Futura o/p; Walke o/p). Dark doings in Umbria.

George Eliot, *Romola* (Penguin). Ponderous tale of fifteenth-century Florence; researched to the hilt, but will probably remain the great unread Eliot novel.

E.M. Forster, *Where Angels Fear to Tread* and *Room with a View* (Penguin; Vintage). The settings are, respectively, San Gimignano and Florence, the milieu uptight Edwardian English society in Forster's two perfectly formed Italian novels.

Nikos Kazantzakes, *God's Pauper* (o/p). Published in 1962, this is a fictionalized account of the life of St Francis as seen through the eyes of a close companion.

Magdalen Nabb, *Death in Springtime, Death in Autumn*, and many other titles (Collins in UK o/p). Florence is the locale for many of Nabb's brilliant thrillers, based on a good knowledge of the city's low life . . . and the Sardinian shepherds who dabble in a spot of kidnapping in the hills.

Michael Ondaatje, *The English Patient* (Picador; Vintage). At the close of World War II, a badly burned English aviator sees out his days in a wrecked Tuscan villa, attended by a cast of characters who come from widely differing backgrounds yet all think and speak in high-flown lyrical language. Some find Ondaatje's prose hypnotic, others think this is one of the most portentous and overpraised novels of recent years.

Barry Unsworth, *After Hannibal* (Penguin; Doubleday). Unsworth lives in Umbria, which is where this black comedy is set. His fiction better evokes the reality of ex-pat existence than the rose-tinted and predictable meanderings of writers such as Lisa St Aubin de Teran (*A Valley in Umbria*, Penguin).

FLORA AND FAUNA

Paul Harcourt-Davies, *Wild Orchids of Britain & Europe* (Chatto). A perfect guide to the orchids you'll find in abundance if you visit Umbria's Piano Grande or other limestone mountains in late May and June. See also the same author's *Wild Flowers of Southern Europe* (Crowood, with R. Gibbons).

Heinzel, Fitter & Parslow, *The Birds of Britain and Europe* (HarperCollins in UK). Best-known general guide, with plentiful maps and illustrations.

Higgins & Riley, *Field Guide to the Butterflies of Britain and Europe* (o/p). Amply illustrated and detailed handbook.

C.J. Humphries, *Trees of Britain and Europe* (Hamlyn). A throughly reliable and straightforward guide for the most demanding of dendrologists.

Oleg Polunin & Antony Huxley, *Flowers of the Mediterranean* (Hogarth Press). Excellent guide, with colour pictures, line drawings and concise reference list as aids to identification.

Thomas Schauer, *Field Guide to the Wild Flowers of Britain and Europe* (Collins in UK o/p). Comprehensive handbook with good drawings and detailed descriptions.

Christopher Grey Wilson & Marjorie Blamey, *Alpine Flowers of Britain and Europe* (HarperCollins in UK). Full account of mountain flora, particularly useful as a handbook for the Monti Sibillini, Orecchiella and Alpi Apuane.

HIKING GUIDES

Stefano Ardito, *A Piedi in Umbria* (Edizione Iter). In the same series as the above titles, written by the doyen of Italian backpackers.

Antonio Arrighi and Roberto Pratesi, *A Piedi in Toscana* (Edizione Iter, 2 vols). Useful route guides for walkers, with basic maps. Widely available in Italy.

WINE AND FOOD

Burton Anderson, *Vino* (Papermac o/p; Little, Brown o/p). The definitive book on Italian wines, detailing production methods, grape varieties, climates and geology, and written in a light-hearted and readable style.

Burton Anderson, *The Pocket Guide to Italian Wines* (Mitchell Beazley o/p; Simon & Schuster o/p). Excellent handbook for selecting rarer or vintage wines on the spot.

Burton Anderson and others, *Chianti* (Edizioni Grafica Comense o/p). Comprehensive handbook to the wines, producers, and restaurants of the region.

Leslie Forbes, *A Table in Tuscany* (Penguin; Chronicle). Regional recipes presented in the format of a facsimile manuscript, illustrated with colourful drawings.

Marcella Hazan, *Classic Italian Cookbook* (Papermac; Ballantine o/p). Marcella features a fair number of Tuscan recipes and issues the kind of instructions that inspire total confidence.

Pino Luongo, *A Tuscan in the Kitchen* (Headline; Clarkson Potter). Serious recipes.

Elizabeth Romer, *The Tuscan Year: Life and Food in an Italian Valley* (Orion; North Point). Mix of recipes and background on countryside traditions.

Janet Ross and Michael Waterfield, *Leaves from our Tuscan Kitchen* (Penguin in UK o/p). Classic vegetarian recipes, first published in 1899.

LANGUAGE

The ability to speak English confers prestige in Italy, and there's often no shortage of people willing to show off their knowledge, particularly in the main cities and resorts. However, in more remote areas you may find no one speaks English at all.

PRONUNCIATION

Wherever you are, it's a good idea to master at least a little Italian, a task made easier by the fact that your halting efforts will often be rewarded by smiles and genuine surprise. In any case, it's one of the easiest European languages to learn, especially if you already have a smattering of French or Spanish, both of which are extremely similar grammatically.

Easiest of all is the **pronunciation**, since every word is spoken exactly as it's written, and usually enunciated with exaggerated, open-mouthed clarity. The only difficulties you're likely to encounter are the few **consonants** that are different from English:

c before e or i is pronounced as in **ch**urch, while **ch** before the same vowel is hard, as in **c**at.

sci or **sce** are pronouced as in **sh**eet and **sh**elter respectively. The same goes with **g** – soft before e or i, as in **g**eranium; hard when followed by h, as in **g**arlic.

gn has the ni sound of our o**ni**on.

gl in Italian is softened to something like li in English, as in stal**li**on.

h is not aspirated, as in **h**onour.

When **speaking** to strangers, the third person is the polite form (ie *Lei* instead of *Tu* for "you"); using the second person is a mark of disrespect or stupidity. It's also worth remembering that Italians don't use "please" and "thank you" half as much as we do: it's all implied in the tone, though if you're in any doubt, err on the polite side.

All Italian words are **stressed** on the penultimate syllable unless an **accent** (´ or `) denotes otherwise, although accents are often left out in practice. Note that the ending -ia or -ie counts as two syllables, hence trattoria is stressed on the i. Generally, in the text we've put accents in whenever it isn't immediately obvious how a word should be pronounced – though you shouldn't assume that this is how you'll see the words written in Italian. For example, in *Maríttima*, the accent is on the first i, but on Italian maps it's often written Marittima.

ITALIAN WORDS AND PHRASES

NUMBERS

1	uno	9	nove	17	diciassette	50	cinquanta	200	duecento
2	due	10	dieci	18	diciotto	60	sessanta	500	cinquecento
3	tre	11	undici	19	diciannove	70	settanta	1000	mille
4	quattro	12	dodici	20	venti	80	ottanta	5000	cinquemila
5	cinque	13	tredici	21	ventuno	90	novanta	10,000	diecimila
6	sei	14	quattordici	22	ventidue	100	cento	50,000	cinquanta
7	sette	15	quindici	30	trenta	101	centuno		mila
8	otto	16	sedici	40	quaranta	110	centodieci		

BASICS

Good morning	Buon giorno	I live in . . .	Abito a . . .
Good afternoon/evening	Buona sera	Today	Oggi
Good night	Buona notte	Tomorrow	Domani
Hello/goodbye	Ciao (informal; to strangers use phrases above)	Day after tomorrow	Dopodomani
		Yesterday	Ieri
		Now	Adesso
Goodbye	Arrivederci (formal)	Later	Più tardi
Yes	Si	Wait a minute!	Aspetta!
No	No	In the morning	di mattina
Please	Per favore	In the afternoon	nel pomeriggio
Thank you (very much)	Grázie (molte/mille grazie)	In the evening	di sera
		Here (there)	Qui/La
		Good/bad	Buono/Cattivo
You're welcome	Prego	Big/small	Grande/Píccolo
Alright/that's OK	Va bene	Cheap/expensive	Económico/Caro
How are you?	Come stai/sta? (informal/formal)	Early/late	Presto/Ritardo
		Hot/cold	Caldo/Freddo
		Near/far	Vicino/Lontano
I'm fine	Bene	Quickly/slowly	Velocemente/Lentamente
Do you speak English?	Parla inglese?	Slowly/quietly	Piano
I don't understand	Non ho capito	With/without	Con/Senza
I don't know	Non lo so	More/less	Più/Meno
Excuse me	Mi scusi/Prego	Enough, no more	Basta
Excuse me (in a crowd)	Permesso	Mr . . .	Signor . . .
		Mrs . . .	Signora . . .
sorry	Mi dispiace	Miss . . .	Signorina . . .
I'm here on holiday	Sono qui in vacanza		
I'm English/Scottish/Welsh/Irish	Sono inglese/scozzese/gallese/irlandese	(il Signor, la Signora, la Signorina when speaking about someone else)	

DRIVING

Left/right	Sinistro/Destro	No entry	Senso vietato
Go straight ahead	Sempre diritto	Slow down	Rallentare
Turn to the right/left	Gira a destra/sinistra	Road closed/up	Strada chiusa/guasta
Parking	Parcheggio	No through road	Vietato il transito
No parking	Divieto di sosta/Sosta vietata	No overtaking	Vietato il sorpasso
		Crossroads	Incrocio
One-way street	Senso único	Speed limit	Limite di Velocità

SOME SIGNS

Entrance/exit	Entrata/Uscita	To let	Affitasi
Free entrance	Ingresso líbero	Platform	Binario
Gentlemen/ladies	Signori/Signore	Cash desk	Cassa
WC	Gabinetto	Go/walk	Avanti
Vacant/engaged	Libero/Occupato	Stop/halt	Alt
Open/closed	Aperto/Chiuso	Customs	Dogana
Arrivals/departures	Arrivi/Partenze	Do not touch	Non toccare
Closed for restoration	Chiuso per restauro	Danger	Perícolo
Closed for holidays	Chiuso per ferie	Beware	Attenzione
Pull/push	Tirare/Spingere	First aid	Pronto soccorso
Out of order	Guasto	Ring the bell	Suonare il campanello
Drinking water	Acqua potabile	No smoking	Vietato fumare

ACCOMMODATION

Hotel	Albergo	Can I see the room?	Posso vedere la camera?
Is there a hotel nearby?	C'è un albergo qui vicino?	I'll take it	La prendo
Do you have a room . . .	Ha una camera . . .	I'd like to book a room	Vorrei prenotare una camera
for one/two/ three people	per una/due/ tre person(a/e)	I have a booking	Ho una prenotazione
for one/two/three nights	per una/due/tre nott(e/i)	Can we camp here?	Possiamo fare il campeggio qui?
for one/two weeks	per una/due settiman(a/e)	Is there a campsite nearby?	C'è un camping qui vicino
with a double bed	con un letto matrimoniale	Tent	Tenda
with a shower/bath	con una doccia/ un bagno	Cabin	Cabina
		Youth hostel	Ostello per la gioventù
with a balcony	con una terrazza	Single room	una camera singola
hot/cold water	acqua calda/freddo	Double room	una camera doppia
How much is it?	Quanto costa?	Room with twin beds	una camera a due letti
It's expensive	È caro	Room with private bathroom	una camera con bagno
Is breakfast included?	È compresa la prima colazione?	Do you have rooms free?	avete camere libere
		I have a reservation	ho una prenotazione
Do you have anything cheaper?	Ha niente che costa di meno?	Could I see another room?	potrei guardare un'altra camera?
Full/half board	Pensione completa/mezza pensione	Porte	il facchino
		Lift	ascensore
		Key	la chiave

QUESTIONS AND DIRECTIONS

Where? (where is/ are . . . ?)	Dove? (Dov'è/ Dove sono)	Can you give me a lift to . . . ?	Mi può dare un passaggio a . . . ?
When?	Quando?	Can you tell me when to get off?	Mi può dire scendere alla fermata giusta?
What? (what is it?)	Cosa? (Cos'è?)		
How much/many?	Quanto/Quanti?	What time does it open?	A che ora apre?
Why?	Perchè?		
It is/there is (is it/is there . . . ?)	È/C'è (È/C'è . . . ?)	What time does it close?	A che ora chiude?
		How much does it cost (. . . do they cost?)	Quanto costa? (Quanto costano?)
What time is it?	Che ora è/Che ore sono?		
How do I get to . . . ?	Come arrivo a . . . ?	What's it called in Italian?	Comè si chiama in italiano?
How far is it to . . . ?	Cuant'è lontano a . . . ?		

TRAVELLING

Aeroplane	Aeroplano	Ferry terminal	Stazione maríttima	Port	Porto
Bicycle	Bicicletta	Ferry	Traghetto	Railway station	Stazione ferroviaria
Bus	Autobus/pullman	Hitchhiking	Autostop	Ship	Nave
Bus station	Autostazione	Hydrofoil	Aliscafo	Taxi	Taxi
Car	Macchina	On foot	A piedi	Train	Treno

A ticket to . . .	Un biglietto a . . .	Where does it leave from?	Da dove parte?
One-way/return	Solo andata/andata e ritorno	What platform does it leave from?	Da quale binario parte?
Can I book a seat?	Posso prenotare un posto?	How many kilometres is it?	Quanti chilometri sono?
What time does it leave?	A che ora parte?	How long does it take?	Quanto ci vuole?
When is the next bus/train/ferry to . . . ?	Quando parte il prossimo pullman/treno/traghetto per . . . ?	What number bus is it to . . . ?	Que número di autobus per . . . ?
		Where's the road to . . . ?	Dov'è la strada a . . . ?
Do I have to change?	Devo cambiare?	Next stop please	La pro'ssima fermata, per favore

GLOSSARY OF ARTISTIC AND ARCHITECTURAL TERMS

AMBO A kind of simple pulpit, popular in Italian medieval churches.

ANFITEATRO Amphitheatre.

APSE Semicircular recess at the altar, usually eastern, end of a church.

ARCHITRAVE The lowest part of the entablature.

ATRIUM Inner courtyard.

BADÌA Abbey.

BALDACCHINO A canopy on columns, usually placed over the altar in a church.

BALUARDO Bastion.

BASILICA Originally a Roman administrative building, adapted for early churches; distinguished by lack of transepts.

BATTISTERO Baptistery.

BELVEDERE A terrace or lookout point.

BORGO Medieval suburb or hamlet.

CALDARIUM The steam room of a Roman bath.

CAMPANILE Bell tower, sometimes detached, usually of a church.

CAMPO Square.

CAMPOSANTO Cemetery.

CANTORIA Choir loft.

CAPITAL Top of a column.

CAPPELLA Chapel.

CASTELLO Castle.

CENACOLO Last Supper.

CHANCEL Part of a church containing the altar.

CHIESA Church.

CHIOSTRO Cloister.

CIBORIUM Another word for baldacchino.

COLLEGIATA Church just below the hierarchy of a cathedral.

CONTRADA Ancient quarter of a town.

CORTILE Galleried courtyard or cloister.

CORNICE The top section of a classical facade.

COSMATI WORK Decorative mosaic work on marble, usually highly coloured, found in early Christian Italian churches, especially in Rome. Derives from the name Cosma, a common name among families of marble workers at the time.

CRYPT Burial place in a church, usually under the choir.

CUPOLA Dome.

CYCLOPEAN WALLS Fortifications built of huge, rough stone blocks.

DECUMANUS MAXIMUS The main street of a Roman town. The second cross-street was known as the Decumanus Inferiore.

DIPTYCH Twin-panelled painting.

DUOMO/CATTEDRALE Cathedral.

ENTABLATURE The section above the capital on a classical building, below the cornice.

EX-VOTO Artefact designed in thanksgiving to a saint. The adjective is ex-votive.

FONTE Fountainhouse.

FORTEZZA Fortress.

FRESCO Wall-painting technique in which the artist applies paint to wet plaster for a more permanent finish.

GONFALONI Painted flags or standards.

INTARSIA Inlaid stone or wood.

LOGGIA Roofed gallery or balcony.

LUNETTE Semicircular space in vault or ceiling.

MAESTÀ Madonna and Child enthroned.

MATRONEUM Women's gallery in early church.

MUNICIPIO Town hall.

NARTHEX Vestibule of a church.

NAVE Central space in a church, usually flanked by aisles.

PALAZZO Palace, mansion, or block of flats.

PALAZZO DEL PODESTÀ Magistrate's palace.

PALAZZO DEL POPOLO, PALAZZO PUBBLICO, PALAZZO COMUNALE Town hall.

PANTOCRATOR An image of Christ, usually portrayed in the act of blessing.

PIANO NOBILE Main floor of a palace, usually the first.

PIETÀ Image of the Virgin mourning the dead Christ.

PIETRA DURE Hard or semiprecious stones used for decorative inlay.

PIEVE Parish church.

PINACOTECA Picture gallery.

POLYPTYCH Painting on several joined panels.

PORTA Gate.

PORTICO Covered entrance to a building.

PREDELLA Small panel below the main scenes of an altarpiece.

PUTTI Cherubs.

RELIQUARY Receptacle for a saint's relics, usually bones. Often highly decorated.

ROCCA Castle.

SALA DEI PRIORI Council chamber.

SANTUARIO Sanctuary or chancel.

SGRAFFITO Decorative technique whereby a layer of plaster is scratched to form a pattern.

SINOPIA Sketch for a fresco, applied to the wall.

STUCCO Plaster made from water, lime, sand and powdered marble, used for decorative work.

TEATRO Theatre

TEMPIO Temple.

THERMAE Baths, usually elaborate buildings in Roman villas.

TONDO Round painting or relief.

TORRE Tower.

TRIPTYCH Painting on three joined panels.

TROMPE L'OEIL Work of art that deceives the viewer by tricks of perspective.

GLOSSARY OF ITALIAN WORDS AND ACRONYMS

ITALIAN WORDS

ALISCAFO Hydrofoil.

ALTO Upper.

AUTSTAZIONE Bus station.

AUTOSTRADA Motorway.

BAGNO Bath or spa.

BASSO (or SCALO) Lower.

BIBLIOTECA Library.

CENTRO Centre.

CENTRO STORICO Historic centre.

COMUNE An administrative area; also the local council or town hall.

CORSO Avenue or boulevard.

ENTRATA Entrance.

FESTA Festival, holiday.

FIUME River.

GIARDINO Garden; GIARDINO BOTANICO (or ORTO BOTANICO), botanical garden.

GOLFO Gulf.

LAGO Lake.

LUNGOMARE Seafront road or promenade.

MARE Sea.

MERCATO Market.

MUSEO Museum.

OSPEDALE Hospital.

PAESE Place, area, or village.

PALIO Horse race (most famously in Siena).

PARCO Park.

PASSEGGIATA The customary early evening walk – sometimes applied to a promenade.

PIANO Plain.

PIAZZA Square.

QUESTURA Main police station.

SENSO UNICO One-way street.

SOTTOPASSAGIO Subway.

SPIAGGIA Beach.

STAZIONE Station.

STRADA Road.

TRAGHETTO Ferry.

USCITA Exit.

VIA Road (always used with name, eg Via Roma).

ACRONYMS

AAST Azienda Autonoma di Soggiorno e Turismo.

ACI Automobile Club d'Italia.

APT Azienda Provinciale di Turismo.

CAI Club Alpino Italiano.

DC Democrazia Cristiana; the Christian Democrat party.

EPT Ente Provinciale di Turismo (provincial tourist office); see also APT and AAST.

FS Italian State Railways.

IVA Imposta Valore Aggiunto (VAT).

MSI Movimento Sociale Italiano; the Italian Fascist party.

PDI Partito Democratica della Sinistra; new name for the Italian communist party.

PSI Partito Socialista Italiano; the Italian Socialist party.

RAI The Italian state TV and radio network.

SIP Italian state telephone company.

SS Strada Statale; equivalent to a British "A" road, eg SS18.

TCI Touring Club d'Italia; map and guide publishers.

INDEX

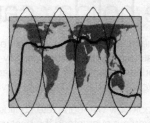